D1162072

(Continued on back endsheets)

Dictionary of Literary Biography® • Volume One Hundred Forty-Six

Old and Middle English Literature

Dictionary of Literary Biography® • Volume One Hundred Forty-Six

Old and Middle English Literature

Edited by
Jeffrey Helterman
University of South Carolina
and
Jerome Mitchell
University of Georgia

A Bruccoli Clark Layman Book
Gale Research Inc.
Detroit, Washington, D.C., London

Contents

Plan of the Series

. . . Almost the most prodigious asset of a country, and perhaps its most precious possession, is its native literary product — when that product is fine and noble and enduring.

Mark Twain*

The advisory board, the editors, and the publisher of the *Dictionary of Literary Biography* are joined in endorsing Mark Twain's declaration. The literature of a nation provides an inexhaustible resource of permanent worth. We intend to make literature and its creators better understood and more accessible to students and the reading public, while satisfying the standards of teachers and scholars.

To meet these requirements, *literary biography* has been construed in terms of the author's achievement. The most important thing about a writer is his writing. Accordingly, the entries in *DLB* are career biographies, tracing the development of the author's canon and the evolution of his reputation.

The purpose of *DLB* is not only to provide reliable information in a convenient format but also to place the figures in the larger perspective of literary history and to offer appraisals of their accomplishments by qualified scholars.

The publication plan for *DLB* resulted from two years of preparation. The project was proposed to Bruccoli Clark by Frederick C. Ruffner, president of the Gale Research Company, in November 1975. After specimen entries were prepared and typeset, an advisory board was formed to refine the entry format and develop the series rationale. In meetings held during 1976, the publisher, series editors, and advisory board approved the scheme for a comprehensive biographical dictionary of persons who contributed to North American literature. Editorial work on the first volume began in January 1977, and it was published in 1978. In order to make *DLB* more than a reference tool and to compile volumes that individually have claim to status as literary history, it was decided to organize volumes by topic, period, or genre. Each of these free-standing volumes provides a biographical-bibliographical guide and overview for a particular area of literature. We are convinced that this organization — as opposed to a single alphabet method — constitutes a valuable innovation in the presentation of reference material. The volume plan necessarily requires many decisions for the placement and treatment of authors who might properly be included in two or three volumes. In some instances a major figure will be included in separate volumes, but with different entries emphasizing the aspect of his career appropriate to each volume. Ernest Hemingway, for example, is represented in *American Writers in Paris, 1920–1939* by an entry focusing on his expatriate apprenticeship; he is also in *American Novelists, 1910–1945* with an entry surveying his entire career. Each volume includes a cumulative index of the subject authors and articles. Comprehensive indexes to the entire series are planned.

With volume ten in 1982 it was decided to enlarge the scope of *DLB*. By the end of 1986 twenty-one volumes treating British literature had been published, and volumes for Commonwealth and Modern European literature were in progress. The series has been further augmented by the *DLB Yearbooks* (since 1981) which update published entries and add new entries to keep the *DLB* current with contemporary activity. There have also been *DLB Documentary Series* volumes which provide biographical and critical source materials for figures whose work is judged to have particular interest for students. One of these companion volumes is entirely devoted to Tennessee Williams.

We define literature as the *intellectual commerce of a nation:* not merely as belles lettres but as that ample and complex process by which ideas are generated, shaped, and transmitted. *DLB* entries are not limited to "creative writers" but extend to other figures who in their time and in their way influenced the mind of a people. Thus the series encompasses historians, journalists, publishers, and screenwriters. By this means readers of *DLB* may be aided to perceive literature not as cult scripture in the keeping of intellectual high priests but firmly positioned at the center of a nation's life.

*From an unpublished section of Mark Twain's autobiography, copyright by the Mark Twain Company

DLB includes the major writers appropriate to each volume and those standing in the ranks immediately behind them. Scholarly and critical counsel has been sought in deciding which minor figures to include and how full their entries should be. Wherever possible, useful references are made to figures who do not warrant separate entries.

Each *DLB* volume has a volume editor responsible for planning the volume, selecting the figures for inclusion, and assigning the entries. Volume editors are also responsible for preparing, where appropriate, appendices surveying the major periodicals and literary and intellectual movements for their volumes, as well as lists of further readings. Work on the series as a whole is coordinated at the Bruccoli Clark Layman editorial center in Columbia, South Carolina, where the editorial staff is responsible for accuracy of the published volumes.

One feature that distinguishes *DLB* is the illustration policy – its concern with the iconography of literature. Just as an author is influenced by his surroundings, so is the reader's understanding of the author enhanced by a knowledge of his environment. Therefore *DLB* volumes include not only drawings, paintings, and photographs of authors, often depicting them at various stages in their careers, but also illustrations of their families and places where they lived. Title pages are regularly reproduced in facsimile along with dust jackets for modern authors. The dust jackets are a special feature of *DLB* because they often document better than anything else the way in which an author's work was perceived in its own time. Specimens of the writers' manuscripts are included when feasible.

Samuel Johnson rightly decreed that "The chief glory of every people arises from its authors." The purpose of the *Dictionary of Literary Biography* is to compile literary history in the surest way available to us – by accurate and comprehensive treatment of the lives and work of those who contributed to it.

The *DLB* Advisory Board

Foreword

The present *DLB* volume, *Old and Middle English Literature,* includes more than fifty entries covering a millennium of literary activity, from the coming of the Angles and the Saxons to England in 449 to about the year 1500. When I began helping with this project in December 1993, most of the material was already in. Jeffrey Helterman had assembled a wide range of essays written by an interestingly diverse group of scholars, some of them older and well established – recognized authorities in their field – and others younger, talented, and standing at the threshold of promising careers. I arranged for a few additional essays, and I wish to thank my colleagues at the University of Georgia and Edmund Reiss for agreeing on short notice to help out. I must also thank Perry T. Patterson, of the University of South Carolina, for reading and critiquing the original group of articles when Professor Helterman became ill. Patterson's queries and comments were invaluable in pinpointing problems that needed to be addressed.

The volume is divided along traditional lines into a smaller group of articles dealing with the Old English period, from the beginnings until the Norman Conquest, and the larger Middle English group beginning with the decades following the conquest and running until about 1500. Each period is preceded by a general introduction. Three articles that did not quite fit into this scheme are in the appendix. The organizational procedure in *Elizabethan Dramatists* (*DLB 62*) has suggested our subdivision of each group into two sections, the first dealing with medieval *authors* in alphabetical order and the second with *works,* when the author is unknown, also in alphabetical order.

As in other *DLB* volumes, the contributors to *Old and Middle English Literature* were requested to gear their work to a readership consisting in large part of advanced undergraduate and beginning graduate students. Not surprisingly, some deviation from this norm was inevitable in a collaborative effort involving fifty-six scholars. If students should find some of the pieces difficult or overly erudite, they will grow into them.

Although this book's title is *Old and Middle English Literature,* the literature of the British Isles during the Middle Ages was multilingual. The importance of Latin during the Old English period is illustrated here by Arthur G. Holder's essay on the Venerable Bede. After the Norman Conquest, French became equally prominent, and even as late as the fourteenth century, when French was beginning to decline, John Gower (Geoffrey Chaucer's "O moral Gower") played it safe with posterity by writing one major work in each of medieval England's three major languages. The importance of French is shown not only in Russell A. Peck's account of Gower's literary career but also in Daniel F. Pigg's essay on the chronicler Robert "Maistre" Wace. The continuing importance of Latin is attested by essays on Geoffrey of Monmouth's *Historia regum Britanniae* (circa 1138) and on John Wyclif, who wrote mainly in Latin. The Anglo-French and Anglo-Latin works discussed in this volume are in fact only a small part of a vast body of literature; Celtic literature must also be reckoned with, because the coming of the Angles and the Saxons did not bring Welsh or Irish literature suddenly to a halt. There is only one college textbook (still in print, fortunately) that presents the literary scene of medieval England as it really was, that is, as a multilingual endeavor: the late D. W. Robertson's *The Literature of Medieval England* (1970).

Except for the important authors just mentioned, the present book does not give detailed attention to individual authors who wrote in French and Latin (or in Welsh or Irish); the emphasis here is on the English literature. The appendixes, however, include general essays on the Celtic and the French influences, and the reader will be aware of various connections. Bede's *Historia ecclesiastica gentis Anglorum* was translated in King Alfred's time into the West Saxon dialect of Old English. Geoffrey of Monmouth purports that he translated his *Historia regum Britanniae* from "a certain very ancient book in the British language" – presumably from Welsh. Wace based his *Le Roman de Brut* (1155) on Geoffrey's *Historia,* and this in turn was the basis for Laȝamon's early Middle English *Brut* (circa 1189–1205). The late-fourteenth-century English lay *Sir Launfal* derives principally from the "Lanval" of Marie de France (who wrote in French in England), and the story has its ultimate roots in a lay recited by some minstrel of Little Britain (Brittany) but never written down in its original language, Breton, which was (and is) closely related to Welsh. The well-known story of the knight and the loathly lady – best represented in late medieval English by Chaucer's "Wife of Bath's Tale," Gower's "Tale of Florent and the Loathly Hag," and "The Wedding of Sir Gawain and Dame Ragnell" – has its roots in Irish legendry.

The essays that follow present a comprehensive picture of Old and Middle English literature in its broader literary and cultural setting. Some neglect, however, of individual poems and authors has been inevitable in a volume that covers one thousand years of literary production. While *The Wanderer, The Seafarer, Caedmon's Hymn, The Fight at Finnsburg,* and other shorter Old English poems receive ample discussion, the reader will not find separate discussions of such poems as *The Ruin, Deor* (or *Deor's Lament*), *The Wife's Lament,* and *The Husband's Message,* although Jonathan Evans touches on some of these in his introduction to the Old English period. While one will find essays on the Breton lays and the so-called Matter of England and Matter of Rome romances, there is no separate account of the Matter of France romances. While the mystical works of Richard Rolle, Walter Hilton, Julian of Norwich, and even Margery Kempe receive ample coverage, there is no separate essay on *The Cloud of Unknowing.* On the other hand, there are entries on interesting authors who are seldom taught or even read, such as John Barbour and John Mirk; and older scholars who peruse this book may be surprised at not only the space allotted to Thomas Hoccleve and John Lydgate but also the sympathetic evaluations of their poetry. This *DLB* volume contains a wealth and variety of material that should satisfy almost any reader's desire for pleasure and profit, for "myrthe and solas." " 'Tis sufficient to say according to the proverb," to quote John Dryden on Chaucer's *Canterbury Tales* (circa 1375–1400), "that here is God's plenty."

A few words about mechanical matters seem in order. Quotations from the Middle English writers treated here are usually in the original language, and they are taken from specified standard editions, with translations of hard words and phrases provided either by the author of the article or by the editors. However, for writers from the early Middle English period and for those who wrote in a difficult dialect of Middle English, translations have been more heavily relied upon and in some cases are used almost entirely, as in William McColly's article on the *Gawain*-Poet. These translations are cited in the text of the article. (When they are not specified, the reader can assume they are the author's.) A similar procedure has been used for the articles on Old English writers, although here the translations are more frequent because of the obvious difficulty of the language. Again

the quoted translations are cited in the article, and if none is specified it is usually the author's. In articles dealing with Anglo-Norman writers, and especially with Latin and Welsh writers, translations are quoted almost to the exclusion of the original languages. In most instances a well-known standard translation is used and is clearly specified, as in Elissa Henken's article on the Celtic background; but sometimes the author (for example, Jane Dick Zatta) has provided the translations. All procedures regarding quotations and translations have been set up and followed primarily for the convenience of readers of this volume, our goal being to give readers an idea of the flavor of the original languages but at the same time to remove, through translations, any barrier to the understanding.

– Jerome Mitchell

Acknowledgments

This book was produced by Bruccoli Clark Layman, Inc. Karen L. Rood is senior editor for the *Dictionary of Literary Biography* series. Sam Bruce was the in-house editor.

Production coordinator is George F. Dodge. Photography editors are Bruce Andrew Bowlin and Josephine A. Bruccoli. The photographic copy work was performed by Joseph M. Bruccoli. Layout and graphics supervisor is Penney L. Haughton. Copyediting supervisor is Bill Adams. Typesetting supervisor is Kathleen M. Flanagan. Julie E. Frick is editorial associate. The production staff includes Phyllis A. Avant, Ann M. Cheschi, Melody W. Clegg, Patricia Coate, Wilma Weant Dague, Brigitte B. de Guzman, Denise W. Edwards, Sarah A. Estes, Joyce Fowler, Laurel M. Gladden, Mendy Gladden, Stephanie C. Hatchell, Leslie Haynesworth, Rebecca Mayo, Kathy Lawler Merlette, Pamela D. Norton, Delores I. Plastow, Patricia F. Salisbury, and William L. Thomas, Jr.

Walter W. Ross, Deborah M. Chasteen, and Robert S. McConnell did library research. They were assisted by the following librarians at the Thomas Cooper Library of the University of South Carolina: Linda Holderfield and the interlibrary-loan staff; reference librarians Gwen Baxter, Daniel Boice, Faye Chadwell, Cathy Eckman, Gary Geer, Qun "Gerry" Jiao, Jean Rhyne, Carol Tobin, Carolyn Tyler, Virginia Weathers, Elizabeth Whiznant, and Connie Widney; circulation-department head Thomas Marcil; and acquisitions-searching supervisor David Haggard.

A Note on the Early English Text Society (EETS)

Most of the articles in this book refer to various Old and Middle English works that have been published by the Early English Text Society, a distinguished, indispensable British series aptly described in a recent list of the society's publications:

The Early English Text Society was founded in 1864 by Frederick James Furnivall, with the help of Richard Morris, Walter Skeat and others, to bring the mass of unprinted Early English literature within the reach of students and to provide sound texts from which the New English Dictionary [now the Oxford English Dictionary] could quote. In 1867 an Extra Series was started of texts already printed but not in satisfactory or readily obtainable editions. In 1921 the Extra Series was discontinued and all publications were subsequently listed and numbered as part of the Original Series. In 1970 the first of a new Supplementary Series was published; unlike the Extra Series, volumes in this series [are] issued only occasionally, as funds allow and as suitable texts become available.

In the nineteenth century the volumes were published in London by N. Trübner or by Kegan Paul, Trench, Trübner and Company. Since about 1915 the publisher has been the Oxford University Press (London and/or Oxford), which has also reprinted many of the older issues, especially when corrections and additions have been made. Other older issues have been reprinted photographically, with authorization of the society, by the Kraus Reprint Company of Milwood, New York.

In order to avoid excessive repetition, most references to this well-known series have been given in an abbreviated form: the Early English Text Society as EETS, the original series as o.s., and the extra series as e.s. Only a few volumes have appeared in the supplementary series, and those that are cited here are clearly indicated as such. If no indication as to which series is given, there is none in the volume itself, and the reader can assume that the original series is meant; in such cases the date of publication is recent, that is, long after the discontinuation of the extra series (in 1921).

A typical citation, then, will read: *The Works of John Metham,* edited by Hardin Craig, EETS, o.s. 132 (1916; reprinted, Kraus, 1973).

Dictionary of Literary Biography® • Volume One Hundred Forty-Six

Old and Middle English Literature

Dictionary of Literary Biography

Old English Literature: An Introduction

Jonathan Evans
University of Georgia

In broad terms the phrase "Old English literature" designates the entire literary output of the inhabitants of England from the first permanent Anglo-Saxon settlements in the fifth century until the demise of Anglo-Saxon culture in the twelfth. The history of this literature began with the composition of the first Anglo-Saxon poem in the British Isles by a permanent Germanic-speaking inhabitant of England; it ended when the last Anglo-Saxon poet died. However, several caveats must be discussed before the overview of Old English literature that follows may be accurately understood. First, precise dates for the beginning and ending of the Old English period are difficult to set; second, the linguistic medium in which Old English literature was composed is not a unitary one; finally, the term *literature* is subject to a variety of definitions.

Exact dates cannot easily be assigned to the beginning of this epoch in English literary history. The traditional date for the beginning of the Anglo-Saxon period of English political history is A.D. 449, the year the Venerable Bede says Anglo-Saxon invaders first entered the island and established permanent settlements. Although Bede was the first English scholar to employ modern historiographic standards, it is nonetheless the case that he could not have known precisely when the first significant Anglo-Saxon migrations occurred. Bede had to rely upon a combination of oral and written popular tradition for knowledge of this series of events. He could not have known for sure that the names he associates with the initial influx of Germanic warriors — two brothers, Hengest and Horsa — refer to actual persons; nor could he be certain that 449 is the exact year in which this influx began. Symbolic martial implications of the name Horsa and the ap-

pearance of a literary character named Hengest in an episode in *Beowulf* cast doubt upon the objective historicity of the account Bede transmits to posterity. Further, recently unearthed archeological findings — primarily grave sites and remains of permanent dwellings — indicate that continental Germanic ethnic groups began arriving in England in fairly large numbers at least several decades before the traditional mid-fifth-century date.

Though the beginnings of Old English literature and Anglo-Saxon political history are both technically undatable, the end point of Anglo-Saxon history can be dated precisely to A.D. 1066, when Duke William "the Bastard" of Normandy mounted a successful military campaign against the English crown, destroying forever the royal aspirations of the noble house of Wessex and the descendants of King Alfred the Great. More precisely, on Saturday, 14 October 1066, sometime after 5:00 P.M., King Harold II died in battle against the Norman invasionary force. And although this military event, the Battle of Hastings, marks the beginning of the end of literary activity in England which can be labeled properly Old English, it would not be correct to say that Old English literature ceased to be composed, recited, or written down in that year. The arrival of Norman French feudal aristocracy permanently altered the political, religious, and cultural life of England; the great tradition of Germanic literature, legend, and folklore that flourished among the Anglo-Saxons was in the end utterly supplanted by material originating in regions of western Europe dominated by the Romance languages and their associated cultures and mythologies. But this process of displacement did not occur suddenly, and speakers of Old English continued to compose literature in their native idiom for many decades after the Norman Conquest, despite the sometimes harsh rule of their French overlords. This literary activity, still essentially Old English both in language and in cultural tradition, continued well into the twelfth century and, technically speaking, ceased only when the last Anglo-Saxon poet breathed the last syllable, or wrote the final letter, of the last poem composed in Old English. In this sense, although the end of Anglo-Saxon England's political history can be precisely delimited, the end of its literary history – much like its beginnings – cannot.

A second problematic issue, related to the first, is that of the linguistic medium in which Old English literature was composed. Currently it is normal to apply the term *Old English* to the earliest phase in the history of the English language, reserving the term *Anglo-Saxon* for matters of political and cultural history. The Old English language was a group of closely associated dialects originating in the coastal regions of southern Jutland, northwestern Germany, and the Low Countries and carried to the British Isles in the fifth century by Germanic settlers – identified by Bede as the Angles, Saxons, and Jutes. These dialects were spoken and written in England until the early twelfth century, when the linguistic effects of the Norman Conquest began to be widely felt. The influence primarily of French but also of the Scandinavian dialects used by Viking settlers mostly in the northeastern portion of the island ultimately produced changes wide enough in scope to mark the beginnings of the second period in English linguistic history – that of Middle English; but even in the Old English period, variations in the language were sufficiently marked to allow the identification of four main Old English dialects: Kentish, Northumbrian, Mercian, and West Saxon. Although literary remains in all four dialects survive, it is in West Saxon, thanks to King Alfred, that the most important and by far the most extensive literature from this period has come down to the modern era. There are notable exceptions: Bede, writing in the eighth century, included Boclæden (scholarly Latin) among the languages of Britain, and much has been preserved in Latin that might earn the valuative term *literary;* literature in medieval Welsh and Scots Gaelic, the languages of the Celtic inhabitants of Britain, also survives. Finally, a select group of Old English prose texts, translated from Latin originals, render their exemplars with varying degrees of faithfulness; while they might not seem to belong to the Old English literary tradition per se, the Old English interpolations and the aesthetic attributes of these texts

sometimes qualify them as genuine contributions to the literature of the Anglo-Saxon period.

A third caveat has to do with the exact designation of the term *literature.* Arguably, the early Anglo-Saxons did not think of themselves as possessing a literature at all. A good deal of poetry – most of it oral in origin – has survived; but traditional oral poetry in preliterate cultures is typically regarded as history, genealogy, encyclopedia, magic, and religious ritual but not as literature in the modern, popular, aesthetic sense. Before the Roman Catholic mission to England in A.D. 597, the Germanic inhabitants of England were for the most part pagan and illiterate. Only with the arrival of Roman Christianity, with its administrative penchant for the keeping of records (for example, births, christenings, baptisms, deeds, and wills) and for the dissemination of sacred writing (Holy Scripture, biblical commentary, sermons, liturgy, saints' lives, and church history), was the need for a writing system thought significant. Monastic and royal scriptoria emerged to meet this need; a direct, early result was the composition of written legal codes harmonizing oral Germanic law with written Christian teaching. A secondary, almost accidental result was the creation and preservation of manuscripts in genres which modern readers would regard as literary. Not until the time of Geoffrey Chaucer did English writers think of vernacular poetry as literature in the classical sense, and not until the Renaissance was prose regarded seriously in England as a suitable mode for literary composition.

Anglo-Saxon England, however, was a culture in transition from orality to literacy, and later in this period some people, especially scholars, probably possessed a conceptual category for *literature.* Most modern students and scholars associate this category almost exclusively with the great monuments of Old English poetry, including *The Dream of the Rood, The Wanderer, The Battle of Maldon,* and preeminently *Beowulf* – indeed, the poems most often anthologized for undergraduate study. The fact that these and other poems were recorded by the Anglo-Saxons at all surely indicates something of an appreciation for native poetry even on the part of ecclesiastical professionals. But indigenous prejudices privileged poetry over prose for artistic composition, while scholarly prejudices promoted by monastic learning recognized Latin alone as the language of literature, with an implied opposition between vernacular poetic discourse and the Latin prose of such genres as history, liturgy, biblical commentary, and hagiography. In addition to the extant poetic corpus a great many poems were probably composed and performed orally but never committed to more permanent forms of discourse; of that which was recorded in durable media – mainly parchment but also, marginally, wood, bone, and stone – no doubt much has been lost. But no Old English poem makes reference to any other poem whether extant or lost; even *Beowulf* is mentioned nowhere else in prose or poetry and lacks any traceable source. One may surmise, then, that there was no contemporary scholarly conception of a native Old English literary tradition; the poetry collections that do survive may seem more like antiquarian curiosities than living contributions to an active tradition.

Enough manuscript evidence has survived into the modern period, though, to give an accurate sense of what Old English written literature was and, vestigially, still is: primarily prose. Regardless of precisely what writers and their audiences in this period considered literary, there are, not only in the poetry but also in the prose of Anglo-Saxon England, recognizable attributes that modern readers would associate readily with the term *literature*. King Alfred's ninth-century translation of Boethius's *De consolatione philosophiae* (circa A.D. 525), for example, includes the earliest English version of the Greek legend of Orpheus and Euridice. The otherwise terse, dry prose of the *Anglo-Saxon Chronicle* includes an episode in the annal for A.D. 755 that is regarded by some as the first short story in the English language. The language of some passages of the Old English version of Bede's *Historia ecclesiastica gentis Anglorum* (Ecclesiastical History of the English People, A.D. 731) is poetic in tone, particularly in the story of the conversion of King Edwin of Northumbria. And it is this same prose history which includes the first account of an English poet, his poetic career, and a rendering of his first poem: *Caedmon's Hymn*.

The preserved record of Old English literature is not particularly extensive. In his *Catalogue of Manuscripts Containing Anglo-Saxon* (1957), N. R. Ker says the number of manuscripts surviving from this period and written mainly or entirely in Old English is "less than 150, including fragments." Adding such categories as Latin/Old English glossaries, Latin texts with complete translation into Old English, and Latin manuscripts with substantial Old English glosses, "the total is still short of 200. In fact more than half the manuscripts containing OE are Latin manuscripts in which the OE takes the form of brief records or notes or of more or less numerous interlinear glosses." Of the 448 manuscripts written prior to A.D. 1200 containing any Old English material at all, only 189 are

regarded as significant. Of these, 125 are devoted largely or entirely to ecclesiastical matters, 42 of which are largely if not exclusively homiletic. The remaining 64 manuscripts are taken up with various subject matters including glossaries, history, law, and trivia such as recipes, herbals, and grammar. In the surviving Old English written record prose is by far the dominant genre of composition. Among the smallest categories of writing represented in the extant manuscripts is that of poetry; four manuscripts alone contain the bulk of Old English poetry: Cotton Vitellius A.xv – *Beowulf;* Oxford, Bodleian Library MS. Junius 11 (5123) – the *Junius* manuscript; Exeter, Cathedral 3501, fols. 8–130 – *The Exeter Book;* and Vercelli, Biblioteca Capitolare CXVII – *The Vercelli Book.*

Regardless of how the manuscript evidence is classified, the Christian doctrinal preoccupations of Old English literature are apparent. By far the largest genre of Old English prose – indeed, of any writing in Old English – is that of the homilies: sermons. Two sermon writers, Wulfstan and especially Ælfric, are highly esteemed as the supreme prose stylists of the Anglo-Saxon period. Ælfric (circa 955–circa 1010) wrote two cycles of homilies designated for use on specific occasions in the penitential and festal seasons of the Christian year, drawing material from a wide variety of mostly Latin sources. His sermons on the Epiphany, the Greater Litany, and the Resurrection are especially highly regarded. Ælfric also composed an extensive cycle of saints' lives written in a rhythmic style modern scholars describe as metrical prose.

Wulfstan's homiletic corpus consists of twenty-one extant sermons. The early homilies are primarily millenarian and eschatological; in the *Sermo lupi ad Anglos* (Sermon of the Wolf to the English), written in 1014, Wulfstan bewails the decrepit state of English morals and spirituality and ascribes the recent upsurge in Danish Viking depredations to the judgment of an offended righteous God. His listing of the English people's offenses is long and colorful. Wulfstan's later work focuses on the sacraments and on practical Christian living.

In addition to the work of these two homilists, a number of anonymous sermons, including the Blickling, Vespasian, Bodley, and Vercelli homilies, survive from the religious life of Anglo-Saxon England. While this category of Old English literature is sometimes neglected in favor of the poetry and the more accessible prose texts, a recent renewal of scholarly attention to the homilies suggests the rise of a more appreciative opinion not only of these sermons' religious and spiritual importance but also of their literary value.

Historical prose, with the exception of the *Anglo-Saxon Chronicle,* is represented for the most part by translations and reworkings of Latin texts. Bede, the most important scholar in England – indeed, in all Europe – in the early eighth century, made the anno Domini system of historical reckoning universal in European culture and sought to move historiography beyond the level of hearsay and popular tradition upon which his predecessors largely depended. Bede attempted to write scholarly, objective history based upon documented sources and eyewitness accounts when possible, cross-checking sources against one another whenever he could. His *Historia ecclesiastica gentis Anglorum* situates English history, especially religious history, in a larger worldwide and cosmic context but emphasizes in the latter portion of that work local events in his own native Northumbria. Passages notable for literary value include Bede's account of Augustine's mission to England in A.D. 597 and the conversion of King Æthelberht of Kent; his accounts of the poet Caedmon and the life of Saint Cuthbert; and the conversion of the Northumbrian king Edwin. Bede's idyllic opening description of the island of Britain sounds like a travel brochure and has been regarded as a conscious attempt to represent England as an Edenic paradise in which Christ's Holy Church would flourish; at the same time, with sobering realism he recounts the miseries wrought upon the earlier Celtic inhabitants by the advancing Anglo-Saxons in the fifth century. The tone of the passage is almost elegiac; the account of Edwin's conversion, which describes human life as a sparrow flying through a lighted hall in winter, achieves an aesthetic beauty in prose equal to the finest elegies in Old English poetry.

Of particular interest to students of Old English literature is a handful of works translated from Latin originals by or at the behest of King Alfred. In his preface to the West Saxon version of the *Cura pastoralis* of Gregory the Great, Alfred bemoans the sorry state of learning in ninth-century England and presents an apologia for his decision to translate several books he considers "niedbeðearfosta . . . eallum monnum to wiotonne" (most needful for all people to know). The surviving collection of Latin texts translated and disseminated under Alfred's royal auspices constitutes a small "library of the classics" and includes the *Cura pastoralis,* the *De consolatione philosophiae* of Boethius, the *Soliloquium* of Saint Augustine, the *Dialogues* of Gregory the Great, and the *Historiarum adversum paganos* of Paulus Oro-

sius. Alfred's prefaces to these works are notable compositions in their own right, and they reveal the subtle fusion of intellectual, political, and spiritual concerns which are the hallmark of his reign. In his preface to Augustine's *Soliloquium,* Alfred develops an extended metaphor describing at once his compositional technique, his intellectual agenda, and an orientation toward future spiritual fulfillment that is representative of the sum of Old English literature. There Alfred likens his studies to the labors of a carpenter/woodcutter gathering sticks, staves, tool handles, and framing timbers in order to "construct many fine houses and build a beautiful homestead out of them, so that [one] can live there pleasantly and comfortably both in winter and summer." Intellectual labor, he implies, should result in knowledge and understanding that real people can actually work with and "live in." Alfred frames this humanistic goal in a larger, spiritual context: "A man is pleased, when he has built a cottage on his landlord's property, and with his help, to be able to rest a while therein and go hunting, fowling, and fishing, and to occupy himself in various ways there both at sea and on land until such time as he earns deeded land and inherited property by the mercy of his lord. So will the Bountiful Giver do, who rules both this transitory dwelling-place and the eternal home. May He who is both Creator and Ruler grant that I may be suited to both: to be useful in this world and indeed to arrive in the next." The rich texture of images interwoven in this passage compares favorably to the metaphysical conceits of such poets as John Donne and Richard Crashaw some eight centuries later and epitomizes the twofold orientation – human and divine – of Old English literature.

Yet, despite the undoubted power of much Old English prose, the heart of Old English literature as it has been traditionally regarded resides in its poetry. In this more narrow sense the history of Old English literature begins with an unknown and unknowable event: the recitation of the first Anglo-Saxon poem in the British Isles by a permanent Germanic-speaking resident of England. Who this poet was, what the poem's subject was, when it was uttered, and in what dialect of Old English it was composed have not been recorded, although fruitful guesses can be made. The first Old English poetic utterance probably occurred sometime in the first half of the fifth century A.D., in all likelihood in the eastern portion of England, probably Kent, and the subject was probably either heroic, commemorating the exploits of a legendary hero under whose inspiration Germanic mercenaries won a local military victory, or perhaps elegiac, lamenting a military defeat. The fact that a probably legendary Jutish warlord named Hengest is associated with Anglo-Saxon settlers in Kent and that an identically named character appears as a Jutish military leader in *Beowulf* just before the Anglo-Saxon migration suggests that he or similar figures may well have furnished the inspiration for early poetry. Other likely figures of foundation legends in early Anglo-Saxon poems include Cerdic and Cynric, the legendary progenitors of the West Saxon dynasty and Germanic counterparts to the legendary Welsh defender against Anglo-Saxon expansion in the fifth century, King Arthur. Offa, a king of the Angles prior to the migrations and a legendary ancestor of both the East Anglian and Mercian royal dynasties, also appears in *Beowulf* and might have offered a suitable subject for this genre. Such speculations, however, resist verification and are perhaps best eschewed in favor of ascertainable, documentary evidence.

As indicated above, the number of manuscripts devoted largely or exclusively to poetry is exceedingly small: *The Exeter Book, The Vercelli Book,* the *Junius* manuscript, and the *Beowulf* manuscript. Of these only the first two contain poetry alone. In these four manuscripts there are 140 poems, with another 45 scattered among prose texts in the rest of the manuscript corpus (excluding 129 translations and fragments of the Psalms). Six of these are entered as poetic annals in various manuscripts of the *Anglo-Saxon Chronicle*. The sum of the entire corpus of Old English poems from whatever sources comes to a scant six volumes, including introductory apparatus and textual commentary, in a modern printed format.

Old English poetry depends upon four main features of verbal patterning for aesthetic effects: stress, alliteration, compounding, and variation in repetition. Like most poetry from the Middle English period onward, Old English poems employ rhythmic arrangements of stressed or accented syllables. But, unlike post-Conquest poetic meters, Old English does not rigidly regulate the number or arrangement of unstressed syllables. The normal Old English poetic line contains four stressed syllables divided by a caesura into two half lines. These two half lines are linked by means of alliteration: the initial sound of the first stressed syllable in the second half line (the root of the Old English poetic line) is also used initially in at least one stressed syllable in the first half line. All vowels and diphthongs alliterate with each other; consonants alliterate only with identical consonants. Within these restrictions, combinations of alliterative patterns and stressed

and unstressed syllables are possible; Old English poems with relative frequency also employ both hypermetric and (more rarely) hypometric lines – lines in which stressed syllables number, respectively, more or less than four.

Common figures of speech based upon underlying similarity of meaning include the epithet and the kenning. The epithet expresses an underlying concept by overt reference to one or more of its attributes: for example, Christ is "Godes sunu" (the "Son of God"). The kenning is produced by compounding two separate words (generally two nouns or a noun and an adjective) into a new linguistic unit in which the relationship between the concept and the verbal compound expressing it is metaphorical and covert: the sea as a *hronrade* (whale pathway); Viking warriors as *wælwulfas* (slaughter wolves). An essentially metaphorical poetic figure, occurring in twelve instances in nine different heroic poems, is the so-called beasts of battle motif in which the wolf, raven, and eagle – carrion-feeding animals – either foreshadow the outbreak of battle or symbolize its fatal consequences for human beings. Another device is litotes, or dramatic understatement: "no need to boast" for "reason to mourn"; "with few companions" for "alone."

Finally, variation in repetition expands the semantic field of a given concept by expressing it in several different ways. In *Caedmon's Hymn,* for example, the concept of the deity is built up and expanded through eight different epithets in which God is described as *heofonrices weard; metod; wuldorfæder; ece dryhten; halig scyppend; moncynnes weard;* and *frea ælmihtig* (guardian of heaven-kingdom; measurer; father of glory; eternal lord; holy shaper; guardian of mankind; and God almighty). F. P. Magoun and others have described Old English poetic tradition as "oral-formulaic," possessing a common stock of words and phrases from which poets could draw freely, combining and inserting them as the exigencies of oral composition required. This creative technique could be said to lie somewhere between memorized recitation and extemporaneous composition. Donald K. Fry has identified common "type-scenes" belonging to the underlying narrative grammar of Old English literary tradition and expressed in divergent verbal terms across the range of Old English narrative poetry. Scholars also have pointed to poetic structures of interlace and ring composition as verbal analogues of the serpentine patterning characteristic of Anglo-Saxon decorative art.

The thematic preoccupations of Anglo-Saxon poets are similar to those of the prose writers. Some sixty of the extant poems are written on explicitly religious themes, including biblical narrative, saints' lives, metrical versions of creeds, and prayers; most of the rest either contain allusions and references to Christian doctrine or, lacking such, embrace a decidedly Christian, Catholic, and monastic worldview. *Beowulf,* for example, while otherwise entirely Scandinavian and pre-Christian in setting and plot, refers nonetheless to the Genesis account of Cain and Abel and the flood of Noah; the great elegies *The Wanderer* and *The Seafarer* include moralizing epilogues that are explicitly Christian in theology and doctrine. Even *Deor's Lament,* which refers exclusively to pagan Scandinavian legendary exempla and makes no biblical or Christian doctrinal allusions, seems to evoke Boethian philosophy, which in turn has often been regarded as Christian, in light of Boethius's other overtly Christian and theological works.

Setting aside speculations concerning its lost oral beginnings, Old English literature might be said to begin with the first recorded poem in the English language, the earliest poem preserved in the earliest manuscript or manuscript tradition. That poem, by scholarly agreement titled *Caedmon's Hymn,* sets the religious agenda for the rest of Old English poetry. A great many Old English poems are reworkings of biblical and hagiographic narrative, exploring not abstract theology, but rather the concrete doctrines of the Christian faith to which all Anglo-Saxon believers, cleric or layperson, simple or sophisticated, may be supposed to have subscribed. Attempting to redirect the earlier emphasis on patristic exegesis promoted in Old English studies by R. E. Kaske, John Gardner, Bernard F. Huppé and others, Judith N. Garde argues in *Old English Poetry in Medieval Christian Perspective: A Doctrinal Approach* (1991), "The poetry does not reflect abstract theology. It might better be understood as an extra-liturgical, vernacular celebration of a singular redemptive fact: that Almighty God chose to descend, incarnate in Christ, to deliver mankind from the bondage of Satan.... " The subjects treated in Caedmon's poetic career, said by Bede to comprehend all of sacred history from Creation to Last Judgment, though all of it is lost except the first poem, serve also as a summary of the whole corpus of Old English religious verse. *Genesis, Exodus,* and *Daniel* in the Junius manuscript expand upon Old Testament narratives in an exegetical tradition emphasizing typological relations between the old Abrahamic covenant and the new covenant in Christ; *Christ and Satan* presents an account of the rebellion and fall of the angels similar to the Miltonic treatment in *Paradise Lost* (1667, 1674); it also describes the harrowing of hell, an apocryphal favorite in medieval literature, and the temptation of Christ in the wilderness – again, the subject of a poem by John Milton, *Paradise Regained* (1671). The Advent, Ascension, and Last Judgment are narrated in three poems from *The Exeter Book: Christ I, Christ II,* and *Christ III,* respectively. The Crucifixion is fully narrated only in *The Dream of the Rood,* a poem from *The Vercelli Book,* and the Resurrection is treated in *Descent into Hell.* In *The Fates of the Apostles,* based on apocryphal material, Cynewulf recounts the apostolic missions and eventual deaths of the twelve apostles of Christ; though the poem is probably mnemonic in intention, its poet also derives consolation from this record of apostolic courage in the face of death. Other apocryphal subjects include those of *Judith,* which treats the Old Testament story (noncanonical, but thought authoritative by the Anglo-Saxons) of Judith's murder and decapitation of the monstrous tyrant Holofernes; *Juliana,* based on a Latin vita of the virgin martyr; *Andreas,* detailing the apostle Andrew's tortures at the hands of the Myrmidonians, and *Elene,* which describes Saint Helen's recovery of the holy cross from concealment in Jerusalem. Cynewulf, the only other Anglo-Saxon poet besides Caedmon (and, nominally, King Alfred) whose name is known, wrote four of these poems (*Fates, Christ II, Juliana,* and *Elene*); his authorship is identified only through the runic acrostics with which the poet signed his works. In a touching autobiographical conclusion to *Elene,* the elderly Cynewulf recounts with elegiac potency his conversion and its salutary effects upon his poetic craft.

Besides biblical and hagiographic narratives, three thematic categories dominate Old English poetry: the heroic, the elegiac, and the gnomic. The specific themes that find expression in this poetry explore positively and negatively the extent and limitations of martial prowess, courage, loyalty, and sacrifice; the transitory nature of earthly wealth, power, and pleasure and the universality of loss; and the value of both existential and spiritual wisdom. These themes seldom occur in pure form but interweave and interplay throughout the Anglo-Saxon poetic record.

The heroic code of ancient Germanic warrior society is implicit in such poems as *The Battle of Maldon, The Battle of Brunanburh,* the surviving lines of *The Fight at Finnsburg,* and fragments of a longer heroic lay, *Waldere. The Battle of Brunanburh* celebrates a decisive battle in A.D. 937 in which Athelstan and Edmund, grandsons of King Alfred, won victory over a confederacy of foreign invaders. Said by the poet to be the greatest battle on English soil since the Anglo-Saxon conquest, it also represents one of the last great victories for the noble house of Wessex, whose long defeat was finalized some one hundred and thirty years later at Hastings. *The Battle of Maldon* recounts the course of a battle in Essex in A.D. 991 and contains perhaps the most concise verbal evocation of the heroic code in Old English. In a battle of defense against a large force of Viking marauders, the surviving warriors of the fallen ealdorman Byrhtnoth mount a desperate last stand, encouraging each other to fulfill their earlier vows against retreat. However, their leader's death and the treacherous flight of several cowards betray the remnant into the hands of their attackers; the Anglo-Saxons lose this battle and are massacred. *The Battle of Maldon* celebrates at once both tragic courage and a glorious defeat.

Poems in which the elegiac mode dominates include *The Wanderer, The Seafarer, The Ruin,* and a handful of others reflecting upon the universal experience of loss. These three poems together present a unified vision of the tragic implications of founding a society upon the heroic ethos. In a stirring *ubi sunt* (where are?) passage, *The Wanderer* laments the loss of horse, rider, treasure, and the pleasures of hall life to "weapons greedy of slaughter." Similarly, *The Seafarer* finds the gauds and pomp of aristocratic city life insufficient consolation for the sufferings of exile and the sorrows of death. In *The Ruin,* ironically a damaged text, the poet — probably viewing decayed Roman buildings in the city of Bath — reflects on the mutability of earthly empires and the proud rulers, gleaming in war gear, who people them. *The Wanderer* commends stoic resignation and a prudent reluctance to make rash vows; *The Seafarer* values moderation and humility in the face of inevitable death. Both derive consolation from knowledge of the Lord in heaven, who alone is immutable.

Gnomic verse, or wisdom poetry, in Old English consists of two collections of aphorisms on the nature of the cosmos (*Maxims I* in *The Exeter Book* and *Maxims II* in Cotton Tiberius B.i); a collection of some ninety-five riddles in *The Exeter Book,* and others. *Beowulf* is full of lines that have been identified as gnomic, or aphoristic. *The Rune Poem* is mnemonic in intention, versifying and giving the meaning of the *futhorc*, the Germanic runic alphabet; *Widsith* recounts the extensive travels of a court poet, giving a long list — probably also a mnemonic device — of the kings, tribes, and emperors he has served. Other poems discussed by Nicholas Howe

in this catalogue tradition include *The Menelogium, The Gifts of Men, The Fortunes of Men,* and *Precepts.* Several Old English translations of the Latin *Distichs of Cato* also survive.

Beyond the intrinsic value of biblical and hagiographic narrative and the heroic, elegiac, and gnomic attitudes preserved in Old English poetry, the subtle interweaving of these themes is sometimes achieved with interesting effect. In *Elene,* for example, the traditional imagery and oral formulas of heroic poetry are adapted to the frankly caustic evangelistic mission of Saint Helen to Jerusalem: Helen's companions are equipped for warfare though they exchange no blows; she herself is described as a *guðcwene* (war queen) even though her battles are rhetorical, not physical. In *The Dream of the Rood,* Christ is called a *hæleð* (young warrior), and his self-sacrifice is presented as a heroic one in which the Hero hastens as if to battle, mounts the cross as if it were a war horse, and then, in the grave, rests after his victorious struggle. The elegies include gnomic reflections on the pagan heroic tradition but point the reader toward a Christian deity. Many other instances of overlapping themes could be cited.

In its 3,182 lines *Beowulf* is the longest Old English poem extant, containing fully 10 percent of the surviving corpus. Its complex interweaving of heroic battle, rich banqueting, mournful lament, and inspiring words of proverbial wisdom, written in a frame of understanding that is unmistakably Christian yet sensitively reticent of overt sermonizing, make it something of an omnibus of many of Old English poetry's most important themes and styles. The poem defies simple generic classification and is perhaps best described as a heroic-elegiac epic. In "*Beowulf:* The Monsters and the Critics" (1936) J. R. R. Tolkien describes its main plot — the young Beowulf's victorious fights against two troll-like monsters and the elderly hero's successful but fatal dragon fight — as "a contrasted description of two moments in a great life, rising and setting; an elaboration of the ancient and intensely moving contrast between youth and age, first achievement and final death." This simple structure is set against a legendary background drawn from a once-rich stock of heroic lays of which *Widsith* and *Deor's Lament* gives only a glimpse. Tolkien regards Beowulf not as "the hero of an heroic lay, precisely. He has no enmeshed loyalties, nor hapless love. *He is a man, and that for him and many is sufficient tragedy.*" The theme is less heroic, says Tolkien, than elegiac: "*lif is læne: eal scæceð leoht and lif somod* [life is transitory: light and life together hasten away].... Its author is still concerned primarily with *man on earth*, rehandling in a new perspective an ancient theme: that man, each man and all men, and all their works shall die. A theme no Christian need despise." Tolkien notes "an intense emotion of regret" in the poem; as "the poet looks back into the past, surveying the history of kings and warriors in the old traditions, he sees that all glory (or as we might say 'culture' or 'civilization') ends in night."

The *Beowulf* poet, undoubtedly a Christian but still an Anglo-Saxon and a product of his age, sees the heroic tradition of his culture's past with a double vision. Much as a Chaucer looks to the ancient Mediterranean world for examples of pagan nobility with which his medieval Christianity might agree, the writer of *Beowulf* looks to the northern world for examples of Germanic excellence. He venerates the heroic tradition's cultivation of courage, loyalty, and noble sacrifice; yet he cannot escape its tragic effects in bloodshed and death. His is a higher calling. A jewel-encrusted sword glittering in firelight in a noble hall attracts his aesthetic admiration; yet the mortal purpose for which swords are forged cannot be forgotten, and in the end this poet seems to turn away sadly from the heroic tradition, to which this poem is an elegiac memorial.

Old English poets sometimes display self-conscious awareness of the nature and implications of poetic composition normally associated with more-recent poetic theory. *Caedmon's Hymn,* for example, casts the divine Creator in the role of a "halig Scyppend" (holy Shaper) who "sceop" (shaped) heaven and adorned earth for the enjoyment of humankind, suggesting an etymological affinity between divine and human creativity. Anglo-Saxon poets were called *scopas* (shapers), and their poetic creativity evokes that of the divine Creator; in the Stoic/Christian philosophical tradition the Logos creates the universe, which can be seen as God's material poem.

The poet of *Deor's Lament* looks for consolation to the wealth of Germanic legend that has been his stock in trade as a *scop;* the solace he derives and the sentiments of the refrain "þæs ofereode, þisses swa mæg" (that passed away; this also may) seem closely akin to the Boethian theme of *consolatio,* though in this instance it is *De consolatione poesiae* rather than *philosophiae.* Another reflection on the role of the poet and the consolations of poetry occurs in *Widsith,* in which the *scop* derives solace by reciting his fabulous career throughout all the eminent courts of the Western world across a span of centuries.

The *Beowulf* poet places some of his most important thematic passages in the mouth of Hrothgar's *scop,* who sings a three-part medley of heroic songs, the first one celebrating Beowulf's victory over Grendel. Here, like some trompe l'oeil devices of experimental fiction, the outer poem *Beowulf* folds self-referentially into its inner analogue. And the anonymous poet of the Cotton Gnomes (*Maxims II*), as if anticipating the postmodern devaluation of pure rationality, records the terse aphorism "soð bið swicolost," often emended to "soð bið switolost" (Truth is most clear). But the original poet probably wrote what he meant: Truth is most tricky. Some verities lie beyond the ken of rational discourse; some truths can be expressed only in poetry.

Despite the problems associated with its initial preservation and subsequent transmission, Old English literature still possesses the ability to speak across the centuries to address the joys, sorrows, and concerns of human beings in this or any other age. Recuperation of its diverse voices requires arduous labor of its students, who must learn, in effect, a foreign language. Preserved in fragile parchment at the end of the first millennium; beleaguered, at the end of the second, in a modern critical tradition that prizes the recent and contemporary over the traditional and historical, there is still no doubt that Old English literature — valued as much in spite of its great age as because of it — will continue to attract the appreciative attention of students and scholars well into the next millennium of human existence and beyond.

Ælfric

(circa 955 – circa 1010)

Eugene Green
Boston University

WORKS: *Catholic Homilies,* series 1 (circa 989) and series 2 (circa 992)

Manuscripts: The earliest extant manuscript, dating from 990, is Royal 7C. xii, in the British Library. Written in two main hands at Cernel (Cerne Abbas) in Dorset, it comprises Ælfric's first series of Catholic homilies. Facsimile: *Ælfric's First Series of Catholic Homilies: British Museum Royal 7C. xii, fols. 4–218,* edited by Norman Eliason and Peter A. M. Clemoes, Early English Manuscripts in Facsimile 13 (Copenhagen: Rosenkilde & Bagger / London: Unwin / Baltimore: Johns Hopkins University Press, 1966). The only manuscript that contains the first and second series in full, their Latin and Old English prefaces, and a final prayer is Cambridge University Library Gg. 3. 28 (circa 1000), written in a single hand. That Ælfric reissued the first series appears from evidence in Corpus Christi College, Cambridge, 188, written in one hand, probably at Eynsham, during the second quarter of the eleventh century.

First publication: *The Homilies of the Anglo-Saxon Church: The First Part, containing the Sermones Catholici, or Homilies of Ælfric, in the Original Anglo-Saxon, with an English Version,* 2 volumes, edited by Benjamin Thorpe (London: Ælfric Society, 1844–1846).

Standard edition: *Ælfric's Catholic Homilies, The Second Series, Text,* edited by Malcolm R. Godden, EETS, supplementary series 5 (1979).

Third Series of Homilies [Lives of Saints] and a *Vita S. Æthelwoldi* (circa 998–1002)

Manuscript: The only extant manuscript of the set as a whole, written mainly in one hand during the first half of the eleventh century, is Cotton Julius E. vii, in the British Library. The Latin *vita* is edited from Bibliothèque Nationale, Paris, Lat. 5362, written circa 1000 by a Norman scribe.

First publications: *Chronicon Monsterii de Abingdon,* edited by Joseph Stevenson, 2 volumes, Rolls series 2 (London: Longman, Brown, Green, Longmans & Roberts, 1858; reprinted, Kraus, 1964); *Ælfric's Lives of the Saints, Being a Set of Sermons on Saints' Days Formerly Observed by the English Church, edited from British Museum Cott. MS. Julius E. VII with Variants from Other Manuscripts,* edited by Walter W. Skeat, EETS, o.s. 76, 82, 94, 114 (1881–1900; reprinted, 2 volumes, 1966).

Standard editions: *Three Lives of English Saints,* edited by Michael Winterbottom, Toronto Medieval Latin Texts (Toronto: Pontifical Institute of Mediaeval Studies, 1972); republished in *Wulfstan of Winchester: The Life of St Æthelwold,* edited by Michael Lapidge and Winterbottom (Oxford: Clarendon Press, 1991).

Remaining *Catholic Homilies*

Manuscripts: Of at least twenty-four manuscripts, seven comprise the substantial sources for the remaining homilies: Corpus Christi College, Cambridge, MSS. 162 and 178, written in two hands, date from the first half of the eleventh century; Trinity College, Cambridge, MS. B. 15.34, written in a single hand, is a compilation of the mid eleventh century; Cambridge University Library MS. Ii. 4. 6, written in two hands, is a homiliary of the mid eleventh century; British Library, MS. Cotton Vitellius C. v. shows evidence of three hands, the first two about the year 1000, the third about twenty-five years later; British Library, MS. Cotton Faustina A. ix., written in the twelfth century, is probably in one hand; Bodleian Library, Oxford. MS. Hatton 115 and University of Kansas, Kenneth Spencer Research Library, Pryce MS. C2: 2, show evidence of two hands, the first ascribable to the latter half of the eleventh century, the second to the twelfth century; Bodleian Library, Oxford, MS. Bodley 343 (2406), written mainly in a single hand, dates from the second half of the twelfth century.

First publications: *Old English Homilies, First Series,* edited by Richard Morris, EETS, o.s. 29, 34 (1868; reprinted in one volume, Kraus, 1973); *Angelsächische Homilien un Heiligenleben,* edited by Bruno Assmann, Bibliothek der angelsächischen Prosa 3 (Kassel: Wigand, 1889); republished, with a supplementary introduction by Peter A. M. Clemoes (Darmstadt: Wissenschaftliche Buchgesellschaft, 1964); *Twelfth-Century Homilies in MS. Bodley 343: Part I, Text and Translation,* edited by Algernon O. Belfour, EETS, o.s. 137 (1909; reprinted, 1962); *Texte und Untersuchungen zur altenglischen Literatur und Kirchengeschichte: Zwei Homilien des Ælfric — Synodalbeschlüsse — Ein Briefentwurf — Zur Überlieferung des Sterbegesanges Bedas,* edited by Rudolf Brotanek (Halle: Niemeyer, 1913).

Standard edition: *Homilies of Ælfric: A Supplementary Collection, Being Twenty-one Full Homilies of his Middle and Later Career for the Most Part Not Previously Edited, with Some Shorter Pieces, Mainly Passages Added to the Second and Third Series,* 2 volumes, edited by John C. Pope, EETS, 259, 260 (1967, 1968).

Heptateuch

Manuscripts: British Library, MS. Cotton Claudius B. iv, written in two hands, dates from the first half of the eleventh century. Several other manuscripts include items useful for collation.

First publication: *Älfrik de Vetere et Novo Testamento, Pentateuch, Iosua, Buch der Richter und Hiob,* edited by Christian W. M. Grein, Bibliothek der angelsächischen Prosa 1 (Kassel: Wigand, 1872).

Standard editions: *The Old English Version of the Heptateuch, Ælfric's Treatise on the Old and New Testament and his Preface to Genesis, Edited together with a Reprint of "A Saxon Treatise Concerning the Old and New Testament . . . by William L'Isle of Wilburgham (1623)" and the Vulgate Text of the Heptateuch,* edited by S. J. Crawford, EETS, o.s. 160 (1922; reprinted, with the text of two additional manuscripts transcribed by Neil R. Ker, 1969).

Letters

Manuscripts: Of several manuscripts containing Ælfric's letters, four comprise the substantial sources for his three in Latin and his six in Old English: Corpus Christi College, Cambridge, MS. 190 has two Latin and two Old English letters for Wulfstan in its part A, dat-

ing from the onset of the eleventh century; part B, written later in the eleventh century, has the Old English letter to Wulfsige. British Library, MS. Cotton Vespasian D. xiv, dating from the mid twelfth century, has the Old English letter to Sigefyrð. Bodleian Library, Oxford, MS. Laud Misc. 509 and British Library, MS. Cotton Vespasian D. xxi, written during the second half of the eleventh century, have Old English letters to Sigeweard and Wulfgeat. Cambridge, Corpus Christi College MS. 265, dating from the mid eleventh century, has the Latin letter to the monks at Eynsham.

First publication: "Excerpta ex Institutionibus Monasticis AEthelwoldi Episcopi Wintoniensis Compilata in usum Fratrum Egneshamnensium per AElfricum Abbatem," edited by Mary Bateson, Appendix 7 in *Compotus Rolls of the Obedientiaries of St. Swithun's Priory, Winchester,* edited by G. W. Kitchin, Hampshire Record Society 7 (London: Simpkin/Winchester: Warren, 1892), pp. 171–198.

Standard editions: *Angelsächische Homilien un Heiligenleben,* edited by Bruno Assmann, Bibliothek der angelsächischen Prosa 3 (Kassel: Wigand, 1889); republished, with a supplementary introduction by Peter A. M. Clemoes (Darmstadt: Wissenschaftliche Buchgesellschaft, 1964); *Die Hirtenbriefe AElfrics in altenglischer und lateinischer Fassung,* edited by Bernhard Fehr, Bibliothek der angelsächischen Prosa 9 (Hamburg: Grand, 1914); republished, with a supplementary introduction by Clemoes (Darmstadt: Wissenschaftliche Buchgesellschaft, 1966); *Early English Homilies from the Twelfth Century MS. Vesp. D. XIV,* edited by Rubie D.-N. Warner, EETS, o.s. 152 (1917; reprinted, Kraus, 1971).

Tracts

Manuscripts: Three manuscripts among several are the major sources: British Library, MS. Cotton Otho C. 1, vol. 2, dating from the first half of the eleventh century, has two tracts. British Library, MS. Cotton Vespasian D. XIV, dating from the mid twelfth century, contains the tract *De Duodecim Abusivis.* British Library, MS. Harley 3271, dating from the first half of the eleventh century, has the tract *Be þam halgan gaste.*

First publications: *Old English Homilies, First Series,* edited by Richard Morris, EETS 29, 34 (1868); "Anglo-Saxonica Minora," edited by H. Logeman, *Anglia,* 11 (1889): 107–110;

Wulfstan: Sammlung der ihm zugeschriebenen Homilies nebst Untersuchungen über ihre Echtheit, I Text und Varienten, edited by A. S. Napier, Sammlung Englischer Denkmäler in kritischen Ausgaben 4 (Berlin: Weidmannsche Buchhandlung, 1883; republished, with a supplementary bibliography, by Klaus Osterheeren, 1967); "Ælfric's Version of Alcuini Interrogationes Sigeuulfi in Genesin," edited by G. E. Maclean, *Anglia*, 7 (1884): 1–59.

Standard edition: *Exameron Anglice, or the Old English Hexameron, Edited with an Introduction, a Collation of all the Manuscripts, a Modern English Translation, Parallel Passages from the Other Works of Ælfric and Notes on the Sources,* edited by Samuel J. Crawford, Bibliothek der angelsächischen Prosa 10 (Hamburg: Grand, 1921; reprinted, Darmstadt: Wissenchaftliche Buchgesellschaft, 1968).

Admonitio ad Filium Spiritualem

Manuscript: The source is Bodleian Library, Oxford, MS. Hatton 76, written in a ragged hand during the first half of the eleventh century.

First publication: *The Anglo-Saxon Version of the Hexameron of St. Basil, or, Be Godes Six Daga Weorcum, and the Anglo-Saxon Remains of St. Basil's Admonitio ad Filium Spiritualem, now first Printed from MSS. in the Bodleian Library, with a Translation, Notes, and an Account of the Presumed Author, Ælfric,* edited by Henry W. Norman (London: Smith, 1848; second edition, 1849).

Standard edition: "AElfric's Translation of St. Basil's Admonitio ad Filium Spiritualem: An Edition," edited by Lawrence E. Mueller, Ph.D. dissertation, University of Washington, 1974.

Colloquy (circa 995)

Manuscript: The manuscript in Latin is British Library, MS. Cotton Tiberius A. iii, written in two hands during the middle of the eleventh century.

First publication: *A Volume of Vocabularies, Illustrating the Condition and Manners of our Forefathers, as Well as the History of the Forms of Elementary Education and of the Languages Spoken in this Island, from the Tenth Century to the Fifteenth,* 2 volumes, edited by Thomas Wright (London, 1857, 1873; second edition, Liverpool: Marples, 1882); revised as *Anglo-Saxon and Old English Vocabularies,* by Richard P. Wülcker (London: Trübner, 1884; reprinted, Darmstadt: Wissenchaftliche Buchgesellschaft, 1968).

Standard edition: *AElfric's Colloquy,* edited by George N. Garmonsway, Methuen's Old English Library (London: Methuen, 1939; second edition, 1947); revised edition, Exeter Medieval English Texts (Exeter: University of Exeter, 1978).

De Temporibus Anni (circa 992)

Manuscript: The major source is Cambridge University Library, MS. Gg. 3. 28 (circa 1000).

First publication: *Popular Treatises on Science Written during the Middle Ages, in Anglo-Saxon, Anglo-Norman, and English,* edited by Thomas Wright (London: Taylor, 1841; reprinted, Ann Arbor, Mich.: University Microfilms, 1959, 1967; London: Dawsons of Pall Mall, 1965).

Standard edition: *Aelfric's de Temporibus Anni, edited from all the known MSS. and Fragments, with an Introduction, Sources, Parallels, and Notes,* edited by Heinrich Henel, EETS, 213 (1942; reprinted, 1970).

Ely Privilege

Manuscript: The principal manuscript for the *Ely Privilege,* dated 970, is Stowe Charter 31 in the British Library, written in the latter half of the eleventh century. Facsimile: *Facsimiles of Anglo-Saxon Manuscripts,* edited by W. B. Sanders, volume 3, no. 32 (Southampton: Ordnance Survey, 1878–1884).

First publication: *Cartularium Saxonicum: A Collection of Charters Relating to Anglo-Saxon History,* 3 volumes, edited by Walter de Gray Birch (London, 1883–1884; reprinted, London: Whiting, 1885–1893; New York: Johnson Reprint, 1964).

Standard edition: *Anglo-Saxon Charters: Edited with Translation and Notes,* edited by Agnes J. Robertson, Cambridge Studies in English Legal History (Cambridge: Cambridge University Press, 1939; second edition, 1956).

Exemplum

Manuscript: Bodleian Library, Oxford, MSS. Hatton 113 and 114 (5210, 5134) were written by several hands at Worcester, during the third quarter of the eleventh century.

Standard edition: Angus McIntosh, "Wulfstan's Prose (The Sir Israel Gollancz Memorial Lecture)," *Proceedings of the British Academy,* 35 (1949): 109–142.

Glossary and Grammar

Manuscript: The principal manuscript is Saint John's College, Oxford, 154, written in two hands at the outset of the eleventh century.

Text for Ælfric's "In natale unius confessoris," or "De uno confessore," on a page from a late-eleventh-century scribal copy of his Catholic Homilies *(University of Kansas, Kenneth Spencer Research Library, Pryce MS. C2:2)*

Standard editions: *Ælfrics Grammatik und Glossar . . . erste Abteilung: Text und Varianten,* edited by Julius Zupitza, Sammlung Englishscher Denkmäler in kritischen Ausgaben 1 (Berlin: Weidmannsche Buchhandlung, 1880); republished, with preface by Helmut Gneuss (Berlin, Zürich, Dublin: Weidmannsche Verlagsbuchhandlung, Max Niehaus Verlag, 1966).

Hexameron

Manuscript: The chief manuscript is Bodleian Library, Oxford, MS. Hatton 115.

Standard editions: *The Anglo-Saxon Version of the Hexameron of St. Basil, or, Be Godes Six Daga Weorcum, and the Anglo-Saxon Remains of St. Basil's Admonitio ad Filium Spiritualem, now first Printed from MSS. in the Bodleian Library, with a Translation, Notes, and an Account of the Presumed Author, Ælfric,* edited by Henry W. Norman (London: Smith, 1848; second edition, 1849).

Exameron Anglice, or the Old English Hexameron, Edited with an Introduction, a Collation of all the Manuscripts, a Modern English Translation, Parallel Passages from the Other Works of Ælfric and Notes on the Sources, edited by Samuel J. Crawford, Bibliothek der angelsächsischen Prosa 10 (Hamburg: Grand, 1921; republished Darmstadt: Wissenschaftliche Buchgesellschaft, 1968).

In the prefaces to *Catholic Homilies,* series 1 (circa 989), Ælfric explains that his purpose is to provide for his unlearned audience an accurate presentation of Christian doctrine in the vernacular. Arranged for masses from Christmas through the second Sunday of Advent, the forty homilies in this first series convey a clear, succinct synthesis of biblical passages and patristic commentary. Although this homiletic series is the first of his substantial works, it manifests the enduring characteristics of Ælfric's writing: his scholarly training and his mastery of prose. What characterizes his training in school and his years of writing is a consistency of approach and order, as if his learning and expression comprise a harmonious integrity.

Fortunately, Ælfric provides some sense of his curriculum and studies in his notes on his years of schooling at Winchester under the leadership of Saint Æthelwold – enough for an overview. These notes appear in his works as scattered items of recollection. Essential to Ælfric's own education and to the method of study that he advocates in his own pedagogical texts is an emphasis on the learning of Latin. Although his life of Saint Æthelwold recalls

pleasurable moments of listening to texts in English, Ælfric's *Colloquy* (circa 995) and Latin grammar aim to help students develop competency in speaking and reading. The *Grammar* assumes an audience of youngsters unfamiliar with Latin, who need as well to learn what the parts of speech are. Assuring his students at the outset that grammar is the key that unlocks the meaning of books, Ælfric designs graded lessons for his text. The initial section relates voice to separate letters and to clusters that comprise syllables and diphthongs; there follows an introduction to the parts of speech, the terms briefly summarized and informally defined, the examples, in English, taken from everyday life. This introductory overview of terms, original with Ælfric and designed for beginners, precedes the bulk of the *Grammar,* a skillful adaptation from the Latin grammars of Priscian and Donatus. Further demonstrating Ælfric's gift as a teacher in his adaptation is his mindfulness, for example, that providing English equivalents for Latin terms is likely to help students learn. Moreover, in the *Grammar* the eight parts of speech have illustrative English and Latin words throughout, buttressed by a bilingual glossary of several hundred words arranged by topic (probably Ælfric's, as well). One hope that Ælfric entertains for his *Grammar,* then, is that his students, as he himself discovered, might find the study of Latin also strengthening their mastery of English.

The *Colloquy,* although entirely in Latin, nevertheless evidences Ælfric's reliance on everyday Anglo-Saxon experience as integral to the advancement of learning, for his dialogues include familiar figures, a teacher, and artisans. The exchanges between the teacher, and, say, a plowman, a hunter, and a merchant on such themes as the worth of one's labor readily encourage students to converse in Latin. As a whole, Ælfric's pedagogical goals express a belief that oblates, sufficiently engaged and trained, could speak in Latin both inside and outside the classroom.

Ælfric's attention to the study of grammar, part of the trivium, probably mirrors as well the investment of his teacher Æthelwold in Englishing Latin texts. Both teacher and student share a fine regard for linguistic structures and for textual interpretation. Just as Æthelwold carefully translated the Benedictine *Rule* into English (circa 970), so Ælfric evinces a sure grasp of how to adapt Latin sources for clear exposition in the vernacular. The approaches to translation by teacher and student, however, differ considerably. Only in his translation of chapters in Genesis (1–3, 6–9, 11–24) and Numbers (13–26) does Ælfric follow Æthelwold's practice of close rendering, occasionally matching an incomprehensible Latin passage with impenetrable Old English. Otherwise the principle for Ælfric, as stated in the first series of his *Catholic Homilies,* is "Nec ubique transtulimus verbum ex verbo, sed sensum ex sensu" (Not to translate word for word, but sense for sense).

Emphasizing the sense of passages, moreover, freed Ælfric to consider relationships among different sources, a practice that access to manuscripts at Winchester probably enabled him to develop. A homily on the Nativity reveals, for example, Ælfric's sureness at integrating passages from both Old and New Testaments and from the works of Bede, Gregory, and Smaragdus. Thus the opening of the homily retells the first chapters of Luke's Gospel as a prelude to what follows – an exposition, consonant with patristic commentary, of particular words and events. Annotating the angelic "Be glory to God in the highest, and on earth peace to men," Ælfric, like Bede, juxtaposes human estrangement from the divine and Christ's saving nativity. What marks Ælfric's practice in this homily from *Catholic Homilies,* series 1, is characteristic, in brief, of his work in general: a schooled dexterity in marshaling and seamlessly aligning sources.

Besides glossing scriptural passages, Ælfric displays in his writing a technique of posing questions and supplying answers, a practice also indicative of his training at Winchester. So in a homily on the holy day of Pentecost Ælfric asks two questions on *bilewitenys* (meekness) and *rihtwisnysse* (righteousness), on whether either attribute is meaningful without the other. What spurs these questions is a desire to account for God's seemingly antithetical appearance in the Gospels as a dove and as fiery tongues. In the form of fiery tongues, God allegorically *onliht* (enlightens) the human heart and makes it as meek as a dove's; he *onælað* (kindles) it with love and wisdom. This instilling of the heart with the meekness of a dove implies a welcome resemblance between the human and the divine. To present such questions and answers to a congregation is to outline as well a catechistic practice learned at school and incorporated in homilies.

Sometimes, as in a sermon on the Lord's epiphany, Ælfric adapts to his writing the academic practice, common enough in school, of imagining an opponent playing the devil's advocate. Thus he tells his audience of heretics who argue that John's baptism was better than "þe nu stent on Godes cyrcan," that which now obtains for them in God's Church. The response immediately given is that John's baptism, divine in origin, did not need to provide for human forgiveness, but enabled him to baptize Christ ("he sceolde Crist fullian"). This linking of baptism in the Gospel according to John with Anglo-Saxon practice through a rhetorical mode of debate contributes a timeliness effective in the classroom and in church.

Ælfric's education at Winchester strongly grounded in the topics of the trivium – grammar, rhetoric, and dialectic – speaks to his development as Anglo-Saxon England's foremost writer of prose. That he also studied astronomy, included with arithmetic, music, and geometry in the quadrivium, accounts for *De temporibus anni* (circa 992), partly concerned with a dispute between the Celtic and Roman churches on when to celebrate Easter. Like the *Catholic Homilies,* this treatise illustrates Ælfric's ability to exploit his sources, in this instance Bede's astronomical works, and to address matters anew, here of cosmography: so besides calculating church festivals, he discusses divisions of time and of the solar year, outlines principles of astronomy, and comments on the nature of the atmosphere.

Living at Winchester from the 970s until 987, probably two years after ordination, Ælfric developed a priestly calling to spread learning in the vernacular. In sum, his love of teaching, abetted by his training in a monastic school, prompted his desire to correct and to educate. For him errors in the liturgical calendar, in interpretations of Scripture (a failing of his first Latin teacher), and in the pages of many English books all required amendment. So in introducing Genesis and *Catholic Homilies* he champions accurate understanding, even urging copyists to take care, lest one "gebringe þa soðan lare to leasum gedwylde" (turn truth to falsity). What constitutes Ælfric's vision, however, also embedded in the pursuit of learning, is to teach as a disciple of God, to instruct as if the Lord had directly guided him. Remembering that God had commanded "his discipulum þæt hi sceoldan tæcan" (his disciples that they should teach) people things that "he sylf him tæhte" (he taught himself), Ælfric began issuing works after leaving Winchester for Cernel (now Cerne Abbas) in Dorset.

After his arrival at Cernel to take up the duties of a teacher and mass priest, the two series of *Catholic Homilies* appeared, the first in 989, the other in 992. The forty homilies in each series, intended for Sundays, festivals, and some saints' days, include expositions of gospel passages, commentary on the Pater Noster, Creed, and Ten Commandments, and hagiographies. A noteworthy difference between the first and second series lies in the formal design of the homilies. Whereas each of the homilies in the

Page from Ælfric's Old English version of the Heptateuch *illustrating the story of Abraham and Isaac — from an eleventh-century manuscript written in two scribal hands (British Library, MS. Cotton Claudius B.iv., fol. 38ʳ)*

first series is a finished whole, eleven of those in the second series have two parts that permit preachers flexibility in selection and arrangement. Thus the homily for Mid-Lent Sunday, series 2, reviews in one part God's covenants with the Israelites, ending with the Ten Commandments and with offerings that foreshadow Christ's passion; the second part relates Joshua to Jesus, paralleling battles against Jericho and against sins, but contrasting their attitudes toward enemies, Joshua as a vanquisher and Christ as urging love. The second series employs two-part structures probably because of Ælfric's willingness to satisfy a variety of needs with a diversity of discourses.

Ælfric's letters to Bishop Wulfsige of Sherborne (992), to Bishop Wulfstan of York (992–1005), and to the monks of Eynsham (1005) attest, as do his homilies, to his educational purposes. The letter to Wulfsige calls for preaching Sundays and mass days in English on the meaning of the gospel to the folk; the letters to Wulfstan repeat the same theme; the letter to the monks, written on his becoming their abbot, offers advice on the night Office and on readings for the Holy Saturday Vigil. In all these, as well as in the two series of homilies, a central concern for Ælfric is catechetical. The design of his homilies, particularly his pre-Lenten and Lenten homilies and those for the Rogationtide festival preceding Ascension Day, share a catechetical hope in guiding souls away from error. To realize this hope Ælfric often entertains essential topics. These include the Godhead – the Trinity and the two natures of Christ; history – the creation and humanity's fall; providence – mortality, judgment, and redemption; and virtuous living.

In the first series of *Catholic Homilies,* the entries for Wednesday in Rogationtide and for Rogationtide Monday inform congregations on the Trinity and on human nature. Committed to strengthening faith, Ælfric would have everyone know ("Wite . . . gehwa") that in respect to memory, understanding, and will the human soul mirrors the Trinity in its three persons. The likeness of the divine and the human resides, for Ælfric, in the united threeness of each: in the faculties of the soul and the persons of the Godhead. This parallelism is also true of human nature and Christ's, as related in the pre-Lenten homily on the Nativity; the mortal body and the immortal soul correspond to the humanity and the divinity of Christ. To persuade auditors that the two natures of Christ are one but not commingled, Ælfric suggests considering a yolk and egg white ("þæt hwite ne bið gemenged to ðam geolcan"). Such topics as the Creation and the Fall

in Judeo-Christian history, partly a design of prefiguration, rely on analogies between human and supernatural experience. The discourse "On the Beginning of Creation" contrasts, for example, the origin and damning of *Leohtberend* (Lucifer) to the fashioning and promised redeeming of Adam and Eve. Ælfric rehearses the basis for this prefigural contrast: although created by God and subsequently damned, Lucifer alone of the three cannot hope for salvation through *eadmodnysse* (humility) and *gehyrsumnysse* (obedience). A further contrast between the devil and the people appears in the homily for Palm Sunday, structured now to distinguish between eternal death and human mortality, forfeiture and remedial justice. The focus of this contrast fixes on the devil, who "tihte þæt folc to Cristes cwale" (instigated people to slay Christ) and *forwyrhte* (forfeited) whoever believed in God. As for the people, the same passage assures the congregation that Christ's innocent death has the power to redeem, so long as one "sylfe ne forpærað" (does not destroy oneself). One effect of these consistent analogies is that Ælfric portrays for his congregation the human condition as held in perspective against that of the divine or supernatural. The acts of mortals and immortals, although of different spheres, nonetheless convey in his catechetical approach a resonance of dramatic commingling.

The second series of *Catholic Homilies* shifts perspective from analogies between the human and the supernatural to an emphasis on the nature of divinely sanctioned realms. Here the issue is whether an earthly kingdom is hopelessly flawed or can in some way resemble the perfection of heaven. The homily for Wednesday in Rogationtide, second series, provides a view of the fallen world: "þeos woruld is micclum geswenct ðurh menigfealdum gedrefednyssum" (this world is much afflicted with manifold troubles). Amidst the corruption of the world the Trinity comes as a power that redeems. Ælfric urges auditors to commit themselves to "micelre lare" (much learning), so that from "wræcfullum life" (a life of exile) they can seek the Redemption of the Holy Trinity. On the other hand, the homily on the Nativity in the second series pictures the world as a human family joined to Christ as a Redemptive parent. In this view everyone is able to have as parents Christ and his bride, the Church, "seoðe dæghwomlice acenð gastlice cild" (which daily bears children in spirit). Throughout this second series, indeed, the idea of a flawed kingdom on earth and of families spiritually joined to God is no paradox but speaks to the possibilities of Redemption. Thus in the homily for Monday in Rogationtide, Ælfric sketches a theological realm for the Anglo-Saxons under the aegis of God, centered on humanity as "Scyppendes frynd" (the Creator's friends). This realm, hierarchically structured, depends on mutual obligations, Christ overseeing all commitments, the king guiding his people, bishops and priests teaching faithfully, judges acting righteously and mercifully. The same homily encourages marital harmony and a due regard of masters and servants for one another. In effect, Ælfric presents a politics endorsed by God, upheld by all classes, and intended to secure redemption through a life of faith and good works.

History in this second series concerns the Creation and Fall but relies on the concept of the earth as a vineyard, reworked from Adam's time until the world's end. The homily for Septuagesima Sunday quotes Isaiah's "Truly, God's vineyard is the house of Israel" and depicts Abel and the last saint as "swa fela winboga" (so many vine boughs). As chief of the household, God calls cultivators, known through the centuries as *heahfæderas* (patriarchs), *lareowas* (teachers), *witegan* (prophets), and *apostalas* (apostles), to undertake the moral instruction of the people. To teach and to welcome a moral life are to "unriht alecgan, and rihtwisnysse fyrðrian" (suppress unrighteousness and further righteousness), thereby helping to prepare people for the kingdom of heaven. Central to this history is Ælfric's exegesis "þæt heofonan rice getacnað ðas andwerdan gelaðunge" (that the kingdom of heaven betokens this present church), a continuity linking the earthly and heavenly.

The individual life within such a historic context, as the homily for the first Sunday in Lent explains, benefits from acts of charity and mercy. Just as the earthly church is an analog for the heavenly kingdom, so is the merciful act a sign of Christ's Redemption. Ælfric concludes, then, that whatsoever we give to God's poor, for love of him, he will "forgylt be hundfealdum" (requite a hundredfold) in the life to come. This homily for Lent has its climactic moment before the judgment seat, when "Cyning Crist" (Christ as king) calls the charitable faithful to the heavenly realm and damns the sinful. The effect is that of a court in which the human soul, accountable for the economy of a mortal life generous or penurious, receives an absolute assessment.

Counting himself among the teachers in Christian history, Ælfric achieves, too, a rhythmic prose style that produces a quality of transcendence. Attuned in his early writings to aspects of alliterative phrasing, verbal repetition, and rhythmical balances

and constrasts, he attains in the second series of *Catholic Homilies* a singular mastery. For example, the homily on the beginning of Creation in the first series, has sequences like this: "*An* angin is *ealra* þinga, þæt is *God Ælmihtig*. He is ordfruma and *ende*, forðin *þe* he wæs *æfre;* he is *ende* butan ælcere ge*end*unge, forðan *þe* he bið *æfre* unge*end*od" (There is one beginning of all things, who is God Almighty. He is source and end, because he has been forever; he is end without any ending, because he is forever unended). The italicized alliteration in this sequence is vocalic; the repetition includes adverbs, nouns, and participles. A two-stress rhythm is palpable in "He is órdfruma and énde, forðí þe he wæs áefre.... "

In the second series, exhibiting Ælfric's realized rhythmic style, appear sequences like that below from a life of Saint Cuthbert (the verse pattern is illustrative, the punctuation original to the manuscript):

Ac an ðæra fugela eft fleogende com
ymbe ðry dagas þearle dreorig
fleah to his foton friðes biddende
þæt he on ðam lande lybban moste
symle unscæððig and his gefera samod.

(But one of the birds, came flying back after three days, alit at his feet, quite miserable, requesting refuge, that he might live on the land ever harmless, together with his mate).

Here the half lines alliterate as before, but the syllable count in each is systematic – none greater than seven nor fewer than four. The figurative phrasing, say, the *fugel* in flight to Cuthbert's foot "friðes biddende," seeking refuge with the saint, complements themes of home, governance, and mercy enunciated elsewhere in the series. Ælfric infuses his image with transcendent force, in the hope of having the spirit match the letter of the word.

This rhythmic style also informs his collection of saints' lives, completed in the decade between 992 and 1002. Intended for well-educated laymen like Æðelmær and Æþelwerd and for monks and bishops, the book and its distinctive style incorporate contemporary events into hagiography as none of the *Catholic Homilies* does. (The saints' lives in the two series of homilies are those commemorated by the whole Church, but the hagiographies in this third collection are those especially that monks commemorate.) In several saints' lives (for example, those of Edmund, Oswald, and Swithin), Ælfric recalls earlier times of peace in the land and likens contemporary disasters, such as heathen successes against Christians, to prophecies on the end of the world. Accounts in Ælfric's collection, not strictly hagiographic, record battles against heathens, the fall of impious kings, the effort to expose traitors, and the need to enlist God's aid to fight enemies. A recurrent issue vital to clergy and laity is the nature of a just war, especially in regard to Vikings. That Ælfric's sense of the contemporary pervades his collection becomes evident, too, in his references to divorce, clerical chastity, and thievery, instances of rupture in contexts of periodic raids.

One sequence of lines, illustrative of these events, colors "The Forty Soldiers, Martyrs" by voicing Anglo-Saxon militance:

Ac þa hæðenan hynað / and hergiað þa cristenan
and mid wælhreowum dædum / urne drihten gremiað
ac hi habbað þæs edlean / on þan ecum witum

(But the heathen vex and plunder the Christians, and with cruel deeds anger our Lord; but they shall have their reward in eternal punishments)[.]

The alliteration here and the proposed caesuras (indicated by a slash mark) help to delimit the half lines, most of which comprise seven syllables. The occurrence of "gremiað" in final position, delayed after the quick succession of "hynað" and "hergiað," exemplifies God's anger, that, once aroused, has irremediable consequences. In Ælfric's implying heavenly punishment for assaulting Christian Anglo-Saxons, he historicizes their sufferings in accord with traditional teaching, supposing eternal joy for believers and a final death for heathen antagonists.

As for disarray in English society, Ælfric portrays – for example, in a life of Saint Edmund – the upheavals brought about by Viking raids:

þæs ic gewilnige and gewisce mid mode
þæt ic ana ne belife æfter minum leofum þegnum
þe on heora bedde wurdon mid bearnum and wifum
færlice ofslægene fram þysum flot-mannum

(I desire and wish this in my heart, that I should not remain alone after my dear thanes, who suddenly in their beds were slain with children and wives by these seamen)[.]

The tone of the Anglo-Saxon spirit here comports with that expressed in *The Battle of Maldon,* a sense of camaraderie in the face of disaster. In the context of a saint's life included in a hagiographic collection, Ælfric's words speak to his evocative power in uniting a people's ethos with a transcendent faith.

The two series of *Catholic Homilies* and the *Lives of Saints* comprise Ælfric's major achievements, directed at providing readings for the liturgical year and for the educated. Their concern with appropriateness of form and theme indicates the strength of Ælfric's sense of order. Their shift of focus from matters of human and divine nature, to governments for the secular and the eternal realms, to an England under siege reflects a systematic continuity. That Ælfric's stylistic development accompanies his formal and thematic undertakings suggests a plan, whether deliberately conceived or not, amounting to a grand unity. The manuscript history argues, after the completion of the saints' lives, for a continued engagement with homiliaries. Two manuscripts – Cambridge, University Library Ii. 4. 6 and British Library, MS. Cotton Faustina A. ix., – follow the liturgical year approximately from Epiphany until the Sunday after Pentecost and mainly contain pieces Ælfric had already written. As compilations each of about forty items, these manuscripts provide homilies for masses and festivals, excepting saints' days. Three other manuscripts – Bodleian Library, Oxford, Bodley 343 (2406); Trinity College, Cambridge, MS. B. 15.34; and British Library, MS. Cotton Vitellius C. v. – contain between fifty-two and eighty items, designed for the Sundays and festivals of an entire year, again excepting saints' days. The items in these three manuscripts, too, are largely copies or modifications of what Ælfric had already written. The principle governing these later compilations is that although Ælfric invested himself in his prose, his abiding concern lay with the spiritual life of his people. What he did he wanted to do rightly for his people, his church, and God. That what he did also speaks to his personal achievement as Anglo-Saxon England's great writer of prose he would have welcomed, but not as a first consideration.

Bibliography:

Luke M. Reinsma, *Ælfric – An Annotated Bibliography* (New York & London: Garland, 1987).

Biographies:

James Hunt, *Ælfric* (New York: Twayne, 1972);

Caroline L. White, *Ælfric: A New Study of His Life and Writings,* Yale Studies in English, 2 (New Haven: Yale University Press, 1898).

References:

Joyce Bazire and James E. Cross, eds., *Eleven Old English Rogationtide Homilies* (Toronto: University of Toronto Press, 1982);

Peter A. M. Clemoes, "Ælfric," *Continuations and Beginnings – Studies in Old English Literature,* edited by Eric G. Stanley (London: Nelson, 1966), pp. 176–209;

Clemoes, "The Chronology of Ælfric's Works," *The Anglo-Saxons – Studies in some aspects of their History and Culture presented to Bruce Dickins,* edited by Clemoes (London: Bowes & Bowes, 1959), pp. 212–247;

Milton McC. Gatch, "The Achievement of Aelfric and His Colleagues in European Perspective," *The Old English Homily & Its Backgrounds,* edited by Paul E. Szarmach and Bernard F. Huppé (Albany: State University of New York Press, 1978), pp. 43–74;

Gatch, *Preaching and Theology in Anglo-Saxon England: Ælfric and Wulfstan* (Toronto: University of Toronto Press, 1977);

Malcom R. Godden, "Aelfric and the Vernacular Prose Tradition," *The Old English Homily & Its Backgrounds,* edited by Szarmach and Huppé (Albany: State University of New York Press, 1978), pp. 99–117;

Godden, "Aelfric's Saints' Lives and the Problem of Miracles," *Leeds Studies in English,* 16 (1985): 83–100;

Godden, "Anglo-Saxons on the Mind," *Learning and Literature In Anglo-Saxon England – Studies Presented to Peter Clemoes on the Occasion of His Sixty-Fifth Birthday,* edited by Michael Lapidge and Helmut Gneuss (Cambridge: Cambridge University Press, 1985), pp. 271–298;

Godden, "The Development of Aelfric's Second Series of *Catholic Homilies,*" *English Studies,* 54 (June 1973): 209–216;

Eugene A. Green, "Aelfric the Catechist," *Preacher and the Word in the Middle Ages,* edited by Thomas L. Amos, Eugene A. Green, and Beverly M. Kienzle (Kalamazoo: Medieval Institute Publications, Western Michigan University, 1989), pp. 61–74;

Stanley B. Greenfield and Daniel G. Calder, *A New Critical History of Old English Literature* (New York & London: New York University Press, 1986);

Eric John, "The World of Abbot Aelfric," *Ideal and Reality in Frankish and Anglo-Saxon Society – Studies Presented to J. M. Wallace-Hadrill,* edited by Patrick Wormald, Donald Bullough, and Roger Collins (Oxford: Blackwell, 1983), pp. 300–316;

John Pope, "Ælfric and the Old English Version of the Ely Privilege," *England Before The Conquest – Studies in Primary Sources Presented to Dorothy Whitelock,* edited by Clemoes and Kathleen Hughes (Cambridge: Cambridge University Press, 1971), pp. 85–113;

Cyril L. Smetana, "Ælfric and the Early Medieval Homiliary," *Traditio,* 15 (1959): 163–204;

Smetana, "Ælfric and the Homiliary of Haymo of Halberstadt [*sic*]," *Traditio,* 17 (1961): 457–469;

P. A. Stafford, "Church and Society in the Age of Aelfric," *The Old English Homily & Its Backgrounds,* pp. 11–42;

Patrick H. Zettel, "Saints Lives in Old English: Latin Manuscripts and Vernacular Accounts: Ælfric," *Peritia,* 1 (1982): 17–37.

King Alfred
(849 – 899)

Allen J. Frantzen
Loyola University of Chicago

MAJOR WORKS: *The Laws of King Alfred* (between 890–899)

Manuscripts: Found in six manuscripts, only two are complete: the earliest is Cambridge, Corpus Christi College 173 (the "A" manuscript of *The Anglo-Saxon Chronicle*), mid tenth century. Facsimile: *The Parker Chronicle and Laws: A Facsimile,* edited by Robin Flower and A. Hugh Smith, EETS, 208 (1941; reprinted, 1973). The other is the *Textus Roffensis* (Rochester Cathedral Library, MS. A.3.4.), written at Rochester between 1115 and 1124. Facsimile: *Textus Roffensis (Rochester Cathedral Library ms A.3.5), Part 1,* edited by Peter Sawyer, Early English Manuscripts in Facsimile 7 (Copenhagen: Rosenkilde & Bagger, 1957).

First publication: In William Lambarde, *Archaeionomia, sive De priscis Anglorum legibus libri, sermone anglico, vetustate antiquissimo* (London, 1568).

Standard edition: In *Die Gesetze der Angelsachsen,* 3 volumes, edited by F. Liebermann (Halle: Niemeyer, 1903–1916).

Edition in modern English: In *The Laws of the Earliest English Kings,* edited and translated by F. L. Attenborough (Cambridge: Cambridge University Press, 1922; reprinted, New York: AMS Press, 1974).

The Pastoral Care of Gregory the Great (between 890–899)

Manuscripts: There are six manuscripts; the two oldest are Bodleian Library, Oxford, Hatton 20, and British Library, MS. Cotton Tiberius B.xi, both written 890–897. Facsimile (Ms. Hatton 20): *The Pastoral Care: King Alfred's Translation of St. Gregory's Regula Pastosalis,* edited by Neil R. Ker, Early English Manuscripts in Facsimile 6 (Copenhagen: Rosenkilde & Bagger, 1956).

The statue of King Alfred at Wantage, the town that stands at the foot of the Berkshire Downs, Alfred's birthplace

First publication (Preface): In *Ælfredi regis res gestae,* edited by Matthew Parker (London, 1574).

Standard editions: *King Alfred's West-Saxon Version of Gregory's Pastoral Care,* 2 volumes, edited by Henry Sweet, EETS 45, 50 (1871–1872; reprinted, with corrections by Neil R.

Ker, 1958); a separate edition of the metrical prologue and epilogue is in *The Anglo-Saxon Minor Poems,* edited by Elliott van Kirk Dobbie, Anglo Saxon Poetic Records 6 (New York: Columbia University Press, 1942; reprinted, 1968).

The Consolation of Philosophy of Boethius (between 890–899)
> **Manuscripts:** Bodleian Library, Oxford, MS. Bodley 180 (twelfth century); British Library, MS. Cotton Otho A.vi (mid tenth century).
> **First publication:** In Christopher Rawlinson, *An. Manl. Sever. Boeth; Consolationis Philosophiae libri V. Anglo-Saxonice redditi ab Alfredo, inclyto Anglo-Saxonum Rege* (Oxford, 1698).
> **Standard editions:** *King Alfred's Old English Version of Boethius De Consolatione Philosophiae,* edited by Walter J. Sedgefield (Oxford: Clarendon Press, 1899); a separate edition of the metrical portions of the text in *The Paris Salter and the Meters of Boethius,* edited by George Philip Krapp, Anglo-Saxon Poetic Records 6 (New York: Columbia University Press, 1932; reprinted, 1970).
> **Edition in modern English:** *King Alfred's Version of the Consolation of Boethius, done into Modern English,* translated by Walter J. Sedgefield (Oxford: Clarendon Press, 1900).

The Soliloquies of St. Augustine (between 890–899)
> **Manuscript:** British Library, MS. Cotton Vitellius A. XV (mid twelfth century).
> **First publication:** In *The Shrine: A Collection of Occasional Papers on Dry Subjects,* by Thomas Cockayne (London, 1864–1870).
> **Standard editions:** *King Alfred's Version of St. Augustine's "Soliloquies,"* edited by Thomas A. Carnicelli (Cambridge, Mass.: Harvard University Press, 1969); *König Alfreds des Grossen Bearbeitung der Soliloquien des Augustinus,* edited by William Endter, Bibliothek der Angelsachsischen Prose 11 (Hamburg, 1922; reprinted, Darmstadt: Wissenschaftliche Buchgesellschaft, 1964).
> **Edition in modern English:** *King Alfred's Old English Version of St. Augustine's Soliloquies, turned into Modern English,* translated by Henry L. Hargrove, Yale Studies in English 22 (New York: Holt, 1904).

The West-Saxon Psalms of the Paris Psalter (between 890–899)
> **Manuscript:** Bibliothèque Nationale, Paris, Fonds Latin 8824 (mid eleventh century). Facsimile: *The Paris Psalter,* edited by John Bromwich, N. R. Ker, Francis Wormald, Kenneth Sisam, Celia Sisam, and Bertram Colgrave, Early English Manuscripts in Facsimile 8 (Copenhagen: Rosenkilde & Bagger, 1958).
> **First publication:** *Libri Psalmorum versio antigua latina; cum Paraphrasi Anglo-Saxonica, partim soluta oratione, partim metrica composita,* edited by Benjamin Thorpe (Oxford, 1835).
> **Standard edition:** *Liber Psalmorum: The West-Saxon Psalms, Being the Prose Portion, or the "First Fifty," of the so-called Paris Psalter,* edited by James W. Bright and Robert L. Ramsay (Boston: Heath, 1907).

Alfred the Great was one of England's most important kings; governing at a time of extreme instability, he stopped Viking invaders and started a process of cultural renewal. He was known as "the Great" by the thirteenth century, and his reputation has never waned. The veneration that began to surround him in the sixteenth century grew to extreme proportions in the Victorian era; but even when that hyperbole is discounted, Alfred remains uniquely important as the king who began unifying England as a nation and simultaneously created the framework for national literature in the vernacular. Alfred is ranked as the preeminent English author of the ninth century; few writers of the Anglo-Saxon period influenced literary history more profoundly, and none equaled Alfred's political achievements.

Alfred ruled the kingdom of the West Saxons from 871 until his death in 899. He was born at Wantage, in Berkshire, in 849, the youngest son of King Æthelwulf. He twice visited Rome, in 853 and 855; on these travels he was welcomed not only at the papal court but also at the court of Charles the Bald. Æthelwulf married Judith, Charles's daughter, as his second wife, thus ensuring the influence of Frankish learning and tradition on the court in which Alfred was raised. In 868 Alfred married Ealhswith, the daughter of a noble family from Mercia. In 871, after a complex sequence of arrangements involving his father, Æthelwulf, and his brothers, Æthelbald, Æthelstan, Æthelred, and Æthelberht, Alfred succeeded to the throne. Æthelwulf had divided the kingdom into two parts, the eastern to be governed by Æthelstan, the western to be ruled by himself. When Æthelstan died, sometime in the 850s, Æthelwulf once again divided the kingdom, assigning Wessex to Æthelbald and the eastern territories to Æthelberht. Æthelberht tried unsuccessfully to gain control of both parts of the kingdom and failed. But when Æthelbald died in 860, Æthelberht assumed control of the entire kingdom; upon his death in 865, Æthelred became king, and upon Æthelred's death in 871 Alfred became king.

Alfred's reign of nearly thirty years (871–899) can be divided into three parts: two periods of Viking resurgence, 871–878 and 892–899; and a middle period of literary productivity. This division indicates that Alfred's life as a ruler and warrior frame his identity as an author. He seems to have pursued scholarship and military leadership simultaneously, and many of the texts attributed to him reveal a thinker deeply concerned with Christian kingship.

The tradition of King Alfred as a lover of literature begins with his biographer and literary associate, the Welsh bishop Asser, whose *Vita Alfredi* (Life of King Alfred, 893) is the most important source of information not only about the events of Alfred's life but about the nature of literary culture at the time. Asser reports that one day Alfred's mother showed her sons a book of English poetry and promised to give it to whoever learned it – that is, memorized it – the fastest. Asser reports that Alfred took the book to a teacher and mastered it; presumably he won the prize. Beyond this engaging incident, matters regarding Alfred's education are not entirely clear; for example, Asser reports that Alfred was "ignorant of letters" until he was twelve, but the king obviously had a teacher to help him learn the book his mother showed him. The references to books and reading in Asser's life do not disclose the process of his education, but they do supply precious, if incomplete, information about reading, teaching, and learning. When his mother displayed the book of English poems, Alfred was particularly "attracted by the beauty of the initial letter in the book." The value of the book depended in part on its material splendor.

Many years later, as king, Alfred read "aloud from a book in English" and enjoyed "above all learning English poems by heart," as he presumably did when a boy; but at this time he still needed tutors to read books in Latin to him, and Asser at one point did so for eight months. Although Asser reports that the king learned to read and translate Latin in a single day, the claim invites skepticism. The king could read English before he understood Latin; he required some works to be read to him, but he read others for himself. It is, therefore, more probable that the king's proficiency in Latin was acquired slowly.

To assess Alfred's place as a major English author it is necessary to distinguish between literary production in his age and modern (that is, postmedieval) notions of authorship. It is highly unlikely that Alfred "wrote," either in the sense of wielding a writing instrument or composing in solitude.

He pursued literary tasks, chiefly translations, with a group of helpers. The degree of their participation in the translations cannot be ascertained. The names of four, in addition to Asser, are known: Wærferth and Plegmund (both bishops) and Æthelstan and Werwulf (both priests). Although Asser stresses that Alfred kept regular company with these scholars, he nowhere offers an extensive description of their working methods. Because Alfred undertook all his translations in concert with these helpers, the texts attributed to him cannot be seen as direct representations of the king's authorial consciousness. Whether or not the king's circle formed a distinct school of translation is uncertain, as is the sequence in which the translations were completed.

At one time a large number of texts was assigned to King Alfred, but modern scholarship regards as certain his authorship of a law code, known as *The Laws of King Alfred* but including collections of laws composed by earlier English kings; *King Alfred's West-Saxon Version of Gregory's Pastoral Care* translated from the *Cura Pastoralis* of Gregory I; *The West-Saxon Psalms*, also known as the *Paris Psalter; The Consolation of Philosophy* of Boethius; and *The Soliloquies of St. Augustine*. Numerous changes, some conspicuous and some subtle, distinguish each of King Alfred's translations from their sources and from each other; it is possible that the translations reflect the influence of other texts, including commentaries, known to the translators and incorporated into the works they helped Alfred produce. In addition to those translations Alfred compiled a handbook, or enchiridion, into which were copied prayers and quotations that especially interested him; this text does not survive, but Asser's reference to it suggests how the king gathered texts for later use. Alfred was also a poet. The epilogue to *The Pastoral Care* survives in both prose and verse forms, and *The Consolation of Philosophy* includes metrical verses. Alfred's original verse is direct and even didactic rather than lyrical. Perhaps because it falls outside the kinds of verse (elegiac and heroic) still favored by critics of Anglo-Saxon literature, Alfred's poetry is seldom ranked among his distinctive contributions to English literature. Scholars have found it difficult to imagine the royal warrior as the author of utilitarian verse; but the king clearly valued the power of poetry, and anyone who remembers Asser's description of Alfred's boyhood enthusiasm for a book of English poems will understand as much.

Of the other texts written about this time and associated with Alfred, but not directly traced to his authorship, *The Anglo-Saxon Chronicle* is the most im-

Alfred's introduction to his translation of Gregory's Regula pastoralis, *from a late-ninth-century manuscript (Bodleian Library, Oxford, MS. Hatton 20 [formerly Hatton 88], fol. 1ʳ)*

portant. Both a contemporary record of events and an attempt to put those events into a historical perspective, the chronicle traces Alfred's kingship back to ancient Rome and the early Christian era. Other texts formerly attributed to the king include the *World History* of Orosius, the Old English *Martyrology,* the Anglo-Saxon translation of Bede's *Ecclesiastical History* and Bald's *Leechbook.* The only text of known authorship from this period is Wærferth's translation of the *Dialogues* of Gregory the Great, which, according to Asser, the bishop undertook "at the king's command." Recent work on the authorship of these texts has made great headway, but it is not uncommon to find some of them, in particular the translation of Orosius, still attributed to Alfred. All of these texts illuminate the cultural milieu of the ninth century. The *Dialogues* and the *World History,* are of special interest, the former for its recasting of the numerous narratives (visions, for example) recounted by Gregory and its use of the dialogue form found in works attributed to Alfred (*The Consolation of Philosophy, The Solioquies*), the latter for its rich and informative geographic descriptions and historical summaries. Both texts have been analyzed with respect to syntax and style, but neither has won anything like the attention its cultural significance merits. The following survey discusses only those texts assigned to Alfred beyond responsible doubt: *The Laws, The Pastoral Care, The Consolation of Philosophy, The Soliloquies,* and the verses of *The Paris Psalter.*

Anglo-Saxon law was primarily customary and unwritten, that is, legal standards were preserved in the memories of counselors who participated in settling disputed claims and determining penalties. The law was also highly specific to regions and districts. Thus, in issuing a written law code, Alfred departed from one tradition but followed another: in proclaiming a "national" legal code, he centralized the tradition in the manner common to ecclesiastical and ancient practice. Alfred's code incorporates the laws of earlier English kings as an essential part of his own code. The most important literary evidence in the legal texts is the introduction to the code. In it Alfred assumes the role of a shaper of tradition who reaches back not only to earlier law collections but to Mosaic law and to the proclamations of early Christian synods at which, Alfred explains, earlier law codes (including the Ten Commandments and Hebrew law) took shape; he then compares these assemblies to synods at which English law was proclaimed. The law code is usually omitted in discussions of Alfred's literary production, and translations routinely omit the introduction entirely. But the laws are particularly important to an assessment of Alfred's belief in the power of the written word. The collection establishes the link between wisdom and power that informs so many of the translations.

Gregory the Great's *Cura Pastoralis* was one of the most influential guides for pastors known in the Middle Ages; some five hundred manuscripts survive. Gregory's chief source for counseling the priest was the Bible, which he quotes hundreds of times. The book admonishes the priest constantly to consider his own worthiness as he advises and directs the spiritual lives of his charges; thus the book sought both to educate the priest and to provide for the spiritual welfare of those in his care. Alfred wrote two prefaces for the text, one in verse, one in prose. The prose translation describes what has come to be called King Alfred's program of education. In it Alfred recalls the high level of learning that characterized the church in his childhood and laments the decline in the present, equating the abundance of learned teachers with material prosperity and the decline of learning with the erosion of national security. He describes how he translated Gregory's text and announces that he will supply all his bishops with copies. Without denying the importance of the preface, it must be said that it has both unduly influenced modern understanding of the level of literacy in Alfred's time and caused neglect of the text of *The Pastoral Care* itself; the preface is included in nearly every introductory Old English textbook ever published, while the main body of Gregory's text, a major source of medieval pastoral theology, goes unread. This circumstance is, interestingly, precisely the reverse of the critical tradition of the law code, the introduction to which is ignored, while the laws themselves are frequently discussed.

King Alfred's translation of *The Consolation of Philosophy,* one of the most famous books of the Middle Ages, is one of the most difficult to discuss. Although he kept to the general five-book structure of the Latin text, in which Lady Philosophy appears to Boethius in prison and engages him in a dialogue about the nature of human suffering, Alfred altered the text extensively, apparently under the influence of Continental commentaries (there are numerous glossed manuscripts of the work) and other theological and philosophical texts. Alfred's major changes were to incorporate many explicitly Christian references, thus significantly altering the character of Boethius's Neoplatonic thought, and to alter the identity of the speakers. At first Alfred refers to Boethius as Mod, Old English for mind; after book 3 Mod becomes Boethius, and later the name is changed again, to I. Lady Philosophy is sometimes known as Gesceadwisness (reason or wisdom) and sometimes as Wisdom. The text, which ranges from philosophy to theology and mythology, allowed Alfred and his assistants to contemplate a wide range of issues. Alfred translated the meters, or poetic passages, in the text and added a verse proem; his translation thus preserves the generic diversity of the original.

Of all the texts translated by King Alfred and his assistants, *The Soliloquies* is surely the most difficult to interpret and to justify as a choice for the king's program of educational reform. Like *The Consolation, The Soliloquies* is a dialogue; Augustine wrote it ten years before he began *The Confessions,* and the earlier work has been seen as an early attempt at self-examination in the context of Platonic and Christian thought. It seems plausible that Alfred translated the Augustinian text because it was included in a manuscript containing the text by Boethius; the two translations contain some similar passages, and the reflective nature of both may have recommended them to the king's introspective side. Oddly enough, although there are few studies of *The Soliloquies,* there are many editions; what critics shy away from, editors embrace: the text may be difficult to interpret, but it is short (and there is only one manuscript). The work is given in three books, with a preface. Supplying a neat and accurate characterization of the distance between the translation and the original text, which grows as the work progresses, Henry L. Hargrove proposes in his edition of the work that Alfred translated the first book, adapted the second, and wrote the third himself. The preface is an extraordinary document; like many of Alfred's texts it employs the scriptural and patristic commonplaces of the timber gatherer and cottage builder in metaphors for the process of selecting and synthesizing texts. In the body of the text, more explicitly than in *The Consolation,* Alfred replaces elaborate figures and analogies with commonsense arguments. A significant example occurs in the first book, when Augustine refers to the Platonic concept that all things eventually return to their point of origin. Alfred notes that some things do not, but are replaced – as apples are replaced on the tree, and "the same ones do not come again to where they were before." Elsewhere Alfred replaces complex analogies with simpler and more direct comparisons; as a translator, Alfred intervenes and mediates more in this text than in any other. Nothing is known about the Latin version of the text known to the king, however, and therefore speculation about the extent of the king's changes is especially risky.

In *The West-Saxon Psalms of Paris Psalter* the first 50 of the 150 psalms were rendered in prose that is now considered to be that of Alfred and his assistants (various means have been used to determine that the prose and verse translations have different authors). The Book of Psalms is one of the most diverse books of the Bible, a series of lyrics reflecting both Hebrew and Christian customs in varying moods and modes. Alfred's translation increases this diversity by adding an introduction to each psalm; the elaborate fourfold interpretive system employed in these introductions has been convincingly traced by Patrick P. O'Neill to an Irish tradition of Psalter commentary employing an unusual fourfold pattern of scriptural exegesis. The wide range of subjects in the Psalter, which is meditative and private rather than hortatory or public in character, invited observations and additions reflective of the king's preoccupations; yet the text was biblical in origin, and the additions and interpolations that Alfred permitted are well within the scope of the work. The psalms were the work of another king – David – whose role as leader and teacher, king and man of prayer, would have held great appeal for Alfred. Observations are made concerning wealth, power, wisdom, and other favorite topics of the ninth-century ruler.

It is not obvious how Alfred, working at a time when learning had declined and when he was occupied with great military and political problems, managed to accomplish so much. Nor is it easy to see how, in such circumstances, he managed to form a canon of works so rich and varied. Scholars disagree about the rationale of Alfred's canon; several have attempted to identify the principles which might have directed his selection of texts for transla-

tion. Alfred's list of translations is, according to Simon Keynes and Michael Lapidge in their *Alfred the Great: Asser's "Life of King Alfred" and Other Contemporary Sources* (1983), "a curious, even idiosyncratic, choice to have served as the basis for a programme of educational reform." It is well to keep their skepticism in mind when reading arguments that Alfred's books were, as he said in the preface to the *Pastoral Care,* "most needful to know." The notion of such a curricular concept is modern, and it is different from the study of the liberal arts as it was known in the early medieval period. Some texts are practical (*The Pastoral Care*) and others abstract and complex (*The Soliloquies*); the diversity is obvious but the coherence is not. Alfred's choices may have been fortunate: that is, that the books available, whether scriptural (the psalms) or attributable to important authors (such as Saint Augustine), were those that Alfred ordered to be translated. It is surely futile to try to demonstrate coherence and logic in what may well have been felicitous rather than systematic choices.

Rather than attempt to forge the works into a system that reflects a coherence beyond the available evidence, readers of King Alfred's texts should be encouraged to examine the texts in various historical and conceptual contexts. These include the relations between writing, reading, and speaking so often referred to in Alfred's works; the processes of both textual production (oral and written) and reception; and the features of cultural diversity and bilingualism characteristic of England in the ninth century, when Irish, Roman, Old English, and Scandinavian languages and cultures were in contact. Manuscripts known to have been written in England or consulted there during or before Alfred's time are the widest and most important register of the king's literary culture; their origins and transmission help trace the relation of the king and his helpers to their chief source of texts and ideas: Continental monastic centers. The relationship of Alfred's circle to Continental centers of learning will become clearer as more is learned about Continental libraries and their practices of textual production and publication. It is, above all, important to resist the temptation of applying biographical criticism to King Alfred's writing. Although remarkably revealing in the Victorian phase of scholarship concerning King Alfred, such an approach assumes answers to questions for which answers are lacking: Alfred's role in each of his works; the order in which they were produced; their sources; their dissemination; and others. King Alfred was idolized at the beginning of Anglo-Saxon scholarship, when

Asser's life and the preface to *The Pastoral Care* were published by Matthew Parker and his assistants in 1574. Later Thomas Jefferson, an avid Anglo-Saxonist, cited Alfred's use of the unit of land measure called the hundred as a model for organizing the counties of the state of Virginia. The place of Alfred and other Anglo-Saxon authors in the thought of later writers is important but widely neglected. But each age has added to understanding of the king and his achievements, and it is not only by grasping the reception of Alfred by all those who have read and written about his texts, not just those who have done so most recently, that readers today can justly estimate his place in English literary history.

Now that recent critical developments have begun to influence scholarship concerning King Alfred, it is appropriate to observe that historical and literary concepts of the late twentieth century can be applied as reductively as any others. One of Alfred's favorite figures of speech compared the mind to a ship: both need to be firmly anchored to avoid being swept away in the current (the figure appears in *The Consolation,* chapter 7; *The Pastoral Care,* chapter 58; *The Soliloquies,* book 1). Just as Alfred read earlier authors in the context of his own time, place, and spirit, readers today contemplate the king's poetry and prose in the context of a critically engaged and culturally diverse world. They would do well to take Alfred's advice and, as they read his writing in the fast-moving mainstream of modern thought, anchor their scholarship firmly in the literary culture of the king's own time.

Biographies:

William Henry Stevenson, ed., *Asser's Life of King Alfred,* (Oxford: Clarendon Press, 1904);

Alfred the Great: Asser's "Life of King Alfred" and Other Contemporary Sources, translated by Simon Keynes and Michael Lapidge (New York: Penguin, 1983).

References:

Janet Batley, "The Nature of Old English Prose," in *The Cambridge Companion to Old English Literature,* edited by Malcolm Godden and Michael Lapidge (Cambridge: Cambridge University Press, 1991), pp. 71–87;

Batley, "Old English Prose before and during the Reign of Alfred," *Anglo-Saxon England,* 17 (1988): 93–138;

Peter Clemoes, "King Alfred's Debt to Vernacular Poetry: The Evidence of *Ellen* and *Cræft,*" in *Words, Texts and Manuscripts: Studies in Anglo-Saxon Culture Presented to Helmut Gneuss,* edited by Michael Korhammer (Cambridge: Brewer, 1992), pp. 213–238;

Eleanor Shipley Duckett, *Alfred the Great: The King and His England* (Chicago: University of Chicago Press, 1956);

Allen J. Frantzen, *King Alfred* (Boston: Twayne/ G. K. Hall, 1986);

Martin Irvine, "Medieval Textuality and the Archaeology of Textual Culture," in *Speaking Two Languages: Traditional Disciplines and Contemporary Theory in Medieval Studies,* edited by Frantzen (Albany: Albany State University of New York Press, 1991), pp. 181–210, 276–284;

Seth Lerer, *Literacy and Power in Anglo-Saxon Literature* (Omaha: University of Nebraska Press, 1991);

H. R. Loyn, *Alfred the Great* (New York: Oxford University Press, 1967);

Patrick P. O'Neill, "The Old English Introductions to the Prose Psalms of the Paris Psalter: Sources, Structure, and Composition," *Studies in Philology,* 78 (Winter 1981): 20–38.

Eric Gerald Stanley, *A Collection of Papers with Emphasis on Old English Literature* (Toronto: Pontifical Institute of Medieval Studies, 1987).

Bede

(circa 673 – 25 May 735)

Arthur G. Holder
Church Divinity School of the Pacific

MAJOR WORKS: *De temporibus liber includens chronica minora* (On Times including A Short Chronicle, 703)

Manuscripts: There are eighty-three extant manuscripts, many dating from the ninth century; some comprise only excerpts. Another ten manuscripts contain the *Chronica minora* only. The standard edition (1980) of *De temporibus liber* is based on eight Continental manuscripts of the ninth century and two twelfth-century English manuscripts; that of the *Chronica minora* is based on four Continental manuscripts from the ninth century and one from the tenth. For each work the oldest extant manuscript is Deutsche Staatsbibliothek, Berlin, 128 (Phillipps, 1831), originally from Verona, circa 800.

First publication: In *Bedae presbyteri Anglosaxonis viri eruditissimi de natura rerum et temporum ratione*, edited by John Sichardus (Basel: Printed by Henri Petrus, 1529).

Standard edition: In *Corpus Christianorum Series Latina*, volume 123C, edited by C. W. Jones (Turnhout, Belgium: Brepols, 1980), pp. 579–611.

De natura rerum liber (On the Nature of Things, circa 703)

Manuscripts: The 131 extant manuscripts represent every century from the ninth through the fifteenth. The standard edition (1975) is based on one late-eighth-century manuscript from northern France (British Library MS. Cotton Caligula A. XV), nine Continental manuscripts from the ninth century, and one twelfth-century English manuscript.

First publication: In *Bedae presbyteri Anglosaxonis viri eruditissimi de natura rerum et temporum ratione*, edited by John Sichardus (Basel: Printed by Henri Petrus, 1529).

Standard edition: In *Corpus Christianorum Series Latina*, volume 123A, edited by C. W. Jones (Turnhout, Belgium: Brepols, 1975), pp. 173–234.

Explanatio Apocalypsis (On the Apocalypse, circa 703–709)

Manuscripts: There are more than seventy extant manuscripts, the earliest of which appears to be Stiftsbibliothek, Saint Gall, 259 (late eighth century).

First publication: In *Secundus operum Venerabilis Bedae . . . tomus, in quo continentur eiusdem commentarii* (Paris: Printed by Jodocus Badius Ascensius, 1521).

Standard edition: In *Patrologia Latina*, volume 93, edited by J.-P. Migne (Paris: J.-P. Migne, 1850; reprinted, Turnhout, Belgium: Brepols, 1980), cols. 129–206.

Partial edition in English: *The Explanation of the Apocalyse by Venerable Beda*, translated by E. Marshall (Oxford: J. Parker, 1878).

De locis sanctis (On the Holy Places, circa 703–709)

Manuscripts: There are more than forty extant manuscripts. The standard edition (1965) is based on seven manuscripts, including two from the ninth century: Bibliothèque publique, Laon, 216, and Staatsbibliothek, Munich, 6389.

First publication: In *Venerabilis Bedae opera omnia* (Basel: Printed by John Herwagen, 1563).

Standard edition: In *Corpus Christianorum Series Latina*, volume 175, edited by J. Fraipont (Turnhout, Belgium: Brepols, 1965), pp. 245–280.

Libri quatuor in principium Genesis (On Genesis, Book 1a, circa 703–709; Books 1b, 2–4, circa 725–731)

Manuscripts: There are seventeen extant manuscripts, eleven of which were the basis for the standard edition; among the oldest are Bibliothèque Nationale, Paris, MS. Latin 13373 (circa 817–835) and Saint Gall, Stiftsbibliothek 255 (early ninth century). Five of the manuscripts transcribe short versions of the text that conclude before the end of Book 1.

Portrait of Bede in a late-twelfth-century transcription of his
Vita sancti Cuthberti metrica *(British Library,*
MS. Yates Thompson 26)

First publication: Book 1a in *Venerabilis Bedae
opera omnia* (Basel: Printed by John Herwagen,
1563); entire work in *Bedae venerabilis opera
quaedam theologica, nunc primum edita, necnon
historica, antea semel edita,* edited by Henry
Wharton (London: Printed by S. Roycroft,
1693).
Standard edition: In *Corpus Christianorum Series Latina,* volume 118A, edited by C. W.
Jones (Turnhout, Belgium: Brepols, 1967).

Liber hymnorum, rhythmi, variae preces (Hymns, circa
703–731)
　　Manuscripts: The most important manuscript
　　is Staatsbibliothek, Bamberg, Misc. Patr. 17
　　(B. II. 10), which includes eight hymns that
　　can be attributed to Bede. The best attested
　　poem is "De die iudicii" (On Judgment Day),
　　which appears in more than thirty manu-
　　scripts.

First publication: In *Hymni Ecclesiastici* (Cologne: Printed by Georgius Cassander, 1556),
which includes eleven poems attributed to
Bede.
Standard edition: In *Corpus Christianorum Series Latina,* volume 122, edited by J. Fraipont
(Turnhout, Belgium: Brepols, 1965), pp. 405–
470.

Vita sancti Cuthberti metrica (Life of Saint Cuthbert, in
verse, circa 706–707)
　　Manuscripts: The standard edition (1935) is
　　based on the nineteen extant manuscripts, the
　　two oldest being Bibliothèque publique,
　　Besançon, 186 (ninth century), and Harley
　　526, in the British Library (ninth or tenth cen-
　　tury).
　　First publication: In *Antiquae lectionis,* volume
　　2, edited by Heinrich Canisius (Ingolstadt:
　　Printed by A. Angermarius, 1604).
　　Standard edition: *Bedas metrische vita sancti
　　Cuthberti,* edited by Werner Jaager in *Palaestra*
　　198 (Leipzig: Mayer & Müller, 1935).

Epistola ad Plegvinam (Letter to Plegwine, 708)
　　Manuscripts: The standard edition (1980) is
　　based on three manuscripts: British Library
　　MS. Cotton Vitellius A. XII; Merton College,
　　Oxford, MS. 49; and Bibliotheca Apostolica
　　Vaticana, Reginensis latinus 123.
　　First publication: In *Venerabilis Bedae epistolae
　　duae, necnon vitae abbatum Wiremuthensium &
　　Girwiensium,* edited by Sir James Ware (Dub-
　　lin: Printed by John Crook, 1664).
　　Standard edition: In *Corpus Christianorum Se-
　　ries Latina,* volume 123C, edited by C. W.
　　Jones (Turnhout, Belgium: Brepols, 1980), pp.
　　613–626.

In Epistolas VII Catholicas (On the Seven Catholic
Epistles, circa 709)
　　Manuscripts: There are more than 110 extant
　　manuscripts. The standard edition (1983) is
　　based on ten Continental manuscripts from
　　the ninth century, two of the earliest of which
　　are Bibliothèque de l'université, Geneva, 99
　　(Latin 21) and Bodley 849 in the Bodleian Li-
　　brary at Oxford.
　　First publication: In *Secundus operum Venerabi-
　　lis Bedae . . . tomus, in quo continentur eiusdem com-
　　mentarii* (Paris: Printed by Jodocus Badius As-
　　censius, 1521).
　　Standard edition: In *Corpus Christianorum Se-
　　ries Latina,* volume 121, edited by D. Hurst
　　(Turnhout, Belgium: Brepols, 1983), pp. 179–
　　342.
　　Edition in English: *Commentary on the Seven*

Catholic Epistles, translated by David Hurst (Kalamazoo, Mich.: Cistercian Publications, 1985).

Expositio Actuum Apostolorum (On the Acts of the Apostles, circa 709)

Manuscripts: There are more than ninety extant manuscripts. The standard edition (1983) is based on fifteen Continental manuscripts that date from the ninth century or, in the cases of Stiftsbibliothek, Saint Gall, 259 and Bibliothèque de l'université, Geneva, 99 (Latin 21), perhaps from the end of the eighth.

First publication: In *Secundus operum Venerabilis Bedae . . . tomus, in quo continentur eiusdem commentarii* (Paris: Printed by Jodocus Badius Ascensius, 1521).

Standard edition: In *Corpus Christianorum Series Latina*, volume 121, edited by M. L. W. Laistner (Turnhout, Belgium: Brepols, 1983), pp. 1–99.

Edition in English: *Commentary on the Acts of the Apostles*, translated by Lawrence T. Martin (Kalamazoo, Mich.: Cistercian Publications, 1989).

In Lucae evangelium expositio (On the Gospel of Luke, circa 709–716)

Manuscripts: There are more than ninety extant manuscripts. The standard edition (1960) is based on six Continental manuscripts from the ninth century and one (Bibliothèque Nationale, Paris, MS. Latin 11681) that dates from the end of the eighth century.

First publication: In *Secundus operum Venerabilis Bedae . . . tomus, in quo continentur eiusdem commentarii* (Paris: Printed by Jodocus Badius Ascensius, 1521).

Standard edition: In *Corpus Christianorum Series Latina*, volume 120, edited by D. Hurst (Turnhout, Belgium: Brepols, 1960), pp. 1–425.

De orthographia (On Orthography, circa 710–731)

Manuscripts: There are nineteen extant manuscripts. The standard edition (1975) is based on six of these, the oldest being Bibliothèque Nationale, Paris, MS. Latin 7530 (circa 779–797).

First publication: In *Venerabilis Bedae opera omnia* (Basel: Printed by John Herwagen, 1563).

Standard edition: In *Corpus Christianorum Series Latina*, volume 123A, edited by C. W. Jones (Turnhout, Belgium: Brepols, 1975), pp. 1–57.

De arte metrica et de schematibus tropis (On the Art of Metrics and On Figures and Tropes, circa 710–731)

Manuscripts: Twenty-one extant manuscripts contain all or part of the first treatise only, and twenty-nine others contain all or part of the second alone. Both treatises appear together in another forty-six manuscripts. The standard edition (1975) is based on sixteen manuscripts, the oldest of which is Stiftsbibliothek, Saint Gall, 876 (late eighth century).

First publication: *Liber Bedae de schemate & tropo* and *Eiusdem vero ars de metris incipit feliciter* (Milan: Printed by Antonius Zarotus, 1473).

Standard edition: In *Corpus Christianorum Series Latina*, volume 123A, edited by C. B. Kendall (Turnhout, Belgium: Brepols, 1975), pp. 59–171.

Edition in English: *Libri II De arte metrica et de schematibus et tropis: The Art of Poetry and Rhetoric*, from Saint Gall, Stiftsbibliothek 876, edited and translated by Calvin B. Kendall (Saarbrucken, Germany: AQ-Verlag, 1991).

In primam partem Samuhelis (On the First Book of Samuel, 716)

Manuscripts: There are eight extant manuscripts. The standard edition (1962) is based on two ninth-century manuscripts: Bibliothèque publique, Lyon, 449, and MS. 335 in the Pierpont Morgan Library in New York City.

First publication: In *Venerabilis Bedae opera omnia* (Basel: Printed by John Herwagen, 1563).

Standard edition: In *Corpus Christianorum Series Latina*, volume 119, edited by D. Hurst (Turnhout, Belgium: Brepols, 1962), pp. 1–287.

In Marci evangelium expositio (On the Gospel of Mark, circa 720–725)

Manuscripts: There are more than ninety extant manuscripts. The standard edition (1960) is based on nine Continental manuscripts from the ninth century, the earliest of which are Bibliothèque Nationale, Paris, MS. Latin 9573; Landesbibliothek, Karlsruhe, Augiensis 62; Saint Gall, Stiftsbibliothek 257; and Nationalbibliothek, Vienna, 767.

First publication: In *Secundus operum Venerabilis Bedae . . . tomus, in quo continentur eiusdem commentarii* (Paris: Printed by Jodocus Badius Ascensius, 1521).

Standard edition: In *Corpus Christianorum Series Latina*, volume 120, edited by D. Hurst

(Turnhout, Belgium: Brepols, 1960), pp. 427–648.

In Tobiam (On Tobit, circa 720–731)

Manuscripts: There are more than seventy extant manuscripts. The standard edition (1983) is based on one late-eighth-century Continental manuscript (Bibliothèque publique, Mons, 635), four Continental manuscripts from the ninth century, and one eleventh-century English manuscript, Hatton 23 in the Bodleian Library at Oxford.

First publication: In *Venerabilis Bedae opera omnia* (Basel: Printed by John Herwagen, 1563).

Standard edition: In *Corpus Christianorum Series Latina*, volume 119B, edited by D. Hurst (Turnhout, Belgium: Brepols, 1983), pp. 1–19.

In Proverbia (On Proverbs, circa 720–731)

Manuscripts: There are more than eighty extant manuscripts of the complete work, and another fifteen that include only the concluding portion, *De muliere forti*. The standard edition (1983) is based on seven Continental manuscripts from the ninth century and one English manuscript (Bodley 819 in the Bodleian Library at Oxford) that was probably written in Northumbria in the late eighth or early ninth century.

First publication: In *Venerabilis Bedae opera omnia* (Basel: Printed by John Herwagen, 1563).

Standard edition: In *Corpus Christianorum Series Latina*, volume 119B, edited by D. Hurst (Turnhout, Belgium: Brepols, 1983), pp. 21–163.

In Habacuc (On Habakkuk, circa 720–731)

Manuscripts: The standard edition (1983) is based on all twelve of the extant manuscripts. Two of these date from the early ninth century: Pembroke College, Cambridge, 81, which was written on the Continent but later came into the monastic library at Bury Saint Edmunds, and Bibliothèque municipale, Orléans, 59 (62), which was written at Fleury.

First publication: In *Bedae venerabilis opera quaedam theologica, nunc primum edita, necnon historica, antea semel edita*, edited by Henry Wharton (London: Printed by S. Roycroft, 1693).

Standard edition: In *Corpus Christianorum Series Latina*, volume 119B, edited by J. E. Hudson (Turnhout, Belgium: Brepols, 1983), pp. 370–409.

In Cantica Canticorum (On the Song of Songs, circa 720–731)

Manuscripts: There are more than sixty extant manuscripts. The standard edition (1983) is based on one manuscript from the eighth century (Bibliothèque Saint Geneviève, Paris, 63), four from the ninth century, and one from the eleventh century.

First publication: In *Venerabilis Bedae opera omnia* (Basel: Printed by John Herwagen, 1563).

Standard edition: In *Corpus Christianorum Series Latina*, volume 119B, edited by D. Hurst (Turnhout, Belgium: Brepols, 1983), pp. 175–375.

Homeliarum evangelii libri II (Homilies on the Gospels, circa 720–731)

Manuscripts: The standard edition (1965) is based on thirteen of the more than twenty extant manuscripts. The full text of all fifty homilies is found only in two Continental manuscripts from the ninth century: Bibliothèque publique, Boulogne, 75, and Zentralbibliothek, Zurich, C. 42.

First publication: In *Homiliae Bedae presbyteri Anglosaxonis . . . aestivales (hyemales) de tempore & de sanctis*, 2 parts (Cologne: Printed by Joannes Gymnicus, 1534).

Standard edition: In *Corpus Christianorum Series Latina*, volume 122, edited by D. Hurst (Turnhout, Belgium: Brepols, 1965), pp. 1–378.

Edition in English: *Homilies on the Gospels*, 2 volumes, translated by Lawrence T. Martin and David Hurst (Kalamazoo, Mich.: Cistercian Publications, 1991).

Vita sancti Cuthberti prosaica (Life of Saint Cuthbert, in prose, circa 721)

Manuscripts: Thirty-six extant manuscripts include this work, and two more include some extracts. The standard edition (1940) is largely based on University College, Oxford, MS. 165 (early twelfth century).

First publication: In *Venerabilis Bedae opera omnia* (Basel: Printed by John Herwagen, 1563).

Standard edition: In *Two Lives of St. Cuthbert*, edited and translated by Bertram Colgrave (Cambridge: Cambridge University Press, 1940), pp. 141–307.

Edition in English: In *The Age of Bede*, edited by D. H. Farmer, translated by J. F. Webb (Harmondsworth: Penguin, 1983), pp. 39–102.

De tabernaculo et vasis eius ac vestibus sacerdotum (On the Tabernacle, circa 721–725)

Manuscripts: There are more than sixty extant manuscripts. The standard edition (1969) is based on five Continental manuscripts from the ninth century, one of the earliest being Bibliothèque publique, Orléans, 62, from Fleury.

First publication: In *Venerabilis Bedae opera omnia* (Basel: Printed by John Herwagen, 1563).

Standard edition: In *Corpus Christianorum Series Latina*, volume 119A, edited by D. Hurst (Turnhout, Belgium: Brepols, 1969), pp. 1–139.

Edition in English: *On the Tabernacle*, translated by Arthur G. Holder (Liverpool: Liverpool University Press, 1994).

De temporum ratione liber includens chronica maiora (On the Reckoning of Times, including a Long Chronicle, 725)

Manuscripts: There are 245 extant manuscripts that include the entire work or portions of it. In the standard edition, the text of *De temporum ratione* is based on fifteen Continental manuscripts from the ninth century; that of the *Chronica maiora* is based on five Continental manuscripts from the ninth century and one from the tenth. For each work the oldest extant manuscript is Deutsche Staatsbibliothek, Berlin, 128 (Phillipps, 1831) from Verona, circa 800.

First publication: In *Bedae presbyteri Anglosaxonis viri eruditissimi de natura rerum et temporum ratione*, edited by John Sichardus (Basel: Printed by Henri Petrus, 1529).

Standard edition: In *Corpus Christianorum Series Latina*, volume 123B, edited by C. W. Jones (Turnhout, Belgium: Brepols, 1977), pp. 239–544.

In Regum librum XXX quaestiones (Thirty Questions on Kings, circa 725)

Manuscripts: There are more than forty extant manuscripts. The standard edition (1972) is based on one manuscript (Koninklijke Bibliotheek 165 at The Hague) that may have been written late in the eighth century, and three ninth-century manuscripts, including Pembroke College, Cambridge, 81, which was written on the Continent but later came into the monastic library at Bury Saint Edmunds.

First publication: In *Venerabilis Bedae opera omnia* (Basel: Printed by John Herwagen, 1563).

Standard edition: In *Corpus Christianorum Series Latina*, volume 119, edited by D. Hurst (Turnhout, Belgium: Brepols, 1972), pp. 289–322.

Retractatio in Actus Apostolorum (Retraction on Acts, circa 725–731)

Manuscripts: There are thirty extant manuscripts. The standard edition (1983) is largely based on seven manuscripts, the most reliable of which is Landesbibliothek, Karlsruhe, Augiensis 77 (ninth century).

First publication: In *Venerabilis Bedae opera omnia* (Basel: Printed by John Herwagen, 1563).

Standard edition: In *Corpus Christianorum Series Latina*, volume 121, edited by M. L. W. Laistner (Turnhout, Belgium: Brepols, 1983), pp. 101–163.

In Ezram et Neemiam (On Ezra and Nehemiah, circa 725–731)

Manuscripts: There are more than thirty extant manuscripts. The standard edition (1969) is based on four Continental manuscripts from the ninth century, including Bibliothèque publique, Lyon, 471, and Stiftsbibliothek, Saint Gall, 253.

First publication: In *Venerabilis Bedae opera omnia* (Basel: Printed by John Herwagen, 1563).

Standard edition: In *Corpus Christianorum Series Latina*, volume 119A, edited by D. Hurst (Turnhout, Belgium: Brepols, 1969), pp. 235–392.

Historia abbatum (History of the Abbots, circa 725–731)

Manuscripts: There are eight extant manuscripts. The standard edition (1896) is largely based on Durham Cathedral Library MS. B. II. 35 (twelfth century) and two manuscripts in the British Library: Harley 3020 (tenth century) and Cotton Tiberius D. III (twelfth century).

First publication: In *Venerabilis Bedae epistolae duae, necnon vitae abbatum Wiremuthensium & Girwiensium*, edited by Sir James Ware (Dublin: Printed by John Crook, 1664).

Standard edition: In *Venerabilis Baedae opera historica*, edited by Charles Plummer (Oxford: Oxford University Press, 1896; reprinted, 1946, 1956), 1: 364–387.

Edition in English: In *The Age of Bede*, edited and translated by D. H. Farmer (Harmondsworth: Penguin, 1983), pp. 183–208.

Martyrologium (circa 725–731)

Manuscripts: There are more than twenty extant manuscripts, including several from the ninth century, such as Staatsbibliothek, Munich, 15818; Stiftsbibliothek, Saint Gall, 451; and Biblioteca, Verona, capitolare 65.

First publication: In *Acta sanctorum quotquot toto orbe coluntur, vel a catholicas scriptoribus celebrantur quae ex latinis et graecis, aliarumque gentium antiquis monumentis*, volume 2, edited by Godefroid Henskens and Daniel van Papenbroeck (Antwerp: Printed by John van Meurs, 1688), pp. viii–xl.

Standard edition: In *Édition practique des martyrologes de Bède, de l'anonyme lyonnais et de Florus*, edited by Jacques DuBois and Geneviève Renaud (Paris: Éditions du Centre national de la recherche scientifique, 1976).

De templo (On the Temple, circa 729–731)

Manuscripts: There are more than forty extant manuscripts. The standard edition (1969) is based on five Continental manuscripts from the ninth century (including Pembroke College, Cambridge, 81, which was later in the monastic library at Bury Saint Edmunds) and one from the eleventh.

First publication: In *Venerabilis Bedae opera omnia* (Basel: Printed by John Herwagen, 1563).

Standard edition: In *Corpus Christianorum Series Latina*, volume 119A, edited by D. Hurst (Turnhout, Belgium: Brepols, 1969), pp. 141–234.

Historia ecclesiastica gentis Anglorum (Ecclesiastical History of the English People, 731)

Manuscripts: More than 150 extant manuscripts include the complete text; many others include excerpts. The standard edition by Colgrave and Mynors (1969, 1991) is based on two classes of early manuscripts. The C group is represented by Landesbibliothek, Kassel, theologicus Q. 2 (Northumbrian, late eighth century); British Library, MS. Cotton Tiberius C. II (Southern England, late eighth century); and an early-eleventh-century manuscript in the Bodleian Library, Oxford, MS. Hatton 43 (4106). The M group includes two Northumbrian manuscripts written soon after the time of Bede: Cambridge University Library Kk. 5. 16 (circa 737) and Public Library, Leningrad, Q. v. I. 18 (circa 747). Facsimiles: *The Moore Bede: Cambridge University Library MS. Kk. 5. 16*, edited by Peter Hunter Blair

and Roger A. B. Mynors, Early English Manuscripts in Facsimile 9 (Copenhagen: Rosenkilde & Bagger, 1959); *The Leningrad Bede*, edited by O. Arngart, Early English Manuscripts in Facsimile 2 (Copenhagen: Rosenkilde & Bagger, 1952). Six extant manuscripts transcribe the Old English version in whole or in part; Miller's edition (1890–1898) is based largely on Tanner 10 (tenth century) in the Bodleian Library at Oxford. Facsimile: *The Tanner Bede: The Old English Version of Bede's "Historia ecclesiastica," Oxford Bodleian Library Tanner 10*, edited by Janet Bately, Early English Manuscripts in Facsimile 24 (Copenhagen: Rosenkilde & Bagger, 1992).

First publications: Latin version, *Historia ecclesiastica gentis Anglorum* (Strasbourg, circa 1475–1480); Old English version, in *Historiae ecclesiasticae gentis Anglorum libri V, a venerabilis Beda presbytero scripti*, edited by Abraham Whelock (Cambridge: Printed by Roger Daniel, 1643); Modern English version, *The history of the Church of Englande compiled by Venerable Bede, Englishman*, translated by Thomas Stapleton (Antwerp: Printed by John Laet, 1565).

Standard editions: *Bede's Ecclesiastical History of the English People*, edited and translated by Bertram Colgrave and R. A. B. Mynors (Oxford: Clarendon Press, 1969; second edition, 1991); *The Old English Version of Bede's Ecclesiastical History of the English People*, edited and translated by Thomas Miller, EETS, o.s. 95–96, 110–111 (1890–1898; reprinted, 1959).

Edition in English: *Ecclesiastical History of the English People, with Bede's Letter to Egbert and Cuthbert's Letter on the Death of Bede*, translated by Leo Sherley-Price, revised by R. E. Latham, with translations of the minor works by D. H. Farmer (London: Penguin, 1990).

Aliquot quaestionum liber (On Eight Questions, circa 731–735)

Manuscripts: There are five extant manuscripts, the earliest of which is probably Bibliothèque publique, Cambrai, 364, from the eleventh or twelfth century. Only the first eight questions are genuine.

First publication: In *Venerabilis Bedae opera omnia* (Basel: Printed by John Herwagen, 1563).

Standard edition: In *Patrologia Latina*, volume 93, edited by J.-P. Migne (Paris: J.-P. Migne, 1850; reprinted, Turnhout, Belgium: Brepols, 1980), cols. 455–462.

Epistola ad Ecgbertum Episcopum (Letter to Egbert, 5 November 734)

Manuscripts: The standard edition (1896) is based on British Library MS. Harley 4688 (twelfth century) and Merton College, Oxford, MS. 49 (fifteenth century). The only other extant manuscript is Koninklijke Bibliotheek 70. H. 7 at The Hague (early tenth century).

First publication: In *Venerabilis Bedae epistolae duae, necnon vitae abbatum Wiremuthensium & Girwiensium*, edited by Sir James Ware (Dublin: Printed by John Crook, 1664).

Standard edition: In *Venerabilis Baedae opera historica*, edited by Charles Plummer (Oxford: Oxford University Press, 1896; reprinted, 1946, 1956), 1: 405–423.

Edition in English: In *Ecclesiastical History of the English People, with Bede's Letter to Egbert and Cuthbert's Letter on the Death of Bede*, translated by Leo Sherley-Price, revised by R. E. Latham, with translations of the minor works by D. H. Farmer (London: Penguin, 1990).

COLLECTED EDITIONS: *Venerabilis Bedae opera omnia*, in *Patrologia Latina*, volumes 90–95, edited by J.-P. Migne (Paris: J.-P. Migne, 1850–1851; reprinted, Turnhout, Belgium: Brepols, 1980).

Bedae venerabilis opera, in *Corpus Christianorum Series Latina*, volumes 118–123, 175–176, to date, various editors (Turnhout, Belgium: Brepols, 1955–).

Bede is chiefly remembered as the author of the *Ecclesiastical History of the English People*, the most important source of information about Anglo-Saxon England prior to 731 (the date of the work's completion). In his own time, however, and throughout the Middle Ages, he was esteemed not only for his historical writings but also for his numerous works on grammar, poetry, chronology, biblical interpretation, and the lives of saints. Although English was his native tongue, all of his surviving works are in Latin, the language of the medieval European church. His vocation was that of a Christian teacher, and his efforts in a variety of literary fields were intended to edify the members (and especially the leaders) of the Church in his own land.

A brief autobiographical account at the end of Bede's *Ecclesiastical History* records that he was born around 673 in Northumbria, on lands that King Ecgfrith would soon thereafter give to Benedict Biscop for the establishment of the twin monaster-ies of Saint Peter's, Wearmouth, and Saint Paul's, Jarrow. All that is known of his family is that they were Christians and English in origin; since he never mentions his parents he may well have been an orphan. When Bede was seven, his relatives brought him to Saint Peter's to be educated, and he probably accompanied the monk Ceolfrith to the new foundation at nearby Jarrow around 682. Except for a few visits to neighboring monasteries, he lived at Jarrow as a monk for the rest of his life.

In the year 686 both Wearmouth and Jarrow were hit by a devastating plague. According to an anonymous *Life of Ceolfrith* that may have been written by Bede, the only ones left to sing the choir offices at Jarrow were Abbot Ceolfrith and a young lad who had been his pupil. If, as is commonly believed, the boy can be identified as Bede, then the episode constitutes a touching picture of him with his mentor, joined in faithful dedication to the life of prayer that was at the heart of the monk's daily routine. Years later, after Bede's death, the Carolingian scholar Alcuin recalled how Bede had believed that angels visited the monastery church at the canonical hours of prayer, saying, "What if they do not find me there among the brothers? Will they not have to say, 'Where is Bede?'"

At the age of nineteen, in 692, Bede was ordained a deacon by John of Beverley, bishop of Hexham. Since the ecclesiastical canons specified twenty-five as the minimum age for diaconal ordination, Bede's pious devotion and aptitude for learning must have been readily apparent to his superiors. Though he became a teacher of renown in the monastic school and was ordained a priest at the age of thirty in 703, Bede never became abbot of his monastery; possibly this was because he did not share the pedigree of noble birth common to most of those elected to that post. His customary occupations as scholar and monk are succinctly described in the *Ecclesiastical History*: "Amid the observance of the discipline of the Rule and the daily task of singing in the church, it has always been my delight to learn or to teach or to write."

The foundation of the monastic curriculum was Latin grammar, so obviously essential for monks who were reading, interpreting, and copying the Bible and other Christian texts. Although Bede's library contained the works of Donatus and many other Roman grammarians, he deemed it advisable to produce three explicitly Christian textbooks of his own for his pupils' use. *On the Art of Metrics* (circa 710–731) is an introduction to the various types of Latin poetry, with an appendix, *On Figures and Tropes*, that deals with stylistic figures of speech, including the forms of allegory so important in medieval biblical exegesis. The third grammatical work was *On Orthography* (circa 710–731), a handbook of word usage which has been compared to Henry Watson Fowler's *A Dictionary of Modern English Usage* (1926). Arranged according to the letters of the alphabet, it lists forms whose spelling or meaning would be likely to cause difficulties for the reader or scribe. Until recently, modern scholars have assumed that Bede was still a deacon when he wrote his textbooks on grammar, but it now appears that these works are considerably more sophisticated than was previously thought. At least in their final forms, they may well be products of his later years.

Bede knew the works of Virgil and some other Roman authors, probably including Cicero's rhetorical handbook *On Invention,* but many of the classical quotations in his grammatical writings are borrowed from the compilations of earlier grammarians. In many cases, however, he substituted passages from the Bible and from Christian poets such as Sedulius and Arator for examples that his predecessors had taken from classical literature. Bede knew that his Anglo-Saxon students were eager to learn Latin primarily because it granted them access to the Bible, the liturgy, and the theology of the Church. Largely due to the emphasis he placed on works of Christian poetry and prose, his grammatical treatises soon became standard texts in the medieval European schools.

Bede's works on nature, number, and time were destined for equal popularity. These topics, classified today under the heading of "science," carried spiritual as well as practical significance for Bede and his contemporaries. In *On the Nature of Things* (circa 703), he drew upon Pliny's *Natural History* and the works of Isidore of Seville to discuss the phenomena of earth, heaven, and ocean as part of God's created order. The short treatise *On Times* (703) and the much longer revision of it entitled *On the Reckoning of Times* (725) deal with the chronology of minutes, hours, days, months, years, centuries, and epochs; both treatises conclude with chronicles of significant events in world history. Here and elsewhere Bede's calendrical computations often dealt with the proper method for calculating the date of Easter, as this had been a long-standing point of controversy between the Roman and Celtic traditions in the Church.

It is ironic that Bede, always so meticulous about matters of chronology, was once accused of heresy as a result of some of his calculations. Following ancient Christian custom, he believed that from the day of creation to the end of time there were six ages of the world, corresponding both to the six days of the Creation in Genesis and to the classical notion of the six stages of human life; the Sabbath rest of the saints was understood to correspond to a seventh age, with Judgment Day expected to inaugurate the eighth age of eternal life. In his treatise *On Times* Bede employs Jerome's Vulgate translation of the Hebrew Old Testament to calculate the number of years from creation to the birth of Christ at the beginning of the sixth age, whereas earlier writers had derived a different figure by using the ancient Greek text of the Old Testament known as the Septuagint. On the basis of this discrepancy, some drunken men at a feast in Hexham suggested to Bishop Wilfrid that Bede was a heretic because he had written that Christ was born in the fifth age of the world, rather than the sixth. His defense is in the *Letter to Plegwine* (708), in which he confesses that he is "as angry as is lawful, and more angry than I am accustomed to be." This letter affords a rare glimpse of Bede as a polemicist publicly maintaining his own cause.

Much more typical of him are the many exegetical works which interpret biblical texts. When he enumerates his writings at the conclusion of the *Ecclesiastical History,* Bede puts the commentaries on the Bible at the head of the list. Even though he modestly describes his role as that of a mere compiler and interpreter of extracts from the writings of the early church fathers, he was actually a highly skilled and creative biblical scholar in his own right. It is true that his commentaries contain many long passages copied verbatim from ancient Christian authors such as Ambrose, Augustine, Jerome, and Gregory the Great. However, he did not hesitate to contradict their authority when he believed his predecessors to be in error. In his commentary *On Genesis* (circa 703–709, circa 725–731), for example, he disagreed with Ambrose by explaining that God rejected the sacrifice of Cain not because a vegetable offering was inferior to an animal sacrifice, but rather on account of Cain's impious attitude of mind. Moreover, a good many of his commentaries were on biblical books that had not received much prior attention; in those instances, he showed himself quite capable of original work very much in the spirit of an earlier age.

For the most part, that meant allegorical interpretation. As he frequently explained, Bede had learned from the fathers that it was possible to interpret Scripture in four different ways: literally, describing historical events; allegorically (in the narrow sense of the term), referring to Christ or the Church; tropologically, yielding moral instruction;

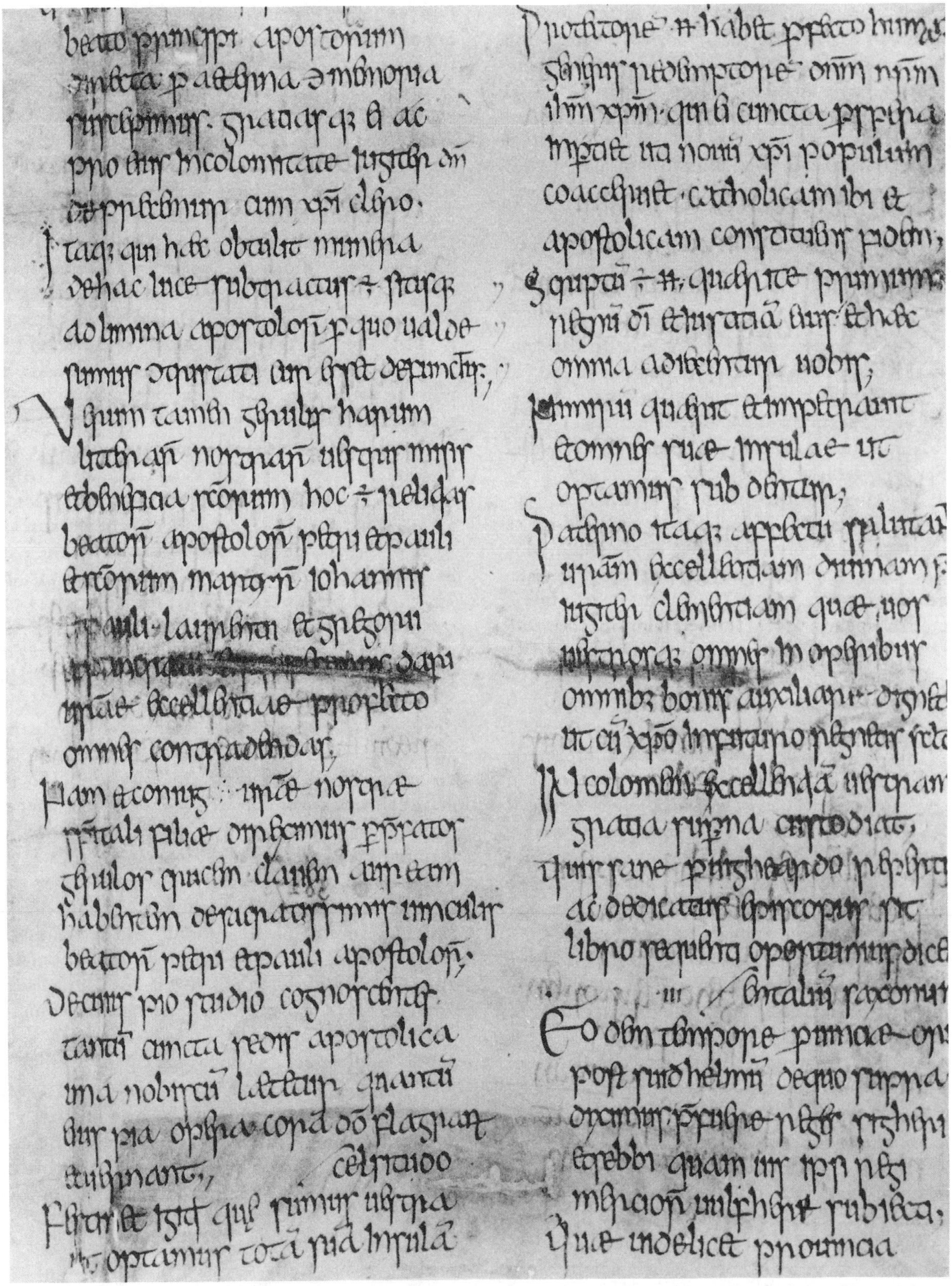

Page from a late-eighth-century transcription of Bede's Historia ecclesiastica gentis Anglorum. *The passage is from the conclusion of Book 3, in which Bede reproduces a seventh-century letter from Wighard at Rome to the Saxon king Oswy (Pierpont Morgan Library, MS. M826).*

or anagogically, pointing to the future joys of heaven and eternal life. Except when expounding this theory of allegorical exegesis, Bede never interpreted a given passage on all four levels. His usual practice was to give a more or less detailed account of the literal meaning, and then to pursue a spiritual meaning on one level or another that would offer his readers inspiration, guidance, or encouragement in the life of faith.

Nearly all of the exegetical works proceed verse-by-verse through the designated portion of the biblical text. Bede's comments were usually based on the Latin Vulgate translation of the Bible executed by Jerome at the end of the fourth century; the Codex Amiatinus, which is the oldest extant manuscript of the complete Vulgate, was prepared in the scriptorium at Bede's monastery during his lifetime. In addition, he referred to several earlier Old Latin versions, as well as to texts of the New Testament in the original Greek. He had no firsthand knowledge of Hebrew, but he did make good use of the Hebrew etymologies and definitions that he found scattered throughout the works of Jerome. He was particularly fond of number symbolism, often remarking that in the Scriptures the number three reminds us of the Holy Trinity, four recalls the four gospels or the four points of the compass, twelve stands for the twelve apostles, and so forth.

Like other ancient and medieval interpreters, Bede believed that every verse of the Bible, indeed every letter, contained spiritual mysteries placed there by divine inspiration. His commentaries were intended to help his readers carry out the program of religious education set forth by Augustine in *On Christian Doctrine,* in which the Bible is seen as the foundation of all true knowledge. Successive generations of Christians must have judged Bede to have been quite successful in this regard, for his commentaries were preserved in an abundance of medieval manuscripts, and many selections from them were taken up into the standard medieval compilation of biblical interpretation known as the *Ordinary Gloss.*

Bede's earliest commentaries dealt with selected books of the New Testament. He began with the last book of the Bible, called the Apocalypse or Revelation (circa 703–709), and then turned to the seven Catholic Epistles (circa 709), the Acts of the Apostles (circa 709), and the Gospel of Luke (circa 709–716). Some years later he wrote a commentary on the Gospel of Mark (circa 720–725) and a second work on Acts which he entitled a *Retraction* (circa 725–731) because in it he corrected some mistakes he had made the first time. Comparing the two works on Acts reveals that Bede's understanding of Greek improved considerably in the intervening period of some twenty years. The same two commentaries give evidence of his interest in biblical geography, which also led him to produce *On the Holy Places* (circa 703–709), an abridgment of the Irish monk Adamnan's account of a pilgrimage to the Holy Land, supplemented with passages taken from Eucherius of Lyons and the Jewish writer Josephus. Bede's work on the New Testament also included an anthology of Augustine's comments on the Pauline epistles (circa 703–731), a treatise *On Eight Questions* (circa 731–735) dealing with specific problems of interpretation, and a collection of fifty homilies (circa 720–731) on the gospel texts appointed to be read in church on the Sundays and major feasts of the liturgical year.

His first completed commentary on the Old Testament was *On the First Book of Samuel* (716), in which he employed the allegorical method to associate each verse with some aspect of the person and work of Christ. He returned to this part of the Bible in a later work entitled *Thirty Questions on Kings* (circa 725), where he concentrated on difficult points concerning the literal meaning of the books of Samuel and Kings. The first part of the commentary *On Genesis,* dealing with the six days of creation, relies heavily on earlier works by the Greek church father Basil and the Latin writers Ambrose, Augustine, and Jerome; this portion seems to have been written quite early in Bede's life (circa 703–709). The remainder of the work, which comes from a later period (circa 725–731), carries the exposition up through the expulsion of Ishmael in Genesis 21:10. Three books completed in Bede's mature years treat the construction of Old Testament houses of worship as symbolic of the building and rebuilding of the Body of Christ; they are *On the Tabernacle* (circa 721–725), *On the Temple* (circa 729–731), and *On Ezra and Nehemiah* (circa 725–731). There are also commentaries on Tobit, Proverbs, the canticle in Habakkuk 3:2–19, and the Song of Songs (all circa 720–731).

Many of Bede's exegetical works were written at the request of individual clergy or monastics who were his friends. In every case, however, he must have had a wider audience in mind. He wrote primarily for his fellow monks, many of whom had neither the ability nor the inclination to read the works of the ancient fathers for themselves. For this reason, he naturally stressed interpretations relevant to those who were striving for perfection in the Christian life under vows of poverty, chastity, and obedience. But he was also mindful that Anglo-Saxon monks in his day were active as pastors, preachers, and teachers, not only within the monastery but among nearby communities of layfolk as well. *The Rule of Saint Benedict* (early sixth century) had not envisioned pastoral activity of this sort on the part of the monks, but Northumbrian monasteries like Wearmouth and Jarrow, though largely Benedictine in spirit, had not yet come to follow that *Rule* in any exclusive fashion. Bede's commentaries, then, offer an ideal vision of the Christian life that is both monastic and pastoral in character.

The same could be said of his hagiographies (saints' lives), which followed the customary and highly stylized form this literature had attained long before the time of Bede. His inspiration came from the Bible, and from classic Christian biographies such as Athanasius's *Life* of the Egyptian monk Antony, Possidius's *Life of Augustine,* and the *Dialogues* of Gregory the Great. Unlike modern biographers, who tend to focus on the distinctive and unique characteristics of their subjects, medieval hagiographers like Bede were primarily concerned to demonstrate how closely the pious lives and courageous deaths of holy men and women conformed to the supreme model of sanctity presented by Jesus Christ himself. Though based on the evidence of historical fact, hagiography was always intended to edify and inspire, as well as to instruct. When Bede wrote that a saint had been wondrously precocious as a child, or had undergone great suffering, or had worked miracles, or had reached the heights of contemplative prayer, he expected his readers to understand such deeds as signs of God's gracious favor not only to that individual, but to the Church as a whole.

The most important of Bede's hagiographical works were two lives of the extremely popular Northumbrian saint Cuthbert (circa 635–687). One of these works was in poetry, the other in prose; it was common practice for writers to treat the same subject in both literary forms, as Bede recognized when he referred to Aldhelm's poetic and prose versions of a treatise *On Virginity* as an "opus geminatum" (paired work). Bede's lives of Cuthbert are largely based on an anonymous prose *Life* (circa 699–705) written by a monk from Cuthbert's monastery at Lindisfarne. This was a simple but effective treatment in four books, each of which covered one period in Cuthbert's career: his childhood and youth; his service in the monastic community; his hermitage on Farne Island; and his brief tenure as bishop of Lindisfarne for two years before returning to the hermitage once again shortly before his death. Both of Bede's versions retain much material from the anonymous *Life* but supplement it with further information, embroider it with more elaborate styles

of writing, and completely recast its structural outline.

The original draft of the metrical *Life of Saint Cuthbert* was written while Bede was preparing his first commentary on the Acts of Apostles, in which he makes frequent use of a paraphrase of Acts in hexameters by the sixth-century Latin poet Arator. Apparently inspired by Arator's method of constructing his exposition as a series of allegorical poetic reflections on brief prose summaries of the main events described in Acts, Bede followed a similar procedure when he wrote his metrical hagiography. The resultant work sacrifices historical detail in favor of symbolic allusion, thereby inviting the reader to ponder the spiritual significance of Cuthbert's life. Bede devotes particular attention to the saint's miraculous powers, of which he believed himself to have some firsthand knowledge. In a dedicatory preface, probably added to the metrical *Life* when Bede made some slight revisions at a later date (circa 710–720), he remarks that he had experienced one of Cuthbert's miracles through the *curationem* of his tongue. This Latin term might designate a physical "cure," but it is more likely that Bede was referring to "guidance" in the form of literary inspiration.

Comprising nearly a thousand hexameter verses, the metrical *Life of Saint Cuthbert* (circa 706–707) was Bede's longest poetic effort; it was not, however, his only contribution to the field. At least thirteen hymns can plausibly be attributed to him, including a long poem *On the Day of Judgment* that also appears in a tenth-century Old English paraphrase. In addition, several short poems are embedded within some of his works of prose. The evidence of these poetic works indicates that he was a competent versifier in a variety of classical Latin forms, but he is not generally regarded as an extraordinarily gifted poet.

The second *Life of Saint Cuthbert* (circa 721) is a prose work in forty-six chapters, written at the request of Bishop Eadfrith and the community of monks at Lindisfarne. In the prologue Bede does not mention the anonymous *Life* from which he drew much of his material, but he does explain that he had obtained information about Cuthbert from some of those who had known him at Lindisfarne. Bede depicts Cuthbert as an exemplary saint in the Celtic tradition of missionary-minded ascetics, but he also makes it clear that Cuthbert was completely devoted to the Roman observance of Easter, which he was reported to have advocated with earnest fervor even from his deathbed. For Bede, Cuthbert's abundant miracles marked him as the model of a reforming bishop whose monastic experience had prepared him first for pastoral service and then for the hermit's life of contemplative prayer. Largely due to the persuasive appeal of Bede's prose *Life,* Cuthbert became, in effect, the patron saint not only of Lindisfarne but of all Northumbria, and one of the most popular of all English saints.

The holy lives of five other Northumbrian monks are the subjects of the *History of the Abbots* (circa 725–731). Based in part on the anonymous *Life of Ceolfrith* (circa 716) that may have been written by Bede as well, this book is more historical biography than hagiography, since it neither reports any miracles worked by the abbots nor describes the development of cults acknowledging them as saints. Its emphasis is on the foundation and growth of the monastery itself. Bede tells of the size of the monastic houses, the extent of their lands, and the magnificence of their buildings and libraries. He also traces the orderly succession of abbots in accordance with Benedict Biscop's directive that his successors should be chosen for their holiness, as prescribed in the *Rule of Saint Benedict,* rather than on account of their kinship to him, as mandated by Anglo-Saxon law. The *History of the Abbots* was a precursor of later medieval monastic chronicles which recorded the privileges and accomplishments of particular monasteries. It also gives a remarkably full picture of monastic life in England at the turn of the eighth century, including the poignant scene in which the monks bid a tearful farewell to Bede's mentor Ceolfrith after he had resigned as abbot in 716 in order to undertake a pilgrimage to Rome.

The *Ecclesiastical History of the English People,* which is Bede's greatest and most enduring achievement, comprises elements of hagiography set within the framework of a larger historical narrative. Like the fourth-century *Ecclesiastical History* by Eusebius of Caesarea, this work tells the story of the Church as it was established and increased by God's providential hand. Unlike Eusebius, however, Bede focuses on the history of a single nation; in this, he was following the example he found in the *History of the Franks* by Gregory of Tours. Even while concentrating on events and personalities in his native Northumbria, Bede consistently affirms that the English, regardless of their diverse tribal origins, are a chosen people united in their allegiance to Christ and their communion with the Roman church. Given the multiplicity of Anglo-Saxon kingdoms in those days, this depiction of a unified England was only an idealized vision, but its influence on later generations certainly helped to create subsequent political reality. It was no accident that the *Ecclesiastical History* was one of the first Latin works translated into English in the ninth century during the reign of Alfred the Great.

In a preface addressed to King Ceolwulf of Northumbria, Bede explains that his history presents the reader with good examples to imitate and bad examples to avoid, a reminder to the modern reader that, despite the care with which Bede acknowledged his sources, his purpose was primarily didactic. He did his best to verify data collated from a variety of sources, including the writings of earlier historians, archival materials from Canterbury and Rome (which he often quoted verbatim), reports from numerous correspondents in other parts of the country, the testimony of eyewitnesses, and the hearsay evidence of common report. But he warns that the inclusion of some of this material could only be justified by a "true law of history," according to which the historian was entitled to report popular opinions that may be unlikely, or even manifestly untrue, as long as they conformed to the expectations of the reading audience and were useful for edification.

Bede divided his history into five books, reminiscent of the Pentateuch, the five books of the law of Moses. Echoing the creation account in Genesis, Book 1 opens with a geographical description of the land of Britain as an earthly paradise. Bede then proceeds to locate his narrative within the framework of Roman history (beginning with Julius Caesar's invasion of Britain), and within the sacred history of the universal Church. By reckoning many dates from the year of Christ's Incarnation, he popularized the anno Domini system of dating, first devised in the sixth century by the Greek monk Dionysius Exiguus and still familiar to us today. Following the British historian Gildas, Bede next tells of the British Christians' fall from grace when they failed to preach the gospel to their Anglo-Saxon conquerors, thereby leaving the conversion of the English to Augustine of Canterbury and his companions, who arrived in 597 as missionaries from Pope Gregory the Great. He describes the baptism of King Æthelberht of Kent and the establishment of Augustine's episcopal monastery at Canterbury in glowing terms, but he does not conclude Book 1 with these milestones. Instead, he shifts his attention north to the land of his birth by appending a final chapter recounting the military defeat of the Irish at the hands of Æthelfrith of Northumbria. The exploits of this pagan king are celebrated in terms that recall both the Old Testament King Saul and the heroic warriors of Anglo-Saxon poems such as *Judith* and *The Wanderer.*

The short biography of Gregory the Great that begins Book 2 includes the famous tale of the pope's encounter with English slave boys, those Angles he admired as having such angelic faces. Subsequent chapters relate the death of Augustine, the struggles and achievements of his successors, and the initial evangelization of Northumbria through the ministry of the Roman missionary Paulinus from Kent. Bede's account of the deliberations over conversion that were held at King Edwin's court provides brief glimpses into the rapidly disappearing world of Anglo-Saxon paganism, such as the high priest Coifi volunteering to be the first new Christian to take up sword and spear for the purpose of profaning a pagan temple, and an unnamed councillor arguing for the new religion by comparing the brevity of human life to the flight of a wandering sparrow through the midst of the king's feasting hall in winter. Stories such as these must have come to Bede as traditions that were already familiar, but modern scholars have noted that his retellings are skillfully constructed to achieve maximum effect. Bede's artistry is also evident in the overall arrangement of the work. Although his narrative often hangs on the succession lists of kings and bishops, he was no slave to chronological arrangement. There are flashes forward and backward in time, capsule biographies of major figures, and thematic clusters of miraculous events.

Book 3 records the renewal of Christianity in Northumbria following the faltering of the Roman mission. The great heroes in this book are the "most Christian king" Oswald and the humble Irish missionary Aidan, whom he invited to become the bishop of Lindisfarne. Bede's admiration for the Celtic spirituality of Aidan, and that of others such as Columba and Colman, was limited only by their refusal to accept Roman customs concerning the date of Easter and the monastic tonsure. To appreciate the significance of these issues for Bede, the modern reader must understand that they symbolized a conflict between two ecclesiastical and political parties. The reason he devoted so much attention to the triumph of the Roman observance at the Synod of Whitby in 664 was that he regarded that assembly as the decisive moment when unity and peace began to prevail in his homeland. However, factional tensions persisted between those Northumbrians who wanted to retain much of the Celtic tradition while correcting its errors and others who preferred to jettison the Celtic past for the Roman future. Bede renders tacit support to the former group by restraining his praise for the Roman partisan Wilfrid and accentuating his admiration for Cuthbert, an Englishman trained in the Celtic tradition.

The vigorous renewal of the English church under Theodore of Tarsus forms the subject of the first several chapters of Book 4. Bede portrays this elderly Greek, who was archbishop of Canterbury from 688 to 690, as an exemplary bishop who instructed many pupils in both sacred and secular learning, convened church councils at Hertford and Hatfield, and made peace between warring kings. The same book contains laudatory accounts of such luminaries as Abbess Hilda of Whitby; Æthelthryth of Ely, who became the virgin queen of Northumbria; and the same Cuthbert whom Bede had memorialized in verse and in prose. Explaining that he had obtained new information since writing the earlier lives of Cuthbert, in this version Bede records two additional miracles said to have been worked by contact with the incorrupt body of the saint. These miracles, like the others he recounts in the *Ecclesiastical History,* he understood as signs of God's providential favor toward faithful Christians, rather than as impressive wonders to convert unbelievers. Especially for miracles that had occurred close to his own time, he is usually careful to cite the sources of his information, often derived from oral tradition.

The fifth and final book records miracles associated with John of Beverley, who had ordained Bede as both deacon and priest. It also tells how the English church, having been fully established by the end of the seventh century, began to send out missionaries of its own. Wilfrid and Willibrord in Friscia, and the two priests named Hewald in Old Saxony, carried the gospel message to their Germanic kinsfolk. Most significantly for Bede, in 716 an Englishman named Egbert was able to persuade the Irish monks at Iona to accept the Roman observance; except for the obstinate Welsh, all the peoples of Britain were at last united in the celebration of Easter. Just prior to a chronological summary of events and the author's autobiographical statement, Bede's *Ecclesiastical History* concludes with his survey of the peaceful and prosperous state of the Church in 731. Noting, however, that a great many Northumbrians of all classes had recently abandoned the art of war for monastic life, he issues an ominous warning: "What the result will be, a later generation will discover."

The cause of this anxiety about the rising tide of monasteries is revealed in Bede's last surviving work, a long letter written on 5 November 734 to a former pupil, another Egbert, who had become bishop of York. Writing from his sickbed because he was too weak to travel, Bede angrily denounces members of the nobility for founding false monasteries on their lands in order to avoid military service. He urges Egbert to correct such abuses, and also to ordain more priests for the country villages, to appoint more bishops to assist him (as Gregory the Great had intended), and to strengthen the spiritual life of the laity by encouraging them to receive communion more frequently and by teaching them to say the Apostle's Creed and the Lord's Prayer in their native tongue.

In the letter to Egbert, Bede acknowledges that he had often found it necessary to provide English translations of liturgical texts even for the clergy, as many of them were ignorant of Latin. This brief remark recalls other instances in which he employed his knowledge of the vernacular, such as his etymologies for the Anglo-Saxon names of the months in *On the Reckoning of Times,* his explication of place-names in the historical works, and, most notably, his famous account of the origins of sacred English poetry through the miraculous inspiration of the cowherd Caedmon. In Book 4 of the *Ecclesiastical History,* Caedmon is described as an illiterate worker on the monastery estate at Whitby who had never been able to take his turn in singing at a feast until an angel appeared to him in a dream and commanded him to "sing about the beginning of created things." Although Bede relates that Caedmon went on to compose English verses about the entire history of salvation, he provides a Latin paraphrase for only one short poem about Creation; fortunately, an Anglo-Saxon version of it is preserved in the margins of two early manuscripts of the *Ecclesiastical History* that were produced at Wearmouth-Jarrow shortly after the time of Bede.

Matters of translation occupied Bede's attention even in his final days, which he partially devoted to rendering a portion of John's Gospel into English. His pupil Cuthbert wrote that the dying man also roused himself enough to instruct his pupils every day and to make some excerpts from Isidore's treatise *On the Nature of Things.* During the rest of his waking hours he chanted psalms and liturgical antiphons, recited an Old English poem about the Day of Judgment, prayed, and wept. On 25 May, the eve of Ascension Day in 735, after distributing a few small gifts to his monastic brethren, Bede declared, "The time of my departure is at hand, and my soul longs to see Christ my King in all his beauty." He directed the young scribe Wilbert to write a final sentence and then asked to be turned so that as he sat on the floor of his cell he might be facing the place where he used to pray. Singing "Glory be to the Father and to the Son and to the Holy Spirit," and with his head cradled in Wilbert's arm, he breathed his last.

After Bede's death, so many monasteries in England and on the Continent requested copies of his writings that the scriptorium at Wearmouth-Jarrow was forced to devise a smaller, more efficient form of handwriting in order to keep pace with the demand. His fame endured throughout the Middle Ages, as numerous Christian authors acknowledged the authority of his teaching and regarded him as a saint. In the eleventh century his remains were moved from Jarrow to Durham Cathedral, where tradition purports that they still lie today. He has been acclaimed as the greatest scholar of his age, the father of English history, and a doctor of the Church. But countless generations of readers across a dozen centuries have known him best by the customary title of a holy priest, simply as "the Venerable Bede."

Bibliographies:

W. F. Bolton, "A Bede Bibliography: 1935–60," *Traditio,* 18 (1962): 436–445;

Henri Ledoyen, "St. Bède le Vénérable," *Bulletin d'histoire Bénédictine,* 10 (1979–1984): 712–718;

Thomas Eckenrode, "The Venerable Bede: A Bibliographical Essay, 1970–81," *American Benedictine Review,* 36 (June 1985): 172–194.

Biographies:

Eleanor Shipley Duckett, "Bede of Jarrow," in *Anglo-Saxon Saints and Scholars* (New York: Macmillan, 1948), pp. 217–336;

Peter Hunter Blair, *The World of Bede* (London: Secker & Warburg, 1970; Cambridge: Cambridge University Press, 1990);

George Hardin Brown, *Bede the Venerable* (Boston: Twayne, 1987);

Benedicta Ward, *The Venerable Bede* (Wilton, Conn.: Morehouse, 1990).

References:

W. F. Bolton, "Bede," in *A History of Anglo-Latin Literature 597–1066,* volume 1: *597–740* (Princeton: Princeton University Press, 1967), pp. 101–185;

Gerald Bonner, "Bede and Medieval Civilization," *Anglo-Saxon England,* 2 (1973): 71–90;

Bonner, ed., *Famulus Christi: Essays in Commemoration of the Thirteenth Centenary of the Birth of the Venerable Bede* (London: SPCK, 1976);

Bonner, David Rollason, and Clare Stancliffe, eds., *St. Cuthbert: His Cult and His Community to AD 1200* (Woodbridge, U.K.: Boydell, 1989);

James Campbell, "Bede," in *Latin Historians,* edited by T. A. Dorey (London: Routledge & Kegan Paul, 1966), pp. 159–190;

M. Thomas Aquinas Carroll, *The Venerable Bede: His Spiritual Teachings* (Washington, D.C.: Catholic University of America Press, 1946);

R. W. Chambers, "Bede," in *Proceedings of the British Academy,* volume 22 (London: Oxford University Press, 1936), pp. 129–156;

H. E. J. Cowdrey, "Bede and the 'English People,'" *Journal of Religious History,* 11 (December 1981): 501–523;

Jan Davidse, "The Sense of History in the Works of the Venerable Bede," *Studi Medievali,* third series 23 (December 1982): 647–695;

Anna Carlotta Dionisotti, "On Bede, Grammars, and Greek," *Revue Bénédictine,* 92, nos. 1–2 (1982): 111–141;

Robert T. Farrell, ed., *Bede and Anglo-Saxon England: Papers in Honour of the 1300th Anniversary of the Birth of Bede, Given at Cornell University in 1973 and 1974,* British Archaeological Reports 46 (Oxford: British Archaeological Reports, 1978);

Walter Goffart, *The Narrators of Barbarian History (A.D. 550–800): Jordanes, Gregory of Tours, Bede, and Paul the Deacon* (Princeton: Princeton University Press, 1988);

Arthur G. Holder, "Allegory and History in Bede's Interpretation of Sacred Architecture," *American Benedictine Review,* 40 (June 1989): 115–131;

Peter Hunter Blair, *Northumbria in the Days of Bede* (New York: St. Martin's Press, 1976);

Martin Irvine, "Bede the Grammarian and the Scope of Grammatical Studies in Eighth-Century Northumbria," *Anglo-Saxon England,* 15 (1986): 15–44;

Charles W. Jones, "Some Introductory Remarks on Bede's Commentary on Genesis," *Sacris Erudiri,* 19 (1969–1970): 115–198;

Calvin B. Kendall, "Bede's *Historia ecclesiastica*: The Rhetoric of Faith," in *Medieval Eloquence: Studies in the Theory and Practice of Medieval Rhetoric,* edited by James J. Murphy (Berkeley: University of California Press, 1978), pp. 145–172;

Margot H. King and Wesley M. Stevens, eds., *Saints, Scholars, and Heroes: Studies in Medieval Culture in Honour of Charles W. Jones,* volume 1: *The Anglo-Saxon Heritage* (Collegeville, Minn.: St. John's Abbey and University, 1979);

M. L. W. Laistner, "Bede as a Classical and a Patristic Scholar," *Transactions of the Royal Historical Society,* fourth series 16 (London: Offices of the Royal Historical Society, 1933), pp. 69–94; republished in *The Intellectual Heritage of the Early Middle Ages,* edited by Chester G. Starr (Ithaca, N.Y.: Cornell University Press, 1957), pp. 93–116;

Laistner and H. H. King, *A Hand-List of Bede Manuscripts* (Ithaca, N.Y.: Cornell University Press, 1943);

Lawrence Martin, "Bede as a Linguistic Scholar," *American Benedictine Review,* 35 (June 1984): 204–217;

Judith McClure, "Bede and the *Life of Ceolfrid*," *Peritia,* 3 (1984): 71–84;

Robert B. Palmer, "Bede as Textbook Writer: A Study of His *De Arte Metrica*," *Speculum,* 34 (October 1959): 573–584;

Roger Ray, "Bede and Cicero," *Anglo-Saxon England,* 16 (1987): 1–15;

Ray, "What Do We Know about Bede's Commentaries?," *Recherches de théologie ancienne et médiévale,* 49 (1982): 5–20;

Joel T. Rosenthal, "Bede's Use of Miracles in *The Ecclesiastical History*," *Traditio,* 31 (1975): 328–335;

J. N. Stephens, "Bede's Ecclesiastical History," *History,* 62 (February 1977): 1–14;

A. Hamilton Thompson, ed., *Bede: His Life, Times, and Writings: Essays in Commemoration of the Twelfth Centenary of His Death* (Oxford: Clarendon Press, 1935);

J. M. Wallace-Hadrill, *Bede's "Ecclesiastical History of the English People": A Historical Commentary* (Oxford: Clarendon Press, 1988);

Dorothy Whitelock, *From Bede to Alfred* (London: Variorum, 1980);

Patrick Wormald, Donald Bullough, and Roger Collins, eds., *Ideal and Reality in Frankish and Anglo-Saxon Society: Studies Presented to J. M. Wallace-Hadrill* (Oxford: Blackwell, 1983);

Neil Wright, "Bede and Vergil," *Romanobarbarica,* 6 (1981–1982): 361–379.

Caedmon

(flourished 658 – 680)

and

The Caedmon School

(circa 660 – 899)

Joy L. Cafiero
University of South Carolina

MAJOR WORKS – by Caedmon: *Caedmon's Hymn*

Manuscripts: Among the seventeen extant manuscripts are the Moore manuscript (dated 737), Cambridge University Library, Kk. 5. 16, fol. 128^v, and the Leningrad manuscript (746 or earlier), Public Library, MS. Lat. Q. v. I. 18, fol. 107; both are available in facsimile: *The Moore Bede,* edited by P. Hunter Blair and R. A. B. Mynors (Copenhagen: Rosenkilde & Bagger, 1959), and *The Leningrad Bede,* edited by O. Arngart (Copenhagen: Rosenkilde & Bagger, 1952). Another important source is Bodleian Library, Oxford, MS. Tanner 10. For exhaustive information on the various manuscripts see Elliott Van Kirk Dobbie, *The Manuscripts of Caedmon's Hymn and Bede's Death Song* (New York: Columbia University Press, 1937).

Standard editions: In *Three Northumbrian Poems: Caedmon's Hymn, Bede's Death Song and the Leiden Riddle,* edited by A. H. Smith (London: Methuen, 1933); in *The Anglo-Saxon Minor Poems (Anglo-Saxon Poetic Records,* VI), edited by E. V. K. Dobbie (New York: Columbia University Press, 1942); in *Seven Old English Poems,* edited by John C. Pope (Indianapolis & New York: Bobbs-Merrill, 1966).

– by the Caedmon School: *Genesis A & B, Exodus, Daniel A & B,* and *Christ and Satan.*

Manuscript: Junius MS. 11, in the Bodleian Library, Oxford, includes the poems of the Caedmon School. Facsimile: *The Caedmon Manuscript of Anglo-Saxon Biblical Poetry,* edited by Sir Israel Gollancz (Oxford: H. Milford for the British Academy, 1927).

First publication: *Caedmonis monachi Paraphrasis poetica Genesios ac praecipuarum sacrae paginae historiarum . . . ,* edited by Franciscus Junius (Amsterdam: Printed by C. Cunradi, 1655).

Standard editions: *Caedmon's Metrical Paraphrase of Parts of the Holy Scriptures, in Anglo-Saxon,* edited and translated by Benjamin Thorpe (London: Society of Antiquaries, 1832); *The Junius Manuscript,* volume 1 of the *Anglo-Saxon Poetic Records,* edited by George Philip Krapp (New York: Columbia University Press, 1931).

Editions of the individual poems: *Die ältere Genesis,* edited by F. Holthausen (Heidelberg: Winter, 1914); *The Later Genesis,* edited by Fr. Klaeber (Heidelberg: Winter, 1913; revised, 1931); *The Later Genesis,* edited by Benno J. Timmer (Oxford: Scrivner Press, 1948; revised, 1954); *Exodus and Daniel,* edited by F. A. Blackburn (Boston: Heath, 1907); *The Old English Exodus,* edited by Edward B. Irving, Jr., Yale Studies in English 122 (New Haven, 1953; reprinted, Archon, 1970); *Christ and Satan,* edited by M. C. Clubb (New Haven: Yale University Press, 1925).

Edition in modern English: *The Caedmon Poems,* translated by Charles W. Kennedy (London: Routledge, 1916).

Caedmon was a Northumbrian poet who composed Christian vernacular verse based on translations of holy scriptures and doctrine. He is widely celebrated as the first English poet, and his is the oldest extant example of Christian song. The origin of the name Caedmon has been a matter of some cu-

An eighth-century scribal copy of Caedmon's Hymn *(Cambridge University Library, Kk. 5.16, fol. 128ᵛ)*

riosity to scholars. The name has no obvious English etymology, although the *Dictionary of National Biography* accepts that it is probably an anglicized form of the common British name Catumanus, which derives from *catu,* meaning "battle." From this it is inferred that Caedmon was likely of Celtic descent, a fact that, if correct, makes it all the more appropriate that he wear the first laurels associated with British poetry. Although all that remains of his work is a single nine-line hymn based on the Creation, it is significant because it provides an early example of Latinate Christian scriptures being transformed into a vernacular and distinctly pagan oral tradition.

The society into which Caedmon was born was a violent and fiercely heroic one. Battle poetry such as *Beowulf* and *The Battle of Maldon,* both of which come from as early as the eighth century, though some scholars now place the former as late as the tenth, exemplify the warlike culture of which they are a product. Life revolved entirely around the battlefield, the mead hall, and the *beot* (boast) through which a warrior proclaimed his loyalty to his lord. From an economic and social standpoint, battle provided a source of income via tribute for the victorious kingdom as well as providing a means of achieving individual fame and status. The presentation of plundered war booty to the king, and his subsequent distribution of gifts to his steadfast retainers, demonstrates the more important aspects of heroic behavior, the *comitatus* (warrior-king contract). Honoring the *comitatus* implied both the excellence of the king's rule and the trustworthiness of the men sworn to serve him. The greatest glory a warrior could attain during those pagan times was to die in battle either defending or avenging his lord, thus fulfilling his boast. To run from battle or even to survive one's lord was considered the supreme act of cowardice.

When Christian missionaries came to these barbaric, if honor-bound, Anglo-Saxon kingdoms, they found it necessary to translate their message of faith and piety into the only language these warlike people could understand, the language of battle, if they were to have any hope of successful conver-

sion. Evidence of this type of hybridization exists in Christian poems such as *The Dream of the Rood* and *Judith,* which re-create the themes of pagan battle poetry by embodying Christ and his servants as brave warriors defending God in the battle against Satan. Based on this evidence, it is believed that England's final conversion to Christianity, which began with Augustine in the sixth century and ended with the Crusades in the eleventh century, was accomplished by integrating theology and scripture into already-existing pagan rituals and heroic traditions. *Caedmon's Hymn* is by no means the most detailed of the works which illustrate this property; however, being the oldest, it does suggest the origins of vernacular religious poetry by providing an example of how such integration may have begun.

Historically speaking, little is known about Caedmon's life other than that he was an illiterate farmhand attached to the monastery at Streoneshealh, later called Whitby by the Danes, for most of his life. He was born a heathen, but sometime during the rule of Abbess Hild (658–680) he entered the monastery and began composing religious verse in his own Northumbrian dialect, based on scripture translated from the Latin. Bede's *Ecclesiastical History of the English People* states that Caedmon sang "about the creation of the world, the origin of the human race, and the whole history of Genesis, of the departure of Israel from Egypt, and the entry into the promised land, and of many other of the stories taken from the sacred Scriptures: of the incarnation, passion, and resurrection of the Lord; of His ascension into heaven; of the coming of the Holy Spirit and the teaching of the apostles. He also made songs about the terrors of future judgment, the horrors of the pains of hell, and the joys of the heavenly kingdom." Although none of the poems allegedly composed by Caedmon on these topics, other than *Caedmon's Hymn,* had survived into modern times, Old English poems on similar subjects exist in a tenth- or eleventh-century manuscript. While these poems contain the essence of Caedmon's work as described by Bede, most scholars believe them to be the work of several later poets, "a Caedmonian School," and maintain that only *Caedmon's Hymn* is realistically attributable to Caedmon.

Virtually everything known about Caedmon comes from the works of the English priest and religious historian Bede. In his *Historia ecclesiastica gentis Anglorum* (731), Bede states that Caedmon was graced by God with the gift of religious song so that "whatever he learned from the Holy scriptures by means of interpreters, he quickly turned into extremely delightful and moving poetry in English which was his own tongue." Many other poets were to imitate him, but none could surpass Caedmon, who "did not learn the art of poetry from men nor through a man but he received the gift of song freely by the grace of God."

Bede goes on to relate how Caedmon had lived in the secular habit for most of his life and had never learned any songs. He was given to attending feasts where singing took place, however. Whenever Caedmon saw the harp approaching him at these banquets, he would immediately flee the hall and return home. It was on one such occasion, Bede relates, that he found himself blessed. Fearing that he would be asked to sing one evening, Caedmon left the hall and entered the barn to do his evening chores. Since it was late, he decided to spend the night there, and while he slept, he dreamed that someone, perhaps an angel, stood over him and called him by name, saying "Caedmon, sing me something," to which Caedmon replied, "I cannot sing; that is why I left the feast and came here." Despite his objections the visitor instructed Caedmon to sing "about the beginning of created things," and "thereupon he began to sing verses which he had never before heard in praise of the Creator."

Bede preserves the sense of the verses but not the order of the words in his Latin translation. Bede manuscripts, however, contain re-creations in Old English of the original Northumbrian verse. The version of *Caedmon's Hymn* found in the Moore manuscript reads:

Nu scylun hergan hefaenricaes uard,
metudaes maecti end his modgidanc,
uerc uuldurfadur; sue he uundra hihuaes,
eci Dryctin, or astelidae.
He aerist scop aelda barnum
heben til hrofe, haleg scepen.
Tha middungeard, moncynnaes uard,
eci Dryctin, aefter tiadae
firum foldu, frea allmectig.

Now must we greet with praise the guard of heaven's realm,
The Maker's might, and of His mind the thought,
The glorious Father's works, and how to wonders all

He gave beginning, He the Eternal Lord!
He at the very first formed for the bairns of men,
He, Holy Shaper! Heaven for their roof;
Then Middle-garth He made: He, of mankind the Ward!
Lord everlasting He! And then He let arise
The earth for man; He is Almighty God!
— translation by Stopford A. Brooke (in his *The History of Early English Literature,* 1892)

When he awoke the next morning, Caedmon remembered these verses and related all that had happened to him to his superior, who, in turn, took him to be examined by the abbess and the learned monks of Whitby. Upon hearing of his miraculous experience, the monks decided to test Caedmon's claims by translating some scripture for him to versify if he could. When he returned the next morning and recited the poem which he had composed, he was immediately accepted into the monastery, whereupon Hild "ordered that he be instructed in the whole course of sacred history." Bede notes that the fervor with which Caedmon composed his songs sprang from his desire "to turn his hearers away from delight in sin and arouse in them the love and practice of good works."

Caedmon's death is described as an unexpected but peaceful event of which the poet seemed to have divine foreknowledge. The exact date of his death is unknown, but some scholars conveniently list it as 680 in accordance with the year of Hild's death. Despite the fact that there is no evidence to the contrary, it has been suggested that such a coincidence, had it occurred, would certainly have been mentioned in Bede.

Poetically, *Caedmon's Hymn,* though brief, exemplifies the alliterative verse pattern of two stressed syllables per half line which is typical of Anglo-Saxon poetry. In addition, translations of the poem reveal, quite significantly, some eight references to God in a work of only nine lines. Many scholars of Old English poetry believe that these references, which seem to be mere repetition in translation, in fact illustrate a complex system of oral composition. In the early nineteenth century Milman Parry and Alfred Lord developed an oral-formulaic theory based on a living oral tradition discovered in the area of present-day Serbia. They suggested that illiterate poets learned songs not by memorization of the whole, but by learning a series of verse units or formulas, each with its own unique set of associations, that could then be assembled orally into a new alliterative structure for each performance. If the theory is correct, the references to the Deity – that now appear to be simple repetition –

at that time would have seemed widely varied because of the different facets of the Deity associated with each formula.

Another issue which is of interest concerning Caedmon's work is its relationship to accepted church doctrine. Since Caedmon was illiterate and even simple scripture had to be translated from Latin for him, his knowledge of church doctrine must have been severely limited. Yet Bernard F. Huppé devotes an entire chapter in his *Doctrine and Poetry: Augustine's Influence on Old English Poetry* (1959) to *Caedmon's Hymn*. The study focuses on Bede's probable interpretation of *Caedmon's Hymn* and on the work's reconciliation of Augustinian teaching and widely accepted church doctrine with the "secular" art of poetry. According to Huppé, Bede had ample precedent for accepting the miracle of Caedmon's song since "the word itself had been connected even by pagans with religious ceremonial in praise of their gods." Moreover, the Bible contains poetry believed to be divinely inspired and uniquely associated with the Creation in the opening lines of Genesis. The underlying meaning of these verses, Huppé says, had become a cornerstone of Christian doctrine, and as such, the Fathers were interested not only in their spiritual meaning, but "with the placing of the best words in the best possible order. For them, poetry was beautiful only because it revealed in a material way the spiritual harmony of the Creator." Huppé argues that *Caedmon's Hymn* falls deliberately into three parts consisting of a theme of praise, a statement of God's creation, and a paraphrase of the first verses of Genesis. In beginning with the theme of praise, "Caedmon emphasizes the importance of man's praise of God's word and works," while the second and last divisions of the poem "reflect the patristic distinction between the creation *in principio* and the creation of heaven and earth for the sons of men, which exists in time."

N. R. Ker's *Catalogue of Manuscripts Containing Anglo-Saxon* (1957) describes approximately one dozen manuscripts preserving *Caedmon's Hymn* which have survived into modern times, including one which was destroyed by fire in 1940. All but one of them are written in the side or bottom margins of copies of Bede's history dating from the eighth to the twelfth centuries, and at least half of them are housed either in the Bodleian Library or in other Oxford libraries. The oldest and perhaps the most famous of these is the early-eighth-century Moore manuscript (named for John Moore, bishop of Ely, who purchased it in the late seventeenth century), which has been housed at Cambridge since

1715. *Caedmon's Hymn* is written on the last page of a copy of Bede. The page was originally blank, and the Old English is a contemporary addition written in a hand similar to the main hand.

Also of importance to scholars is the tenth- or eleventh-century Caedmon or Junius XI Manuscript of Anglo-Saxon biblical paraphrases, which is currently housed in the Bodleian Library. In the seventeenth century the manuscript belonged to James Ussher, archbishop of Armagh (1581–1656), and was presented to Francis Junius (1589–1677), librarian to Thomas Howard, second Earl of Arundel, as a gift in about 1651. After Junius's death the manuscript found its way along with his other books to the Bodleian, where it has been housed since 1678. The manuscript is particularly fascinating because the works contained in it use the same biblical sources, namely Genesis, Exodus, Daniel, and the battle between Christ and Satan, which Bede claims for Caedmon's works. Based on this coincidence and a marked similarity between *Caedmon's Hymn* and the opening lines of the *Genesis* paraphrase, the poems contained in the manuscript were initially ascribed to Caedmon in the mid seventeenth century. Scholars now believe that they have found enough linguistic and paleographic evidence to link these poems not only to different authors, but to separate periods as well. Several other poems have also been erroneously associated with Caedmon over the years, including *Judith* and *The Dream of the Rood,* both of which are currently associated with the ninth-century poet Cynewulf, whose writings reveal significantly more ecclesiastical learning and a more sophisticated skill than the so-called Caedmonian poems and reflect the New Testament rather than the Old. Although only *Caedmon's Hymn* is now seriously attributed to Caedmon, the poems contained in the Junius XI Manuscript do contain the essence of Caedmon's alleged canon and as such form the basis of what is commonly known as the school of Caedmon or the Caedmonian cycle.

Typically scholars divide the 229-page manuscript into two distinct parts. The first part comprises a single alliterative work in fifty-five fits, or numbered sections, which contains paraphrases of most of Genesis, several chapters of Exodus, and the first part of Daniel. The second part contains the poem *Christ and Satan* in twelve fits. In *The Caedmon Poems* (1916) Charles W. Kennedy agrees with Henry Bradley that these numbered sections "represent the separate sheets of the archetypal MSS." The text of the initial 212 pages appears to be in a uniform hand, while the concluding 17 pages

Page from the Caedmon School's Genesis, with an illustration of Noah's Ark — from a tenth- or eleventh-century manuscript of Anglo-Saxon biblical paraphrases (Bodleian Library, Oxford, Junius MS. 11)

show the work of three distinct hands. Full- and half-page illustrations occupy roughly the first hundred pages of the text, and various corrections have been made throughout.

Genesis is the most interesting of the poems in terms of structure. The poem consists of 2,935 lines, occupies the first forty-one sections of part 1 of the manuscript, and consists of two distinct works fused together. Lines 1–235 and 852–2935 comprise the Anglo-Saxon portion of the poem known as *Genesis A,* while lines 235–851, identified by Eduard Sievers in 1875 to be derived from Old Saxon, are called *Genesis B.* Sievers was the first to suggest multiple authors for *Genesis* based on internal evidence, and portions of an Old Saxon original found in the Vatican Library in the 1890s confirmed his suspicions. In contrast, Kennedy suggests that *Genesis A* may be the older of the two pieces, citing especially the research of Adriaan Jacob Barnouw, who dated it at 740. Regardless of which part is older, however, Kennedy writes that "much that is of Teutonic origin in manners and customs, character and feeling, is blended with the biblical elements of *Genesis A* and *Genesis B* alike." Kennedy notes, for example, the similarities between Anglo-Saxon battle and the war between good and evil. "The angels are the vassals of God," who is, in turn, the "dispenser" of life. Several scholars have also noted the similarities between *Genesis* and John Milton's *Paradise Lost* (1667, 1674). It is possible that Milton may have had some acquaintance with Junius and known of the Caedmon manuscript, but the theory has yet to be successfully proved.

Exodus follows *Genesis* in the manuscript and is a poem of 589 lines occupying sections 42–49 of the first part. Gollancz remarks upon the distinction between the two poems in terms of style, diction, and technique, and he focuses primarily on the education of the poet, who he believes may have been influenced by Neo-Latin verse. The work relates the story of Moses, the parting of the Red Sea, and the destruction of the Egyptians, and its principal source is the Vulgate *Exodus.* Because of the linguistic evidence, scholars tend to target the mid eighth century for its composition, and James W. Bright (quoted also by Kennedy) discusses its originality of structure with regard to "interweaving of tradition with sacred history" and "observing the demands of a central theme." Kennedy suggests some additional sources for the poem.

The remainder of part 1 is occupied by *Daniel,* a work of 764 lines. Like *Exodus,* the poem is principally dependent on the Vulgate Version, although other sources are evident, and Kemp Malone, in his essay on Old English literature for Albert C. Baugh's *A Literary History of England* (1948), states that "the poet does not follow his source slavishly; he leaves much out." Structurally, the poem resembles *Genesis,* though it is composed of only six fits. The third of these splits the poem into what are known as *Daniel A* (lines 1–278, 362–764) and *Daniel B* (lines 279–361). *Daniel A* is written in an old style which presumably goes back to early Northumbria and includes material from a canticle preserved in the *Vespasian Psalter* in the form of a lyric known as "The Song of the Three Youths." *Daniel B* is taken from a poem called *Azariah* which survives in the *Exeter Book.* As a whole the poem tells the story of David and Nebuchadrezzar II, but because of a defect in the manuscript the account of Belshazzar's Feast is incomplete.

A single 733-line work in twelve fits known as *Christ and Satan* comprises the entire second part of the Junius XI (or Caedmon) Manuscript. The text is faulty, owing to textual errors and corruption, but it is for the most part complete. The poem is structured according to a series of laments by Satan and the fallen angels, followed by a homily detailing the joys of heaven and the sorrows of hell. The story of Christ's temptation and Satan's vanquishment to hell concludes the work. Sir Israel Gollancz notes the anomalies in the text, and Malone concurs, suggesting that the awkward chronology may be intended to emphasize the poem's message rather than its narrative qualities: "The fate of Satan and his crew serves as the supreme object-lesson by which mankind may take warning." No immediate sources have been found for the work, but Malone attaches it to the ninth century and remarks upon the possible influence of Cynewulf.

Caedmon's Hymn illustrates a significant move by the early church to incorporate sacred doctrine into the secular literature of a pagan society in order to promote mass conversion. As the oldest piece of extant Christian song, *Caedmon's Hymn,* as well as the fantastic story of its author, still exerts a tremendous influence over how scholars perceive the conversion of Britain. Though only a fragment of his original work survives, Caedmon's art reveals not only the expression of a divinely inspired will, but also the creation of a seminal work instrumental in shaping the verse of succeeding generations of poets from Cynewulf to Milton.

Bibliography:

Stanley B. Greenfield and Fred C. Robinson, *A Bibliography of Publications on Old English Literature to*

the end of 1972 (Toronto: University of Toronto Press, 1980).

References:

George K. Anderson, "The Old English Christian Epic," in his *The Literature of the Anglo-Saxons* (Princeton: Princeton University Press, 1949), pp. 105–123;

Henry Bradley, "The Numbered Sections in Old English Poetical MSS.," *Proceedings of the British Academy,* 7 (1915): 165–183;

James W. Bright, "The Relation of the Caedmonian *Exodus* to the Liturgy," *Modern Language Notes,* 27 (April 1912): 97–103;

Stopford A. Brooke, *English Literature from the Beginning to the Norman Conquest* (New York & London: Macmillan, 1898);

Brooke, *The History of Early English Literature* (New York & London: Macmillan, 1892);

John Burke, *An Illustrated History of England,* second edition (London: Collins, 1985);

Bertram Colgrave and R. A. B. Mynors, eds., *Bede's Ecclesiastical History of the English People* (Oxford: Clarendon Press, 1969);

E. Talbot Donaldson and Alfred David, eds., "The Old English Period," in *The Norton Anthology of English Literature,* fifth edition, volume 1 (New York: Norton, 1986);

John Gardner, *The Construction of Christian Poetry in Old English* (Carbondale: Southern Illinois University Press, 1975);

Bernard F. Huppé, *Doctrine and Poetry: Augustine's Influence on Old English Poetry* (New York: State University of New York Press, 1959);

Charles W. Kennedy, *The Earliest English Poetry* (London & New York: Oxford University Press, 1943);

N. R. Ker, *Catalogue of Manuscripts Containing Anglo-Saxon* (Oxford: Clarendon Press, 1957);

Francis P. Magoun, "Bede's Story of Caedmon: The Case History of an Anglo-Saxon Oral Singer," *Speculum,* 30 (January 1955): 49–63;

Kemp Malone, "The Old English Period (to 1100)," in *A Literary History of England,* edited by Albert C. Baugh (New York: Appleton-Century-Crofts, 1948; revised, 1967);

Barbara C. Raw, *The Art and Background of Old English Poetry* (London: Edward Arnold, 1978);

G. Shepherd, "The Prophetic Caedmon," *Review of English Studies,* new series 5 (1954): 113–122;

C. L. Wrenn, "The Poetry of Caedmon," *Proceedings of the British Academy,* 32 (1946): 277–295.

Cynewulf

(circa 770 - 840)

Alexandra Hennessey Olsen
University of Denver

MAJOR WORKS: *Christ II* (circa 800–825?)

Manuscript: *Christ II* is found in the *Codex Exoniensis* (commonly known as the *Exeter Book*), MS. Ker 116 in the Chapter Library of Exeter Cathedral, where it was bequeathed by Leofric, the first bishop of Exeter (died 1072). The *Exeter Book* is written in a single attractive hand and is usually dated 960–980. Facsimile: *The Exeter Book of Old English Poetry,* edited by R. W. Chambers, Max Förster, and Robin Flower (London: Lund, Humphries, 1933).

First publication: *Codex Exoniensis. A Collection of Anglo-Saxon Poetry, from a Manuscript in the Library of the Dean and Chapter of Exeter, with an English Translation, Notes, and Indexes,* edited by Benjamin Thorpe (London: Society of Antiquaries, 1842).

Standard editions: *The Christ of Cynewulf,* edited by Albert S. Cook (Boston: Ginn, 1909); *The Exeter Book,* edited by George Philip Krapp and Elliott Van Kirk Dobbie (New York: Columbia University Press, 1936).

Edition in modern English: *Christ,* translated by R. K. Gordon, in *Anglo-Saxon Poetry* (London: Dent, 1970).

Elene (circa 800–825?)

Manuscript: *Elene* is found in the *Codex Vercellensis* CXVII (commonly known as the *Vercelli Book*), a manuscript preserved in the Eusebian Archives of the Cathedral Library of Vercelli, Italy. Some scholars believe that the entire manuscript was copied by a single scribe whereas others see two or even three hands therein. On paleographical grounds, the manuscript can be dated between 960 and 980. Facsimile: *Codex Vercellensis. Die ags Handschrift zu Vercelli in getreuer Nachbildung,* edited by Richard P. Wülker (Leipzig: Veit, 1894).

First publication: *Andreas und Elene,* edited by Jakob Grimm (Cassel: Fischer, 1840).

Standard editions: In *The Vercelli Book,* edited by George Philip Krapp, Anglo-Saxon Poetic Records 2 (New York: Columbia University Press, 1932); *Cynewulf's 'Elene,'* edited by P. O. E. Gradon, revised edition (Exeter: University of Exeter, 1977).

Editions in modern English: *Elene,* translated by R. K. Gordon, in *Anglo-Saxon Poetry* (London: Dent, 1970); in *Judith, Juliana, and Elene: Three Fighting Saints,* translated by Marie Nelson (New York: Lang, 1991).

Fates of the Apostles (circa 800–825?)

Manuscript: *Fates of the Apostles* is found in the *Vercelli Book.*

First publication: In *The Poetry of the Codex Vercellensis, with an English Translation,* part 2, edited by John M. Kemble (London: Ælfric Society, 1856).

Standard editions: In *The Vercelli Book,* edited by George Philip Krapp, Anglo-Saxon Poetic Records 2 (New York: Columbia University Press, 1932); *Andreas and The Fates of the Apostles,* edited by Kenneth R. Brooks (Oxford: Clarendon Press, 1961).

Edition in modern English: *The Fates of the Apostles,* translated by R. K. Gordon, in *Anglo-Saxon Poetry* (London: Dent, 1970).

Juliana (circa 800–825?)

Manuscript: *Juliana* is found in the *Exeter Book.*

Standard editions: In *The Exeter Book,* edited by George Philip Krapp and Elliot Van Kirk Dobbie (New York: Columbia University Press, 1936); *Cynewulf's 'Juliana,'* edited by Rosemary Woolf (Exeter: University of Exeter, 1977).

Edition in modern English: *Juliana,* translated by R. K. Gordon, in *Anglo-Saxon Poetry* (London: Dent, 1970).

Old English poems are the written versions of oral and oral-derived works, and like all compositions of tradition-dependent societies, they are primarily anonymous. Because of the influence of the

Christian missionaries and of monasticism, Anglo-Saxon England was a period of transition from oral culture to literate culture, as attested by the existence of the vernacular poems in manuscript form. The names of five vernacular poets are known, although the poems of King Alfred (849–899) and Aldhelm (circa 640–709) have been lost. To Bede, who lived between 673 and 735 and who was the author of many important Latin works, including *Historia ecclesiastica gentis Anglorum* (731), is attributed a five-line poem known as "The Death Song." Bede's Latin history recounts the biography of Caedmon, who lived at the monastery of Whitby during Hild's abbacy (658–680). Bede considers Caedmon to have been the first poet to compose Christian vernacular poetry in England. Although Bede relates that Caedmon composed many works that were copied by monastic scribes, only the nine-line poem known as *Caedmon's Hymn* can be attributed to him with certainty. The third vernacular poet is Cynewulf.

Cynewulf is the author of four substantial poems, *Christ II* and *Juliana* in the manuscript known as the *Exeter Book* (960–980), and *Elene* and *Fates of the Apostles* in the *Vercelli Book* (960–980). Unlike Bede and Caedmon, nothing is known of Cynewulf except his name despite the fact that his corpus comprises twenty-six hundred lines of the extant thirty thousand lines of Old English poetry, about 11.5 percent of the whole. At the ends of his poems Cynewulf incorporated his name in runes, the letters of the Teutonic alphabet (the futhark). Since each runic letter stands for a thing, and modern scholars are not certain what each rune stands for, there is much debate about what the runic letters mean in the poems. In *Christ II* and *Fates of the Apostles,* the name is spelled *Cynwulf* and in *Elene* and *Juliana, Cynewulf.* The section of each poem bearing the runic signature is known as the epilogue. In the *Vercelli Book, Elene* consists of fifteen numbered sections. Section 14 ends with *finit* (it is finished), which suggests the scribe saw the epilogue as an addendum to the poem. The epilogue occupies section 15 and ends with Amen. The end of *Fates of the Apostles* typifies the runic signatures. The speaker says, "her mæg findan foreþances gleaw, / se ðe hine lysteð leoðgiddunga, / hwa ðas fitte fegde" (here may the one wise of perception, he who delights in songs, discover who composed this poem). Many critics believe that the epilogues give genuine autobiographical information. Jackson J. Campbell's words may stand as a summary of this consensus: in the epilogues Cynewulf is "speaking to his au-

dience directly as one man to another.... Even if the poem were being read aloud to a group a hundred years after his death, the same effect would be produced on the auditors."

An edition of *Elene* was first produced by Jakob Grimm in 1840, and an edition of the *Vercelli Book* appeared in two volumes (1843, 1856), edited by John M. Kemble. An edition of the *Exeter Book* was produced by Benjamin Thorpe in 1842. In his edition Grimm notes that the runes in *Elene* show that the poet was named Cynevulf, but he does not develop his insight. In a study of runes published in 1840, however, Kemble discusses the runes that appear in *Elene, Christ II,* and *Juliana,* asserting that these poems are by a single author named Cynewulf. He attempts to identify Cynewulf as "the Abbot of Peterborough who flourished in the beginning of the eleventh century, who was accounted in his own day a celebrated poet, both in Latin and Anglo-Saxon, whose works have long been reputed lost." In 1888 Arthur S. Napier identified the runes in the conclusion of *Fates of the Apostles,* adding a fourth poem to the corpus of works by Cynewulf. Since the runic passage is on a different folio from the rest of the poem and since the folio could have been misplaced, the runic passage may have originally belonged to a different poem. Most scholars, however, accept it as the conclusion of *Fates of the Apostles.*

The arrangement of the runes differs in the four poems, and there has been much disagreement about how the runes are to be interpreted, because the same rune can represent different words. In a seminal lecture given to the British Academy in 1932, Kenneth Sisam pointed out that Cynewulf uses the names of the runes as words in the poems, so that the runes would affect an audience of listeners as well as one of readers: "An Anglo-Saxon hearing *cen, yr,* would know at once that he was dealing with runes; his attention would be directed at once to the task of solution because runes sometimes played a part in Old English riddles; and he would listen closely for the succession." The poems appeal equally to an audience of auditors and to an audience literate in both the Roman and runic alphabets.

In *Juliana* the runes are used as letters that spell out the name Cynewulf, although the runic letters are arranged in three groups that seem to have double meanings. The first set states "Geomor hweorfeð / C, Y, ond N" (Sadly CYN [mankind] will depart); the second set states "synnum fah / E, W, ond U acle bidað" (EWU [The sheep], stained with sins, will await in terror); the third set states

"L, F beofað" (LF [The body] will tremble), assuming that LF is an acrostic for lic-fæt (body). In contrast the epilogues to *Christ II* and *Elene* weave individual runes into the passages, necessitating that one read the word that the rune represents to understand the sentence; then the runes themselves must be interpreted in order to determine the name of the author. The epilogue of *Christ II* reads, "C [*cene* or *cen*] cwacað" (The bold one [or] The torch will tremble), "þendan Y [*yfel* or *yr*] ond N [*nied*] yþast meahtan / frofre findan" (while misery / [or] anger and sorrow, distress, or necessity will find consolation), "Bið se W [*Wynn* or *Wen*] scæcen," (delight [or] hope has departed), "U [*ur*] wæs longe / L [*lagu*] flodum bilocen, lifwynna dæl / F [*feoh*] on foldan" (Our portion of the joys of life has departed, enclosed by water floods, Wealth on Earth). The epilogue to *Elene* reads "A wæs secg oð ðæt / cnyssed cearwelmum C [*cen*] drusende" (Until then the man was always tossed about by waves of sorrow, The torch was drooping), "Y [*yr*] gnornode / N [*nied*] gefera" (The bow or harp mourned, the companion of sorrow, distress, or necessity), "þær him E [*eoh*] fore / milpaðas mæt" (although for him the horse measured the mile-paths), "W [*wyn*] is geswiðrad" (Hope or Delight is lessened), "U [*ure*] wæs geara / geogoðhades glæm" (Ours was formerly the splendor of youth), "swa L [*lagu*] toglideð" (so the waters departed), "F [*feoh*] æghwam bið / læne under lyfte" (The wealth of each is transitory under the sky).

All the epilogues suggest, in the words of *Juliana,* that Cynewulf needs the prayers of readers because he is "synnum fah" (stained with sins). Ernst Robert Curtius, however, warns against making overly simplistic interpretations of such poetic statements. He shows that requests for prayer are common in Christian poetry and speculates that they enabled an author "to put in his name" because he was proud of his poem and are not to be interpreted literally. Even the use of runes, although unique in Anglo-Saxon poetry, has parallels. Dolores Warwick Frese points out that "clerical copyists – especially those connected with the Alcuinian 'diaspora' – had instituted something of a rage for the insertion of runic inscription into their manuscripts." It is possible that the traditional meaning of the runes – for example, *nied* (sorrow, distress, or necessity) for *N* – rather than the sinfulness of the historical Cynewulf produced the emphasis on sorrow and sin in these epilogues. Furthermore, as P. O. E. Gradon, the most recent editor of *Elene,* points out, poetic parallels to the discussion of sin and judgment can be found in writers like Hrabanus Maurus and Bede, so there is "no reason to suppose that the epilogue is autobiographical."

The epilogue to *Fates of the Apostles* is especially interesting because it is an acrostic; the reader must both interpret the names of the runes in order to read the sentences and unscramble the acrostic in order to determine the name of the poet. The epilogue reads "F [*feoh*] þær on ende standeþ" (Wealth comes at the end), "U [*ur*] sceal gedreosan / W [*wynn*] on eðle" (Our pleasure shall pass away in our land), "L [*lagu*] toglideð" (water glides away), "þonne C [*cene*] ond Y [*yfel*] cræftes neosað" (Then the bold one and the wretched one will seek help), "on him N [*nied*] ligeð" (on them sorrow, distress, or necessity rests). Although it stands first in the acrostic, the *F* rune is especially riddling because it "on ende standeð" (comes at the end) of Cynewulf's name. The statement gives readers and auditors a clue to interpret the name. Like the other epilogues, this one includes statements that have been interpreted biographically. The lines "Ic sceall feor heonan, / an elles forð, eardes neosan, / sið asettan, nat ic sylfa hwær, / of þisse worulde" (I must go far hence, go elsewhere alone, seek a country, set forth on a journey from this world, I myself do not know whither), for example, have suggested to critics that at the time of the poem's composition Cynewulf was elderly and about to die and have promoted the Cynewulf legend. The riddling quality of the acrostic emphasizes the playful side of the Cynewulf poems, their link to riddles in Latin and the vernacular, a quality largely ignored by scholars. It also de-emphasizes the biographical significance of the passages.

Passages like 109b–112a of *Fates of the Apostles* can be interpreted in a literary way; Roberta Bux Bosse and Norman D. Hinton have recently suggested an "apocalyptic reading of the runic passage in *Fates,*" and they argue that the acrostic itself reinforces their interpretation. All four epilogues can be interpreted as literary works rather than biographical. Although there is manuscript precedent for calling the sections of the poems that include the runic signatures epilogues, so doing often prevents scholars from perceiving the poems as the unified pieces they actually are. George Philip Krapp says of the epilogue to *Elene,* for example, that "nothing in the content of this runic passage connects it inescapably with *Elene,*" and Varda Fish calls the epilogue to *Elene* "a mere appendix" to the poem. In contrast, Frese argues that Cynewulf is the last of the converts in the poem, including Constantine, Elene, Symon, and Judas, "all of whom, like Cynewulf, grow from scant to deep knowledge of the cross in the course of poetic events."

Cynewulf's runic signature appears a third time in the *Vercelli Book* in the same acrostic form in which it is found in the epilogue of *Fates of the Apostles:* "FWULCYN." The acrostic appears in the margin of folio 84ʳ, facing *Vercelli Homily* 15, but no one has suggested that the homily was actually composed by Cynewulf. Even Bosse and Hinton state that it is unlikely that "Cynewulf himself entered the acrostic," arguing that a reader of the manuscript, "struck by the thematic resemblance between *Homily* 15 and the Cynewulfian treatment of the Last Days in *Fates of the Apostles* and *Elene,*" must have added the runic signature. It would be as reasonable to speculate that Cynewulf was the author of the homily as to write biographies of him based only on the evidence of the epilogues.

Throughout the late nineteenth century scholars attempted to identify Cynewulf and date his works precisely. Kemble's suggestion that Cynewulf was the abbot of Peterborough was not generally accepted for two reasons. First, the poems seem to be earlier than the eleventh century, and second, the abbot's name, Cenwulf, is an unlikely variant of Cynewulf even though the rune C (*Cene* [The bold one] or *Cen* [Torch]) forms part of the runic signatures. Because the name Cynewulf appears in documents from the Old English period, and because the four signed poems give evidence of the author's familiarity with Latin learning, many scholars, such as Carleton Brown, tried to identify Cynewulf with a historical cleric like Bishop Cynewulf of Lindisfarne, who died in 783. Albert S. Cook and others identified Cynewulf as the priest named Cynulf who signed a document at the Council of Clovesho in 803. The attempts to identify Cynewulf have become less widespread since Frederick Tupper observed in 1911 that Cynewulf was so common a name that attempts to identify the poet in the absence of new discoveries are futile.

Looking at the identifications suggested by Brown and Kemble reveals the range of dates that have been attributed to Cynewulf, from 783 to 1006. Two runic signatures spell the name Cynewulf and two Cynwulf, but the spellings could be scribal rather than authorial. Medieval scribes were notoriously careless about copying texts faithfully, and Frese's discussion of the "clerical copyists" of "the Alcuinian 'diaspora' " suggests that the runes may have been inserted by scribes. The identification of Cynewulf depends on dating the poems and identifying the dialect thereof. According to Sisam, early scholars suggested that the poet must have lived when unstressed *i* was beginning to weaken to *e*, assumed to be around 750 because "in Cynewulf 's day two spellings recorded with such deliberate care indicate alternative pronunciations." Although the

dialect of the *Vercelli Book* is West Saxon, the rhymes in *Elene* suggest that Cynewulf wrote an Anglian dialect (that is, either Mercian or Northumbrian). Gradon provides the most persuasive discussion of the rhymes available, although there are alternate interpretations of the evidence. Gradon suggests that a Northumbrian provenance for the poems is unlikely because the alternation of *i* and *e* occurs only in the Mercian dialect of Anglian, not in the Northumbrian. This fact, coupled with the evidence of the rhymes, suggests that Cynewulf was Mercian. Since the exact period at which the change appeared is unclear, and since it is uncertain in which dialect area Cynewulf lived, the evidence of the spelling is difficult to interpret. Many recent scholars argue that Cynewulf lived in the early ninth century. Derek Pearsall dates him and the poems between 775 and 825; in the "Notes on Individual Writers, Works and Sources" in his 1987 study of medieval literature, Michael Swanton says simply "*fl.* 800."

Although attempts to identify the author of the four signed poems with a historical man have failed, interpretations based on poems that do not bear the runic signature have produced imaginary but seemingly factual biographies of Cynewulf. Heinrich Leo, for example, interpreted the poem now known as *Wulf and Eadwacer* as a riddle by Cynewulf. The word *wulf* (wolf) appears five times, and Leo interpreted "wælreowe weras" (fierce men) as a riddle indicating *cene* (fierce). He combined *wulf* and *cene* and argued that the solution of the riddle is *Cynewulf*. On the basis of the runic signature of *Elene,* which indicates that the poet received gifts of "æplede gold" (dappled gold), Leo hypothesized that Cynewulf was an itinerant scop and attributed to him a wife named Cyneburh. Leo's interpretation received the backing of other scholars for years until Henry Bradley argued that the poem was not by Cynewulf and ruled out the riddling interpretation. The epilogue to *Elene* reads, "Ic wæs weorcum fah, / synnum asæled" (I was stained because of my deeds and bound by my sins). These lines and others, such as 705b of *Fates of the Apostles,* have led scholars to hypothesize that Cynewulf lived a decadent youth. Because the epilogue later states that God "me lare onlag þurh leohtne had" (gloriously bestowed teaching on me), scholars hypothesized that Cynewulf experienced a religious conversion. Leo assumed that Cynewulf applied his poetic talents to religious poetry after his conversion; Richard P. Wülker interpreted the same material to indicate that Cynewulf became a poet only after he experienced his conversion. The disagreement reveals

Page from Cynewulf's Elene, *in the* Vercelli Book, *a tenth-century manuscript (Vercelli, Italy, Cathedral Library,*
Eusebian Archives, Codex Vercellensis CXVII, fol. 133)

the difficulty of interpreting the allusive poetic material of the epilogues as factual biography. Gradon points out that a conventional poetic topos is the receipt of a divine poetic gift in old age and that it appears in both Bede's story of Cædmon and the Old Saxon *Heliand*. Earl R. Anderson suggests that "the view of poetic composition that we have seen implicit in Bede's account of Cædmon becomes explicit in Cynewulf's account of himself." The very conventionality reduces the likelihood that actual biographical details can be determined from the epilogues.

Although it is impossible to interpret the epilogues in a way that brings conviction to all readers, and although the epilogues are conventional and probably fictional, even recent scholars make authoritative statements about the poet based on them. Two common "facts" are that Cynewulf lived near the sea and received gifts in the mead hall. According to Swanton, Cynewulf "cannot be identified with any known historical personage, but if a purportedly 'autobiographical' epilogue to *Elene* be taken at face value, the poet may have lived for a time as a warrior in well-to-do circumstances before experiencing a conviction of sin and religious conversion." Despite his careful use of the subjunctive mood, Swanton basically perpetuates the traditional Cynewulf legend, which is derived from poems that, despite their autobiographical aura, cannot be assumed to be truly autobiographical. One sensible answer to the question of autobiography is the view expressed by Stanley B. Greenfield and Daniel G. Calder that Cynewulf's runic signatures illustrate that the poet had "a self-consciousness about his craft and his creations" regardless of their inclusion of genuine autobiographical details.

Postmodern criticism provides an alternative approach to the issue. Michel Foucault argues that the historical existence of a writer is of little importance but that "the fact that several texts have been placed under the same name indicates that there has been established among them a relationship of homogeneity, filiation, [or] authentication." Such a relationship was perceived by whatever person put the acrostic in the margin of folio 84[r] of the *Vercelli Book,* who linked the apocalyptic homily to the four epilogues. If the homily is not by Cynewulf, it is important that an Anglo-Saxon reader thought that it might be. Fred C. Robinson argues that Anglo-Saxonists pay insufficient attention to the manuscript contexts of Old English works, and the runic marginalia might repay study more than the repetition of pseudobiographical facts derived from the epilogues.

Bosse and Hinton, noting that "no other extant Old English poems end with a 'coda' which contains the name of the poet spelled out by means of runes," argue that Cynewulf "was a more urbane and sophisticated man of his times than has been previously supposed" and that he was "close to the center of England's political and cultural interests." Bosse and Hinton use the epilogues not to write a fictional biography of Cynewulf but to place him and his work in the culture of Anglo-Saxon England and indeed in the Latinate culture of the early Middle Ages in general. It is important to note that the four poems (and perhaps *Homily* 15 as well) form a coherent unit. Foucault points out that "the coming into being of the notion of 'author' constitutes the privileged moment of *individualization* in the history of ideas, knowledge, literature, philosophy, and the sciences." Whether Cynewulf was an actual person or whether the runic signatures are fictional, the fact that he was conceived of as an individual in the modern sense of the word is important in the history of ideas and Western civilization.

The relationship among the poems is more important than the question of who Cynewulf may have been. Many recent students of Cynewulf say that it is the works themselves that are of interest, not least because they provide an opportunity to compare four works by a single Old English poet. The fact that there are four poems attributable to a single author has ramifications for the criticism of Old English poetry. For example, oral-formulaic studies involve the comparison of formulaic poetry within a single tradition. Some scholars, such as Ann Chalmers Watts, argue that a poet's work should be compared only to his or her own corpus, although Albert B. Lord points out that it is useful to compare *Beowulf* and the religious poems in order to understand the Old English formulaic tradition. Anonymous medieval poetry makes the oral-formulaic method difficult to apply, but the four signed poems can be compared to each other. Such an approach permits the reader to compare Cynewulf's formulaic language to poems outside the Cynewulfian corpus and helps clarify the effectiveness of this method of composition.

Just as modern *Beowulf* criticism was initiated by a lecture given to the British Academy by J. R. R. Tolkien in 1936, so modern Cynewulf studies began with Sisam's 1932 lecture. Sisam surveys previous discussions of Cynewulf and his writings and makes sensible judgments of the evidence. In the 1940s two books on Cynewulf appeared, one by Satyendra Kumar Das and the other by Claes Schaar, but serious literary criticism of book length did not commence until the 1980s, when three such works were published. The first was Calder's *Cynewulf* (1981), a volume in the Twayne's English Authors series. Despite 140 years of discussion of the works of Cynewulf – especially the works of Sisam, Das, and Schaar – Calder comments that his book "prefaces Cynewulfian studies, because they are yet in their infancy," primarily because of the emphasis on trying to identify Cynewulf. Like other volumes in the Twayne series, Calder's gives brief summaries of the poet's biography and achievement, as well as what might be called "state-of-the-art" interpretative essays of the poetry, discussing sources, poetic unity, and criticism.

In 1983 Anderson's *Cynewulf: Structure, Style, and Theme in His Poetry* appeared. Anderson's study breaks new ground because it provides serious literary analysis and emphasizes "the unity of the Cynewulf corpus: a unified subject matter; a commitment to book learning; a style of composition that combines native formulaic techniques with the conventions and patterns of the Latin rhetorical tradition; and a conceptual development that maintains two complementary dimensions – a concern for the welfare of the community as a Christian *ordo,* and a commitment to a fundamentally mystical religious experience."

While Anderson emphasizes the Christian Latin context of Cynewulf's four poems, Alexandra Hennessey Olsen's *Speech, Song, and Poetic Craft: The Artistry of the Cynewulf Canon* (1984) discusses the context of vernacular poetry, especially the oral-formulaic quality of the verbs of speech-act. Olsen studies the verbal phrases both in the signed poems and in the poems of the canon. Because her study isolates specific strands within Old English formulaic diction, it lays the groundwork for reconsideration of whether the poems of Cynewulf and of his "School" share more than a merely inherited diction.

Calder helps readers appreciate the state of Cynewulf studies before the 1980s, and Anderson and Olsen provide new directions for research and provide excellent bibliographies of work published before 1984. To date, no other book-length study of Cynewulf has appeared, although substantial articles have been published in major journals and as chapters in books. Two 1990 essays (one by Bosse and Hinton, and one by Charles D. Wright) discuss Cynewulf 's use of the Judgment Day theme. Robert E. Bjork discusses *Elene* and *Juliana* as part of a 1985 study of Old English hagiographic poetry; a 1989 work by Marie Nelson provides a fresh reading of *Juliana* using a methodology derived from speech-act theory; and John P. Hermann (1989) discusses *Elene* and *Juliana* in the light of postmodern literary criticism. Such studies show growing critical interest in the poems of Cynewulf.

Cynewulf is a shadowy figure, known by name and by nothing else, and his "School" is even more shadowy. Sisam observes that "at one time or another the bulk of Old English poetry has been attracted to his [Cynewulf 's] name." Kemble originally assumed that Cynewulf was the author of the entire Exeter and Vercelli books, but few other scholars accepted this idea, and Henry Morley made the first argument for accepting only the signed poems as authentically Cynewulfian. As in the case of determining Cynewulf 's biography from the epilogues, the evidence for the authorship of the unsigned poems can be interpreted in antithetical ways. Arthur Fritzsche and Friedrich Ramhorst both examined the sources and style of *Andreas,* the former arguing that *Andreas* could not have been written by Cynewulf, and the latter, that it was definitely the work of Cynewulf. Linguistic studies in the late nineteenth and early twentieth centuries eventually convinced Anglo-Saxonists that only the signed poems were Cynewulfian. Although modern scholars only accept the attribution of the four poems to Cynewulf himself, several of the anonymous poems (*Christ I* and *III, The Dream of the Rood, The Phoenix, Guthlac A* and *B,* and *Andreas*) have always reminded readers of the signed poems because of their style, diction, and choice of subject matter. They are therefore usually known as the Cynewulf "School" (as in Wrenn), "Canon" (in Das), or "Group" (in Schaar). Anderson points out that the formulaic nature of Old English poetry "gave rise to similarities in diction and style among the so-called Cynewulfian poems" and suggests that "to allude to a 'Cynewulfian school' . . . is to distort the realities of literary history." The formulaic nature of Old English poetry means that careful consideration of the tradition needs to inform judgments on poetic schools.

Christ I and *III* were originally attributed to Cynewulf because the middle poem, *Christ II,* bears the runic signature and because scholars found it difficult to decide where the sections of the poem were. In his 1842 edition of the *Exeter Book,* Thorpe attached the signature to the beginning of *Christ III,* and only in 1892 was the manuscript division accepted. *Christ* is not a unified poem, and the text in the *Exeter Book* includes the capitalization that indicates major divisions in the manuscript after lines 439 and 866 as well as after line 1664, indicating that the three poems are separate. The poems have been seen as forming a triptych and have been given the names "The Advent," "The Ascension," and "The Last Judgment," and *Christ I* is considered "Cynewulfian" but *Christ III* is not. Olsen notes that both poems "show little interest in speech" but that this fact does not identify the author because *Christ II* and *Fates of the Apostles* have a similar lack of interest in speech.

Like *Christ, The Dream of the Rood* and *The Phoenix* are lyrical poems. Early editors ascribed both of them to Cynewulf on the basis of dictional and thematic similarities. *The Dream of the Rood* was perceived as Cynewulfian because of the subject: it is about the Crucifixion, and *Elene* is about the Invention (Finding) of the True Cross. In addition, the speaker describes himself as "synnum fah" (stained with sins), a formulaic half-line that duplicates *Juliana* 705b and echoes *Elene* 1242b, "weorcum fah" (stained because of my deeds). It may be one of the earliest extant Old English poems because the Northumbrian runic inscription on the late-seventh- or early-eighth-century Ruthwell Cross in Dumfriesshire, Scotland, includes lines 39 to 49 and 56 to 64 of *The Dream of the Rood*. The existence of the runic inscriptions coupled with a runic inscription on the Brussels Cross has led scholars such as Krapp to theorize that "these inscriptions were extracted from the text of the poem" and that "it is not improbable" that the poem "was written by Cynewulf." Olsen, however, questions this assumption, pointing out that most of the verbs of speech-act "are simple and introduce speeches without calling attention to the nature thereof or the relationship of thought and speech."

According to Krapp, early editors attributed *The Phoenix* to Cynewulf because of "the many verbal and stylistic resemblances between the poem and the signed works of Cynewulf." Even before the widespread acceptance of the oral-formulaic theory of poetic composition made it unlikely that such verbal similarities alone indicated authorship, Krapp notes that "the absence of a runic signature puts a heavy burden of proof upon those who argue for Cynewulf's authorship." Anderson finds *The Phoenix* similar to *Christ II* because both consist of "explicit narration . . . followed by meditative discourse"; Olsen argues that the poet "demonstrates an interest in poetic craft reminiscent of that of Cynewulf." Despite the formulaic nature of Old English poetry, it seems reasonable to speak of *The Phoenix* as a poem of a "Cynewulf School."

Guthlac A and *B* are two poems about Saint Guthlac of Croyland, and the conclusion of *Guthlac*

B and the beginning of *Azarias,* which follows it in the extant *Exeter Book,* have been lost. Some scholars believe *Guthlac A* derives from oral tradition rather than from a precise Latin source as Cynewulf's poems do. But because of the diction, the poet's use of his source (Felix's *Life of St. Guthlac*), and the hagiographic subject matter, other scholars hypothesize that the lost ending of *Guthlac B* included a runic signature and that the poem was by Cynewulf. Although it is futile to speculate about the content of a lost ending, it is possible to make careful literary judgments that locate the *Guthlac* poems in the "Cynewulf School." For example, Olsen argues that the *Guthlac* poets, like Cynewulf, use formulaic verbs of speech-act such as "ongean þingode" (he addressed) to translate simple Latin verbs of speaking.

Other than in *Christ,* the most interesting problems of the "Cynewulf School" are posed by *Andreas,* which has affinities with *Beowulf* as well as with the Cynewulfian poems. Olsen has suggested that the *Andreas* poet is, like Cynewulf and the *Phoenix* poet, a self-conscious poet concerned with poetics. *Andreas* precedes *Fates of the Apostles,* a brief poem of less critical interest than *Elene, Juliana,* and *Christ II,* and the poems are separated in the manuscript in the same way that sections of a single poem are separated. Some scholars therefore propose that *Fates of the Apostles* is actually the conclusion of *Andreas.* Other scholars argue that, because the epilogue of the *Fates of the Apostles* is on a folio separate from the remainder of the poem, the folio should follow *Andreas.* Krapp points out that "nothing in the manuscript record justifies such an assumption," especially since *Andreas* and *Fates of the Apostles* have different sources. Calder suggests that "the collator" of the manuscript juxtaposed the two poems. Although Kenneth R. Brooks, the most recent editor of *Andreas* and *Fates of the Apostles,* concedes that "there remains the possibility that *Andreas* may be an unsigned work of Cynewulf," he observes, "in the total absence of external evidence, the supporters of this view have been obliged to argue mainly from similarities of phraseology . . . [and] the formulaic character of Old English verse makes it practically impossible to establish genuine parallels." After reviewing the available evidence, Brooks concludes that *Andreas* is "later than the signed poems of Cynewulf."

Das's study of the "Cynewulf School" had the simple purpose "of ascertaining whether any of the Unsigned poems can be looked upon as his in the light of certain tests, (mainly, metrical and stylistic), derived from a study of the Signed ones." He also criticizes previous scholars for paying too much attention to linguistic and metrical matters and ignoring "the art and ideals of Cynewulf." Because of its attention to literary matters and its attempt to settle the question of authorship on literary grounds, his study marks a new era in Cynewulf studies. Das questions the existence of a "Cynewulf School" and concludes that "the Signed Poems should be placed in a class by themselves" for both literary and linguistic reasons. Sharon Elizabeth Butler questions Das's assessment, arguing that Das's evidence ultimately "offers no support to either side of the question," although as Anderson notes, the oral-formulaic theory gives a pragmatic reason not to attribute the unsigned poems to Cynewulf.

Schaar is more concerned with literary matters, and he discusses both "the hagiographic or homiletic tradition underlying the poems" and "the poets' independence of this tradition . . . [and] how far events and episodes are described in terms of Anglo-Saxon civilization and ideology." Although more than forty years old, the study remains the fullest stylistic investigation into the poems of Cynewulf and his "School." Schaar adopts a methodology initiated in the nineteenth century and compares the Old English poems and their probable Latin sources, and this methodology is still used. Schaar argues that Cynewulf's style "is distinguished by elaborateness combined with moderation and variety." He concludes that *Christ III, Guthlac A, Andreas,* and *The Phoenix* "cannot be the work of Cynewulf" but that *The Dream of the Rood, Christ I,* and *Guthlac B* must have been composed either by Cynewulf or by poets "whose style and manner had much in common with Cynewulf's."

Olsen's 1984 work argues that "whether the signed poems and the poems of the Cynewulf canon are by a single author or whether they are simply works that derive from a common formulaic tradition, one interested in literary artistry should examine the poems of the canon because their use of the mixed tradition of Old English poetry illuminates the use thereof by Cynewulf." Calder believes that the poems of Cynewulf are "the first example of processes that established themselves firmly in the history of English poetry: the reworking of foreign literatures in the native language, and consequent attention to form, genre, surface, and technique." Olsen finds such processes in the poems of the canon as well, and she argues that Cynewulf and the poets of his "School" are "literary artists concerned with the quality and effectiveness of the 'wordcræft' (word-art) each of them 'wæf' (has woven)."

Schaar's final words stand as a summary of the question of the biography of both Cynewulf and the poets of his "School": "The poets, about whose lives and destinies we know nothing, give us, unconsciously, some important characteristics of their poetic personalities, even though the ancient vernacular and the new Latin traditions abundantly supplied them with matter as well as with form."

References:

Earl R. Anderson, *Cynewulf: Structure, Style, and Theme in His Poetry* (Rutherford, Madison & Teaneck: Fairleigh Dickinson University Press, 1983);

Robert E. Bjork, *The Old English Verse Saints Lives: A Study in Direct Discourse and the Iconography of Style* (Toronto: University of Toronto Press, 1985);

Roberta Bux Bosse and Norman D. Hinton, "Cynewulf and the Apocalyptic Vision," *Neophilologus,* 74 (April 1990): 279–293;

Henry Bradley, Review of Henry Morley's *English Writers I: The Writers Before Chaucer, Academy,* 31 (1887): 197–198;

Carleton Brown, "The Autobiographical Element in the Cynewulfian Rune Passages," *Englische Studien,* 38, no. 2 (1907): 196–233;

Sharon Elizabeth Butler, "The Cynewulf Question Revived," *Neuphilologische Mitteilungen,* 83, no. 1 (1982): 15–23;

Daniel G. Calder, *Cynewulf* (Boston: Twayne, 1981);

Jackson J. Campbell, "Cynewulf's Multiple Revelations," *Medievalia et Humanistica,* new series 3 (1972): 257–277;

Ernst Robert Curtius, *European Literature and the Latin Middle Ages,* translated by Willard R. Trask, Bollingen Series, 36 (Princeton, N.J.: Princeton University Press, 1973);

Satyendra Kumar Das, *Cynewulf and the Cynewulf Canon* (Calcutta: University of Calcutta, 1942);

Varda Fish, "Theme and Pattern in Cynewulf's *Elene,*" *Neuphilologische Mitteilungen,* 76, no. 1 (1975): 1–25;

Michel Foucault, "What is an Author?," translated by Josue V. Harari, in *Modern Criticism and Theory: A Reader,* edited by David Lodge (London: Longman, 1988), pp. 197–210;

Dolores Warwick Frese, "The Art of Cynewulf's Runic Signatures," in *Anglo-Saxon Poetry: Essays in Appreciation, for John C. McGalliard,* edited by Lewis E. Nicholson and Frese (Notre Dame: University of Notre Dame Press, 1975), pp. 312–334;

Arthur Fritzsche, "Das ags Gedicht 'Andreas' und Cynewulf," *Anglia,* 2 (1879): 441–496;

James M. Garnett, "The Latin and the Anglo-Saxon *Juliana,*" *PMLA,* 14, no. 3 (1899): 279–298;

Gordon Hall Gerould, "The Old English Poems on St. Guthlac and Their Latin Source," *Modern Language Notes,* 32 (February 1917): 77–89;

Otto Glöde, "Cynewulf's *Juliana* und Ihre Quelle," *Anglia,* 11 (1899): 146–158;

Israel Gollancz, ed., *Cynewulf's Christ: An Eighth Century English Epic* (London: Nutt, 1892);

Stanley B. Greenfield and Calder, *A New Critical History of Old English Literature* (New York: New York University Press, 1986);

John P. Hermann, *Allegories of War: Language and Violence in Old English Poetry* (Ann Arbor: University of Michigan Press, 1989);

John M. Kemble, "On Anglo-Saxon Runes," *Archaeologia,* 18 (1840): 360–364;

Charles W. Kennedy, *The Earliest English Poetry* (London: Oxford University Press, 1943);

Heinrich Leo, *Quae de se ipso Cynevulfus (sive Cenevulfus sive Coenevulfus) poeta Anglosaxonicus tradiderit* (Halle: Hendelius, 1857);

Albert B. Lord, "Perspectives on Recent Work on Oral Literature," *Forum for Modern Language Studies,* 10 (1974): 187–210;

Morley, *English Writers I: The Writers Before Chaucer* (London: Cassell, 1864);

Arthur S. Napier, "The Old English Poem *The Fates of the Apostles,*" *Academy,* 34 (1888): 153;

Marie Nelson, *Structures of Opposition in Old English Poems* (Amsterdam: Rodopi, 1989);

Alexandra Hennessey Olsen, *Speech, Song, and Poetic Craft: The Artistry of the Cynewulf Canon* (New York: Lang, 1984);

Derek Pearsall, *Old English and Middle English Poetry,* Routledge History of English Poetry, 1 (London: Routledge & Kegan Paul, 1977);

Milton Henry Riemer, "The Old English *Andreas:* A Study of the Poet's Response to His Source," Ph.D. dissertation, University of Texas, 1965;

Fred C. Robinson, "OE Literature in its Most Immediate Context," in *OE Literature in Context,* edited by John D. Niles (Cambridge: Brewer, 1980), pp. 11–29, 157–161;

H. L. Rogers, "Rhymes in the Epilogue to *Elene*: A Reconsideration," *Leeds Studies in English,* 5 (1971): 47–52;

Gregor Sarrazin, "Beowulf und Kynewulf," *Anglia,* 9 (1886): 515–550;

Claes Schaar, *Critical Studies in the Cynewulf Group* (Lund: Gleerup, 1949; New York: Haskell, 1967);

Kenneth Sisam, "Cynewulf and His Poetry," *Proceedings of the British Academy,* 18 (1932): 1–28;

Godfrid Storms, "The Weakening of Old English Unstressed *i* to *e* and the Date of Cynewulf," *English Studies,* 37, no. 2 (1956): 104–110;

Michael Swanton, *English Literature before Chaucer,* Longman Literature in English Series, 1 (London: Longman, 1987);

J. R. R. Tolkien, "*Beowulf:* The Monsters and the Critics," *Publications of the British Academy,* 22 (1936): 245–295; republished in *An Anthology of Beowulf Criticism,* edited by Lewis E. Nicholson (Notre Dame: University of Notre Dame Press, 1963), pp. 51–103;

Frederick Tupper, "The Philological Legend of Cynewulf," *PMLA,* 26, no. 2 (1911): 235–279;

Ann Chalmers Watts, *The Lyre and the Harp: A Comparative Reconstruction of Oral Tradition in Homer and Old English Epic Poetry,* Yale Studies in English, 169 (New Haven: Yale University Press, 1969);

Charles L. Wrenn, *A Study of Old English Literature* (London: Harrap, 1967);

Charles D. Wright, "The Pledge of the Soul: A Judgment Theme in Old English Homiletic Literature and Cynewulf's *Elene,*" *Neuphilologische Mitteilungen,* 91, no. 1 (1990): 23–30;

Richard P. Wülker, "Ueber den Dichter Cynewulf," *Anglia,* 1 (1878): 483–507.

The Anglo-Saxon Chronicle
(circa 890 – 1154)

Jolyon Helterman

Manuscripts: Corpus Christi College, Cambridge, MS. 173 (A'); British Library Cotton MS. Otho B.ix (A). Facsimile: *The Parker Chronicle and Laws,* edited by Robin Flower and Hugh Smith, EETS, o.s. 208 (1941); British Library MS. Cotton Tiberius A.vi (B); British Library MS. Cotton Tiberius B.i (C); British Library MS. Cotton Tiberius B.iv (D); Bodleian Library, Oxford, MS. Laud 636 (E); British Library MS. Cotton Domitian A.viii (F); British Library MS. Cotton Domitian A.ix (H); British Library MS. Caligula A.xv (I).

Editions: *Two of the Saxon Chronicles Parallel* (MSS. A' & E), edited by Charles Plummer, based on the edition by John Earle (1865), 2 volumes (Oxford: Clarendon Press, 1892–1899; reprinted, 1952, 1965); *An Anglo-Saxon Chronicle* (MS. D), edited by E. Classen and F. E. Harmer (Manchester: University Press / London: Longmans, Green, 1926); *The Parker Chronicle: 832–900* (MS. A'), edited by A. H. Smith (London: Methuen, 1935); *The C-Text of the Old English Chronicles,* edited by Harry August Rositzke, Beiträge zur Englischen Philologie 34 (Bochum-Langendreer: Heinrich Pöppinghaus, 1940; reprinted, Johnson, 1967); *The Peterborough Chronicle* (MS. E), edited by Dorothy Whitelock (Copenhagen: Rosenkilde & Bagger, 1954); *The Anglo-Saxon Chronicles,* edited and translated by Anne Savage (London: Phoebe Phillips/Heinemann, 1982); *The Anglo-Saxon Chronicle: A Collaborative Edition,* volume 3 (MS. A'), edited by Janet M. Bately (Cambridge: Brewer, 1986).

Editions in modern English: *The Anglo-Saxon Chronicle,* translated by G. N. Garmonsway (London: Dent / New York: Dutton, 1954); *The Anglo-Saxon Chronicle: A Revised Translation,* edited by Dorothy Whitelock, David C. Douglas, and Susie I. Tucker (New Brunswick, N.J.: Rutgers University Press, 1962).

The seven surviving manuscripts and two fragments known collectively as the *Anglo-Saxon Chronicle* are valuable as a primary source for historical, literary, and linguistic studies of early England. Spanning the years from the birth of Christ to A.D. 1154, the end of the reign of the last Norman ruler, King Stephen – and briefly summarizing sixty years before that in two prefaces – the chronicle consists of annal entries that are most often prose accounts of particular events of the year, although several annals employ some form of poetic verse. *The Anglo-Saxon Chronicle* was begun some time during the reign (871–899) of King Alfred of Wessex, one of the seven Anglo-Saxon kingdoms into which England was divided at the time, and was disseminated into its various versions from a single manuscript that originated, some scholars believe, at a monastery at Winchester, Wessex.

The original compilation of this chronicle was part of the cultural revival that was associated with Alfred's reign, and the king – who had himself contributed to the literary world with his several translations from Latin into English – may even have commissioned the undertaking of the chronicle by his scholars in the monasteries. In any case, the time and place were right for such a literary endeavor; since the early 800s the Danes had been raiding the various kingdoms of England, and each had been effectively quelled into submission except for Alfred's Wessex. It is significant that the impetus to compile a registration of historical events occurred in a time when, finally, events in England were characterized by not only relative peace but by actual triumph.

Also, there was at the time more of a "national" unity in England than ever before. Although not until after Alfred's reign would England be completely unified, the most pressing concern for the remaining separate kingdoms was no longer the battles among themselves for piecemeal political control, although this internal fighting still occurred frequently. The much greater threat of powerful forces from abroad effected an ad hoc cooperation that gradually became more and more permanent. The kingdoms became more developed and effective militarily, especially Wessex, and this resultant relative stability allowed for more cultural, especially literary, pursuits: England had become enough of a nation to make the compilation of its history seem an appropriate undertaking in the eyes of its scholarly leaders.

The *Anglo-Saxon Chronicle* is of historical importance also in its use of the English vernacular rather than Latin for the text of its entries. Latin had been almost exclusively the language of choice for scholarly writing, and, in fact, the chronicle is the first known example of historical prose written in any Germanic language. G. N. Garmonsway attributes this choice of the vernacular to the general decay in the knowledge and study of the Latin language in England by the time of the ninth century, when the first version of the chronicle was compiled; this was a significant change from the days of the Venerable Bede and other prominent English medieval literary figures who wrote in Latin. During the almost three hundred years of the compilation of the chronicle, English emerged as the dominant scholarly and literary language and then was replaced once again by Latin in the last twelfth-century entries of the work.

That English was used for this extended period of time allows the critical reader to study the development of the Old English language as a medium for literary expression. Together, the versions of *The Anglo-Saxon Chronicle* contain six annals that are in a sufficiently regular meter to be called poetry, the majority of these making use of the Old English poetic convention of unrhymed alliterative verse. Other, later entries show a tendency toward this regularly metered style while still remaining basically prose. Garmonsway credits the account of the conflict between Cynewulf and Cyneheard – the annal for the year 757 – as being the first English short story. Occasionally the entries are personal and emotional in nature – such as some of the early poems; the description (annal 1083) of the massacre of the monks at Glastonbury; and the biographical sketch (annal 1087) of William the Conqueror, the longest entry, which spans more than one hundred lines – but a large number of the annals are merely a single sentence or two, giving a brief camera-obscura account of an event. The entry for the year 873, "Her for se here on Norþhymbre. Ond he nam wintersetl on Lindesse aet Turecesiege, ond þa namon Mierce friþ wiþ þone here" (In this year the army went into Northumbria. It took up winter quarters at Torksey in Lindsey, and then the Mercians made peace with the army), is typical in format and length for many of the years, especially earlier in the chronicle.

However, the modern retrospective tendency has been to emphasize a hierarchical distinction among the different annalistic styles as determined by measurement against some literary-historical yardstick – a tendency that belies a misunderstanding of the motivations for the compilation of the chronicle. For the monastic writers the purpose was not to compose works of high literary value, although some of the more ambitious scribes inadvertently approached this end, nor was it even to provide a particularly methodical reduction of important events, either for contemporary historical value or for the sake of posterity. According to Charles Plummer, in an often-repeated description from his edition *Two of the Saxon Chronicles Parallel* (1892–1899), the annalistic entries *characterized* the receding series of years, each by a mark and sign of its own, so that the years might not be confused in the retrospect of those who had lived and acted in them. . . . To posterity they present merely a name or two, as of a battlefield and a victor, but to the men of the day they suggested a thousand particulars, which they in their comrade-life were in the habit of recollecting and putting together. That which to us seems lean and barren, was to them the text for a winter evening's entertainment."

On the other hand, the fact that the annalistic framework was chosen at all is notable. In medieval times a chronological format was often avoided due to the difficulties in achieving a precise and consistent dating system. Records from the Middle Ages reveal the use of several different dates for the first day of the year, including 1 January; 25 March, the Annunciation; 1 September, the Greek or Byzantine indiction date; 24 September, the Caesarian indiction date; and, most frequently, 25 December. Also significant is the rarity of precedence for the use of the annalistic format. Although it had been used in Europe at least as early as the fourth century in the works of Eusebius of Caesarea, Saint Jerome, and Isidore of Seville, those works were not readily available to English readers until much later. Bede's works sometimes make use of this framework, but not as strictly and consistently. The compilers of *The Anglo-Saxon Chronicle* were remarkably conscientious in maintaining the precision of the historical chronology, but dating problems still occurred with some frequency: scribes sometimes omitted or misread the long roman-numeral dates when copying the original, and later scribes would often go back and "correct" those mistakes or omissions; annals left blank (not every year has an entry) were sometimes unaccounted for, putting that particular manuscript a year or two behind; and dates were sometimes repeated.

When the compilers of *The Anglo-Saxon Chronicle* first began their endeavor (circa 890), they at-

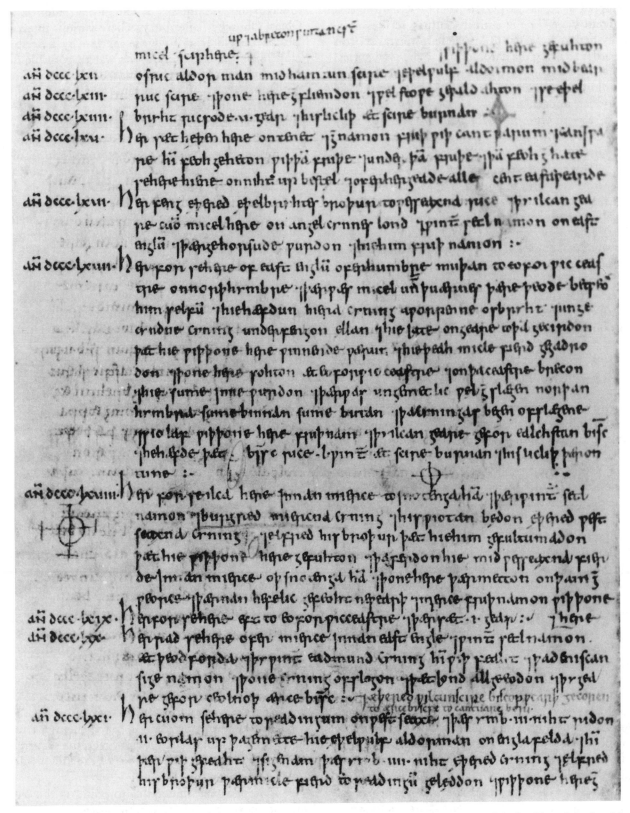

Page from the Winchester Chronicle, also known as the Parker Chronicle. Begun in the late ninth century, it is the oldest of the chronicle manuscripts (Corpus Christi College, Cambridge, MS. 173).

tempted to cover the period from 60 B.C. up to that current year. The late-ninth-century scribes naturally had to make use of available historical sources in order to bring the chronicle up to date. Historical data were extracted from a variety of sources, including regnal and episcopal lists, genealogies, Frankish annals, possibly earlier West Saxon annals, an epitome of world history, and certainly Bede's *Historia ecclesiastica gentis Anglorum* (Ecclesiastical History of the English People, 731).

The various versions of the *Anglo-Saxon Chronicle* were kept and maintained at monasteries and other religious houses throughout England, but all derived from some single, original manuscript (now lost) most likely compiled at Winchester, Wessex. In any case, copies of the original manuscript were in Winchester and had been distributed to a monastery in Abingdon and to a northern monastery either by the end of the ninth or the beginning of the tenth century. Some efforts were made to keep these various copies of the chronicle up to date, and possibly consistent, as "continuations" were periodically sent from Winchester to these new locations with supplemental entries. However, the scribe, or scribes, at a particular religious house would frequently add to its copy of the manuscript certain events of local interest, often using some local annals or registers and sometimes substituting completely for the "official" supplemental material. The two large continuations are generally referred to by scholars as Cont.1 (material up to 924) and Cont.2 (material from 925 to 975).

Manuscript A' (Corpus Christi College, Cambridge, MS. 173) was begun at Winchester and is believed by some scholars to be the source for the chronicle copies that were circulated to the various monasteries. It is also called the Winchester Chronicle and, alternately, the Parker Chronicle, after Matthew Parker, archbishop of Canterbury, who later had possession of the manuscript and bequeathed it, on his death, to the college. It is the oldest of the surviving manuscripts, having been written in one late-ninth-century hand until annal 891 and then continued in various hands. The preface to this version of the chronicle consists of a regnal list and genealogy and is followed by a brief paragraph summarizing the sixty years before the birth of Christ — the time that the chronicle proper begins in an annalistic format. Manuscript A' remained at Winchester until at least the mid tenth century, so the two continuations that were distributed were available to its scribes firsthand; it may have been the original manuscript to contain these additional annals. By the late eleventh century, probably after

the Norman Conquest, it had been removed to Christ Church, Canterbury, where various interpolations and alterations were made — by a scribe, most likely the same scribe who was responsible for compiling manuscript F (British Library MS. Cotton Domitian A.viii) at that same location.

Fortunately, a copy was made of the Winchester Chronicle before it was tampered with at Canterbury; manuscript A (British Library MS. Cotton Otho B.ix), an eleventh-century transcription, consists of only three leaves of this copy; the rest was destroyed in the fire at the Cottonian Library in 1731. However, manuscript A served as the basis for Abraham Wheloc's 1644 edition of *The Anglo-Saxon Chronicle,* so its basic content differences can be studied indirectly.

Manuscript A' contains the first four of the six annals in poetic meter — including accounts of the Battle of Brunanburh (annal 937), the most famous of the chronicle's poems; the capture of the five boroughs (annal 942); Edgar's coronation (annal 973); and King Edgar's death (annal 975). After 975 there are only a few scattered entries, the last of which is 1070.

The Battle of Brunanburh seems an anomaly in comparison to the other, rather mundane concerns of *The Anglo-Saxon Chronicle:* annual reports of kings going to pay their tithes and flat recountings of military victories. The genre of this poem is that of a *gielp,* a boastful formulaic telling of deeds of heroism yoked together with scornful mockery of the defeated enemy. The mockery is couched in what would appear to be the most tasteful of literary devices — understatement.

The poet takes a small incident, a battle at Brown's fort, and puts it on a cosmic scale so that the setting sun, "Godes condel beorht" (God's bright candle), becomes the divine witness to the overwhelming defeat of England's enemies. The poem is filled with the conventional topoi of Anglo-Saxon battle poetry, especially the beasts of the battlefield: the wolf, the raven, and the kite. As the beasts take over the field after the bloody battle, the theme of the valor of the warriors is replaced by a much darker view of war. The end of warfare is supposed to be the distribution of the enemy's treasury; at the end of this battle, however, the scavenging beasts distribute the corpses of the fallen warriors.

The poet uses metaphor to point up the ironies of the situation. Early in the poem swords are called, in a conventional phrase, "hamora lafan" (the leavings of hammers — that is, what is left when the smith takes his hammer from the newly forged steel blade). Later in the poem the few remaining enemy warriors are called "daratha laf" (the leavings of spears – that is, what is left of the Scandinavian army when the English spears are through with them). But it is particularly the *Schadenfreude,* or gleeful malice, masked by understatement that marks the *gielp*. An instance of this device comes when the poet states that the enemy "hlehhan nethorfton" (had no reason to laugh [exult]) that it had performed boldly on the battlefield. And in the portion that perhaps approaches the most offensive in nature, the name of the genre is invoked as the poet mocks the rival king on the death of the latter's son on the battlefield: "gelpen ne thorfte" (he had no reason to *gielp*) at that clashing of swords. All through the poem the invaders are marked as cowards, while the courage of the English is applauded.

In addition to its heightened emotional discourse when compared to most other annals of the chronicle, the poem is remarkable for its early recognition of England as a geopolitical entity. England was composed of seven kingdoms that were almost tribal in nature, but the poem celebrates the defense of what is now called England by a combined force of Mercians and West Saxons against an invasion led by Olaf Guthfritharson, the Scandinavian king of Dublin, and Constantinus III, the king of Scotland.

As an incipient national poem, *The Battle of Brunanburh* shows little sign of the *comitatus* relationship between ring giver and hearth companion that is typical of Anglo-Saxon war poetry such as *The Battle of Maldon* and *Beowulf*. The opposing forces seem to be national armies rather than heroic individuals tied by personal loyalties to a warlord. The poet insists on this distinction when he closes the poem by telling his reader that there has been no greater battle recorded in old books since the arrival of the Angles and Saxons from the East, that is, from the beginning of what we would call English history. That he would invoke old books written by wise, old men rather than earlier poems sung by poets (*scops*) suggests an awareness of his poem's place in *The Anglo-Saxon Chronicle* – as written history rather than oral legend.

Another copy of the original chronicle is thought to have been sent to a monastery at Abingdon. In any event, manuscripts B (British Library MS. Cotton Tiberius A.vi) and C (British Library MS. Cotton Tiberius B.i) were at Abingdon and are eleventh-century copies twice removed from this lost exemplar. Neither manuscript makes use of the original genealogical preface attached to the Winchester manuscript, although manuscript B has

pages missing from the beginning and is thought to have once included this text. Abingdon apparently received both continuations from Winchester, but, after entering the first part of Cont.1 (to annal 915), the scribe opted to insert en bloc a set of annals known as the *Mercian Register,* which covers the years 902 to 924; because there was no attempt to conflate the entries with already-existing annals, some chronological problems occur in these manuscripts. The entries for the two manuscripts proceed in close, often exact, agreement, but in some places C appears to have preferred the reading of some other source. Manuscript B ends at annal 977, while manuscript C continues to annal 1066, at which point the manuscript has been mutilated. The Abingdon manuscripts include the four occasional poems also found in manuscript A'.

Manuscript D (British Library MS. Cotton Tiberius B.iv) is a mid-eleventh-century copy of a lost original, which is thought to have been compiled at York or Ripon using one of the copies of the chronicle sent from Winchester. This manuscript, known as the Worcester Chronicle due to its eventual location and possibly also its place of compilation, represents the northern recension of the chronicle, as it includes many events of particularly northern interest and occasionally makes use of Northumbrian annals to supplement the entries. Manuscript D incorporates the *Mercian Register,* but, unlike the Abingdon chronicles, it dovetails the text throughout the entries already received in the supplements from Winchester, attempting, with mixed results, to preserve some sense of chronological integrity. In place of the genealogical preface of A', D inserts a brief history and description of the island of England based on Bede's history. It includes the first two poems (annals 937 and 942) but gives a prose summary of the accounts of Edgar's coronation and death (annals 973 and 975), which are in alliterative verse in other copies. Manuscript D also contains two other poetic entries, including an account of the death of Alfred (annal 1036) and of the death of Edward (1065); the former entry is not in regularly alliterative verse like the other five poems existing in the various versions of the chronicle but is a combination of prose and irregular rhymed verse. This manuscript includes details on Queen Margaret of Scotland not found in any other version. The last entry is annal 1079, except for the later addition of the events of 1130, incorrectly marked as 1080.

Manuscript E (Bodleian Library, Oxford, MS. Laud 636) was initially copied in the eleventh century from a version of *The Anglo-Saxon Chronicle* based on D – a version that was possibly removed from the north in the mid tenth century and included items of northern interest. Manuscript E is also called the Peterborough Chronicle, for the location of the monastery at which it was copied and then continued, and is the longest running of the manuscripts, its last entry describing King Stephen's death in 1154. Its many accounts of events of northern interest naturally occur in the earlier (pre-eleventh-century) entries, for which its archetype was most likely following D. Interestingly, E substitutes prose accounts for the six annals in poetic verse found in other versions of the chronicle, despite the fact that other material from the two Winchester continuations, which contained four of those poems, was available to E or its exemplar. Manuscript E contains the account of the political disorder of King Stephen's reign (1135–1154) – not available in any other manuscript – describing in vivid detail the acts of torture and subjugation inflicted upon the people of England. It uses, as does D, the preface based on Bede rather than the original genealogical preface.

Manuscript F (British Library MS. Cotton Domitian A.viii) was copied in the late eleventh and early twelfth centuries from possibly the same archetype of E, but its scribe also included some interpolations from A'. This manuscript has each entry written in both Old English and Latin, foreshadowing impending full-circle change back to Latin as the language of historical documents. Its last entry is that for 1058.

In addition to these more complete versions of *The Anglo-Saxon Chronicle,* some fragments of a single to a few leaves each have been uncovered; studies have followed, often with convincing theories as to their place in the complex history underlying the circulation of the chronicle. Some scholars have recognized the distinctness of certain of the chronicle versions to call them collectively the "Anglo-Saxon Chronicles," in the plural.

In final note, *The Anglo-Saxon Chronicle* is remarkable for its function as a literary-historical mirror placed in the background of a nearly three-hundred-year period of turbulent English history. That it managed to maintain such continuity as its compilers withstood internal battles among kingdoms, invasions from the Danes, numerous changes in political and religious leaders, the Norman Conquest, as well as the horrors of King Stephen's reign, is remarkable, especially in light of all the valuable literary, historical, and cultural material for study that it has preserved.

References:

Alistair Campbell, ed., *The Battle of Brunanburh* (London: Heinemann, 1938);

G. N. Garmonsway, Introduction, *The Anglo-Saxon Chronicle,* translated by Garmonsway (London: Dent / New York: Dutton, 1954), pp. xv–xliv;

N. Kershaw, ed. and trans., *Anglo-Saxon and Norse Poems* (Cambridge: Cambridge University Press, 1922);

Elliott Van Kirk Dobbie, ed., *The Anglo-Saxon Minor Poems* (New York: Columbia University Press, 1942);

Dorothy Whitelock, Introduction, *The Anglo-Saxon Chronicle: A Revised Translation,* edited by Whitelock, David C. Douglas, and Susie I. Tucker (New Brunswick, N. J.: Rutgers University Press, 1962), pp. xi–xxxii.

The Battle of Maldon

(circa 1000)

Marie Nelson
University of Florida

Manuscript: The six folios comprising *The Battle of Maldon* in Cotton Otho A.xii were destroyed by the Cotton Library fire in 1731. The only extant transcription, made circa 1721 by David Casley, is in the Bodleian Library, Oxford (Rawlinson B. 203, fols. 7ʳ–12ᵛ).

First publication: *Johannis Confratris et Monachi Glastoniensis Chronica sive Historia de Rebus Glastoniensibus,* volume 2, edited by Thomas Hearne (Oxford: e theatro Sheldoniano, 1726).

Standard editions: *The Battle of Maldon,* edited by E. V. Gordon (London: Methuen, 1937); In *The Anglo-Saxon Minor Poems,* edited by E. V. K. Dobbie, Anglo-Saxon Poetic Records 6 (New York: Columbia University Press, 1942); *The Battle of Maldon,* edited by D. G. Scragg (Manchester: Manchester University Press, 1981).

The Battle of Maldon, after *Beowulf* the most important expression of the Anglo-Saxon heroic ethos, is wrapped in scholarly mysteries about its subject and text transmission due to its near destruction in the 1731 fire at the Cotton Library, which destroyed many Old English texts. Fragments of the manuscript remain and are in the British Library, under its Cottonian listing, Otho A.xii (which refers to the name of the emperor whose bust was on the bookcase, and identifies the shelf and the position on the shelf of the volume). The first textual problem is the question of who copied the unique manuscript before it was destroyed by fire. The eighteenth-century antiquarian book dealer Thomas Hearne attributes the transcribed copy to John Elphinston, a sublibrarian of the Cotton Library, but more recent examination identifies the hand as that of David Casley, Elphinston's successor as sublibrarian.

The opening and closing lines of *The Battle of Maldon* had already been lost when the poem was copied, and the name of its composer, which probably was never attached to the poem (since poets who wrote in Old English seldom signed their poems), has long been lost as well. Other contemporary records of the battle such as those included in the Latin *Vita Oswaldi,* (Life of Oswald) which was written between 997 and 1105, and in the *Liber Eliensis* (Book of Ely), with a surviving copy dating back to 1170, give at least some hint about who their authors were. The *Vita Oswaldi* has been attributed to Byrhtferth, a monk associated with the monastery of Ramsey; and a monk named Thomas of the monastery at Ely may have based the part of his *Liber Eliensis* that deals with the Battle of Maldon on the earlier work of Richard, another monk known to have a particular interest in the deeds of English heroes.

The hero of the poem, an English earl named Byrhtnoth, had no direct heirs, so he left most of his estate to religious houses in Essex, particularly the monastic foundation at Ely. For this reason the monks at Ely paid much attention to their patron, whom they memorialized in *Liber Eniensis* and the *Vita Oswaldi,* and the *Maldon* poet has traditionally been associated with this monastery. Some readers have also assumed that he was first a warrior and later a man of the church. A man who had been a warrior would have a personal understanding of the value system embodied in the poem, and the lives of a great many Anglo-Saxons of high rank followed this pattern. It is no longer believed, however, that the poet was actually present when the battle was fought or that he necessarily wrote his account soon afterward. For that matter, twentieth-century scholars have pointed out that the poet neither had to be a monk to be associated with a monastery nor did he have to have war experience to write about a battle. Indeed, it is most unlikely that formal speeches of the kind we find in his poem could have been made in the heat of battle.

The poet, then, could have been associated with a monastery, either as a monk or a layman, but all that is certain is that he knew the area of Essex

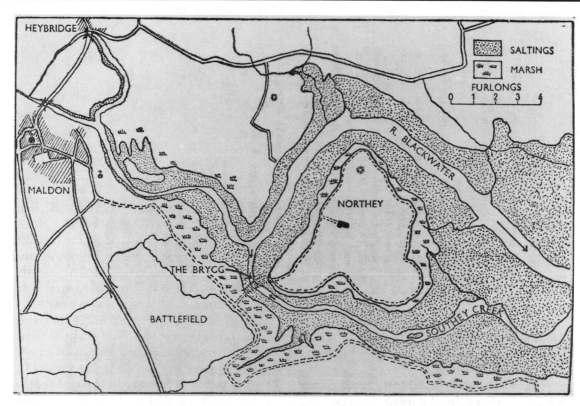

Map of the area where the Battle of Maldon took place in or around 991 (from E. V. Gordon, ed., The Battle of Maldon, *1937)*

where Byrhtnoth, the hero of his poem, held land and contributed to the support of monasteries. He had to know the lay of the land to establish the setting of the battle, which took place circa 991 and was a Viking raid in Essex in the estuary of the Blackwater River. Since the raid precedes the millennium by less than a decade, the Viking raiders have special significance in the sermons of the time: they are the offspring of the Antichrist, who will arise, as predicted in Revelation, immediately before the end of the world.

The 325 lines of the poem that survive begin with Byrhtnoth telling his young men to prepare for battle and giving them instructions about where they must stand and how they must hold their weapons, but the *Anglo-Saxon Chronicle* relates that sometime before this a strong Viking force had sailed up the Blackwater River to Northey Island, which was surrounded by marshes and coastal lands subject to flooding.

As the *Maldon* poet tells the story, a Viking messenger shouts a challenge to Byrhtnoth from the eastern side of the *brycg* (bridge or causeway). The poet, who seems familiar with the site of the battle, left scholars in a quandary over its location, searching for the *brycg* over which the Vikings are permit-

ted to cross. Historians believed that if they could find evidence of a bridge over the Blackwater, they would know the place of the battle. Various bridges which did not fit all the details of the poem were found and rejected until it became clear that the *brycg* was not an architectural structure but a narrow causeway or land bridge that connected the shore of the Blackwater to the channel island Northey. The messenger gives Byrhtnoth two choices: he can pay the Vikings to go away; or he can refuse to pay tribute and suffer loss of life. Byrhtnoth refuses to pay tribute. He sends a man named Wulfgar to defend the causeway, and Wulfgar, with the help of only two other men, successfully defends it.

Byrhtnoth and his men had the topographical advantage over the Vikings. When the Blackwater River and Southey Creek come together at high tide, the causeway is completely flooded, and crossing it is impossible. At low tide the Vikings could cross, but the English would have opportunity to pick them off almost one by one as they forded the river. Arguing that the two forces must meet on solid ground in order to fight a proper battle, the Viking messenger requests permission to cross the *brycg*. Byrhtnoth surrenders his advantage by allowing the Vikings to cross unmolested: "Nu eow is gerymed: gað ricene to us, / guman to guþe" (Now the way is open to you: come quickly to us, / men to battle). The reason Byrhtnoth allowed the Vikings to use the causeway without interference is given by the poet: "Ða se eorl ongan for his ofermode / alyfan landes to fela laþere ðeode" (Then the earl [Byrhtnoth] began because of his great pride / to allow too much land to the hateful people).

The great thematic problem of the poem is why Byrhtnoth allows the Vikings to cross. Many modern scholars attribute Byrhtnoth's error to *ofermod,* which is seen as Aristotelian hubris or Christian pride. J. R. R. Tolkien, for example, provides this rendering of the two lines into modern English: "Then the earl in his overmastering pride actually / yielded ground to the enemy, as he should not have done." For the same lines Kevin Crossley-Holland has the following: "Then, in foolhardy pride, the earl allowed / those hateful people access to the ford." These are scholars trying to make a warrior ethos bow to reason and good sense, but in the poem Byrhtnoth laments that the Vikings might go away *unbefohtene* (unfought with). The English have spent every waking breath learning to be warriors; this is the moment they have been training for all their lives. Nothing could be worse than an enemy that just goes away.

In addition, the poet obviously has great respect for Byrhtnoth, and it is reasonable to believe that his respect was based, at least in part, on his judgment of Byrhtnoth's capabilities as a leader of fighting men. One mistake, if it was a mistake, does not make a commander unworthy of the loyalty of his men. Nor does it make a hero unworthy of the praise of the poet who tells the story of what he did when faced with the challenge of invasion.

On the other hand, the poet has nothing good to say about the Vikings. He first refers to them with neutral words like *sæmen* (seamen) and *brimliðend* (sailors), but as the battle progresses they become *laðe gystas* (hateful strangers), *wælwulfas* (slaughter wolves), and, even worse, *helsceaðan* (fiends from hell). Just as he is consistently unpositive about the Vikings, the poet, with the possible exception of his *ofermod* reference, is consistently positive about Byrhtnoth and his men. He respectfully refers to his hero by rank, calling him *se eorl* (the earl), *folces ealdor* (lord of the people), and *æþelan Æþelredes þegen* (the noble thane of Ethelred). He also calls Byrhtnoth a *har hilderinc* (gray-haired warrior), and this reference also carries positive associations. The *eorl* or þegen or ealdorman of Anglo-Saxon times had a responsibility to defend his land and people, and this meant that, young or old, he

personally led his warriors in battle. Finally, the *Maldon* poet calls Byrhtnoth *Byrhtelmes bearn* (Byrhthelm's son), an epithet Tolkien utilizes in the title of his "Homecoming of Beorhtnoth Beorhthelm's Son," a modern English continuation of the story (collected in *The Tolkien Reader: Stories, Poems, and Commentary by the Author of The Hobbit and The Lord of the Rings,* 1966).

Like Byrhtnoth, the names of some of the warriors of *The Battle of Maldon* can also be found in other documents from the Old English period. Wulfstan, son of Ceol, who earns a place for himself in history by bravely defending the causeway during the first stage of the battle, is one of these warriors. Wulfmær, the young son of Thurstan who distinguishes himself by pulling a spear from the body of his leader and hurling it back at the Viking who threw it, is another. The name and lineage of Ælfwine, the son of Ælfric, whose character is established with indelible clarity in *The Battle of Maldon,* are also to be found elsewhere. What is remarkable about the characterization of Ælfwine in *The Battle of Maldon,* though, is the fact that the speech he makes after the death of Byrhtnoth is presented as a direct quotation. That speech, in which Ælfwine encourages his fellows to fight on, provides a model for heroic behavior. No one will ever have reason to reproach him, Ælfwine says, for leaving the field of battle because his leader lies dead.

Offa, like Ælfwine and the other named speakers of *The Battle of Maldon,* establishes his identity through reference to his relationship to his lord. He says he will return alive with Byrhtnoth or he will not return at all. Leofsunu, who also encourages the men of the Anglo-Saxon force to fight on after the death of Byrhtnoth, is not provided with a patronymic. He identifies himself instead by referring to the place from which he came. The men from around Sturmer will have no reason to reproach Leofsunu because he fled from battle. Even Dunnere, a simple man who is identified neither by reference to lineage nor to place of origin, shows his essential character when he says, "Ne mæg na wandian se þe wrecan þenceð / frean on folce, ne for feore murnan" (He who intends to avenge his lord among the people cannot turn away or have concern for his life). Equally courageous are Eadward the tall, who is reported to have said that he would not flee one footstep when his lord lay dead, and many other loyal warriors.

There were, however, a few who fled the battle, and the poet sees to it that their names live in infamy. He identifies Godric the son of Odda as the first to flee, and names Godric's brothers Godwin and Godwig as well. But what comes through most strongly in his account is his praise of the courage of Byrhtnoth and the loyalty of his men. Perhaps the best demonstration of that loyalty is to be found in the words attributed to a man named Byrhtwold, who is identified simply as an *eald geneat* (old retainer). Uttering the last speech of the poem, Byrhtwold says in heroic defiance of the inevitable,

> Hige sceal þe heardra, heorte þe cenre,
> mod sceal þe mare, þe ure mægen lytlað.
> Her lið ure ealdor eall forheawen,
> god on greote. A mæg gnornian
> se ðe nu fram þis wigþlegan wendan þenceð.
> Ic eom frod feores; fram ic ne wille,
> ac ic me be healfe minum hlaforde,
> be swa leofan men, licgan þence.

> (Courage must be the more resolute, heart the bolder,
> mind must be the stronger, as our strength grows less.
> Here lies our lord, all cut down,
> the good man on the ground. He who intends
> to turn now from this war-play must mourn forever.
> I am old; I will not turn;
> I intend to lie by the side of my lord,
> by the side of the loved man.)

It has been easy enough for historians and literary scholars who have the advantage of hindsight to say that Byrhtnoth should have simply paid the protection money the Vikings requested. The story of Viking victories is told in a long series of entries in the *Anglo-Saxon Chronicle*. The general military-political situation for the time when Byrhtnoth responded to the Viking challenge is made clear in an entry that says a man named Unlaf came with ninety-three ships to Folkestone, then moved on to Sandwich, then to Ipswich, harrying and plundering all the way until he turned toward Maldon and met Byrhtnoth. The chronicler may have been mistaken about the number of ships, but there was no mistaking the awesome naval power of the Vikings. They made their demands from a position of strength. In fact, in 991, the same year that Byrhtnoth fought and died, the Vikings were paid one thousand pounds to go away by an archbishop named Siric.

What could Byrhtnoth have expected to gain by taking on opponents like these? The *Maldon* poet provides no answer for this question, other than his identification of Byrhtnoth as Ethelred's earl, an officer of the king, a man with a responsibility to protect the land and people entrusted to his good government. But this could mean that what he expected to gain was the satisfaction of doing what he was obligated to do. Tolkien, however, provides a different answer to the question of what Byrhtnoth could

expect to gain. In his "Homecoming of Beorhtnoth Beorhthelm's Son," Tolkien has Tidwald, an older and wiser man, say that Byrhtnoth sacrificed his own life and the lives of his men to gain glory. This would hardly be an admirable, or even intelligent, way of carrying out his responsibility to defend the people of Essex and the lands of Ethelred.

On the other hand, from Byrhtnoth's standpoint, there *was* reason to fight. Defending his territory was a responsibility that went with his rank. In addition, it should be pointed out that the battle was not as great a defeat for the Anglo-Saxons as *The Battle of Maldon,* which breaks off before it reaches its conclusion, makes it seem. Other sources verify that Maldon, a defensive establishment that went back to the days of King Alfred, did not fall into the hands of the Vikings; and one early historian reported that the Vikings were so severely mauled by the Anglo-Saxons that they could barely make it back to their ships.

Finally, again considering other reports from this time period, it does not seem reasonable to believe that the Vikings Byrhtnoth confronted were likely to go away and stay away unless they were forcefully opposed. Here it may be useful to refer to a word from the request that led to Byrhtnoth's display of *ofermod.* That word is *lytegian,* and it is agreed that it means "to use guile." The poet's use of *lytegian* has been read as a statement that the Vikings tricked Byrhtnoth into giving them room to fight, but it can also be read as a comment on the sincerity of their promise to go away. The Viking strategy was to persuade Anglo-Saxon leaders to pay them, and pay them, and pay them again to go away. Byrhtnoth may have seized an opportunity to make the Vikings stay and fight for once. Once the Vikings had crossed the stream, their opportunities for escape, should the battle turn against them, would be drastically diminished. The tide would rise, and the two joined streams could just as easily keep the Vikings from fleeing to safety as they prevented their earlier crossing.

Two questions have been given a good deal of attention by the readers of *The Battle of Maldon.* Did Byrhtnoth make a mistake when he gave unimpeded access to the Vikings? Was Byrhtnoth a good military leader? Neither can be answered with finality, though the poet, through his portrayal of the loyalty of Byrhtnoth's followers, seems to have meant for Byrhtnoth to be judged as a good leader. As for questions concerning the poet's identity, it does not seem likely that his name will ever be known. The author probably considered his own name much less important than the names of the men whose courage he immortalized. Nevertheless, by writing Byrhtnoth, Byrhtwold, Offa, Ælfwine, and a host of other names into literary history to be honored for their heroic defense of their land, the anonymous *Maldon* poet has proved himself capable of giving enduring expression to the values of a heroic tradition.

References:

Earl R. Anderson, "*The Battle of Maldon:* A Reappraisal of Possible Sources, Date, and Theme," in *Modes of Interpretation in Old English Literature: Essays in Honour of Stanley B. Greenfield* (Toronto: University of Toronto Press, 1986), pp. 247–272;

Janet Backhouse, D. H. Turner, and Leslie Webster, *The Golden Age of Anglo-Saxon Art* (London: British Museum, 1984);

Jess B. Bessinger, "*Maldon* and the *Oláfsdrápa:* An Historical Caveat," in *Studies in Old English Literature in Honor of Arthur G. Brodeur,* edited by Stanley B. Greenfield (Eugene: University of Oregon Press, 1963), pp. 237–252;

Norman F. Blake, "The Genesis of the Battle of Maldon," *Anglo-Saxon England,* 7 (1978): 119–129;

W. G. Busse and R. Holtei, "*The Battle of Maldon:* A Historical, Heroic, and Political Poem," *Neophilologus,* 65 (October 1981): 614–621;

Cecily Clark, "On Dating *The Battle of Maldon:* Certain Evidence Reviewed," *Nottingham Mediaeval Studies,* 27 (1983): 1–22;

George Clark, "The Hero of Maldon: *Vir Pius et Strenuus,*" *Speculum,* 54 (April 1979): 257–282;

James E. Cross, "Mainly on Philology and the Interpretative Criticism of *Maldon,*" in *Old English Studies in Honor of John C. Pope,*" edited by Robert B. Burlin and Edward B. Irving (Toronto: University of Toronto Press, 1974), pp. 235–253;

Kevin Crossley-Holland, *The Anglo-Saxon World: An Anthology* (New York: Oxford University Press, 1984);

A. N. Doane, "Legend, History and Artifice in *The Battle of Maldon,*" *Viator,* 9 (1978): 39–66;

Helmut Gneuss, "*The Battle of Maldon* 89: Byrhtnoth's *ofermod* Once Again," *Studies in Philology,* 73 (April 1976): 117–137;

John McKinnell, "On the Date of The Battle of Maldon," *Anglo-Saxon England Medium Ævum,* 44, no. 2 (1975): 121–136;

Charles Plummer and John Earle, *Two of the Saxon Chronicles Parallel* (Oxford: Clarendon Press, 1892);

Fred C. Robinson, "God, Death, and Loyalty in *The Battle of Maldon,*" in *J. R. R. Tolkien, Scholar and Storyteller,* edited by Mary Salut and Robert T. Farrell (Ithaca, N.Y.: Cornell University Press, 1979), pp. 76–98;

H. L. Rogers, "*The Battle of Maldon:* David Casley's Transcript," *Notes and Queries,* 32 (June 1985): 147–155;

John Scattergood, "The Battle of Maldon and History," in *Literature and Learning in Medieval and Renaissance England: Essays Presented to Fitzroy Pyle,* edited by Scattergood (Dublin: Blackrock, 1984), pp. 11–24;

J. R. R. Tolkien, *The Tolkien Reader: Stories, Poems, and Commentary by the Author of The Hobbit and The Lord of the Rings* (New York: Ballantine, 1966);

Michael Wood, *In Search of the Dark Ages* (New York: Facts on File, 1987);

Rosemary Woolf, "The Ideal of Men Dying with Their Lord in the *Germania* and in *The Battle of Maldon,*" *Anglo-Saxon England,* 5 (1976): 63–81.

Beowulf

(circa 900–1000 or 790–825)

Jeffrey Helterman
University of South Carolina

Manuscript: The only extant transcription, in the hands of four scribes and dating from circa 975–1025, is in the British Library (Cotton Vitellius A. xv). Facsimile: *Beowulf: Reproduced in Facsimile from the Unique Manuscript, British Museum MS. Cotton Vitellius A. xv, with a Transliteration and Notes by Julius Zupitza, Second Edition, Containing a New Reproduction of the Manuscript,* with an introduction by Norman Davis, EETS, o.s. 245 (1967).

First publication: *De Danorum rebus gestis secul. III & IV. Poëma danicum dialecto anglo-saxonica. Ex bibliotheca cottoniana Musaei britannici,* edited by Grimur Johnson Thorkelin (Havniæ: Typis T. E. Rangel, 1815).

Standard edition: *Beowulf and The Fight at Finnsburg,* edited by Friedrich Klaeber (Boston & New York: Heath, 1922; third edition, with supplements, 1950).

The knotty problem of the date of *Beowulf* reveals a great deal about how modern readers think of the past and the kinds of assumptions that are made in confronting history. In the first edition of the poem (1815), Grimur Johnson Thorkelin identified the historical events as occurring in the third and fourth centuries, and the poem, because of the detail in such allusions, as having been written not more than a century later. This date is the earliest that has been assigned to the poem. The last composition date for the poem, the *terminus ad quem*, is the date of the unique manuscript for the poem. Based on the two copyists' hands, this manuscript date has been established, with some certainty, as around 975–1025. The last date would put the poem within half a century of the Norman invasions and the consequent end of the Old English language. The date of the manuscript is accepted by most scholars, but until recently most of them have argued that the poem predates the manuscript by at least two hundred years. This assumption has led to some interesting attitudes toward the manuscript.

Thorkelin's early date for the poem derives from a bias that controlled the response to it in the nineteenth century. Following investigations showing how the Homeric poems were based on earlier shorter poems that reflected the spirit of the ancient Greek people, there was a movement in early studies of *Beowulf* to see it as derivative of the Germanic *Volk.* Any Christian attitudes in the poem were presumed to be monkish interpolations. Such a reading of the poem allowed Thorkelin to ignore the date of 597, the year when Saint Augustine of Canterbury carried out his missionary work and undertook the conversion of England to Christianity (there are no direct New Testament references and no naming of Christ, though the frequent Old Testament references make it seem clear that the poet was a Christian); free of missionary zeal, it would seem likely that the poem was written at least several generations after the conversion, which would put the earliest date for the composition of the poem at about 700. At this point, the subject matter of the poem comes into play.

This English epic has no action which takes place in England; the bulk of the action takes place in Denmark, the home of the Vikings, who were raiding the English coast from 834 to the end of the disastrous reign of Aethelred the Unready (978–1016). Until recently, all those who dated the poem started with the basic assumption that *Beowulf* could not have been composed in this period, so if its language predates this period and the manuscript is eleventh century, there must be two hundred years between the manuscript and the composition of the poem. This "Viking age Englishmen must hate poems about Scandinavia" attitude is based on assumptions about grudge holding that are not evidenced explicitly in the period. There were already Danes who owned English farms in the ninth and tenth centuries, and the Viking raids, though an ever-present threat, were not constant. It does not seem impossible that a pro-Danish poem could have been written in this period, though a pro-Viking one is a different matter.

The poem has been dated by internal evidence, using linguistic forms, primarily case endings, which are then matched against externally datable texts. Such analysis reveals oddly contradictory evidence, as if a modern formal, printed text included the fifteenth-century form *axeth* (asks), the seventeenth century *thou saist,* and the only recently acceptable *ain't.* One way to account for these discrepancies was to posit that the poem went through the hands of several copyists who lived at different times and in different regions in England. This assumption is made by Friedrich Klaeber, whose 1922 edition of the poem is still the standard school text. Because Klaeber assumes that the poem has gone through at least four copyists, the manuscript is fair game for any linguistically justifiable emendation, the assumption always being that the copyist mistook a form he did not recognize. This explanation is given even when the reading of the manuscript is clear. It should be noted that the arguments against the composition of the poem in the Viking period militate even more heavily against the copying of the poem in this period (the time when Klaeber says it was done). The copying of a long poem was not a matter of interest or preference but an institutional event that took place in copying rooms called scriptoria. The copying of a text such as *Beowulf* would be an official act assigned by one monk, probably with the approval of at least one superior, to another. Since the extant *Beowulf* manuscript is in two hands, it is likely the decision to copy it this one time needed the approval of at least four men, which would have been the case each time the poem was copied before. If one would not be likely to compose a pro-Dane poem in the Viking period, it would be more unlikely that one could copy it.

Recent criticism has argued for a late date of composition for the poem, probably closely coinciding with the date of the manuscript. These scholars view the existence of antique linguistic forms in *Beowulf* as part of a poetic word stock rather than as a reflection of the composition date of the poem.

The oral-formulaic theory of the composition of Anglo-Saxon poetry supports the possibility of a late date for *Beowulf:* this theory states that most Anglo-Saxon poetry, even epics as long as *Beowulf,* were composed orally. The basic poetic unit is a four-stressed line in which three of the four stressed words alliterate. The poetry is filled with appositions and frequent modification by adverb and adjective so that a poet could instantly turn a sentence into verse. For example, the Old English bard, or scop, could look at the headline "Bush defeats Hus-

sein in Kuwaiti desert" and turn it into the following:

Bold-hearted Bush. Bravest of Men
Kicked the Iraqi, most Craven of Cowards,
Saddam slipped away, scudding into infamy.

The only full surviving discussion of Anglo-Saxon poetic creation is Bede's story of the inspiration of Caedmon, an illiterate cowherd who was told by an angel to sing (to make up a song). Caedmon responded with a nine-line alliterative hymn of creation. The monks at the local monastery were so impressed with this gift that they kept feeding Caedmon doctrine which he transformed into poetry. The monks wrote down his every word. The story, no matter how apocryphal, tells of a culture where the composition of poetry was thought to be oral and writing it down was already seen to be copyists' work. Caedmon's poems, however, are lyrics, and it is not certain that an epic could be composed this way. Early oral-composition theories of *Beowulf* portrayed it as an aggregate of episodic lays, poems of the same size and kind as *The Fight at Finnsburg,* in which the Danish scop makes up a song of "Beowulf," praising the hero's victories over Grendel and his mother. A very different notion of the possibilities of oral composition followed the researches of Albert Bates Lord and Milman Parry in the mountains of Yugoslavia. In *The Singer of Tales* (1960) Lord reports on Yugoslav folk poets who could compose extemporaneously epics longer than *Beowulf.* None of these poems, however, is nearly as good as *Beowulf.* A problem that has not been addressed in the oral theory of composition is how the poems were then written down. Caedmon had a small army of monks writing down his every word, but these were lyrics. How could a long oral secular poem be written down as it was being recited in a day of quill pens and vellum? The poem would either have to be written by someone who had the whole poem in his head, either the scop himself, which would mean he could not be unlettered like Caedmon, or else by some literate man, most likely a cleric, who had learned or was an apprentice at the art of oral composition. In either case the poem as literary artifact would be different from the oral poem, if it ever existed. The likelihood of an oral stage of the poem would help explain the existence of antique words and case endings in the poem. Contrary to expectation, illiteracy is far more conservative than literacy. A phrase such as "wait *on* opposing traffic" or a pronunciation of "hep" for "help" will survive from grandfather to grandson as long as it is not exposed to the printed word. Oral generation of the text tends to preserve antique locutions even in fairly late tellings of a story.

In any case the Viking-gap theory of dating the composition of *Beowulf* assumes that the poem is strongly pro-Danish in its leanings. This assumption is based on many "brave Spear-Dane" phrases and the reports of the splendors of the Danish court, but those who accept this theory ignore the plot and setting of the Grendel episodes. Rather than existing triumphantly, the Danes are moping around impotently while they await a stranger who will defeat the monster that has rendered their glorious mead hall useless. One of the difficult determinations in this text is the establishing of tone of the war poetry of this period. *Beowulf* has often been linked with elegiac poetry, such as *The Wanderer* and *The Seafarer,* which laments the loss of the glories of the hall and the hearth companions. In fact, *Beowulf* may be closer to a *yielp* such as *The Battle of Brunnanburh,* which mocks the defeat of one's enemies. *The Battle of Brunnanburh* says that the losers have no need to laugh or boast of their victory, a statement which implies that the winners do laugh and boast. That, in fact, is the point of the *yielp.* The spirit of *Schadenfreude,* joyful malice, is everywhere. It is quite possible to imagine that an audience which has just heard about a Viking attack on the English coast in *The Battle of Maldon* would greet the story of Grendel's meal of one fully armed Dane with uproarious laughter. In fact, the epic depths of *Beowulf* seem to intertwine the elegiac with the military *yielp,* but it is quite difficult to tell where one ends and the other begins.

The threefold structure of Beowulf's confrontations with the monsters must give the reader pause since the three battles — with Grendel, with Grendel's mother, and with the dragon — seem anticlimactic. Though the dragon in "real life" may be more powerful than either of the Grendels, he is clearly less original or fearsome. Beowulf's battles with the monsters must be read in an oddly foregrounded context. The background to these battles is in the stories and songs often told in celebration of victory or told as exempla: "You should not be as hardhearted as X who...." The so-called digressions produce an anecdotal portrait of the Germanic society out of which the Anglo-Saxon society arose. Beowulf's battles tell of the collapse of that society — a society based on the principle of feud. Such a society is out of harmony with the principles of Christianity — a point that is too often ignored. Other poems, such as *The Wanderer* and *The Seafarer,*

come to the same conclusion, but then include a specific moral: "thus should a man...." *Beowulf* has no such moral, though its characters do moralize, and it is perhaps for this reason, as much as any other, that the poem is set in the pre-Christian past. The values of the society in *Beowulf* will have to stand or fall on their own merits.

These values are based on the interrelations of the *comitatus,* the king and his warrior household. In the ideal society, the king (gold friend, ring giver) gives treasure to his thanes and they, in turn, give service to their king. There is no sense of payment here but of generosity on both sides. In order to distribute treasure, the king must have a center of power, a mead hall with a giving chair (throne) at its very center. He must also have treasure in the form of rings (gold armbands) or ancient and often famous arms and armor. This treasure is obtainable from three primary sources: directly from military victories, indirectly from the subjugation of neighboring tribes in the form of tribute, or from inheritance, though it should be noted that this last requires ancestors who have done the first two, and *no one ever forgets.* In the beginning of *Beowulf* the eponymous founder of the Danish (Scylding) line, Scyld Scefyng, starts his nation by subjugating his neighbors and leaving a large treasure for his son. For this he earns simple but unqualified praise from the poet: that was a good king.

The mead hall is the social and spiritual center of the Anglo-Saxon culture, and the loss of the joys of the hall is seen as a fate worse than death. In the hall the king distributes treasures to his hearth companions, and they in turn pledge their loyalty to him. The fact that these pledges are made with the mead cup in hand is not lost on the Anglo-Saxon poet: the value of the *beot* (pledge) is based on its successful completion. If a man fulfills his *beot,* it is an "oath," and he is a man of his word; if he fails, his *beot* is merely a "boast," and his courage in the mead hall was no more than the liquor talking. The most basic pledge was not to outlive the ring giver on the battlefield, and the greatest cowards, like the sons of Offa in *The Battle of Maldon,* are those who flee before the battle is done. The duty imposed on the survivors (those who were not there, in fact, even those who were not born yet) is to pay back those who killed their kinsmen. It is then the duty of *their* relatives to get even for the deaths of their kin. Everywhere the principle of feud is kept alive; a sword taken two generations earlier from an ancestor is enough to ignite it again.

In theory there are two ways of escaping from this endless cycle of feud. The first is the payment

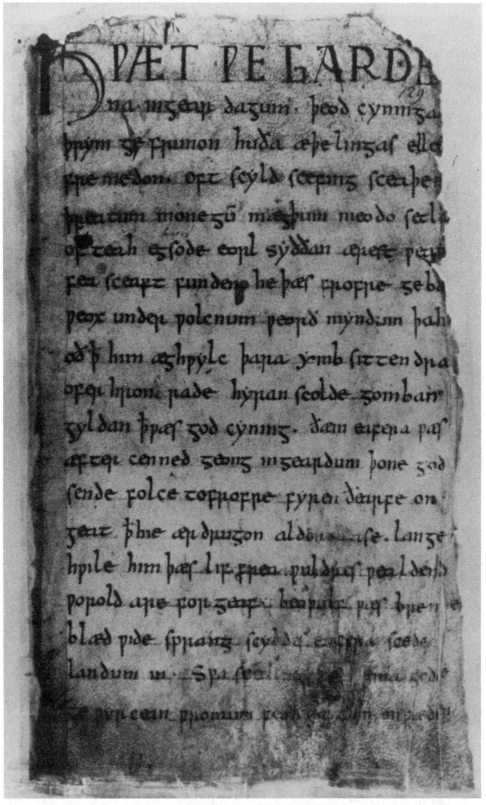

First page of the only surviving manuscript for Beowulf, *a copy made by two scribes circa 975–1025 (British Library, MS. Cotton Vitellius A. xv)*

of *wergeld* (a man's price). Each man in the society was given a price based on his rank in society. Upon the receipt of this amount the aggrieved family was supposed to give up the need to continue the feud. The second solution was a marriage between important representatives of the feuding parties, the equivalent of the prince and princess of feuding tribes marrying. The woman was seen as the bringer of peace in these circumstances, and two words for *woman* in Anglo-Saxon, which translate as "peace weaver" and "peace contract," attest to this function.

In *Beowulf* both these methods to disengage the feud mentality are measured and found wanting. Their inherent failure is seen first in Beowulf's trip to Denmark and then, even more poignantly, in his return home. The end of his reign almost certainly marks the end of the Geatish nation, which has become inextricably bound in international feud.

As a hero, Beowulf goes to the court of Hrothgar, the man who has apparently mastered the system only to discover that his mastery is for nought. Hrothgar, King of the Danes, has built the ultimate mead hall, a place from which he can distribute treasure and fulfill his function as ring giver. Hrothgar's hall, Heorot (the hart, stag), is the biggest that has ever been, but it has been rendered useless by the incursions of Grendel, who occupies it at night and has killed and eaten thirty Danish thanes. In his role as wanderer of the trackless fens and as a creature of night, "forscrifen . . . / in Caines cynne" (proscribed as a member of the race of Cain), Grendel appears to represent all of the aspects of chaos in Anglo-Saxon society. For that reason, it is not surprising that he is enraged by the song of the scop. The scop sings the song of creation, which is probably similar to the song known as *Caedmon's Hymn*. To Grendel the ordering of chaos is anathema, and he attacks its center and the hall joys from which he has been excluded. Perhaps the greatest irony is that, despite Grendel's epic depredations, it is not he who destroys Heorot. Beowulf will save the mead hall this time, but the end of Heorot is predicted. It will be destroyed by the uncle of Hrothgar's son. The man who will burn it is, in fact, at dinner when Beowulf comes. Beowulf can protect Heorot from monstrous, maneating enemies; he cannot defend it against friends and relatives.

One of the odd situations of Beowulf's rescue mission is how difficult the Danes make it for Beowulf to kill their monster. Beowulf is stopped by a Coast Guardian, then by a Hall Guard, and then finally he is challenged by Unferth, the spokesman (*thyle*) of the Danish court. Unferth's basic question is, Who are you to presume to challenge our monster? At this point the Danes expect Beowulf to lose, and in a world where reputation is everything, they do not want him getting cheap — even at the price of his life — glory. Even a loss to Grendel would go down in song and story, and such a glorious end is not to be earned lightly. Unferth, as *thyle,* seems to be the court insulter, whose job is to test Beowulf in the two things that count in Anglo-Saxon culture: words and works. Unferth says that Beowulf has no reason to challenge Grendel since he was not even able to defeat the warrior Breca in a swimming race. Beowulf replies that it was not a swimming race, but two men testing themselves against the sea and its monsters. In the process Beowulf defeated many monsters, reopening the seas to commerce, an act which establishes him as a civilizer versus chaos, a principal symbolic role he will take on in his struggle against Grendel. Beowulf's answer also puts Unferth and the Danes in their place. If you are so brave, he asks Unferth, why are you still safely alive while the monster is ravaging your kingdom? Then, in a final turn of the screw, Beowulf notes that Unferth's only act of courage was the murder of his own brother. This fratricide makes Unferth, like Grendel, of the race of Cain and casts Grendel's shadow on the whole Danish court.

In his fight with Grendel, Beowulf disdains armor, stating rather gentlemanly reasons for his decision. The monster does not know the use of armor so the hero, too, will refrain from wearing it. The odd turn is that Beowulf later uses armor against Grendel's mother, who supposedly is weaker than her son. Beyond his stated reason of courtesy, Beowulf's decision not to wear armor allows the audience to confuse man and monster in the description of the fight with Grendel, which does not happen in the fight against Grendel's mother. The hand-to-hand combat of Grendel and Beowulf appears to be a fair one. Grendel has eaten thirty men, and Beowulf has the strength of thirty in his arm. The immediate effect of Beowulf's not wearing armor or carrying a sword is that he does not kill Grendel outright; he merely tears off his arm. Both of these situations — the confusion of Beowulf and Grendel in the tangle of flailing opponents and the hanging up of Grendel's arm as a token of victory in Heorot — point to the same thing: that Grendel is less alien to the Danish society than anyone would like to admit. His being of the race of Cain (there is a tradition that the mark God put upon Cain after he killed Abel was some kind of monstrous malformation) puts Grendel only one generation from the ancestry of all of mankind. Nothing is said about the naming of Heorot (the stag), but it would not be unlikely that a stag's horns might be used to mark the spot. It is clear that, when Beowulf puts up Grendel's Grip as a token (though he never says what it betokens), Grendel has in a real sense co-opted Heorot by becoming the fratricidal spirit of the place – even though he has lost the fight and run back to his lair to die.

Though Grendel's mother quickly redeems her son's arm, one can imagine the unlettered Danish tourist looking for the memorial of the great battle. Where can I find Grendel's Grip?, he might ask, and in a few years the great mead hall would be known as Grendel's. Though Grendel's mother retrieves the hand, it will soon be replaced by Grendel's head, so the tourist's question will hardly change. He had better hurry though, for the hall will be destroyed within this generation by internecine familial hate. The spirit of Cain is the equal possession of the Grendels and the Danish royal family.

The place of Grendel's mother arises out of the function of women and mothers in this society and is related to three stories about women that are told in the time surrounding her descent upon the mead hall. The first of these women is Wealhtheow, the wife of Hrothgar, who seems to be the ideal queen and woman, but her danger to Beowulf stems from this idealness. It is Wealhtheow who cements the bond between the Danes and their not-quite-welcome guests by passing the mead cup among them. Later, when Beowulf defeats her enemies, she gets him to pledge his support for her sons, in case any new enmity should come to them. The reader does not know if she already suspects the uncle's treachery, and the poem does not tell of Beowulf coming to their aid, but it is important that Beowulf has bound himself for the first time in the web of feud. At this point Wealhtheow is designated as *frithowebbe* or weaver of peace.

At the same time two stories are told about the failure of marriage as a way to end feud. In both cases the woman's presence becomes the spark for new violence rather than the ender of the old. In the first, a sketched version of events which are also told in *The Fight at Finnsburg*, Hildeburh, the daughter of the Danish king Hoc is married to Finn, the king of the enemy Frisians, to cement peace between two warring tribes. A generation later, Hnaef, now king of the Danes, goes to visit his sister at Finn's fortress. As a king, Hnaef does not travel alone, but with a band of armed retainers. Their presence rekindles the old flames, and war breaks out. Hnaef and Hildeburh's warrior son are killed. These deaths, in turn, are avenged when Hengest, Hnaef's chief thane, spends the winter in Finn's land (a thing never done among Scandinavian tribes) and, with the coming of spring, slays his host and enemy.

The other marriage story is told by Beowulf on his return home to his own country. He tells his king, Hygelac, that the Danish princess Freawaru is about to marry Ingeld, the king of the Heathobards, in another of these peace-insuring unions. Then, in a tricky piece of narration, Beowulf tells what will happen to this marriage. The events he foretells are in fact history to the audience, and what is shocking about Beowulf's narration is the detail in which he recounts the future. The story he tells is as follows: Freawaru will come to the Heathobard court, and one of her retainers will be wearing a sword taken from the grandfather of one of the young men in the court; an old man will recognize the sword and will incite the young man to murder with an incendiary speech. Then Beowulf provides verbatim the words of a speech that has not yet been made. The poet seems to be saying that the pattern of woman as institutional peacemaker is so flawed that one can predict exactly how it will go wrong in the future. Within this pattern of woman as the net that binds together the corrosive energy of society, Grendel's mother appears. If Grendel is the deadly force that implements the murderous acts of feud, then she is the institution itself, and so it is that her killing of one man is not the unmotivated wrath and hunger of her son, but rather an act sanctioned by the society she attacks. She had been content to dwell in her lair, but the code of retribution demands that she take one life for her son's.

After Beowulf's return home, the historical digressions shift from a generalized vision of the Anglo-Saxon way to the specific history of the Geatish line which leads to Beowulf's becoming king. The history of the Geatish royal line provides a paradigm for the self-destruction inherent in the feud system. Beowulf's grandfather, Hrethel, is a successful warrior king. He rules over the *comitatus* with the aid of his three sons, all proven warriors. Then his eldest son, Herebeald, is killed in an archery accident. In the normal state of affairs Hrethel could then claim *wergeld* in lieu of punishment from the family of his son's slayer. This solution will not work, nor will the option of feud, since his son's slayer is also his son and now the heir to the throne. Hrethel suffers the ultimate frustration of a tribal leader – an unavenged son. The poet writes that Hrethel's grief drove him from the world; that is, he either died from morbid sorrow, or he took his grief into the monastery, where he then died. In any case the options and obligations of revenge incumbent on a tribal leader are closed to him.

Beowulf's actual reign of fifty years is never discussed; only the conditions – a series of disastrous wars against the Swedes which remove the three-man line for the throne ahead of him and allow him to become king – are mentioned. When the reader meets Beowulf as king, his reign of half a hundred years (fifty years seems to indicate that he has ruled his whole life rather than to designate the specific length of his reign) is almost at an end. The strength of Beowulf's right arm has apparently guaranteed the Geats a reign of tranquility despite their being surrounded by powerful neighbors waiting to swallow them up. This peace is shattered by the awakening of a dragon that has held its own peace for three hundred years. Once again it is the mechanism of the feud system which causes the uproar in the land of the Geats. The dragon is disturbed by someone designated as "niththa nathwylc" (no one in particular), a man who steals a plated cup from the dragon's treasure hoard, presumably for the purpose of paying off *wergeld*.

The dragon, therefore, puts Beowulf in the position of Hrothgar, a king whose kingdom is besieged by a monster, but Beowulf does not wait for a hero. Instead he seeks out the dragon himself. As has been his custom, Beowulf goes with an armed troop of men, and this time he carries an iron shield. Beowulf, still operating in the heroic rather than royal mode, tells his men that the dragon is his fight, not theirs. They conveniently accept this determination and skulk off to the wood to hide. That their action is wrong is confirmed by Wiglaf, the one warrior who comes to Beowulf's aid. Wiglaf condemns Beowulf's hearth companions, both before the dragon fight and after. He accuses them of failure to do service for ring giving. His condemnation of these men is a condemnation of the system itself and renders Beowulf's tragic end pathetic. Beowulf's death in the face of the dragon's fiery wrath is inevitable. He is already an old man, but he does accomplish, with Wiglaf's help, the killing of the dragon. This feat is all Beowulf could hope for, but he hopes for more. He wants the treasure to leave to his people so that a ring giver – someone like Wiglaf – could rule over his people the way the original Scyld ruled over the Danes. Beowulf, literally on his deathbed, holds on long enough to luxuriate in the treasure he has won for his people. But

all is in vain; the treasure is cursed and will prove useless. With all his virtues Beowulf has left the Geats neither an heir with a strong right arm (which Hrethel did in begetting Haethcyn and Hygelac) nor a treasure for ring giving (as Scyld did for his son, the first Beowulf). As the treasure is returned to the earth, Wiglaf's condemnation reminds us of the pathetic decline of the whole enterprise. Even if the treasure remained to be distributed, it would have been left to men like these, who were too craven to honor the treasure they had been already given.

The Beowulf manuscript, which provides the basis of all editions, has led a kind of charmed life. It survived from its tenth-century birth until the sixteenth century almost certainly in some monastic library. During the terrible depredations upon monastic holdings during the reign of Henry VIII (1509–1547), it came into the hands of the antiquarian scholar Laurence Nowell, whose name, and the date 1563, are written on the manuscript. Soon after it became the property of Sir Robert Cotton (1571–1631), in whose library it was listed as Cotton Vitellius A. xv (in the Cottonian library, in the book press under the bust of the Roman Emperor Aulus Vitellius, first shelf down, fifteenth volume in). The library remained in the Cotton family for several generations, until it was donated to the British nation in 1700. The Cottonian Library was eventually designated as the manuscript collection of the British Museum when that library was founded in 1753.

By 1722 the Cotton house was considered so dilapidated that the library was moved to Essex House, and then – because this building was considered unsafe – the collection was taken to Ashburnham House, which burned in 1731. The codex survived, and the manuscript, which was bound between several other works, remained remarkably intact. The manuscript, whose importance no one recognized, should have been rebound after the fire, but no one knew its significance, and the fire-damaged vellum began to decay. Fortunately, the Danish scholar Thorkelin had some sense of what the manuscript was, and had it hand-copied in 1790. Thorkelin eventually produced an edition and a Latin translation. Though the many inaccuracies of Thorkelin's edition were recognized by the first great *Beowulf* scholar, N. F. S. Grundtvig, the Thorkelin transcription of the manuscript has proved invaluable in preserving readings lost by the gradual deterioration of Cotton Vitellius A. xv. It was not until the mid nineteenth century that the manuscript was rebound, so that it could be once again available to scholars.

References:

Stephen C. Bandy, "*Beowulf:* the Defense of Heorot," *Neophilologus,* 56 (January 1972): 86–92;

Adrien Bonjour, *The Digressions in Beowulf* (Oxford: Blackwell, 1950);

Arthur G. Brodeur, *The Art of Beowulf* (Berkeley: University of California Press, 1959);

Alan K. Brown, "The Firedrake in *Beowulf,*" *Neophilologus,* 64 (July 1980): 439–460;

Allen Cabaniss, "*Beowulf* and the Liturgy," *Journal of English and Germanic Philology,* 54 (April 1955): 195–201;

R. W. Chambers, *Beowulf: An Introduction to the Study of the Poem,* third edition, with a supplement by C. L. Wrenn (Cambridge: Cambridge University Press, 1959);

Robert P. Creed, "A New Approach to the Rhythm of *Beowulf,*" *PMLA,* 81 (March 1966): 23–33;

Norman E. Eliason, "Beowulf's Inglorious Youth," *Studies in Philology,* 76 (April 1979): 101–108;

Margaret E. Goldsmith, "Christian Perspective in *Beowulf,*" *Comparative Literature,* 14 (Winter 1962): 71–90;

Stanley B. Greenfield, "A Touch of the Monstrous in the Hero, or Beowulf Re-Marvellized," *English Studies,* 63 (1982): 294–300;

Marie Padgett Hamilton, "The Religious Principle in *Beowulf,*" *PMLA,* 61 (June 1946): 309–330;

Jeffrey Helterman, "*Beowulf:* The Archetype Enters History," *ELH,* 35 (March 1968): 1–20;

Bernard F. Huppé, *The Hero in the Earthly City: A Reading of Beowulf* (Binghamton: Medieval & Renaissance Texts & Studies, State University of New York at Binghamton, 1984);

Edward B. Irving, Jr., *A Reading of Beowulf* (New Haven: Yale University Press, 1968);

Stanley J. Kahrl, "Feuds in *Beowulf:* A Tragic Necessity?," *Modern Philology,* 69 (February 1972): 189–198;

R. E. Kaske, "*Sapientia et Fortitudo* as the Controlling Theme of *Beowulf,*" *Studies in Philology,* 55 (July 1958): 423–456;

Kevin S. Kiernan, *Beowulf and the Beowulf Manuscript* (New Brunswick, N.J.: Rutgers University Press, 1981);

Albert Bates Lord, *The Singer of Tales* (Cambridge, Mass.: Harvard University Press, 1960);

Kemp Malone, "Young Beowulf," *Journal of English and Germanic Philology,* 36 (January 1937): 21–23;

M. B. McNamee, "*Beowulf* – An Allegory of Salvation?," *Journal of English and Germanic Philology,* 59 (April 1960): 190–207;

Charles Moorman, "The Essential Paganism of *Beowulf,*" *Modern Language Quarterly,* 28 (March 1967): 3–18;

John D. Niles, *Beowulf: The Poem and its Tradition* (Cambridge, Mass.: Harvard University Press, 1983);

Milman Parry, "Studies in the Epic Technique of Oral Verse-Making, I: Homer and Homeric Style," *Harvard Studies in Classical Philology,* 41 (1930): 73–147;

Donald H. Reiman, "Folklore and Beowulf's Defense of Heorot," *English Studies,* 42 (August 1961): 231–232;

James L. Rosier, "The Uses of Association: Hands and Feasts in *Beowulf,*" *PMLA,* 78 (March 1963): 8–14;

Kenneth Sisam, *The Structure of Beowulf* (Oxford: Clarendon Press, 1965);

J. R. R. Tolkien, "*Beowulf:* The Monsters and the Critics," *Proceedings of the British Academy,* 22 (1936): 245–295;

Jacqueline Vaught, "*Beowulf:* The Fight at the Center," *Allegorica,* 5 (Winter 1980): 125–137;

Dorothy Whitelock, *The Audience of Beowulf,* corrected edition (Oxford: Clarendon Press, 1958).

The Blickling Homilies

(circa 971)

Margaret Pyne Monteverde
Belmont University

Manuscript: The only manuscript is Scheide MS. 71, at the John H. Scheide Library, Princeton, New Jersey. It is written in two hands and dated 971 in the text of Homily XI. The manuscript was known as Lord Lothian's Manuscript, because until 1932 it was at the library of the Lothian home, Blickling Hall in Norfolk, after which the homiliary was named. The manuscript is missing leaves in several places and was damaged and disordered as a result of rebinding sometime between 1607 and 1827; in the 1950s it was reconstructed, restoring the homilies to liturgical order. Facsimile: *The Blickling Homilies,* Early English Manuscripts in Facsimile 10, edited by Rudolf Willard (Baltimore, London, Copenhagen: Rosenkilde & Bagger, 1960).

First publication: *The Blickling Homilies of the Tenth Century,* edited and translated by Richard Morris, EETS, o.s. 58, 63, and 73 (1874, 1876, 1880; reprinted, one volume, 1907).

The Blickling Homilies are a late-ninth-century collection of eighteen (two fragmentary) sermons in the vernacular tied to the major feast and saints' days of the Church's calendar. The year 971 is mentioned in the text of Homily XI, a sermon for Holy Thursday (Ascension Day): "þonne sceal þes middangeard endian & þisse is þonne se mæsta dæl agangen, efne nigon hund wintra & lxxi in þys geare" (then shall this world end and of this then the greatest portion has gone by, even nine hundred winters and seventy-one in this year). Most critics agree, however, that 971 is the date of the manuscript rather than the date of the sermons themselves or even of their compilation into a homiliary. According to Marcia Dalbey, the Blickling Homilies are the product of an unknown homilist or, more probably, homilists, judging by their eclectic subject matter and variations in dialect vocabulary. In language and style they predate the more scholarly and polished sermons of Ælfric and Wulfstan, which may explain why they have received little critical attention other than dialect and source studies.

C. L. Wrenn, in *A Study of Old English Literature* (1967), categorizes the Blickling Homilies as "good examples of what was probably successful popular rhetoric with little discipline of language." The homilies provide an "often entertaining picture . . . of the kind of popular beliefs which might be exploited by a less educated preacher." J. Elizabeth Jeffery, the author of the only book-length treatment of the Blickling Homilies, sees the less scholarly nature of the sermons as a result of the aural quality of the Anglo-Saxon homiletic tradition and the noncourtly, nonmonastic, and less homogeneous audience being addressed. Comparing several of the homilies to their sources, Dalbey notes in *The Old English Homily and Its Backgrounds* (1978) exegetical weaknesses but concludes that they may stem as much from disinterest as from an inability "to explain points of dogma, to speculate on Christian mysteries, and to develop intricate exegetical arguments" even when working from exegetically based sources.

Whatever the cause, it is clear that the style and audience of the homilies are more popular than learned, as is evident, according to Milton Gatch, in the use of catechesis rather than exegesis in presenting matters of church doctrine, as well as in the creation of passages of often vivid, original imagery, and the building of aural resonances through the use of verbal, thematic, and structural repetition. As Jeffery points out, several basic themes recur, often unexpectedly, throughout many of the homilies: blindness and seeing; soul and body; Mary's miraculous pureness of body; the hope of unending bliss with Christ and the coming of the last days; and even narrative parallels between the four hagiographic sermons.

Through the use of such simple and universal devices, the homilies seem designed to resonate in the ears of their audience beyond the particular moment. The universal quality of the references in the Blickling Homilies as a whole has led Gatch to conclude that without further source study and a much more detailed knowledge of "how Latin, ecclesiastical – often, indeed monastic – conventional materials were prepared and transmitted to serve the needs of Anglo-Saxon Christians. . . . we have to accept that the audience for the Blickling sermons is 'unknowable,'" if indeed the homilies in their current form reflect the needs of a single audience at all. It seems quite probable, as Gatch implies, that the audience of the homilies changed between the time of writing and the time of compilation, and such changes are probably reflected in the texts of the homilies themselves.

The date of the manuscript, just twenty-nine years before what many Christians believed would be the end of time, may account in part for the apocalyptic tone of many of the homilies. The focus is less on the particulars of belief and more on the community and the power of Christ. According to Jeffery, the purpose of the homilies, if not at the time of composition then certainly by the time of compilation, was to pull all believers firmly back to the community of Christ through concrete images and topoi that were aurally accessible. In her *Neuphilologische Mitteilungen* article Dalbey contends that almost half the Sunday (rather than saint's day) homilies are hortatory, that is, designed "to persuade rather than to explicate," though not with an eye toward inspiring fear but rather toward leading "their congregations by loving exhortation into the paths of good Christian behavior and belief." Not surprisingly, many of the sermons turn on stories drawn from popular hagiographies, the Apocrypha, and the more fantastic elements of the New Testament. According to Dalbey, the sermons are most effective when "making vivid and immediate . . . the rewards for virtue and the punishments for iniquity."

Because so little critical attention has been directed toward the Blickling Homilies, many important questions regarding their provenance remain unanswered, and few questions beyond this issue have even been posed. Until the work of Dalbey and Jeffery, most studies of the collection focused on three areas of concern: the date and place of composition; the sources of the individual homilies; and proposed textual emendations to supplement Richard Morris's edition (1874–1880). The numbering of the homilies in most literary studies follows that of Morris's edition and so is in keeping with the pre-1950 order rather than the current, reconstructed order of the manuscript and facsimile; Willard's introduction to the facsimile provides a concordance between the manuscript folios and Morris's page numbers, a restructuring which Morris had admitted was desirable.

By modern standards Morris's edition of the manuscript is remarkably untechnical, as is to be expected in a work that predates all of the major philological research tools – grammars, dictionaries, dialect studies – available to editors today. Although Morris confidently attributes the homilies to the tenth century in the title of his edition and does not speculate on the place of origin for the collection, he does comment on what he terms the "more archaic" vocabulary that seems more in accord with "the English of the 9th century" or with "later poetical literature," which by its style is more conservative in vocabulary. Because the dialect of the only extant manuscript is primarily late West Saxon, the homilies for a long time were seen as part of the flowering of tenth-century vernacular prose following Alfred. Closer studies of the vocabulary have revealed many Anglian elements, leading some critics to conclude that many of the homilies may be Mercian rather than West Saxon in origin. While this has lead some critics to propose a date of composition prior to Alfred, Jeffery argues convincingly for an early-tenth-century date for the compilation of the homiliary as a whole. This attribution in no way precludes the possibility that Robert J. Menner is correct in asserting that most of the homilies in their original form "were a product of Mercian learning and Mercian piety."

Until quite recently, the primary area of concern for most critics of the Blickling Homilies has been determining the scriptural and homiletic sources for the individual sermons. As Morris points out in his introduction, the subjects of the homilies are rarely unique; for sixteen of them, other Anglo-Saxon homilies on the same subjects survive. Later scholars have also traced a large number of the homilies to, among a variety of Apocrypha, the New Testament of James, the Apocalypse of Thomas, the Visio Pauli, and the Gospel of Nicodemus, as well as to the Latin sermons of Gregory the Great and Caesarius of Arles.

Three of the Blickling Homilies have also been shown to have significant ties to Old English po-

Page from the only extant manuscript for the Blickling Homilies. Known as Lord Lothian's Manuscript (after a previous owner), it is written in two scribal hands and dated 971. (John H. Scheide Library, Princeton University Library, Scheide MS. 71).

etry. The best-known parallel undoubtedly occurs in Homily XVII, "To Sanctae Michaheles Mæssan" (Dedication of St. Michael's Church), in which a description derived from the Visio Pauli gazing into a terrible place of "hremige bearwas" (frosty woods), dark mists, and monsters is reminiscent of a passage in *Beowulf* describing Grendel's mere. This discovery enabled Morris to propose a now-accepted reading, "hrimge bearwas," for the textual corruption, "hrinde bearwas," in line 113 of *Beowulf.* Homily X, on the end of the world, bears some resemblance in language and tone to the elegiac passages of *The Wanderer* and *The Seafarer,* but Gatch points out that these themes were commonplaces of the time and can in part be traced directly to earlier homiletic sources.

Homily XIX, however, has the most important tie to Old English vernacular poetry, its text being a close analogue, though much briefer, of the poetic hagiography *Andreas.* The popular story of Andrew's experiences among the cannibalistic Anthropophagi in Marmadonia survives in Greek (probably the original language), Latin, and Anglo-Saxon versions. Blickling XIX and *Andreas,* however, are neither drawn from each other nor from the same source. The Blickling version is much closer than the poem in style, content, and emphasis to the Latin recension, *Recensio Casanatensis,* which is generally held to bear the greatest similarity of detail to the original Greek. In *Andreas* the greatest emphasis is placed on Andrew's doubt and subsequent personal testing by Christ, who is disguised as the pilot of a ship during the journey to rescue Matthew from the cannibals. In *Recensio Casanatensis* and Homily XIX, however, Andrew's blindness in not recognizing Christ is yet one more example of God's almighty power, a recurring theme of the final six hagiographic Blickling Homilies.

As a whole the Blickling Homilies can be divided into two groups based on order and subject matter. The first twelve are sermons for the major Sundays and holy days of the liturgical year. In Morris's edition this section begins with a sermon for the Annunciation. Although this sermon is placed before Lent, Jeffery contends that it would have been delivered on 25 March, during Lent. The twelve sermons for the Temporale conclude with the homily for Pentecost. Although in the current form of the manuscript no homilies are given for Advent and Epiphany, most critics agree that originally the Blickling homiliary would have spanned the complete liturgical year, a conclusion supported by the absence of com-

plete quires in places where these sermons would normally occur. Homily II, for Shrove Sunday, addresses Luke 18:31–43 in which Christ prepares his uncomprehending disciples for his passion and then heals a blind beggar. Its source is Gregory the Great's "Homilia II in Evangelica," according to Dalbey, and it introduces three important themes that will be developed throughout the collection: the correspondence of soul and body; human blindness; and the potential of good people to achieve unending bliss through Christ.

The next four sermons are for the first, third, fifth, and Palm Sundays in Lent; there is no indication that sermons for the second and fourth Sundays were ever part of the collection. As both Jeffery and Dalbey point out, the first three of these homilies are unified thematically by their concerns with Lenten customs of fasting, tithing, repentance, and punishment, placing these actions in the larger context of living a life of Christian charity leading to an eternal life with Christ. Of these sermons, Homily IV, for the Third Sunday in Lent, is perhaps the most interesting. In *Philologica: The Malone Anniversary Studies* (1949) Rudolf Willard describes this "tithing homily" as "the longest and most persuasive treatment" of tithing "in the vernacular." Based on the sixth-century Latin sermon of Caesarius of Arles, Homily IV ties together the spiritual and practical purposes of tithing with a long discussion of clerical responsibility. A similar text in Old English is also found in MS. Junius 86, which dates from the eleventh or early twelfth century. Homily V, which discusses the cost of sinful action, is followed by one of the few Blickling Homilies for which there is no known source or analogue: Homily VI, for Palm Sunday, which provides several topoi of virtuous action before turning to an apocalyptic description of the destruction of Jerusalem forty years after Christ's death, a demonstration of the cost of sinful action.

The remaining six homilies of the Temporale begin with Easter Sunday and conclude with Pentecost. Two of these, both for Rogationtide, are fragmentary. From a combination of joy at Easter and admonition regarding what should be done before the end of the world, the six sermons build to a climax best expressed by the final lines of the sermons for Ascension Thursday and Pentecost: "teolian we þonne þeos halige tid eft cume . . . þe se lifge þæt he betre sy þonne he nu is" (let us take care that when this holy season shall return . . . that he who is alive may be better than he is now . . . [Homily XI]) because "eac us is alefed edhwyrft to þæm ecean life, & heofena rice to gesittenne mid eallum halgum & mid Drihtne sylfum" (to us also is permitted a way of return to everlasting life, and to occupy heaven's kingdom along with all saints and with the Lord himself [Homily XII]).

The final six homilies of the collection (excluding a fragment that Morris numbers separately as XVI) form a Sanctorale, providing sermons for special saints' days to complete the church calendar: Homily XIII, "The Assumption of the Virgin Mary"; Homily XIV, "The Birth of John the Baptist"; Homily XV, "The Story of Peter and Paul"; Homily XVII, "Dedication of St. Michael's Church"; Homily XVIII, "Festival of St. Martin"; and Homily XIX, "St. Andrew." The rationale behind the choice of these particular subjects remains unclear, especially in the case of the last three sermons, although Willard proposes in his introduction to the facsimile that they are arranged in terms of their thematic importance to the Incarnation. Nevertheless, correspondences in miraculous subject matter, structure, and theme clearly tie these homilies not only to each other but also to the homilies of the Temporale.

One of the more interesting aspects of the Blickling homiliary taken as a whole is the emphasis placed on Mary, who is the main subject of two of the sermons – Homily I, on the Annunciation, and Homily XIII, on the Assumption – and is mentioned prominently in several others, such as Homily II, which opens the Lenten season, Homily VII, for Easter, and Homily XIV, on the birth of John the Baptist. Mary's relevance to the apocalyptic themes of the collection is particularly evident in Homily XIII. As Willard shows in his article in *Review of English Studies* (1938), great and conflicting emphasis is placed in this homily on how Mary's soul is reunited with her body. This focus reflects what Jeffery identifies as a recurring theme throughout the homilies, the reaching of the soul through the reunion of the Word and the body, culminating in the resurrection of a body "purified of all distinctions." Jeffrey points out that in Morris's edition the two homilies dedicated to Mary are out of liturgical order; each should occur later than they do, unless, as Willard suggests, the organizing principle for the collection is both liturgical and thematic. If this is true, then perhaps the placement of a sermon concerning Mary at the start of each of the two main divisions in the homiliary, either at the time of compilation or at a later date, may be further evidence of

what is now recognized as a growing cult of the Virgin in Anglo-Saxon England.

Many questions regarding the Blickling Homilies remain unanswered: Who wrote them and when? What were the guiding principles behind their collection and arrangement? What do they tell about Anglo-Saxon piety and learning in the later ninth and early tenth centuries? Undoubtedly, these questions and others could be more easily addressed if a new edition of the Blickling homiliary were made available. In 1989 Gatch reported that he was working on an edition based on a typescript of the text by Collins, but Collins's death and some differing opinions regarding the type of critical apparatus necessary have hindered the project.

References:

Mary Clayton, "Blickling Homily XIII Reconsidered," *Leeds Studies in English,* 17 (1986): 25–40;

Rowland L. Collins, "Six Words in the Blickling Homilies," in *Philological Essays: Studies in Old and Middle English Language and Literature in Honour of Herbert Dean Meritt,* edited by James L. Rosier (Paris: Mouton, 1970), pp. 137–141;

J. E. Cross, "Blickling Homily XIV and the Old English Martyrology on John the Baptist," *Anglia,* 93 (1975): 145–160;

Cross, "The Dry Bones Speak – A Theme in Some Old English Homilies," *Journal of English and Germanic Philology,* 56 (1957): 434–458;

Cross, "On the Blickling Homily for Ascension Day (No. XI)," *Neuphilologische Mitteilungen,* 70, no. 2 (1969): 228–240;

Marcia Dalbey, "Hortatory Tone in the Blickling Homilies: Two Adaptations of Caesarius," *Neuphilologische Mitteilungen,* 70, no. 4 (1969): 641–658;

Dalbey, "Patterns of Preaching in the Blickling Easter Homily," *American Benedictine Review,* 24 (December 1973): 478–492;

Dalbey, "Structure and Style in the Blickling Homilies for the Temporale," Ph.D. dissertation, University of Illinois, 1968;

Dalbey, "Themes and Techniques in the Blickling Lenten Homilies," in *The Old English Homily and Its Backgrounds,* edited by Paul E. Szarmach and Bernard F. Huppé (Albany: State University of New York Press, 1978), pp. 221–239;

Milton Gatch, "The Unknowable Audience of the Blickling Homilies," *Anglo-Saxon England,* 18 (1989): 99–115;

J. Elizabeth Jeffery, *Blickling Spirituality and the Old English Vernacular Homily: A Textual Analysis* (Lewiston, N.Y.; Lampeter, Wales & Queenston, Ontario: Edwin Mellen, 1989);

Clare Lees, "The Blickling Palm Sunday Homily and its Revised Version," *Leeds Studies in English,* 19 (1988): 1–30;

Robert J. Menner, "The Anglian Vocabulary of the *Blickling Homilies*," *Philologica: The Malone Anniversary Studies,* edited by Thomas A. Kirby and Henry Bosley Woolf (Baltimore: Johns Hopkins Press, 1949), pp. 56–64;

Claes Schaar, *Critical Studies in the Cynewulf Group,* Lund Studies in English, 17 (Lund: Gleerup, 1949);

D. G. Scragg, "The Homilies of the Blickling Manuscript," *Learning and Literature in Anglo-Saxon England,* edited by Michael Lapidge and Helmut Gneuss (Cambridge: Cambridge University Press, 1985), pp. 299–316;

A. E. H. Swaen, "Notes on the Blickling Homilies," *Neophilologus,* 25 (1940): 264–272;

Rudolf Willard, "The Blickling-Junius Tithing Homily and Caesarius of Arles," in *Philologica: The Malone Anniversary Studies,* pp. 65–78;

Willard, "An Old English *Magnificat,*" *Studies in English,* 20 (8 July 1940): 5–28;

Willard, "On Blickling Homily XIII: *The Assumption of the Virgin,* the Source and the Missing Passages," *Review of English Studies,* 12 (January 1936): 1–17;

Willard, "The Two Accounts of the Assumption in Blickling Homily XIII," *Review of English Studies,* 14 (January 1938): 1–19;

Charles D. Wright, "Blickling Homily III on the Temptation in the Desert," *Anglia,* 106 (1988): 130–137.

The Germanic Epic and Old English Heroic Poetry: *Widsith, Waldere,* and *The Fight at Finnsburg*

Richard David Wissolik
Saint Vincent College

Widsith (late seventh century)

Manuscript: *Widsith* exists in one manuscript only, Liber/Codex Exoniensis, carrying the pressmark 3501 in the Library of the Dean and Chapter, Exeter Cathedral — known as the *Exeter Book*. The text of *Widsith* begins with the eleventh line of fol. 84^r and ends with the eighth line of fol. 87^r. Facsimile: *The Exeter Book of Old English Poetry,* edited by R. W. Chambers, Max Förster, and Robin Flower (London & Lund: Humphries, 1933).

Standard editions: *The Exeter Book,* edited by George Philip Krapp and Elliott Van Kirk Dobbie, Anglo-Saxon Poetic Records 3 (New York: Columbia University Press, 1936); *Widsith: A Study in Old English Heroic Legend,* edited by R. W. Chambers (Cambridge: University Press, 1912); *Widsith,* edited by Kemp Malone, second edition, Anglistica 13 (Copenhagen: Rosenkilde & Bagger, 1962).

Waldere (circa 750)

Manuscripts: *Waldere* survives in two fragments in the Royal Library of Copenhagen and is catalogued as MS. NY Kgl. S. 167b.

Standard editions: *Waldere,* edited by Fred Norman, second edition (London: Methuen, 1949); *Waldere,* edited by Arne Zettersten (Manchester: Manchester University Press, 1979).

The Fight at Finnsburg (circa 750)

Manuscript: *The Fight at Finnsburg* (The Finnsburg, or Finnsburh, Fragment) survives only in a 1705 transcript by George Hickes, which he included in his *Thesaurus.* The original, a flyleaf in a volume of homilies from the Library of Lambeth Palace, is briefly described in Humphrey Wanley's *Catalogue* (Oxford, 1705). The fragment is lost, but the volume of homilies from which it came may be either MS. 487 or MS. 489 in the Lambeth Collection.

First publication: In George Hickes, *Linguarum Veterum Septentrionalium Thesaurus, grammatico-criticus et archaeologicus,* (Oxford, 1703–1705; reprinted, Hildesheim: Olms, 1970).

Standard editions: In *Beowulf and the Fight at Finnsburg,* edited by Fr. Klaeber, third edition (Boston: Heath, 1950); in *Beowulf: With the Finnesburg Fragment,* edited by C. L. Wrenn (London: Harrap, 1953; revised, 1958); *Finnsburh Fragment and Episode,* edited by Donald K. Fry (London: Methuen, 1974); in J. R. R. Tolkien, *Finn and Hengest: The Fragment and the Episode,* edited by Alan Bliss (London: Allen & Unwin, 1982).

COLLECTED EDITION: *Leo : Six Old English Poems — A Handbook,* edited by Bernard James Muir (New York: Gordon & Breach, 1989) — includes *Widsith, The Finnsburh Fragment,* and *Waldere.*

COLLECTED EDITIONS IN MODERN ENGLISH: Francis B. Gummere, *The Oldest English Epic: Beowulf, Finnsburg, Waldere, Deor, Widsith, and the German Hildebrand. Translated in the Original Meters with Introductions and Notes* (New York: Macmillan, 1909);

Kemp Malone, *Ten Old English Poems, Put into Modern English Alliterative Verse* (Baltimore: Johns Hopkins University Press, 1941) — includes *Finnsburg Fragment* and *Widsith;*

Charles W. Kennedy, *An Anthology of Old English Poetry* (New York: Oxford University Press, 1960);

Beowulf Together with Widsith and the Fight at Finnsburg in the Benjamin Thorpe Transcription and Word-for-Word Translation, introduction by Vincent F. Hopper (Woodbury, N.Y.: Barron, 1962).

In general, an epic is a narrative presenting a central hero whose adventures assume importance to the historical identity of a particular race or nation. Distinctions between folk epics and art epics are currently less rigidly defined, but epics that focus on the life of a noble hero, have an unknown or uncertain author, establish an ethnic or national history, and are founded on early or primitive traditions and beliefs are usually called folk epics (*Beowulf, Iliad, Odyssey*), while art epics generally have a known author (Dante, *Divina Comedia;* Virgil, *Aeneid;* Milton, *Paradise Lost*) and are rather more consciously artistic, idealized, and technically sophisticated. All epics, however, share common characteristics: the central hero is larger-than-life, of high position, usually world-renowned, and able to trace his lineage to significant historical or legendary figures; the hero may be assisted or hindered by supernatural entities, who often intervene in the action; superhuman strength and courage are necessary qualities of the hero; the deeds of the hero are usually reported with objectivity; settings usually are limitless, and the action may take the hero across international boundaries, even into the realm of the underworld; style is elevated, yet simple. In addition, epics may share other devices or conventions: an opening in medias res; an invocation to a Muse or other inspirational figure; catalogues of gods, heroic predecessors, armies; extended, rhetorical speeches by the hero and other main characters; expository passages throughout.

The themes and action of the Germanic epic, though perhaps influenced by classical forms and exhibiting many of the characteristics outlined above, specifically reflect a distinct ethos, common to the Germanic peoples of European history, which is clearly defined by the first-century Roman historian Tacitus in his *Germania*. The Germans, Tacitus writes, were a fierce race of warriors who set courage and renown in battle above all other virtues. They were supposedly visited by Hercules, and it was of him they sang before any military engagement, in a chant they called *baritus,* performed by allowing the sound of their voices to reverberate in their shields. They augured the outcome of the battle by the nature of the sound they produced, a sound which might have terrified themselves or the enemy. There are legends that Ulysses, who came via the North Sea, as well as Mars and Mercury, also visited Germanic lands.

The Germans fought on foot and horse, but their main battle formation was the shield wall, a virtually impenetrable defense constructed by the interlocking shields of the warriors. In the eyes of the Germans a coward suffered the deepest shame; retreat from battle was acceptable only if it was a cunning prelude to counterattack. Leaders among the Germans were chosen on the basis of their abil-

ity to be role models, which they demonstrated specifically through manifested courage and prowess. Tacitus further relates that the Germans had a profound belief in fate (*wyrd* in Old English) and augury, that they came to meetings of their assemblies (Old English *witan*) fully armed, and that their youths became men when they were publicly given arms, but this only after having shown proof of courage in battle. Of great importance to the Germans was the *comitatus,* a group of warriors gathered around a single, courageous, and generous chief to whom they owed unswerving devotion and obedience and whose own reputation and power were enhanced by their own deeds. It was not politic for one of the retainers to outclass the chief on the battlefield, nor to allow an enemy to do likewise. Members of the *comitatus* were required to die on the battlefield rather than leave it, especially if the chief was slain. Such attitudes are clearly shown in the Old English battle poem *The Battle of Maldon:*

> Heart the braver, courage the bolder,
> Mood the sturdier, as our strength grows less!
> Here on the ground my good lord lies
> Bloody with wounds. Always will he rue
> Who turns now from battle [even] thinks to turn back.
> I am grown old in years; [yet] I will never relent,
> Here at the last next to my lord
> By this leader beloved I wish to lie.

Tacitus explains that the German warriors loathed peace, and if they did not find war at home, they sought it elsewhere. Moreover, the German warriors were given to plundering those things of most value to them – horses, arms, armor, and ornaments. They lived not in organized towns, but in scattered, communal dwellings. They displayed a definite reverence for women, who exhorted them in battle and to whom they ascribed holiness and gifts of prophecy.

When not engaged in warfare, the German males enjoyed the fruits of idleness, disdaining regular employment and preferring to leave the care of farm and home to women, old men, and weaklings. Hunting was an important activity, but Tacitus points out that the men were most content when sleeping and eating.

Blood feud and kin loyalty were common among the Germans, and heirs were expected to continue the feuds and friendships of their kinsmen. Feuds, though often mutually ruinous, did not continue to be forever unreconciled. Payment for injury – even murder – in the form of money and goods (Old English *wergeld*) often sufficed to end a feud, allowing at least a temporary restoration of honor to injured parties. Such matters form an important part of the narrative and thematic structure of *The Fight at Finnsburg.*

According to Tacitus, drinking and feasting were important to the social life of the Germans, and hospitality was an honored custom, even to uninvited guests. Drinking bouts lasted all day and continued through the night. Though many bloody quarrels broke out during drinking bouts, the time was profitably used (because then the heart and mind were more expansive) for the ending of feuds, the adoption of new chiefs, the elevation of youths to warrior status, settlement of the issues of war and peace, and the arrangement of marriages.

To the Germanic peoples death was a necessary end, and the bodies of famous men were buried with appropriate kinds of wood, from which pyres were made and upon which were cast the possessions of the dead man including, sometimes, his warhorse (Old English *eoh*). At such times the men nursed grief only in their own hearts, while the women were allowed to make a public show of grief. Until the late 1930s and the important archaeological discoveries at Sutton Hoo, in East Anglia, the various descriptions of Germanic burial as they were described in Old English poetry, especially those of Scyld Scefing and the title character of *Beowulf,* were often relegated to the realm of fantasy.

The Germans, then, were strong, rugged, warlike people who placed emphasis on the fame of one's name, on personal courage – the one enduring virtue – yet who trusted in fate, that to which all things material were subject. These qualities are manifested in the literature of the Germanic peoples who settled the British Isles and who sang of them long before they came to be preserved in writing.

Though Tacitus wrote seven centuries before the Anglo-Saxons set down in writing the old heroic songs, his *Germania* reveals much about the old traditions from which they grew. Thus, in such works as *Beowulf, The Battle of Maldon, The Battle of Brunnanburgh, Widsith, Waldere,* and *The Fight at Finnsburg,* the figures of Tacitus's descriptions reappear – warrior clans bound by the ties of blood, allegiance, and mutual duty between chief and retainer who, through strong ties of kinship and devotion to courage, stand against an inexorable, universal fate, fearing only loss of courage and the degradation of an honored name. The hero's courage grows as the situation becomes more hopeless. He stands fast behind his shield wall, defiant in the face of overwhelming odds, often with a laugh on his lips. Since his reputation for honor is dependent on the opinion of others, he feels compelled to protect it at all costs. Hence he is sensitive to the dictates of a social code which requires fidelity to the dictates of blood kinship and loyalty to his war chief, two factors which often come into conflict with each other. The hero yearns for the glory and dignity that can be gained only through war, and he dreads the coming of old age, when the opportunity for glory will lessen, when the old comrades will be gone, and when the great mead halls will come to ruin through the ravages of war, the devastation wrought by the blood feud, or the relentless progress of time and chance.

Unfortunately, the only extant epic written in German (though there is a much larger body preserved in Scandinavian languages) is the *Hildebrandslied,* a fragment which probably derives its themes from sources common to *Waldere* and *The Fight at Finnsburg.* The motif in the *Hildebrandslied,* that of a father unwillingly placed in the position of killing his son, is an old one, and it appears in many other works, even in modern literature. The poem also extols the virtue of loyalty to one's lord or comrade, to the extent that it overshadows loyalty to one's kin. Hildebrand must choose between the two loyalties not once, but twice. The poem opens with Hildebrand and Hathubrand facing each other in battle. Hathubrand, unaware of his opponent's identity and thinking his father to be dead, first reveals himself to be the son of Hildebrand and then tells the story of how Hildebrand abandoned and dispossessed him, when years before he fled eastward to escape from the wrath of Odoacer and Theodric. Hildebrand then identifies himself to the unbelieving Hathubrand. After some attempts by Hildebrand to dissuade his son from battle, the two meet in combat:

> Let him who under fate must fight
> Now try himself, and see if his armor be taken from him,
> Or whether both shields become his.
> First charging with ash-spears, that splintered,
> They carved hateful blows with swords
> Until the linden shields grew small,
> Worn with weapons....

The Old English *Widsith, Waldere,* and the fragment *The Fight at Finnsburg* are early works which illuminate the continental background of the Germanic invaders of England and help in the understanding of all Old English heroic poems, especially *Beowulf,* by placing them in historical, intellectual, social, and artistic perspective. The old themes would also find their way into the Old English la-

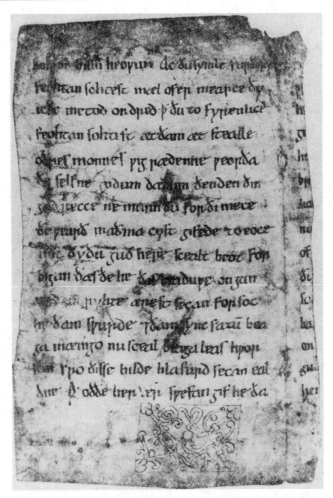

Fragment from a manuscript dating circa 1000, with text from Waldere
(Royal Library, Copenhagen, Ny Kgl. S. MS. 167b)

ments and elegies — *The Wanderer, The Seafarer, The Ruin,* and *Deor* — and of these things the *scop* (bard, from *scieppan,* "to shape, to create") sang.

The evidence of Old English heroic poetry is enough to indicate that knowledge of the stories of the Germanic heroic age did not pass with the coming of Christianity and that audiences entertained by scops were entirely familiar with allusions to the ancient traditions, battles, feuds, and heroes. A good example of this is the "Lay of Finnsburg" in *Beowulf,* which would certainly not have been understood without knowledge of the historical event, and it is likely that the Hengest of the lay would have been associated with the Hengest of Anglo-Saxon history, as Dorothy Whitelock suggests.

In the poem *Widsith* a scop, Widsith, the "far traveler," tells of his visits to the lands of acclaimed Germanic kings, whom he praises for the gifts they give him for his works. Such generosity toward scops by kings was understandable since, through

the songs of these oral poets, the kings were assured of a certain immortality through succeeding generations, who would come to marvel at their deeds. Indeed, many of the scops were professionals whose livelihood depended upon employment in the service of some lord. The poetic utterances of scops were important in Anglo-Saxon England, primarily because they kept alive a heroic tradition that touched the myth consciousness of listeners long after the advent of Christianity. The scop sang of the old heroes and their deeds, of the hardships of life, and of the pains of death. He made the point, again and again, that even if defeat must ultimately occur, the good fight is always worth making. *Widsith* preserves the career of one of these singers of myths, or gleemen.

The structure of *Widsith* consists of a prologue (9 lines) and an epilogue (9 lines), between which falls a speech by Widsith (125 lines) which has as its core three *thulas* (a metrical catalogue of names) and one *thula* fragment. The name catalogues list many of the personages and places found in *Beowulf*, including Eormenric the Goth, the Franks, Breca the Bronding, Finn the Frisian, Hnaef the Hocing, the Wylfings, Ongentheow the Swede, the Hetware, Offa the Angle, Hama, the Geats, the South Danes, and Heorot, where Hrothgar and his nephew Hrothulf vanquished Ingeld and the Heatho-Bards, a conflict which Beowulf predicts.

Widsith's speech may be divided into five parts: an introduction, three main divisions (fits), and a conclusion. Each fit consists of a *thula* and some passages added by the author. The *thulas* demonstrate Widsith's knowledge of historical events, Germanic culture, and heroic themes. Other passages highlight the singer's professional success and status and his access to primary historical information. The poem relates that Widsith sang to the accompaniment of a harp, the name of which, W. J. Sedgefield conjectures, might have been Scilling.

It is clear from the text that Widsith is both performer and composer. He sings in mead halls about his own life and praises his patroness, Queen Ealhild. The relationship between scop and patron is described in the epilogue.

The *Widsith* poet undoubtedly drew upon much of the body of oral verse common in his day, though he almost certainly invented parts of the poem himself. The arguments raised by early scholars concerning the scop's longevity – his visits are separated historically by nearly two hundred years – are of limited consequence to both the poem's speaker and purpose. Only because of his "longevity" was Widsith able to travel to the lands of the famous kings he served. The poet's purpose was to arouse, through allusion to the great kings of the past, the imagination of the hearer/reader. Apparent fictional aspects aside, Widsith, who had a lord, a homeland, and a professional life, becomes, under the poet's hand, a paradigm of scops – a respected historian who was well traveled, praiseworthy, experienced, and authoritative, one who kept alive the traditions of his Germanic heritage. Kemp Malone especially defends the persona of Widsith as paradigm.

An intriguing theory advanced by David A. Rollman argues that *Widsith* may well be a poem about poetry itself, a sort of Old English "defense of poetry," thus fulfilling one of the three "vital functions of poetry," the didactic. This, plus the other functions of the "experiential" and the "ability to add something to life itself by endowing immortality," governs the poem and even determines the nature of the catalogues of kings. The three functions

also form "the basis of the poet's plea, which is not for himself, but for his art." More recent scholarship, for the most part, has come to see a greater value in the poetics of *Widsith*, rather than dismissing the poem as a negligible work, valuable mostly for its lists of famous kings.

Waldere (circa 750), a fragment of heroic poetry in Old English, exists in complete form in other languages, the most commonly cited being the tenth-century Latin *Waltharius*. The Latin version was written in hexameters, possibly at the monastery of Saint Gall, and was probably a compositional exercise. The story of Walter was undoubtedly popular among the Germanic peoples. *Waldere* carries the only reference to it in Old English, and because of this Frederick Norman (1969) maintains that the Old English poem can only be discussed in comparison with *Waltharius*, without which it would be basically incomprehensible.

In the *Waltharius*, Attila the Hun makes war on the western kingdoms of Frankland, Burgundy, and Aquitaine, which submit without much struggle, offering him hostages. The hostages – Hagano, Waltharius's comrade in arms and son of the Frankish king Gibicho; Hiltgunt, daughter of the Burgundian king Heriricus; Waltharius, betrothed of Hiltgunt and son of the Aquitainian king Alpthere – are humanely treated by the Hun leader. Gibicho dies, and his successor, his son Guntharius, refuses to continue paying tribute to the Huns. Eventually Hagano escapes without being pursued and is later followed by Waltharius and Hiltgunt, who manage to take with them a considerable treasure. Attila is unable to find pursuers even after promises of reward. Later the hostages are ferried across the Rhine River. The ferryman is given unfamiliar fish in payment, which are seen by Guntharius, who then deduces that Waltharius has returned. Hearing of Attila's stolen treasure, Guntharius, against Hagano's advice, decides to rob Waltharius and Hiltgunt. When overtaken by Guntharius, Waltharius makes two offers of rings, which Guntharius refuses. Guntharius and Hagano ambush Waltharius and Hiltgunt, and in the ensuing struggle the king loses a leg and Waltharius his right hand. Using his sword in his left hand, Waltharius blinds Hagano in one eye and knocks out several of his teeth. The fight ends, and Hiltgunt nurses the combatants. Guntharius and Hagano, their friendship with Waltharius renewed, return to their homeland, Waltharius marries Hiltgunt, and they reign in Aquitaine for three decades.

The Old English *Waldere* consists of two speeches. In the first Hildeguth (Hildegunt) cheers

Waldere, assuring him that his combat will be successful and that God will preserve him from fear. In the second *Walthere*, in what constitutes a typical Germanic boast, recalling the exchange between Byrhtnoth and the Vikings in *The Battle of Maldon*, points to his coat of mail and dares Gunthere (Guntharius) to strip it from his shoulders.

The Fight at Finnsburg (circa 750) is a forty-seven-line fragment in Old English concerning a conflict between the Frisians and the Danes, and it is generally held to have particular value in relationship to the whole Finnsburg story and its special place in *Beowulf* as the "Lay of Finnsburg," sung by Hrothgar's scop. The fragment concentrates on the actual heroic struggle taking place in the great hall, while the longer treatment in *Beowulf* exhibits the tragic overtones of the struggle between the Frisians and the Danes.

The Fight at Finnsburg is all too lightly dismissed by scholars. If it had been written in a later age, the poem (undoubtedly epitomizing older Germanic poetry) would have been an excellent short, compressed, heroic narrative – a *lai*. The fragment, moreover, does not seem to have been intended to be moralistic but appears to be the work of a singer who knew his traditions and his craft, one who reached the point quickly (a recounting of the battle) by taking from his "word-hoard" the most stirring and perfect of epic formulas.

Originating in oral form, the fragment recounts early stages of the Frisian-Danish struggle, when the Frisians attacked King Hnaef. Hnaef and a band of sixty Danes were visiting Queen Hildeburh (Hnaef's sister) and her husband, King Finn, when they were betrayed by Jutes (Eotens) in the service of Finn. The beginning of the fragment is missing, but it may be deduced that a Danish sentinel becomes aware of the attack when he sees light reflected from the swords of the attackers, for Hnaef responds in terms classic to the rhetoric of war: "This is no daylight dawning from the east, nor flying dragon, nor gables of the hall afire; but there they bring (arms), birds (of prey) sing, the grey-coated one (wolf) howls, the battle wood resounds, shield answers shaft." The narrative continues with equally classic images: "many a golden thane girded on his sword"; "Then was the noise of battle in the hall." The Danes take up defensive positions at the two doors of the great hall and hold out, with no loss to themselves, for five days. The fragment ends when a Dane (or, according to some scholars, a Frisian) suffers a wound and is questioned by Hnaef (or perhaps Finn) as to the fate of other warriors.

Through a collation of the fragment and the "Lay of Finnsburg" from *Beowulf*, it is possible to form a fairly complete narrative of the feud that occurred between the Frisians and the Danes. The reason for the feud is never told, but it seems likely that the visit described in the fragment happened during an interlude of peace, during Yuletide. While the fragment includes only the conflict described above, the "Lay of Finnsburg" relates that Hengest, Hnaef's successor, concludes a tenuous peace with the Frisians. For many months Hengest is torn between honoring the peace and avenging the early attack, an internal conflict which illustrates one kind of choice confronting a hero in an heroic setting – the kind of choice, though free, which carries opposing values and consequences. Such conflict of choice is discussed in detail in W. G. Busse and R. Holtei's study of heroic poetry and *The Battle of Maldon*. Ultimately Hengest resumes the feud, and in a battle Finn is slain and the Frisians are defeated. Hengest rests contented, knowing that he has avenged his countrymen and fulfilled the dictates of loyalty to kin.

References:

Alan Bliss, "The Aviones and *Widsith* 26a," *Anglo-Saxon England,* 7 (1978): 119–129;

W. G. Busse and R. Holtei, "The Battle of Maldon: A Historical, Heroic and Political Poem," *Neophilologus,* 65 (October 1981): 614–621;

Alistair Campbell, "The Old English Epic Style," in *English and Medieval Studies Presented to J. R. R. Tolkien on the Occasion of His Seventieth Birthday,* edited by Norman Davis (London: Allen & Unwin), pp. 13–26;

Benjamin H. Carroll, Jr., "An Essay on the Walther Legend," *Florida State University Studies,* 5 (1952): 123–179;

Robert Creed, "Widsith's Journey through Germanic Tradition," in *Anglo-Saxon Poetry: Essays in Appreciation,* edited by Lewis E. Nicholson and Dolores Warwick Frese (Notre Dame, Ind.: University of Notre Dame Press, 1975), pp. 376–387;

Joseph Dane, "Finnsburh and *Iliad* IX: A Greek Survival of the Medieval Germanic Oral-Formulaic Theme, The Hero on the Beach," *Neophilologus,* 66 (1982): 443–449;

Stefan Einarsson, "The Hero on the Beach in *Finnsburh*," *Neophilologische Mitteilungen,* 67 (March 1966): 27–31;

Einarsson, "The Location of Finnsburh: *Beowulf* 1125–29a," *English Language Notes,* 8 (September 1970): 2–3;

Einarsson, "Two Voices in *Widsith*," *Mediævalia*, 6 (1980): 37–56;

W. H. French, "Widsith and the Scop," *PMLA*, 60 (September 1945): 623–630;

J. M. Fritz, "Chronological Impossibilities in *Widsith*," *Germanic Notes*, 6, no. 4 (1975): 50–52;

Donald K. Fry, "*Finnsburh* 34a: *Hwearflicra Hwær*," *English Language Notes*, 6 (June 1969): 241–242;

Fry, "*Finnsburh*: A New Interpretation," *Chaucer Review*, 9 (Summer 1974): 1–14;

G. N. Garmonsway, "Anglo-Saxon Heroic Attitudes," in *Medieval and Linguistic Studies in Honour of Francis Peabody Magoun, Jr.*, edited by J. B. Bessinger, Jr. (London: Allen & Unwin, 1965), pp. 139–146;

Stanley B. Greenfield, " 'Folces Hyrde,' *Finnsburh* 46b: Kenning and Context," *Neuphilologische Mitteilungen*, 73 (April 1972): 97–102;

Joyce Hill, "*Widsith* and the Tenth Century," *Neuphilologische Mitteilungen*, 85, no. 3 (1984): 305–315;

Ida M. Hollowell, "Was Widsith a *scop?*," *Neophilologus*, 64 (1980): 583–591;

Bernard F. Huppé, "The Concept of the Hero in the Early Middle Ages," in *Concepts of the Hero in the Middle Ages and the Renaissance*, edited by N. T. Burns (Albany: State University of New York Press, 1975), pp. 1–26;

Gosta Langenfelt, "Some Widsith Names and the Background of Widsith," in *VI. Internationaler Kongress für Namenforschung* (Munich, 1958);

William W. Lawrence, "Beowulf and the Tragedy of Finnsburg," *PMLA*, 30, no. 2 (1915): 372–431;

Lawrence, "Structure and Interpretation of *Widsith*," *Modern Philology*, 4 (1906–1907): 329–374;

Francis P. Magoun, Jr., "Two Verses in the OE *Waldere* Characteristic of Oral Poetry," *Beiträge zur Geschichte der deutschen Sprache und Literatur*, 80 (1958): 214–218;

Magoun and H. M. Smyser, *Walter of Aquitaine: Materials for the Study of His Legend*, Connecticut College Monographs 4 (New London: Connecticut College, 1950);

Kemp Malone, "The Franks Casket and the Date of *Widsith*," in *Nordica et Anglica* (The Hague: Mouton, 1968), pp. 10–18;

Malone, "The Old Tradition: Courtly Poetry," in *A Literary History of England*, edited by Albert C. Baugh (New York: Appleton-Century-Crofts, 1948), pp. 45–59;

R. Meindl, "The Artistic Unity of *Widsith*," *Xavier University Studies*, 3 (1964): 19–28;

Frederick Norman, "Early Germanic Background to Old English Verse," in *Medieval Literature and Civilization: Studies in Memory of G. N. Garmonsway*, edited by D. Pearsall (London: Athlone, 1969), pp. 3–27;

Norman, "The Evidence for the Germanic Walter Lay," *Acta Germanica*, 3 (1968): 21–35;

Norman, "The OE *Waldere* and Some Problems in the Story of Walther and Hildegunde," in *Mélanges pour Jean Fourquet* (Paris, 1969), pp. 261–271;

David A. Rollman, "*Widsith* as an Anglo-Saxon Defense of Poetry," *Neophilologus*, 66 (July 1982): 431–439;

W. J. Sedgefield, "Scilling," *Modern Language Review*, 26 (January 1931): 75;

Michael Swanton, "Heroes, Heroism and Heroic Literature," *Essays and Studies*, 30 (1977): 1–21;

Tacitus, *The Agricola and the Germania*, translated by H. Mattingly, revised by S. A. Handford (Harmondsworth: Penguin, 1970);

Dorothy Whitelock, *The Audience of Beowulf* (Oxford: Clarendon Press, 1951);

Rosemary Woolf, "The Ideal of Men Dying with Their Lord in the *Germania* and in *The Battle of Maldon*," *Anglo-Saxon England*, 5 (1976): 63–81;

Lamar York, "A Reading of *Widsith*," *Midwest Quarterly*, 20 (1979): 325–331.

Judith
(circa 930)

Katherine E. Krohn
Texas A&M University

Manuscript: British Library, MS. Cotton Vitellius A.xv, fols. 202^r–209^b. Transcription: Bodleian Library, Oxford, MS. Junius 105 (SC 5216), made by Franciscus Junius (died 1677). Facsimile: *The Nowell Codex: British Museum Cotton Vitellius A.xv, Second Manuscript,* edited by Kemp Malone, Early English Manuscripts in Facsimile 12 (Copenhagen: Rosenkilde & Bagger, 1963).
First publication: *Heptateuchus, Liber Job, et Evangelium Nicodemi, Anglo-Saxonice. Historiae Judith Fragmentum,* edited by Edward Thwaites (Oxford: e theatro Sheldoniano, 1698).
Standard editions: In *Beowulf and Judith,* edited by Elliot van Kirk Dobbie, Anglo-Saxon Poetic Records 4 (New York: Columbia University Press, 1953); *Judith,* edited by B. J. Timmer, revised edition, Exeter Medieval English Texts (Exeter: University of Exeter Press, 1978).

Judith occurs as the fifth of five articles in British Library, MS. Cotton Vitellius A.xv, a document originally made up of two distinct manuscripts. The first of this pair, the Southwick Codex, was produced in the twelfth century. The Nowell Codex ("the *Beowulf* manuscript") is approximately 150 years older and commonly dated between roughly A.D. 980 and 1020. The manuscripts were combined in the seventeenth century, it being clear that the second scribe of *Beowulf* also wrote down the *Judith.* Like much of the Cotton Library, the manuscript was damaged in the 1731 fire at Ashburnham House.

The damaged manuscript has been the source of much conjecture concerning the length of the original poem and the relation of the extant fragment to the whole. Other critical speculation deals with the significance — in the context of the male-dominated militarist culture in which the poem was written — of this version of the biblical story of a woman who takes a sword and beheads her would-be ravisher. The search continues for historical models for Judith, for martial and religious allegorical interpretations and for the meaning of gender-role reversals, since Holofernes covets Judith's maidenhead, but, to the horror of his men, she claims his head instead.

Judith is incomplete; the 349-line fragment that survives begins in midthought. (The modern notion of "sentence" does not accurately describe units in the appositive style of Old English verse.) A key debate concerns the original length of the poem. B. J. Timmer, the modern editor of *Judith,* advocates one school of thought — that what remains of the poem represents perhaps one-quarter of an original verse of "about 1,344" lines. Other scholars have equal confidence that far less than three-quarters of the poem has been lost. Based on calculations of section length in the poem, it may be that only around 98 lines of *Judith* have been lost, meaning that as much as 78 percent survives. Obviously critical and aesthetic appreciation of the work is strongly affected by apprehension of it as either a coherent near whole or a mere tattered fragment.

The primary evidence cited by the "incomplete" camp resides in the section or fit numbers affixed to the work that begin just before line 15 with Roman numeral *X,* suggesting that there were once nine more sections of *Judith. Beowulf,* which survives in its entirety, also has fit numbers; these begin at *i.* The numbers may mark spurts of poetic inspiration, or something as prosaic as stints of copying.

The *Judith* scribe, perhaps copying from an incomplete exemplar, may have guessed at the amount lost, numbering the poem according to events in the apocryphal book, which would account for the numerals' close correspondence to it; conceivably the scribe worked from an earlier version of the manuscript which included other works, already lost, and with which *Judith* had been numbered in sequence. Three of the only six Old English poems having fit numbers are numbered seriatim, suggesting that the missing sections may not all have been part of *Judith.*

Page from Judith in the only extant manuscript for the work, a transcription (circa tenth century) that also includes the text for Beowulf (British Library, MS. Cotton Vitellius A.xv)

The opposition to this point of view argues that the poems numbered seriatim have clear organizing principles about them, such as the three parts of *Christ* (Advent, Ascension, Judgment) in *The Exeter Book,* and the episodes in the Junius Manuscript of *Christ and Satan* (Fall of Angels, Harrowing of Hell, Christ's Temptation). Other possibilities include the section numbers being equivalent to *lections,* or daily readings, which are used in monastic study or a program of reading, and are not structurally significant.

Physical evidence suggesting that *Judith* may not always have been next to *Beowulf* also affects the question of its original length. Cotton Vitellius A.xv comprises five works: *Christopher, Marvels of the East, Alexander's Letter, Beowulf,* and *Judith. Beowulf* appears at one time to have been at the end of an unprotected volume. Its last page is rubbed and dirty. Worm holes that do not penetrate *Judith* are observable in the last quire of *Beowulf.* (A quire, section, or gathering consists of sheets of writing material folded so as to produce pairs of conjugate leaves, each side of which is a page. The book is made up of quires sewn together through the folds, which form the spine of the volume.)

Certainty about the original location of the poem in the manuscript could shed light on the original length of the work. Not only physical indications, such as the layout of the five articles in the various quires, but also linguistic evidence indicate that *Judith* was probably once at the beginning of the manuscript. *Beowulf,* for example, was laid out so as to conclude at the end of the quire. *Judith* does not conclude at the end of a quire, opening the possibility that there once was an outer bifolium that included the beginning as well as the end material that has since been appended to the last surviving page.

The difference in how *eo/io* spellings of words are handled merits examination. In late West Saxon, *eo* and *io* were no longer pronounced differently. The usual spelling became *eo.* Current opinion holds *io* spellings to have come from or through Mercia rather than from Wessex. Of the five articles in this manuscript, *Marvels of the East, Alexander's Letter,* and *Beowulf* include 194 *io* spellings in 207 manuscript pages, whereas *Christopher* and *Judith* have none in a total of twenty-five manuscript pages. *Marvels of the East, Alexander's Letter,* and *Beowulf* may have formed a *Liber de diversis monstris,* or "monster collection," while the other two have no monsters at all. For these reasons one might suspect that *Christopher* and *Judith* were originally copied from one exemplar and the other works from a different one.

The Book of Judith, although translated by Saint Jerome in the fourth century for his Vulgate Bible, is now included in the Old Testament Apocrypha. Bernard Huppé's *The Web of Words* (1970) traces the history of the book's canonical status. Ælfric wrote a metrical paraphrase of the entire Book of Judith more than a century after the poem was written. The apocryphal version and the metrical paraphrase provide the most interesting comparisons with the Old English *Judith.* Thomas Gregory Foster and Alessandra Rapetti provide comparisons of the poem with the Greek Septuagint, and Middle High German and Middle English redactions respectively.

Aspects of the poem that differ from the Apocryphal and metrical paraphrase versions hold interest for their literary value and for their parts in the debate as to the primary meaning of the poem as allegory or political persuasion. In the Old English poem Judith is a maiden rather than a widow. The poem omits the exultant Song of Judith found in the Vulgate (16:1–21) as well as any account of her later life. The biblical cast of characters undergoes significant truncation in the poetic version. Leading characters that appear in the Vulgate but not in the Old English version include Joachim, Achior, Ozias, Bagao, Holofernes' eunuch, and Nebuchadnezzar.

In the poem far less emphasis rests upon Judith's adornment of her person to entice Holofernes than in the Old Testament telling. Nor does she speak ambiguous words designed to mislead him into believing that his amorous attentions meet with acquiescence, as in a passage from the Vulgate where Judith asks, "who am I, that I should gainsay my lord? for whatsoever shall be pleasing in his eyes I will do speedily" (Judith 12:14); her speech fails to clarify whether the lord to whom she refers is God or Holofernes. In the Old English version, Holofernes has no conversation with her but simply orders her brought to his bed. His doom comes to him not as a result of her seductiveness but as a consequence of his own drunken debauchery.

Nor does the Old English heroine appear at the feast, as she does in the Vulgate (Judith 12:19). Thus the poem omits the relation of how, at Holofernes' banquet, Judith eats only the kosher food brought by her maidservant; this would have been most uncivil conduct on the part of a guest. In further consequence of not having been there to consume Holofernes' provender, the Old English Judith avoids the affront of harming a person with whom she had broken bread.

The poem brims with inversions. While later Christian writers regarded feasting as the locus of gluttony and inebriation, early Germanic peoples saw the banquet as central to maintaining a strong bond among members of the tribe, particularly between a lord and his retainers. Holofernes displays the reverse of proper conduct toward guests. He forces wine upon the warriors until they become intoxicated, thus leading them into spiritual, as well as physical, death. Judith, in praying for strength, refers to him as *morðres bryttan* (distributor of murder), inverting the usual epithet for a lord, *sinces brytta* (distributor of treasure). Later, when the Hebrews rout their camp, the Assyrians are anxious to inform Holofernes of the disaster but fear disturbing him during his presumed "enjoyment" of the holy maiden. Such feelings are in complete opposition to the trust and affection that normally flourished between retainers and their lord.

Judith's use of the (phallic) sword to decapitate Holofernes, an act symbolic of castration, constitutes a shocking reversal, as Holofernes' men had been led to expect that she, not he, would be violently penetrated on the bed. Even the *fleohnet* (flynet) surrounding the bed seems a mockery, recalling the veil in Exodus 26:33: "The veil shall divide unto you between the holy place and the most holy." Holofernes' golden net, transparent from within but opaque from without, makes him appear to be an all-seeing, unseen god, until his men discover him deprived of any vision at all, having lost his head. Soon the beasts of battle — ravens, wolves, and eagles — gather, and the carrion eaters replace the Assyrian revelers in an ironic inversion of mead-hall hospitality: the feasters have become the feast.

The martial aspects of the story receive different handling in the various accounts. In the Apocrypha, no battle actually ensues; the Hebrews threaten attack, and the Assyrians retreat. The poem highlights the battle, which, far from simply feeding an Anglo-Saxon appetite for fierce fighting, separates the characters into "God's people" and "God's enemies."

Whereas in the Vulgate Judith is awarded the Assyrian leader's bedcover and pots and pans, "a woman's trophies," in Ælfric's metrical paraphrase she is offered his helmet, byrnie, rings, and other war gear, which she refuses, not wanting to be in any way associated with Holofernes' sinfulness. The heroine of the Old English poem, however, gives every indication of following the ancient custom of retaining the visible symbols, the reminders, of her triumph over her vanquished foe.

Conversely, none of the accounts using Judith's story for exemplary ends includes the memorable narrative details of the Old English verse. Neither the elaborate feast, the hair seizing and two-stroke decapitation of Holofernes, the bag for the head, the calling of the men to the wall, the farcical attempt at waking the dead general, nor the extended plundering of the Assyrians is included in the Latin analogues, which are brief, exclude other characters, and stress Holofernes' slaying and Judith's celebration.

The Old English *Exodus* pares its biblical source selectively and presents it heroically, establishing a precedent for the short, focused form of *Judith*. It also highlights particular biblical themes without displaying the entire panorama of surrounding events. Some scholars refute the *Exodus* argument, noting that a poet who glories in describing hand-to-hand combat would unlikely be able to resist the temptations of the biblical Judith. The conquests of Nebuchadnezzar, Holofernes' great army approaching Israel, the fortification of her passes and mountain tops, and the long siege of Bethulia would all inspire rousing scenes in an epic war song.

Critics note marked similarities between *Judith* and *Beowulf*, such as the Bethulian guards anxiously awaiting Judith's return, and Beowulf's *duguð* (band of retainers) keeping watch as he descends into the mere to do battle with Grendel's *moðr*. Further similarity appears in the handing round of drink at the respective feasts. Several possible borrowings of words, phrases, and lines from *Elene, Andreas, Juliana, Dream of the Rood, Genesis, Exodus,* and *Christ,* as well as several ostensibly borrowed from *Judith* by the author of the poem *The Battle of Brunanburh* (937), are recorded. Given the large number of *hapax legomena* (uniquely attested words) that present themselves in Old English, either through accidents of survival or neologistic design, one might wonder how many of these "borrowings" could be kennings (formulaic tropes), such as *hwalrad* ("whale-road," for "sea"), or simply common features of Anglo-Saxon epic adventures.

Literary techniques in *Judith* have also attracted critical attention. The four-part theme of the hero(ine) on the beach, one of many oral-formulaic substructures, features a hero(ine), retainers, a flashing light, and a journey. This theme functions, similarly to other such structures, as an organizing unit in composition and reception. Researchers observe not simply contrasts in the poem but paired contrasting scenes. The first (surviving) scene has its analogue at the end of the poem, the second scene its penultimate counterpart, and so on. The pairs reach a summit at the center of the work, where Judith unleashes the potential energy accumulated by her efforts in the first half of the epic, the momentum carrying her people forward to victory in the second half.

Donald K. Fry describes another narrative unit which he calls the typescene: a "stereotyped presentation of conventional details used to describe a certain narrative event requiring neither verbatim repetition nor specific formula content." Other critics examine battle-related typescenes and the mock-heroic variations on them used throughout the poem. Huppé's *The Web of Words* analyzes *Judith* and three other Old English poems, establishing a set of structural units which describe the nonlinear style of Anglo-Saxon poetry, called variously pyramidal, appositive, and interlaced.

Alain Renoir's "*Judith* and the Limits of Poetry" (1962) uses the analogy of the cinematograph as a basis for analyzing the visual effects that the poet achieves in bringing the audience into the battle scene. The modern reader would do well to read this study in light of Walter J. Ong's *Orality and Literacy: The Technologizing of the Word* (1982). Ong makes a strong case for the mind of a literate person in a long-literate culture perceiving the world in ways fundamentally more visual than that of a person in an oral culture. From such findings the reader may infer that the "naturalness" of a cinematographic analogy comes not from the work under examination but from the well-trained vision of the examiner.

Those *Judith* scholars embracing the cinematic analogy, however, point out that the armaments described by the scop are named as one would see them upon approaching the battle: first banners and helmets, then shields and distance weapons (arrows), which one would see outside the ranks. These are followed, as if upon closing in, by shorter-range projectiles (spears) and finally hand weapons (swords). A similar effect may be noted in *Beowulf,* where sailors see land, then cliffs, then hills, and finally headlands as they approach the shore.

The hypermetric lines in *Judith* pose another provocative problem. These lines, which include more than the normal four stresses per line, attract attention to themselves, but to precisely what end critics disagree. It has been proposed that they distinguish between narrative (normal) and "reflective or psychological passages" (hypermetric).

Constance B. Hieatt calls attention to the echoing of words from earlier in the poem in the hypermetric lines. These echoes she views as framing or linking passages together, forming "envelope patterns." Other scholars, also marking the pleonastic quality of the lines, regard these passages as rife with "sheer padding." However, in many places the scop uses hypermeter for heights of elevated rhetoric and also as "a kind of rhythmic brake" when the poet wishes to dwell with "a kind of slow relish" upon a particular moment. Studies on the hypermetric lines in *Beowulf,* such as John C. Pope's classic *The Rhythm of Beowulf* (1942), provide further discussion.

The poem's use as political propaganda or as a Christian allegory receives wide comment. Those scholars favoring the allegorical approach read the poem as using military idiom to betoken spiritual warfare. Those in the "political" camp see the verse as a literal call to arms for the Anglo-Saxons, who were at the time in conflict with the Danes.

Patristic critics of *Judith* perceive in this apocryphal narrative an allegory wherein Judith prefigures Christ. Judith also stands for Ecclesia, the Church; it is for this reason that she is described as bright and shining. Holofernes, by contrast, is sinful and devilish. The verb *cirman,* emphasizing this point, refers to the shrieking of devils or evildoers in *Guthlac, Genesis, Christ,* and *Andreas.* The Assyrians drowning in wine may stand allegorically for the Egyptians drowning in the Red Sea. Anglo-Saxons commonly used the image of crossing the sea to indicate the life journey. The absence of Joachim, the high priest who praises Judith, and Achior, dramatically converted by Judith's deed, argues against such interpretation. The omission of both the Christ figure and the pagan convert suggests a poet deliberately avoiding allegory.

Both the twin attributes of *sapientia et fortitudo* (wisdom and courage), associated with Christ, are attributed to Judith only in the Old English verse. Although this Judith appears stronger and less duplicitous than her Latin and prose English counterparts, the commentators pursuing this line of reasoning understand the theme as emphasizing the power of God to make a "weak woman" the instrument of the delivery of her people.

Helen Damico's studies of the military associations for several of the words used to describe Judith and other Anglo-Saxon females (both in terms of appearance and mental capabilities), as well as her tracing of the reflex of warrior women in old Icelandic literature, suggest that the poem reflects less the tradition of God's choosing unlikely souls through whom to act than that of the Valkyries.

A great deal of the poem's understandable appeal to feminist critics stems from its recounting of the brave deeds of a woman celebrated for her wisdom and determination. Even the incident of her having to smite Holofernes twice in order to decapitate him underscores her strength of purpose rather than demonstrating physical frailty. Particularly since the narrator's foreknowledge ("daring shield-warriors doomed to death") contrasts with Holofernes' lack of ordinary foresight, and physical incapacity brought about by moral weakness, it would seem that the poet emphasizes strength of character, not breadth of biceps.

Those reading the poem as an incitement to political action quote Ælfric's *On the Old and New Testament* (circa 1075), which tells the reader that he has translated the Book of Judith "as an example to you people that you should defend your land with weapons against the invading army." One controversial interpretation sees the poem as an exhortation to the Anglo-Saxons to protect their women from rape by invading Danes. This could provide motivation for de-emphasizing Judith's much-vaunted chastity; presumably Anglo-Saxon wives and daughters would have an easier time identifying with a maid than a chaste widow. Wulfstan's *Sermo lupi ad Anglos* (1014) depicts the oppressed condition of Anglo-Saxon women at that time.

Æthelflæd, the "Lady of the Mercians," is often proposed as inspiration for the Old English *Judith*. Born circa 870, widow of Æthelred of Mercia and sister to King Edward, Æthelflæd ruled Mercia for eight years. She built ten fortresses for Mercian defense against Danish incursion and led troops into battle in 916 and 917. None of these possibilities proves compelling in light of linguistic and cultural evidence, however.

The poem may, alternatively, have been written to honor a real Judith. Rabanus Maurus, author of the earliest complete commentary (834) on the Book of Judith, dedicates his work to the empress. The exegesis, concentrating upon the allegorical level of the book, views the eponymic character as representing the Holy Church. Isidore of Seville and Saint Jerome also see her, with the great emphasis placed on her chastity, as standing for the Holy Church, "Christ's new household." Following this example, the Anglo-Saxon poet may have written in celebration of the deliverance of Wessex, honoring the Judith whom Æthelwulf, father of Alfred, wed in 865. This Judith was also the granddaughter of the empress.

Ann W. Astell and Mary Flavia Godfrey weave several current approaches together in essays demonstrating that the leitmotiv of headship becomes reified in Holofernes' own head, the object of capital wordplay, which itself functions as a sign designed to spur the auditors to action. The embedded allegory, rather than nullifying the literal meaning of military action, supports it, presenting it as holy warfare. Astell comments that their enemy "is at once historical and eternal, political and religious, Danish and demonic."

This anonymous text, formerly believed to be either Caedmonian or Cynewulfian, merits further study on several points. The effects, if not the de-

signs, of the end rhymes and hypermetric lines continue to draw debate. The intriguing crux at line 90, where Judith pulls Holofernes to her *bysmerlice* (disgracefully), awaits satisfactory explication. Her needing two strokes to part Holofernes from his head, even after prayer, deserves elucidation. With the emergence of feminist criticism and gender studies, the *Judith* assumes a new prominence in the Old English canon. The advent of other poststructuralist theoretical approaches, such as those attempted in John P. Hermann's *Allegories of War* (1989), provides fresh methodologies for reading Judith, and indeed, all of Old English literature.

References:

The Apocrypha: Translated out of the Greek and Latin Tongues: Being the Version set Forth A.D. 1611 Compared with the Most Ancient Authorities and Revised A.D. 1894 (London: Oxford University Press, 1926);

Ann W. Astell, "Holofernes's Head: *Tacen* and Teaching in the Old English *Judith*," *Anglo-Saxon England*, 18 (1989): 117–133;

Carl T. Berkhout and James F. Doubleday, "The Net in *Judith* 46b–54a," *Neuphilologische Mitteilungen*, 74 (1973): 630–634;

Arthur G. Brodeur, "A Study of Diction and Style in Three Anglo-Saxon Narrative Poems," in *Nordica et Anglia: Studies in Honour of Stefán Einarsson*, edited by A. H. Orrick (The Hague: Mouton, 1968), pp. 98–114;

Jackson J. Campbell, "Schematic Technique in *Judith*," *English Literary History*, 38 (1971): 155–172;

David Chamberlain, "*Judith*: A Fragmentary and Political Poem," in *Anglo-Saxon Poetry: Essays in Appreciation: For John C. McGalliard*, edited by Lewis E. Nicholson and Dolores Warwick (Notre Dame, Ind.: University of Notre Dame Press, 1975);

Jane Chance, *Woman as Hero in Old English Literature* (Syracuse, N.Y.: Syracuse University Press, 1986);

Helen Damico, *Beowulf's Wealhtheow and the Valkyrie Tradition* (Madison: University of Wisconsin Press, 1984);

Damico and Alexandra Hennessy Olsen, eds., *New Readings on Women in Old English Literature* (Bloomington: Indiana University Press, 1991);

James F. Doubleday, "The Principle of Contrast in *Judith*," *Neuphilologische Mitteilungen*, 72 (September 1971): 436–441;

Christine Fell, *Women in Anglo-Saxon England* (Bloomington: Indiana University Press, 1984);

Thomas Gregory Foster, *Judith: Studies in Metre, Language and Style, with a View to Determining the Date of the Oldenglish Fragment and the Home of Its Author,* edited by Bernhard Ten Brink and Wilhelm Scherer, Quellen und Forschungen zur Sprach, Kulturgeschichte der Germanischen Volker 71 (Strassburg, 1892);

Raymond-Jean Frontain and Jan Wojcik, eds., *Old Testament Women in Western Literature* (Conway: University of Central Arkansas Press, 1991);

Donald K. Fry, "The Heroine on the Beach in *Judith,*" *Neuphilologische Mitteilungen,* 68 (June 1967): 168–184;

Fry, "Imagery and Point of View in *Judith* 200b–231," *English Language Notes,* 5 (March 1968): 157–159;

Malcolm Godden, "Biblical Literature: The Old Testament," in *Cambridge Companion to Old English Literature,* edited by Godden and Michael Lapidge (Cambridge: Cambridge University Press, 1991);

Mary Flavia Godfrey, "*Beowulf* and *Judith*: Thematizing Decapitation in Old English Poetry," *Texas Studies in Literature and Language,* 35 (Spring 1993): 1–43;

Stanley B. Greenfield, *The Interpretation of Old English Poems* (London: Routledge, 1972);

Fredrik J. Heinemann, "*Judith* 236–291a: A Mock Heroic Approach-to-Battle Type Scene," *Neuphilologische Mitteilungen,* 71 (March 1970): 83–96;

John P. Hermann, *Allegories of War: Language and Violence in Old English Poetry* (Ann Arbor: University of Michigan Press, 1989);

Hermann, "The Theme of Spiritual Warfare in the Old English *Judith,*" *Philological Quarterly,* 55 (Winter 1976): 1–9;

Constance B. Hieatt, "*Judith* and the Literary Function of Old English Hypermetric Lines," *Studia Neuphilologica,* 52 (1980): 251–257;

Bernard Huppé, *The Web of Words* (Albany: State University of New York Press, 1970);

R. E. Kaske, "*Sapientia et Fortitudo* in the Old English *Judith,*" in *The Wisdom of Poetry: Essays in Early English Literature in Honor of Morton W. Bloomfield,* edited by Larry D. Benson and Siegfried Wenzel (Kalamazoo: Medieval Institute Publications, Western Michigan University, 1982);

Peter J. Lucas, "*Judith* and the Woman Hero," *Yearbook of English Studies,* 22 (1992): 17–27;

Lucas, "The Place of *Judith* in the *Beowulf*-Manuscript," *Review of English Studies,* new series 41 (November 1990): 463–478;

Hugh Magennis, "Adaptation of Biblical Detail in the Old English *Judith:* The Feast Scene," *Neuphilologische Mitteilungen,* 84, no. 3 (1983): 331–337;

Jane Mushabac, "*Judith* and the Theme of *Sapientia et Fortitudo,*" *Massachusetts Studies in English,* 4 (Spring 1973): 3–12;

Marie Nelson, "Judith: A Story of a Secular Saint," *Germanic Notes,* 21, no. 1-2 (1990): 12–13;

Nelson, *Judith, Juliana, and Elene: Three Fighting Saints* (New York: Peter Lang, 1991);

Olsen, "Inversion and Political Purpose in the Old English *Judith,*" *English Studies,* 63 (August 1982): 289–293;

Walter J. Ong, *Orality and Literacy: The Technologizing of the Word* (London: Routledge, 1982);

John Collins Pope, *The Rhythm of Beowulf: An Interpretation of the Normal and Hypermetric Verse-Forms in Old English Poetry,* revised edition (New Haven: Yale University Press, 1966);

Ian Pringle, "Judith: The Homily and the Poem," *Traditio,* 31 (1975): 83–97;

Edna Purdie, *The Story of Judith in German and English Literature* (Paris: Champion, 1927);

Burton Raffel, "*Judith:* Hypermetricity and Rhetoric," in *Anglo-Saxon Poetry: Essays in Appreciation: For John C. McGalliard;*

Alessandra Rapetti, "Three Images of Judith," *Études de Lettres,* 2-3 (1987): 155–165;

Alain Renoir, "*Judith* and the Limits of Poetry," *English Studies,* 43 (June 1962): 145–155;

Richard J. Schrader, *God's Handiwork: Images of Women in Early Germanic Literature,* Contributions in Women's Studies, 41 (Westport, Conn.: Greenwood Press, 1983);

Donald C. Scragg, "The Nature of Old English Verse," in *Cambridge Companion to Old English Literature;*

Mary W. Smyth, "The Numbers in the Manuscript of the Old English *Judith,*" *Modern Language Notes,* 20 (November 1905): 197–199;

F. M. Stenton, *Anglo-Saxon England,* third edition, Oxford History of England, 2 (Oxford: Clarendon Press, 1971);

Elizabeth M. Tyler, "Style and Meaning in *Judith,*" *Notes and Queries,* new series 39 (March 1992): 16–19;

R. E. Woolf, "The Lost Opening to the *Judith,*" *Modern Language Review,* 50 (April 1955): 168–172.

The Old English Riddles

(eighth–tenth centuries)

Andrew Welsh
Rutgers University

Manuscript: The only extant manuscript of the Old English riddles is in the *Exeter Book,* the largest of the four important manuscript collections of Old English poetry, which is preserved in the library of Exeter Cathedral (Exeter Cathedral Library, MS. 3501). A version of one of the *Exeter Book* riddles appears in the Northumbrian dialect of Old English in a manuscript of the University Library at Leiden (Leiden Univ. MS. Voss. Q. 106) and is known as the Leiden Riddle. Facsimile: *The Exeter Book of Old English Poetry,* with introductory chapters by R. W. Chambers, Max Förster, and Robin Flower (Bradford, U.K.: Percy Lund, Humphries & Co., 1933).

First publication: *Codex Exoniensis: A Collection of Anglo-Saxon Poetry, from a Ms in the Library of the Dean and Chapter of Exeter,* edited by Benjamin Thorpe (London: Published for the Society of Antiquaries of London, 1842) – includes an English translation.

Standard editions: *The Exeter Book. Part II: Poems IX–XXXII,* edited by W. S. Mackie, EETS, o.s. 194 (1934; reprinted, 1958; reprinted, Kraus, 1973); *The Exeter Book,* edited by George Philip Krapp and Elliott Van Kirk Dobbie, The Anglo-Saxon Poetic Records 3 (New York: Columbia University Press / London: Routledge & Kegan Paul, 1936); *The Old English Riddles of the "Exeter Book,"* edited by Craig Williamson (Chapel Hill: University of North Carolina Press, 1977); *Die altenglischen Rätsel des Exeterbuchs: Text mit deutscher Übersetzung und Kommentar,* edited by Hans Pinsker and Waltraud Ziegler (Heidelberg: Carl Winter, 1985).

Editions in modern English: *Anglo-Saxon Riddles of the Exeter Book,* translated by Paull F. Baum (Durham, N.C.: Duke University Press, 1963); *The Riddles of the Exeter Book,* translated by H. H. Abbott (Cambridge: Golden Head,

1968); *The Exeter Riddle Book,* translated by Kevin Crossley-Holland (London: Folio Society, 1978); republished as *The Exeter Book Riddles* (Harmondsworth: Penguin, 1979); *A Feast of Creatures: Anglo-Saxon Riddle-Songs,* translated by Craig Williamson (Philadelphia: University of Pennsylvania Press, 1982).

The invaluable codex of Old English poetry known as the *Exeter Book* apparently was given to Exeter Cathedral by Leofric, the first bishop of Exeter, who died in 1072. It is almost certainly the "mycel englisc boc be gehwilcum þingum on leoðwisan geworht" (big book in English concerning all sorts of things made into poetry) mentioned in a list of Leofric's donations to the cathedral. The *Exeter Book* appears to have been written sometime around the period 970–990 by a single scribe, whose work preserved for us a large body of Old English poetry, including the justly famous elegiac poems of *The Wanderer, The Seafarer, Deor, The Wife's Lament,* and *The Ruin.* Some of the less well known poems in the *Exeter Book* can be loosely grouped into the category of "wisdom literature," including such poems as *Precepts* (a father's admonitions to his son), *The Gifts of Men* and *The Fortunes of Men* (catalogues of the various talents and destinies allotted to people), *Maxims* (a series of proverblike gnomic statements about the nature of the world and the norms of human conduct), and a large number (from ninety-one to ninety-five, depending on how they are edited) of literary riddles. The riddles appear in the manuscript in three separate groups – two large groups and a third group consisting of only two riddles. The second large group comes at the end of the manuscript, where the final pages have suffered serious damage, and as a result some of those riddles are only fragmentary.

The riddles appear to have been composed by various authors and could have been written (as distinct from when they were copied into the *Exeter*

> Mın hlıfoð ıſ homene gehunfh rtıpo pıla puno
> ſponffh ſeole oft ıcbegıne þıcɫme ongɫın fıcað þon
> ıchnıcan ſctul hpıngum gehoeð hcıpoe pıð hcıpoū
> hınoan þpıel poſð aſcuſın þıcɫ mınſh ſnıcın moo · p ·
> fncðþað mıooel mlhcum · hpılꝩm ıc unoſh bɫt bnꝪoe ·

Part of riddle 87 in the Exeter Book, *a late-tenth-century codex that includes the only exant manuscript of the*
Old English Riddles (Exeter Cathedral Library MS. 3501)

Book) anytime between the eighth and the tenth centuries. A date sometime in the eighth century has seemed most likely, not because of any direct evidence but because that was a time when various English churchmen were particularly active in composing literary riddles in Latin. It is to that learned tradition, rather than to a folk tradition, that the Old English riddles belong.

The medieval Latin tradition of riddle-poems began with a collection of one hundred riddles composed by Symphosius, a late-classical author of whom nothing else is known. Sometime late in the seventh century the great English scholar Aldhelm composed one hundred Latin riddles – probably intended as part of his treatise on Latin prosody – in which he acknowledges the influence of Symphosius. In the early eighth century Tatwine, archbishop of Canterbury, composed forty riddles, which were combined with sixty riddles by "Eusebius" (who may have been Hwætberht, abbot of Wearmouth) to make another collection of one hundred. Among other English authors of Latin riddles at that time was Saint Boniface, the famous missionary bishop, who wrote twenty riddles on the Virtues and the Vices. The Latin tradition clearly had some influence on the Old English riddles: three of the *Exeter Book* riddles derive from Symphosius, two are translated from Aldhelm, and others are on the same subjects as Latin riddles. The compiler of the *Exeter Book,* or the source from which he was copying, may have intended to gather one hundred Old English riddles in all, following the model of the Latin collections. But the Old English riddles also differ markedly from the Latin riddles in many ways. One immediately obvious difference is that, unlike the riddles of Symphosius and Aldhelm, the *Exeter Book* riddles do not have titles giving the solutions to the riddles, which has left modern readers in the position of grappling, not always successfully, with these puzzles made long ago.

The riddles are written in the standard West Saxon literary dialect of Old English, with occasional archaic Anglian or Northumbrian dialect forms, which is consistent with the rest of the manuscript. A few of the riddles also have runes in their texts – characters from the twenty-four letters of the runic alphabet – which can be read backward or otherwise rearranged to spell out clues or the answer itself. As poems, the riddles generally conform to the traditional meter of Old English poetry, a four-stress alliterative line with medial caesura, though again metrical irregularities occasionally appear (as in the first onion riddle). Why they were written and what function they served is unknown. Latin riddles such as Aldhelm's were used in medieval schools for exercise in Latin grammar, whether or not that was the reason for their composition; it is unlikely, however, that the Old English riddles served any such purpose. Posing and solving riddles is a universal human activity, and the Old English riddles were probably written as literary entertainments, meant for enjoyment rather than pedagogy. Their inclusion in the *Exeter Book* shows that they were valued as poetry as well.

The subjects of the riddles range widely, from the battlefield to the monastic scriptorium, from the natural world of sky, sea, and field to the domestic world of hall, kitchen, and bedroom. There are weapons of warfare such as the sword, the bow, the shield, the coat of mail, the battering ram, and the ballista (a kind of large bow for hurling projectiles such as big rocks). There are implements and products of the scriptorium: fingers using a quill pen; an inkwell made from a stag's horn; a sacred book written on parchment; and the book moth that ultimately destroys the book, "imbibing wisdom, but not at all wiser for it." Other riddles present a storm at sea, a ship carrying its cargo, an anchor struggling against the forces of wave and wind, the fearsome beauty of an iceberg. Birds of the air fly again in these poems – the jay and the cuckoo, the wild swan and the barnacle goose, a swirling flock of swallows – and in the fields below are a badger, a young bull, a fish in the river, a cock with a hen, a plow, a rake. In a hall a horn hangs on the wall, a bagpipe plays for men feasting there, and wine and mead confuse their thoughts. In the kitchen an onion is being chopped, dough is rising, an oyster is opened, and bellows are blowing up the fire. The familiar creatures and simple objects of the world are seen in a new light and become puzzling, mysterious, absurd marvels. In two of the riddles the idea of creation itself is celebrated (one, much longer than the other riddles, being a translation of Aldhelm's final riddle), along with the Creator of infinite imagination who governs and guides its broad plenitude.

The techniques and moods of the riddles also range widely. The "shield" riddle, for example, like other *Exeter Book* riddles, is both a riddle and a poem. As a riddle it is essentially a metaphor with one term concealed. Speaking in the first person, the shield describes itself as a warrior, a scarred veteran of numerous battles. As a poem it elaborates on that central metaphor with images of the "warrior" in action. There are quick, vivid glimpses of the battlefield and of the stronghold under attack, of weapons and of wounding. Most of all, however, the poem develops the voice of the weary speaker and his melancholy sense of being isolated in a hostile world:

> Ic eom anhaga,   iserne wund,
> bille gebennad   beadoweorca sæd,
> ecgum werig.   Oft ic wig seo,
> frecne feohtan –   frofre ne wene,
> þæt me geoc cyme   guðgewinnes
> ær ic mid ældum   eal forwurðe;
> ac mec hnossiað   homera lafe,
> heardecg heoroscearp   hondweorc smiþa,
> bitað in burgum.

> (I am alone, weapon-wounded,
> sword-slashed, sick of battle-work,
> weary of sword-edge. Often I see war,
> dangerous fighting – I expect no help,
> no assistance to come to me in the struggle,
> before among men I perish completely;
> but the forged swords strike,
> the handiwork of smiths, hard-edged and fearfully sharp,
> in the fortified towns they bite into me.)

The world of the speaker is one of endless war, of wounds that do not heal, and of inevitable defeat. Nevertheless, in the best tradition of Anglo-Saxon battle poetry, the warrior faces his fate with grim fortitude, heroic because he knows there is no hope:

>   ic a bidan sceal
> laþran gemotes.   Næfre læcecynn
> on folcstede   findan meahte
> þara þe mid wyrtum   wunde gehælde,
> ac me ecga dolg   eacen weorðað
> þurh deaðslege   dagum ond nihtum.

>   (I must ever await
> a more grievous meeting. There is no doctor
> for me among the dwellings of people,
> one of those who with herbs heals wounds,
> but for me the wounding by swords only increases
> from death-blows by day and by night.)

The paradox of wounds that cannot be cured arises from the basic metaphor which sees the shield as a warrior, and it reminds us that the poem is a riddle. The reader may also sense that this warrior, awaiting ever fiercer battles, endures far more wounding than human flesh could take. In many ways the shield is like a human warrior, but in this passage it is not, and these contradictory elements in the description are the key that unlocks the puzzle. The subject of the riddle is "shield"; the subject of the poem is the dark world that shield and warrior both inhabit.

The *Exeter Book* collection includes both first-person riddles, in which the hidden subject itself speaks the riddle, and third-person riddles, in which another speaker describes the hidden subject. Both forms frequently use opening or closing formulas as a traditional way of signaling that the poems are, in fact, riddles. First-person riddles may begin with the words "Ic eom wunderlicu wiht" (I am a remarkable creature), as do the riddles for jug, sword, magpie or jay, and onion. A large number of the first-person riddles conclude with a formulaic command (or appeal) to the reader to give the name of the speaking subject. The nightingale, barnacle goose, ox, bow, gimlet, horn, gold, and personified creation all say to the reader, "Saga hwæt ic hatte" (Say what I am called), and the horn (in another riddle), anchor, sacred book, and mead similarly challenge, "Frige hwæt ic hatte" (Find out what I am called). Third-person riddles use analogous formulas. A description of the moon begins, "Ic wiht geseah wundorlice" (I saw a marvelous creature); someone who saw an iceberg says, "Ic þa wiht geseah on weg feran" (I saw the creature traveling on the way); another observer, who saw the bagpipe, says, "Ic seah sellic þing singan on ræcede" (I saw a strange thing singing in the hall). The closing formulas in third-person riddles are especially varied and interesting – challenging, teasing, cajoling, and pleading with the reader to solve the puzzle. A riddle for ship ends: "Rece gif þu cunne, / wis worda gleaw,   hwæt sio wiht sie" (Explain, if you can, wise one skillful of words, what that creature could be). The conclusion of another riddle, the solution to which has never been agreed upon, says quite truly: "Micel is to hycganne / wisfæstum menn hwæt seo wiht sy" (What that creature may be is much for wise men to think about).

Another conventional technique of riddle making in the Old English poems is the juxtaposition of contrasting states of a single subject. Different stages of the subject's existence that occur at different times are brought together in one enigmatic picture of something whose fundamental nature contradicts itself. The reed describes itself as standing fixed and alone in a remote spot (when it is growing by the sea), but also as a mouthless singer in a festive hall where men sit at the mead bench (when it is formed into a flute), and again as the bold speaker of a silent message heard by only one person (when it is formed into a pen). In another riddle the speaker describes how it travels on foot and tears the earth when it is alive (as an ox pulling the plow), but when it is dead it binds captives, gives drink to warriors, is stepped upon by the proud bride, and is intimately caressed in the dark nights by the drunken servant-girl (as ox-hide thongs, wineskin, shoes, and shirt). The onion similarly conflates its "living" and "dead" states in one description. Alive, it is a helpless victim of atrocities, but once it is dead it fights back:

Cwico wæs ic – ne cwæð ic wiht;   cwele ic efne
      seþeah.
Ær ic wæs – eft ic cwom;   æghwa mec reafað,
hafað mec on headre,   on min heafod scireþ,
biteð mec on bær lic,   briceð mine wisan.
Monnan ic ne bite   nympþe he me bite:
sindan þara monige   þe mec bitað

(I was alive and said nothing; even so, I die.
I was before – I came again; everyone plunders me,
imprisons me, cuts off my head,
bites my bare body, breaks my nature [or stalk],
I do not bite anyone unless he bites me:
there are many who bite me)[.]

In presenting the voice of a single identity that takes on multiple forms, such riddles can become poems of metamorphosis and rebirth; both continuity and change, they say, are intrinsic to existence.

The onion riddle puns on the Old English noun *wise,* which can mean "manner" or "nature" (applying to the human victim), as well as "sprout"

or "stalk" (applying to the onion). Playing with such ambiguities in language is another fundamental technique of riddle making. Among the Old English riddles, eight are especially notorious for employing double meanings. These are usually classed as obscene riddles, though perhaps it would be more accurate to speak of obscene readers, for the riddles themselves maintain a studied innocence. By means of ambiguous wording and sly innuendo, however, the riddles for key, dough, churn, helmet, gimlet or poker, and bellows trick the reader into giving answers rather less innocent. Another example is a different riddle for onion:

Ic eom wunderlicu wiht,   wifum on hyhte,
neahbuendum nyt.   Nængum sceþþe
burgsittendra   nymþe bonan anum.
Staþol min is steapheah;   stonde ic on bedde,
neoþan ruh nathwær.   Neþeð hwilum
ful cyrtenu   ceorles dohtor,
modwlonc meowle,   þæt heo on mec gripeð,
ræseð mec on reodne,   reafað min heafod,
fegeð mec on fæsten.   Feleþ sona
mines gemotes   seo þe mec nearwað,
wif wundenlocc –   wæt bið þæt eage.

(I am a wonderful creature, made to delight women,
useful to neighbors. I injure none
of the citizens, except my slayer alone.
I stand up in bed, my foundation is high,
and I'm hairy down below. At times the beautiful
peasant's daughter, a high-spirited woman,
rushes onto my redness, ravages my head, ventures to
    grab onto me,
places me in confinement. Our meeting
she soon feels, she who forces me in,
the curly-haired girl – her eye becomes wet.)

Onions, planted in a raised mound of loose dirt, grow in a high "foundation" and stand in a "bed," usually without shocking (or so vividly delighting) anyone. This form of riddle appears unambiguously to describe one thing, but the words actually apply to something else entirely. Meaning is doubled, and the riddle as a whole can be thought of as an extended pun.

Opinions have varied on the nature and the achievement of the Old English riddles. A reader such as F. H. Whitman, for example, writing in the journal of medieval scholarship *Neuphilologische Mitteilungen,* finds that with a few exceptions most of the riddles are "modest" in their aspirations, "undistinguished" in the quality of their language, and – because "they take their inspiration from the mundane world, the home and commonplace experience" – limited in their subject matter. They are, in short, "intellectual and trivial," and in this they share in the "gradual degeneration in poetic sensibility" from classical times that can be seen in the medieval Latin riddle tradition, a decline in which "the artificial came to be preferred over the natural and the aim came to be surprise and astonishment." A reader such as John F. Adams, on the other hand, writing in the journal *Criticism,* sees their minute examination in verse of the things of the mundane world as having provided "a medium and form for lyric expression which was otherwise, as a distinct literary conception, non-existent." The riddles, that is, represent the missing lyric tradition of Old English literature, and "many of the riddles deserve to be read in fact as first rate lyrics." From that perspective the appeal of these verses, for those who feel it, is modern as well as medieval. Baroque intellectual exercises they sometimes may be, but at their best they are nature poems, imagist poems, and metaphysical poems as well as riddle-poems – for the fundamental techniques of riddle making are also fundamental techniques of poetry making. In both forms metaphors reveal something in light of something else, rhetorical conventions provide familiar literary signals with which to approach unfamiliar ideas, the poet's wordplay explores double meanings in language to search for hidden connections between things in the world, and tough, precise, even obscene puzzles are posed that challenge and expand the reader's customary ways of knowing that world.

Bibliographies:

Patrizia Lendinara, "Gli Enigmi del Codice Exoniense, Una Ricerca Bibliografica," *AION,* 19 (1976): 231–329;

Stanley B. Greenfield and Fred C. Robinson, *A Bibliography of Publications on Old English Literature to the end of 1972* (Toronto: University of Toronto Press, 1980), items 4067–4183 (*Exeter Book* Riddles), items 3899–3909 (Leiden Riddle);

Donald K. Fry, "Exeter Book Riddle Solutions," *Old English Newsletter,* 15 (Fall 1981): 22–33;

Bernard J. Muir, *The Exeter Book: A Bibliography* (Exeter: University of Exeter Press, 1992).

References:

John F. Adams, "The Anglo-Saxon Riddle as Lyric Mode," *Criticism,* 7 (1965): 335–348;

James E. Anderson, *Two Literary Riddles in the Exeter Book: Riddle 1 and The Easter Riddle* (Norman: University of Oklahoma Press, 1986);

Nigel F. Barley, "Structural Aspects of the Anglo-Saxon Riddle," *Semiotica,* 10 (1974): 143–175;

Stanley B. Greenfield and Daniel G. Calder, *A New Critical History of Old English Literature* (New York: New York University Press, 1986), pp. 269–273;

Agop Hacikyan, *A Linguistic and Literary Analysis of Old English Riddles* (Montreal: Casalini, 1966);

Elaine Tuttle Hansen, *The Solomon Complex: Reading Wisdom in Old English Poetry* (Toronto: University of Toronto Press, 1988), pp. 126–143;

Marie Nelson, "The Rhetoric of the Exeter Book Riddles," *Speculum,* 49 (1974): 421–440;

Nelson, *Structures of Opposition in Old English Poems* (Amsterdam: Rodopi, 1989);

Fred C. Robinson, "Artful Ambiguities in the Old English 'Book-Moth' Riddle," in *Anglo-Saxon Poetry: Essays in Appreciation for John C. McGalliard,* edited by Lewis E. Nicholson and Dolores Warwick Frese (Notre Dame, Ind.: University of Notre Dame Press, 1975), pp. 355–362;

Archer Taylor, *The Literary Riddle Before 1600* (Berkeley: University of California Press, 1948);

Frederick Tupper, Jr., Introduction to *The Riddles of the Exeter Book* (Boston: Ginn, 1910), pp. xi–c;

F. H. Whitman, "Medieval Riddling: Factors Underlying Its Development," *Neuphilologische Mitteilungen,* 71 (1970): 177–185;

C. L. Wrenn, *A Study of Old English Literature* (New York: Norton, 1967), pp. 170–175.

The Wanderer

and

The Seafarer
(circa 970)

Sarah Lynn Higley
University of Rochester

Manuscript: Both texts are found in the *Codex Exoniensis* (commonly known as the *Exeter Book*), Exeter, Cathedral Library, MS. 3501 (76^b–78^a and 81^b–82^a). Paleographic and linguistic evidence places the poems in the last third of the tenth century.

Standard editions: *The Wanderer,* in the *Exeter Book, Part I,* edited by Israel Gollancz, EETS, o.s. 104 (1895; reprinted, Kraus, 1973), pp. 286–292; *The Seafarer,* in *The Exeter Book, Part II,* edited by W.S. Mackie, EETS, o.s. 194 (1934; reprinted, Kraus, 1973), pp. 1–8; *The Wanderer* and *The Seafarer,* in *The Exeter Book,* edited by George Philip Krapp and Elliott Van Kirk Dobbie (New York: Columbia University Press, 1936), pp. 134–136, 143–146; *The Wanderer,* edited by Roy F. Leslie (Manchester: University Press, 1965); *The Wanderer,* edited by T. P. Dunning and A. J. Bliss (New York: Appleton-Century-Crofts, 1969); *The Seafarer,* edited by Ida L. Gordon (London: Methuen, 1960); *The Wanderer* and *The Seafarer,* in *The Old English Elegies: A Critical Edition and Genre Study,* by Anne Lingard Klinck (Montreal: McGill-Queen's University Press, 1992).

Edition in modern English: *The Wanderer* and *The Seafarer,* in *Anglo-Saxon Poetry,* edited and translated by S. A. J. Bradley (London: Dent, 1982), pp. 320–325, 329–335.

The Wanderer and *The Seafarer* are the modern titles given to two of the best-known and most poignant and controversial elegies included in the Old English *Exeter Book.* Compared to the narrative texts, these are short, reflective poems (115 lines for *The Wanderer,* 125 for *The Seafarer*) written in the classic Old English style of two-stressed couplets

(with an occasional use of hypermetric lines) linked by alliteration. Both have inspired heated diatribes over speech boundaries, divisions, origins, imagery, allegory, and genre. *The Seafarer* can boast Ezra Pound among its many translators. Since most scholarly discussions of these texts do not usually include their context within the curious manuscript that contains them, a brief background of the contents of the *Exeter Book* will be provided here before closer examination of the poems.

"Mycel englisc boc be gehwilcum þingum on leoðwisan geworht" (A great English book on all sorts of things wrought in verse): thus is the late-tenth-century *Codex Exoniensis* or *Exeter Book* described in an eleventh-century inventory of items donated by Leofric to Exeter Cathedral, England, during his appointment there as first bishop (1050–1071) and where it remains to this day in the Cathedral Library. As the anonymous description indicates, the texts comprising this manuscript are hardly homogeneous: they range from the hagiographic to the gnomic, from the sacred to the secular, from the homiletic to the elegiac. There are no manuscript illuminations, no rubric, a few ornamental capitals, and a few drawings scratched with a dry quill. It is in remarkably good shape for a book that was burned by a poker or some hot instrument, which scorched its last sections.

In his history and description of the *Exeter Book,* Patrick W. Conner has shown that the manuscript seems to be made up of three distinct codices sewn together, which he identifies as booklets: the first booklet (8^a–52^b) begins with *Christ I* and ends with *Guthlac B;* the second (53^a–97^b) begins with *Azarias* and ends with *The Partridge;* and the third (98^a–130^b) begins with *Homiletic Fragment III* and ends with Riddle 95. Conner carefully notes the physical evidence of these divisions – soiled outer leaves, differences in the quality of the vellum, variations in the script — but remarks that "the effect of this manuscript structure on our perceptions of the poetry contained within it" is especially important to interpretive study or any attempt to understand category and textuality in Anglo-Saxon times.

The Wanderer and *The Seafarer* are in the second booklet, a small codex which offers so much of its own variation as to make it a model of the diversity of the *Exeter Book,* thwarting further efforts to find some kind of unifying integrity. *The Wanderer* follows *Juliana,* a poem of some seven hundred lines recounting the spiritual agony and martyrdom of a Roman saint, and it precedes *The Gifts of Men,* a predominantly gnomic poem detailing in listlike fashion various human skills and attributes. Then comes *Precepts,* another gnomic poem sometimes given the title *A Father's Instruction,* and finally *The Seafarer.* What makes *The Wanderer* and *The Seafarer* stand out like emeralds in a field of pearls is the extraordinary depth of feeling along with the multifaceted quality of imagery and contradiction expressed in them. Read separately from the diversely organized *Exeter Book,* these two poems are already richly ambiguous and perplexing.

Most scholars look upon these poems as companion pieces, of a sort, although it is not at all clear that the same author composed them or that separately they are the products of single authors, composing and writing as we know it today. Both *The Wanderer* and *The Seafarer* concern a solitary wayfarer, an exile from his clan either voluntarily or by accident, who travels the earth and the sea. Both poems are filled with splendid natural imagery: each speaker recounts in detail the alienating sights and sounds of gulls that are poor replacements for human companionship; each speaker describes the physical hardships of one who is homeless; and each ponders human mortality and the transient nature of life. Both poems describe a psychological process by which their speakers find consolation for their condition, moving from largely secular concerns to spiritual wisdom. In *The Seafarer* this process takes the form of an extended Christian homily at the end of the poem, a conclusion that some early scholars found inconsistent with the poem's seemingly secular character. Indeed, the interpretive problems have been in identifying the tone of the speaker, especially in *The Seafarer,* where the narrator seems now cold, now hot for the hardships of a life on sea, and its relationship to the developing traditions of literacy and monasticism that inspired someone to record them in the *Exeter Book* in the first place.

Indeed, the shifts in mood and style in both poems have led early scholars to argue that they were products of pagan culture, the Christian elements having been added by scribal interpolation. This view has been replaced by the more accepted theory that they are entirely the products of the flowering of monasticism in tenth-century England but imbued with the strong elements of an older Germanic philosophy and poetic tradition. Nonetheless, the polyphonous aspect of so much Old English contemplative poetry has occasioned a great deal of discussion. The ambiguous nature of speech boundaries in *The Wanderer,* for instance, or the unclear but persistent use of "for þon" ("therefore," "because," "indeed," and so forth) in *The Seafarer* has given rise to many studies on the unity of the poems. An enormously influential school of criticism — the debates about oral formula and the theories of orality and literacy — has left its mark on the way these poems are read today. Following the pagan/Christian controversy that occupied scholars in the nineteenth century, Milman Parry's discovery in 1930 of the techniques of oral formula in Homeric verse led to vigorous examination in the twentieth century of such traces in Old English poetry, starting with Francis Peabody Magoun's 1953 article on *Beowulf.* Whether *The Wanderer* or *The Seafarer* show elements of preliterate oral formulas has been polemical: how long before they appear in the *Exeter Book* were these poems composed? How much of the pagan Germanic philosophy do they express? How did they come to be written down? Had they been in oral circulation and recorded later? Or were they written by clerics for the *Exeter Book* who naturally used the poetic traditions available to them? The social structure of the pre-Christian Germanic *comitatus,* described by Tacitus, did not disappear overnight when England was converted in the sixth century; it stressed the loyalty of a thane to his chieftain and treated exile and outlawry as the most tragic lots that could befall one. This secular sense of loss is keen in *The Wanderer.* On the other hand, the *ubi sunt* motif found in this poem has an obvious connection to Latin Christian texts on mutability and *contemptus mundi,* as Michael J. B. Allen and Daniel G. Calder point out, and the *perigrinus* (pilgrim), the wayfarer in search of the City of God, is an established topos in Christian literature. For background on the debates over oral formula, interested scholars will want to consult John Miles Foley's *Oral-Formulaic Theory and Research: An Introduction and Annotated Bibliography* (1985) and to read Carol Braun Pasternack on the question of the semiotics of *The Wanderer* in a transitionally literate society.

Finding a generic category for these poems has also been difficult: are they elegies as tradition has termed them, and, if so, are they thematically united to the other so-called elegies of the *Exeter Book* – *The Wife's Lament, The Husband's Message, Resignation* A and B, and *The Ruin?* Examination reveals vastly differing poems that defy easy categorization, the one linking element being a general mood of contemplation and loss. In *Continuations and Beginnings: Studies in Old English Literature* Stanley B. Greenfield defines the Old English elegy as "a relatively short reflective or dramatic poem embodying a contrasting pattern of loss and consolation, ostensibly based upon a specific personal experience or observation, and expressing an attitude towards that experience." Some of the so-called elegies, however, are less elegiac than others: *The Husband's Message* may be the solution to the preceding Riddle 60; *The Ruin* is devoted to the examination of the Roman remains at Bath and does not express a subjective point of view. In short, the elegies are a diverse and contradictory lot, the most recent discussion and definition being that by Anne Lingard Klinck, who attempts to refine previous definitions: "Old English elegy is a discourse arising from a powerful sense of absence, of separation from what is desired, expressed through characteristic words and themes, and shaping itself by echo and leitmotiv into a poem that moves from disquiet to some kind of acceptance."

Trying to fit *The Wanderer* and *The Seafarer* into the more specific category of what P. L. Henry terms the "penitential lyric" has proved to be difficult as well, for, as Allen J. Frantzen notes, these poems do not "contain explicit exhortations to repent," nor do they name any sin that the speaker wishes to be absolved of. Set against prose works that include rules for daily living and praying, such as *The Exhortation to Christian Living, A Summons to Prayer,* and other texts that counsel salvation through disclosure of sin, *The Wanderer* counsels silence and a stoicism that "dignifies circumstances which poems about penance seek to transcend." Nor does the reader ever learn just why it is that the mariner has taken to sea in *The Seafarer.* Frantzen suggests that we call them "Wisdom Poems," a term that would put them more in league with the gnomic texts that surround them. Rosemary Woolf puts them in the rhetorical genre of *planctus,* or plaint poems spoken by a *figura* of the ascetic or the exile, and more than one scholar has noted the similarity in tone, mood, and imagery to certain ninth-century Welsh poems of lament, in particular the *Canu Llywarch Hen* (Songs of Llywarch the Old), as

well as a text called *Claf Abercuawg* (The Leper of Abercuawg). Ernst Sieper notes that the sad cuckoo of *The Seafarer* occurs nowhere else in medieval British literature except in this last Welsh poem and *The Husband's Message.* Few scholars now maintain that these poems describe the specific experiences of actual persons. Eric G. Stanley points out that fact and figure are often not clearly distinguished in Old English poetry, a feature which, while inconvenient to interpretation of these poems, greatly enhances their pleasing quality of double-voicedness. His article inspired a host of other studies examining the use of nature imagery in Old English poetry to represent states of mind, storm and winter being classic symbols of mental duress, contest, or bereavement; meanwhile, the "mind" and "soul" words in Old English have come under particular scrutiny for what they reveal about how Anglo-Saxons conceptualized thought and its power to act within the world.

These lines open *The Wanderer:*

Oft him anhaga   are gebideð
metudes miltse   þeah þe he mod-cearig
geond lagu-lade   longe sceolde
hreran mid hondum   hrim-cealdne sæ
wadan wræc-lastas   wyrd bið ful aræd
swa cwæð eardstapa,   earfeþa gemyndig
wraþra wælsleahta   winemæga hryre
oft ic sceolde ana uhtna gehwylce
mine ceare cwiþan

(Often for himself does the lone-dweller await grace,
the mercy of God, although sick at heart
through watery paths he must long
stir with his hands the ice-cold sea,
tread the tracks of exile. Fate is fully fixed.
Thus spoke the earth-walker, mindful of hardships,
of cruel slayings, of the downfall of kinsmen.
Often, each dawn, alone I had to
bewail my care.)

The "lone-dweller" and "earth-walker" is pictured here as one for whom fate is predetermined. A critical feature of *The Wanderer* is the fact that speech boundaries are so undetermined. The narration slips from third person to first and back again in a confusing way. Editors find it difficult to punctuate. One question that confronts them is whether or not the first five lines are the reported speech of the recluse. "Swa cwæð" (thus spoke) often introduces direct discourse, but the discourse in question seems to start in line eight with the introduction of the first-person speaker "oft ic . . ." (often I . . .), and most editors put quotation marks here and not around the opening five lines. But in the reported discourse that follows, the speaker continues to

Opening lines of The Wanderer *in the* Exeter Book, *a late-tenth-century codex*
(Exeter Cathedral Library MS. 3501, fol. 76ᵇ)

refer to his plight in the third as well as the first person: "There is no one now alive to whom I may dare reveal my heart," he declares and goes on to say that it is a "noble custom" to "bind the soul-enclosure fast," to "guard the treasure chest" of one's heart, just as the wanderer has covered his dead lord and kinsman with the "darkness of the earth." These images of burial stand in vivid contrast to the image of the open ruin described in lines 73 to 105, which form the rhetorical point of focus for the reflections of the speaker. It is almost as if *The Wanderer* shares with another *Exeter Book* elegy, *The Ruin,* the general subject of "Discourse Upon a Fallen Citadel" and has taken it to imaginative lengths not explored in the other poem. The here and now of *The Wanderer* is situated in the scrutiny of a particular site:

Se þonne þisne weal-steal   wise geþohte
and þis deorce lif   deope geond-þenceð
frod in ferðe   feor oft gemon
wæl-sleahta worn·   and þas word acwið·
hwær cwom mearg·   hwær cwom mago·

(Then, wise in thought, he deeply contemplates
this foundation wall and this dark life,
experienced in spirit, recalls from long-ago
many bloody battles, and speaks these words:
"What has become of the horse? What has become of the kinsman?")

The exposed, windswept walls of the ruin are identified with *þis deorc lif* through which the wanderer must navigate, while the poem, like an opened coffer, articulates eloquently what the noble custom must repress. It contrasts the memories of the speaker with his present condition: although he dreams of his lord's friendly embrace, he awakes to the outspread feathers of seabirds. In a typically gnomic list the poem tells what wisdom the speaker has amassed: "Therefore, a man may not become wise before he has had his portion of winters in the world. A man of wisdom must be patient: neither too hotheaded nor too hasty of speech, nor too feeble as a warrior, nor too reckless, nor too fearful, nor too eager, not too greedy for reward, nor too ready to boast before he is well aware." The last natural image in the poem depicts a ragingly hostile winter, which, in a passage reminiscent of *The Seafarer,* sends "from the north fierce hailstorms in malice to men," and it concludes with the conventional reminder that all security resides with our Father in Heaven. The final reference to direct discourse has been much disputed: "Swa cwæð snottor on mode, gesæt him sundor æt rune" (Thus

spoke the wiseman in his mind [or, thus spoke the one wise in mind], he sat himself apart in secret counsel). This passage raises the question of single or double narrators; does the reader know these things because of access to the unspoken mind of the speaker or is the "one wise in mind" uttering his wisdom to a second speaker? His sitting "apart in secret counsel" echoes the image of solitude stressed at the beginning of the poem, but throughout, the frequent shifts in person, the gnomic lists, the shifting location of the speaker (on board ship; standing before a ruin; sitting apart in secret counsel), and the commingling of secular and Christian values have led early scholars to find fault with the poem's unity. Pasternack criticizes this essentially modern expectation of a premodern poem and emphasizes an aesthetic of modularity and disjunction, what she calls the "polyphonous" nature of the poem's textuality. Thus postmodern critical theory with its emphasis on the dialogic and the plural "may bring us closer to the earliest English texts than we have been since Anglo-Saxon studies began."

The following passage from *The Seafarer* demonstrates why its disjointedness poses more of a problem to modern readers than that of *The Wanderer:*

For þon nu min hyge hweorfeð   ofer hreþerlocan
min modsefa   mid mereflode
ofer hwæles eþel   hweorfeð wide
eorþan sceatas   cymeð eft to me
gifre ond grædig   gielleð anfloga
hweteð on [h]wælweg   hreþer unwearnum
ofer holma gelagu.   For þon me hatran sind
dryhtnes dreamas   þonne þis deade lif
læne on londe

(Therefore my mind passes over the heart-enclosure,
my spirit with the floodtide
over the whale's country passes far and wide
the expanses of the earth; it comes back to me,
eager and greedy: the lone-flyer yells,
whets onto the whale-way [or, road of the dead] the
    heart irresistibly
over the sea's tract. Therefore [or, Because] to me
the joys of the Lord are hotter than this dead life,
fleeting on land.)

The narrator seems to make an inexplicable shift from abhorrence for a life at sea and its miseries (along with an apparent envy of the man who lives a pleasant life on land) to an ascetic and spiritual hunger for seafaring. Earlier, in the often-debated lines 33[b]–34, the speaker makes his first presumably contradictory statement when he declares that his "heart's thoughts compel him to explore the high seas," after having described in bone-chilling detail the physical and emotional privations of the mariner. It would seem that the hardships described in the first half of the poem, even the fear the speaker expresses of "what the Lord may wish to do to him," are not necessarily abhorrent to him, in the way that they would be to modern readers.

Rather, the speaker experiences a kind of out-of-body experience in which his soul leaves its heart-enclosure in a journey over the ocean. In direct contrast to the tender heart of *The Wanderer,* which must be protected from the ravages of the world, the soul of the Seafarer pursues its vision aggressively, yells like a seabird, urges his heart onto either the ocean or the path of the dead. The rest of the poem counsels readers to find their true home in God's kingdom, and all further references to the sea are abandoned. The conjunction *for þon* occurs eight times in *The Seafarer* in varying degrees of unclarity. For instance, is it "because the joys of the Lord are hotter to him than this dead life" that his mind urges his heart outward, or is the heart urged, and *therefore* the joys of the Lord are hotter?

Such ambiguities lead some scholars to consider the poem a dialogue between a headstrong youth and an old man, as M. Rieger proposes, to include more than one speaker, as John C. Pope suggests, or to dismiss the second half of the poem as a piece of didacticism tacked on by a mediocre homilist, as F. Kluge states. Others reconcile the two halves of the poem with elaborate allegorical interpretations: G. Ehrismann wrote that *The Seafarer* is the expression of a "monastic asceticism" whereby the dangerous voyage represents the afflictions of life which the man of God willfully embraces for his soul's sake. His opposite is the fortunate man on shore given to worldly materialism. S. Olaf Anderson suggests that the sea voyage is to be taken symbolically but not necessarily as a symbol of monastic life. It may stand for "the life of the pious on earth . . . as well as the road to Eternity," through death. E. V. Smithers cites the metaphors of the *peregrinus* in medieval ecclesiastical writings, especially Augustine's *City of God*. The *peregrinus* has made himself an alien on earth in order to be a member of the city of God, and it is in this sense that Smithers takes the "elþeodigra eard" of line 38, which he believes to be a symbol for Heaven: "the land of 'aliens in this world.' " Blickling Homily 2 would seem to substantiate this identification in its principal figure of pilgrimage: "we synd on þisse worlde ælþeodige" (we are exiles in this world). John Vickrey interprets the sea voyage described in the

first half of the poem as the life of the sinner, drawing upon the conventional image of the human heart as a tempest-tossed ship given us by Gregory in his *Dialogues:* "ic eom gecnyssed mid þam stormum pære strangan hreohnesse in þam scipe mines modes" (I am beaten by the storms of the harsh tempest in the ship of my heart); indeed, *The Seafarer* abounds with imagery of conflict: the ship that "knocks" by the cliffs ("be cliffum cnossað"), the "thoughts of the heart" that "urge" or literally "beat" upon the speaker ("cnyssað nu / heortan geþohtas"). Opposition to the allegorical interpretation begins with Dorothy Whitelock's objection that "we are given no hint of any kind that the beginning of the poem is anything other than a realistic description." Stanley argues that the poem is "neither realism nor allegory," but "an imagined situation, invented to give force to the doctrine which forms the end of the poem and is its purpose"; in his article in *Speculum* (April 1955), Greenfield suggests that the ambiguous quality of the poem is a direct reflection of the speaker's own uncertainty and conflict, and Peter Orton notes that the poem describes a kind of rite de passage wherein the values of a secular life are harshly examined. At the very least, the references to *sylf* (self) and the question it raises about the subjectivity of *The Seafarer* are intriguing and fraught with controversy. Whatever interpretation one decides will make *The Seafarer* and *The Wanderer* coherent to a modern readership, it is chiefly their capacity to create so much modern dialogue that remains the best tribute to their complexity, mystery, and beauty.

Bibliographies:

Fred C. Robinson and Stanley B. Greenfield, eds., *A Bibliography on Publications of Old English Literature to the End of 1972* (Toronto: University of Toronto Press, 1980);

Bernard James Muir, ed., *The Exeter Book: A Bibliography* (Exeter: University of Exeter Press, 1992).

References:

Michael J. B. Allen and Daniel G. Calder, *Sources and Analogues of Old English Poetry: The Major Latin Texts in Translation* (Cambridge: Brewer, 1976), pp. 133–153;

S. Olaf Anderson, "*The Seafarer:* An Interpretation," *K. Humanistika Vetemskapssamfundets i Lund Arsberättelse,* 1 (1937–1938): 1–49;

Frederick G. Cassidy and Richard N. Ringler, eds., *Bright's Old English Grammar and Reader,* third edition (New York: Holt, Rinehart & Winston, 1971), pp. 323–337;

S. L. Clark and Julian N. Wasserman, "The Imagery of *The Wanderer*," *Neophilologus*, 63 (April 1979): 291–296;

Peter Clemoes, "*Mens absentia cogitans* in *The Seafarer* and *The Wanderer*," in *Medieval Literature and Civilization: Studies in Memory of G. N. Garmonsway*, edited by Derek A. Pearsall and R. A. Waldron (London: Athlone, 1969), pp. 62–67;

Patrick W. Conner, *Anglo-Saxon Exeter: A Tenth Century Cultural History* (Woodbridge: Boydell, 1993);

Conner, "A Contextual Study of the Old English Exeter Book," Ph.D. dissertation, University of Maryland, 1975;

Conner, "The Structure of the Exeter Book Codex (Exeter, Cathedral Library, MS 3501)," *Scriptorium*, 40, no. 2 (1986): 233–242;

G. Ehrismann, "Religionsgeschichtliche Beiträge zum germanischen Frühchristentum," *Beiträge zur Geschichte der deutschen Sprache und Literatur*, 35 (1909): 209–239;

John Miles Foley, "Genre(s) in the Making: Diction, Audience and Text in the Old English *Seafarer*," *Poetics Today*, 4, no. 4 (1983): 683–706;

Foley, *Oral-Formulaic Theory and Research: An Introduction and Annotated Bibliography* (New York: Garland, 1985);

Foley, "Texts that Speak to Readers Who Hear: Old English Poetry and the Languages of Oral Tradition," in *Speaking Two Languages: Traditional Disciplines and Contemporary Theory in Medieval Studies*, edited by Allen J. Frantzen (Albany: State University of New York Press, 1991), pp. 141–156;

Frantzen, *The Literature of Penance in Anglo-Saxon England* (New Brunswick, N. J.: Rutgers University Press, 1983);

M. R. Godden, "Anglo-Saxons on the Mind," in *Learning and Literature in Anglo-Saxon England: Studies Presented to Peter Clemoes on the Occasion of his Sixty-fifth Birthday*, edited by Michael Lapidge and Helmut Gneuss (Cambridge: Cambridge University Press), pp. 271–298;

Stanley B. Greenfield, "Attitudes and Values in *The Seafarer*," *Studies in Philology*, 51 (1954): 15–20;

Greenfield, *Continuations and Beginnings: Studies in Old English Literature*, edited by Eric G. Stanley (London: Nelson, 1966), pp. 142–175;

Greenfield, "The Formulaic Expression of the Theme of 'Exile' in Anglo-Saxon Poetry," *Speculum*, 30 (April 1955): 200–206;

Greenfield, "*Min, Sylf*, and 'Dramatic Voices in *The Wanderer* and *The Seafarer*,' " *Journal of English and Germanic Philology*, 68 (1969): 212–220;

Greenfield, "*The Wanderer*: A Reconsideration of Theme and Structure," *Journal of English and Germanic Philology*, 50 (1951): 451–465;

Elizabeth A. Hait, "The Wanderer's Lingering Regret: A Study of Patterns of Imagery," *Neophilologus*, 68 (April 1984): 278–291;

P. L. Henry, *The Early English and Celtic Lyric* (London: Allen & Unwin, 1970);

Sarah Lynn Higley, *Between Languages: The Uncooperative Text in Early Welsh and Old English Nature Poetry* (University Park: Pennsylvania State Press, 1993);

Higley, "Lamentable Relationships? 'Non-Sequitur' in Old English and Middle Welsh Elegies," in *Connections Between Old English and Medieval Welsh Literature*, edited by Patrick K. Ford and Karen G. Borst (Lanham, Md.: University Presses of America, 1985), pp. 45–66;

Higley, "Storm and Mind in Anglo-Saxon Poetry: A Hard Lesson," *In Geardagum*, 9 (September 1988): 23–39;

Sally C. Hoople, "*Stefn*: The Transcendent Voice in *The Seafarer*," *In Geardagum*, 11 (1990): 45–55;

Colin A. Ireland, "Some Analogues of the O.E. *Seafarer* from Hiberno-Latin Sources," *Neuphilologische Mitteilungen*, 92, no. 1 (1991): 1–14;

Nicolas Jacobs, "Syntactical Connection and Logical Disconnection: The Case of *The Seafarer*," *Medium Ævum*, 58, no. 1 (1989): 105–113;

Anne Lingard Klinck, *The Old English Elegies: A Critical Edition and Genre Study* (Montreal: McGill-Queen's University Press, 1992);

F. Kluge, "Zu altenglischen Dichtungen: I. 'Der Seefahrer,' " *Englischen Studien*, 6 (1883): 322–327;

Roy F. Leslie, "The Meaning and Structure of *The Seafarer*," in *The Old English Elegies: New Essays in Criticism and Research*, edited by Martin Green (Rutherford: Fairleigh Dickinson University Press, 1983), pp. 96–122;

Francis Peabody Magoun, "The Oral-Formulaic Character of Anglo-Saxon Narrative Poetry," *Speculum*, 28 (July 1953): 446–467;

Clair McPherson, "The Sea a Desert: Early Spirituality and *The Seafarer*," *American Benedictine Review*, 38 (June 1987): 115–126;

Bruce Mitchell and Fred C. Robinson, eds., *A Guide to Old English*, revised fourth edition (Oxford: Blackwell, 1986), pp. 252–266;

Peter Orton, "The Form and Structure of the Seafarer," *Studia Neophilologica,* 63, no. 1 (1991): 37–55;

Milman Parry, "Studies in the Epic Technique of Oral Verse-Making, I: Homer and Homeric Style," *Harvard Studies in Classical Philology,* 41 (1930): 73–147;

Carol Braun Pasternack, "Anonymous Polyphony and *The Wanderer's* Textuality," *Anglo-Saxon England,* 20 (1991): 99–122;

John C. Pope, "Dramatic Voices in *The Wanderer* and *The Seafarer,*" in *Franciplegius: Medieval and Linguistic Studies in Honor of Francis Peabody Magoun, Jr.,* edited by Jess B. Bessinger, Jr., and Robert P. Creed (New York: New York University Press, 1965), pp. 164–193;

Gerald Richman, "Speaker and Speech Boundaries in *The Wanderer,*" *Journal of English and Germanic Philology,* 81 (October 1982): 469–479;

M. Rieger, " 'Der Seefahrer' als Dialog hergestellt," *Zeitschrift für deutsche Philologie,* 1 (1869): 334–339;

Robinson, " 'The Might of the North': Pound's Anglo-Saxon Studies and 'The Seafarer,' " *Yale Review,* 71 (Winter 1982): 199–224;

Ernst Sieper, "Keltische Einflusse," in his *Die altenglische Elegie* (Strassburg: Trübner, 1915), pp. 55–77;

E. V. Smithers, "The Meaning of *The Seafarer* and *The Wanderer,*" *Medium Ævum,* 26 (1957): 137–153;

Stanley, "Old English Poetic Diction and the Interpretation of *The Wanderer, The Seafarer* and *The Penitent's Prayer,*" *Anglia,* 73 (1955): 413–486;

John Vickrey, "Some Hypotheses Concerning *The Seafarer:* Lines 1–47," *Archiv für das Studium der neueren Sprachen und Literaturen,* 219, no. 1 (1982): 57–77;

Dorothy Whitelock, "The Interpretation of *The Seafarer,*" in *The Early Cultures of Northwest Europe,* edited by Sir Cyril Fox and Bruce Dickens (Cambridge: Cambridge University Press, 1950), pp. 261–272;

Rosemary Woolf, "*The Wanderer, The Seafarer,* and the Genre of *Planctus,*" in *Anglo-Saxon Poetry: Essays in Appreciation for John C. McGalliard,* edited by Lewis E. Nicholson and Dolores Warwick Frese (Notre Dame: University of Notre Dame Press, 1975), pp. 192–207.

Middle English Literature: An Introduction

William Provost
University of Georgia

The great variety to be found in Middle English literature is evident and appealing but poses problems for the reader seeking to become familiar with it and the writer of a brief introduction to it. What are the shared characteristics of the large body of literature composed over a period of more than four centuries; influenced by a variety of Germanic, Classical, Romance, Celtic, and biblical cultures; representing many genres and sui generis forms; and addressed to significantly different kinds of audiences? How can those characteristics be isolated, defined, and presented in a relatively simple, but accurate and useful, way to readers looking for some help with the material?

In attempting to meet these challenges, this introduction to the literature of the Middle English period is only to a limited extent an essay with a sharply defined controlling thesis. To a greater extent it is a series of points related to various matters – historical, philosophical, social, cultural, literary, and intellectual – aimed at helping to focus for modern readers some of the more potentially troublesome differences between modern worldviews and those of medieval times. It may also highlight some of the essential human similarities between the two cultures and, in so doing, increase the reader's appreciation and understanding of medieval authors, audiences, and the literature they shared.

The four centuries that constitute the Middle English period contain a typical mix of both cataclysmic historical events and less-dramatic, but often far-reaching, changes. The Norman invasion, when William the Conqueror defeated the last Anglo-Saxon king, Harold II, near Hastings on an October afternoon in 1066, was clearly a dramatic turning point in British history. The changes that it began – or at least served as a sharply defined point from which to mark those changes – continued and spread throughout the period (see especially "Anglo-Norman Literature in the Development of Middle English Literature" in the Appendix to this volume). The Battle of Bosworth Field in late August of 1485, when Henry VII became the first Tudor monarch and so concluded the long strife between the great families of York and Lancaster, certainly did not finish the complex tapestry of effects the Norman invasion had on British culture, but it did serve as a convenient marking point: this time for the ending of the medieval period in England and the beginning of the long decline that followed. For all its horrors (to modern sensibilities), limitations, and idiosyncrasies, the Middle English period was arguably the last era in Western cultural history when a strong, clear, pervasive sense of belonging was shared by a whole people. That sense was certainly strained at times – perhaps especially in the fourteenth century with the unparalleled devastation of the bubonic plague that began in 1348. Nonetheless, this sense of belonging characterized the era as a whole, and an understanding of it is important for reading the literature well. The points that are touched on in the following pages focus some of its components.

Religion and the Roman Catholic church were central to the lives and thus to the literature of all Middle English people, but neither of these terms meant quite what they mean today. Religion was a universal, complex, and inclusive mix of faith, superstition, formal practices (liturgy), system of knowledge, point of reference, and source of structure. Indeed, the term *religion* would not have been used with its common modern connotations of a special, limited, very personal matter, essentially in opposition to "the real world." To suggest to a person of this period that religion was something that could, should, or ever would be separable from life itself in all its aspects would have been to suggest a strange idea. Religion's centrality to – or even identity with – life itself does not imply that medieval people were morally or ethically better than moderns (nor does it imply that they were worse), but rather that their essential orientation was significantly different from that of most people today. Of course, sometimes it seems not to have made any difference at all: the lazy anchoress of *Ancrene Riwle* (circa 1200–1225), the disrespectful servant of the Towneley *Mactacio Abel* (The Killing of Abel) pageant, and the food-loving friar of William Langland's *Piers Plowman* (circa 1360–1390) are universally familiar characters whose faults are as easily recognized now as they were by their original audiences. But whereas readers of today would probably see the faults essentially as individual traits, describable in terms of psychological, cultural, or environmental forces, the faults would at that time have been immediately and clearly understood as willful disruptions of the divine order and harmony that really and significantly exist. On the one hand, modernist tendencies to see the individual as a product of society constitute a surface similarity with medieval outlooks. However, the nature and significance of the social orders of the two eras are radically different. One of the etymologies of *religion* relates it to the idea of a binding, and for the folk of the Middle Ages, their individualities were understood as points in the great binding of love that was God's creation and providence.

The specific religion of the period was, of course, Roman Catholicism. (For a time, under William I and his immediate successors, a small number of Jews were encouraged to come into the country, and some served important functions as Norman feudalism began to edge toward a money-based economy. But royal support of their presence eventually waned, and in 1290 all Jews were formally expelled.) The church throughout the period, though, tended to be more English than Roman. This was largely true even during those periods in the thirteenth century, under the Kings John and Henry III, when England was made a fief of the pope and had to provide him with extensive financial support. Even then, and more so at other times, encyclicals, bulls, and other official pronouncements from Rome (or, during most of the fourteenth century, when the papal court was ensconced at Avignon, from France) were received and eventually promulgated; but the archbishops of Canterbury and York tended to be somewhat independent. The English church was relatively uninvolved with the many struggles and intrigues between popes and princes that are such a dominant part of the history of Continental Catholicism from the twelfth through the fifteenth centuries. So, in terms of their sense of being Christians, Middle English people certainly thought of themselves as belonging, but belonging to a church distinctly their own: a relatively local, familiar, insular body.

The pervasiveness of the appendages of that body would be difficult to overestimate. The majority of the works discussed in the following essays are written by people with some official connection to the church. All of those works – from the most

learned to the most homely, from the most sacred to the most carnal – simply assume universal familiarity with basic ecclesiastical structures, rites, and terminology. In addition – and this is especially important for the modern reader to understand – they assume a general acceptance of ecclesiastical authority. With the possible and then only partial exception of John Wyclif, the strongest criticisms, satires, or parodies of clerics or their practices found in the literature of the period must be seen in the context of that universal familiarity and acceptance. At least most (and some readers would say all) of the literature explores, explains, and celebrates the truth and beauty that was known to have come from God, and of which the church was the greatest earthly repository. It held the keys, not only to the kingdom of heaven, but also, through its responsibility and power of teaching (referred to often as the magisterium), to God's two books: Nature and the Bible. For the entire medieval period, incidentally, the standard text of the Bible was Saint Jerome's Latin translation, known as the Vulgate. What was for many years the standard modern Bible in English for Roman Catholics, the Douai/Rheims version, is basically a translation of the Vulgate, unlike the King James version or many other contemporary translations which are based on the Greek Septuagint; hence, the Douai/Rheims version is probably for modern readers the most accessible translation of what was essentially the form of the Bible known then.

The full magisterium of the church is an immensely complex philosophical and theological construct, involving great quantities of Latin commentaries, interpretations, and codifications. No one in the medieval period knew it all, based as it was on centuries of writings going back ultimately to Scripture and proceeding through the likes of Saint Ambrose, Saint Augustine, Saint Jerome, Boethius, Saint Thomas Aquinas, and many others. But that it did exist was known and that it was authoritative was accepted. Further, it was, despite its complexity and Latinity, a living and present constituent of the thinking and understanding of many people, even among the most unlearned and unsophisticated of the day. The means of transmission of this body of knowledge was the physical presence of the church. Just as the literal church building itself visually focused and dominated the life of practically every individual in the England of the Middle Ages, from the villagers whose houses surrounded the parish church to the city dwellers for whom the sight and sounds of the great cathedrals were omnipresent, so too did the spiritual and intellectual structure of which that building was a sign. In the paintings, statuary, stained glass, and carvings of their churches, the people of the Middle English period had many elements of its complex teaching visually before them. In the sermons they regularly heard within the walls of the church, or from wandering friars in the thirteenth and fourteenth centuries, or in the plays they attended from the twelfth century on, they heard these elements explained again and again. They must have developed an extensive, and even sophisticated, understanding of many details of the theology and philosophy which their learned superiors were reading, debating, and producing. Also absorbed from their cultural environment would have been at least something of an understanding of the methods of the system itself: those principles of exegesis that the church used in its reading of and commentary on God's books.

There is no need to go into the details of medieval exegetical systems; they were complex, and modern interpretations of them are probably even more complex. However, corollaries and implications especially important for a reading of Middle English literature derive from some of these points relating to religion and the church, and these can be usefully summarized. Perhaps the most basic is the pervasive sense of the unity, the oneness that characterizes creation in all its aspects. The differences between this life and the life to come, between spirit and flesh, were obvious to the people of the time. These differences are often sharply focused and emphasized by writers. But the essential oneness of all God's creation was clearly seen as subsuming the differences. A sense of unity, and of belonging in a precisely defined way within that unity, was the invariable starting point for writers, whatever their immediate theme or subject might be. And it was a starting point they could count on their audience sharing with them.

This understanding goes a long way toward explaining a characteristic of many Middle English writings that often surprises modern readers: the tendency to include within a single work tones, subjects, and styles that seem discordant to modern sensibilities formed on modern literary conventions. Marked examples of such discordances are abundant in the literature of the period: from the blending of simple, homely practical advice with profound spiritual commentary in *Ancrene Riwle;* to the sometimes seemingly chaotic stylistic, generic, and narrative jumps in *Piers Plowman;* to the low, farcical, even scatological humor that is such a frequent element of the profoundly moral lessons about saving our souls that are insistently taught in

the drama. It also helps reveal how the intricate romances of the Arthur stories or the fantasies of Mandeville or the myth/histories of Wace are at once engagingly creative narratives and serious spiritual lessons. It provides a way of appreciating as something other than a kind of burlesque or blasphemous parody the tendency of so many medieval lyrics which celebrate sex or drinking to be written with the same style and diction as those on highly sacred subjects. And, though Geoffrey Chaucer is probably the most "modern" of Middle English writers – the one who requires the least effort for modern readers to understand – this basic idea supplies a way of seeing the *Canterbury Tales* (circa 1375–1400), with its radically unfinished appearance and its manifold disparities of subject, style, and genre, as a coherent, unified poem according to perceptions typical of the medieval worldview. Anything could fit in a human production because everything was part of God's creation.

Understanding medieval confidence in the essential oneness of all things can help modern readers respond more fully to aspects of the literature at levels other than those of structure, genre, and style. Allegory in particular is a frequently encountered element of Middle English literature that is sometimes difficult to appreciate. It is best thought of not so much as a genre but rather as a mode of thinking and writing. It is a highly analytical and intellectual mode that allows the bewildering complexity of human experience to be artificially dissected by the mind in order to see parts and relationships more clearly. Thus, it might show the innate human tendency toward wrongdoing as if that tendency were seven individuals, each with appropriate traits and physical appearances, who accompany, or try to accompany, a person on life's journey: the seven deadly sins. Or it shows the instant of death, the final moment of physical consciousness and free will, as if it were an extended period of time: the amount of time it takes to play *Everyman* (circa 1500). Allegory accomplishes such "as ifs" through the mind's creative, analytical powers. It assumes an audience that is aware of these powers, is willing to use them, and understands both the artificiality and the validity of the procedure. It is not so much a matter of whether the character of Sloth, for example, is "real" or not as it is a matter of whether such a character's actions and appearance within the narrative context where he exists effectively show and explain what happens when a person begins neglecting responsibilities. This mode of thinking/writing is highly sophisticated and involves some of the kinds of pleasures many modern readers readily recognize in working out the puzzles of mystery stories; it ultimately depends on the assumption that artifice is part of the truth of creation.

Figurative language in some form is presumably at the heart of all literature, that of the modern period certainly being no exception. Today's readers are accustomed to metaphor, simile, and other figures, and also to the device of symbolism. But moderns trying to read medieval literature well require some adjustment to their ideas about these literary techniques. First, it may be best to forget about symbolism entirely. Perhaps, simplistically, symbolism can be understood as a technique of language used to suggest some less-than-precisely definable link between an element (for example: a place, name, object, person, and so on) of the "real" world and an idea or a meaning separable from it. Linkages and the signs thereof are certainly a part of the medieval view of the world, but not the ephemeral, open-ended, quasi-mystical sorts of linkages that symbols imply. Likewise, if a metaphor is now seen as essentially a linguistic or rhetorical trick – a skillful manipulation of words to say something that is understood as not really true but rather cleverly suggestive – then it is viewed rather differently from the way it was seen and used then. Once again, the modern reader must remember that within the medieval worldview, the whole of creation was real and ultimately one. The medieval delight in categorizing, in arranging the elements of human experience, knowledge, and understanding according to wonderfully complex hierarchies and compartments, was not an attempt to provide the *appearance* of order for a random or absurd universe, but rather an acknowledgement of the reality of order that was confidently accepted. The ability of the mind to see and note linkages is at once a part of the order and a proof of it. So metaphors calling the king a lion, or tree sap a virtue, or perseverance a castle, or life a wheel were not simply linguistic exuberances – though they were definitely enjoyed as such. They were more: statements of truth, affirmations of what everyone understood to be the way things really were. The frantic energy in the "violent yokings" of seventeenth-century metaphysical conceits is the last desperate attempt by English poets to recapture what was an easy meld of simplicity and complexity for the people of the Middle Ages. The power of figurative language for Nicholas of Guildford or Julian of Norwich or the York Realist was one with the power that began and sustains creation in its entirety: the power of love itself. A good metaphor reveals, for an instant, part of the mystery of creation.

Two additional matters need to be touched on at least briefly. The first is the importance of Boethius's *De consolatione philosophiae* (The Consolation of Philosophy, circa 525), and especially the idea of Fortune deriving from it, to the medieval worldview. The *Consolation* was known and revered throughout the period. It provided the central model for dealing with the obvious fact of human suffering as a part of a world created and run by love. In that model, Fortune represents the principle of change as that principle governs human existence within the sublunary portion of the universe. Lady Philosophy teaches Boethius that the wise human being comes to understand that Fortune is indeed an essential part of the divine plan; human lives, in their earthly state, are subject to change. The things the world gives and takes are good, but they are not lasting and must be understood in this way. Failure to do so means the submission of reason to the senses, and this inversion of the divine hierarchy can lead only to suffering and tragedy. A person in any work of Middle English literature who rails against Fortune – calling her names, cursing her, referring to her as a traitor who seeks and takes pleasure in human suffering – is understood in two ways simultaneously: first, as a fellow human who is experiencing and voicing something everyone has felt and who is thus an object of sympathy; and second, as a fool, someone who has failed to learn or has forgotten the ultimate reasonableness of God's Providence. As the *Consolation* shows in its final book, the temporariness of time itself is also a matter that the reasonable human being can come to understand, however hard that matter may sometimes be to accept.

A typical and frequently occurring example of those who rail against Fortune in works of Middle English literature is the courtly lover, and the literary convention of courtly love is worthy of brief consideration here. Passionate love between men and women is a subject treated often in this literature, the subject matter being one of the ways it differs markedly from the literature that has survived from the preceding Old English period. The treatment of this subject varies, but often its presentation entails specific motifs which are referred to collectively by the modern phrase *courtly love*. These motifs include a lover (male) who is powerfully and instantly stricken by the beauty of the beloved (female), sometimes after he has decided to follow the "craft" of love. A long period of silent, private suffering ensues for the lover before he eventually musters the courage – sometimes with the help of someone, perhaps a friend who has discovered his pitiful state – to reveal his love to the beloved. He is rejected, suffers more, finally reapproaches her, and is accepted on a kind of probation as a love servant. After his long and faithful service, the two become lovers. The entire proceeding is usually extramarital, though sometimes, especially in its English versions, marriage can be the outcome. The participants are of the courtly estate, and the affair is conducted according to the highest levels of decorum and manners. It is typically beautiful, erotic, and doomed to tragedy. The tragedy is not the result of hubris in the classical sense, nor is it specifically because of some heroic flaw in the Renaissance sense. It comes about, rather, because the lover has forgotten that for all her God-given beauty, the beloved is finally mortal and thus subject to the mutability of Fortune. He would have her be immortal, as his language in praise of her often clearly shows, but she cannot be immortal and still be the creature she is.

The details of this formulaic presentation vary; they frequently occur, however, and constitute a recognizable literary convention. The history of its development is complex, and scholars do not universally agree on it, but it seems to involve source lines going back through early medieval Provençal and Spanish literature, perhaps even to Arabic love poetry before that, and making its way gradually north and west to the England of Henry II (reigned 1154–1189) and his queen, Eleanor of Aquitaine. The convention is used in many different kinds of Middle English writing, and apparently even a cryptic allusion to one or more of its elements would have been recognized and would have evoked a distinct set of responses from its audience. Exactly how fixed that set was and exactly how readers should understand it are matters about which late twentieth-century medievalists are still uncertain. This much is clear: writers of the period knew that passionate love was an engaging literary subject – that it was, like all love, potentially an element of the divine, but like all things human also

open to misuse. Often, and maybe always, the occurrence of the convention would imply an inordinate degree of love, a perversion of the divine hierarchy of love which humans understand but regularly fail to achieve.

The beliefs, understandings, and assumptions of any culture are always at least somewhat curious when examined from the perspectives of a different one. It is not difficult to find examples of Middle English worldviews that seem limited, restricting, and ignorant. No doubt medievals would hold the same opinions of many modern beliefs, understandings, and assumptions. But it would be a mistake to retreat into simplistic relativism. Reading the literature or thoughtful descriptions of the literature of the Middle English period does not mean the modern reader must – even if he or she could – become a medieval person. Readers of today need to bring to the reading of this literature that which they are and believe. And they need to be able to see in medieval literature the intelligent, learned, thoughtful, often passionate attempts of the authors to speak of what they knew, felt, believed, and wanted. Readers certainly can come to understand the rigid hierarchies that were so basically a part of the systems medieval people lived by, and disagree. It is possible to learn something of the amount and kind of violence and physical suffering so constantly a part of their lives, and sympathize. Modern readers may also be able to comprehend the grandeur and beauty of the creation medievals so confidently knew themselves to be an important part of – despite the suffering and the rigidity – and wonder. Theirs was a hard world, but one that made sense. It had love as its center and energy, and it could be understood, if not completely. It was a world *where* they belonged, though they knew they must not belong *to* it, and it fascinated them. Modern readers can see this fascination if they look honestly at the literature. And if nothing else, strong, clear, lively human fascination is always fascinating.

John Barbour

(circa 1316 – 1395)

Phoebe A. Mainster
Wayne State University

MAJOR WORK: *The Bruce* (1375)

> **Manuscript:** The text of *The Bruce* has been preserved in two manuscripts, one signed "J. de R." and dated 1437, in the Library of Saint John's College, Cambridge, and another signed "Johannes Ramsay," the Edinburgh MS., dated 1489 and bound up with *The Wallace* by the same hand, in the Advocates' Library, Edinburgh. No trace of the original manuscript is known to exist.
>
> **First publication:** *The Bruce* (Edinburgh: Printed by Andrew Hart, 1616).
>
> **Standard edition:** *The Bruce: Or the Book of the Most Excellent and Noble Prince, Robert de Broyss King of Scots, Compiled by Master John Barbour, A.D. 1375,* edited by Walter W. Skeat, EETS, e.s. 11, 21, 29, 55 (1870–1889); reprinted as one volume (1968).
>
> **Edition in modern English:** *The Bruce: An Epic Poem,* edited and translated by Archibald A. H. Douglas (Glasgow: Maclellan, 1964).

Scotland's political identity is linked to its transition to nationhood during the fourteenth century. It was an era of political controversy, with power struggles for the succession and guardianship of the Scottish kingdom. John Barbour's historical narrative, *The Bruce* (1375), pays homage to the emerging national unity as symbolized in the heroic qualities of virtue, prowess, and leadership. Despite Barbour's significant literary contribution, few facts are known of his life. Magister Iohannes Barber Archdiaconus Aberdonensis (Master John Barbour, Archdeacon of Aberdeen), often referred to as the father of Scottish poetry, was born about 1316 and died 13 March 1395. The exact date of his birth is unknown. A marble memorial stone, which once marked his grave, is now on the inner wall of Aberdeen Cathedral. Nothing is known about his parentage or ancestry, and there is no record that Barbour left any descendants. There is no mention by any-

one of his appearance, personality, or character. Little is known about him except through references in various records from the reign of Robert the Bruce's son David II (1329–1371). These sources reveal that Barbour had passports (1357 and 1364) from Edward III of England allowing him to journey to Oxford with certain scholars and knights for purposes of study. He had similar permits in 1365 and 1368 allowing him to travel through England to France for scholarly purposes. From 1357 until his death Barbour held the title of archdeacon of Aberdeen.

Barbour composed his verse narrative, *The Bruce,* commemorating the achievements of Robert the Bruce (born 1274, reigned 1306–1329), during the reign of his grandson Robert II (1371–1390), founder of the Stewart dynasty. Robert the Bruce, a courageous fourteenth-century Scottish patriot, fought with unflinching heroism for the legitimate ascension to the Scottish throne in a national war of liberation against England. In telling the story, Barbour affirms the legitimacy of the Bruce/Stewart line by recounting the origins of the Royal House of Stewart. The events take place in the early part of the fourteenth century in Scotland, Northern England, and Ireland and tell of Scotland's Wars of Independence. As literature with a political agenda, *The Bruce* serves as a model for the role of a good king and as a warning of what may happen when a nation is undermined by factionalism and disloyalty. The historical verse narrative purports to be a true record of events from Robert Bruce's ascension to the Scottish throne in 1306 to his death in 1329. The tale follows Bruce, his friend James Douglas, his brother Edward Bruce, and his nephew Thomas Randolph as the Scottish king sets out to win the great victory over England, going from danger and adversity to fame and success.

Invoking the intimate tone of a storyteller surrounded by a congenial audience, Barbour announces that his purpose in writing *The Bruce* is to entertain by telling a "suthfast story" about Scottish patriots – the author seems to have shared in the general belief that these stories were substantially true. It may be assumed that he spent many years collecting oral histories, folklore, ballads, and detailed chronicled information of the events he describes. As Barbour was approximately fifty-five years old when he wrote the poem, most of the events in his story happened during his lifetime. According to Barbour, the work was completed in 1375. While it is one of the principal sources of the historical information it relates, *The Bruce* contains several historical errors, primarily related to the sequence of certain events or to names and titles. Most noticeably, Barbour makes no reference to Sir William Wallace, whose rebellions against English domination took place at the time of the events alluded to in the opening section of the poem. Although subsequent Scottish writers accepted Barbour's interpretation and used it either as a source for their historical writings or as an inspiration for "true" tales, Barbour's "suthfast story" is hardly equal to what modern historians would consider veracity. To the medieval historian, truth generally allowed for the flexibility of building a fictionalized work around a historical fact, figure, or legend so as to make the event serve either didactic or political ends.

The Bruce is the earliest major verse narrative in the vernacular of eastern and southern fourteenth-century Scotsmen, referred to as "Braid Scots" or literary Lowland Scots. The language at this time was still in the process of evolution from its Scandinavian, Anglo-Saxon, and Norman-French ancestry. *The Bruce,* written in octosyllabic rhymed couplets, marks a shift which occurred in the fourteenth century from unrhymed, alliterative poetry to the rhymed verse and metered lines characteristic of Continental poetry.

Barbour seems to have been familiar with the Continental romances. He derived his inspiration and models from the heroic romance cycles of Arthur, Charlemagne, *The Romance of Fierabras* (Farmer MS. fourteenth century), and the *Romans d'Alixandre* (by Tors and Bernay, thirteenth century). Barbour's panegyric on freedom, his portrait of James Douglas, and his description of spring at Bruce's setting forth from Arran are some of the poetic passages reminiscent of the romances.

He refers to his poem as a romance, yet it is not about mythical, magical, or legendary heroes. In the tradition of the Charlemagne and Alexander romances, it is a narrative of heroic deeds. *The Bruce* tells of Scottish heroes and real events which had happened between forty and sixty years prior to the

King Robert Bruce, the subject of Barbour's poem (portrait by de Witte; Holyrood House, Edinburgh)

poem's composition. When Barbour's story begins, Robert Bruce is about thirty or thirty-one and has refused to accept a titular kingship as vassal to Edward I of England. Bruce is determined to assert his right to be the king of an independent Scotland. Barbour develops his hero's career and achievements in detail, through all his years of adversity and success until his death. Like a chronicle, *The Bruce* describes Scotland under English domination and tells of select incidents chosen for their patriotic and didactic values.

In his re-creation of historic events, Barbour reveals his familiarity with the historical rhyming chronicles of the early fourteenth century. Andrew Wyntoun followed the same example and wrote a metrical history of early Britain, possibly based upon the Anglo-Norman *Le Roman de Brut* (1155) of Wace, the Norman-French trouvère, or perhaps on the *Historia regum Britanniae* (circa 1138) of Wace's predecessor, Geoffrey of Monmouth, a work that described the legendary descent and deeds of the Scottish kings, from Brutus, great-grandson of Aeneas, to his own day. Continuing in this tradition, in 1386 Barbour is reputed to have written *The Brut*. In 1388 Barbour received an annual pension of ten pounds, possibly in recognition of his third poem, *The Stewartis Orygenalle,* a fictitious account of the origins of that royal house, attributed to Barbour on Wyntoun's authority. Neither manuscript has survived.

Book 1 of *The Bruce* is devoted to two prominent figures in the narrative, King Robert of Scotland and Sir James of Douglas. The story begins with the deaths of King Alexander III, who fell over a cliff and into a crag at Kinghorn on 16 March 1286, and of his granddaughter, the Maid of Norway, who died on 7 October 1290. The Scottish barons' subsequent dissension over the right of succession involved the claims of John Baliol, grandson of the eldest daughter of David, Earl of Huntingdon. This claim was denied by the Bruce faction, who argued that succession could not succeed through a female while any male was to be found of equal descent. Omitting the details of twelve years of Bruce/Baliol factionalism and warfare, Barbour conflates the three Roberts – the grandfather, Robert the Competitor; his son, Robert the Bruce, Earl of Carrick; and Barbour's hero, King Robert, also Earl of Carrick – and proceeds directly to the disastrous events surrounding the barons' efforts for a peaceful solution. Misguidedly trusting the friendship of Edward I of England, the barons apply to him to decide the question of succession.

In Barbour's story Edward's duplicity begins as he offers the crown to Robert the Bruce. In exchange for the crown, Bruce must swear that he and his offspring will forever hold Edward as overlord. Bruce refuses, but John Baliol, who receives the same offer, accepts. Baliol's victory is shortlived as Edward sets out to disgrace and ultimately to arrest and to imprison him. With Baliol out of the way, Edward sends in the troops and quickly seizes and suppresses all of Scotland. Barbour then turns to James Douglas, beginning with Edward's imprisonment of James's father, Sir William, Lord of Douglas, and the disposition of the Douglas lands that have been awarded to the Englishman, the lord of Clifford. In the course of the narrative James Douglas becomes Clifford's chief adversary and, historically, the predecessor of a long line of Scotsmen who harrass the borderlands between Scotland and England.

With the heroes' early histories accounted for, the exposition ends, and the reader is informed that "The Romanys now begynnys her." Bruce is returning from Stirling when his cousin John Comyn proposes a deal in which one of them would become king of Scotland in exchange for turning over all lands now in possession. Bruce agrees to pledge his bond in writing, a covenant by which he will be king and Comyn will get possession of the Bruce land. Treacherously, Comyn goes to Edward I and tells of the pact he has made with Robert Bruce. Edward summons Bruce. In Barbour's narrative this summons sounds ominous, but historically the relationship between Edward and Bruce had been cordial. Among his omissions, Barbour fails to mention Bruce's bond with the English through his marriage to Elizabeth de Burgh, daughter of the earl of Ulster, a follower of Edward. This was Robert Bruce's second marriage; his first, to Isabella, daughter of Donald, Earl of Mar, produced a daughter, Marjory, who in turn married Walter Stewart, and their son, Robert II, became the first Stewart monarch of Scotland.

The events of book 2 lead to the Battle of Methven. At Dumfries, Bruce meets Comyn at the high altar of the Greyfriars' church where Comyn has taken sanctuary. Despite the privilege of sanctuary, Bruce kills Comyn, his brother Edmund Comyn, and several of their followers. Soon after, Bruce summons his friends and followers and proclaims himself king. Barbour does not dwell on the sacrilegious murder of Comyn or the hopelessness of Bruce's decision to claim a kingdom but instead turns the spotlight on Bruce's devoted follower, Bishop Lamberton, whose response to Bruce's proclamation is symbolic in two ways: first, Lamberton's positive reaction indicates the general community's willingness to accept Bruce as king; second, Lamberton recalls Thomas of Erceldoune's prophecy, which symbolizes the ultimate hope for the Scots. Douglas, in response to Bruce's proclamation, leaves the service of Bishop Lamberton to join the self-proclaimed king. Douglas sees this as his chance to win back his own lands from Clifford. Bruce enthusiastically receives Douglas, marking the beginning of a long friendship.

The narrative turns to Aymer de Valence, accompanied by two other English knights, Philip the Mowbray and Ingram the Umphraville, chief administrators in Scotland at that time, sent by Edward I of England to capture Bruce. At Methven, Bruce's men are overrun, and Thomas Randolph, Bruce's nephew, is taken prisoner. Mowbray seizes the reins of Bruce's horse and cries for help to capture the "new-made king." Christopher Seton attacks Mowbray and rescues Bruce. Learning of his men's fate, Bruce mourns for the captured and slain.

In book 3 King Robert is a fugitive. Events begin near Tay, where the lord of Lorne (John MacDougall), Comyn's uncle and Bruce's deadly enemy, sets out to take Bruce by surprise. Bruce, alerted to the danger, fights well against Lorne's men. He next encounters Lorne's henchmen, the MacIndrosser brothers and a third assailant, who attempt to ambush him in a narrow pass, but he dispatches all three with brutal precision.

Through the winter Bruce and his men wander the Highlands. To escape the hardships, he plans to go to the isle of Cantyre off the mainland. He sends Neil Campbell to reconnoiter and gather boats and supplies from his kinsmen. For three days Bruce and his company wait, but, fearing the enemy, they seek to cross Loch Lomond. Douglas finds a small sunken boat that is used to ferry three men at a time. During this progress Bruce keeps their spirits up with tales from the romance of Fierabras.

When in book 4, Edward I hears how Neil Bruce, Robert's brother, had held Kildrummy against his son, and he sets out for Scotland. En route he falls ill and stops at a nearby hamlet. Deathly ill, he is taken to the church called "Jerusalem in Vy Laterane," as related by Wyntown (bk vi. c. xii), in the Burgh in the Sand (Burgh-on-Sands at the Solway Firth), which he construes as an ironic twist to the prophecy that he would not die until he had taken the burgh of Jerusalem. On his deathbed Edward has the Kildrummy prisoners brought to him. Grinning, he orders them hanged and drawn. Edward dies, and his son, Edward of Carnarvon, becomes king. Historically, the twenty-three-year-old sportsman and patron of the arts, Edward II, did not attempt to emulate his father's hammering of the Scots. Then, in replacing Aymer de Valence, Edward II removed Bruce's second most feared adversary and allowed Bruce to consolidate the territory he had won and to establish himself among his countrymen throughout Buchan, Argyll, and Galloway.

Meanwhile, in Barbour's narrative, Bruce has taken refuge in Rathlin. From there he sends a spy, Cuthbert, to Carrick to assess the allegiance of the Scots. If they are friendly toward Bruce and his cause, Cuthbert is to light a signal fire at Turnberry Point. But Cuthbert learns of their fear of Bruce and opposition to him. Carrick is a land full of the enemy, under the rule of Henry Percy, garrisoned at Turnberry Castle. Cuthbert decides not to fire the signal but to return to Bruce to report. Nevertheless, Bruce thinks he sees a fire, and his men concur. Joyfully, they set out.

In book 5 King Robert and three hundred men set out from Arran to Carrick, rowing at night with the fire as the only guide in the dark night. Cuthbert also has seen the fire and is now afraid to put it out, so he waits to meet Bruce. Despite Cuthbert's bad news, Bruce's carefully planned night attack succeeds. He learns from a kinswoman in Carrick about the deaths of his brother, Neil Bruce of Seton, and of the earl of Athol, as well as the imprisonment of Bruce's queen. He swears revenge.

Douglas proposes that he be allowed to challenge the English, specifically Clifford and the men holding his lands in Douglasdale. Douglas captures the castle, and what he cannot take, he destroys. He beheads the prisoners, mixing the mess of blood, meal, malt, and wine into what afterward is known as the "Douglas Larder." Then he fouls the well with salt and dead horses and burns down everything that is not stone. To balance the prowess of his heroes, Barbour concludes this book with the account of Bruce's one-eyed kinsman and his two powerful sons who are bribed into treasonable service for forty pounds worth of land. Bruce defeats the traitors and then laments the wasted valor of the three dead men.

Book 6 recounts how a group of men from Galloway plan to catch Bruce in Carrick by tracking him with a bloodhound. Forewarned, Bruce reconnoiters for a narrow pass where the men must proceed in single file. Bruce kills the first horseman, and the remainder come on in a furious rush. He kills so many that the passage is jammed with dead horses and men. Seeing fourteen men dead, Bruce's men praise God for such a valiant leader, and the news of his deed of valor brings him additional followers.

The Bruce also relates many of Douglas's heroic exploits. Barbour's inclusion of this material was undoubtedly due to the important role James Douglas played during the lifetime of King Robert I, but it may also be due to the fact that the Douglas family was still powerful in Robert II's lifetime. Therefore, it was prudent that the Douglas family not be offended by omission, unlike the poem's neglect of the part William Wallace played during the early fourteenth century or of the reign of David Bruce during the mid fourteenth century.

In the narrative the cunning Douglas ambushes Thirlwall and his garrison outside the castle walls. The plan goes well: Thirlwall is slain, and the rest of his men flee in terror. Douglas then rejoins Bruce, reporting that Aymer has returned and is seeking Bruce in Cumnock, but Bruce decides to remain. Aymer's assembled forces include Thomas Randolph and John of Lorne. This time Lorne uses Aymer's prize bloodhound to hunt for Bruce. Lorne sets the hound on Bruce's track, which Bruce and his brother escape from by retreating into a nearby forest.

Book 7 continues the tale of escapes and surprises. Bruce and a foster brother leave the forest for the upland moors. The two meet three suspicious-looking men with swords and axes. One man has a sheep draped across his shoulders and around his neck. That night, at a farmhouse, the three villains attack Bruce with swords, but his armor protects him, and he slays all three. Unfortunately, his foster brother is killed in the fray. Lamenting his death and cursing the villains, Bruce sets out for a pre-arranged meeting with his men. Aymer learns of Bruce's whereabouts and sets out to surprise him in Glen Trool. He sends a female spy into Bruce's camp. Suspicious of strangers, Bruce has his men seize her, and she confesses. Then, gathering his three hundred men to his banner, Bruce leads the charge, and the English forces retreat. Disgraced that they have been beaten by a handful of Scots, the English knights fall out arguing; Clifford and Vaux even come to blows. Aymer parts them, dismayed that so many Englishmen of such renown displayed so little prowess in battle.

Book 8 tells of the Battle of Loudoun Hill. Confident that his greater forces will win, Aymer sends Bruce a challenge of open combat at Loudoun Hill on the tenth day of May. Bruce dislikes Aymer's haughtiness and accepts. Aymer's three thousand men are well armed and equipped in knightly fashion, with shields flashing in the sun. Bruce cautions his men to discount their grandeur, because if the Scots can fiercely repulse the foremost, the rest will break rank. As predicted, the English vanguard is overcome, and the rear guard falls back. Aymer is unable to turn the flight, and he, too, flees the field, returning to Bothwell. Ashamed, Aymer resigns the wardenship.

In book 9 Bruce is in Inverury, where he becomes too sick to eat, drink, ride, or walk. While he is recovering, his enemy, John Comyn, the earl of Buchan, and his men assault. Bruce's revenge is to raze the region, so that fifty years later the event is still known as the "Ravage of Buchan." In the course of events Edward Bruce, Robert's brother, sets out to recover Galloway from the English. Barbour states that he cannot even begin to tell a tenth part of Edward Bruce's prowess, and this disclaimer highlights a complex interplay of heroic models. Unlike the successful raids of Douglas and

Robert Bruce, Edward Bruce's daring and reckless behavior does not add anything to Scotland's political and economic well-being. In episodes that portray the tension between the brothers, Barbour sets up the situation so that in a pattern of resolved stresses, Edward Bruce represents serious actions which turn out disastrously, so that his errors serve as the foil for Robert Bruce's successes. Barbour portrays Edward Bruce's deeds as admirable and of importance to those who love chivalry but of no real importance to the survival of Scotland. Ultimately the nonchivalric but successful strategies of Robert Bruce and Douglas prove who the best knights really are. The selection, treatment, and ordering of events in the narrative determine and emphasize the distinctive differences between diverse kinds of leadership. Like Bruce, Douglas is always in control – of his men, his integrity, and his destiny. In the Forest (the historic haunt of sixth-century Merlin) Douglas maintains control. He captures Thomas Randolph and Alexander Stewart, who are kin to Bruce and to Douglas, respectively.

Book 10 reports the capture of several castles. Bruce captures the castle at Dunstaffnage and takes control through his own warden. Alexander of Argyll, seeing his land destroyed, makes peace with Bruce, while his son, John of Lorne, remains rebellious and flees with his ships to sea. Returning to Perth, Bruce reconciles with Thomas Randolph and makes him the earl of Moray. Randolph settles his own lands and comes to help his uncle by going to Edinburgh to lay siege to the castle. In the meantime, Douglas sets out to take Roxburgh. Bruce sends his brother Edward with instructions to destroy the castle at Roxburgh and to pacify Teviotdale. When Randolph hears about Roxburgh, he follows suit at Edinburgh. Outnumbered, Randolph's men fight a bloody combat, but they finally take the castle. Meanwhile, Edward Bruce wins Galloway and Nithdale, working his way toward Stirling, which is under warden Philip the Mowbray. He lays siege to Stirling, but Mowbray gets him to agree to a one-year truce, at the end of which there is to be a decisive battle to win or to yield Stirling castle.

Book 11 recounts the events leading up to the Battle of Bannockburn. Initially Bruce is upset at Edward Bruce's covenant, because the Scots are too few and the enemy too many, but Edward Bruce is undaunted, and Robert ultimately agrees to the challenge. In this crucial encounter Edward II brings together the greatest array of feudal power. In contrast, Bruce's small army is divided into four.

Dunfermline Abbey, the burial place of Robert Bruce

Randolph heads the vanguard with the banner, Edward Bruce leads the second division, and the third division has coleaders, Walter Stewart and Douglas. Robert Bruce takes the rear guard.

Book 12 begins with the first stroke of the fight. Bruce, his crown set on his leather hat, arrays his men into battle formation. Henry of Bohun, cousin to the earl of Hereford, spots Bruce and heads toward him. Bruce rides out and kills Bohun with the first blow of his ax. The Scots are inspired by this bold action. After defeating the English, the Scottish lords are distressed at Bruce for the danger to himself and the potential ruin of Scotland, but Bruce only laments his broken ax handle. His example of personal courage inspires his men in the ensuing Battle of Bannockburn.

At daybreak the Scots hear mass and ready their divisions. Stewart, Douglas, and others are knighted on the field according to their degree. The English, shining bright as angels, are in one throng and not arrayed in divisions as the Scots are, except for the large vanguard that stands separately. Edward II has the trumpets sound, and the English

vanguard heads straight at Edward Bruce. Mowbray leads the other nine English divisions into the fray. The ground steams with blood. Randolph's men join in, ten against one.

In book 13 Bruce's men attack the enemy's flank, fighting like unstoppable madmen. With the Scots' axes against the English weapons of steel, there is a horrid roar of men and metal. Edward Bruce's men overthrow the English vanguard. At that moment Bruce's "small folk" of yeomen, swains, and camp followers choose one of their own as captain, and with sheets on poles for banners and spears, fifteen thousand or more march toward the battleground. From the distance the English see and hear shouts of what seems a great company and are frightened. Bruce sees the English hesitancy and presses on. Edward II is upset at the disarray of the English forces and takes flight. With Aymer and Edward II gone, the English troops scatter.

At Stirling, Bruce has the dead buried honorably and then has the castle and tower destroyed. He sends Edward Bruce to Bothwell to make a treaty with England to exchange the earl of Hereford for three prisoners: Robert, the blind bishop; Bruce's queen; and Lady Marjory, Bruce's daughter. Near the close of book 13 Barbour notes that Lady Marjory marries Walter Stewart, and their son, Robert, named after his grandfather, becomes King Robert II after his uncle David's forty-two-year reign. The poet offers a prayer that the offspring will uphold and keep safe the people of Scotland, maintaining their rights and their loyalty as it was in the time of the Bruce. Book 13 concludes with Robert I at fortune's height, as he publicly proclaims that all who hold land or fee in Scotland should come and claim it within the year and swear allegiance to the king.

In book 14 Edward Bruce leaves for Ireland. Compared to the bold and restless leopard, he has no desire to be at peace. In his mind Scotland is too small for both brothers, so he decides to become king of Ireland. He enters into a treaty with the Irish to overcome English rule there. King Robert consents to this adventure, and in May, Edward sets out with Randolph and Philip Mowbray and numerous other Scottish knights.

In book 15 the narrative returns to Robert Bruce, who has gone to the Isles while Edward is in Ireland. The people of the Isles all pay homage to him except John of Lorne, who is then imprisoned. Ultimately Lorne dies in captivity. While Bruce subdues the Isles, Douglas is in the Forest. At this time Edmond de Calion, a Gascon knight serving with the English in Berwick, has been ravaging Teviotdale and Merse and then fleeing back to Berwick. Douglas sets up an encounter at the ford and a fierce melee ensues in which Calion dies.

Robert Neville, envious of Douglas's reputation, vows to kill him should he appear. Douglas takes the boast as a challenge and comes to Berwick. Neville and Douglas meet in single combat, and Douglas, the tougher and more accustomed to fighting, kills Neville. Douglas's reputation spreads, and he is widely feared. Barbour interjects that mothers threaten their children into good behavior with the dread of Black Douglas.

Book 16 tells of Robert Bruce's journey to Ireland, the king having left Stewart and Douglas as wardens in his absence. Up to that time Edward Bruce had achieved nineteen victories in less than three years. Edward greets the king and Randolph, and they march victoriously from one end of Ireland to the other. In Limerick they are about to march when they hear a woman's cry. They discover that a laundress is in labor, and King Robert halts the army and commands that she be sheltered in a tent, where the child is born. He then orders

that the woman be carried with the army, and Barbour praises the courtesy of this great and mighty sovereign for a poor, humble laundress. Completing the march, Bruce recrosses Ireland, now going north.

Book 17 tells of the siege of Berwick. King Robert returns to Scotland, and soon north and south are under his rule, except Berwick, which is under the brutal control of the English. Aided by a burgher named Sym of Spalding, the Scots win the town and its spoils. Bruce decides not to destroy the walls but instead to garrison the town. He leaves Stewart to prepare the defenses. Meanwhile, Edward II of England gathers his forces to lay siege at Berwick. When Bruce hears of the siege, he gathers an army and plans an alternate strategy. He sends Randolph and Douglas into England on a rampage to force the English to return to protect their own lands and to leave the siege. Randolph and Douglas lay waste to the country, but the English at Mitton gather twenty thousand men, with the archbishop of York as captain. The English come ready for the clash, but they panic and run.

The Scots march and pillage while the English troops are still at Berwick waiting for an assault. By morning the English learn of the raids in Mitton, and Edward II calls a council to decide whether to stay or to rescue England. The lords of the north and south argue. Angry, Earl Thomas of Lancaster leaves without permission, taking one-third of the army with him (Edward later gets revenge at Ponefract and has Thomas beheaded and then hanged and drawn). With Thomas gone, Edward II disbands the English troops.

In book 18 Edward Bruce, restless, without restraint, and against the advice of his council, prepares for battle. The Scots are soon overwhelmed, and Edward Bruce is slain. Planning to avenge the English further, Edward II gathers his forces, intending to destroy all of Scotland. In turn, Bruce gathers his forces and crosses the Scottish Seas, marching toward England in pursuit of Edward II. At Byland, Bruce surprises and defeats the English army. Edward II flees southward as Walter Stewart pursues him to the gates of York. At the Abbey of Byland and nearby Rievaulx, the Scots share the spoils of battle. Leaving Byland, Bruce marches southward, pillaging and destroying his enemies as far south as the Wolds. He then turns northward and returns home with the booty, much to Edward II's dismay at the turn of events in his own country.

In book 19 Bruce works toward a peace with England, while factionalism within Scotland erupts. William Soulis and his followers attempt a conspiracy to assassinate Bruce. Soulis confesses before Parliament and is sent to Dunbarton, where he ultimately dies in captivity. Other conspirators are hanged, drawn, and quartered, in keeping with the punishment for treason. When Bruce sends a message to Edward II to arrange for a peace treaty, Edward accepts. After two and a half years of the thirteen-year truce, Bruce breaks the treaty as a result of English violations at sea. Soon after, Edward II dies (murdered at Berkeley Castle), and his young son Edward of Windsor is crowned. The eighteen-year-old Edward III marches north from York against the Scots.

In book 20, because of his unsuccessful pursuit of Bruce and through the advice of his mother and her favorite counselor, Roger Mortimer, Edward III requests a peace. The terms are that Bruce's five-year-old son, David, marry Edward's seven-year-old sister, Joan of the Tower, and that England give up its claims to Scotland, resulting in Scotland's total independence. The rest of book 20 relates the deaths of the heroes of *The Bruce*. Bruce, too sick to attend the wedding, sends Randolph and Douglas to Berwick. With great pomp and solemnity David is crowned. An ordinance is drawn that proclaims that if David should die without a male heir, Robert Stewart, Bruce's grandson by his daughter Marjory, shall be king. All the lords sign the order of succession. If both princes should die, Randolph and Douglas are to govern jointly. All lords swear oaths to the two wardens. Deathly sick at Cardross, Bruce calls the lords to witness his deathbed testament. He asks them not to grieve, as his sickness and pain are his reward for his trespasses. In repentance, he requests that his heart go into battle on a crusade against the enemies of God. The lords choose Douglas to take the journey. Bruce dies, and his people mourn; they also fear that his death means the end of their defense and of the peace.

Bruce is buried at Dunfermline, and Randolph governs the country. Thereafter Douglas receives Bruce's heart and places it in an enameled box that he wears around his neck. He then travels to Seville to fight for the king of Spain. In a fierce battle against the Saracens, Douglas throws Bruce's heart into the battlefield and follows it into combat. Douglas dies in the melee. Subsequently, his men bring home his bones, along with Bruce's heart. Douglas is buried in Saint Bride's Kirk of Douglas, and Archibald, Douglas's son, builds an alabaster tomb in his honor. Randolph has Bruce's heart buried at Melrose Abbey. Thereafter Randolph governs until his death, seemingly by poison. In clos-

ing, Barbour offers a benediction for Bruce's offspring that they may govern well and all of their lives emulate their noble forefather's excellence.

Barbour's poem was not only immediately accepted at court, it was received at once into the popular literature of the country and adopted as authentic history. The historical perspective of *The Bruce* partly accounts for the work's lasting status as a relevant product of Scotland's literary heritage. When its primary poetic form as a romance was no longer in vogue, it assumed the alternate role of chronicle, in which it was viewed as a significant contribution to Scottish literature. The pervading contribution of *The Bruce,* however, is neither its literary style nor the credibility of the historical data, but the political attitudes it expresses. It characterizes, probably for the first time in Scottish literature, the nationality of the Scots. The poem sets a trend that may be traced through the country's literature from the time of William Dunbar and the makars to that of Robert Fergusson and Robert Burns. Dunbar, in his "Lament for the Makaris," included Barbour in his roll call of Scottish poets. Fact or fiction, *The Bruce* became an important Scottish emblem of national unity.

Barbour's imaginative view of history, then, is a fictionalized recollection of certain historical persons and events. The short prologue to the narrative explains the purpose of the poem: to tell a true story that will preserve for posterity the noble deeds of Scotland's heroes in their fight against injustice. One purpose of the poem, then, is to point out the value of history. Its second purpose is to provide an appropriate literary vehicle that will be informative and entertaining. In the closing lines of the prologue Barbour promises that, with the grace of God, he will "say nocht bot suthfast thing!" His claim to tell a "suthfast" story and his concern with the practical utility of "aulde storys" indicate a moral purpose, but they also suggest another consideration for the author. As a court poet and the teller of a true story, Barbour had to take into consideration both political and historical implications. He was writing historical fiction, and the historical content of the work had to appear factual, representing a series of political events that had existed in an age apart from the immediate audience, but whose political consequences had lasting results with which succeeding generations could identify.

As literature, the poem continued to have an effect on future generations of readers who could still respond to it – particularly those writers of history and fiction who wanted to imitate, praise, or refute it. The "truth" of Barbour's text has been judged by the discriminations and perspectives of its immediate as well as its subsequent audiences at various points of retrospect. The narrative itself calls for the continuous refocusing of expectations and intentions. It attempts to correlate and interpret the truth and the integrity of its data as it seeks to bring meaning and value to its numerous patterns of interaction and to the mingling of dramatic and real situations that make up the historical fiction.

References:

G. W. S. Barrow, *The Kingdom of the Scots* (London: Edward Arnold, 1973);

Barrow, *Robert Bruce and the Community of the Realm of Scotland* (Los Angeles: University of California Press, 1965);

J. A. W. Bennett, *Middle English Literature 1100–1400,* edited and completed by Douglas Gray (Oxford: Clarendon Press, 1986);

Caroline Bingham, *The Stewart Kingdom of Scotland 1371–1603* (London: Weidenfeld & Nicolson, 1974);

Piero Boitani, *English Medieval Narrative in the 13th and 14th Centuries* (Cambridge: Cambridge University Press, 1982);

Lois A. Ebin, "John Barbour's Bruce: Poetry, History, and Propaganda," *Studies in Scottish Literature,* 9 (April 1972): 218–242;

Alexander M. Kinghorn, "Scottish Historiography in the 14th Century: A New Introduction to Barbour's Bruce," *Studies in Scottish Literature,* 6 (January 1969): 131–145;

Phoebe A. Mainster, "How To Make a Hero: Barbour's Recipe: Reshaping History As Romance," *Michigan Academician,* 20 (Spring 1988): 225–238;

Jacqueline Trace, "The Supernatural Element in Barbour's Bruce," *Massachusetts Studies in English,* 1 (Spring 1968): 55–65.

Geoffrey Chaucer
(1340? – 1400)

Jeffrey Helterman
University of South Carolina

MAJOR WORKS: Guillaume de Lorris, *The Romance of the Rose*, translated by Chaucer (early 1360s)

Manuscript: The only Middle English manuscript is *Romaunt of the Rose*, MS. V.3.7, in the Hunterian Museum, Glasgow.

First publication: In *The Workes of Geffray Chaucer Newly Printed, with dyuers Workes neuer in print before,* edited by W. Thynne (London: Printed by T. Godfray, 1532).

The Book of the Duchess (circa 1368–1369)

Manuscripts: There are three extant transcriptions, included in three manuscripts in the Bodleian Library, Oxford: Fairfax 16 (circa 1450), Tanner 346 (circa 1450), and Bodley 638 (circa 1430–1440).

First publication: In *The Workes of Geffray Chaucer Newly Printed, with dyuers Workes neuer in print before,* edited by W. Thynne (London: Printed by T. Godfray, 1532).

The Canterbury Tales (circa 1375–1400)

Manuscripts: Of the more than eighty whole or partial transcriptions of *The Canterbury Tales,* the bases for most editions are two of the earliest: the Hengwrt Manuscript at the National Library of Wales and the Ellesmere Manuscript at the Henry E. Huntington Library, both dating from 1400 to 1410 and thought to be the work of the same copyist, working under different editors. While some recent scholars consider the Hengwrt Manuscript to be the more accurate of the two, the Ellesmere Manuscript is the more complete, and its ordering of the tales is widely accepted. John M. Manly and Edith Rickert, editors of the comparative edition based on all known manuscripts of *The Canterbury Tales,* see the Hengwrt Manuscript as the earliest attempt — after the death of Chaucer — to arrange the unordered tales, and so closest to Chaucer's intentions. N. F. Blake, in *The Textual Tradition of the Canterbury Tales* (1985), has presented the strongest case for the primacy of the Hengwrt Manuscript. The Ellesmere Manuscript, more regular in spelling and dialect — as well as more complete — remains the choice of most modern editors.

First publication: *wHan that Apprill with his shouris sote* (Westminster: Printed by William Caxton, 1477).

The House of Fame (circa 1378–1381)

Manuscripts: There are two texts. Two manuscripts at the Bodleian Library, Bodley 638 (circa 1430–1440) and Fairfax 16 (circa 1450), both include transcriptions in the hand of the "A" copyist, while Pepys 2006 (circa 1450–1500) at Magdalene College, Cambridge, includes a copy in the hand of scribe "B." Most modern editions are based on the "A" text.

First publication: *The Book of Fame Made by G. Chaucer,* edited by William Caxton (Westminster: Printed by William Caxton, 1483).

The Parliament of Birds (circa 1378–1381)

Manuscripts: All of the fourteen extant manuscripts seem deficient. Modern editions are largely based on the texts in Cambridge University Library Gg 4.27 (circa 1420–1440) and in Fairfax 16 (circa 1450), in the Bodleian Library.

First publication: In *The lyf so short the craft so loge to lerne* (Westminster: Printed by William Caxton, 1477?).

Boethius, *Consolation of Philosophy (Boece)*, translated by Chaucer (circa 1380s)

Manuscripts: There are ten extant manuscripts, including two at Cambridge University Library — Ii.i. 38 and Ii.iii. 21 — on which modern editions are largely based.

First publication: *Boecius de consolacione* (Westminster: Printed by William Caxton, 1478?).

Miniature of Geoffrey Chaucer in the Ellesmere Manuscript of The Canterbury Tales, *a transcription dating from 1400 to 1410 (Henry E. Huntington Library and Art Gallery, EL 26 C9, fol. 153ᵛ)*

Troilus and Criseyde (circa 1382–1386)

Manuscripts: There are twenty extant manuscripts of which four represent fragments. Most modern editions are based on Corpus Christi College, Cambridge, MS. 61 (circa 1400) or Pierpont Morgan Library MS. 817 (formerly the Campsall Manuscript), a transcription made for Henry V when he was Prince of Wales (1399–1413).

First publication: *tThe [sic] double sorrow of Troylus to telle* (Winchester: Printed by William Caxton, 1483).

The Legend of Good Women (circa 1386)

Manuscripts: Modern editions are usually based on the transcriptions in Fairfax 16 (circa 1450) at the Bodleian Library and Gg 4.27 (circa 1420–1440) at Cambridge.

First publication: In *The Workes of Geffray Chaucer Newly Printed, with dyuers Workes neuer in print before,* edited by W. Thynne (London: Printed by T. Godfray, 1532).

COLLECTED EDITIONS: *The Complete Works of Geoffrey Chaucer,* edited by F. N. Robinson (Boston: Houghton Mifflin, 1933); revised as

The Works of Geoffrey Chaucer, Second Edition (Boston: Houghton Mifflin, 1957); revised as *The Riverside Chaucer, Third Edition,* edited by Larry D. Benson (Boston: Houghton Mifflin, 1987);

The Text of The Canterbury Tales, Studied on the Basis of All Known Manuscripts, 8 volumes, edited by John M. Manly and Edith Rickert (Chicago: University of Chicago Press, 1940);

The Complete Poetry and Prose of Geoffrey Chaucer, edited by John H. Fisher (New York: Holt, Rinehart & Winston, 1977; second edition, 1989);

A Variorum Edition of the Works of Geoffrey Chaucer, 3 volumes to date, Paul G. Ruggiers, general editor (Norman: University of Oklahoma Press, 1979–).

Perhaps the modern reader must first realize what a curious phenomenon it is that Geoffrey Chaucer became the first English author. It would have been surprising in the fourteenth century for anyone to think of writing in his native tongue, and this was particularly true for Chaucer's role models. The first impulse for a medieval writer who was writing something he wanted remembered was to write it in Latin. Latin was considered to be the *grammatica,* the language which would not change, the indestructible language. Cicero wrote in it a millennium and a half ago, and Cicero is still read, so it is not surprising that around 1307–1314, when Dante started out to write the *Commedia,* he started in Latin. Fortunately, he started in Hell, not in Heaven, because when he discovered he did not know enough Latin words for mud, dirt, and most political intrigues, he found that he could write it better in Italian.

Though Petrarch wrote his sonnets about his beloved Laura in Italian, he expected to be remembered for his Latin epic poems. In England during Chaucer's time, Latin was not so much the language of choice as was French. Since the Normans had ruled England for three hundred years, everyone who was anyone spoke and wrote in French. Chaucer's friend and rival, "moral Gower," wrote a treatise in Latin, the *Vox Clamantis* (circa 1379–1381), and one in French, the *Mirour de l'Omme* (circa 1376–1378), to match his great English work the *Confessio Amantis* (circa 1386). And so it was not at all assumed that an English writer would write in English, especially not someone in the odd personal circumstances of Chaucer.

Chaucer was probably quite comfortable with Latin since he translated Boethius's *Consolation of Philosophy* into English, and yet there is no reason to suspect that he did not have John Gower's fluency. For example, he often used French translations of Latin texts: the French *Livre Griseldis* instead of Petrarch's Latin version of the story of Griselda or the *Ovide Moralise* instead of the Latin *Metamorphoses*. Though his Latin was certainly better than that of William Shakespeare, whom Ben Jonson twitted about his small Latin and less Greek, it seems unlikely that he had the fluency even if he had the desire to write in Latin. That Chaucer did not write in French is more surprising; his French must have been quite good. In addition to the evidence of his translation of *The Romance of the Rose*, it is clear that the upper class of England still spoke French in their daily lives. They were still Normans, and their French separated them from the lower-class Saxons. Though Chaucer was not of the upper class, he married into it and shockingly high up. His wife, Philippa, was the sister of Katherine Swynford, the third wife of John of Gaunt, and so Chaucer was the brother-in-law of the most powerful man in England, even, as Shakespeare reminds us in *Richard II* (1595), more powerful than the king himself.

Because of Chaucer's unlikely alliance with the center of Norman power, one might suppose that he would write in French to impress his in-laws and their circle. After all, he could never be as rich or powerful as John of Gaunt, but he could write better – even in French – than his Norman relatives. Chaucer was apparently of an age with Gaunt, who was born in 1340, and both were married to daughters of the French knight Sir Paon de Roet. For Chaucer the marriage appears to have been a small step up; for Gaunt, this marriage, his third, was such a long step down that many of the wives of his peers refused to appear in court any longer. Gaunt had married his mistress of many years, probably to legitimize the offspring of their union (all the English kings after Henry VI came from this line). No one was shocked at his having a mistress, but they were horrified that Gaunt married the daughter of a poor French knight. Some historians suggest that he had gotten both sisters pregnant, and that Chaucer's marriage to Philippa, on or before 12 September 1366, helped Gaunt out of some difficulty. Though some critics have attributed Chaucer's perceived bitterness toward the institution of marriage to this loveless union, one might better understand his motives by realizing that marriages, even at Chaucer's relatively low social level, had nothing to do with love and everything to do with property and rank. Despite the views of Anya Seton's romantic novel, John did not marry his mistress out of love, but to legitimize her sons.

Chaucer must have seen his own marriage as a way into the world of the aristocracy. Of all the Canterbury pilgrims (and there is a "Chaucer"), the one who most closely approximates his situation is the social-climbing Franklin, a man heartily concerned with the gentility of his son. Chaucer's own son, Thomas, became one of the richest men in London, and *his* great-grandson (who died on the battlefield) was named heir apparent to the throne of England.

Chaucer had all these incentives to write in French, but he chose instead to write in English, the language of Saxon England. As Sir Walter Scott pointed out, the Saxon language can name only barnyard animals on the hoof. If one fed a domestic animal, one called it by its Saxon name, *sheep*, but if one ate it, one called it by its French name, *mouton*, which soon became *mutton*. This distinction is linguistic class distinction in Chaucer's England: if one raised a farm animal, one was a Saxon and called it by its English name; if one were rich enough to eat it, one named it in French: *calf/veau* (veal); *chicken/poulet* (pullet); *pig/porc* (pork). Chaucer did not try, however, to impress his relatives with his French, and when he wrote about farm animals he stood Scott on his head. True to Scott's model, the widow who raises Chauntecleer and Pertelote lives in a world of one-syllable Saxon words, "Milk and broun breed, . . . / Seynd bacoun, and somtyme an ey [egg] or tweye," while her Norman chickens exist in a Frenchified world where the "faire damoysele Pertelote" is "Curteys . . . , discreet, and debonaire, / And compaignable." But Chaucer gives the Saxons their first revenge for 1066. Chauntecleer, for all his French words and fancy manners, escapes only the French fox, Reynard; one day he will be stuffed and roasted for the widow's table.

One of the best ways of imagining the world in which Chaucer grew up is to picture him as a character in Shakespeare's *Richard II*. Although Chaucer belonged to the previous generation, the world of Richard's uncles, Duke Lionel and John of Gaunt, it is important to understand that he was always on the fringes of this world of political intrigue. There is still a nineteenth-century image of Chaucer in his father's London tavern preparing to write *The Canterbury Tales* (circa 1375–1400) by analyzing the customers. The fact that he was the descendant of a man named Le Taverner certainly plays a part in this misconception, and the poet himself has fostered this image by his self-portraits in *The Book of the Duchess* (circa 1368–1369) and *The House of Fame*

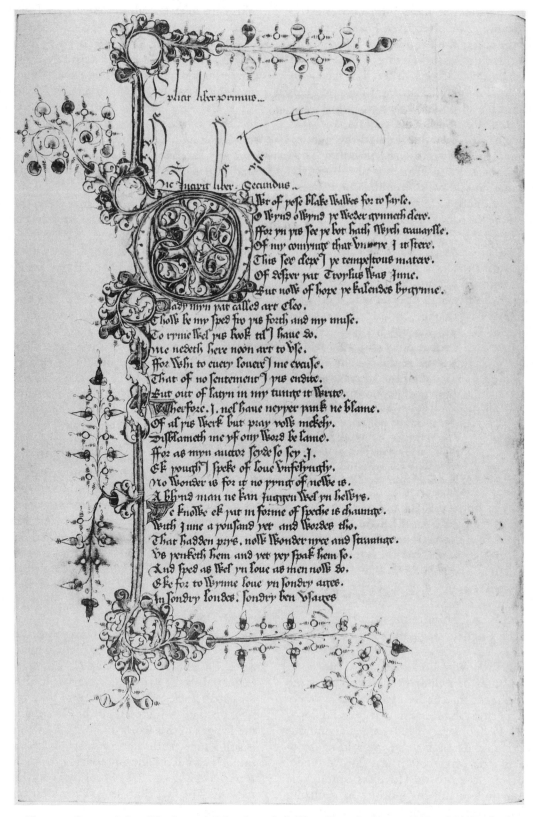

First page of a transcription of Troilus and Criseyde *made for Henry V sometime between 1399 and 1413, when he was Prince of Wales (Pierpont Morgan Library, Lewis Cass Ledyard Fund, MS. 817)*

(circa 1378–1381) as an innocent, overweight bookworm. Nothing could be further from the truth.

The son of John and Agnes (de Copton) Chaucer, Geoffrey Chaucer was descended immediately from two generations of wealthy vintners who had everything but a title, a thing that no imagined amount of money could buy. What could be bought was position, and in 1357 Chaucer began pursuing this assiduously as a squire in the court of Elizabeth, Countess of Ulster, the wife of Lionel, Earl of Ulster (later Duke of Clarence). Also in service at this court was Philippa Pan, probably his own age; that is, both were teenagers. She is probably the same Philippa, daughter of Paon (hence Pan) de Roet, whom Chaucer eventually married in 1366. As an esquire Chaucer would have served as a gentleman's gentleman in a time before this phrase designated a butler. A young man in this position would be in service to the aristocrats of the court. His duties would include such butlerly tasks as making beds and fastening shirts. Since there were always twenty young men on duty in this household, such duties could not have been very onerous, and it is likely that one of the burdens that fell on these young men was the entertainment of nobles. The way must have opened quickly for a young man who could both tell stories and compose songs. The countess was French, so French poets such as Guillaume de Machaut and Eustache Deschamps provided an early inspiration, and his earliest poems, *The Book of the Duchess* and *The Parliament of Birds,* rest on a heavy French base. At the duchess's castle at Hatfield, Chaucer made the acquaintance of the man who would most deeply influence his political career, John of Gaunt, Duke of Lancaster.

Chaucer's first major work, *The Book of the Duchess,* is an elegy on the death of Blanche, John of Gaunt's first wife. For this reason the poem can be dated with some certainty. Blanche died of the plague in 1368, and Gaunt married Constance of Castile in 1372. The poem must have appeared between these two dates for Gaunt to be portrayed as an inconsolable widower.

The poem, though filled with traditional French flourishes, develops its originality around the relationship between the narrator, a fictionalized version of the poet, and the mourner, the Man in Black, who represents Gaunt. Though there has been some interest in the source of the allegory – the death of Blanche is seen as the loss of a game of chess – Chaucer's originality is seen in his handling of the naive narrator. In all his incarnations, this narrator is always meant to be a cartoon version of Chaucer (in *The House of Fame* he is called Geoffrey), and his naiveté is a tool that Chaucer exploits everywhere.

In *The Book of the Duchess* the narrator seems to miss the point of everything. He reads the story of Ceys and Alcione, a story whose point is consolation, and appears to think that it is a story about cures for sleeplessness. The narrator's chief naiveté is in relation to the Man in Black. Although he hears the Man complain that Death has taken his Lady, he acts as if he has never heard this lament. He becomes particularly obtuse when the Man in Black says that he has lost a game at chess at Fortune. The obtuseness, however, forces the Man in Black to face his loss without the comfortable protection of allegory. The narrator's naiveté becomes a sounding board against which the Man in Black must assert both the value of his love and the reality of losing her.

In *The Book of the Duchess,* especially through the instrument of the naive narrator, Chaucer begins to develop a concealment model of the language of fiction rather than a communication model. What becomes most interesting and, oddly enough, most useful to characters is what they misunderstand. At the beginning of this poem, the narrator is suffering from an unknown malady (which is presumably unrequited love). Since he cannot deal with the malady, the narrator sets out to deal with the symptom – sleeplessness. From here on, he always misinterprets. He reads a story of consolation but finds in it only a sleeping potion; he dreams of a hunt where the "hert" (stag) disappears and thinks he has missed the "hert-huntyng." For this reason, he is content to follow a puppy instead of the hounds, but the puppy leads him to the Man in Black whose "herte" (heart) is in hiding. The narrator acts as if he thinks the Man in Black is mourning the lost hart, while he finds (invents) a tale to recover the man's lost heart.

It is at this point that the reader begins to realize that the narrator's mistakes are necessary. For example, if he sees the issue of consolation in Ceys and Alcione, the problem will be settled before he gets to the Man in Black. If he openly acknowledges that the Man in Black's loss is his heart, he will only be able to offer empty words of consolation. Instead, his irritating misunderstanding forces the Man in Black to re-create his love, to de-allegorize his loss (Blanche as the "goode faire White" was too easy to allegorize as the losing side in a chess game), and finally to recognize that it would have been a greater sorrow never to have loved her than to have loved her and lost her. In searching (cleansing) the Black Knight's wound, the narrator finally faces his own; that is, the love that he seeks is worth the pain that it costs in the seeking. Thus when the narrator says near the end of this poem, "al was doon, / For that tyme, the hert-huntyng," he is no longer talking about deer hunting, but about the cure for a broken heart.

Chaucer also makes use of the naive narrator in *The House of Fame,* a poem which has been tied by scholars to events in the courts of Richard II, of Gaunt, or of Lionel, but none of these theories has been convincing enough to refute the others. What is clear is that Chaucer had been reading Dante, and he provided a comic version of the guide-narrator relationship of Dante and Virgil in the *Commedia.* The talkative Eagle guides the naive "Chaucer" just as the naive Dante is guided by the gossipy Virgil. There are many comic touches as the Eagle gives new meaning to the term *captive audience.* Though it seems as though the Eagle's lecture is going to be boring, "Chaucer," in the grasp of the Eagle's talons, is hardly in a position to say "no, I'm not interested in your story."

In this poem Chaucer tries on the role he would use more effectively in *Troilus and Criseyde* — the historian of love who is himself a failure in love. The Eagle takes him to the House of Fame (Rumor), which is even more the house of tales. Here Chaucer makes a case for the preeminence of story. The inhabitants of the House of Fame are asked whether they want to be great lovers or to be remembered as great lovers, and all choose the latter: the story is more important than the reality.

A third dream-vision poem, *The Parliament of Birds* (circa 1378–1381), has been tied to several occasions and corresponding dates. As with *The House of Fame,* there is much disagreement over what these events are. Perhaps the accuracy with which *The Book of the Duchess* can be dated has led literary historians to expect too much of the allegory. *The Book of the Duchess* is datable because of the elaborate puns on "Blanche" and "Lancaster" in the poem. There is no comparable evidence in either *The House of Fame* or *The Parliament of Birds,* so scholars have had to look for parallel situations where the primary question is "In what ways is Anne of Bohemia like this bird?" The problematics of such an approach has led some critics to see the poem as a beast fable with no particular occasional reference and only a debate about the running of parliamentary government.

The Parliament of Birds has as its subject a flock of birds of the noble class (eagles and hawks) arguing over who has priority in a love match with a female eagle. After a long wrangle in which the lower orders of birds get involved, the hoped-for wedding is put off. This conclusion has led historians to try to figure out to which delayed betrothal contract the poem refers. The occasion for the poem has been seen as the negotiations for the betrothal of Richard II to Marie, Princess of France, in 1377 or his successful betrothal to Anne of Bohemia in 1379, or the end of further negotiations which culminated in the marriage in 1381. Taking a different approach to dating (whose end is establishing the order of composition of the texts), it has been noted that in *The Parliament of Birds* Chaucer changed from the eight-syllable couplets he was using in *The Book of the Duchess* and *The House of Fame* and started using the seven-line pentameter stanza that he would use in *Troilus.* If one assumes that the change is an abandonment of an old form and style, then the order of these poems is *The Book of the Duchess, The House of Fame, The Parliament of Birds,* and *Troilus and Criseyde* (circa 1382–1386).

Despite frequent echoes from Guillaume de Lorris's section of *The Romance of the Rose, The Parliament of Birds* seems to be an indictment of courtly love as Chaucer had found it in the French poem, so that when the dreamer enters the Garden of Love he finds it filled with allegorical figures such as Foolhardiness, Bribery of Servants, and Flattery and Jealousy, who represent the worst aspects of love. Opposed to Venus, the guardian spirit of courtly love, is Nature, who hopes to effect the marriage of all the birds so that they can go out and propagate their species and by extension all nature. Their marriages are prevented, however, by the failure of the noble birds to settle their differences over a matter of courtly love: who has priority in love? Each of the male eagles has a different answer: the one who loves first; the one who loves most; or the one who suffers most. The other birds, exasperated by the courtly love quandary of the noble birds, get into the act with views of love that represent their social classes. Chaucer appears to have divided the birds into four classes that match the standard medieval conception of the social hierarchy. The hunting birds (eagles, hawks) represent the nobles, the worm eaters (cuckoos) represent the bourgeois, the water fowl are the merchants, and the seed eaters (turtledoves) are the landed farming interests. Each class is given a distinctive voice, so that when the sparrow hawk complains sarcastically about the "parfit resoun of a goos," the reader knows what he means: the goose, in his examples of, and metaphors for, love has made love mercantile and goose foolish.

The disorder caused by courtly love ruins the scheme of "commune profyt" that would keep this commonwealth of birds functioning, and as such it touches one of Chaucer's favorite social issues: in

The beginning of "The Knight's Tale" in the Ellesmere Manuscript (Henry E. Huntington Library and Art Gallery,
EL 26 C9, fol. 10ʳ)

"The Clerk's Tale" Walter forgoes the "commune profyt" of his realm so that he can pursue his obsessive testing of Griselda's love. In *The Parliament of Birds* Chaucer examines themes that will pervade his later work. The conflict between Nature and courtly love will be a major issue in *Troilus and Criseyde* and especially in "The Knight's Tale," where Palamon and Arcite's argument about who has priority in loving Emily comes right out of the arguments for the "hand" of the female eagle. Perhaps more significant is the experiment with different voices for all the characters and social classes of birds. Such differentiation would become the benchmark of *The Canterbury Tales*.

As a courtier of some rank, Chaucer found his service to the nobility quickly escalating beyond making beds. In the late 1350s he was in military service in France with John of Gaunt. Chaucer was soon to serve England in peace as well as war, as part of several embassies to France and Italy. These often involved delicate personal matters of the royal family, such as the betrothal of Richard II, who succeeded his grandfather, Edward III, to the throne in 1377 at the age of nine.

By 1374 Chaucer was firmly involved in domestic politics and was granted the important post of controller of customs taxes on hides, skins, and wool. In addition to the direct income of ten pounds a year, the position had the added remuneration of fees and fines for those who tried to evade customs. The position was no sinecure, and Chaucer had to keep the records himself as well as oversee the collectors. It is notable that the collectors themselves became important men in the business life of London, with at least one of them becoming lord mayor. These were prosperous times for Chaucer; his wife had gotten a large annuity, and they were living rent free in a house above the city gate at Aldgate. Thus Chaucer would have felt comfortable with the men of substance on the Canterbury pilgrimage, where he would have ridden in company with the Merchant, Franklin, and Man of Law.

Chaucer's love affair with the Italian language, nurtured by his visits in 1372–1373 to Genoa and Florence and in 1378 to Lombardy, flowered in the following decade with his composition of *Troilus and Criseyde*. This poem, considered by some to be the first English novel, takes its story line from Giovanni Boccaccio's *Il Filostrato* (1335–1340), but its inspiration from Dante's love for Beatrice as told in the *Convito* (1307) and from Petrarch's love for Laura as manifested in the sonnets. Though many critics have insisted that the poem presents an ironic view of romantic love in

which Troilus confuses passion (*cupiditas*) with celestial love (*caritas*), Chaucer is presenting a case for ennobling passion which fits with the French romances he had read in his youth; only in *Troilus and Criseyde* this romance takes a particularly Italian turn. The most telling demonstration of this development is an odd piece of borrowing done by Chaucer, in which a passage from Boccaccio is deliberately put in the wrong poem.

When Chaucer borrowed his plot for "The Knight's Tale" from Boccaccio's *Teseida* (1341), he left out the apotheosis of Arcite. In *Teseida* Arcite's spirit ascends to a sphere of a classical heaven. Not only does Chaucer leave out Arcite's flight to heaven, but the knight claims that his source says nothing about the fate of Arcite's soul. It has been suggested that Chaucer left out Arcite's ascent to heaven because heaven has no place at the beginning of *The Canterbury Tales* and only becomes significant as the pilgrims approach Canterbury.

Chaucer, however, did not forget the passage, and he inserted it, not in "The Knight's Tale," but into *Troilus and Criseyde,* immediately after Troilus's death. At this point in his poem he is translating almost word for word from Boccaccio. The result of this insertion is that a situation which is desperate in *Il Filostrato* becomes sublime in *Troilus and Criseyde*. In *Il Filostrato* Troilo is killed, and the narrator says over and over that this is the end of Troilo's "ill-conceived" love for Criseyda. In the English poem Troilus is killed; then Chaucer inserts the passage from the *Teseida,* so that Troilus ascends to heaven (with words meant originally for Arcite); then the narrator says such an end Troilus had for love, but this end is now triumph, not tragedy. If books were not so expensive, one could imagine Chaucer cutting out the passage from the *Teseida* and pasting it in the appropriate spot in *Il Filostrato*.

This alteration allowed Chaucer to use brilliantly the naive narrator in this poem. The narrator considers himself above love and sets as his task to tell the double sorrow of Troilus in love: the pain of falling in love with Criseyde and the pain of losing her. The narrator's standpoint is that of a moral, Christian man who has forsaken earthly love for the hope of divine love. His assumption is that Troilus has sacrificed heaven for his ill-conceived love for Criseyde. After all, he has read Boccaccio's version where Troilo simply dies – better to eschew love and go to heaven. Nevertheless, the narrator is sorely tried when he watches Troilus and Criseyde consummate their love, and he, who was once proud of his lack of experience in love, says "O blisful nyght of hem so longe isought, / . . . / Why nad I swich oon with my soule ybought / . . . ?" Yet this gasp of desire is stifled by his knowledge that ultimately he is right and Troilus is wrong. Imagine his surprise when he finds Troilus in heaven. This was not supposed to happen; the story – Boccaccio's story – says that Troilus just dies, but Chaucer has changed the ending, and the morally superior narrator is in for a shock when he discovers that Troilus has his love and heaven, too.

The claim that *Troilus and Criseyde* is the first English novel is based on the way Chaucer handled the psychology of the main characters. They are always operating at two levels of response, verbal and intellectual. For Criseyde, this usually comes out as a she thought/she said duality, which happens so often that the reader comes to wonder what she is thinking anytime she says anything. This duality is less common in the men, but only because they have each other to confide in. Their duality is between what they say to Criseyde and what they say to each other.

The poem analyzes the artifices of love as well as the complex motivations of lovers. This analysis often has been seen as an ironic view of romantic love, but this interpretation assumes that falling in love is as simple as it is for Tristan and Isolde. The first half of the poem, the seduction of Criseyde, is necessitated by the literary models followed by Pandarus, her uncle. There is, for example, no good reason why the love of Troilus and Criseyde has to be secret. Unlike Tristan and Isolde or Launcelot and Guinevere, there is no adultery involved. Pandarus, however, has been getting his notion of love from literary models such as Andreas Capellanus's *Art of Courtly Love* (circa 1174). Andreas insists there can be no love between partners in an arranged marriage and so sets up an elaborate system for adulterous love. Pandarus, a self-confessed failure in love, promotes the affair by the book until his involvement pushes the limits of vicarious pleasure, "And so we may ben gladed [gladdened], alle thre."

The seduction of Criseyde is programmed to exploit her tenuous position as the daughter of a traitor and to force her to turn to Troilus for protection. Two plots are set in motion: the Poliphete plot, in which rumors are spread that Poliphete wants her, as the traitor Calchas's daughter, out of Troy; and the Horaste plot, in which she is accused of being the lover of Horaste (Orestes). Both plots put Troilus, Criseyde, and a bed in the same place. In each case Troilus is set up as a rock in a stormy sea of politics. Criseyde is never allowed to forget

that Troilus is the king's son and, after Hector, the strongest man in Troy. While Pandarus and Troilus are manipulating her, Criseyde is in many ways their match. She is, for example, always aware that they are less than frank with her. Criseyde is actually more experienced than either of the men. She is, after all, a widow, not a virgin, and her responses to Pandarus's devices are always complex. In this situation Troilus is the emotional virgin. He is the one who swoons first and who falls in love at first sight. In a typical reaction, when Pandarus tells Criseyde that Troilus must see her at night, she agrees because his condition seems wretched, because she loves Troilus more than anything, because the dark night will hide his coming, and because he is coming through a secret entrance. She is always both passionate and practical.

Perhaps Pandarus's most despicable device is his reifying of the metaphor of heartbreak. It is given of the Petrarchan view of love as well as of *The Romance of the Rose* that the lady's coldness will break the lover's heart. Pandarus accuses Criseyde of desiring Troilus's death. One might say that Pandarus is overplaying the metaphor, but then he makes the metaphor real by drawing his dagger and threatening to stab himself if Troilus dies of a broken heart due to Criseyde's coldness. Whatever she thinks of the metaphoric "death" of Troilus, her uncle's threat is with a real knife. In this way guilt is added to Criseyde's fear in an effort to destabilize her and throw her into the arms of Troilus.

The elaborate fictions that have been used to establish this romance become the reason for its destruction. When Calchas demands his daughter in exchange for a Trojan prisoner of war, only Hector stands up to the Trojan council. He equates the giving up of Criseyde with the sanctioning of prostitution, "We usen here no wommen for to selle," and it is clear that if Troilus added his voice to his brother's then Criseyde would not be sent to the Greek camp. The secrecy – unnecessary in its origins – of the affair makes it impossible for Troilus to stand up for Criseyde, and she is sent to her father.

It has been said that she falls too quickly for the Greek warrior Diomedes, but her actions are entirely explainable by the way Troilus and Pandarus have programmed her behavior. They have deliberately undermined her sense of security and stability so that she would fall for Troilus as a tower of strength, a strong man in an enemy camp. Diomedes simply pushes the same buttons, and she is his. In a comic scene the huge Greek champion echoes Troilus, the swooning swain. Diomedes quavers and blushes as he proffers his

*Miniature of the Wife of Bath in the Ellesmere Manuscript
(Henry E. Huntington Library and Art Gallery, EL 26
C9, fol. 72ʳ)*

love: love becomes a wall of steel, the stone of certainty, and he becomes the lover of Love. Finally, Troilus goes beyond both of his mentors to something at once higher and lower. He loves Criseyde for herself, for no reason at all. This love is not shaken by Pandarus's doubts or by Criseyde's betrayal; he says "I ne kan nor may . . . unloven yow a quarter of a day" at a point where Boccaccio's Troilo condemns and curses her.

Troilus goes essentially from being Romeo in love with Rosaline to Romeo in love with Juliet, a distinction already made by Petrarch. Petrarch's *rime* (poems) to Laura are in two groups divided by a simple fact, her death. The sonnets in "Vita di ma donna Laura" are artificial, conventional poems filled with such tropes as oxymoron, antithesis, hyperbole, and conceit. The style was so conventional that the French poets had a verb, *Petrarquizer,* to write like Petrarch. The sonnets change radically after Laura's death, as the artifices fall away in his attempt to re-create the true Laura. The same change occurs in Troilus after the absence of Criseyde. He has been a Petrarchist, who in fact spouts Petrarch. His first song, *Cantus Troili,* is a sonnet of Petrarch's, but after Criseyde's absence these artifices will not serve to re-create the missing Criseyde, and, in fact, the first physical description of Criseyde occurs only in book 5. Until this point, she had merely been the ideal beloved. Only in the last book does she become a real woman. She even has a flaw in her beauty: her eyebrows are too close together. Through his trials Troilus learns, as have Dante and Petrarch before him, that loving a real woman is the only real love.

In the prologue to *The Legend of Good Women* (circa 1386), Chaucer castigates himself for doing a disservice to love by publishing the unfaithfulness of women. In this poem the poet figure responds to this charge from the god of love by telling stories of faithful women, love's martyrs. It was at about this time that Chaucer's friend John Gower was writing his work on a similar theme, *Confessio amantis* (The Lover's Confession, circa 1390–1392), and there is some sense of rivalry between the two poets. Gower, however, turned his poem into his masterpiece, while Chaucer seemed to tire quickly of *The Legend of Good Women* and left it unfinished. The most original and interesting part of this poem is the prologue, which, among other things, names and sometimes critiques the poems that Chaucer had written up to this time. The list is particularly interesting because it includes some works, such as *Troilus and Criseyde,* that critics see as stylistically more advanced than *The Legend of Good Women.* If

tender love to Criseyde with small nods and gestures.

Though the subtlety of the love games and the deviousness of the player are greater than in Boccaccio, Chaucer's understanding of love takes on a new quality when he leaves that model altogether. Both Dante and Petrarch begin by seeing love as artifice and then show how love breaks free of that artifice. In the *Convito* Dante tells of using a screen lady when he becomes enamored of Beatrice. This is a woman who sits between him and Beatrice at church. Because of her position, Dante can pretend to be looking at her while in fact he is looking at Beatrice. Then Dante writes sonnets to this lady. He has to learn to be a love poet before he can be Beatrice's poet. Dante then reports that he becomes Love's poet, that is, the celebrant of Cupid and love in the abstract. Finally, a voice tells him it is time to put away simulacra, and he becomes the poet in love with Beatrice. Troilus follows three similar steps. Under Pandarus's guidance he becomes a courtly lover by the book, who uses all the conventional attitudes expected of lovers. Then Troilus emulates Criseyde's metaphysical expectations of critics see this poem as more primitive than poems that certainly antedate it by virtue of being on this list, then the list calls into question the whole enterprise of the dating of Chaucer's works by cues such as style or literary influence (a French or Italian period). The legends themselves, of such martyrs to love as Dido, Cleopatra, and Ariadne, are treated with such an unsympathetic voice that some critics have seen the poem as a parody of such collections of stories of martyred women that Chaucer left off when the joke got old.

Although there has been movement in this century to see the finished (Chaucer would say "parfit") *Troilus and Criseyde* as his masterpiece, it is *The Canterbury Tales* that is the measure of his greatness. Though this fact is not surprising, the reasons for it may be. Although unfinished, the work is a brilliant advance on the frame tale as practiced by Boccaccio in *The Decameron* (1349–1351). It should be noted that Petrarch, who knew Boccaccio fairly well, did not know of *The Decameron,* so there is no certainty that Chaucer knew of its existence either. Since, in the days before printing, fragments of a manuscript were gathered with no concern for a whole work or even an individual author, it would be possible to prove that Chaucer knew a tale from *The Decameron* without assuming he was aware of the whole book. This seems to be the case with Petrarch, who knew Boccaccio from his Latin works. Both Italians were prouder of their Latin achievements than their work in the vernacular. Chaucer's favorite works of Boccaccio, *Teseida* (source of "The Knight's Tale") and *Il Filostrato* (source of *Troilus and Criseyde*), are in Italian, and it makes sense that Chaucer, avid book collector that he was, would have sought a copy of *The Decameron* if he knew of its existence. In any case, it is helpful to set out *The Decameron* as a model of the frame-tale narrative in order to see what Chaucer is doing in *The Canterbury Tales.*

The pretext for storytelling in Boccaccio is a plague in Florence which sends a group of ten nobles to the country to escape the Black Death. For each of ten days, they each tell a tale. Each day's tales are grouped around a common topic or narrative subject. Boccaccio, perhaps straitened by the need to tell ten tales on the same topic, has one escape valve each day: one teller who can improvise a subject. The tales, all one hundred of them, are completed; the plague ends in Florence; and the nobles return to the city.

Set against this model, Chaucer's innovation is revealed. Far from being noble, his tale-tellers run the spectrum of the middle class, from the Knight to the Pardoner and the Summoner. The Knight and the wealthy ecclesiastics (Prioress, Monk, Friar) are introduced first. The Summoner, who tells an obscene tale, and the Pardoner, from whom one is expected, are described last. If this list were mere reportage of the events, the Miller, who leads them out of town, should be the first person described, and the Reeve, who brings up the rear (partly to stay away from the Miller), should be the last. When the tales begin it looks as if this social order will be followed. Though straws are drawn to determine the first teller, Chaucer gives the first straw to the Knight, and when he is finished, place is given to the Monk, one of the high-ranking ecclesiastics. But the Monk is not destined to tell his story at this point.

Though George Lyman Kittredge, the dean of American Chaucerians, sees most of the tales as centering on discussions of marriage, what may be occurring in the frame tale of Canterbury storytelling is the social-climbers' revenge. "The Knight's Tale," for all its Italian origins, is a tale that Jean Froissart, the chronicler of Edward III and the Hundred Years' War, would approve – it is an upper-class entertainment. Though it is nominally set in ancient Greece, the details, especially of the tournament, are fourteenth-century English. It is unlikely that Chaucer would have been aware of this anachronism, but he would have been aware that "The Knight's Tale" is just the kind of tale that Froissart might have told to the approval of Chaucer's father-in-law, Sir Paon de Roet, and that this sort of tale was the typical entertainment in the courts of Duke Lionel, and of the king. When "The Knight's Tale" is finished, it is established as a noble tale, one, in fact, that the better class of pilgrims should memorize. In a sense it would seem that the storytelling contest is over before it begins. Yet before the Knight is allowed to rest on his laurels, the Miller interrupts with a "noble" tale of his own. His tale – among other things, a lower-class parody of the plot outlined in "The Knight's Tale" (two apparently similar men fight over the same woman) – becomes the first tale motivated by answering the previous tale. The Miller's word *quite* (require) becomes the energizing force behind the tale-telling. Each character uses his tale as a weapon or tool to get back at or even with the previous tale-teller. Compare this linkage with *The Decameron,* where the tales of the day hang statically on the pegs of topic; not even the plague impacts much on Boccaccio's tale-telling. His tales, clever as they are, just sit there.

Not so in Chaucer. Once the Miller has established the principle of "quiting," each tale generates the next. The Reeve, who takes offense because

"The Miller's Tale" is about a cuckolded carpenter (the Reeve had been a carpenter in his youth), tells a tale about a cuckolded miller, who also gets beaten up after his daughter is deflowered. As in many of the tales, subtle distinctions of class become the focal point of the story. The social-climbing miller, Simkyn, is upset mostly that his daughter has slept with the wrong class of man. It is not so much that she has been deflowered, but disparaged (had sex with a man of a lower social class). From this point in the tale-telling, each tale becomes the motive for the tale or several tales which follow it.

The neatest example of this quiting principle is seen in the group of tales beginning with the Wife of Bath's and ending with the Clerk's. In her long prologue the Wife stirs up first the Pardoner and then the Friar, but she also issues a challenge to the Clerk saying that clerks, because they are men, are incapable of praising women. Therefore, she challenges the Clerk to tell a tale which praises women. After the Wife's tale, the Friar and Summoner have at each other, the Friar telling of a rascally summoner and the Summoner of an evil friar. In their tales the two tellers reflect the personalities ascribed to them in the "General Prologue." "The Friar's Tale" is as elegant as he is, and the gross, garlic-eating Summoner tells an obscene tale filled with ill winds of all kinds. The last turn in this grouping is the Clerk's tale of patient Griselda. Though the Clerk does nothing but praise Griselda, thus responding to the Wife's challenge, he does it in such a way that Griselda's wifely virtue, her perfect obedience to her husband, seems a monstrous kind of womanly and motherly behavior. Though Chaucer provides a framework in which Griselda's behavior – allowing her children to be taken to what she believes to be their deaths according to her husband's whim – is acceptable, he will then undercut this frame with another ending. Chaucer first offers what is essentially Petrarch's idea of the tale, which reads Griselda's behavior allegorically: Griselda's incomprehensible obedience to Walter is a model for man's unquestioning acceptance of God's judgments. Just when Griselda's behavior is normalized as allegory, Chaucer adds a second ending, which warns men that they had better not test their wives the way Walter tested Griselda because they may find that they have married not Patient Griselda but the irritable Alice of Bath.

Chaucer's refusal to let his tale end conventionally is typical of the way he handles familiar stories. He wants to have it both ways, and he reminds the reader of this constantly. In "The Nun's Priest's Tale," for example, he argues both against an alle-gorical reading of the tale, "My tale is of a cok," and for it, "Taketh the fruyt, and lat the chaf be stille."

At work in the presentation of Griselda as a good woman is an important Chaucerian device, a false syllogism based on the movement from the specific to the general back to the specific again, although the specific now occupies a new moral ground. The Clerk praises Griselda, who as a good wife (specific) is also a good woman (general). The Clerk never spells out the inference that results from the movement back to the specific. Griselda, the good wife and woman, leaves her children to be murdered. If she is a bad mother, then she should also be a bad woman, but the Clerk, in his "contract" with the Wife, will never dispraise women, so he never completes the syllogism.

Almost every time Chaucer offers a list of examples, he is playing with this disparity between the general and the specific. In "The Merchant's Tale," when January, in his haste to get married, offers examples of good women from the Bible, he misses the fact that all of his good women were deceivers or destroyers of their husbands or lovers. Rebecca deceived her husband, as did Esther, and Judith chopped off the head of Holofernes; good women certainly, but not, as January thinks, a very convincing argument to get married. Chaucer often combines this trick with a basic notion about the way stories are used to avoid confrontations with the truth. In "The Franklin's Tale" Dorigen promises the squire Aurelius that she will sleep with him if he accomplishes the impossible task of removing the rocks from along the coast of Brittany. By a trick, Aurelius removes the rocks, and Dorigen, a married woman, sees only one out: death before dishonor – but then, instead of plunging the blade into her breast, she begins regaling herself with tales of good wives who chose death before dishonor. Gradually her list drifts to good wives who chose death after dishonor, and finally, moving from the specific to the general, stories of good wives. She then concludes that, since good wives are obedient to their husbands, she will run and ask her husband what to do, hoping he will not recommend death before dishonor. Dorigen spends three days "purposing ever" to die, and then, as a good wife, she runs and asks her husband for guidance, even though, in a unique arrangement, he had made her sovereign in their marriage.

As Chaucer worked against the impossibility of finishing *The Canterbury Tales* according to the original plan – 120 tales, 4 told by each of thirty pilgrims (in the Middle Ages, which had many systems based on 12, 120 was as round a number as the 100 of *The Decameron*) – he began to consider the nature of finishing an act of storytelling. In *The Canterbury*

Tales, in addition to several unfinished tales (the Cook's, the Squire's), there are two tales that are interrupted by other pilgrims: Chaucer's own "Tale of Sir Thopas" and "The Monk's Tale." In handling these tales, Chaucer moves into issues, particularly that of closure, that are only now appearing in the theory of fiction. In "The Franklin's Tale" Chaucer had shown how Dorigen avoids the moral imperative of suicide by telling tales about the moral imperative of suicide. "The Monk's Tale" includes a complicated meditation on what a tale is: when does an episode or an embedded tale become a tale itself? The Monk had been chosen as the second teller but had been interrupted and silenced. When he is invited, later on in the pilgrimage, to take his turn and tell his story, he promises to tell a collection of stories, which have in common the fact that they are all tragedies. He says he has a hundred of these stories, and he will tell them all as his tale. Perhaps this is his payback for being interrupted by the Miller. Though such a project would be as long as *The Decameron,* no one interrupts the Monk at first because his tales, the Fall of Lucifer and the Fall of Adam – that is, the plot of John Milton's *Paradise Lost* (1667, 1674) – are only a stanza long. Gradually, however, his tales begin to get tales embedded within them (the tale of Hercules has twelve labors, each a potential tale) so that they become multistanzaic. Finally, the Knight has to interrupt the Monk. Though the Knight says that the dreariness of the tragedies is the reason for the interruption, the reader remembers that the Knight, in his own tale, insisted on not adding digressive embedded tales because he wants everyone to get a chance to tell his tale. The Monk is interrupted because his tale is potentially endless, and his hundred tragedies could scuttle the whole Canterbury tale-telling enterprise.

Conversely, the pilgrim Chaucer's "Tale of Sir Thopas" is filled with problems of not knowing how to start a tale and, for that reason, presents as much of a hazard to the tale-telling as the Monk's. "Chaucer's" tale-telling constantly suffers narrative letdown as sentences and stanzas build up to jarring anticlimaxes. As the knight errant, Sir Thopas, rides out in search of adventure, the phrase "Ther spryngen" promises a tiger or at least a panther, but typical of the pattern of the story, the only things that leap out at the doughty knight are grass and weeds: "Ther spryngen herbes grete and smale." If "The Monk's Tale" is interrupted because he does not know how to end it, then Chaucer's tale is interrupted by Harry Bailey because "Chaucer" does not know how to begin it. The poet Chaucer, with sto-

Early miniature portrait of Chaucer, commissioned by Thomas Hoccleve for a manuscript of his Regement of Princes *(1411–1412), which includes a tribute to Chaucer (British Library, MS. Harley 4866, fol. 88)*

ries told in different styles by distinct storytellers, plays games with the idea of narration. He tells tales such as the Clerk's and then offers conflicting interpretive conclusions to the tale. The second interpretation is based on a completely different way of reading the tale; it is to be read as an allegory / it is not to be read as an allegory.

Chaucer worries both about what a story can mean and what a story can be. The Wife of Bath – whose tale follows the Man of Law's claim that Chaucer has used up all the stories and that he, the Man of Law, is going to tell the last available story – seems to want to tell her own life as an original story. The men on the pilgrimage refuse to allow her life to be a story for several reasons. The most important is that stories *exist;* people did not make up stories in the Middle Ages, they retold them – they offered new versions of old stories. The Monk says he has a hundred stories in his cell; he is planning on drawing on his stock of old stories, not on making up new ones. The second reason for the protest against the Wife's use of her life as a story – "This is a long preamble of a tale!" – is that in the Middle Ages, one's life was not a story. Painters did not paint self-portraits, and writers did not write autobiographies. Perhaps Augustine's autobiography was accepted by the Middle Ages because it was called a confession. Clearly no one on the Canterbury pilgrimage would have accepted it as an entry in Harry's storytelling contest.

When he invents a way for the Miller to use his tale as a weapon against the Knight, Chaucer moves toward a very modern conception of the function of speech. In a book with an oddly primitive title, *How To Do Things with Words* (1962), J. L. Austin points out that there are certain acts that one can perform with words: one can promise, swear, threaten, curse, and so forth. These speech acts are so solid that they often acquire legal standing, so that one can be sued for breach of promise, and all testimony must be preceded by an oath because perjury is not lying in court but rather breaking one's oath to tell the truth. In considering the ramifications of an invented teller telling about other invented tellers telling stories whose main purpose is to get back ("quite") at other tellers, Chaucer finds himself with a new conception of fiction. This idea of the use of story puts him at odds with the patristic tale readers of his day as well as those modern critics who use the methods of the Church Fathers to read medieval fiction. The Fathers (Augustine, Ambrose, Jerome, and the millennium of scholars who followed them) asked exclusively what does a story mean ultimately? – to the extinction of the story itself. "Taketh the fruyt, and lat the chaf be stille," in "The Nun's Priest's Tale," refers to this doctrine. The meaning of the story was the fruit, or kernel of the wheat, and the story was the chaff, to be blown away by the wind once one had gotten the meaning out. Chaucer, seeing the Miller take up his story in arms against the Knight, is impressed by the power of the story-act. The Miller's weapon, the cudgel, would be useless against the Knight's lance, but his noble tale puts him on equal footing with the noble tale of the Knight.

Once this principle is established, it is often more fruitful to ask about each pilgrim's tale, what is he doing with it rather than what does it mean. This can be seen in one of the most vexing of the tales, the Pardoner's, which raises many questions about the meaning and characterization of the teller. "The Pardoner's Tale" is one of several (the others are the Wife of Bath's and the Canon's Yeoman's) which include an extensive confessional self-portrait as a prologue to the tale proper. In his prologue the Pardoner confesses to being a vicious, evil man who cheats his customers, the purchasers of his pardons. There has been much speculation about the reason for this confession, usually centering around the likelihood that he is drunk, or that he is mimicking the Wife's confession of her lustfulness, or that the confession of evil is a way to assert his suspect masculinity. Though there is some validity to each of these claims, one must consider what the Pardoner was trying to do with his tale. One of the notable aspects of the pilgrims is their perfection – the Knight is "parfit," the physician is a "parfit praktisour," and the Friar is the best beggar in his house. It is important to note that this concept does not at all designate moral perfection, but only completion; the perfect one is whatever he is to the nth degree. This is most easily seen in the designation of the Friar as the best beggar. He is a member of a mendicant order whose essence, therefore, is begging. To be the best beggar is to be able to beg the most money and, even better, in the smallest begging district. This notion of expertise, of being the best at whatever one does, is everywhere in *The Canterbury Tales*. The Wife is the best wife, if being good at being a wife means marrying and subjugating the greatest number of husbands.

In the tales the best example of such a character is the Summoner in "The Friar's Tale." For him, summoning means using his ecclesiastical office to gouge parishioners through the threat of a summons to the archdeacon's court. When the Summoner finds himself in the company of a devil, he does not try to run as do all the characters in his position in analogous tales. Rather he stays to show up the devil, to outsummon him. When he sees the devil fail to get a horse that a carter has consigned to the devil, the Summoner is filled with condescension. He tells the devil that he may be good at what he does in his neck of the woods, but if he wants to see how it is done, he should watch the Summoner at work. This spirit of expertise energizes many of the pilgrims and their characters: they are so good at what they do that they can outdo the devil, even if it is doing evil.

The Pardoner then raises this notion of doing evil to new heights. His plan is to use the Great Magician's trick of showing his audience how he does the trick, then pulling it off anyway. In this case, the ultimate act of a pardoner would be to tell the pilgrims how he sells his pardons dishonestly, then sell them pardons anyway. In this tale the Pardoner plans the ultimate act of requital; he wants to get back at the whole pilgrimage. That he has been designated as the lowest of the low is seen in his position in the "General Prologue." He is the last pilgrim to be introduced in a sweep that goes down the social order to him. This scorn is resurrected at the beginning of his tale when the "gentils" put strictures on him, insisting that he "Telle us som moral thyng," with the implication that an obscene story is to be expected from such a low, obscene fellow. What better revenge than to sell these people his pardons? For them to buy the pardons after he has told them the tricks of his trade would certify them as fools. And the genius of the Pardoner is that he almost pulls it off.

Walter Clyde Curry has argued that the Pardoner's confession works partly as a smoke screen for his real secret, that he is a eunuch. Most critics have accepted this analysis and have noted that many of his actions come out of an attempt to hide his true nature. It is for this reason that the Pardoner interrupts the Wife's prologue to announce that he is about to get married. Also for this reason he confesses to a desire to have a wench in every town; that is, he is proclaiming he can do that which nature has left him unable to do. Though there is a moral dilemma for the Pardoner in his eunuchry because he believes eunuchs are cursed in the Bible and therefore unpardonable, Chaucer will use his condition for the last twist in his use of language as a weapon.

The Pardoner's trick in selling pardons to his usual flock is to tell them that his pardons will work only for people who have not committed vicious sins, like adultery. Since his usual trade is families out for market day, both husband and wife rush up to buy his pardons. Once one couple comes up to purchase pardon, the rest will fall in line. Silence or inactivity appears to admit guilt. The Pardoner plans the same method of attack in his plot to sell his pardons to the pilgrims: he needs just one pilgrim to bite, and they will all fall into his net. He determines that Harry Bailey is his target, and this version of his tale has only one purpose: to force Harry into purchasing pardon. The interest in the tale is in what it does rather than what it means.

The interruption of the pilgrimage by the Canon and his Yeoman signifies a radical change in the narrative plan for *The Canterbury Tales*. The introduction of a teller who does not belong to the original company assembled at the Tabard Inn breaks down all notions of what the finished *Tales* should be. In contrast to *The Decameron,* a collection of tales named for the number of sets of tales (ten) which it comprises, *The Canterbury Tales* will not now be so easily rounded off. The medieval reader liked the roundedness of *The Decameron:* ten tellers times ten days equals one hundred tales. But Chaucer's symmetry breaks down with the arrival of the Canon's Yeoman. Suddenly, simply multiplying the number of pilgrims by the number of tales will not yield the number of tales that there are supposed to be. It is not clear if the new teller is to be included in the number of pilgrims or if he will be expected to tell four tales and be a legitimate entrant in the storytelling contest. Furthermore, the number of tellers is no longer stable. There is nothing to prevent another stranger from joining the pilgrimage, or, in fact, to keep an original pilgrim from leaving.

As if to underscore how radical the change is, Chaucer does not have the interrupter tell the tale, but rather his assistant. Everyone expects the Canon to tell the tale; as if to qualify him as a storyteller, the Canon is introduced with an elaborate description of the kind given to the pilgrims in the "General Prologue." When the Canon is frightened away, the Yeoman tells his master's tale, the story of alchemy. The Yeoman is the only pilgrim who does not present himself as an expert. In fact, one of the points he makes in delivering his lecture on alchemy is how little he knows about the subject. Though the Yeoman is not an expert, he is in a position to claim expertise. He has served his master for seven years, which is the time it takes for a journeyman to become the master of a trade, and with his master fled he could claim the position of master himself. Instead, he rejects the art he has almost mastered, swears off alchemy, and advises everyone else to do the same.

"The Canon's Yeoman's Tale" then marks a major turning point in *The Canterbury Tales,* so by the end of the next tale (the Manciple's), the narrator announces, "Now lakketh us no tales mo than oon" to "knytte up wel a greet mateere." Chaucer is bringing things to an end, though the tales have not gone the original distance planned. In fact, not all of the pilgrims have told even one tale.

There is much speculation as to why Chaucer left *The Canterbury Tales* unfinished. One theory is that he left off writing them in the mid 1390s, some five or six years before his death. At that time he was about fifty-five years old and, from the record of his business activities, apparently in good health. Since he was writing tales, rather than a long unified work like *Troilus and Criseyde,* there would not seem to be a problem of getting stuck in a narrative. It is possible that the enormousness of the task overwhelmed him. He had been working on *The Canterbury Tales* for ten years or more, and he was not one quarter through his original plan. He may have felt he could not divide his time successfully between his writing and his business interests.

Chaucer himself offers an explanation in the "Retraction" which follows "The Parson's Tale," the last of *The Canterbury Tales*. In it Chaucer disclaims apologetically all of his impious works, especially "the tales of Caunterbury, thilke that sowen into synne." There has been some speculation of "deathbed confession" about the "Retraction": Chaucer in ill health confesses his impieties; and some belief that the "Retraction" is merely conventional: the apologetic voice allows Chaucer to list all his works while taking on the persona of the humble author, a stance favored in the Middle Ages.

If the reader is to take Chaucer at his word, he seems to suggest that his works were being misread, that people were mistaking the sinful behavior in *The Canterbury Tales* for its message (for example, seeing the Wife's lechery – instead of the empty life to which it leads – as the point of her tale). If this is the case, then he must, like his favorite Latin poet, Ovid (in the Tristia, A.D. 8–18), disclaim all the works that he believed could be read immorally. It may be that a more anguished version of the calm, valedictory tone of the "Retraction" is found in "The Manciple's Tale," where Apollo takes away the voice and tears out the feathers of the crow because he has told the truth. The crow seems to be exactly like Chaucer, the poet of *The Canterbury Tales,* when it is said that he could "countrefete the speche of every man / . . . when he sholde telle a tale." The crow's problem is that his truths are mistaken, and the conclusion of "The Manciple's Tale" proclaims, "be noon auctour newe / Of tidynges, wheither they been false or trewe." As in the "Retraction," Chaucer excludes explicitly didactic works, but here the flaw is seen in the misreading of the tales; in the "Retraction," Chaucer, in the guise of the humble author, puts the blame on himself.

The last thirteen years of Chaucer's life correspond almost exactly to the span of years covered by Shakespeare's *Richard II,* that is, the period marked by Richard's claiming his majority (he had become king at age nine) and his assumption of the power of the throne in 1389 until his deposition and death in 1399. Though the realm was marred by the power struggles of the Lancastrian (Gaunt and his son, the eventual Henry IV) and Court (Richard) parties, it must be remembered that in presenting this strife Shakespeare squeezes thirteen years of intrigue into one five-act play. Chaucer had connections in both camps, and over a dozen years it was possible to be of the court without being Gaunt's enemy. That Chaucer was able to do this is indicated by the fact that Henry renewed annuities granted to Chaucer during Richard's reign.

Nonetheless, these appear to have been financially trying times for Chaucer. His wife received the last payment of her annuity in 1387, which suggests she died in the following year. Although Chaucer lost his post as controller of customs in 1386, he had been appointed justice of peace for the County of Kent in 1385, and in 1389, following the coming to power of Richard, Chaucer was named clerk of public works. This post, which amounted to being a kind of general contractor for the repair of public buildings, was more lucrative than the controller's job that he had lost, but it caused him no end of headaches. One of the duties of this position required him to carry large sums of money, and in 1390 he was robbed of both his and the king's money three times in the space of four days. Though there was no direct punishment of Chaucer, he was appointed subforester of North Pemberton in Somerset. It appears that in 1390 or 1391 he was eased out of his clerk's job and rusticated. In a short poem from this period, "The Letter to Scogan," Chaucer says, "thynke I never of slep to wake my muse, / That rusteth in my shethe stille in pees." Chaucer eventually got into financial trouble. In 1398 he borrowed against his annuity and was sued for debt. His last poem, "The Complaint to his Purse," is a letter asking King Henry for money. It is not surprising that at least one manuscript of this poem calls it the "Supplication" to King Richard. It is quite likely that in the last years of his life, he was constantly asking the king, whoever he was, for money. The poem, or his connections to the Lancastrians, must have worked because Chaucer was granted a sizable annuity by Henry. Nonetheless, Chaucer moved to a house in the Westminster Abbey Close because a house on church grounds granted him sanctuary from creditors. And so, from the fact of Chaucer's debts comes the tradition of burying poets, or erecting memorials to them, in Westminster Abbey. Chaucer died in 1400, the year after the accession of Henry to the throne and also the year after the death of John of Gaunt, the king's father, Chaucer's almost exact contemporary and once the most powerful man in England. That Chaucer was buried in Westminster Abbey was due primarily to the fact that his last residence was on the abbey grounds. So important was he deemed as a poet that the space around his tomb was later dubbed the Poets' Corner, and luminaries of English letters were laid to rest around him.

Bibliographies:

Eleanor P. Hammond, *Chaucer: A Bibliographical Manual* (New York: Macmillan, 1908);

Dudley David Griffith, *Bibliography of Chaucer, 1908–1953* (Seattle: University of Washington Press, 1955);

William R. Crawford, *Bibliography of Chaucer, 1954–63* (Seattle: University of Washington Press, 1967);

Lorrayne Y. Baird, *A Bibliography of Chaucer, 1964–1973* (Boston: G. K. Hall, 1977);

Lorrayne Baird-Lange, *A Bibliography of Chaucer, 1974–1985* (Hamden, Conn.: Archon, 1988).

Biographies:

Marchette Chute, *Geoffrey Chaucer of England* (New York: Dutton, 1946);

Martin M. Crow and Clair C. Olson, eds., *Chaucer Life-Records* (Oxford: Clarendon Press, 1966; Austin: University of Texas Press, 1966);

John C. Gardner, *The Life and Times of Chaucer* (New York: Knopf, 1976);

Derek Brewer, *Chaucer and His World* (New York: Dodd, Mead, 1977);

Donald R. Howard, *Chaucer: His Life, His Work, His World* (New York: Dutton, 1987).

References:

Ruth Ames, *God's Plenty: Chaucer's Christian Humanism* (Chicago: Loyola University Press, 1984);

C. David Benson, *Chaucer's Drama of Style: Poetic Variety and Contrast in The Canterbury Tales* (Chapel Hill: University of North Carolina Press, 1986);

N. F. Blake, *The Textual Tradition of the Canterbury Tales* (London: Arnold, 1985);

Muriel Bowden, *A Commentary On the General Prologue to the Canterbury Tales* (New York: Macmillan, 1948);

Derek Brewer, *Chaucer in his Time* (London: Nelson, 1964);

W. F. Bryan and Germaine Dempster, eds., *Sources and Analogues of Chaucer's Canterbury Tales* (Chicago: University of Chicago Press, 1941);

Nevill Coghill, *The Poet Chaucer* (London & New York: Oxford University Press, 1949);

Walter Clyde Curry, *Chaucer and the Mediæval Sciences* (New York & London: Oxford University Press, 1926);

Alfred David, *The Strumpet Muse: Art and Morals in Chaucer's Poetry* (Bloomington: Indiana University Press, 1976);

Rodney Delasanta, "The Theme of Judgment in *The Canterbury Tales*," *Modern Language Quarterly,* 31 (September 1970): 298–307;

Bert Dillon, *A Chaucer Dictionary* (Boston: G. K. Hall, 1974);

Carolyn Dinshaw, *Chaucer's Sexual Poetics* (Madison: University of Wisconsin Press, 1989);

John Ganim, *Chaucerian Theatricality* (Princeton: Princeton University Press, 1990);

John Gardner, *The Poetry of Chaucer* (Carbondale: Southern Illinois University Press, 1977);

Jeffrey Helterman, "The Dehumanizing Metamorphoses of the Knight's Tale," *ELH,* 38 (December 1971): 493–511;

Richard L. Hoffman, *Ovid and the Canterbury Tales* (Philadelphia: University of Pennsylvania Press, 1966);

Donald Howard, *The Idea of the Canterbury Tales* (Berkeley: University of California Press, 1976);

Bernard Huppé and D. W. Robertson, Jr., *Fruyt and Chaf: Studies in Chaucer's Allegories* (Princeton: Princeton University Press, 1963);

Robert M. Jordan, *Chaucer and the Shape of Creation: The Aesthetic Possibilities of Inorganic Structure* (Cambridge, Mass.: Harvard University Press, 1967);

Stanley J. Kahrl, "Chaucer's *Squire's Tale* and the Decline of Chivalry," *Chaucer Review,* 7 (Winter 1973): 194–209;

R. E. Kaske, "The Knight's Interruption of the Monk's Tale," *ELH,* 24 (December 1957): 249–268;

Robert Kellogg, "Oral Narrative, Written Books," *Genre,* 10 (Winter 1977): 655–665;

George Lyman Kittredge, *Chaucer and His Poetry* (Cambridge, Mass.: Harvard University Press, 1915);

V. A. Kolve, *Chaucer and the Imagery of Narrative: The First Five Canterbury Tales* (Stanford: Stanford University Press, 1984);

W. W. Lawrence, *Chaucer and the Canterbury Tales* (New York: Columbia University Press, 1950);

C. S. Lewis, *The Allegory of Love: A Study in Medieval Tradition* (Oxford: Clarendon Press, 1936);

R. M. Lumiansky, *Of Sondry Folk: the Dramatic Principle of The Canterbury Tales* (Austin: University of Texas Press, 1955);

Francis P. Magoun, Jr., *A Chaucer Gazetteer* (Chicago: University of Chicago Press, 1961);

John Matthews Manly, *Some New Light on Chaucer* (New York: Holt, 1926);

J. Mitchell Morse, "The Philosophy of the Clerk of Oxenford," *Modern Language Quarterly,* 19 (March 1958): 3–20;

Charles Muscatine, *Chaucer and the French Tradition: A Study in Style and Meaning* (Berkeley: University of California Press, 1957);

Charles A. Owen, Jr., "The Problem of Free Will in Chaucer's Narratives," *Philological Quarterly,* 46 (October 1967): 433–456;

Russell A. Peck, "Chaucer and the Nominalist Questions," *Speculum,* 53 (October 1978): 745–760;

Robert A. Pratt, "Chaucer and the Hand that Fed Him," *Speculum,* 41 (October 1966): 619–642;

Edmund Reiss, "Medieval Irony," *Journal of the History of Ideas,* 42 (1981): 209–226;

D. W. Robertson, Jr., *A Preface to Chaucer: Studies in Medieval Perspectives* (Princeton: Princeton University Press, 1962);

Beryl Rowland, *Blind Beasts: Chaucer's Animal World* (Kent, Ohio: Kent State University Press, 1971);

Paul Ruggiers, *The Art of the Canterbury Tales* (Madison: University of Wisconsin Press, 1965);

James Sledd, "The Clerk's Tale; The Monsters and the Critics," *Modern Philology,* 51 (1954): 73–82;

Paul Strohm, *Social Chaucer* (Cambridge, Mass.: Harvard University Press, 1989);

Joseph Westlund, "The Knight's Tale as Impetus for Pilgrimage," *Philological Quarterly,* 43 (October 1964): 526–537;

Trevor Whittock, *A Reading of the Canterbury Tales* (London & New York: Cambridge University Press, 1968);

Arnold Williams, "Chaucer and the Friars," *Speculum,* 28 (July 1953): 499–513;

Chauncey Wood, *Chaucer and the Country of the Stars: Poetic Uses of Astrological Imagery* (Princeton: Princeton University Press, 1970).

William Dunbar

(circa 1460 – circa 1522)

Deanna Delmar Evans
Bemidji State University

WORKS: *Poems* (circa 1485 – circa 1517)

Manuscripts: Aberdeen Minute Book of Seisins, ii (1503–1507), iii (1507–1513), Town Clerk's Office, Aberdeen, contains three poems by Dunbar; Arundel Manuscript 285, British Library, contains three religious poems by Dunbar including *The Passioun of Crist;* Asloan Manuscript (circa 1515), Malahide Castle, Dublin, contains four poems by Dunbar including "Ane Ballat of Our Lady" and "The Passioun of Crist"; Bannatyne Manuscript (circa 1568), National Library of Scotland, Edinburgh, contains forty-five poems by Dunbar including *The Golden Targe,* "The Dregy of Dunbar," *The Thistle and the Rose,* and *The Flyting;* Maitland Folio Manuscript (circa 1570–1586), Pepysian Library, Magdalene College, Cambridge, contains fifty-nine poems by Dunbar including the *Treatise of the Two Married Women and the Widow, The Golden Targe,* and *The Flyting;* Reidpeth Manuscript (1622–1623), Cambridge University Library, is the only authority for some eight poems by Dunbar.

First publications: [*The Flyting of Dunbar and Kennedy*]; *The Ballade of ane Right Noble Victorius & Myghty Lord Barnard Stewart; Here Begynnys ane Litil Tretie Intitulit the Golden Targe* (Edinburgh: Printed by Walter Chepman & Androw Myllar, 1508); *The Poems of William Dunbar,* 3 volumes, edited by John Small, Scottish Text Society, 2, 4, 16, 21, 29 (Edinburgh: Blackwood, 1884–1889).

Standard editions: *The Poems of William Dunbar,* 5 volumes, edited by Jakob Schipper (Vienna: Kaiserliche Akademie der Wissenschaften, 1891–1894); *The Poems of William Dunbar,* edited by W. Mackay Mackenzie (London: Faber & Faber, 1932; reprinted, with corrections by Bruce Dickins, 1960); *The Poems of William Dunbar,* edited by James Kinsley (Oxford: Clarendon Press, 1979).

It has been said with some justice that the most vibrant and interesting poetry of the fifteenth and early sixteenth centuries in Europe was written in Scotland. Of those Scottish makars William Dunbar merits highest praise, although his reputation rests on no lengthy major work but on approximately eighty shorter poems, many associated with the court of the Scottish king James IV (reigned 1488–1513). Written records of Dunbar's birth, death, and parentage have not been found. Nevertheless, a reasonable outline of his life and career can be sketched from the official records along with the presumed record of his university attendance and statements in his verse and that of his contemporaries.

William Dunbar was born in about 1459 or 1460, this probable date being provided by the records of the University of Saint Andrews, in which a William Dunbar is "determinant" in 1474 and master of arts in 1479. The university entrant had to have reached his fourteenth year; the recipient of the M.A., his twentieth. The poet is regularly described as "Maister William Dunbar" in the *Accounts of the Lord High Treasurer of Scotland* and in titles and colophons of several poems. To fill in important details about Dunbar's life upon leaving the university, clues must be sought in the poetry. Some critics, it must be noted, reject this method, either arguing that authorial self-reference in medieval poetry is always conventional, or defining first-person discourse as part of the fictional world of "the text." Nevertheless, scholars like J. W. Baxter and Matthew P. McDiarmid have found clues in the poetry that can be corroborated by historical facts, and from their work it is possible to formulate a reasonable biography of Dunbar.

An object of such research is *The Flyting of Dunbar and Kennedy* (circa 1492–1493), Dunbar's entry in an energetic poetic duel of verbal abuse with his poetic rival, Walter Kennedy. Kennedy's many attacks on Dunbar's family and activities must have had some basis in fact — a barb not strengthened by fact carries no bite. Yet James

Kinsley, Dunbar's most recent editor, advises against giving much heed to the attacks.

Concerning Dunbar's parentage there is little evidence. In one of his moral poems Dunbar makes some claim to being of "nobill strynd" (noble ancestry), and in a later complaint poem he protests that "churllis" (churls) should be advanced before him at the court of James IV. According to Kennedy, he belongs to one of the "four branchis" of the ancient house of Dunbar.

Dunbar's activities after leaving Saint Andrews remain somewhat of a mystery. Earlier scholars suggested that Dunbar became a friar on the basis of his own statement in the satiric vision, "How Dunbar was desyrd to be ane Freir," and Kennedy's gibes in *The Flyting* that Dunbar was "prestyt and ordanit be Sathan" and "beggit wyth a pardoun" in many churches of England and France. There is no other evidence for these claims, and yet one notes that he knew French, for it has been shown that he was acquainted with works by Hélinant and Deschamps. It has been argued much less convincingly, indeed fancifully, that he attended a French university or served in France or, as Jean-Jacques Blanchôt suggests, as a member of the Scots Guard.

Dunbar next appears on ambassadorial voyages in the ship *Katryne,* perhaps acting both as priest and secretary. One of these voyages is described in *The Flyting,* the mission of 1492 to Denmark when the ship was blown off course and forced to land its passengers on the Norwegian coast. Who the paymaster of Dunbar was during these years is also unknown, for the earliest mention of his name in the *Accounts* is 1500. Presumably payment came from the person in charge of an embassy, in the Danish case the earl of Ogilvy. The early date of *The Flyting* seems fixed by the poet's address in it to Sir John the Ross. This reference surely is to Ross of Montgrenan, who as the king's chief secretary would have had dealings with Dunbar and who died in 1493. In addition, both poets refer to the Danish embassy of 1492. By that date Dunbar would have been in his early thirties and surely would have begun writing poetry. In fact, Matthew P. McDairmid argues convincingly that some of Dunbar's most famous poems, including the "Dance of the Seven Deadly Sins," *The Flyting,* and *The Golden Targe,* were written during that early period.

Dunbar's life from 1500 to 1513 was spent at the court of James IV. Entries in the *Accounts* provide concrete evidence that Dunbar was a "servitour" of the king's household, his duties most likely being clerical, since there is no evidence that James maintained a resident poet laureate. Dunbar is first mentioned in the entry for 15 August 1500 showing that he was awarded a pension. The *Accounts* also offer proof that Dunbar was an ordained priest, for he received an offering for celebrating his first mass on 17 March 1504. This entry does not preclude the possibility that Dunbar had been ordained earlier, as Kennedy says; it could refer simply to the first mass he celebrated at court or for the queen. Further evidence of Dunbar's priestly vocation is indicated by a legal document of 1509; Dunbar's name is listed as a witness to a property resignation in Edinburgh where he is called chaplain. The *Accounts* show that on 26 August 1510 the king granted Dunbar a pension of eighty pounds per year, a most generous sum at the time, being twice the stipend paid in the same year to the scholar Hector Boece as principal of Aberdeen University. Plainly the increasing pension, alongside Dunbar's many complaints about receiving no benefice, indicate the king's wish to keep his poet-priest at court.

Dunbar is last mentioned in the *Accounts* for 14 May 1513, the entry showing that he received a partial payment "in his pensioun," though the records of the *Accounts* between August 1513 and June 1515 are not extant, a result of the disruption caused by the war with England. In September 1513 James, along with the flower of his nobility, was killed at the Battle of Flodden, a battle which, in his better judgment, he had wished to avoid and fought only to honor a pledge made to his ally France, which recently had been invaded by the armies of Henry VIII. For years James had collected artillery for just such an occasion, artillery sometimes alluded to in Dunbar's poetry. But when war came James did not use it, and English muskets took their terrible toll.

It has been suggested that Dunbar lost his life alongside his king. Yet, considering the poet's age at the time, it seems unlikely. In addition, some poems written after Flodden have been attributed to Dunbar, and at least two are plausible. A poem on the duke of Albany, "Quhen the Governour Past in France," not at all flattering to the new governor who tried to rule for only three years before leaving for France in June 1517, is assigned to Dunbar in the Maitland collection made a generation later. It has been rejected from the canon of his work on the grounds that it is technically inferior. Yet the poem's stanzaic pattern and refrain are characteristic of Dunbar's work, and its plainer style and serious tone seem natural in an older poet, especially one who had recently experienced a traumatic event like Flodden. Another poem, apparently written for the young widowed queen, is untitled and anonymous in the Bannatyne Manuscript but was attrib-

Apon thy cors vengeance vengeance thay cry
Thou art the cause thay may not rest nor ly
Thou sais for thame few psaltris psalmis or cred
Bot geris me tell thair trentalis of my dedis
And thair ald sin wyth new schame certify

    Insensuate sow cesse false Eustale air
And knaw kene scald I hald of alathya
And cause me not the cause lang to declare
Off thy curst kyn deulber and his Allya
Cum to the croce on kneis and mak acrya
Confesse thy crime hald kenydy the king
And wyth ane hauthorne scurge thy self and dyng
Thus dree thy penaunce wyth deliquisti quia

    Pas to my conmissare and be confest
Cour before him on kneis & cum in will
And syne ger Stobo for thy lyf protest
Renounce thy rymis bath ban and birn thy bull
Heve to the heuyn thy handis ande hald the still
Do thou not thus bogane thou salbe brynt
Wyth pik fire ter gun puldre or lynt
On Arthuris sete or on ane hyar hyll

    I perambalit of pernaso the montayn
Enspirit wyth Mercury fra his goldyn spere
And dulcely drank of eloquence the fontayne
Quhen it was purifit wyth frost and flowit clere
And thou come kule in marche or februere
Thare till a pule and drank the padok rod
That gerris the ryme in to thy termes glod
And blaberis that novis menis eris to here
Thou lufis nane irische elf I vnderstand
Bot it suld be all trew scottis menis lede
It was the gud langage of this land

Page from William Dunbar's The Flyting of Dunbar and Kennedy, *from a series of pamphlets printed circa 1508 by Walter Chepman and Androw Myllar*

uted to Dunbar by the nineteenth-century editor David Laing, and the many correspondences between this poem and others that are indisputably Dunbar's have persuaded Kinsley to accept the attribution. If Dunbar wrote the poem for the dowager queen, he definitely lived after Flodden; if he wrote the Albany poem, then he was still alive in 1517. But he most certainly is dead by 1530 when Sir David Lindsay speaks of Dunbar as dead in the *Testament of the Papyngo.*

If there is a single word to describe Dunbar's poetic achievement, it is *variety.* Dunbar is both an innovator and experimenter in verse forms, and he displays great diversity in subject matter. In his many short poems he presents a variety of themes, pictures, and moods, all vividly human. In many scenes there is a dimension of fantasy. To achieve such variety, Dunbar employs many kinds of diction – from the most splendid, the so-called aureate diction consisting of Latinate words, to colloquial Scots including slang and obscenities. Some of those poems written in the colloquial are said to convey Dunbar's eldritch voice where, as C. S. Lewis noted, "the comic overlaps with the demoniac or terrifying." Yet, in all of Dunbar's poetry there is a conscious human voice speaking. To illustrate the above-mentioned diversity, this essay will refer to certain notable examples of his kinds of verse, while attempting to avoid that common error of one type of modern criticism that sees all Dunbar's poems as exercises in a particular form, discounting the self that each work expresses.

Surely the most important of Dunbar's early poems is *The Golden Targe.* Its date can be surmised, for Kennedy seems to allude to it in *The Flyting,* where he refers to himself as "of Rethory the Rose" and describes Dunbar's craft as "imperfyte." Gavin Douglas also alludes to Dunbar's poem in the *Palice of Honour* (1500–1501). *The Golden Targe* is an ambitious work, probably Dunbar's most courtly and formal, written in the high style and the elaborate nine-line stanza of the *compleynt* of Geoffrey Chaucer's *Anelida and Arcite.* It concludes with a tribute to Chaucer, as "rose of rhethoris [rhetoricians] all," and then adds praise for Gower and Lydgate. This tribute seems the work of a younger poet trying to gain recognition by associating himself with the tradition established by earlier English poets.

It is a May morning love vision in which Dunbar depicts the failure of Reason with its shield of gold to defend a dreamer from Venus's fighting force. It seems that only a poet who had himself experienced the pain of romantic love could create a protagonist who laments:

> Quhy was thou blyndit, Resoun? quhi, allace!
> And gert ane hell my paradise appere,
> And mercy seme quhare that I fand no grace.
>
> (Why were you blinded, Reason? Why, alas!
> And made a hell appear as my paradise
> And mercy seem where I found no grace.)

Yet interwoven into an allegorical *psychomachia* (a battle between personified elements of the human psyche) of love are self-conscious comments about the writing of allegorical love poetry. The narrator, drawing upon the inexpressibility topos, states that he would describe the fields with the white lilies but has difficulty finding the words and adds that even Homer and Tullius (Cicero) could not. In the final tribute he states that "reverend" Chaucer with his "fresch anamalit [enameled] termes" could have "illumynit" the matter of the poem far better. Dunbar's choice of this latter term to describe Chaucer's writing is significant, for he suggests that in poetry of the highest style the language should make the subject matter shine.

Dunbar's short love poems also appear to be early works. There is no way of knowing the poet's source of inspiration for them, but the reader cannot assume that because Dunbar was a priest they are merely formal exercises. At least one, the allegory of "Bewty and the Presoneir," most probably was written around the time of *The Golden Targe,* for its narrator similarly complains of becoming beauty's prisoner and describes his pain in a similar allegorical *psychomachia.* Some of Dunbar's love poems were perhaps written for musical accompaniment, such as "Sweit Rois of Vertew," in rondeau form, containing a description of a lady's garden where only "rew" (pity) is missing. In another, "My hartis tresure and swete assured fo," Dunbar describes the woes of a courtly lover, including "intollerabill pane" and "passioun dolorous."

As already noted, *The Flyting* is an early poem, probably written circa 1492–1493. Deriving from a genre of Gaelic origins, *The Flyting* seemed to have been instigated by Kennedy, who was from Carrick, in great part a Gaelic-speaking area. Dunbar, in fact, early in the poem dissociates himself from the tradition of the Gaelic bard by saying that he is ashamed to be "flyting" which "is nowthir wynnyng nor rewaird." Nevertheless, Dunbar displays great vitality in his attacks on Kennedy, concluding his final portion of the poem with a catalogue of insults – "Heretyk, lunatyk, purspyk [pickpocket]" – which climaxes in a victor's challenge: "Cry coc, or I sall quell the [slay you]."

Dunbar's most famous satiric dream vision, "Dance of the Seven Deadly Sins," was probably also written during this period, considering the narrator's comment that the Fastern Eve vision took place on 15 February. As McDiarmid has shown, 1491 was only year when Ash Wednesday fell on 16 February during the reign of James. Here, in his eldritch voice, Dunbar reveals the seven deadly sins dramatically in a dance set in hell on Fastern's Eve, the last day before Lent. Although the dance is performed in hell for the amusement of devils, it suggests a type of Mardi Gras celebration. But the poem is also a notable example of the medieval grotesque, forcing laughter at human torment.

The tail-rhyme stanzas provide a sprightly, dancing rhythm, and there is vivid iconographic detail in the depictions of the individual sins:

> Than Yre [Wrath] come in with sturt and stryfe;
> His hand was ay upoun his knyfe –
> He brandeist lyk a beir [conducted himself like a bear].

The poem also provides comedy at the expense of the Highlanders, for after the dance, a Highland pageant is requested, but the resultant noise proves too much for even the devil. Yet there is a serious side to this comedy, for the dancers in the poem are the unshriven, tortured souls of the damned, a fate Dunbar and his contemporaries took seriously. Hence his use of the obscene and the comic here serves a moral purpose.

"Dance of the Seven Deadly Sins" is actually either part of a tripartite poem or a trilogy. "The Turnament," in similar stanzaic style, begins, "Nixt that a turnament was tryid." An antichivalric burlesque, rich in scatological imagery and again expelling robust energy, it describes a tournament between a cobbler and a tailor. Its concluding line, "now believe this if you wish," suggests its absurdity. It is followed by "The Amendis," a parodic dream-vision that is a tongue-in-cheek apology to cobblers and tailors. Its narrator relates that an angel from heaven came to say that the highest place in heaven, next to God's in dignity, is reserved for these two professions since they "do amend" what "God mismakkis." The refrain bestows a blessing on them.

Impossible to date but also quite likely to be early is "The Tway Cummeris" (The Two Old Gossips), another comic Lenten poem; it is recorded in the earliest manuscript source of Dunbar's poetry, the Aberdeen Minute Book of Seisins ii (1503–1507). Written in colloquial Scots, it depicts two older women, obvious tipplers, irreverently drinking malmsey (a rich wine) "right early" on Ash Wednesday morning, the very time that the Church demands fasting. One, rest-

ing "on cowch besyd the fyre," complains to the other that this long Lent makes her lean, but the behavior of both women suggests that neither is likely to become slender during the forty days.

Dunbar's court poems were probably written after the 1500 pension, although only a few can be dated. Two seem to have been written during a visit made to England in 1501 to honor the wedding of James IV to Margaret Tudor, daughter of the English king Henry VII. A note in the *Accounts* places Dunbar in England in 1501, and it is believed that Dunbar was a part of the Scottish delegation sent to negotiate the marriage. At least two occasional poems, one in honor of London and another on the theme of "Learning vain without guid life" with the subtitle "Written at Oxinfurde," were perhaps the poems for which King Henry VII rewarded "the Rhymer of Scotland" on 31 December 1501 and again on 7 January 1502. Similarly, Dunbar's "Welcome to Queen Margaret" and *The Thrissill and the Rois* were written in 1503, the year of James's marriage.

The Thrissill and the Rois, Dunbar's third longest poem, is just under two hundred lines. This elegant courtly epithalamium honors the marriage of James and Margaret. Since the wedding took place on 8 August 1503, the date of this poem's composition can be determined with some degree of accuracy, especially since the narrator says that he wrote it on the ninth of May. Written in the seven-line rime royale stanza of Chaucer's *Troilus and Criseyde* and the *Kingis Quair* by James I, the poem consists of many conventions of courtly love poetry. But *The Thrissill and the Rois* also displays Dunbar's creativity, for in it he forces his readers to confront the unreality of the conventions. The narrator, a sleepy poet, is awakened on a May morning and commanded by a personified May to go and write something in her honor. In a humorous dialogue, the poet-narrator resists, arguing that he has found nothing worth writing about in this particular spring with its unwholesome atmosphere and the blustery winds of Lord Aeolus. May then leads the reluctant poet into an allegorical garden. Dunbar's allegory throughout the poem is enriched by political expectations for the marriage.

In the garden the narrator discovers three heraldic parliaments – those of beasts, birds, and flowers. Dame Nature presides over all three, and King James is represented as reigning in each, first as the red Scottish lion standing majestically on a field of gold encircled by fleurs-de-lis, then as the royal eagle, and finally as the Scottish thistle betrothed to the Tudor rose. Dame Nature has advice for James in each parliament, reminding him in the last that he should behave as a king and "be discreet" and

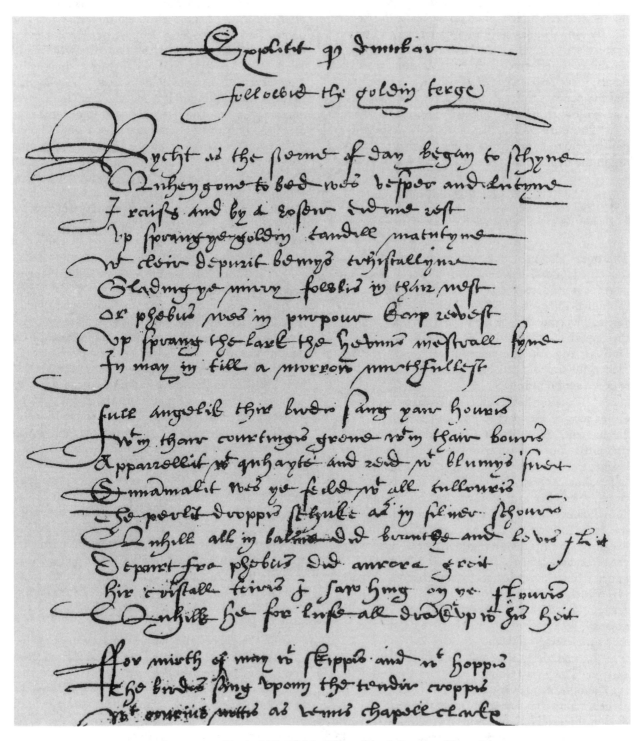

The beginning of Dunbar's The Golden Targe, *from the Bannatyne Manuscript
(National Library of Scotland, Adv. MS. 1. 1. 6)*

not hold any other flower in such high esteem as the rose. After Dame Nature's last speech to the king, the birds sing a paean of praise for the rose and conclude with a prayer: "Christ save thee from all adversity." Then the sound of combined voices of all the birds grows so loud that the dreamer awakens and proceeds, he says, to write the poem.

Dunbar wrote several other official poems in the courtly style, and some of these with reference to particular events can be dated conjecturally. One written for the queen begins, "Gladethe thoue, queyne of Scottish regioun," and celebrates the approaching birth of the first child of James and Margaret in February 1506 or 1507. Dunbar also honored the city of Aberdeen in a poem after the queen visited it in May 1511. Two of Dunbar's official poems were written in honor of the military hero Lord Bernard Stewart, the Sieur d'Aubigny, who was welcomed by James in May 1508. Dunbar's "Welcome" poem, a ballade in which he compares d'Aubigny with the Nine Worthies, was undoubtedly intended for that celebration. When d'Aubigny died about a month later, Dunbar wrote an elegiac ballade, employing the same intricate stanzaic form, and a note in the *bursa regis* indicates that on 26 June 1508 Dunbar received special payment, presumably for these two poems.

About twenty of Dunbar's court poems are known as petitionary or "begging" poems, and his requests are surely personal. These poems tend to be short and witty, generally written in a four-stress line, a simple verse form, and colloquial diction. In one, no doubt inspired by the well-known "Complaynt of Chaucer to His Purse," Dunbar addresses the king as "Saint Salvator," urging him to "send silver sorrow" (money) to relieve the painful prickling of his empty purse. Among the most witty of Dunbar's petitionary poems is one written as a Christmas carol. Its central image suggests that it was written during Dunbar's later years at court. Addressed to the king, it begins by asking that it never be told in town that the poet Dunbar is a "Yule's yald." (A *yald* was an old horse, but the phrase meant a person without a new Christmas garment.) Dunbar then builds around this image, describing himself as an old horse who has long run forth in field with his mane having turned to white. The final verse attached to the poem is a response by James IV, commanding the treasurer, "Tak in this gray hors, auld Dumbar" and to "busk [dress] him lyk ane bischopis muill [mule]." Such humorous petitions have much in common with Dunbar's comic court poems.

Since so much of Dunbar's poetry relates to his life at court, it is hardly surprising that some of his comic poems refer specifically to people he lived and worked with there. In one short poem he describes a dance in the queen's chamber, in which many individuals are listed as dancers, and "Than cam in Dunbar the mackar; / On all the flur thair was nane frackar [readier]." In two others Dunbar plays upon the name of the queen's wardrober, James Dog. In another Dunbar describes a court jester as a knight, "Sir Thomas Norny." This short burlesque, written in modified tail-rhyme stanzas, is most certainly a parody of Chaucer's *Tale of Sir Thopas,* but while Chaucer was satirizing a literary tradition, Dunbar again creates a joke at the expense of someone he knew personally. Another chivalric burlesque is Dunbar's contribution to the "Black Tournament" held by James IV in 1507 and repeated in 1508, which featured the "jousting of a wild knight for the black lady." The poem describes the black lady as a courtly love heroine and is evidence of James's love of tournaments as well as the fascination with the exotic, including dark-skinned people. Dunbar, a product of his time and environment, shows no sensitivity toward the feelings of the woman so honored.

Among Dunbar's most memorable comic court poems are two which appear to grow out of the medieval goliardic tradition in which divine offices, prayers, and creeds were parodied. In these Dunbar interweaves Latin words and phrases for parodic effect. "The Testament of Maister Andro Kennedy," with alternating lines of Scots and Latin, offers parody of a familiar legal document, the last will and testament. The object of Dunbar's satire leaves his soul to his lord's wine cellar and requests that no priests sing the traditional service for the dead at his funeral. The other goliardic poem, "The Dregy of Dunbar," is among the best of Dunbar's comic poems. In this irreverent parody of the Office of the Dead, complete with Latin responses, Dunbar humorously contrasts his state of living in the "paradise" of Edinburgh, "We that ar heir in hevins glory," with the king's "purgatory," the Franciscan Observantine house James had had built at Stirling, where the king was then in religious retreat.

Dunbar's satire is almost certainly personally motivated in his two parodic dream-visions mocking John Damian, an Italian court physician, who unsuccessfully attempted to fly with wings from Stirling Castle to France in September 1507 and suffered a broken thigh for his efforts. James IV, who had an interest in science and in replacing depleting funds in the royal treasury, had provided Damian with money and equipment to practice alchemy, and in 1504 had rewarded Damian by naming him abbot of Tungland in Kirkcudbrightshire. Dunbar attacks Damian in one satiric vision written as an eschatological prophecy: Lady Fortune appears to a dreamer and says that an abbot in feathers, looking like a horrible griffin, flies up into the air and there is attacked by a huge female dragon; together among the clouds they beget the Antichrist. In his other satiric vision against Damian, a "ballat" about the "Fenyeit Frier Of Tungland," Dunbar's narrator accuses the abbot of having murdered many in Scotland with his phony medicine and then reports that birds, confused about the identity of the winged physician in the sky, attack, and the "feigned friar" then defecates in the air before he is brought down in a comic scene of feathers, dirt, and noise.

Dunbar's longest poem, *The Tretis of the Tua Maritt Wemen and the Wedo,* most probably was written for some type of oral presentation at court. Although it cannot be dated, it is relatively early, for it was one of Dunbar's first poems to be printed. Although this comic fantasy displays some debts to Chaucer's portrait of the Wife of Bath and his "Merchant's Tale," it is also one of the last medieval poems to be written in the quite un-Chaucerian unrhymed alliterative line.

This comic masterpiece recounts the Midsummer Eve adventure of a male narrator who hides *en cachette* in the shrubbery outside a garden to witness the candid conversation of three ladies — two women married to lords and a twice-married widow. The women, dressed in elvish green, the color often conveying sexual associations in medieval poetry, have literally let down their hair, and while indulging in rich wine, they discuss the trials of marriage in frank detail. Although the plot of the poem is simple, the overall structure is complex; in it Dunbar blends together several literary conventions, including parody of the *chanson d'aventure* and the love *débat,* and demonstrates his mastery at balancing contrasting styles and dictions even as he contrasts the artifices of *amour courtois* with the realities of marriage and the sexual relationship. The opening and concluding descriptive passages are memorably lush and sensual:

> I muvit furth allane neir as midnicht wes past
> Besyd ane gudlie grein garth full of gay flouris
> Hegeit of ane huge hicht with hawthorne treis.
>
> (I moved forth alone just after midnight
> Beside a lovely green garden full of gay flowers
> Hedged by a high hedge of hawthorn trees.)

The voices of the women, on the other hand, are "heard" in a colloquial Scots well seasoned with slang and obscenities.

The widow establishes herself as the authority and opens the debate by asking the other two if they have found bliss in that "blessed bond" of wedlock or if they wish instead the freedom of birds to choose a new mate each year. Both married women indicate a preference for the latter option. The first describes her marriage to an old husband, emphasizing his impotence with a series of epithets, such as "old caterpillar" and "bag of phlegm," and in great detail explains her repugnance at his sexual advances; his embraces cause her physical pain, especially his stiff beard and "hurcheone scyne" (hedgehog skin) rubbing against her delicate face. The second married woman states that her fate is worse, for she was deceived by her husband's younger age. This "hugest whoremaster on earth" was worn out from an earlier life of unrestrained lechery. He had the gleam of gold but proved to be only glass.

After the married women's disclosures, the widow presents her tale of woe, taking up more than twice the space of the others combined. To reveal her grotesque hypocrisy, Dunbar parodies the literary forms of both the medieval sermon and saint's legend. The widow prays that God will inspire her so that her preaching will pierce the hearts of the other two and make them "meeker to men," and when she concludes, she refers to her tale as "the legend" of her life, although clearly she is no saint. But what the widow actually teaches is how to deceive and use men. Her advice to be as fierce as dragons but to outwardly appear mild as doves seems to parody a saying by Christ (Matthew 10:16). Using her life as exemplum, she describes how she sat in the kirk, "as foxe in lambis fleise," and wet her face with a sponge to feign widow's tears while contemplating young men most likely to provide sexual pleasure. The climax of her preaching occurs when she describes her fantasy of "the best game," a brothellike scenario where she is surrounded by men ("baronis and knychtis / And othir bachilleris blithe, blumyng in youth"). In this fantasy all want to serve her, and she comforts each one with a perverse notion of *caritas,* saying that there is no living man so low in degree that shall love her and not be loved in return. She boasts that she is so "mercifull in mynd" that her soul will be safe when the Lord comes to judge all.

In spite of the hypocrisy and blasphemy of the widow, Dunbar's overall purpose in *The Tretis of the Tua Marritt Wemen and the Wedo* seems less misogynistic or moral than comic. The husbands, like their wives, are caricatured and dehumanized, yet the beauty of the setting and the spirit of medieval carnival ultimately triumph. Such matter should repel, and yet in the end it is the enormity of the jest fitting for Midsummer carnival and the beauty of the setting that stay with the reader. Any seriousness that the poem seems to convey disappears with the concluding question to the "auditoris," namely, "which one would you choose for your wife if you should wed one?"

Although the majority of Dunbar's poems in some way connect with his life at court, several are not written on secular themes but reflect his priestly vocation, including some that derive from courtly models. In an interesting bird debate between a merle and a nightingale, Dunbar adopts the orthodox Christian attitude toward profane love. The merle argues in favor of "a lusty lyfe in luves service," but the nightingale, who always speaks afterward, is given the last word with variations on the refrain, "All luve is lost bot upone God allone." The merle concedes the point, and "Than sang thay both with vocis lowd and cleir" the same refrain.

Most of Dunbar's poems on moral themes are short, simple verses with Latin or English refrains that reiterate familiar truths, often scriptural in nature. Dunbar's greatest concern in his moral poems is with mutability in the world and the fact of human mortality. In a poem beginning with the line "I seik about the warld unstabille," a poem without a refrain, the narrator observes that yesterday the season was "soft and fair" but today stings like an adder. Dunbar also portrays life as a pilgrimage in several poems, including his shortest work, a poem of only one stanza that begins with the observation that life is but a straight way to death. In another, with the words from Ecclesiastes for its Latin refrain, "Vanitas Vanitatum, et omnia Vanitas," Dunbar includes this directive: "Walk furth, pilgrame, quhill thow hes dayis licht," and in another poem the Latin refrain reminds the reader that all humanity is but earth and ash.

This concern with mutability is the theme of one of Dunbar's most personal poems, a meditation upon winter, in which the speaker complains that the dark and "drublie" days trouble his spirit and remind him of his own mortality. Only the thought of summer with its flowers can relieve his depression. This same theme is repeated in Dunbar's greatest moral poem, a poetic *danse macabre* known by its Latin refrain, "Timor mortis conturbat me" (The fear of death greatly disturbs me). In this nearly perfect poem Dunbar makes use of several medieval conventions and at the same time personalizes and makes immediate the inescapable fact of death, even in the opening lines:

> I that in heill [health] wes and gladnes,
> Am trublit now with gret seiknes
> And feblit [made feeble] with infermite.

The narrator observes that no estate on earth stands secure: Death takes the knights in the field and spares no lord for his power, nor clerk for his intelligence. Then the narrator notes the fate of poets:

> I se the makaris amang the laif [crowd]
> Playis heir ther pageant, syne gois to graif [grave];
> Sparit is nought ther faculte [talent].

A roll call of individual poets follows, poets with whom Dunbar most identifies, beginning with Chaucer. The Scottish poets are listed chronologically, and the list includes some familiar names: Barbour, Blind Hary, Robert Henryson. The list grows more personal as it winds down to the names of Dunbar's friends, "gentill Stobo and Quintyne Schaw," and finally his erstwhile antagonist, "Gud Maister Walter Kennedy," who is said to lie at point at death. With syllogistic logic the narrator climatically concludes:

> Sen he [Death] has all my brether tane
> He will naught lat me lif alane;
> On force [therefore] I man [must] his nyxt pray [prey] be.

Considering Dunbar's religious vocation, a surprisingly small number of religious poems are in his collected canon. Some undoubtedly have been lost, and others may have been destroyed during the Reformation. Nevertheless, Dunbar seems to have written religious poems throughout his life, some of which must be considered as among the greatest of all his poems.

One work that has been thought to be quite early is his ornate hymn to the Virgin Mary, "Ane Ballat of Our Lady." Deriving ultimately from the tradition of the Latin hymns of Saint Bernard of Clairvaux, this hymn, in which Dunbar interweaves Latin words and phrases with Scots, is perhaps the most aureate in the language: "Hale, sterne superne; hale in eterne / In God's sicht to schyne." It has a complicated stanza form and contains triple internal rhyme and supplementary alliteration. Its intricate structure and gilded diction contribute to its meaning, for with them Dunbar emphasizes the holiness of his subject, the Queen of Heaven.

Dunbar's poems on the life, passion, and Resurrection of Christ also constitute a remarkable trilogy. Lewis believed Dunbar's nativity hymn the greatest of its type in the language. Dunbar's hymn contains Latin lines of the Advent service and their English translations:

> Heavens distill your balmy schouris [showers]
> For now is rissen the brycht day ster
> Fro the ros Mary, flour of flouris.

Each stanza rises to a triumphant close with the Latin refrain, "Et nobis Puer natus est" (and unto us a son is given), a part of the introit for Christmas Day. Around the liturgical lines Dunbar weaves a hymn of welcoming praise for the Christ child, calling on all creation to welcome "the cleir sone quhome no clud [cloud] devouris."

Dunbar's passion poem emerges out of the late medieval tradition that focuses on the suffering of Christ. Dunbar makes real for the reader Christ's agony by having the poem's narrator in a Good Friday dream-vision witness the events. The beautifully moving refrain of the *visio* stanzas, "O mankind, for the love of thee," emphasizes the significance of Christ's suffering for every individual.

Dunbar's triumphant Resurrection ballad is ageless. Written in colloquial diction, it is known by its Latin refrain, "Surrexit Dominus de sepulchro" (Christ is risen from the grave). This ballad is one of Dunbar's greatest poems. Its rhythm, alliteration, and structural form recall Anglo-Saxon poetry, as does its depiction of Christ as warrior-king dramatically descending into hell, then building to a crescendo and climax as he slays the evil dragon Satan, and emerges as the victorious Savior of mankind:

> Done is a battell on the dragon blak;
> Our campioun Christ confoundit hes his force:
> The gettis of hell ar brokin with a crak.

In spirit a different poem from the preceding, "The Tabill of Confessioun" appears to be a late work, perhaps composed after Flodden. It is a great if neglected poem. The "Confessioun" may speak for much in Dunbar's life but is offered as one that should be made by each lord of Scotland. Refrain follows refrain with a terrible urgency to the last, "I cry the marcy and laser to repent."

Dunbar's poetic corpus, then, exhibits wide variety while each poem displays marked qualities of the immediate and the personal. Judging from the few poems that it is possible to date, it seems that Dunbar tended to write in a plainer style as he matured. Those heavily aureate poems such as *The Golden Targe* seem to belong to those years when he was experimenting with various styles and trying to establish his reputation as a poet. Dunbar's work also indicates that the poet was interested in the

world around him, for he often wrote about real people and events, and often for the purpose of satire or moral correction. Yet, in spite of Dunbar's attention to detail, his obvious perfectionism, and his fascination with language, his poems are more than ornate exercises, for Dunbar puts something of himself, his experience, into each poem. Indeed, in all of his poetry can be seen the moving expression of a mind that can be both worldly and religious, a richly various yet always human personality.

Bibliographies:

William Geddie, *A Bibliography of Middle Scots Poets*, Scottish Text Society 61 (Edinburgh: Blackwood, 1912);

Peter Heidtmann, "A Bibliography of Henryson, Dunbar, and Douglas, 1912–1968," *Chaucer Review*, 5 (Summer 1970): 75–82;

Florence H. Ridley, "Middle Scots Writers," in *A Manual of the Writings in Middle English 1050–1500,* edited by A. E. Hartung, volume 4 (New Haven: Connecticut Academy of Arts and Sciences, 1973), pp. 1005–1060, 1204–1284;

William Russell Aitken, "William Dunbar (1460?–1513?)," in *Scottish Literature in English and Scots: A Guide to Information Sources, American Literature and World Literature in English,* volume 37, edited by Aitken (Detroit: Gale Research Company, 1982), pp. 33–35;

Jean-Jacques Blanchôt, "Dunbar and his Critics: A Critical Survey," in *Scottish Language and Literature, Medieval and Renaissance,* edited by Dietrich Strauss and Horst W. Drescher, Scottish Studies 4 (Frankfurt am Main: Lang, 1986), pp. 303–336;

Walter Scheps and J. A. Looney, *Middle Scots Poets: A Reference Guide to James I, Robert Henryson, William Dunbar and Gavin Douglas* (Boston: Hall, 1986).

Biography:

J. W. Baxter, *William Dunbar: A Biographical Study* (Edinburgh: Oliver & Boyd, 1952).

References:

Priscilla Bawcutt, "Aspects of Dunbar's Imagery," in *Chaucer and Middle English Studies in Honour of Rossell Hope Robbins* (Kent, Ohio: Kent State University Press, 1974);

Bawcutt, *Dunbar the Maker* (Oxford: Clarendon Press, 1992);

Bawcutt, "William Dunbar and Gavin Douglas," in *The History of Scottish Literature,* volume 1, Origins to 1660, edited by R. D. S. Jack (Aberdeen: Aberdeen University Press, 1988);

Eileen Bentsen and S. L. Sanderlin, "The Profits of Marriage in Late Medieval Scotland," *Scottish Literary Journal,* 12 (November 1985): 5–18;

Lois A. Ebin, *Illuminator, Makar, Vate: Visions of Poetry in the Fifteenth Century* (Lincoln: University of Nebraska Press, 1988);

Ebin, "The Theme of Poetry in Dunbar's 'Golden Targe,' " *Chaucer Review,* 7 (Fall 1972): 147–159;

Elizabeth Eddy, "Sir Thopas and Sir Thomas Norny: Romance Parody in Chaucer and Dunbar," *Review of English Studies,* new series 22 (November 1971): 401–409;

Deanna Delmar Evans, "Ambivalent Artifice in Dunbar's *The Thrissill and the Rois,*" *Studies in Scottish Literature,* 22 (1987): 95–105;

Evans, "Dunbar's *Tretis:* The Seven Deadly Sins in Carnivalesque Disguise," *Neophilologus,* 73 (January 1989): 130–141;

Denton Fox, "The Chronology of William Dunbar," *Philological Quarterly,* 39 (October 1960): 413–425;

Fox, "Dunbar's *The Golden Targe,*" *English Literary History,* 26 (September 1959): 311–334;

Fox, "The Scottish Chaucerians," in *Chaucer & Chaucerians: Critical Studies in Middle English Literature,* edited by D. S. Brewer (University: University of Alabama Press, 1966);

Louise O. Fradenburg, *City, Marriage, Tournament: Arts of Rule in Late Medieval Scotland* (Madison: University of Wisconsin Press, 1991);

David V. Harrington, "The 'wofull prisonnere' in Dunbar's *Goldyn Targe,*" *Studies in Scottish Literature,* 22 (1987): 173–182;

A. D. Hope, *A Midsummer Eve's Dream: Variations on a Theme by William Dunbar* (Canberra: Australian National University Press, 1970);

Jack, "Dunbar and Lydgate," *Studies in Scottish Literature,* 8 (1970–1971): 215–227;

A. M. Kinghorn, "Dunbar and Villon – A Comparison and a Contrast," *Modern Language Review,* 62 (April 1967): 195–208;

C. S. Lewis, "The Close of the Middle Ages in Scotland," *English Literature in the Sixteenth Century, Excluding Drama* (Oxford: Clarendon Press, 1954);

Roderick J. Lyall, "Moral Allegory in Dunbar's 'Golden Targe,' " *Studies in Scottish Literature,* 11 (1973): 47–65;

Alasdair A. MacDonald, "Dunbar in Paraphrase," in *A Day Estivall: Essays on Music, Poetry and History of Scotland and England and Poems Previously Unpublished in Honour of Helena Mennie Shire,* edited by Alisoun Gardner-Medwin and Janet Hadley Williams (Aberdeen: Aberdeen University Press, 1990), pp. 112–123;

Matthew P. McDiarmid, "The Early William Dunbar and his Poems," *Scottish Historical Review,* 59 (October 1980): 138–158;

Steven R. McKenna, "Drama and Invective: Traditions in Dunbar's 'Fasternis Evin in Hell,' " *Studies in Scottish Literature,* 24 (1989): 129–141;

Edwin Morgan, "Dunbar and the Language of Poetry," *Essays in Criticism,* 2 (January 1952): 138–158;

Wilhelm F. H. Nicolaisen, "Line and Sentence in Dunbar's Poetry," in *Bards & Makars,* edited by Adam J. Aitken, McDiarmid, and Derick S. Thomson (Glasgow: Glasgow University Press, 1977), pp. 61–71;

Joanne E. Norman, "Sources for the Grotesque in William Dunbar's 'Dance of the Sevin Deidly Synnis,' " *Scottish Studies,* 29 (1989): 55–75;

Norman, "William Dunbar: Scottish Goliard," in *Selected Essays on Scottish Language and Literature: A Festschrift in Honor of Allan H. MacLaine,* edited by McKenna (Lewiston, N.Y.: Edwin Mellen Press, 1992);

Roy Pearcy, "The Genre of William Dunbar's *Tretis of the Tua Mariit Wemen and the Wedo,*" *Speculum,* 55 (January 1980): 58–74;

Edmund Reiss, *William Dunbar* (Boston: G. K. Hall, 1979);

Florence Ridley, "Scottish Transformations of Courtly Literature: William Dunbar and the Court of James IV," in *The Expansion and Transformation of Courtly Literature,* edited by N. B. Smith and J. T. Snow (Athens: University of Georgia Press, 1981), pp. 171–184;

Ian Simpson Ross, *William Dunbar* (Leiden: E. J. Brill, 1981);

Walter Scheps, "Chaucer and the Middle Scots Poets," *Studies in Scottish Literature,* 22 (1987): 44–59;

Tom Scott, *Dunbar: A Critical Exposition of the Poems* (Edinburgh: Oliver & Boyd, 1966);

Pamela K. Shaffer, "The Relationship of Syntax and Semantics in Three Poems of William Dunbar," *Fifteenth-Century Studies,* 12 (1987): 165–173.

The *Gawain*-Poet

(flourished circa 1350 – 1400)

William McColly
University of South Carolina

WORKS: *Sir Gawain and the Green Knight; Pearl; Cleanness* (or *Purity*); and *Patience*

Manuscript: The four poems attributed to the *Gawain*-Poet are in a unique manuscript: British Library MS. Cotton Nero A.x. (late fourteenth century). Facsimile: with introduction by Sir Israel Gollancz, EETS, o.s. (1923 [i.e. 1922]; reprinted, 1971).

First publications: *Sir Gawain,* edited by Sir Frederic Madden, Bannatyne Club Publications 61 (London: Printed by R. & J. E. Taylor, 1839); *Pearl, Purity,* and *Patience,* in *Early English Alliterative Poems,* edited by Richard Morris, EETS, o.s. 1 (1864; revised edition, 1869; reprinted, 1965).

Standard editions: *The Pearl,* edited by Charles G. Osgood, Jr. (Boston: Heath, 1906); *Pearl,* edited by E. V. Gordon (Oxford: Clarendon Press, 1953); *Cleanness* (*Purity*), edited by Robert J. Menner, Yale Studies in English 61 (New Haven: Yale University Press, 1920); *Patience: A West Midland Poem of the Fourteenth Century,* edited by Hartley Bateson (Manchester: Manchester University Press, 1912; revised edition, 1918; reprinted, Folcroft Press, 1970); *"Patience": An Alliterative Version of Jonah by the Poet of "Pearl,"* edited by Sir Israel Gollancz (London: Oxford University Press, 1913; revised edition, 1924); *Patience,* edited by J. J. Anderson (Manchester: Manchester University Press, 1969); *Sir Gawain and the Green Knight,* edited by Gollancz, EETS, o.s. 210 (1940 [i.e. 1938]; reprinted, 1951, 1957, 1964, 1966); *Sir Gawain and the Green Knight,* edited by J. R. R. Tolkien and Gordon, second edition, revised by Norman Davis (Oxford: Clarendon Press, 1967); *The Works of the "Gawain"-Poet,* edited by Charles Moorman (Jackson: University Press of Mississippi, 1977); *Pearl, Cleanness, Patience, Sir Gawain and the Green Knight,* second edition, edited by A.

C. Cawley and Anderson (London: Dent, 1978).

Editions in modern English: *Pearl,* translated by Marie Boroff (New York: Norton, 1977); *Sir Gawain and the Green Knight,* translated by Theodore H. Banks (New York: Crofts, 1929); *Sir Gawain and the Green Knight,* translated by Borroff (New York: Norton, 1967); *The Complete Works of the Gawain-Poet,* translated by John Gardner (Chicago: University of Chicago Press, 1965); *The Pearl-Poet: His Complete Works,* translated by Margaret Williams (New York: Random House, 1967); *The Complete Works of the "Pearl" Poet,* edited by Malcolm Andrew, Ronald Waldron, and Clifford Peterson, translated by Casey Finch (Berkeley: University of California Press, 1993).

The works said to be by a single anonymous author known as the *Gawain*-Poet (sometimes called the *Pearl*-Poet) are *Sir Gawain and the Green Knight, Pearl, Cleanness* (or *Purity*), and *Patience.* If they indeed are the work of one man, these four poems mark the so-called *Gawain*-Poet as one of the three greatest English writers of the later Middle Ages — along with Chaucer and the author of *Piers Plowman.* It is proper to refer to the *Gawain*-Poet as so-called. There is no firm evidence to prove even that these four poems are the works of one man. They might have been written by the same poet, but, on the other hand, they might have been written by two, three, or four different poets who imitated a common source or who imitated each other.

Even so, the idea of a *Gawain*-Poet is accepted by most Middle English literary scholars on the basis of circumstantial evidence they find compelling. The most obvious circumstance is the survival of *Sir Gawain, Pearl, Cleanness,* and *Patience* in a unique manuscript, the Cotton Nero A.x., in the British Library. The manuscript is unique because

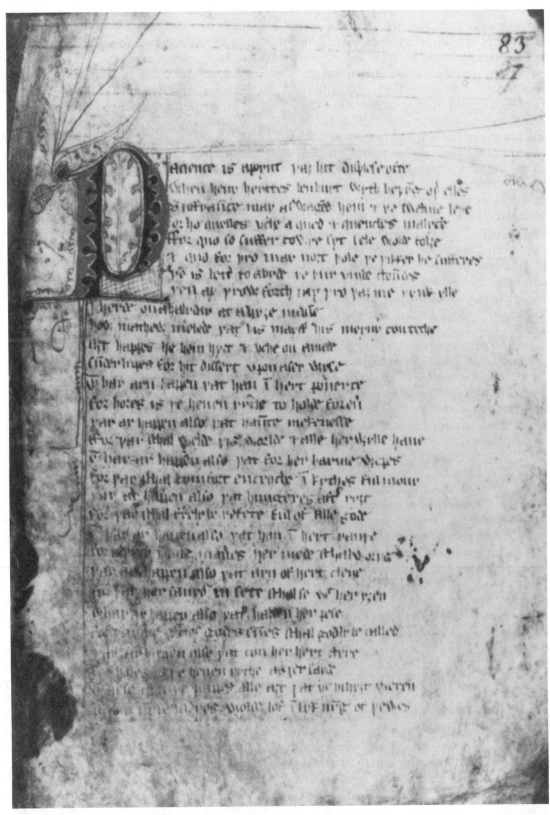

The beginning of Patience, *from the late-fourteenth-century manuscript that preserves all four works of the* Gawain-*poet (British Library, MS. Cotton Nero A.x., fol.87)*

only these four works are in it, and they exist in no other known manuscript. Cotton Nero A.x. was written by a single copyist, whose handwriting has been dated as late fourteenth century. Evidence such as vocabulary, morphology, inflections, and terms for and descriptions of objects and artifacts such as clothing suggests that the poems of the Cotton Nero A.x. were written between 1350 and 1400, most probably in the last third of the century. All four poems are in the same dialect, which has been identified as that of fourteenth-century southeast Cheshire. The dialect of the copyist might have been that of the poet or poets, but, if not, it was probably similar.

Further, the four poems have important stylistic similarities. *Sir Gawain, Patience,* and *Cleanness* are in the strong-stress meter of alliterative long lines. Alliteration – the repetition in the same line of identical or similar stressed sounds – survived as a metrical device from the Old English into the Middle English period. Even the different types of alliterative lines that metrists can identify in Old English verse survived, except that by the fourteenth century alliterative poets wrote lines that in general have more unstressed syllables than in Old English and which therefore are longer lines. *Pearl,* though its meter is iambic tetrameter, uses alliteration in most lines as ornament. A second distinct quality of Middle English alliterative verse that the four poems share is the amount of vocalic alliteration (repetition of stressed vowel sounds). Popular in Old English verse – in *Beowulf* one of every six lines is of this type – its use declined so that few Middle English alliterative poems have more than one in twenty lines with vocalic alliteration. This is the rate of occurrence, in fact, in *Sir Gawain, Pearl, Cleanness,* and *Patience.* (J. P. Oakden discusses these metrical matters in great detail.) Moreover, several rare words appear in two or more of these poems that surface in few or, in some cases, no other Middle English writings. Finally, the content of the poems, especially of *Pearl, Cleanness,* and *Patience,* shares a common ground of serious Christian orthodoxy.

The assumption of a single *Gawain*-Poet instead of two or more poets is so strong that scholars such as Henry L. Savage and Charles Moorman have written books about this legendary figure. In his *The Pearl-Poet* (1968) Moorman's argument for single authorship is typical. In a chapter titled "The Anonymous Poet," he says that scholars who believe in single authorship are an overwhelming majority. Also, Moorman says, in the four poems "one is conscious of a wholly unified and individual

point of view and of the presence of an author whose central concern is with the trials of life." From an objective standpoint, however, the argument for common authorship of the *Gawain*-poems is tenuous, and the counterarguments seem reasonable. A majority – even of scholars – can be wrong, and literary attribution by acclamation is risky. Medieval poets who were preoccupied with Christian doctrine are bound to reflect much unity, and it can be said that English poets in general have been concerned with the trials of life. Further, each of the four poems shares characteristics of vocabulary with poems besides its companions of the Cotton Nero A.x. manuscript. Such sharing, in fact, might have been the product of a school of poets or of an intense poetic tradition. The vocabularies of these poems have even been subjected to statistical analysis, with vague results except in one study: using function-word frequencies, William McColly and Dennis Weir demonstrated that the existence of a single poet is impossible to prove through a statistical analysis of internal evidence.

In a more recent introductory study than Moorman's, David Lawton reviews the single-authorship controversy with insight and common sense. Taking a cue from Lawton, the reader may be prudent to remember that to refer to the work of the *Gawain*-Poet is safe only when speaking of *Sir Gawain and the Green Knight,* but with the other three poems *Gawain-Poet* is a term of convenience. Such being the case, it would seem better to call these four poems the "*Gawain*-group." This is no handicap. The author of each of the poems – whoever he was – wrote a work of distinction in which he left a distinctive biographical mark.

In spite of the lack of believable evidence, however, and the uncertainty and ambiguity that arise from trying to attribute the *Gawain*-poems to a single author, let alone a specific identifiable author, scholars work continually to do the latter. The most recent attempts focus on cryptographic evidence in *Pearl* and *Sir Gawain and the Green Knight,* but these studies inspire skepticism. Those who argue in favor of such evidence claim to have found the name Massey encoded in these poems. Massey was a common name in Cheshire in the later fourteenth century, a time during which it appears that one John Massey was indeed a poet. Among the problems with this hypothesis are that the encoding so far identified is not as convincing as it should be and that more than one John Massey existed in Cheshire at that time. Those who argue for the Massey attribution are Erik Kooper, William Vantuono, and Barbara Nolan and David Farley-

Hills. The skeptics are Thorlac Turville-Petre, Edward Wilson, and Clifford J. Peterson. Until firmer evidence of the names of any poets responsible for the *Gawain*-poems is forthcoming, it would seem wisest to admit that such an identity or identities are not provable and that any so-called *Gawain*-Poet is a legendary figure.

Examining each of the four poems singly reveals material from which to speculate about its poet. There is much in *Patience* to tempt the reader. *Patience* is the shortest and simplest poem of the *Gawain* group — a narrative homily of 531 alliterative long lines — less than half the length of the next shortest of these four works, *Pearl*. Some critics would date *Patience* as the earliest of the group, finding it somewhat primitive in comparison with the others. Such a view, however, is an oversimplification. The brevity and simplicity of *Patience* reflect merely its more limited scope, within which the poet nevertheless created a sophisticated rhetorical exercise memorable for the imaginative elaboration of his source. Whether *Patience* is an earlier or later effort than the others is a moot point. To pursue this matter can lead only to speculation about the aesthetic, technical, and intellectual development of a poet whose existence is legendary at best and who in reality might have been two or three or four poets.

The *Patience*-Poet took as the text for his sermon the eighth beatitude from the Sermon on the Mount as given in Matthew 5:10 — blessed are the patient, those who suffer persecution for the cause of righteousness. As his exemplum, he uses the story of Jonah and the whale from the Old Testament. He animates this brief and bare-bones story with vivid details that reveal a playful mind often devoted to drollery for its own sake. The poet foreshadows his distinctive poetic voice with obvious care in his exordium. He personalizes his posture by reporting that he heard his text at high mass on a holy day. Then, after summarizing each of the eight beatitudes in their order in Matthew, he observes with typical understatement that even though a person is lucky if he enjoys one of these conditions, he is better off if he has all eight. Since (he continues wryly) he himself is forced to be poor, he will be patient with his poverty and enjoy patience as well. He personifies the beatitudes as Dame Poverty, Dame Patience, and so on, and he observes that Poverty will not be put off but will appear wherever she pleases. Thus, he says, a man must forbear his impatience with poverty and suffer much on its account.

The poet's transition to the particular application of the Jonah story is by way of remarking about the necessity of forbearance. In his own case

he asks if his liege lord should send him to Rome on an errand, what good would grumbling about it do except to invite more trouble? Readers may ask whether these remarks are true and therefore autobiographical. If so, why was the poet poor? Was he in regular orders — a monk or a mendicant — sworn to the vow of poverty? Was he a priest with only a meager living? Or was he in minor secular orders, an unfortunate supernumerary clerk stuck in the rut of penury? Bearing on these questions is the poet's remark about not begrudging his liege lord if the latter should ask him to go to Rome. Any trip to Rome at that time suggested a pilgrimage, and the medieval English (including Chaucer's Wife of Bath) were inveterate Roman pilgrims. If the poet's reference is to a pilgrimage, his liege lord was God (a common metaphor), but the idea of forbearance is ironic because a pilgrimage was a form of penance to be undergone gladly as a step in the purification of the soul. If a pilgrimage is not meant, a trip to Rome could well have been on business, in which case the liege lord most likely was an ecclesiastic with the rank of a peer — a member of the group of lords spiritual. In the poet's time bishops were the equivalent of earls and abbots the equivalent of barons.

A problem with such speculation is that the poet might have fictionalized so as to make the Jonah story more vivid and compelling. His comment about impatiently resisting a lord's bidding foreshadows Jonah's resistance to God's command. To say that the poet follows the Old Testament closely is misleading. The biblical version is a short and matter-of-fact narrative that the poet embellishes not only with lively details but also with much wit. In *Patience,* as Jonah starts for Tarshish, where he plans to hide and escape God's order to go to Nineveh to denounce the city for its wickedness, he rationalizes absurdly, as though oblivious of God's omniscience. God's throne is so high, Jonah reasons, that God worries little whether Jonah is "taken in Nineveh and stripped naked, / Shredded on a cross by many ribalds" (translation by A. C. Cawley and J. J. Anderson, from their 1978 edition; all subsequent quotations are from this edition unless otherwise indicated). Jonah also ignores God's omnipotence. On board a ship bound for Tarshish he rejoices that he deftly escaped God's dangerous mission and feels secure because, he says, God "has no power to grieve a man in that sea." Yet the poet, as if unsure that his audience would understand the irony of Jonah's foolish acts and thoughts, makes the point explicit. Jonah is a "witless wretch" to think that, because he has left Samaria, God "sees no further." Even though the truth is otherwise, as David made clear in a psalm, Jonah in the dotage of old age has no fear, for he is "far in the flood" rushing to Tarshish.

The poet's humor intensifies when the whale appears. The sailors throw Jonah overboard in hope of calming the rough sea. With the men still holding Jonah by the feet, the whale opens his gullet, and Jonah tumbles into its throat without touching a tooth. Here the poet approaches the absurd level of modern black humor. Standing up in the whale's stomach, Jonah, the man who will suffer no hardship, "builds his bower." He looks for the best place "in each nook of his [the whale's] navel" but finds no rest – only "muck and mud . . . in whichever gut he goes to." When God relents and orders the whale to deposit Jonah on dry land, the poet adds this understatement: "It may well be that he needed to wash his mantle."

The rest of the poem follows the Old Testament story closely but with characteristic added details. When the whale disgorges Jonah, instead of merely commanding him again to go to Nineveh, God remarks, "will you never go to Nineveh by any known route?" God's Old Testament phrase "denounce it [Nineveh] in the words I give you" becomes, in the poet's version, "Listen, my lore is locked within you – release it therein." The poet elaborates Jonah's message to the Ninevites as well. The city shall fall to the ground, he tells them: "Upside down you shall be dumped deep into the abyss, / To be swallowed swiftly by the black earth." The Ninevite king's simple proclamation in the Old Testament that no man or beast is to taste food or drink water becomes dramatic in *Patience*: "Children shall cease their suckling, howsoever it may sorrow them." Beasts cannot chew on broom or grass, go to pasture, or top shrubs, nor can oxen eat hay or horses drink water, and "Everybody shall cry out from hunger with all our clear strength; / The noise shall rise to Him Who shall have pity."

After telling the rest of the story, which he elaborates in the same fashion, the poet concludes with a short peroration of eight lines. His message, that one should be quiet and patient in pain and in joy, is capped with an apt proverb: he who is too quick to tear his clothes must go to more trouble to sew them together. This conclusion and the brief expostulation of the introduction reflect an intention to create vivid dramatic narrative at the expense of ratiocination. Thus, even though the theme of *Patience* is doctrinal and the poet's matter is biblical, he was, it seems, first of all a storyteller and almost incidentally a preacher.

Cleanness (or *Purity*), also a narrative homily, in some respects is a companion poem to *Patience*. All of *Patience* and much of *Cleanness* are in units of four lines each that can be considered unrhymed stanzas. Markings in the manuscript support this view of their stanzaic form. Their use of function words makes their vocabularies more alike than are any other companion of the four poems of the *Gawain* group. *Cleanness*, however, is much longer (1,812 lines) than *Patience* and is theologically more complicated, but it is less playful and witty. The poet's tone, in fact, is always stern and sometimes grim.

The title of the poem reflects its theme, which the poet pursues with compulsive rigor. After a short introduction (52 lines) he moves swiftly from scene to scene, with intervals of expostulation, beginning with an attack on impure priests. If priests approach the altar and "handle there His own body and use it both" (administer the sacrament of communion as well as partake of it) and are pure, they are rewarded. If they are counterfeit, outwardly honest but inwardly filthy, they defile God's vessels and are therefore sinful and inspire him to anger. After noting the beatitude "blessed are the pure in heart," the poet remarks that even an earthly lord is offended by a filthy guest at a feast. Here the poet shares the fondness for vivid detail that marks the *Patience*-Poet. Such a guest, the *Cleanness*-Poet says, with a ragged tabard, trousers torn at the knees, and his toes out of his shoes, would be dragged to the hall door and thrown out, perhaps beaten, and forbidden to go to that house again on pain of imprisonment. If such a filthy man offends an earthly noble, he is even more loathsome to God.

Immediately the poet tells the parable of the wedding feast from Matthew 22:1–14 and Luke 14:16–24 but adds lively touches that require well over 100 lines. In proclaiming the feast for his son's wedding, the lord speaks not only of his bulls that are slaughtered but also of pen-fed poultry and partridges, cranes, and swans that are broiled and roasted and ready to be eaten. After the lord's retainers have scoured the neighborhood to find guests, the hall still is not full. The lord sends them far into the countryside, searching the gorse and thickets, to bring anybody – bold or timid, whole or lame, hobbling cripples, blind or one-eyed – they are all welcome so that the hall will be full. The unclean guest, as in the gospel, is mute when the lord confronts him, but for the *Cleanness*-Poet he is shamed by the lord's angry words, and he hangs his head, looking at the ground. He is so frightened at the prospect of punishment that he knows not what to say. The poet's version of the parable omits from the Matthew version the mistreatment and murder of the king's messengers and the lord's severe punishment of the killers, reflecting the poet's intention to focus on the virtue of purity.

After this parable the poet expostulates on its significance. Christ, he says, compares this earthly feast to the kingdom of heaven, to which all are called. Thus, the poet warns, make sure you are clean when you approach God. Your deeds are your garments lined with the feelings in your heart, he explains, and if your clothes are clean, you will see the Savior and his rich throne, but for many faults you can forfeit this pleasure. Here the poet catalogues sins and vices in an impetuous and haphazard way: sloth; vanity, boasting, and pride; envy, cowardice, and crooked deeds; perjury, manslaughter, and drunkenness; theft and quarreling; robbery, ribaldry, and lying; stealing women's dowers; adultery; protecting criminals; treason, treachery, and tyranny; and slander and false laws.

The purpose of this catalogue seems clear. The poet has read and has heard many great clerks say that God is displeased with all sin, but he has never heard or read that God's vengeance was so great as it was for filth of the flesh. To get to the subject of the sin of filth, the poet first remarks about Satan's revolt in heaven, which is an upshot of the sin of pride. This leads to the story of Adam and Eve and Original Sin. God punished Satan with banishment, and Adam and Eve with the loss of paradise — in each case a milder sentence than the vengeance he reserved for sins against cleanness. The sin of filth, hinted at in Genesis, was expanded by medieval theologians into the cause of the Flood. The poet follows this tradition, speaking of men who "enjoyed filth in fleshly deeds, / And against nature contrived perverted practices." The devils saw "How the daughters of men were exceedingly beautiful, / And began to consort with them in human fashion, / And engendered on them a race of giants." The poet then tells the story of Noah, with characteristic vividness, and concludes it by mentioning God's remorse for having destroyed most of mankind.

After an exhortation to his audience to abjure the sin of filth, the poet moves to his next exemplum. The outline of his story follows closely the scriptural account of God's destruction of Sodom and Gomorrah, from Genesis 18–19, except for heightened dialogue and descriptive elaboration. The poet's own contribution is most striking when he specifies the sins of the Sodomites. Through his angels God says to Abraham that these sinners "Have learned a practice that ill pleases me, . . .

Daniel, Baltassar, and the queen; an illustration from the manuscript for Cleanness *(British Library, M S. Cotton Nero A.x., fol. 60*^{b}*)*

Each male makes his mate a man like himself, / And they join together foolishly in the manner of females." God taught mankind a natural skill, through which, in the married state, "Between a male and his mate such pleasure should come / That pure paradise itself might prove no better." But now, the angels tell Abraham, "They [the Sodomites] have spurned my skill and scorned nature, / And caught in contempt a usage unclean." Subsequently the poet describes what replaced the ruined cities — a dead, stinking lake with sulphurous shores, into which any man thrown to be killed will live forever in a sinful state.

The poet got his account of this lake from a popular medieval work, Sir John Mandeville's *Travels* (1356–1357). For part of the discourse that follows, the poet was indebted to a passage in Jean de Meun's *Romance of the Rose,* an influential thirteenth-century French allegorical poem. In de Meun's passage, Reason advises the Lover to woo his lady by doing what pleases her best. The *Cleanness*-Poet applies this to a Christian's attempt to please Christ. Christ is the pure pearl of greatest value, and the soul of greatest value to Christ is the pure soul. The exhortation is workaday doctrine given the elevated inspiration of the pearl image. "You may shine through shrift, though you have served shame, / And purify yourself with penance until you become a pearl," says the poet, but he continues, "beware, if you wash with the water of confession, / And are polished as plainly as smooth parchment," be sure to sin no more. Once a soul is reconciled with God it is his. Thus, "Beware then of his vengeance once his wrath is aroused, / If that which was once His should then become unclean."

This message has a ring of finality, and if *Cleanness* were to end here these lines would be taken as a peroration meant to be conclusive. Thus many critics think that the continuation of the poem was a mistake, that it creates a disjunctive break and weakens the structure of the whole. This view of the poem's disintegration is reinforced by the brief and abrupt transition to the next exemplum. "Though it be a basin, a bowl, or a cup, / A dish or a plate, that God once served," the poet warns, "To defile it . . . He forbids, / . . . And that was borne out in Babylon in Balshazzar's time." "If you give me a chance," the poet tells his audience, "I will tell the story" – as if to prepare them for the length of what was to come. Before he gets to Belshazzar, however, he must describe the conquest of the idolatrous Zedekiah by Nebuchadnezzar, a story he takes not from the "dialogues of Daniel," as the poet says, but from Jeremiah 52:1–27.

The Bible's bare account of the sack of Jerusalem by Nebuzaradan, the captain of Nebuchadnezzar II's guard, the poet expands with some relish. The Babylonians under Nebuzaradan, he relates, would spare no one, not even the sweetest maidens or the children, the "Bairns bathed in blood, with their brains spilled." They "Cut up the wombs of wives and wenches / That their bowels burst out into the ditches." They went to the temple, where they pulled out the priests by the crown and beheaded them, as well as the deacons, clerks, and maidens. In the temple "They ran to the relics like robbers gone wild." Here the poet describes the victor's expropriation of the holy objects, which they took to Babylon, but he adds to Jeremiah's catalogue of these artifacts such symbolic details as God the light giver, reflected in "The chief chandelier, charged with the light." Nebuchadnezzar refused to defile these treasures but "Trussed them in his treasury, in a tried place," as the poet remarks, "with reverence." Nebuchadnezzar's prudence in so doing is not mentioned by either of the prophets Daniel or Jeremiah, but it was traditional in medieval biblical exegesis.

Nebuchadnezzar's wisdom on this occasion is crucial to the poet's exemplum, for it contrasts with the folly of Belshazzar during his well-known feast, a description of which preoccupies the poet for nearly all of the poem's remaining 450-odd lines. As a transition from the story of Nebuchadnezzar to that of Belshazzar, the poet prefaces his treatment of the banquet with a unique account of Belshazzar's sinful state, his idolatry in rejecting God and worshiping images of the devil, "False phantoms of fiends formed with hands," which he called gods. Belshazzar thus was arrogant and proud, and, although he had a wife, he lived in lust with concubines. He was also vain and gluttonous "In noting of new meats and of nice get-ups." Having prepared his audience for Belshazzar's folly, the poet expands the few lines of the Book of Daniel into a long passage (lines 1385–1532) describing the banquet, during which Belshazzar angered God by using the holy vessels as drinking cups. The impression left by the banquet description is of a poet's rushing headlong through a catalogue of the events, dishes, and artifacts of a fourteenth-century English aristocratic feast. Cawley and Anderson's translation of lines 1402–1406 reflects well this quality: "[There was] a loud blast of trumpets, clamour in the hall; everywhere along the walls flourishes burst out, and [there were] great banners on the trumpets, gleaming of gold."

The poet describes the upshot of Belshazzar's reckless transgressions swiftly: the handwriting on the wall, his queen's wish that Daniel be consulted, Daniel's prophecy, and the sack of Babylon by Darius the Medean. The poet follows these passages with a brief conclusion, which is hardly hortative and whose calm message contrasts notably with the strident trenchancy of his other expostulations. These final 8 lines seem inappropriately short as the peroration to an exemplum of more than 600 lines, much less to a homily of 1,812 lines. They may well demonstrate the soundness of what many critics have argued, that the stories of Nebuchadnezzar, Belshazzar, and Daniel seem to be an afterthought to a poem that should have ended with the poet's moralizing on the destruction of Sodom and Gomorrah. In his 1987 study of the vocabulary of *Cleanness* McColly identifies a significant contrast between the frequencies of many words in the first part (through line 1144) and in the rest of the poem. This contrast indicates, moreover, a shift in modality between the two parts. Part 1 is quite dramatic, while part 2 is conventional narrative. Indeed, this division is so striking that the reader may wonder whether two poets wrote *Cleanness*. But in the absence of any evidence to the contrary and since different modes (dramatic and narrative) exercise different constraints on the vocabulary even of the same author, it is assumed that *Cleanness* is the work of one poet. Although the poem seems divided aesthetically, it is unified through its theology and the symbolic elaboration of its doctrinal themes as Charlotte Morse, and T. D. Kelly and John T. Irwin argue.

Critics have no reservations about the structure of *Pearl*. Its structural and thematic unity, in fact, does much to make it one of the most distinctive works of English literature. The poem consists of 101 twelve-line stanzas in iambic tetrameter, with alliteration as ornament in about three-fourths of the lines. These devices along with the rhyme scheme (*ababababbcbc*) and the stanza form create much structural intensity. The poet grouped the stanzas into sections of five stanzas, except for section 15, which has six. The stanzas of each section are linked, and the last line of each section is linked with the first line of the next through the repetition of a key word. None of the poet's formal devices is unique, for other Middle English poems with the same stanza form survive, but his handling of these devices shows an almost perfect mastery of Middle English prosody.

In its rhetorical structure *Pearl* is a dream-vision allegory and, at the same time, some critics believe, an elegy. In order to read *Pearl* as an elegy it is necessary to accommodate an autobiographical interpretation to certain conventions of medieval symbolism, in particular as applied to pearls, as well as to medieval conventions of the creation of poetic personae. To read the poem as autobiography assumes that the narrator is the poet speaking in his own voice as he describes the loss through death of a pearl, which he personifies as a small girl of less than two years, and with whom he implies a close blood relationship. Critics in the autobiographical school believe that the pearl represents the poet's daughter. They base this interpretation on the narrator's comment that the pearl "was nearer to me than aunt or niece." In his edition of *Sir Gawain and the Green Knight* E. V. Gordon points out that the word *nearer* in the poet's day referred to blood relationship. Thus the autobiographical hypothesis is that, because the narrator's expression of sorrow is so profound, he refers to a daughter and not to a sister.

Alternative views, however, seem just as logical. First is the fact that the conventional symbolic gender of medieval pearls was feminine. The poet's choice of a small girl (of less than two years) as a symbol may be in part a reflection of this standard of femininity. More important is the commonsense view that autobiographical proof that depends on the depth of feeling a narrator shows is bound to be tenuous when the poet is a genius, as in the case of *Pearl*. The greater the emotion is, the greater the effect, and of course the greater the work as well. Intensity of feeling from the pen of a master runs deep on a printed page whatever the source — personal or gratuitous. Further, the dream-vision mode invites fictionalizing, in which poets may indulge as freely as playwrights or novelists. No critic would argue that Chaucer experienced the aerial episode described by the narrator of *The House of Fame*. By the same token, simply because the dreamer of *Pearl* is earthbound, in a garden, there is no more reason to assume that the dreamer and the narrator and the poet are one and the same and that the pearl-maiden, the other character in the poet's drama, represents a figure from the poet's real-life world.

To read *Pearl* autobiographically and to take the pearl-maiden as the poet's daughter would make the primary intention of the poem elegiac, in which case the Christian message becomes a device used by a particular man in a situation unique to him that might have been known to his immediate audience but that is now irrecoverable. To read the poem in this way subordinates the doctrinal themes to occasional lyricism, and doing so may distort the poem's intention. The doctrinal meaning is not only timeless but also prepossessing as the poet treats it. When the reader responds to this thematic urgency and views the poet's theological demonstration as his main intention, the personal element becomes in effect part of an exemplum. Whether the pearl-maiden is fictional or representational or some combination of the two makes little difference in a doctrinal interpretation and hence in the poem as a whole.

What does matter is whether the dreamer is identified with the poet or taken as a fictional persona. To see the dreamer as the poet creates a contradiction and a critical impasse, for the dreamer is boorish and obtuse, a dramatic agent who serves as a foil to the theologically sophisticated pearl-maiden. How can the dreamer be real (that is, represent the poet) and also be simultaneously ignorant and knowledgeable — knowledgeable enough to create the doctrinal message that the pearl-maiden preaches? The answer is elementary: the poet has license to fictionalize himself. Yet this recognition clouds the autobiographical view: if the poet fictionalized one thing, he could just as easily have fictionalized everything. Thus the autobiographical hypothesis resembles a house of cards: it may stand up, but the chances are that it cannot.

The pearl-maiden tries to teach the dreamer-narrator the necessity for patience as an antidote to despair and therefore as necessary to a state of grace, as well as the orthodox belief that baptism alone is enough to achieve a state of grace and therefore divine acceptance of the soul in heaven. The narrator is in a sinful state, and his soul is in danger because of the inconsolable loss of his pearl in a garden, which he now visits. As the reader soon learns, the dropped pearl symbolizes the loss of the small girl, and the spot where the narrator dropped it symbolizes her grave. He explicitly acknowledges his despair and the failure of his faith to provide consolation: the throng of thoughts in his brain includes an awareness of the teachings of Christ, but his willfulness ("my wreched wylle") distorts them. In this passage the narrator may imply – if one interprets as symbolic his statement that if the garden is fair to look at so also is the fragrance fair – that he seeks consolation through sensual relief. But it is risky to go so far as to make this interpretation explicit, as Marie Borroff does in adding to her 1977 translation of the work the phrase "the fragrance that my senses sought."

This point bears on the autobiographical question. In the maiden's expostulation to the dreamer, who likens himself to a jeweler, she advises him to reject the mad world and purchase his matchless pearl, that is, his soul. Some critics believe that the maiden's advice to forsake the world implies that the poet was not in a religious order, whose members ipso facto forsake the world. This view is unwarranted, however, for in the poet's day it was believed that even priests needed to withdraw from the world from time to time and cloister themselves to renew their faith. Such is one explanation of Piers Plowman's resolution to become a contemplative after he cultivates his half acre. And the contemplatives themselves, of course, were notoriously worldly, as with Chaucer's monk in *The Canterbury Tales* (circa 1375–1400). Thus the narrator's response to the garden's sensual pleasures is symbolic of worldly weakness in general because the garden in which he sleeps symbolizes the world, and the meaning is that everyone is susceptible to worldly impurity through the senses, the gates to the soul.

To help purify the soul through patience so as to achieve salvation is the immediate message of the pearl-maiden. As a vehicle for this instruction, the poet employs the dream vision, whose agent, the uninstructed dreamer-narrator, impatiently wishes to join the maiden in heaven. Clearly what he dreams of seeing across the river (of life, or death) is heaven, contrasted with the world, the place from where he sees the maiden. It is from heaven that the maiden speaks across the river to the dreamer, and through their dialogue she instructs him. At the outset of this dialogue the key symbolism is the soul as a pearl and the dreamer as its jeweler. The soul-as-jewel image is almost archetypal, but the poet makes his context distinctive with the pearl-maiden, whose loss the dreamer mourns despairingly.

The poet creates a paradoxical mourner who, once inconsolable but now rejoicing at the discovery of his lost maiden, risks further loss (of his soul). The dreamer exposes his endangered soul when he tells the maiden that he is now consoled because he has found her and can join her on the other side. This simplistic and self-gratifying remark arouses the maiden, who rebukes him for believing what he sees. Believing the eye tempts men to take the proud stance of putting things to the test of reason alone, the maiden proclaims, implying that the ultimate test is not reliance on reason but faith in the word of God. The dreamer must die first, she tells him, in order to join her. With her remonstrance he becomes inconsolable again, saying he must pine away for having both found his pearl and lost it again – a thought that reveals his ignorance and therefore the imminence of his unregeneracy. He recovers somewhat, however, with the maiden's lesson that to complain bitterly over smaller sorrows is to risk ignoring the greater (that is, the loss of the soul). Man's obligation, therefore, through joy and pain alike, is to worship God and seek his mercy, which is the true source of consolation. In reply the dreamer protests that he means not to offend God, though sorrow gushes from his heart as water from a well. In the same speech, however, the dreamer asks the maiden to console him as both his bliss and his sorrow, yet claims that Christ's mercy is the "grounde of alle my blisse." Thus the dreamer's confusion of earthly and divine joy reveals a mind and soul not yet fully reconstructed.

The poet emphasizes the dreamer's cloudy awareness of his precarious state through the dreamer's petulant complaint that, because he is mournful while his pearl is blissful, she pays too little attention to his sorrow. Even so, the dreamer is glad that her condition seems honorable and prosperous, and he asks her to describe her life. His request moves the discussion from its focus on the interdependency of faith, mercy, sorrow, patience, and consolation to the mutual functions of baptism, Original Sin, good works, God's grace, and salvation. The dreamer responds incredulously to the maiden's statement that she is one of the elect in heaven and a bride of Christ and accuses her of presumption. Thus he reveals his doctrinal ignorance. She corrects him with the orthodox view, which she elaborates in detail in response to the dreamer's obtuse incredulity, that baptism is enough for the salvation of infants, whose only sin is Original Sin, and reinforces her lesson with the parable of the workers in the vineyard from Matthew 20:1–16. Rounding out the poet's successful creations of these contrasting characters – the naive and opaque dreamer and the learned maiden – is material in the latter's speeches from several biblical sources but mostly from Revelation.

The dialogue ends with the dreamer's request to see the heavenly city, or city of God, which the dreamer describes in passages which owe much to Revelation. This description has gemological importance – sometimes overlooked – in the twelve precious stones in the foundation of the New Jerusalem (jasper, sapphire, chalcedony, emerald, sardonyx, ruby, chrysolite, beryl, topaz, chrysoprase, jacinth, and amethyst). These jewels symbolize the foundations of Christianity: faith, hope, repentance, atonement, regeneration, good works, and the teachings, sacrifice, and rebirth of Christ. They complement symbolically the pearls so pervasive in the poem, from the single large one worn by the maiden symbolizing Christ and her status as his bride to the gravel of pearls in the path the dreamer follows until he can see the maiden.

Of significance as well is the poet's numerical symbolism. In a puzzling variation from his source for the description of the New Jerusalem, however, the poet gives its cubic dimension as twelve furlongs per side, whereas the biblical text has twelve thousand. In her translation Borroff changes the poet's number to the latter, but this change seems unjustified. As Gordon points out in a note to this line, the poet's variation might well have been deliberate in view of his pervasive use of combinations of the number twelve: twelve lines per stanza, the duplication of the number twelve in the total number of lines (1,212), and the square root of the first three digits of 144,000 – the number of virgins in the apocalyptic vision of the New Jerusalem, which the poet repeats from his source. The accepted critical interpretation is to take the poet's use of twelve as a symbolic device that echoes the number of apostles, the number of days from the birth of Jesus to his epiphany, and the product of the mystical numbers three (the holy or heavenly Trinity) and four (the elements presumed in the Middle Ages to be the

Illustration from the manuscript for Pearl, *showing the dreamer and the pearl-maiden (British Library, MS. Cotton Nero A.x., fol. 42)*

physical matter of which earthly things, including mankind, are comprised). Such symbolic complexity reflects the fact that the poet overlooked little in making *Pearl* a doctrinal enterprise exemplary in its intensity.

Sir Gawain and the Green Knight is a poetic jewel of a different type. Many critics consider it the most perfect in structure of all Middle English romances. *Sir Gawain and the Green Knight,* too, is in a stanzaic form, consisting of groups of unrhymed alliterative long lines followed by five short rhyming lines. The number of unrhymed long lines in each stanza varies from twelve to thirty-eight. The poem has four divisions, indicated in the manuscript by large ornamental colored capital letters. This partitioning may be evidence that the poem was meant originally to be read aloud publicly, in stages. If so, such a recitation must have been to an audience that shared the poet's dialect. Only an audience familiar with most of the words in the poet's esoteric vocabulary could have followed an oral reading with satisfaction. The poem has not only rare words but also words used in arcane senses because of the constraints of alliteration. Who this audience might have been as well as the particular appeal of the poem and the time of composition are discussed by McColly in "*Sir Gawain and the Green Knight* as a Romance à Clef" (1988).

More important to the case for *Sir Gawain and the Green Knight* as a work originally meant for recitation is that above all it is vernacular entertainment. The poet, to be sure, was an orthodox Christian whose work reflects a pervasive Christian intention, but he was also a lively humorist who created social comedy with almost-sublime dramatic irony. He might or might not have written another poem or other poems of the *Gawain* group. Looking for his benchmark elsewhere, one should more likely find it in *Patience* and *Pearl* than in *Cleanness,* whose author highlights its grim matter with much irony but without humor. On the other hand, the inventive wit that underlies *Sir Gawain and the Green Knight* could no doubt have created the puckish drollery of either Jonah or the narrator in *Patience,* or the gauche, naive, and petulant dreamer in *Pearl.* But whether the author of *Sir Gawain and the Green Knight* also wrote *Pearl* and/or *Patience* is an obscure and pedantic question. The *Gawain*-Poet adequately reflects his genius in *Sir Gawain and the Green Knight* alone.

Most generally, *Sir Gawain and the Green Knight* is a poem about chivalry, the ideals and the ideal customs and traditions of medieval knighthood. As it was idealized, chivalry never really existed, and thus *Sir Gawain and the Green Knight* is an ideal reflection of an ideal world. Here knightly virtue is tested through the testing of the most renowned knight, Gawain. Renown in the poet's vocabulary meant reputation in the most positive sense, not just fame or notoriety — a knight's renown was based on his quotient of the knightly, or chivalric, virtues. Not only is Gawain the most renowned knight, but also Arthur's court is the most renowned court, and hence the testing of Gawain is the testing of Camelot as well. This testing, as the Green Knight reveals at the poem's end, is a result of the jealousy felt toward Guinevere by Morgan le Fay, the sorceress (Arthur's half sister), who disguises Sir Bertilak (sometimes spelled Bercilak) as the Green Knight and sends him to Camelot to terrorize Guinevere. The poet fails to give the reason for this jealousy, but in the Arthurian tradition lurked the suspicion that Arthur and Morgan had once had an incestuous relationship.

The testing motif dominates the motivation of the plot, so that alert readers (or listeners) are al-ways mindful of the most significant question, whose delay in being answered is the main source of suspense: will Gawain fail as a chivalrous knight? In a scene whose importance to the testing motif is often overlooked, the Green Knight challenges a knight of Arthur's court to behead him, on the condition that the knight take a similar blow from the Green Knight a year hence. Gawain accepts and strikes off the Green Knight's head, but to the astonishment of the court, the latter picks up his head and departs, adjuring Gawain to meet him in one year, when he will take his turn. Though the Green Knight's challenge is rather vague, a case can be made for his wanting to trade literally just a blow for a blow — that is, a second blow (the Green Knight's) exactly like the first blow (the challenger's). The evidence for this is the Green Knight's peaceful aspect. Many critics would make him a hostile and ogreish character and adopt a mythic reading of the poem, an interpretation that depends on making the Green Knight into a figure whose appearance at New Year's time symbolizes the so-called archetypal vegetation, or rebirth, myth. In this kind of reading, the Green Knight is considered a stock character known as the Green Man or Wild Man of traditional midwinter folk festivals — a descendant of the nature god or god of vegetation — a less then noble figure. Larry Benson argues at length for characterizing the Green Knight as a churl.

But the status of the Green Knight, though his manner may seem to belie it, is far from churlish, and, further, he seems to be on a benign mission. He is not, as the proper term is, armigerous. As he tells the court at Camelot, he has armor and weapons and retainers at home if his purpose were to fight. But he carries a holly branch — symbolic of peace — and, if Norman Davis's gloss of the poet's word *scholes* (line 160) is correct, he even wears no shoes. A shoeless knight was traditionally a knight riding peacefully. Relying on the now-obsolete first edition of the poem by J. R. R. Tolkien and Gordon, Borroff translates *scholes* as "footgear well-fashioned," which misses the point of the Green Knight's unwarlike costume. Elsewhere Borroff translates the Middle English words *runisch* and *runischly* as "roisterous" and "roisterously." To roister means to indulge in carousing and noisy revelry, but in Middle English the word *runisch* simply means fierce. Such details as these questionable translations help create a negative bias toward the Green Knight that he does not deserve.

On the contrary, the poet's intention seems to be to present the Green Knight as a man of great worth, and his audience probably viewed him as such. The poet wrote in an age that took the idea of virtue so literally, at least in theory, that outward attractiveness reflected inward beauty. A conventional device in medieval romance plots, in fact, is for a knight to be recognized as such because of his comeliness, as is the case when Isolde recognizes the nobility of Tristram. Hence, when the poet describes the Green Knight as the fairest who might ride, with strong back and chest and slender waist and belly, he endows him with a nobility of appearance the audience would have easily recognized. Thus, at the Green Knight's invitation to trade blow for blow, if Gawain is absolutely courteous and charitable – two of the chief knightly virtues – he will strike less than a mortal blow and spare his adversary. After all, it is New Year's Day and a season for games, and the visitor is on a peaceful mission. If, then, one considers Gawain's first temptation, the first test of his chivalry, to be the Green Knight's challenge, why does Gawain fall short? Because of Arthur, who induces Gawain to behead the Green Knight by saying that if he minds his cutting he will be able to withstand the other's blow later. Arthur is young and headstrong, with "a wild brain" (to use the poet's phrase), and the Green Knight stings him with taunts. Further, Arthur will not banquet on New Year's until he has some entertainment: a marvelous story or a joust to the death ("life for life"). Ironically, the Green Knight's game is just such a marvel, but it puts Arthur in a ridiculous position, to which he overreacts. This gesture is less than magnanimous and chivalric, and it casts Arthur in a negative light. The poet reinforces this image shortly, at the end of the first section of the poem, when Gawain sets out for the Green Chapel. Gawain's friends at Camelot protest that Arthur would have been wiser to invest Gawain with a dukedom than to send him on this journey, to be beheaded by an elvish man for pride and vanity. But the pride and vanity are Arthur's, as can be seen when the courtiers ask who ever knew of a king who would cavil with knights in a Christmas game. This less-than-exalted portrait of Arthur is not unusual. In many Arthurian stories he is weak, foolish, or even stupid, in contrast to someone who approaches knightly perfection – such as Gawain here and Lancelot elsewhere. But to pursue the point of Gawain's chivalric lapse at Camelot leads to an impasse. His is a fated act, its necessity fixed by Morgan and without which the plot could not develop. Thus his fault at Camelot is small, extenuated by his loyalty to Arthur and obscured by the grand plan of the romance, and it is important

only because it highlights Arthur's inhospitable gesture.

When Gawain resolves to keep his promise against the advice of Camelot, he passes his next test. For his quest he is well prepared: his coat of arms, which can be blazoned *gules mullet d'or* (in heraldry a *mullet* is a five-pointed star), symbolizes his knightly virtues, and the image of the Virgin Mary on the inside of his shield reminds him of his patroness. Each point of the star on Gawain's shield likewise has five points. Point one, that Gawain is faultless in his five senses, has the subpoints sight, touch, taste, smell, and hearing. To be faultless in these points is to withstand sensual pleasures, which are admitted through the senses, so as to concentrate on devotion to God. Point two, that Gawain never fails in his five fingers (the subpoints), symbolizes Gawain's strength, which in turn symbolizes virtue in general. Point three, that all his faith is fixed on the five wounds of Christ, has the subpoints of the two hands, the two feet, and the side. Point four is that all Gawain's force (his courage) is founded on the five joys of the Virgin: the Annunciation (the revealing of the Incarnation), the Nativity, the Resurrection, the Ascension, and the Assumption (into heaven of the Virgin Mary). The fifth point comprises the knightly virtues of beneficence, brotherly love, pure mind, pure manners, and compassion.

Gawain's arms are ascribed to him in no other known story. This may mean that the poet created them especially for this work and for their effect on his immediate audience. They emphasize Gawain's status in this poem as the most renowned knight, or, in other words, as the most perfect knight. As such, Gawain overcomes the obstacles he meets in traveling through Logres (England) and North Wales to look for the Green Chapel, and in this way he passes another test. But however much the hardships of his journey tempt him to renege and turn back, these tests are easy compared to what he must survive in Bertilak's castle and later at the Green Chapel.

The location of this castle and chapel inspires much research and speculation, but the castle and chapel may be fictional. It seems likely, however, that the poet intended the setting, even if fictional, to be somewhere in Cheshire. The poet's only specific contemporary reference is to a district there, the Wirral. His phrase, the "wilderness of Wirral," means the forest of Wirral, a promontory of the county between the Dee and the Mersey. His remark that few men live there who love either God or man with a good heart had a special meaning for

Cestrians alone. In the poet's day the Wirral was a secular sanctuary (where guilty men were immune from apprehension and prosecution by outsiders) populated by outlaws. Obviously this remark meant more to a local audience than it did to an audience elsewhere. Thus Bertilak's castle and the chapel should probably be imagined as being near the Wirral, an inference that makes sense when the passage that follows the poet's remark is read as a summary of Gawain's adventures before he reaches the Wirral, and not after he leaves it.

On Christmas Eve Gawain prays to the Virgin Mary to guide him to some dwelling. On that morning (Borroff translates the poet's phrase "on the morn" as "next morning," which would make Gawain's arrival on Christmas Day – but that is wrong, the phrase meaning *in* or *during* the morning) he sees the magnificent castle, whose lord is Bertilak, though Gawain does not recognize him as the undisguised Green Knight. The status, manner, appearance, and character of Bertilak are critical to a basic interpretation of the poem. The poet foreshadows these qualities in his earlier description of the Green Knight at Camelot. Bertilak is a noble, a potentate, a great lord. The poet emphasizes this status by calling him the "beloved lord" and the "noble lord." Only a man of great estate and high degree could rule such an impressive domain: a castle of sophisticated (for that day) architecture and furnishings; accommodations and entertainment for other guests besides Gawain; enough servants to manage such an opulent household; and the territory and retainers necessary – including a hundred huntsmen – for hunting the great beasts of the forest (boars and deer).

Bertilak is not only a great noble, he is also a chivalric knight, whose virtues he clearly displays. Perhaps the cornerstone of knightly chivalry is courage, which Bertilak summons in particular during the boar hunt. He dismounts and wades into a stream across which the boar stands to confront his pursuers. The boar rushes toward him, but he kills it by thrusting his sword into the heart. His courage is matched by his courtesy, which he shows mainly through hospitality, a virtue important as a knight's gesture of charity toward fellow human beings. He harbors Gawain from Christmas Eve through New Year's morning, treats Gawain with the respect due the most renowned knight, and entertains him appropriately as the most honored guest.

He proposes to Gawain that they exchange their daily winnings and invites Gawain to sleep in the morning while he hunts. In medieval England hunting was a preventive for the temptations of sloth, gluttony, and luxury. A vigorous and demanding activity, hunting required good physical conditioning reinforced with early rising and temperate dieting. While Gawain sleeps, Bertilak eats only a sop and arrays the hunting party for the chase before daybreak. By sleeping in a comfortable bed until after daylight shines on the walls (a late hour on 28 December in the poet's latitude), Gawain creates a situation in which his soul is in danger. Bertilak's wife visits his bedroom and tells him he is an unwary sleeper to let her steal in. The symbolic meaning is that Gawain's five senses, in which he is presumed faultless, have been dulled because of his compromising position as a luxurious sleeper. When the body sleeps, the soul does likewise. The poet's audience were therefore well prepared for the drama of the first bedroom scene, whose humorous irony suddenly burst upon them when the lady offers Gawain her body for him to take at his pleasure.

The lady's bluntness gives the bedroom scenes a fabliaulike quality, which is tempered by the great status of both characters and especially by Gawain's success in resisting her. Readers should remember, however, that a fourteenth-century audience hearing the poem for the first time would be unsure at this stage of the narrative that Gawain would be able to do so. Earlier, when Gawain had met the lady (who is accompanied by Morgan le Fay) on Christmas Eve, they had asked to be his acquaintances, and he in turn asked to be their servant, if they will accept him. Gawain may not have meant love service, but to a contemporary audience able to understand this sophisticated poem, its significance in Gawain's remark was at least tacit. After this the poet makes a point of telling the reader that Gawain and the lady dally in a courtly conversation so brilliant it outshines the games played by others. Further, in the Arthurian romances Gawain is not always a perfect knight. In fact, in the *Alliterative Morte Arthure* – a work of the alliterative revival contemporary with *Sir Gawain* – Gawain is rash, foolish, and unpredictable. For these reasons the reader is unsure whether Gawain, already attracted to the lady and now lying naked in bed with her sitting on the bed by his side, can withstand the temptations of this seductress.

The poet reinforces the potential sexuality of his bedroom scenes with Gawain and Bertilak's complementary exchange of gifts, a stroke of superb plotting worthy of a well-structured fabliau. On the first two days, as Gawain gives Bertilak his winnings, first one and then two kisses, the poet's audience surely asked themselves what Gawain would

Gawain's temptation by Bertilak's wife; illustration from the manuscript for Sir
Gawain and the Green Knight *(British Library, MS. Cotton Nero
A.x., fol. 129)*

do next time if the lady were to succeed in seducing him. Thus Gawain faces three problems in the series of bedroom temptations. The most important is to save his soul by keeping his sexual purity. Next he must remain honorable and courteous to his host by not making love to his wife. This problem becomes a dilemma, of course, with Gawain's wish to remain loyal to his host and at the same time avoid being discourteous to the lady. Last is Gawain's more serious dilemma of what to give Bertilak as his winning and still remain pure and honorable, if his dalliance with the lady develops into more advanced sexual play. In creating for Gawain this problem with its commingling of religious sublimity and implications of sexual inversion, the poet is worthy of comparison to Chaucer and William Shakespeare in his mixing of modes for humorous effect.

Even though the lady offers herself to Gawain at the outset of the first meeting, with each visit her temptations become more dangerous. In the first scene are two important exchanges. First she assures him that there are ladies who would rather have her place (beside Gawain) than their gold and jewels. Gawain responds easily that her praise comes not from his reputation but her courtesy. Her next sally, that she would have no other than Gawain for a husband, he dismisses by saying she is married to a better man – an ironic foreshadowing of the Green Knight's similar comparison at the Green Chapel. The next day the lady reproaches Gawain at length for not having talked of love. He evades the subject by saying that he would be foolish to do so with someone who knows much more about it than he does. No matter how slyly she tries to seduce him, the poet adds, Gawain withstands her and remains faultless. The third day is marked by less dialogue, but the poet explains that the lady's dress (open in front and back), her fair features, and the beguiling talk make desire well up in Gawain's heart. He is in great peril, but the Virgin Mary remembers her knight, and he does not succumb. He does accept a magic girdle from her as a favor, however, which she claims will protect him.

Paralleling these scenes are the three days' hunting, which contrast the active Bertilak, who keeps his body fit as the portal of the soul, and the inactive Gawain, who vitiates his physical defenses through sloth. A commonplace of criticism is to analogize the progression from a deer to a boar to a fox to the increasing danger of the lady's temptations. A boar is more dangerous prey than deer, of course, but a fox is not. Nevertheless, critics explain a fox analogy to the third bedroom scene as being due to its cunning, which reflects the lady's rather vixenish reproach that Gawain must reject her because he has another love, which in turn leads to Gawain's taking the girdle. Critics have less to say about the long passage that describes the breaking of the deer, except to praise it for its vividness and technical brilliance. The passage is unusual, such detailed descriptions of deer breaking being found elsewhere in Middle English literature only in the romance *Sir Tristrem* and the dream-vision allegory *The Parliament of the Three Ages*. The poet's audience were hunters and probably enjoyed this descriptive interlude, but how does it fit into the poem's dynamic plot and logical structure, otherwise without false starts and loose ends? First, it would seem, the frenzied action of this breaking emphasizes the salutary benefits of hunting. And second, this action contrasts in particular with Gawain's inaction, as do the hunting episodes in general contrast with Gawain's predicament as an unwary sleeper. When the lady leaves, Gawain (wearing the girdle) goes to confession, where a priest absolves him of his sins, both the greater and lesser. Since he conceals the lady's gift, whether Gawain's confession is justified inspires much critical discussion, but obviously the poet felt that Gawain acts as a righteous Christian.

Bertilak again demonstrates his chivalric nature with his treatment of Gawain at the Green Chapel during the New Year's confrontation where he reveals his dual identity. Necessary ingredients of knightly courtesy are mercy and forbearance, which the Green Knight/Bertilak shows when he spares Gawain with just a nick and forgives him for concealing the green girdle.

Altogether Bertilak is remarkable for his energy, his virility, his courage, his intelligence, his diplomacy, and above all his courtesy, hospitality, and charitableness. In a sense he, rather than Gawain, is the perfect knight, a point the poet drives home with much irony at the Green Chapel. Bertilak says that at Camelot he calmly watched his head fly to his feet, while Gawain is now terrified after a feinted blow, so that therefore he (Bertilak) should be called the better man. Having thus become Gawain's chivalric superior, Bertilak serves as Gawain's confessor. He tells Gawain that the latter absolved himself of the guilt of withholding the girdle when he freely admitted his shortcomings and that Gawain should take the nick on his neck as due penance. Gawain's last temptation, to take and conceal the magical girdle, proves overwhelming. In failing to honor his promise to exchange this winning, Gawain lacks, as Bertilak reminds him, a little in loyalty. This lack of loyalty (to his host) is a defect of knightly honor. Yet Gawain is merely human while Bertilak has been given magical powers. Thus Bertilak's judgment of Gawain's reason for faltering in concealing the girdle was only that he loved his life, a forgivable motive. Bertilak also confesses to Gawain that he arranged (obviously through the constraint of Morgan le Fay) Gawain's tempting by his wife.

Some critical dissatisfaction arises from Gawain's suggestion at the Green Chapel that his fault was due to the wiles of a woman, putting him in a class with Adam, David, Samson, and Solomon. Other critics, however, take Gawain's tone in this passage as more matter-of-fact than petulant. The fact is that he does fail to resist temptation altogether because of the blandishments of Bertilak's wife. He ends his statement with the modest observation that, if these great men could be so beguiled, he thinks his lapse may be excused. Gawain returns to Camelot, having passed the tests of knighthood and chivalry the Green Knight imposed on him, but he is nevertheless a chastened knight, wearing a green sash as a reminder of his fault.

Bibliographies:

Helaine Newstead, "Arthurian Legends," in *A Manual of the Writings in Middle English, 1050–1500*, volume 1, edited by Jonathan Burke Severs (New Haven: Connecticut Academy of Arts & Sciences, 1967), pp. 54–57, 238–243;

Marie P. Hamilton, "The *Pearl* Poet," in *A Manual of the Writings in Middle English*, volume 2, edited by Severs (New Haven: Connecticut Academy of Arts & Sciences, 1970), pp. 339–353, 503–516.

References:

Ian Bishop, *Pearl in Its Setting: A Critical Study of the Structure and Meaning of the Middle English Poem* (Oxford: Blackwell, 1968);

Robert J. Blanch, ed., *"Sir Gawain" and "Pearl": Critical Essays* (Bloomington: Indiana University Press, 1966);

J. A. Burrow, *A Reading of Sir Gawain and the Green Knight* (New York: Barnes & Noble, 1966);

John Conley, ed., *The Middle English "Pearl": Critical Essays* (Notre Dame, Ind.: University of Notre Dame Press, 1970);

Marie P. Hamilton, "The Meaning of the Middle English *Pearl*," *PMLA,* 70 (September 1955): 805–824;

Donald R. Howard and Christian K. Zacher, eds., *Critical Studies of Sir Gawain and the Green Knight* (Notre Dame, Ind.: University of Notre Dame Press, 1968);

P. M. Kean, *"The Pearl": An Interpretation* (London: Routledge & Kegan Paul, 1967);

T. D. Kelly and John T. Irwin, "The Meaning of *Cleanness:* Parable as Effective Sign," *Medieval Studies,* 35 (1973): 231–260;

George Lyman Kittredge, *A Study of Gawain and the Green Knight* (Cambridge, Mass.: Harvard University Press, 1916);

Erik Kooper, "The Case of the Encoded Author," *Neuphilologische Mitteilungen,* 83 (1982): 158–168;

David Lawton, Introduction to *Middle English Alliterative Poetry,* edited by Lawton (Cambridge: Brewer, 1982);

William McColly, "*Sir Gawain and the Green Knight* as a Romance à Clef," *Chaucer Review,* 23, no. 1 (1988): 78–92;

McColly, "Style and Structure in the Middle English Poem *Cleanness,*" *Computers and the Humanities,* 21 (July–September 1987): 169–176;

McColly and Dennis Weir, "Literary Attribution and Likelihood-Ratio Tests: The Case of the Middle English *Pearl* Poems," *Computers and the Humanities,* 17 (June 1983): 65–75;

Sister Mary Madeleva, *Pearl: A Study in Spiritual Dryness* (New York: Appleton, 1925);

Charles Moorman, *The Pearl-Poet* (New York: Twayne, 1968);

Charlotte Morse, "The Image of the Vessel in *Cleanness,*" *University of Toronto Quarterly,* 40 (Spring 1971): 202–216;

Charles Muscatine, "The *Pearl* Poet: Style as Defense," in his *Poetry and Crisis in the Age of Chaucer* (Notre Dame, Ind.: University of Notre Dame Press, 1972), pp. 37–69;

Barbara Nolan and David Farley-Hills, "The Authorship of *Pearl:* Two Notes," *Review of English Studies,* new series 22 (August 1971): 295–302;

James Parker Oakden, *Alliterative Poetry in Middle English,* 2 volumes (Manchester: University of Manchester Press, 1930, 1935);

Clifford J. Peterson, "The *Pearl*-Poet and John Massey of Cotton, Cheshire," *Review of English Studies,* new series 25 (August 1974): 257–266;

Henry L. Savage, *The Gawain-Poet: Studies in His Background and His Personality* (Chapel Hill: University of North Carolina Press, 1956);

Hans Schnyder, *Sir Gawain and the Green Knight: An Essay in Interpretation* (Bern: Francke, 1961);

A. C. Spearing, *The Gawain-Poet: A Critical Study* (Cambridge: Cambridge University Press, 1970);

Thorlac Turville-Petre and Edward Wilson, "Hoccleve, 'Maistir Massy' and the *Pearl* Poet: Two Notes," *Review of English Studies,* new series 26 (May 1975): 129–143;

William Vantuono, "John de Mascy of Sale and the *Pearl*-Poems," *Manuscripta,* 25 (July 1981): 77–88;

David Williams, "The Point of *Patience,*" *Modern Philology,* 68 (November 1970): 127–136.

Geoffrey of Monmouth

(circa 1100 – 1155)

Maureen Fries
State University of New York College at Fredonia

WORKS: *Prophetie* [or *Prophetiae*] *Merlini* (*The Prophecies of Merlin*, before 1135)

Manuscripts: Eventually published as part of *Historia regum Britannie*, *Prophetie Merlini* survives separately in almost eighty independent manuscripts and as an insertion in almost a dozen others.

Historia regum Britannie [or *Britanniae*] (*The History of the Kings of Britain*) – Vulgate version (circa 1138), Variant version (before 1155)

Manuscripts: *Historia regum Britannie* survives in at least 215 Latin manuscripts, separable into versions called the Vulgate and the Variant. The most important of these include, for the Vulgate (which encompasses the majority), Cambridge University Library MS. 1706, fols. 1^r–128^v (twelfth century); Bürgerbibliothek (Stadtbibliothek), Bern, MS. 568, fols. 18^r–83^r (early twelfth century); and Trinity College, Cambridge, MS. 1125, fols. 5^r–117^v (late thirteenth or early fourteenth century). For the Variant (only eight of the total), the most important are British Library MS. Harley 6358, fols. 2^r–58^v (late twelfth or early thirteenth century), and Bibliothèque de l'Arsenal, Paris, MS. 982 (7.H.L) fols. 168vb–188rb (second half of fourteenth century).

First publication: *Britannie utriusque regum et principum origo et gesta insignia ab Galfrido Monemutensi*, edited by Ivo Cavellatus (Paris: Jodocus Badius Ascensius [Josse Bade], 1508; revised edition, 1517).

Standard editions: Vulgate version: *The Historia Regum Britanniae of Geoffrey of Monmouth*, edited by Acton Griscom and R. E. Jones (London: Longmans, Green, 1929); *La légende Arthurienne*, volume 3, edited by Edmond Faral (Paris: Champion, 1929), pp. 64–303; *The Historia Regum Britannie of Geoffrey of Monmouth*, volume 1, edited by Neil Wright (Cambridge: Brewer, 1985). Variant version: *Geoffrey of Monmouth: Historia Regum Britanniae: A Variant Version*, edited by Jacob Hammer (Cambridge, Mass.: Medieval Academy of America, 1951); *The Historia Regum Britannie of Geoffrey of Monmouth: The First Variant Version; A Critical Edition*, volume 2, edited by Wright (Cambridge: Brewer, 1988).

Vita Merlini (*Life of Merlin*, after 1140)

Manuscript: *Vita Merlini* survives independently in one complete manuscript and in extracts of various lengths. The complete version appears in British Library MS. Cotton Vespasian E. iv, fols. 112^b–138^b (late thirteenth century), which is also the earliest.

First publication: *Gaufridi Arthurii Archidiaconi postea vero episcopi Asaphensis, de vita et vaticiniis Merlini Calidonii carmen heroicum*, edited by William Henry Black (London: Printed by William Nicol for the Roxburghe Club, 1830).

Standard editions: *The Vita Merlini*, edited and translated by by John Jay Parry (Urbana: University of Illinois Press, 1925); *Life of Merlin*, edited by Basil Clarke (Cardiff: University of Wales Press, 1973).

Of both the life and the works of Geoffrey of Monmouth more is known than is usual about an author of the twelfth century, but this information has often been the subject of controversy, both in his own and in later times. Geoffrey was probably born about 1100, and he almost certainly died in 1155. That he styled himself for most of his life as "of Monmouth" has led to suggestions that he was born there and/or that he resided in or was educated there at a Benedictine priory, founded by Wihenoc, one of the Breton lords of Monmouth, some years before Geoffrey's birth. Since he also bears a Norman name, sought Norman patronage, and shows intense interest in Welsh pseudohistory and legend, a mixed Norman- or Breton-Welsh background is also possible. Scholars have argued, often chau-

Page from an early-twelfth-century manuscript of the Vulgate version of Historia regum Britannie *(Bürgerbibliothek [Stadtbibliothek] Bern, MS. 568, fol. 43ʳ)* vinistically, for each of these origins, but none of these arguments is conclusive. Moreover, none of the various signatures of a Geoffrey in the Monmouth priory documents is provably that of the author in question.

Authentic signatures dating from 1129 to 1151 do appear, however, in witness to six different charters connected with various religious houses at or near Oxford. From these an early career is constructible: Geoffrey was perhaps a secular canon at the College of Saint George's, which he had joined in 1129 and where he may have taught (although Oxford was not yet a university). Archdeacon Walter, from whom Geoffrey claimed to have received both written and verbal sources for the *Historia regum Britannie* (circa 1138), was provost, and Robert de Chesney, to whom he dedicated the *Vita Merlini* (after 1140) after Robert became bishop of Lincoln in 1148, was a canon of Saint George's, which was terminated in 1149. In the Oxford period Geoffrey composed his three extant works – the *Prophetie Merlini* (before 1135), the *Historia regum Britannie,* and the *Vita Merlini* – before finally gaining the preferment sought in his dedications. Made bishop-elect of Saint Asaph's in 1151, he was at last ordained priest at Westminster in February 1152 and consecrated bishop at Lambeth eight days later, but he apparently never visited his see. This, and his witnessing in late 1153 the Treaty of Westminster between King Stephen and Henry Fitz Empress [Matilda], later Henry II, suggests a residence in London during the last four years of his life. The Welsh chroniclers (whose reliability has been questioned) say he died in 1155, perhaps in Llandaff, Wales.

If even these bare facts of Geoffrey's death and life have been disputed, so much more has been the provenance of his *Historia regum Britannie*. Unlike the *Prophecies of Merlin* and the *Life of Merlin,* which have attracted little concentrated study and little controversy, this most important of his extant works has generated disagreement over the sources, the dates, and the intra- and intertextual relationships of its Vulgate and Variant versions. Discussion of Geoffrey's sources – including also works by the earlier chroniclers Gildas, Nennius, Bede, and Geoffrey's near contemporaries William of Malmesbury and Henry of Huntington, as well as Welsh and Breton legend and myth – has centered upon the "certain very ancient book" he claims in the *Historia regum Britannie* to have received as principal source from his friend Walter the archdeacon. Variously characterized, usually upon very little evidence, as a Welsh (as Acton Griscom and R. E. Jones posit in their 1929 edition of *Historia regum Britannie*) or Breton or Breton-Latin text or as a met-

aphor for folkloric sources (as Lewis Thorpe suggests in his 1966 translation) or as the Variant *Historia regum Britannie* itself (as Hans Erich Keller claims in a 1977 article) or – most fancifully of all – as a lost history of an actual British Continental conqueror called "Rhiothamus" (so asserts Geoffrey Ashe in a 1981 essay), this supposed original has never been reliably identified. More likely Geoffrey uses the term to suggest a prior "authority," or canonical written antecedent, similar to Chaucer's "Lollius" or numerous other pseudosources cited by medieval authors.

More-recent arguments have centered upon priority of authorship of the Vulgate and Variant versions of the *Historia regum Britannie*. At issue is whether the Variant was composed before or after the Vulgate, whether it was authored by Geoffrey or someone else, and whether Wace's *Roman de Brut* (1155) inspired it or was inspired by it. The Variant version of the *Historia regum Britannie* was identified first by Jacob Hammer; he later called it the First Variant. Subsequent investigators have confirmed his findings that this version differs from the Vulgate – the text previously regarded as standard – in important respects: its use of additional, sometimes older sources; changes in the length, form, and content of speeches; a toning down or omission of narrative unpleasantness; and a simpler style and mode of expression. Hammer assumed the Variant was later than the Vulgate, but subsequent scholars have argued otherwise. R. A. Caldwell claims not only that the Variant was Wace's source for the *Roman de Brut,* but that the Vulgate itself was a reworking of the Variant. But Pierre Gallais, while agreeing on stylistic grounds with Caldwell, Hammer, and others that the Variant could not have been written by Geoffrey, maintains that the Variant drew on Wace rather than vice versa, mandating a date after 1155 for the former. In attacking these arguments, Keller agrees with Caldwell on Wace's (and Geoffrey's) use of a pre–Vulgate Variant and further posits two separate, Latin sources for the two versions. R. W. Leckie's study of Geoffrey's impact upon other twelfth-century authors leads him to ratify the primacy of both the Vulgate and a (later) Variant over Wace's *Roman de Brut,* an order affirmed by Neil Wright, the best and most recent editor of both versions of the *Historia regum Britannie*.

Wright believes that Geoffrey was not the author of the Variant, of which his Vulgate served as the primary source. But no one has questioned Geoffrey's authorship of the two works inspired by the figure of Merlin, the com-

Games at Arthur's court in Caerleon; illustration from a medieval transcription of Geoffrey's Historia
regum Britannie (*Bibliothèque royale, Brussels, MS. 9243, fol. 45*)

position and publication of which bracket the *Historia regum Britannie.* Geoffrey says he has translated *The Prophecies of Merlin* "from the British tongue into Latin" at the urging of many people. Taking time off from his composition of the *Historia regum Britannie,* he published *The Prophecies of Merlin* for Alexander, bishop of Lincoln, including an extended prefatory compliment. This initiates a pattern of dedication to influential superiors: to ecclesiastics here and in the *Vita Merlini* and to Norman aristocrats for the *Historia regum Britannie,* which was designed to gain him the churchly preferment he eventually achieved. Merlin, conflated from the "marvelous boy" Ambrosius of Nennius's *Historia Britonum* and the wild man Myrddin of Welsh legend, is one of Geoffrey's most provocative creations. His prophecies result from a vatic seizure induced by his explanation of the red (British) and white (Saxon) dragons beneath Vortigern's collapsing tower. Not just explicating the battling dragons but offering also a panoramic (if largely allegorical) his-

tory of Britain, the seer recites a dense series of political vaticinations grounded in animal symbolism and designed initially to ratify the subsequent contents of Geoffrey's own *Historia regum Britannie.* To these self-fulfilling prophecies he adds an ambitious remainder, ever more obscure in meaning and relentlessly continuing through actual historical events to doomsday itself. The terminus ad quem for the composition of the *Prophetie Merlini* is 1135, since there is no mention in the dedication or text of the death of Henry I in that year; and a contemporary reference by Orderic Vitalis to his own use of a "libellus Merlini" confirms the actual publication of Geoffrey's first Merlin book as a separate entity, even had not the surprising number of separate manuscripts survived, and it also marks the first independent witness to the *Prophetie Merlini.*

In their eventual placement as chapter 7 of the *Historia regum Britannie* the prophecies of Merlin stand as a striking prelude to the career of Arthur which embodies the spiritual center of Geoffrey's narrative. Covering a period of nearly two thousand years, from the fall of Troy to the death of Cadwallader, the *Historia regum Britannie* begins with the flight of the eponymous Brutus, either grandson or great-grandson to Priam of Troy; Brutus gathers up colonies of Trojans with whom he founds Britain. Much of the subsequent rehearsal of the island's fortune consists of lists of kings punctuated by tales of love, war, and derring-do. Geoffrey dilates upon some of these, including the stories of Sabrina (later taken up by John Milton in his *Comus,* 1637) and Leir (a source for William Shakespeare's *King Lear,* 1606). Three personalities dominate this panorama: Brutus, the founding father of Britain; Belinus, said to have captured and sacked Rome; and Arthur, the greatest king. In the prelude to Arthur's history, beginning in book 6, Vortigern usurps the high kingship from the rightful progeny of Constantine and employs Merlin to interpret what is, in reality, Vortigern's own death sentence. Through Merlin's magic arts Uther fathers Arthur upon Igerna, wife to Gorlois of Cornwall. Arthur succeeds to the high kingship at the traditional age of fifteen and, subsequent to defeating his domestic enemies and marrying Guinevere, conquers Norway, Denmark, and Gaul. While celebrating his victories in a recrowning at Caerleon, Arthur is challenged by Emperor Lucius of Rome, which he therefore determines to conquer. Leaving one nephew, Modred, in charge of his queen and his country, he sails with another, Gawain, and other notable followers to Brittany. His single combat with the giant of Mont-Saint-Michel, who has raped and killed Helena, the niece of Arthur's kinsman Hoel, is succeeded by the defeat and death of Lucius. But, as he is preparing to march on Rome, Arthur learns that Modred has seized both the throne and Guinevere. On his return home he faces Modred and an army of his domestic enemies — Scots, Picts, Saxons, and Irish — and finally defeats them in Cornwall, where he was born and where Modred and most of the leaders on both sides are killed. Guinevere becomes a nun out of penitence, and Arthur, wounded *letaliter* (deadly), is borne to Avalon to be healed.

The reigns of Constantine, Arthur's kinsman who conquers the sons of Modred and the Saxons, and his successors form an anticlimax to Arthur's story in the remainder of the *Historia regum Britannie.* Brief victories by Malgo, and particularly Cadwanus and his son, Cadwallo, who conquers the Saxons and enjoys a long rule at London, give way to Cadwallader's flight to Brittany and his becoming a monk at Rome. On his death he can bequeath to his son Ivor and his nephew Iny only the rule of Wales; thus ends the story of the British kings.

That it was not really the British but the Norman dynasty which Geoffrey wished to flatter, however, has been noted by scholars who seldom otherwise agree on the provenance of the *Historia regum Britannie.* Like his other works, this one bears dedications to contemporary power wielders — in fact, the several forms of dedication existing in the various manuscripts reflect the political struggles of the time. Of the dedications that seem to be Geoffrey's own composition, three are important: one to Robert of Gloucester alone, one to Robert and Waleran of Meulan, and one to King Stephen and Robert. Robert was the illegitimate son of Henry I, and Waleran the son of an important adviser to that king and a favorite of his successor Stephen, Henry's nephew who wrongfully seized the throne in 1135, breaking his oath to support the designated heir, the king's daughter, Matilda. Not only are the changing dedications an important index to the dates of the *Historia regum Britannie* — Robert and Stephen broke decisively with each other in 1138, and Robert joined Matilda in an unsuccessful civil war against the king in the following year, making a joint dedication to the two no longer politic, but they indicate Geoffrey's awareness of the Norman dynasty's desire for legitimation of their possession of Britain. Down to Tudor times Arthur, to whom Geoffrey linked Henry I's name in his dedication, served as an ideal distinguished ancestor for every line of the kings of Britain.

Turning once again to ecclesiastical patronage, Geoffrey dedicated his final work, the *Vita Merlini,* to his friend Robert de Chesney, who had become bishop of Lincoln and who succeeded an incumbent unfavorable to its author's ambitions. Apparently intended for a learned audience that would have been familiar with his scholarly and hagiographic sources, rather than the popular one envisaged for the *Historia regum Britannie,* this life of Merlin is founded on Celtic, postclassical, and what Basil Clarke in his edition of the poem calls exotic sources. Merlin takes to the Caledonian forest out of grief at the death of brother companions in battle. Wooed out of the woods by music, he reveals a queen's adultery and, giving his wife permission to remarry, moves once again to the forest. Returning with deer as a wedding present for her, he kills her new husband on a whim. Taken captive, he spouts prophecies, which are ratified as true, and then returns to the forest, where his sister Ganieda at his request builds him a dwelling with a large staff of astronomers. Again he prophesies, this time about Britain's fate. He meets and talks with Taliesin, a fellow bard who tells him of Arthur's voyage to Morgan le Fay's island, Avalon, for treatment of his deadly wound. Cured of his madness by washing and drinking at a newly flowing spring, Merlin now converses about the delights of nature with Taliesin. The arrival of a new madman, Maeldin, also cured by the spring, disrupts the plot, which climaxes with Merlin, Taliesin, Maeldin, and Ganieda determining to spend their lives in spiritual pursuits in the forest. Ganieda, says Merlin, will inherit his power as prophet.

As with his previous works, Geoffrey's *Vita Merlini* had a political purpose, here more closely tied to his ambitions than even the *Prophetie Merlini* and the *Historia regum Britannie*. His readers would have made the connection between Taliesin and perhaps even Merlin and the legend of Saint Kentigern, for whose disciple, Asaph, his newly organized Welsh diocese (Geoffrey was its second bishop) had been named.

But while Geoffrey's purpose, in writing all of his works, was both broadly (in terms of his Norman patrons) and narrowly (in terms of his own quest for churchly preferment) political, the narratives and characters he gave world literature in the Arthurian section of the *Historia regum Britannie* and in the *Vita Merlini* have come to have an existence on their own that has produced the largest and most continuous corpus devoted to a single theme in literary history. Its vitality has outlasted the Middle Ages, when it inspired the fourteenth-century romances of Chrétien de Troyes and such splendid poems as *Sir Gawain and the Green Knight*, the *Alliterative Morte Arthure* and the *Stanzaic Morte Arthur*, and Sir Thomas Malory's *Le Morte Darthur* (1451–1470), to name some of the most striking examples, and the Renaissance, when its political uses would be revived by Edmund Spenser's *Faerie Queene* (1596).

After a brief period of neglect, it would fuel both the nineteenth-century Arthurian revival, with works by Alfred Tennyson, Mark Twain, and a host of others, and the continuing twentieth-century Arthuriana, especially motion pictures (almost three dozen) and novels (more than two hundred since 1884) which have exhibited such strikingly original modifications of their sources. All of this vitality is owing to Geoffrey of Monmouth, whose handling of the medieval genre of *historia* and bundling together of themes and characters which had previously existed only fragmentarily were the decisive influences in initiating Arthurian literature. This achievement belies criticism both in his own time (as in William of Newburgh) and in the recent past (as in Hammer) that would brand him a liar. More than these critics, Geoffrey understood the creative potential of his material. To him goes credit for writing the first biography of Arthur, with its tragic

shape of rise and fall and yet enough flexibility to include the possibility for comedy as well. He is also responsible for the characters of Guinevere and Gawain, Bedivere and Modred (Mordred), Kay and Morgan le Fay, as well as the fleshed-out Arthur himself. If this story and its actors are not true, then, as Sir Winston Churchill noted, they ought to be, and their creator, Geoffrey of Monmouth, must be recognized as the superlative creator of imaginative literature he was.

Bibliography:
Julia C. Crick, *The Historia Regum Britannie of Geoffrey of Monmouth: A Summary Catalogue of the Manuscripts*, volume 3 (Cambridge: Brewer, 1989).

References:
Geoffrey Ashe, "A Certain Very Ancient Book," *Speculum*, 56 (1981): 301–323;

R. A. Caldwell, "The Use of Sources in the Variant and Vulgate Versions of the *Historia Regum Britanniae* and the Question of the Order of the Versions," *Bibliographical Bulletin of the International Arthurian Society*, 9 (1957): 123–124;

Caroline D. Eckhardt, "The *Prophetia Merlini* of Geoffrey of Monmouth: Latin Manuscript Copies," *Manuscripta*, 26, no. 3 (1982): 167–176;

Edmond Faral, ed., *La Légende Arthurienne*, volume 3 (Paris: Champion, 1929), pp. 64–303;

Robert Huntington Fletcher, *The Arthurian Materials in the Chronicles, Especially Those of Great Britain and France* (New York: Burt Franklin, 1958);

Maureen Fries, "Boethian Themes and Tragic Structure in Geoffrey of Monmouth's *Historia Regum Britanniae*," in *The Arthurian Tradition*, edited by Mary Flowers Braswell and John Bugge (Tuscaloosa: University of Alabama Press, 1988), pp. 29–42;

Pierre Gallais, "La *Variant Version* de l'*Historia Regum Britanniae* et le *Brut* de Wace," *Romania*, 87, no. 1 (1966): 1–32;

Robert W. Hanning, *The Vision of History in Early Britain from Gildas to Geoffrey of Monmouth* (New York: Columbia University Press, 1966);

Hans Erich Keller, "Wace et Geoffrey de Monmouth: Problème de la chronologie des sources," *Romania*, 98 (1977): 379–389;

R. W. Leckie, *The Passage of Dominion: Geoffrey of Monmouth and the Periodization of Insular History in the Twelfth Century* (Toronto: University of Toronto Press, 1981);

Lewis Thorpe, ed. and trans., *The History of the Kings of Britain* (Baltimore: Penguin, 1966).

John Gower

(circa 1330 – 1408)

Russell A. Peck
University of Rochester

MAJOR WORKS: *Cinkante Balades* (circa 1350–circa 1400)

Manuscript: Trentham Hall (Duke of Sutherland, Dunrobin Castle, circa 1400).

First publication: In Thomas Warton, *The History of English Poetry from the Eleventh to the Seventeenth Century* (London, 1774–1781) – includes *balades* 20, 34, 36, and 43; first complete edition, *John Gower: Balades and Other Poems, Printed from the Original Manuscript of the Marquis of Stafford at Trentham* (London: Roxburghe Club, 1818).

Standard edition: In Macaulay (1899–1902).

Mirour de l'Omme (circa 1376–1379); also known as *Speculum Hominis* and *Speculum Meditantis*.

Manuscript: Cambridge University Library MS. Additional 3035 (dated before 1400).

First publication: In *The Complete Works of John Gower,* edited by George C. Macaulay, volume 1: *The French Works* (Oxford: Clarendon Press, 1899), pp. 1–334.

Standard edition: In Macaulay's collected edition (1899–1902).

Edition in English: *Mirour de l'Omme,* translated by William Burton Wilson (East Lansing, Mich.: Colleagues Press, 1992).

Vox clamantis (circa 1377–1381)

Manuscripts: The work survives in twelve manuscripts, which John Fisher in his 1964 biography of Gower divides into three groups: an A-version, written before the Peasants' Revolt, without the Visio on the revolt, which becomes Book I; a B-version, which includes the Visio and is written after the Peasants' Revolt; and C-versions, after 1400, which include at the end the "Cronica Tripertita." Modern printed editions base their texts on All Souls College, Oxford, MS. 98 (circa 1400). Other important manuscripts include the Bodleian MS. Digby 138 (early fifteenth century), which mixes A- and C-versions) and British Library Cotton Tiberius A.iv. (circa 1408).

Miniature portrait of John Gower from a fifteenth-century transcription of his Confessio amantis *(British Library, Egerton MS. 1991)*

First publication: *The Vox Clamantis of John Gower,* edited by Rev. H. O. Coxe (London: Roxburghe Club, 1850).

Standard edition: In Macaulay (1899–1902).

Confessio amantis (circa 1390–1392)

Manuscripts: There are forty-nine manuscripts of the complete poem and an additional eight that contain various parts of it. Bodley, Fairfax 3, MS. 3883 (late fourteenth century) comes from Gower's own scriptorium and seems to bear revisions by the poet. Most modern editors (including Macaulay) follow this manuscript as their copy text.

First publication: *Confessio amantis,* edited by William Caxton (London: Printed by Caxton, 1483).

Standard edition: In Macaulay (1899–1902).

Traitié (circa 1397)

> **Manuscripts:** The work survives in ten manuscripts, the best being at the Bodleian Library, Fairfax 3 (late fourteenth century), where the *balades* are appended to *Confessio amantis*.
>
> **First publication:** In *John Gower: Balades and Other Poems, Printed from the Original Manuscript of the Marquis of Stafford at Trentham* (London: Roxburghe Club, 1818).
>
> **Standard edition:** In Macaulay (1899–1902).

"Cronica Tripertita" (circa 1400)

> **Manuscripts:** The work is found in five manuscripts. Four versions are appended to *Vox Clamatis:* All Souls College, Oxford, 98; Glasgow Hunterian Museum T.2,17; British Library Cotton Tiberius A.iv; and British Library Harleian 6291. The work exists separately in Bodley, Hatton 92 (4073).
>
> **First publication:** In *Political Poems and Songs,* volume 1, edited by Thomas Wright, Rolls Series 14 (London: Longman, Green, Longman & Roberts, 1859), pp. 417–454.
>
> **Standard edition:** In Macaulay (1899–1902).

Laureate Poems (circa 1400) – "Rex celi deus," "O recolende," "Carmen super multiplici viciorum pestilencia," "De lucis scrutinio," "Ecce patet tensus," "Est amor in glosa pax bellica," "Eneidos bucolis," "O Deus immense," and "Quicquid homo scribat."

> **Manuscripts:** These poems are included in all five manuscripts in which *Cronica tripertita* appears.
>
> **First publication:** "Rex coeli deus," "Ecce patet tensus," and "Henrici quarti," a variation of "Quicquid homo scribat," in *John Gower: Balades and Other Poems* (London: Roxburghe Club, 1818); "Quicquid homo scribat," "Eneidos bucolis," and "O Deus immense" in *The Vox Clamantis of John Gower,* edited by Coxe (London: Roxburghe Club, 1850); "Carmen super multiplici vitiorum pestilentia" and "De lucis scrutinio" in *Political Poems and Songs,* edited by Wright (London, 1859); "Laureate Poems," in *The Complete Works of John Gower,* edited by Macaulay, volume 4: *The Latin Poems* (Oxford: Clarendon Press, 1902).
>
> **Standard edition:** In Macaulay (1899–1902).

In Praise of Peace (circa 1400)

> **Manuscript:** Trentham Hall manuscript.
>
> **First publication:** In *The Works of Geffray Chaucer* (London: Thomas Godfrey, 1532).
>
> **Standard edition:** In Macaulay (1899–1902).

COLLECTED EDITION: *The Works of John Gower,* 4 volumes, edited by George C. Macaulay (Oxford: Clarendon Press, 1899–1902; reprinted, Grosse Pointe, Mich.: Scholarly Press, 1968).

COLLECTED EDITION IN MODERN ENGLISH: *The Major Latin Works of John Gower: The Voice of One Crying and The Tripartite Chronicle: An annotated Translation into English with an Introductory Essay on the Author's Non-English Works,* translated by Eric W. Stockton (Seattle: University of Washington Press, 1962).

John Gower is one of the three or four major poets of the English fourteenth century. The canon of his writings is large, and the influence of his work on subsequent generations of writers is substantial. He is still read today with delight by a large number of admirers. To readers in the fifteenth and sixteenth centuries, Gower stood with Geoffrey Chaucer as the originator of English poetry. They are the makers who introduced into English vernacular poetry the melifluous meters of the classical tradition.

Literary and historical evidence indicates a long-standing friendship between the two poets. In 1378, when Chaucer traveled to Italy on business for the royal household, he gave Gower power of attorney over his estate. A few years later Chaucer paid his friend high tribute by dedicating a work that some critics consider his greatest literary masterpiece, *Troilus and Criseyde* (circa 1382–1386), to him:

> O moral Gower, this bok I directe
> To the, and to the, philosophical Strode,
> To vouchen sauf ther nede is to corecte
> Of youre benygnites and zeles goode.

Ralph Strode was a philosopher of Merton College, Oxford, who had moved to London to take up law practice. Strode lived near Chaucer at Aldgate, directly across the Thames from Southwark, where Gower lived. According to John Leland, Strode also wrote poetry. There appears to be here a literary circle of considerable talent and sophistication that took pride in each other's craftsmanship and achievements.

Of the three Chaucer was the first to achieve distinction as a poet in the vernacular. By around 1385 he had written his exquisite dream visions and numerous lyrics, and he had translated Boethius's *Consolation of Philosophy* sometime in the 1380s and Guillaume de Lorris's *Romaunt of the Rose* in the early 1360s. Also he had worked for several years on his

Troilus and Criseyde, revising and polishing it. Such care suggests an audience whose opinion the poet must have admired and whom he sought to please. Gower, likewise, was known by 1385 to be a writer of considerable stature, the author of two great poems, one in French – the *Mirour de l'Omme* (circa 1376-1379), and the other in Latin – the *Vox clamantis* (circa 1377-1381). These major works are in a voice quite different from Chaucer's, more hortatory and moralistic. Instead of satire, Gower writes complaint – earnest, foreboding, precautionary, even apocalyptic, but always with a powerful conviction that people have it within themselves to rise above their errors to right the mess they have made. Chaucer's dedication of *Troilus* to Gower is clear evidence that Gower must have been a crucial part of his London audience, the critic and confrere whose voice and opinion the writer works for and also against.

Approximately five years after *Troilus* was published, Gower paid tribute to Chaucer in his first effort in the vernacular, a frame poem of the magnitude of Chaucer's *Canterbury Tales* (circa 1375-1400), which proved to be Gower's finest achievement, the *Confessio amantis* (circa 1390-1392). At the end of Gower's poem, the goddess Venus, as she departs from Amans, the lover-poet for whom the stories are told, says to him: "And gret wel Chaucer whan ye mete, / As mi disciple and mi poete." Venus asks Amans to tell Chaucer to "sette an ende of alle his werk" as Venus's "owne clerk," apparently alluding to Chaucer's unfinished *Legend of Good Women,* a frame narrative dedicated to the praise of Cupid's saints (women who die for love) that Chaucer had begun in 1386, about the time Gower was beginning the *Confessio amantis.* Some have thought that the two poets set out in the mid 1380s to write frame narratives celebrating cupidity with a mocking wit – Chaucer in his *Legend of Good Women* and Gower in his *Confessio amantis.* Chaucer left his poem unfinished to work instead on *The Canterbury Tales.* In *Confessio amantis,* through "Gower" the lover who has finished writing his frame narrative, Venus encourages Chaucer to finish his earlier undertaking.

In the early 1390s, perhaps in response to Gower's reference to his unfinished work, Chaucer alludes in a witty repartee to Gower's completed poem in the prologue to the "Man of Law's Tale." The Man of Law, a lawyer-purchaser like Gower, complains that there are no poems left for him to tell, since Chaucer has already told them all. He allows, however, that Chaucer has not told sinful tales of wretched incest such as the stories about

Canacee, who "loved hir owene brother synfully," or "the cursed kyng Antiochus," who bereft his own daughter of her maidenhead – both stories told by Gower in *Confessio amantis.* The joke appears to be a takeoff on an implicit juxtaposition of moral Gower and bawdy Chaucer, a joke which Chaucer gives one further twist by having the Man of Law then proceed to tell the story of Custance, one source of which is "Gower."

This is the last mention either makes of the other. But it is evident that the friendship was a long one which must have continued to the end of their lives. Some scholars have thought there may have been a breach in the friendship in the early 1390s, when Gower shifted his allegiance from Richard II to Henry of Lancaster, and that Chaucer may have had Gower in mind in creating the old fool Januarie in the "Merchant's Tale," who marries late when he should be turning his thoughts to holiness. But the dates do not match up well for such an analogy to be compelling. Gower did marry in 1398, when he was well beyond sixty years of age and on the verge of blindness. But Chaucer had written his "Merchant's Tale" several years before (circa 1394), only a couple of years after Gower had completed his revision of *Confessio amantis.* Moreover, Chaucer appears to have been on good terms with John of Gaunt and his Lancastrian descendants throughout his life. There is no good evidence to indicate that the friendship and mutual regard between Chaucer and Gower dwindled at the end of their lives except insofar as the infirmities of old age isolate people. When Chaucer died in 1400, Gower was essentially confined as an elderly blind man to his residence at Saint Mary Overeys, where he died in 1408.

For two hundred years Gower and Chaucer are named together as England's greatest poets – John Lydgate calls them "erthely goddes two"; the *Kingis Quair* refers to them as progenitors "of Rethorike" in England; and Erasmus, comparing them to Dante and Petrarch in Italy, names them the source of delight within a national literature for the English people. They are regularly cited, sometimes along with John Lydgate, for the freshness of their rhetoric, their craftsmanship, and their felicitous influence in stimulating the writing of English poetry. Gower is usually the first named in such accolades, not so much for being the superior poet as for being the older of the two. His seniority led his earliest biographers to portray him as Chaucer's mentor as in some ways he may have been, though it was Chaucer who first excelled as a poet in the vernacular.

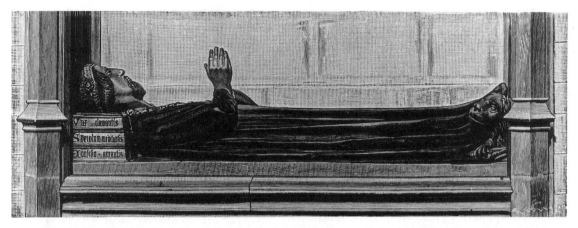

Gower's effigy in Saint Saviour's Church, Southwark. The poet's head rests on three volumes: Vox clamantis, Speculum
meditantis *(also known as* Mirour de l'Omme*), and* Confessio amantis.

Chaucer's phrase "moral Gower" has become indelibly attached to his friend. Gower has been commonly praised for his sententiousness and wisdom, attributes less admired in poetry of the eighteenth, nineteenth, and early twentieth centuries. In more recent times, however, readers have again discovered the felicities of his verse and have rehistoricized his work in light of his social and political commitments.

Of the two poets Gower is the more sonorous and predictable and thus, initially at least, the more imitated, though not necessarily the more admired. The pairing of the two continued into the seventeenth century. Caxton published both the *Canterbury Tales* and Gower's *Confessio amantis* in 1483. And as William Thynne published the collected works of Chaucer in 1532, in that same year Thomas Berthelette published *De confessione amantis*. Gower's poem was sufficiently popular to be reissued in a second edition in 1554, the edition read by Sir Philip Sidney, Edmund Spenser, and William Shakespeare. But after that a complete edition of Gower's great English poem was not reprinted until Alexander Chambers included it in the second volume of his twenty-one-volume *The Works of the English Poets* (1810). An edition by Reinhold Pauli appeared in 1857, and at the end of the century George C. Macaulay's edition appeared in four volumes titled *The Works of John Gower* (1899–1902), the standard edition of Gower's work. But in his nineteenth- and twentieth-century revival Gower was usually set in opposition to Chaucer and represented as a markedly inferior poet – less dramatic, dull, and long-winded – in contrast to his brilliant contemporary. It is only in the later twentieth century that Gower has once again come into his own

as a poet of unique merits and with a stature independent of his famous contemporary.

Information about Gower's biography is sparse by modern standards, though by medieval standards there is quite a bit. Besides references to his relationship with Chaucer, there are two kinds of information – documentary materials and evidence within the poetry itself. There are more than eighty known documents pertaining to Gower's life – a marriage license dated 25 January 1398 which permits his marriage without further publication of banns to Agnes Groundolf; his will dated 15 August 1408 and proved on 24 October of that year; his twice-moved tomb, which was originally in the now-nonexistent chapel of Saint John the Baptist in Southwark Cathedral (formerly Saint Mary Overeys Priory and Church); legal documents pertaining to property and inheritance; family seals and heraldic details; real estate transactions, royal grants, and notes of protection; and the record of power of attorney granted him by Chaucer. In addition, his writings, though never autobiographical in the way that Thomas Hoccleve's seem to have been, nonetheless tell a great deal about his social and intellectual concerns, his reading, his literary background, his political sensibilities, and his psychological temperament.

To a modern biographer these scraps of evidence pertaining to Gower's life must seem perplexingly sparse. What is unknown far exceeds what is known. For example, who Agnes Groundolf was and why he chose to marry her when he was nearly seventy years old remains puzzling. Perhaps it was a marriage of convenience or of gratitude. Gower's poetry reveals that he was blind and infirm: perhaps he needed someone to look after him.

The marriage would have permitted Agnes to live in the priory with him. Or maybe she was someone who had looked after him for years, his attendant upon whom he now wished to secure an inheritance. In his will he leaves her one hundred pounds of "lawful money"; three cups; one "cooperculum"; twelve silver spoons and two saltcellars; beds; chests; furniture of hall; pantry, and kitchen along with all the vessels and utensils; and all the rents due from his manors of Southwell in Northampton and Multoun in Suffolk – altogether a considerable inheritance for a decade of cohabitation. According to Leland, Agnes was also buried in the Saint John the Baptist Chapel, but in a lower tomb. The date of her death is not known. It is also possible that Agnes was Gower's second wife. There are hints in the *Mirour de l'Omme* (in lines 8794 and 17649) that he may have been previously married, but there are no documents to confirm such a marriage.

Scholars usually estimate Gower's date of birth to be about 1330. Nothing is known for certain about his birthplace nor his childhood or formal education. John Gower is a common name in fourteenth-century county records. In his edition of Gower's works, Macaulay cites five different John Gowers who appear contemporaneously in the records of Kent alone. On the basis of the poet's crest scholars conjecture that he was born either in Kent or Yorkshire, into an upper-middle-class family of considerable wealth who held land in Kent, Yorkshire, Norfolk, and Suffolk. As John H. Fisher discusses in his 1964 biography of Gower, real estate dealings and similarities in coats of arms link the poet to Sir Robert Gower of Brabourne (perhaps an uncle) who was kin to the powerful Langbargh Gowers of the North Riding of Yorkshire. In 1332 David Strabolgi, Earl of Athol, granted Sir Robert the manor of Kentwell in Suffolk, property that the poet bought from Sir Robert's heirs in 1368. As further evidence of a possible family connection, the coats of arms of Sir Robert, the Langbargh Gowers, and the poet share the colors of argent and azure, a chevron, and three animal heads or hounds (a "gower" is a hunting dog). Hounds also appear in the Langbargh Gowers' shield and in both of the surviving seals of the poet. And according to John Stow a hound appeared on the crest on Gower's tomb, a crest which is no longer extant.

Gower's earliest biographers, Stow (in his *A Survey of London,* 1598) and John Leland (in his *Comentarii de Scriptoribus Britannicus,* 1709), imply that he made his way as a lawyer, though they wrote long after the poet's death. He knows legal terms intimately, is always precise in his numerous discussions of lawyers, and refers to himself as wearing a garment with striped sleeves in the *Mirour de l'Omme,* implying some sort of affiliation with civil service. Fisher imagines that by about 1350 he would have been "old enough to enter the Inns of Court, and by 1368 have made enough money to buy Kentwell Manor from Robert Gower's heir." In the next decade there are records of several real estate dealings involving the poet, enough to suggest that Gower, as was common with lawyers in his time, was a "purchasour" who made money through the buying and selling of land. There is also some evidence that he may have had investments in the wool trade.

One real estate exchange involving "William, son of William de Septvanz, knight," was sufficiently messy to convince Macaulay, who more than any other is responsible for the revival of interest in Gower in the twentieth century, that Gower was "a villainous misleader of youth" who encouraged "a young man to defraud the Crown by means of perjury, in order that he might purchase his lands from him at a nominal price." Fisher has studied the details of the case with great care, however, and demonstrates that there is nothing "nefarious in Gower's behavior; indeed the records indicate just the opposite, that he was unusually scrupulous.... Certainly there is nothing in the record.... to suggest that [the purchase] was in any way illegal." Fisher asserts, however, that there is plenty of evidence to indicate that Gower "knew what he was doing" when he had writs and charters recorded in Chancery.

According to Leland, Gower helped finance the restoration, completed by 1377, of Saint Mary Overeys Priory and Church, which had been destroyed by fire a century and a half earlier. Documents pertaining to his marriage to Agnes Groundolf confirm that in 1398 he was living there, presumably in quarters on the close, and other evidence establishes that he was buried in the Saint John the Baptist Chapel of the Priory church. Just when he took up residence at the priory is not known, but that residence has much bearing upon his literary career since there was a scriptorium associated with the priory which produced some of Gower's manuscripts. It is perhaps reasonable to conjecture that Gower had his quarters built during the restoration and took up residence there at about that time. This is also the time that his literary productions begin to appear in earnest. Fisher notes that the colophon appended to many manuscripts of the *Vox clamantis* and the *Confessio amantis* asserts: "John Gower, desirous of lightening somewhat the account for the intellectual gifts God gave to his keeping, while there is time, between work and leisure, for the knowledge of others, composed three books of instructive material" – the third of the three books would have been *Speculum meditantis* (that is, the *Mirour de l'Omme*). It may be that from about 1377 until his death Gower entered into some sort of semiretired life at the priory to devote himself to his studies and his writings. The residence placed him near his friend Chaucer and the London literary scene. Gower's writings, like Chaucer's, are bookish. The priory might have had library holdings of the kind he draws upon so extensively in his three "meditational" poems, though he might by this time in his life (mid seventies) have had a library of his own. He may even have given books to the priory.

All three of his greatest poems were written later in life. It seems likely that Gower was already known as a poet before establishing himself in Southwark, however. Toward the end of *Mirour de l'Omme* he claims in his youth to have dressed as a courtier and to have composed "les fols ditz d'amours" (foolish love poems) to which he sang and danced. Similarly, in the first book of the *Confessio amantis* the "poet" claims, in the guise of the lover addressing Venus, to have written rondels, balades, and virelais for his lady which he sang "in halle and ek in chambre aboute, / And made merie among the route." Such passages may be autobiographical, or they could be simply rhetorical poses suitable to the requirements of the device.

Gower appears to have been very much a Londoner. He knows all phases of the city well, refers to it as "our city," and, even more than Chaucer or Langland, depicts the ways and thoughts of its merchants, victuallers, and guildsmen. Fisher makes a compelling case for Gower's having been involved in the Pui, a religious, charitable, convivial musical organization whose regulations are described in the records of the guildhall in London. A member was exempted from the twelve pence dues if he brought to the meeting a new song. It is possible that some of Gower's love poems may have been written for such occasions, though it must be acknowledged that the Pui was an all-male organization which, though it often celebrated women, barred them from its company. The resulting festivities would hardly have been conducive to dancing. It is possible, of course, that the love songs he mentions could have been written in French and performed at courtly occasions quite different from those at the guildhall, although Gower was not affiliated with the royal court to the extent that Chaucer was.

There can be no doubt about Gower's piety, however. In his will he endows the saying of prayers on his behalf in perpetuity. According to Berthelette's *De confessione amantis* the prayers were still being said in the mid sixteenth century. Gower was a man who thoroughly believed in medieval principles of social gradation within society, but at the same time he upheld Christian principles of equality in the afterlife. He detested corruption in all forms wherever it was to be found. He saw society as a great organism, responsible to God and itself. Although it brings doom upon itself through sin, it has, nonetheless, the capacity to reform and uphold the common good. Repeatedly in his writings Gower abhors war and debases chivalry. Though he denounces the Lollards, he shares in their reform-mindedness of individual character, if not of social structures.

Apart from whatever balades, carols, and virelais Gower may have written in his youth, none of which have been identified, his earliest datable poem is the *Mirour de l'Omme,* a French moral treatise of about thirty-one thousand lines set in stanzas of twelve octosyllabic lines rhymed aabaab/bbabba, a stanzaic form commonly used by French poets of the moral school. The pauses in the stanza normally follow the rhyme divisions, with a break often occurring at the middle of the stanza and a moral tag at the end. The quality of the French is excellent. That Gower could sustain his tightly rhymed stanza without repetitiousness or sonorous cliché through so long a poem is a tribute to his thorough knowledge of the language. The verse is syllabic, in the French manner, but the rhythm is, nonetheless, unmistakably English.

Gower appears to have composed the poem between 1376 and 1379, perhaps completing it after taking up residence at the priory about 1377. For centuries the poem was known only through its representation as one of three volumes supporting the head of Gower's effigy on his tomb, where it is identified by the name *Speculum meditantis,* and in the colophons to several of the Gower manuscripts where it is referred to by the title *Speculum hominis.* In 1895 Macaulay identified the poem in Cambridge University Library Additional MS. 3035, where it is given the title *Mirour de l'Omme.* The quality of this unique copy of the poem is excellent – it is so accurate, in fact, that Macaulay thinks it must have been corrected under the poet's supervision and was probably his own copy. Unfortunately the manuscript is somewhat mutilated: the first four leaves of the poem have been cut out along with seven other leaves at various places in the manuscript (totaling

Page from Gower's Vox clamantis *in a fourteenth-century manuscript (British Library, Cotton Tiberius A. iv., fol. 9)*

about fifteen hundred lines), and a few leaves at the end also appear to be missing.

The *Mirour de l'Omme* is an ambitious undertaking, intended to cover the whole domain of man's moral nature and religious obligation. The manuscript begins with an announcement which divides the poem's contents into ten parts. This division does not reflect at all the proportions of the poem, but rather its topics. It has many subdivisions, identified by prose rubrics which describe briefly the subject matter of what follows.

Basically the *Mirour de l'Omme* is a complaint against the ills of the world. The first ten thousand or so lines describe the seven deadly sins. Gower imposes upon what might be a dull exercise in classification a rather subtle allegory of how Sin gained its status as the greatest power in the world. His scheme reminds modern readers of John Milton's genealogy of Sin and Death in *Paradise Lost* (1667, 1671). In the *Mirour de l'Omme,* Lucifer, after his precipitous fall, gives birth to a daughter named Sin, who is evil, ugly, and vile. The fiend raises her, teaching her guile and treachery. She becomes so beguiling that she seduces her father, who engenders upon her a son named Death. She then espouses her child. Ugliness breeds ugliness as they engender seven daughters to set upon the world.

The *Mirour de l'Omme* rivals Spenser's *The Faerie Queene* (1596) as it describes the grand procession of the seven daughters to their new home on earth – Pride first, riding a lion, gayly arrayed; Envy next, dressed in purple embroidered with burning hearts and serpent tongues, riding a dog and carrying a moulting sparrow hawk; then Ire, riding a boar, bearing a cock on her fist and wearing a coat of armor with a thousand knives hanging from her sides. Ire is followed at some distance by Sloth with her leaden couch, riding slowly upon an ass and holding an owl attached by a cord; then there is Avarice, with ten purses of gold, riding a dappled pony and carrying a falcon and goshawk, who hunts and brings her prey even as she rides. Next Gluttony, led by Drunkenness, rides a wolf and carries a kite on her fist; and finally Lechery, the most cunning, is dressed wantonly, seated upon a goat and carrying a dove, which many admire. They are all espoused to the World, with Hell as their dowry. After his wedding feast the World engenders upon each of the seven five more offspring – hermaphroditic monsters, each more ugly than the others, but all fraudulently dressed to seduce the Soul, which they do with great subtlety.

Nearly a third of the *Mirour de l'Omme* is devoted to the enumeration of Sin's grandchildren. It, along with the next eight thousand lines on the appropriate remedies for the thirty-five subdivisions of sin, becomes a main source for Gower's subsequent poetry, particularly the *Confessio amantis,* which draws much of its structure and ideological framework from these subdivisions. Gower's representation of the sins is rich with anecdotes, bits of wisdom pertaining to nature as he compares sinners to animals, and biblical material, especially Job, Psalms, Ecclesiastes, Proverbs, the Song of Songs, and the Gospels. This portion of the work is akin to manuals of virtues and vices designed for the preparation of persons for confession.

In the next ten thousand or so lines Gower examines the various estates of human endeavor, from popes, cardinals, bishops, and lesser ecclesiastical officials to secular rulers of the world, men of law, merchants, artificers, victuallers, and laborers. For each degree and class of people the dominant forms of corruption are described along with their effects against mankind in general. Gower is decidedly conservative in his moral estimation of human activities, looking back to a former age when people behaved more honestly and were less motivated by greed or adept at deceit. It is in this section that he describes most assiduously life around him in London. He holds a mirror up to the world and finds it overwhelmed by fraud. "Ah, World, wherefore art thou gone astray?" he laments. The answer to the painful question, he insists, lies not in the world as such, but in the actions of people. Blame not the elements or the stars. The evil that causes the ills is engendered in the sinful hearts of men and women. If people transgress against God, by their sins they undo everything – earth, water, air, and fire – the very elements themselves.

The last three thousand or so lines turn inward, as the observer of the world shifts to the first person to put aside the foolish love songs and ditties of his youth to sing a new song of disenchantment. Since mankind is so wretched, the only hope lies in "Jhesu Christ et ... sa doulce Miere la Vierge gloriouse," who offer humankind their only remedy. By telling the life of Mary the poet offers an example of purity and piety that guarantees the greatest satisfaction through virtuous fruition. In the life of Jesus he exemplifies a justice and love of such potency as to redeem the fallen Adam, despite the devil and "sa merdaille" (his filthy wretches). No woman ever had so great a love or so great a lover as Mary, nor did anyone ever suffer so. Yet, at the end, neither had anyone experienced such joy as she. Mary is the model of compassion and the assurance of joy for humankind, and the poem ends with a celebration of her name.

The *Mirour de l'Omme* is not a great poem, but it possesses many remarkable features. It provides the first statement of moral Gower, shooting his barbs at the world to expose its fraudulence. The poem is rhetorically sophisticated, particularly in its use of admonitorial devices. Although he was, as Macaulay so aptly says, "a man of stereotyped convictions, whose thoughts on human society and on the divine government of the world tended constantly to repeat themselves in but slightly varying forms," his pellucid style anticipates the artistic refinements so characteristic of both his later long poems. The poem is rich in proverbial lore and wise sayings, and it offers, through its examples, an abundance of insights into fourteenth-century everyday life, particularly life in the busy streets and hidden chambers of London.

Gower's next major work, the *Vox clamantis* (The Voice of One Crying), is a moral essay of 10,265 lines arranged in seven books and written in Latin elegiac verse. The title is prophetic and comes from Isaiah and the Gospel accounts of John the Baptist – the voice crying in the wilderness, admonishing humankind to change its ways. The poem draws heavily upon the *Mirour de l'Omme,* which may explain why Gower never had that poem recopied but instead used it as a source for his subsequent poetry. Originally Gower seems to have planned a different structure from the seven-part scheme he ended up with. The prologue and much of what is now book 2 initially may have been a preface to a treatise in five books declaiming the evils of the time. After the Peasants' Revolt, Gower separated his first book into a prologue and book 2 and added a more compelling first book with an apocalyptic vision of the hurling time, plagued by a bestial displacement of humankind. Eighteen years later, after the ascension of Henry IV to the throne, he rewrote passages dealing with the "boy king" and added as a continuation the "Cronica Tripertita" (Tripartite Chronicle), another beast allegory on the last days of Richard's reign and the bringing of that king to judgment.

Like William Langland's *Piers Plowman* (circa 1360–1390), the message and composition of Gower's great Latin poem was always growing, even to the latter days of his life. But where the several stages of *Piers Plowman* seem to demarcate the personal and social growth of the poet-persona, preoccupied with himself and his society, the several stages of *Vox clamantis* reflect primarily the changing

political scene of England and little of the poet's relationship to it, except as an admonisher.

In the preface to *Vox clamantis* Gower identifies himself through a riddle, claiming as his guide Saint John of the Apocalypse, whom he calls his namesake. Macaulay suggests that the tone of the *Mirour de l'Omme,* where "Les bons sont bons, les mals sont mals" (the good are good and the bad are bad), is that of a perpetual Last Judgment. The same may certainly be said of the tone of the *Vox clamantis*. Gower presents his book as that of a visionary – a Daniel or a Joseph – whose will is good and whose mission is to help man "better understand the conditions of time." He writes at a "tearful time" so that posterity may benefit from the mournful example.

Book 2 announces the poem's title and examines how it is that man has achieved such misery. The blame lies not with Fortune, as people commonly assert, but rather with the wanton behavior of mankind. God created all things; He alone should be contemplated. Books 3 and 4 offer a bold diatribe against the corrupt clergy and religious orders who, more than any, are in their worldliness culpable for neglect of their sacred offices. Book 5 is an attack on the estate of knighthood and its failure to uphold temporal affairs, mainly because of its devotion to Venus and is an attack on those committed to agriculture who through avarice, usury, fraud, and malice ignore the common good. Book 6 assails the chicaneries of ministers of the law – lawyers, judges, and sheriffs – who plunder the populace with their thirst for money, twisting the law to their advantage and corrupting even the king, to whom Gower offers much sound advice on good rule in a mirror for magistrates' tradition. Book 7 reviews mankind's desperate condition and brings the poem to its apocalyptic conclusion by recounting Nebuchadrezzar II's dream of the monster of degenerative time and reviewing the seven deadly sins which corrupt all worldly estates.

Book 1, written last, provides a brilliant dramatization of the consequences of irresponsible behavior throughout society. By means of a dream fable, Gower depicts the nightmarish world of a society gone berserk, where even the common men, in whom Gower elsewhere has great faith, turn themselves into plagues of beasts ravaging each other. Gower draws skillfully on a host of Ovidian materials in shaping his account of the sinful mutations. The effect is to encapsulate within a literary tradition what he took to be a horrendous moment in the history of England.

Book 1 ends with an emblem of chaos in which common profit has been totally obliterated.

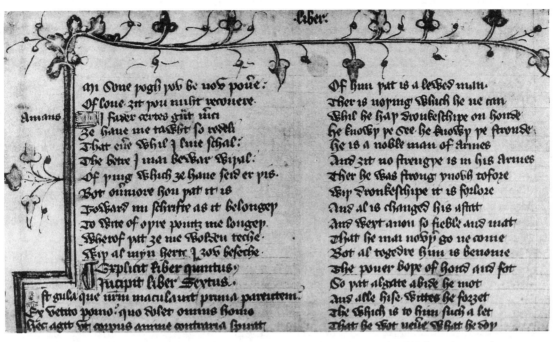

Part of a page from a late-fourteenth-century manuscript of Confessio amantis *produced by Gower's own scriptorum (Bodleian Library, Oxford, Fairfax 3, MS. 3883, fol. 125ᵛ)*

In a dramatically memorable scene the narrator, unwillingly caught up in his narrative, finds himself isolated in a wilderness, afraid of all men about him, who seem surely bent upon his destruction. This book should not be understood simply as an attack on the commons in revolt against hierarchy, but rather as a dramatic statement of the consequences of a whole society in disintegration, the causes of which Gower has analyzed in the remaining six books. To Gower the Peasants' Revolt must have seemed veritable proof of the validity of his prophetic attack on corrupt religious and civil authorities.

In composing *Vox clamantis* Gower draws extensively on other Latin writers from whom he borrows sometimes in passages of eight, ten, or even twenty lines. His main sources are Peter Riga's *Aurora,* for much of his biblical lore; Alexander Neckam's *De vita monachorum,* for many of his criticisms of corruption within the monasteries; the *Speculum stultorum,* for many of his animal and nature descriptions; Godfrey of Viterbo's *Pantheon,* for various stories about the ancient gods and priestly behavior; and various writings of Ovid. Gower knew well the full range of Ovid's works and draws shrewdly upon them. Such borrowings are not so much plagiarisms as wise compilations, part of Gower's faith in the continuity of moral probity despite history and its weird events.

In Gower's world everything good has its place. Given the beast allegories of book 1 of *Vox clamantis,* the "Cronica tripertita" fits well as a conclusion to Gower's complaint. In *Vox clamantis,* book 1, in a twisted Ovidian manner, men turn themselves into beasts and set upon one another in hateful destruction. But in the "Cronica tripertita" a few good (allegorical) animals and one good prince, though all sorely put upon, rise up with Christ's guidance to restore order on earth. The concluding piece begins:

It is the work of man to pursue and seek out peace. The three nobles of whom mention is made below did this, as there was good faith among them. It is the work of hell to disturb peace and to slay a kingdom's just men. The headstrong Richard was not afraid to do this, through devious trickery. It is a work done in Christ to depose haughty men from the throne and to exalt the humble. God did this. He cast the hateful Richard from his throne and He decided upon the glorious elevation of the pious Henry, who was a man most pleasing in the estimation of all.
– translation by Eric W. Stockton from *The Major Latin Works of John Gower,* 1962)

This time the good beasts – the Swan (Gloucester), the Bear (Warwick), and the Horse (Northumberland) – work as a team to restrain the misguided king and his minions. But the foxlike king slays the

Swan, exiles the Bear, and flays the Horse. Without their restraint the evil king becomes molelike, undermining and spoiling the land, until Henry, the noble man, returns with Christ's help to restore rule in the kingdom. Gower concludes, "Here ends the Chronicle, which is to be heeded with a watchful heart by kings both present and future."

Between the time that he completed the *Vox clamantis* and then added the "Cronica tripartita," Gower wrote the *Confessio amantis,* his great poem in English that likewise went through several stages of composition. *Confessio amantis* differs markedly in its tone from Gower's previous efforts in French and Latin. The poet now chooses a "middel waie" – "somewhat of lust, somewhat of lore" – designed to entertain as well as instruct. The result is truly delightful. In fact, given the somber effect of both *Mirour de l'Omme* and *Vox clamantis* the achievement of *Confessio amantis* would be difficult to predict. Its complex narrative design reveals powers of poetic invention in degrees of sophistication not seen in Gower's other poems. His capacities as a storyteller and his masterful sense of irony are utterly enchanting in this more playful creation. The theme concerns love in all its manifestations – natural, sublime, cosmic, personal, social, and divine – all cast in eight books, framed with a prologue, Latin epigrams, marginal glosses, and an Explicit.

In the first recension of the poem, begun perhaps about 1386 and completed about 1390, Gower tells how, while rowing his boat on the Thames, he was invited aboard the king's barge and encouraged to write "som newe thing . . . Which may be wisdom to the wise / And pley to hem that lust to pleye." Gower takes on the commission gladly and dedicates the ensuing poem to the king:

> A bok for king Richardes sake,
> To whom belongeth my ligeance
> With al myn hertes obeissance
> In al that evere a liege man
> Unto his king may doon or can.

Thirty-one of the forty-nine known manuscripts of *Confessio amantis* follow this recension. It was popular because of its priority, because of the charming dedication to the king with its lively autobiographical moment, and because it concludes with Venus's admonition to Chaucer to finish his love poems.

Between 1390 and 1392 Gower revised the *Confessio amantis,* reworking books 5, 6, and 7, adding new material, some of which was subsequently cut, and rearranging old. In 1392 Richard had a falling out with the city of London, imposing taxes which the city refused to pay. Gower rewrites the opening commission of the poem – "A bok for Engelondes sake" instead of "Richardes" – and dedicates the poem "unto myn oghne lord, / Which of Lancastre is Henri named." Although this might seem a fickle or, given Richard's temper and vindictive memory, an impolitic thing to do, it is doubtful that the king ever knew of the new direction of Gower's loyalty, though Chaucer might have. Furthermore, Gower's admiration of Henry had always been great, and his loyalty to him never flagged. To Gower, Henry is the ideal ruler, "Ful of knyhthode and alle grace," the embodiment of conscientious behavior.

In 1393, "the yer sextenthe of kyng Richard," Gower completed his third recension, the best exemplar of which is the Bodleian Fairfax 3 manuscript, the correction of which Gower seems to have personally supervised. In this final version of the poem, the leave-taking of Venus in book 8 is altered: instead of Venus's address to Chaucer, the goddess simply says "adieu" and vanishes, leaving the poet astonished and reflective, smiling upon his cupidity before he turns homeward. Then, instead of a prayer for King Richard, the author prays for England, admonishes against the evils of division within the land, reminds the king of his duty within the state, chastises tyranny, and insists, as he did in *Vox Clamantis,* upon the king's personal responsibilities: "First at hym self he mot begynne, / To kepe and reule his owne astat." The dedication to Henry of Lancaster from the second recension remains, as does some of the rearranging of material, but in this final recension he drops the "Tale of Lucius and the Statue," which he had added to book 5, and, in book 7, Dante's rebuff of a flatterer, a passage on the importance of pity in kings, and the "Tale of the Jew and the Pagan," all of which had been added in the second recension.

The layout of *Confessio amantis* is clever. Although the prologue, some portions of book 7 and the conclusion are in the analytic voice of his earlier works, defining the ideals and failures of the states of England and Christendom, the heart of the poem is a delightful fiction in which the poet poses as a lover who has gone to the woods to lament his frustration and to invoke Venus's aid. The goddess appears, wonders about so unlikely a candidate, and, in a sort of parody of last rites, sends the failing lover to Genius, "myn oghne Clerk," for confession.

Genius is an amusing combination of one's attendant spirit, imagination, ingenuity, natural reason, and procreativity. He is subservient to Nature and resents all "unkynde" (unnatural) behavior.

And, though he appears to be bound to Venus as a kind of priest, he is often impatient with her caprices and seems quite aware of the contradictions of his service to her and her selfish son Cupid and to Nature and the commonweal. But he accepts most cheerfully his task of shriving the disconsolate lover and does so with an irrepressible enthusiasm and thoroughness.

To effect a full confession whereby nothing will be left out or mistimed, Genius first exorcises the senses, through which confusions sometimes arise, then takes the lover on an instructive road trip through the seven deadly sins. For each definition, problem, or remedy, Genius tells stories by way of example. Between the stories is dialogue between Genius and the lover, which Gower wittily manipulates as both discussants impose their immediate or partial understandings upon the issues. Although Genius's intention is always good, he has his own blindnesses and limitations with which Gower plays. The lover certainly has his blind spots as well, though he too is good-hearted and wishes for the best, imagining the best to be what he wishes.

In the prologue Gower frames his fiction of the distraught lover with a moral essay on the degeneration of the three estates. Using the figure from Nebuchadrezzar II's dream (Daniel) of the composite statue with golden head, silver breast and arms, belly of bronze, legs of iron, and feet of iron and clay to epitomize the current state of history, Gower juxtaposes the world's present state, amalgamated with sin, with a former time, a time of peace and common profit, accessible now only through a penitential turn of mind. In introducing this penitential process through the myth of Arion, who with his music saves children from drowning and brings accord between commoner and lord, Gower projects a crucial role for art and the imagination in the salvific process. Genius and his stories, along with more specific instruction on good rule of self and kingdom in book 7, bring the lover to a reexamination of himself, through the dreams of fiction and its authorities, which enables him to leave the woods and return a healthy citizen of England, dedicated to advancing its welfare in the sight of God.

But although the overall conception and framework of *Confessio amantis* is admirably wrought and subtly conceived, the strength of the poem lies in its stories, which range in length from a few lines to over eighteen hundred. Most notable are, from book 1, the tales of Mundus and Paulina, of Florent (a source for Chaucer's "Wife of Bath's Tale"), of Albinus and Rosemund, and the tale of Three Ques-

tions; from book 2, the tale of Constance (a source for Chaucer's "Man of Law's Tale"); from book 3, the story of Canace and Machaire; from book 4, the tale of Rosiphelee; from book 5, the stories of Jason and Medea and of Adrian and Bardus; from book 6, the tales of Ulysses and Telegonus and of Nectanabus; and from book 8, that of Apollonius of Tyre (the source for Shakespeare's *Pericles, Prince of Tyre,* 1608).

Toward the end of his life Gower completed two *balade* sequences in French. The first, *Traitié pour Essampler les Amantz Marietz,* completed prior to his marriage to Agnes Groundolf in 1398, is a sequence of eighteen *balades* celebrating marriage. They consist of three rhyme royal stanzas each; to the eighteenth an envoy is added. The *Traitié* is found in ten manuscripts and usually, but not always, appended to *Confessio amantis.* A heading to the sequence announces that the poet, having written in English about the folly of lovers, will now write in French a book to instruct married lovers in fidelity.

Upon the accession of Henry IV, Gower dedicated his second sequence, *Cinkante Balades* (circa 1350–circa 1400), to the king. In return he received from Henry the golden "S" collar, which is depicted in his effigy. The *Cinkante Balades* survive in a single manuscript, first discussed by Thomas Warton in his *History of English Poetry* (1774–1781). Fisher argues that several of the *balades* may have been the "fols ditz d'amours" of Gower's youth, though some were clearly written for the occasion of Henry's enthronement. There are fifty-one *balades* in all. Many are elegant in their simplicity.

After completing *Confessio amantis* Gower wrote three shorter Latin poems: "Carmen super multiplici viciorum pestilencia"; "O Deus Imennense"; and "De lucis scrutina." After Henry's coronation he also wrote three laureate poems praising the king in whom he placed such high hope: "Rex celi deus"; "H. aquile pullus"; and "O recolende." His last poem, "To Henry the Fourth: In Praise of Peace," is in English, a poem of 385 lines in rhyme royal stanzas, written, perhaps, after the poet was blind. Its theme, which links peace with good rule, was one Gower sounded throughout his life.

John Gower was a master craftsman and a highly intelligent thinker – a man shrewdly in touch with the moral and social issues of his day. His wit is subtle and his genius for conveying that wit deliberately and deceptively plain. He was a writer cleverly in touch with the literary conventions of his day, particularly Latin conventions, who, in the *Confessio amantis,* brings to the vernacular a range of stylistic options surpassed only by Chaucer and

Langland. Even more than they, he takes both care and pride in his melifluous literary style, ingenious voicing, and structural design. He wrote for the ages to come, and his voice has been heard, especially in the fifteenth and sixteenth centuries.

Bibliographies:
Robert F. Yeager, *John Gower Materials: A Bibliography through 1979* (New York: Garland, 1981);
Peter Nicholson, *An Annotated Index to the Commentary on John Gower's Confessio Amantis* (Binghamton, N.Y.: Medieval and Renaissance Texts and Studies, 1989).

Biography:
John H. Fisher, *John Gower, Moral Philosopher and Friend of Chaucer* (New York: New York University Press, 1964).

References:
Denis N. Baker, "The Priesthood of Genius: A Study of the Medieval Tradition," *Speculum,* 51 (April 1976): 277–291;
Linda Barney Burke, "Women in John Gower's *Confessio Amantis,*" *Mediaevalia,* 3 (1977): 238–259;
George R. Coffman, "John Gower in his Most Significant Role," in *Elizabethan Studies & Other Essays in Honor of George F. Reynolds,* University of Colorado Studies, series B: Studies in the Humanities, II, no. 4 (1945), pp. 52–61;
Coffman, "John Gower, Mentor for Royalty: Richard II," *PMLA,* 69 (September 1954): 953–964;
Sian Echard and Claire Fanger, *The Latin Verses in the Confessio Amantis: An Annotated Translation* (East Lansing, Mich.: Colleagues Press, 1991);
John H. Fisher, "A Calendar of Documents Relating to the Life of John Gower the Poet," *Journal of English and Germanic Philology,* 58 (January 1959): 1–23;
Patrick J. Gallacher, *Love, the Word, and Mercury: A Reading of John Gower's Confessio Amantis* (Albuquerque: University of New Mexico Press, 1975);

C. S. Lewis, *The Allegory of Love* (Oxford: Oxford University Press, 1936), pp. 198–222;
Masayoshi Ito, *John Gower: The Medieval Poet* (Tokyo: Shinozaki Shorin, 1976);
A. J. Minnis, ed., *Gower's Confessio Amantis: Responses and Reassessments* (Cambridge: Brewer, 1983);
James J. Murphy, "John Gower's *Confessio Amantis* and the First Discussion of Rhetoric in the English Language," *Philological Quarterly,* 41 (April 1962): 401–411;
Peter Nicholson, ed., *Gower's Confessio Amantis: A Critical Anthology* (Cambridge: Brewer, 1991);
Alexandra Hennessey Olsen, *"Betwene Ernest and Game": The Literary Artistry of the Confessio Amantis* (New York: Lang, 1990);
Kurt Olsson, *John Gower and the Structures of Conversion: A Reading of the Confessio Amantis* (Cambridge, U.K.: Brewer, 1992);
Derek Pearsall, *Gower and Lydgate* (London: Longmans, Green, 1969);
Pearsall, "Gower's Narrative Art," *PMLA,* 81 (December 1966): 475–484;
Russell A. Peck, *Kingship and Common Profit in Gower's Confessio Amantis* (Carbondale: Southern Illinois University Press, 1978);
Peck, "The Phenomenology of Make Believe in Gower's *Confessio Amantis,*" *Studies in Philology,* 91 (July 1994): 250–269;
J. D. Pickles and J. L. Dawson, *A Concordance to John Gower's Confessio Amantis* (Cambridge: Brewer, 1987);
Maria Wickert, *Studies in John Gower,* translated by Robert J. Meindl (Washington, D.C.: University Press of America, 1981);
Robert F. Yeager, ed., *John Gower: Recent Readings* (Kalamazoo: Western Michigan University Press, 1989);
Robert F. Yeager, ed., *Chaucer and Gower: Difference, Mutuality, Exchange* (Victoria, B.C.: University of Victoria Press, 1991);
Yeager, *John Gower's Poetic: The Search for a New Arion* (Cambridge: Brewer, 1990).

Robert Henryson

(1420s or 1430s – circa 1505)

Edwin D. Craun
Washington and Lee University

MAJOR WORKS: *The Moral Fables*

Manuscripts: The Bannatyne Manuscript, Adv. MS. I.I.6 (dated 1568) in the National Library of Scotland includes ten of the thirteen fables. Facsimile: *The Bannatyne Manuscript* (New York: Scolar Press, 1980); The Harleian Manuscript, MS. Harley 3865 (dated 1571), is in the British Library.

First publication: *The Morall Fabillis of Esope the Phrygian* (Edinburgh: Printed for Henry Charteris, 1569).

Standard editions: In *The Poems of Robert Henryson*, edited by Denton Fox (Oxford: Clarendon Press, 1981); *The Moral Fables of Aesop*, edited and translated by George D. Gopen (Notre Dame: University of Notre Dame, 1987).

The Testament of Cresseid

Manuscript: No manuscript for the work exists.

First publication: *The Testament of Cresseid* (Edinburgh: Printed by Henry Carteris, 1593).

Standard edition: In Fox's edition (1981).

Orpheus and Eurydice

Manuscripts: The work survives in the Bannatyne Manuscript and in the Asloan Manuscript, Accession 4233 in the National Library of Scotland (dated between 1513 and circa 1530).

First publication: *Here Begynnis the Traitie of Orpheus Kyng* . . . (Edinburgh: Printed by Walter Chepman and Androw Myllar, 1508). Facsimile: *The Chepman and Myllar Prints: Nine Tracts from the First Scottish Press, Edinburgh 1508,* edited by William Beattie (Edinburgh: Edinburgh Bibliographical Society, 1950).

Standard edition: In Fox's edition (1981).

Although Robert Henryson was the major poet of late-fifteenth-century Scotland, his life is even more difficult to construct than the texts of his poems, which must rest on prints or manuscripts made over seventy years after his death. Only one certain reference by a near contemporary survives, fittingly in a poem. In his "Lament for the Makars" (circa 1505), William Dunbar lists Henryson among two dozen dead poets: "In Dunfermelyne he [Death] hes done roune [whisper] / With Maister Robert Henrisoun." Dunfermline was a flourishing market town in western Fife, long a royal burgh and site of a royal palace where the poet-king James I was born. Although Robert Henryson was a common name in Fife, several city records, together with sixteenth-century prints of Henryson's poems, indicate that the poet was schoolmaster in the grammar school of the town's wealthy Benedictine abbey. Like his successors in this prestiguous position, he was probably also a notary public with some legal training. Almost certainly he had taken an M.A. degree at a Scottish university or abroad.

The Middle Scots in which Henryson wrote was the language, spoken and written, of most Scots, including the powerful and the well educated. Although introduced into the Scottish Lowlands by Northumbrian raiders and colonizers in the early Anglo-Saxon centuries, Scots had evolved independently of English as it gained dominance over both the native Celtic language, Pictish, and, finally, Gaelic. By the late Middle Ages, Gaelic culture was confined to the Highlands, inaccessible to Lowland Scots writers such as Henryson because of political, geographical, and linguistic barriers. Middle Scots was the vernacular of their country. It was also the language of their major poets: John Barbour in the national epic, *The Bruce* (1375); the romancers; and James I in *The Kingis Quair* (circa 1424).

Middle Scots heroic poetry, in Henryson's own time (as in Henry the Minstrel's *Wallace*, circa 1460) and for at least a century before, had advanced a communal vision of national life. Derived, perhaps, from the ancient Celtic cult of kin-

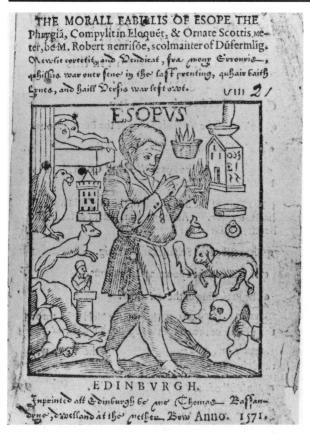

THE MORALL FABILLIS OF ESOPE THE
Phrygiã, Compylit in Eloquét, & Ornate Scottis meter, be M. Robert Henrisõe, scolmaiter of Dúfermlig.

ESOPVS

EDINBVRGH.

*Title page for an early publication of Henryson's adaptations of the
fables of Aesop*

ship, it presented Scotland as a network of relations, almost familial, between king and lords and commons and church. During Henryson's lifetime this honored model was violated repeatedly by acts of political treachery. James I was assassinated in 1437 by nobles who objected to his attempts to centralize power, attempts which seemed to them to abrogate the customary power sharing of a king who was merely a popular leader and of his barons. The barons' struggles with the Stuart kings were exploited by England, which contested the Borders and the Lowlands throughout the century. James III, who ruled for much of Henryson's adult life (1460–1488), was killed by rebellious barons who objected (among many other things) to his alliances with England through marriage. James II and James IV were enthroned as minors, precipitating struggles between barons marked by near civil war, ambushes, and feuds so bloody that some families were nearly exterminated.

Henryson's *Moral Fables,* probably from the 1480s, were written for an audience concerned with the disintegration of communal life at all levels. At the center of this carefully structured set of thirteen

beast fables, Henryson placed "The Lion and the Mouse," which treats political and social relations the most fully. Its importance is marked by a separate prologue, by a dream vision in which the narrator's "gude maister" Aesop appears, majestic and authoritative, to converse with him about the value of fables, and by Aesop's narration of this fable. Henryson's version of this ancient tale explores the need in an uncertain world for mutual help and dependence, even by the powerful: the mice chew the ropes that bind the lion. His *moralitas,* the generalized, reflective interpretation which follows each narrative as an integral part of the fable, argues for a political reading: the lion signifies a ruler; the mice, the common people. Both fable and *moralitas* also develop the central duty of a ruler, executing a justice in which mercy mitigates the rigor of the law.

This central fable is also about wise listening and reading, about virtuously apprehending and applying discourse. Fables may be fictive, the narrator remarks to Aesop, but they offer their audiences "prudence and moralitie." Prudence, the highest of the cardinal virtues, is realized in two traditional ways by the lion when he accepts the mouse's arguments for showing mercy: he shows foresight in governing his own life and he recognizes consciously the moral course of action.

In the *moralitas* of the first fable, "The Cock and the Jasp," prudence is signified by the jasper stone which the cock rejects as he scratches food out of a trash heap. It is at once worldly wisdom, the pragmatic sense of how to act popularly associated with Aesopian fable, and "science," the moral knowledge of why a certain action is good. What prevents the Cock from understanding the moral value of the jasper is his inability to see beyond its materiality. Henryson lets the reader apprehend the jasper first from the Cock's point of view: it is only a resplendent social ornament, meant for a king, of no use to him in his search for food. Opposed to his interpretation and his choice is the narrator's: his *moralitas* reads jewel and story alike as "figure of ane vther thing," attending to "inward sentence and intent." "Ga seik the iasp, quha will," exhorts the narrator, advancing his figurative, moral interpretation as a model for reading the whole text.

Henryson's most expansive fable on prudence, "The Preaching of the Swallow," is the inverse of "The Lion and the Mouse," serving as its companion at the center of the fables. The Swallow's eloquent warnings that the fowler's flax is growing into material for nets are ignored by other birds, bent like the Cock on satisfying their appetites of the moment. Like the Mouse, the Swallow argues for prudence, in this case for strenuously applying past experience to the present in order to avoid future suffering. The changing seasons of the tale suggest the inevitable changes of all natural life, but the birds apprehend only the pleasure they offer.

Henryson's *Moral Fables* as a whole is constructed with the conviction that, to paraphrase a medieval schoolboy's Latin dictum, every created thing is like a book or a picture in which humans may see themselves. For the medievals this was especially true of animals. They, like people in other cultures that have prized stories about animals, lived close to them and observed different inclinations in different kinds of animals: in "The Cock and the Fox," the crafty and dissimulating fox and the vain and therefore gullible cock. The beast fable uses these stock types in order to instruct in a pleasing way, much as biblical proverbs and other types of wisdom literature do, though it has the rhetorical advantage of a short, memorable story. For example, the riotous story of the cock's ensnarement by the fox and then his escape (also told by Geoffrey Chaucer in "The Nun's Priest's Tale") is followed by a simple *moralitas* instructing readers in the dangers of vainglory and flattery.

By Henryson's time the beast fable was of great antiquity, as were many of his source stories; he presents Aesop as an ancient Roman. Originally a Greek literary type, Aesopian fables were composed in both verse and prose in late Latin culture, where they entered the schoolroom as a basic text for the study of grammar and rhetoric. This learned Latin tradition of storytelling was revived in the twelfth century by sophisticated writers such as Marie de France and homilists such as Odo of Cheriton. Henryson almost certainly used as a source the anonymous late-twelfth-century version of the fables in verse (ascribed to Gwalterus Anglicus, "Walter the Englishman"), but he also drew on the mock-epics of Reynard the Fox and popular, probably oral, Scottish traditions. His is the oldest known collection of beast fables in Scots.

The central device of the fable, of course, is the use of talking animals. Not only does it realize the ancient human longing to overhear animals speaking and to speak with them, but it also presents amusing incongruities, such as the "burges mous" of the second fable speaking in the idiom of a prosperous Scottish merchant. The distance created by such incongruities enables the fabulist to present, in a comic way, conflicting ways of life, such as the agrarian, mean estate of the rural mouse and the

mercantile luxury of the "burges mous." The two mice of this fable may also illustrate the main literary effect of talking animals: that the reader recognizes the animalistic in himself, here the drive to lord it over one's less successful kin or the fear of powerful predators.

Henryson's exposure of the animalistic in human conduct is realized most fully in those fables taken from the tradition of Reynard the Fox, where it is the main element in harsh social and political satire. From at least the twelfth century, Reynardian stories were used to satirize conniving climbers in the feudal system and hypocritical monks (and later friars). In them the fox is the cynical trickster who gulls everyone, human as well as animal, and rejects all moral or social norms. In Henryson's "The Fox and the Wolf," for instance, the fox inveigles the friar/wolf into assigning him an absurdly light penance for his misliving, although he is sorry only that he has not slain more hens or lambs. Since the fox is forbidden meat until Easter as his penance, when the sly Lowrance ("the lowerer") steals a kid, he baptizes it in the river, christening it a salmon as he drowns it. Thus the fox abuses two sacraments by manipulating the speech on which they depend, subverts the friar (a doctor of divinity), and cheerfully violates two of the Ten Commandments.

For all this, Henryson's fox is not the feckless and triumphant antihero of many Reynardian tales. Driven to confession by astrological signs of a shameful death, Lowrance murders the kid because of what the *moralitas* terms "carnall sensualitie" but what the fox and the wolf excuse as need which "may haif na law." More concerned with justice than other tellers of the same tale, Henryson has his fox slain for persisting in evil habits.

The second half of the collection, Reynardian and Aesopian tales alike, becomes progressively darker. In the ninth and the tenth, just after the pivotal "Preaching of the Swallow," the fox is the successful plotter who steals from hardworking, nearly impoverished humans, although the wolf's comic misadventures somewhat lighten the endings. The eleventh and twelfth present not only an insecure world without justice but one in which even the most persuasive speech fails to save an innocent victim's life. The quaking lamb of the penultimate fable resists the patently lawless accusations of the wolf with learned and eloquent arguments from law, natural science, and Christian Scripture, only to madden his powerful adversary. A blunt *moralitas* applies the tale to oppressors of the laboring poor — "fals peruerteris of the lawis," armed men, and greedy landlords – and prays for the king to banish those who deprive the poor of the necessities of life.

The final fable, "The Paddock and the Mouse," leaves the reader with animals driven by their appetites to abuse speech and every social bond: the mouse is so eager to feed on the grain across the river that she consents to the frog's offer of a ride, even though she knows its oath to ferry her over safely will prove false. As in many other tales, gruesome detail (their skin pulled over their heads by a kite which devours their guts) images the violence of a world in which imprudent acts lacking foresight or bereft of a sense of morality quickly lead to destruction.

Henryson achieves variety and complexity in *The Moral Fables* not only through narrative detail but through expansive *moralitates*. In the Aesopian tradition such moral closure is usually brief and monological, advancing popular virtues of daily life, such as the moderation of Henryson's rural mouse. Sometimes a Henryson *moralitas* offers multiple interpretations, each allowed by some narrative detail: "The Paddock and the Mouse" warning against "fals intent vnder ane fair pretence," producing a second warning against giving up freedom for bonds, and then allegorizing the frog as the body, the mouse as the soul, the river as the world, and the kite as death. These different perspectives suggest that the *moralitas* does not claim to give the complete, exclusive significance of the tale. Recent critics have been even more interested in the disjunctive *moralitates*. "The Trial of the Fox," for example, tells how a royal lion assembles all beasts in parliament, save the oppositional gray mare, and then how the lion/king deals justice to the murdering fox. Given the king's justice, the figurative *moralitas* is wholly unexpected: with the lion as the world in all its grandeur and the mare as the solitary contemplative who rightly rejects the empty world. Such a disjunctive *moralitas* jolts the reader into recognizing how rich and varied (some critics would say arbitrary) moral, especially figurative, interpretations of a narrative can be: even that which seems contrary to the drift of the whole can be prompted by textual details and fit perfectly. Altogether the direct, multiple, and dissonant *moralitates* prod readers to reflect upon how to read, how to think and act morally.

Like his Aesopian fables, Henryson's longer narratives, *Orpheus and Eurydice* and *The Testament of Cresseid,* are stories which he believed to be classical and which were immensely popular in the late Middle Ages. In the last few decades scholars have debated whether or not Henryson can be considered a humanist. John MacQueen has demonstrated that several of Henryson's Scottish contemporaries, especially those who had studied or traveled in Italy, were devoted to the "new learning." Unfortunately nothing remains of Henryson's library or his Latin style. He was certainly a learned man who could cite Aristotle's *Metaphysics* and Boethius's *Consolation of Philosophy,* but both had been fundamental texts for centuries; it has not been proven that he knew any text by a humanist writer.

Henryson's vital and sustained interest in antiquity was less like Petrarch's than like Chaucer's in *Troilus and Criseyde* (circa 1382–1386) and "The Knight's Tale." In *Orpheus and Eurydice* and *The Testament of Cresseid* he sought to construct an antique culture in which the characters comprehend the world and their own experience in pagan terms. Although both poems contain medieval anachronisms (Cresseid prays in the oratory of the kirk of Venus and is housed in a leper's "spitall"), there are no explicitly Christian references.

The Testament of Cresseid is the finest narrative tragedy in medieval and Renaissance Scottish literature. Like the fables, it sees humankind as vulnerable, victimized by the appetites of the powerful but also by its own lack of wisdom or prudence. It is also the most Chaucerian of Henryson's poems. Like the fables and *Orpheus and Eurydice,* it is written in the rhyme royal of Chaucer's tragic poem *Troilus and Criseyde,* the flexible seven-lined stanza rhyming *ababbcc,* equally apt for narration, description, and formal speech (also known to Henryson as the verse form of the most ambitious and sophisticated of Scottish narratives about love and fortune, *The Kingis Quair* [circa 1424] by James I). Moreover, Henryson's poem is introduced as a sequel to Chaucer's. Like the sleepless narrators of so many medieval dream visions, Henryson's speaker takes up a book, *Troilus and Criseyde,* manifesting the poem's intertextuality and the influence of "worthie Chaucer glorious."

This ostentatious gesture toward Chaucer, with its two-stanza summary of the last book of *Troilus and Criseyde,* conveys Henryson's aspiration to write sophisticated narrative tragedy. Such gestures, along with Henryson's practice of writing in verse forms and genres used by Chaucer, have prompted literary historians to group him with James I and Dunbar as a "Scottish Chaucerian." Such a label suggests not only indebtedness but derivative work. Moreover, it ignores Henryson's avowedly independent choices as a writer. His narrator registers the limitations of the ending of Chaucer's poem: its preoccupation with Troilus's sorrow and his virtues, its omission of the "fatall destenie / Of fair Cresseid," despite the earlier extensive and sympathetic portrayal of her.

Although Henryson questions Chaucer's treatment of the story, he follows Chaucer in disclaiming any definitive authority for his own version: the narrator bases his account on a mysterious "vther quair," for whose authority he cannot vouch. Moreover, the narrator is portrayed as an aging devotee of Venus, longing for the green love of youth, who is determined to establish that Cresseid's misfortunes were not at all caused by her own guilt. So while Henryson marks off his own narrative territory, he creates a "Chaucerian" text, at once self-consciously relative and innovative.

After this prologue the narrative alternates plain-style reports of brutal facts with three elaborate formal utterances in which Cresseid labors to interpret her suffering: her blasphemy against Venus and Cupid, her complaint among the lepers, and her dying lament with its testament. In the events she is acted upon by powerful men or the gods; in the laments she acts with words. Unlike Chaucer's treatment and that in other medieval tragedies, which are, in the words of Chaucer's translation of Boethius's *Consolation of Philosophy,* "dite[s] of a prosperite for a tyme, that endeth in wrecchidnesse," this account narrates only Cresseid's suffering, invoking past happiness only to heighten or fathom it.

The account begins with her abrupt rejection by Diomede and her isolation, as an alien and a shameful "common woman," in the Greek camp. Diomede is presented simply as a coldly exploitative sexual predator who turns to a new woman "Quhen [he] had all his appetyte / And mair, fulfillit of this fair ladie." In response Cresseid, fearing both loss of beauty and of the male companionship and protection on which she had come to depend, blames her own gods: Cupid is false and Venus blind because they once responded oracularly "That I suld be the flour of luif in Troy."

In contrast to her blasphemy, Henryson develops in the planetary deities, the intelligences governing the seven planets, the natural forces to which Cresseid, like all other natural beings, is bound. Some medievals thought that these planets, along with the stars, governed events and people's bodies through their influence. So, while Cresseid's vision of the gods suggests how a pre-Christian might have imagined the cosmic powers, their attributes also figure forth the laws of the physical world which control humans in all cultures. While Jupiter's attributes represent growth and the prime of physical

beauty (crystal eye, blond hair, clear voice), his father Saturn, first among the gods, is aged, ugly, and diseased. And the Venus to whom Cresseid has entrusted her life is, like the classical and medieval figure of Fortune, "full of variance," half green and half black in dress, betokening love's sudden shifts from joy to sorrow. Physical decay and mutability of love are the laws from which Cresseid believes she should be exempt.

While Henryson uses Cresseid's vision of the gods to counter her initial interpretation of her misfortune, he also has them punish her so severely – with disfiguring leprosy, then often thought to be a venereal disease – that critics have often questioned their justice. These critics usually focus on Cresseid's leprosy, ignoring Cupid's legal complaint of blasphemy: that she has slandered the gods, misrepresenting their natures in proclaiming that he is false and Venus blind, projecting her own promiscuity and lack of moral understanding onto them.

Henryson returns to a concise, plain style to convey the painful facts of Cresseid's leprosy and her grief in facing it, often using understatement to suggest its magnitude. Juxtaposed to this restrained account is Cresseid's complaint in the leper house, set off by its nine-line stanza and a title. In the mode of late medieval complaints, she expresses loss and suffering through the *ubi sunt* topos, which counterpoints details of her lost life of beauty, status, luxury, and companionship with her present isolation, poverty, degradation, and disfigurement. With these formal, alliterated antitheses, she transcends her earlier self-absorption, recognizing that mutability (personified in Fortune) is an irresistible force, that she exemplifies a universal law.

The unwitting agent for Cresseid's third stage in her progression from ignorance to self-knowledge is Troilus, who enters the story as the fully realized knight and lover of the early books of Chaucer's *Troilus and Criseyde.* Although he does not recognize her because of her disfigurement, Cresseid stirs his memory enough that he throws gold and jewels into her lap. Cresseid perceives his character in the action, his generosity, and above all his constancy in love; in her final lament she reconceives of herself in contrast: "O fals Cresseid and trew knicht Troylus." As a beautiful, highborn woman, she failed to value his love and loyalty, turning to Diomede simply out of lust. By abandoning and betraying him, she entrusted herself to the "fickill quheill" of fortune and became the worker of her own fate: "Nane but my self as now I will accuse." What she saw first as a tragedy of divine betrayal

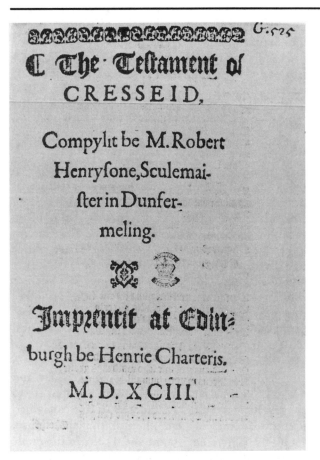

Title page for the first publication of Henryson's narrative tragedy

and then as a tragedy of fortune she sees anew as a tragedy of character.

The testament, with which Cresseid concludes her lament, was a popular medieval genre because it displayed the final disposition of the soul at death. Cresseid's disgust for her conduct directs her to leave her body to be rent by toads and worms; her longing for chastity and her spirit to Diana; her renewed love and her ring to Troilus. However, even in this remorse she is made to face irremediable loss: she dies recalling that Troilus's tokens of true love are still in Diomede's possession.

Although the self-accusatory lament and testament carries great weight as the last of Cresseid's interpretations of her misfortunes, it, like her other laments or the narrator's choric interjections, is a highly emotional response to a specific, overwhelming event, not a cumulative, definitive interpretation of what constitutes her loss, let alone what causes it. Diomede's exploitation, like the gods' harsh vengeance, remains part of her tragedy, even if she omits both in her fierce acceptance of responsibility. In the antique world Henryson creates, one without revealed religion, acquiring wisdom is a painful and

incomplete process, and it provides prudence only for its audience, as in many of the fables.

Henryson's other narrative in rhyme royal, *Orpheus and Eurydice,* also recounts the loss and suffering of a famous lover of antiquity. Henryson's version of this popular story, based on meter 12 in book 3 of Boethius's *Consolation of Philosophy,* is cast as a mythological fable, with grand encyclopedic and cosmological episodes and with an extended allegorical *moralitas* reminiscent of the fables.

The marriage of the lovers and Eurydice's taking by Proserpine are narrated with the stark simplicity of ballad and popular romance, both vital genres in medieval Scottish literature. Likewise, as Douglas Gray observes, Orpheus's perilous journey through the heavens and the underworld to seek her has all the appeal and emotional power of the romance quest. However, unlike its counterpart in Middle English romance, *Sir Orfeo,* Henryson's story ends with Orpheus's loss of the wife whom "he had bocht so dere," simply because his love prompted the forbidden backward glance.

The archetypal simplicity of this story is overlaid periodically with learned, rhetorical set pieces that develop its moral significance. The prologue on the exemplary force of ancestral story suggests that Orpheus the King will embody every human's capacity to rule his life, and the strengths with which Orpheus is endowed by his divine origin – nobility, eloquence, and knowledge of music – are introduced in the catalogue of the muses and recalled in his journey through the heavens. As a musician/ruler he practices brilliantly the craft of music (as his lament for Eurydice stresses), but he also achieves harmony with the "other" in marriage and with the natural world.

Henryson justifies his 218-line *moralitas,* marked off by a subtitle and change in verse form (to couplets), by appealing first to Boethius's aim of telling "this feynit fable" "for oure doctryne and gude instruction" and then to the "gude moralitee" to which the tale was applied by the English Dominican Nicholas Trivet, the author of the most popular commentary on the *Consolation of Philosophy* at the time. Although more elaborate than any *moralitas* in the *Fables,* it functions similarly: to draw attention to some moral dimensions of the tale. Orpheus figures forth the intellectual power of the soul; Eurydice, the appetitive power; their marriage, the harmonious relation of the two; Orpheus's attempted rescue in hell, the intellect's drive to reunite itself with the affections seduced by the material world. Such allegorizing formulates what the details suggest. However, Henryson also constructs some of his allegory through opposites: Arestyus the would-be rapist signifies moral virtue with its longing to be joined to the human appetites. Unfortunately most of the *moralitas* is given over to the denizens of hell, who are interpreted painstakingly as various worldly appetites. This disproportionate treatment enervates the *moralitas,* depriving it of the rhetorical force which should be given to the tragic, irremediable (in this world) loss of union between human intellect and appetite.

In addition to *The Fables,* the *Testament of Cresseid,* and *Orpheus and Eurydice,* twelve or thirteen disparate shorter poems, most of considerable artistry, have been included in twentieth-century editions of Henryson's work. Since all are in conventional late medieval genres, with fairly standard poetic diction and rhetoric, internal evidence – rhymes, epithets, proverbs – linking them to each other or the three narrative texts cannot convincingly establish authorship. However, Denton Fox's painstaking edition (1981) prints twelve, all attributed to Henryson in one or more manuscripts.

Of these twelve two share the poet's central concern in *The Testament of Cresseid:* how to interpret adversity and how to take arms against it with words. "The Abbey Walk" offers an inscription as consolation for the "changeng and grit variance" of earthly life. Its remedies of patience in adversity and humble detachment in prosperity are uttered with simple diction, with conventional metaphors, and with an unvaried refrain befitting commonplaces. Although also written in eight-line stanzas rhyming *ababbcbc,* "Ane Prayer for the Pest" is as different in style as could be. Against the plague, that recurrent horror of the late Middle Ages that shattered human community ("[We] de as beistis without confessioun / That nane dar mak with vdir residens"), the poem offers the common stance: it is punishment for sin from an omniscient and omnipotent God. But it also offers the common recourse, prayer for God's mercy, with a formal eloquence which climaxes in the final three stanzas. There Henryson brilliantly employs internal rhymes, together with the polysyllabic Latinate diction called "aureate" by his contemporaries: "Superne lucerne, guberne this pestilens." This most elaborate of late medieval Scottish styles creates a sense of urgency but also suggests the Christian God of power who can deliver his people.

Three of the remaining shorter poems, all in eight-line stanzas, are cast in traditional "getting of wisdom" genres. "Against Hasty Credence" presents advice to lords about talebearing, while "The Praise of Age" celebrates closeness to heaven's bliss in a sinful and mutable world. As a debate poem,

"The Ressoning betuix Aige and Yowth" is more complexly constructed. After listening to a young man boast about his strength, sexual gamesmanship, and health and to an old man counter each boast with sour statements of loss and self-loathing, the speaker judges both of the positions valid.

A more powerful debate poem, "The Ressoning betuix Deth and Man," ends in a victory. Against an unnamed speaker's menacing lists of those who cannot understand his destructive power, Man asserts his confidence that no one can overmaster him. Yet at the speaker's revelation that he is Death, Man's defiance collapses, he recalls his mortal sins, and he humbly seeks the shelter of Death's cloak. A second poem warning humans of the inevitability of death and the need to repent, "The Thre Deid Pollis" is of an equally traditional genre: the memento mori. In it the mirror presented to the living is the three heads, all peeled and hollow-eyed, signifying that death and decay erase all the distinctions on which the living pride themselves.

While these seven moralizing poems are all written in an eight-line stanza (and all of them in tetrameter except "The Abbey Walk"), four of the remaining five are cast in stanzas in which *a*-rhymed tetrameter lines alternate with *b*-rhymed trimeter lines. The most balladlike of these four is "The Bludy Serk," the common late-medieval story of a knight who liberates his lady from a giant's dungeon and, mortally wounded in the battle, leaves his bloodied shirt as a reminder. A short *moralitas* gives the expected allegory: Christ's winning of the human soul from Satan's power. Akin in its simplicity of style and diction is "The Garmont of Gud Ladeis," which glosses items of dress as virtues which a woman should "put on." Also in this group is an Annunciation lyric which treats the event as a supreme example of the power of love before it delivers the traditional paradoxes of the Virgin Birth and the Incarnation and the typology of Mary.

The last of these poems is the pastoral narrative and debate "Robene and Makyne," balladlike, too, in its direct and ingenuous style. Unlike its French cousin the *pastorelle,* in which a powerful man, knight or clerk, attempts to seduce a shepherdess, "Robene and Makyne" gives voice to a young man and woman of the same class, allowing Henryson to focus on the shifting dynamics of desire and rejection. In these rural speakers love exhibits its all-consuming but unpredictable power, driving the woman to take the initiative and driving both to open declarations of desire, shame, and pain, as well as to arguments characteristic of courtly literature.

In "Robene and Makyne," as in his longer poems, Henryson appropriates a common genre of late-medieval writing, modifying it with considerable wit to explore painful reversals and victimization in a world dominated by powerful human appetites. The romance quest of *Orpheus and Eurydice* ends abruptly in irremediable loss when its hero cannot resist the pull of "grete affection," condemning himself to live as a "wofull wedow." Henryson's Cresseid also experiences loss of love, but as the victim of a predatory male and at the beginning of her tragedy, in which her passionate refusal to accept inevitable painful changes instigates further losses of physical beauty, erotic power, luxurious living, and life itself. If the animal kingdom of the *Moral Fables* presents some protagonists who escape traps through the verbal dexterity, foresight, and awareness of communal bonds commended to the reader, the darker second half of the collection portrays imprudent and helpless animals – even humans – who are at the mercy of wily, powerful, and ravenous adversaries. All the more forceful and incisive for their simplicity of language and situation (contrasted by the occasional pyrotechnic setpeice), these three major works reveal that Henryson was the most gifted of narrative poets writing in Middle Scots amid the political distintegration of the fifteenth century.

Bibliographies:

Louise O. Fradenburg, "Henryson Scholarship: The Recent Decades" in *Fifteenth-Century Studies,* edited by Robert F. Yeager (Hamden, Conn.: Archon, 1984), pp. 65–92;

Walter Scheps and J. Anna Looney, *Middle Scots Poets: A Reference Guide to James I of Scotland, Robert Henryson, William Dunbar, and Gavin Douglas* (Boston: G. K. Hall, 1986).

References:

C. David Benson, "O Moral Henryson" in *Fifteenth-Century Studies,* edited by Robert F. Yeager (Hamden, Conn.: Archon, 1984), pp. 215–236;

J. A. Burrow, "Henryson: 'The Preaching of the Swallow,' " *Essays in Criticism,* 25 (January 1975): 25–37;

Edwin Craun, "Blaspheming Her 'Awin God': Cresseid's 'Lamentatioun' in Henryson's *Tes-*

tament," Studies in Philology, 82 (Winter 1985): 25–41;

Douglas Duncan, "Henryson's *Testament of Cresseid," Essays in Criticism,* 11 (April 1961): 128–135;

Douglas Gray, *Robert Henryson* (Leiden & New York: Brill, 1979);

Ian Jamieson, " 'To Preive Thare Preching Be a Poesye': Some Thoughts on Henryson's Poetics," *Parergon,* 8 (April 1974): 24–36;

Robert L. Kindrick, *Robert Henryson* (Boston: G. K. Hall, 1979);

Gregory Kratzmann, "Henryson's *Fables:* 'The Subtell Dyte of Poetry,' " *Studies in Scottish Literature,* 20 (1985): 49–70;

R. J. Lyall, "Politics and Poetry in Fifteenth and Sixteenth Century Scotland," *Scottish Literary Journal,* 3 (December 1976): 5–29;

John MacQueen, *Robert Henryson: A Study of the Major Narrative Poems* (Oxford: Clarendon Press, 1967);

Matthew P. McDiarmid, *Robert Henryson* (Edinburgh: Scottish Academic Press, 1981);

McDiarmid, "Robert Henryson in His Poems" in *Bards and Makars: Scottish Language and Literature: Medieval and Renaissance,* edited by A. J. Aitken (Glasgow: Glasgow University Press, 1977), pp. 27–40;

Daniel M. Murtaugh, "Henryson's Animals," *Tennessee Studies in Language and Literature,* 14 (Fall 1972): 405–421;

Lee Patterson, "Christian and Pagan in *The Testament of Cresseid," Philological Quarterly,* 52 (October 1973): 696–714;

Marianne Powell, *'Fabula Docet': Studies in the Background and Interpretation of Henryson's Fables* (Odense: Odense University Press, 1982);

Florence Ridley, "A Plea for the Middle Scots," in *The Learned and the Lewed: Studies in Chaucer and Medieval Literature,* edited by Larry D. Benson (Cambridge, Mass.: Harvard University Press, 1974), pp. 175–196;

Jennifer Strauss, "To Speak Once More of Cresseid: Henryson's *Testament* Re-considered," *Scottish Literary Journal,* 4 (December 1977): 5–13;

Harold E. Toliver, "Robert Henryson: From *Moralitas* to Irony," *English Studies,* 46 (1965): 300–309.

Walter Hilton

(died 23 March 1396)

Toni J. Morris
University of Indianapolis

WORKS: *The Scale of Perfection* (circa 1380–1395)

Manuscripts: Of the forty-seven whole or partial transcriptions of the work, the best appear to be Bodleian Library, Oxford, Eng. poet. a. I, Vernon (1380–1400); Corpus Christi College, Cambridge, R. 5 (368); and British Library, Harley 6579.

First publication: *Scala Perfectionis* (London: Wynkyn de Worde, 1494).

Editions in modern English: *The Scale of Perfection,* edited and modernized by Evelyn Underhill (London: Watkins, 1923; reprinted, 1948); *The Stairway of Perfection,* edited and modernized by M. L. Del Mastro (Garden City, N.Y.: Doubleday, 1979).

Epistle on the Mixed Life (circa 1380–1395)

Manuscripts: There are sixteen complete, extant transcriptions of Hilton's *Epistle on the Mixed Life.* The standard edition (1985) is based on Lambeth Palace 472, fols. 193^r–213^r. Other manuscripts used for the standard edition include Bodleian Library, Oxford, Rawlinson A 356, fols. 83^r–90^v; Cambridge University Library, Ff. v 40, fols. 1–14^v; and British Library, Harley 2397, fols. 73^r–85^r.

First publication: *Yorkshire Writers,* 2 volumes, edited by Carl Horstman (London: Sonnenschein, 1895; New York: Macmillan, 1895).

Standard edition: *Walter Hilton's Mixed Life Edited from Lambeth Palace MS 472,* edited by S. J. Ogilvie-Thomson, Salzburg Studies in English Literature (Salzburg: Institut für Anglistik und Amerikanistik, 1985).

Of Angels' Song (circa 1380–1395)

Manuscripts: Six manuscripts have been found of the work: British Museum, Add. MS. 27592; Lincoln Cathedral Chapter Library, MS. 91, A. i. 17; Cambridge University Library, MS. Dd. v. 55; Cambridge University Library, MS. Ff. v. 40; MS. Takamiya 3, ff. 170–173; and Bodleian Library, Oxford, MS. Bodley 576.

First publication: *Of Angel's Song* (London: Printed by Henry Pepwell, 1521).

Standard editions: In *Yorkshire Writers,* edited by Carl Horstman (1895); "Of Angels' Song," edited by Toshiyuke Takamiya, in *Studies in English Literature* (Tokyo), English number (1977): 3–31.

Editions in modern English: In *Eight Chapters on Perfection and Angels' Song,* translated by Rosemary Dorward (Oxford: SLG, 1985).

Louis de Fontibus, *Eight Chapters on Perfection,* translated by Hilton (circa 1380–1395)

Manuscripts: The work survives in MS. anglais 41, Bibliothèque Nationale, Paris, and in Petyt 524, Library of the Inner Temple of London.

Standard edition: *Walter Hilton's Eight Chapters on Perfection,* edited by Fumio Kuriyagawa (Tokyo: Keio Institute of Cultural and Linguistic Studies, 1967).

Qui habitat (circa 1380–1395)

Manuscripts: Bodleian Library, Oxford, Vernon, Lambeth MS. 472.

First publication: In *Minor Works of Walter Hilton,* edited by Dorothy Jones (London: Burns, Oates & Washbourne, 1929).

Standard edition: *An Exposition of Qui Habitat and Bonum Est in English,* edited by Bjorn Wallner, Lund Studies in English 23 (Lund: Gleerup, 1954).

James of Milan, *The Goad of Love,* translated by Hilton (circa 1380–1395)

Manuscripts: The work survives in ten complete and six partial manuscripts, including British Library, Harley 2415; British Library, Harley 2254; and Durham University, Cosin MS. V. III. 8.

First publication: *The Goad of Love,* edited by Clare Kirchberger (New York: Harper, 1951; London: Faber & Faber, 1952).

Page from Walter Hilton's Scale of Perfection, *in a fifteenth-century transcription (Columbia University Library, MS. Plimpton 257, fol. 99ʳ)*

Standard edition: *The Prickynge of Love,* edited by Harold Kane (Salzburg: Institut für Anglistik und Amerikanistik, 1983).

Few hard facts are available about Walter Hilton except that he died on the Vigil of the Annunciation, 23 March 1395 (1396 by the current calendar) and that he was a canon of Saint Augustine in the priory at Thurgarton, near Southwell, in Nottinghamshire. He may have spent some time as a recluse, but it seems reasonable to assume, given the character of his works, that he understood the contemplative life and experience well. In modern times he is probably best known as one of the English mystics of the late fourteenth century. This flowering of mysticism included Richard Rolle, Julian of Norwich, and the author of the *Cloud of Unknowing* (circa 1350–1400) and its related treatises.

Despite his duties at Thurgarton and his own spiritual life, he found time to be a director of contemplative souls. This he does in the three English works that can be attributed to him with certainty: *The Scale of Perfection, Epistle on the Mixed Life,* and *Of Angels' Song,* all composed between 1380 and 1395. Many scholars also attribute an English translation of the *Stimulus Amoris* (The Goad of Love) to Hilton. Two Latin treatises – *De imagine peccati* and *Epistola aurea* – and four short English treatises – *Eight Chapters on Perfection, Qui habitat, Bonum est,* and *Benedictus* – all dating from the same period, have also been attributed to Hilton, but there is some contention among scholars about the authorship of these works (*Eight Chapters on Perfection* is probably a translation of the work of a Spanish friar resident at Cambridge in 1383). Latin letters ascribed to Hilton in manuscripts and close in theological outlook and subject matter are *Epistola ad quemdam seculo renunciare volentem, Epistola ad solitarium,* and *Epistola de utilitate et prerogatiuis religionis* (all dating from the early fifteenth century). As with many works of the medieval period, especially religious works, definite authorship is uncertain.

Walter Hilton is certainly best known for a long treatise entitled *The Scale of Perfection. The Scale of Perfection* is often described as a mystical classic, but, like many other mystical works, it is as much concerned with moral and ascetic life as it is with contemplative exercises. It is, as editor Evelyn Underhill has said, a road map for a soul traveling to the spiritual Jerusalem. *The Scale of Perfection* had a wide and enduring influence, circulating for over a century in numerous manuscripts. It was translated into Latin by 1400 (presumably to make sure it was preserved) and was printed rather early (first publi-

cation in 1494). The work is long for a Middle English devotional treatise, book 1 having ninety-three chapters and book 2 (probably written much later) with forty-six chapters.

In terms of its rhetorical stance, *The Scale of Perfection* sounds as though it were addressed to one individual, a "sister," probably an anchoress just embarking on her spiritual work. Hilton posits this reader for his book through several explicit references to her and her circumstances, notably at the beginning and the end. He usually focuses on this hypothetical reader, but he has within his peripheral vision a wider potential audience – one to which he refers from time to time. If a work of devotional instruction were helpful, naturally it would be passed on to other like-minded individuals. *Epistle on the Mixed Life* and *Of Angels' Song* are tailored to a specific reader, a particular audience.

Hilton's opinion of how *The Scale of Perfection* should be taken is summed up nicely at the end of book 1. He ends, of course, with a blessing and a warning that the advice contained in the book applies only to those who have adopted the contemplative lifestyle and not at all to those who pursue the active lifestyle. This passage also conveys the tone of the work, for while much of the treatise is instructional, didactic, or tutorial in tone, the relationship to the reader is warm and immediate rather than distant. Hilton states:

> I've told you a little of what I think, first about what the contemplative life is, and then about the ways which, through grace, lead to it. Not that I have experienced and can do what I have been describing! Nevertheless, by these words (such as they are) I would first rouse myself from my own negligence that I might do better than I have done. Second, my purpose is to stir you (or any other man or woman who has taken on the contemplative state of life) to labor more diligently and more meekly in that way of life, using such simple words as God has given me grace to say.
>
> And therefore, if there is in this book anything which motivates you to love God more, or comforts you, thank God, for it is through His gift, not from my words, that it comes. And if something does not comfort you or you're not yet ready to accept it, don't waste too much time on it. Put it aside until another time.... Take it as it will come – and not all at once.
>
> And don't take these words I write too strictly, but where it seems to you in your good judgment that I have spoken too briefly I beg you fix it – but only where it needs it.
>
> – translation by M. L. Del Mastro (in his edition of *The Stairway of Perfection,* 1979)

The organization of *The Scale of Perfection* has been a matter of much scholarly controversy over the years. The metaphor of the scale, or ladder, is not really an appropriate description of the contents. The contemplative individual does ascend spiritually in a sense. As Underhill notes in her 1923 edition of *The Scale of Perfection,* this ladder is a conventional symbol and stands for a conception of the spiritual life. The work, however, is chiefly concerned with metaphorically portraying "man's soul as the image of God, defaced by sin, which has impressed on it another pattern or dark image." The reformation of the image of God in the soul and how to achieve it are the real themes of the book. It is a long, hard job to make the tarnished internal image of God more like its divine correspondent. The reformation of the soul in faith and experience is a state of being clean of heart, meek, humble, and charitable, and the soul must freely choose to accept the reformation God offers. Most of the work is devoted to this topic and the ideas surrounding it. *The Scale of Perfection* deals with the deepening of the union of the contemplative to God through contemplation as a focus of life. Practical spiritual advice – on the daily practice of prayer, and on dealing with emotions, such as pride, that will assail the meditator – abounds.

Underhill describes Hilton as "discursive rather than methodical." David Knowles sees the organization as having its share of "medieval digression and disorder." Mainly, critics and editors note the repetitions, the lapping back to previously treated subjects, though Joseph E. Milosh defends the work's order at some length. Del Mastro sees the structure as a staircase which spirals upward and which has landings or interludes. Thus it covers the same ground, so to speak, more than once, but each time at a higher level. In a 1982 essay Michael G. Sargent demonstrates that Hilton uses a basic scholastic method in organizing *The Scale of Perfection.* Each question posed in the work is first distinguished by its parts, then the relationship of each part to the whole is explored, and finally each part is treated individually.

Book 1 begins by setting forth the concept of the active and contemplative lives and the way of life connected with each. The stages of contemplation are discussed in ascending levels. He warns against overdoing physical penance. The contemplative must be humble and understand the nature of prayer. When the image in the soul is reformed, the conscience must testify to the full forsaking of sin and true turning of the will to good living. The inward is always stressed over the outward. There is a constant emphasis on turning away from worldly things and toward spiritual experience of God. The full fire of love and experience and knowledge of God, however, come only after death in Heaven, Hilton assures his readers.

Book 2 seems to cover the same ground as book 1 in greater depth and detail. Hilton stresses how hard the reformation of the image in the soul is to perform and how the sacraments figure in the contemplative's life. The final chapters of book 2 speak specifically about the desire to experience the spiritual love and presence of Jesus in the soul. How should one respond to these touchings of grace? What will it be like to hear the voice of Jesus sounding in the soul? What is the nature of the gracious illuminations made in the soul? Hilton tries to answer these questions about the essentially ineffable experience of God: however, he confesses, "A soul clean and stirred by grace may see more in an hour than might be written in a great book of this spiritual matter." At the end he dwells on the contemplative experience of God and of the presence of grace, using traditional imagery referring to Jesus as the spouse and the wooer. Hilton's book of spiritual advice was extremely popular in its own time and for two centuries after, as the number of manuscripts indicates.

A much shorter work and probably the next best known after *The Scale of Perfection* is Hilton's Middle English *Epistle on the Mixed Life.* As an Augustinian canon, Hilton had contact with secular life yet some opportunity for contemplation; thus he has some basis for the advice he gives. Hilton tailors this work to a nobleman, focusing on the special spiritual problems of his state. Although no recipient is named, two manuscripts indicate that *Epistle on the Mixed Life* is addressed to a man in temporal estate. It is unusual in this feature, since Hilton's other treatises all seem to be addressed to other contemplatives. The author seems cognizant that not everyone can pursue the contemplative life. Noble persons have duties they must carry out even if they are extremely devout. The epistle has the same friendly, personal, yet tutorial tone of Hilton's other works. His intimate rhetorical stance enables him to demonstrate how the devotional life applies to a particular Christian living in a given set of circumstances.

The letter dwells on the particular pitfalls which present themselves to those involved in worldly activities who yet aspire to spiritual perfection. He draws careful distinctions between the active, contemplative, and mixed lives, pointing out that Christ led a mixed life. Work, he tells his reader, should be viewed as a sacred duty, as a worship to God, especially since God has knowingly put the nobleman in that state and his will should be fulfilled.

The advice is sound, and the tone assuages the conscience of Hilton's correspondent at his inability to devote himself fully to the contemplative life. Deeds of mercy performed for others in truth and charity please God, the writer points out. Deeds are a token of moral virtue without which spiritual work cannot begin. As in *The Scale of Perfection*, the reader is urged to break down a love of worldly things and to avoid fleshly desires. Interestingly, Hilton warns that even charitable works need to be used with discretion because "unruled charity" can turn to vice. Bible quotations are frequently brought in to support the arguments. He refers conventionally to the story of Mary and Martha, and he also uses Saint Gregory for support. The simple, homely imagery is not dependent on a knowledge of theological texts or allusions or obscure biblical knowledge. Hilton is by no means arguing for a novel concept in advocating the mixed life. His division of lives demonstrates the medieval tendency to formalize and categorize every aspect of experience.

Another short treatise on mystical life also in the epistolary mode is *Of Angels' Song*. It is addressed to a "brother in Christ." The subject is that which would interest only contemplatives at a fairly advanced level – the reader who wishes to know more about the sound heard by those deep in contemplative prayer when grace comes to them. The problem is in discerning the true from the false. The human soul and God must accord in perfect charity. This oneness is truly achieved when the soul is reformed by grace to the dignity and the state of the first condition. Then the soul is comforted with the song of angels, which is "not like anything bodily and above all manner of imagination and reason." The mind must be ravished out of the sense or mind of earthly things into great fervor of love and light of God. But one must beware the false soundings resulting from an overworked imagination. The essential joy is in love of God by himself and for himself.

Eight Chapters on Perfection, a translation ascribed to Hilton, is a treatise much in keeping with the subject matter of his other works. The intended audience is someone advanced in the life of contemplative prayer. Within this context the advice is practical. The work is addressed to believers who are not beginners in the contemplative enterprise. The contemplative who would achieve perfection is advised to "set then all thy study and thy business for to make ready a place and a privy chamber for thy Lord Jesu Christ, thy spouse in thy soul, by

sweet meditation, by continual orisons." The author mentions perils to be avoided by a holy man. For example, contemplatives are to beware of those who speak pleasantly but lack real virtue. One should look beneath the outward show. He also warns that spiritual love for other people must be guarded with "armours of discretion" lest it turn to fleshly love. Hilton, following Fontibus, describes the five degrees a soul passes through in contemplation. In the first degree the contemplative feels sorrow for sin, a repulsion for vice, and a determination to stand against wickedness. The second degree is one of great fervor and desire to please Christ and to love him with all the powers of the soul. The burning desire of this stage cleanses the conscience. The third degree is a state of wonderful sweetness because the grace of the holy spirit touches the soul. In the fourth degree the soul is asleep to the world as the thoughts are ever on Christ. In the fifth degree the contemplative has a glimmering of heavenly bliss.

Qui habitat is likewise addressed to the devoutly religious. Though it laments "the prison of this life," it is fundamentally an uplifting discussion of the experience of grace in the soul. It is similar in style, subject, and rhetorical procedure to *The Scale of Perfection, Bonum est.,* and *Benedictus.* Hilton's discussions are entirely orthodox and reflect the integral role of the church in the life of the mystic. *The Goad of Love* (also titled *The Prickynge of Love*) is a free translation of the thirteenth-century *Stimulus Amoris* by James of Milan. After some discussion of Christ's Passion, this treatise discusses how a person becomes a contemplative and the joys of a life of prayer and meditation. It is a manual for the novice mystic.

In recent years the works of Walter Hilton (along with those of other medieval mystics, Continental as well as English) have received increased attention from readers and critics. Modernizations of most of his Middle English works are in print. Scholarship has focused recently on the production of solid scholarly editions from the manuscripts and on style as well as on some of the major concepts of the treatises. Hilton's subject range is narrow, to be sure, but the spiritual quest of striving for union with God that his works explore seems to be one of enduring appeal.

Bibliographies:

Valerie Lagorio and Ritamary Bradley, eds., *The Fourteenth-Century English Mystics: A Comprehensive Annotated Bibliography* (New York: Garland, 1981);

Alastair Minnis and A. S. G. Edwards, "*The Cloud of Unknowing* and Walter Hilton's *Scale of Perfection*," in *Middle English Prose: A Critical Guide to Major Authors and Genres* (New Brunswick, N. J.: Rutgers University Press, 1984).

References:

Walter H. Beale, "Walter Hilton and the Concept of the 'Medled Lyf,' " *American Benedictine Review,* 26 (1975): 381–394;

A. J. Bliss, "Two Hilton Manuscripts in Columbia University Library," *Medium Ævum,* 38 (1969): 157–163;

J. P. H. Clark, "Image and Likeness in Walter Hilton," *Downside Review,* 97 (1979): 204–220;

Clark, "Intention in Walter Hilton," *Downside Review,* 97 (1979): 69–80;

Clark, "The 'Lightsome Darkness' – Aspects of Walter Hilton's Theological Background," *Downside Review,* 95 (1977): 95–109;

Clark, "Walter Hilton and 'Liberty of Spirit,' " *Downside Review,* 96 (1978): 61–78;

Helen L. Gardner, "The Text of *The Scale of Perfection*," *Medium Ævum,* 5 (1936): 11–30;

Gardner, "Walter Hilton and the Mystical Tradition of England," *Essays and Studies by Members of the English Association,* 22 (1937): 103–127;

Marion Glasscoe, ed., *The Medieval Mystical Tradition in England,* Exeter Symposium IV (Cambridge: Brewer, 1987);

S. S. Hussey, "Latin and English in the *Scale of Perfection*," *Medieval Studies,* 35 (1973): 456–476;

Hussey, "The Text of *The Scale of Perfection, Book II*," *Neuphilologische Mitteilungen,* 65 (1964): 75–92;

Hussey, "Walter Hilton: Traditionalist?," in *The Medieval Mystical Tradition,* edited by Glasscoe (Exeter: University of Exeter Press, 1980);

David G. Kennedy, *Incarnational Element in Hilton's Spirituality* (Salzburg: Institut für Anglistik und Amerikanistik, University of Salzburg, 1982);

David Knowles, *The English Mystical Tradition* (London: Burns & Oates, 1961);

Fumio Kuriyagawa, ed., "The Inner Temple Manuscript of Walter Hilton's Eight Chapters on Perfection," *Studies in English Literature* (Tokyo), English number (1971): 7–34;

Joseph E. Milosh, *The Scale of Perfection and the English Mystical Tradition* (Madison, Milwaukee & London: University of Wisconsin Press, 1966);

Joy Russell-Smith, "Walter Hilton," *Month,* 207, new series 21 (1959): 133–148;

Russell-Smith, "Walter Hilton and a Tract in Defense of the Veneration of Images," *Dominican Studies,* 7 (1954): 180–214;

Michael G. Sargent, "Hilton's Scale of Perfection: The Manuscript Group Reconsidered," *Medium Ævum,* 52, no. 2 (1983): 189–214;

Sargent, "The Organization of the *Scale of Perfection*," in *The Medieval Mystical Tradition in England,* edited by Glasscoe (Exeter: University of Exeter Press, 1982), pp. 231–261;

Gerard Sitwell, "Contemplation in *The Scale of Perfection*," *Downside Review,* 67 (1949): 276–290; 68 (1950): 21–34; 69 (1950): 271–289;

Toshiyuke Takamiya, "The Luttrell Wynne MS of Walter Hilton," *Reports of the Keio Institute of Cultural and Linguistic Studies,* 7 (1975): 171–191.

Thomas Hoccleve

(circa 1368 – circa 1437)

Douglas J. McMillan
East Carolina University

MAJOR WORKS: "The Letter of Cupid" (May 1402)

Manuscripts: "The Letter of Cupid" appears in eleven manuscripts and one early printed version based on a twelfth manuscript now lost; of the surviving manuscripts Durham University MS. Cosin V. iii. 9 and Huntington Library MS. HM 744, autograph (holograph) are the most important.

First publication: In *The Workes of Geffray Chaucer,* edited by W. Thynne (London: Printed by T. Godfrey, 1532).

Standard editions: In *Hoccleve's Works: The Minor Poems,* edited by Frederick J. Furnivall and I. Gollancz, volume 1, EETS, e.s. 61 (1892; reprinted, 1937), pp. 72–92; volume 2, EETS, e.s. 73 (1925 for 1897), pp. 294–308; revised by Jerome Mitchell and A. I. Doyle, 1 volume (London: Oxford University Press, 1970).

The Regement of Princes (1411–1412)

Manuscripts: *The Regement of Princes* survives in forty-five manuscripts; those used for standard editions include British Library MS. Arundel 38; British Library MS. Harley 4866; British Library MS. Royal 17. D. vi; and Huntington Library MS. HM 135 (formerly Phillips 8980).

First publication: *The Regement of Princes,* edited by T. Wright (London: Roxburghe Club, 1860).

Standard editions: *Hoccleve's Works: The Regement of Princes and Fourteen Minor Poems,* edited by Frederick J. Furnivall, volume 3, EETS, e.s. 72 (1897; reprinted, Krause, 1973), pp. 1–197; *Thomas Hoccleve: Selected Poems,* edited by Bernard O'Donoghue (Manchester: Carcanet, 1982).

"How to Die" (1421–1422)

Manuscripts: "How to Die" survives in six manuscripts; Huntington Library MS. HM 144 is particularly valuable.

Standard edition: In *Hoccleve's Works: The Minor Poems* (1892), I: 178–212.

"Prologue and a Miracle of the Blessed Virgin" (before 1430)

Manuscripts: This poem survives in three known manuscripts, including Huntington Library MS. HM 744.

Standard edition: In *Hoccleve's Works: The Minor Poems* (1892), II: 290–293.

"Mother of God" (before 1430)

Manuscripts: "Mother of God" survives in three known manuscripts, including Huntington Library MSS. HM 111 and HM 744.

Standard edition: In *Hoccleve's Works: The Minor Poems* (1892), I: 52–56.

It is time for Thomas Hoccleve (or Occleve) to come out from under the shadow of his beloved master, Geoffrey Chaucer, and to be recognized as the excellent poet that he is. His four best-known short poems are usually entitled "The Letter of Cupid" (1402), "How to Die" (1421–1422), "Prologue and a Miracle of the Blessed Virgin" (before 1430), and "Mother of God" (before 1430). Hoccleve's major long poem is *The Regement of Princes* (1411–1412). These five poems stand out from the total of thirty-eight poems by Hoccleve because of their artistic and aesthetic merit. They deserve to be called Hoccleve's best in the various genres he used. Indeed, they can serve as a sampler for the remainder of Hoccleve's poetry, which includes a significant number of additional fine poems.

Hoccleve was born about 1368 or 1369, possibly in Hockliffe, Bedfordshire, about thirty-five miles northwest of London. In 1387 he began a thirty-five-year career as a clerk in the Privy-Seal Office in the city of Westminster (now a borough of Greater London). King Richard II granted Hoccleve a corody in the Priory of Hayling between 1395 and 1399. When Hoccleve was a little over thirty, in 1400, his poetical inspiration and friend Chaucer died. Numerous poems by Hoccleve were com-

Page from a scribal copy of Thomas Hoccleve's Regement of Princes, *with an illustration of the author presenting the work to Prince Henry (British Library, MS. Royal 17. D. vi)*

pleted in the decade after Chaucer's death: "The Letter of Cupid" in May 1402, "The Ill-Regulated Youth" ("La Male Regle de T. Hoccleve") late in 1406, "The Court of Good Company" about 1410. Having given up the hope of being ordained as a priest, Hoccleve married (his wife's name is unknown) in 1410 or 1411. This was followed in 1411–1412 by the completion of his major work, *The Regement of Princes,* for Henry, Prince of Wales; also during the years 1411–1412 Hoccleve commissioned a portrait of Chaucer for inclusion in *The Regement of Princes,* and in 1413 the poem's patron became King Henry V. About 1414 Hoccleve completed his "Balade to My Gracious Lord of York," and in 1415 or 1416 he completed his "Balade to King Henry V," sometimes called "Victorious King," after King Henry's return to England from Agincourt. From about 1416 to 1421 Hoccleve was probably unable to serve in the Privy-Seal Office full-time, but he still drew his annuity regularly; he was suffering from a nervous breakdown. He returned during 1421–1422 for a short time to his regular routine at the Privy-Seal Office and wrote the so-called Series poems. In 1422 Henry V died; the infant Henry VI succeeded him. Hoccleve's annuity was continued in 1423; however, he was referred to in official documents as "late one of the clerks of the Privy-Seal Office." In 1424 he was awarded yearly sustenance of about twenty pounds during the remainder of his life in retirement at, or from, the Austin Canon's Priory of Southwick in the county of Hampshire, about sixty miles southwest of London. The year 1426 marks the last known appearance of Hoccleve's name in official government documents: the Pell's Issue Roll notes payment of Hoccleve's final half-year's annuity on 11 February. Some scholars now think that he died in 1426, but he may have died as late as 1437.

Hoccleve's longest poem is also his masterpiece, as well as his most popular poem. *The Regement of Princes* appears on the surface to be yet another handbook for the correct conduct of a ruler or ruler to be. Although the work is partly such a handbook, in this case addressed to Henry, the Prince of Wales, it is also much more. At its core it is one of Hoccleve's major autobiographical poems, in which he begs for pay owed him, for an annuity, and for a pension; he also appears to reveal much about his own troubled life, about his high regard for Chaucer, and about the daily activities in the London and Westminster in which he both lived and worked.

The poem is in 777 rhyme royal stanzas plus an envoi of three eight-line stanzas directing (dedicating) the book to Prince Henry, bringing the total length of the poem to 5,463 lines. (Rhyme royal, rhyming *ababbcc,* was made popular in English by Chaucer, but it derives its name from *chant-royal* and from the royal user of the Chaucerian form, King James I of Scotland.) Hoccleve's three main sources are an eighth-century work, the *Secreta secretorum* (Secret of Secrets), once erroneously thought to be letters of advice from Aristotle to Alexander the Great; and two thirteenth-century works, *De regimine principum* (The Regiment of Princes) of Aegidius Romanus; and *De ludo scacchorum* (The Game of Chess) of Jacobus de Cessolis.

Hoccleve's poem opens with a sixteen-stanza prologue in which the persona-Hoccleve meditates on a sleepless night and on his own confused thoughts about fame and fortune and falls therefrom, especially as they apply to princes (that is, rulers). This is followed by another "prologue" of 272 stanzas comprising a long dialogue between the persona-Hoccleve and an old beggar whom he meets the day after this sleepless night. In the dialogue the old man tries to console Hoccleve in his troubles and guides him in his attempt to write his handbook of advice for a ruler. Also included in this section is major praise of the poets Chaucer and John Gower as models and inspiration for Hoccleve's poetical attempts.

The Regement of Princes proper begins with stanza 289 and continues through stanza 777. Stanzas 289–301 form a proem (yet another prologue) addressed to the prince, after which come the poem's major topics: the dignity of a king; the keeping of coronation oaths; truth; cautious speech; justice, observing laws; pity; mercy; patience; chastity; magnanimity; poverty; generosity; avarice; prudence; the taking of good advice; and peace. These topics are illustrated by interesting, skillfully wrought stories of varying length. The general flow suggests that virtues practiced and vices avoided lead to peace and tranquillity in individuals and in communities. The entire poem concludes with an envoi of three stanzas in which Hoccleve directs his book toward the good it may do for the prince.

In addition to being a highly autobiographical poem, *The Regement of Princes* also contains some famous lines in praise of Chaucer, as well as the so-called Hoccleve portrait of Chaucer. The central part of Hoccleve's praise reads:

> O, maister deere, and fadir reverent!
> Mi maister Chaucer, flour of eloquence,
> Mirour of fructuous entendement,
> O, universel fadir in science!
> Allas! that thou thyn excellent prudence,

In thi bed mortel mightist naght by-quethe;
What eiled deth? allas! whi wolde he sle the?

(O, master dear, and father reverent!
My master Chaucer, flower of eloquence,
Mirror of fruitful intellect,
O, universal father in learning!
Alas! that you your excellent prudence,
In your mortal bed might not bequeath;
What ailed death? alas! why did he want to kill you?)

Four special characterizations are presented within *The Regement of Princes:* two are apostrophized and discussed (Prince Henry and Chaucer); two are the major speakers (the persona-Hoccleve and the unnamed and unidentified old man). The poem is addressed to Prince Henry; he is asked to support Hoccleve now and in the future, and he is given excellent advice for his own current and future success. Chaucer is remembered by his pupil and fellow government worker in a poetical and pictorial way. Hoccleve portrays himself in a realistic, honest, and humorous way. He seems less a persona and more a person here than he appears in some of his other poems. He knows that he has troubles (financial, mental, religious, social), and he admits that he has them and, therefore, in a way is coping and possibly curing himself of some of them. The old man or beggar, however, is the most interesting character in the poem. He too is portrayed realistically as he remembers his youthful faults and traces his pilgrimage to God via poverty. Hoccleve consistently calls him father, and the old beggar man calls Hoccleve son. Stanzas 280–282 are devoted to Chaucer, approximately twelve stanzas after the old man asks Hoccleve his name and mentions Hoccleve's acquaintance with Chaucer. Stanzas 712–714 are devoted to Chaucer, including a discussion of the poet's portrait, which appeared in many manuscript versions of the work. Hoccleve may be suggesting that the old man is the spirit of Chaucer come in a dream to counsel him, allegorically expressing additional praise and admiration for the greatest medieval English poet.

The Regement of Princes is a minor masterpiece. It is well written and adds to the modern reader's understanding of the London area in Hoccleve's and in Chaucer's day. It also contains facts about Chaucer and reveals much about Hoccleve himself. Finally, it offers appropriate advice for anyone who wishes to live a good life.

"The Letter of Cupid," "Prologue and a Miracle of the Blessed Virgin," and "Mother of God" were for many years attributed to Chaucer. These poems and "How to Die" are certainly worthy of

Chaucer, and that reflects well on Hoccleve's ability as a poet. The subjects of these poems – questions of love, of death, and of spiritual assistance – are perennial themes of intense interest to all humanity. The intensity and depth of Hoccleve's writing still forcefully speak to modern readers.

The full title of "The Letter of Cupid" is "The Letter of Cupid to Lovers, His Subjects." In the manuscripts the title varies, with Latin and French forms: "Litera Cupidinis, dei Amatoris, directa subditis suis amatoribus" and "Lepistre de Cupide." The poem is in the form of a five-part letter, and the general theme relates to courtly love – the mistreatment of women by men. The earliest of Hoccleve's known datable poems, "The Letter of Cupid" has sixty-eight rhyme royal stanzas totaling 476 lines and is an adaptation of Christine de Pisan's *L'epistre au dieu d'amours* (1399). Christine must have been to the fourteenth century someone much like the twentieth-century Simone de Beauvoir, both being spokespersons not only for the France of their times but for the world. It is to Hoccleve's credit that he thought Christine's message so important that it needed to be put into an English version. Most upper-class English people could probably understand French in Hoccleve's day. It is fair to assume, therefore, that Hoccleve put Christine's poem into English for a wider audience, the general populace of England. "The Letter of Cupid" was included in W. Thynne's collected edition of Chaucer's works, and again in J. Stowe's 1561 edition of Chaucer. The work was also attributed to Chaucer by Hakluyt in 1598 and modernized by G. Sewell as Chaucer's poem in 1718. There is agreement among scholars now, however, that "The Letter of Cupid" is Hoccleve's poem. W. W. Skeat in his edition of Chaucer and Frederick J. Furnivall in his edition of Hoccleve give careful consideration to the work's vocabulary, syntax, meter, and style. They conclude that this poem is Hoccleve's. It perhaps seems too long for most modern readers, whose taste probably would be satisfied with a poem of about half its length, leaving out repetitions and long descriptions. However, Hoccleve's audience, who typically enjoyed explanations, exemplifications, and dilation, may have thought his poem too short. He could, for example, have told the life histories of all or some of the persons mentioned in the poem. Poetry was a, if not *the,* major form of entertainment and instruction in the Middle Ages, comparable to the long and sometimes highly repetitive novels of modern times. Through his vivid presentation of Cupid, his careful arrangement of the parts of his argument, and especially his moving treatment of an eminently important theme, Hoccleve has produced a memorable poem which deserves to be considered one of his best contributions to English literature.

"How to Die" (called in the manuscripts "Ars sciendi mori") is about preparing for death and is in the form of a dialogue between the poet (called the Disciple) and Wisdom. Within this frame-dialogue is a longer dialogue between the poet (Disciple) and an imagined dying sinner, and the poem is followed in the manuscripts by a link and by a prose continuation. "How to Die" is an integral part of Hoccleve's "Series," which includes also his "Complaint," his "Dialogue with a Friend," and two verse translations from the Anglo-Latin *Gesta Romanorum*. "How to Die" comprises 131 rhyme royal stanzas plus a three-stanza-rhyme-royal link, totaling 938 lines. Its main source is Henry Suso's *Horologium sapientiae*, composed about 1327–1328. Hoccleve translated freely and doubled the length of his source through moralizing additions and through what appear to be personal references. Again, as was the case with Christine's *L'epistre au dieu d'amours*, it is to Hoccleve's credit that he chose a superior work as a source for his English poem. Suso's work was very popular. Europe in the fourteenth and fifteenth centuries was greatly concerned with mysticism and its direct divine (spiritual) revelations of truth, and Suso was a leading European mystic with an international influence. Hoccleve knew what his contemporaries enjoyed and were interested in, and he provided his own English version so that English readers who did not understand Latin would be able to share this mystical insight into learning how to prepare to die. The theme is neither Suso's nor Hoccleve's exclusively; it is *the* medieval theme. Despite his use of a source, Hoccleve's English poem is certainly an original work, and a good, even excellent one.

Equally excellent is Hoccleve's "Prologue and a Miracle of the Blessed Virgin," a legend in the genre to which the well-known French folktale "Our Lady's Juggler" also belongs. At one time this poem too was thought to be Chaucer's: in at least one manuscript this poetic legendary miracle is presented as "The Ploughman's Tale" of Chaucer's *The Canterbury Tales* (circa 1375–1400). "The Prologue" is in three rhyme royal stanzas, twenty-one lines, and "The Miracle" is in fifteen rhyme royal stanzas, 105 lines. A written source for the poem is not known; the legend might correctly be placed in the context of oral literature (folklore), for it floated freely about from person to person by word of mouth. Hoccleve's version is a form of the earlier

legend called "Coment le sauter Noustre Dame fu primes cuntrove," an English work, despite the French title, found in Digby Manuscript 86 (circa 1275) in the Bodleian Library, Oxford. It is thought that the Psalter of Our Lady, or more commonly now, the Rosary, was the counterpart in the Middle Ages to the Divine Office read daily by the priests. It was, in effect, the illiterate lay brothers' and sisters' Divine Office, which they could say from memory. The legend as composed by Hoccleve is also called "The Monk and Our Lady's Sleeves" or "The Story of the Monk Who Clad the Virgin By Singing *Ave Maria*" or "The Legend of the Virgin and Her Sleeveless Garment." The theme of the poem is revealed through every word: Mary, mysteriously, is a person's only salvation. All, literate and illiterate, need to worship her; she in turn will save her faithful through her Son and through the Father. The excellence and appeal of this poem are in its theme and brevity. Rarely does Hoccleve or any other medieval poet say so much so movingly yet so succinctly.

Hoccleve's "Mother of God," also called "Ad Beatam Virginem," is in the form of a prayer invoking the Virgin to intercede with her Son for the salvation of the soul of the poet and for the salvation of all persons. The poem comprises twenty stanzas in rhyme royal, totaling 140 lines. It survives in three known manuscripts, two of which ascribe the poem to Chaucer. The Latin lyric *O Intemerata* is the source of the last six stanzas of Hoccleve's poem. "Mother of God" is sometimes still affectionately called "Chaucer's 'Mother of God,' " although it is agreed that this is Hoccleve's poem. The theme is the standard, conservative, but pious medieval one: I need help, Mary (and Saint John, and Jesus); pass my prayer on from one to the other so it may be heard by the Father and the Holy Spirit and so that with you and them my soul will live on forever in Heaven. Again, it is the immediacy, the high theme, and the brevity that in combination make this a gem of Middle English literature.

A study of Hoccleve's work, then, reveals that he was at times an excellent poet. His themes are high and important and as appealing to modern readers as they were to his contemporaries. His structuring is carefully done, appropriate, and moving. The core of his poems – his characterizations of medieval people and spiritual beings – also are thoughtfully created, appropriate, and moving.

Hoccleve probably should have been allowed to become a priest as he had wanted to for most of the earlier part of his life. He is much like Chaucer's poor parson; they both searched their own souls, learned sacred truths, and were thereby fully prepared through their lives to preach and teach others. In a special way, however, Hoccleve was a "priest." His daily routine as a clerk in the Privy-Seal Office, copying and writing documents, was similar to the copying and writing activities in a monastic scriptorium. Moreover, as a poet, he did preach and teach; and he was good, yet modest, as J. A. Burrow observes in a 1982 essay: "The poet's own confession that he was 'dull' and learned 'little or nothing' from his master Chaucer is still commonly accepted as a fair summary of his achievement; but such self-depreciation is itself eminently Chaucerian, and I want to suggest that the disciple's poetry in fact displays, at its best, a lively intelligence and a command of English verse which give the lie to his talk of incompetence and stupidity."

Hoccleve is orthodox, conservative, and naive, unlike Chaucer, who saw through hypocritical surfaces to reality, to the human comedy. He is typical of the medieval mind of his own day and earlier, and it is just this that makes him a worthy subject of careful investigation; Chaucer, again by contrast, appears as an early Humanist, an early Modern living in the medieval world. Hoccleve, on the other hand, is an important and representative *medieval* English poet, as his literary output demonstrates.

Bibliographies:

Caroline F. E. Spurgeon, *Five Hundred Years of Chaucer Criticism and Allusion 1357-1900,* 3 volumes (London, 1914–1924; revised edition, Cambridge, 1925; New York: Russell, 1960);

William Matthews, "Thomas Hoccleve," in *A Manual of the Writings in Middle English,* volume 3, edited by Albert E. Hartung (New Haven: Connecticut Academy of Arts and Sciences, 1972), pp. 746–756, 903–908;

Jerome Mitchell, "Hoccleve Studies, 1965–1981," in *Fifteenth-Century Studies: Recent Essays,* edited by Robert F. Yeager (Hamden, Conn.: Archon, 1984), pp. 49–63.

Biography:

Diane Fincher Horne, "Thomas Hoccleve: A Biographical Study," M.A. thesis, East Carolina University, 1978.

References:

J. A. Burrow, "Autobiographical Poetry in the Middle Ages: The Case of Thomas Hoccleve," *Proceedings of the British Academy,* 68 (1982): 389–412;

David R. Carlson, "Thomas Hoccleve and the Chaucer Portrait," *Huntington Library Quarterly,* 54 (Fall 1991): 283–300;

Albrecht Classen, "Hoccleve's Independence from Chaucer: A Study of Poetic Emancipation," *Fifteenth-Century Studies,* 16 (1990): 59–81;

Frederick J. Furnivall, ed., *A Parallel-Text Edition of Chaucer's Minor Poems,* part 2 (London: Trübner, 1878);

D. C. Greetham, "Self-Referential Artifacts: Hoccleve's Persona as a Literary Device," *Modern Philology,* 86 (February 1989): 242–251;

C. S. Lewis, *The Allegory of Love* (London: Oxford University Press, 1936);

Douglas J. McMillan, "The Single Most Popular of Thomas Hoccleve's Poems: *The Regement of Princes,*" *Neuphilologische Mitteilungen,* 89 (1988): 63–71;

Jerome Mitchell, *Thomas Hoccleve: A Study in Early Fifteenth-Century English Poetic* (Urbana: University of Illinois Press, 1968);

Derek Pearsall, "The English Chaucerians," in *Chaucer and Chaucerians,* edited by D. S. Brewer (University: University of Alabama Press, 1966);

William A. Quinn, "Hoccleve's *Epistle of Cupid,*" *Explicator,* 45 (1986): 7–10;

Malcolm Richardson, "Hoccleve in His Social Context," *Chaucer Review,* 20 (1986): 313–322;

Anna Torti, "Specular Narrative: Hoccleve's *Regement of Princes,*" in *The Glass of Form: Mirroring Structures from Chaucer to Skelton* (Cambridge: Brewer, 1991), pp. 87–106;

Rosemary Woolf, *The English Religious Lyric in the Middle Ages* (Oxford: Clarendon Press, 1968).

Julian of Norwich

(1342 – circa 1420)

Elizabeth Psakis Armstrong
University of Cincinnati

WORKS: *Revelations of Divine Love*

Manuscripts: Four manuscripts of the work are known: one of the short text, British Library, MS. Additional 33790 (Amherst) and three of the long text, two in the British Library, Sloane 2499 and 3705, and one in Paris, Bibliothèque Nationale, Fonds Anglais, 40.

First publication: *XVI Revelations of Divine Love, Shewed to a Devout Servant of Our Lord, called Mother Juliana an Anchorete of Norwich: Who Lived in the Dayes of King Edward the Third,* edited by R. F. S. Cressy (London, 1670).

Standard editions: *Julian of Norwich's Revelations of Divine Love,* edited by Frances Beer (Heidelberg: Winter, 1978); *A Book of Showing to the Anchoress Julian of Norwich,* 2 volumes, edited by E. Colledge and James Walsh (Toronto: Pontifical Institute of Medieval Studies, 1978); *A Revelation of Love,* edited by Marion Glasscoe (Exeter, U.K.: Exeter University Press, 1989).

Edition in modern English: *Revelations of Divine Love,* translated by M. L. del Mastro (Garden City, N.Y.: Doubleday, 1977).

Julian of Norwich's writings are centered in a vision of Christ's Crucifixion which she experienced while seriously ill – a vision so compelling and complex that it filled her life. She recovered from the illness to spend the next twenty years in meditation and study, writing two different narratives, one much longer than the other, which describe and analyze the event. The only absolutely solid fact known about Julian's life is the date of this vision, which she carefully records in the *Revelations of Divine Love:* it was "the year of our Lord 1373, the 8th day of May . . . when I was thirty years old and a half." She was born, then, in 1342, close to the time of Geoffrey Chaucer's birth. She was still alive in 1416, when she was the beneficiary of a will so dated, but the year of her death is unknown. The very name "Julian" is not that of the writer but that of a church in the city where she lived.

For centuries the *Revelations of Divine Love* was known only to a small number of readers, people with traditional kinds of religious training and devotion. But today's revival of interest in spirituality brings new kinds of readers to her – charismatics, members of New Age movements, and, in the academy, scholars of literature, religion, and feminism. Departments of literature in universities, which not too long ago read and taught only those texts that can be loosely described as fictional and secular, now customarily include in their curricula some of the great spiritual texts, and so broaden their range not only in genre, but in gender, since the majority of writing by medieval women was on religious subjects.

Despite this democratizing of readership, it is certainly still true that religious texts, particularly medieval, are much less accessible to modern readers than secular writings. The difficulties a student might have with Chaucer's parodies of courtly love are easier to solve than the barriers a text such as *Revelations of Divine Love* will raise against twentieth-century tastes and sensibilities. Readers may find the subject matter, fixed in its early chapters in graphic descriptions of Christ's Passion, too stern, even grotesque and morbid. Concerning the author, the few known biographical facts are precisely those which many readers will find most disconcerting and puzzling. She lived as a religious recluse, not in the way modern readers would find familiar. She was not a hermit, a vocation that still has some romantic appeal. She was not a cloistered nun or a member of an order or organization – though she was under the general supervision of church authorities, she remained a layperson all her life. Instead she lived alone, permanently sealed in a room with only limited contact with the world outside. The word *anchorite* was the common word for this kind

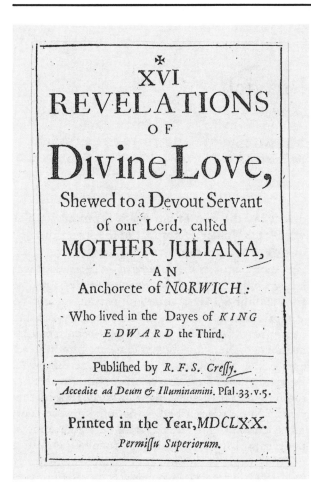

XVI
REVELATIONS
OF
Divine Love,
Shewed to a Devout Servant
of our Lord, called
MOTHER JULIANA,
AN
Anchorete of *NORWICH:*

- Who lived in the Dayes of *KING
EDWARD* the Third.

Publiſhed by *R. F. S. Creſſy.*

Accedite ad Deum & Illuminamini. Pſal.33.v.5.

Printed in the Year, MDCLXX.
Permiſſu Superiorum.

Title page for the first publication of Julian of Norwich's writings

of recluse throughout the Middle Ages in England; it is derived from a Greek word meaning "to withdraw" and has an ancient usage in early Christian writing.

This freely chosen enclosure explains not how odd Julian was but how much her life was modeled on one of the most dynamic circumstances of her time — the creative and varied participation in religious life by lay folk, particularly by women. In late medieval times women who wished to live a spiritual life outside of both social and religious norms had several options. Many organizations, particularly on the European continent, catered to lay women's spirituality: single and widowed working women, called Beguines, lived in communes. The Brothers and Sisters of the Common Life and the Friends of Jesus were assemblies of lay people who continued to work at jobs in the world, sometimes in communal houses, sometimes meeting in study groups. The fourteenth century is also remarkable for the number of clerics writing religious texts for

people living secular lives, as well as for the number of secular people writing religious texts, and, most amazingly, for the number of women writing and being written to. Walter Hilton and Richard Rolle in England and Heinrich Suso, Johannes Tauler, and Meister Eckhart in Germany all direct their attention to women through their preaching or writing. Although some of this attention is explained by traditional clerical associations — for instance, the one between male and female Dominicans — the frequency of such relationships is remarkable. There are notable examples as well of women's freelance enterprises. In Rome a Swedish widow, Bridget, worked in the soup kitchens, wrote a journal about her mystical experiences, founded an order of nuns called the Bridgettines, and achieved sainthood. A young mystic in Siena named Catherine became a third-order Domincan, continued to live at home with her mother, and also wrote (or dictated) a narrative of her spiritual life; she also was canonized. Margery Kempe, an English middle-class wife and mother, like Julian a native of East Anglia, wrote the first autobiography in English about her spiritual adventures. In these closing years of the Gothic age, lay people, especially women, had an unprecedented freedom of choice in the conduct of their religious lives.

Julian's decision to immure herself in a room attached to Saint Julian's Church in Norwich was, in the context of her own times and in the larger history of Christianity, not uncommon at all, especially in England, where records show that over two hundred anchorites lived in various anchor holds during the fourteenth and fifteenth centuries. Ann Warren's recent book on anchorites gives the statistical history of the vocation and also facilitates an understanding of it: "In the Middle Ages the anchorite was viewed as living the sanest of lives, a life more perfect than any other. Far from being neurotics, solitaries led the most authentic life considered possible for the Christian." Late-medieval anchorites had many models from the first centuries of Christianity in the men and women who took themselves to the deserts of the Middle East to practice prayer and penance alone or in quasi-monastic groups. There are also many records of hermits living reclusive but itinerant lives in all parts of England, including London, until the Reformation. Among their haunts was a famous hermitage near Aldgate in the city wall where Chaucer lived on the floor above street level. Rolle fled the student's life at Oxford for a hermit's existence in the forest and then in a benefactor's house. It is clear that the vocation was full of creative spirits who knew, as

Rolle knew, that a retreat to the desert could mean living in the "quiet of the heart."

There is still at Norwich in Saint Julian's Church a reconstruction of a recluse's room like the one occupied by Julian probably from 1373 to her death; the site is maintained by a group called the Friends of Julian of Norwich, and it draws pilgrims from all over the world. The one contemporary mention of Julian outside of her own writing and legal documents is in *The Book of Margery Kempe,* which describes a visit to her at this anchor hold. The visit has a charisma for students of medieval mysticism that might be compared to what Chaucerians would feel if a journal by John Gower were discovered describing a visit from Chaucer to his lodgings at Saint Mary's Overy. Here for the first time in medieval literary history are two secular women writers talking together. There are records of precious few such meetings for centuries after this one. Beset on every side by hostile responses to her public displays of religious emotion by men of civil or ecclesiastic authority – aldermen, mayors, priests, friars, bishops – Kempe sought Julian for advice and comfort. "Great was the holy conversation that the anchoress and this creature [Kempe's consistent third-person self-identification] had through talking of the love of our Lord Jesus Christ for the many days that they were together" (translation by B. A. Windeatt, in *The Book of Margery Kempe,* 1985). Although it was Kempe's constant habit to seek approval from all kind of authorities to balance out the plentiful disapprovals, the manner and speech of the Julian she describes is like the Julian of the *Revelations of Divine Love.* The quiet Julian offers the hectic Kempe advice, love, and wisdom, encouraging her to receive her spiritual experiences as affirmations, signs of God, not of the devil: "Holy Writ says that the soul of a righteous man is the seat of God, and so I trust, sister, that you are" (translation by Windeatt).

The story of this meeting provides a dramatic image of the diversity of religious practice in the late Middle Ages because Kempe and Julian, in life and work and writing, are as different as two Christian mystics can be. On the one hand, Julian wrote as lucid and intellectual a report of mystical experience as was ever penned; on the other hand, Kempe's mysticism was centered in her weeping and shouting ecstasies in church during the Eucharist. Julian's vision lasted one day, but Kempe for years spoke daily to God, and, as with Saint Catherine of Siena and Saint Bridget of Sweden (whose book she knew), he was a constant companion in her life, paying attention to what she should eat and what clothes she should wear. Julian lived enclosed in her anchor hold; Kempe went about England preaching the good news, an office forbidden to women by Paul, and she came close several times to being declared a heretic. Many readers of Chaucer's *Canterbury Tales* (circa 1375–1400) see her as a religious type of Alison of Bath, filled with the vitality and vigor of antipatriarchal dissent. Kempe's displays were so unconventional and embarrassing that her writing still inspires contempt and derision in some readers.

Although Kempe's kinds of public displays were unusual in England, the idea that God can be reached by the human lover through emotional intensity is part of a long tradition. In England the most famous exponent of the emotional way to God is Rolle, whose writings compare his mystical experiences to sensory perceptions, as, rapt in devotion, he hears music, feels heat, and smells sweet things. This center in feeling brings him closer to Kempe than to other men, who, while educated in Latin like Rolle, wrote solidly in the dominant penitential tradition. Hilton's *The Scale of Perfection* (circa 1380–1395), a handbook for the practice of contemplation, is an example of that tradition. Though it recognizes the possibility of mystical contact with God, its emphasis is on the difficulty of any human becoming pure enough to stand before God, and its continual admonitions about sin sometimes quite overwhelm the positive message. Another fourteenth-century English text, the anonymous *Cloud of Unknowing* (circa 1350–1400), resembles Hilton's work in its address to a student of contemplation; it is different, however, from both the ecstatic and penitential traditions in its teaching of the negative way to God through the practice of sensory and intellectual deprivation: to make contact with God, one concentrates not on prayer, language, ritual, or penance – these being relevant only to the neophyte – but on emptiness.

In this diverse group of English mystics, Julian, sharing aspects of thought with all of them and taking many ideas and themes from the tradition of Christian writing, composes a way of her own. There are three areas which most distinguish her work from others: the all-encompassing joy of her message and its freedom from the pedagogue's tone; her combination of steely logic of explanation with the ecstasy of her visionary experience; and the climax of the message in a feminization of Christ. These perspectives are woven together in the text in a way which is unlike any other in the tradition of spiritual writing.

The initiating event of the narrative in *Revelations of Divine Love* is Julian's total concentration on a crucifix that her curate brings to her during what they both believe are her dying moments. The image on the crucifix devolves into a slowed-time enactment of Christ's Passion, delineating the changes in Christ's body from the beginning in flowing blood to the ending in the drying of the blood and flesh. From that point on, Julian and the reader are joined in a mutual adventure of the experience and interpretation of the vision as it happens and as it spreads from ocular to aural acts and as it moves from the Passion to other dramatizations of God's love. The reader sees and hears what Julian does and participates in her developing discoveries about God's relationship with his creation. The process of discovery is painstaking but never dull; it has some setbacks, some passages of brilliant intellectualism, and some epiphanies of insight. Because the vision and its interpretation are presented as ongoing processes, Julian never becomes simply the teacher/preacher to the student/reader. Because she presents the dilemmas of comprehension she faced at the time of the vision in the context of her still-continuing practice of analyses, her text is free from the admonitory, cautionary tone that so often permeates didactic texts, even those written by mystics. This is largely due to the two elements which together create the work – God's demonstrations of love and the intellectual energy of the human to understand everything it is possible to understand about that love.

Julian sees and causes the reader to see God dying, but not so much to cue repentance as to fix the human mind and soul on the Passion as the epitomizing image of Christ's love for humanity. From the beginning of the vision, the point is God's joyful willingness to die for his creation and to do so in the most tender and humble way: "At the same time that I saw the vision of his bleeding head, our Lord gave me spiritual insight into the unpretentious manner of his loving. I saw that for us he is everything that is good, comforting, and helpful; he is our clothing, who, for love, wraps us up, holds us close; he entirely encloses us for tender love, so that he may never leave us, since he is the source of all good things for us" (translation by M. L. del Mastro, 1977). It is as if a medieval painter had painted a crucifix that showed a laughing Christ. Julian's message is informed at every turn by the fact, often lost in texts which teach much of sin and penance, that God created the world and found it good. Julian wishes her readers to recover, as she did, a joyful sense of the amazing grace of God's love. She daringly insists that everything about humans, including the bowels enclosed in the body

created in God's image, is witness to his care and love. God does not "disdain to serve us in the simplest requirements the nature of our body demands, seeing that its necessary functions are accomplished" (translation by del Mastro). Our souls, she says, are enclosed in our bodies "as in a beautiful purse. In time of necessity, the purse is opened and closed again, quite properly"; so God "comes down to us to the lowest part of our need, for he has no contempt for what he has made." And "as the body is clad in . . . clothes, and the flesh in the skin, and bones in flesh, and heart in the whole, so are we, soul and body, clad and enclosed in the goodness of God" (translation by del Mastro).

The connecting of God's love to the seemly operation of the bowels is the most startling of a variety of evocative images that can be described by one of Julian's favorite words, *homely*. Homely can be variously rendered as unpretentious, humble, plain, unassuming, or down-to-earth, but never in its modern denotation of ugliness. The earthy, homely vitality of these images – hazelnuts, herrings, eaves on a roof, seashores, breasts full of milk – recalls the pastoral vocabulary of the Gospel parables and, like them, belies an apparent simplicity in the manifold significances which they yield in interpretation. Both Julian and Christ speak in images like these. The purse of the body and the comparison of God's love to warm clothing in chapter 6 are spoken in Julian's voice, while in chapter 5 Christ invents an apt and homely image, a hazelnut to represent the smallness of all creation compared to God's immensity. Julian calls God "the only doer," and her visions consistently present him as actor/director. He gestures from the cross, and he appears in a pantomime of two characters, master and servant. He moves Julian along in her thinking by enacting small, discreet pieces of the Gospel drama. It is as if he is composing for her an anthology of touchstone passages which he causes her to work into her own intellectual and imaginative schema.

In chapter 5, immediately after Julian sees the vision of the bleeding head and understands it to be a homely demonstration of God's loving, he shifts the scene: "And with this insight [of the bleeding head] he also showed me a little thing, the size of a hazelnut, lying in the palm of my hand" (translation by del Mastro). Christ puts into her understanding that this tiny round ball represents all created things. How can this survive, she thinks, and the answer that comes to her is that it lasts through the love of God, who protects it. The negative image of vulnerability is enclosed in an overwhelmingly positive one: the things of creation are small and fragile, but they exist within three properties: "The first is that God made it. The second is that God loves it. The third is that God keeps it" (translation by del Mastro). The bleeding head of Christ and the hazelnut in the palm of Julian's hand become a coherent, if mysterious, emblem of God's love as she is able to synthesize the visual elements. Then the perception expands to a further dimension as, in this context of divine positiveness, Julian sees how necessary it is "for us to know the littleness of creatures in order to reduce them to nothingness in our judgement, so that we may love and have the uncreated God. The reason we are not fully at ease in heart and soul is because we seek rest in these things that are so little and have no rest within them, and pay no attention to our God, who is . . . the only real rest" (translation by del Mastro). She comes to the same philosophic position about human dependency on God that the tradition of scholarly exegesis had long made clear, but the route she takes to that point through intellectual cogitation and dramatic imagery is of her own creation. Her text is produced by the combined efforts of Christ, the actor, and Julian, the exemplary audience who receives each scene with the greatest intellectual intensity.

Sometimes Christ's dramas overwhelm Julian's comprehension, as in chapter 11, when he presents himself to her "in a point." This "point" is an inclusive graphic representation of God's totality, and the vision causes great anxiety in Julian because in showing her only God and only love it fails to give space to sin and fails to explain the origin or the reason for sin. This episode constitutes a crux because, for some interpreters, Julian's experience of God seems to present a heterodox version of the ancient doctrines of original sin and God's plan for sinning humans. Scholarly debate on this issue continues and has not yet reached a consensus. It is certainly true, however, that sin and its eschatological ravages of fear and guilt do not occupy much space in the *Revelations of Divine Love*. The notice that Jesus takes of Julian's uneasiness about the point without sin and her "foolish" wish (her description, not his) that sin had never existed is characteristically kind, if inconclusive: "Sin is necessary," he says, "but all shall be well, and all shall be well, and all manner of things shall be well" (translation by del Mastro). Of all of God's words in Julian's work, this utterance is the most evocative of his role in the visions as consoler and loving counselor. Like many of God's words, it reappears throughout the book, its significance becoming larger and denser as it does so.

The culmination of this exposition of the joy and bliss and absolute love that this humble, unpretentious, and tender God extends to his creation is in Julian's rendering of Christ as mother. Here the rational, analytic modes of explanation give way to a psalmic tone of delight. Although maternal images of God were invoked before Julian, none of them has the specificity, the power, and the inclusiveness of the extended description in her work. Ritamary Bradley points out that one of the ways this image is unique in Julian is that it does not divide God into the stern father and kind mother, as earlier tradition had done. Indeed, in *Revelations of Divine Love,* the Trinity is a unity of love. In chapter 59 of the long text, which introduces the exposition of Christ as mother, this tripled compassion is delivered in one of Christ's lyric and emotional speeches. Working from the "I am" of the Hebrew Torah, it is like a new litany: "I am the goodness of the fatherhood; I am the wisdom of the motherhood. I am the light and the grace that is all blessed love. I am the trinity. I am the unity. I am the goodness of all manner of things. I am the one who makes you love. I am the one that makes you yearn. I am the endless fulfilling of all true desires" (translation by del Mastro). These images of love are attached to the specific physical and emotional work of motherhood. "Christ births us to joy and eternal life. . . . a human mother may give her child her breast to suck, but our precious mother Jesus, he feeds us with himself full curiously and full tenderly with the blessed sacrament. . . . The mother may lay the child tenderly to her breast, but our tender mother Jesus, he leads us into his blessed breast through his sweet open side [where we] are secure in endless bliss in his assurance as he says, 'Lo, how I love you' " (translations by del Mastro). Jesus as mother exceeds all earthly mothers in his capacity to love the child unconditionally: he keeps us "as tenderly and as sweetly and as securely in our times of failure as he does in our good times." The presentation of this image of God has many theological and literary implications, as Bradley suggests in this summary from her book *Julian's Way* (1992): "Julian sees in her mother-Christ not only female functions, such as birthing, and female stereotypes, such as tenderness, but also . . . steadfastness, which was often denied women in the Middle Ages. It is precisely as 'mother' that Christ has this quality of trustworthiness, not as a trait coming from his maleness. Hence the very image of woman [Julian attributes] to Christ is already revised from its medieval forerunners. . . . The image is not a form of androgyny but is of a unique order, suggesting the restoring of both men and women to full humanity."

Julian's contributions to the twentieth century are in both religious and literary topics. The *Revelations of Divine Love* has become a major text for religious feminists seeking greater roles for women in church governance and the inclusion of the feminine in liturgies and devotions. For students of English literature Julian's writing can be compared in significance to Metaphysical poets such as Thomas Traherne and George Herbert, whose renderings of the religious experience share with hers a vital inventiveness. Like them, she thinks in terms that combine the low and the lofty; like them, she creates a blend of intellect and passion. As readers of Metaphysical poetry must do, Julian's readers must engage all their faculties to understand the layers of implication in word and image.

Bibliographies:

Michael E. Sawyer, *A Bibliographical Index of Five English Mystics* (Pittsburgh: Clifford E. Barbour Library, Pittsburgh Theological Seminary, 1978);

Valerie Marie Lagorio and Ritamary Bradley, *The 14th-Century English Mystics. A Comprehensive Annotated Bibliography* (New York: Garland, 1981).

References:

A. M. Allchin, "Julian of Norwich and the Continuity of Tradition," in *The Medieval Mystical Tradition in England,* edited by Marion Glasscoe (Exeter: University of Exeter Press, 1980), pp. 72–85;

Allchin and Sisters of the Love of God, *Julian of Norwich: Four Studies to Commemorate the Sixth Centenary of the Revelations of Divine Love* (Oxford: Fairacres, 1975);

Ritamary Bradley, "In the Jaws of the Bear: Journeys of Transformation by Women Mystics," *Vox Benedictina,* 8 (Summer 1991): 117–175;

Bradley, *Julian's Way: A Practical Commentary on Julian of Norwich* (London: HarperCollins, 1992);

Caroline Walker Bynum, *Jesus as Mother* (Berkeley: University of California Press, 1982);

J. P. H. Clark, "Nature, Grace and the Trinity in Julian of Norwich," *Downside Review,* 100 (July 1982): 203–229;

Marion Glasscoe, "Vision and Revisions: A Further Look at the Manuscripts of Julian of Norwich," *Studies in Bibliography,* 42 (1989): 103–120;

James Janda, *Julian: A Play Based on the Life of Julian of Norwich* (New York: Seabury, 1984);

Margery Kempe, *The Book of Margery Kempe,* translated by B. A. Windeatt (New York: Penguin, 1985);

Margot H. King, "Julian of Norwich: A Saint for the Nineties," *Vox Benedictina,* 8 (Summer 1991): 55–89;

Valerie M. Lagorio, ed., *Mysticism Medieval and Modern* (Salzburg, Austria: Institut für Anglistik und Amerikanistik, Universität Salzburg, 1986);

Robert Llewelyn, ed., *Julian, Woman of Our Day* (London: Darton, Longman & Todd, 1985);

Roland Maisonneuve, "The Visionary Universe of Julian of Norwich," in *The Medieval Mystical Tradition in England,* edited by Glasscoe (Exeter: University of Exeter, 1980), pp. 86–98;

Brant Pelphrey, *Christ Our Mother. Julian of Norwich* (Wilmington, Del.: Glazier, 1989);

Paul Renaudin, *Quatre Mystiques Anglais* (Paris: Editions du Cerf, 1945);

Anna Maria Reynolds, "Courtesy and Homelinesss in the *Revelations* of Julian of Norwich," *Fourteenth-Century English Mystics Newsletter,* 5 (June 1979): 12–20;

Jill Riatt, ed. *Christian Spirituality: High Middle Ages and Reformation* (New York: Crossroad, 1989);

Ann Warren, *Anchorites and their Patrons in Medieval England* (Berkeley: University of California Press, 1985).

Margery Kempe
(circa 1373–1438)

Denise L. Despres
University of Puget Sound

MAJOR WORKS: *The Book of Margery Kempe* (circa 1436–1438)

Manuscript: British Library Add. MS. 61823, copied by a scribe within a few years of Margery Kempe's dictation of her *Book,* is the only extant manuscript.

First publication: *A Shorte Treatyse of Contemplacyon* (London: Printed by Wynkyn de Worde, 1501).

Standard edition: *The Book of Margery Kempe,* edited by Sanford B. Meech and Hope Emily Allen, EETS, o.s. 212 (1940; reprinted, 1961).

Edition in modern English: *The Book of Margery Kempe,* translated by Barry A. Windeatt (Harmondsworth, U.K.: Penguin, 1985).

Margery (Burnham) Kempe was a fifteenth-century Englishwoman known in her own time as a mystic and exemplar of the apostolic life of contemplative prayer and charitable works. Her life story, *The Book of Margery Kempe* (circa 1436–1438), recorded in two volumes by two priests during her lifetime, is a rich and controversial document that has provided literary, social, and religious historians with insights on medieval spirituality, the role of literacy in regard to authorship, and the role of women in late-medieval society.

Born in Bishop's Lynn (now King's Lynn), Norfolk, a prosperous, mercantile town, Margery belonged to a prominent family. Her father was mayor five times, an alderman of the merchant guild, coroner, justice of the peace, and a member of Parliament six times. Margery does not mention her mother in her *Book.* Around 1393, at the age of twenty, Margery married a burgess of Lynn named John Kempe. Shortly thereafter she became pregnant with the first of her fourteen children. At this point in her life, however, she departed from the ordinary course of life of a middle-class, medieval laywoman. After a difficult delivery she experienced a severe illness of a spiritual nature, brought on by her sense of her own sinfulness and fear of damnation. Fear of her confessor, a stern and impatient priest, prevented her from receiving the absolution necessary for her comfort and emotional well-being.

This event resulted in a period of despair and madness, during which time she was isolated and incarcerated to prevent her from harming herself or others. Margery's healing was initiated by a vision, which began the process of religious conversion in her life and her unique religious vocation. Her life of pilgrimage, penance, and contemplation, unusual for a married woman in late-medieval England, is the subject of her spiritual autobiography.

Margery's record of her life conforms to various patterns of religious life set forth in the hagiographic, devotional, and mystical writings that were so influential in her day, including the three-fold mystic way of purgation (penance), illumination, and mystical union. During the first stage of penance Margery decided that celibacy was necessary for her new vocation. Although the medieval church considered celibacy superior to marriage, and thus nuns necessarily holier than laywomen, it insisted upon conjugal rights once men and women married. Margery's desire to be an exception to the rigid, hierarchical conception of sanctity and order was often perceived by her community and churchmen as hypocritical, eccentric, and even dangerous in a period of Lollard heresy. The Lollards, early Wycliffites, believed that laypeople, including women, should have access to Scripture and be able to preach and teach. Although Margery's eucharistic devotion and frequent pilgrimages prove that she did not share the Lollards' beliefs, she confused both the learned and unlearned in her defiance of the roles and expectations held conventional for medieval women.

Nonetheless, in her travels throughout her own country, Margery gathered many supporters who were moved by her desire to imitate Christ. Among these was Philip Repyngdon, bishop of Lincoln, before whom Margery and her husband took formal vows of chastity sometime between 23 June

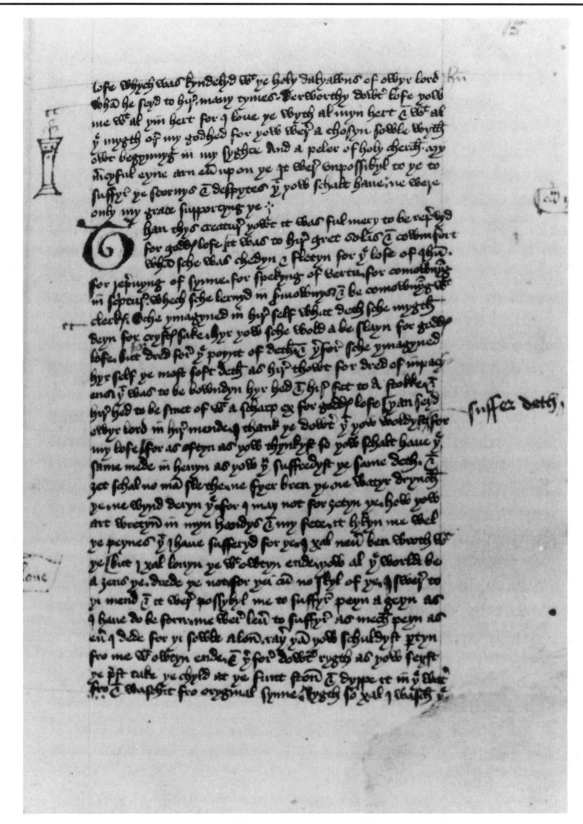

Page from the only extant manuscript for Margery's works (British Library Add. MS. 61823, fol. 15a)

1413 and 19 February 1414, after twenty years of married life, although the bishop refused her requests to wear a mantle and ring, outward signs of the religious life he clearly thought unsuitable for a married woman. Thus, at or near the age of forty Margery began her independent life as a pilgrim, a life fraught with danger and hardship. Several times in her *Book* Margery tells of her arrests and imprisonments in England, where she traveled to shrines or to visit famous holy persons like the anchoress Julian of Norwich, a more conventional model of English female sanctity. When Margery journeyed to the Holy Land, Rome, Assisi, and Santiago de Compostela, the most popular medieval pilgrimage routes, she often had difficulty obtaining a traveling companion, a necessity for a woman whose virtue was always suspect since she had left the protection of her husband. In addition, other pilgrims mocked the white clothing she eventually donned as a sign of her vocation, considered presumptuous since she was not a virgin or nun.

Margery's visit to the Holy Land in 1413–1414 is extremely important for an understanding of her typically late-medieval desire to imitate Christ literally. Like other holy personages in the late middle ages, she believed that a special grace and illumination would come to her if she walked in Christ's footsteps. By meditating on Christ's Passion, his suffering and death, she could experience more fully her own commitment to an apostolic life. On Calvary, therefore, Margery first experienced the sympathetic response to Christ's Passion that baffled her fellow travelers and seems strange to modern readers – but her violent cries and weeping would distinguish her thereafter.

In fact, the gift of holy tears has its origins in the well-known iconographic tradition of the Mother of Sorrows, who weeps at the foot of the cross. Like many medieval people, Margery viewed Mary Magdalene and Mary, Christ's mother, who witnessed and participated in Christ's suffering, as models of devotion. Tears and prayer were connected in late-medieval devotion as a preparation for penance and the sacrament of confession or as a sign of compunction for sin. Margery's tears were thus part of a religious tradition and not a unique sign of sanctity. Nevertheless, English spiritual expression was considerably more restrained than Continental spiritual expression; furthermore, there was a rich and influential tradition of feminine spiritual expression on the Continent that influenced the well-traveled Margery but of which her compatriots were largely ignorant. On the Continent, for example, women like Marie d'Oignies, who also

had the gift of tears, formed religious communities in the thirteenth century called beguinages; the Beguines, like Margery, lived a mixed life of contemplation and service to the poor. This is the kind of life Margery lived when she visited Rome. When she returned to England, however, her loud cries were considered a nuisance and public embarrassment; they continued for more than ten years, to the discomfort of both Margery and her community. Even after the cries departed, she continued her penitential weeping until she died.

Margery's status as a mystic has been debated by numerous scholars and was certainly open to question in her own day, despite the support she received from powerful churchmen. As stated earlier, most mystics proceed through the threefold experience of purgation, illumination, and union with God; the latter stage occurs only after a period of spiritual fatigue and a suffering from God's absence, known as "the dark night of the soul." Margery describes in her book an experience she had in a Roman church during prayer, in which she envisioned herself being married to Christ in a ceremony much like that of a contemporary English wedding. This "mystical wedding" is similar to the experience of infusion of the self with a divine Godhead, described by Continental women mystics. An illiterate laywoman, Margery had neither the vocabulary to describe such matters nor more-than-limited insight into them, unlike other mystics who were theologically knowledgeable and could express mystical experiences in a traditional, poetic language. It should not be concluded, however, that because she did not have the means to write a mystical treatise of the depth and power of Julian's *Revelations of Divine Love* her witnessing was therefore insincere or self-conceived. Margery's visions, prophetic powers, and public prayer were accepted, albeit with caution, by authorities in her own day. The single extant copy of her *Book* was preserved in a Carthusian monastery in Yorkshire in the fifteenth century. In addition, seven pages of extracts from *The Book of Margery Kempe* were printed in pamphlet (or popular) form by Wynkyn de Worde in 1501. Both facts attest that Margery's spiritual experience was considered by late-medieval people, whether lay or cleric, helpful guidance in the individual search for salvation. Clearly her religious conviction, open criticism of clerical corruption, and the dangerous paths she chose to tread distinguished her as an extraordinary woman.

That Margery was conscious of her own limitations is indisputable. Although she had the trained memory of an orally literate person, she hungered for the formal education available predominantly to nuns and noblewomen in her own day, demonstrated in the written works by and about religious women with whom she was familiar, such as Saint Bridget of Sweden, Marie d'Oignies, and Saint Elizabeth of Hungary. Margery's confessors, particularly Master Robert of Spryngolde, a parish priest who was also a bachelor of law, read to her from contemplative and theological treatises and the Bible. Like other holy women, she was reluctant to tell her story, for mystical experience was a problematic distinction for medieval women: it gave them a special authority and voice recognized by the church but simultaneously invited the male religious hierarchy to scrutinize the source of unusual religious experience. Such women might be embraced by their communities as seers and vessels of divine power, or condemned as heretics, as in Joan of Arc's case. Surely Margery was aware of the statute *De heretico comburendo,* passed by Parliament in 1401, sending heretics to the stake. Its first victim, William Sawtrey, a parish priest of Saint Margaret's Church in Margery's city, was burned on 2 March 1401. That she exercised caution in relating her spiritual autobiography, a privilege hither to be enjoyed by saints and aristocrats, is therefore hardly surprising. The religious climate did not encourage feelings of freedom, experimentation, or security.

That Margery's *Book* was written at all, let alone that it was preserved through the English Reformation, is somewhat miraculous. She dictated her life to two scribes and began after she was sixty years old to reconstruct her multifarious experiences without the benefits of notes, maps, or diaries. Having only her memory to consult, Margery acknowledges at the very beginning that her story will lack a chronological framework. This does not mean, however, that the *Book* has no shape or order at all. As Maureen Fries notes, the *Book* conforms to other patterns more in keeping with the function of a spiritual autobiography than a typical autobiography. In addition to the tripartite mystical structure, Margery's work demonstrates other themes and elements of medieval religious writings. For example, the *Book* opens with the experience of sickness and conversion – a common pattern in hagiography and mystical writings. The narrative, like medieval romance, has the cyclic form of quest or pilgrimage and return. Most important of all, Margery's *Book* incorporates the pattern of Christ's own life – his call in midlife to service and contemplation, his suffering and journeys, his poverty, and finally his death. The *Book* thus takes its place with popular Franciscan hagiography, Dante's *Divine Comedy*

(1321), William Langland's *Piers Plowman* (circa 1360–circa 1390), and the Middle English *Pearl.* Still, the construction of the *Book* presents difficulties to the modern reader that stem from the peculiar circumstances in which it was written.

Book 1, the first, lengthy part of the spiritual autobiography, consisting of eighty-nine chapters, was written by one scribe. Book 2 consists of ten chapters written by a second scribe who rewrote the first section. The first scribe was an Englishman who had lived in Germany for some time and could barely compose in English or German. Furthermore, his handwriting was so poor that the priest who rewrote it in 1436 had great difficulty reading the original. Margery was fortunate to find a literate second scribe who would undertake the task of revision, but he did so with some hesitation. Apparently he felt uncomfortable with the contents of her *Book* and waited four years before he would begin the work.

Ironically, *The Book of Margery Kempe* caused nearly as much trepidation when it was rediscovered in 1934 by William E. I. Butler-Bowdon in his family library in Lancashire. Scholars familiar with the extracts printed by de Worde and reprinted in 1521 by Henry Pepwell in a small devotional book of mystical writings assumed, as Pepwell had, that Margery was an "anccchoress" of King's Lynn, rather than a mother of fourteen children. Even modern scholars doubted the sincerity and integrity of a woman as boisterous, independent, and complex as Margery Kempe. The eloquent, learned notes of Hope Emily Allen in the 1940 edition of the manuscript published by the Early English Text Society first provided modern readers with information on late-medieval feminine spirituality necessary to place Margery Kempe in a social, religious, and historical context. Much of this scholarship was ignored, however, since early criticism focuses on the same issues of feminine behavior and propriety that preoccupied medieval authorities. With the revival of mystics studies in the 1980s, a large body of insightful scholarship has appeared, enabling the student of Margery Kempe to understand and appreciate this remarkable woman.

References:

Clarissa W. Atkinson, *Mystic and Pilgrim: The Book and the World of Margery Kempe* (Ithaca: Cornell University Press, 1983);

Sarah Beckwith, "Problems of Authority in Late Medieval English Mysticism: Language, Agency, and Authority in *The Book of Margery Kempe,*" *Exemplaria,* 4 (Spring 1992): 171–199;

Eric Colledge, "Margery Kempe," *Month,* 28 (July 1962): 16–29;

Louise Collis, *Memoirs of a Medieval Woman: The Life and Times of Margery Kempe* (New York: Crowell, 1964);

Denise L. Despres, "The Meditative Art of Scriptural Interpolation in *The Book of Margery Kempe,*" *Downside Review,* 106 (October 1988): 253–263;

Susan Dickman, "Margery Kempe and the Continental Tradition of The Pious Woman," in *The Medieval Mystical Tradition in England,* edited by Marion Glasscoe (Cambridge: Brewer, 1987), pp. 150–167;

Maureen Fries, "Margery Kempe," in *An Introduction to the Medieval Mystics of Europe,* edited by Paul Szarmach (Albany: State University of New York Press, 1984), pp. 217–235;

A. E. Goodman, "The Piety of John Brunham's Daughter of Lynn," in *Medieval Women,* edited by Derek Baker (Oxford: Blackwell, 1978), pp. 347–358;

Valerie M. Lagorio, "Defensorium Contra Oblectratores: A 'Discerning' Assessment of Margery Kempe," in *Mysticism: Medieval and Modern,* edited by Lagorio (Salzburg: University of Salzburg, 1986), pp. 29–48;

Karma Lochrie, "*The Book of Margery Kempe:* The Marginal Woman's Quest for Literary Authority," *Journal of Medieval and Renaissance Studies,* 16 (Spring 1986): 33–55;

Ute Stargardt, "The Beguines of Belgium, The Dominican Nuns of Germany, and Margery Kempe," in *The Popular Literature of Medieval England,* edited by Thomas J. Heffernan (Knoxville: University of Tennessee Press, 1985), pp. 277–313;

Hope Phyllis Weissman, "Margery Kempe in Jerusalem: Hysteria Compassio in the Late Middle Ages," in *Acts of Interpretation: The Text in Its Contexts, 700–1600,* edited by Mary T. Carruthers and Elizabeth D. Kirk (Norman, Okla.: Pilgrim Books, 1982), pp. 201–217.

William Langland

(circa 1330 – circa 1400)

Rosanne Gasse
Brandon University

MAJOR WORK: *Piers Plowman* (circa 1360–circa 1390)

Manuscripts: *Piers Plowman* survives in fifty-two known manuscripts. Robert Crowley's first printing of 1550 represents a lost manuscript, and Crowley's second and third printings represent still another lost manuscript and three fragments that do not derive from any known surviving copy. Of the surviving complete texts, ten are of the A-text, twelve of the B-text, and eighteen of the C-text. The remainder are composites. The most recent critical editions of the three versions are corrected from other manuscripts but based upon the following: [A-text] Trinity College Cambridge R.3.14, also known as T, a conjoint AC manuscript (C after A, X1) written in one good English vernacular hand about 1400; [B-text] Trinity College Cambridge B.15.17, also known as W, written in one *anglicana formata* hand about 1400; [C-text] Huntington Library HM 143, also known as X. Facsimile: *Piers Plowman: The Huntington Library Manuscript (HM 143)* (San Marino, Cal., 1936). Bodleian Library, Oxford, MS. Bodley 851 (Z) and Huntington Library, MS. 114 (Ht) possibly represent other textual traditions but are more likely to be pastiches.

First publication: *The Vision of Pierce Plowman* (London: Printed by Roberte Crowley, [1550]).

Standard editions: *The Vision of William Concerning Piers Plowman,* 5 volumes, edited by Walter W. Skeat, EETS, o.s. 28, 38, 54, 67, 81 (1867–1885); *The Vision of William Concerning Piers the Plowman in Three Parallel Texts,* 2 volumes, edited by Skeat (Oxford: Clarendon Press, 1886; reprinted, with additional bibliography by J. A. W. Bennett, 1954); *Piers Plowman: The A Version. Will's Vision of Piers Plowman and Do-Well,* edited by George Kane (London: Athlone Press, 1960); *Piers Plowman: The B Ver-sion. Will's Visions of Piers Plowman, Do-Well, Do-Better and Do-Best,* edited by Kane and E. Talbot Donaldson (London: Athlone Press, 1975); *Piers Plowman: An Edition of the C-text,* edited by Derek Pearsall, York Medieval Texts, second series (London: Edward Arnold, 1978).

Edition in modern English: *Piers the Plough-man,* translated by J. F. Goodridge (Harmondsworth: Penguin, 1959).

The earliest publishers of *Piers Plowman* assumed that there was one version of the poem. By the early nineteenth century it had become evident that there are three different versions of *Piers Plowman,* known as the A-text, the B-text, and the C-text since Walter W. Skeat's editions of 1867, 1869, and 1873 respectively. The A-text is the earliest and shortest of the three versions, being roughly 2,400 lines long. The B-text is an extensive reworking of the A-text: the original 2,400 lines are transformed into 3,200 lines, and more than 4,000 lines of new material are added. The B-text is the most poetic of the three versions, and the majority of criticism (including this essay) is based upon it. In comparison, the C-text is more prosaic. C is almost a total revision of B, except for the last two *passus* which are untouched (the various sections of all three versions are called by the Latin word *passus;* the singular spelling is the same as the plural). Elsewhere, the cuts, additions, and shifting of passages result in a slightly longer poem (7,338 lines), but one which is radically different in style and effect.

There has been much debate regarding the dates of composition for the three recensions, but the A-text is usually dated as completed by 1370, while the B-text seems to be the product of the mid to late 1370s. The "Parliament of Rats" in the prologue likely refers to the Good Parliament of 1376, and the later *passus* contain several possible allusions to the Papal Schism of 1379. The C-text is the hardest to date, but some changes made to it strongly suggest a date shortly after the Peasants' Revolt of 1381. The C-text, then, may be dated between 1382 and 1387. *Piers Plowman* is thus the product of nearly thirty years' labor, as its author wrote and revised the poem in a near-constant fashion.

Although Skeat claimed that all three versions were written by one individual, the question of whether the three recensions are the product of single or multiple authorship was long a point of contention. After George Kane's thorough study of the available internal and external evidence in his *Piers Plowman: The Evidence for Authorship* (1965), single authorship is now generally, though not universally, accepted. The author's name may appear within the text at B, 15, 152 in the first person narrator's remark, "I have lyved in *londe*, . . . my name is *Longe Wille*." Read in reverse order the emphasized words form the "name" Wille Longe londe, leading to speculation that the author's name was William Langland. As some manuscript attributions use this name, "William Langland" has come to be accepted as that of the author.

Beyond this, little can be said with any certainty about the author of *Piers Plowman*. He was probably a cleric, but if he was married, as is the narrator within the text, he could only have been in minor orders. The knowledge the narrator displays suggests that Langland possessed some higher education, but the Latin quotations from the church fathers and the Latin and vernacular tags he employs probably came from the numerous handbooks and manuals that collated such material into convenient sources. He also had some legal background. *Piers Plowman* was the lifework of Langland as a writer. No other text can be attributed to him.

The geography and verse form can also tell the reader something about the historical Langland. He was a writer who belonged both to the western Midlands, situated near the Malvern Hills where the poem begins, and to the city of London. The dual nature of Langland's life can be seen in the wide scope of his vision of English society, from the pomp and majesty of the trial of Lady Meed at the King's court to the wretched poverty of life on Piers Plowman's half-acre. The poem also demonstrates its dual nature in its verse form, the alliterative line and circular structure characteristic of the alliterative revival of the northwest.

Practically no aspect of English medieval life passes without comment in *Piers Plowman*. The text draws upon a number of literary forms – among them the beast fable, sermon, and debate – but Langland is primarily a satirist working within a complex allegorical dream vision. In it Langland grapples with the most serious questions of his generation, so he must be viewed in the context of the religious, social and economic upheavals sweeping mid- to late-fourteenth-century England. *Piers Plowman* is a series of quests, of searches for answers as the dream narrator Will goes from authority to authority. The object of the search, however, changes as the poem proceeds. First the search is for what is expected of the Christian living in the world, then its object becomes Truth and salvation, and this transforms into a quest for Dowel, Dobet and Dobest (that is, do well, do better, and do best), which becomes in turn a vision of Faith, Hope, and Charity, which at length returns the Dreamer to the human world. The poem concludes with the beginning of yet another quest as Conscience vows to become a pilgrim "and walken as wide as the world lasteth, / To seken Piers the Plowman." The fact that *Piers Plowman* concludes with a new quest makes it clear that Langland is concerned with searching; he does not offer any hard and fast solutions. Will the Dreamer is always directed toward a new path. The point is clear: the Christian quest for salvation is never ending.

The opening lines of the prologue set the work in the familiar context of the dream vision: it is a usual May morning when the narrator, exhausted from his wanderings, falls asleep. The interesting aspect is the narrator's state of dress. He is in "shroudes as [he] a sheep were, / In habite as an heremite unholy of werkes." These details are symbolic of the narrator's uncertain spiritual condition. The sheep represents the saved Christian in the New Testament, but the wording here suggests that the narrator might be a wolf in sheep's clothing instead. Hermits are men and women who have renounced the world and devoted their lives to God in contemplation, but they can only do so at the expense of others. Other people must endow the monasteries or support hermits with alms. The potential for abuse is great, as the lazy individual dons the garb of the contemplative and lives comfortably off alms from the pious without giving anything in return. The false contemplatives are thus a drain on the resources of the community and also a threat to its spiritual health. The false contemplatives are wolves in sheep's clothing, having the appearance of holiness – the habit – but none of the substance. Will thus puts himself into a position at the beginning of the poem that only raises questions. As a hermit in sheep's clothing, is he part of the problem or the solution? What kind of hermit is he? How does one tell the true contemplative from the false?

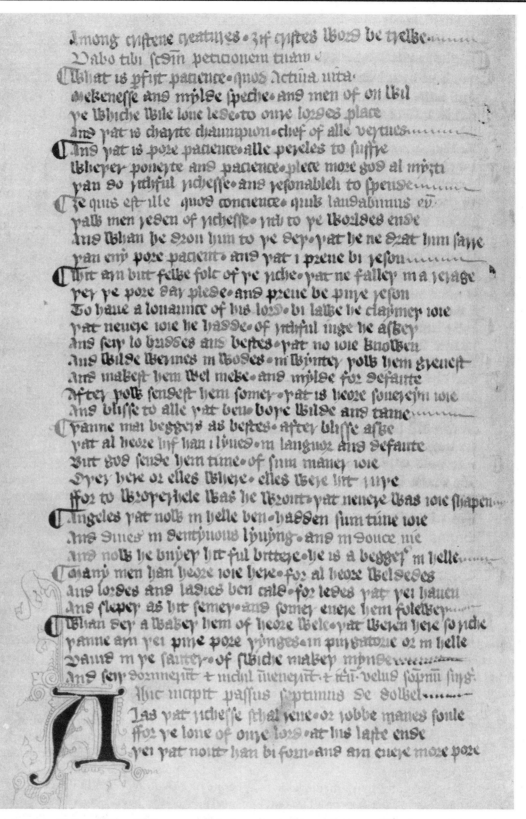

Page from the C-text of Piers Plowman, *a scribal transcription dated circa 1390–1400 (British Library, MS. Cotton Vespasian B.xvi, fol. 64ᵛ)*

A solution to this last question is implied in Will's description of himself as "unholy of werkes." The expression does not mean that Will is evil. It is part of Langland's emphasis throughout *Piers Plowman* on the spirit of James 2:2 (quoted at B, 1, 187a) – that faith without good works is dead. Later, during the quest for Dowel, Dobet, and Dobest, one cannot forget the verbal action implied in those terms. The Christian is to *do* well, not simply be well, for Christian faith must be expressed in actions before it is valid. Will, however, is "unholy of werkes" at the beginning – which means that he has performed no works at all and is metaphorically a child. By the end of the poem he will be an old man on the verge of death. The majority of the poem traces Will's development through life as he chooses between doing good and bad works. To some degree this life journey can be seen as autobiography, but primarily it is allegory. Will is not just William; he is the human will personified in human flesh – *will* being the intellectual faculty which enables an individual to make a choice and put it into action. The protagonist is thus an Everyman figure whose struggles represent the human struggle for salvation.

The dream landscape into which Will enters furthers this idea of choice. Again the details are symbolic. The wilderness is the earth and the unknown dangers it entails. The tower on a "toft" in the east is heaven; the deep dale and its dungeon are hell. These two put the poem in a cosmic perspective. What lies between the two extremes of heaven and hell is Langland's major concern: namely, the Field Full of Folk which represents the Christian community. The presence of heaven and hell reminds the reader that choices made during the transitory life on earth have eternal consequences. One is, in effect, challenged to choose between heaven and hell.

The complete social spectrum is portrayed in the Field Full of Folk: the three estates, the rich and the poor, men and women. At once the element of choice appears. The people are "werking and wandering as the world asketh." Clearly the world's demand is interpreted in two different ways: there are those who work hard and obey the strictest dictates of their social position and estate, and there are those who selfishly accumulate material goods. Yet Langland is not being morally ambiguous, for the distinction between the right choice and the wrong choice is clear-cut. Hardworking plowmen, anchorites and hermits who keep to their cells, and guiltless minstrels are the sort who are bound for heaven. The rest – gluttons, hermits in a heap, and

friars, just to name a few – are the sort who are bound for hell. They have made the world and its pursuits their all. Notably, of those who have chosen worldliness, half are from the clerical estate. This spiritual rot undermines the Christian community throughout *Piers Plowman* and causes its final collapse.

The feudal spectrum of the Field Full of Folk is incomplete until the introduction of the King. There has been considerable disagreement over Langland's political views as expressed in the prologue, ranging from those who believe Langland's political views are democratic in the B-text to those who argue that Langland is an absolutist. Some critics argue that Langland's political leanings can be seen to change in the three versions; others argue that he was consistently conservative in preferring absolute rule of a king to that of a sycophantic mob. The system established by Kynde Wit (common sense) is the ideal scenario of all three social estates working in unison for the common good. The set-up described by the angel and goliard is also an idealized scenario: the King is granted unlimited power and the people commit themselves willingly to obey. This unrestricted power, however, presents problems which are illustrated in the political fable of the Parliament of Rats. The predatory cat who torments the rats represents royal authority at its worst: capricious, arbitrary, and cruel. The rats desire to curb this royal tyranny by belling the cat, but not one of them volunteers to do so, and they opt instead for the status quo. They must wait for their opportunity when the cat dies and a kitten takes its place. Yet Langland makes it clear that he is not advocating the rule of the rats over the rule of the cat. The rats are cowardly, destructive creatures who have no self-restraint; their rule would be chaos. The rats do not represent the oppressed masses; they represent the selfish (and therefore destructive) forces in society – the gluttons, false hermits, and other social parasites – who are only kept in check by an equally selfish and destructive force – the King. The ideal may be the three estates working in harmony according to the dictates of common sense, but the reality is once again a choice between tyranny or social collapse. Selfishness is the cause of this uncomfortable choice on both a social and spiritual scale: first, individuals putting their wants and desires before the common good; and second, individuals putting themselves before God. This human devotion to the self is underscored by the end of the prologue as the scene dissolves with an appeal to the pleasures of the flesh.

The prologue sets up the situation into which Will is metaphorically born. With the appearance of Holy Church in the opening lines of *passus* 1, Will is ready to begin his education. Holy Church is a familiar character in medieval literature. She is a wise woman counselor in the tradition of Lady Philosophy from Boethius's *Consolation of Philosophy* (circa 525). She represents *Ecclesia,* the eternal and divine Church untouched by human corruption and weakness, and she functions as Will's catechist, teaching him the rudiments of his Christian faith and the basics of Christian behavior. She especially emphasizes the need to be wary of the body's desires. The body cannot be trusted, for, unlike the soul which is taught by the divine Church and guided toward moderation by Reason, the body is taught by the World, the Flesh, and the Fiend (the familiar anti-Trinity) and is immoderate in all things. Thus, Will is again presented with a demand that he make a choice: the body and soul are in constant struggle for dominance, and what is good for one is invariably not good for the other. Will must find the balance between the conflicting physical desires of the body and the spiritual desires of the soul. Life on earth means that a human must by necessity be concerned to some degree about material things in order to stay alive, but even this concern for the good of the body distracts the soul. The balance is Truth, the best treasure, which allows three things in moderation: clothes (shelter in general), food, and drink.

Reason and moderation are important agents of self-control in *Piers Plowman*. The problem of self-rule has thus a simple solution: reasonability, but it is typical of the medieval perspective that the difficulty does not lie in not knowing what one should do but in acting upon what one knows. Even at this early point in *Piers Plowman* Will does not need any more education; he already knows all that he needs to know. Kynde Wit tells him what is commonsensical, Reason tells him what is reasonable and moderate, Holy Church tells him the rudiments of his faith, and Truth through Holy Church tells Will what is expected of him: he must be true of tongue, true of work, and true of intention. Will therefore *knows* the truth, but he is not yet able to *act* upon this knowledge. This inability is due in part to his being a typically obtuse dream-vision narrator. But Will's inability to act goes back to his allegorical nature as the human will, the intellectual faculty of choice and action, neither of which is this Will seemingly capable.

Before Will can understand fully what Truth is, he needs to know what it is *not:* that is, Falseness. This is the subject of *passus* 2. Holy Church does not explain the nature of Falseness to Will; instead,

it is demonstrated to him by the story of Lady Meed, the first of several ambivalent characters in the text. On the one hand, she is the bastard daughter of False and about to be wed to Fals Fikel-tonge. Her description, especially her scarlet robe, recalls the Whore of Babylon in Revelation. She also looks like Alice Perrers, the extravagant and much-hated mistress of Edward III. This aspect of Lady Meed represents the corruptive influence of money (bribery, simony, prostitution), and she is everywhere. She is even as intimate with the papacy as Holy Church. On the other hand, she is the legitimate daughter of Amendes and is intended by God to wed Truth. This aspect of Lady Meed represents the legitimate uses of money in such matters as payment for work and material restitution. The problem with Lady Meed is that she can be used by anyone and is thus very dangerous. Even with the best of intentions, money may come to be used for illegitimate purposes.

Lady Meed's impending marriage to Fals Fikel-tonge is prevented by Theology, who insists that the King decide whom Lady Meed should marry. The scene shifts back to the royal court as Lady Meed and her entourage travel to London riding on the backs of various legal officials. The King, however, is a good ruler. He listens to Conscience, swears he will have nothing to do with wickedness, and plans to punish the evildoers. The latter are warned of the King's good intentions and abandon Lady Meed. *Passus* 2 concludes with Lady Meed all alone, her fate in the King's hands.

The King has already demonstrated promise in listening to Conscience, yet at the start of *passus* 3 there are ominous signs of trouble. He states his intention to "assayen" Lady Meed, to investigate the sort of character she is, but he also decides "if she werche bi wit and my wil folwe I wol forgyven hire this gift." The King intends for Lady Meed to follow his will, ultimately expressed by his wish that she marry Conscience – the ability to know the right from the wrong. The King's desire is well-intentioned. He thinks that by joining Conscience and Lady Meed he will subsequently reward only those who deserve it. Yet the King does not realize that Lady Meed's nature is ambivalent, that he cannot use her solely for good, since even when the donor has the best of intentions she always has the potential to corrupt. Lady Meed is likely to destroy quickly a person's sense of right and wrong. The King is confident that he can control Lady Meed, but Conscience points out that it is she who would soon control him.

Lady Meed quickly corrupts those in the legal system, those looking for promotion at court, those involved in trade, and, most ominously, the friars. The latter are accused of perverting the sacrament of penance, the means by which the sinner is reconciled to God and the sacrament in which the sinner admits responsibility and expresses a desire to amend. Penance, thus, should both renew the sinner's relationship with God and function as a means by which society as a whole can be transformed. The friars undermine both roles of the sacrament by turning it into a financial transaction, accepting money as proof of contrition as well as the required satisfaction. Lechery, for example, is no longer a serious moral offence that alienates the sinner from God but a small offence that is easily paid for. The rich in particular have no motivation to improve their lives morally or socially since they can do what they please if they can afford to pay for it in the confessional. The friars' corruption of the sacrament of penance will undermine the Christian community. It will be critical in the unfolding of events at the poem's end.

Lady Meed debates her merits with Conscience, pointing out the good things about her nature, while Conscience emphasizes the bad and underscores her essential ambivalence. Lady Meed appeals to scriptural authority with a quotation from Proverbs 22:9 that at first glance seems to support her side: "Honorem adquiret qui dat munera" (He who gives riches receives honor and victory). Yet Lady Meed has not quoted the entire line, and Conscience triumphantly finishes it: "Animam autem aufert accipientium" (But he carries away the soul of the receiver). Lady Meed's own words betray that whatever benefits she may bring, like worship and victory, come at a very high and dubious price: the freedom of the soul.

Conscience wins the debate, but the King is still not convinced of Lady Meed's dangerous nature and tries to reconcile them forcibly by ordering Conscience to give her the kiss of peace. Conscience refuses unless Reason assents first. The King again demonstrates his potential for good by agreeing to Conscience's request that Reason (the ability to weigh the pros and cons of a situation) be summoned. Immediately a test of the King's justice is presented to the court in the legal case of Peace versus Wrong. Wisdom and Wit, figured as lawyers, argue a course of action seconded by Lady Meed: Wrong should be allowed to buy his way out of the charges against him — which include rape, murder, and theft. Reason argues for harsh punishment. In the end, the King realizes the right and acts reasonably: Wrong is punished, Lady Meed is recognized for the troublesome quality she is, and Conscience

and Reason are accepted as the King's counselors. This is political wishful thinking, an idealized court where the King, if not absolutely perfect, does successfully balance conflicting forces and acts upon the advice of Conscience and Reason. He is a portrait of a good king, a strong, but not abusive, authority. There is only one problem, noted by Conscience: "But the commune wol assente, / It is ful hard, by myn heed, herto to brynge it, / And alle youre lige leodes [people] to lede thus evene."

This King is an idealized king of England, but the message of the passage is more general. Conscience and Reason are faculties that all humans possess to some degree. The conflict between Peace and Wrong is a common one, if not always as extreme as that in the poem. The problem presented by Lady Meed is also a universal one. The King's dilemma is not an abstract one limited to those of royal blood. The King is another Everyman, and his dilemma is one all humans must face.

The scene returns to the Field Full of Folk at the start of *passus* 5 as the Dreamer wakes up and then falls asleep again. The link is the figure of Reason, dressed as a bishop, who advises the people to repent and reform. One of the most memorable sections of the text follows: the confession of the Seven Deadly Sins. Each of the Sins confesses, yet there are many signs that there has been no inner spiritual renewal. Repentance, for example, asks Covetousness if he has ever repented or made restitution. Covetousness does not even know what restitution means, and he certainly does not understand its importance to the sacrament. The confession has the correct outward form but little evidence of any inner sense of conversion. Reason has led the people to repent, repentance has led the people to Hope, and Hope has led the people to the first quest in *Piers Plowman* – that for Truth. Yet the people are lost on this spiritual journey. They "blustreden forth as beestes" and need to ask for directions. The point is that humans need more than Reason to advise them; they need faith as well, which is absent here.

Just how lost the people are is evidenced when they first seek direction. They ask someone who has the correct outward form: a man who is dressed as a pilgrim and who has been to most of the major shrines. But this guide knows the way to Truth no better than the rest, for he is a professional pilgrim whose journeys have been physical adventures, not spiritual ones. There is no substance in the form.

At this point someone who does know the way to Truth suddenly appears: Piers Plowman, whose identity is very complex. Literally, he is a simple

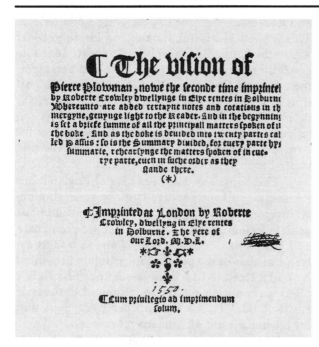

Title page for the earliest extant edition of Langland's poem

plowman of the third estate, the lowest of the low on the social scale. Unlike the professional pilgrim, who looks as if he would know something, Piers looks least likely to know anything. He is proof that spirituality has nothing to do with social status. But Piers is also meant to be taken symbolically as the good priest who harvests Christian souls, who plows the Gospels to prepare their message for his congregation, and who uses his tongue as a plowshare in his sermons. Later visions reveal that Piers Plowman is Truth/Good Samaritan/Christ/Eucharist, but at first such connections are only suggested. Piers is seen here as a follower of Truth. Through him the importance of good works is again stressed since Piers follows Truth through labor and not pilgrimages to far-off lands. His directions to Truth indicate an inner spiritual journey through Meekness to Conscience, over to the obedience of the Ten Commandments, to the moat of Mercy, through the walls of Wit, past Grace the porter, to arrive at Truth, which in the end is sitting "in thyn herte." In spite of very clear directions, not all the people accept Piers's guidance. Some still prefer to put their trust in such external paraphernalia as indulgences and bulls.

Passus 6 returns to the discussion of the world's demands of the individual. Piers becomes, in effect, a king, as he equitably divides labor between the estates, social classes, and sexes. In this idealized scheme everyone has duties and responsibilities so that the whole can function smoothly:

women make cloth and plowmen produce food. Langland uses the events of *passus* 6 to demonstrate the differences between how feudalism should be and the corrupted reality of the fourteenth century. This is clearly illustrated in the role of the knight whose role as protector of society is emphasized. He plights his troth to defend feudalism against what the rats and mice of the prologue represent, both literally and figuratively: real animals, and wasteful, wicked human parasites. For a time all is well; then Piers discovers that some will not or cannot work. He is willing to support out of Christian charity those who really do need help, but he is unwilling to support parasites, the professional beggars, false hermits, and so on. When Piers confronts these parasites, they simply refuse to work. He then turns to the knight to fulfill his pledge to defend society from such a threat. True to his word, the knight tries to enforce the law, but is ignored and insulted. Conscience's cautionary words to the King in *Passus* 4 are now self-evident: without the cooperation of the people governed, political authority is ineffective. Unless the knight is willing to play the tyrant like the cat of the prologue, he cannot fulfill his role in society.

In anger, Piers calls upon Hunger to help him, a strategy that quickly puts the parasites to work; but as soon as Hunger no longer poses a threat, they return to their wasteful ways. It may appear peculiar that Piers Plowman, the representative of Truth and later the human manifestation of Christ the Good Samaritan, would call upon something so seemingly uncharitable as Hunger, yet this would be to misunderstand the episode. Hunger is not to be seen as an evil or even amoral force. It is first of all the logical extension of human action: if too few produce, soon all will starve. But it is also a moral force for the good, as is demonstrated in Hunger's conversation with Piers where it reinforces, first, Piers's own belief that the needy must be supported and the parasites ignored; second, Holy Church's earlier insistence upon moderation; and third, Kynde Wit's message that work is necessary. Hunger is shown to be part of the larger good but is limited because it is coercive and external to the individual.

Passus 7 concerns the pardon sent from Truth to Piers Plowman and therefore to the whole Christian community, represented by the Field Full of Folk. The pardon absolves both *a poena et a culpa,* that is, from punishment and guilt. As such, it does not have the usual form or function of a pardon. It combines the function and powers of an indulgence, since it will enable the recipient "thorugh purgatorie to passen ful lightly," and the sacrament of penance, the only orthodox means by which absolution from guilt can be obtained. The pardon's combination of the sacrament and the indulgence strengthens the connections between Christ, Truth, and Piers Plowman, as well as between Piers Plowman and the priesthood.

Although the pardon cannot be used in this life, it shows the importance of work in Langland's vision. Those included in Truth's pardon are those who work hard and use their talents to support the less fortunate. Truth's pardon very carefully and explicitly includes those who cannot work, such as the old, the pregnant, the sick, the blind, and the crippled. Those who can work but refuse are pointedly left out. Corrupt friars, false contemplatives (especially in the C-text), and professional beggars are excluded from Truth's pardon and any claim upon the charity of others.

Passus 7 contains what is probably the most controversial scene in all of *Piers Plowman:* the confrontation between Piers and a priest over this pardon. The episode begins when a priest in the crowd asks to see the pardon so that he can "construe" it, that is, interpret its meaning in the medieval exegetical fashion. The priest's demand is, on one level, well-intentioned, as he is offering to put the pardon's Latin text into words that simple plowmen and others can understand. On another level, given the deeper meanings behind Piers Plowman as the Good Priest, Truth, and Christ, the priest's actions are a challenge and lead to conflict. When the priest reads the pardon he sees only a worthless scrap of paper – no pardon at all. When Piers's interpretation is contradicted by the priest, Piers rips the pardon in two and swears off sowing, "swynking," and belly joy in favor of prayers, penance, and weeping. The two men become embroiled in a heated exchange, and the Dreamer abruptly wakes up.

There are several points of contention in this scene, and there is no general consensus on any of them. The first dilemma is whose interpretation of the pardon is correct, that of Piers or of the priest. Most critics favor Piers, but some support the priest. In the literal sense the priest is right. The pardon does not have the correct form and in legal terms that would invalidate it. Nor does it actually pardon anything since the text is really just a simple statement about the consequences of human actions: if one does well, one goes to heaven; if one does evil, one goes to hell. On the other hand, the usual medieval belief was that no one deserved heaven as a reward. Thus, in a sense the document is a pardon, as it commutes the sentence from certain damnation to conditional salvation. The argument that the pardon does not have the correct form actually works against the priest since the idea of "form" recalls previous instances in the poem of the opposition of form to substance.

More difficult to resolve is Piers's tearing of the pardon. The reader should consider two factors. First, it is unlikely, given his symbolic value, that Piers is meant to be doing the wrong thing in this scene. It could be that the tearing of the pardon is meant to be seen as wrong from a limited, human point of view, yet right from the omniscient, divine point of view. Second, the Dreamer's musings on the scene cannot be taken as Langland's thoughts, for the Dreamer's spiritual education is far from complete. Another consideration is that, although the tearing seems to be a critical moment in the B-text, it does not appear in the C-text. C follows B closely up to the priest's rejection of the pardon; it then abruptly ends the scene with Piers and the priest beginning to argue. If the tearing of the pardon was so crucial to Langland's conception of the poem, then why (assuming single authorship) did he choose to cut the scene from the C version? It could be simply that Langland did not feel the scene to be all that important. More likely, the changes in the C-text reflect Langland's fears about misinterpretation. Perhaps he realized that the episode was far too ambiguous – certainly the mass of contradictory critical interpretations of the tearing scene attests to its lack of clarity. One reason why Langland would have had to make changes here was the Peasants' Revolt of 1381, in which the peasant rebels murdered Simon Sudbury, the archbishop of Canterbury. The revolt was a traumatic experience for the ruling class, and, in light of it, the scene in the B-text, in which a peasant reacts with violence to a clergyman, takes on a significantly different dimension. Langland likely distanced himself as quickly as possible from any dangerously subversive suggestion that he approved of the peasant rebels.

There is also a possible connection between Piers's tearing of the pardon and the rejection of the Active Life in favor of the Contemplative Life. The concept of the Active and Contemplative Lives is a very common motif grounded in the New Testament story of Martha and Mary. The Active Life of Martha is concerned with physical labor, but within a Christian perspective. The Contemplative Life of Mary is a turning away from the physical to the spiritual. The Active Life is good, but the Contemplative Life is better, although more difficult to maintain. Piers's vow sounds like a transition from the physical to the spiritual, the Active to the Contemplative. Some critics object that the stress remains on *doing* things and that Piers's vow thus cannot be a rejection of the Active Life, but such reasoning is based on false premises. The Active Life is described as active because it obviously entails hard, active labor, but that does not mean the Contemplative Life must be passive and involve no work. After all, faith without good works is dead. Langland's conception here is of a very aggressive spirituality. Piers shall continue to plow, only his materials and mode change from the physical to the spiritual. Even so, Piers's vow is not technically the same as the transition from the Active to the Contemplative Lives, for these were very precise terms in the Middle Ages. In any case, the tearing of the pardon and Piers's renunciation of his past life do mark the point at which *Piers Plowman* changes its focus from the social to the individual as the search for Truth on a social scale turns into the Dreamer's individual quest for the "Three Lives" of Dowel, Dobet, and Dobest.

Will's quest marks an improvement in his character that is underscored by the echoes between the beginnings of the prologue and *passus* 8. At the beginning Will wandered about without direction to hear wonders; in *passus* 8 he is still wandering, but this time with a specific goal in mind. There is also an echo of the beginning of the search for Truth, which had almost ended before it began with the Field Full of Folk turning to a false authority — the professional pilgrim — for guidance. Here Will's search is nearly sidetracked by the two friars he meets who claim that Dowel lives with them, but he recognizes the exaggeration of their claim and continues his search. He encounters a series of allegorical authority figures such as Thought, Wit, Study, Clergy, Scripture, Imaginatif, Patience, and Anima, who all offer definitions of Dowel, Dobet, and Dobest. Most of these figures are manifestations of faculties possessed by every human; therefore, Will is in a sense meeting aspects of his own self, a fact that emphasizes the individual, internal nature of the quest yet maintains its universality. This may explain why the divisions between speakers in this section are so obscure: in a sense they are all the same person.

What Dowel, Dobet, and Dobest represent is another point of contention. There have been many attempts to equate them with the triad of the Active, Contemplative, and Mixed Lives or with the triad of the Illuminative, Purgative, and Unitive stages of mysticism. To some degree these schemata have merit, yet neither fits the context exactly. For exam-

ple, Thought defines the Three Lives, with Dowel being honest labor, Dobet being compassion for others, and Dobest being the reprimand of sinners. This can fit neatly into the Active-Contemplative-Mixed triad if Dowel is equated simply with the Active Life, Dobet the Contemplative, and Dobest with the Mixed — the Mixed Life being a combination of the physical deeds of action and the prayerful deeds of contemplation seen in the role and function of a bishop, and it is noteworthy that Dobest bears a bishop's crook. Nevertheless, Langland makes no mention of the Mixed Life by name even when ample opportunity arises, as in the C-text when Will specifically states without contradiction that there are but two Lives (8.81). Moreover, examination of the details in Thought's description reveals that they are not specific to any one of the traditional lives. Does the reader believe that only bishops can reprimand sinners? The description of Dobet in particular does not fit its place in the triad very well. It begins with preaching and interpreting the Bible which were indeed exclusive functions of the clergy; but it also includes the prevention of financial abuse and the distribution of wealth to the poor which surely are activities as open to the laity as the clergy.

What is truly important is the pattern that Langland consistently builds between the three lives. Dowel's focus is on what one must do for oneself. Dobet puts the person into the larger context of a community and focuses on what one must do to meet the physical needs of other people. Dobest also functions within the context of a larger community; however, the focus this time is upon how one must act to meet the spiritual needs of other people. The three stages build upon one another: to care for another's spiritual needs one must first care for that person's physical needs. Dobest therefore entails the other two. Wit's definition (9.200-207) is similar. Dowel is self-contained: personal obedience to the Ten Commandments. Dobet includes others: love of friend and foe. Dobest goes even farther, since it expresses that love in action by giving to, caring for, healing, and helping friend and foe. Always the definitions entail doing more than one has done before, and thus ultimately the quest for Dowel, Dobet and Dobest will give way to the Dreamer's vision of Faith, Hope, and Charity in the guise of Abraham, Moses, and the Good Samaritan/Christ in *passus* 16 and *passus* 17.

Although the definitions given to Will have a consistent pattern, his journey is not a smooth one. He is sidetracked in *passus* 11 by Fortune and taken to the land of longing and love where he is persuaded by the three temptations of the Lust of the Flesh, the Covetousness of the Eyes, and the Pride of Life to enjoy a materialistic life. He is warned of his folly by Old Age, but Will at this point is at the height of his health and wealth and trusts in friars to ensure he will be saved at a later date, only to be deserted by them when his wealth fails.

If salvation cannot be bought, how can it be gained? Langland spends some time discussing a problematic theological point in the fourteenth century: the fate of the righteous heathen. Scripture offers the strict interpretation: only the Christian is saved through faith. (The A-text ends approximately at this point.) However, Scripture is contradicted by the example of the Roman emperor, Trajan, who was not saved by faith yet nevertheless broke out of hell through the uprightness of his life. Langland raises the subject to emphasize the importance of action. Will is a baptized Christian, and baptism is an expression of Christian faith, but baptism alone does not guarantee salvation. The onus is always on the individual to act in a Christian manner, for faith without good works is dead. The dilemma of the salvation of the heathen is solved in *passus* 12 by Imaginatif, who first points out that there are levels of reward in heaven and that Trajan could never attain the same closeness to God a baptized Christian can.

Langland firmly grounds the ability to maintain a Christian life in divine grace. Imaginatif quotes, "salvabitur vix iustus in die iudicii; ergo – salvabitur!" (The just man will scarcely be saved on the day of judgment; therefore – he will be saved!) The Latin employs a common pun in exegetical writing. The literal text emphasizes that no one, even the righteous, deserves to be saved. Yet *vix* (scarcely), which literally seems to exclude most people, actually offers hope for all since it is an allusion to Christ's Passion. *Vix* refers to the five wounds of Jesus Christ suffered on the cross (V = Roman numeral five; I = Latin letter I in Iesus; X = the Greek letter chi in Christ). Humans are thus saved by God's divine grace.

Passus 13 begins with the Dreamer awakening to contemplate his experiences and then again falling asleep. It is largely taken up by two episodes: the Feast of Patience and Will's encounter with Haukyn the Active Man. Six people attend the Feast: Conscience; Clergy and his wife, Scripture; Patience; Will; and a Master of Divinity. The latter is a friar and theologian. The rich foods he eats and the good wine he drinks are metaphors for elaborate exegetical interpretations of the Bible which serve only to obfuscate its meaning. Will and

Patience's food, in contrast, is very simple. It is also allegorized, since the dishes are named as Latin quotations which encourage the sacrament of penance. The Feast reminds the reader of the importance of the sacrament, and it also attacks current practices of exegesis and implicitly connects friars again with the corruption of penance.

Will next meets Haukyn the active man, a personification of the Active Life. Like Will, Haukyn is cast into ambivalent roles. He is a "minstral," but the prologue talks of good and bad minstrels. He is also a waferer, but could sell either bread for the body or bread for the soul (that is, the Eucharist). Haukyn represents what is good about the Active Life – its hatred of idleness, for example – but mostly he underscores its limitations, symbolized by his coat, which is then described at great length. Like Will's clothing, Haukyn's coat is a metaphor for his spiritual condition. Each sin committed stains his coat, which is then cleansed by the sacrament of penance, yet no sooner is it clean than it is again soiled. Patience offers guidance, extolling the benefits of patient poverty. Haukyn responds with genuine contrition, and Will awakens at the end of *passus* 14.

Passus 15 begins with Will characterized as a fool. This may seem derogatory, but it actually marks progress, for the word *fool* recalls 1 Corinthians 4:10. Will is a fool from the world's limited point of view, and in that state of mind he falls asleep and meets the last of the major allegorical figures, Anima (Liberum Arbitrium in the C-text), who points out to Will the importance of putting into action all that he has learned. He supports Patience's advice on poverty and especially stresses the importance of charity. Anima thus prepares Will for a vision of the Tree of Charity in *passus* 16, a vision granted and explained to Will by Piers Plowman himself. This tree is an image of fallen humanity. Its three kinds of fruit are human souls in the states of wedlock, widowhood, and virginity, and it is supported by three planks – the Trinity. Yet the Tree is under constant threat by Covetise, the Flesh, and the Fiend. The Devil eagerly snatches up the fallen, unredeemed fruit despite Piers's efforts to save it, for humanity will only be redeemed when Jesus Christ jousts with the Devil for the fruit. Langland reenters historical time at the moment of Incarnation and quickly summarizes the life and death of Christ. The Dreamer encounters Faith, Hope, and the Good Samaritan, who is visualized as a knight riding off to a joust in Jerusalem and who pauses to explain to Will the limitations of Faith and Hope as well as the nature of the divine.

He then leaves Will to awaken once again at the end of *passus* 17.

In *passus* 18 Will is dressed like a "reccheles renk," a penitent man careless about the things of this world. His change in dress reveals that he has learned from his experiences. He falls asleep again, sleeping through Lent to Palm Sunday, during which time he dreams of a knight who has a "semblance to the Samaritan, and somdeel to Piers the Plowman" riding on an ass toward Jerusalem. The events of Holy Week unfold as Langland conflates history, the ecclesiastical year, and allegory into one. The effect is that Will does not briefly hear of Christ's triumph over the Devil as he did in *passus* 16; instead, he is an eyewitness to these sacred events as they unfold in detail. The Triumphant Entry into Jerusalem, the trial before Pilate, the Crucifixion and Death, blind Longinus and his spear, the Debate of the Four Daughters of God, and the Harrowing of Hell are all recounted. *Passus* 18 concludes with Will waking up to the bells ringing on Easter Sunday.

At the start of *passus* 19 Will goes to mass on Easter Sunday and, during the middle of mass, falls asleep and dreams of Piers Plowman, this time "peynted al blody / And com in with a cros bifore the comune peple, / And right lik in all lymes to Oure Lord Iesu." Piers is identified this time as the eucharistic Host at the moment of consecration during the Mass when the bread and wine become the Body and Blood of Christ. The mystery of transubstantiation is illustrated by the sudden appearance of Piers before the people. Will turns to Conscience for an explanation of the mystery. In answer, Conscience reviews the life of Jesus in terms of the sacraments. The miracle at Cana involves the changing of water into wine, a type of wine turning into blood in the Eucharist. The whole episode is not only an allusion to the Eucharist, it is also explicitly related to Dowel. Thus, the Three Lives are put into the perspective of the ministry of Christ, and the message is clear: it is impossible to do well, do better, and do best without divine grace, and this grace is available to all through the sacraments, especially the Eucharist and penance. If Dowel is the sacramental wine, Dobet is the eucharistic bread, as it is paralleled to the miracle of the loaves and fishes.

When Conscience tells the story of Christ's Passion and Resurrection, the focus is significantly different from before. Unlike *passus* 18, where the focus was on the divine, *passus* 19 puts its focus on the human: the Jews, Mary Magdalene, Peter, James, John, and doubting Thomas. The focus is on the human element because Langland's concern here is to narrate the founding of the Christian church so he can review its entire history as a human institution from its beginnings here to the apocalyptic coming of Antichrist in *passus* 20. Langland has not, however, forgotten Dobest, which he associates with the power to forgive sins – in other words, the sacrament of penance. As the last sacrament instituted by Christ and the only one to grant the baptized Christian absolution of sin, it is made the cornerstone of the Christian community in Langland's text. It should not be forgotten that during the Middle Ages frequent reception of the Eucharist was strongly discouraged. Most people received it only once a year, preferably at Eastertime. The rest of the year the laity was encouraged to adore the eucharistic Host on display in a monstrance in the church. Frequent reception of the sacrament of penance, in contrast, was strongly encouraged. It was canon law since the Lateran Council of 1215 that confession be made at least once a year, preferably immediately before Easter, but the Christian was encouraged to confess as often as possible. Given this context, it is no wonder that Langland places penance above the Eucharist and that the corruption of the newly founded Church will come to rest on the friars' corruption of it.

That Piers is granted the power of binding and unbinding sins reflects back upon the early association of Piers and the Good Priest. *Piers* is a variation of *Peter,* suggesting the apostle and first pope. Piers remains behind after the Ascension, and it is to him that Grace gives the four oxen (the four Evangelists) and the four "stottes" (the church fathers). The connection of Piers as Christ and as the Good Priest implies that the priesthood is a part of the eternal, divine Church. It is noteworthy that the forces of Pride wait to attack until Piers has made his final appearance in the poem. The suggestion is clear: there are no good priests left by the end.

The coming of Grace on Pentecost Sunday reassures the reader that the human community is not abandoned. Grace acts as a counselor to Piers and Conscience, and it enables both Conscience to know right from wrong and the good priest to remain faithful. It also calls the people together and distributes to them talents for particular occupations, actions which recall the events of *passus* 6 where Piers distributes labor among the people. In many ways, in fact, the last two *passus* repeat earlier events in the poem, but there is one fundamental difference: the tone is now much darker.

The Barn of Unity that Grace advises Piers to build is another image of the whole Christian community. But just as the Tree of Charity is under constant threat, so too is the Barn of Unity. Pride's agents attack at the first opportunity and target Penance. Their aim is to confuse Conscience with their sophistry so that he cannot tell right from wrong or Christian from heathen. On Conscience's advice the Christians retreat for safety to the barn and prepare for a siege. Among the preparations is the reception of the sacraments of penance and the Eucharist. So long as people listen to their consciences, the faithful can with God's grace resist evil. However, this does not happen. Representatives from each estate – a brewer, a vicar, and a lord and a king – refuse to submit to the authority of Conscience, and so collapse from within seems inevitable.

In *passus* 20 events become even more grim. Will is accosted by Need, another ambivalent quality. It can be a humbling factor, but it can also be a convenient excuse for doing what one wants to do rather than what one ought to do. Will falls asleep after being reproached by Need and dreams of the coming of Antichrist. As a defense, Conscience calls upon Kynde (Nature) and its associates – Old Age and Death – for help, echoing Piers's summons of Hunger earlier in the poem. The outcome is again a momentary success, as the enemy forces are thrown into confusion. But as soon as the coercive force ceases, the vices renew their attack with increased vigor.

In spite of the grimness of the scene, there are humorous moments, as when Old Age hits Will who promptly becomes bald, deaf, toothless, goutish, and impotent. But when Death approaches, Will begs Kynde for aid. Kynde's advice is for Will to learn the craft of love, advice almost identical to that of Holy Church in *passus* 1, where Truth is defined in terms of love. The implication is that Will knew the answer all along and was just unable to act upon the information. In *passus* 20 Will is finally able to choose. He chooses to undergo contrition and confession and so enter the Barn of Unity.

In desperation Conscience calls upon Clergy for help. He is answered by the friars. This scenario illustrates Langland's attitude toward the fraternal orders. Allusions to Saint Francis of Assisi and Saint Dominic demonstrate Langland's acceptance of their initial purpose, the spiritual rejuvenation of the people. Nevertheless, Langland as a writer within the larger antifraternal tradition sees more potential for abuse. Envy, rather than a spiritual impetus, is depicted as sending friars to the university to become philosophers and theologians.

When Conscience calls for a "leche" (a leech, that is, a physician), it is a friar for whom the people ask, against Conscience's better judgment. The "leche" is part of a physical/spiritual metaphor common to medieval writing, sin being a disease. The physician image is also one that is used with two earlier figures: Christ, the "Leech of Lyf" (16.118) and Satan, the "Doctor of Death" (18.365). When the physician-friar appears, a question is understood: is he aligned with the Leech of Life or the Doctor of Death? As a friar in an openly antifraternal text, one answer is obvious: friars are the favorite agents of Antichrist and this one will be no exception. Nevertheless, a potential for goodness exists if the friar chooses to follow Christ instead.

The friar's name is Sire Penetrans-Domos, an allusion to 2 Timothy 3:6–7, which describes the false preachers of the last days and which was interpreted in antifraternal literature as referring to friars. The name suggests his invasive nature. When he penetrates the Barn of Unity, instead of groping the sinner's conscience, he, like Judas, gropes for silver. The sacrament becomes a financial transaction, and contrition, the sense of remorse for sin, is paralyzed. The people no longer fear sin or dread its consequences. Pride and Sloth see their advantage and attack. Nothing can stop them now.

For such a long and complex poem, *Piers Plowman* concludes very abruptly. Conscience vows to undertake another quest, this time to find Piers Plowman, and he calls upon Grace for help. Then the Dreamer simply wakes up and that is the end. There is considerable debate about whether the conclusion of the poem should be regarded as pessimistic or optimistic. The forces of evil seem triumphant, but things are not entirely bleak, as revealed by Conscience's final thoughts about the friars. Although his attitude toward them has been consistently negative, Conscience finally urges not their abolishment but their reformation. Conscience's aim in searching for Piers is in fact twofold: Piers Plowman as Christ / Good Priest will destroy Pride just as he once destroyed Satan; Piers Plowman will also ensure that the friars be granted a "finding," endowed resources of their own, so that they will not be forced by ambivalent Need to beg for a living. There is still hope that the friars can realize their spiritual potential. There is also hope for humanity at large because Conscience still functions, Grace is still present, and Piers Plowman still exists. The reader only has to find him.

Bibliography:

A. J. Colaianne, *Piers Plowman: An Annotated Bibliography of Editions and Criticism, 1550–1977* (New York: Garland, 1978);

Vincent Di Marco, *Piers Plowman: A Reference Guide* (Boston: G. K. Hall, 1982);

Derek Pearsall, *An Annotated Critical Bibliography of Langland* (Ann Arbor: University of Michigan Press, 1990).

Biography:

E. Talbot Donaldson, *Piers Plowman: The C-text and Its Poet* (New Haven: Yale University Press, 1949);

George Kane, *Piers Plowman: The Evidence for Authorship* (London: Athlone Press, 1965).

References:

John A. Alford, ed., *A Companion to Piers Plowman* (Berkeley, Los Angeles & London: University of California Press, 1988);

Robert J. Blanch, ed., *Style and Symbolism in Piers Plowman: A Modern Critical Anthology* (Knoxville: University of Tennessee Press, 1969);

Morton Bloomfield, *Piers Plowman as a Fourteenth-Century Apocalypse* (New Brunswick, N. J.: Rutgers University Press, 1961);

Mary Carruthers, *The Search for St. Truth: A Study of Meaning in Piers Plowman* (Evanston, Ill.: Northwestern University Press, 1973);

T. P. Dunning, *Piers Plowman: An Interpretation of the A-text* (Dublin: Talbot Press, 1937);

David Fowler, *The Bible in Middle English Literature* (Seattle: University of Washington Press, 1984);

R. W. Frank, *Piers Plowman and the Scheme of Salvation* (New Haven: Yale University Press, 1957);

Pamela Gradon, "Langland and the Ideology of Dissent," *Proceedings of the British Academy,* 66 (1980): 179–205;

Britton J. Harwood, *Piers Plowman and the Problem of Belief* (Toronto: University of Toronto Press, 1992);

S. S. Hussey, ed., *Piers Plowman: Critical Approaches* (London: Methuen, 1969);

Anne Middleton, "The Audience and Public of *Piers Plowman,*" in *Middle English Alliterative Poetry and Its Literary Background,* edited by D. A. Lawton (Woodbridge: Boydell & Brewer, 1982), pp. 101–123;

Pamela Raabe, *Imitating God: The Allegory of Faith in Piers Plowman B* (Athens & London: University of Georgia Press, 1990);

D. W. Robertson and Bernard Huppé, *Piers Plowman and Scriptural Tradition* (Princeton: Princeton University Press, 1951);

A. C. Spearing, "The Art of Preaching and *Piers Plowman,*" in *Criticism and Medieval Poetry,* second edition (London: Edward Arnold, 1972), pp. 107–134;

Penn Szittya, *The Antifraternal Tradition in Medieval Literature* (Princeton: Princeton University Press, 1986);

Edward Vasta, ed., *Interpretations of Piers Plowman* (Notre Dame, Ind.: University of Notre Dame Press, 1968).

Laȝamon

(flourished circa 1200)

Elizabeth J. Bryan
Brown University

MAJOR WORK: *Brut* (circa 1189–1236)

Manuscripts: Two manuscripts are extant, both copied during the second half of the thirteenth century: British Library MS. Cotton Caligula A.ix (referred to as C hereafter), in two scribal hands; and British Library, MS. Cotton Otho C.xiii (referred to as O hereafter), in a single scribal hand. O was damaged by the 1731 fire at Ashburnham House. C is fully described in N. R. Ker's introduction to *The Owl and the Nightingale: Reproduced in Facsimile from the Surviving Manuscripts Jesus College Oxford 29 and British Museum Cotton Caligula A.ix,* EETS, 251 (1963).

First publication: *Laȝamons Brut, or Chronicle of Britain; A Poetical Semi-Saxon Paraphrase of the Brut of Wace, Now First Published from the Cottonian Manuscripts in the British Museum, Accompanied by a Literal Translation, Notes and a Grammatical Glossary,* 3 volumes, edited by Sir Frederic Madden (London: Society of Antiquaries of London, 1847).

Standard edition: *Brut: Edited from British Museum MS. Cotton Caligula A.ix and British Museum MS. Cotton Otho C.xiii,* 2 volumes to date, edited by G. L. Brook and R. F. Leslie, EETS 250 and 277 (1963, 1978).

Editions in modern English: *Laȝamon's Brut,* translated by Donald Bzdyl (Binghamton, N.Y.: MRTS, 1989); *Brut,* translated by Rosamund Allen (London: Dent, 1992).

Laȝamon's *Brut* is a 16,095-line early Middle English verse narrative that traces the genealogical descent of British (Celtic) kings from Brutus, the great-grandson of Aeneas of Troy, through King Arthur, to the last British king, Cadwalader. It is the earliest extant text in the English language to tell the stories of King Lear and of King Arthur. The work was produced from the midst of sweeping but still inadequately understood political, cultural, and linguistic change in late-twelfth- and early-thirteenth-century England, and critics of the text have historically sought literary and linguistic categories to accommodate its straddling of cultural borders.

Nothing is known of the author or the conditions of the work's composition beyond what is said in a prologue that introduces each of the two manuscript versions (C and O). The best evidence for the date of composition is the past-tense reference to Eleanor of Aquitaine, "Ælienor þe wes Henries quene," in the prologue of C. This puts the date between 1189 (the death of Henry II) and 1236 (the date when Henry III married Eleanor of Provence, making the qualifier meaninglessly ambiguous). Sometime around 1205–1206, shortly after Eleanor of Aquitaine's death in 1204, is generally accepted as the date of composition.

Both prologues name the compiler (C has "Laȝamon," while O has "Laweman") as a priest who lived at Areley (Areley King's) on the Severn River, thus locating the place of writing near the political border of Wales and England. Other details include Laȝamon's father's name (in C, Leouenað; in O, Leuca) and the place-name Redstone (in C, Radestone; in O, Radistone), where Laȝamon read books. The prologues differ on exactly where in Areley Laȝamon lived (C has him at the great church; O, with the good knight). In both, Laȝamon was not a monk but a secular clergyman, a "priest among the people," who presumably carried out priestly duties such as reading the office and hearing confession and who traveled widely to find the sources for his history.

The prologues emphasize Laȝamon's project of writing as a process of synthesis, which has implications not only for issues of political and linguistic difference but also for the role of the writer himself. Having gotten the idea of telling the ancestry of those who first possessed the English land, Laȝamon is described as gathering together three books and compiling the "truer words" of them all into his one book. While the prologues differ on exactly what these three books were, they both stress the multilingual nature of the author's sources. In C, one book is in English (by "Saint Bede"; presumably the Alfredian English translation of Bede's *Historia ecclesiastica gentis Anglorum,* 731), one is in Latin (by "Saint Albin and the fair Au[gu]stine [of Canterbury]"), and one is in French (by Wace, a "French clerk"). In O, English and Latin sources are named, as Albin and Austin are said to have made separate books, and Wace is not mentioned at all. Modern textual comparisons leave no doubt that Laȝamon's *Brut* was primarily a translation of the French *Roman de Brut* (1155) by Wace, though it also drew from Geoffrey of Monmouth's *Historia regum Britanniae* (circa 1138) in the Merlin section and Bede's *Historia ecclesiastica* for some Anglo-Saxon material. Neither prologue is completely accurate in naming these sources, but it was common for medieval texts to represent an authorial "pedigree" that did not necessarily represent accurate authorial attribution according to modern standards. While O's omission of Wace and C's implication of even distribution of source material both misrepresent the actual sources, there is an important cultural message that this text meant to bring together cultures, languages, histories, and prior writings into something unified.

The language of Laȝamon's *Brut* is an early form of Middle English that retains much Old English diction and traces of Old English grammar. The verse form is a prosodic mix of alliterative long lines derived from Old English and rhyme and assonance patterns derived from Latin or French. Explanations for the historical development of this verse form have been sought in the influence of French verse on Old English poetic conventions, in a "popular" (that is, nonaristocratic) alliterative verse postulated by Dorothy Everett as Laȝamon's literary milieu, and in the pervasive presence of what N. F. Blake terms "rhythmical alliteration" in devotional and homiletic writing of the period. Carolynn Van Dyke Friedlander has cogently analyzed the prosody of Laȝamon's *Brut,* describing its "stylistic variety" without "systematic complication," and argues persuasively for both Old English poetry and church "rhythmical alliteration" as major influences on Laȝamon's verse form.

The two manuscripts use this verse form and, to a greater extent, this early Middle English language differently. Many verse lines in C that offer rhetorical repetition in the style of Old English poetic envelope patterns are excised in O as part of the latter's overall condensing of a C-like text. Also as part of the condensation project, O omits lines that

do not offer information, including some details in formulaic alliterative descriptions most reminiscent of Old English poetry (for example, battle descriptions); nevertheless, O retains enough of these passages to give the flavor of the Old English alliterative formulas. O does not systematically alter the verse form, in other words; it condenses the text, and the cuts have almost random effects on the verse form. The greater difference is with the language of the two versions. O often substitutes words of French derivation where C has terms derived from Old English. This phenomenon has prompted both linguistic explanations – that each manuscript reflects a linguistic stage of development of Middle English and/or reflects dialectal differences – and rhetorical explanations such as E. G. Stanley's argument that the language of C is deliberately archaized. Linguistic arguments for developmental stages must now consider that there is no evidence for a measurable time interval between the copying of the two manuscripts.

It was once thought that C was copied around 1200 and O about fifty years later, but in 1963 N. R. Ker revised the copy date of C to post-1250 on the basis of traits in its Gothic *textura* script. It now appears on the basis of scripts that both texts were copied in the second half of the thirteenth century, although the ornate initials in O were added not before the late fourteenth century. Neither C nor O is an author's autograph. One of C's two scribes mistakenly repeats a passage in a manner that indicates the scribe was copying from a written exemplar, and Robert Millar has demonstrated a significant grammatical shift in article usage in C that is best explained by linguistic habits of two different scribes in a preceding exemplar. At least two manuscript generations probably exist, therefore, between C and "Laȝamon's original." The text of O is a tight condensation of a version resembling C but is not derived from C itself. There is no evidence to reveal whether the scribe of O was the condenser or was copying from another manuscript already containing the condensed version. Without other extant manuscripts for comparison, C and O carry equal textual authority from the point of view of manuscript stemmata.

Laȝamon's *Brut* is a history, albeit employing a kind of medieval providential historiography alien to modern, positivist approaches. As history, it was almost certainly controversial in its own time, when the veracity of Arthurian narratives as first recorded by Geoffrey of Monmouth was under attack by such twelfth-century Anglo-Latin historians as William of Newburgh. The textual tradition of histories of Britain, of which Laȝamon's *Brut* is a thirteenth-century example, includes Gildas's sixth-century *De excidio et conquestu Britanniae,* the seventh-to-ninth-century *Historia Brittonum* attributed to Nennius, Geoffrey of Monmouth's *Historia regum Britanniae,* and Wace's *Roman de Brut.* Laȝamon's *Brut* is the first in a proliferation of vernacular Middle English chronicles of Britain.

Lesley Johnson observes that many of the critical issues surrounding this poem – the political sympathies of the author, class influence on the production of the text, the classification of the work's linguistic medium and verse form, and the identification of its genre – have been debated largely in terms of binary oppositions. Were Laȝamon's sympathies Celtic or Anglo-Saxon? Anglo-Saxon or Norman? Was the text's production popular, as opposed to aristocratic? Is the apparently unsystematic mixture of alliteration, assonance, and rhyme a poetic degeneration or continuation? Is the language reflective of contemporary speech or rhetoricized? Was the text regarded as fact or fiction? Johnson points out that some of these polarities now seem inadequate, and the current revival of scholarly interest in Laȝamon's *Brut* focuses on ways in which this text manifests literary-historical, textual, linguistic, political, and cultural complexities.

Though the text is not sectioned in any formal way, its narrative structure relies on a sequence of genealogical lines, sometimes continuous and sometimes interrupted, that effectively form five structural units. Lines 1–2023 comprise the first such unit, which explains Brutus's Trojan ancestry through his great-grandfather Aeneas, details his exile from Italy for patricide and his divinely guided journey to the island of Albion, and traces the descent of twenty-four rulers of Albion (renamed "Brutaine"), from Brutus to Porreus and Fereus. This line ends in fratricide (Poreus slays Ferreus), infanticide (Iudon dismembers her surviving son Poreus), murder (a gathering of men drown Iudon), and civil war (brothers kill brothers, and hunger and hate pervade the land). From Brutus's accidental killing of his father to Iudon's avenging one son's death by slaying her other son, this first series of British rulers is thematically linked by emphasis on kin-conflict, treachery, and self-destruction.

The story of Leir, the basis of William Shakespeare's *King Lear* (1604–1605), unfolds in this context. It follows the story of Locrin, Brutus's son, who was killed in battle by his wife, Gwendoleine, after he repudiated her and her son Madan

in favor of his foreign lover, Astrild. It also presents the story of Membriz, Madan's son, who slew his brother, Malin. Laȝamon's Leir provides another variation on intrafamily treachery and violence, with three daughters in potential rivalry for rule of Britain. Leir disinherits the third daughter, Cordoille, and splits his kingdom between his two older daughters, Gornoille and Regau, only to be ousted by them. Cordoille has told "the truth," that the basis of her love is that of daughter to father and that others will love Leir only to the extent of what he possesses and rules, whereas Gornoille and Regau have told "lies," that they love Leir more than their life. Laȝamon's narrative has Leir returning to rule with Cordoille's help. Cordoille later succeeds him as ruler of Britain, only to be imprisoned by her treacherous nephews Morgan and Cunedagius (or Cunedagies). She commits suicide. Cunedagius beheads Morgan, his only remaining rival, and then rules uncontested for thirty-three years. The complex of betrayal and killing of family members receives pointed emphasis with the detail that Romulus and Remus's building of Rome and subsequent fratricide occurred during Cunedagius's reign. Such interpolation of contemporary world historical events draws on conventions of universal history employed by Laȝamon's sources. The events function not only as measurements of time but also as thematic pointers, in this case to the theme of fratricide among rulers.

The second genealogically based structural unit of Laȝamon's *Brut,* lines 2024–5117, provides the thematic antithesis of fratricide: strength through familial unity. The second line of British rulers rises from the ashes of civil war and continues through sixty kings to end with the arrival of Christianity during the reign of Luces. In this section, lists and synopses of successive reigns alternate with three prominently elaborated narratives that highlight the political advantages of intrafamily accord: the story of Belin and Brenne, the story of Cassibellaunus and Julius Caesar, and the story of Arviragus and Genuis. A major issue of the section is the unfolding relationship between Britain and Rome, with its varying roles of the quasi-ancestral home of Brutus, the powerful political rival of Britain, and the eventual seat of Christianity.

The brothers Belin and Brenne are able to conquer Rome, but only after their initial bloody feud transforms into reconciliation and alliance at the instigation of their mother, Tonwenne. This long narrative episode details the exploits in which Brenne, the younger brother goaded by evil counselors, gains control of foreign armies through mar-

Page from Laȝamon's Brut *in a thirteenth-century scribal copy, one of the two extant manuscripts for the work (British Library, MS. Cotton Caligula A.ix, fol. 3ʳ)* riage. At the brink of battle between Brenne's Burgundian army and Belin's British troops, Tonwenne intercedes, barefoot and dressed in rags, to plead with Brenne to put down his weapons and make peace with his brother. Tonwenne's speech is touching and powerful, including reminders that her one body produced and suckled the two brothers. Her role is clearly a variation on the female peace weaver figure, which has precedents in Old English poetry, and the iconographical function of her character as nurturer of the nation will later be counterpointed by the broken body of the failed foster mother in the Arthurian episode at Mont-Saint-Michel. Belin and Brenne, moved to reconciliation, wage a successful campaign against Rome, where Brenne remains as ruler while Belin returns to rule Britain. The text pointedly contrasts Belin and Brenne's brotherly union to the fratricide of Romulus and Remus.

Forty-nine British kings later, Britain's political relationship with Rome reverses when Julius Caesar, rebuffed twice by united British armies under Cassibellaunus, successfully invades on the third try because of a falling-out between King Cassibellaunus and his nephew Androgeus. The narrator intones:

The while that they were settled in conciliation (sæhte), and their men united (on some)
This land fared very well; with brotherhood they held it
But when they became wrathful, it turned for the worse,
Such that the Roman people came to this nation,
And collected taxes on this land both in silver and gold,
They who never before in life dared to travel here.

Caesar, drawn to conquer every land he can see, invokes common Trojan ancestry with the British through Brutus and claims that his demand for silver and gold from Britain is justified by Belin and Brenne's previous removal of gold from Rome. Cassibellaunus refuses to pay, demanding instead that Rome pay Britain. Caesar attacks but is repelled; he attacks thirteen months later and must withdraw in defeat again. British victory celebration erupts in hostility, however, when the king's man Herigal is killed by Androgeus's man Ævelyn. Androgeus, the king's nephew, refuses to surrender Ævelyn. King Cassibellaunus orders Androgeus's men to leave, and Androgeus, in spite, offers his alliance to Caesar. Battle ensues, and only when his army is pinned between those of Caesar and Androgeus does Cassibellaunus regret his unwilling-

ness to reconcile with his nephew. The outcome is Britain's forced agreement to pay yearly tribute to Rome. Although this agreement marks Britain's political subjugation, it also invokes ancient kinship between the two powers.

Three generations later, the story of Arviragus and Genuis layers onto the Rome-Britain fraternal kinship a marital model of political union, as the genealogical lines of Rome and Britain become remingled. British kings Wither and Arviragus stop payment to Rome and endure invasion by the Roman "kaiser" Claudius as a result. When King Arviragus is finally forced to negotiate a truce, the settlement includes his marriage to Genuis, daughter of Claudius. A parallel Roman-British love match between Claudius and a British woman produces a son, Gloi, for whom Gloucester is named and whose eventual posterity includes Saint Helena, Queen of Jerusalem. At Claudius's death Arviragus again stops payment to Rome, and a second Roman "kaiser," Vespasian, invades Britain. In a scene reminiscent of Tonwenne's reconciliation of Belin and Brenne, Queen Genuis rides out between the poised armies of Britain and Rome and pleads that her Roman kin and her married British kin not destroy each other. Genuis's peace weaving results in a strong accord between Britain and Rome, betokened by Genuis and Arviragus's son, Maurus, becoming the second Roman-educated ruler of Britain (Kinbelyn was the first).

These three narratives all emphasize the ideal of sæhtnesse (agreement, settlement, peace) and some (agreement, arbitration, togetherness) for relations within Britain as well as relations between Britain and Rome. In all cases, recognition of proper relationships is necessary for that accord. The disappointment of an injured party – whether younger brother Brenne, nephew Androgeus, or defeated Cassibellaunus, Arviragus, or even Britain – must be offset by the memory of the origin or the marriage that bonds. These explorations of the nature of political accord, in terms of fraternal kinship, nephew-uncle kinship, relation by marriage, and connection through ancient ancestor, are accompanied by the arrival of Christianity.

The structure of the poem's second section suggests that the emphasis on achieving friendship parallels the entrance into history of the Christian values of love and mercy, and to Britain's political relationship with Rome is added a religious relationship. The birth of "Iesu Crist" is announced during the reign of Kinbelyn, nephew of Androgeus and first British ruler to benefit from Roman education. Peter's arrival in Rome from Antioch to spread

Christianity is announced strategically after Claudius's accord with Arviragus. Luces, the last king of this line, is portrayed as the greatest British king since Brutus, because he brings Christianity to Britain. Indeed, the story of his inviting Dunian and Fagan, two bishops from Rome, to convert the British people to Christianity and their pagan temples to Christian churches is reminiscent of Bede's description in his *Historia ecclesiastica* of Augustine's later mission to the Anglo-Saxons in 597. Luces dies without heirs – "neither sister nor brother, / nor queen nor other kin" – in the year 106, bringing his genealogical line to an end at the precise historical moment of British conversion to Christianity. Political and military history interlink with the history of salvation, and one aspect of the poem's presentation of that link resides in the shifting political and religious roles of Rome in relation to Britain.

The third section of La3amon's *Brut*, lines 5118–6431, chronicles a period of genealogical discontinuity. In this section, violence and regicide account for the succession of kings far more often than kinship (four of the first six kings kill their predecessors), and the text chronicles rulers of not one but three interacting political entities, Britain, Britain-the-lesser (Brittany), and Rome. Rome's military and political presence in Britain starts out strong under the rule of Severus but ends up nonexistent, as the Romans under Febus finally withdraw from Britain, plagued by the vacillating support and hostility of the natives.

Rome's religious role reverses in this section as well. Diocletian persecutes British Christians, and Saint Alban is martyred. Britain provides Rome with a Christian leader, Constantine, whose ancestry traces to Claudius and his British wife through Gloi, and whose British mother, Elene (Saint Helena), takes on legendary status as "Queen of Jerusalem" and finder of the "true Cross." Elene's line of Christian British-Roman rulers comes to an end with her cousin Maximien (distinct from Diocletian's brother Maximian), leaving Britain exposed to pagan incursion. After prominently displaying British Christian saints throughout this section, the text figures the pagan invasion of Britain through a gruesome secularization of the legend of Saint Ursula and the eleven thousand virgins: pagan outlaws Melga and Wanis intercept fourteen ships of British women en route to Brittany, and they rape, humiliate, or kill all the women starting with Ursele, Conan's intended bride. In an episode that draws a parallel between Ursele's body and the British land, Melga and Wanis proceed to ravage Christian Britain. Rome at first wards off the pagan threat but then ends its role as protector.

Britain-the-lesser replaces Rome as both political and religious ally of Britain, even though its colonization is partly to blame for Britain's vulnerability. Formerly named Armoriche, it is conquered and repopulated with British by Maximien and Conan. The exporting of its best earls and kings, however, leaves Britain open to strife at home and invasion by Melga and Wanis. Unlike Rome, Britain-the-lesser remains loyal to Britain. A second Constantine, this one a son of Conan, returns from Britain-the-lesser, kills Melga and Wanis, and becomes the new ruler of Britain. Thus ends a period of Roman occupation and contested rule, and a new dynasty allied with Britain-the-lesser begins that unites the interests of Christianity and British power.

The fourth and by far the longest section of La3amon's *Brut*, lines 6431–14297, follows the descent of kings from Constantine, son of Conan, to King Arthur, a lineage beset by threat of Anglo-Saxon occupation but finally triumphant over even Rome before it abruptly self-destructs. Constantine is succeeded by each of his three sons, Constance, Aurelius Ambrosius, and Uther, although Constance's steward Vortigern and his son Vortimer usurp rule for twenty-five years between Constance and Aurelius. King Arthur succeeds his father Uther Pendragon to become the last of this line. The Arthur of La3amon's *Brut* is not at all the courtly lover of romance, but a military hero and a Christian king who purges the land of pagans and who fosters fraternal peace among British Christians. He is the subject of prophecies by Merlin, and his conception, birth, and final leavetaking (not death) are attended by either Merlin or elves. Providential allegories of history that merge national with Christian interests, epic delight in the high-flown rhetoric of battle tales, and contemplative exploration of coexisting supernatural agencies and their signs all are brought together in detailed and elaborate narratives of this line of kings and especially of King Arthur's rule.

In fostering British strength through unity, this Christian British dynasty from Conan to Arthur typologically parallels and surpasses that of the pre-Christian British line of Belin and Brenne in section 2. From Constantine to Uther, this dynasty is threatened by the presence in Britain of non-Celtic and non-Christian peoples initially invited as guests or allies. Picts kill both Constantine and Constance, and three generations of Anglo-Saxons battle the British for their land: Hengest with his army, welcomed to Britain by the usurper Vortigern, betrays the latter, has Vortimer killed, massacres British earls at Stonehenge, and is finally beheaded in Aurelius's reign. Aurelius, in turn, is poisoned by a Saxon mercenary; Ebissa, Ossa, and Hengest's son Octa harass British kings until they are slain by Uther Pendragon, who is then poisoned by Anglo-Saxon knights. King Arthur avenges his father's death by killing Saxons Colgrim, Baldulf, and Childrich (although later a Saxon called Childrich is invited in by the treacherous Modred) after fierce battles at York, Lincoln, and Bath. Having constructed the Saxons as a religious and quasi-national "Other," the opposites of the British, the text presents Arthur's expulsion of the pagan Saxons as a turning point. Having thus defined his land as essentially Christian and British, Arthur's task of leadership turns outward toward gathering many lands under his British rule.

In sequence, Arthur establishes Britain's sovereignty over the North Atlantic (Scotland, Ireland, Iceland, the Orkney Islands, Gutland, and Winetland) and over France and other European lands (Norway and Denmark). The repute of Arthur's Round Table and his victory over Frollo of France bring him to the attention of Rome, whose demand that Arthur reinstitute payment to Rome is answered by war. Britain marshals all the forces of its diverse possessions into a unified, and victorious, military campaign against Rome. The text lavishly catalogues battles, knights, and kings, and in the end the Roman "kaiser Luces" is killed. But just before Arthur enters Rome in a triumphant restoration of British rule unknown since the days of Belin and Brenne, a messenger arrives with news that Arthur's nephew Modred and Arthur's wife, Wenhaver, have betrayed him. The mightiest and most expansive Britain in history to that time is undermined by treachery of kin at home, as Arthur returns to fight for his own kingship. Modred and all the knights of Arthur's Round Table die, and the wounded Arthur leaves for Avalon to be healed by Argante, the Elf Queen. He designates a third Constantine, this one the son of Cador of Cornwall, to succeed him. Arthur's imperialism has been figured as an act of gathering and unification, albeit violent, that, by implication at least, meets a Christian agenda as well as one which is almost national. All the peace weaving and fraternal military strength are undone by Modred's and Wenhaver's violation of kinship bonds, the problem that has troubled the British from Brutus's original line of descent.

Besides the genealogical linkage, Merlin's prophecies and their fulfillment provide a second structuring mechanism for the fourth section. Laȝamon's *Brut* gives Merlin more prominence and credibility than does Wace's *Roman de Brut*. The character is first introduced as a boy whose parentage consists of a Christian nun and the golden incubus that impregnated her. Sought out by Vortigern, Merlin discredits the predictions of Ioram, Vortigern's adviser, by accurately predicting the presence of two dragons fighting next to an underground pool at Mont Reir. In Laȝamon's *Brut,* Merlin continues to make predictions that are confirmed by the playing out of events, a convincing display that Merlin's prophetic power is real, though it derives from an ambiguous spiritual source. Often accompanying Christian ceremony and purpose, Merlin is twice linked with the Sibyl, the prophet of classical epic appropriated by medieval iconography as a pre-Christian medium for the Christian God. The suggestion here and elsewhere is that Merlin's prophecies are divinely inspired and reflect purposes of Christian salvation. These prophecies include Vortigern's downfall and great slaughter by Saxons; the succession of Aurelius, Uther, and Uther's son; rule over Rome by Uther's son; the death of Aurelius by Vortigern's kin; Uther's son and daughter; Uther's begetting on Igerne a son who will never die; Arthur's subjugation of all he sees; great sorrow at Arthur's going forth; the fall of Roman walls before Arthur; and the destruction of Winchester (in Arthur's battle with Modred). Except for an open-ended promise that Arthur will not die, all these predictions come to pass in section 4 of the poem. Laȝamon's heavy use of Merlin's prophecies draws on Geoffrey of Monmouth's *Vita Merlini* and *Historia regum Brittaniae,* texts frequently copied and translated in this period, all testifying to a medieval readership keenly interested in Merlin's prophecies.

This section continues a conventional pattern of using female characters in part to figure the condition of the British land and people. Rouwenne, daughter of the Anglo-Saxon Hengest whom Vortigern weds in a pagan ceremony and who poisons Vortigern's son Vortimer, combines the threat of the foreign with the treachery of the biblical Eve. The Scottish women who appeal to Arthur to make peace with their besieged husbands act as peace weavers, with the innovation that accord is based not on blood kin or marriage but on the bond of shared belief in Christianity. The story of Arthur's battle with the giant of Mont-Saint-Michel reworks elements of the holy virgin martyr, the Old English peace weaver, and the nurturing mother of the nation in the two characters of Eleine and her foster mother. The young maid Eleine has died in response to the giant's sexual assault, evoking the dynamic of the virgin martyr's life without the spiritual triumph, and the old foster mother has (like Ursele) been repeatedly raped and brutalized; she has failed to sustain the life of her entrusted charge, her own body is broken, and there is neither death nor hope to comfort her. She is the inverse of Tonwenne, mother of Belin and Brenne, and presages the condition of Britain after Arthur. Finally, Wenhaver's violation of marriage vows to Arthur through alliance with Modred reverses the peace weaving process and figures the breakup of society. The text unequivocally damns Wenhaver to hell along with Modred.

The loss of the Round Table is the loss of a fraternal relationship without hierarchy, a table at which all knights are equal. Laȝamon's version of the making of the Round Table is one of the most reflective passages in the whole poem. The historian observes that narratives frequently have bias, either of hate or love, arising from loyalties. He then posits the possibility of transcendent Truth, asserting that his history is the truth about Arthur because it is written (not oral) and because it is the whole story, not just a fragment out of context. True narrative, like the Round Table, finds a way to transcend particular interests in the service of a higher loyalty. For Laȝamon, that higher loyalty and transcendent purpose are Christian, and the British are most glorious when they ally themselves with a Christian agenda.

The fifth and final section of Laȝamon's *Brut*, lines 14298–16095, chronicles the struggle and decline of British rule after Arthur. This post-Arthurian section provides a carefully structured closure to an allegorical historiography that has depicted British political events as figurations of the history of Christianity, and at the same time offers tales memorable for their supernatural, grotesque, or romance details. Among the latter is the story of God's miraculously inflicting the inhabitants of Dorchester with fish tails in retaliation for their humiliation of Augustine, as well as stories of Brien, nephew of Cadwadlan, who restores the health of his uncle by feeding him a piece of Brien's own thigh.

As a Christian providential history, Laȝamon's *Brut* concludes with the story of the conversion of the Anglo-Saxons to Christianity and their supplanting of the British people as God's chosen possessors of Britain. The British genealogical line in this final section begins with familiar names – for example, Constantin and Conan – who are antitypes of their namesakes (this Constantin violates

church sanctuary in order to kill Modred's two sons, and this Conan, like Modred, betrays his mother's brother, Constantin). Despite protracted struggles, British king Carric or Kinric cannot defeat pagan African invader Gurmund, and for 105 years Christianity is suppressed in the land (figured by graphic descriptions of mutilation). Five Anglo-Saxon kings receive rule of the land from Gurmund. The return of Christianity comes with Austin (Augustine of Canterbury), whose story of being sent by Pope Gregory to convert the "angel-like" Angles is taken from Bede's *Historia ecclesiastica*. Austin converts Æðelbert, king of Kent, and then the whole of Anglo-Saxon England, but the few remaining British clerics refuse to ally with the newly Christianized Anglo-Saxons, and at this turning point British "national" loyalty becomes an obstacle to Christian unity.

Subsequent political struggles between the British and Anglo-Saxons produce one period of brotherly *sæhte* (togetherness), in the reigns of Anglo-Saxon Æluric and British Cadwan, but war breaks out between their sons Edwine and Cadwaðlan. Cadwaðlan prevails and reigns forty-seven years as the last British king to rule over the whole land. During his reign, the Anglo-Saxon king Penda, in the service of Cadwaðlan, kills the Anglo-Saxon king Oswald (later Saint Oswald) in a treacherous breach of truce. Before dying, Oswald had planted a cross at Hoven-feld (Heavenfield) and asked God to enact Vengeance if Penda broke the truce. Plagues beset the land afterward, during the reign of Cadwaðlan's son Cadwalader, so that all inhabitants flee abroad. Anglo-Saxons resettle the land after eleven years under Æðelstan, the first English ruler of all Britain. Cadwalader, intent on returning to challenge Anglo-Saxon rule, receives a vision from God instructing him to go instead to Rome and confess to the pope. The dream prophesies that the British will yield possession of Britain to the "Alemainisce" – the English – who will rule until a time when the British will find Cadwalader's bones in Rome and return them to Britain, a prophecy that has been made by both the Sibyl and by Merlin.

Rome, at the end of this long poem, is important as the seat of Christian power rather than civic or national power. It is the resting place for Cadwalader's bones and the holding area for British hope of resurrection of power in England, and taxes paid from Anglo-Saxon England – "Peter's pence" – go to the pope, not the kaiser. In this allegorical history of salvation, in which Christianity is the main character, the status of the chosen people passes from Celts to Anglo-Saxons. The history closes with the statement that the British still live in Wales, ruled over by English kings, that the day has not yet come when they will rule again as prophesied, and that the future will be as it will be, according to God's will.

Laȝamon's history of the Bruts shapes rhetoric and structure to understand the meaning of differences among peoples, territories, and language. It would be anachronistic to apply to Laȝamon's *Brut* the term *national identity* in the sense of post-eighteenth-century nation-states and twentieth-century models of subjectivity and identity, but it would be equally mistaken to deny that Laȝamon's *Brut* explores precisely those serious historical issues in exploring what it means to be "English" when the territorial borders contain people of diverse ancestral groups, diverse languages, and diverse access to political power. The question of Laȝamon's political sympathies is unresolved in terms of his loyalties to one "national" group over another. What is absolutely clear from the shape of his history is a philosophy that Christian unity transcends national difference. In bringing together languages, forms, symbols, and narratives from several groups, Laȝamon's *Brut* embodies that unity, drawing from the old while subverting its meanings to create the new.

References:

N. F. Blake, "Rhythmical Alliteration," *Modern Philology,* 67 (1969): 118–124;

G. L. Brook, "A Piece of Evidence for the Study of Middle English Spelling," *Neuphilologische Mitteilungen,* 73 (1972): 25–28;

Daniel Donoghue, "Laȝamon's Ambivalence," *Speculum,* 65 (1990): 537–563;

Dorothy Everett, "Laȝamon and the Earliest Middle English Alliterative Verse," in *Essays on Middle English Literature,* edited by P. Kean (Oxford, 1955), pp. 23–45;

Carolynn Van Dyke Friedlander, "Early Middle English Accentual Verse," *Modern Philology,* 76 (1978): 219–230;

Robert W. Hanning, *The Vision of History in Early Britain: From Gildas to Geoffrey of Monmouth* (New York: Columbia University Press, 1966);

Lesley Johnson, "Tracking Laȝamon's *Brut,*" *Leeds Studies in English,* new series 22 (1991): 139–165;

W. J. Keith, "Laȝamon's *Brut:* The Literary Differences between the Two Texts," *Medium Ævum,* 29 (1960): 161–172;

Francoise H. M. Le Saux, *Laȝamon's* Brut: *The Poem and Its Sources,* Arthurian Studies, 19 (Cambridge: Brewer, 1989);

Angus McIntosh, "Early Middle English Alliterative Verse," in *Middle English Alliterative Poetry,* edited by David Lawton (Woodbridge, 1982), pp. 20–33;

Robert Millar, "The Realization of the 'Simple' and 'Compound' Demonstrative Pronouns in Laȝamon's *Brut* and *The Owl and the Nightingale,*" Ph.D. dissertation, King's College, London, 1991;

Herbert Pilch, *Laȝamon's 'Brut': Eine Literarische Studie* (Heidelberg, 1960);

E. G. Stanley, "Laȝamon's Antiquarian Sentiments," *Medium Ævum,* 38 (1969): 23–37;

Theodore Stroud, "Scribal Editing in Lawman's *Brut,*" *JEGP,* 51 (1952): 42–48;

J. S. P. Tatlock, *The Legendary History of Britain: Geoffrey of Monmouth's* Historia Regum Britanniae *and its Early Vernacular Versions* (Berkeley: University of California Press, 1950);

Henry Cecil Wyld, "Laȝamon as an English Poet," *Review of English Studies,* 6 (1930): 1–30.

John Lydgate

(circa 1370 – 1450)

Jerome Mitchell

and

Judith Davis Shaw
University of Georgia

MAJOR WORKS: *The Temple of Glas* (1403?)

Manuscripts: Alain Renoir and C. David Benson (1980) list nine manuscripts; John Norton-Smith's 1966 text is based on Bodleian Library MS. Tanner 346.

First publication: *The temple of glas* (Westminster: William Caxton, 1477?).

Standard editions: *The Temple of Glas,* edited by Joseph Schick, EETS, e.s. 60 (1891; reprinted, 1924, 1973); also in *John Lydgate: Poems,* edited by Norton-Smith (Oxford: Clarendon Press, 1966), pp. 67–112, 176–191.

Reson and Sensuallyte (circa 1408)

Manuscripts: Bodleian Library MS. 3896 (Fairfax 16) and British Library MS. Additional 29729.

Standard edition: *Reson and Sensuallyte,* edited by Ernst Sieper, 2 volumes, EETS, e.s. 84 & 89 (1901–1903; reprinted, 1965).

The Life of Our Lady (1409–1411?)

Manuscripts: Alain Renoir and C. David Benson list forty-seven manuscripts, the best of which (according to Norton-Smith) is Durham University MS. Cosin V.ii.16.

First publication: *tHis book was compyled by dan John lydgate . . . in thonoure glorye & reuerence of the byrthe of our moste blessyd lady, mayde wyf, and moder of our lord Ihesu cryst,* edited by William Caxton (Westminster: William Caxton, 1484?).

Standard edition: *A Critical Edition of John Lydgate's Life of Our Lady,* edited by Joseph A. Lauritis, Ralph A. Klinefelter, and Vernon F. Gallagher, Duquesne Studies, Philological Series 2 (Pittsburgh: Duquesne University Press, 1961).

Troy Book (1412–1420)

Manuscripts: This long poem exists in more than twenty manuscripts; Henry Bergen's text (1906–1935) is based on British Library MS. Cotton Augustus A.iv, collated with British Library MS. Arundel 99 and Bodleian Library MSS. Digby 230 and Digby 232.

First publication: *The hystorye, Sege and dystruccyon of Troye* (London: Richard Pynson, 1513).

Standard edition: *Troy Book,* edited by Henry Bergen, 4 volumes, EETS, e.s. 97, 103, 106, and 126 (1906–1935; reprinted, 1973).

The Siege of Thebes (1420–1422)

Manuscripts: Alain Renoir and C. David Benson list thirty manuscripts; the standard EETS edition is based on British Library MS. Arundel 119.

First publication: *The Storye of Thebes* (London: Wynkyn de Worde, 1496?).

Standard edition: *The Siege of Thebes,* 2 volumes, edited by Axel Erdmann and Eilert Ekwall, EETS, e.s. 108 (1911; reprinted, 1960) and e.s. 125 (1930; reprinted, 1973).

The Serpent of Division (1422)

Manuscripts: Alain Renoir and C. David Benson list five manuscripts of this prose treatise.

Standard edition: *The Serpent of Division,* edited by Henry Noble MacCracken (London: Frowde / New Haven: Yale University Press, 1911).

The Pilgrimage of the Life of Man (1426–1430)

Manuscripts: British Library MSS. Cotton Vitellius C.xiii, Cotton Tiberius A.vii (a fragment), and Stowe 952; and Worcester Cathedral MS. C.i.8 (a fragment).

Standard edition: *Deguileville's Pilgrimage of the Life of Man,* 3 volumes, edited by Frederick J.

John Lydgate (probably third from left) and pilgrims leaving Canterbury; an illustration from a late-fifteenth-century transcription of Lydgate's The Siege of Thebes *(British Library, MS. Royal 18.D.ii, fol. 148)*

Furnivall and Katharine B. Locock, EETS, e.s. 77, 83 & 92 (1899–1904; reprinted, 1973).

The Dance of Death (or *The Daunce of Machabree*) (1426–1430)

Manuscripts: Alain Renoir and C. David Benson list fifteen manuscripts, eight with and seven without the five-stanza prologue; the standard EETS edition is based on Ellesmere MS. 26.A.13 (in the Huntington Library) and Lansdowne MS. 699 (in the British Library).

Standard edition: *The Dance of Death,* edited by Florence Warren and Beatrice White, EETS, o.s. 181 (1931; reprinted, 1971).

Fall of Princes (1431–1439)

Manuscripts: Alain Renoir and C. David Benson list thirty-four manuscripts plus numerous manuscripts of extracts; Henry Bergen's text is based on Bodley MS. 263, collated throughout with British Library MSS. Royal 18.D.iv and Harley 1245, and in part with other manuscripts.

First publication: *Here begynnethe the boke*

calledde John bochas descriuinge the falle of princis . . . (London: Richard Pynson, 1494).

Standard edition: *Fall of Princes,* edited by Henry Bergen, 4 volumes (Washington, D.C.: The Carnegie Institution, 1923–1927); and EETS, e.s. 121–124 (1924–1927; reprinted, 1967).

The Lives of Saints Edmund and Fremund (1433)

Manuscripts: Alain Renoir and C. David Benson list thirteen manuscripts.

Edition: "John Lydgate's Saint Edmund and Saint Fremund: An Annotated Edition," edited by James I. Miller, Ph.D. dissertation, Harvard University, 1967.

The Lives of Saint Albon and Saint Amphabel (1439)

Manuscripts: The poem exists in more or less complete form in five manuscripts; both standard editions are based on Lansdowne MS. 699 (in the British Library).

First publication: *Here begynnethe the glorious lyfe and passion of seint Albon prothomartyr of Englande / and also the lyfe and passion of saint*

Amphabel / whiche conuerted saint Albon to the fayth of Christe (St. Albans: J. Hertford, 1534).

Standard editions: *The Life of Saint Alban and Saint Amphibal,* edited by J. E. van der Westhuizen (Leiden: Brill, 1974); *The Life of Saint Alban and Saint Amphibalus,* edited by George F. Reinecke, Garland Medieval Texts no. 11 (New York & London: Garland, 1985).

Secrees of the Old Philosoffres (with Benedict Burgh) (1446?)

Manuscripts: Alain Renoir and C. David Benson list twenty manuscripts; Steele's text is based on Sloane MS. 2464 (in the British Library).

Standard edition: *Secrees of the Old Philosoffres,* edited by Robert Steele, EETS, e.s. 66 (1894; reprinted, 1973).

The Testament of Lydgate (1448–1449)

Manuscripts: The poem exists in whole or in part in about a dozen manuscripts; Henry Noble MacCracken's text is based on British Library MS. Harley 218.

First publication: *Here begynneth the testament of John Lydgate monke of Berry: which he made hymselfe / by his lyfe dayes* (London: Richard Pynson, 1515?).

Edition: *The Testament of Dan John Lydgate,* in *The Minor Poems of John Lydgate,* edited by Henry Noble MacCracken, volume 1, EETS, e.s. 107 (1911; reprinted, 1962), pp. 329–362.

COLLECTED EDITIONS: In *English Verse between Chaucer and Surrey,* edited by Eleanor Prescott Hammond (Durham, N.C.: Duke University Press, 1927; reprinted, Octagon, 1965), pp. 77–187;

The Minor Poems of John Lydgate, edited by Henry Noble MacCracken, 2 volumes, EETS, e.s. 107 (1911; reprinted, 1962) and o.s. 192 (1934; reprinted, 1961);

John Lydgate: Poems, edited by John Norton-Smith (Oxford: Clarendon Press, 1966).

When John Lydgate died in the middle of the fifteenth century, he had long been the most important and most sought-after poet of his time. Geoffrey Chaucer had died in 1400, John Gower in 1408, and the only poet of his own generation with whom he can reasonably be compared is Thomas Hoccleve, who had died in 1426. In the second half of the century and throughout the entire sixteenth century and indeed until the early 1600s, Lydgate, Chaucer, and Gower were grouped together and their praises sung by well-known poets including Gavin Douglas, William Dunbar, Stephen Hawes, Sir David Lindsey, and John Skelton; by lesser-known poets such as George Ashby, Osbern Bokenham, and John Metham; and by many other writers including the important scholar of William Shakespeare's day, Francis Meres. But worldly fame, indeed everything in this life, is transitory, as Lydgate knew and often stated. Before the middle of the seventeenth century his fame had evaporated and his name was all but forgotten. Few writers even mentioned him in the eighteenth century, although the few included Thomas Gray and Thomas Warton, both of whom had kind things to say about him.

Unfortunately this early attempt at rehabilitation was thwarted in 1802 by "scholar-at-arms" Joseph Ritson in one of the most brutally negative critiques ever written. To him Lydgate was a "voluminous, prosaick, and driveling monk" whose "stupid and fatiguing productions . . . by no means deserve the name of poetry . . . are neither worth collecting . . . nor even worthy of preservation." Although pedantic, contentious, and eccentric, Ritson nevertheless was an indefatigable scholar and a meticulous editor of earlier English poetry. His forcefully expressed opinion of Lydgate was to influence critical opinion for the next 150 years. Scholars are still not totally free of it, although they now know, or *should* know, better. Joseph Schick's thoughtful introduction to *The Temple of Glas* (1891) gives a kinder, better-informed view of its poet and can be said to be the beginning of modern Lydgate studies. On the whole Lydgate has been better regarded by his editors than by nineteenth- and early-twentieth-century critics and literary historians, who usually did little more than to repeat in their own words what they had read *about* him in previous histories of literature. Finally, in the third quarter of this century, Lydgate received fair and informed critical appraisal in book-length studies by Walter F. Schirmer, Alain Renoir, and Derek Pearsall. There have been new editions, numerous articles, and even another book (Lois A. Ebin's) in the past twenty years or so. It is true that Lydgate was no Chaucer, but he deserves to be read. Readers with an open mind might actually find that they like him.

John Lydgate was born in or around the year 1370 in the village of Lidgate, in Suffolk, eight miles west of the Benedictine abbey of Bury Saint Edmunds. When he was about fifteen he became a novice at this great monastery with which he would be associated for the rest of his long life. He received his education first at the monastery – which had at that time an impressive library of some seven hundred volumes – and later probably at Oxford. In 1389 he became a subdeacon, in 1393 a deacon, and in 1397 he was ordained a priest. He is believed to have founded a school of rhetoric at Bury Saint Edmunds, where he taught the sons of noble families. To the first decade of the fifteenth century belong his so-called courtly poems: *The Complaint of the Black Knight, The Flour of Courtesye,* and *The Temple of Glas* (1403?) – which show the influence of Chaucer's dream poems – and his unfinished poem of seven thousand lines, *Reson and Sensuallyte* (circa 1408), a moralistic allegory on the subject of love. Toward the end of this period he may have written his *The Life of Our Lady* (1409–1411?), commissioned by Prince Hal (later King Henry V), but some scholars date it later. In 1412 he began his long translation in verse of Guido delle Colonne's *Historia Destructionis Troiae,* titled *Troy Book,* which was also commissioned by Prince Hal, and when Lydgate finished it in 1420, the prince had been king for seven years.

Lydgate's admiration of Chaucer was immense, as his several tributes to his predecessor show, scattered as they are among longer works, and his literary indebtedness to Chaucer is well documented. While he never knew Chaucer personally, he did know the great poet's son Thomas and granddaughter Alice. Thomas Chaucer was a prominent figure on the political scene of the early century, and his home in the village of Ewelme, south of Oxford, was a gathering place for the social and cultural elite. Lydgate belonged to this circle, and it was there that he could have met the king's colorful brother Humphrey, Duke of Gloucester, who was later to be the patron of Lydgate's *Fall of Princes* (1431–1439). Alice Chaucer would later commission his *Virtues of the Mass* (circa 1435). One of Lydgate's most attractive occasional poems is his *Ballade at the Departyng of Thomas Chaucer into France* (1417?).

The years between 1420 and 1434 might be called Lydgate's high-noon period. It began with the composition of his fine Canterbury tale, *The Siege of Thebes* (1420–1422), and his one important prose treatise, *The Serpent of Division* (1422). In 1423 he became prior at Hatfield Broad Oak in Essex, and he apparently resided there until 1426, when he went to Paris on official government business. Henry V had died in 1422, leaving an heir who was only an infant. During the absence from France of England's official regent, John of Lancaster, Duke of Bedford (another brother of the late king), Lydgate was asked by Bedford's representative Richard de Beauchamp, the fifth Earl of Warwick, to write the

relatively short poem known as *The Title and Pedigree of Henry VI* (1427). Also while in Paris he was commissioned by Thomas Montacute, the fourth Earl of Salisbury and second husband of Alice Chaucer, to translate Guillaume de Deguileville's *Pèlerinage de la Vie Humaine* (1330–1331; translated as *The Pilgrimage of the Life of Man,* 1426–1430). He returned to London in 1429 for the coronation of Henry VI, spending his time in the following years there, at Windsor, at Bury Saint Edmunds, and occasionally perhaps at Hatfield Broad Oak, but he gave up his priorate in 1434.

Between 1431 and 1439 Lydgate was engaged in writing his greatest historical work, the *Fall of Princes.* In 1433 he completed his *Lives of St. Edmund and St. Fremund* for presentation to young Henry VI on the occasion of his official visit at Bury Saint Edmunds. In 1439 he wrote *The Lives of Saint Alban and Saint Amphibal* for John Whethamstede, Abbot of Saint Albans, the great Benedictine abbey just north of London. Lydgate's last years, which he spent at Bury Saint Edmunds, were quieter. He translated much of the *Secreta Secretorum* as *Secrees of the Old Philisoffres* (1446?), but it had to be completed by Benedict Burgh. In the late 1440s he wrote his *Testament,* a religious poem in which he reveals, among other things, a glimpse of his mischievous boyhood days when he neglected his studies and stole apples from the monastery garden. The personal details are attractive to the present-day reader, but they are probably more conventional than genuinely autobiographical. Lydgate died in late 1449 or in 1450 and was buried at Bury Saint Edmunds.

With a corpus totaling almost 150,000 lines, Lydgate was one of the most voluminous of all English poets. His two great historical works, the *Troy Book* and the *Fall of Princes,* contain 30,000 and 36,365 lines respectively. *The Pilgrimage of the Life of Man* is not far behind with its nearly 25,000 lines. Of the legendary lives of holy people *The Life of Our Lady* is the longest, with some 6,000 lines. By contrast, his Chaucerian romance about the siege of Thebes seems almost short, with only 4,716 lines. Even shorter are courtly poems like *The Temple of Glas,* with a "mere" 1,400 lines, and there are almost countless truly short poems and poems of medium length. Lydgate tried his hand at almost all the literary genres of the time. In addition to those already mentioned, one finds fables (such as his translation of Aesop) and his delightful satirical fable about the two beasts Bycorne and Chichevache: the latter fed on patient wives and was always lean, while the former fed on patient husbands and was fat. There were other relatively short satirical poems, various political poems (such as *The Title and Pedigree of Henry VI* and the *Ballade to King Henry VI on His Coronation*), didactic poems about table manners and about food and drink, didactic poems of a moralistic nature (for example, *As a Mydsomer Rose,* included in John Norton-Smith's collection of Lydgate's *Poems*), numerous religious lyrics and prayers of one sort or another (including the excellent *Ballade in Commendation of Our Lady*, beginning "A thowsand storiis kowde I mo reherse" – analyzed by Schirmer in a pioneering essay and also included in the Norton-Smith volume), and the mummings, that is, poems intended to be recited during pantomimes. Lydgate wrote these mummings not only for nobility and the court but also for prominent citizenry: he did a *Mumming for the Mercers of London* in honor of the Lord Mayor, and another for the goldsmiths of London performing before the same Lord Mayor, and still another honoring the sheriffs of London at a dinner (entitled *Mumming at Bishopswood* by Schirmer and *Balade Sente to the Shirrefs Dyner* by Norton-Smith). The corpus, then, is not only vast in bulk but also in scope and variety. If the position of Poet Laureate had existed in the fifteenth century, it would have been held without question by John Lydgate, the Monk of Bury.

Of the shorter long poems *The Siege of Thebes* (circa 1421) is perhaps the most appealing to modern readers. It begins with a prologue of 176 lines in which Lydgate imagines himself joining Chaucer's pilgrims in Canterbury, where he speaks with the Host (Harry Bailey) and agrees to tell the first tale on the homeward journey. The opening lines are a series of subordinate *when* clauses, in obvious imitation of the opening of Chaucer's General Prologue, but Lydgate's imitation goes far beyond its model in length and complexity; indeed, the reader is hard put to find just where the main clause begins (if it ever does). There are brief references to the Cook, the Miller, and the Reeve, and also to the Pardoner, "beerdlees al his Chyn, / Glasy-Eyed and face of Cherubyn, / Tellyng a tale to angre with the frere" – whom Lydgate partly confuses with the Summoner, in an apparent slip of memory. He goes on to describe himself in terms somewhat reminiscent of the Clerk, but it is in his depiction of Chaucer's self-assured, plainspoken Host where he is most convincing. Bailey's direct discourse rings amazingly true with its lack of delicacy, its interspersed oaths and earthy humor, and its echoes of Chaucer's diction and phraseology.

The story that Lydgate tells as the pilgrims depart from Canterbury is meant to be a companion piece to "The Knight's Tale." It relates the momentous events that occurred before Duke Theseus of Athens, in Chaucer's opening lines, encounters the Greek ladies dressed in black who are bewailing the deaths of their husbands and loved ones and the fact that Creon, who is now king in Thebes, will not allow them to bury or cremate the bodies of men who had fought against the city. In three parts, Lydgate's tale is a free translation in 2,270 iambic pentameter couplets of a medieval French prose romance adapted from the late-twelfth-century metrical *Roman de Thebes,* but the story itself goes back to Statius' *Thebaid* (of the first century). In part 1 Lydgate gives all the necessary background information. He tells of the founding of Thebes by King Amphioun and then relates the complete story of Oedipus and his ill-fated marriage to Jocasta, his mother. The subsequent dispute over the kingship between their sons, Eteocles and Polyneices, brings about the siege that turns out to be devastating to both sides. At appropriate places along the way, Lydgate gives advice to contemporary princes. Amphioun successfully won the esteem and affection of his subjects because of his humility and gentle demeanor; he is someone to be emulated. The story of Oedipus, on the other hand, shows (rather too obviously) what can happen if a prince makes a bad marriage. When Oedipus discovers who he really is, his sons treat him despicably, but children ought to honor their parents, and those that do not will come to an "vnhappy ende."

Although it has been argued that Lydgate's retelling of the Oedipus story shows an improvement over his immediate sources, most readers find it bland and colorless in comparison with Sophocles' play. However, the differences in detail between the medieval account and *Oedipus Rex* are sometimes intriguing. Lydgate tells precisely why the infant Oedipus's ankles were pierced (Sophocles is vague on the point); huntsmen of King Polybus find the babe hanging from a tree (there are no shepherds); the oracle of Apollo advises Oedipus to go to Thebes to discover his parentage, instead of intimating that he is doomed to kill his father and sleep with his mother; Oedipus slays his father in a tournament rather than at a place where three roads meet. The riddle of the Sphinx is stated and explained fully. Creon and Teiresias are not mentioned, nor are the Thebans suffering from the plague. When the final revelation of Oedipus's identity comes, Lydgate's Jocasta does not hang herself; she is alive and well in Thebes during the siege and tries, without success, to negotiate peace between her sons.

Part 2 tells of the events prior to the siege. According to a formally accepted agreement, Eteocles

First page of Lydgate's The Lives of Saints Edmund and Fremund *in a fifteenth-century scribal copy. The illustration shows Lydgate presenting the volume to Henry VI (British Library, MS. Harley 2278, fol. 6ᵃ).*

becomes King of Thebes after Oedipus's death because he is the older brother. He is to reign for a year while Polyneices must go off to seek his fortunes elsewhere. At the end of the year the brothers are to exchange roles. Although having grave doubts about his brother's designs, Polyneices does depart from the city. While seeking shelter during a storm, he encounters the Caledonian prince Tydeus, the real hero of Lydgate's poem, who is in exile for having accidentally killed his own brother. In trying to escape the storm, the two men have unwittingly stumbled upon the castle of King Adrastus, who befriends them and, being without a male heir, is pleased to have them marry his daughters. He agrees to help Polyneices in his dispute with Eteocles. Graciously offering to be Polyneices' ambassador, even though the mission is dangerous, Tydeus goes to Thebes to find out whether Eteocles will abide by the agreement. When it is clear that he will not relinquish the kingship, Tydeus roundly and publicly denounces him and then departs. Enraged, Eteocles sends fifty knights out after him to kill him, but Tydeus defends himself valiantly and kills all of them but one, whom he orders to go back and report to Eteocles the outcome of his deceit. The man does so, and then suddenly grabs a sword and kills himself. Eteocles' conduct, unbecoming of a ruler, leads Lydgate into reflections on the importance of a prince's being true to sworn agreements. Eteocles listens to flatterers and decides to keep the throne for himself, despite much good advice to the contrary. Clearly Lydgate believes that the false cause to which he was dedicated brought about his ruin: "For this the fyn: falshede shal not availe, / Ageynes trouth in feeld to hold batayle"; and again: "Ageynes trouthe falshed hath no myght" – lines curiously anticipating by some 225 years John Milton's famous remark in the *Areopagitica* (1644): "Let [Truth] and Falsehood grapple; who ever knew Truth put to the worse in a free and open encounter."

In part 3 the Greeks decide to embrace Polyneices' cause and to make war on Thebes, despite the admonition of their respected soothsayer, Amphiorax, that war will prove devastating. He foresees also that he will meet with his own death if he accompanies the Greek forces. As the men move toward Thebes, they run out of water, and their enterprise nearly ends at the outset in disaster until they are helped by the princess Ipsiphyle, who is in the service of King Lycurgus. However, in leaving the king's infant son unattended while she shows the Greeks the way to a river, she makes a serious error in judgment, for the infant is bitten by a snake

and dies. The grateful Greeks are not about to leave her in the lurch. Mindful of her timely help, Adrastus pleads on her behalf before Lycurgus, who, although grieved beyond words, spares her life. This whole episode is something of a digression, but it does present in a favorable light the leaders of the forces against Thebes. (Also, the consolation offered to Lycurgus by Adrastus recalls the words of Theseus and his father Egeus in "The Knight's Tale" after the death of Arcite.)

When the Greeks arrive at the walls of Thebes, Eteocles belatedly asks his followers for advice. Almost all of them try to persuade him to abide by the previous agreement, Jocasta telling him plainly that he will be held accountable for the many people who will be slain for his sake. Eteocles then offers terms for peace, which are conveyed to the Greek leaders by Jocasta herself, but they are much too unrealistic to be acceptable. Amphiorax warns again that war will be a disaster for everyone, but the war begins, ironically, when a pet tiger of Thebes gets loose and frightens the Greeks, who kill it, and Thebans retaliate by coming out from the city and killing Greeks. In the final pages of the story, Lydgate has plenty of occasion to comment both directly and indirectly on the evil, the horror, and the absurdity of war. Amphiorax meets with his expected death when the ground opens and swallows him up. Many of the Greeks are so discouraged that they wish to discontinue the siege, but Adrastus and his advisers decide that it would be too great a loss of honor and fame if they should pack up and go home. As the fighting resumes, Tydeus is killed by an arrow shot by a Theban defending the city. His death is followed by the deaths of Eteocles and Polyneices, who engage in close combat and kill each other. Finally only Adrastus and King Campaneus are left alive among the Greek leaders. No Theban knights are alive, and Creon (not identified as Jocasta's brother) is elected king by the Theban parliament. In the meantime news has spread throughout Greece of the tragedy, and multitudes of ladies "clad all in blak and barfoot euerychon" wend their way toward Thebes.

This is the point at which Chaucer's "The Knight's Tale" begins. Creon refuses to allow the ladies to dispose properly of the bodies of their loved ones. Theseus arrives on this stark scene of death and grief; he kills Creon, defeats the Theban host, and destroys the city. The ladies are now free to burn the bodies of the fallen Greeks – Lydgate dwelling in some detail on the pagan obsequies while pretending to pass over them (in an obvious imitation of Chaucer's similar use of *occupatio* in the

Knight's description of Arcite's funeral pyre). Jocasta and her daughters Antigone and Ismene are taken to Athens as prisoners; Theseus returns to Athens; Adrastus returns home and dies soon thereafter. "Lo, her the fyn of contek and debat. / Lo, her the myght of Mars the froward sterre. / Lo, what it is for-to gynne a werre." (Lydgate's sentence structure here recalls the third-from-the-last stanza of Chaucer's *Troilus and Criseyde*.) The Christian monk has further appropriate observations on the horrors of war, which he believes is caused primarily by covetousness and false ambition. He looks forward to a time when "Martys swerd shal no more menace" and when love and peace shall prevail.

The Siege of Thebes succeeds and pleases for a number of reasons. The subject matter in itself is interesting: the story is a good one, with many a memorable scene, and the lessons it conveys about the horror and absurdity of war are profound and of perennial concern. The poem is long, but not too long. Lydgate has managed to eschew prolixity and the parading of encyclopedic knowledge that some modern readers find tedious about his other long poems. In conceiving of this poem as an additional Canterbury tale, he has filled it with numerous specific references to Chaucer and "The Knight's Tale" and with almost countless echoes of Chaucer's diction and phraseology; sometimes he has consciously borrowed Chaucer's rhetoric and sentence structure. *The Siege of Thebes* is obviously written by a poet who was utterly fascinated with Chaucer's works and who had read Chaucer as closely as anyone of his time. While the prologue in Canterbury contains one of Lydgate's set tributes to Chaucer, the poem as a whole is his supreme tribute to the earlier, greater poet. All in all, it is one of the most eminently readable poems surviving in Middle English.

Many consider the *Fall of Princes* (1431–1439) Lydgate's magnum opus; at 36,365 lines, it is certainly his longest work. Although the *Fall of Princes* is often described as a history of Fortune, it is actually more like an encyclopedia of cautionary tales, gathered from myth as well as from classical, biblical, and medieval history, recounting the tragic histories of illustrious men and women whom "from hih estat [men] cast in low degre." Lydgate begins with the Fall of Adam and Eve and ends, eight books later, with the almost contemporary account of the capture of King John of France at the Battle of Poitiers in 1356. The *Fall of Princes* is a translation of a French prose translation of Giovanni Boccaccio's *De casibus virorum illustrium* (1355–1360) which Lydgate undertook at the behest of his patron Humphrey, Duke of Gloucester, brother to Henry V and protector of England during the minority of Henry VI. In the Prologue to the *Fall*, Lydgate states that Humphrey considered *De casibus virorum illustrium* "onto pryncis gretli necessarie / To yive exaumple how this world doth varie." According to Lydgate it was Humphrey who requested that the poet follow "everi tragedie" with an envoy specifically directed to princes, making clear how "by othres fallyng [thei myht] themsilff correcte." This taste for illustrative tales from history is typical of kings and nobles of the fifteenth century, many of whom kept such reading material by their bedside in the belief that "reedyng off bookis bryngith in vertu, / . . . / Makith a prynce to have experience, / To knowe hymsilff, in many sundri wise."

A prince looking to escape the vagaries of Fortune would, however, have found conflicting advice in the *Fall of Princes*. At one extreme, Lydgate argues fatalistically that the entire world is at the mercy of Lady Fortune, from whom there is no escape, even for the virtuous. Elsewhere in the poem, however, he maintains, as did Boethius in *The Consolation of Philosophy* (circa 525), that the remedy for Fortune lies in contempt for the things of this world. Book 3 of the *Fall of Princes* opens with a debate between Fortune and Glad Poverty in which Poverty claims that she need not fear Fortune's changeableness for the simple reason that she does not seek those worldly gifts and honors which are under Fortune's control. Chaucer also warns about putting too much trust in the things of this world in the palinode to *Troilus and Criseyde*, his own Boethian tragedy. However, in the final lines of that poem, the narrator goes beyond this *contemptus mundi* to an explicitly Christian understanding that the only source of true felicity and permanence is God. Lydgate the monk seems to resist this final step in the Boethian solution. In its place he offers yet another explanation of the workings of Fortune, which, although it flatly contradicts earlier formulations, offers a less ascetic but more worldly and manageable explanation of Fortune's caprices. According to this view, Fortune is simply an instrument of God's justice here on earth; as such, she rewards men according to their deserts. Thus, virtuous men can expect to enjoy good fortune and the honors and material prosperity that go along with it while sinful men cannot complain of their fate since bad fortune is but another name for the punishment of sin.

This last view of Fortune gives form to a number of biographies of individual princes in the *Fall of Princes*. In the majority of these, Lydgate has reworked his sources in order to underscore the inter-workings of sin and fate. One such tragic biography is that of Theseus in book 1. Lydgate actually relates the details of Theseus's life in two separate sections of the book; in each instance, he is careful to identify the fatal flaw in Theseus's character that leads to his eventual fall. Lydgate's first mention of Theseus comes while he is recounting the history of the Minotaur and the kings of Thebes. Theseus, of course, escaped the labyrinth of the Minotaur with the help of the king of Thebes's two daughters, Ariadne and Phaedra. Despite his promise to marry Ariadne, the older of the two, in return for her help, Theseus eventually deserts her on an island in order to run off with her younger sister, whom he eventually marries. Chaucer gives a poignant account of Ariadne's grief and sense of betrayal at Theseus's desertion in his *Legend of Good Women* (circa 1386), but he makes no attempt to integrate this image of Theseus-the-seducer with his portrait of Theseus-the-ideal-knight-and-king in "The Knight's Tale." Lydgate, on the other hand, takes pains to rectify the two accounts, for even though the emphasis of his story is on the incident involving the Minotaur, he is careful to mention Theseus's later kindness to the Athenian widows in an obvious reference to the opening scene of "The Knight's Tale." According to Lydgate this chivalry is all for naught because "froward Fortune in a-wait eek lay, / For his diffautis to hyndre hym yiff she may." Later when he is king of Athens, Theseus makes another fatal mistake, again involving a woman. In this instance, according to Lydgate, Theseus believes Phaedra's accusations against Hippolytus, her stepson. These accusations eventually prove false, but not before Hippolytus dies fleeing his father's wrath and Phaedra kills herself. Theseus sees all of this as fit punishment for his desertion of Ariadne. Lydgate, however, cannot pass up the opportunity to warn as well against listening to women's counsel.

Lydgate continues to give flesh-and-blood shape to his concept of Fortune in other moralized biographies, scattered throughout the *Fall of Princes*. One of the most notable is his account of the life and death of King Arthur in book 8. He portrays Arthur as the ideal Christian chivalric king, whose reign ushers in a new golden age for Britain; nonetheless, in Lydgate's little Arthuriad, Arthur too comes to a tragic end because of his choice of Mordred, a treacherous kinsman, as protector of the realm during his absence. Certainly, the Arthur of legend is, like Theseus, deserving of punishment, but Lydgate's Arthur has no fatal flaw, no adulter-ous wife, no illegitimate son. Instead, he seems to be the victim of the doubleness and discord endemic to this world; he is the tragic figure of the good king, doomed to fall by virtue of active service to the world.

With the division of the kingdom of Britain following Arthur's death, the lessons of the *Fall of Princes* come full circle, for Lydgate began the poem with a detailed history of the Theban kings, a history (as the account in *The Siege of Thebes* reveals) that is rife with incest, patricide, quarrels and blood-letting between kinsmen, and the subsequent division of the kingdom. In a famous envoy at the end of book 2, Lydgate warns that Rome too will fall as a result of its foundation in robbery, murder, and the quarrel between Romulus and Remus (a history that plays itself out in subsequent books of the poem). Thus, in the *Fall of Princes,* as in *The Siege of Thebes* and Lydgate's other chronicle, the *Troy Book,* individual exempla give way to a more generalized theory of history, which, while it focuses on individual moral choice, also addresses larger cyclical patterns, the rise and fall of civilizations, that result from man's continuing failure to amend his behavior despite very obvious lessons from the past. One is reminded of the fourteenth-century poet John Gower's assertion in the prologue to the *Confessio Amantis* (circa 1390–1392) that "man ... is as a world in his partie, / And whan this litel world mistorneth, / The grete world al overtorneth."

The *Fall of Princes* became one of Lydgate's most popular works, a popularity that continued throughout the Renaissance, culminating in the publication of the *Mirror for Magistrates* (1559), a source for William Shakespeare's history plays. Although the *Fall of Princes* was printed in four editions between 1494 and 1555, nearly ten times that number of manuscripts containing selections from the poem existed during this same time. Ironically, although the Renaissance considered Lydgate's poem a fairly reliable translation of Boccaccio, it was the envoys, those moralizing passages requested by Duke Humphrey and dutifully added by Lydgate, that were most frequently excerpted and therefore best known in the Renaissance as the legacy of Boccaccio and Lydgate.

Almost from the time of his death, and in an association that soon became formulaic, Lydgate's name was linked with that of Chaucer and his contemporary Gower as one of the "primier poetes of this nacion." Certainly, the number of extant manuscripts and, after the advent of printing, of printed editions of Lydgate's works (most particularly of the *Troy Book* and the *Fall of Princes*) attests to his importance and continuing popularity throughout the fifteenth and sixteenth centuries and even into the beginning of the seventeenth century. Indeed, as late as 1559 John Bale, in his influential *Scriptorum Illustrium Majoris Brytannie Quam nunc Angliam et Scotiam Vocant: Catalogus,* refers to Lydgate as first among the early English poets in eloquence and erudition. In a famous encomium to Lydgate in the opening lines of *The Pastime of Pleasure* (1509), Stephen Hawes, addressing King Henry VII, singles out these same qualities along with "fruitfulness" or productivity as meriting special praise, qualities which the Renaissance in general prized in Lydgate:

Nothynge I am / experte in poetry
As the monke of Bury / floure of eloquence
Whiche was in tyme / of grete excellence

Of your predecessour / the .v. kynge henry
Vnto whose grace / he dyde present
Ryght famous bokes / of parfyte memory
Of his faynynge / with termes eloquent
Whose fatall fyccyons / are yet permanent
Grounded on reason / with clowdy fygures
He cloked the trouth / of all his scryptures

Lydgate also sees himself as a follower of Chaucer, albeit a humble one. He would undoubtedly have agreed wholeheartedly with those Renaissance critics who saw him as the heir to Chaucer's rhetorical style, a style that he praises time and again and that he tries to imitate. In contrast, Lydgate mentions Gower only once in the *Fall of Princes* and then in connection with the philosophical Strode in a line that obviously has its origins in the palinode to Chaucer's *Troilus and Criseyde.* Nonetheless, it is generally acknowledged that Lydgate's tale of Canace in the *Fall of Princes* closely follows Gower's version in the *Confessio Amantis,* as is probably the case with the first half of the life of the Emperor Constantine in book 8, and yet of this indebtedness Lydgate makes no mention. Despite this silence, the subsequent linking of Lydgate to Gower seems particularly apt since Lydgate is in many ways more Gower's heir than Chaucer's.

Ironically, the ornate rhetorical style that Lydgate claims most closely identifies him with Chaucer and that subsequent centuries repeatedly point to as shared by the two poets, actually distinguishes the two. Those very features that distinguish Lydgate's aureate style – ornate, sonorous Latinate words, or what one critic referred to as "changyd Latin," and the use of figures and rhetorical flourishes for their own sake – also distinguish it from Chaucer's style, as any comparison of similar passages from the two poets demonstrates. John Skelton alone among Renaissance poets recognized this difference between the two poets and in a criticism that proved prophetic accused Lydgate of being "too haut" or ornate as well as too verbose. In this regard, Lydgate differs from Gower as well, who was known for his plain style, described by C. S. Lewis as "direct and genuine." If, then, Lydgate does not share aureate style with Chaucer and Gower, in what sense might he claim to be their heir, if not their equal?

Much more is known about Lydgate's reliance on Chaucer than on Gower, in large part because Lydgate himself is always reminding his readers of the similarity; however, Lydgate's account of the extent and nature of Chaucer's influence is not entirely reliable. Despite his frequent claims that he will refrain from telling a certain story because Chaucer told it before him (for example, in the *Fall of Princes* when he says it would be presumptuous of him to tell the story of Philomena or of Lucrece), in truth he offers his own version of practically every one of Chaucer's major poems; in this sense, he models his poetic career after Chaucer's. Thus, for the *Book of the Duchess* (circa 1368–1369), there is Lydgate's *The Complaint of the Black Knight;* for Chaucer's *House of Fame* (circa 1378–1381), Lydgate's *The Temple of Glas;* for *Troilus and Criseyde,* Lydgate's *Troy Book;* for the *Legend of Good Women* and "The Monk's Tale," the *Fall of Princes;* and for the *Canterbury Tales* (circa 1375–1400), Lydgate's own tale, *The Siege of Thebes.* Yet despite this repetition, Chaucer and Lydgate are very different poets, particularly in their approach to history and in their conception of the role of the poet. In both these instances it could be said that Lydgate is modeling himself after Gower, not Chaucer.

Both Gower and Lydgate share the same conception of the role of the poet. Lydgate frequently compares himself to Amphioun, the legendary founder of Thebes, who with "his harpyng made folk of louh degrees, / As laboreres, tenhabite first cites; – / And so bi musik and philosophie / Gan first of comouns noble policie." There are obvious echoes here of Gower's claim in the *Confessio Amantis* that he is the new Arion, who, through his harping, will cause the lord to agree with the shepherd, the lion to lie down with the lamb, thereby establishing peace (also a common theme of the two poets) where there was previously only division. The theme of division also runs throughout the two poets' works (Lydgate even wrote a prose work about it: *The Serpent of Division*); both poets agree that division is the cause of the lamentable state of

Illumination showing Lydgate praying at the shrine of Saint Edmund; from a fifteenth-century scribal copy of
Lydgate's The Lives of Saints Edmund and Fremund *(British Library, MS. Harley 2278, fol. 9)*

the world. As Lydgate says of Thebes and certainly by extension of his own England, "Kyngdamys devyded may no while endure." Like Gower, Lydgate also maintains in the *Fall of Princes* that division in man, for which sin is but another name, is the ultimate cause of the world's woes. Both poets feel that the way to heal this division is to recall for man, and more particularly for princes, examples from the past to serve as a corrective on current excesses. In keeping with this view Gower approaches history as a vast storehouse of illustrative tales, a veritable "Mirour of ensamplerie," as he calls it. Lydgate also approaches history in this way, even in his historical chronicles, where he prizes the exemplary incident over the sweep of historical event. In contrast, Chaucer demonstrated an uneasiness with collections of moral exempla all making the same point in "The Monk's Tale," where this prolixity was seen as a failure of the Monk's character, as well as in the *Legend of Good Women,* which he abandoned, much to Gower's distress. Certainly, in his role as "public poet" and advisor to kings, Lydgate takes on the moralizing voice of Gower, not the ironic voice of Chaucer.

Born in about the same year, Lydgate and Hoccleve never knew each other personally, and apparently neither was cognizant of the other's work, but as poets they resemble one another in several respects, especially as they relate to Chaucer. Both

wrote essentially in the East Midland dialect of Middle English, which was the language of Chaucer and the basis for modern English. They both occasionally echo Chaucer's diction and phraseology, Lydgate more so than Hoccleve. Both have a predilection for the seven-line rhyme-royal stanza that Chaucer used in *Troilus and Criseyde* and several of the Canterbury tales. Although both adopted Chaucer's favorite meter, iambic pentameter, rather than the alliterative verse of the *Pearl* Poet and of William Langland, they have used it with more freedom, especially noticeable in the so-called broken-backed lines, in which two heavily accented syllables come together in the middle of a line. In larger structural matters Hoccleve reveals his indebtedness to Chaucer in his "Series"-group of five poems joined together by a framework, while Lydgate shows his indebtedness most conspicuously in his own Canterbury tale, *The Siege of Thebes.* If Hoccleve is more noted for his lively direct discourse, which is certainly Chaucerian, Lydgate is closer to Chaucer in his humorously satirical attitude toward women. He sometimes translates a blatantly antifeminist passage from Latin or French with great relish and embellishment while pretending that he must be true to his source.

With only about thirteen thousand lines of poetry to his credit, Hoccleve is no match for Lydgate, who wrote over ten times as much. Along with the greater bulk is a wider variety. While both poets wrote hymns to the Virgin, other prayers, begging poems, political poems, and occasional poems, Hoccleve wrote no saints' legends, no verses to accompany religious processions, no rhymed sermons, no fables, and no mummings. Both wrote important didactic verse, but in different modes. Hoccleve's magnum opus is his *Regement of Princes* (1411–1412), a traditional manual of instruction for princes in verse in which various qualities that a prince should or should not have are illustrated by stories. Lydgate preferred to give instruction to princes not in a typical *De Regimine Principum* but rather in his tale of the siege and fall of Thebes, which he interrupts at several appropriate places to offer comments on behavior befitting or not befitting a prince or king, and of course in his *Fall of Princes,* where he offers very sensible advice that would behoove any ruler to heed and follow.

In two realms Hoccleve and Lydgate are as different as day and night. Even when Hoccleve's reputation in literary histories was at its lowest ebb, he was admired for his poems of self-revelation: *La Male Regle* (1406), the prologue to the *Regement of Princes,* his *Complaint* (1422), and his *Dialogue with a Friend* (1422). Poems of this sort, in which a clear, individualized portrait of their creator emerges, are virtually unique in Middle English literature. Lydgate, like Chaucer, says little or nothing about himself that is not largely conventional. Both Hoccleve and Lydgate wrote Marian hymns and lyrics, but the results are markedly different. Hoccleve describes the Virgin in human terms, especially when he imagines her at the foot of the Cross lamenting the death of her son; the simple, unadorned diction of his one *planctus Mariae* very effectively depicts her grief. Lydgate, in contrast, prefers to think of Mary as the Queen of Heaven, enthroned in glory and magnificence, and for this conception he resorts to the aureate diction for which he is famous, as in the opening stanza of his *Ave Regina Celorum:*

> Hayle luminary & benigne lanterne,
> Of Ierusalem the holy ordres nyne,
> As quene of quenes laudacion eterne
> They yeue to thee, O excellente virgyne!
> Eclypsyd I am, for to determyne
> Thy superexcellence of Cantica canticorum,
> The aureat beames do nat in me shyne,
> Aue regina celorum!

Despite Lydgate's pose that the aureate beams do not shine in him, they did, and he knew it. This is a good example of what has been called the "new religious style" of the fifteenth century; Lydgate was its foremost proponent and practitioner. Whatever the reader may think about the poetic merits of this style, Lydgate in any case is important in the history and development of the English language because of his having introduced into it a large number of polysyllabic Latinate words that have since become standard vocabulary.

Lydgate's place in the annals of English literature has risen very noticeably, if not dramatically, in the past forty-five years. Walter F. Schirmer's *John Lydgate* (1952, translated, 1961), the first of the important book-length studies, is still the most useful because of its careful placement of Lydgate in historical and literary-historical context. Alain Renoir's *The Poetry of John Lydgate* (1967) is especially noteworthy for its detailed and excellent treatment of *The Siege of Thebes*. The other long poems are discussed, but not as fully, and Renoir perhaps overstates the case that Lydgate was a precursor of the Renaissance. Derek Pearsall's *John Lydgate* (1970) provides well-balanced analyses of the major poems and is refreshingly critical in its approach, but it does not say a lot that was not known already. Lois A. Ebin's 1985 Twayne book is conspicuous for its helpful analysis of Lydgate's poetic technique. The past forty-five years have seen the publication of so many fine notes and articles on various aspects of the poet's vast output that the references that follow are necessarily selective. While John Lydgate will never hold the high place he once did, at present his work has rightfully become a subject of serious scholarly inquiry. The best of him may eventually be standard reading in courses on medieval literature.

There is no book-length biography of Lydgate as such, but much biographical material can be gleaned from the pages of Schirmer's *John Lydgate;* and although written over a century ago, Joseph Schick's introduction to his 1891 edition of *The Temple of Glas* is still useful in this regard. Manuscripts of Lydgate's many and often lengthy works are so numerous that a complete listing is beyond the scope of this study. The reader is referred to Carlton Brown and Rossell Hope Robbins, *The Index of Middle English Verse* (1943), and to Robbins and J. L. Cutler, *Supplement to the Index* (1965), for information of this sort; to Alain Renoir and C. David Benson's section on Lydgate in *A Manual of the Writings in Middle English, 1050–1500* (1980); and to the introductions of the standard editions, especially the prefatory material to Henry Noble MacCracken's edition of Lydgate's *Minor Poems* (1911), which is useful not only for manuscript information but also for MacCracken's pioneering establishment of the Lydgate canon. In the past many poems were attributed to Lydgate that he probably did not write; indeed, the exact Lydgate canon is still a matter of uncertainty and dispute.

Bibliographies:

Alain Renoir and C. David Benson, "John Lydgate," in *A Manual of the Writings in Middle English, 1050-1500,* volume 6, edited by Albert E. Hartung (Hamden: Archon/Shoe String Press for the Connecticut Academy of Arts and Sciences, 1980), pp. 1809-1920, 2071-2175;

A. S. G. Edwards, "Lydgate Scholarship: Progress and Prospects," in *Fifteenth-Century Studies: Recent Essays,* edited by Robert F. Yeager (Hamden, Conn.: Archon/Shoe String Press, 1984), pp. 29-47.

References:

Robert W. Ayers, "Medieval History, Moral Purpose, and the Structure of Lydgate's *Siege of Thebes,*" *PMLA,* 73 (December 1958): 463-474;

C. David Benson, *The History of Troy in Middle English Literature* (Ipswich: Brewer, 1980), pp. 97-129;

Carlton Brown and Rossell Hope Robbins, *The Index of Middle English Verse* (New York: Columbia University Press, 1943);

Richard A. Dwyer, "Arthur's Stellification in the *Fall of Princes,*" *Philological Quarterly,* 57 (Spring 1979): 155-171;

Lois A. Ebin, *John Lydgate* (Boston: Twayne, 1985);

A. S. G. Edwards, "The Influence of Lydgate's *Fall of Princes* c. 1440-1559: A Survey," *Mediaeval Studies,* 39 (1977): 424-439;

R. D. S. Jack, "Dunbar and Lydgate," *Studies in Scottish Literature,* 8 (1971): 215-227;

John Norton-Smith, "Lydgate's Changes in the *Temple of Glas,*" *Medium Ævum,* 27, no. 3 (1958): 166-172;

Derek Pearsall, "Chaucer and Lydgate," in *Studies in Honour of Derek Brewer,* edited by Ruth Morse and Barry Windeatt (Cambridge: Cambridge University Press, 1990), pp. 39-53;

Pearsall, *John Lydgate* (London: Routledge & Kegan Paul / Charlottesville: University Press of Virginia, 1970);

Alain Renoir, *The Poetry of John Lydgate* (Cambridge, Mass.: Harvard University Press / London: Routledge & Kegan Paul, 1967);

Rossell Hope Robbins and J. L. Cutler, *Supplement to the Index of Middle English Verse* (Lexington: University of Kentucky Press, 1965);

Walter F. Schirmer, *John Lydgate: A Study in the Culture of the XVth Century,* translated from the 1952 German edition by Ann E. Keep (London: Methuen / Berkeley & Los Angeles: University of California Press, 1961);

Schirmer, "Der Stil in Lydgates Religiöser Dichtung," in his *Kleine Schriften* (Tübingen: Niemeyer, 1950), pp. 40-56;

A. C. Spearing, "Lydgate's Canterbury Tale *The Siege of Thebes* and Fifteenth-Century Chaucerianism," in *Fifteenth-Century Studies: Recent Essays,* edited by Robert F. Yeager (Hamden, Conn.: Archon/Shoe String Press, 1984), pp. 333-364;

Elfriede Tilgner, *Die Aureate Terms als Stilelement bei Lydgate,* Germanische Studien no. 182 (Berlin: Ebering, 1936).

Sir Thomas Malory

(circa 1400–1410 – 14 March 1471)

Jeffrey Helterman
University of South Carolina

WORKS: (1451-1470)

Manuscript: The only extant manuscript, a transcription in the hands of two scribes and dating from circa 1475, is the Winchester Manuscript in the British Library (Add. MS. 59678). Facsimile: *The Winchester Malory: A Facsimile,* edited by N. R. Ker, EETS, supplemental series 4 (1976).

First publication: *Thus endeth thys noble and Ioyous book entytled le morte Darthur* [colophon] (Westminster: Printed by William Caxton, 1485; facsimile, New York: Scolar, 1976).

Standard edition: *The Works of Sir Thomas Malory,* 3 volumes, edited by Eugène Vinaver (Oxford: Clarendon Press, 1947); third edition, revised by P. J. C. Field (Oxford: Clarendon Press, 1990).

The central issue of Malory scholarship and, therefore, of critical interpretation is whether the body of his work is a "hoole booke" or a collection of diverse tales centering in the Arthurian court. From the publication of William Caxton's edition in 1485 until this century, it was assumed that the body of work was a whole book that should be given the name of the last tale, "Le Morte Darthur." It was not until the discovery of the Winchester Manuscript of Malory by W. F. Oakeshott in 1934 that the unity of the work was seriously questioned. The manuscript, which predates Caxton, seems closer to Malory's original than does Caxton's printed text, based on another manuscript that is no longer extant. The Winchester Manuscript is a handwritten transcription, while the Caxton text, with a fulsome, rather moralistic preface, seems much more the *edition* by England's first printer. A study of the Winchester Manuscript by Eugène Vinaver indicates that Caxton made changes in chapter rubrics and linkages that create more unity among these Arthurian tales than Malory intended. Vinaver's edition (1947), which has become the

standard edition of the text, insists that the collection of tales be called *The Works of Sir Thomas Malory* and not be given *Le Morte Darthur* as an inclusive title. Criticism of Malory since Vinaver's edition, especially the collection of essays *Malory's Originality* (1964), has worked to reestablish the unity of Arthur's story, while making allowances for the anachronisms and inconsistencies (such as dead characters appearing in later tales). The resurfacing of the Winchester Manuscript reminds us that Malory's literary career ended right at the cusp that separated hand copying of manuscripts from printing. When Malory died (perhaps of the plague) in 1471, he could not have imagined any other transmission of his text than by the labor of hand copying. Given the length of the manuscript, one can imagine that very few such copies were made. Yet when, less than fourteen years later, Caxton set out to print the book, he guaranteed not only that Malory would be vilified for the so-called immorality of the popular book, but also, since Caxton set up as what would now be considered a publisher rather than simply a printer, that the book would be launched by a preface that trumpeted the book's morality. "I . . . have doon sette it in enprynte to the entente that noble men may see and lerne the noble actes of chyvalrye. . . ."

Certainly the Winchester Manuscript is full of small inconsistencies which could well be explained by the checkered career of the author even if he were trying to write a unified book. Sir Thomas Malory, a knight of Warwickshire, was born between 1400 and 1410 to Sir John Malory and his wife, Philippa, and came into his father's holdings in 1433. He fought at Calais in 1436 and late in his life was involved on the side of Richard Neville, Earl of Warwick, in the Wars of the Roses. Warwick, as William Shakespeare records it in *Henry VI,* part 3 (circa 1590-1592), and *Richard III* (circa 1591-1592), was a traitor to Edward IV and went over to the Lancastrian side in 1468-1469 – and

Sir John Malory and his wife, Philippa, the parents of Sir Thomas Malory. This sketch of a stained-glass window that was once in Grendon Church was first published in William Dugdale's Antiquities of Warwickshire Illustrated *(1656).*

presumably so did Malory. Malory was already a well-known ne'er-do-well, who had been accused of ambushing and attempting to murder Humphrey Stafford, Duke of Buckingham, in 1450, of raping (or perhaps only seizing) the wife of another man twice in that same year, and of twice robbing the Cistercian Abbey of Blessed Mary Coombe in 1451. Over the years, beginning in 1451, Malory was jailed eight times, escaping twice by violent means. During this time Malory wrote most of what are now called his collected works. Prisoners then could use their own resources to fit themselves out well. Malory seems to have been fairly comfortable in prison, and while he was in Newgate (1460–1462) he had access to a nearby monastic library. In such turmoil, even if Malory intended to unify his works, it would seem unlikely that he could do it neatly. Even Shakespeare, only under the exigency of getting out a play in time, nodded often. He introduces Cassio as "a fellow damned in a fair wife," but in

the text of *Othello* (1604), Cassio's wife disappears. So Malory, writing between brief bouts of freedom, is unlikely to be able to hold onto the details that would make the work seamless. It is also unlikely that the work, which comes to some nine hundred pages in the Oxford edition, was ever revised.

It is Malory who gave Arthur to England, who shaped the legend so that there could be Alfred Tennyson's *Idylls of the King* (1855–1885) and T. H. White's *Once and Future King* (1958). Arthur began as little more than a tribal chieftain. He was elevated by Geoffrey of Monmouth (who still claimed to be writing history) in his *Historia regum Britanniae* (circa 1138) into a great and tragic hero whose queen is coveted by Mordred. The story grew to huge proportions through the vast prose romances, a "Holy Grail," a "Lancelot," a "Merlin," and a "Death of Arthur" written in France in the thirteenth century. Malory knew these French sources, but it is his vision that gives the Arthurian legend its mythic quality, as he tells of men (and women) who are doomed because they love each other too much. It is likely that Malory began his reworking of this material with a rather pedestrian handling of a story of Arthur at war, the book that turns up finally as book 5, the story of the war between Arthur and Emperor Lucius. This book, different in kind and mood from the rest of Malory's output, is based on a native source, the fourteenth-century *Alliterative Morte Arthure,* rather than the French romances which support the rest of the work. In this tale Arthur and his knights seem much more warriors than courtiers, and there is little sense that Malory put his individual stamp on these characters.

From this handle on Arthurian story, Malory went back to the begetting of Arthur, and with the story of Uther Pendragon he began to explore the delicate lines that separate, and also link, love and hate. In a pattern that Arthur will follow with desperate results, Uther begets Arthur on Igrayne, the wife of his greatest enemy. It is by Merlin's sorcery that Uther is able to accomplish this act, and only by additional treachery is Arthur born in wedlock, though conceived out of it. Such are the unpromising beginnings of a man who would be the greatest king in Christendom. Even as Arthur begins a pattern of virtuous activities, he also repeats his father's sin by begetting a child on Margawse, the wife of King Lot and also Arthur's half sister (she is Igrayne's daughter by her first husband), thereby adding incest to the stain of adultery. The product of this union, Mordred, will finally destroy Arthur and his kingdom.

Arthur, with the conspicuous aid of Merlin, becomes a victorious king and — in a theme that was picked up by Tennyson — the civilizer of the uncivilized. Arthur begins with a signal victory over the five kings, but Malory soon starts to pull at the threads that will destroy the fabric of knighthood everywhere. Arthur's early knights embrace chivalry with unbridled passion and rush off on a series of quests that lead to unmitigated disaster. Clearly, just having the right intentions is not enough. In one early episode three knights pursue three quests with the purpose of avenging the deaths of Gawain's dogs and Pellinor's horse. In furious determination to follow the quest, Pellinor ignores the needs of a wounded knight and his lady. When Pellinor returns from achieving his quest, only the knight's head remains, and the damsel ends up carrying it home. The unsuccored damsel turns out to be Pellinor's own daughter. Pellinor's son, Torre, ends up beheading a man through the ploy of the unexamined boon: the situation in which a knight

pledges his word to an individual to do anything that person asks. Since a knight's word is an oath, to break it would be perjury. Under such constraints Arthur's knights commit many felonies because it is the honorable thing to do. The man whom Sir Torre kills is Abelleus, identified provisionally as the son of a cowherd. The third knight who rides out in this trio of quests is Sir Gawain, supposedly the best of the pre-Lancelotian knights. He beheads a lady by accident and is forced to carry the head with him when he returns from his quest. The toll for this vengeance over the deaths of some dogs and a horse is two beheaded men and one beheaded lady. Abelleus turns out to be another son of Pellinor, not the son of a cowherd but perhaps of a coward. Seeing these disastrous results, Arthur institutes a code of behavior which stresses always succoring ladies, damsels, gentlewomen, and widows — and never taking up battles for a wrongful cause. Now the real trouble starts. Up to this point mayhem has been random and chaotic. Now it is institutionalized, and destructive and self-destructive acts will be carried out because they are the knightly thing to do.

By the time he gets to the story of Balin, or "the Knight with Two Swords," Malory, a witness to, and probable participant in, the Wars of the Roses, has found his theme: divided loyalties, epitomized in the struggle of brother against brother. Balin, like Arthur, can draw a sword that no other man can, a sword that will go only to the best knight, but Balin is warned that with this sword he shall kill the man he loves most in the world. In the narrowest context (of the tale) the target of the sword is his brother Balan, who is slain in a mutual case of mistaken identity; but in a larger context Balin is also the one who will strike the Dolorous Stroke (of the Fisher King legend) and so imperil all Western culture; and, on another backdrop, Balin's drawing this sword marks the beginning of the end of Arthur's world. Malory connects Balin's sword, which kills his brother Balan and delivers the Dolorous Stroke with the sword that Lancelot later uses to kill Gawain, a death that does what not even the adultery of Lancelot and Guinevere can do: it separates Arthur and Lancelot. Malory uses a piece of syntactic maneuvering so that it appears that Lancelot will discover Balin's sword. In fact, it is Galahad who discovers Balin's sword, but the deliberate uncertainty of the locution (at various times — all in the future — Lancelot and Galahad will each be the Best Knight in the World) allows it to appear that Lancelot will have *this* sword and that with it he will kill Gawain: "there shall never man handyll thys swerde but the beste knyght of the worlde, and that shall be sir Launcelot other ellis Galahad, hys sonne. And Launcelot with [t]hys swerde shall sle the man in the worlde that he lovith beste: that shall be sir Gawayne."

After the establishment of the code of courtesy and Arthur's signal victory over Emperor Lucius, it appears that Arthur's world is headed for the order that is largely established in "The Tale of Sir Gareth." This tale of a youth growing into maturity – literally earning his spurs – is the kind of tale told of the two greatest knights, exclusive of Lancelot, of Arthurian legend. In the Middle High German romances, Parzifal and Tristram are polar opposites. Tristram is the prodigy, the child who knows everything – warfare, the code of the hunt, music, and love talk; and Parzifal is the bumpkin, a lad so benighted that he thinks knights in their armor are angels. Both are alike in one thing: they are the subjects of huge romances which record their upbringing. "The Tale of Sir Gareth" is the story of a young man growing up, but significantly, his hero-model, Lancelot, does not share the luxury of a bildungsroman. Lancelot is, when initially presented, the best knight in the world, and he will continue to be plagued by this designation throughout Malory's writings. Gareth, on the other hand, gets a chance to earn the right to use his name only when he is able to shed the mocking nickname Bewmaines, given him by Sir Kay (Bewmaines, which means fair hands, may refer to the fact that when Gareth is put to work as a kitchen knave he has fair, smooth hands rather than the red, rough hands of his supposed lowborn origins). Though Gareth begins as a kitchen knave, he soon meets and defeats a series of different colored knights, one black, one blue, one red, and one green, and then a second red knight, the Red Knight of the Red Launds. It has been suggested that these defeated opponents make Gareth into an astrological hero who defeats the rainbow and then the sun (the Red Knight of the Red Launds, like the sun, grows stronger until noon) and then, in the conquest of the sisters Lyonette and Lyonesse, two representations of the moon (luna). There is no suggestion that Malory was aware of these origins in his sources, only that they are likely to be there.

Though it is not unlikely that the original of Gareth was some kind of conqueror of the heavens, a more satisfying explanation of the colored knights and the marriage with the moon is found in the language of alchemical lore, which would explain both the presence of the Black Knight and the existence of a second red knight. Medieval alchemical texts were usually allegorized so that metals and the reagents with which they were mixed were described as human beings, and the final act of the base metal–protagonist was a marriage. Each of the metals was identified with a heavenly body: copper was Venus, iron Mars, and silver the Moon. The base metal would go through a series of struggles with the personified reagents. In such a system Gareth's meeting with the Black Knight would be the "mortifying" of the original reagent, and his confrontation with the Red Knight would be immersion into the "waters rubifying." In a pattern of alchemy, the defeat of the second red knight, the Red Knight of the Red Launds, would signify "conclusion" of the alchemical process, the base metal becoming gold (in the Middle Ages gold was thought to be red, not yellow, in color).

Gareth's stint as a kitchen knave would increase the likelihood of this alchemical reading, since alchemical experiments were seen as literally "cooking things up," thus the term for the alchemical brew, *concoction*, coined in the Renaissance. Whether Malory would be aware of the alchemical imagery in his tale is uncertain, but it is worthy to note that early in his life there was a flurry of interest in alchemy in England which led to the publication of English (in English, not merely Latin texts written in England) alchemical texts. What might have struck Malory about these texts was the inclusion of Geoffrey Chaucer, because of "The Canon's Yeoman's Tale," as an alchemist. The alchemical reading of "The Tale of Sir Gareth" would reinforce the theme of the growth of the hero so that he can reclaim his name, earn his knighthood, and marry his bride. At the tournament which ends "The Tale of Sir Gareth," events are ordered so that all appears right in Arthur's world. On the three successive days of the tournament, the prize is won by the three best knights in the world with results that confirm both their greatness and their ranking. The third-best knight in the world, Lamerok, wins the first day, defeating thirty knights; the second-best knight in the world, Tristram, wins on the second, defeating forty knights; and, on the final day, the Best Knight in the World, Lancelot, wins, defeating fifty knights. All is right with Arthur's world, but the reader is only halfway through the book. At this point Malory, a man living on the edge and a liegeman of the earl of Warwick, the real-life Best Knight in the World, knows where his book has to go.

After "The Tale of Gareth," Malory's book becomes Lancelot's, even though the next book is the huge, shapeless, and unfinished "Tale of Sir Tristram." From here on Lancelot wrestles with the irritating designation as the Best Knight in the

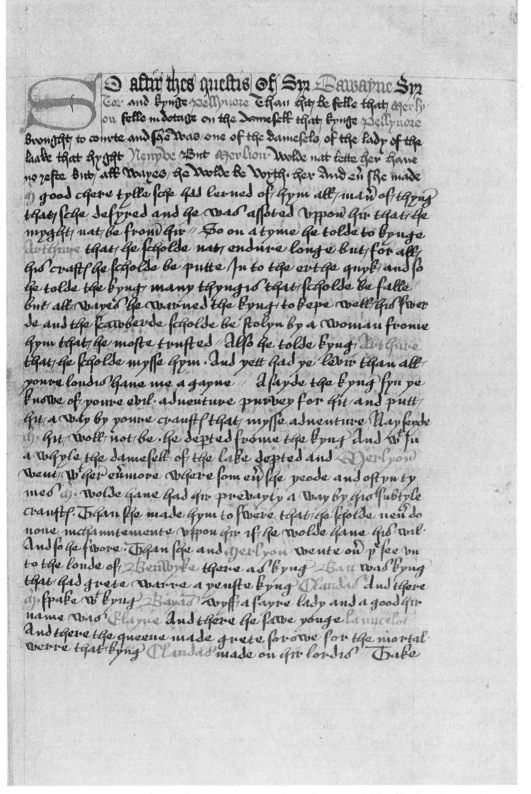

First page of "The Death of Merlin" in the Winchester Manuscript of Malory's works (British Library, Add. MS. 59678, fol. 45)

World. A stranger meets Lancelot, hears his name, and says, Oh you are the Best Knight in the World. In this context appears the significance of Lancelot's not being accorded the bildungsroman granted to his protégé, Gareth, as well as (in other texts) those two paragons Tristram and Parzifal. In a fiercely competitive world, perhaps best exemplified by Sir Palomides, knights pursue combat in the hope of gaining in the world's estimation or worship. Therefore, if the sixth-best knight in the world defeats a better, that is, higher-ranking, knight, he moves up in the world's estimation. For Lancelot this is impossible; he begins — for the reader and for himself — as the Best Knight in the World, so that no victory will change anyone's estimation of him. In order to get beyond his designation, he has only two paths: transcendence or transgression, that is, going beyond the order of things or going below. In "The Tale of Sir Tristram," a vast confused work, Lancelot tries several petty transgressions as a way to cope with one of the inconveniences of being the Best Knight in the World: no one will joust with him once they know who he is. In order to get some competition he pretends to be the worst knight in the world, the craven Sir Kay. Throughout the tale knights, especially Lancelot, refuse to acknowledge who they are and, perhaps worse, allow others to take on their identities. In order to get a combat out of the cowardly King Mark, Lamerok dresses as the even-more-cowardly Kay. Then, to mock Mark even further, Dagonet, the court fool, is dressed as Lancelot, which causes Mark to flee shamefully. But such confusions are made easy because Lancelot has taken to not acknowledging his name. He fights with covered shield, that is, with his coat of arms hidden. The reason for this begins as the pragmatic but soon becomes symbolic. Since the Knights of the Round Table are not supposed to joust against each other, and they include most of the best knights, the only challenge for a knight, such as Lancelot, who wants to be tested would be to fight against them anyway. For this reason Lancelot twice covers his shield and fights against Arthur's knights, but even this transgression pales against his decision to don a gown and fight in the guise of a woman. Even worse, with the gown over his armor, he defeats Sir Dinadan, the most decent of knights, and then Lancelot has his men dress Dinadan in the gown. This behavior makes him more mean-spirited than Sir Kay at his worst.

Yet the aggregate of such aberrant behavior does not begin to match his treatment of the mother of his son in the tale that became the favorite of Tennyson as well as of the Pre-Raphaelite painters.

In "Lancelot and Elaine" Lancelot has a chance to shed officially the title of Best Knight in the World. In a reversal of Sir Gareth's bildungsroman he starts as a man with a proud name and ends with a nickname that epitomizes his opprobrium. For this reason Malory chose to tell the story within the frame of his version of Tristram and Isolde.

In "The Book of Sir Tristram" Malory describes the decline of Arthurian knighthood. Here it is revealed that the three greatest knights in the world are also the three greatest adulterers: Lancelot with Guinevere, Tristram with Isode, and Lamerok with Margawse. From the time of the medieval romance by Gottfried von Straßburg to the Liebestod of Richard Wagner's music drama, the tragic romance of Tristram and Isode was treated with sublimity. Not so in Malory, where it is little more than a pathedy of manners in which Tristram tries in vain to give a little dignity to the hapless Cornish knights of which he is one. Because Malory cuts off Tristram's tale before it ends, the tragic conclusion is simply not forthcoming. Instead, there are many pointless jousting and pathetic outcomes, such as the great Sir Lamerok accidentally killing a man he has just saved and Tristram foolishly marrying the wrong woman because she is also named Isode. More and more both the quest and the joust seem pointless. The symbol of frustration in the book is a shield that the evil Morgan la Fay gives to Tristram to bring as a present to Arthur's court. The shield depicts a king and a queen on a red field with a knight standing above them with a foot on each of them. Morgan only says it represents Arthur and Guinevere and a knight who holds them in bondage. This shield turns out to be the public recognition of Lancelot and Guinevere's adultery, though not even Morgan yet knows Lancelot is guilty of it. Instead, she trusts in her philosophy of believing the worst of everyone, and in this case she is right. Tristram does not understand the message on the shield but carries it to Arthur anyway because he has given Morgan his word that he would. When Tristram reaches Arthur, he has no name (a knight's family name should be represented on his shield). Instead, since he uses Morgan's shield, he unwittingly fights in the name of Lancelot's adultery. In this guise he defeats Arthur, who shatters his lance on the telltale shield. Arthur's impotence against the shield foreshadows the changes that will come to the court once the adultery is made public.

Another of Morgan's devices links the adultery in the two courts with the failure of the greatest knights. In order to embarrass Arthur and Guinevere, Morgan sends a bejeweled drinking horn to

Camelot. No woman can drink wine from this horn without spilling it unless she is faithful to her husband. Morgan expects Guinevere to shame Arthur but is intercepted by Lamerok (whose mistress, Margawse, would not be able to pass the horn test) and sent instead to Mark's Cornish court, where Isode is put to the test and fails. Unfortunately, so do ninety-six of the hundred ladies who try to drink from the horn. The Cornish court decides that either the horn does not work or the results are too demeaning to accept.

The formal history of Lancelot's transgression reaches its peak in the story of Lancelot's begetting of Galahad upon Elaine. As with the begetting of Arthur, it is a matter of lust cooperating with deceit to produce goodness. This time Malory overlays the case with moral ambiguities. The avowed purpose of the tale is to tell of the begetting of the preeminent Grail Knight, Galahad. Even though Elaine is his mother, events are manipulated so that he is born out of the adulterous lust of Lancelot and Guinevere. Since the tale is a prelude to the Sankgreal (Holy Grail) episode, the Grail appears to the two men, Bors and Percival, who will, in addition to Galahad, become Grail Knights. It is also declared that Galahad will become the primary achiever of the Grail. In an omen that tempts the reader into believing redemption is possible for Lancelot, the Grail also appears to Lancelot, the one man of these four who does not achieve it. Furthermore, Lancelot is told that if it were not for his carnal sin with Guinevere he could be the Best Knight in the World in regard to spiritual as well as worldly matters.

Malory loves the ironies inherent in the begetting of Galahad, an event which will complete the Round Table because Galahad is the only knight who can fill the Siege Perilous; yet the moment of Galahad's completing the Round Table also marks the beginning of the end since his arrival marks the opening of the quest for the Grail, which will dismember the Round Table.

Lancelot's deflowering of Elaine is the first of a series of events which will stand moral certainties on their heads. Elaine knows she is fated to be the mother of Lancelot's child, and she is in love with him as well. Lancelot, however, is the faithful lover of another man's wife, so Elaine has to use sorcery to make herself look like Guinevere. Then she sends a message to Lancelot that she, "Guinevere" (really Elaine), wants him to come to her. Lancelot arrives and begets Galahad on the transformed Elaine. In the morning the spell is broken, and Lancelot realizes he has slept with the wrong woman. Then he angrily accuses Elaine of treachery, resulting in the spectacle of a knight – who has just deflowered a maiden when in fact he intended to commit adultery against the best man in Christendom – indicting the deflowered virgin with whom he thought he was betraying his best friend. When Guinevere hears that Lancelot has had a son by another woman, she is outraged but forgives Lancelot when she discovers the circumstances of his betrayal.

This event could stand by itself as another of the rapes through transformation that bring about the most significant births in Camelot: Uther begetting Arthur on Igrayne and Arthur begetting Mordred on his half sister, Margawse. Instead, the act is repeated, this time with no genealogical significance so that the emotional impact alone is at issue. Elaine, her dynastic function completed, comes to Camelot, where she is acknowledged as the fairest woman in the world, not excluding Guinevere. Guinevere, who knows of Elaine's relation to Lancelot, jealously indicates that she will send for him (mostly because she wants to make sure he is not sleeping with Elaine). Elaine's guardian sorceress anticipates the queen's message and goes to Lancelot to tell him "Guinevere" is waiting for him. Lancelot falls for the same trick again, goes to Elaine whose face is hidden in the dark, and spends the night with her. When Guinevere sends for Lancelot, her servant finds his bed is cold, but he can be found in the castle because of his habit of "clattering" in his sleep about Guinevere. This time perhaps because he thinks that he has just slept with Guinevere he jabbers louder than usual, and Guinevere finds him in Elaine's bed. This time he has no sorcery for an excuse, and he escapes from Guinevere's verbal abuse by leaping out the window. He strips off his clothes, and for two years he exists as a clownish (rustic) madman – thereby embodying all the playful transformations he had practiced in trying to escape his designation as the Best Knight in the World.

In his rustic madness, where he often fights naked and with bare fists, he takes on the appearance of a country bumpkin or villein; he has been transformed from heroic to "villeinous." When Lancelot finally recovers his sanity, he realizes what he has done. At this point he gives up the name Lancelot and calls himself by a shameful epithet, "le shyvalere Mafete," the knight who has trespassed. In this he reverses the history of two young knights, Gareth and Brewne le Noyre, who have, through their deeds, earned the right to give up their clownish nicknames, Beawmayns, and La Cote Male

¶ Capitulum primum

It befel in the dayes of Uther pendragon when he was kynge of all Englond / and so regned that there was a myghty duke in Cornewaill that helde warre ageynst hym long tyme / And the duke was called the duke of Tyntagil / and so by meanes kynge Uther send for this duk / chargyng hym to brynge his wyf with hym / for she was called a fair lady / and a passynge wyse / and her name was called Igrayne /

So whan the duke and his wyf were comyn vnto the kynge By the meanes of grete lordes they were accorded bothe / the kynge lyked and loued this lady wel / and he made them grete chere out of mesure / and desyred to haue lyen by her / But she was a passyng good woman / and wold not assente vnto the kynge / And thenne she told the duke her husband and said I suppose that we were sent for that I shold be dishonoured Wherfor husband I counceille yow that we departe from hens sodenly that we maye ryde all nyghte vnto oure owne castell / and in lyke wyse as she saide so they departed / that neyther the kynge nor none of his counceill were ware of their departyng Also soone as kyng Uther knewe of theire departyng soo sodenly / he was wonderly wrothe / Thenne he called to hym his pryuy counceille / and told them of the sodeyne departyng of the duke and his wyf

¶ Thenne they auysed the kynge to send for the duke and his wyf by a grete charge / And yf he wille not come at your somons / thenne may ye do your best / thenne haue ye cause to make myghty warre vpon hym / Soo that was done and the messagers hadde their ansuers / And that was thys shortly / that neyther he nor his wyf wold not come at hym /

Thenne was the kyng wonderly wrothe / And thenne the kyng sente hym playne wordes agayne / and badde hym be redy and stuffe hym and garnysshe hym / for within xl dayes he wold fetche hym oute of the byggest castell that he hath /

¶ Whanne the duke hadde thys warnynge / anone he wente and furnysshed and garnysshed two stronge Castels of his of the whiche the one hyght Tyntagil / & the other castel hyght

a j

First page of text in the Pierpont Morgan Library copy of William Caxton's first edition of Malory's works. The only other surviving copy of this edition, printed in 1485, is in the John Rylands Library in Manchester.

Tayle (the ill-fitting surcoat). Perhaps, if William Matthews is right when he says in *The Ill-Framed Knight: A Skeptical Inquiry into the Identity of Sir Thomas Mallory* (1966) that Malory is not a surname but an epithet attesting to its owner's evil, then Sir Thomas is telling the story of a knight like himself, whose violent acts were always ill regarded.

The degradation born of confusion, even the official self-shaming of Lancelot, is nothing compared to the destruction brought about by the quest for the Holy Grail, which gives the court a purpose even as it tears at its very roots. Though Arthur's court is built on Christian ideals, Arthur realizes that the ideal of moral perfection that underlies the Grail quest will subvert the more worldly, yet noble, pursuits of the Round Table; so when the quest is taken up, Arthur laments the end of his enterprise in one of the most poignant speeches in English literature: "I am sure at this quest of the Sankegreall shall all ye of the Rownde Table departe, and nevyr shall I se you agayne holé togydirs, therefore ones shall I se you togydir in the medow [of Camelot], all holé togydirs . . . to juste and to turney, that aftir youre dethe men may speke of hit that such good knyghtes were here, such a day, holé togydirs."

Though all of the Round Table pursues the Grail, Malory focuses on five knights to explain the options open to man. There are three Grail Knights, that is, those who will achieve the Grail: Galahad, Percival, and Bors. They are symbolized by a vision in which there are 150 bulls in a meadow; all are black except three; of these, two are completely white, and one is white with a black spot. The two white bulls are Galahad and Percival, two virgin knights, and the spotted bull is Bors, who has lapsed once in his chastity. Lancelot's son, Galahad, temporarily takes the pressure off his father because now that he has achieved knighthood, he has also put on the mantle of the Best Knight in the World. After Galahad comes to Camelot, an old wise man chaffs Lancelot with the fact he does not have the name (of the Best Knight) that he had in the morning. The wise man does not realize that for Lancelot a great burden has been lifted. Galahad is the best not merely in prowess but in moral perfection as well. For this reason Galahad is also the most boring character in the book since he always does the right thing. Eventually he will take his perfection out of Arthur's worldly kingdom into the otherworld of the heavenly kingdom, leaving Lancelot with the possibility of being the Best Knight *in* the World.

Unlike the unerring Galahad, Percival does the right thing purely by chance throughout his quest for the Grail. For example, once he is about to be seduced by a demon who has taken the shape of a beautiful woman, but at the very moment of his yielding, he sees the crucifix in his sword hilt, crosses himself, and his naked, would-be paramour disappears in a cloud of black smoke. The accidental nature of his virtue suggests that no amount of reason will help in uncovering the mystery of the Grail. Bors is significant mostly for what his presence implies about the situation of Lancelot; that is, one can have been unchaste and still become a Grail Knight.

The other two knights who are significant in the book of the Holy Grail are Gawain and Lancelot. Gawain is the worldly knight who always makes the wrong choice almost the way Percival accidentally makes the right one. Gawain is also the first of the 147 worldly knights who elects to pursue the Grail, and his departure opens the floodgates for the "departition" of the Round Table. After he takes up the quest, all the other worldly knights decide to try also. Interestingly, Arthur calls Gawain a traitor for changing the Round Table's focus from knightly pursuits to those of Christian perfection. Arthur reprimands Gawain for seeking the truth, but Lancelot is not scolded for carrying on a twenty-four-year-long adulterous affair with Guinevere.

Gawain finds himself unable to maneuver through the arbitrary allegorical landscape of the Grail world. For example, he takes up for a group of white knights against a group of black knights. It turns out the white knights represent hypocrisy (as in "whited sepulchres"), so that he should have counterintuitively taken up for the black knights. If paths diverge in the allegorical landscape, Gawain always takes the wrong fork. He is the worldly knight who is destined to fail on a spiritual quest.

As usual, Lancelot has the most interesting story of all the knights in the book. He is the only one of the worldly knights who is capable of achieving the Grail, but he does not. The case of Sir Bors shows that Lancelot's past of indiscretion with Guinevere does not in itself prevent Lancelot from reaching the Grail. In fact, Lancelot confesses, then disavows, his love for Guinevere, and then he spends twenty-four hours in a steaming room: one hour for every year of the adultery. He emerges cleansed of his past sins and therefore is capable of achieving the Grail. Lancelot knows that if he achieves the Grail and Galahad leaves the world, he would once again become the Best Knight in the World, an appellation he has worked so hard to erase. Unlike Gawain, Lancelot does see the Grail, but unlike the Grail Knights, he does not get to touch it or to share in its feast.

By the end of the Grail episode Malory has embarked on a tragic story of transgression that will go far beyond the formal statement of trespass that ends "Lancelot and Elaine." There, Lancelot may have been wrong, but there was little emotional weight because the trespass was against the apparent form of things. He twice betrayed Guinevere only because he thought the woman he was sleeping with was Guinevere. Furthermore, since he was, in fact, sleeping with Elaine, he was not at those times technically guilty of the adultery that was in his heart.

All this changes after his unsuccessful quest for the Grail. The tale that follows Galahad's success begins with the striking fact that Lancelot's failure was not due to his past sin with Guinevere, but to the sin he would do with her in the future. Lancelot's sin takes on the dimension of Original Sin, by which mankind is punished with death not for the sin it has done but for the sin it will do. Lancelot tells Guinevere how much her love has cost him: "if that I had nat had my prevy thoughtis to returne to you[r]e love agayne as I do, I had sene as grete mysteryes as ever saw my sonne, sir Galahad, Percivale, other sir Bors." The history of the romance of Lancelot and Guinevere is now tightly plotted through interlocking incidents. Malory shows how this love brings down Arthur's court and how knightly behavior will destroy knighthood.

Lancelot's relation to Guinevere and Arthur is formulated and reformulated in a series of three trials in which Lancelot becomes the champion of Guinevere. In each trial the breach between the letter and the spirit of the law widens until finally Lancelot destroys the system of chivalry altogether.

The trials begin when Guinevere is falsely accused of poisoning one of the Knights of the Round Table, a matter that has to be settled by judicial combat. Unfortunately, Guinevere has already sent Lancelot packing, mostly to quash the rumors of their affair. Arthur reprimands her severely for leaving herself without a champion. Fortunately, Lancelot returns in the nick of time to be her defender. His success should cause no surprise, since she is innocent according to the letter and spirit of the law.

The second trial occurs when Malory tells a streamlined version of Chrétien de Troyes's romance "The Knight of the Cart" (circa 1177–1181). In Malory's version the evil Meleagaunt has captured Guinevere and some of Arthur's knights, who

have been wounded. Guinevere is kept in the same donjon cell with the wounded knights, but in the night Lancelot tears the bars off the window (cutting his hand as he does), enters the donjon, sleeps with Guinevere, and leaves. In the morning Meleagaunt sees the blood on Guinevere's sheets and accuses Guinevere of being unfaithful to her husband with one of the wounded knights. To shame Arthur's court, Meleagaunt decides to put Guinevere on trial. Lancelot comes forward to be her champion on this specific charge. Meleagaunt, evil though he is, believes in the principle behind judicial combat: God will defend the right. He, therefore, thinks that with the help of divine justice he can defeat Lancelot, especially when Lancelot agrees to fight with a quarter of his armor removed and, literally, with one hand tied behind his back, so he can neither hold a shield nor swing a broadsword properly. Nonetheless, Lancelot easily defeats Meleagaunt because Guinevere is innocent, even if it is only according to the letter of the law, and, therefore, in the eyes of God. What Malory, the greatest scofflaw in England, made of these proceedings is left unrecorded.

Meleagaunt's comeuppance is not lost on the most evil characters in Arthur's court: Arthur's son, Mordred, and Gawain's brother Aggravayne. They are determined to catch Guinevere in the act of adultery with Lancelot so that the long-rumored infidelity can be brought into the open and a trial can result in direct and deadly conflict between Lancelot and Arthur.

In these proceedings the disposition of Gawain's family is vital: there is one evil brother, Aggravayne; two good brothers, Gaheris and Lancelot's protégé, Gareth; the leader of the clan is Gawain, whose place as Arthur's nephew is insisted upon. In the later books Malory works to upgrade the character and reputation of Gawain. Throughout the Grail episode, Gawain is the epitome of the boorish worldly knight, often with more courage than sense, but in the later tales he becomes the fairest man in Camelot, Arthur's trusted counselor, and Lancelot's staunchest supporter, a man not given to wrath or rash action. Much of the last book is devoted to a single, simple question: what will it take to turn Gawain against Lancelot? He refuses to join his evil brother in the plot to entrap Lancelot, and even when Lancelot kills Aggravayne and two of Gawain's sons when they are trying to catch him in the act of adultery with Guinevere (the reader is never told if he is in the queen's chamber for that reason this time), Gawain defends Lancelot saying that his brother and his sons received their just deserts.

Though the entrapment fails, Arthur's knights prevail upon him to put Guinevere to the stake for her adultery. When he is urged to put the issue of Guinevere's guilt up to a judicial combat, Arthur denies the whole point of knightly combat, all the jousting and tourneying for which his court is famous. Arthur's court has operated under the principle that right makes might, but Arthur now realizes that Lancelot will win no matter what side he is on, so that the operative principle is might makes right: "Lancelot trustyth so much uppon hys hondis and hys myght that he doutyth [fears] no man. And therefore for my quene he shall nevermore fyght, for she shall have the law."

Nonetheless, it is expected that Lancelot will try to rescue the queen, and a cordon of Knights of the Round Table is assigned to defend against her rescue. Among them are the brothers Gaheris and Gareth. They refuse to wear armor against Lancelot, the man who made Gareth knight, so they take their place in the cordon unarmed. Lancelot is troubled by the idea of going against Arthur, so he asks his cousins what he should do, and they invoke the original chivalric code: always defend ladies in distress, and so Lancelot goes "knightly" to rescue the queen. In riding to her rescue he unwittingly rides down Gaheris and Gareth, thereby committing the most dastardly of acts: killing unarmed knights. Before, in his rural madness, he was a villein; now he is a villain. This act is enough to set the long-suffering Gawain against Lancelot. In a wonderfully pathetic moment Gawain looks for his brothers immediately after declaring that Lancelot was only doing his knightly duty in rescuing the queen. Gawain's rage over the death of Gareth forces Lancelot to leave the court, and Gawain has him officially declared "false recreayed [recreant] knyght." Lancelot has now become, in a way he never expected, the Worst Knight in the World. In some of the coldest lines in literature, Arthur notes that he is brokenhearted, not for Guinevere, but for the Round Table: "I am soryar for my good knyghtes losse than for the losse of my fayre quene; for of quenys I myght have inow, but such a felyship of good knyghtes shall never be togydirs in no company."

Lancelot's retreat from the court means that the king's strongest champion is away when Mordred comes to wound Arthur fatally and destroy the kingdom. As the Dolorous Day unfolds, Malory orchestrates events to a tragic conclusion. The fated end of Arthur and his Round Table is inherent in the New Testament message cited as early as "The Knight with the Two Swords": "And that knyght that hath encheved the swerde shall be destroyed thorow the swerde." Arthur, like Balin, is a knight who has achieved the sword, and, like Balin, his death is caused by a misunderstood sign. The sign that will break the fragile truce between the armies of Arthur and those of Mordred is the drawing of a sword. If the truce holds, then Lancelot will be able to come in time to succor the king. However, in an echo from Eden, an adder stings one of Arthur's knights, who "drew hys swerde to sle the addir, and thought none othir harme." With the flash of the sword the truce is broken, and Mordred and Arthur slay each other. Lancelot, who has always come in time to rescue the queen, comes too late to save the king. Malory closes his book at this point and asks the reader to pray for his deliverance (probably from prison). He calls this "the ende of the hoole book of kyng Arthur and of his noble knyghtes of the Rounde Table," and it is clear that Caxton made the book somewhat more whole than the manuscript he had.

The fact that Caxton would typeset a book as huge as Malory's testifies to the popularity of the Arthurian legend at the end of the fifteenth century. Arthur was the key to an important piece of political mythology. After ending the Wars of the Roses by defeating Richard III and marrying the daughter of the Yorkist line, Henry VII worked on establishing the Tudor myth, one of whose linchpins was the claim that he was descended through his Welsh ancestors from King Arthur and, therefore, belonged to a royal line even older than the Norman Plantagenet one. To this end he named his eldest son (who did not survive) Arthur. Though it is likely that Caxton had a small circle of paying customers for a great Athurian epic, he seems also to have expected to cash in on the popularity of the figure. Certainly since the great victory over the French at Agincourt (1415), there had been much interest in an authentic English hero. Malory was a boy when Henry V defeated the French in the greatest victory in English military history. His lifetime saw the aftermath of that victory, the bloody Wars of the Roses, in which brothers and cousins killed each other in the name of honor. It is out of this world that Malory wrote his tale of Arthur and the internecine struggle that destroyed the Round Table.

Bibliography:

Page West Life, *Sir Thomas Malory and the Morte Darthur: A Survey of Scholarship and Annotated Bibliography* (Charlottesville: Published for the Bibliographical Society of the University of

Virginia by the University Press of Virginia, 1980).

Biography:

William Matthews, *The Ill-Framed Knight: A Skeptical Inquiry into the Identity of Sir Thomas Malory* (Berkeley: University of California Press, 1966).

References:

Stephen C. B. Atkinson, "Malory's 'Healing of Sir Urry' Lancelot, the Earthly Fellowship, and the World of the Grail," *Studies in Philology,* 78 (Fall 1981): 341–352;

J. A. W. Bennett, ed., *Essays on Malory* (Oxford: Clarendon Press, 1963);

Larry D. Benson, *Malory's Morte Darthur* (Cambridge, Mass.: Harvard University Press, 1976);

Muriel C. Bradbrook, *Sir Thomas Malory* (London & New York: Published for the British Council by Longmans, Green, 1958);

R. T. Davies, "Malory's Launcelot and the Noble Way of the World," *Review of English Studies,* 6 (November 1955): 356–364;

Bert Dillon, *A Malory Handbook* (Boston: G. K. Hall, 1978);

Murray J. Evans, "The Explicits and Narrative Division in the Winchester MS: A Critique of Vinaver's Malory," *Philological Quarterly,* 58 (Summer 1979): 263–281;

P. J. C. Field, *Romance and Chronicle: A Study of Malory's Prose Style* (London: Barrie & Jenkins, 1971; Bloomington: Indiana University Press, 1971);

Sandra Ness Ihle, *Malory's Grail Quest: Invention and Adaptation in Medieval Prose Romance* (Madison: University of Wisconsin Press, 1983);

Tomomi Kato, *A Concordance to the Works of Sir Thomas Malory* (Tokyo: University of Tokyo Press, 1974);

Beverly Kennedy, "Malory's Lancelot: 'Trewest Lover, of a Synful Man,' " *Viator,* 12 (1981): 409–456;

Edward D. Kennedy, "Malory's King Mark and King Arthur," *Mediaeval Studies,* 37 (1975): 190–234;

Mark Lambert, *Malory: Style and Vision in Le Morte Darthur* (New Haven: Yale University Press, 1975);

R. M. Lumiansky, ed., *Malory's Originality: A Critical Study of Le Morte Darthur* (Baltimore: Johns Hopkins Press, 1964);

Terence McCarthy, *An Introduction to Malory* (Cambridge: D. S. Brewer, 1988; corrected edition, 1991);

Elizabeth Pochoda, *Arthurian Propaganda: Le Mort Darthur as an Historical Ideal of Life* (Chapel Hill: University of North Carolina Press, 1971);

Edmund Reiss, *Sir Thomas Malory* (New York: Twayne, 1966);

Felicity Riddy, *Sir Thomas Malory* (Leiden & New York: E. J. Brill, 1987);

Toshiyuki Takamiya and Derek Brewer, eds., *Aspects of Malory* (Cambridge: D. S. Brewer, 1981);

Muriel A. Whitaker, *Arthur's Kingdom of Adventure: The World of Malory's Morte Darthur* (Cambridge: D. S. Brewer, 1984);

Robert H. Wilson, "The Fair Unknown in Malory," *PMLA,* 58 (March 1943): 1–21.

Sir John Mandeville

(mid fourteenth century)

Iain Higgins
University of British Columbia

WORKS: *Mandeville's Travels* (circa 1360)

Manuscripts: Some 275 manuscripts (including fragments and excerpts) in ten languages are still extant, about 80 of which belong to the Insular as against the Continental tradition of transmission. Of the Insular manuscripts some 44 are in English, 21 or 22 in French, 12 in Latin, and 3 in Irish, and all ultimately descend from an Anglo-French version of the French original. The English manuscripts, none of which can be dated to before circa 1400, represent four prose versions (Bodley, Cotton, Defective, and Egerton) as well as a metrical version and a stanzaic fragment. The two verse redactions survive in a single manuscript each, as do the important Cotton and Egerton Versions (British Library MSS. Cotton Titus C.xvi and Egerton 1982, respectively). The Bodley Version survives in two manuscripts (Bodleian Library MSS. e Musaeo 116 and Rawlinson D 99), while the Defective Version is extant in some thirty-eight. There is no facsimile of any manuscript in any language.

First publications: Defective Version: *Here endeth the boke of John Maunduyle, knyght of wayes to Jerusalem & of marueylys of ynde and of other countrees* [colophon] ([London]: Printed by Richard Pynson, 1496?) Facsimile (Exeter: University of Exeter Printing Unit, 1980). Cotton Version: *The Voiage and Travaile of Sir John Maundevile, Kt. . . .* (London, 1725). Egerton and Insular French Versions: *The Buke of John Maundeuill . . . ,* edited by George F. Warner (Westminster, 1889).

Standard editions: *The Bodley Version of* Mandeville's Travels, edited by M. C. Seymour, EETS, 253 (1963); Cotton Version: *Mandeville's Travels,* edited by Seymour (Oxford: Clarendon Press, 1967); Defective Version collated with the Cotton Version: *The Voiage and Travayle of Syr John Maundeville Knight* (London: Dent, 1928); The Bodleian Version, modernized Egerton text, and the Continental French Version: *Mandeville's Travels: Texts and Translations,* edited by Malcolm Letts, Hakluyt Society, second series 101–102 (London, 1953); *The Metrical Version of* Mandeville's Travels, edited by Seymour, EETS, 269 (1973).

Editions in modern English: Egerton text: *The Travels of Sir John Mandeville,* translated by C. W. R. D. Moseley (Harmondsworth, U.K.: Penguin, 1983).

Mandeville's Travels is the modern editorial title of a prose treatise that initially circulated under several medieval titles, most commonly *The Book of John Mandeville*. By its own account this variously titled book was put together by a certain John Mandeville, knight, of Saint Albans, a town just north of London. Having left his native country on Michaelmas Day 1322, the English knight spent some thirty-four years traveling throughout Asia and northern Africa, only ceasing his travels when the physical infirmities of increasing age finally caught up with him. His world travels thus ended, Sir John took comfort in his gouty retirement by setting down in writing some of his memories from his years abroad. In general, these "memories" have little to do with the knight's own experiences as a traveler, and so they are organized not as a first-person narrative recounting a personal itinerary, but as an informative and largely third-person exposition based on a geographical scheme that proceeds roughly from west to east, from Constantinople toward the Earthly Paradise (a real place in medieval thought and one which Columbus would later believe he had located).

According to the prologue, the book was produced especially for pilgrims intending to go to Jerusalem, a claim apparently confirmed by the text,

Portrait of Mandeville from a fifteenth-century manuscript of Michel Velser's translation of Mandeville's Travels *(New York Public Library, Spencer Collection, MS. 37)*

which devotes about half of its considerable length to tracing different routes from Europe to the Holy Land as well as to describing important historical and sacred sites in, around, and en route to Jerusalem. Yet the same prologue also tempts its readers with the promise of information about the larger and more diverse world beyond the biblical East, and the book appropriately spends its latter half describing the distant places only recently made familiar to the Christian West by the travel memoirs of missionaries and merchants such as John of Plano Carpini and Marco Polo (Friar John produced his Latin *History of the Mongols* in 1245, while Polo dictated his *Description of the World* in about 1298). In its unique account of both the old East and the new, *Mandeville's Travels* offers its audience more than just a guidebook and a geography lesson; it also offers details from local and world history, accounts of curious fauna, flora, and minerals, descriptions of the diversity of human appearance, language, customs, and religious practices, the odd story, and even a few anecdotes about Sir John himself: one learns, for instance, that he received as a gift one of

the thorns from Christ's crown of thorns, that he once drank from a healing fountain which some call the Fountain of Youth (and felt the better for it), that through his renewed piety he survived a horrible passage through a mysterious far-eastern valley called the Vale Perilous, that he was not worthy to reach the Earthly Paradise, and that he served as a soldier under both the sultan of Egypt and the great khan of Cathay, the former even offering him a large inheritance and a Muslim princess in marriage, if he would only give up his Christian faith (he would not).

Not surprisingly, given such material, *Mandeville's Travels* was one of the most popular and widely circulated books produced anywhere in Europe before the advent of printing and one of the few such books to have had an almost continuous afterlife in print. Like Polo's account, only more so, Sir John's memories of the East were clearly of profound interest to medieval European audiences, and the book was copied, translated, and recopied so many times that it survives in some 275 manuscripts representing ten languages (Czech, Danish, Dutch, English, French, German, Irish, Italian, Latin, and Spanish). The last of these many translations, from English into Irish, was made in 1475, just as *Mandeville's Travels* was about to find an equally enthusiastic readership in print. By 1480 printed editions were available in at least three languages (French, German, Italian), and by 1515 it had been issued in another five (only the Irish and Danish translations remained unprinted at the time, as they would until the late nineteenth century when they were issued in scholarly editions). By the middle of the sixteenth century, however, as news of the Americas was radically transforming medieval conceptions of the world, interest in *Mandeville's Travels* began to wane.

Not all of the surviving medieval manuscripts tell their readers in what language *Mandeville's Travels* was originally composed, but those that do usually agree in naming French. With one important exception none of the English manuscripts says anything at all about the language of composition, nor do any of the English editions published before the eighteenth century, leaving their readers to suppose that the text at hand represented the author's original. The sole exception is British Library MS. Cotton Titus C.xvi, which was first published in London in 1725 and has since had a disproportionate influence on the book's popular and scholarly reception. According to the Cotton manuscript, the English knight originally produced his travel memoirs in three languages, setting them down first in

Latin, next translating them into French, and finally translating the French text into English so that everyone of his nation could read them. For more than two hundred years after 1725 the book's readers took this claim at face value, and by the late nineteenth century some scholars had even enthroned this trilingual Mandeville (a sort of worldly John Gower) as the "Father of English prose." At almost exactly the same time, however, other scholars irrefutably demonstrated that *Mandeville's Travels* was originally set down in French and that its author was not responsible for any Latin or English versions whatsoever (some recent readers – Mary B. Campbell and Donald R. Howard, for example – have nevertheless continued to take the Cotton manuscript's claim at something like its word on the author's responsibility for an English translation).

In addition, these same nineteenth-century scholars showed that the book was not what it claimed to be, and, somewhat scandalized by their discovery, they labored to cast doubt on the existence of a John Mandeville, knight, world traveler, and author. On closer examination the self-proclaimed travel memoir turned out to be a skillful compilation of material borrowed from other writers, some of them genuine travelers. The compilation's two most important sources were the pilgrimage itinerary written in 1336 by William of Boldensele, a German Dominican, and the memoir dictated in 1330 by Odoric of Pordenone, a Franciscan missionary who traveled in India and China during the 1320s. But the book's author also drew on sources such as the *Letter of Prester John* (late twelfth century), Johannes Sacrobosco's treatise on the sphere (circa 1220), Vincent of Beauvais's encyclopedia (circa 1256–1259), and William of Tripoli's account of Muslim beliefs (1273). Clearly an author who did so much reading must have had little time for travel, except to a good library, and he gave himself away to modern scholars by claiming to have done certain things at the wrong historical time. Having discovered what they themselves anachronistically called plagiarism, these scholars also found evidence to suggest that the famous English knight might have been neither a knight nor an Englishman, but rather one of two Continental authors hiding under an assumed name: either Jean de Bourgogne, otherwise Jean à la Barbe (flourished mid fourteenth century), a Liège physician and the author of an influential plague treatise, or Jean d'Outremeuse (1338–1400), a prolific and not especially scrupulous Liège chronicler and romance writer. Early-twentieth-century scholars were quick to endorse the findings of their predecessors, and

P. Hamelius went so far as to use his EETS edition of the Cotton manuscript (1919–1923) to enshrine Jean d'Outremeuse as author.

By midcentury, however, there was something of a counterreaction to such hostile treatment of the life of the English knight, and two scholars wrote books devoted in part to reestablishing an English John Mandeville as both knight and author. The first of these books, Malcolm Letts's *Sir John Mandeville: The Man and his Book* (1949), offers assertions rather than arguments, but the second, Josephine Waters Bennett's *The Rediscovery of Sir John Mandeville* (1954), makes a careful, if not entirely convincing, case based on the evidence of manuscripts and archival material, and some scholars have accepted her conclusion that *Mandeville's Travels* was probably composed in England by an Englishman called John Mandeville. More recently, M. C. Seymour, the current authority on the English manuscripts, has advanced "anonymous" as the best candidate for authorship and shifted this nameless figure back to the Continent. Seymour's claim is by no means decisive, but it does have the merit of accommodating both positive and negative evidence with the fewest leaps of faith. Barring the unlikely discovery of new evidence to the contrary, "Sir John Mandeville" is probably best thought of as an "authorizing" name attached to a popular medieval book and long accepted as genuine. Indeed, it would be useful if scholars were to distinguish between Sir John, the English knight and occasional tour guide created by text, and the Mandeville-author, the probably pseudonymous figure actually responsible for compiling the book.

As for the book, the manuscript evidence suggests that it was composed shortly after 1356, probably somewhere in the northern French-speaking regions of the Continent (this evidence says nothing one way or another about the author's nationality). Bennett's hypothesis that the original French text was composed in England and subsequently carried to the Continent in one of the many diplomatic exchanges between England and France following the battle of Poitiers (1356) is a plausible alternative explanation but is unprovable. In any case, the earliest dated manuscript, Paris, Bibliothèque Nationale MS. nouv. acq. franç. 4515 (the basis for Letts's 1953 edition), which is almost certainly the earliest extant manuscript, is a Continental French copy made at the royal court in Paris in 1371, and the relatively poor state of its text points to an original already at some remove. The earliest dated Insular manuscript, Leiden University MS. Vulcan 96, is a Latin translation from the French; it was copied in

1390, but in a 1964 article Seymour suggests that its French source may have been circulating in England as much as twenty years earlier. Clearly the textual history of *Mandeville's Travels* is especially complicated, and it has yet to be fully studied, let alone definitively traced.

Building on the work of their nineteenth-century predecessors, who were usually more interested in questions of authorship and sources, three scholars (Bennett, Seymour, and Guy De Poerck) agree on a credible account of the work's early transmission in French and English. In their view the extant French manuscripts fall into three larger groups defined by the nature of the text: those of the Continental Version (thirty-one or thirty-two manuscripts), the Interpolated Continental (or Liège) Version (seven manuscripts), and the Insular Version (twenty-one or twenty-two manuscripts). Although the Liège Version is ultimately descended from the Continental, it stands apart from both the Continental and Insular Versions by virtue of numerous interpolations, especially those devoted to the exploits of Ogier the Dane (a figure from the twelfth-century *Chanson de Roland*). The latter two versions are distinguished from each other by only a few minor textual differences, the most important of which concerns Sir John's passage through the Vale Perilous (the Insular Version offers a considerably shorter account than the Continental). Between them the two Continental texts gave rise either directly or indirectly to versions in Czech, Danish, Dutch, German, Italian, Latin, and Spanish, while the Insular Version similarly gave rise to versions in English, Irish, and Latin. As usually happened with medieval texts, the book's translators, redactors, and scribes felt free to adapt "Sir John's memoirs" as they saw fit, and the resulting versions can vary considerably. Indeed, it could be argued that there is no single, authoritative version of *Mandeville's Travels*, that it is really a fascinating medieval multitext produced not so much by a single person as by an entire culture.

In general this multitext was less transformed in England than it was on the Continent. Just as the Insular French Version differs but little from the Continental, so three of the four independent Insular Latin translations constitute generally faithful translations of their French source, while only the fourth abridges its source considerably. The English Bodley Version, translated from a Latin source, also represents an abridged text, turning *Mandeville's Travels* into a kind of Eastern story-book. In contrast, the three remaining English prose renderings are quite faithful to their French source,

and they appear to represent a single translation made shortly before 1400 and twice revised. It is not clear which was the first translation, but it is certain that the Egerton Version, which may have been made between 1410 and 1425, represents the second revision; Seymour reverses the opinion of his nineteenth-century predecessor J. Vogels in making the Defective rather than the Cotton Version the original English translation, but the evidence is equivocal. Whatever the case, the Defective Version is the least appealing of the three texts, characterized as it is by frequent omissions, in particular a large lacuna known as the "Egypt gap." It is, however, the only English rendering to have given rise to another translation (into Irish). The related Cotton Version is a literal translation which occasionally misconstrues its source but still offers a pleasant, readable text, whereas the Egerton Version represents a subtle, thoroughgoing, and intelligent redaction of its English and French sources into a flexible northern English prose. It is the best rendering from a literary point of view. The two verse redactions have little literary interest, yet they show very clearly the extent of medieval interest in "Mandeville's travels."

Whoever was responsible for inventing the man and compiling the book may not have been the literary genius that some modern critics have thought him to be, but neither was he the shameless plagiarist depicted in nineteenth-century criticism. Rather, the author was someone with a profound, sympathetic, and imaginative interest in both the larger world and the moral state of medieval Christendom, and out of that interest and others' writings he made a book that continues to inform and delight, not least because of the unforgettable character of Sir John himself.

Bibliographies:

Ernst Bremer, "Mandeville, Jean de (John, Johannes von)," *Die deutsche Literatur des Mittelalters: Verfasserlexikon,* second edition, edited by Kurt Ruh and others, volume 5 (Berlin & New York: de Gruyter, 1985), columns 1201–1214;

Christian K. Zacher, "Travel and Geographical Writings," in *A Manual of the Writings in Middle English 1050–1500,* volume 7, edited by Albert E. Hartung (New Haven: Connecticut Academy of Arts and Sciences, 1986), pp. 2452–2457.

Biography:

Josephine Waters Bennett, *The Rediscovery of Sir John Mandeville* (New York: MLA, 1954);

Rita Lejeune, "Jean de Mandeville et les Liégeois," in *Mélanges de linguistique romane et de philologie médiévale offerts à Maurice Delbouille,* volume 2 (Gembloux, France: Duculot, 1964), pp. 409–437.

References:

Mary B. Campbell, *The Witness and the Other World: Exotic European Travel Writing, 400–1600* (Ithaca, N.Y.: Cornell University Press, 1988), pp. 122–161;

Guy De Poerck, "La tradition manuscrite des 'Voyages' de Jean de Mandeville: à propos d' un livre récent," *Romanica Gandensia,* 4 (1955): 125–158;

Christiane Deluz, *Le livre de Jehan de Mandeville: Une "géographie" au XIVᵉ siècle,* Textes, Etudes, Congrès, 8 (Louvain-la-Neuve: Institut d'Etudes Médiévales de L'Université Catholique de Louvain, 1988);

Stephen Greenblatt, *Marvelous Possessions: The Wonder of the New World* (Chicago: University of Chicago Press, 1991), pp. 26–51;

Ralph Hanna III, in "Mandeville," in *Middle English Prose: A Critical Guide to Major Authors and Genres,* edited by A. S. G. Edwards (New Brunswick, N. J.: Rutgers University Press, 1984), pp. 121–132;

Iain Higgins, "Imagining Christendom from Jerusalem to Paradise: Asia in *Mandeville's Travels,*" in *Discovering New Worlds: Essays on Medieval Exploration and Imagination,* edited by Scott D. Westrem (New York: Garland, 1991), pp. 91–114;

Donald R. Howard, "The World of Mandeville's Travels," *Yearbook of English Studies,* 1 (1971): 1–17;

Howard, *Writers and Pilgrims: Medieval Pilgrimage Narratives and Their Posterity* (Berkeley: University of California Press, 1980), pp. 53–76;

Malcolm Letts, *Sir John Mandeville: The Man and His Book* (London: Batchworth Press, 1949);

Dorothee Metlitzki, *The Matter of Araby in Medieval England* (New Haven: Yale University Press, 1977), pp. 220–239;

C. W. R. D. Moseley, "The Metamorphoses of Sir John Mandeville," *Yearbook of English Studies,* 4 (1974): 5–25;

Moseley, "The Availability of *Mandeville's Travels* in England, 1356–1750," *Library,* fifth series 30 (June 1975): 125–133;

M. C. Seymour, "The Scribal Tradition of Mandeville's *Travels:* The Insular Version," *Scriptorium,* 18, no. 1 (1964): 34–48;

Seymour, "The English Manuscripts of *Mandeville's Travels,*" *Transactions of the Edinburgh Bibliographical Society,* 4 (1966): 169–210;

Christian K. Zacher, *Curiosity and Pilgrimage: The Literature of Discovery in Fourteenth-Century England* (Baltimore: Johns Hopkins University Press, 1976), pp. 130–157.

Robert Mannyng

(flourished 1303 – 1338)

Kathleen Gaines McCarty
University of South Carolina

WORKS: *Handlyng Synne* (circa 1303–1317)

Manuscripts: Idelle Sullens's 1983 edition lists nine manuscripts; Frederick J. Furnivall's edition of 1901 and 1903 is based on Bodley MS. 415 (Bodleian Library, Oxford University), Harley MS. 1701 (British Library, London), and Dulwich MS. XXIV (Dulwich College Library, London).

Standard editions: *Robert of Brunne's 'Handlyng Synne,'* edited by Frederick J. Furnivall, EETS, o.s. 119 and 123 (1901, 1903; reprinted as one volume, Kraus, 1973); *Robert Mannyng of Brunne: Handlyng Synne,* edited by Idelle Sullens, Medieval & Renaissance Texts & Studies 14 (Binghamton: State University of New York, 1983).

Chronicle of England (1338)

Manuscripts: The work survives in three manuscripts – Lambeth MS. 131 (Lambeth Palace Library, London); Petyt MS. 511, vol. 7 (Inner Temple Library, London); and R. Rawlinson Miscellany D. 913 (Bodleian Library, Oxford University).

Standard editions: Part 1: *The Story of England by Robert Manning of Brunne,* edited by Frederick J. Furnivall, Rolls Series 87 (London: Longmans, 1887); Part 2: *Peter of Langtoft's Chronicle, as Illustrated and Improved by Robert of Brunne, from the Death of Cadwallader to the End of King Edward the First's Reign,* 2 volumes, edited by Thomas Hearne (Oxford: Printed at the Theatre, 1725).

Robert Mannyng is an important transitional figure in the history of English poetry. His major work, *Handlyng Synne* (circa 1303–1317) provides a link between the penitential writing in Latin and French sparked by the church reform in the thirteenth century and the great English confessional poetry of the later Middle Ages, while his metrical experimentation in his *Chronicle of England* (1338) and his use of the Midland dialect helped, in some part, to establish the shape and dialect of the English that was to become standard. In Mannyng's emphatic compassion for the poor and the oppressed and his disgust at the corruption of those in power an early William Langland, in his adept combination of the trouvère and the moralist on sin an early John Gower, and, most important, in his love for illustrating serious morals with lively tales and his flair for telling them in a conversational, down-to-earth style, scholars have seen an early Geoffrey Chaucer. His dedicated purpose of writing for the "lewed" helped to solidify the rise of the English vernacular as a language fitting to replace Latin and French. Although his reputation as a poet in his own right is certainly no match for those who succeeded him, it is still rather surprising that a man with such consistent praise as a literary figure remains relatively unknown and unread.

What is known of Mannyng's life comes directly from his poetry, and the personal information he does supply is more complete than usual for most writers of his time. In the prologue to *Handlyng Synne* he states that he is a native of Brunne, or Bourne, in Kesteven, Lincolnshire, and that for fifteen years he has dwelt six miles away at the priory of Sempringham, the founding house of the Gilbertine Order. There he began his "englyssh ryme" in the year 1303, while Dan Philip was master. In the prologue to his *Chronicle of England* he adds that he is Robert "Mannyng," under commission from Robert of Malton to translate Peter of Langtoft's version, by which time he is residing at another Gilbertine house in Sixhills. Also in the *Chronicle of England* Mannyng makes a reference to some time spent in Cambridge, attending a commencement feast given by Robert I, before he became king of Scotland, for his brother Alexander. In the last two lines of the work he gives the exact date of its completion, 15 May 1338.

From this information and from the contemporary figures listed in the verse it is most likely that Mannyng lived in Sempringham from 1303, the starting date of *Handlyng Synne,* until at least 1317, when he wrote his prologue to *Handlyng Synne,* and that when he arrived at Sempringham, he came with an education from Cambridge (he certainly could not have been at the university after 1306, when Robert I became king). As for his position at the priory, there can be little doubt that Mannyng was a canon and not a lay brother, as his earlier editors have suggested, since by Gilbertine rule no lay brothers were allowed to read or to be taught to read books (let alone write them). This fact provides some interesting possibilities on what exactly Mannyng meant by the "lewed" men he wished to inform: as Idelle Sullens points out in her 1983 edition, the unlearned could be the parishioners of the churches in the area served by such Gilbertine canons as Mannyng, or they could be the lay brethren at the priory, or both. In any case it is fairly certain that both *Handlyng Synne* and the *Chronicle of England* were written under similar circumstances, in that a prior at the head of the order commissioned, or at the very least approved, a learned canon's work meant to edify the ignorant.

Handlyng Synne is easily the more important of the two works in literary terms. This 12,638-line poem in octosyllabic verse is a translation and adaptation of a popular contemporary homiletic poem, the *Manuel des Péchiez,* generally attributed to William of Wadington, an English cleric writing in Anglo-French for an Anglo-Norman audience. Both *Handlyng Synne* and its source were types of a new genre, the confessional guidebook, created out of the church reforms of the early thirteenth century. The Fourth Lateran Council in 1215 put a new priority on private confession, and this led to a proliferation of texts systemizing the points of faith, the types of sins, and the various duties of the confessor. When the itinerant friars began winning over parishioners by using common language and lively stories in their sermons, reform-minded bishops, such as Robert Grosseteste and John Peckham, issued "Constitutions" requiring the parish clergyman to teach the new classifications to the laity in a language they could understand, to produce confessional guidebooks for the common man, not the priest. The resulting genre was a widespread success, and as D. W. Robertson demonstrates in a 1947 essay, a confessional guidebook of essentially the same form is still in use by the church.

It was Mannyng's role to provide the first such book for an English audience, and in so doing he would far surpass his source. He asserts twice in his prologue that his version will be in the "englyssh tongue," for the benefit of the unlearned men of his native land who know no Latin or French. Knowing that these men delight in the kind of "talys & rymys" which often lead them into "velanye," "dedly synne or outher folye," Mannyng endeavors to provide stories that will entertain and morally instruct them, guiding them to recognize and understand their sins so that they can adequately "handle" them at confession and find God's grace. After the prologue he moves through a series of homilies, illustrated with exempla from a variety of sources, on the Ten Commandments, the seven deadly sins, the sin of sacrilege, the Seven Sacraments, the Twelve Points of Shrift, and the subsequent Twelve Graces of Shrift.

The work is hardly the dry catalogue it sounds, however, and while Mannyng follows the general scheme of the *Manuel des Péchiez* and employs some of the tales from that source, his departures, variations, and amplifications call attention to his superiority as a storyteller. As a general rule, the least remarkable parts of his poem occur where he adheres most closely to his source (also true of the *Chronicle of England*), and the passages that have received the most critical note are usually either Mannyng originals, fleshed-out versions of rather skeletal outlines in the *Manuel des Péchiez,* or exempla taken from different sources. His style is marked by simplicity of language, colloquialism, and a vividness of detail, a style that any reader of Chaucer will easily find comfortable. One of his more famous tales, an original used to illustrate the First Commandment, is "The Witch and Her Cow-Sucking Bag," a story that opens in style sounding like the simplest folktale:

> Lo, heyr a tale of a wycche
> þat leuyd no better þan a bycche.
> þer was a wycche & made a bagge,
> A bely of leþer, a gret swagge.

The ultimate moral, that words spoken without belief are empty and worthless, is a sincere one, but there is certainly no small irony or sense of enjoyment in the picture of the bishop's, trying in vain to make the spell work for himself. Vividness of detail often turns into a penchant for the grotesque, as it does in "The Bloody Child" episode, in the depiction of the worms of gluttony feeding on the bloated rich man, and especially, as might be expected, in the pictures of hell found in the Knight's vision of the Bridge of Hell and Saint Fursey's Descent. Overall, his detail, directness, and colloquialism

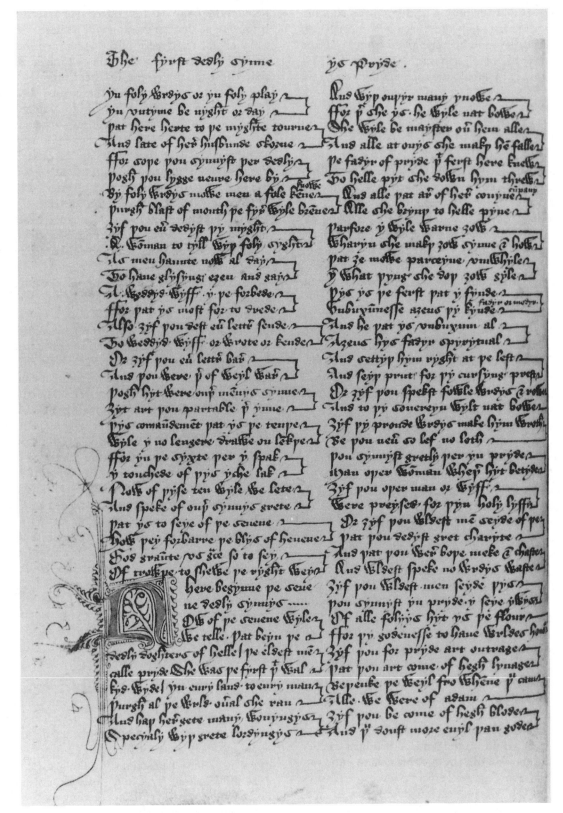

Page from Mannyng's Handlyng Synne *in a scribal copy from circa 1400 (Bodleian Library, Oxford, Bodley MS. 415, fol. 19ᵛ)*

give a kind of fabliaux feel that shows a narrator with a keen sense of his audience in mind.

One of the more intriguing tales in the work is "The Dancers of Colbek." Although the tale appears in the *Manuel des Péchiez,* Mannyng thought the version too colorless and turned instead to a second Latin source of the story. On Christmas Eve a group of carolers sing and dance in the churchyard, ignoring the warnings of the priest who insists they attend mass. In return for their sacrilege he curses them to dance perpetually for a year. In one of his typical asides Mannyng adds that "Yn þe latyne þat y fond þore, / He seyþ nat twelfmonth but euermore." The bitter twist of the story is that the priest's own daughter, Ave, is one of the dancers, and when her brother tries to pull her out of the reeling group, her arm breaks off, as dry and withered as a branch. After a year all of the dancers recover while Ave dies, and in his grief the father soon follows her. The arm becomes a token in Rome of the dangers of the sin of sacrilege. The ultimate effect of the story is remarkable, and Mannyng's skillful use of the sources and flowing narrative have made it the best-known tale of the entire work.

Mannyng also modifies his translation of the *Manuel de Péchiez* by localizing his stories, often providing invaluable commentary on life in England in his day; as Frederick J. Furnivall remarks in his 1901 edition of the work, "his chronicle is fiction; his *Handlyng Synne* is history." Two of the tales in Mannyng's section on the sin of avarice, "The Cambridge Miser Parson" and "The Wicked Kesteven Executors," reflect the poet's concerns over a type of greed he sees as bearing an English stamp, particularly in the case of the executors:

> Of alle false þat beren name,
> False executours are most to blame.
> þe pope of þe courte of rome
> Aȝens hem ȝyfþ he hard dome,
> And curseþ hem yn cherches here
> Foure tymes yn þe ȝere.
> Of alle executors þat men fynde,
> Werst are þyn owne kynde.

His general hatred of those taking advantage is nowhere more fervent than in his remarks on the social abuses of the poor at the hands of the privileged. Knights often come under attack, and Mannyng specifically names tournaments as the root of all seven of the deadly sins. His reputation as an early social reformer can clearly be drawn from such a tale as "The Norfolk Bondman," in which a bondman rather bravely reproves a knight

for allowing his beasts to defile the graves in a churchyard. When the knight indignantly responds that the graves contain only "cherles bones," the bondman replies:

> þe lord þat made of erþe erles,
> Of þat same erþe made he cherles.
> Erles myg22t and lordes stut,
> As cherles shal yn erþe be put.
> Erles, cherles, al at ones,
> Shal none knowe ȝoure fro oure bones.

The knight takes the lesson to heart, leaving Mannyng to close the tale by adding, "Lordynges þyr are ynowe of þo: Of gentyl men þyr are but fo." Members of the church do not fare much better, and a man from Suffolk's cry for "A prest, a prest, of clene lyff!" could serve as a refrain for many characters in the poem.

What must be kept in mind when examining passages such as these is Mannyng's primary purpose in writing the work, a purpose of which he never loses sight. The tendency to read him as a storyteller alone ignores the fact that Mannyng carefully balances each tale with commentary on the nature of the sin involved and instruction on how to be shriven of it. While he is obviously sincerely outraged at the mistreatment of the lower classes, he has little tolerance for the moral transgressions of his "lewed" audience. He is a moralist, and in many respects a quite conservative one, regardless of his often modern feel. He was strongly opposed to the popular amusements of the day and condemned mystery plays save those dealing with Christ's Birth and Resurrection. His criticism of women is harsh and fairly constant, markedly more pronounced than in his source. Still, the impression with which one is left after reading the poem is one of a man dedicated to his moral purpose, with a true pleasure in telling a good story and an instinctual knack in relating to his audience.

The *Chronicle of England,* Mannyng's lesser work, is primarily known for its metrical experimentation, although there are still some passages of the characteristic Mannyng voice that are noteworthy. The *Chronicle of England* is in two parts, the first tracing the ancestry of British kings from Brut's arrival in Britain to the time of the English invasion in the latter half of the fifth century, and the second from the invasion to the end of the reign of Edward I. Although commissioned to translate Peter of Langtoft's chronicle, Mannyng instead goes straight to Peter's source, Robert Wace's *Roman de Brut* (1155), complaining that Peter often skips over the Latin in the work of Geoffrey of Monmouth while

Wace "alle redes." In the second part he keeps his earlier promise to return to Peter at the point where Wace's version ends, and for the most part he adheres to his source. His characteristic flair for variation in his earlier poem is much less apparent in the *Chronicle of England,* although he still exhibits his combination of the moralist and the lover of stories: he puts a distinctly moral cast on Wace's version, emphasizing the fact that the Britons must pay for their sins, while at the same time he criticizes those authors who downplay or ignore the importance of the Arthurian stories.

Metrically, the *Chronicle of England* is quite interesting. Mannyng's customary octosyllabic verse used in the first part of the story as well as in the prologues to both parts was not well suited for the alexandrine lines of Peter's French version, and Mannyng's continual attempts in the second part to find a proper line resulted in what George Saintsbury calls "a metrical jumble." His alexandrines sometimes suffered from his natural inclination to condense the line and became decasyllabic, while his attempts at the single rhyme of the original ended up as couplet rhyme. As awkward as much of his efforts at new forms were, Saintsbury sees here the beginnings of the heroic couplet as perfected by Chaucer.

A third work, a translation of Saint Bonaventura's *Medytacyuns of the soper of our lord Iesu,* has been erroneously attributed to Mannyng by J. Meadows Cooper, who edited the work for the Early English Text Society in 1875. His dialect comparison, supported by Kington-Oliphant in the afterword to the text, has since been discredited by the discrepancy in source manuscripts.

Both of Mannying's works were written at a crucial, formative time in the history of the language, the formation of the vernacular as a literary medium. The particular combination of his position in the clergy, his affinity for the common man, and his ear for what made up popular narrative led Mannyng to graft an oral-vernacular language onto a literary form at the height of its popularity, a confessional genre that had already been granted a position of high regard by the church. There is no direct proof that Langland, Gower, or Chaucer ever had before them a copy of *Handlyng Synne,* but they certainly drew upon an idea of literature that its author helped to implant. And though Mannyng remains virtually unnoticed by students and critics, his use of the Midland dialect helped to shape Standard English.

Biography:
Ruth Crosby, "Robert Mannyng of Brunne: A New Biography," *PMLA,* 57 (March 1942): 15–28.

References:
Robert W. Ackerman, "*The Debate of the Body and the Soul* and Parochial Christianity," *Speculum,* 37 (1962): 541–565;

E. J. Arnould, *Le Manuel des Péchés: Etude de littérature religieuse anglo-normande (xiiime siècle)* (Paris: Droz, 1940);

Charlton G. Laird, "Character and Growth of the *Manuel des Pechiez,*" *Traditio,* 4 (1946): 253–306;

Laird, "Manuscripts of the *Manuel des Pechiez,*" *Stanford Studies in Language and Literature,* volume 1, edited by Hardin Craig (Stanford, Cal.: Stanford University Press, 1941), pp. 99–123;

D. W. Robertson, Jr., "Certain Theological Conventions in Mannyng's Treatment of the Commandments," *Modern Language Notes,* 61 (December 1946): 505–514;

Robertson, Jr., "The Cultural Tradition of *Handlyng Synne,*" *Speculum,* 22 (April 1947): 162–185;

George Saintsbury, *The History of English Prosody,* volume 1 (New York: Macmillan, 1906), pp. 112–115;

R. A. Shoaf, " 'Mutatio Amoris': 'Penitentia' and the Form of *The Book of the Duchess,*" *Genre,* 14 (Summer 1981): 163–189.

Dan Michel of Northgate

(circa 1265 – circa 1340)

John Felicien Lorio, Jr.
University of South Carolina

WORK: *Ayenbite of Inwyt* (1340)

> **Manuscript:** Dan Michel's one work exists in a unique autograph manuscript: British Library MS. Arundel 57, fols. 13–94.
> **First publication:** *The Ayenbite of Inwyt,* edited by Joseph Stevenson (London: Nichols, 1855).
> **Standard editions:** *Dan Michel's Ayenbite of Inwyt or Remorse of Conscience,* edited by Richard Morris, EETS, o.s. 23 (1866); revised edition, volume 1, with corrections by Pamela Gradon but with Morris's editorial apparatus omitted (1965); volume 2, edited by Gradon, EETS, 278 (1979).

About Dan Michel of Northgate little is known, and much of what is known about him comes from his only work, which was completed in 1340. The *Ayenbite of Inwyt* (remorse of conscience, or, literally, again-biting of inner wit) is not an original work, but rather a prose translation of *Somme des Vices et Vertus* (1279), better known as the *Somme le Roi,* a widely read work by the French friar Lorens (Laurentius Gallus). Dan Michel's translation is rather literal, and it may appear unremarkable to someone first approaching it. To date, the primary importance of the *Ayenbite of Inwyt* has been its language – it remains the best extant specimen of the Kentish dialect. However, this text has other ramifications in the study of the English language that have yet to be explored.

Throughout the thirteenth century English church fathers were confronted with the problem of widespread ignorance among their priests. Many priests knew only "singing Latin" – that is, they could recite the Latin mass but could not tell their parishioners what the words meant. Some priests did not even know basic doctrinal matters, much less Latin. In 1281 the archbishop of Canterbury, John Peckham, set out to rectify this matter by issuing what are known today as *Peckham's Constitutions.* In them Peckham listed the doctrinal matters which he felt priests should be teaching the people; more important, he commanded that church doctrine be taught in English. *Peckham's Constitutions* were the foundation for a special category of English prose works, the manuals of sins, or the *manuel des péchés,* as their French counterparts were known. The seminal works in this category were Raymond of Pennafort's *Summa casuum poenitentiae* (1235) and Guillaume de Perrault's *Summa de vitiis* and *Summa de virtutibus* (circa 1261). Perrault's work was also the basis for Friar Lorens's *Somme le Roi.* Important manuals of sins in English are the *Lay Folks' Catechism* (fourteenth century) of the archbishop of York John Thoresby, the *Sermon* of Dan John Gaytryge, Robert Mannyng's *Handlyng Synne* (circa 1303–1317), the anonymous *Book of Vices and Virtues,* and Dan Michel's *Ayenbite of Inwyt.*

The meager biographical information that survives concerning Dan Michel is chiefly in the *Ayenbite of Inwyt.* In the preface he writes, "þis boc is dan Michelis of Northgate / y-write an englis of his oȝene hand. þet hatte: Ayenbite of inwyt. And is of þe boc-house of saynt Austines of Canterberi." At the conclusion of the book he adds: "Ymende [Take note]. þet þis boc is uolueld [fulfilled, completed] ine þe eue of þe holy apostles Symon an Iudas / of ane broþer of þe cloystre of sanynt austin of Canterberi / Ine þe yeare of oure lhordes beringe. 1340." Dan Michel, then, was a brother of the cloister of Saint Augustine's, Canterbury, where he completed the manuscript of the *Ayenbite of Inwyt* on 27 October 1340. Pamela Gradon notes that Dan Michel "was probably born in the parish of St. Mary Northgate in Canterbury" and "as a brother of St. Augustine's . . . would have been a Benedictine monk." A. B. Emden and other sources offer more conjectural information about Dan Michel – for instance, that he was ordained a deacon in 1295 and a priest in 1296. When he completed the *Ayenbite of Inwyt,* he was between seventy and seventy-six years old. In his introductory verses Dan Michel states that he is "Blind. and dyaf. and alsuo domb. Of zeuenty yer al uol rond," which would lead one to believe that he was indeed seventy at the time he completed the

Page from the only extant manuscript for Dan Michel's Ayenbite of Inwyt, *written in the author's hand and dated 1340 (British Library, MS. Arundel 57, fol. 84)* text. But Gradon points out that this statement logically conflicts with his earlier statement that the text was written in his own hand, which he certainly could not have done blind. This introduces another point of contention – the actual role of Dan Michel in the creation of the *Ayenbite of Inwyt*. There is evidence which might lead one to believe that Dan Michel was only the copyist of a translation of the *Somme le Roi*, rather than the actual translator himself. Richard Morris observes that at no point in the text does Dan Michel ever mention that his work is a translation or that it borrows from other works; in fact, not until Joseph Stevenson's edition of 1855 was it ever known that the *Ayenbite of Inwyt* was not an original English text. Dan Michel's statements about his role in the production of the text are ambiguous: this book, he says, was "uolueld by him," which could refer to either the translation of a French text or merely the copying of an English one. Gradon notes that Dan Michel was "a practised copyist"; his hand has survived in several extant manuscripts from the library at Saint Augustine's, some of which (including the *Somme le Roi*) he owned himself. She further points out that there are instances in the *Ayenbite of Inwyt* where Dan Michel assigns not only wrong meanings but also wrong constructions to words in the French. Was he copying errors from an English translation or possibly mistranslating a French text? It is generally assumed that the translation is his.

The grammatical peculiarities of the *Ayenbite of Inwyt* are quite extensive – while most are common to all southern texts, many are unique to Kentish texts and to the *Ayenbite* in particular. Morris's work and Fernand Mossé's *A Handbook of Middle English* provide useful information regarding the differences between southern and Kentish aspects of the *Ayenbite of Inwyt*, and aspects of the more widely used and uniform northern dialect. The most immediately obvious differences are orthographical. In the *Ayenbite of Inwyt* *z* replaces *s* (*zenne* for *sinne*), and *v* replaces *f* (*vingre* for *fingre*, *vor* instead of *for*). Morris asserts that the *Ayenbite of Inwyt* marks the only appearance of the *z* for *s* substitution in the fourteenth century. Also found in the text is the use of *ch* for *k* (*smech* for *smek*, *thench* for *think*), *g* for *y* (*begge* for *bye*, *segge* for *saye*), and *b* for *v* (*libbe* for *live*, *habbe* for *have*). Finally the *sh* sound is represented by *ss* (*ssarp* for *sharp*, *ssipe* for *ship*). There are notable changes in nouns in the *Ayenbite of Inwyt*, especially the use of *ya* for *ea* (*dyad* for *dead*, *byam* for *beam*), *ie* or *ye* for *eo* (*diere* or *dyere* for *deore*), and *e* for *i* (*skele* for *skill*, *uelthe* for *filth*). There are numerous plural nouns in the *Ayenbite of Inwyt* which end not with *s*,

but with *en* – *cherchen* (churches), *hurten* or *heorten* (hearts), and *saulen* or *zaulen* (souls), just to name a few. Finally, personal pronouns such as *ich* or *uch* are used instead of *ik* or *I*.

Little has been written on the *Ayenbite of Inwyt* in recent years, although avenues of further study are still open. The paucity of information on Dan Michel, as well as the persistent question of his true involvement in the creation of the text, would seem to indicate that there is still room for biographical and authorial examination. Also, based on linguistic evidence, Morris asserts that Geoffrey Chaucer may have been familiar with Dan Michel's work; perhaps there are as-yet-undiscovered connections between it and other later Middle English works such as Chaucer's. Perhaps the most important remaining avenue of study is that of its status as a political and social document. Despite the fact that the one copy of it appears never to have circulated outside the monastery, it was intended to have been a public document. Dan Michel says as much when he writes near the end, "þis boc is y-write mid engliss of kent. / þis boc is y-mad uor lewede men / vor uader / and uor moder / and uor oþer ken." This statement – indeed, the mere existence of the text in English – raises questions. Considering the fact that English, despite having long been the de facto language of England, was still made up of distinct dialects, one might ask what part this Kentish text played in the development of a standard English vernacular. One might also ask what this text reveals about the relocation of English ecclesiastical power from the north to the south – that is, might the texts from this period such as the *Ayenbite of Inwyt* be used to establish the demographic facts of this relocation? There is also the issue of power within the church itself. By translating this text into Kentish, might Dan Michel have been privileging the spiritual (and cultural) needs of his people – his Kentish "ken" – and thus refuting the church's symbolic power as invested in the Latin mass? Or is Dan Michel, in stating that his text is "y-mad uor lewede men," being disingenuous, allying himself with the church by acknowledging the ignorance of his illiterate countrymen? After all, the *Ayenbite of Inwyt* is nothing if not a guide to good (that is, meek, mild, and unquestioning) behavior, and one can very well concur with Albert C. Baugh's statement in his well-known *Literary History of England* that the phrase "for lewd men" was often inserted into texts by authors who wished to have nothing whatever to do with the uneducated "rabble" for whom their work was intended. There also remains the issue of the literal and thus unremarkable nature of Dan

Michel's translation. A linguist, or someone schooled in comparative literature, might examine the choices Dan Michel made in his rendering of the *Somme le Roi* and thereby discover important, previously unrecognized differences in his translation and the original text. One might then infer any of a variety of motives behind his translation, or mistranslation.

Unfortunately, recent inquiry into Dan Michel's *Ayenbite of Inwyt* is hard to find, most scholars apparently being of the opinion that nothing remains to be said about it. Admittedly, it is a minor text in the canon of Middle English literature. However, to relegate it to the status of a footnote to Middle English literature is a mistake, if for no other reason than the fact that any religious text is a comment on the culture which produced it. Dan Michel's text, being in an uncommon and perhaps esoteric English dialect, may have more to say than anyone has yet acknowledged.

References:

Albert C. Baugh, *A Literary History of England* (New York: Appleton-Century-Crofts, 1948);

Wilhelm Rudolf Dolle, *Graphische und lautliche Untersuchung von Dan Michels 'Ayenbite of Inwyt'* (Bonn: University of Bonn, 1912);

Alfred B. Emden, *Donors of Books to St. Augustine's Abbey, Canterbury* (London: Oxford Bibliographical Society, 1968);

Max Förster, "Die Bibliothek des Dan Michael von Northgate," *Archiv,* 115 (1905): 167–169;

W. Nelson Francis, "The Original of the 'Ayenbite of Inwyt,' " *PMLA,* 52 (September 1937), 893–895;

W. Heuser, "Zum kentischen Dialekt im Mittelenglischen," *Anglia,* 17 (1895): 73–90;

Hans Jensen, *Die Verbalflexion im "Ayenbite of Inwyt,"* (Kiel, 1908);

Ulf Magnusson, *Studies in the Phonology of the "Ayenbite of Inwyt,"* Lund Theses in English 1 (Lund: Lund University, 1971);

Fernand Mossé, *A Handbook of Middle English,* translated by James A. Walker (Baltimore: Johns Hopkins University Press, 1952);

Herbert Senff, *Die Nominalflexion im "Ayenbite of Inwyt"* (Jena: Biedermann, 1937);

Hermann Varnhagen, "Beiträge zur Erklärung und Textkritik von Dan Michel's 'Ayenbite of Inwyt,' " *Englische Studien,* 1 (1877): 379–423; 2 (1879): 27–59;

Johannes K. Wallenberg, *The Vocabulary of Dan Michel's 'Ayenbite of Inwyt'* (Uppsala: Appelberg, 1923).

John Mirk

(died after 1414?)

Joel Fredell
Southeastern Louisiana University

MAJOR WORKS: *Festial* (circa 1382–1390)

Manuscripts: Forty manuscripts include the *Festial* sermons in some form: twenty-six include all or most of the sermon collection, organized by the church calendar (Group A texts) or divided into *sanctorale* and *temporale* holy days (Group B texts). The earliest extant manuscript including a Group A text of the *Festial* and the *Instructions for Parish Priests* is British Library, MS. Cotton Claudius A II. Fourteen manuscripts include *Festial* sermons abridged, excerpted, or substantially revised by later hands.

First publication: *Incipit liber qui vocatur festialis* (Westminster: William Caxton, 1483).

Standard editions: Group A text: *Mirk's Festial: A Collection of Homilies by Johannes Mirkus (John Mirk)*, edited by Thomas Erbe, EETS, e.s. 96 (1905). Revised text: *The Advent and Nativity Sermons from a Fifteenth-Century Revision of John Mirk's Festial*, edited by Susan Powell (Heidelberg: Winter, 1981).

Instructions for Parish Priests (circa 1382–1390)

Manuscripts: The work survives in seven manuscripts; the earliest extant text is in British Library MS. Cotton Claudius A II.

First publication: *Instructions for Parish Priests*, edited by Edward Peacock, EETS, o.s. 31 (1868); revised by F. W. Furnivall (1902).

Standard edition: *John Mirk's Instructions for Parish Priests*, edited by Gillis Kristensson (Lund: Gleerup, 1974).

Manuale sacerdotis (circa 1414)

Manuscripts: The work survives in thirteen manuscripts; Bodleian Library, Oxford, MS. Jesus College 1 may illustrate Mirk's original conception of the work — as a *vade-mecum* for active pastors.

John Mirk, Augustinian canon of Lilleshall Abbey, was one of the most widely read and influential religious writers in fifteenth-century England.

Mirk's first readership early in that century certainly consisted of his fellow clergy. By the late fifteenth century, however, Mirk's *Festial* (circa 1382–1390) was regularly published and reissued in new editions for a much wider audience. This Middle English collection of sermons, originally intended as an anthology for use by poorly equipped priests, was adopted for private reading by the merchant class and aristocracy, whose tastes favored devotional writing in their vernacular tongue. Within its first one hundred years the *Festial* found a general public hungry for its blend of sacred but fascinating topics: biographies, brief histories of holiday origins and doctrines, stories infused with shocking behaviors and supernatural events, and local legends.

The *Instructions for Parish Priests* (circa 1382–1390) is a basic how-to manual aimed at the same clergy the *Festial* tried to help and may originally have been a companion volume for the sermons. The *Instructions for Parish Priests* never achieved the popularity of the other work and did not appear in print until the nineteenth century. The *Manuale sacerdotis* (circa 1414), a Latin handbook encouraging proper conduct for priests, has not yet been published. Neither work was likely to have reached outside clerical circles in the later middle ages, but today they are finding a secular audience. The *Instructions for Parish Priests* provides an intimate view of religious life in rural England, as well as specifics on how the parish priest functioned as an agent for social control. The *Manuale sacerdotis* details the common abuses of the day among the regular clergy, as well as the threats posed by Lollardy.

The historical traces left by John Mirk are few. The earliest manuscript of his Middle English writings (London, British Library MS. Cotton Claudius A II) includes both the *Festial* and the *Instructions for the Parish Priests*. This manuscript, in a colophon to the *Instructions for the Parish Priests*, identifies John Mirk as the author and a canon regular of the monastery of Lilleshall, an abbey near Shrewsbury and the Welsh border in the West Midlands county of

Shropshire. In the preface to the *Manuale sacerdotis* Mirk refers to himself as prior of the Lilleshall canons. No other records which refer to Mirk have been found, but internal evidence and what is known about the Augustinian canons of Lilleshall yield a more complete portrait.

Some rhyming words from the couplets that make up the *Instructions for Parish Priests* (virtually the only evidence of Mirk's own dialect likely to survive "translation" into the dialects of whatever scribes happened to have copied the manuscripts) are clearly from the north of England. Though this evidence is very slight, Mirk may have grown up or lived in Yorkshire or nearby, regions with strong traditions of religious learning and lay piety. His name does not appear among surviving lists of university students, but he had enough schooling to be an accomplished reader of many Latin authors. There is evidence of brother canons near to Mirk in place and time doing university study. One Lilleshall canon, William of Longdon, was licensed in 1400 to study at Oxford or Cambridge. A nearby Augustinian house, Haughmond Abbey, placed a group of Augustinian canons at Oxford, an establishment which later became Saint Mary's College, but Mirk and the canons of Lilleshall were not necessarily involved. Lilleshall Abbey was founded by Arrouasians, an austere and contemplative monastic order later absorbed into the much larger and more powerful Augustinian order. The Lilleshall canons of Mirk's day were thus Augustinians, but not under the jurisdiction of the Augustinian general chapters nor under any obligation to maintain a canon at a university. Consequently there is no reason to assume Mirk studied at Oxford or Cambridge however much his reading knowledge may suggest such study.

What can be more firmly established is Lilleshall's benefits for Mirk as an active scholar and writer. Established around 1148 by Richard de Belmeis, the abbey apparently ranked as a royal foundation and was one of the few Augustinian houses privileged to have an abbot, rather than a lower-ranking prior, at its head. Mirk's own citation of many authors in his writing suggests that among the abbey's advantages was a substantial library. Lilleshall flourished, though it was not consistently prosperous, drawing income in Mirk's time from the lease of properties, sheep, grain mills, fulling mills, and tanneries.

Lay support for Lilleshall was substantial during Mirk's years there. Among the great names of laypersons admitted into the fraternity of the abbey in 1398 are John of Gaunt, his wife Catherine, and his squire William Chetwind. An unidentified canon of Lilleshall also recorded the great historical events of the day (in Corpus Christi College, Cambridge, MS. 332.ii, fols. 47–47^v) including the ascension to the throne of Edward III and Richard II, and Richard II's visit to Lilleshall in 1398. The flurry of visits by the great in that year, probably witnessed by Mirk, was occasioned by the Shrewsbury Parliament. A few years later Mirk's abbey was near an even more momentous event. On 21 July 1403, a few miles northeast of Lilleshall Henry IV and Prince Hal defeated the rebel forces of Henry (Hotspur) Percy and killed Percy himself in the Battle of Shrewsbury.

These historical landmarks do not show up directly in Mirk's writing, but some larger historical forces behind them do. In the Great Revolt of 1381, rural and urban workers threatened England's structure of governance and controlled England for some days; but this uprising is only the most dramatic of a long series in the late fourteenth century. The causes for this instability are many and complex, but among the responses of the governing classes are clerical condemnations of social and political rebels. An excommunications formula in some manuscripts of Mirk's *Instructions for Parish Priests* curses a sweeping range of such violators of the secular order. In the *Festial* sermons there is the less obvious shepherding of moral instruction and obedience, but Mirk does characterize the Flemish, the immigrant clothworking population attacked in the Great Revolt, as nothing more than thieves.

A more long-term danger, one which may have prompted Mirk's writing in the first place, developed in the aftermath of the Black Death. This combined epidemic of bubonic, pneumonic, and septicemic plagues devastated England in waves from about 1349 through the end of the century. Although estimates of the death toll vary widely, the clergy were particularly hard hit because of their obligations to serve the sick and the dying. As much as 40 percent of the English clergy may have died in this period. Badly trained replacements were pressed into service to fill the needs of the church, particularly in poor rural areas. Mirk's vernacular handbooks, as he says himself in his preface to the *Festial,* are intended to provide sound, authoritative support for his underequipped brethren. Many of them were operating without reference books of any kind in English, the one language they could read, to guide them.

Although Mirk lived a monastic life at Lilleshall, and a relatively ascetic life if the Arrouasian influence was still strong during his time there, it is not surprising that he devoted his writing to the needs of parish priests. Augustinian (or "Austin") canons lived and worked in the pastoral as well as the contemplative world. The canons were monks in that they renounced all private property and followed the rule of Saint Augustine. However, the name *canon regular* refers to the fact that Augustinian canons all took the holy orders of priesthood and were included on the official canon of the church's clergymen. In addition to their contemplative life and duties at their house, Augustinian canons were expected to preach at neighboring churches and in parishes where their abbey or priory had substantial holdings. They also served as pastors in churches where two or more canons were resident. Lilleshall was responsible for appointing pastors in some parishes, and its canons probably served as pastors themselves, particularly in Mirk's earlier years when there was a shortage of clergy for rural parishes. In 1381 Lilleshall had ten canons, Mirk probably among that number, enough to send off at least a few to pastoral duties.

Mirk apparently preached at the nearby Saint Alkmund's Church in Shrewsbury, a church whose endowments had been turned over to Lilleshall Abbey in 1244. The sermon on Saint Alkmund in the *Festial* refers to the saint as patron of "this church" and a founding legend which corresponds exactly with that of Saint Alkmund's, Shrewsbury. The familiarity with the particular needs of pastoral duty Mirk shows, particularly in his two Middle English works, also suggests some direct experience with his own flock of souls. The sheer variety of methods Mirk uses to compose his sermons in the *Festial* suggests that it is a working collection taken from his own series of sermons delivered to the kind of provincial parishioners he would have served. The *Instructions for Parish Priests* shows a remarkable knowledge of the fundamental questions a provincial pastor would need answered. Mirk may have gleaned this information from his brethren returning from the field or other vicars associated with Lilleshall, but in either case a central part of his life as an Augustinian canon was concerned with the proper performance of pastoral duties in the churches associated with his abbey.

Mirk's writings are part of a broad movement in the church to educate the laity. This movement was made official in the Western church by a decree of the Fourth Lateran Council (1215) that all Christians should confess annually to their parish priests. This decree, and existing pastoral concerns, produced a body of practical treatises for parish priests on the techniques of confession and penance. In En-

gland this movement was bolstered by Archbishop of Canterbury John Peckham's six-point program of instruction, issued (in Latin) in the Lambeth Constitutions (1281). These points of instruction included the Lord's Prayer or Pater Noster, the fourteen Articles of Faith, the Ten Commandments and the two precepts of the Gospels, the seven sacraments, the seven deadly sins, the seven remedial virtues, and the seven acts of mercy.

Closer to Mirk's time Archbishop Thoresby of York in 1357 issued similar instructions to his clergy but provided an English translation essential for the many parish priests and the vast majority of their flock. Following Thoresby's manual, now known by the inaccurate title *The Lay Folks' Catechism,* came a number of handbooks in English similar to Mirk's *Instructions for Parish Priests:* the *Speculum Christiana* (circa 1360), *Pore caitiff* (circa 1375), *Memoriale credenciam* (circa 1400–1425), *Speculum vitae* (circa 1380, one of several English translations of the *Somme le Roi* circulating in the fourteenth and fifteenth centuries), and various treatises on individual points of instruction. The seven deadly sins was a particularly popular topic, and many of these works became general reading among the laity.

Mirk's *Instructions for Parish Priests* differs from these translations by his pragmatism and focus on the minutiae of priestly duties, which may have doomed the *Instructions for Parish Priests* to a specialist audience. Mirk details the proper conduct of a pastor and his flock, Latin and English formulae for rituals, translations of the seven sacraments, and appropriate methods to deal with crises ranging from mice gnawing the communion wafers to spiders falling into the consecrated wine during the Eucharist to administering the host to dying parishioners afflicted with nausea. Mirk states that the *Instructions for Parish Priests* is a translation from the Latin of the second part of the *Oculus sacerdotis* (circa 1320–1328) by William of Pagula. However, the work draws on all three sections of the *Oculus sacerdotis* and is not a literal translation of any substantial part of the Latin work. Mirk has combined various materials mined from this source with other sources and practical experience.

The *Instructions* begins with a discussion of proper priestly behavior and ends with appropriate methods for dealing with both standard and exceptional circumstances and for conducting the mass and other rituals. Within this frame Mirk arranges his material according to the sacraments as they occur in a parishioner's life from birth to death, beginning with baptism and ending with extreme unction. Mirk moves efficiently through baptism, con-

Page from the earliest extant transcription of Mirk's Instructions for Parish Priests *(British Library, MS. Cotton Claudius A II, fol. 130ʳ)* firmation, and marriage, but keeps his attention on the practical. Along with Latin and English formulae for the rite of baptism is a strong encouragement to teach these formulae to midwives and expectant parents who may have to do an emergency baptism for an endangered newborn. The procedure for proclaiming an upcoming marriage, the wedding banns, is succinctly laid out, but far more time is taken to explain the rules of consanguinity: what degree of kinship is allowable for marriage. Since godparents were considered cousins to their godchildren and to the parents of their godchildren, small parishes already faced with inbreeding problems would need thorough guidance to obey the rules of the church.

Mirk then moves into a discussion of the appropriate conduct for parishioners and provides translations of the Pater Noster, the Hail Mary, the Creed, the fourteen Articles of Faith, and the seven sacraments. After instructions on baptism and confirmation, the "Great Sentence" of excommunication appears in two manuscripts (Oxford, Bodleian Library MS. Douce 60 and MS. Douce 103). Another version of this substantial (one hundred lines) passage occurs separately between the *Festial* and the *Instructions for Parish Priests* in the earliest-known manuscript (British Library, MS. Cotton Claudius A II, fol. 123[v]). This version is printed in F. W. Furnivall's revised edition of the *Instructions for Parish Priests* (1902); Erbe gives the Douce version in the original (1868) edition of the *Instructions for Parish Priests*. The remaining manuscripts do not have the Great Sentence, though gaps in most of these (following line 674) suggest that the scribes were aware of a problem at that point. It is not clear whether the scribes excised the long cursing ritual or simply recognized a gap in the exemplar manuscript. There is no way to tell which of the two versions might be closer to Mirk's own, nor whether Mirk wrote either excommunication passage. What is clear is that these lines were in the manuscript tradition at the earliest date known and that the coverage of the cursing pronouncements is thorough. The priest is enjoined to perform this ritual a few times a year to excommunicate whole categories of sinners rather than individuals. Any sinners who fell into these categories would be cut off from salvation and all benefits of the community of the faithful until they confessed in a state of true contrition and began to fulfill the terms of their penance. Not surprisingly, sacrilege, witchcraft, and heresy are included among the actions that deserve cursing by bell, book, and candle. Less obvious are child abandonment, perjury, and usury. Most interesting in this period is the cursing of traitors to the king, disturbers of the peace, and dishonest merchants. All of these actions are regularly included in contemporary discussions of deadly sin and as such deserve the condemnation of the church. Nonetheless, these last problems are among the crucial issues of social control during Mirk's time. Excommunication is intended to support secular efforts to maintain law and order.

Mirk's next topic in the *Instructions for Parish Priests* is the sacrament of confession. He cautions priests to temper with mercy the just penance required by the seriousness of the sin. Too strict a penance may drive a sinner into despair. The priest should also assign a penance appropriate to the parishioner's social class, sex, and particular sin. This consideration prompts a discussion of the seven virtues, each of which remedies one of the seven deadly sins. A brief review of which cases should be sent on to the bishop, and the prayers for absolution to be recited by sinner and priest complete the section.

The life cycle of sacraments ends with a short treatment of the rites of extreme unction. After considering some miscellaneous problems, Mirk closes with a request that the priest-reader pray for his soul, then declares that he has written this manual for those priests who have no books of their own. Though Mirk may have decided to fulfill these needs at any time, the most likely period for him to have done so was during the worst shortage of competent clerics in the late fourteenth century, when the younger canon Mirk was most likely to be sent out to serve rural parishes. The *Festial* was probably produced some time between 1382 and 1390; the appropriateness of the *Instructions for Parish Priests* as a companion volume and its concern with the basics of pastoral duties place its most likely date of composition around the same period.

Eventually Mirk became prior of Lilleshall Abbey. He was probably a claustral prior, appointed by the abbot to take over whatever supervisory duties the abbot delegated. The work in which Mirk reveals this promotion, the *Manuale sacerdotis,* also contains in one early manuscript a dedication to "Johannis de .S. vicario de .A." John of Sotton was appointed vicar of Saint Alkmund's in 1414 and no other applicable group of initials associated with Lilleshall has been found, so Mirk may have dedicated the *Manuale sacerdotis* (or one copy of it) to this John of Sotton around the time of the latter's appointment: a cautionary present to the new vicar of a parish in which Mirk had some personal experience and interest. Again this evidence allows only speculation, but it represents some basis for dating the *Manuale sacerdotis* as Mirk's latest work around 1414 and for seeing him as an active figure whose importance grew from the 1380s to the second decade of the fifteenth century.

Mirk's second handbook for priests is not simply a rewrite of the *Instructions for Parish Priests*. His use of Latin in the *Manuale sacerdotis* targets a more learned readership. Again he relies on William of Pagula's *Oculus sacerdotis,* but transforms and adds extensively to it. Once more Mirk raises problems of priestly conduct and unforeseen crises during mass. The *Manuale sacerdotis,* however, has little of the type of material at the center of the *Instructions for Parish Priests:* the administration of the sacraments, the expansive discussion of confession and penance, and the essentials of lay religious instruction ordained by Archbishops Peckham and Thoresby. Instead, the *Manuale sacerdotis* concentrates on reforming the moral and professional outlook of the priesthood.

Mirk provides a set of exhortations to the priest, as he does in the *Instructions for Parish Priests,* functioning as a frame for the practical-methods outline that qualifies the *Manuale sacerdotis* as another handbook. At its center are directions on the proper conducting of the mass and solutions to problems such as the communion wine freezing in the chalice. The sermon-like frame for these directions includes a description of proper conduct balanced by memorably scandalous examples of improper behavior. Then Mirk presents a system of six virtues necessary for priests, laying out their many branches or subdivisions in detail with more sensational examples of priestly failings. At the other end of the frame Mirk develops a comparison of worldly and spiritual conduct with illustrations of the consequent infernal torment or heavenly joy.

One other topic crops up in the *Manuale sacerdotis.* A host of diverse religious beliefs and opinions verging on an early Reformation divided the English church, particularly after 1380. The orthodox countered by condemning them all with a single epithet, "Lollardy," but suppression of the heresies was a major struggle in the first half of the fifteenth century. Mirk attacks Lollards twice in the *Festial* sermons in what may be the earliest known use of the term. The temperate tone and small number of such references indicate that Lollards were a minor concern for Mirk at this point; later works by other orthodox writers are far more strident. If the *Manuale sacerdotis* was produced around 1414, Mirk was writing during one of the most intense periods of struggle with the shrillest rhetoric, but his main

interest is not another polemical attack on the Lollards. In keeping with his pragmatic character he tries to assure orthodoxy by attacking clerical abuses himself. Mirk's discussion of the priesthood in the *Manuale sacerdotis,* shielded from appropriations by Lollards or other outside critics by his use of Latin, unflinchingly details priestly failings in its first two sections by attacking worldliness in the clergy with the peculiar vigor and enthusiasm to be expected from a man who has combined pastoral service with the austere life of Lilleshall Abbey. He also provides specific remedies for proper conduct, demanding personal morality more fervently than competence in serving mass.

These two handbooks achieved some circulation in England, as the number of remaining manuscripts and their diverse dialect "translations" attest, and so had the kind of success Mirk must have intended. The *Festial,* however, was a far greater success for an audience he may never have expected. This anthology provided short sermons for a full year's liturgical cycle of holy or feast days (known as *temporales*) commemorating the lives of Christ and the Virgin Mary, and days (known as *sanctorales*) dedicated to the saints and martyrs. One measure of the work's first wave of popularity, generated among a clerical readership, is that the version apparently closest to Mirk's original, in the manuscripts collectively known as Group A, was promptly reorganized into a new form recorded by the Group B manuscripts. The Group A texts have a straightforward organization. *Sanctorale* and *temporale* sermons simply follow the calendar year in order from Advent Sunday to the feast of Saint Katherine, and Mirk provides an appendix of sermons for funerals, weddings, and other occasional use. He also addresses two "sermons" or instructional pieces to the priests themselves. Between Good Friday and Easter sermons he provides a set of answers to the most common questions about the various celebrations leading up to Easter. Only a few of the *sanctorale* sermons are designed for reading on the saint's day. Most are for delivery on the Sunday before the feast days as spiritual preparation and advance instruction for the observances during the week. Group B texts separate the *sanctorale* and *temporale* sermons, probably for easier reference in the hands of those priests who did not have to rely on Mirk to provide them with homiletic material each successive Sunday.

The *Festial* thus became the sort of widely-used reference that Mirk relied on. In his colophon to the *Festial,* the author says he has translated the *Legenda aurea* (before 1298), a source famous throughout medieval Europe for its sacred stories, "with some adding to." In fact Mirk called upon a wide variety of different authors and works, some of which he names, including John Beleth, Alexander Neckam, the *Gesta Romanorum* (circa 1250?), and the "Gestes of France" (possibly the *Gesta Francorum,* circa 1130). Nonetheless, most of his sources, as well as particular passages in those sources he names, remain to be identified. Mirk's method of compilation from various sources may have been that indicated by one thirteenth-century manuscript of the *South English Legendary,* another important vernacular collection of saints' lives. This manuscript (Oxford, Bodleian Library MS. Corpus Christi 148), apparently from a Cistercian monastery, includes an annotated calendar. Each holy day is given a list of references to books in the monastery's library that contain appropriate stories for the feast celebrated that day. Mirk may well have had such an aid for Lilleshall's library to help write the sermons Augustinian canons were expected to deliver. The *Festial* quickly seems to have been added to clerical libraries for similar purposes. In addition to the Group B reorganization, which adapted Mirk's collection for quick occasional reference, many manuscripts reveal clerical writers in the fifteenth century abridging, excerpting, and rewriting *Festial* sermons for their own purposes.

Among these diverse forms of the *Festial* the Group B text was sufficiently well established to become the basis for all the printed editions up to 1532, and the work's second wave of popularity was among the upper-class audiences for early publishing in England. William Caxton produced the first printed edition in Westminster in 1483. Caxton and his successor, Wynkyn de Worde, subsequently published a number of editions, clearly indicating the commercial success of the *Festial.* Another printer, Theodore Roode, published his own edition in 1486, apparently trying to break out of academic printing in Oxford and into a broader market. This attempt is interesting for its imitation of Caxton (Roode's typefaces are very close to those of Caxton) and its use of many woodcut engravings that seem more appropriate to the *Legenda aurea,* another of Caxton's successes. An illustrated popular edition of this kind dramatizes how far the *Festial* had come from its original role as a preacher's reference.

The *Festial* still deserves a general readership for its crisp narrative and its scandalously vivid use of short narratives, known as exempla, to support its moral and doctrinal arguments. Virtually absent are the penitential instructions on the deadly sins,

the articles of faith, and other essentials recommended for the laity by Archbishops Peckham and Thoresby. One explanation for this absence may be that the *Instructions* was intended as a companion text. If so, Mirk considered one-to-one instruction and review, particularly at the confessional, to be more effective than a sermon presentation. There is one sermon dedicated to the Pater Noster and instructions on teaching the Hail Mary, the two most basic prayers to be taught to the faithful. The stages of penance are discussed several times, though not in any clear formulaic terms, and various deadly sins get condemned. Some fundamental instruction thus appears in sermon form, but, except for the Pater Noster, Mirk never takes up the essentials covered in the *Instructions for Parish Priests* for systematic treatment in his preaching.

Often Mirk structures his sermon by narrating a holy life, followed by some exemplary miracles, with only a brief exposition of any moral point being made at beginning and end. More frequently he begins by carefully explaining the historical basis for a holy day and often uses a format regularly recommended by contemporary manuals on the art of preaching: an introduction which points out a few points of significance, an exposition which expands each point, and exemplary stories to illustrate these points. The sermon for Corpus Christi day, for instance, begins with an explanation of the feast's history and purpose, discusses the body of Christ miraculously contained in the Eucharistic communion wafer or host, then elaborates four skills offered to humanity by the Eucharist: its help in achieving salvation, in remembering Christ's passion, in revealing God's love, and in receiving God's grace. These points are developed with some spectacular exempla: a copiously bleeding host squelching the doubts of a skeptic, the host "swallowed" by abdominal incision when its dying recipient was afflicted with severe nausea, and a pillar of fire locating a consecrated host lost along a country road. Mirk also uses this opportunity to attack Lollard iconoclasts who viewed crosses, sculptures, and paintings of holy figures as a form of idolatry. He takes the orthodox position that these representations are "books for the illiterate," an understandable but fairly oblique argument for the Eucharist as a reminder of Christ's Passion.

The most constant feature of the *Festial* is its striking exempla; they may not perfectly suit the point being made, but undoubtedly they can hold an audience's attention. Mirk is enough of a fire-and-brimstone preacher that his opening sermon of the collection, on the joyous occasion of Advent

Sunday, moves promptly to Christ's Second Coming and the horrific events of the Apocalypse accompanying that return. Gruesome details of martyrdoms and cruel torturers are not spared in his sermons, nor are visions of damnation. Believers in necromancy, ubiquitous fiends, talking idols, diabolical Moslems, and wicked Jews would find extensive support for their views. The number of lively Christian icons bleeding, crying, and embracing penitents in these exempla would yield plenty of fodder for any iconoclastic Lollard's attack. These sensational aspects, nonetheless, should not obscure Mirk's consistent efforts in his sermons to give parishioners the basic information they need to understand the complex cycle of worship and prayer demanded from all of them.

The importance of the *Festial* extended at least into the Elizabethan period, when one unfortunate lay preacher was arrested in 1591 for delivering a sermon out of Mirk's collection. Recently Mirk's virtues as a vernacular writer and a representative of popular religious experience in the age of Geoffrey Chaucer have been recognized once more. There are a number of other sermon collections from around Mirk's time: the *Fasciculus morum* (circa 1320?) John Bromyard's *Summa praedicantium* (circa 1390), and the sermons (1373–1389) of Bishop Thomas Brinton are among the best known. These Latin collections are key witnesses to religious thought surrounding Mirk and his contemporaries. Still, they do not have much direct role in the early history of what is now called English literature. Mirk's *Festial* may have been the most important sermon collection, and one of the most important pieces of native religious writing, in a period when Caxton and other early printers were establishing the first canon of English literature. The relationship between religious writing and the "high art" of poets like Chaucer and John Gower working in Mirk's lifetime is still poorly understood. How much these writers knew or considered the very different literary environments in which their contemporaries operated is not clear and largely undiscoverable when they do not refer to or copy each other directly. More fruitful questions could be asked about why both kinds of authors were published and read by the same people in later fifteenth-century England or what kinds of people might have been reading both religious and "high art" authors during the great formative period of literature in English at the end of the fourteenth century.

It is nonetheless possible to imagine Mirk's development over three decades at Lilleshall. The practical vernacular handbooks, the *Festial*, and the *Instructions for Parish Priests* may have come out of an earlier period of preaching and some acquaintance with pastoral work in the unsettled years following the Black Death, from the Great Revolt of 1381 through the deposition of Richard II in 1399. Mirk's primary concern in this time was the pressing need for basic competence among rural pastors, a need the canons of Lilleshall could not fill by themselves. The *Manuale sacerdotis,* a Latin handbook with more sophistication and learned authority, was probably produced during his later years as prior or during his grooming for that position. In this period domestic political unrest was far less revolutionary than during Richard's reign, the numbers of well-trained clergy increased steadily, and Lilleshall's chronic budget troubles finally subsided. However, another major challenge to the clergy arose in the 1380s and gathered force throughout Mirk's time at Lilleshall: Lollardy. Mirk apparently saw the heresies abroad as less harmful than the often accurate criticisms of the church which lent authority to the proclamations of the Lollards. He may have saved his discussion of sensitive topics raised by critics of the church for the limited-circulation context of his Latin *Manuale sacerdotis,* a tactic appropriate throughout his career. However, the overview of the clergy and its problems and his choice of Latin with its broader yet more learned audience suggest that Mirk wrote the *Manuale sacerdotis* from a position of long experience, institutional authority, and removal from the daily concerns of pastors. The promotion to prior Mirk notes in his preface to the *Manuale sacerdotis* would suit all these qualities and mark the manual as a capstone work for his lifelong interest in what priests need to lead their flocks. That Mirk's reference works became an important part of commercially produced literature for general use can tell modern readers much about the formative years of English literature and the audiences for that literature.

References:

Margaret Aston, *Lollards and Reformers: Images and Literacy in Late Medieval Religion* (London: Hambledon, 1984);

L. E. Boyle, "The *Oculus Sacerdotis* and Some Other Works of William of Pagula," *Transactions of the Royal Historical Society,* fifth series 5 (June 1955): 81–110;

Alan J. Fletcher, "John Mirk and the Lollards," *Medium Ævum,* 56, no. 2 (1987): 217–224;

Fletcher, "The Manuscripts of John Mirk's *Manuale Sacerdotis,*" *Leeds Studies in English,* new series 19 (1988): 106–139;

Fletcher, "Unnoticed Sermons from John Mirk's *Festial*," *Speculum*, 55 (July 1980): 514–522;

Fletcher and Susan Powell, "The Origins of a Fifteenth-Century Sermon Collection: MSS Harley 2247 and Royal 18 B XXV," *Leeds Studies in English*, new series 10 (1978): 74–96;

Angus McIntosh and Martyn Wakelin, "John Mirk's *Festial* and Bodleian MS Hatton 96," *Neuphilologische Mitteilungen*, 83, no.4 (1982): 443–450;

G. R. Owst, *Literature and Pulpit in Medieval England* (Oxford: Blackwood, 1961);

Owst, *Preaching in Medieval England* (Cambridge: Cambridge University Press, 1926);

W. A. Pantin, *The English Church in the Fourteenth Century* (Cambridge: Cambridge University Press, 1955);

H. G. Pfander, "The Medieval Friars and Some Alphabetical Reference-Books for Sermons," *Medium Ævum*, 3, no. 1 (1934): 19–29;

O. S. Pickering, "Notes on the Sentence of Cursing in Middle English: or, A Case for the Index of Middle English Prose," *Leeds Studies in English*, new series 12 (1981): 229–244;

Powell, "John Mirk's *Festial* and the Pastoral Programme," *Leeds Studies in English*, new series 25 (1991): 85–102;

Powell, "Lollards and Lombards: Late Medieval Bogeymen," *Medium Ævum*, 59, no. 1 (1990): 133–139;

Powell, "A New Dating of John Mirk's *Festial*," *Notes and Queries*, new series 29 (December 1982): 487–489;

Lillian L. Steckman, "A Late Fifteenth-Century Revision of Mirk's *Festial*," *Studies in Philology*, 34 (January 1937): 36–48;

Victoria History of the Counties of England. A History of Shropshire, 2 volumes, edited by A. T. Gaydon (London: Oxford University Press, 1973), II: 70–80;

Wakelin, "The Manuscripts of John Mirk's *Festial*," *Leeds Studies in English*, new series 1 (1967): 93–118.

Richard Rolle

(circa 1290–1300 – 1349)

William F. Pollard
University of Evansville

WORKS: (1322?–1348)

Manuscripts: There are well over 450 extant manuscripts of Rolle's Latin and English writings dating roughly from 1390 to 1500. The 2 major manuscripts containing the English works are Cambridge University MS. Dd.v.64 (early fifteenth century) and MS. Longleat 29 (early to mid fifteenth century).

First publications of English writings: *English Prose Treatises of Richard Rolle de Hampole,* EETS, o.s. 20, edited by George G. Perry (1866; revised, 1921) – contains some spurious works; *The Psalter or Psalms of David and Certain Canticles,* edited by H. R. Bramley (Oxford: Clarendon Press, 1884); *Yorkshire Writers: Richard Rolle of Hampole, An English Father of the Church, and His Followers,* 2 volumes, edited by Carl Horstman (London: Swan Sonnenschein, 1895–1896; reprinted, Cambridge: D. S. Brewer, 1978).

Standard editions: *The Fire of Love and the Mending of Life or the Rule of Living of Richard Rolle,* edited by Ralph Harvey, EETS, o.s. 106 (1896); *English Writings of Richard Rolle, Hermit of Hampole,* edited by Hope Emily Allen (Oxford: Clarendon Press, 1931; reprinted, 1963); *Richard Rolle: Prose and Verse, from MS. Longleat 29,* edited by S. J. Ogilvie-Thomson, EETS, o.s. 293 (1988).

Editions in modern English: *Rolle: The Fire of Love,* translated from Latin by Clifton Wolters (Harmondsworth, U.K.: Penguin, 1972); *Richard Rolle, The English Writings,* edited and translated by Rosamund S. Allen (New York: Paulist Press, 1988).

Richard Rolle and his followers have left considerable information about his life, including autobiographical comments in Rolle's Latin and English writings and the *Officium de Sancto Ricardo,* compiled by hagiographers in the 1380s in anticipation of a never-realized canonization. The lessons and antiphons of the *officium* tell of Rolle's birth at Thornton in Yorkshire, his years as a student at Oxford, and his flight from that city and from sin at age nineteen. Considerable attention is then given to his encounter with his sister and his request for two of her garments – one gray and one white – to make a tunic before his next flight to the life of a hermit. As he runs in this makeshift habit, covered with his father's rain hood, his sister gives him his first unsympathetic reading: "Frater meus insanit. Frater meus insanit" (My brother is mad. My brother is mad). Subsequent responses through the next 650 years have covered the spectrum from veneration to outright disdain, from claims of sanctity in the fourteenth-century *officium* to a denial of his mystical authenticity. Clearly the hagiographers were the chief proponents of the cult of "Saint" Richard, which flourished from his death in 1349 to the sixteenth-century recusants, who preserved and cherished his writings. The incident of the makeshift habit and his sister's startled response is a detail paralleling the call to vocation experienced by Saint Francis of Assisi.

As with Saint Francis, the stripping and the clothing are symbolic of a spiritual movement from the old man (*vetus homo*) to the new (*novus homo*). Indeed, there is a distinctive Franciscan element in Rolle's thought that combines with and directs his appropriation of the rich traditions of Anselm, Bernard of Clairvaux, and Richard of Saint Victor. As evidence of Rolle's similarity to the great thirteenth-century synthesizer of these monastic traditions and the successor to Francis, Margaret Deanesly notes in a 1914 essay the confusion of the Quaracchi editors in printing Rolle's *Incendium amoris* (translated as *The Fire of Love,* 1434) as Bonaventure's *De triplici via* (The Triple Way, 1259). Bonaventure visited England in 1259 and was offered but declined the archbishopric of York in 1265. The spirit and tone of the Seraphic Doctor, nevertheless, remained a dominant force and was transmitted to Rolle, the Yorkshireman often called "the English Bonaventure."

The next important details of Rolle's life have to do with the care of souls. As to whether the sister's view of her brother's mental state ever softened, the record is silent, but he was taken seriously by his family's overlord, John de Dalton, and by Thomas de Neville, a future archdeacon of Durham who maintained Rolle during his Oxford years. After leaving Oxford without a degree and thus without the possibility of taking holy orders, the would-be hermit returned to Dalton's estate after the episode with his sister's tunics. It was at the Dalton residence in Pickering that Rolle probably felt the first stirrings of mystical experience. After about three years on his benefactor's manor, he left for his hermitage at Hampole and for the permanent status of hermit. At this point his care of souls generated a collection of Latin and English writings that remain among the most influential of the late medieval period. The extant English works include two meditations of the life of Christ, a psalter commentary, seven independent lyrics, four short prose pieces, and three epistles. All the English pieces were probably written for women, if not for a particular woman, Margaret Kirkby, a recluse of Ainderby in Yorkshire. Rolle had been called to her side during one of her seizures and, after allowing her to lay her head on his shoulder, promised that she would not suffer again while he was alive. The prophecy held true, for the recluse did not suffer another convulsion until she heard of her spiritual guide's death during the plague of 1349. Richard's life as a hermit is thus framed by two associations with women, his sister and the recluse.

Many of the less sympathetic readings of Rolle focus upon the judgmental tone frequent in his Latin writings. But the English writings present a more sympathetic figure and encapsulate the themes of the Latin works while giving them a more tempered and caring tone. Certainly his English Psalter (circa 1330s), the *Meditations on the Passion,* his lyrics, and the epistles were immediately influential beyond most fourteenth-century English texts. The Lollards appropriated elements of the Psalter, and his language of "heat," "song," and "sweetness" (*calor, canor,* and *dulcor*) found its way into pious compilations, prayers, and lyrics through the fifteenth century and into the recusant literature of the sixteenth. Rolle's Latin works have been continuously in print since the fifteenth century, and some were circulated in manuscript translations. Richard Misyn translated the *Incendium amoris* as *The Fire of*

Miniature portrait of Richard Rolle from a manuscript for The Desert of Religion, *an anonymous poem that has been ascribed to Walter Hilton (British Library, MS. Cotton Faustina, B. VI. Pt.ii, fol. 8b)*

Love in 1434 and the *Emendatio vitae* as *The Mending of Life* in 1435. Furthermore, an anonymous English version of Rolle's treatment of the Holy Name was excerpted from his commentary on the Song of Songs and had a wide circulation. Beyond influencing others, the hermit's Latin compositions first influenced his own English texts.

Those portions of the hermit's life highlighted in the *officium* are accurate guides to the themes and concerns of medievalists, who have followed in his sister's wake as critics. Studies of the hermit address the question of mystical authenticity; they grapple with antifeminist elements in the Latin works in the light of his English writings for Margaret Kirkby; they examine his well-known triad of *calor, canor,* and *dulcor* and discuss his sources; they discover characteristic image patterns; and they deal with the sheer volume of his writings in Latin and English and with his influence on fifteenth-century devotional works and compendiums.

The English Psalter includes all 150 psalms and dates from the 1330s. It follows a much earlier Latin commentary dating from Rolle's early career shortly after his departure from Oxford. Much of his work with the psalms depends upon the traditional exegesis of Peter Lombard, but the language of Rolle, an idiosyncratic mixture of Franciscan and Victorine spirituality, shines through with regularity. A good example of the hermit's contribution to psalter commentary may be seen in his treatment of Psalm 39:4:

> '*Et immisit in os meum canticum novum: carmen deo nostro.* And he sent in my mouth a new sange: ympyn [hymned] til oure lord god.' When he had taken me fra syn and fra all bisynes of erth, and stabild me in luf and vertus, thain he sent in til the mouth of my hert and of my body alswa a new sange, that is the melody of the tone of heven, that nane may synge bot his derlyngs.

In many ways this early work of commentary sets the tone also for the discussion of song in all of Rolle's English writings. His Latin commentaries on the Psalter and the Canticles from the previous decade place Rolle in the tradition of Bernard of Clairvaux and Bonaventure, and this language is carried over into the works of instruction and devotion written for Margaret Kirkby. This particular comment on Psalm 39:4 coalesces the dual thrusts of Franciscan spirituality, affective piety and ecstatic joy – all in terms of celestial harmony. For Rolle it is the imagery of heavenly song which represents – as fully as language permits – the final union between God and his lover.

Giving pride of place to *canor* is in the tradition of the *jubilius* theme so central to Franciscan writings. Bonaventure's *Vitis mystica* (The Mystical Vine), for instance, presents Christ as the "plen-titude of Grace blazing anew in the fullness of time with the flames of burning love." His treatise continues to center on the metaphor of love's fire as preparatory to the *Canticum novum,* or new song, of Christ's Passion as an instrument prefiguring the perfect tone of heaven, where God's elect gaze eternally upon Christ in majesty. As the inheritor of this tradition, Rolle would need to look no further than the images of *The Mystical Vine* or *The Triple Way* to find his three in one: his *calor, canor,* and *dulcor.* The metrical preface appended to the English Psalter acknowledges that the Lollards had appropriated Rolle's work on the psalms. In fact, the preface indicates that two such Lollard versions of the hermit's commentary had been discovered to be "grafted in with heresy." The importance of the "ungrafted" original version of Rolle is attested by its being the only accepted English translation of the Bible for over two hundred years. There are more than twenty extant manuscripts of the Psalter, not counting those versions interpolated by Lollards.

It is generally supposed that Rolle's somewhat leaden treatment of the Ten Commandments was composed shortly after the English Psalter. It is preserved in two manuscripts – in one of which the decalogue commentary follows a copy of the Psalter. There has been some debate about Rolle's authorship of this piece, despite both manuscripts making the attribution, despite similarities with the later epistle, *Ego dormio,* and despite the treatment of the third commandment, an epitome of Rolle's teaching on the three degrees of love. Of this commandment to keep the Sabbath holy, Rolle says there are three "manners":

> [The] firste generally that we sesse [cease] of all vyces. Sithen [then] speciali, that we cesse of alle bodili werkis that lettys [hinder] devocyone [devotion] to God in prayenge and thynkynge. The thyrde es specyall, als in contemplatyfe mene that departis thayme fra all werldly thynges swa that they hally gyfe thayme till God.

This is the triad of insuperable, inseparable, and singular love adapted from Victorine thought and more fully developed in the subsequent English epistles.

Rolle's *Meditations on the Passion* exist in longer and shorter versions. They are Anselmian in their emphasis upon the observer's ironic sense of alienation from those very events re-created in the mind for spiritual participation at the foot of the cross: "I knowe wel, gloryouse Lord, that I was nevere worthi to be thi modur [mother's] felowe, to stonde at thi passyoun with hyre and with Johan" (from the shorter version). The great tradition of meditations on the Passion of Christ often focuses upon the sufferings of Mary. In this regard Rolle uses James of Milan's *Stimulus amoris* (circa 1300) in a series of prayers directed to the Virgin:

> A, Lady, for that mercy, that modur art of mercy, socoure of al sorewe, and bote [remedy] of alle bale [evil], modur mad [mother appointed] of wrecchys and of wooful, herken to this wrecche, and vysyt thy chyld. Soue [sow] in myn herte, that is hard os ston, a sparcle of compassyoun of that dere passyoun, a wounde of that reuthe to souple it with [from the shorter version].

The two versions of Rolle's *Meditations* also reflect the pseudo-Bonaventuran *Meditations on the Life of Christ* (circa 1250) now thought to be the work of John of Caulibus. Certainly a Franciscan and Bernardine thrust flows through the hermit's re-creation of the Passion events and gives a traditional flavor to his efforts at this popular genre of devotion. Especially reflective of these two predecessors is the emphasis in the longer version on Christ's wounded body as a heaven full of stars, as a net and a dove house full of holes, and as a honeycomb full of cells. Rolle also employs the image – popular in fifteenth-century Carthusian manuscripts – of Christ's body as "a boke written al with rede ynke. . . ." Finally the wounded body is like "a medow ful of swete flours and holsome herbes . . . swet savorynge to a devout soule, and holsome as herbes to euch synful man" (from the longer version).

Dating from the early 1340s are three short prose pieces often anthologized as examples of the northern dialect. They have some merit in their own right, but they mostly reflect themes and ideas developed in the longer Latin works such as the *Incendium amoris* or in the more substantial English epistles and the more fervent English lyrics. "Ghastly Gladnesse" (Spiritual Gladness) was associated by Hope Emily Allen with a vision granted Richard on 1 February 1343, telling him that he would live for another twelve years. This record of his response to the vision reflects the characteristic longing for death so central to the *Meditations*, to his later epistles, and to the lyrics. Here a personified Death is welcomed though he will not come: "It war na wonder if dede [death] war dere, that I myght se hym [Christ] that I seke. Bot now it is lenthed [lengthened] fra me, and me behoves lyf here, til he [Death] wil me lese [release]."

In the second of these short pieces, "The Bee and the Stork," Rolle borrows from the popular genre of the bestiary to make his point about the superior love of the contemplative. Rolle cites Aris-

totle as a source. Either Aristotle's *History of Animals* or Pliny's *Natural History* supplies the information for the bee. The material for the stork comes from Aristotle, and the moral derives from Gregory's *Moralia* on Job (circa 590), most likely via the highly influential *Ancrene Riwle* (Rule for Anchoresses, circa 1200–1225). The latter uses "stork" for "ostrich" as does Rolle, who admonishes those who would be true lovers to fly like a bee and not like the stork "that has wenges, and it may noghte flye for charge of body."

The third of this group of short prose pieces, "Desyre and Delit," speaks of three factors that elevate delight in God: restraining physical desire, repressing the inclination to sin and the temptations of the will, and controlling and lifting up the heart through the illuminative powers of the Holy Ghost. Without using the term in this instance, Rolle is speaking of the singular love of the contemplative. He cites "skyll," or reason, as the source of one's turning from sensuality to "pure delight," but this reason, or "skyll," must be used meekly in the service of prayer, in meditation, and in reading holy books. This short treatise does not develop the relationship between reason and affection. It does, however, clearly indicate a subordination of mental powers to the inclination of the heart – a subordination central to Rolle's more complex Latin writings and especially to the English epistles.

The most substantial segment of Rolle's English writings are the *Ego dormio, The Commandment,* and *The Form of Living.* These three epistles are remarkable for their language and for their codification of traditional theology into the idiosyncratic themes and emphases of the hermit. The title of the first of the three English letters is taken from Song of Songs 5:2: "Ego dormio et cor meum vigilat" (I sleep, and my heart wakes). There are twelve extant manuscripts of the *Ego dormio,* and all but four cite Rolle as the author. As with the other two letters, this epistle follows the example of the *Ancrene Riwle* in addressing a female audience. The colophon of one manuscript identifies the recipient as a nun of Yedingham. Near Pickering on the border between the North and East Ridings of Yorkshire, this town and its nunnery were a mere mile from Dalton's manor at Foulbridge, where Rolle was first given protection as a hermit. Although there has been some debate about her identity, the nun was most likely Margaret Kirkby, for whom he assuredly wrote *The Form of Living.* In its discussion of the second degree of love, this letter emphasizes the need to abandon the world and separate from father and mother. While this seems an unlikely emphasis for a letter to one already in holy orders, Rolle may simply be celebrating the abandonment of the world by the nun or recluse. Furthermore, the *Ego dormio* could have been written to Margaret early in her religious career when an emphasis on separation from family would be a timely reminder of her sacrifice and an affirmation of her vocation.

The three degrees of love, insuperable, inseparable, and singular, are not named in the epistle, although they are clearly its organizing principle. Rolle takes on the persona of the lover from the Song of Songs and suggests that anyone wishing the perfection of love should follow a progression through its three stages to final love of the seraphim. One of the most significant elements of the *Ego dormio* is its early mention of the nine orders of angels, culminating with the seraphs, emblems of the contemplative order. The name "seraphim" means burning, and those who are received into this order are those who least covet the world, feel the most sweetness in God, and possess hearts which are the most burning in his love. The prose letter is punctuated by four lyrics, two short and two long. This approach is characteristic of Rolle and demonstrates his emphasis on song as the unifying element of his characteristic triad of *calor, canor,* and *dulcor.* The first of the longer lyrics is "Meditation on the Passion of Christ," provided as a defense against idleness. It borrows from Rolle's own *Incendium amoris,* which in turn borrows from two Latin meditations, "Respice in Faciem Christi" (Look into the Face of Christ) and "Candet Nudatum Pectus" (White Was His Naked Breast). Rolle's use of the second of these meditations was taken from an early-fourteenth-century English version beginning "Wit was his nakede brest" rather than from the Latin source ascribed to Anselm.

It is the second long lyric of the *Ego dormio,* however, that best demonstrates Rolle's debt both to standard liturgical material and to the spiritual tradition of England. The forty-eight-line "Cantus Amoris," or "Song of Love," that ends the epistle continues the theme of love longing from the Passion lyric. As with its predecessor, it uses the language of the "Jesu Dulcis Memoria" and recapitulates in English Rolle's Latin treatment of the unrequited lover in chapter 34 of the *Incendium amoris.* Deriving ultimately from the Song of Songs 2:5 and 5:8, the "quia amore langueo" refrain has a rich tradition in the devotional literature of the late Middle Ages. In an English lyric entitled "Quia Amore Langueo," it is Christ as bridegroom who laments the errant human soul. In Bernardine exegesis the languishing of the bridegroom for the bride, of Christ for the human soul, is reciprocal. It is this tradi-

tion which is reflected in both Bonaventure and Rolle:

Jhesu my savyoure, Jhesu my comfortoure,
Of al my fayrnes flowre, my helpe and my sokoure,
When may I se thi towre? . . .
Jhesu, my dere and my drewry [sweetheart], delyte ert
 thou to syng.
Jhesu, my myrth and melody, when will thow com, my
 keyng?

In these lyric invocations the hermit draws particularly from Anselm's *Meditation 18* (actually written by John of Fécamp) and from the early-thirteenth-century Anselmian *Wohunge of Ure Lauered* (Wooing of Our Lord) and the related *Ureisun of Oure Louerde* (Prayer of Our Lord).

There is no doubt that Rolle's second English epistle, *The Commandment,* was written for a nun. Although one manuscript associates this nun with the village of Hampole, Hope Emily Allen does not believe she could be Margaret Kirkby since that would mean that Rolle had addressed two similar letters to the same person — his third and last epistle, *The Form of Living,* deals with the same subject of the three degrees of love and clearly names Margaret Kirkby as its recipient. It seems plausible, however, as Rosamund Allen contends, that a nun removing herself to an enclosure might leave behind such a work for the benefit of her sisters and might then be the recipient of another version from her spiritual guide. The importance of this work, regardless of intended audience, is its clear exposition in English of Rolle's hierarchy of love. Unlike the *Ego dormio, The Commandment* gives the names insuperable, inseparable, and singular to the three degrees of love. In this Rolle is borrowing from Richard of Saint Victor's *De quattuor gradibus violentae caritatis* (The Four Grades of Violent Love), where these terms are used but capped by a fourth degree, insatiable. Bernard's influential *De diligendo Deo* (On Loving God) also uses four degrees, as does Rolle in his Latin *Melos amoris* (Song of Love).

But the three degrees work best for Rolle and figure prominently in the Latin works as well as in the English epistles. There is, however, no clear parallel between the progression of these three degrees and Rolle's other triad of *calor, canor,* and *dulcor.* Rolle calls love insuperable when nothing overcomes it, neither prosperity nor woe, ease nor anguish, lust of the flesh nor love of the world. This degree of love proceeds always in good thoughts, regardless of temptation, "and it hates all syn, sa that na thyng may slokken [slacken] that lufe." The next stage of love, inseparable, is characterized by a gathering together of all thoughts and inclinations which are then "festend haly [wholly] in Jhesu Criste, swa that thou may na tyme forgete hym." The final degree, of singular love, is reached "whan al thi delyte es in Jhesu Criste, and in nane other thyng fyndes joy and comforth." In this third degree love is "stalworth as dede" (as resolute as death) and "hard as hell," for as death kills all living things, so perfect love kills all fleshly desires and worldliness in the human soul. And, as in hell, none of the dead is spared, but all are tormented; so a person in experiencing singular love not only "forsakes the wretched solace of this lyf, bot alswa he covaytes to sofer [suffer] pynes for Goddes lufe."

Though this treatise does not mention the seraphim as patterns for the final degree of love, Rolle clearly has them in mind when he speaks once more of the Passion as the means of spiritual pilgrimage or as the goad of love: "It [the death of Christ] wil rayse thi thoght aboven erthly lykyng, and make thi hert brennand in Cristes lufe, and purches in thi sawle delitabelte and savoure of heven." At the end of *The Commandment*, Rolle repeats an earlier emphasis in this work on the praise of the Holy Name. Here he borrows from his own early treatment of the theme in a Latin commentary on the Song of Songs. The popular "Encomium Nominis Jesu" was extracted from his treatise and circulated separately in Latin and in a later English translation not by Rolle but included in Carl Horstman's 1895–1896 edition. Those who think continuously on his name "er taken up intil the orders of awngels, to se hym in endles joy that thai have lufed."

The third and last of Rolle's epistles contains the themes and language of the *Ego dormio* and *The Commandment*. *The Form of Living* (1348) was the most popular of Rolle's English works and circulated widely after the death of Margaret Kirkby, for whom it was written. There are thirty-eight surviving manuscripts, not counting a poetic version of its first six chapters and two fragmentary texts of a translation into Latin. In the complete letter of twelve chapters, Rolle outlines a pattern for the perfect life, with the last five dealing most explicitly with the interior life of the mystical experience. There were actually only eleven chapters to the original letter, but a scribe inserted an earlier piece by Rolle as chapter 11, and modern editors have kept this addition. *The Form of Living* is Rolle's final work and the final example in medieval England of a tradition beginning with the *Ancrene Riwle* in the late twelfth or early thirteenth century. Even though Rolle has organized his treatise with the natural break at the end of the sixth chapter, his rule for the

fourteenth-century anchoress Margaret Kirkby is not as carefully balanced as its predecessor in separating external, practical matters in the first half from internal, personal matters in the second. Records indicate that Kirkby was enclosed in her cell on 12 December 1348 – only ten months before Rolle's death – providing a fairly accurate date for this work, which follows the other English epistles by at least six years.

In many ways the penultimate paragraph of *The Form of Living* is the finest passage of an epistle that Hope Emily Allen calls "the finest of Rolle's English works." Not only is its description of contemplative life a masterpiece of concision and clarity, its English prose is also an epitome of the hermit's figurative language and speaks eloquently for Rolle as an authentic mystic – perhaps the most influential of the fourteenth century. After ordaining a man or a woman to a contemplative life, God speaks to the hearts of his lovers, and, in the words of the prophet Hosea, "He gifs tham at sowke the swetnes of the begynnyng of lufe." God then gives the gifts of prayer, meditation, and tears of compunction. God's final gift to the contemplative is the same opening of heaven's door so central to Rolle's vocation and to the hagiographical account of his conversion quoted from the *Incendium amoris* in the *officium*. The account in *The Form of Living* is Augustinian in its imagery of the heart's eye, but its fervor is Rolle's:

> [Finally, God] opens til the egh [eye] of thair sawls the gates of heven, swa that the ilk egh lokes intil heven. And than the fire of lufe verrali ligges [lies] in thair hert and byrnes tharin, and makes clene of al erthly filth. And sithen forward thai er contemplatife men, and ravyst in lufe. For contemplacion es a syght, and thai se intil heven with thar gastly [spiritual] egh. Bot thou [Margaret] sal witt [know] that na man hase perfite syght of heven whils thai er lifand bodili here; bot als sone als thai dye, thai er broght before God, and sese hym face til face and egh til egh, and wones with hym withouten ende. For hym thai soght, and hym thai covayted, and hym thai lufed in al thar myght.

This passage describes the nature and rewards of singular love and contains in small compass the language of *calor, canor,* and *dulcor*, Rolle's characteristic emphasis on binding and fastening, and the sense he has of life lived as contemplative prayer or pure harmony.

It remains only to speak of the songs Rolle composed, possibly as experiments in the *canor* so central to his mystical theology. They are by their very genre most akin to the celestial harmony of which he speaks in the *Incendium amoris* (chapter 15) after heaven had opened its door:

> In my prayer I was reaching out to heaven with heartfelt longing when I became aware, in a way I cannot explain, of a symphony of song, and in myself I sensed a corresponding harmony at once wholly delectable and heavenly, which persisted in my mind. Then and there my thinking itself turned into melodious song, and my meditation became a poem, and my very prayers and psalms took up the same sound.
> – translated by Clifton Wolters (in *Rolle: The Fire of Love*, 1972)

The seven lyrics existing separately from the epistles are now generally believed to be authentic works of Rolle, though some critics have felt them to be from his "school." The colophons of two manuscripts name Rolle as their author, and it is fairly safe to accept those early notations. The lyrics are in tone and substance at one with Rolle's Latin and English prose and with the occasional songs that punctuate them. The titles of the seven lyrics are supplied by Hope Emily Allen: "Exhortation," "A Song of Mercy," "A Song of Love-Longing to Jesus," "A Song of the Love of Jesus," "A Salutation to Jesus," "The Nature of Love," and "Thy Joy Be in the Love of Jesus." These titles suggest the general focus of the lyrics on the Holy Name and the singular love of the contemplative.

The first sixty lines of Rolle's longest lyric, "A Song of the Love of Jesus," are closely translated from the Latin of the *Incendium* and are related to the passion lyric from the *Ego dormio*. The "quia amore langueo" of the Song of Songs informs the imagery of all Rolle's lyrics, but the love longing precipitated by meditation on the crucified Christ quickly gives way to the joy of consummation:

> Sigh and sob, bath day and night, for ane sa fayre of hew.
> Thar es na thyng my hert mai light, bot lufe, that es ay new.
> Whasa had hym in his syght, or in his hert hym knew,
> His mourning turned til joy ful bryght, his sang intil glew [glee].

Singular love is permanent love. The binding and fastening imagery of the lyrics is nowhere better expressed than in one remarkable line from this same "Song of the Love of Jesus": "In lufe lacyd he [Jesus] hase my thoght, that sal I never forgete." In binding sinful man to him, Christ is the true "luf-lace," and Rolle's use of this term is within the mystical tradition of the love knot, or *nodus amicitiae* dating in England from the mid twelfth century and

Aelred of Rievaulx's *Speculum charitatis* (Mirror of Love). Rolle's frequent use of the love knot, or *cingulo amoris*, in his Latin and English writings is a bridge between the spiritual writings of the early Cistercian tradition and the devotional writings dating from shortly after his death to the dissolution of the monasteries in the sixteenth century.

The following passage from an anonymous nun's fifteenth-century prayer cycle (Bodleian Library, Oxford, MS. Holkham Misc. 41) is evidence of Rolle's influence:

> O Ihesu Lord ful of al goodnesse that were thus peinefulli festnid to the cros for love of mankende, have mercy and pite on al yowre peple that ye bowth [bought] so dere. And race [erase] from us al wikkidnesse and *knytte* us so faste to yow with a *love knotte* that the *knotte* be never *on knyt* ne we fro yow disseverid.

For both Rolle and the nun who authored "The Festis and Passion of Oure Lord Ihesu Crist," the tradition of Saint Bernard and the language of Aelred of Rievaulx fuse Christ as Lover and Spouse of the Soul with the crucified Christ whose wounded body is a flowered meadow, a starry heaven, a honeycomb, a dovecote, or a rock with clefts of refuge. The many manuscripts containing Rolle's writings, the fifteenth-century translations of selected Latin texts, and the echoes of his language and emphases in those who wrote devotional treatises through the Tudor period all attest to the impact of Rolle upon the thought and language of late medieval and early modern England.

Bibliography:

Valerie Lagorio and Ritamary Bradley, *The Fourteenth-Century English Mystics: A Comprehensive Annotated Bibliography* (New York: Garland, 1981), pp. 53–80.

Biography:

Francis Comper, *The Life of Richard Rolle, Together with an Edition of His English Lyrics* (London & Toronto: Dent, 1928; reprinted, New York: Barnes & Noble, 1969).

References:

John A. Alford, "Biblical *Imitatio* in the Writings of Richard Rolle," *English Literary History*, 40 (Spring 1973): 1–23:

Hope Emily Allen, *Writings Ascribed to Richard Rolle, Hermit of Hampole, and Materials for his Biography*, Modern Language Association Monograph Series 3 (London: Oxford University Press, 1927);

Rosamund Allen, " 'Singular Lufe': Richard Rolle and the Grammar of Spiritual Ascent," in *The Medieval Mystical Tradition in England, Papers Read at Dartington Hall, July 1984,* edited by Marion Glasscoe (Cambridge: Brewer, 1984), pp. 28–54;

J. P. H. Clark, "Richard Rolle as Biblical Commentator," *Downside Review,* 104 (July 1986): 165–213;

Rita Copeland, "Richard Rolle and the Rhetorical Theory of the Levels of Style," in *The Medieval Mystical Tradition in England, Papers Read at Darlington Hall, July 1984,* pp. 55–80;

Margaret Deanesly, "The *Incendium Amoris* of Richard Rolle and St. Bonaventure," *English Historical Review,* 29 (January 1914): 98–101;

Vincent Gillespie, "Mystic's Foot: Rolle and Affectivity," in *The Medieval Mystical Tradition in England, Papers Read at Dartington Hall, July 1982,* edited by Glasscoe (Exeter: Exeter University Press, 1982), pp. 199–230;

Margaret Jennings, "Richard Rolle and the Three Degrees of Love," *Downside Review,* 93 (1975): 193–200;

David Knowles, *The English Mystical Tradition* (New York: Harper & Row, 1961);

Mary F. Madigan, *The Passio Domini Theme in the Works of Richard Rolle: His Personal Contribution in its Religious, Cultural, and Literary Context,* Salzburg Studies in English Literature, Elizabethan and Renaissance Studies 79 (Salzburg: Institut für Anglistik und Amerikanistik, 1978);

The Officium et Miracula of Richard Rolle of Hampole, edited by Reginald Woolley (London: SPCK, 1919);

William F. Pollard, "The 'Tone of Heaven': Bonaventuran Melody and the Easter Psalm in Richard Rolle," in *The Popular Literature of Medieval England,* edited by Thomas J. Heffernan (Knoxville: University of Tennessee Press, 1985), pp. 252–276;

Wolfgang Riehle, *The Middle English Mystics* (London: Routledge & Kegan Paul, 1981);

Dennis Rygiel, "Structures and Style in Rolle's *The Form of Living,*" *Fourteenth-Century English Mystics Newsletter,* 4 (1978): 6–15;

Nicholas Watson, *Richard Rolle and the Invention of Authority,* Cambridge Studies in Medieval Literature 13 (Cambridge: Cambridge University Press, 1991);

Rosemary Woolf, *The English Religious Lyric in the Middle Ages* (Oxford: Clarendon Press, 1968).

John Trevisa

(circa 1342 – circa 1402)

Anthony S. G. Edwards
University of Victoria

WORKS: Ranulf Higden, *Polychronicon,* translated by Trevisa (circa 1385–1387)

Manuscripts: This work is found in at least fourteen complete manuscripts, and selections appear in others. British Library MS. Cotton Tiberius D. vii is now held to be the most authoritative of these manuscripts. The standard edition was based on Corpus Christi College, Cambridge MS. 354 and British Library MS. Additional 24194.

First publication: *Policronicon* (Westminster: Printed by William Caxton, 1482).

Standard edition: *Polychronicon Ranulphi Higden Monachi Cestrensis; Together with the English Translations of John Trevisa and of an Unknown Writer of the Fifteenth Century,* 9 volumes, edited by Churchill Babington and J. R. Lumby, Rolls Series 41 (London: Longman, Green, Longman, Roberts & Green, 1865–1886).

Richard Fitzralph, *Defensio Curatorum,* translated by Trevisa (circa 1385–1387)

Manuscripts: This work appears in six manuscripts of the *Polychronicon,* including British Library MS. Cotton Tiberius D. vii.

Standard edition: In *Dialogus inter Militem et Clericum. Fitzralph's Sermon: 'Defensio Curatorum' and Bygynnyng of the World,* edited by Aaron J. Perry, EETS, o.s. 167 (1925), pp. 39–93.

Dialogus inter Dominum et Clericum and Epistola (circa 1385–1387)

Manuscripts: Either or both of these works appear in six manuscripts of the *Polychronicon* including British Library MS. Cotton Tiberius D. vii.

First publication: Both appear in Caxton's edition of the *Polychronicon* (Westminster, 1482).

Standard edition: "Trevisa's Original Prefaces on Translation: A Critical Edition," edited by Ronald A. Waldron in *Medieval English Studies Presented to George Kane,* edited by E. D.

Kennedy, Waldron and J. Wittig (Woodbridge, Suffolk: D. S. Brewer, 1988), pp. 285–300.

William of Ockham, *Dialogus inter Militem et Clericum,* translated by Trevisa (circa 1385–1387)

Manuscripts: This brief work appears in six manuscripts of the *Polychronicon,* including British Library MS. Cotton Tiberius D. vii.

First publication: *Dialogus inter Militem et Clericum* (London: Thomas Berthelet, [1533?]).

Standard edition: In *Dialogus inter Militem et Clericum. Fitzralph's Sermon: 'Defensio Curatorum' and Bygynnyng of the World,* edited by Aaron J. Perry, EETS, o.s. 67 (1925), pp. 1–38.

Bartholomaeus Anglicus, *De Proprietatibus Rerum,* translated by Trevisa (1398)

Manuscripts: This work is found in at least ten complete manuscripts or fragments, and selections from it appear in others. The standard edition is based on British Library MS. Additional 27944. The first publication was based, at least in part, on Columbia University Library MS. Plimpton 263.

First publication: *Bartholomomeus de proprietatibus rerum* (Westminster: Printed by Wynkyn de Worde, 1495).

Standard edition: *On the Properties of Things. John Trevisa's translation of Bartholomaeus Anglicus De Proprietatibus Rerum,* 3 volumes, edited by M. C. Seymour and others (Oxford: Clarendon Press, 1975–1988).

Aegidius Romanus, *De Regimine Principum,* translated by Trevisa (date unknown)

Manuscript: The only manuscript is Bodleian Library, Oxford, MS. Digby 233.

Gospel of Nicodemus (date unknown)

Manuscripts: There are three manuscripts, of which the earliest is probably British Library MS. Additional 16165.

Standard edition: "*The Gospel of Nichodemus,* translated by John Trevisa," edited by H. C.

Page from Trevisa's translation of the Polychronicon, *in a fifteenth-century transcription (British Library, MS. Add. 24194)*

Kim, Ph.D. dissertation, University of Washington, 1963.

Although the sheer volume of his output would seem to make John Trevisa a figure of comparable stature to his poetic "Ricardian" contemporaries, Geoffrey Chaucer, John Gower and William Langland, his achievements have not received the same sort of critical and scholarly attention. This situation is due in part to the pattern of Trevisa's life and career, in part to the forms of literary activity he undertook, and in part to the lack of modern critical editions of most of his various works, editions that would facilitate a full appreciation of his achievement.

Trevisa differs from these major contemporary poets in various ways: unlike them, he lacks any significant connection with London and with late-fourteenth-century metropolitan culture; his career was exclusively provincial, confined to the West Country and to Oxford; and his entire life was lived within the relative stability and seclusion of academic and clerical appointments. Trevisa was most likely born in the early 1340s in Cornwall, where he was initially educated before proceeding to Exeter College, Oxford, in 1362. He removed to Queen's College in 1369 and became a priest in the following year. He also became a fellow of Queen's, remaining there until 1378, when he was expelled under obscure circumstances. He subsequently held various ecclesiastical preferments in the gift of Thomas, Lord Berkeley. He was Thomas's chaplain and also vicar of Berkeley, Gloucestershire and a nonresidentiary canon of Westbury-on-Trym, near Bristol. Most of his later life seems to have been spent in the West Country, at Berkeley, although there are references in his works which suggest that he had traveled abroad in his earlier years, and he was granted permission for such travel again in 1390. He was dead by May 1402.

Trevisa's relationship with Thomas, Lord Berkeley, was undoubtedly of crucial significance to his career. Berkeley was a magnate of great power and influence in southwestern England. He was also a man of evident literary interests. He is named as Trevisa's patron in his three major works, the prose translations from the Latin into Middle English of the *Polychronicon* (circa 1385–1387), the *De Proprietatibus Rerum* (1398), and the *De Regimine Principum*. Apart from these the clearly established body of Trevisa's work includes only a few other short prose undertakings: translations of Archbishop Richard Fitzralph's *Defensio Curatorum* (circa 1385–1387), William of Ockham's *Dialogus inter Militem et*

Clericum (1385–1387), and the apocryphal *Gospel of Nicodemus,* and his original works, the *Dialogus* and *Epistola,* which preface the *Polychronicon* translation. Such an involvement with prose translation once again differentiates Trevisa from his more famous poetic contemporaries.

The earliest of these translations, the *Polychronicon,* was begun in 1385 and completed by 1387. It is a translation of a popular Latin universal history compiled by Ranulf Higden, a monk at Saint Werburgh's Abbey, Chester, from the 1320s until his death in 1364. Higden's history is divided into seven books, representing the seven ages of the world, and presents an account of the world from creation to his own age; it examines English and world history, both secular and religious.

Trevisa's other datable translation is of Bartholomaeus Anglicus's *De Proprietatibus Rerum* (Concerning the Properties of Things) which was completed in February 1398, toward the end of his life. This is a translation of another popular medieval work, an early-thirteenth-century Latin encyclopedia, compiled by an English Franciscan (Bartholomew the Englishman) living in Paris. It is divided into nineteen separate books, each concerned with some aspect of the spiritual, human, or natural worlds.

Trevisa's third major translation, also from the Latin, was the *De Regimine Principum* (Concerning the Rule of Princes) of Aegidius Romanus (Giles of Rome), a work done in the 1280s by an Augustinian friar in Paris to provide comprehensive instruction for rulers. As with the other Latin works Trevisa translated, this was extremely popular. Many manuscripts survive both from the Continent and England, although Trevisa's translation survives only in a single manuscript. It cannot be precisely dated, but its length suggests that it was undertaken between his other major translations.

Among Trevisa's shorter translations those of Ockham's *Dialogus inter Militem et Clericum* (Dialogue between a Knight and a Clerk) and of Fitzralph's *Defensio Curatorum* (Defense of Curates) appear only in various of the manuscripts of his *Polychronicon* translation. The former is a debate on the limits of power and privilege attached to temporal and spiritual authority. The latter is a justification of the prerogatives of secular clergy in their jurisdictional disputes with the friars. His translation of the *Gospel of Nicodemus* is one of the surviving Middle English versions of this apocryphal New Testament narrative. Trevisa's version seems to have had a limited circulation and is chiefly noteworthy because it provides the only certain example of his translation of biblical material.

In addition to his known works, Trevisa has been associated circumstantially with another biblical translation project, the Early Version of the Wyclif Bible. Trevisa was at Queen's College, Oxford, at the same time as John Wyclif, the late-fourteenth-century religious controversialist whose name has been identified with the first full Middle English translation of the Bible. Also at Queen's College at the same time was Nicholas Hereford, one of the named translators of the Early Version. There is a tradition, dating from the late fifteenth century, that Trevisa was involved in a Bible translation at the behest of Berkeley. But most subsequent discussions of this translation in the sixteenth and seventeenth centuries specifically differentiate this translation from the Wycliffian Bible translation. There is, however, a unique passage in one manuscript of Trevisa's *Polychronicon* translation which seems to have some correspondences with the Early Version. The evidence for Trevisa's involvement in this undertaking is tenuous. Yet, given his situation in the 1360s and his subsequently demonstrated abilities as a translator, it remains tempting to speculate on Trevisa's possible connection with the Bible translation. But the case has yet to be satisfactorily established.

The attribution to Trevisa of a translation into Middle English of another Latin work, the *De Re Militari* (Concerning Martial Matters) of Vegetius, can be more confidently discounted. Although done for Trevisa's patron, Berkeley, it seems to have been undertaken after Trevisa's death.

Trevisa's translational technique helped to ensure the popularity of his major translations. In general, he seems to have been a faithful, but not slavish, translator. He gives a useful statement of his way of proceeding in the prefatory letter to the *Polychronicon* to Berkeley:

> For to make þis translacion cleer and pleyn to be knowe and vnderstonde, in some place Y schal sette word vor word and actyue for actyue and passyue vor passyue ... without changyng of þe ordre of wordes. Bot yn som place Y mot change ... þe ordre of wordes and sette þe actyue vor þe passiue and aȝenward. And yn som place Y mot sette a reson vor a word to telle what hyt meneþ. Bot vor al such chaungyng, þe menyng schal stonde and noȝt be ychanged.

Trevisa seems to have usually been faithful to these flexible principles in all his translations. They are generally characterized by the attempt to reflect the original that he claims here. From time to time he

makes interpolations, which are generally prefaced by his name: Trevisa. They are normally based on either personal observation or his own reading. Perhaps the most famous of these is his comment in the *Polychronicon* on Higden's account of the status of English. Whereas in Higden's time children "beeþ compelled for to leue hire owne langage, and for to construe hir lessouns and here þynges in Frensche." Trevisa notes that now "children leueþ Frensche and construeþ and lerneþ an Englische." Other comments are drawn either from direct observation (as in his comment that Thomas Hayward of Berkeley is able to "breke strong dores wiþ his heed" or that William Wayte of Berkeley "sigh a childe wiþ tweye hedes") or from further reading (he cites, for example, Nicholas of Lyra and Aristotle, as well as additional biblical authorities), as well as several cross-references. Similar added passages, although far fewer in number, can be found in the *De Proprietatibus Rerum;* some of these are virtually identical to additions in the earlier work.

Apart from such interpolations, Trevisa's translations are fluent and accurate reflections of his Latin originals, without being overly constrained by a literal fidelity to their syntax or construction. At its best his prose is supple and lucid, as in this passage from *De Proprietatibus Rerum:*

> In þe dawinge for maistrie of blood sleep is swete and holsom. Also most þat tyme kokkes beþ excitid to crowe. And in þe dawinge Lucifer 'þe day sterre' arisiþ and warneþ of þe sonne risynge and of his sone comynge.

Apart from the Latinate inversion of the final phrase "sone comynge" and the separation of adverb ("most") from verb ("excitid"), the translation is idiomatic and accurate.

This passage also indicates another characteristic of Trevisa's prose-translation techniques, his use of doublets: the rendering of a single Latin word by two English ones. The technique is apparent in the above passage in such collocations as "swete and holsom" or "arisiþ and warneþ." Doublets are also found in the *Polychronicon* – "commandede and het" (translating *jussit*); "taking and bondage" (translating *captivitate*) – and in the *De Proprietatibus Rerum* – "taboures and tymbres" (translating *tympanis*); "norische and fede" (translating *nutrire*).

Another distinctive feature of Trevisa's work is the number of apparent neologisms he introduced into the English language, often anglicizations of technical Latin terminology, particularly in the *De*

Proprietatibus Rerum translation. But apart from the creation of new technical language, the simple volume of Trevisa's English prose helps to establish the currency of existing native diction and idiom and hence contributes to the consolidation of English as a literary language that took place in the latter part of the fourteenth century.

That Trevisa's translations, particularly those of the *Polychronicon* and *De Proprietatibus Rerum,* were able to make such a contribution to the establishing of English is demonstrated by their evident popularity in the later Middle Ages in England. They circulated in relatively high numbers of manuscripts for such large and expensive works. Some fourteen of the *Polychronicon* and ten of the *De Proprietatibus Rerum* survive either in complete or fragmentary form. In addition, there are various manuscript selections from both works, which provide further testimony to the care with which they were studied.

The popularity of Trevisa's translations is also reflected in evidence of their influence. Trevisa's *Polychronicon* seems to have been known to various fourteenth- and fifteenth-century writers, including Chaucer and John Lydgate. Later in the fifteenth century William Caxton's printed edition, with his own continuation, gave the work renewed currency. It was reprinted by Wynkyn de Worde in 1495 and by Treveris in 1527.

The *De Proprietatibus Rerum* translation also had an influential posterity. Writers and works of various kinds drew upon it, and its popularity extended into the Renaissance, partly due to various printed editions. The first of these was by de Worde in 1495. It was reprinted in 1535 by Thomas Berthelet and, in an expanded and updated form, by Thomas East in 1582. This last edition seems to have proved particularly influential in ensuring that knowledge of Trevisa's translation continued on into the seventeenth century and became a source, albeit a minor one, used by such writers as William Shakespeare and John Milton.

It is, then, through his translations that Trevisa achieved his importance in late-medieval literary history. They establish him as the most prolific and versatile English translator of the Middle Ages. His actual output amounts to around two million words, virtually all concerned with rendering Latin into Middle English prose. Such an unremitting commitment to massive programs of translation makes him a figure of importance in the linguistic and literary history of Middle English prose. His extensive translations helped to make prose an idiomatic and utilitarian means of written communication. The attendant neologisms materially enlarged the lexicon of English. And the actual material he made available attracted a wide audience. If Trevisa's achievement has not been fully acknowledged by literary historians of the period, it is because few of his works are available in trustworthy modern texts. Although this state of affairs makes it difficult to appraise Trevisa's full importance, his work and influence on the period are clearly substantial.

Bibliography:

Anthony S. G. Edwards, "John Trevisa," *Middle English Prose: A Critical Guide to Major Authors and Genres*, edited by Edwards (New Brunswick, N. J.: Rutgers University Press, 1984), pp. 133–146.

References:

Anthony S. G. Edwards, "Bartholomaeus Anglicus and Medieval English Literature," in *Archiv für das Studium der neueren Sprachen und Literatur,* 222 (1985): 121–128;

David C. Fowler, *John Trevisa* (Aldershot, U.K.: Variorum, 1993; Brookfield, Vt.: Ashgate, 1993);

Fowler, "John Trevisa and the English Bible," *Modern Philology,* 58 (1960): 81–98;

Fowler, "More About John Trevisa," *Modern Language Quarterly,* 32 (1971): 243–264;

Fowler, "New Light on John Trevisa," *Traditio,* 18 (1962): 289–317;

David C. Greetham, "Models for the Textual Transmission of Translation: The Case of John Trevisa," *Studies in Bibliography,* 37 (1984): 131–155;

Ralph Hanna III, "Thomas Berkeley and His Patronage," *Speculum,* 64 (1989): 878–916;

Traugott Lawler, "On The Properties of John Trevisa's Major Translations," *Viator,* 14 (1983): 267–288;

Aaron J. Perry, "Trevisa as Translator," *Manitoba Essays* (Toronto: Macmillan, 1937), pp. 277–289;

Ronald A. Waldron, "John Trevisa and the Use of English," *Proceedings of the British Academy,* 74 (1988): 171–201;

Waldron, "The Manuscripts of Trevisa's Translation of the *Polychronicon* Towards a New Edition," *Modern Language Quarterly,* 51 (1990): 281–317.

Thomas Usk

(died 4 March 1388)

John C. Hirsh
Georgetown University

WORKS: *The Appeal of Thomas Usk Against John Northampton* (1384)

Manuscript: *The Appeal of Thomas Usk Against John Northampton* is preserved in a unique manuscript in the Public Record Office, London, E163 5/28, number 9; there is an abbreviated Latin translation also in the Public Record Office in a coram regis roll, KB 27/507, mem. ff. 40 *et seq.*

First publication and standard edition: In *A Book of London English 1384–1425,* edited by R. W. Chambers and Marjorie Daunt (Oxford: Clarendon Press, 1931; reprinted, 1967), pp. 18–31.

The Testament of Love (circa 1385–1388)

Manuscript: There are no known manuscripts of *The Testament of Love.*

First publication: In *The Workes of Geffray Chaucer Newly Printed, with Dyuers Workes Which Were Neuer in Print Before as in the Table More Playnly Dothe Appere* (London: Thomas Godfray, 1532; reprinted, 1542; reprinted, [circa 1550]); republished as *The Woorkes of Geffrey Chaucer, Newly Printed with Diuers Addicions Which Were Neuer in Print Before* (London: John Stowe, 1561). Facsimiles: *The Works of Geoffrey Chaucer and Others, Being a Reproduction in Facsimile of the First Collected Edition of 1532 from the Copy in the British Museum,* edited by Walter W. Skeat (London: Alexander Moring & Oxford University Press, 1905); Geoffrey Chaucer, *The Works, 1532, with Supplementary Material from the Editions of 1542, 1561, and 1602,* edited by Derek Brewer (Menston, Yorkshire: Scholar, 1969).

Standard edition: In *Chaucerian and Other Pieces, Being a Supplement to the Complete Works of Geoffrey Chaucer,* edited by Walter W. Skeat (Oxford: Oxford University Press, 1897; reprinted, 1935, 1959), pp. 1–145.

Thomas Usk is best known for his participation in political intrigues that led to his execution and for a long prose work, *The Testament of Love,* once attributed to Geoffrey Chaucer and preserved only in William Thynne's 1532 edition of Chaucer and in later reprints; no manuscripts of the work are known to exist. In certain official documents of the period Usk is referred to as a scrivener, though it is a mistake to identify him simply as a writer of manuscripts. At one time he worked as a confidential agent for one of the more powerful men in London; at another he held office at the direction of the king. In addition, many of the literary allusions that have been found (sometimes too readily) in *The Testament of Love,* together with the impressive list of antiphons, prayers, and other devotions that the *Westminster Chronicle* reports that Usk recited from memory while being taken to his execution, suggest that his education went beyond what he would have been able to recall from copying, and indicate a degree of clerical education. In addition, some of the documents associated with Usk's trial refer to him as "clericus," though Paul Strohm insists that the word must mean clerk or secretary rather than cleric. Whether or not this is the case, there is much about Thomas Usk that simply is not known, and the question of his education must be regarded as unresolved.

Usk's willingness to engage in certain activities in search of advancement suggest that he came from a family of no high standing, almost certainly in London, the city in which, as he remarks in *The Testament of Love,* "I was forth growen." Hard facts are few, but there are indications that he was, and represented himself as being, something of a "New Man" – intelligent, literate, ambitious, and in search of a future – one who in less dangerous times might well have made his way in the city or at court.

Whatever Usk's origins and education, he springs vividly to life in *The Appeal of Thomas Usk Against John Northampton,* a document of 1384 preserved in the Public Records Office in London. In it, he turns against his former patron, John of Northampton (or John Northampton), formerly lord mayor of London, and charges him with treason. Northampton had a following among certain of the London guilds such as the Drapers' and the Mercers' and in the poorer parts of the city. He seems also to have had Wycliffite associations and to have received limited support from John of Gaunt, one of the most powerful men of England, with whom Chaucer had associations as well.

But Northampton and his party were opposed by other guilds, primarily those associated with food provision such as the Grocers' and the Fishmongers'; the opposition was led by Sir Nicholas Brembre, who had connections to King Richard II. In 1381 Northampton was elected mayor and proceeded to cause the king to enact certain popular measures, allowing, for example, previously excluded merchants into the city, a device that increased the supply of food and so drove down prices. Northampton was no doubt seeking personal and party advantage, but it is impossible not to regard with interest what he accomplished both for himself and for the most disadvantaged persons in the city. Violating custom, he accepted the office of lord mayor again in 1382, but in 1383 Brembre was returned with the all-but-official backing of the king. Brembre caused the king to withdraw some of the edicts he had issued at Northampton's urging, and when he did so, strife between the two men increased.

Never without a large following among the poor, on 7 February 1384 Northampton appeared in Cheapside with what seemed to be a particularly large crowd of supporters, possibly intending to seize power. If he had been planning an insurrection it miscarried, and according to one account he quickly withdrew into a church, claiming he had come only to hear mass. Northampton was not known for his devotions and was soon arrested, though he put up no resistance. Shortly thereafter he was tried before the king at Reading, where the chief evidence against him was supplied by a formerly trusted lieutenant, Usk.

Usk's evidence, his appeal, gives a fascinating glimpse of political life in fourteenth-century London. In it he recounts his meeting with Northampton "in J[ohn] Willynghames taverne in the Bowe," plotting to undermine his adversaries in the Fishmongers' guild and generally doing what he could to gain power. It is not clear exactly what, apart from the usual threats, caused Usk to change sides, though an interview with King Richard II

seems to have been a deciding factor. The king fully pardoned Usk of all offenses in September 1384, and in 1387, at Richard's direction and perhaps to serve writs on nobles opposed to him, Usk was made Under-Sheriff of Middlesex and titled Sergeant-at-Arms of the king. Richard may have intended Usk to serve writs on nobles opposed to him.

The evidence Usk offered at Northampton's 1384 trial was devastating. Not only had the former lord mayor plotted against the current one, but the appeal also suggests that Northampton had allied himself with those in court who were opposed to the king. The accused tried to brush the charges aside, but Richard, in a fury, was about to order his execution when the queen intervened and obtained a sentence of life imprisonment instead, a sentence that in 1387 was commuted to allow him to move freely about the countryside, provided he did not come within eighty miles of London; in 1390 even that condition was relaxed. Meanwhile Brembre was elected mayor for three increasingly disastrous terms. By November 1387 a small group of powerful "Lords Appellant," against whose interests and persons Richard had been industriously working, seized power, protesting their loyalty to the king and their determination to rid him of those advisers whom they judged to have misled him. On 3 February 1388 they produced their accusations, naming their five most powerful enemies, including Brembre. Subsequently they did the same both to Usk and to John Blake, who had also assisted Richard against the appellants' interests, charging both men with treason against the king, *not* against Northampton or the appellants: they were said to have betrayed Richard by having induced him to act against the interests of those now in power.

Under the circumstances created by the Lords Appellant, the law became more or less what pleased them: Brembre was hanged, and Usk and Blake were first condemned to be hanged, then taken down alive and beheaded; in Usk's case his head was then to be displayed at Newgate. The sentence was carried out the same day that it was handed down. As J. A. W. Bennett remarks, Chaucer must have seen Usk's head, and it is not unreasonable to believe that Usk's fate may have deepened Chaucer's reluctance to become involved in the politics of his day, particularly since he also had associations with Brembre and may have been in danger because of them.

The executions carried out by this "Merciless Parliament" (as it became known) and the forfeitures of land and property that went with them were so blatantly illegal that Commons produced a statute declaring that, among other things, all accusations, judgments, and executions of the then-present Parliament could not be used as future precedents under common law and that no judge had authority to give judgments in cases of treason further than they did before the seating of this Parliament. The best early student of these extraordinary trials, M. V. Clarke, remarks in her "Forfeitures and Treason in 1388" (1937) that this last clause in particular "proves that the irregularity of the whole proceeding was understood." Parliament was concerned that some of its own practices – particularly those relating to treason and forfeiture – might be used against its own members at a later date. Even by contemporary standards, Usk's death on 4 March 1388 was a judicial murder, not an execution.

During the period between December 1384 and June 1385, however, Usk was in Brembre's custody awaiting trial, and it may have been then that he began to write the work known as *The Testament of Love,* though he probably continued it later, perhaps until his second arrest in 1387. Hard evidence is lacking, but Ramona Bressie's proposal that the work was completed between December 1384 and June 1385 almost certainly comprises too brief a time span. *The Testament of Love* is an unusual work in many ways. Part apologia, part complaint, part allegorical dream-vision, and part philosophy, it reveals, too, a somewhat muted theological dimension, often overlooked in a text referred to, if at all, as one of the earliest English prose works of secular philosophy. Its audience is uncertain, though May Newman Hallmundsson's suggestion that it was directed toward members of the court at Chancery is possible, even though it has evident literary and courtly aspirations as well, and may equally be aimed at what Strohm calls Usk's "new associates."

The Testament of Love draws on Boethius's *Consolation of Philosophy* (circa 525), though whether from Chaucer's Middle English translation (as Walter W. Skeat thought), from the Latin original (as C. S. Lewis believed), from the barest memory of either text (as Bennett urged), or from a French translation (as Strohm asserts) has yet to be demonstrated. Usk's putative reference in book 3, chapter 6 to the Tree of Charity in the C-version of William Langland's *Piers Plowman* (circa 1360–circa 1390) has been called into question, most recently by Malcolm Godden. (The matter is of some importance for students of *Piers Plowman,* since if Usk knew the C-Version of *Piers Plowman,* it must have been in circulation by about 1385, and there is reason to be-

lieve it may not have been completed as early as that.) Saint Anselm's discussion of free will in *De concordia praescientiae et praedestinationis* (eleventh century) clearly influenced book 3 deeply, again indicating the clerical depth of Usk's reading, his philosophical and theological purpose, and his ability to adapt his sources freely.

Taken together, the first letter of each chapter constitutes a carefully constructed acrostic which reads: MARGARETE OF VIRTW HAVE MERCI ON THIN VSK. Skeat, the work's first (and so far only published) editor, discovered a jumbled form of the acrostic, which was finally explained by Henry Bradley, who saw that it was confused by certain of the chapters having been misplaced; restored to their proper order they identified the author, whose well-attested life matches the one recorded in *The Testament of Love* beyond any reasonable doubt.

The Testament of Love comprises three books, but the structure of the work has not been much studied even though an understanding of its structure is essential. Each book has its own form and direction, but it is also related to the other two, and at the beginning of book 3 the narrator, who maintains a voice very different from that of Usk, the prisoner and protagonist, pauses to explain the direction of the structure of his work. "This world," he says, "is three times divided": by "Deviacion, that is to say, going out of trewe way" – from the time of Adam to the coming of Christ; the "tyme of Grace" – from Christ to Domesday; and the time of "Joy, glorie and rest, both body and soule" – the time which shall follow. His three books, he avers, are like these times, showing first the "Errour of missegoinge," then "Grace in good waye proved," and finally "Joy and blisse, graunted to him that wel can deserve it, and hath savour of understandinge in the tyme of grace."

Remarking that *The Testament of Love* will treat of philosophy (the love of wisdom) and law (which maintains peace), Usk notes that with these "love must nedes acorden." He then proceeds to draw an important distinction that also influences the structure of *The Testament of Love.* There are for Usk three kinds of philosophy: first, natural philosophy, which treats all things in the world including the quadrivium: arithmetic, geometry, music and astronomy, the first four liberal arts; second, moral philosophy, which "by reson proveth vertues of soul most worthy in our living" including the cardinal virtues of prudence, justice, temperance and fortitude; and third, a philosophy that "turneth in-to reson of understanding al things to be sayd soth and

Page from the first publication of Usk's The Testament of Love *in a 1532 edition of Chaucer's works. The work was mistakenly attributed to Chaucer until the mid nineteenth century.*

discussed," which includes art and rhetoric, here representing the trivium, the second group of the seven liberal arts: logic, grammar and rhetoric. Usk insists that "the Margarit in vertue" – the pearl, at once natural and divine, that is the complex object of his search – is "lykened to Philosophy with her three speces [kinds]." The first two of these (natural and moral) accord with human reason, the third with the divine. In book 3, Usk adds, he will treat the right and custom of law which comes both by God's ordinance and the working of nature.

These distinctions are by no means original nor does Usk follow them slavishly, but they do define and inform the focus and meaning of *The Testament of Love* and provide a good way of addressing a text whose difficulty is as much structural as thematic. Thus book 1 is far more autobiographical than its "dream-vision" opening suggests. The pro-

tagonist finds himself separated from his "Margarite," which he understands to be a person, but who is finally shown to be the pearl of Matthew 13:45–46 and to resemble the symbolic order present in the Middle English poem *Pearl,* written in the northwest Midlands at roughly the same time. Like Boethius in the *Consolation of Philosophy,* the protagonist is in prison, lamenting his hard lot, when suddenly he is confronted by his patroness, Love, who comes to comfort him. He tells her that, wandering through the woods one late October or early November day, he was set upon by some animals, now turned wild. He boards a ship named *Travail* (Danger) to escape them, but finds the ship manned by Lust, Thought, Sight, and Will, who take him to an island where he catches a glimpse of a "precious Margarite," the woman-pearl, whom he at once loves. Protesting his love for the Margarite-pearl, he blames Fortune for his present predicament, which

308

has been brought about by his act of betrayal, and which he describes with some care, protesting, however, that he acted out of his high regard for London and a desire for stability and peace.

In his edition of the work, Skeat dismisses this explanation as "vague, shifty and unsatisfactory." But the point is that book 1 does not offer a final word on anything, least of all Usk's actions. The *Testament* is a philosophical and theological work, not a defense brief, and the narrator is at pains to establish that the protagonist has mistaken his ground. In book 2 the difficulties he faces are placed on a different plane, as Usk considers at length how he, now repentant, may understand and grasp what Love describes as "the knot in the hert." This "knot," which has evident spiritual resonances, reappears throughout book 2 and has been understood variously: by Claes Scharr as an echo of Alan of Lille's *De planctu natura,* (mid to late twelfth century), and by Bennett as a scrivener's term, "an intricate design of crossing lines" representing "an image of true felicity." But the image also appears in Chaucer's *Troilus and Criseyde* (circa 1382–1386), a work Usk knew much better than is usually believed and which had a marked thematic influence on his work. In Chaucer's poem, just before the *Canticus Troili,* a song based on Boethius and dedicated to Love, the narrator remarks that Criseyde's "net" was so fixed "[a]boute his [Troilus's] herte" that no quality in any other woman could so much as a single "knotte unbynde." It would be like Usk to take up the reference to *knot* and to *heart* but to alter the image so as to allude not only to the depth of a deeply set devotion but also to the more spiritual resonances it contains.

Yet in dealing with divine grace, as he does in book 2, Usk treats the role of the church with some care, beginning with his rejection of Northampton's Lollardy. The Latin word for cockle is *lolia,* and here as elsewhere in the literature of the period cockle alludes to the Lollards, followers of the philosopher Oxford Don and reformer John Wyclif (died 1384), who sought the reformation of the church and society and who was largely distrusted by the church and state alike. Repenting his earlier association with the group (an association Northampton shared), Usk credits King Richard's grace and pardon for having brought him to the place where "moral vertue groweth," thus lifting the errors and illusions of book 1 to a higher plane, that of moral virtue, and preparing, in the praise of the divine grace as taught by the Holy Church which the pearl has now come to represent, for the more universal explanation of book 3.

In book 3 Usk returns to the philosophical and personal reflections which have run through books 1 and 2, but the ground changes once again to a concern with fate and freedom freely adapted from Boethius, Chaucer, and the eleventh-century philosopher Saint Anselm of Canterbury. Early in book 3 Love reminds the protagonist that anyone who desires the bliss of perfect joy must follow virtue. But now the protagonist is brought to understand that "the comune sentence of the people in opinion, that every thing after destenee is ruled, false and wicked is to beleve." The role of fate and free will figures importantly in book 3 as Usk returns to a consideration, in markedly philosophical terms, of the events that had brought him down. He moves away from the treatment of philosophy according to nature, which he had treated in book 1, and even from the moral considerations of book 2. Book 3 shows him freed from the illusions which had previously blinded him, the illusion of being trapped by position and fate first among them, so that he now can see, as Love tells him, that "'heven is goddes being; although he be over al by power, yet there is abydinge of devyne persone; in whiche heven is everlastinge presence, withouten any movable time.'"

This consideration leads to one of the most quoted passages in *The Testament of Love,* the praise of Chaucer in book 3, chapter 4, lines 248–259, in which Love refers to "a tretis that he [Chaucer] made of my servant Troilus," a treatise in which philosophical matters are well discussed. Love then praises Chaucer as "Myne owne trewe servaunt," and adds, "Certaynly, his noble sayinges can I not amende; in goodnes of gentil manliche [manly] speche, without any maner of nycetè [folly] of storiers [story tellers'] imaginacion, in witte and in good reson of sentence [meaning] he passeth al other makers [poets]. In the boke of Troilus, the answere to thy question mayst thou lerne." The question referred to concerns whether God's foreknowledge of evil deeds implies that God is equally their author and so should not punish them, and it has implications for Thomas Usk, prisoner, as much as for Troilus. The praise of Chaucer as a philosophical poet capable of addressing such issues is important in establishing the concern of *The Testament of Love* for a meaning beyond that which immediate events seem to indicate and for the faithfulness in Love's service that both Troilus and Usk are said to represent. Human faithfulness, which in the case of both Troilus and Usk ended in sorrow, brings together the several meanings of Margarite-pearl that both protagonist and author have been considering, and indicates that, whatever happens in the end, faithfulness in human love resonates with the divine.

The search for "parfit joye" will not lead to position or to worldly goods, as Thomas Usk, prisoner, had believed in book 1. Instead the searcher must turn to the cardinal virtues and to the Holy Church which will lead him through reason and will, though Usk insists in book 3 that both reason and will are within the soul, but they are not the soul itself. His emphasis on rectitude ("trouthe or els rightwisnesse") allows him both to warn against false affection and to locate an appropriate way to serve God in the faithfulness that human love requires. Such love is a "testament," which in medieval Latin (*testamentum*) can mean not only a witness but also a charter or a proof, and in the context of the book becomes a witnessing or a showing of divine grace. The Margarite-pearl thus becomes the source both for the realization that human love has moral and spiritual resonances that reason and will can direct and for the joy that springs from the knowledge to which it leads.

Finally, there is the question as to whether *The Testament of Love* clarifies its author's secular conversion, his changing of sides in 1384 which brought about the series of events that led at once to his book and his death. Again, Usk was something of a "New Man," concerned with getting ahead, and the quest for advancement no doubt played its part. But his interview with Richard II, whose character could induce the most extraordinary sort of attentiveness in those who responded to him, seems to have offered him something beyond the scramble of party and the quest for gain, perhaps something that appeared to be eternal. The course of events soon overtook that illusion, and the realization that followed may help to account for the nature of the quest, the sense of loss, and the elegiac tone that inform *The Testament of Love*.

Thomas Usk believed that, like Troilus, he had served Love and rejected mere Fate in favor of an ideal of service and devotion which began in this world but which ended in another. This consciousness may have sustained him in his final hours, of which the *Westminster Chronicle* provides this description:

Sentence of drawing and hanging was passed on 4 March [1388] in full parliament on John Blake and also on Thomas Usk, who met his death with great contriteness of heart and supreme penitence, reciting with utmost piety, as he was drawn to the gallows, the Placebo and Dirige, the Seven Penitential Psalms, the Te Deum, Nunc dimittis, Quicumque vult, and other hymns that bear upon devotion in the hour of death. His contrition was an example to others to amend their lives by drawing back from evil and turning forthwith to good. Eventually Thomas Usk was hanged and immediately taken down and, after about thirty strokes of the axe, beheaded. To the very end he refused to admit having wronged John Northampton, of whom he maintained that every word was true that he had spoken at Reading in the previous year.

Bibliography:

Robert R. Raymo, "XX. Works of Religious and Philosophical Instruction," in *A Manual of the Writings in Middle English, 1050-1500,* volume 7, edited by Albert E. Hartung (New Haven: Connecticut Academy of Arts and Sciences, 1986), item no. 191, pp. 2346–2347, 2551–2552.

Biographies:

May Newman Hallmundsson, "The Community of Law and Letters: Some Notes on Thomas Usk's Audience," *Viator,* 9 (1978): 357–365;

T. F. Tout, "Literature and Learning in the English Civil Service in the Fourteenth Century," *Speculum,* 4 (1929): 365–389.

References:

J. A. W. Bennett, *Middle English Literature,* edited by Douglas Gray (Oxford: Clarendon Press, 1986);

Ruth Bird, *The Turbulent London of Richard II* (London: Longmans, Green, 1949);

Ramona Bressie, "The Date of Thomas Usk's *Testament of Love,*" *Modern Philology,* 26 (1928): 17–29;

J. D. Burnley, "Chaucer, Usk and Geoffrey of Vinsauf," *Neophilologus,* 69 (1985): 284–293;

M. V. Clarke, "Forfeitures and Treason in 1388," in *Fourteenth Century Studies,* edited by L. S. Sutherland and M. McKisack (Oxford: Clarendon Press, 1937), pp. 115–145;

Janet Coleman, *English Literature in History; 1350–1400, Medieval Readers and Writers* (London: Hutchinson, 1981);

John Conley, "The Lord's Day as the Eighth Day: A Passage in Thomas Usk's 'The Testament of Love,'" *Notes and Queries,* new series 17 (1970): 367–368;

Conley, "Scholastic Neologisms in Usk's 'Testament of Love,'" *Notes and Queries,* new series 11 (1964): 209;

Malcolm Godden, *The Making of Piers Plowman* (London & New York: Longman, 1990);

Anthony Goodman, *The Loyal Conspiracy, The Lords Appellant under Richard II* (London: Routledge & Kegan Paul / Coral Gables, Fla.: University of Miami Press, 1971);

S. K. Henninger, Jr., "The Margarite-Pearl Allegory in Thomas Usk's *Testament of Love*," *Speculum*, 32 (1957): 92–98;

P. L. Heyworth, "The Punctuation of Middle English Texts," in *Medieval Studies for J. A. W. Bennett*, edited by Heyworth (Oxford: Clarendon Press, 1981), pp. 139–157;

C. S. Lewis, *The Allegory of Love: A Study in Medieval Tradition* (Oxford: Clarendon Press, 1936), pp. 222–231;

Stephen Medcalf, *The Later Middle Ages* (London: Methuen, 1981);

Medcalf, "Transposition: Thomas Usk's *Testament of Love*," in *The Medieval Translator: The Theory and Practice of Translation in the Middle Ages*, edited by Roger Ellis (Cambridge: Brewer, 1989), pp. 181–195;

Pearl, edited by E. V. Gordon (Oxford: Clarendon Press, 1953);

Edmund Reiss, "The Idea of Love in Usk's *Testament of Love*," *Mediaevalia*, 6 (1980): 261–277;

George Sanderlin, "Usk's *Testament of Love* and St. Anselm," *Speculum*, 17 (1942): 69–73;

Claes Schaar, "Notes on Thomas Usk's *Testament of Love*," *Lunds Universitets Arsskrift*, 46, no. 2 (1950): 3–45;

Schaar, "Usk's Knot in the Heart," *English Studies*, 37 (1956): 260–261;

Margaret Schlauch, "Thomas Usk as Translator" in *Medieval Literature and Folklore Studies: Essays in Honor of F. L. Utley* (New Brunswick, N. J.: Rutgers University Press, 1971), pp. 97–103;

Myra Stokes and John Scattergood, "Travelling in November: Sir Gawain, Thomas Usk, Charles of Orleans," *Medium Ævum*, 53 (1984): 78–83;

Paul Strohm, "Politics and Poetics: Usk and Chaucer in the 1380s," in *Literary Practice and Social Change in Britain, 1380–1530*, edited by Lee Patterson (Berkeley & Los Angeles: University of California Press, 1990), pp. 83–112;

Strohm, "The Textual Vicissitudes of Usk's Appeal," in his *Hochon's Arrow: The Social Imagination of Fourteenth-Century Texts* (Princeton: Princeton University Press, 1992), pp. 145–160;

The Westminister Chronicle, 1381–1394, edited and translated by L. C. Hector and Barbara F. Havey (Oxford: Clarendon Press, 1982).

Robert ("Maistre") Wace

(circa 1100 – circa 1175)

Daniel F. Pigg
University of Tennessee at Martin

La Vie de Sainte Marguerite (The Life of Saint Marguerite, circa 1135)

Manuscripts: There are 3 manuscripts containing the saint's life. Two date from the thirteenth century and one from the fourteenth century. Bibliothèque municipale, Troyes, 1905 and Bibliothèque de l'Arsenal, Paris, 3516 are the best copies. The Troyes manuscript forms the basis for the 1990 edition of Hans-Erich Keller.

First publication: *La Vie de Sainte Marguerite* (Clairvaux: Printed by Jean Bouhier, 1781).

Standard editions: *La Vie de Sainte Marguerite,* edited by Elizabeth A. Francis (Paris: Champion, 1932); *La Vie de Sainte Marguerite,* edited by Hans-Erich Keller (Tübingen: Niemeyer, 1990).

La Conception Nostre Dame (The Conception of Our Lady, 1130–1140)

Manuscripts: There are 18 manuscripts containing sections of the entire text in different dialects. Bibliothèque municipale, Tours, 927, a thirteenth-century manuscript, is the best as it contains the entire poem. The first publication was based on Bibliothèque nationale, Paris, Fonds Français 25532 (thirteenth century).

First publication: *La Conception Nostre Dame* (Caen: Mancel & Trébutien, 1842).

Standard edition: *The Conception Nostre Dame of Wace,* edited by William Ray Ashford (Chicago: The University of Chicago Libraries, 1933).

La Vie de Saint Nicolas (The Life of Saint Nicholas, circa 1150)

Manuscripts: There are 5 manuscripts, with Bodleian Library, Oxford, Douce 270 and Bibliothèque nationale, Paris, Fonds Français 902 being the best versions and the ones on which editions of the *Vie* are constructed.

First publication: *La Vie de Saint Nicolas* (Bonn: Delius, 1850).

Standard edition: *The Life of Saint Nicholas,* edited by Mary Sinclair Crawford (Philadelphia: University of Pennsylvania, 1923).

Le Roman de Brut (The Story of Brutus, 1155)

Manuscripts: There are 22 manuscripts from the thirteenth through the fifteenth century typically found in collections with other chronicle histories, with British Library Sous le n 13.A.XXI (thirteenth century) being among the best. Facsimile: *Le Roman de Brut; a Reproduction of MS. 2603, folios 1–100b in the National Library Vienna* (New York: Modern Language Association of America, 1927).

First publication: *Le Roman de Brut,* edited by Le Roux de Lincy, 2 volumes (Paris: Frère, 1836–1838).

Standard edition: *Le Roman de Brut,* edited by Ivor Arnold, 2 volumes (Paris: Société des Ançiens Textes Français, 1938–1940).

Edition in English: In *Arthurian Chronicles,* translated by Eugene Mason (London: J. M. Dent and Sons, 1962); "The Birth and Rise of Arthur," in *The Romance of Arthur: An Anthology of Medieval Texts in Translation,* revised edition, edited by James J. Wilhelm (New York: Garland Publishing, 1994).

Le Roman de Rou (The Story of Rollo, 1174)

Manuscripts: There are four manuscripts, two from the thirteenth and one from the fourteenth century, with British Library, Royal 4.c.XI and Bibliothèque nationale, Paris, fr. 375 being the earliest and best.

First publication: *Le Roman de Rou et des Ducs de Normandie,* edited by Frederic Pluquet (Rouen: Frère, 1827–1829).

Standard edition: *Le Roman de Rou,* edited by A. J. Holden, 3 volumes (Paris: Picard, 1970–1973).

Editions in English: *Master Wace: His Chronicle of the Norman Conquest,* translated by Edgar Taylor (London: William Pickering, 1837; reprinted, New York: AMS Press, 1975); *The*

Conquest of England, translated by Alexander Malet (London: Bell & Dadly, 1860).

Robert Wace, or "Maistre Wace" as he refers to himself in several of his works, is one of the most intriguing figures associated with literature between the Old and Middle English periods. While all of his works were written in French and at least one under the patronage of the court of Henry II of England, he deserves greater recognition in the literary canon of intermediate texts written for Anglo-Norman courtly consumption. Of greatest influence to English literature was his *Le Roman de Brut* (1155), a translation and reshaping of Geoffrey of Monmouth's *Historia Regum Britanniae* (1136). The work added several new accretions to the Arthurian legend, particularly in its treatment of Arthur and in the development of theories surrounding the form and significance of the Round Table. Wace was a writer deeply enmeshed in the development of philosophical and literary ideas of the twelfth century, and these ideas shape the forms of his fictions from the early saints' lives to *romanz* (romance) to historical chronicle.

Much of Wace's biography can be reconstructed from lines in his last work, *Le Roman de Rou* (abandoned in 1174). He was born around 1100 on the island of Jersey, located in the English Channel and strategically and ideologically located between France and England. He was educated first at Caen, near the coast in northern France – a village whose schema is noted in *Le Roman de Rou.* As Margaret E. Houck notes, Caen was an important site for Anglo-Norman ideology as it was the favorite city and subsequent burial place for William the Conqueror. That Wace would devote a large portion of the *Le Roman de Rou* to William's rise to monarchy shows on one level how deeply civic mythology can circulate among the threads of a literary text. Urban Tigner Holmes, Jr., suggests that the writer must have been educated in Caen at Psalter and grammar schools. Wace notes he was further educated in Paris, most likely in circles that gave rise to the city's becoming one of Europe's most renowned sites for education in the arts and theology. Which literary, philosophical, and theological figures Wace may have known is uncertain, but his texts reflect some of the issues arising in Platonism, from political theorists such as John of Salisbury, and from the ecclesiastically sanctioned models that define social organization according to the tripartite model (clergy, nobility, and peasantry).

Wace next notes that he returned to Caen, where he wrote *romanz* – a designation, according to

Nancy Vine Durling, that refers to writing in the vernacular, rather than to a specific generic classification. While there he wrote several saints' lives: *La Vie de Sainte Marguerite, La Conception Nostre Dame,* and *La Vie de Saint Nicolas* (likely written in this order). He also wrote one of his most extended works, *Le Roman de Brut.* He later notes in *Le Roman de Rou* that because of the favor of Henry II, he was assigned the position of canon at Bayeux. His position, however, seems more connected with writing and teaching than with religious duties. In 1160 he was commissioned by Henry II to write a history (*Le Roman de Rou*) of the Norman dukes that would justify Norman rule beginning with Rollo and continuing through the contemporary reign of Henry II; however, Henry withdrew his commission and subsequent financial support in 1174. The last traces of Wace appear in records of 1175, although there is no exact record of his death date.

While *Le Roman de Brut* and *Le Roman de Rou* are his most important works, Wace's early saints' lives reveal important aspects about his developing poetic sensibilities. *La Vie de Sainte Marguerite,* as Edward Montgomery observes, manifests the poet's preoccupation with the symbolic order, particularly in the use of numbers and directional movements. Such a treatment would reflect not only aspects of realist philosophy, based upon the Augustinian notion of signs but also the flowering of Platonic thought in the twelfth century. As Montgomery further notes, the poet's contemplation of the saint's name, the symbolism of the pearl at the beginning of the poem and the underlining of Marguerite's moral rectitude are also part of this emphasis to turn the poem to cosmic dimensions. That twelfth-century grammarians also bring rectitude to the fore as a point of consideration may be reflected in Wace's plot development. While some critics, such as Hans-Erich Keller, following the influential study of Charles Homer Haskins, see Wace as a "precursor" to the Renaissance writers' notion of the individual, this text and the other two identifiable saints' lives reflect linguistic and theological positions purely "medieval" in their placement of the individual within social institutions in a way which valorizes the external forms. As A. J. Minnis shows, medieval writers from the twelfth century on were also conscious of the textual construction of authors. The tripartite structure of *La Conception Nostre Dame* and the numerology and triadic form in *La Vie de Saint Nicolas,* as Gerald F. Carr observes, lend some indication of Wace's artistic and ideological formation as a poet engaging with materials that are only slightly altered in plot, but are given the voice of Wace's philosophical discourse.

Wace seems to have favored subjects based on national, theological, and patronal motivations. *La Conception,* as William Ray Ashford notes, was likely written to encourage the celebration of the feast of the Immaculate Conception in France. The life of Saint Nicholas under the patronage of Robert the Magnificent, according to Mary Sinclair Crawford, celebrates a saint who was developing in Normandy as a regional hero. Wace's poems thus participate in a network of social and religious relationships.

Of the works attributed to Wace, *Le Roman de Brut* has attracted the most significant attention and has the greatest impact on an English literary tradition. Robert Huntington Fletcher (1906), E. K. Chambers (1927), J. S. P. Tatlock (1950), Charles Foulon (1959), Peter Korrel (1984), Jean Blacker-Knight (1988), and Durling (1989) have provided the most extended studies of the poem in connection with its principal written source, the *Historia Regum Britanniae.* To understand the importance of Wace's adaptation of the Arthurian tradition, the modern reader needs to examine some of the major cruces that reveal the author's unique artistry.

The structure of *Le Roman de Brut* parallels that of Geoffrey's *Historia Regum Britanniae* in what Fletcher labels the form of "free paraphrase." The poem treats events from the founding of Britain by Brutus to the death of the last Briton leader, Cadwallader. There are, however, several changes to the original source in Wace's text, particularly in the section treating the history between Constantine and the death of Arthur, which reshape the ideology of the text in concert with twelfth-century philosophical speculation about language and its relationship to truth.

One of the first changes in the "Arthurian section" is Wace's refusal to translate Merlin's prophecies found in Geoffrey's work. Wace implies that he will not translate them because he cannot interpret them. For him the entire interpretive loop is essential; signs have referents, and they must be traced and decoded. In Geoffrey's text Merlin delivers an extensive series of prophecies concerning warfare and the future state of the Britons against the Saxons under typical apocalyptic signs of animal imagery. Wace, instead, weaves into his narrative, in the section that follows his refusal, Merlin's image of the boar of Cornwall, which he identifies with Arthur. Durling argues that Wace refuses because there are "no external texts to support Merlin's Prophecies, and this makes the interpretation of them problematic." The refusal, however, seems to have more to do with Wace's overall explo-

King Arthur's arrival at court; an illustration from a fourteenth-century transcription of Wace's Le Roman de Brut *(British Library, MS. Egerton 3028, fol. 42)*

ration of the nature of fiction, including its relation to and his desire to alter the image of Arthur. At least in the case of Arthur, Wace finds Merlin's prophecy understandable.

While interpretive reduction is one of Wace's most frequently practiced methods, he does, however, build into his narrative a sense of drama and intrigue. The meeting of King Uther with his guests, Gorlois, Earl of Cornwall, and his wife, Igerne, is an example. At the meeting in Wace's depiction, Uther focuses his visual attention on Igerne, who, while she does not favor or deny his attention, does complete the circuit of what some psychoanalytic critics term the "male gaze." An aspect of power beyond the mere aspect of ceremonial gift-giving, also noted by Geoffrey, can be seen here. It is precisely that power that circulates between the visual perceptions of Uther and Igerne that prompts Gorlois and Igerne to leave the feast and for Uther to follow in order to gain his object of desire – Igerne. Wace's addition is a significant one, because it adds another aspect of causation to the text, suggesting that twelfth-century writers of the literary and philosophical traditions were beginning to consider casual relationships in greater detail. At the very least, Wace's development of his text approaches the notion of verisimilitude – again blurring the distance between a potential human action and fiction.

Of the developments in *Le Roman de Brut,* the presentation of the Round Table is one of the poet's most significant in terms of symbolism. This section of the narrative grows out of the intersection of fact and fiction and oral and written texts. The notion of the Round Table was already present in Celtic sources, which Wace may have known. Wace's addition is significant for several reasons. First, it contributes a symbolic dimension to the narrative and becomes part of the verbal emblem defining Arthur's knights. Subsequent medieval treatments strengthen this tradition, so that by the late fifteenth century Malory's designation of a knight as a member of the Round Table imparts a sense of community – a community fractured by internal feuds which bring an end to this symbolic order. Second, the Round Table creates the appearance of equality through the obvious orchestration of a proxemic code (one that governs space and location). Much of Wace's *Le Roman de Brut* is infused with feudalism. The overwhelming majority of the episodes show the establishment of the lord/vassal relationship, which Arthur creates through a show of military force. The paradigm is overtly monolithic. With the Round Table Wace negotiates a position within the established form of feudal custom and practice. Again, the symbolic import is unity, but it also provides an example of a primitive society refashioned through the eyes of a poet grounded in feudal ideology. Third, the Round Table is also described as multinational. Wace notes that Britons, Frenchmen, Normans, Angevins, Flemings, Burgundians, and Loherians are seated there. Such a union across international boundaries is significant for Arthur's base of power, but it is also significant for Anglo-Norman ideology as well. The uniting of Norman and English interests under William the Conqueror and his descendants created at least for a few years a substantial base of monarchical power, which in turn supported the writing of history that circulated this ideology.

On a more global scale, *Le Roman de Brut* reshapes the image of Arthur, not just into a medieval king, but also into a more courteous, humane leader than in Geoffrey's *Historia Regum Britanniae*. Korrel and Fletcher both observe the poet's subduing the harshness of conquest against the Saxons, Irish, Scots, Picts, and Norwegians in most cases through an obvious curtailing of description. Sometimes, however, this intention seems to be at odds with the narrative. For example, in the moment when the religious community of the Scots approaches Arthur with bodies of their slain saints and relics and at the same time recount the massive destruction that Arthur's forces have wrought among them, Arthur's perfunctory display of compassion seems slightly less than humane, given their condition.

Wace's tendency to expand the narrative moment might do more to deconstruct his image of Arthur than to enhance it; at the least, his motive seems indeterminate. Throughout, Wace's intention seems to be to show Arthur as a man of action as well as a gifted statesman, putting together workable political/military alliances.

One of the most intriguing aspects of the Arthurian legend in any form is the treatment of Arthur's death and his anticipated return. On these issues Wace seems purposely evasive, again in keeping with a poetic strategy that scorns speculation. Wace differentiates between oral and written sources. Taking the prophecy of Merlin as his authority, he refuses to say more than that Arthur's ending is hidden in dark shadows. Wace chooses to celebrate the power of the living Arthur, and he seldom raises him above a human being. Readers desiring a more romanticized version of Arthur must look to the end of the Middle Ages and the speculations of Malory, who longs for the lost age of Arthur.

The apparent success of *Le Roman de Brut* won for Wace royal favor and a commission in 1160 to write a history of the Norman dukes for Henry II. This work proved to be far more demanding ideologically for Wace, perhaps so much so that he could not finish it. Numerous references in the poem suggest that he spent most of the next fourteen years in some measure of want, or at least with a level of support that he did not mind pointing to in less-than-complimentary terms. His complaints strike readers more strongly than do Geoffrey Chaucer's. That his personal fortunes change in 1174 can be clearly discerned from the ending of *Le Roman de Rou* where Wace notes he was supplanted by Benoît de Sainte-Maure in writing the propagandistic history. As Jean Blacker notes, the author's failure to write a history supporting the image of the Normans as the rightful possessors of the English throne may have been the reason for the withdrawal of patronage. There are, however, other possibilities.

While *Le Roman de Rou* traces Norman history from the time of the Viking Rollo, the first Duke of Normandy, to the early reign of Henry I, the portion which treats events surrounding the Norman Conquest of England shows Wace's attempt to justify Norman succession on the throne of England. Earlier in *Le Roman de Rou* Wace shows William's great military strength in defeating opponents and moving them to perform fealty and homage. Included are descriptions of the monstrous defeats of the king of France at Mortemer and Varaville. William is represented simultaneously as both a skillful leader militarily and diplomatically. He forms ties with powerful leaders in "France" and with the papacy. Readers of *Le Roman de Rou* encounter many examples of the poet's admissions that he does not know all the details surrounding an event and his tendency to suggest all possible readings of an event. As in his earlier works, Wace is concerned with the representation of truth – one which can never be arbitrary. Wace might in one sense be called a precursor to a modern journalist: he works with several sources, isolates gaps within narrative units, and subsequently refuses in a traditional formulaic manner to speculate beyond what he can verify with his senses or find in other sources, whether written or oral.

Critics cite events recorded in *Le Roman de Rou* that problematize the text for its intended reading audience, Henry II. Blacker observes that Wace chooses to follow an English version of the events surrounding the granting of Edward's throne to William. Wace has Harold Godwinson, William's rival for the throne, make a trip to Normandy to secure the release of some hostages. In the Norman version, as Blacker notes, Harold travels to Normandy to demonstrate to William that William is the rightful heir. The choice is significant because narrative sympathy is blurred. William is seen as manipulative, while Harold is seen as having no position but to swear an oath to William in order to be released from prison. In a text commissioned to display Norman power, such ambiguity in the portrait of William the Conqueror, while perhaps more accurate from the poet's perspective since truth probably lies more clearly in the fusion of English and Norman ideological versions, fails to support the ruling order. That Wace has William admit on his deathbed that he has no rights to England and that his son William may only inherit it as a result of ecclesiastical action further underscores this highly problematic retelling of history. In a power struggle between Henry I and his brother Robert for control of the throne Wace seems to support the right of Robert and the losing faction. Certainly, these two episodes do not suggest that Wace was a writer of literary/historical treason, but that he saw in the writing of history in particular – and all composition in general – the way that language generates its own sense of truth, perhaps one not always connected to an external, verifiable reality. For a poet working in a period when philosophical realism was dominant, such a dilemma would, without question, have an impact upon the production of his texts.

Traditionally, Wace scholarship has taken two very decided directions. As an intermediate figure between a Latinate and a vernacular English tradition, Wace has been placed within an evolutionary chain. In addition, historical-critical scholarship as represented by several textual editors focused on his development of metrical and linguistic forms. Beginning in the 1980s under the influence of structuralist and post-structuralist strategies, scholarship began to view Wace as a writer whose merits were much greater than those of a mere translator and political propagandist. In fact, recent criticism isolates Wace's tendencies to speculate on the nature of his fictive enterprise and his often ambivalent treatment of historical sequences in Norman history that seem to undermine the supposed intention in light of his socio-economic position. At the same time, studies note that Wace is able to affirm and deny the cultural values of Anglo-Norman institutions.

Wace made an almost-immediate impact on English literature and continued to have influence until the fourteenth century. Shortly after 1200 Laȝamon translated *Le Roman de Brut,* where he claimed that Wace gave a copy of his original poem to Queen Eleanor. In the fourteenth century Robert Mannyng of Brunne based a portion of his *Chronicle* (1338) on Wace's *Le Roman de Brut.* As Fletcher notes, manuscript evidence in England from the fourteenth century shows that Wace maintained a reading population, but subsequent "medievalizations" of Arthurian materials from the fourteenth and fifteenth centuries as much as linguistic difficulties must have brought Wace's influence into decline. A poet caught up in the world of Anglo-Norman rule and social custom, Wace stands as the supreme example of the interplay between French and English culture and language.

References:

Jean Blacker, "'La geste est grande, longue et grieve a translater': History for Henry II," *Romance Quarterly,* 37 (November 1990): 387–396;

Jean Blacker-Knight, "Transformations of a Theme: The Depolitization of the Arthurian World in the *Roman de Brut,*" *The Arthurian Tradition: Essays in Convergence,* edited by Mary Flowers Braswell and John Bugge (Tuscaloosa: University of Alabama Press, 1988), pp. 54–74;

Blacker-Knight, "Wace's Craft and His Audience: Historical Truth, Bias, and Patronage in the *Roman de Rou,*" *Kentucky Romance Quarterly,* 31 (November 1984): 355–362;

Leger Brosnahan, "Wace's Use of Proverbs," *Speculum,* 39 (July 1964): 444–473;

Arthur C. L. Brown, *The Round Table Before Wace,* Harvard Studies and Notes in Philology and Literature 7 (Boston: Ginn, 1900), pp. 183–205;

Gerald F. Carr, "The Prologue to Wace's *Vie de Saint Nicholas,*" *Philological Quarterly,* 47 (January 1968): 1–7;

E. K. Chambers, *Arthur of Britain* (1927; reprint, New York: Barnes and Noble, 1964);

Nancy Vine Durling, "Translation and Innovation in the *Roman de Brut,*" *Medieval Translators and Their Craft,* edited by Jeanette Beer (Kalamazoo: Western Michigan University, 1989), pp. 9–39;

Najaria Hurst Esty, "Wace's 'Roman de Brut' and the Fifteenth Century 'Prose Brut Chronicle': A Comparative Study," Ph.D. dissertation, Ohio State University, 1978;

Robert Huntington Fletcher, *The Arthurian Material in the Chronicles* (New York: Burt Franklin, 1906);

Charles Foulon, "Wace," in *Arthurian Literature in the Middle Ages: A Collaborative History,* edited by Roger Sherman Loomis (Oxford: Clarendon Press, 1959), pp. 94–103;

Charles Homer Haskins, *The Renaissance of the Twelfth Century* (Cambridge, Mass.: Harvard University Press, 1927);

Urban Tigner Holmes, Jr., "Norman Literature and Wace," *Medieval Secular Literature,* edited by William Matthews (Berkeley: University of California Press, 1967), pp. 46–67;

Margaret E. Houck, "Sources of the *Roman de Brut* of Wace," *University of California Publications,* 5 (April 1938): 161–356;

Hans-Erich Keller, "The Intellectual Journey of Wace," *Fifteenth-Century Studies,* 17 (1990): 185–207;

Amy Kelly, *Eleanor of Aquitaine and the Four Kings* (Cambridge, Mass.: Harvard University Press, 1950);

Peter Korrel, *An Arthurian Triangle* (Leiden: Brill, 1984);

Mary Dominica Legge, *Anglo-Norman Literature and Its Background* (Oxford: Clarendon Press, 1963);

A. J. Minnis, *Medieval Theory of Authorship: Scholastic Literary Attitudes in the Late Middle Ages* (London: Scolar, 1984);

Edward Montgomery, "Structure and Symbol in Wace's *Vie de Sainte Marguerite,*" *Kentucky Romance Quarterly,* 24 (November 1977): 301–309;

Sidney R. Packard, *Twelfth-Century Europe: An Interpretive Essay* (Amherst: University of Massachusetts Press, 1973);

Jeff Rider, "The Fictional Merlin of the *Brut,*" *Modern Philology,* 87 (August 1989): 1–12;

Josiah C. Russell, *Twelfth-Century Studies* (New York: AMS Press, 1978);

William Sayers, "The Jongeleur Taillefer at Hastings: Antecedents and Literary Fate," *Viator,* 14 (1983): 77–88;

J. S. P. Tatlock, "Wace," *The Legendary History of Britain: Geoffrey of Monmouth's Historia and Its Early Vernacular Versions* (Berkeley: University of California Press, 1950), pp. 463–482;

Paul Zumthor, *Toward a Medieval Poetics,* translated by Philip Bennett (Minneapolis: University of Minnesota Press, 1992).

John Wyclif

(circa 1335 – 31 December 1384)

Thomas A. Goodman
University of Miami

WORKS: (circa 1357–1384)

Manuscripts: More than four hundred Latin titles, numbered individually, are attributed to Wyclif. They include multipart collections in philosophy and theology, as well as biblical commentary, minor tracts, and sets of sermons and letters. Whole works attributed to the author, some of which have many substantial parts, number about 120. Around 240 manuscripts are extant throughout Europe; the majority are in collections in Vienna and Prague; some are in British libraries, while others appear in places as diverse as Dublin, Stockholm, and the Vatican.

First publication: *Trialogus* (Basel [?], 1525).

Standard edition: *Johannis Wyclif Latin Works,* 36 volumes (London: Trübner, 1883–1922; reprinted, New York & London: Johnson Reprint / Frankfurt am Main: Minerva, 1966).

John Wyclif deserves a place in a volume of Old and Middle English writers and writing not because of any works in English that may be ascribed to him with certainty. He should be included, rather, because of the influence of his Latin writings both in England, where they inspired adherents to write in the vernacular, and on the Continent, particularly in Bohemia. There they engaged the interest of the reformer Jan Hus, among many others, because of Wyclif's philosophical realism and his harsh criticisms of the institutional church. As a doctor of theology at Oxford University, Wyclif taught and wrote on problems of logic, the Bible, and theological issues. His rejection of current explanations of transubstantiation in the Eucharist, as well as his ultimate antisacerdotalism, which undermined the necessity of the priestly and papal offices in the life of the Christian, was the leading point in the eventual condemnation of his teachings. The acrimony of his expression in his later writings no

doubt contributed as well to the negative reception of his views by church authorities.

Wyclif may be counted among English writers of the later Middle Ages in that he was an Englishman and a prolific writer. Surviving evidence suggests that none of the Middle English writings that express ideas similar to his may be confidently attributed to him; scholars' understanding of his connection to these vernacular writings may change, however. One hundred years ago there were fewer doubts about the matter, and the modern student of Wyclif should read early editions of Wyclif's so-called English writings as Wycliffite productions of his followers. Like most medieval academics, Wyclif wrote in Latin for other scholars, though it is likely that, as did some of his Oxford contemporaries, he sometimes preached in English, and he certainly advocated an English translation of Scripture. It was his adherents and successors, first at Oxford and later well outside the university, who translated Scripture and spread Wyclif's ideas, putting into practice Wyclif's sometimes startlingly egalitarian statements about scriptural translation and the community of faithful readers. While these followers, called Wycliffites or, derisively, Lollards (from the Middle Dutch word *lollen,* "to mumble"), and their texts are not of primary concern here, a list of sources and studies concerning the Wycliffites follows the references on Wyclif at the end of this article.

Wyclif's reputation in modern times has veered toward one of two poles: he has either been seen as a vigilant precursor of the Protestant Reformation of the sixteenth century or as the heretical product of decrepit medieval scholasticism, reflecting the social and intellectual disintegration of the later Middle Ages. The former view was the product of Protestant polemics, stemming particularly from John Bale's entry in his *Illustrium scriptorum majoris Britanniæ* (1548) in which he referred to Wyclif as the "stella matutina" (morningstar) of the

Woodcut portrait of Wyclif, from John Bale's Illustrium scriptorum
majoris Britanniae *(1548)*

Reformation; this view of Wyclif as proto-Protestant prevailed throughout much nineteenth-century scholarship. The less sanguine view of Wyclif arose under the primacy of Thomas Aquinas as the medieval mind par excellence among some scholars of the nineteenth and twentieth centuries. Compared to Aquinas's, Wyclif's Latin and systematic organization have been judged much inferior. Wyclif scholars today have placed him on more-level ground due to more-critical reading of condemnatory medieval chroniclers and to careful work on all the sources, including the registers of bishops who were responsible for looking into heretical ideas among their flocks and who thus left rich records. Despite repeated efforts to burn his writings, Wyclif's works survive in a great volume of texts reflective of his analytical scholastic training and communicates the stridency of his opinions regarding clerical endowment, fitness for office, and the nature of the Eucharist. He is remarkable as well for the diverse and somewhat surprising longevity of his influence among people far removed from his Oxford circle.

Wyclif's origins remain obscure; no information survives concerning his birth or early years. There is an uncertain case for his being a member of the Wyclif family from the North Riding in Yorkshire; he may have come from that area at any rate. The earliest firm biographical evidence is in an Oxford record of 1356, listing Wyclif as a probationary first-year fellow of Merton College, having graduated as a bachelor of arts. The curriculum for this degree included the seven liberal arts, comprising the trivium, including grammar, rhetoric, and, particularly, logic, and the quadrivium, including arithmetic, astronomy, geometry, and music. From the date of his degree scholars have guessed at the year of Wyclif's birth — anywhere from the late 1320s to 1338. By 1360 he was the master of Balliol College, having also achieved the academic rank of *magister,* or master. For part of the next three years Wyclif was away from Oxford while holding clerical livings, but by 1363 he was back at the university to study theology, a course extending eight or nine years for a doctorate. This was one of the three graduate programs available in the medieval university, the other two being medicine and law. By 1372 Wyclif had achieved his doctorate, though he had been writing and teaching for more than a dozen years.

Wyclif's career at Oxford up to the early 1370s was typical, focused on the study of and commentary on standard school texts and subjects, even while he earned a great reputation. The precise dates of Wyclif's written works are a matter of conjecture for editors and scholars, who base their guesses on limited references within the works to known historical events or to preceding works; most such dates are only approximate. Works on logic date from the late 1350s and early 1360s, just after he finished the arts course, including his time as a master lecturing on logic, a subject much concerned at the time with the grammatical functions of words. His *On Logic,* written before 1362, is distinctive in part, as Anthony Kenny has remarked, because of Wyclif's claim at the outset to be writing on the logic of sacred Scripture; there is no easy separation between issues of philosophy and of theology in Wyclif's mind.

Also, in the third treatise of this work, Wyclif gives attention to what would be his lifelong concern with universals, those terms which speak to common features of a class of things, predicating something shared by every member. Some famous examples include the general term *animal* and the general proposition "Humans are animals." What exactly does it mean when one says that dogs, cats, and humans are all animals? Are their commonalities real; that is, does the term *animal* refer to something real that all these have in common, or does the word lack direct reference, serving only as a linguistic shorthand for all those individuals who make up the category? William of Ockham, whose presence had been important in Oxford theology in the 1320s, held something close to the latter view (though the subtleties of his analysis deserve much fuller exposition than present space allows). His ideas are often termed *nominalist* (though no such term would have been familiar to him) because of his skeptical attitude towards the ontological status of general nouns (names) such as *animal* and toward the status of those qualities by which two things are deemed similar. He had left Oxford in 1324; subsequently many of his ideas were attacked, and no clear school furthering his views is apparent among succeeding students.

To Wyclif, however, as he would later say in *On Universals* (circa 1374), "intellectual and emotional confusion concerning universals is the cause of all the sin reigning in the world"; the rhetorical flavor of this claim suggests Wyclif's stridency in his later writings. Wyclif espoused a so-called Realist position, arguing (among many other things) that the qualities of similarity between two objects have real existence and are not just convenient abstractions. For Wyclif, then, the "animalness" an

observer perceives in order to draw a similarity between a dog and a cat has real being. No matter the historical case for or against Ockham's influence: these so-called doctors of signs or moderns were the first enemies Wyclif attacked in his writings; in *On Universals* he names "Ockham and many other doctors of signs" who, because of weak understanding, deny the reality of universals. This issue remained at the heart of Wyclif's concerns throughout his career, reaffirmed in the late work *Trialogus* (1382–1383), which summarizes and attempts to synthesize his philosophical, theological, and political views via a "trialogue" among Truth, Lies, and Wisdom. Philosophical concerns with logic, language, and being, then, laid the foundation for the theological views he would expound in later works.

After his return to Oxford by 1363, when he was allowed to hold his clerical appointments, or benefices, in absentia in order to draw their income and pursue his studies, Wyclif rented rooms in Queen's College until he left Oxford in 1381 – with one interruption. For a few years he was the warden of Canterbury College, but this experience ended with his being driven out due to conflicts among the members of the hall. Meanwhile, between 1363 and 1374 he progressed toward the doctorate in theology, adding to and then gathering together the philosophical works, including his early logical treatises, that make up his *Summa de ente,* concerned with the problems of being. These efforts were capped by the substantial work *On Universals,* to date the only important treatise by Wyclif to have been translated into present-day English. Toward the end of this period he was lecturing and, probably at the same time, writing a commentary on the entire Bible. This commentary, as yet largely unpublished, while it draws heavily on the work of Nicholas of Lyra, is the only such full-scale work produced in England during the fourteenth century. As a writer Wyclif ambitiously sought to express himself in every avenue of philosophy and theology.

While lecturing on the *Sentences* (circa 1157–1158) of Peter Lombard, a standard text in theology, as part of his work towards the doctorate, Wyclif produced *On the Blessed Incarnation* sometime around 1371–1372. The text reveals the theological importance of Wyclif's dispute with the "moderns" on the nature of the universals in linguistic use. It is important to Wyclif's understanding of the Incarnation to see Christ as the Word who took on humanity in two real senses: first, as the real, essential humanness that makes all members of the species human; second, as a real, particular individual.

Playing on language to make his point, Wyclif writes that Christ in his Incarnate "form reformed the deformed" souls of humans. He accuses the moderns (who typically remain unnamed as individuals) of denying Christ's created nature and of obfuscating the matter with empty arguments against the logic of Scripture, whose authority, along with the Fathers, is superior. These sources, and such expression, were the touchstones of much of his later writing.

By the early 1370s John Wyclif was well established as a lecturer and writer on logical, metaphysical, and theological matters. He was remarkable as well for the vehemence with which he expressed his views that, at least at the time, were accepted as orthodox, though some early ideas on predestination were subsequently criticized. His energies turned to new directions as he completed his doctoral degree and compiled his philosophical writings to that date. First Wyclif embarked on an extended series of works in theology to complement his efforts in philosophy. Those writings are often grouped together as the *Summa de ente,* while the theological treatises form his second *Summa.*

By 1371 Wyclif also began to participate in the affairs of state. At issue during this period was the right of the papacy to tax the English clergy and to appoint clergy to important (and remunerative) posts in the English church, for which appointments the papacy exacted a substantial payment. These practices denied power and revenue to an English crown desirous to finance military campaigns in France – the long and intermittent series of battles comprising the Hundred Years' War. Large claims were made on the English clergy simultaneously by King Edward III and Pope Gregory XI in 1371–1372, when Wyclif attended Parliament and witnessed two Augustinian friars from Oxford making the case for the Crown to tax the English clergy, instead of the papacy. Soon after this time Wyclif was a member of a delegation sent to Bruges to meet with representatives of the pope; the mission was not very successful. But Wyclif's participation, the beginning of a career outside the Oxford schools, coincides with the new treatises addressing themselves to the issue of power and who has the right to exercise it, marking the inception of Wyclif's move away from strict theological issues in writings where he circumscribes the power of the church government and the papacy; such views were sure to win him enmity in Rome.

Given that the medieval church and the royal government – in whatever area of medieval Europe – constituted sometimes rival political systems, it is not surprising that the relations of the two formed a central problem for medieval society. Clerical appointments, taxation, and the dispensation of justice were consistent areas of dispute. The Thomas Becket case is probably the most famous incident in the latter area in English history. In the English disputes with the papacy of the 1370s Wyclif sided with the Crown. His motivations for doing so are uncertain; perhaps he was hoping for further involvement in political and diplomatic affairs. Patronage of a royal court or of the papal court were key paths to preferment, of course, and distinguished works in theology – and useful partisan views – were often means to such preferment. (Legal studies soon began to take precedence as a career path.) As an apparent result of his minor diplomatic participation, as well as his publicized disputes with two Benedictine monks about the proper relationship of princes over prelates, Wyclif received the moderately lucrative church holding of Lutterworth via the government in 1374. Some have speculated that Wyclif's disappointment in procuring a profitable benefice in England, perhaps even a bishopric, from Pope Gregory XI in the next year turned him into a strident antipapalist. The case has been made by M. J. Wilks that the young Wyclif was in fact strongly supportive of papal prerogative and that he later abjured this youthful error. In any case, he held the Lutterworth benefice in absentia, a practice he later criticized in clergymen, and it was to Lutterworth that he retired from Oxford in 1381.

In his long treatise on the subject of power, *On Civil Dominion* (1375–1376), Wyclif argues that the Church is subject to the Crown, rather than vice versa, since it falls to the state to order secular matters, including all matters of taxation. To begin with, Wyclif maintains that no one can rightly exercise dominion unless he or she is in a state of grace. This argument is, as so often for Wyclif, a logical conclusion from Augustine's view that anyone in a state of sin cannot properly be said to have the use of anything, since he or she is not using the thing for the good. Conversely, those in a state of grace possess lordship of the world – in an ideal world, of course, wherein all people might be lords if all things were held in common. Such arguments lay the ground for circumstances in which the secular authority may deprive the clergy of money and materials. There remains the problem of how to know who is in a state of grace; the uncertainty of this knowledge certainly limits any practical employment of the view, but Wyclif does not here address the issue directly. In making a case for the superior-

Lutterworth Church, to which Wyclif retired after 1381

ity of civil over ecclesiastical authority in matters of taxation and property – the obvious reason for the longest work he wrote – Wyclif expresses another ideal that would become more and more insistent in succeeding works. This is the view that the law of the Gospel is superior to civil or ecclesiastical codes, which of course take shape in a fallen world. The idea is hardly radical, but Wyclif would use it later as a litmus test for rejecting the promulgations of what he saw as a corrupt papacy, in particular, and a generally worldly church. In the text at hand, he lays the ground for a more serious rejection of institutional church authority by defining the church proper as the entire community of those elected to be saved by predestination. These members may decide as a community to redirect their free donations for the poor away from the hands of any fallen clerical agent. Wyclif further outlines the fallibility of the pope and the college of cardinals, especially limiting the power to excommunicate.

With this work Wyclif entered the political scene prominently. On the one hand, John of Gaunt, Duke of Lancaster, the son and leading councillor of Edward III, engaged Wyclif to preach in London on the state's supremacy over the clergy in ordering secular matters and on the worldliness of contemporary bishops. On the other hand, all of the main points of *On Civil Dominion,* having been examined by the pope, resulted in a bull censuring his views and ordering his arrest. It is a testimony to the power of his university and court supporters that the decree was not carried out for a year; by that time Edward III had died, and Richard II was a ten-year-old king in his minority with his uncle Gaunt as regent. The only results of the pope's efforts to curb Wyclif were investigations – in Oxford by university officials and in London by the bishops he opposed – that resulted in no condemnations or penalties. At the inquiry in London he had the support of Gaunt and of the Queen Mother, as well as the sustaining presence of four representatives of the orders of friars, whose ideal of apostolic poverty Wyclif admired. Pope Gregory XI died in 1378, and soon thereafter the Great Schism broke out over who was the true pope – a situation that lasted until the church's Council of Constance (1414–1418), where Wyclif, long dead, was finally condemned by name. At the least the schism confirmed for Wyclif the instability of papal dominion.

His writing over the next few years, while it turned more vitriolic and condemnatory both of the papacy and of clerical possession of worldly goods, included ideas that resulted finally in his retirement from Oxford. During the period from 1378 to 1381 Wyclif, who could number Benedictine monks and the pope – or popes – among his enemies, also alienated the royal councillors and the friars who had hitherto supported him. His two major works of this period are *On the Truth of Sacred Scripture* (1377–1378) and *On the Eucharist* (1380); the former forwarded his view of the ultimate and unquestionable primacy of Scripture; the latter introduced a logical analysis of the sacrament that brought forth condemnation of his teaching.

The precedence Wyclif gives to "scriptura sola" (scripture alone) has sometimes been interpreted simplistically as fundamentalism. The senses of the Word and of the letter, however, offered in *On the Truth of Sacred Scripture* suggest greater complexity than a simple reliance on a clear and apparent literal meaning. That was only one of the senses of Scripture understood by Wyclif. In Wyclif's view Scripture resides not only in the words on the page, the codex, but in an aggregate of the words and a devout understanding; to this interpretive effort the writings of the early Fathers of the Church are useful supplements. He stresses that one needs to learn the logic of the Bible, not the arguments of sophists. Throughout the work Wyclif rails against such enemies of the truth of Scripture, whether real or rhetorical inventions, and continues the invective against fallen clergy that he began in earlier works. He defends the inerrancy and truth of Scripture at great length; having established its primacy in the life of the Christian, he goes on to argue that it must be made available to all Christians, male and female, clergy and laity, in whatever language they speak. (All languages, he argues elsewhere, being of human origin, are all distant from the true Word and are of equal value for communicating it.) The study of Scripture makes a true priest, and priests and bishops, who should study it especially, must preach on it. The tone of the work is urgent, and Wyclif is much concerned with addressing the shortcomings of the contemporary clergy. Correlative with his idealistic projection of common property holding in *On Civil Dominion,* Wyclif imagines all the faithful who study Scripture as priests. He comes close to placing the book in the hands of the laity in order to emphasize priestly preaching and teaching.

The importance of Scripture expressed in this treatise seems a logical outgrowth of the great biblical commentary completed a few years earlier. At the same time, the critical reformative attitude points the way to Wyclif's ecclesiology, an idea of the church that informs two works immediately following *On the Truth of Sacred Scripture – On the Church* (1378–1379) and *On the Power of the Pope* (1379). The rigorous definition of the true Church as including only those predestined to be saved dominates both texts; the idea may stem from the opening lines of *On Dominion,* in which Wyclif states that only those in a state of grace may properly exercise the use of anything. The correlative is that those not in a state of grace, such as bad priests, may be rightfully deprived of the use of the faithful's donations. The prerogative given to secular rulers in *On Civil Dominion* is enlarged in a companion work, *On the Office of King* (1379). These definitions of the true Church and of righteous dominion, taken to logical ends in circumstances of priestly corruption, undermine the role of the institutional church. Knowing who is in a state of grace seems no longer at issue; it is easier and more urgent to act against (or to ignore) those who are, in his view, clearly not in such a state. By the time that Wyclif wrote about the power of the pope, his doubts include not only individual popes such as Gregory XI and Urban VI, but the very office of the papacy, for which he cannot find scriptural support. As in his exclusive and noninstitutional definitions of church and of priests, Wyclif defines the true pope of the Church as he who lives in the most holy manner. He argues that it falls to the king – who should be obeyed no matter what his character – to order the contemporaneous chaos of papal dispensation and to reform the Church.

None of Wyclif's ideas, expressed however critically, effected a break with church doctrine before his treatise *On the Eucharist* (1380). Here in no uncertain terms he rejects explanations, though not the teaching, of transubstantiation, which address Christ's real presence in the Eucharist. Different teachings and challenges concerning transubstantiation coexisted throughout the thirteenth and most of the fourteenth centuries, developed thoroughly in the theologies of mendicants, or friars, such as the Dominican Thomas Aquinas, and the Franciscans Bonaventure and John Duns Scotus. But the absolutist tenor of Wyclif's objections occasioned the condemnation of his views. His teaching lost him the protection of Gaunt and the court, as well as the allegiance of the friars, whom he had already begun to attack; they took Wyclif's correction of fraternal theologians badly. The importance of the topic is evident from five other, shorter treatises on the subject; it became a new touchstone of faith for him.

Wyclif objects to the explanation of transubstantiation on philosophical as well as spiritual and theological grounds. Based on his realist views of being, which he had expressed more than twenty years earlier, he believes that matter cannot be destroyed and rejects the argument that in transubstantiation the substance of the bread is annihilated. Being, maintains Wyclif, cannot be destroyed, since all being in reality lies in God. Thus the idea of annihilation is even impossible for God, according to Wyclif.

The argument of annihilation was not part of every explanation of transubstantiation, but every such account included the premise that the substance of the bread was at least absent. Such a state of things made no sense to Wyclif, for he could not see how the consecrated host could maintain all the characteristics of bread, called accidents, if the substance of bread was now gone in the change to Christ's body. Assigning the phenomenon to God's omnipotence, according to one explanation, made God appear to Wyclif as a kind of trickster. While never denying Christ's real presence in the host bread, Wyclif disputes the nature of that presence, primarily by attacking the absence of the substance of bread itself. If accidents can exist alone without a present substance, one's senses cannot truly identify anything nor affirm its existence, and one is left with a world of sensory appearances. The question of just which accident underlies the host invites

Wyclif's satirical treatment of some historical and some straw-man explanations. Among them is the unattested one that the essence lies in the host's characteristic of "whiteness" – but this, he says, is a belief held in the Welsh mountains and in Ireland, where people say they see the dead. The tenor of most of the treatise, however, is a good deal more dour and condemnatory of the current ills in the institutional church. Wyclif's own explanation for Christ's presence is that he is in the host spiritually, though not in his own body, through the sacramental transformation enacted in consecration, even while the substance of the bread also remains.

On long-maintained philosophical grounds, then, Wyclif might have voiced this critique of transubstantiation at any point in the previous decades. The explanation of why he did not may lie in his unwillingness to contradict the institutional church on this important, if still controversial, teaching while he retained some respect for the church's authority. His great disaffection with the papacy and with institutional church authority is apparent, however, from his writings in 1378 and 1379. Thus his other objections to transubstantiation are theological: bad priests could consecrate the host and gull the people. More properly, these works argue, holiness, not office, was the prerequisite for clerical status. Thus devout lay people had more right to perform consecration than bad priests. Moreover, no scriptural precedent could be found for the various explanations. It must be added that Wyclif's explanation for Christ's spiritual presence in the host reduces the efficacy of the priest, who is not now changing the substance of bread in consecration but effecting a sacramental sign.

By this time in 1380 the university did not hesitate to act against Wyclif, fearing perhaps that the academic freedom of the whole corporation would be threatened if he were allowed to teach his ideas on the Eucharist. A commission appointed by the chancellor of the university condemned Wyclif's arguments that the substances of bread and wine remained after consecration and that Christ was not bodily present in the sacrament. The findings of the commission, which decided the issues by a vote of only seven to five – so Wyclif himself reports – were read out to him as he sat disputing with students. No one was to teach these ideas, the commission ordered. Wyclif's subsequent efforts to defend himself in writing, and by appealing to the court of Richard II, were of no avail.

It did not help matters that early in the spring of 1381 common men rose against taxation, killing Sudbury, archbishop of Canterbury, burning John of Gaunt's residence, and murdering many Flemings, who were accused of ruining the cloth trade. According to chroniclers writing after Wyclif's death, one of the leaders, John Ball, was supposedly a student of Wyclif's ideas. This claim is questionable, but it may have been circulated in 1381 to associate Wyclif with the rebels. Silenced within the university on issues of great importance to him, Wyclif left Oxford for Lutterworth.

Immediately after the rising, Sudbury's successor Archbishop William Courtenay worked for further sanctions against Wyclif's ideas, now promulgated at Oxford by men such as Nicholas Hereford and Philip Repton. In London, Courtenay convened a group of theologians, half of whom held Wyclif's rank of doctor and who were also mostly friars. This group condemned a list of twenty-four items, judging ten as heretical and fourteen as erroneous. Their meetings at Blackfriars in London were interrupted by an earth tremor, and Wyclif called the proceedings the "Earthquake Council," seeing God's hand at work against his enemies. It is important to note that the condemnations in London were much broader than those at Oxford, which spoke only to Wyclif's teachings on the Eucharist. Those ideas were condemned in London as well, but the Blackfriars council included items relating to Wyclif's limitation of papal and clerical prerogative, clerical possession of worldly goods, and the sinfulness of the religious orders, as well as the view that no one could exercise dominion if not in a state of grace. The findings of the council were clearly influenced by the loyalties of its members and by fears stemming from the recent insurrection. Strikingly, Wyclif was not named in the council's decrees, to which the university was forced to capitulate.

The condemnation of Wyclif's leading ideas at Oxford and London did nothing to stop his pen – nor was he further harassed at Lutterworth, where he was probably helped by a secretary, John Purvey, following a stroke in 1382. Besides editing his sermons, which are in many parts free of the argumentative tone and content of his theological treatises, Wyclif summarized his ideas in the *Trialogus,* and he reiterated his attacks on clerical corruption, attacks that included every variety of clergy in texts such as *On Simony.* Wyclif was particularly relentless with regard to the friars, whom he saw as leading the final attacks on him at Oxford and London; he vilified them for falling away from the ideals of their founders such as Francis and Dominic. Typical of his writing style in this period are the acrimonious acronyms he devises. The orders of the friars

Wyclif's monument at Lutterworth (illustration from Lewis Sargent, John Wyclif: Last of the Schoolmen and First of the English Reformers, *1893)*

are to be associated with Cain (*Caim* in Latin), he says, from the initials of each of the four orders: *C*armelites, *A*ugustinians, *I*acobites (for Dominicans), and *M*inorites (for Franciscans). The correspondence Wyclif finds here, however speciously and satirically, suggests in a sense his understanding of how this world and its words may be read as reflecting a higher reality.

Wyclif suffered a second stroke on 28 December 1384; he died on the last day of the year. At the international church's Council of Constance that concluded in 1418, Hus was burned at the stake, Wyclif's ideas were broadly condemned, and his bones were ordered exhumed and likewise burned, according to the penalty for heretics. Philip Repton, the bishop of the diocese including Lutterworth who first received such orders, had once been an adherent of Wyclif. His recantation paved the way to a successful career in the church, but apparently he could not bring himself to carry out the promulgations of Constance. A long ten years later these orders were effected by Bishop Richard Fleming, and Wyclif's ashes were thrown into a stream near Lutterworth.

It is difficult to judge Wyclif's character and motivations. His writings suggest someone tenacious and tendentious, colorful and temperamental.

If he intended a career at the royal or papal court, he would not seem to have made a diplomatic presence, though he clearly impressed his contemporaries as a teacher and a scholar. His intentions also remain unclear: did he advocate holy laity over corrupt clergy mainly in order to spur the latter to reform? Or did he intend a reformation so radical that, among many other changes, absentee clergy such as he would be removed from places of privileged study by a new and potentially broad priesthood of devout laity? Modern students cannot have clear answers to such speculations.

The near-contemporary monastic chroniclers are, not surprisingly, severely condemnatory in their accounts of him, linking Wyclif to the Rising of 1381 and naming him as the translator of the Bible; neither of these attributions has good foundations, though his impetus may be felt behind the translation effort. The vehemence with which Wyclif himself attacked his enemies, whether "modern" logicians, monks, friars, or the pope, probably contributed to the bitter judgment of him by others. It is fairly representative that in one sermon he refers to an inimical monk as a "canis niger" (black dog) and calls his adherents "barking whelps." An entry in the *Vetus catalogus* (Old Catalogue), com-

The *Alliterative Morte Arthure* and the *Stanzaic Morte Arthur*

(circa 1350 – 1400)

R. A. Shoaf
University of Florida

Alliterative Morte Arthure (circa 1400)

Manuscript: The only extant copy is the Thornton Manuscript (Lincoln Cathedral Library MS. 91 [4,346 lines]) which was compiled circa 1440. Facsimile: *The Thornton Manuscript (Lincoln Cathedral MS. 91)*, with an introduction by D. S. Brewer and A. E. Owen (London: Scolar Press, 1975; revised edition, 1977).

First publication: *Morte Arthure: The Alliterative Romance of the Death of King Arthur,* edited by James O. Halliwell (Brixton Hill: Privately printed, 1847).

Standard editions: *King Arthur's Death: The Middle English "Stanzaic Morte Arthur" and "Alliterative Morte Arthure,"* edited by Larry D. Benson (Indianapolis: Bobbs-Merrill, 1974); *The Alliterative Morte Arthure,* edited by Valerie Krishna (New York: Burt Franklin, 1976); *Morte Arthure: A Critical Edition,* edited by Mary Hamel (New York: Garland, 1984).

Editions in modern English: *The Alliterative Morte Arthure: A New Verse Translation,* translated by Valerie Krishna (Lanham, Md.: University Press of America, 1983); in *King Arthur's Death,* translated by Brian Stone (Harmondsworth: Penguin, 1988).

Stanzaic Morte Arthur (circa 1350–1400)

Manuscript: The only extant copy is British Library MS. Harley 2252 (3,969 lines); the poem occupies fols. 86–133. The manuscript was compiled in the early sixteenth century, but these folios can be dated to the period between 1460 and 1480.

First publication: In George Ellis, *Specimens of Early English Metrical Romances,* 3 volumes (London: Longman, Hurst, Rees & Orme, 1805); republished, edited by James O. Halliwell (London: Bohn, 1848), pp. 154–187.

Standard editions: *King Arthur's Death: The Middle English "Stanzaic Morte Arthur" and "Alliterative Morte Arthure,"* edited by Larry D. Benson (Indianapolis: Bobbs-Merrill, 1974); *Le Morte Arthur: A Critical Edition,* edited by P. F. Hissiger (The Hague: Mouton, 1975).

Editions in modern English: *The Stanzaic "Morte": A Verse Translation of "Le Morte Arthur,"* translated by Sharon Kahn (Lanham, Md.: University Press of America, 1986); in *King Arthur's Death,* translated by Brian Stone (Harmondsworth, U.K.: Penguin, 1988).

Anonymous works of literature frustrate modern readers, who have a natural desire to know who wrote influential stories and poems. This is especially true of the *Alliterative Morte Arthure* (circa 1400) and the *Stanzaic Morte Arthur* (circa 1350–1400) since they are both poems that mattered a good deal to another reader, Sir Thomas Malory. He uses them extensively in his version of the Arthurian legends – the former in the "Noble Tale of King Arthur and the Emperor Lucius" (book 5 in Caxton's edition), the latter in "The Tale of Lancelot and Guinevere" and "The Morte Arthur Saunz Guerdon" (Caxton's books 18–21). Scholars would obviously like to know who wrote these poems that figure so significantly in one of the most important and enduring monuments of English literary history.

And yet not only do they not know who wrote them, they are also unsure as to when or where they were written. The *Stanzaic Morte Arthur,* which survives in only one manuscript, was probably written about the middle of the fourteenth century (but possibly as late as 1400) in the north Midlands; the surviving manuscript was copied by two different scribes writing in two different dialects (neither the same as the poet's) somewhere toward the end of the fifteenth century.

The *Alliterative Morte Arthure* also survives in only one manuscript, which was copied about 1441 (but possibly, as Mary Hamel conjectures in a 1990 essay, as early as the 1420s) by Robert Thornton (a Yorkshireman); to be sure, there is a prose version of the poem in the Winchester Manuscript of Malory's work, but it still remains most accurate to speak of only one manuscript of the poem. The poem itself was written around 1400, possibly in the west Midlands, although there is a strong case to be made for a provenance in the east or northeast Midlands — "it is not implausible, finally, that the poet was a Lincolnshire man," concludes Hamel. At one time, the author was thought to be a northerner named "Huchown of the Aule Ryale," following the attribution of the chronicler Andrew of Wyntoun, but this ascription is no longer taken seriously. Both Larry D. Benson (1976) and Hamel have argued for a date roughly between 1398 and 1402, with 1402 as a strong preference. Neither argument can be considered conclusive, though both are interesting.

The language of both poems is Middle English of the non-Chaucerian sort — that is, northern, not southern, English of the fourteenth century. In appearance this language resembles Old English more than it does Chaucer's English, and therefore it often strikes modern readers as more difficult than Chaucer's, especially in *The Canterbury Tales* (circa 1375–1400); it is, however, less difficult than it appears and is as Middle English as Chaucer's language is. Recently translations or "modernizations" of both poems have appeared, and each provides a helpful introduction to the poem with an extensive summary of its plot.

The most distinctive feature of both poems, alliteration, is intimately connected with their northern origin. The *Alliterative Morte Arthure,* considered a monument of the so-called Alliterative Revival, is actually composed in the alliterative mode, although it is perhaps distinctive in that mode for its use of alliterative groups larger than the traditional pairs, comprising from three to ten lines linked by alliteration. The *Stanzaic Morte Arthur,* though composed in a form much more obviously of French or Romance origin, still makes extensive use of alliteration — in nearly half of its lines, in fact. Given the eight-line stanza with four-stress lines, rhyme scheme *abababab,* and a largely iambic beat, so much alliteration attests to the dominance of this tradition over a poet

from the north even when he is working with romance forms.

The Alliterative Revival represents a complex scholarly problem. Already resolved in the phrase is an opinion of supposed obsolescence, at some point, followed by rejuvenation at a later point. The phrase assumes that the Old English tradition of alliterative poetry died down, presumably because of and in the years after the Norman Conquest, but did not ever completely die out, especially in the north, the region further removed from Norman influence, where, eventually, interest in the tradition (presumably preserved orally) led to its gradual revival, the late fourteenth century proving to be the period of maximum florescence (with, for example, the works of the *Gawain*-Poet and William Langland's *Piers Plowman*). Among the assumptions of the phrase, then, is one of minimum continuity between the Old English period and the fourteenth century. This may well be correct; it is also possible, however, that there was never a "revival," that there was greater continuity than the phrase *Alliterative Revival* allows, and that, in short, poems like the *Alliterative Morte Arthure* and *Sir Gawain and the Green Knight* emerge from an unbroken, if only partially recorded, tradition of alliterative poetry in English extending from before the conquest to the end of the Middle Ages. Scholars will probably never know for sure which is the case; and commentary, therefore, on such matters as sources, influences, audience, transmission, and so on, must remain tentative and qualified.

In particular, the question of audience remains and apparently must remain vexed. Scholarly consensus favors the opinion that the primary audience and hence patrons of alliterative poetry in the fourteenth century were the lesser nobility or landed gentry of the north Midlands. Hamel, basically in agreement with this opinion, refines it by suggesting that: "the less exalted members of the magnatial staff and retinue would have been a sizable and appropriate audience . . . men . . . of essentially the same class as the country gentry and minor clergy who are later known to have possessed copies of the alliterative poems — men, one infers, of the poet's own class." However, the consensus, it must be remembered, is based on incomplete evidence and a good deal of inference because the origins of the Alliterative Revival remain shrouded in darkness.

Similarly speculative and inferential are our tentative conclusions about the immediate historical contexts of the *Alliterative Morte Arthure* and the *Stanzaic Morte Arthur.* This issue is much more relevant to the former since it in some ways gives the appearance of being a roman à clef – in effect, a barely concealed commentary on the reign of Edward III that finally judges that reign harshly. Certainly much about the reign of Edward III could contribute to such a judgment: the Hundred Years' War, the ravages of the Black Plague, the economic crises resulting from the plague, baronial unrest at perceived corrupt influences on Edward in the court in his later years, and so forth. However, to attempt to decode the poem as a systematic *à clef* reference to any of these matters is, as most recent scholarship on the poem recognizes, to distort it seriously, the more so in that our uncertainty about the date of the poem renders any such decoding suspect from the start. A moderate approach is probably best: the poem contains episodes and themes generally consonant with historical events between roughly 1340 and 1400, but specific references to a specific event are unlikely and almost impossible to prove conclusively.

At the same time, the *Alliterative Morte Arthure* does contain such episodes and themes, and one of its more important features might be called its "generic compendiousness." Although the exact genre of the work is a matter of considerable dispute, still, within its genre, however defined, it gives comprehensive evidence of many different themes, episodes, images, figures, and ideas. Its compendiousness ranges from what is probably the most famous presentation of the idea of the Nine Worthies in English literature before the Renaissance, to detailed itineraries of pilgrimage routes in medieval Europe, to minutely detailed descriptions of armorial bearings, to accurate reenactments of diplomatic negotiations, to blood-chilling descriptions of battles and the damage done in them to human bodies. Whether or not any or all of this is topical, it does add up to one of the most complete, as well as most relevant, extant poetic representations of late-Middle English chivalric culture.

The *Alliterative Morte Arthure* opens with Arthur secure in his kingdom and successful. Challenged suddenly by Lucius, Emperor of Rome, who demands the ancient tribute owed by Britain, Arthur refuses to pay and sends Lucius's ambassadors back to Rome with a promise of war. Arthur then leaves for France to engage the emperor, appointing Mordred regent in his absence. During the voyage he has the first of two crucial dreams. It involves a fierce contest between a dragon and a bear and obscurely forecasts not only the outcome of the impending war with Lucius but also Arthur's own fate. On landing in France, he learns of the ravages of the giant of Mont-Saint-Michel, whom he attacks and eventually slays, single-handedly.

The poem now turns to the battles between Lucius and Arthur. These involve skirmishes and a main engagement. The first skirmish occurs when Gawain, as an ambassador, approaches Lucius with Arthur's demand that the Romans leave France immediately; fighting breaks out, and Gawain and his comrades are victorious. The second skirmish occurs when Cador is escorting the prisoners from the first skirmish to Paris; ambushed, Cador and his men must fight against great odds and, though Cador is victorious, many of Arthur's best knights perish – Arthur later expresses keen displeasure at Cador's foolhardiness in staying to fight against such odds. Next, the battle with Lucius takes place. Arthur is victorious, Lucius is slain, and Arthur sends the bodies of the slain Romans back to their native city, disdainfully labeling them the tribute Britain owes Rome.

After his victory over Lucius, Arthur decides to attack the duke of Lorraine, who has proved traitor to him. During the siege of Metz, Gawain sets out to forage for supplies and, in an episode that seems lifted directly from romance, encounters a knight, Priamus, whom he overcomes in single combat and who thereupon asks for confession and last rites.

After his conquest of Metz, Arthur determines to conquer all of Italy. He begins his march down the peninsula and wins so many victories that the Romans offer him the imperial crown. At this juncture Arthur has the second of his two dreams, involving a vision of Fortune and her wheel and the Nine Worthies, or greatest heroes of the West. Arthur in fact is one of these Worthies, and he is also one of Fortune's victims in the dream. Arthur's "philosophers" interpret the second dream as a portent of his impending doom and downfall, and, soon thereafter, Arthur meets a British knight on a pilgrimage to Rome who reveals that Mordred has proved traitor, seizing both the Crown of England and Arthur's queen, Guinevere, with whom he has joined in adultery.

Arthur hurriedly returns to Britain in order to avenge himself on Mordred. After a naval battle with some of Mordred's allies, in which Arthur is victorious, Gawain rushes ashore to engage the enemy in yet another skirmish that involves British knights fighting against insurmountable odds. This time Arthur's knights cannot overcome the odds; Gawain is slain by Mordred. Arthur is beside himself with grief, searches out Gawain's body, laments him in one of the most moving scenes of personal grief in Middle English poetry, and then vows not

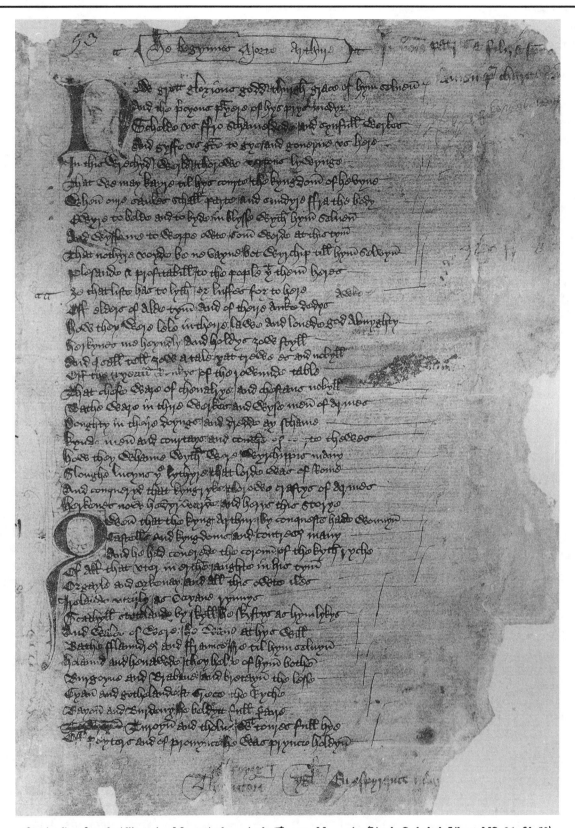

Opening lines from the Alliterative Morte Arthure *in the Thornton Manuscript (Lincoln Cathedral Library MS. 91, fol. 53)*

to rest until Mordred is slain in punishment. The poem then concludes with the final battle between Arthur and Mordred, in which each receives his death wound from the other. Just before he dies Arthur appoints Constantine his successor, and he is then buried in Glastonbury.

Several important features emerge from this summary. First, and most important, is the fundamental change in Arthur's mood and behavior after the defeat of Lucius: whereas before this decisive moment Arthur was a king defending his land and people (note the emphasis on defense of his people also in the episode of the giant of Mont-Saint-Michel), after his defeat of Lucius, Arthur begins to indulge war for the sake of aggression and conquest, culminating in his desire to conquer all of Italy. He moves from a justifiable war of defense to unjustifiable, or at least questionable, acts of aggression. This movement defines a narrative arc which some scholars have identified as tragic: after a fairly consistent rise in success and glory, Arthur experiences a fall, forecast by his second dream, which leads eventually to the loss of his country, his most beloved knight, and finally his life.

The second noteworthy feature of the poem follows directly from the first. For the Middle Ages, the king's career most nearly resembling the career of Arthur is that of David, King of the Jews; and, as most scholars observe, there is an obvious parallel between, on the one hand, David and Goliath, and, on the other, Arthur and the giant of Mont-Saint-Michel – this parallel serves to reinforce the assimilation of Arthur's rise and fall to David's rise and fall. Arthur, like David, is a great king who is nonetheless flawed (by overweening aggressiveness) and who suffers for his flaw.

The parallel between Arthur and David further suggests that the *Alliterative Morte Arthure* is concerned not just with the story of a famous king but also with the nature and duties and liabilities of kingship. This in turn justifies the common scholarly speculation that the poem is a kind of *Fürstenspiegel* (mirror for princes), a very popular and important genre of the later Middle Ages in which a counselor attempts to provide guidance for the education and training of a king. The possible relation between the *Alliterative Morte Arthure* and the *Fürstenspiegel* also coheres with the generally accepted notion that the former aligns much more with the chronicle tradition of the Arthurian matter than with the romance tradition: both the mirrors for princes

and the *Alliterative Morte Arthure*, like the chronicle tradition (descending ultimately from Geoffrey of Monmouth's *Historia regum Britanniae*, circa 1138), emphasize the dealings of chivalric life more than the fantastic adventures and amorous encounters of the romance tradition (though the Priamus episode chastens any global assumption that the *Alliterative Morte Arthure* is strictly chroniclelike, and there is crossover between both the chronicle and the romance traditions).

These comments lead to one last summary observation: all readers of the *Alliterative Morte Arthure* note its remarkable, even astounding, descriptions of battle and the bloody results of it. They are some of the most vivid and arresting descriptions in the whole poem. These descriptions, and numerous other tendencies of the poem that emphasize "realistic" (for want of a better word) details, suggest that the work is as much a cultural archive as it is a version of a traditional story. In other words, the poem not only tells a story; it also archives a complex set of cultural codes, manners, procedures, dress, and ritual activities.

A concrete sense of the *Alliterative Morte Arthure*, its tone and sweep and thematics, may best be collected, briefly, by concentrating on two passages in particular: part of Arthur's lament over the fallen Gawain and Arthur's lament for himself, for his own fallen kingliness. In both passages we encounter the poem's emphasis on what in the older Anglo-Saxon tradition would have been called *ofermode* (in Homeric epic, hubris) and in this poem is called *cirquytrie*, pride or overreaching of the limits imposed on human beings:

"Freke," sais the philosophre . . .
"Thow has schedde myche blode   and schalkes distroyede,
Sakeles, in cirquytrie,   in sere kynges landis.
Schryfe the of thy schame   and schape for thyn ende!"

In identifying *cirquytrie* as the recurrent failing of Arthur and his knights – as in the numerous instances of a British soldier or group of soldiers fighting recklessly against overwhelming odds – the poem by no means lapses into sermonizing; but it does describe an ethic, complex and subtle but palpable, of self-knowledge as self-restraint, in the breach of which ruin is inevitable.

In his long and poignant lament over Gawain's corpse, Arthur, though advised by his loyal knights to relent ("þis es botles bale"), resolutely refuses:

"For blode," said the bolde kynge   "blinn sall I neuer,
....
Was neuer so sorowfull a syghte   seyn with myne
    eyghen!
He es sakles, supprysede   for syn of myn one!"

In assuming full guilt for Gawain's death, Arthur begins to acknowledge not only that he has erred, but that his error has been contagious: he is, after all, *the* model for his knights; he is king (in part) because they want to imitate him. Hence, if various of them undertake fights against seemingly insurmountable odds, they only do as their king has already done in undertaking to refuse Lucius the tribute and to carry the battle directly to him and his empire. Arthur's *cirquytrie* is, at least in part, just this desire for overwhelming odds (he fights the monstrous giant of Mont-Saint-Michel *alone*).

There is, then, a certain compelling if also sobering appropriateness about the terms and images in which Arthur laments his own doom and ultimate defeat:

"Kyng comly with crowne,   in care am I leuyde!
All my lordchipe lawe   in lande es layde vndre,
....
I may helples on hethe   house by myne one,
Alls a wafull wedowe   þat wanttes hir beryne."

Arthur imagines himself at the end alone, helpless as a widow in want of her man. In a sense his tragedy expresses his and his followers' error, the error of *ofermode* or *cirquytrie,* namely, unrestrained singularity or the desire for personal glory. Though the mainstay of his success was the "house" of knights acting in concert, the constant opposing force was his and their desire for singularity, uniqueness, personal glory. And, finally, Arthur could not counter this force, for himself or for his knights (and this, of course, is a constant theme of Arthurian legend in many different versions). Hence, his doom is to "helpless one hethe house by [his] one."

No single perspective on the work can exhaust its thematics, but the view from the angle of perverse singularity probably provides the clearest vision of the poem's sense of the Arthurian (and the poet's own contemporary) worlds. It also helps a good deal to make sense out of a certain ambiguity in the exordium, which has proved somewhat puzzling to critics in the past. Although the exordium is commonplace enough and largely consonant with fourteenth-century mores, it nonetheless hints at strains and flaws in the Arthurian (and, by implication, contemporary) culture:

3e that liste has to lyth   or luffes for to here
Off elders of alde tym   and theire awke dedys,
How they were lele in theire lawe   and louede God
    Almyghty,
Herkynes me heyndly.

Awke is an awkward word: its usual meaning is "perverse" (it derives from an Old Norse word that means "turned the wrong way"). Most scholars prefer the decision of the Oxford English Dictionary and Middle English Dictionary that here, in the *Alliterative Morte Arthure,* however, it means "strange" or "marvelous." Hamel tries to control the sense of the word by arguing that "the poet's introductory summary extends only to line 3217 of the poem.... [his] apparently deliberate avoidance of ominous foreshadowing in introducing his story argues in favor of the ameliorative interpretation of *awke.*" Plausible as this seems, it does not conclusively eliminate the negative tones of *awke* and hence the suggestion that the exordium adumbrates the conflicting interpretations of the "elders ... deeds" – actions of either heroic or reckless *cirquytrie.*

The *Stanzaic Morte Arthur* much more straightforwardly condemns the pride of the Arthurian court (and of Lancelot especially). The plot of the poem is more complex than that of the *Alliterative Morte Arthure,* partly because there are more numerous central protagonists. However, the story is much more familiar to most modern readers because of their familiarity with Malory, especially the conclusion of his work.

The poem opens soon after the events of the quest for the Holy Grail. Arthur, concerned about the effects of that quest on the Round Table and his knights, calls a major tournament at Winchester. When he leaves for Winchester, Lancelot lingers behind, as does Agravayne, who suspects him and Gaynor, Arthur's queen. Finally, Lancelot decides to leave, before any discovery is made.

Lancelot plans to attend the tournament in disguise. He lodges with the Earl of Ascolot, whose daughter quickly falls in love with him. When one of the earl's sons proves too ill to fight, Lancelot fights in his arms, wearing the sleeve of the Maid of Ascolot as a token (although he has insisted that he cannot love her), and defeats all knights who encounter him.

He is, however, sorely wounded and returns to the earl's castle to recuperate. There, hearing that Arthur has called another tournament, he tries to rise to attend it but succeeds only in opening his wound, whereupon he must return to his rest. Arthur, learning of the severity of the mysterious knight's wound, calls off the tournament and returns to Camelot. Not finding Lancelot there, he agrees that Bors, Ector, and Lionel should go in search of him. They find him at the earl's castle, and he tells them that he was the mysterious knight who fought with them and defeated them at the earlier tournament. They are reconciled, and the three knights return to Camelot to inform Arthur that Lancelot will soon return.

Gawain, however, wishes to see Lancelot as soon as possible and sets out in search of him. Arriving at the Earl of Ascolot's castle, he learns that Lancelot has already departed and that he has left his armor behind, in effect, as a gift for the Maid. Gawain returns to Camelot and reports this news, whereupon Gaynor becomes incensed, thinking Lancelot has betrayed her for another. Thus, when Lancelot appears and finds Gaynor enraged, not knowing of Gawain's report, he thinks he has fallen out of Gaynor's favor and departs from Camelot immediately.

His departure proves ominous when Gaynor is implicated in the death of a Scottish knight who perishes by a poisoned apple. She is in peril of dying at the stake unless she can find a champion. With Lancelot away, however, and Arthur and his knights convinced that Gaynor drove him away, she has great difficulty in finding a champion. Her dilemma is compounded by the sudden arrival of a barge carrying the corpse of the fair Maid of Ascolot who has died for unrequited love of Lancelot. With her corpse is a letter in which she explains that Lancelot never returned her love. Gaynor becomes even more forlorn since she now understands that she unfairly drove away the very champion she needs. At long last she is able to persuade Bors to defend her, but finally it becomes unnecessary for him to do so since Lancelot, having heard of her peril, appears to champion her and defeats the knight who has accused her. The real perpetrator of the death by poisoning, a certain squire, is discovered and put to death.

The story now turns to developments that would later figure in the conclusion of Malory's work, "The Morte Arthur Saunz Guerdon." Gawain's brother, Agravayne, is determined to expose Lancelot and Gaynor, although Gawain and his other brothers counsel against this. Nonetheless, he catches Lancelot in Gaynor's chamber, where Lancelot, defending himself, slays Agravayne and all his companions except Mordred, who survives to tell Arthur what has happened. With Lancelot in flight, Gaynor is condemned to burn at the stake. Lancelot returns for her, however, and in saving her from the stake, accidentally kills Gawain's brothers, Gaheriet and Gaheris.

Gawain now turns against Lancelot, implacable in his desire for revenge. He and Arthur attack Lancelot, who defeats them. The pope, hearing of the internecine strife in England, commands an end to it, else he will put the whole kingdom under interdict. Arthur and Lancelot agree to a peace, and Lancelot returns Gaynor to Arthur; but Gawain refuses any reconciliation, and Lancelot is forced to leave Britain for his own Benwick.

There Arthur and Gawain assault him again, laying waste to his lands and harming his people. Lancelot, ever courteous, attempts to reach a truce, but again Gawain will have none of it. In fact, he challenges all of Lancelot's people to single combat and wounds or slays many of them. Finally, he challenges Lancelot, calling him a coward; Lancelot can no longer endure such insults and agrees to fight him. Eventually, Lancelot inflicts a terrible wound on Gawain's head that he soon reopens in another single combat. After healing, Gawain prepares to meet Lancelot yet again, but word reaches Arthur's camp that Mordred has usurped the throne in Britain and declared his intent to marry Gaynor.

Arthur and Gawain hasten back to engage Mordred and forestall further treason (Gaynor has already fled). Mordred's and Arthur's forces meet in battle, first at Dover, then at Barlam Downs; on both occasions Arthur is victorious, but in the second battle Mordred slays Gawain, striking him on the wound Lancelot had given him. Having agreed on a date to meet Mordred in battle again, Arthur has two dreams the night before, the first a dream of Fortune's wheel, the second a dream in which Gawain appears to him and warns him against immediate battle with Mordred, urging him to wait until Lancelot can arrive. Obeying Gawain's suggestions in the dream, Arthur seeks a truce with Mordred. They agree to meet, each with fourteen knights, to discuss it.

At this meeting, however, a knight draws his sword to kill an adder that has struck him, and the assembled hosts, seeing the sword, construe it as an attack and set about full-scale hostilities. It proves to be the last battle: countless men die, including Mordred, though not before he has given Arthur his death blow. Knowing he is dying, Arthur gives Excalibur to Bedivere, with instructions for its disposal. When eventually Bedivere casts it into the lake, a hand mysteriously rises from the depths to grasp it. Arthur is subsequently carried away on a ship piloted by ladies, to be healed in Avalon.

Alone, Bedivere comes upon a chapel the next day where he learns that a body was brought the night before for burial. He realizes that it is Arthur and decides to stay and pray for his king. Gaynor, having learned of Arthur's death, has entered a monastery; Lancelot later follows her lead and finishes his life in a monastery, praying and repenting of his sins. Several years later Lancelot dies and is buried at Joyous Gard. At about the same time, Gaynor dies and is buried beside Arthur in Glastonbury Abbey.

The author of the *Stanzaic Morte Arthur* is not only a translator of his French source, the *Mort Artu* (circa 1215–1235), but also an abbreviator; he significantly reduces the length of the French work and in the process also renders it less philosophic and didactic. In particular, he seeks explanations for events and their consequences in human motives and behavior. For example, he carefully emphasizes the role of pride in the Arthurian world, and especially in Lancelot. Although he never sermonizes, he periodically mentions the court's pride or this or that knight's pride and refers to Lancelot's on enough occasions to suggest that, if Lancelot is the best knight in the world, even the best knight in the world is not immune to the desire for self to the exclusion of others.

Again, in the character of Gawain, the poet searches the human motive precipitating eventful behavior. As A. V. C. Schmidt and Nicolas Jacobs observe, after Lancelot slays his brothers, "the change in Gawain can be interpreted as a relapse from the quality of *corteisé* which Bors discerned in Lancelot . . . to the ethic of the earlier 'heroic' stage of society, in which revenge of slain kinsmen . . . constituted the paramount claim upon a man." Gawain gives in utterly to the desire for revenge and becomes ultimately the victim of that desire.

The poet's interest in human motives, finally, partly explains his addition of the episode near the end of the poem of Lancelot and Gaynor's last meeting with each other. This episode appears to originate with the *Stanzaic Morte Arthur*. It is a powerful scene, and the effect clearly arises from the poet's emphasis on the humanness of Lancelot and Gaynor, both their capacity for greatness and their susceptibility to error; the latter, in particular, is acknowledged poignantly in the scene when Gaynor refuses to kiss Lancelot one last time before his final departure:

> "Nay," sayd the quene, "the wyll I not.
> Launcelot, thynke on that no more;
> To absteyne us we muste have thought
> For suche we have delyted in ore.
> . . . .
> Thynke on thys world how there is noght
> But warre and stryffe and batayle sore."

Both the *Alliterative Morte Arthure* and the *Stanzaic Morte Arthur* remain of interest and appeal to modern readers. Moreover, the former is by common consent one of the most important poems in fourteenth-century English literature, ranked usually only slightly behind *Sir Gawain and the Green Knight* in overall artistic excellence and achievement. Both poems will continue to appeal to modern readers, despite their occasional difficulties, because they reach so near to that contradictoriness between the human and the ideal which indelibly marks representation of character in the Arthurian legend and which Alfred Tennyson perhaps expresses best in his analysis of Lancelot from *Idylls of the King* (1842): "His honour rooted in dishonour stood, / And faith unfaithful kept him falsely true."

Bibliography:

Michael Foley, "The Alliterative *Morte Arthure*: An Annotated Bibliography, 1950–1975," *Chaucer Review,* 14 (1979): 166–187.

References:

W. R. J. Barron, *English Medieval Romance* (London: Longman, 1987), pp. 138–147;

Larry D. Benson, "The Date of the Alliterative *Morte Arthure*," in *Medieval Studies Presented in Honor of Lillian Herlands Hornstein,* edited by Jess B. Bessinger, Jr., and Robert K. Raymo (New York: New York University Press, 1976), pp. 20–29;

Karl Heinz Göller, ed., *The "Alliterative Morte Arthure": A Reassessment of the Poem* (Cambridge: D. S. Brewer, 1981);

Mary Hamel, "Adventure as Structure in the Alliterative *Morte Arthure*," *Arthurian Interpretations,* 3 (Fall 1988): 37–48;

Hamel, "Arthurian Romance in Fifteenth-Century Lindsey: The Books of the Lords Welles," *Modern Language Quarterly,* 51 (September 1990): 341–361;

David Lawton, ed., *Middle English Alliterative Poetry and its Literary Background: Seven Essays* (Woodbridge: Boydell & Brewer, 1982);

Angus McIntosh, "The Textual Transmission of the Alliterative *Morte Arthure*," in *English and*

Medieval Studies Presented to J. R. R. Tolkien, edited by Norman Davis and C. L. Wrenn (London: Allen & Unwin, 1962), pp. 231–240;

William Matthews, *The Ill-Framed Knight: A Skeptical Inquiry into the Identity of Sir Thomas Malory* (Berkeley: University of California Press, 1966), pp. 213–221;

Matthews, *The Tragedy of Arthur: A Study of the Alliterative "Morte Arthure"* (Berkeley: University of California Press, 1960);

Lee Patterson, "The Romance of History and the Alliterative *Morte Arthure,*" in his *Negotiating the Past: The Historical Understanding of Medieval Literature* (Madison: University of Wisconsin Press, 1987), pp. 197–230;

Russell A. Peck, "Willfulness and Wonders: Boethian Tragedy in the Alliterative *Morte Arthure,*" in *The Alliterative Tradition in the Fourteenth Century,* edited by Bernard S. Levy and Paul E. Szarmach (Kent, Ohio: Kent State University Press, 1981);

A. V. C. Schmidt and Nicolas Jacobs, *Medieval English Romances, Part Two* (London: Hodder & Stoughton, 1980);

R. A. Shoaf, "The Alliterative *Morte Arthure:* The Story of Britain's David," *Journal of English and Germanic Philology,* 81 (April 1982): 204–226;

John J. Thompson, "The Compiler in Action: Robert Thornton and the 'Thornton Romances' in Lincoln Cathedral MS. 91," in *Manuscripts and Readers in Fifteenth-Century England: The Literary Implications of Manuscript Study,* edited by Derek Pearsall (Woodbridge: Boydell & Brewer, 1983), pp. 113–124;

Thorlac Turville-Petre, *The Alliterative Revival* (Cambridge: Cambridge University Press, 1977).

Ancrene Riwle

(circa 1200 – 1225)

Nancy Coiner
Middlebury College

Manuscripts: There are eight manuscripts in English, two in French, and four in Latin, as well as some manuscript fragments. Of the manuscripts in English, the most important are the five copied in the thirteenth century: Corpus Christi College, Cambridge, MS. 402; British Library, MS. Cotton Cleopatra C. vi; Caius College, Cambridge, MS. 234; British Library, MS. Cotton Nero. A. xiv; British Library, MS. Cotton Titus D. xviii. There are also two complete fourteenth-century manuscripts in English: the Vernon MS. in the Bodleian Library and Pepys MS. 2498 at Magdalene College, Cambridge.

First publication: *The Ancren Riwle,* edited by James Morton (London: Camden Society, 1853).

Standard editions: *The English Text of the Ancrene Riwle,* edited by Mabel Day, EETS, 225 (1952); *The English Text of the Ancrene Riwle,* edited by J. R. R. Tolkien, EETS, 249 (1962); *The English Text of the Ancrene Riwle,* edited by E. J. Dobson, EETS, 267 (1972).

Editions in modern English: *The Ancrene Riwle,* translated by M. B. Salu (Notre Dame, Ind.: University of Notre Dame Press, 1956); *Anchoritic Spirituality: Ancrene Wisse and Associated Works,* translated by Anne Savage and Nicholas Watson (New York: Paulist Press, 1991).

The *Ancrene Riwle* (Rule for Anchoresses), or *Ancrene Wisse* (Guide for Anchoresses), was originally composed by an anonymous cleric sometime in the early thirteenth century for three sisters who had chosen to live solitary religious lives. As various manuscripts were copied and even translated into other languages, the *Ancrene Riwle* was read by ever-expanding groups of anchoresses and eventually laypeople in England. Though arguments have been made for the priority of the Latin or French versions of the *Ancrene Riwle,* James Morton's contention in his 1853 edition that it was originally composed in English has been borne out by recent work on manuscript affiliations.

Written in a rhythmic, alliterative prose, the *Ancrene Riwle* is notable for its simplicity and informality of style, for its intimacy of tone, and for its densely packed structures of imagery. In the context of its time the *Ancrene Riwle* takes a radically new approach to the idea of a "rule" governing religious life: it emphasizes an "inner rule," the right ruling of the unruly heart, over an "outer rule" prescribing diet, dress, and the daily round of devotions. For a modern audience the *Ancrene Riwle* is rich in details of the daily life and temptations of female recluses in early medieval England. In general, the work presents readers with a complex understanding of a rich, interior religious life, as the author integrates everyday experience with abstract religious precepts at a high level of psychological and literary sophistication.

Nothing certain is known about the identity of the author or audience of the *Ancrene Riwle* except through the internal evidence offered in the work itself. The best and earliest manuscripts derive from the early thirteenth century, probably from between 1220 and 1230; their dialect is that of the southern and western Midlands, probably that of Herefordshire. In *The Origins of the Ancrene Wisse* (1976) E. J. Dobson argues that it was composed at Wigmore, an abbey of the Victorine congregation of Augustinian secular canons located along the Welsh Marches. The earliest manuscripts are linked to Wigmore Abbey and are in a remarkably consistent dialect known as the AB dialect (also the dialect of another important group of early Middle English texts, the "*Katherine*-group" which includes *Hali Maidenhed*).

While the *Ancrene Riwle* might have been written any time after about 1200 (because one source stems from 1197), and though many of the author's intellectual interests stem more from the late twelfth century than from the early thirteenth, Dobson suggests a date after the Lateran Decrees of 1215, which not only mandated regular, annual attendance at mass, but also emphasized the need for frequent and thorough confession of sins. This date suits the iconography of the text, its advanced liturgical practices, and its concern with confession and penance. After composing the original version, the author of the *Ancrene Riwle* may have revised and copied the text again for other groups of readers. Dobson speculates somewhat tentatively that the Cleopatra manuscript includes revisions and additions in the author's own hand and that the Corpus Christi manuscript represents an even later state of revision by the author: the uniformity of language of the early-thirteenth-century manuscripts does suggest that they were composed and copied locally, perhaps under supervision of the author.

The relatively large number of manuscripts of the *Ancrene Riwle* testifies to its popularity and adaptability, as do the passages quoted from it in later Middle English religious works. It is quoted in such fourteenth-century texts as *Chastising of God's Children, Gratia Dei, Adam and Eve,* and *The Poor Caitiff* and even in the fifteenth-century *Treatise of Love.* It may also have influenced the allegories and visions of Julian of Norwich's visionary *Showings of Divine Love* (circa 1373–1393).

The author's use of quotations and sources reveals that he was a cleric well versed in Scripture and the writings of the church fathers. He addresses his audience as three young "well-bred women . . . sought after by many for your goodness and generosity, and sisters of one father and one mother" (translation by Anne Savage and Nicholas Watson in their *Anchoritic Spirituality: Ancrene Wisse and Associated Works,* 1991) who have already taken up the life of religious recluses and who have requested that he write them a rule. Dobson places the anchorhold of the original three sisters near Wigmore Abbey, at either Deerfold or at Limebrook Priory, where contemporary documents attest that groups of religious sisters lived; he further speculates that the author was their brother, Brian of Lingen, a canon of Wigmore Abbey, who also may have been their spiritual director and who may have supervised and edited later copies of the *Ancrene Riwle.*

The author has sometimes been described as a benevolent and tolerant older man, and frequently anthologized passages support this view. He allows the anchoresses to keep a cat; he recommends that they not wear penitential garments of hair, iron, or hedgehog skin; he advises that they rest for three days after a bloodletting and do nothing more strenuous than exchange edifying tales with their maidservants. Yet the regimen of prayer he prescribes is severe. He offhandedly assumes that the anchoress will discipline herself physically at least on the fifteen occasions each year when she prepares to take communion, and he puts heavy restrictions on the anchoress's speaking and eating with others, even with visiting religious men or with her servant. Despite the austerity of the life recommended by the author, his tone of personal warmth is noteworthy.

There were several ways to take up the religious life in England in the first decades of the thirteenth century. Men or women could join a monastic community or could choose religious solitude; some solitaries, usually known as hermits, wandered around freely or chose to live in remote places, while others took a vow of stability of abode. For those who chose enclosure, a cell of one or several rooms was often built alongside a church, under the eaves, presumably along one side of the nave, with one window into the church for viewing the altar during mass. Each of the three sisters for whom the *Ancrene Riwle* was originally composed had two other windows, one opening into the quarters of an indoor maid, who fixed the meals, and one opening to the outside. Religious solitaries were sometimes sealed into their cells as a symbol that they were now dead to the world. One analogy the author of the *Ancrene Riwle* uses for the cells of the three sisters is that of a sepulchre, and one ritual of enclosure, nearly contemporary with the *Ancrene Riwle,* involved extreme unction, the sprinkling of dust and the sealing of the doorway as of a living tomb.

Controversy over two proposed titles for the work has prompted discussion of exactly what kind of guidance the author is offering. When Morton edited the Cotton Nero manuscript for publication in 1853, he used *The Ancren Riwle* as a title; with a corrected genitive plural form, *Ancrene Riwle* was adopted by the Early English Text Society for its subsequent editions (1952, 1962, and 1972). Furthermore, the author states in the opening section of the text that he has been requested to furnish a rule for three sisters and gives them advice and counsel throughout the text. Yet the Corpus Christi Cambridge manuscript, a later and revised version copied in what Dobson has convincingly argued may be the author's own hand, is titled *Ancrene Wisse* (A Guide for Anchoresses), and Linda Georgiana has suggested that this emphasis on guidance rather than on absolute prescriptions indicates the flexible nature of the "rule" given.

The author implies that the sisters have been under pressure from local churchmen to define their dedication to solitude in terms of some traditional rule of religious life. (This detail suggests that

Page from the Ancrene Riwle *in a thirteenth-century scribal copy (British Library, MS. Cotton Nero A. xiv, fol. 16)* the sisters entered their cells as laywomen, devoid of monastic training.) He chooses not to adapt for them either the Benedictine Rule, which governed most monastic life until the rise of new orders in the early thirteenth century, or the so-called Rule of Saint Augustine, which guided the life of secular canons. He suggests instead that the sisters call themselves the Order of Saint James, after a scriptural verse (James 1:27) that specifies the righteous life as the assistance of widows and orphans (primarily the task of priests) and keeping oneself uncontaminated by the world (the task of monastic religious and recluses). He advises the three sisters to take solemn vows only for chastity, obedience, and stability of abode; all other rules, he says, are "monnes fundles" – man's inventions – and may vary from person to person and time to time. In like manner he distinguishes between an outer rule and an inner: the outer rule, furnishing guidelines for the conduct of the body, serves as the handmaiden of the inner rule, which is the lady who governs the soul. This inner rule is governed by God's Commandments in the Bible and aims toward an unblemished conscience.

After the introduction, which defines the nature of a rule and an "order," eight sections follow. In accord with the author's distinction between an inner and outer rule, sections 1 and 8 are concerned primarily with the regulation of daily life: the first book lays out the recluse's rounds of devotions, while the last book examines her dealings with the outside world, including servants, visitors, and even animals. These two sections present the details of the daily life of an enclosed anchoress. The author prescribes for the three sisters a strict regimen of devotions broken only by reading in the Scriptures and the *Ancrene Riwle,* by sewing ecclesiastical vestments or simple garments for the poor, and by occasional visitors. Though contemporary records suggest that some recluses were quite active in the life of their village communities, the author of the *Ancrene Riwle* discourages much contact with people other than the recluse's maidservant; he discourages even school teaching and the giving of spiritual advice, especially to men.

On the other hand the sisters seem to have been allowed several servants: each had an indoor maid, who lived in the cell attached to the recluse's cell, and probably another servant as well, who was freer to go about the village on errands. Clothing, the author advises, should be sensible – coarse but reasonably comfortable; the plain and sparse furniture should include an altar with a crucifix; meals should be simple and infrequent (once a day in winter, twice a day in summer except on fast days). Though he allows the sisters to keep a cat if they choose, the author discourages the keeping of a cow, because it will require too much worldly business.

These fairly brief sections on the "outer rule" stand like the walls of the recluses' cells, sheltering and enclosing the more complex, discursive sections that analyze the interior life of a religious solitary. Sections 2 through 7 move both inward and upward along a spiraling path of spiritual development; beginning with the proper guardianship of the five senses (2), the *Ancrene Riwle* moves to the regulation of the emotions (3), then through temptation (4), confession (5), penance (6), and finally the love of God (7). Despite this implied narrative of spiritual progress, however, the author stresses not so much motion toward moments of mystical union with God but a steady resistance to temptation. He seems to conceive of religious life as a continuing and daily process of maintaining a state of virtue, with repetitive cycles of temptation, sin, confession, penance, and renewed devotion to God. In section 6, for example, the author sets out three images for a life of dedication to God: a pilgrim, a dead person, and a person being crucified. The pilgrim, an emblem of steady spiritual progress, was to become by the fourteenth century very popular in works of religious guidance; for the author of the *Ancrene Riwle,* however, the pilgrim is the least appropriate metaphor for the life of a recluse. He prefers the two other images, denoting immobile suffering, because they suggest so clearly the recluse's retirement from the ordinary world and her willingness to suffer pain for the sake of her devotion. Similarly, although the central sections of the *Ancrene Riwle* move in a kind of narrative progress from temptation to penance and then to love, the fundamental organization of the book is the enclosed and static shape of the recluse's cell, with the "outer rule" in the first and last sections sheltering the "inner rule."

This concentration of the *Ancrene Riwle* on the ascetic themes of bodily austerity and steadfast resistance to sin rather than on the mystical progress of the spirit toward God may seem surprising to readers more familiar with the better-known devotional treatises of the fourteenth century, which are intensely preoccupied with contemplative prayer in its various forms. The author of the *Ancrene Riwle* does posit the steadfast love of God as the source and goal of the life of a recluse; yet his attention is focused on the temptations offered the anchoress even in her secluded life. His aim is not so much to praise the joys of the life of prayer as to guide the anchoress toward a life of obedient, quiet chastity and to keep her attention withdrawn from the worldly life around her and turned toward God. The author makes a traditional comparison of the life of a recluse to the lives of Mary and Martha (the sisters of Lazarus with whom Christ visited), reminding the anchoresses that Christ praised Mary's quiet attention to his words over Martha's bustle; yet even here he emphasizes Mary's quietness and her withdrawal from the ordinary business of a female life in the world rather than her sitting at Christ's knee or her enraptured listening to his words. That is, he emphasizes the embrace of the virtues of the enclosed life and barely suggests the possibilities of rapturous mystical contact with God in this life.

However ascetic the life of the recluse, the text furnishes a wealth of images to enrich the life of her imagination. The most common images include sin as a wound or a disease, the soul as a castle or tower under siege or buffeted by high winds, life as a journey from this world to the next, and the recluse herself as a bird or animal. In section 3, on the regulation of the emotions, for example, the author draws on the Psalms and the medieval bestiaries to compare the life of a religious solitary to various birds: the recluse should be an eagle who brings back an agate (Christ) to her nest to protect it from harm, a swallow who sits alone and is subject to the "falling sickness" of temptation, a pelican who will kill her young if she gives way to anger. Other images are more unexpected. In the section on temptations, organized around the seven deadly sins, each sin is not only analyzed in terms of a beast (the lion of pride, the serpent of envy), but more unusual, each kind of sinner is assigned a role in the devil's court: the proud man is his trumpeter; the wrathful man, his knife thrower; the avaricious man, his fire tender; and so forth. Again, in section 7, the author compares the love of God to Greek fire, which can only be quenched with urine (sin), sand (idleness), and vinegar (a sour heart).

The author's intrinsic love of analogy is seen in his easy movement between an object's literal and allegorical significances. He recommends that the curtain over the recluse's public window be black and says that the black will function symbolically to show that "you are black and unworthy, and that the true sun has burnt you outwardly, and so made you as outwardly unlovely as you are, with the gleams of his grace." Moments later he adds sensibly that black cloth is also "less harmful to the eyes and is thicker against the wind and harder to see through, and keeps its color better against the wind and other things" (translations by Savage and Watson).

The author of the *Ancrene Riwle* lingers over the window because, once the door to the recluse's cell has been sealed, the window becomes the boundary between the recluse's inner world of her devotions and the busy outer one, full of dangers and temptations. Throughout the *Ancrene Riwle* the author distinguishes between inner and outer, always with the implication that whatever is inside is of more importance than whatever is outside. For example, outer temptations, which arise from the body (sickness, bodily harm) and from the world (shame, misfortune), are less to be feared than temptations that arise from within the self, such as the seven deadly sins. In discussing the prayers devoted to the Annunciation, the author emphasizes that Jesus was conceived inside Mary's body and suggests that the recluse should pray, "Make me count every outward joy little; but comfort me within" (translation by Savage and Watson). In general, the author stresses that one must look inward to see God; the more one looks outward at the world, the less one sees the inward light.

Like many other aspects of the *Ancrene Riwle,* the author's discussion of the window as a dangerous boundary is tailored very carefully to his female audience: he addresses the three original sisters not only as religious recluses, but as women. Thus, in his analysis of the control of the five senses (section 2) he chooses women from Scripture as his primary examples. His negative models reflect culturally prevalent notions about women as daughters of Eve and magnets for sexual temptation. To support his recommendations that the sisters not look out their windows, he cites Eve's glance of desire at the apple, which led to the Fall, and Dinah's glance outside at strange women, which eventually led to her rape and to the downfall of her people. The author also cites a traditional analogy between the face of a woman and an open pit: just as the owner of an uncovered pit can be held liable for the loss of an animal who falls into it, so will a woman be held spiritually responsible for the sin of a man whose animal nature falls into desire for her beauty. The author's positive models for the sisters' behavior are also predominantly female. In his discussion of the proper governance of speech, he contrasts the garrulity of Eve, who "held a long discussion with the serpent, told him the whole lesson about the apple that God had taught her and Adam; and so the enemy understood her weakness right away through her own words, and found a way into her for her destruction," with the quietness of Mary, who "did not discuss anything with the angel, but asked him briefly about what she did not understand" (translation by Savage and Watson). Later in the book he cites as a model for the recluse Queen Esther,

George Ellis, in G. L. Way, *Fabliaux or Tales . . . ,* volume 2 (London: Bulmer, 1800).
Standard edition: In *Ancient English Metrical Romances,* volume 1; *Thomas Chestre: Sir Launfal,* edited by A. J. Bliss (London: Nelson, 1960).

COLLECTED EDITION: *The Breton Lays in Middle English,* edited by Thomas C. Rumble (Detroit: Wayne State University Press, 1965).

The term *Breton lays* refers to a surviving group of over thirty short romances produced between about 1150 and 1450, most of which in one way or another purport to be written versions of lays sung by ancient Bretons to the accompaniment of the harp. The best known of these are the twelve written by the Anglo-Norman author Marie de France during the mid to late twelfth century. About a dozen others are anonymous Old French lays that are modeled, with varying degrees of success, on those of Marie and produced between about 1160 and 1270. The remainder are English poems, eight in all, dating from the late thirteenth or early fourteenth to the early fifteenth century.

At issue in any study of this group of English poems is the accuracy and usefulness of their designation as Breton lays. In the prologue to "The Franklin's Tale" (circa 1393) from Geoffrey Chaucer's *The Canterbury Tales* (circa 1375–1400) the Franklin tells the pilgrims:

Thise olde gentil Britouns in her dayes
Of diverse aventures maden layes,
Rymeyed in her first Briton tonge,
Whiche layes with her instrumentz they songe,
Or elles redden hem for hir plesaunce;
And oon of hem have I in remembraunce.

This passage condenses the description found in two fifteenth-century manuscripts at the start of *Sir Orfeo* (circa 1300) and in these lines from the Auchinleck manuscript at the beginning of *Le Freine* (circa 1300):

We redeth oft, and findeth ywrite,
And this clerkes wele it wite [know],
Layes that ben in harping,
Ben yfounde of ferli [wondrous] thing:
Sum bethe of wer and sum of wo,
And sum of joie and mirth also,
And sum of trecherie and of gile,
Of old aventours that fel while [befell long ago];
And sum of bourdes [jests] and ribaudy
And many ther beth of fairy;
Of al thinges that men seth,
Mest o love, forsothe, thai beth.

In Breteyne, bi hold [olden] time,
This layes were wroughte, so seith this rime.
When kinges might our [anywhere] yhere
Of ani mervailes that ther were,
Thai token an harp in gle and game,
And maked a lay and gaf it name.

Cited with remarkable frequency as a suitable definition of the genre, this passage in fact does little to differentiate the Breton lays from most other medieval tales. Apart from the fact that they are all short verse romances, perhaps the only thing they have in common is an evocation of the Breton/Celtic past, either because they claim to be lays, because they are set in Brittany – the region in France and Normandy inhabited by Armorican Celts – or because they derive from one of Marie's lays. Otherwise they are as varied in their subjects, themes, and styles as the opening lines of *Le Freine* suggest. Even the earliest English lays from the Auchinleck manuscript illustrate this variety. *Sir Degare* (circa 1300) has as its hero Degare, the son of a maiden who had been raped by a fairy knight. It focuses on the boy's successful attempt to discover his heritage through a series of adventures, ranging from a near-incestuous reunion with his mother to a Sohrab and Rustem–like battle with his father. Expanding this central story line into 998 lines are fights that Degare has first with a dragon who imperils an old earl and then with a giant who is tyrannizing a maiden. The poem is essentially a romance of adventure in which the hero regains a lost status. Though Degare's father is a fairy and, according to the Breton lay prologue, technically gives the poem a Breton flavor, his supernatural status matters little to the sense of the poem: by the end the poet has apparently forgotten that Degare's father is not mortal. *Sir Degare* has no identifiable source, though its early sections borrow liberally from the English *Le Freine*.

A 408-line translation of Marie de France's *Fresne* (1155–1170), *Le Freine* tells the simple story of the separation and reunion of twins. The twins are separated at birth, and one is lost. She later becomes the mistress of a knight, who, giving in to the pressure of his followers, must marry the other twin sister. Like Chaucer's Griselda in "The Clerk's Tale," the mistress faithfully helps to prepare for the wedding of her knight to the unknown woman. During these selfless preparations, her mother discovers who she is by recognizing a mantle in which she had originally wrapped her discarded child. By virtue of this happy coincidence the family is reunited, the mistress married to the knight and her sister to another knight living in that region. No brushes with patricide or incest here, no quests through wild forests or battles with monstrous foes, only the depiction of a quietly faithful love and the playing out, through a set of coincidences, of a separation and reunion story pattern. As a faithful translation of one of Marie's lays, *Le Freine* retains Marie's general disregard for external action and adventure. However, like the other English lays, *Le Freine* differs from Marie's poems in its less aristocratic tendencies; its increased piety; its heavier accumulation of concrete, sensory detail; its tendency to rationalize or naturalize events; its preference for the external rather than the internal experience; and its de-emphasis of the symbolic value of objects.

Though it also involves the separation-and-reunion pattern of these other two English lays, *Sir Orfeo* tells quite a different story. In this poem of 603 lines Orpheus and Euridice have been translated into King Orfeo and his wife Herodis, who is suddenly and magically abducted to the otherworld by a fairy king despite all the warriorlike preparations against the anticipated event on the part of Orfeo and his knights. Apparently in despair over losing his wife, but perhaps as much over a recognition of his powerlessness, Orfeo leaves his kingdom to his steward and wanders off into the wilderness with his harp, where he becomes a wild man, a typical representation in medieval literature of madness. Unaccountably he sees Herodis in this setting, whereupon he follows her through a cave and into the fairy world. There Sir Orfeo uses his expert harp playing to win her back from the fairy king. Unlike his classical namesake, he does not look back at Herodis as he returns to his kingdom. Because the steward is faithful and recognizes the disguised Orfeo, Orfeo regains his kingdom and lives happily with Herodis.

An impressive and intriguing poem, *Sir Orfeo* includes many of the features mentioned in the Breton lay prologue. It centers around love, not only the marital love of Orfeo for Herodis but also the aggressive, tyrannical love of the fairy king; it touches on war in its descriptions of Orfeo's preparations against the fairy king's promised abduction of Herodis; it treats joy and mirth; it depends on *ferli*, or marvelous, events; and it makes the fairy element – the king, his knights, his otherworld, and his magic powers – integral parts of the poem's meaning. Furthermore, the fact that Orfeo plays the harp and performs before a king – as if he were some ancient Breton – suggests almost that the poem's author intentionally tried to design a poem to match the criteria in the prologue. Versions of that prologue, in fact, preface *Sir Orfeo* in two fifteenth-century manuscripts, and a torn leaf just before the poem in the Auchinleck manuscript suggests that it began *Sir Orfeo* there, as well.

Unlike *Le Freine, Sir Orfeo* is not a translation of any identifiable source, though two references to a *Lai d'Orphey* survive in Old French literature. Ultimately the story derives from books 10 and 11 of Ovid's *Metamorphoses,* which tell of Euridice being mortally bitten by a snake and Orpheus attempting unsuccessfully to bring her back from the underworld. In book 3 of *The Consolation of Philosophy* (circa A.D. 525), likely a strong influence on *Sir Orfeo* or its source, Boethius treats the story of Orpheus and Euridice as an illustration of the way in which man's desire for light and God can be undermined by attachment to earthly concerns, to the things that cause him to turn his head toward hell. In keeping with this Boethian source of the story, scholars who practice patristic criticism read *Sir Orfeo* as a kind of Christian allegory in which Orfeo represents the reasonable element that must rescue the flesh, symbolized by Herodis, from the clutches of hell, depicted by the fairy king and his region. However, the poem resists such moralistic, religious interpretations. What these commentators see as an underworld and thus an image of hell is actually an otherworld, a region paralleling Orfeo's Thrace but neither better nor worse than it. And though readers frequently speak of Orfeo as journeying from his kingdom in search of Herodis, as if the poem were just a retelling of the classical account of Orpheus's search for Herodis, Orfeo actually goes into the wilderness without purpose. The chief problem that readers face in interpreting *Sir Orfeo,* then, is accounting for apparently arbitrary events – the fairy king's sudden appearance before Herodis in her dream, Orfeo's aimless retreat into the wilderness and Herodis's appearance there, and Orfeo's ability to see the fairy king late in the poem when he could not perceive him earlier – without distorting what the poem actually describes and without treating the poem as primitive or quaint. The work's meaning emerges through its careful narration, with its sudden shifts in setting, its use of the fairy realm as a reflection upon the real one, and its dependence on such symbols as the battlements of a castle, a harp, and torn, scarred bodies. Though it does not possess the wit and the highly self-conscious wordplay of Marie's lays, it nevertheless resembles these earliest literary examples of this subgenre of romance in its minimalist, but richly suggestive, surface. Because of these features, it has attracted more scholarly attention than any poem in this group except "The Franklin's Tale."

Chaucer's tale of Averagus's near loss of his wife, Dorigen, because of the squire Aurelius's adul-

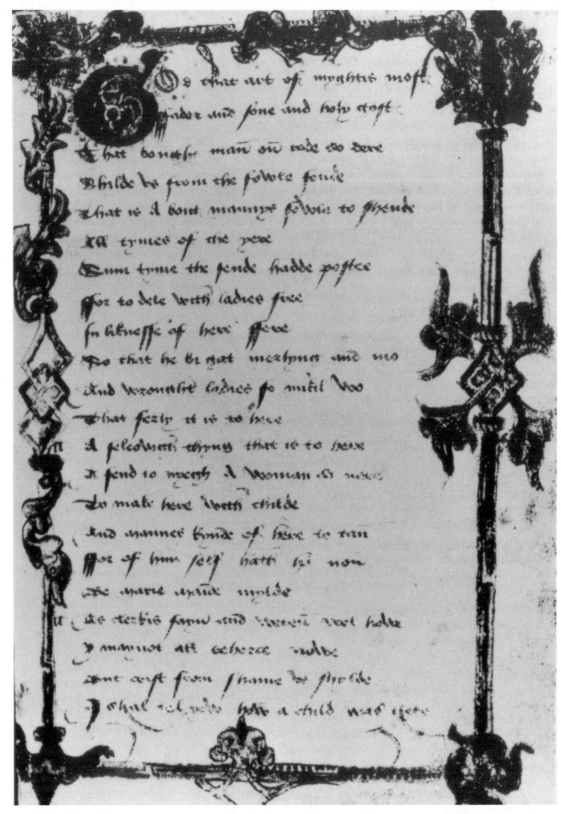

Page from Sir Gowther *in the only extant manuscript, a transcription dating from the second half of the fifteenth century (British Library, MS. Royal 17. B.43, fol. 116ᵃ)*

terous love is well known. "The Franklin's Tale," along with the tales of the Wife of Bath and the Merchant, suggests that Chaucer might have read the Breton lay prologue in the Auchinleck manuscript and perhaps the lays themselves. However, the tale he calls a lay differs greatly from these earlier samples, not only because its 916 lines are written in ten- rather than eight-syllable couplets but also because it is more sophisticated: its characters make longer, more ornate speeches; it contains a rich array of classical allusions, as in Dorigen's meditation on suicide; and its events are far more rationalized than those in, say, *Sir Orfeo*. The disappearance of the rocks from the sea, for instance, is a learned clerk's illusion rather than a Celtic form of magic. What in these earlier lays are sudden appearances and unexplained coincidences, in "The Franklin's Tale" are more carefully motivated, probable occurrences. In fact, this difference between Chaucer's tale and these others might reveal more about some essential features of the Breton lays than its claim to a literary kinship with them: the Breton lays depart from the typical romance in their folkloric disregard for coherent, motivated, and elaborated action and in their maintenance of a flat narrative surface depending for its meaning on sharp oppositions of characters in nonpolitical, if occasionally geographically real, landscapes.

Consideration of "The Franklin's Tale" as a Breton lay is also complicated by the fact that Chaucer situates it within the dramatic framework of *The Canterbury Tales,* which repeatedly calls into question the reliability of the tale-teller. When the Franklin claims that he will tell a Breton lay, for instance, he is betraying his old-fashioned tastes more than accurately defining a genre. The assumption is that between 1350 and 1400 the Breton lay was out of fashion, Chaucer having had no familiarity with the form other than through his acquaintance with the lays in the Auchinleck manuscript from the early part of the century. Another important view, however, is that "The Franklin's Tale" merely continues an uninterrupted tradition and that the Franklin's claim that his tale is a lay amounts to an attempt to appeal to the fashionable tastes of a sophisticated audience. The assumption behind this view is that the surviving lays do not constitute an accurate picture of the currency of that form. In fact, one late-thirteenth-century manuscript, Shrewsbury School MS. vii, f. 200, names many lays that are no longer extant, suggesting that "The Franklin's Tale" was either part of a fashionable revival of the form, in which the other English lays of the late fourteenth and early fifteenth century participated, or part of a continuous, strong tradition, of which survives a small and perhaps even unrepresentative sample.

If these later lays participated in a continuous, strong tradition, that tradition underwent immense transformations, not the least of which is that from the eight-syllable couplet to tail-rhyme stanza, which Chaucer mocks in his *Tale of Sir Thopas. The Erle of Tolous* (early fifteenth century), *Emare* (circa 1400), and *Sir Gowther* (late fourteenth century) hardly resemble the lays from the Auchinleck manuscript; and Thomas Chestre's *Sir Launfal* (1350–1400), as a version of Marie's *Lanval* (1155–1170), is often seen as a gross misrepresentation of the form, at least if Marie's lays and *Sir Orfeo* are seen as its models. The longest of these poems, at 1,224 lines, *The Erle of Tolous* has nothing of the strange or fairy element in it, and its sequence of events is surprisingly coherent and the motives for its characters' actions reasonably well delineated. It tells the story of Sir Barnard falling in love with the wife of his enemy, the Emperor of Germany, and finally marrying her. It involves interesting scenes of disguise in which Barnard dresses as a hermit in order to see the emperor's wife and then as a monk in order to hear her confession just before the Emperor's supporters are to burn her on false charges of adultery. The tale ends with a trial by combat through which Barnard rescues the lady from her false accusers. More typical of the love in English romances than of that in French ones, the relationship is not adulterous: Barnard waits three years for the Emperor to die before consummating his love within marriage.

Tenuous as it is, this poem's claim to being a lay is perhaps more deserved than that made by the author of *Emare:* "Thys ys on of Brytayne layes." Resembling Chaucer's story of Constance in "The Man of Law's Tale," the story focuses on pious material, something excluded even from the broad definition in the Breton lay prologue. After being exiled in an open boat because she refused her father's proposal of marriage, Emare finally washes up on the shore of a land called Galys, whose king falls in love with and marries her, despite his mother's disapproval. Because of her stepmother's plotting, Emare is put to sea in an open boat again, this time with her newborn son. Seven years after being rescued off the coast of Rome by a merchant, she is reunited with the King of Galys, who has come to Rome to do penance for having been part of what he thinks is Emare's death. The happiness of their reunion is increased by their discovery that the Emperor, Emare's father, is also in Rome doing penance. The marvelous in this tale does not emanate from a Celtic otherworld but rather from a Christian God.

The same is true for the apparently magical elements in *Sir Gowther,* a poem of 696 lines whose structure most closely resembles that of a saint's life. An offspring of a fiend, Sir Gowther must do penance for a series of nasty deeds ranging from killing his wet nurses to forcing priests to jump off cliffs. He becomes a dumb fool in the German Emperor's court and there proves that he is blessed by defeating the Saracens, who want to take the Emperor's beautiful but dumb daughter. The magic in the tale occurs when God sends Gowther three marvelous sets of armor on three successive days and when the Emperor's daughter suddenly begins speaking in order to identify Gowther as the knight whose prowess has saved her from the heathens. The pope takes her speech as a divine sign and absolves Gowther of his former sins. Gowther then marries the Emperor's daughter, rules Germany, and acts as a model Christian. After his death he is considered a saint because his corpse, which lies in a "shryne of gold," works miracles for those desiring help.

The most problematic of these later Middle English lays, *Sir Launfal* concerns one of Arthur's knights who goes into self-imposed exile after being shunned by Queen Guinevere. Through the agency of a fairy queen, however, he regains his chivalric reputation, which in this poem has more to do with wealth than prowess. Tryamour, Launfal's fairy mistress, endows him with great riches and guarantees his victory in battle. She also promises to appear to him in private whenever he wants her to, all so long as he never boasts of her to anyone. When Launfal returns to Arthur's court, he becomes the object of Guinevere's sexual advances. Angered that he is not attracted to her, Guinevere insults him, remarking not only that he is a coward but that he is incapable of loving or being loved by any woman. Launfal angrily responds that he does have a lady and that her ugliest maid is prettier than Guinevere. This hasty remark causes Guinevere to charge Launfal with treason. Only Tryamour's appearance at his trial saves him. The poem ends with the blinding of Guinevere and a description of Launfal's happy life with Tryamour in her otherworld away from Arthur's court.

This story has six surviving Middle English versions, three of them whole and three of them fragments. Chestre's *Sir Launfal,* or *Launfal Miles* as it is also called, is the longest version, its tail-rhyme stanzas and its addition of both a tournament scene and a fight between Launfal and Sir Valentine stretching it to 1,038 lines, 400 more than *Sir Landaval* and *Sir Lambewell,* the two shorter, eight-syllable couplet versions from the first half of the fourteenth century. Though they derive from separate translations of *Lanval,* one of Marie's lays, these earlier poems do not advertise themselves as Breton lays and therefore are not always considered as such. *Sir Launfal* also derives from an early translation of Marie's lay that combined features of her version with elements from *Graelent,* an anonymous romance. In Chestre's hands the tale becomes what most commentators regard as a monstrous expression of bourgeois values, obsessed with gifts, fantasies of unlimited wealth, and envy of status and possessions. The efficiency of Marie's lay gets lost in the jangling tail rhymes and the superfluous action and adventure that two additions concerning combat bring to the material. Chestre's claim that his poem is a lay amounts to a grabbing for an aristocratic status that his poem, interestingly enough, ends up rejecting: its style, subject matter, and tone ignore the courtly suggestiveness of Marie's lay, and his hero turns from Arthur's unappreciative, aristocratic court to the fairy world of Tryamour, where there is little delay between desire and fulfillment.

Despite scholars' depreciation of *Sir Launfal,* it has drawn considerable attention. It serves as an illuminating focus for questions related to the intersection of the oral and written cultures of the period and for those concerned with the appropriation of an aristocratic genre by a developing middle class. It has also attracted thematic analyses, especially those trying to justify or criticize Chestre's expansion of Marie's lay, but also others documenting surprising instances of Chestre's playfulness as a narrator, and even his attempt to burlesque the romance tradition and such values as largesse. Unfortunately, nothing is known about Chestre's life, and only this poem remains to suggest his habits as a writer, so conjectures about tone are difficult to prove.

Whatever the critical judgment of the poem, however, *Sir Launfal* stands as a fascinating conjunction of the lay and the tail-rhyme romances not only because of the difference between the lay's quieter interest in internal conflicts and the tail rhyme's devotion to external adventure and conflict but also because both of these types claim for themselves a kind of performative authority — the tail-rhyme version's narrator repeatedly reminding his audience that he is telling his tale and not lying and the Breton lay version's narrator simply putting into writing a story that originally was sung to the music of the harp.

Bibliographies:

Thomas C. Rumble, "Select Bibliography," in *The Breton Lays in Middle English* (Detroit: Wayne State University Press, 1965), pp. 261–269;

A Manual of the Writings in Middle English, 1050–1500, edited by J. Burke Severs and Albert E. Hartung, volume 1: Romances (New Haven: Connecticut Academy of Arts and Sciences, 1967).

References:

Dorena Allen, "Orpheus and Orfeo: The Dead and the *Taken,*" *Medium Ævum,* 33, no. 2 (1964): 102–111;

Earl R. Anderson, "The Structure of *Sir Launfal,*" *Papers on Language and Literature,* 13 (Spring 1977): 115–124;

Mortimer J. Donovan, *The Breton Lay: A Guide to Varieties* (Notre Dame, Ind.: University of Notre Dame Press, 1969);

Penelope B. R. Doob, *Nebuchadnezzar's Children: Conventions of Madness in Middle English Literature* (New Haven: Yale University Press, 1974);

John Finlayson, "The Form of the Middle English Lay," *Chaucer Review,* 19 (Summer 1985): 352–368;

John Block Friedman, *Orpheus in the Middle Ages* (Cambridge, Mass.: Harvard University Press, 1970);

Thomas B. Hanson, "*Sir Orfeo,* Romance as Exemplum," *Annuale Mediaevale,* 13 (1972): 135–154;

D. M. Hill, "The Structure of 'Sir Orfeo,'" *Medieval Studies,* 23 (1961): 136–153;

Kathryn Hume, "Why Chaucer Calls the *Franklin's Tale* a Breton Lai," *Philological Quarterly,* 51 (April 1972): 365–379;

Alice E. Lasater, "Under the ympe-tre in *Sir Orfeo,*" *Southern Quarterly,* 12 (July 1974): 353–363;

Laura Hibbard Loomis, "Chaucer and the Breton Lays of the Auchinleck MS," *Studies in Philology,* 38 (January 1941): 14–33;

B. K. Martin, "*Sir Launfal* and the Folktale," *Medium Ævum,* 35, no. 3 (1966): 199–210;

M. Miles, "The Composition and Style of the 'Southern' *Octavian, Sir Launfal,* and *Libeaus Desconus,*" *Medium Ævum,* 31, no. 2 (1962): 88–109;

Carol J. Nappholz, "Launfal's 'Largesse': Word-Play in Thomas Chestre's *Sir Launfal,*" *English Language Notes,* 25 (March 1988): 4–9;

Timothy D. O'Brien, "The 'Readerly' *Sir Launfal,*" *Parergon,* 8 (June 1990): 33–45;

G. V. Smithers, "Story-Patterns in Some Breton Lays," *Medium Ævum,* 22, no. 2 (1953): 61–92;

A. C. Spearing, "Marie de France and Her Middle English Adapters," *Studies in the Age of Chaucer,* 12 (1990): 117–156;

William C. Stokoe, Jr., "The Double Problem of *Sir Degare,*" *PMLA,* 70 (June 1955): 518–534;

Paul Strohm, "The Origins and Meaning of Middle English *Romaunce,*" *Genre,* 10 (Spring 1977): 1–29;

Susan Wittig, *Stylistic and Narrative Structures in the Middle English Romances* (Austin: University of Texas Press, 1978).

The Castle of Perseverance
(circa 1400 – 1425)

Carol Falkenstine
Berea College

Manuscript: The work survives in one extant manuscript, Folger MS. V. a. 354 (circa 1440) in the Folger Library in Washington D.C. Facsimile: *The Macro Plays: The Castle of Perseverance, Wisdom, Mankind,* edited by David Bevington (New York: Johnson Reprint, 1972).
First publication: *The Macro Plays,* edited by F. J. Furnivall, with an introduction by A. W. Pollard, EETS, e.s. 91 (1904).
Standard edition: *The Macro Plays,* edited by Mark Eccles, EETS 262 (1969).

The Castle of Perseverance is one of three morality plays that have been traditionally grouped and referred to as the Macro Plays. The manuscripts of *The Castle of Perseverance, Mankind,* and *Wisdom* were acquired by the Reverend Cox Macro of Bury Saint Edmunds in the eighteenth century; while in Macro's possession, these three along with three other manuscripts were bound together. When Macro's collection was sold in 1820, Hudson Gurney bought the manuscripts of *The Castle of Perseverance, Mankind,* and *Wisdom* and bound the three of them into one volume. Since then they have been known as the Macro Plays, even after the Folger Library purchased them in March 1936.

There is some question as to the geographical provenance of the play; F. J. Furnivall believes it was written in Norfolk, while Walter K. Smart and Jacob Bennett contend that the play is from Lincoln. Mark Eccles maintains that *The Castle of Perseverance* could not have been written in Lincoln, due to vocabulary and stylistic considerations; he states that it is more likely to have come from near Norfolk.

The exact date when the play was written is also uncertain, though the surviving manuscript is from approximately 1440. Most scholars believe that *The Castle of Perseverance* was written near the beginning of the fifteenth century, frequently dating it between 1400 and 1425. It is generally agreed that *The Castle of Perseverance* is the earliest complete En-glish morality play in existence (only *The Pride of Life,* which survives as a fragment, is earlier). As such, *The Castle of Perseverance* serves as a kind of reference book to all later moralities, since it includes in its plot the fate of Mankind from birth to death and beyond, and the basic accompanying theme of birth/temptation/fall/redemption, as well as all the stock characters of the morality-play genre: the World, the Flesh, and the Devil; the Seven Deadly Sins; the Seven Moral Virtues; God on his scaffold; and, of course, Mankind.

The banns of *The Castle of Perseverance* suggest that it was a traveling play, produced in various towns by a touring company of actors. The banns, which were meant to be read aloud by an actor, provide a plot summary of the play and announce that it would be performed in one week's time. The name of the town is left blank, so that the actor could insert the name of whatever town the company planned to visit. There has been disagreement, however, as to whether or not the banns should be considered part of the play, and several scholars have suggested that they are a later addition.

A difficulty faced by the performers was that of taking such a massive play from place to place, with its thirty-three characters and elaborate staging requirements. The play would have been performed outdoors, in a round *platea,* or playing place, surrounded by a ditch, and there would have been various structures to build, including a tower to represent the Castle of Perseverance, as well as five scaffolds (some scholars believe that each scaffold would have had a curtain, to be opened only when the scaffold's occupants were directly involved in the action of the play).

One of the most interesting aspects of the manuscript of *The Castle of Perseverance,* and one that has caused a great deal of speculation in terms of how medieval plays, and this play in particular, were staged, is the well-known diagram that encompasses a full leaf of the manuscript and provides a fascinating indication of how the play was to be staged. The drawing shows a round performance area surrounded by a ditch, ideally full of water. In the center of the circle is a castle, the Castle of Perseverance (drawn as a single tower, open underneath to show Mankind's bed and Avarice's cupboard). Various scaffolds, belonging to the most powerful characters, are placed outside of the ditch: God's scaffold is to the east, in the direction of Jerusalem; Covetousness, the most persuasive of the Deadly Sins in this play, has his own scaffold, to the northeast; Belyal (the devil) is placed due north; the World's scaffold is to the west; and Flesh is situated to the south.

According to Richard Southern in *The Medieval Theatre in the Round* (1975), the ditch would mark the outer boundary of the outdoor theater, and the audience, after paying an admission fee, would enter the playing place and seat themselves on the dirt that had been thrown up by the digging of the ditch. However, many scholars have seen problems with this interpretation and have made countersuggestions. Whether or not Southern's suppositions are correct in every detail, *The Castle of Perseverance* diagram clearly shows that the area was to be circular and also indicates that the audience should not sit too close to the castle. This round "theater" would have meant that the characters engaged in much physical action, moving from one place to another, and probably were involved in lively interaction with the audience on all sides. Much of the medieval love of procession and spectacle must have been present in the performances. There are stage directions for music, including trumpet fanfares; directions are included for the processional singing of *Eterne rex altissime,* when the Seven Virtues enter the Castle of Perseverance with Mankind; and several of the characters' costumes and props are described in enough detail to show that they were considered important: the four daughters of God are to wear richly colored mantles; Flesh is to be draped in costly tapestries and flowers; Pleasure clothes Mankind in a splendid robe hung all over with golden coins; during the battle scene between the Virtues and Vices, Lechery carries a bucket of burning coals, which Chastity appropriately douses with water; and Belyal is arrayed in a costume which includes pipes full of burning gunpowder sticking out from his ears, hands, and rear.

The term *morality play* generally refers to a late-medieval or early-Renaissance play which has a moral theme and allegorical characters. The moralities have much in common with sermon literature of the time and seem to arise from the same impulse. The moralities endeavor to teach their audiences a lesson about life, along with its temptations and pitfalls, and how life should be lived. *The Castle of Perseverance* includes the fullest, most inclusive moral lesson of any surviving English morality play, beginning with Mankind's birth and ending after his death with the disputation among the four daughters of God concerning the fate of Mankind's soul. There are thirty-three characters, including: Mankind, Mankind's Good Angel and Bad Angel; the three enemies of man, the World, the Flesh, and the Devil; the Seven Deadly Sins — Covetousness (or Avarice), Pride, Wrath, Envy, Gluttony, Lechery, and Sloth; the opposing Seven Virtues — Generosity, Humility, Patience, Charity, Abstinence, Chastity, and Busyness; the additional characters of Backbiter, Confession, and Penitence; the four daughters of God — Mercy, Righteousness, Truth, and Peace; and finally, God himself.

The action of the play can be divided into four basic parts: the birth of Mankind and his almost-immediate fall into temptation and sin; Mankind's repentance, his installation into the Castle of Perseverance, and his protection therein by the Seven Virtues, even through an assault by the Seven Deadly Sins; Mankind's succumbing to the temptation of Covetousness and leaving the Castle of Perseverance, with his subsequent death; the disputation among the four daughters of God concerning the ultimate fate of Mankind's soul, with Mankind's final redemption. The play begins with World (*Mundus*) holding forth from his scaffold, using the alliterative technique common throughout the play. In three thirteen-line stanzas (the thirteen-line stanza is by far the most common, used in 235 of the play's 318 stanzas), World identifies himself, brags about his character and power, introduces his "treasurer," Sir Covetousness, and threatens any who would speak against him. The Devil (*Belyal*) follows suit; his personal servants are Pride, Wrath, and Envy, and Belyal makes clear his intent to cause Mankind to be damned. Flesh (*Caro*) is next; his "children" are Gluttony, Lechery, and Sloth. In the third of his three thirteen-line stanzas, Flesh claims:

> Behold þe Werld, þe Deuyl, and me!
> Wyth all oure mythis we kyngys thre
> Nyth and day besy we be
> For to distroy Mankende
> If þat we may.

Mankind (*Humanum genus*) enters at this point, naked and shivering; he, too, takes three thirteen-line stanzas to identify himself and state his plight.

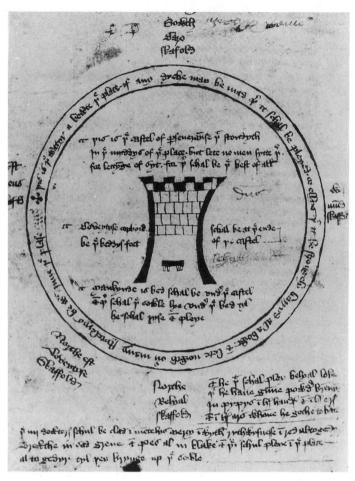

Staging diagram in the only extant manuscript for The Castle of Perseverance, *a transcription dating from circa 1440 (Folger Shakespeare Library, MS. V.a. 354)*

He has nothing; he does not know where to go; he expresses confusion about why he was born:

> Whereto I was to þis werld browth
> I ne wot, but to woo and wepynge
> I am born and haue ryth nowth
> To helpe myself in no doynge.

Mankind explains to the audience that two angels have been assigned to him, one good, and the other bad, and he finally prays to God for guidance.

The Good Angel then speaks, giving, as one might expect, good advice: that Mankind serve Lord Jesus, heaven's king, throughout his life. The Bad Angel gives bad advice, luring Mankind with riches, delicious foods, beautiful women, and luxurious clothing. He suggests that Mankind is too young to be good; he will have plenty of time to repent when he is older:

> Wyth þe Werld þou mayst be bold
> Tyl þou be sexty wyntyr hold.
> Wanne þi nose waxit cold,
> þanne mayst þou drawe to goode.

Mankind is won over by the enticements of the Bad Angel and goes off with him to meet World, Flesh, the Devil, and the Seven Deadly Sins, to whom Mankind pledges loyalty and friendship. After Mankind has welcomed the Sins to his acquaintance, he turns to the audience and implicates them in his own fall: "I se no man but þey vse somme / Of þese seuene dedly synnys." He continues in the next stanza, saying that there are neither rich nor poor who will forsake all seven Sins, but "In synne iche man is founde."

At this point the Good Angel bemoans Mankind's fall and apparent fate; though he is continually striving to bring Mankind's soul into bliss, his charge seems determined to damn himself. Confession hears the Good Angel's lament and goes to

Mankind to try to convince him to change his ways. Mankind replies that Confession has come too early and suggests that he return on Good Friday, because at the moment Mankind has other things to do. Penitence then enters the scene and pierces Mankind with a lance that represents sorrow for his sins. Mankind repents, asks for mercy and grace from God, and promises to amend his life. Confession shrives Mankind and tells him where he can go to be safe from sin: the Castle of Perseverance.

Mankind joyfully goes to the Castle, accompanied by the Seven Moral Virtues: Charity (*Caritas*), Abstinence (*Abstinencia*), Chastity (*Castitas*), Busyness (*Solicitudo*), Generosity (*Largitas*), Patience (*Paciens*), and Humility (*Humilitas*). Humility promises to keep Mankind safe from his foes if he stays within the castle:

> Stonde hereinne as stylle as ston;
> þanne schal no dedly synne þe spylle. . . .
> þis castel is of so qweynt a gynne
> þat whoso euere holde hym þerinne
> He schal neuere fallyn in dedly synne;
> It is þe Castel of Perseueranse.

As soon as the Bad Angel sees that Mankind means to change his ways and live a virtuous life, he sends Backbiter to tell World, Flesh, and the Devil of their loss. Backbiter, true to his name, sows discord among all the evil characters, causing them to turn on one another and blame each other for the loss of Mankind. Finally, they decide to launch an attack on the Castle of Perseverance and to drag Mankind out if he will not come out on his own. In an episode reminiscent of Prudentius's *Psychomachia* (405) the Seven Deadly Sins array themselves for battle, and head for the castle with many a vulgar epithet. Belyal's forces attack first, and each Sin goes up against its opposing Virtue: Pride against Humility, Wrath against Patience, and Envy against Charity. The Virtues defeat the Sins soundly by throwing roses at them, the rose being a symbol of Christ's Passion and the blood of Redemption. The Sins retreat, with much comic complaining about the wounds they have received. Flesh is the next to send in his troops: Gluttony against Abstinence, Lechery against Chastity, and Sloth against Busyness. Again the Virtues triumph by pelting the Sins with roses.

The last to approach the Castle is World's servant, Covetousness, who uses a different approach than the other Sins. Rather than confront and attempt to overcome a Virtue, which is impossible, Covetousness speaks directly to Mankind, avoiding Generosity altogether. Mankind resists at first, but since he is old and worried about his comfort, he eventually gives in to the temptings of Covetousness and leaves the safety of the Castle of Perseverance for the promise of riches. The Good Angel calls to the Virtues to help Mankind, but the Virtues point out that Mankind has free will to turn from God and goodness and to damn himself; this is unreasonable behavior on his part, they say, but Mankind has the freedom to make an unreasonable choice, and they are not to blame. Avarice instructs Mankind to be insatiable, to want more and more, and never to share with another, no matter what his need may be. Mankind agrees to this and forsakes God:

> If I myth [might] alwey dwellyn in prosperyte,
> Lord God, þane wel were me.
> I wolde, þe medys [in return], forsake þe
> And nevere to comyn in heuene.

Immediately after Mankind has made this speech, Death appears. In his opening lines he comments on how Mankind has misspent his life; then, in an analogue of the dance of death motif of the period, moves to a discussion of his own character, emphasizing that all – rich and poor, great and small – are brought equally low by him. Saying that he will teach Mankind a new lesson, Death strikes him. Mankind immediately cries out to World to save him, but World coldly abandons him, saying that he wishes Mankind were already in the grave and sending a page boy to take all of Mankind's wealth. Mankind has not yet died when the boy arrives. Mankind sees that the boy is no kin to him:

> What deuyl! þou art not of my kyn.
> þou dedyst me neuere no maner good.
> I hadde leuer sum nyfte or sum cosyn
> Or sum man hadde it of my blod.

In spite of Mankind's desire that some of his blood kin inherit the money, the boy seizes it, telling Mankind that his name is "I Wot Neuere Whoo."

Mankind finally realizes his error, gives a verbal lesson to the audience, and prays to God for mercy:

> To helle I schal bothe fare and fle
> But God me graunte of hys grace.
> I deye certeynly.
> Now my lyfe I haue lore.
> Myn hert brekyth, I syhe sore.
> A word may I speke no more.
> I putte me in Goddys mercy.

The Soul, which would have been played by a child actor, rises from under the bed where the Body lies,

A scene from the 1979 Poculi Ludique Societas production of The Castle of Perseverance, *which followed the staging diagram in the Folger manuscript (from Paula Neuss, ed.,* Aspects of Early English Drama, *1983)*

reproaches the Body for its sinful behavior, and asks the Good Angel for advice. (At this point there is a leaf missing from the manuscript.) When the action resumes, the Bad Angel is preparing to carry the Soul to hell. After five stanzas of moral instruction to the audience concerning the evils of being covetous and listening to bad counsel, the Bad Angel hoists the Soul onto his back and says to the audience: "Haue good day! I goo to helle."

The last part of the play, which also uses a common motif of the time — the trial in heaven — begins with one of the daughters of God, Mercy (*Misericordia*), hearing Mankind's call. She wishes to save his soul from hell, and tells her sister Righteousness, who in turn replies that saving him would not be just. He deserves to be damned for his misdeeds — after all, he died in a state of sin, only calling out for mercy at the very last moment. Another sister, Truth, agrees with Righteousness, but their sister Peace agrees with Mercy that Mankind should be saved. The four sisters ascend to God's scaffold to let him judge the case. After each of his daughters has been heard, the Father determines that, since he is above all a merciful God, Mankind should be saved, brought to heaven, and seated at his right

hand. The play ends with the four daughters of God bringing the Soul of Mankind up to God's scaffold and presenting him to the Father. God is given the final four stanzas of the play in which to present a minisermon to the audience, telling them to follow good and amend their misdeeds.

With its collection of common medieval motifs and characters and its basic plot of birth/temptation/fall/redemption, *The Castle of Perseverance* is useful in making sense of the morality plays that follow it. It emphasizes the necessity of persevering in virtue, making virtue a way of life rather than putting it off until old age. Though long (3,649 lines) and at times somewhat long-winded, this well-thought-out, carefully crafted, symmetrically structured play provides a fascinating insight into the early fifteenth century, its beliefs, and its likes. With its serious moral lessons and flamboyant costumes, music, and staging, the play seems to take seriously the old Horatian adage that the purpose of poetry is both to teach and to delight.

Bibliography:

Sidney E. Berger, *Medieval English Drama: An Annotated Bibliography of Recent Criticism* (New York: Garland, 1990).

References:

Catherine Belsey, "The Stage Plan of *The Castle of Perseverance*," *Theatre Notes,* 28, no. 3 (1974): 124–132;

Jacob Bennett, "The 'Castle of Perseverance': Redactions, Place, and Date," *Mediaeval Studies,* 24 (1962): 141–152;

David Bevington, " 'Man, Thinke on Thine Endinge Day': Stage Pictures of Just Judgment in *The Castle of Perseverance*," in *Homo Memento Finis,* edited by Bevington (Kalamazoo: Western Michigan University, 1985), pp. 147–177;

Philip Butterworth, "Gunnepowdyr, fyre and thondyr," *Medieval English Theatre,* 7, (December 1985): 68–76;

W. A. Davenport, *Fifteenth-Century English Drama: The Early Moral Plays and Their Literary Relations* (Cambridge: Brewer, 1982);

Clifford Davidson, *Visualizing the Moral Life: Medieval Iconography and the Macro Morality Plays* (New York: AMS Press, 1989);

John S. Farmer, ed., *The Castle of Perseverance* (London & Edinburgh: Tudor Facsimile Texts, 1908);

Merle Fifield, "The Arena Theatres in Vienna Codices 2535 and 2536," *Comparative Drama,* 2, no. 4 (Winter 1968–1969): 259–282;

Fifield, "The Assault on the *Castle of Perseverance* – The Tradition and the Figure," *Ball State University Forum,* 16 (Autumn 1975): 16–26;

Fifield, *The Rhetoric of Free Will: The Five-Action Structure of the English Morality Play* (Leeds: University of Leeds, School of English, 1974);

Peter Happé, ed., *Four Morality Plays* (New York: Penguin, 1979);

S. E. Holbrook, "Covetousness, Contrition, and the Town in the *Castle of Perseverance*," *Fifteenth-Century Studies,* 13 (1988): 275–289;

Michael R. Kelley, *Flamboyant Drama: A Study of "The Castle of Perseverance" and "Wisdom"* (Carbondale: Southern Illinois University Press, 1979);

Alan H. Nelson, *The Medieval English Stage* (Chicago: University of Chicago Press, 1974);

Nelson, " 'Of the seuen ages': An Unknown Analogue of *The Castle of Perseverance*," in *Studies in Medieval Drama in Honor of William L. Smoldon on His 82nd Birthday,* edited by Davidson, and others (Kalamazoo: Western Michigan University, 1974), pp. 125–138;

Ann Eljenholm Nichols, "Costume in the Moralities: The Evidence of East Anglian Art," *Comparative Drama,* 20 (Winter 1986–1987): 305–314;

David Mackenzie Parry, "*The Castle of Perseverance:* A Critical Edition," Ph.D. dissertation, University of Toronto, 1983;

Steven Irvin Pederson, "The Staging of *The Castle of Perseverance:* A Re-Analysis," *Theatre Notes,* 39, no. 2 (1985): 51–62;

Pederson, "The Staging of *The Castle of Perseverance:* Testing the List Theory," *Theatre Notes,* 39, no. 3 (1985): 104–113;

Alfred W. Pollard, ed., *English Miracle Plays, Moralities and Interludes* (Oxford: Clarendon Press, 1904);

Robert A. Potter, *The English Morality Play: Origins, History, and Influence of a Dramatic Tradition* (London & Boston: Routledge & Kegan Paul, 1975);

Michael E. Ralston, "The Four Daughters of God in *The Castle of Perseverance*," *Comitatus,* 15 (1984): 35–44;

Milla Cozart Riggio, "The Allegory of Feudal Acquisition in *The Castle of Perseverance*," in *Allegory, Myth, and Symbol,* edited by Morton W. Bloomfield (Cambridge, Mass.: Harvard University Press, 1981), pp. 187–208;

Edgar Schell, *Strangers and Pilgrims: From* The Castle of Perseverance *to* King Lear (Chicago: University of Chicago Press, 1983);

Natalie Crohn Schmitt, "The Idea of a Person in Medieval Morality Plays," *Comparative Drama,* 12 (Spring 1978): 23–34;

Schmitt, "*Perseverance*," *Theatre Survey,* 18 (November 1977): 96–98;

Schmitt, "Was There a Medieval Theatre in the Round?: Part II," *Theatre Notes,* 24 (Winter 1969): 18–25;

Walter K. Smart, "The 'Castle of Perseverance': Place, Date, and a Source," in *The Manly Anniversary Studies in Language and Literature* (Chicago, 1923), pp. 42–53;

Richard Southern, *The Medieval Theatre in the Round: A Study of the Staging of "The Castle of Perseverance" and Related Matters,* second edition (London: Faber & Faber, 1975);

Betsy S. Taylor, *Selections from the Castle of Perseverance* (Sydney: University of Sydney, Drama Studies Unit, Department of English, 1977).

The Chester Plays

(circa 1505 – 1532; revisions until 1575)

Shearle Furnish
West Texas A&M University

Manuscripts: Eight extant manuscripts witness fragmentary or major portions of the Chester play cycle. The five full-cycle compilations among them are *Hm,* or Huntington 2 (1591), in the Henry E. Huntington Library and Art Gallery, San Marino, California; *A,* or Additional 10305 (1592), in the British Library; *R,* or Harley 2013 (1600), part of the Randle Holme Collection, British Library; *B,* or Bodley 175 (1604), in the Bodleian Library, Oxford; and *H,* or Harley 2124 (1607), in the British Library. Facsimiles: *The Chester Mystery Cycle: A Facsimile of MS. Bodley 175,* edited by Robert Lumiansky and David Mills, Leeds Texts and Monographs, Medieval Drama Facsimiles 1 (Leeds, 1973); *The Chester Mystery Cycle: A Reduced Facsimile of Huntington Library MS 2,* edited by Lumiansky and Mills, Leeds Texts and Monographs, Medieval Drama Facsimiles 6 (Leeds, 1980); *The Chester Mystery Cycle: A Facsimile of British Library MS Harley 2124,* edited by Mills, Leeds Texts and Monographs, Medieval Drama Facsimiles 8 (Leeds, 1984).

First publications: Partial: *Chester Mysteries: De Deluvio Noe. De Occisione Innocentium,* edited by J. H. Markland (London: Bensley, 1818). Complete: *The Chester Plays,* edited by Thomas Wright (London: Printed for the Shakespeare Society, 1843–1847; reprinted, 1853).

Standard edition: *The Chester Mystery Cycle,* edited by R. M. Lumiansky and David Mills, EETS, supplementary series 3 (1974).

Edition in modern English: *The Chester Mystery Plays: Seventeen Pageant Plays from the Chester Craft Cycle,* edited and translated by Maurice Hussey (London: Heinemann, 1957).

In the course of the twentieth century the Chester cycle of mystery plays has undergone a profound change in scholarly perception. Once seen as the earliest and most primitive of the four surviving English cycles – the York Cycle, the Wakefield or Towneley Plays, the Chester Plays, and the N-Town Plays – the extant Chester plays are now generally considered a Tudor achievement and among the last to reach their most developed state. Although evidence of dramatic performance in some form at Chester dates from 1422, and the nature of that evidence suggests a tradition already underway, the dramatic design of a Corpus Christi cycle spanning biblical history from Creation to doom may not have been performed there before the sixteenth century. In Chester a fifteenth-century tradition of single-day performances, staged on the feast of Corpus Christi, may have involved little more than a Passion play. The expansion and revision of the Chester Plays into the extant cycle occurred during the first quarter of the sixteenth century and coincided with a shifting of the performance from Corpus Christi to Whitsuntide, when three days were given over to the event. In records of the Corpus Christi Day performances, the body of pageants is regularly referred to in the singular as a play. With the expansion and modifications of the early sixteenth century, the cycle comes to be styled as plays.

The move from Corpus Christi to Whitsun may have been related to the sponsors' desire to stage multiple performances at various locations different from the stations along the traditional Corpus Christi processional route. The Corpus Christi procession of clergy and congregants, led by the priest displaying the elevated Host, commenced at the altar, passed various prominent locations of the city, and returned to the altar again. Mobile staging on pageant wagons, a technique already associated with the Corpus Christi procession, answered the need of multiple performances in different locations. Motivations for the expansion of the play and the shift to Whitsun may include desires to associate the plays more emphatically with the city than with the church, to avoid competition with the Corpus Christi productions in other cities, and to increase the commercial value of the plays. Civic authorities and the guilds (occupational or trade fraternities) struggled through the Reformation decades to continue regular performances and frequently amended the contents of the cycle to accommodate Protestant objections until opposition from the archbishop of York finally put an end to the plays in 1575. The surviving manuscripts recording the entire cycle, for the most part antiquarian projects, were written down in the last decade of the sixteenth and the first decade of the seventeenth centuries.

The Chester Plays employ only a few rhyme schemes, including a cross rhyme, or alternating rhyme, and a few passages of rhyme royal, but one scheme, a tail-rhyme stanza, or *rime couee,* predominates throughout the body of pageants. This nearly uniform rhyme scheme and the heavy influence on many of the plays of *A Stanzaic Life of Christ* (a work in verse also of Chester origin) are among features which suggest that one master reviser may have orchestrated the expansion of Chester's fifteenth-century Passion play into the sixteenth-century cycle of salvation history preserved in the extant manuscripts. Many of Chester's twenty-four pageants are within themselves groups of distinct episodes, and the remarkable use of *A Stanzaic Life of Christ* to expand or supply certain of these episodes, in addition to rhyme-scheme variations and external records attesting to fifteenth-century performances, enables scholars to perceive within the extant cycle the outline of the "Old Play" associated with Corpus Christi. Accompanied by the names of the Chester guilds that staged them, the twenty-four pageants of the extant cycle are (titles are those of the standard edition):

1. *The Fall of Lucifer* – the Tanners
2. *Adam and Eve; Cain and Abel* – the Drapers
3. *Noah's Flood* – the Waterleaders and Drawers of Dee
4. *Abraham, Lot, and Melchysedeck; Abraham and Isaac* – the Barbers
5. *Moses and the Law; Balaack and Balaam* – the Cappers
6. *The Annunciation and the Nativity* – the Wrights
7. *The Shepherds* – the Painters
8. *The Three Kings* – the Vintners
9. *The Offerings of the Three Kings* – the Mercers
10. *The Slaughter of the Innocents* – the Goldsmiths
11. *The Purification; Christ and the Doctors* – the Blacksmiths
12. *The Temptation; the Woman Taken in Adultery* – the Butchers
13. *The Blind Chelidonian; the Raising of Lazarus* – the Glovers
14. *Christ at the House of Simon the Leper; Christ and the Money-lenders; Judas' Plot* – the Corvisors
15. *The Last Supper; the Betrayal of Christ* – the Bakers
16. *The Trial and Flagellation* – the Fletchers, Bowyers, Coopers, and Stringers
16a. *The Passion* – the Ironmongers
17. *The Harrowing of Hell* – the Cooks
18. *The Resurrection* – the Skinners
19. *Christ on the Road to Emmaus; Doubting Thomas* – the Saddlers
20. *The Ascension* – the Tailors
21. *Pentecost* – the Fishmongers
22. *The Prophets of Antichrist* – the Clothworkers
23. *Antichrist* – the Dyers
24. *The Last Judgement* – the Websters.

In terms of its general sketch of salvation history, Chester's treatment of Christ's Passion is somewhat slight by comparison to the other cycles, and its ministry and eschatological episodes are rather more developed. However, anyone who compares the outlines of the cycles needs to avoid making judgments about an event's emphasis or significance in a particular cycle based only on the length of its development or whether it is set off in a pageant of its own. It is still not clear, for instance, to what degree logistical and environmental factors such as the number, size, and strength of guilds may have entered into decisions affecting the artistic construction of a city's cycle. By comparison to the others, Chester shows a tendency to cluster numerous significant events of scripture within the bounds of one pageant, and the Chester cycle is sometimes deliberately and effectively spare and austere.

The generic likeness of the four extant cycles resides in more than just the shape of the collection of individual pageants, stretching as they do from Creation to doom. It can also be seen in the governing and unifying motif of the Body of Christ, a feature which suggests that the original impetus of the great cycles was the institution of the Corpus Christi feast in 1311. This emphasis on the Eucharist makes it appropriate to call the cycles collectively the plays of Corpus Christi, even though, as in Chester, it is not always clear that performances were limited or even dedicated to the feast day. Along with the sometimes massive Marian content in the other cycles and the tendency in all to augment scriptural story with nonscriptural elaboration, this sacramental theme also presents one of the genre's inevitable challenges to Reformation policy. All four cycles exhibit typological interpretations of biblical history, that is, an exegetical view of Old Testament books that locates and emphasizes prefigurations of the Incarnation, ministry, Passion, or Resurrection of Christ. Important examples of such *figurae,* or "types," are Abraham's readiness to sacrifice Isaac (seen as prefiguration of divine self-sacrifice in the Passion), Noah's labor on the ark to save humanity from the Flood (seen as prefiguration of the founding of the Church and its sacraments), and Melchysedeck's offering of wine and bread to Abraham (seen as prefiguration of the Last Supper and the Eucharist). The selection of biblical episodes to be played in any cycle depends enormously on their potential to magnify the crucial moments of salvation history, including moments in the history of the sacrament of the Blessed Body. Perhaps even more than the municipal records of performance extending back into the late Middle Ages, this essential Roman Catholic sacramentalism of the great cycles explains the propriety of considering them medieval phenomena even when the surviving manuscripts and much of the artistry within them may be demonstrably Tudor.

For all their generic likeness, however, each of the cycles is distinctive in certain ways, and Chester's distinctive traits are vivid and crucial to its total achievement. Among its clear distinctions is its antifeminism. In Chester, Eve and the serpent are paired as the villains of the Fall, and no playwright who worked on extant portions of the succeeding action made any effort to cast Eve's life into an ameliorating context, whereas Adam is systematically recuperated as the cycle progresses. Woman's propensity for lechery is a commonplace in Chester, and the role of Mary is much smaller than in other cycles. In connection with Mary, Chester seems preoccupied with the question of what male has her in charge at any moment – first Joseph and later the disciple John, who leads her away from the Crucifixion before her son is dead.

Foremost among the distinctions of Chester is the theme of divine power and Christ's divinity. The other cycles seem by contrast to concentrate almost as decisively on Christ's humanity, and indeed the genre of mystery plays generally bears the marks of Franciscan emphasis on the humanity of Jesus and of late-medieval affective piety. Chester, however, takes a much more conservative, perhaps deliberately archaic position, emphasizing the divinity and omnipotence of Christ to such a degree that the influences of antischolastic and nominalist theology and of neo-Romanesque aesthetics have been seen in the cycle. Divine power is dramatized throughout the Chester cycle; indeed, the cycle's unity derives from the abundant iterations of that theme. Some emphatic instances are in its first play, the Tanners' *Fall of Lucifer,* which focuses on the omnipotence and benevolence of the Creator God;

the fifth play, the Cappers' episodes of the Commandments and *Balaack and Balaam* (the latter episode is unique to Chester among the great cycles); and the ministry plays, comprising plays 12 through 14. Chester's ministry sequence is the most developed of all the cycles, and these plays focus on the miracles of Jesus as demonstrations of power.

Another distinction of Chester is the occasional appearance of a narrator or expositor, variously called Preco, Nuntius, Doctor, and Expositor. The theme of divine power and the strategic use of the Expositor work in especially close harmony in the Cappers' pageant, where the alternating pattern of dramatization and exposition clearly reveals the playwright's chief interest in the material. After Moses receives the Commandments and descends to reveal the Law to the people (whose role was supplied by the audience of each performance), the Doctor summarizes the source material, which explains the original smashing of the tablet of the Law. After this passage God appears to Moses and orders the carving again of the Ten Laws. The Doctor's appeal to brevity is curious, for, among other business, he includes a summary of the action that follows his exposition. To decline to dramatize the faithlessness of the people, the testing of Moses, the smashing of the tablets, and the second inscription might seem by modern standards a rather antidramatic decision, especially in view of the redundancies of the passage. Chester instead chooses to dramatize twice the giving of the Law in scenes more like *tableaux vivants,* simple verbal transactions between Moses and God. Sandwiched between these two static images stands another verbal transaction, the explanation delivered by the Doctor to the performance audience (implicitly acknowledged as such by Doctor). The play makes clear that its interest lies in the Law as such: as commandments, power, words, and writing that bind community by requiring observance. In the Cappers' episode of *Moses and the Law* the same law is given three times to the same people, the contemporary audience of performance, in a deliberate redundancy emphasizing that this law pertains to contemporary Christians as well as to historical Jews. A different artist engaged in another project – Geoffrey Chaucer, for instance, or Hieronymus Bosch – might have been as interested in the fecklessness and stubbornness of Moses' people, and other mystery-play dramatists were interested in such material, as can be seen in the way Noah's wife, the shepherds, and the tormentors of Jesus are typically handled. The Doctor's abridgment, joining the two dialogues of Moses and God, however, makes unmistakable

Illustration of a Corpus Christi procession in a fifteenth-century manuscript (National Széchényi Library, Budapest, MS. Cod. Lat. 424, fol.69 ᵛ)

Chester's interest in this biblical material: the codification of divine law.

The construction of the episode of *Balaack and Balaam,* in the same play, sheds more light on Chester's central themes. Here there is more dramatic embellishment than in the episode of Moses. Balaack's grandeur as an earthly monarch is displayed in pomp and flourishes, and the moment of Balaam's confrontation with the angel of the Lord, complete with a balking ass who then miraculously speaks to his master, is fully played. Clearly the supernatural power represented by the angel and by the beast's use of speech accounts for the lavish development in this episode as compared to the treatment of Moses. Although the Expositor is thus not needed to emphasize the theme of divine power, he does appear near the end of the pageant when Balaam counsels Balaack to undermine the people of God with harlotry. Here the Doctor speaks nine

unbroken stanzas in which he first summarizes the success of Balaam's advice, then describes the vengeance wrought by Moses and Phineas, mentions the death of Balaam, and finally reminds the audience of Balaam's key prophecy:

> a sterre of Jacobb springe shall,
> a man of Israell,
> that shall overcome and have in bond
> all kinges and dukes of strange land;
> and all this world have in his hand.

The Doctor subsequently closes Chester's Old Testament pageants by linking Balaam's prophecy to its fulfillment in the visit of the magi, thus providing a transition to the New Testament pageants.

But there is a greater function served by the Doctor than abridgement and transition, and that is his way of standing apart from the dramatized history to point out its critical significance, freeing the playwright from resorting to anachronism. Other cycles freely and deliberately contrive to have their Old Testament characters speak of the Christian import of their deeds, but Chester eschews this technique, using the Expositor instead, standing outside the historical frame of staged actions, to mediate between those actions and the audience and to clarify and emphasize their Christian relevance.

Associated with this rejection of anachronism is another distinctive feature of Chester's Old Testament pageants. Although the cycles generally rely on typology as a device of selection and unification, Chester does so less than the others, and in its Old Testament pageants typology is deliberately underplayed. Rather than a body of material whose ultimate significance is projected into later actions, Chester's Old Testament pageants develop an interpretation of history and focus more on the condition of pre-Christian humans than on the prefigurations of Christianity among them. Chester's most emphatic typology occurs in play 4, in the episode *Abraham and Isaac.* Just before the intervention of God's angel, when Abraham is on the point of slaying his only son to fulfill the command of the Lord, the two characters exchange remarks that testify to the correspondence of Old Testament *figurae* (Abraham and Isaac) to New Testament fulfillments (divine Father and Son in the opening events of the Passion). Isaac's willingness and dedication is identical to and reminiscent of Christ's resolve concluding the agony in the Garden.

The passage is less typical of Chester, however, than it would be of the Wakefield and York cycles. The five pageants opening Chester have been seen as dividing Old Testament time into two ages: a period of natural law followed by a period of written law. The relative underplaying of typology in the Drapers' *Adam and Eve; Cain and Abel* (play 2) and also in the Waterleaders and Drawers' pageant of *Noah's Flood* (play 3) is consistent with the Expositor's absence from those pageants and the playwright's apparent decision not to relate early history to his Christian audience by any "prophetic principle" but rather by dramatizing the darkness of the first age through its radical lack of enlightenment. Only with the development of Hebrew culture, institutions, and especially written law, as dramatized in the Barbers' and Cappers' plays, does the Expositor appear and the employment of typology and prophecy accelerate. Thus the cycle's sequential process accounts for its audience's contemporary situation as the culmination of historical forces shaped to evolve humanity's spiritual enlightenment. That movement is both encapsulated in

and reiterated by the cyclic nature of the performance.

The idea of transition is a principal thematic aim of Chester pageants 6 through 9, the Nativity sequence. Much of the cycle's brilliant use of the *Stanzaic Life of Christ* for a unique effect lies in the Nativity sequence, where an older and more concise flow of action is slowed and spread out among newer passages to highlight various characters in various places of the earth as they are profoundly affected at the threshold moment between Old Testament and New Testament time. Joseph and Salome the midwife are converted from doubt to faith, and Octavian from paganism to Christianity (play 6). The shepherds of the fields are seen living brutal and clownish lives but then led by the star to inspired vocations of ministry (play 7), and the three kings undertake their arduous journey to enjoy, as they stand in the presence of the Child, a perfect understanding of the mystery they have sought. Herod is destroyed, reduced from pompous majesty to madness and futile infanticide, which ultimately engulfs his own child. At the end Herod's corpse is carried off to hell by a demon. The Innocents are slaughtered, but Jesus is saved by flight into Egypt (play 10), and Simeon's faith in the prophecies of Christ is perfected and rewarded by contact with the Child. Those who have kept the law of Moses, the doctors in the temple, affirm the authority of and are astonished by the One come to renew the Law (play 11). No significant human character in the Nativity pageants survives unchanged by the Incarnation.

The Painters' play of *The Shepherds* (play 7) is similar to the others of the Nativity sequence in the way it dramatizes the threshold moment of the Incarnation, but it is unique in its temporal perspective. Like the treatment of the shepherds in the Wakefield Plays, Chester Play 7 dramatizes contemporary English shepherds and thus underscores the recurrent threshold moment, the possibility of salvation through pastoral and sacramental mediation, for which the Nativity is the archetype. The shepherds have English names and evoke English places and customs. Their original state is nonetheless a pre-Christian benightedness, as shown by their earthly leechcraft ("henbane and horehounde, / tybbe, radishe, and egermonde," and other herbs), by the "dyrte" and "grubbes" on their food, and by the "wrastlinge and wakinge" that typifies their working lives. When the star and the angel appear to them and they progress across the playing surface to adore the Child in the creche, they cross the threshold and enter into reformed lives, which they dedicate explicitly to religious vocation.

The Chester ministry sequence, plays 12 through 14, is perhaps the most forceful expression of the theme of divine power. With few exceptions its episodes have their source in the Gospel of John, and recent appraisals of the thoroughgoing Johannine tone of Chester have done much to restore appreciation for the coherent fideistic purpose of this cycle, which was previously regarded as underdeveloped and purposeless. The combination and arrangement of episodes throw into sharp relief Jesus's attributes of divinity – judge, victor, and king – most obviously by dramatizing the miracles, but also by dramatizing other manifestations of divine power. Among other attributes upon which the Chester playwright insists is knowledge of men's (and demons') hearts. The Butchers' pageant of *The Temptation* is constructed to suggest simultaneously that Christ is never actually tempted by Satan's proposals and that he exposes himself to them as an act of supreme autonomy. Jesus vanquishes the devil by exposing to him the inadequacy of his categories for understanding God. Christ is able not only to read the sins in the hearts of the adulterous woman's accusers (and in Judas and Peter) but also her and Mary Magdalene's capacity for repentance. The range of his miraculous deeds is remarkable. The restoration of the blind man's sight with earth and spittle recalls the Creation of Man, and the raising of Lazarus proves Christ's power over death and hell; thus the pairing of these episodes in the Glovers' play 13 links what one might call the original power with the final and suggests the absolute sweep of Christ's attributes. Between the two episodes Chester dramatizes the preparation of the Pharisees to stone Jesus and his escape from them. The stage direction calls for them to collect stones and then states that "statim evanescit Jesus" (Jesus disappears instantly). The phrasing of this direction and the surprised reactions of Primus and Secundus Judeus suggest that the scene was constructed to make Jesus' disappearance a moment of astonishing stage technique and thus a theatrical metaphor of Christ's absolute power over the natural order. A similar moment occurs in the episode *Christ on the Road to Emmaus* (play 19) when Jesus disappears from the company of Cleophas and Lucas.

In the complex arrangement of episodes belonging to the Corvisors' play 14 (known in the civic records as the "Jerusalem Carriage") are set the homage by Mary Magdalene, the rebuke of Simon and Judas, the triumphal entry into Jerusalem, the scourging of the temple, and Judas's plot. The busy activity and multiple parts of this pageant have been adduced as evidence of Chester's uncertain purpose and loose construction, but attention to its Johannine character reveals a deliberate strategy in the author's selection and ordering of episodes. For all of its heterogeneous material, the pageant maintains a sharp focus on Jesus and presents him in all his attributes – Christ the merciful (with Magdalene), Christ the judge (with Simon, Judas), Christ the victor (with the money lenders), and Christ the king (in the entry and in the temple). Chester's Christ-centered attitude is consistent and thorough; it accounts in great part for the cycle's general tendency towards brevity and spareness of style.

In the Passion sequence especially – which in other cycles is lavish, elaborated at length, spectacular, and highly affective in manner – Chester keeps a rigorous and restrained focus on Christ. The episodes of *The Last Supper; The Betrayal of Christ* (play 15) are composed as close to unelaborated scripture as English mystery cycles come. The stage directions of the Bakers' *The Last Supper* suggest a ritualized performance reminiscent of liturgical drama (the same is also true of *The Ascension,* play 20), but they also emphasize Jesus as the first celebrant of the Holy Sacrament, thus making the pageant's most important exegetical point in a medium entirely aside from speech and requiring no extrascriptural composition. Even where the pageants of *The Trial and Flagellation* (play 16) and *The Passion* (play 16a) seem to dwell on other characters – such as Pilate, Simon of Cyrene, Dymas the converted thief, the centurion and Longinus, Joseph of Arimathea, and Nicodemus – a general pattern remains fixed: at first neutral or objective (as opposed to the unmitigated hostility of Christ's accusers and tormentors), these characters come to recognize and testify to Christ's powers, thus deflecting the play's attention back to its central focus – Jesus.

The typical sequence of pageants following the Crucifixion is in any cycle a concatenation of "minor" or partial climaxes, beginning with the Harrowing of Hell (the epic victory of Christ over Satan), continuing with the Resurrection (the victory over the tomb), the Ascension and Pentecost (the victory perceived and enjoyed by the disciples), and at length the Judgment (the victory of the original paradisal creation which was compromised by the Fall). The grand climax of Chester, however, comes at Pentecost, a point of particular didactic significance to the audience, related in-

Map of Chester circa 1577 (from Georg Braun and Francis Hohenberg, Civitates Orbis Terrarum, *1612–1617)*

trinsically to the Passion, Harrowing of Hell, Resurrection, and Last Judgment, but superior in that it relates these other events directly to the audience and knits them together in the problem of faith, which must be the abiding programmatic concern of Chester's emphasis on unapproachable, otherworldly, and inscrutible divine power. The Fishmongers' play of *Pentecost* (play 21), then, dramatizes the sending of the Holy Spirit to the disciples and their preparation to take up Christian ministry. In light of the cycle's previous focus on Christ, this play dramatizes a particularly human victory in emphasizing the disciples' growth in confidence and mission and their full arrival in their vocations. The principal evidences of this growth are the Apostle's Creed, indicating their understanding of the sacred life and ministry, and their new, extraordinary powers of language, indicating the action of the Spirit within them. But most significant about the play is

the elaborate statement of the creed, both in the familiar Latin and in English verse paraphrase and gloss. This extensive passage more directly relates to the audience the whole sweep of the cyclic process than any other single element of the play. The twelve articles rehearse events and words of scripture which are for the most part dramatized in the cycle. Furthermore, they make explicit the audience's fundamental responsibility as practicing Christians – to believe – and enumerate what things in particular the audience should believe. Consequently, *Pentecost* may be seen as the didactic climax of the cycle – the implicit exhortation to the audience to participate in the epic deeds dramatized by the twenty-four pageants and alluded to obliquely in the twelve articles of the creed.

At this point in their recitation of salvation history, other cycles take up the Last Judgment, but Chester supplies an innovation that emphasizes the audience's moment in time, a moment synonymous with the cycle's transition between biblical past and eschatological future. Chester's penultimate plays, the Clothworkers' *The Prophets of Antichrist* (play 22) and the Dyers' *Antichrist* (play 23), mitigate any complacency in the audience arising from a perception that they live in a time of victory and easy grace. When Antichrist, through his imitations of Christ in word and deed, succeeds in winning the allegiance of several kings, the members of the audience are warned of their own dilemma, their need not simply to be faithful in the midst of worldly distractions but also to discern the proper objects of faith. In the play the imposture of Antichrist is revealed when those he has raised from the dead are thwarted by the appearance of the Eucharistic wafer in the bread given them to eat by Enoch and Elias. The didactic point is clear: the audience is to put its faith in the sacraments of the holy church.

The death of Antichrist supplies, therefore, another of the cycle's considerable array of minor, incremental climaxes. Chester's trio of plays touching upon the Eschaton has prompted Martin Stevens's observation that the cycle has a highly developed "sense of an ending," or aesthetics of closure, consistent with the generic demand that the plays as a whole imitate the complete sweep, or fullness, of time. Because Antichrist's power lies in imitation and in the power of images, some recent commentators are also convinced that those plays indicate the cycle's artistic self-consciousness and moral self-examination. Does the eventual defeat of Antichrist constitute an affirmation of Christian art or a victory of faith and grace over sense and reason? Does Antichrist represent the essential problem of images and imitation, and does the pageant thus constitute a deep ambivalence about the kind of art that the mystery play involves? Interpretations of these problems vary, but it is evident to most critics that the Antichrist pageants reveal the playwright's awareness of the iconoclastic disputes that attended Lollardy and Puritanism.

It may be no simple accident that the Chester Plays enjoyed production well into Elizabeth I's reign, surviving Protestant opposition. Not only were the Chester city fathers vigorous in defense of their grand midsummer production, the plays also lacked the Marian elements of other cycles, and the expanded cycle that emerged during the reign of Henry VIII appears to diminish without removing the typical sacramentalism of Corpus Christi by building up beside it a substantial emphasis on the articles of faith and prophecies of the latter days. These, having clear scriptural authority and as direct a reference to the individual believer as to the church, are more congenial to the reformation temperament than are the ecclesiastical invention of the Corpus Christi feast and the exegetical interpretations which support it.

The Chester playwright – that master who effected most of the Tudor revision and expansion – may be the best Bible scholar of all the cycle masters, and his plays are more fideistic than theirs. It would be a mistake, however, to conclude that his sparer, briefer cycle is less effective as dramatic art when it is less affective in temper, less satisfying when it is less elaborate, or less significant when it is less attentive to the ordinary human condition. Chester's appeals to divine power are powerfully drawn, its demand of faith as compelling as the demands of compassion in the other cycles, the sweep of its cyclic process as sustained and coherent (if not perhaps more so), and its particular artistic techniques and aesthetic designs as aptly chosen for the purposes of dramatic performance, civic celebration, and spiritual enrichment.

References:

Mary D. Anderson, *Drama and Imagery in English Medieval Churches* (Cambridge: Cambridge University Press, 1963);

Kathleen M. Ashley, "Divine Power in Chester Cycle and Late Medieval Thought," *Journal of the History of Ideas,* 39 (July–September 1978): 387–404;

Marianne G. Briscoe and John C. Coldewey, eds., *Contexts for Early English Drama* (Bloomington: Indiana University Press, 1989);

E. K. Chambers, *The Mediaeval Stage,* 2 volumes (Oxford: Clarendon Press, 1903);

Lawrence M. Clopper, ed., *Chester: Records of Early English Drama,* volume 3 (Toronto: University of Toronto Press, 1979);

Clopper, "The History and Development of the Chester Cycle," *Modern Philology,* 75 (1978): 219–246;

Hardin Craig, *English Religious Drama of the Middle Ages* (Oxford: Clarendon Press, 1955);

Richard K. Emmerson, *Antichrist in the Middle Ages: A Study of Medieval Apocalypticism, Art, and Literature* (Seattle: University of Washington Press, 1981);

Emmerson, ed., *Approaches to Teaching Medieval English Drama* (New York: Modern Language Association, 1990);

Judith Ferster, "Writing on the Ground: Interpretation in Chester Play XII," in *Sign, Sentence, Discourse: Language in Medieval Thought and Litera-*

ture, edited by Julian N. Wasserman and Lois Roney (Syracuse: Syracuse University Press, 1989);

Harold Gardiner, *Mysteries' End: An Investigation of the Last Days of the Medieval Religious Stage* (New Haven: Yale University Press, 1946);

R. W. Hanning, " 'You Have Begun a Parlous Pleye': The Nature and Limits of Dramatic Mimesis as a Theme in Four Middle English 'Fall of Lucifer' Cycle Plays," *Comparative Drama,* 7 (Spring 1973): 22–50;

O. B. Hardison, Jr., *Christian Rite and Christian Drama in the Middle Ages: Essays in the Origin and Early History of Modern Drama* (Baltimore: Johns Hopkins University Press, 1965);

Kevin J. Harty, "The Unity and Structure of *The Chester Mystery Cycle,*" *Mediaevalia,* 2 (1976): 137–158;

V. A. Kolve, *The Play Called Corpus Christi* (Stanford, Cal.: Stanford University Press, 1966);

R. M. Lumiansky and David Mills, *The Chester Mystery Cycle: Essays and Documents* (Chapel Hill: University of North Carolina Press, 1983);

Alan H. Nelson, *The Medieval English Stage: Corpus Christi Pageants and Plays* (Chicago: University of Chicago Press, 1974);

Eleanor Prosser, *Drama and Religion in the English Mystery Plays: A Re-evaluation* (Stanford, Cal.: Stanford University Press, 1961);

Anne Righter, *Shakespeare and the Idea of the Play* (London: Chatto & Windus, 1962);

A. P. Rossiter, *English Drama from Early Times to Elizabethans: Its Background, Origins and Developments* (London: Hutchinson University Library, 1950);

F. M. Salter, *Mediaeval Drama in Chester* (Toronto: University of Toronto Press, 1955);

Martin Stevens, *Four Middle English Mystery Cycles: Textual, Contextual, and Critical Interpretations* (Princeton: Princeton University Press, 1987);

Jerome Taylor and Nelson, eds. *Medieval English Drama: Essays Critical and Contextual* (Chicago: University of Chicago Press, 1972);

Peter W. Travis, *Dramatic Design in the Chester Cycle* (Chicago: University of Chicago Press, 1982);

Glynne Wickham, *Early English Stages, 1300 to 1600,* 3 volumes (London: Routledge & Kegan Paul, 1959–1981);

Wickham, *The Medieval Theatre* (New York: St. Martin's Press, 1974);

Arnold Williams, *The Drama of Medieval England* (East Lansing: Michigan State University Press, 1961);

Williams, "Typology and the Cycle Plays: Some Criteria," *Speculum,* 43 (October 1968): 677–684;

Robert H. Wilson, "The *Stanzaic Life of Christ* and the Chester Plays," *North Carolina Studies in Philology,* 28 (July 1931): 413–432;

Rosemary Woolf, *The English Mystery Plays* (London: Routledge & Kegan Paul, 1972).

Cursor Mundi
(circa 1300)

Sally C. Hoople
Maine Maritime Academy

Manuscripts: None of the original manuscript versions of the work survives, though nine transcriptions are extant: British Library, MS. Cotton Vespasian A. iii (circa 1340); Göttingen University, theol. 107 r (1350–1400); Bodleian Library, Oxford, Fairfax 14 (late fourteenth century); Edinburgh Royal College of Physicians (late fourteenth century); College of Arms, London, Arundel LVII (circa 1400); Trinity College, Cambridge, R.3.8 (circa 1400); British Library, MS. Additional 31042 (mid fifteenth century); British Library, MS. Additional 36983 (1 January 1442); and Bodleian Library, Laud Misc. 416 (25 October 1459).

First publication and standard edition: *Cursor Mundi,* 7 volumes, edited by Richard Morris, EETS, o.s. 57, 59, 62, 66, 68, 99, 101 (1874–1893; reprinted, 1961–1966).

Standard edition: *The Southern Version of* Cursor Mundi, Sarah M. Horrall, general ed., 4 volumes to date, volume 1 edited by Horrall, volume 2 edited by Roger R. Fowler, volume 3 edited by Henry J. Stauffenberg, volume 4 edited by Peter H. J. Mous (Ottawa: University of Ottawa Press, 1978, 1990, 1985, 1986).

Cursor Mundi is an anonymous English poem of unknown date and location. However, one may make certain inferences about the author and origin of this salvation epic written in rhyming couplets and comprising approximately twenty-four thousand lines plus an additional six thousand lines of devotional writings. Scholarship places authorship in late-thirteenth-century northern England, near the Scottish border, and the poet demonstrates a wide-ranging knowledge of the Bible, biblical exegesis, and literary sources in English, French, and Latin. He also evinces a keen awareness of his reading audience. Directing his didactic message to the common people, he announces that

þis ilke book is translate
Into englisshe tonge to rede
For þe loue of englisshe lede
For comune folke of engelonde
Shulde þe better hit vndirstonde.

Declaring his intention "al þis world" to "ouer rynne," the author produces an encyclopedic work in honor of the eternally faithful Virgin Mary, aiming to rival the appeal of contemporaneous romances about powerful but worldly figures such as King Arthur, Tristan and Isolde, Charlemagne, Roland, Julius Caesar, and Alexander.

Securely grounding his work upon "the holy trinite," the poet organizes his history into seven ages. Following the prologue (lines 1–270), the first age (lines 271–1626) begins with God's creation of heaven and earth and concludes when God, angry at the wickedness of Cain's offspring, decides to inundate the world. The second age (lines 1627–2314) opens with the Lord's instructions to Noah to build an ark and ends with God's punishment for the forbidden construction of the Tower of Babel. Establishing Abraham as the root of Christian law and a progenitor of the Virgin Mary ("Oure lady wex out of his sede"), the poet spans in the third age (lines 2315–7860) the period from Abraham to the death of Saul and a reiteration of the lineage from Abraham to David, once again establishing the genealogy of the Virgin Mary. The fourth age (lines 7861–9228) runs from the accession of David to the throne to the successors of Solomon and to the Babylonian captivity, and the fifth age (lines 9229–12712) links Isaiah's prophecies in the Old Testament to the births of the Virgin and Jesus in the New Testament and narrates legends of Christ's childhood. Opening with John's baptism of Christ, the sixth age (lines 12713–21846) deals with the ministry of Christ and the Apostles and concludes with the discovery of the Holy Cross. The seventh age (lines 21847–23908) runs from the Antichrist to Doomsday, and four short poems in honor of the

Page from the Cursor Mundi *in a transcription dating from circa 1340 (British Library, MS. Cotton Vespasian A. iii)*

Virgin and Saint John follow, as well as additional poems with New Testament themes.

The *Cursor Mundi* poet relies upon a multitude of sources, which include the Vulgate, particularly the New Testament; Herman de Valenciennes's Old French *Histoire de la Bible* (twelfth century); an anonymous Old French poetic narrative about the wood of the crucifix and an account of Genesis and Exodus; *Vita Prothoplausti Ade* (the *Legende*), a Latin version of the cross-wood story; Petrus Comestor's *Historia scholastica evangelica* (twelfth century); Honorius Augustodunensis's *De imagine mundi, Speculum Ecclesiae,* and *Elucidarium;* Robert Grosseteste's *Chateau d'amour* (thirteenth century); Robert Wace's *L'Établissement de la fête de la conception Notre Dame dite la fête aux normands* (1130–1140); *Pseudo-Matthaei evangelium* (eighth or ninth century); *Gospel of Nicodemus;* Isidore of Seville's *Etymologiarum;* and Jacobus de Voragine's *Legende aurea* (circa 1260) and *The Bestiary.* Editors of *The Southern Version of Cursor Mundi* cite numerous studies of sources.

The result of this derivative approach is a remarkable, and generally coherent, compilation of diverse materials. For example, the myth of Seth, the third son of Adam, reveals a combination of biblical sources, and in the *Cursor Mundi* it typologically links the Old and New Testaments. In the Bible Seth appears only briefly. Genesis 4:25 refers to his birth and his mother's words: "For God . . . hath appointed me another seed instead of Abel, whom Cain slew." Genesis 5:3 states that Adam, at the age of 130 years, "begat a son in his own likeness, after his image; and called his name Seth." According to Genesis 5:6–7, Seth begat Enos and other sons and daughters and died at the age of 912 years. In 1 Chronicles and Luke 3:38 the genealogies listing Seth lead to the birth of Christ. The *Cursor Mundi,* however, narrates an elaborate legend in which ancient Adam bids Seth to go to Eden, ask the cherubim guarding the gate when Adam "shal fro þis world wende," and seek "þe oyle of mercye" that God, when he expelled Adam and Eve from Eden, promised to send to Adam "sum tide."

Seth immediately responds to his father's request and journeys "to paradyse þat same day." Kathleen M. Skubikowski places this trip in the context of the journey motifs appearing in diverse medieval writings and cultures. Citing the Latin *Legende* as a source, she notes the thematic shift from peril to reconciliation. When Seth arrives at the gate of Eden, he explains to the angel, Michael, that Adam finds life unendurable and urgently wishes to die. The angel grants Seth three views of Eden: the first revealing a veritable paradise of won-

drous flowers, fruits, sweet aromas, and a remarkable well from which "renne stremes foure" that water all of the earth. Beyond the well, however, appears a dry tree, which has become withered "for adam synne." A second view reveals a serpent encircling the tree. The New Testament theme of redemption appears with Seth's third view of Eden: in the top of the tree, which extends to the sky, lies a newborn babe wrapped in swaddling clothes. The angel explains to Seth that the child "is goddis sone," weeping for Adam's sins that in the future he "shal clense . . . Whenne þe plente shal come of tyme."

When Seth returns to his father with the angel's gift of three seeds from "þat tre . . . þat his fadir eet of adam," he instructs him to put them "vndir his tunge roote" and conveys the angel's message that "þe oyle may to þe wende / þourȝ birþe of a blissed childe / þat shal þe world fro shame shylde." Thus the child in the treetop and the oil of mercy foretell the New Testament promise of redemption. Skubikowski notes the link between the oil and baptism, "the eventual Christianization of the birth myth," and the reemergence of the Seth legend in the nonbiblical harrowing of hell. After Adam understands that he has been baptized in the river Jordan, he calls upon his son to tell the story of his quest. Seth repeats the angel's promise to give Adam the holy oil when at the end of the world Adam's "cors he shal vp reise," and through baptism "goddes sone . . . þi fadir shal he brynge . . . Fro helle to paradys þat blis."

Just as the Bible says little about Seth, it offers scant information about the childhood of Jesus. Thus the *Cursor Mundi* poet draws upon numerous sources for legends to fill the void. Those legends abound in miracles that the Christ child performs, while often portraying Jesus as a somewhat unappealing character. More than once his words and actions force Joseph and Mary into the undesirable roles of fearful parents of the neighborhood holy terror. For example, when one of his playmates maliciously destroys clay dams that Jesus has constructed on the river, Jesus causes the child "þat sibbe was to satanas" to fall down dead. The parents accost Joseph and Mary: "þei seide ȝoure sone wantoun & wylde / Wiþ his cursyng haþ slayn oure childe." This accusation fills Joseph and Mary with "Soore dredde," and they ask Jesus what the child had done to deserve to die. Jesus arrogantly replies, "worþi is he / Wh[e]nne he wolde not suffer to stond / þe werke made of my honde." After abusively smiting the corpse, Jesus grudgingly bids the child rise, but chides him, "þou wast neuer ny art worþi / In my fadir riche [kingdom] to be set / For þou hast my dedis let [destroyed]."

Jesus also offends the Jews by fashioning twelve mud sparrows and infusing life and flight into them on the Sabbath. Later, when the son of a wrathful priest destroys with a wand the lakes and dams that Jesus has created, Christ curses him with sterility, and the boy falls down dead. On the way home Jesus repeats his mortal curse upon a child who maliciously attacks him; the child's accusing friends question Joseph about the nature of one who "þus may do þat his wille is / And þat he biddeþ also soone / Wiþouten lettying [impediment] hit is done." In response to threats from the Jews, Jesus restores life to the corpse. Later, in pedagogical arguments, Jesus offends his teachers and other learned men by exposing them as blind fools who try to teach what they themselves do not know. Claiming that he existed "ar [before] þe lawe was founden" and that he has "no fadir erþely," Jesus declares himself not bound by earthly laws. While the *Cursor Mundi* poet obviously uses these legends demonstrating Jesus' total power over life and death to reinforce belief in the divinity of Christ, in human terms the image of a capricious young tyrant, albeit one whose aim is to stamp out evil, is unsettling.

Nevertheless, the author does relate more agreeable legends that demonstrate Jesus' divine power. Christ wins the respect of his peers when he restores to life a young boy whom another child has fatally struck, and during the flight into Egypt, the infant Jesus miraculously produces fruit and water for his suffering mother. En route from Jericho to the river Jordan, eight-year-old Jesus tames a threatening lioness and her cubs and creates a charming image when he sits among them:

> Aboute his feet þe whelpes ron
> Pleyinge wiþ him on her manere . . .
> þese oþere leouns þat were olde . . .
> Honoured him wiþ faunnyng tail.

The sources of those apocryphal legends are complex and often elusive. Tracing some of them, Roger R. Fowler cites as the *Cursor Mundi* poet's primary source the eighth- or ninth-century Latin *Pseudo-Matthaei evangelium* and its retelling of the childhood miracle stories from the second-century Greek *Gospel of Thomas*. In most cases the accounts are direct translations or close paraphrases. Among other uncanonical New Testament materials are reports concerning the disposition of the remains of John the Baptist. During the Middle Ages there were conflicting claims by the clergies of both Constantinople and Amiens and also by the monks of Angers that they possessed the head of Saint John the Baptist. In Matthew 14:12 the disciples bury the body, though Herod, when he hears of the deeds of Jesus, fears that he is John risen from the dead. According to the *Cursor Mundi* poet, however, Herodias, fearing that John's holiness might revive him, has the head "saltid in a wal" to prevent its rejoining his body, which, as a double precaution, she has burned "to poudir." Fowler identifies a direct correspondence between the *Cursor Mundi* reference to John's head and that in Herman's Bible.

Scholars have also given considerable attention to sources of the apocryphal *Cursor Mundi* account of the death of Herod the Great. The Gospel of Matthew simply mentions the death. Miriam Skey, however, examines possible sources for the greatly expanded report in the *Cursor Mundi,* which paints a vivid picture of God's vengeance upon the flagrant evildoer Herod, who even receives historically unsubstantiated blame for the Slaughter of the Innocents. He develops a palsy on one side of his body, his head begins scaling, and the itching "scab over-gas his bodi all." Ulcers pierce his body, and gout attacks his foot. Recurring fever and dropsy intensify the torment, "His teth ut of his heved" fall, pus and matter ooze out everywhere, "And wormes" crawl "here and there." Because his doctors cannot help him, he has them killed. His household and friends flee from him, and, because of his stench, no one can approach his bed. His son Archelaus reports that "The roting that him rennes ute, / The stink that ai es him abute, / Ne mai na liveand [living] man it thole [endure]." Finally, the son, assisted by doctors and barons, thrusts his father headfirst into boiling pitch and oil. With a vow that Herod would hang no more men, they send "him quar [where] he feris werr [fares worse] — / Werr than he fard ever ar [before]." According to Skey, the *Cursor Mundi* poet relied upon Josephus and Comestor for details about Herod's ailments and agonies. The actual murder, however, appears to be a medieval creation with a close parallel between Herman's Bible and the *Cursor Mundi*.

An important unifying element in the *Cursor Mundi* is the rood-tree legend, which springs from numerous and extremely complex sources. Skubikowski and Sarah M. Horrall trace this legend from the three seeds that the angel sends to Adam via Seth in the Old Testament to the New Testament cross upon which Christ is crucified. According to the *Cursor Mundi,* three saplings from the seeds grow out of Adam's mouth and endure through many generations until Moses, recognizing that "þei bitokenen persones þre / And o godhede in vnite," uproots them, sweetens the bitter water in the wilderness with their divine power, and later hides them on Mount Sinai. Scholars attribute the basis for the *Cursor Mundi* story of Adam and the saplings to the Latin *Legende,* and Horrall notes that details from the *Legende* are interspersed with material from the *Traduction anonyme de la Bible entière,* another major source. Carolyn E. Jones examines pre-Christian and Christian origins of the rood-tree legend, finds in *Post peccatum Adae* an important source, and links the tree leading to man's downfall in the Garden of Eden to the cross of Christ's Crucifixion, which redeems mankind:

> þourȝe a tre as ȝe haue herde
> was mankynde made þralle
> And þourȝe þe holy rode tre
> fredome coom vs alle.

Henry J. Stauffenberg points to a number of unusual characteristics of the cross wood: its composition of cedar, cypress, and pine (or "palme," according to *Cursor Mundi*), which strongly suggests a Trinitarian interpretation; an odor "wondir swete," a popular medieval attribution; and a strength that requires two hundred men (three hundred, according to other legends) to move it. Further evidence of its power is shown when Christ kisses it, and after the crucifixion the Jews sequester "þe crosse vnder erþe."

Not only are the *Cursor Mundi* sources numerous, complex, and often elusive, but also the various versions of the work are complicated. It does not survive in an original manuscript version, though nine of the many fourteenth- and fifteenth-century copies still exist. Richard Morris and his colleagues produced the first complete modern transcription of four different manuscripts (Cotton Vespasian A. iii, Fairfax 14, Göttingen, and MS. R.3.8 of Trinity College, Cambridge), arranged in four parallel columns on the page, published by the Early English Text Society between 1874 and 1893. For almost a century this edition, with Morris's critical commentary, was the only version readily available to readers. As Horrall and Skubikowski indicate, four of Morris's transcriptions are in Northern or Northeast Midland dialects; the fifth is East Midland.

During the past century scholarship has unearthed many new sources of the *Cursor Mundi* and increased knowledge of the dialects and historical context. Under Horrall's general editorship, scholars have transcribed the Southern Version, analyzed the text, and developed invaluable biblical exegesis and other annotations. Challenging Morris's

dismissal of the fourteenth-century southern manuscript as a corrupt, relatively useless copy of the original work, Horrall notes that the south central Midlands scribe preserved material lost in the northern versions, revised the poem significantly, and in effect created a new poem. Thus it would be erroneous to regard the Southern Version as a twentieth-century revised edition of Morris's work.

Scholars have also disagreed about the identity of the *Cursor Mundi* poet. Morris assumes that the writer must have been a learned cleric, arguing that the literary scope of the *Cursor Mundi* would have been out of the layman's reach. Also, the poet identifies himself in the epilogue as a pastor: "Amang thaa hirdes [shepherds] am I." Skubikowski views the work as the unified product of one author who felt a compelling responsibility to educate and communicate God's message to the common people. In some cases the *Cursor Mundi* affords glimpses into the medieval mind that may disturb a late-twentieth-century audience. One heated diatribe, for example (with no evident sources, so it appears to express the poet's opinion), names, starting with Adam, the biblical characters who succumbed to evil, "Folwynge wicked wommonnes wille." The powerful Samson "was bigyled þourȝe a wyf"; King David, for the illicit love of Bathsheba, sent her husband to his death; and even wise Solomon was beguiled by women. "In þis world of wicke wommon," any man under the control of an evil female "She bryngeþ to confusion." Therefore, the poet concludes, the man who is not subject to her dominion is blessed. The author does moderate his diatribe when he exempts good women, especially those following the example of the Virgin Mary, from his condemnation.

Repeated anti-Semitic execrations also permeate the *Cursor Mundi,* especially the New Testament section. Although "God loued þe iewis long biforn / þat his swete sone was born / . . . þat ilke cursed sede" fled from God. "Ful of enuye / To god & mon myche contrarye," "þis cursed folk wiþ þis mystrow [disbelief] / Wolde ihesus slee." The poet becomes vehement when he speaks of Jesus' love for the recalcitrant Jews who

> Bitauȝte [assigned] to þe fend grym
> Noon edder more ful of venym
> Of wicked wille & euel mood
> Aȝeyn her owne flesshe & blood . . .
> þei would not leue for his good dede
> Til þei had made his sides blede.

Yet the poet should not be judged in the context of late-twentieth-century political correctness.

Little is known about anti-Semitism in medieval England, and there is disagreement about Geoffrey Chaucer's Prioress in *The Canterbury Tales* (circa 1375–1400) and about Chaucer's own attitudes toward the Jews. And while fallible mortal women pose a threat to the poet's moral sense, he lavishly praises the flawless Virgin:

> I am and euer shal been hir þral . . .
> For þou3 my tunge were of steele
> And þat I loued noþing so wele
> And I bigon hir worshepe speken
> A þousande 3eer my3t I not reken
> þou3e I dude noon oþere þinge
> þe tenþe part of hir lovuynge.

He resolves, therefore, to worship her for the rest of his life. Seeking a receptive audience for his powerful Christian message, the *Cursor Mundi* poet offers a panoramic overview of religious history, both biblical and apocryphal, and vivid insight into the medieval mind.

References:

Zygfryd Marjan Arend, "Linking in *Cursor Mundi*," *Transactions of the Philological Society* (1925–1930): 200–259;

Paul E. Beichner, "The *Cursor Mundi* and Petrus Riga," *Speculum* (April 1949): 239–250;

Lois Borland, "Herman's *Bible* and the *Cursor Mundi*," *Studies in Philology,* 30 (July 1933): 427–444;

Carleton Brown, "The *Cursor Mundi* and the Southern Passion," *Modern Language Notes,* 26 (January 1911): 15–18;

Philip Buehler, "The *Cursor Mundi* and Herman's *Bible* – Some Additional Parallels," *Studies in Philology,* 61 (July 1964): 485–499;

Sarah M. Horrall, "The 'Cursor Mundi' Creation Story and Hugh of St. Victor," *Notes and Queries,* new series 23 (March 1976): 99–100;

Horrall, "An Old French Source for the *Genesis* Section of *Cursor Mundi*," *Mediaeval Studies,* 40 (1978): 361–373;

H. Hupe, "*Cursor Mundi*," *Anglia Beiblatt,* 1 (1890–1891): 133–136;

Hupe, "Zum Handschriftenverhältniss und zur Textkritik des Cursor Mundi," *Anglia,* 11 (1889): 121–145;

Carolyn E. Jones, "*Cursor Mundi* and *Past Peccatum Adae:* A Study of Textual Relationships," Ph.D dissertation, Miami, 1976;

Max Kaluza, "Zu den Quellen und dem Handschriftenverhältniss des *Cursor Mundi*," *Englische Studien,* 12 (1889): 451–458;

Kaluza, "Zum Handschriftenverhältniss und zur Textkritik des *Cursor Mundi*," *Englische Studien,* 11 (1888): 235–275;

Kirsti Kivimaa, "*Bitwix and* in *Cursor Mundi*," *Neuphilologische Mitteilungen,* 73, no. 1 (1972): 134–142;

Jacob Justin Lamberts, "The Noah Story in Cursor Mundi (vv. 1625–1916)," *Mediaeval Studies,* 24 (1962): 217–232;

Henning Larsen, "*Cursor Mundi* 1291," in *Philologica: The Malone Anniversary Studies,* edited by Thomas A. Kirby and Henry Bosley Woolf (Baltimore: Johns Hopkins Press, 1949), pp. 164–166;

Ernest G. Mardon, *The Narrative Unity of the* Cursor Mundi (Glasgow: William MacLellan, 1970);

Kari Sajavaara, "The Use of Robert Grosseteste's *Château d'amour* as a Source of the *Cursor Mundi*," *Neuphilologische Mitteilungen,* 68, no. 2 (1967): 184–193;

Miriam Skey, "The Death of Herod in the *Cursor Mundi*," *Medium Ævum,* 57, no. 1 (1988): 74–80;

Kathleen M. Skubikowski, "A Readers' Edition of *Cursor Mundi*," Ph.D. dissertation, Indiana University, 1985;

Otto Strandberg, *The Rime-Vowels of* Cursor Mundi (Uppsala, Sweden: Almqvist & Wiksells Boktryckeri, 1919);

John Thompson, "Textual Interpolations in the Cotton Manuscript of the *Cursor Mundi*," *Neuphilologische Mitteilungen,* 92, no. 1 (1991): 15–28.

The Matter of England

(1240–1400)

Sharon Stevenson

King Horn (circa 1240)

Manuscripts: The three extant manuscripts are Bodleian Library, Oxford, MS. Laud Misc. 108 (circa 1290), fols. 219^b–228^a; Cambridge University Library MS. Gg. 4.27 (2) (circa 1300), fols. 6^a–13^a; and British Library MS. Harley 2253 (circa 1340), folios 83^a–92^b. Facsimile: *Facsimile of British Museum Manuscript Harley 2253,* edited by N. R. Ker, EETS 225 (1964).

First publication: in *Ancient English Metrical Romance,* volume 2, edited by Joseph Ritson (London: Nicol, 1802), pp. 91–155.

Standard editions: *King Horn: A Middle-English Romance,* edited by Joseph Hall (Oxford: Clarendon Press, 1901); *King Horn: An Edition based on Cambridge University Library MS Gg.4.27(2),* edited by Rosamund Allen (New York: Garland, 1984).

Havelok the Dane (circa 1280)

Manuscripts: Bodleian Library, Oxford, MS. 1486, also called Laud Miscellany 108 (circa 1300), fols. 204^a–219^b includes the only extant nearly complete version of *Havelok the Dane.* Cambridge University Library MS. Additional 4407 (19) (circa 1350–1400) contains fifty-seven fragmentary lines, twelve of which do not appear in the Laud text.

First publication: *The Ancient English Romance of Havelok the Dane,* edited by F. Madden (London: Roxburghe Club, 1828).

Editions: *The Lay of Havelok the Dane,* edited by Walter W. Skeat, EETS, e.s. 4 (1868); second edition, revised by K. Sisam, 1915; reprinted, 1973; *Havelok,* edited by G. V. Smithers (New York: Oxford University Press, 1987).

Guy of Warwick (circa 1300)

Manuscripts: The earliest extant version appears in folios 108^a–175^b in the National Library of Scotland, Edinburgh, Advocates MS. 19.2.1, better known as the Auchinleck manuscript (circa 1330); Caius College, Cambridge,

MS. 107 (circa 1475) includes a short version; Cambridge University Library MS. Ff. 2.38, formerly no. 690 (circa 1450–1500), fols. 161^a–239^a includes a complete version of the story; two fragments also exist: Sloane 1044 no. 625 (circa 1375–1400), fols. 345^a–345^b; and British Library, MS. Add. 14409 (circa 1325–1350), fols. 74^a–77^b. Facsimiles: *The Auchinleck Manuscript,* edited by Derek Pearsall and I. C. Cunningham (London: Scolar Press, 1979); *Cambridge University Library Manuscript Ff. 2.38,* edited by Frances Mcsparran and P. R. Robinson (London: Scolar Press, 1979).

First publication: *The Booke of the moste victoryous Prynce, Guy of Warwick* (London: Printed by William Copland, [1560]).

Standard editions: *Romance of Guy of Warwick: The Second or 15th-Century Version,* edited by Julius Zupitza, EETS, e.s. 25 and 26 (1875, 1876); *Romance of Guy of Warwick: The First or 14th-Century Version,* edited by Zupitza, EETS, e.s. 42, 49, and 59 (1883, 1887, and 1891).

Beves of Hamtoun (circa 1300)

Manuscripts: Complete or nearly complete versions of the tale appear in the following: Advocates MS. 19.2.1 (the Auchinleck manuscript, circa 1330), fols. 176^a–201^a; British Library, Egerton MS. 2862, often referred to as the Sutherland manuscript (circa 1375–1400), fols. 45^a–94^b; Cambridge University Library, MS. Ff.2.38 (circa 1450–1500), fols. 102^b–133^b; Royal Library, Naples, MS. XIII. B. 29 (dated 1457), pp. 23–79; Chetham Library, Manchester, MS. 8009 (circa 1450–1500), fols. 122^a–187^b. Facsimile: *The Auchinleck Manuscript,* edited by Derek Pearsall and I. C. Cunningham (London: Scolar Press, 1979). Fragmentary copies are included in Caius College, Cambridge, MS. 175 (1300–1350), fols. 131^a–156^b; and Trinity College, Cambridge, MS. 1117 (IV) (fifteenth century), fols. 149–152.

First publication: *Beues of Hamtoun* (London: Printed by Rycharde Pynson, [1503]).

Standard edition: *The Romance of Sir Beues of Hamtoun,* edited by Eugen Köbling, EETS, e.s. 46, 48, and 65 (1885, 1886, 1894).

Richard, Coer de Lyon

Manuscripts: Six manuscripts and two fragments are extant: British Library, Egerton MS. 2862, formerly the Sutherland manuscript (circa 1400), fols. 1ª–44ᵇ; Caius College, Cambridge, MS. 175 (1425–1450), fols. 1–98; British Library MS. Add. 31042, formerly the Fillingham manuscript (circa 1425–1450), fols. 125ª–163; College of Arms MS. HDN 58, formerly Arundel manuscript (circa 1448), fols. 250ª–275; Bodleian MS. 21802, formerly Douce 228 (1475–1500), fols. 1ª–40ᵇ; British Library, Harleian MS. 4690 (1475–1500), fols. 106ª–115; and the fragments: National Library of Scotland, Edinburgh, Advocates MS. 19.2.1, better known as the Auchinleck manuscript (circa 1330), fols. 326–327; and Badminton House MS. 704.1.16.

First publication: *Rycharde cuer de Lyon* (London: Printed by Wynkyn de Worde, 1509).

Standard edition: *Der Mittelenglische Versroman Über Richard Löwenherz,* edited by Karl Brunner (Vienna & Leipzig: Wilhelm Braumüller, 1913).

Jean Bodel's twelfth-century poem *Chanson des Saisnes* divided the content of medieval romances into the Matter of Rome, those having classical heroes; the Matter of France, the Charlemagne romances; and the Matter of Britain, the Arthurian cycle. Nearly a hundred years after Bodel's poem, however, a body of romances written in English and celebrating English heroes became popular. Modern bibliographers adopted Bodel's method of classification and added a category, the Matter of England, to designate those romances dealing with British heroes: *King Horn* (circa 1240), *Havelok the Dane* (circa 1280), *Guy of Warwick* (circa 1300), *Beves of Hamtoun* (circa 1300) and *Richard, Coer de Lyon.* These romances are all metrical, use rhyme rather than alliteration, use chivalric conventions to varying degrees, deal with a historical or legendary English personage, and, with the exception of *Richard, Coer de Lyon,* utilize an exile-and-return motif. Although the works may have been composed earlier, the extant manuscripts all date from about 1290 to 1400, a time when the popularity of such verse forms was waning on the Continent in favor of prose.

Contemporary scholars are critical of Bodel's system of classification because it obscures the genres, which cross subject-matter boundaries and help to elucidate authorial intent and innovation. Consequently, the dominant trend in recent literary criticism has been to delineate what medieval poets and audiences may have understood by terms such as *romaunce, geste, cronicle,* and *legende,* for example, or how poets were using already established types such as historical romance (*chanson de geste*), the romance of adventure (*chanson d'aventure*), the *lai,* and saints' lives. No classification system has emerged that would tidily group all the English medieval romances by form, but the many analyses of narrative form and structure show that the romances in the Matter of England group often clothe their subjects in techniques, themes, and motifs more readily associated with other genres or types. For example, part 2 of *Guy of Warwick* blends chivalric romance with saints' lives; *Richard, Coer de Lyon* combines chronicle and legend into romance; *King Horn* casts a romance of adventure into modified *lai* format; *Havelok the Dane* injects social-estates material into chivalric romance; and *Beves of Hamtoun* draws motifs from a potpourri of sources – even the fabliau. The intentional blurring of genres, possible only because such forms had already been established, was used as a strategy to enervate the waning courtly romance, to satisfy patrons, families who wanted an ancestor of historical importance glorified as heroic, pious or egalitarian, and to bolster a growing national consciousness among the English by developing literary forms and tastes distinctly different from those of the French.

Although some scholars believe these Middle English romances were created for a lower-class rather than an aristocratic or courtly audience, the ownership of the manuscripts points in other directions: clerical libraries, well-to-do families, and the duke of Sutherland. On the other hand, most of the tales appear in compendiums of rather pedestrian works, probably because the works were not seen in the same artistic category as great works such as *Sir Gawain and the Green Knight* or *Piers Plowman.* The octosyllabic couplet forces a closure that does not promote the development of extended metaphor, ornate description, or sophisticated thought often found in long-line alliterative verse or iambic pentameter. The lack of erudition, an egalitarian tone, and the confounding of genres combine to make these romances the "popular culture" of the late medieval period.

King Horn is the earliest of the romances in the Matter of England group. Although scholars dis-

The opening lines of King Horn *in a transcription dating circa 1340 (British Library, MS. Harley 2253)* agree about the date of the Cambridge manuscript (MS. Gg 4.27[2]), Joseph Hall argues in his 1901 edition of the poem that the characters' names prove the tale is from much earlier than 1290 and is probably of English, not French, origin. *King Horn* is a brief work, running to only about 1,550 lines. When compared to its French counterpart, *Horn et Rimenhild,* the English poem favors action and dialogue over description, detailed social ritual, or motivation. The meter, an irregular iambic trimeter with frequent alliteration, gives it a strikingly lyrical quality and links it to the *lai,* a French narrative form often sung, but MS Harley. 2253 records each couplet as one line, suggesting that the rhyme may have been an innovation introduced into an earlier alliterative long-line source for purposes of adapting it to a romance format.

The work employs chivalric conventions, but battles, ritual, and courtly manner are diminished in favor of an emphasis on noble behavior. Since the overall motif of the poem is exile and return, the chief narrative complication focuses on the restoration of King Horn's kingdom, a matter which requires maturation, circumspect behavior, courage, and quick wit. In the opening episode when pagan raiders invade Suddene (an area Walter Oliver identifies as modern southwestern Scotland), kill King Muri (Horn's father), and set the youngster with his twelve companions adrift at sea, the chief of the invaders explains that if Horn is not drowned, he will be sure to seek revenge when he is grown, a foreshadowing of subsequent events. The narrative emphasis is not on what happens next at any given point, but on *how* it will come about, the key to which lies in the character of the hero.

Horn first demonstrates courage – despite fear and threatening currents, he rows bravely through the night and lands at Westernesse. The author does not attribute this safe landing to divine intervention or good fortune, but to resolute action on the part of the hero. In fact, when Horn reaches land, he thanks not Mary or Christ or fortune but the boat for refusing to break up or take on water. The poet demonstrates his hero's maturation through repetition of events. When Horn's home country of Suddene is attacked, for example, he is unable to confront the invaders; but later, when his adoptive country Westernesse is invaded, he successfully defends the kingdom. In fact, this defense is the first act of his new knighthood. His circumspect behavior is shown in his relationships with women. When King Aylmar's daughter Rimenhild falls madly in love with him, he is prudent enough to keep his promise to the king's steward not to take advantage of the princess's eager advances. When King Thurston of Ireland offers him both a kingdom and his daughter, Horn carefully replies that he will take the daughter only when he longs for her but that he will serve Thurston as knight and protector for seven years, an apprenticeship period evidently meant to demonstrate the characteristics of service and loyalty, until he reaches the age of twenty-two.

Horn endures three exiles in the poem. In the first he loses his social position and power, moving from prince to cupbearer, but makes knighthood a condition of his love for Rimenhild so that with her help he begins to regain his status. Unfortunately the treacherous Fikenhild, one of Horn's own companions, tells King Aylmar of Horn's love affair, and for the second time the hero finds himself exiled. He sails to Ireland, but because he has not been able to clear his name he must use a disguise. He introduces himself as Cutberd and lives for six years without his proper identity. He retains the heroic character he developed in Westernesse because that quality cannot be stripped from him as can identity, position, and property. After he has served most of his apprenticeship, however, Rimenhild sends a message that she is being forced into marriage with King Modi. Horn seizes the opportunity to clear his name, requests troops from Thurston, and successfully completes his first military foray. He forces himself into a kind of self-exile when he declares that he will not claim his bride, despite the fact that he has won her, until he has liberated his own country, Suddene, and reestablished his status as a king in his own right. Thus the three exiles Horn experiences reveal his strong character. The self-exile also creates a dramatic surprise for the audience.

The romantic element shows that the prince must learn to ferret out treachery and deal with palace intrigue. When Horn celebrates too long in recapturing Suddene, Fikenhild, his old enemy, forces Rimenhild to marry him and sequesters her in an impregnable tower. The hero, using the skills he learned as cupbearer, poses as a singer to gain entrance to the tower with his men. In their previous encounter Horn was not able to deal with Fikenhild's treachery because he could not see it. By making treachery the last obstacle to be overcome, the poet implies that overcoming deceit is the most difficult of leadership skills. The romantic element also introduces the use of two symbolic motifs. One is a fairly standard ring device, but the other employs the image of a fish, which first appears in Rimenhild's dream but which changes throughout the poem and is a kind of barometer of the couple's love.

King Horn is a deceptively simple tale that relies on repetition, and although this technique is sometimes seen as a mark of immature artistry, in this work it is used to develop a kind of handbook for princes. The foreshadowing devices that occur throughout, the repetition that builds in intensity, the lyrical line, and the complex use of symbols all indicate an artistic level not often attributed to Middle English romance.

Another romance in the Matter of England group, *Havelok the Dane* is unique partly because it combines the idea of social-estates literature with historical romance. The story probably reflects events of an eighth-century line of Anglo-Saxon kings recorded in Geoffrey Gaimar's Anglo-Norman *L'Estoire des Engleis* (circa 1135–1140). But the romance is memorable for its humble hero and its portraits of various social practices. Havelok, who is stripped of his kingdom by a treacherous guardian, is introduced as one who was "naked" in youth but who became the strongest man around, good in a crisis, and welcome in any company. He is not described in terms of knightly prowess, adventure, courtly manner, or religiosity, but in terms of his changing condition.

The hero journeys through much of the secular feudal class system from dispossessed orphan to fisherman's helper, porter, kitchen scullion, merchant, knight, and finally king of both Denmark and England. When the hero is a fisherman, the poet includes a lively description of the fish caught, a paean to the bountiful resources off the coast of England. Unemployed, he stands by the Lincoln Bridge and waits to hear the call, "Berman, Berman" (Porter, Porter). His true identity unknown, he makes his mark in an athletic event by "putting the stone" further than anyone, and, as a reward, he is married to Goldeboru, the dispossessed heir to England's throne. Becoming a merchant, Havelok bribes Ubbe, a justiciar, to let him sell his wares in Denmark, and he wins his knighthood not with a lance but with a door tree: when robbers break down the door of his temporary lodging, Havelok picks up the massive wooden lock bar and kills sixty-one men. This portrait of the homely hero, not the infallible knight, is another trait that makes the poem unique among romances.

The work also includes descriptions of aristocratic practices. When Godrich is sworn in as Havelok's guardian, the ceremony with its pomp and legal stipulations is described in detail, and Athelwold's death is portrayed as an orderly process: confession, last rites, self-flagellation, and clear disposition of property. These scenes, along with the judgment episodes at the end, give the poem a focus on orderly legal action and administration that most romances do not have.

Modern readers are sometimes surprised to find nascent capitalist values in this medieval poem, in which Havelok's hard work is presented as a moral virtue. He knocks down nine or ten men to answer the call for work; he carries four times as much as others; he never rests "longer than would a beast"; and he performs the heaviest and lowliest tasks without being told. To underscore the point that work is good for the would-be king, the narrator exclaims, "For it is no shame for to swinken!" The ideal King Athelwold is praised because he keeps order by ensuring that thieves, robbers, and outlaws are brought to the gallows, and he creates free trade for chapmen throughout the realm. Social mobility is also stressed. Grim, the Danish fisherman who refuses to drown the young Havelok, moves from serfdom to freeman by selling all his goods and sailing under the cover of night to Lindsey. Because Grim's three sons help him defeat the evil Godard, the hero makes them landed barons in Denmark. A cook befriends Havelok in Lincoln by giving him not only a job but a new set of clothes and shoes for his bare feet, and Havelok makes him the earl of Cornwall. A judge named Ubbe recognizes Havelok as the rightful heir and charges the people to swear homage to him, and in return the hero makes Ubbe justiciar of Denmark.

Despite the value it places on hard work, protection of free trade, punishment for theft of property, and social mobility, the romance does not celebrate egalitarianism. It clearly supports the concept of divine right: Havelok has a royal birthmark — a red cross on his shoulder — and a strange light emanates from his mouth when he sleeps that others identify as a special providential sign. He does not gather an army to regain his kingdom. He depends on others to recognize his royalty, to acquiesce to it, and to restore his status and property. Those who act on these values are rewarded; those who do not are punished. In this way *Havelok the Dane* is very different from *King Horn*. The earlier romance focuses on character and the behavior that will allow the hero to regain his kingdom through purposive action, whereas *Havelok* focuses on the values of work, justice, and private property, leaving the matter of the restitution of the kingdom to those who recognize the providential marks, believe in the social order, and can bring about justice.

The plot is built on a doubling effect. When Athelwold, mortally ill, must provide for his infant daughter, Goldeboru, and his English realm, his council of nobles selects Godrich, Earl of Cornwall,

Guy of Warwick battling the giant; an illustration from The Booke of the Moste Victoryous Prynce, Guy of Warwick *(1560), the first publication of the work*

The engaging style of *Havelok the Dane* is created by the persona of the poem's speaker. The work was intended for recitation, but the final lines, wherein the speaker asks the audience to say a Pater Noster for the poet who stayed up many nights to make the rhyme, clearly separate the speaker from the poet. Throughout the poem the poet gives the speaker lines that create familiarity: he asks for a cup of ale before he begins; he swears his favorite oath "datheit" (a curse on anyone who . . .); he moralizes; and he sometimes refuses to relate an action. Since at least half the lines are dialogue, the speaker appears to be a familiar gossip who repeats conversations. Such a tone complements the egalitarian subject matter and the humility of the hero.

Guy of Warwick is the longest of the Matter of England romances, running to nearly twelve thousand lines. The many surviving manuscripts and printed versions are evidence of its popularity among the aristocracy during the late Middle Ages, and it remained popular down to the nineteenth century. For modern readers the work lacks aesthetic unity, but this problem arises partly from the medieval compilation of different versions of the poem into one manuscript and partly from the limitations of modern editions. Cambridge University Library MS. Ff. 2.38, which carefully follows its Anglo-Norman source, *Gui de Warewic* (circa 1240), contains the complete story from the rise of the hero through the exploits of his son, but the Auchinleck manuscript presents a conflation of three separate romances. The first, done in octosyllabic couplets, describes the hero's rise from lowly cupbearer to world-renowned knight, ending with Guy's return to England, where he fights a dragon for King Athelstan. The second, done in tail-rhyme stanza, details Guy's chivalric service for God, beginning with his marriage and ending with his death and a prayer. The third, also done in tail-rhyme stanza, contains the exploits of Guy's son, Reinbrun. This division breaks the story into units of about seven thousand, thirty-five hundred, and fifteen hundred lines respectively, lengths that more closely approximate the other romances in the Matter of England. The three units also exhibit differences in form: part 1 is a fairly conventional chivalric romance, part 2 is an exemplary or hagiographic romance, and part 3 is a romance of adventure. Considered in this way, *Guy of Warwick* demonstrates aesthetic unity and coherent form, although repetition is sometimes a problem and devices for generating various episodes are not sophisticated.

The unifying principle in the first part is the main character's motivation to win his lady by be-

as guardian, but he immediately covets the kingdom for his son. This pattern is repeated (doubled) in Denmark with Birkabeyn, Havelok's father, but the detail of the process is shortened in favor of painting Godard's treachery. After seeing his sisters slain, Havelok begs for a tradesman's deal: his kingdom and his promise not to attempt to regain the crown in exchange for his life. Godard agrees, but he strikes a bargain with Grim to drown the boy in exchange for freedom from thralldom. Once the Grim episodes begin, the doubling stops, and the plot focuses on Havelok's fortunes.

The plot begins to double again when Godard is brought to justice. The council decrees that he shall be flayed alive and hanged with two ropes. Likewise, when Godrich's treachery is exposed, in England, the council there decrees that he shall be publicly displayed and burned at the stake in a little square on the south side of Lincoln. Although doubling is not a sophisticated device, the poet handles it well, varying the situations and collapsing and suggesting rather than repeating detail. The point of nearly all the doubling events is the orderly administration of social and legal processes, including justice.

coming the greatest knight. Felice is the type of distant heroine more typical of Continental than English romance. Unlike Rimenhild, in *King Horn,* who calls the hero to her bower or the impetuous Josain who runs off with Beves in *Sir Beves of Hamtoun,* Felice spurns the hero at least three times because his station is too lowly or his renown is not great enough. Like the other two heroines, however, Felice is the means by which the hero gains his knighthood, and the knighting ceremony is given in great detail. Indeed, part 1 celebrates chivalry and chivalric exploits rather than romantic intrigue. Guy fights a tournament honoring the emperor of Germany's daughter, survives an ambush by Earl Lambard, breaks the emperor of Germany's siege of Duke Segwin, saves Emperor Ernis of Constantinople from his enemy the sultan, helps Sir Tyrry win Ozelle and her kingdom, kills the son of the earl of Florentine because the young man unjustly demanded the hero's hunting horn, and returns to England to slay a dragon and claim his bride and her kingdom. The episodes are often linked with a standard device: the hero hears of an injustice or an opportunity to prove himself. The episodes do not build in intensity, however, nor do they distinguish between the relative worths of different kinds of undertakings or even skillfully interweave the fates of a set of heroes and villains.

Several episodes provide memorable interludes to the fighting: Duke Segwin's walking through the streets while stripped of all his symbols of nobility so that he may ask forgiveness of the emperor, the lion who is so grateful to Guy he will not leave the hero, the palace intrigue at Constantinople, the "soul-animal" that runs out of Tyrry's mouth to the treasure, and Guy's rescue of Ozelle just as she arrives at the church to be married against her will. These episodes underscore the exotic nature of such faraway places and the hero's admirable conduct in relation to Continental aristocracy, showing that a steward's son from backwater England can mediate justice in the great Continental empires both east and west.

The second section of *Guy of Warwick* blends chivalric adventure with hagiography. The hero leaves his wife and unborn son to fight, not for personal fame or the love of a woman but for the glory of God. When he fights the giants Ameraunt, Barrard, and Colbrond, however, he fights disguised as a beggar; for this reason the romance is often compared to the legend of Saint Alexis, who also posed as a beggar, but the comparison is tenuous since Alexis was not a warrior. Guy becomes God's instrument for establishing earthly justice.

When he fights Ameraunt to establish the innocence of King Triamour's son, he is given Alexander's helmet and Hector's sword, signifying that he is the Christian culmination of all that the virtuous pagan heroes prefigured. His enemy Ameraunt is described as "the devil and no man," and he carries Hercules' sword which had been "put in the water of hell." Thus the episode invokes a religious symbolism not present in the first section of the romance, and it deepens to the miraculous in the battle with Barrard, fought to prove the innocence of Guy's good friend Sir Tyrry, who spends the entire sequence in the chapel, praying for the poor pilgrim who will fight for him. Guy is described as divine: "Guy was no earthly man: / He was no man earthly, / He was an angel, sekerlye [truly]." When the battle lasts all day and the combatants are given to protectors for the night, Barrarde has four men throw the sleeping Guy, bed and all, into the sea, proving that the emperor, Guy's protector, is not infallible. A fisherman rescues the hero, protects him for the rest of the night, and announces him in court the next day. The fisherman symbolizes Christ's commitment to the pious warrior, suggesting that secular life can be as worthy as the religious.

The importance of the religious warrior for England is underscored in Guy's battle with Colbrond, an African giant in the service of the Danes. When Athelstan stands to lose England, he prays for a warrior who can fight the giant. In a dream an angel tells Athelstan where he can find a beggar to fight for the nation's cause. Athelstan enlists Guy's aid, and the battle is engaged. Guy resists the promises of material goods offered to him by Colbrond during the fight, defeats the giant, and frees England forever from Danish threat. Afterward the hero retires to a hermitage, where he spends the rest of his life in anonymity. Signs of saintliness accompany his death: the body cannot be removed from the spot, a sweet odor with healing properties emanates from it, and a religious house is established there.

The tale of Guy's son Reinbrun affirms the continuation of the chivalric tradition into the next generation, but the hagiographic elements are dropped in favor of adventure and fantasy. Reinbrun is kidnapped by Russian merchants who are shipwrecked in Africa, where Reinbrun is given to King Argus's daughter. When Sir Harrad, Guy's teacher and friend, goes in search of the boy, he is thrown in prison and made to fight against King Argus's army. He discovers that the young man he cannot best is Reinbrun. The two are reunited and on the way home participate in an adventure to save

Guy's friend Amis from an elvish knight in a fairy grotto with a magic underground river. The pattern of youth perpetuating the chivalric tradition doubles as Harrad and Reinbrun meet a young man who exacts passage from them but will not give his name. The mysterious young man turns out to be Harrad's son, Aslak, who has gone off to find his father. One difference between the secular and the religious man lies in the former's ability to perpetuate his values through his offspring; consequently Reinbrun continues the argument for the value of the active warrior hero.

Sir Beves of Hamtoun, another popular Matter of England romance, enjoyed an international reputation. There are versions in French, Irish, Italian, German, Russian, Romanian, Yiddish, Welsh, and Norse. Its popularity was probably due to its emphasis on a fast-moving plot and adventurous intrigue. Its revenge framework, which bears similarities to William Shakespeare's *Hamlet* (1603), begins when Beves's mother, a young Scottish princess, sends Beves's aged father on a hunting trip, where her lover murders him. Because Beves attempts revenge, his mother orders him sold to Saracen merchants, who take him to the court of King Ermin. There he grows up, proves his knighthood, and falls in love. In a later episode Beves carries a note ordering his own execution, but King Brademond chooses to imprison him rather than carry out the execution order. As when Gertrude dies accidentally at the end of *Hamlet,* so when Beves's mother is made to watch her lover's torture and death by hot pitch, brimstone, and lead she accidentally falls and breaks her neck. These similarities are too vague to establish a source relationship between the two; rather, they probably attest to the persistence of the motifs in the popular imagination.

Although the romance is nearly forty-five hundred lines long, the outrageous plot events never seem to be repeated and are quickly paced, each episode being motivated by preceding events so that no awkward linking devices are needed. Short summaries of the action occur about every nine hundred lines, suggesting that the romance was intended for reading or oral recitation. Although the story has the trappings of chivalry – the hero wins his famous sword, Morgelai, by striking its owner with a boar's head; his faithful horse Arundel will let no Saracen ride him; and he has a knightly peer, Sir Terri, who is in the end given a kingdom for his good service – the romance is really not composed to glorify the chivalric code. Indeed, sometimes it strays from this code. The heroine Josaine, like

Rimenhild in *King Horn,* forces her love on the hero, and it is he, not she, who dictates that he must prove himself before he can claim her love. Josaine is no fainting female: she refuses to believe her father when he tells her that Beves has gone back to England to marry a king's daughter; she calls Beves a churl when he refuses to marry her; she wears a magic ring to protect herself from intercourse with Brademond; she offers to hold one lion while Beves fights the other; she hangs Earl Miles, an evil suitor who forces her to marry him, using a towel she finds in their bedchamber; she eats herbs to make herself leprous so the giant Ascopard cannot give her to Brademond; and, when Beves's faithful friend Saber becomes ill, she disguises herself as a minstrel to make money. Josaine is not the aloof, disdainful, aristocratic woman of the standard chivalric romance.

Although he grew up in pagan lands, the hero is unswervingly Christian. He is not tempted to worship Apollo even though King Ermin promises him all of Ermonie if he will do so. On Christmas Day Beves slays all the Saracens who ridicule his God. He also slays the infidel priests in Damascus and goes for confession to the patriarch in Jerusalem. He ultimately makes his home in Momebrant and Christianizes the land. But he is not described as angelic or saintly, and he does not renounce worldly fame and pleasures as Guy of Warwick does. Nor is Beves infallible. He fails to open the letter ordering his own execution although he is advised to do so. When he escapes Brademond's prison, he is so tired that after seven miles he must rest. But when he wakes up and rides off again, he rides the wrong way, back to the enemy. He argues with the giant's wife and so must fight her husband. Beves is appealing precisely because he is rash, makes mistakes, and is not inhumanly pious. He is different from Horn, who announces what he will do and then does it, or Havelok, who bumbles into his predestined fortune, or Guy, who is motivated by pious intentions and the love of a disdainful woman.

The romance includes miraculous passages that seem more suited to saints' lives than to this earthy adventure. When Beves escapes from prison, for example, Brademond's men chase him over a cliff, but the miraculous horse, which the hero has stolen, swims all day and night to carry him to safety. Later, when Josaine, Bonefas, and Beves hide in a cave, lions attack and kill Bonefas but will not attack Josaine because she is a virgin (the patriarch had commanded that Beves marry a virgin). When Beves fights the dragon at the request of the bishop of Cologne, he is so seriously wounded he cannot continue, until he falls in the well of the Virgin and is made whole again. All of these motifs appear elsewhere in hagiography and legend. Because they appear in this poem between Beves's imprisonment and his return to England — an easy place to add material — and because they are out of keeping with the framework of the romance, they probably represent medieval accretions. The adaptor indicates before the dragon fight that the episode proves Beves to be the equal of many other heroes, Guy of Warwick included. Because many of the possible accretions are pious in nature, it may be that the adaptor of Beves was trying to imitate the kind of alterations done to *Guy of Warwick* to make it hagiographic in nature. The adaptor of *Guy of Warwick* seems to have been aware of French forms and to have altered his material at the end so that he did not destroy the unity of the original. The *Beves of Hamtoun* adaptor chooses a much more difficult strategy, inserting the miraculous episodes into the middle of a secular, pseudohistorical and probably politically motivated narrative.

Much more in keeping with the tone of the romance are the many clever ruses or tricks gone awry. The first prison guard, who angrily slides down the rope to put an end to Beves's Christian prayers, meets the hero's fist and dies, and the second guard descends the rope and is impaled on the first one's upraised sword. Saber is able to regain Arundel from thieves by getting the water boy to show him the horse's hindquarters, whereupon Saber leaps on the horse and rides off. When the evil stepfather finds that Beves has tricked him, he throws a knife at Beves's messenger but misses and kills his own son instead. This motif occurs elsewhere, but it is integrally related in this case when the messenger makes a crude joke, claiming that the stepfather has "groped" his wife too long at night so that he might not see to throw "aright." Such fabliau material set beside the miraculous underscores the idea that the tale has been reworked by an adapter or adapters.

The headiest episode appears at the poem's conclusion, when Beves takes on the entire population of London and wins. King Edgar's steward treacherously organizes the citizens to gather their clubs and chain off the streets so the hero with his six men must fight sixty knights in the narrow Godes Lane in Cheapside. The citizens shout, "Aӡilt, aӡilt" (Surrender, surrender), and the hero cries, "I will surrender only to God that sits in trinity." He slays thousands so that the Thames runs red with blood, and the London Bridge is burned.

King Richard; illustration from Wynkyn de Worde's 1528 edition,
Rycharde cuer de Lyon

Fortunately Beves's sons save the day, and Beves and Edgar are reconciled. There seems to be no corresponding historical event in King Edgar's reign, but Judith Weiss makes a convincing argument that this episode is a veiled political analogy to the stormy relationship between Henry III and his barons and that it was probably composed in support of the barons.

Richard, Coer de Lyon exists in two distinct manuscript versions. The Auchinleck manuscript, Egerton 2862, Harley 4690, the Arundel manuscript, and Douce 228 represent a shorter, more historical version than those of the British Library MS Add. MS. 31042 and the Cambridge MS. 175, which include several fabulous and unsavory episodes. The poem refers throughout to a French source, but none is extant to help modern editors understand the different natures of the two sets of manuscripts. The shorter version begins with Pope Urban's call for the Third Crusade to regain Surreyland (Syria) and to recover a portion of the Holy Cross. After dispatching his navy, Richard travels by land to rendezvous with King Philip of France in

Messina, Sicily. The treachery begins when Philip sends a letter warning King Tancred of Sicily that Richard plans to attack. Philip's deceit is exposed, but on Christmas Day, when thirty-six of Richard's men are killed in Messina, he retaliates by besieging the city using the "Mate-Griffon" (Greek-killer) siege tower. Peace is restored only after the archbishop intervenes.

On the way to Acre, Richard's ships break up at sea, and the king of Cyprus kills some of the survivors and loots the supplies. When Richard's demands for restitution are denied, he attacks and conquers Cyprus. He then conquers a freighter carrying supplies to the Saracens. At Acre a great chain lies across the bay, but Richard breaks it and sails into port where he celebrates by setting off fireworks. At night he builds a huge lighted figure with bloody eyes and horns that gives off a terrible grinding sound from the rocks rigged inside. The enemy in Acre believes the devil has arrived, and Richard wins a psychological battle. Richard sets about mining the city walls and constructing a new Mate-Griffon for showering arrows and a Robinet for catapulting stones and beehives into the city, all of which brings about Acre's surrender. When the terms of the peace agreement cannot be worked out, Richard kills his prisoners in full view of the city, a historical fact, but the poet embroiders it with an angel that emerges from a cloud and commands "Seynyours, tuez, tuese, / Spare them nought, beheadeth these!"

Richard then marches south to capture Caphyas (Haifa) and Arsour (Arsuf), where he argues with Philip over who will be named as steward of Jerusalem. Philip returns home on his doctor's advice, and Richard moves on to take Joppe (Jaffe) and Chaloyn (Ascalon), where he begins a new enmity with the duke of Austria over stopping to fortify the walls of Ascalon. Word comes to him of his brother John's treachery at home. He returns to Joppe to create a sort of self-defense force and goes on to Acre, intending to leave for England, but Saladin attacks Joppe, and Richard ultimately returns, where he is nearly taken by Saladin in a surprise raid. Richard, knowing he must return to England, bargains a truce whereby pilgrims may pass to the holy sites for three years. He finally returns home, where he receives a mortal wound to the head while he is storming Gaillard, a castle between Rouen and Paris.

The emphasis of the shorter versions of this romance is on military exploits; they portray Richard as an impetuous, courageous, charismatic leader who is also a brilliant military strategist, using the technology of the period and promoting himself as a devil. At the same time, the supernatural qualities of the short version are angels, dreams, and a vision of Saint George, but these are devices associated with the historical epic rather than the marvels of the romance, as Finlayson has shown. The poet mentions specific knights' names – Aleyn Trenchemere, Richard's naval captain; Hubert Gawtry, the nephew of the archbishop of Canterbury; Jake de Neys, a Flemish crusader; and his sons – perhaps to please patrons, but more likely as a kind of epic device to preserve history and create authenticity. Not all the material is factual, however, and Karl Brunner in the introduction to his 1913 edition attempts to separate the history from the pseudohistory and the marvelous. The material does not coincide with that in any extant chronicles that antedate the romance; the poet may have been working with materials that are now lost, or he may have relied on oral tradition.

The longer manuscript versions, however, present some fabulous and unsavory accretions. The first suggests that Richard was the offspring of an evil sorceress, a legend actually circulating at the time that was exploited by Richard in convincing the Saracens that he was the devil. The second accretion is a three-day tournament in which a disguised Richard jousts with Fulk D'Oilly and Thomas Moulton to test their prowess. The third accretion is the story of Richard's capture, imprisonment, and subsequent ransoming in Germany, a historical event which occurred after, not before, the Third Crusade. The quarrel with the duke of Austria at Ascalon included in this episode is probably an indication that it originally occurred at the end of the romance. Adapters may have moved it to the beginning to establish the epithet "Lionheart" since it relates how Richard saves himself from death by reaching down a lion's throat, pulling out its heart, and salting and eating it before the emperor of Germany. But it may also be included at the beginning so that the romance can end with Richard's triumphant exploits.

Another set of accretions deals with Richard's cannibalism. When he becomes ill in Acre (he actually suffered from malaria) and wants pork, the cook, having none, serves him Saracen flesh. It heals Richard, and he subsequently asks for the head of the swine, forcing his cook to confess, at which Richard laughs heartily and says that his troops will never go hungry so long as there is an enemy. Later when Saladin sends messengers to negotiate for the release of prisoners at Acre, Richard has several noble prisoners slaughtered and boiled to feed the messengers. These accretions are usually seen as an unfortunate reflection of the religious zeal of the period.

A final set of accretions can be found after the victory at Acre. The longer versions add battles that deal with the heroism of Fulk D'Oilly and Thomas Moulton and single combat between Richard and Saladin in which Saladin sends Richard a devil horse that will begin to suckle when it hears the mare's cry. An individual combat or even a meeting between the two men never took place, but Richard requested such opportunities on more than one occasion.

The two versions contain two different romantic elements, but neither is typically chivalric: Richard does not become lovesick, nor are his actions motivated by love for a woman. In the longer, more fabulous versions there is a woman named Margery, daughter of the emperor of Almayne. When Richard is captured, she forms a liaison with him, tells him of her father's plot to turn the lion on him, and supplies him with the forty scarves he needs to wrap his hand and arm so that he might reach down the lion's throat to extract its heart. She does all this after Richard kills her brother in a game of buffets so that the emperor complains that Richard has killed his son and "forleyn" his daughter. In this version the woman is simply a means to establish Richard's reputation and further his military prowess. She is not mentioned again.

The shorter versions present a woman named Berengaria, daughter of the duke of Navarre, whom Richard's mother, Eleanor of Aquitaine, brings to him at Christmastime in Sicily. He declares that he will not be married to her until Easter, if he is still alive. He is firmly in control of Cyprus at Easter and so does marry Berengaria (a historical fact), but there is no celebration of the festivities. Johanna, Richard's widowed sister, and Berengaria accompany Richard to the Holy Land, and at one point Richard tries to bargain with Saladin by offering him Johanna in marriage (another historical fact). The events in the short versions are historically accurate, and the romantic element functions, as it does in epic, strictly for the good of empire building. Richard, as a hero, does not look on a ring and sigh for his ladylove as Horn does nor return to her for approval as Guy does.

The action of this romance is almost wholly violent, and the recurring themes are treachery and revenge. Although most of the actions in the poem are done for the glory of Christ, the tone is not pious but coarse. While the narrator of *Havelok* swears his mildly comic "datheit," the characters in *Richard* engage in name-calling ranging from "heathen hounds" or "devils of hell" to "taylardes," which in its most innocent reading means having a tail, an epithet most often reserved for the French. In a historical setting wherein Saladin poisons the rivers with Christian corpses and Richard commands his army to bludgeon to death some three-thousand hostages, including three hundred women and children, the poet and his adaptors have probably captured the mindset accurately.

Although the Matter of England romances do not have a single, well-defined subject (as do those of Charlemagne, Arthur, and the classical heroes), each of them presents a secular, English hero involved in international events or intrigue and whose status moves from unheralded or destitute to worthiest of all. The versification of these romances breaks with the traditional Anglo-Saxon alliterative long line in favor of imitating Continental rhyme forms, and their narrative structures mix genres that had already peaked on the continent. Their plots emphasize adventure, travel, and social success. The inordinate amount of dialogue in these works creates a sense of present action and a gossipy intimacy with momentous affairs. Humor, heroic ingenuity, and solid morality coupled with the outrageous, impossible, or marvellous apparently appealed to a wide, not simply a learned, pious, or female, audience. In fact, these English heroes clothed in Continental cultural forms who overcome their national and international rivals are probably a barometer of the popular English aspirations of the period to create an adventurous national identity and a culture comparable to that on the continent. Modern readers may find the verse form too simplistic and the action interminably repetitive, but for medieval audiences who heard a few hundred lines at a time, read aloud or sung, these romances were probably heady entertainment.

Bibliographies:

Laura Hibbard Loomis, *Medieval Romance in England* (New York: Burt Franklin, 1960), pp. 83–155;

J. Burke Severs, ed., *A Manual of the Writings in Middle English 1050–1500,* volume 1 (New Haven: Connecticut Academy of Arts and Sciences, 1967);

Lillian Herlands Hornstein, "Middle English Romances," in *Recent and Middle English Scholarship and Criticism: Survey and Desiderata,* edited by J. Burke Severs (Pittsburgh: Duquesne University Press, 1971), pp. 55–95.

References:

Henk Aetsen, "*Havelok the Dane:* A Non-Courtly Romance," in *Companion to Early Middle English Literature,* edited by Aertsen and N. Veldhoen (Amsterdam: Free University Press, 1988), pp. 31–51;

Susan Crane, *Insular Romance* (Berkeley & London: University of California Press, 1986);

Susan C. Dannenbaum, "*Guy of Warwick* and the Question of Exemplary Romance," *Genre,* 17 (Winter 1984): 351–374;

John Finlayson, "Definitions of Middle English Romance," *Chaucer Review,* 15 (Summer 1980): 44–62; (Fall 1980): 168–181;

Finlayson, "*Richard, Coer de Lyon:* Romance, History or Something in Between?" *Studies in Philology,* 87 (1990): 156–180;

Kenneth Gadomski, "Narrative Style in *King Horn* and *Havelok the Dane,*" *Journal of Narrative Technique,* 15 (Spring 1985): 133–145;

John Ganim, "Community and Consciousness in Early Middle English Romance," in *Style and Consciousness in Middle English Narrative* (Princeton: Princeton University Press, 1983), pp. 16–24;

Robert W. Hanning, "The Audience as Co-Creator of the First Chivalric Romances," *Yearbook of English Studies,* 11 (1981): 1–28;

Hanning, "*Havelok the Dane*: Structure, Symbols, Meaning," *Studies in Philology,* 44 (July 1967): 586–605;

Harriet Hudson, "Middle English Popular Romance: The Manuscript Evidence," *Manuscripta,* 28 (July 1984): 67–78;

M. Dominica Legge, *Anglo Norman Literature and Its Background* (Oxford: Clarendon Press, 1963);

Dieter Mehl, *Middle English Romances of the Thirteenth and Fourteenth Centuries* (New York: Barnes & Noble, 1968);

Walter Oliver, "*King Horn* and Suddene," *PMLA,* 46 (March 1931): 102–114;

Derek Pearsall, "The Development of Middle English Romance," *Mediaeval Studies,* 27 (1965): 91–116;

Velma B. Richmond, "The Most Popular Hero: *Guy of Warwick,*" in her *The Popularity of Middle English Romance* (Bowling Green, Ohio: Bowling Green University Popular Press, 1975), pp. 149–193;

Anne Scott, "Plans, Predictions, and Promises: Traditional Story Techniques and the Configuration of Word and Deed in *King Horn,*" in *Studies in Medieval English Romance: Some New Approaches,* edited by Derek Brewer (Cambridge: Brewer, 1988);

Judith Weiss, "The Major Interpolations in *Sir Beues of Hamtoun,*" *Medium Ævum,* 47, no. 1 (1978–1979): 71–76;

Susan Wittig, *Stylistic and Narrative Structures in Middle English Romances* (Austin: University of Texas Press, 1978).

The Matter of Rome

(early twelfth – late fifteenth century)

George R. Keiser
Kansas State University

WORKS ON TROY: *The Seege or Batayle of Troye* (circa 1300–1325)

Manuscripts: This work is extant in four manuscripts of the fourteenth and fifteenth centuries: British Library, MS. Egerton 2862 and MS. Harley 525; College of Arms, London, MS. Arundel 22; and Lincoln's Inn, London, MS. 150.

First publication: "Zwei me Bearbeitungen der Historia de Excidio Trojae des Phrygiers Dares," edited by A. Zeitsch, *Archiv für das Studium der neueren Sprachen und Literaturen,* 72 (1884): 11.

Standard edition: *The Seege or Batayle of Troye,* edited M. E. Barnicle, EETS, o.s. 172 (1927).

The Gest Historiale of the Destruction of Troy (circa 1350–1400)

Manuscript: This work is found only in one mid-fifteenth-century manuscript, University of Glasgow, MS. Hunterian 388.

First publication and standard edition: *The Gest Historiale of the Destruction of Troy,* 2 volumes, edited by George A. Panton and David Donaldson, EETS, o.s. 39, 56 (1866, 1874).

The Laud Troy Book (circa 1400)

Manuscript: This work is found only in an early-fifteenth-century manuscript, Bodleian Library, Oxford, MS. Laud 595.

First publication and standard edition: *The Laud Troy Book,* 2 volumes, edited by J. Ernst Wülfing, EETS, o.s. 121, 122 (1902, 1903).

John Lydgate, *Troy Book* (1420)

Manuscripts: This work exists in at least 23 manuscripts of the fifteenth and early sixteenth centuries.

First publication: *The hystorye Sege and dystruccyon of Troye* (London: Printed by Richard Pynson, 1513).

Standard Edition: *Lydgate's Troy Book,* 4 volumes, edited by Henry Bergen, EETS, e.s. 97, 103, 106, 126 (1906–1935; reprinted, 1973).

The Sege of Troy (circa 1425)

Manuscript: This work exists in one manuscript from the mid fifteenth century, Bodleian Library, Oxford, MS. Rawlinson misc. D.82.

First publication: "The Sege of Troy," edited by N. E. Griffin, *PMLA,* 22, no. 1 (1907): 174–200.

Standard edition: "Zwei mittelenglische Prosaromane: The Sege of Thebes und The Sege of Troy," edited by Friedrich W. D. Brie, *Archiv für das Studium der neueren Sprachen und Literaturen,* 130 (1913): 47–52, 269–285.

William Caxton, *The Recuyell of the Historyes of Troy* (1473–1474)

Manuscripts: No known manuscript of this work exists.

First publication: *The Recuyell of the Historyes of Troy* (Bruges: Printed by William Caxton, 1473–1474).

Standard edition: *The Recuyell of the Historyes of Troy . . . translated and printed by William Caxton,* 2 volumes, edited by H. Oskar Sommer (London: Nutt, 1894).

William Caxton, *The History of Jason* (1477)

Manuscripts: No known manuscript of this work exists.

First publication: *The History of Jason* (Westminster: Printed by William Caxton, 1477).

Standard edition: *The History of Jason,* edited by J. Munro, EETS, e.s. 111 (1913).

William Caxton, *Eneydos* (1490)

Manuscripts: No known manuscript of this work exists.

First publication: *Eneydos* (Westminster: Printed by William Caxton, 1490).

Standard edition: *Caxton's Eneydos, 1490,* edited by Matthew T. Culley and Frederick J. Furnivall, EETS, e.s. 57 (1890).

WORKS ON ALEXANDER: *Kyng Alisaunder* (circa 1300)

Manuscripts: This romance exists in three manuscripts, including Bodleian Library, Oxford, MS. Laud misc. 622 (circa 1400) and Lincoln's Inn, London, MS. 150 (circa 1500). The most interesting is National Library of Scotland, Advocates 19.2.1 (known as the Auchinleck manuscript), a miscellany of romances and other writings that was produced in London around 1330. It has been suggested that Geoffrey Chaucer might have known this miscellany. Two leaves from this volume were discovered in a binding at the library of the University of Saint Andrews, Scotland, and are in the collection there.

First publication: *Kyng Alisaunder* (London: Printed by Richard Faques, [1525]).

Standard edition: *Kyng Alisaunder,* 2 volumes, edited by G. V. Smithers, EETS, o.s. 227, 237 (1952, 1957).

Alexander A, or *Alisaunder of Macedoine* (circa 1350)

Manuscript: Bodleian Library, Oxford, MS. Greaves 60.

First publication: In *The Romance of William of Palerne; The Gestes of the Worthie King and Emperour, Alisaunder of Macedonie,* edited by Walter W. Skeat, EETS, e.s. 1 (1867; reprinted, Kraus, 1973).

Standard edition: *Gests of King Alexander of Macedon,* edited by Francis P. Magoun (Cambridge: Harvard University Press, 1929).

Alexander B, or *Alexander and Dindimus* (circa 1350)

Manuscript: Bodleian Library, Oxford, MS. Bodley 264.

First publication: *The Alliterative Romance of Alexander,* edited by J. Stevenson (London: Roxburghe Club, 1849).

Standard edition: In *Gests of King Alexander of Macedon,* edited by Francis P. Magoun (Cambridge: Harvard University Press, 1929).

Wars of Alexander (circa 1400)

Manuscripts: Bodleian Library, Oxford, MS. Ashmole 44, and Trinity College, Dublin, MS. 213.

First publication: *The Alliterative Romance of Alexander,* edited by J. Stevenson (London: Roxburghe Club, 1849).

Standard edition: *The Wars of Alexander,* edited by Hoyt N. Duggan and Thorlac Turville-Petre, EETS, supplementary series 10 (1989).

Prose Alexander (circa 1425)

Manuscript: The only manuscript copy of this romance is in Lincoln Cathedral MS. 91, an important miscellany compiled by Robert Thornton, a member of the minor gentry in mid-fifteenth-century England.

First publication and standard edition: *The Prose Life of Alexander,* edited by J. S. Westlake, EETS, o.s. 143 (1913).

The Dicts and Sayings of the Philosophers – translated by Stephen Scrope, revised by William Worcester; an anonymous translator; and Anthony Woodville, Earl Rivers (1450–1475)

Manuscripts: The Scrope translation and the revised version are extant in nine fifteenth-century manuscripts. The anonymous translation is preserved in only one, Lord Tollemache's MS. in Helmingham Hall. Copies of the entire Earl Rivers translation appear in three manuscripts, all copied from the first printed edition by Caxton: London, Lambeth Palace Library, London, MS. 265; British Library, MS. Additional 22718; and Newberry Library, Chicago, MS. Ry.20. The Lambeth manuscript is an elegant copy presented to Edward IV on 24 December 1477.

First publication: Earl Rivers translation: *The Dicts and Sayings of the Philosophers* (Westminster: Printed by William Caxton, 1477).

First publication and standard edition: Scrope translation and anonymous translation: in *The Dicts and Sayings of the Philosophers,* edited by Curt Bühler, EETS, o.s. 211 (1941; reprinted, 1961).

WORKS ON THEBES: John Lydgate, *Siege of Thebes* (1422)

Manuscripts: This work exists in at least thirty manuscripts of the fifteenth and early sixteenth centuries.

First publication: *The Storye of Thebes* (London: Wynkyn de Worde, 1496?).

Standard edition: *Lydgate's Siege of Thebes,* 2 volumes, edited by Alex Erdmann and Eilert Ekwall, EETS, e.s. 108 (1911; reprinted, 1960) and e.s. 125 (1930; reprinted, 1973).

The Sege of Thebes (circa 1450)

Manuscript: The work exists in one manuscript from the mid fifteenth century: Bodleian Library, Oxford, MS. Rawlinson misc. D.82.

First publication and standard edition: "Zwei mittelenglische Prosaromane: The Sege of Thebes und The Sege of Troy," edited by Friedrich W. D. Brie, *Archiv für das Studium der neueren Sprachen und Literaturen,* 130 (1913): 47–52, 269–285.

The best known and most admired of Middle English romances, *Sir Gawain and the Green Knight* (circa 1350–1400), begins and ends with references to the siege and assault of Troy. Similarly, late-medieval English heraldic treatises assert that heraldry began with the Trojan War. In his *Aeneid* Virgil had told of the founding of Rome by the Trojan prince Aeneas, who was directed by the gods to leave the great city of Troy as it was about to fall to the Greeks and to journey to Italy and establish the city of Rome. Like most other European kingdoms, later-medieval England nurtured a legend of its founding by other Trojan heroes and their descendants, which permitted Englishmen to exploit a claim to a heritage and a destiny as great as that of Rome.

In England this legend, as developed by Geoffrey of Monmouth in *Historia regum Brittaniae* (The History of the Kings of Britain, circa 1138), told of the founding of Britain by Brut, who had been conceived in a secret affair between Silvius, grandson of Aeneas, and a woman of Italian nobility who died in childbirth. After Brut, at age fifteen, killed his father in a hunting accident, he went into exile in Greece, where he met the descendants of Aeneas's brother, Helenus, and other Trojans who had been captured at the fall of Troy. Rescuing them from their captivity, Brut led these descendants of Troy to the isle of Albion, which he renamed Britain, and established its capital, Troia Nova (the New Troy), later renamed London. This story had a long circulation in vernacular translations and adaptations in both French and English. Its widest circulation was in a prose chronicle, the *Brut,* compiled in the Anglo-Norman language shortly after 1272 and still extant in at least 47 manuscripts. This work was translated, with additions, into an English version in about 1400, and it survives in at least 172 manuscripts.

Medieval Europe saw itself as an inheritor of the traditions and learning of the ancient world, and stories of antiquity were often the subject of romances and other narratives in vernacular languages. In English literature these stories, classified under the general heading "The Matter of Rome," are primarily narratives of the Trojan War and its consequences or of Alexander the Great, though there are also accounts of Thebes, the city of Oedipus, and other loosely associated stories.

The medieval knowledge of the fall of Troy did not derive from the *Iliad* and the *Odyssey* of Homer, for these were unknown in western Europe, where a knowledge of Greek was largely lost during the Middle Ages. Rather, the official histories of Troy consisted of the *Ephemeris belli Trojani* of Dictys of Crete and the *De excidio Troiae historia* of Dares

the Phrygian. While they may have had Greek originals from an earlier period, these two late Latin works date from the fourth and sixth centuries respectively; both purport to be translations of eyewitness reports, Dictys's story told from the Greek perspective and Dares's from that of an ally of Troy.

In his *Roman de Troie* (circa 1160) Benoit de Sainte-Maure conflated the information he found in the accounts of Dares and Dictys to produce a romantic epic of about thirty thousand lines, which he dedicated to Eleanor of Aquitaine. Benoit tells the story of the Trojan War in terms suited to the tastes of his courtly dedicatee and their contemporaries. Its chivalric heroes fight in numerous battles; the narrator sympathizes with Hector and scorns Achilles. The love stories of Jason and Medea, Helen and Paris, Troilus and Briseida, and Achilles and Polyxena are presented in detail. Furthermore, Benoit embellishes his narrative with material from such classical writings as Ovid's *Metamorphoses* (circa A.D. 8), as well as with lengthy rhetorical descriptions and exotic, marvelous, and magical elements found in contemporary romantic narratives.

About a century after its composition, Benoit's poem was turned into Latin prose by Guido delle Colonne, a judge of Messina, Sicily, who completed his work in 1287 and who never acknowledged his indebtedness to Benoit. Guido's *Historia destructionis Troiae* (History of the Fall of Troy) was soon accepted as an authentic history derived from Dares and Dictys, and it is the principal source of other accounts of the Trojan War throughout the later Middle Ages. To produce a work of seemingly historical character, Guido removes the elaborate descriptive detail in Benoit's battle scenes and transforms the love stories by reducing their courtly elements and overlaying them with ponderous moralizing, especially about the frailties of women. In Guido's version the story of the fall of Troy is not the noble tragedy of Benoit's poem but a skeptical, even pessimistic, account of treachery, deceit, and death.

Of the Middle English versions of the story of Troy, *The Gest Historiale of the Destruction of Troy* is the most faithful and accurate translation of Guido's history. This poem consists of 14,044 alliterative long lines, the work of a competent poet who probably composed it in the Northwest Midlands during the second half of the fourteenth century. It begins, as Guido's narrative does, with the story of Jason's quest for the Golden Fleece and his ultimately treacherous love affair with Medea, who teaches him how to overcome the bulls and the dragon that protect the Fleece. On his way to this adventure Jason had been refused hospitality by King Laomedon

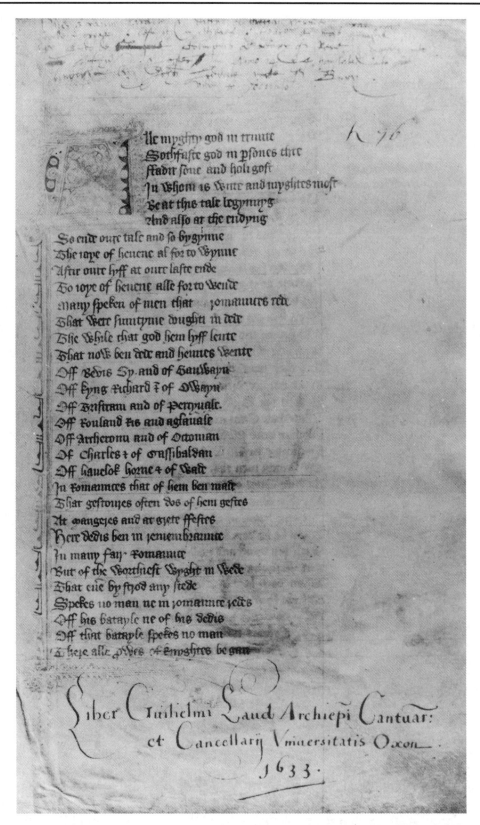

First page of The Laud Troy Book *in the only extant manuscript of the work (Bodleian Library, Oxford, MS. Laud 595, fol. 1ʳ)*

of Troy; after obtaining the Fleece, Jason returns to Troy and, with the aid of Hercules, destroys the city. King Priam, Laomedon's son, rebuilds the city and in time seeks the recovery of his sister Hesione, who had been abducted by Jason. When a mission by Antenor meets with failure, Priam sends his son Paris to abduct a Greek woman, whom the Trojans will exchange for Hesione.

While in the Greek islands Paris recognizes that the Greek Telamon will not part with Hesione without a war; with that excuse Paris determines that abducting Helen, with whom he has fallen in love, will inflict most injury on the Greeks. Negotiations for the return of Helen fail, and the Greeks determine to make war upon the Trojans. The remainder of the work describes the lengthy series of battles, which culminate in the destruction of Troy. During the narrative of the decade-long siege, two other love stories are recounted – that of the Trojan prince Troilus, from whom his lover Briseis is taken, and the love of Achilles for Priam's daughter Polyxena, both of which end in the treacherous destruction of the heroes. The fall of Troy is brought about by the treachery of Antenor and Aeneas, who contrive a false peace with the Greeks; the bronze horse, in which the Greek warriors have hidden, is brought into the city, and destruction ensues.

The alliterative poet has been faulted by some modern readers for a rigidly conventional handling of alliterative verse and for an uncritical response to his source, which he reproduces almost unquestioningly. This can be explained as a desire to provide a faithful account of what he believed to be a factual history. He does, however, reduce Guido's moralizing, modifying the Sicilian's spirited condemnation of women's frailties and eliminating a lengthy digression on idolatry. The poet, clearly lacking a sound historical sense, introduces anachronistic detail, such as an engaging catalogue of tradesmen whose occupations are clearly those with which he and his audience would be familiar. Such detail gives the story a sense of immediacy and reality in detail and dialogue and would surely have made his narrative more meaningful for a contemporary audience.

In contrast to the poet's faithfulness to his source for *The Gest Historiale of the Destruction of Troy* is the freedom with which the poet of *The Laud Troy Book* (circa 1400) handles Guido's narrative, dispensing with digressions on morality and learned matter. This poem of 18,664 lines in four-stress couplets was intended to be a romance of Hector. While the poet remains faithful to the historical narrative of his source, he expands the battle scenes

with conventional romance material and emphasizes the deeds of Hector in battle, drawing a sharp contrast between his bravery and the dishonorable cowardice of Achilles. Like so many of the authors of Middle English romance, this poet shows some remarkable skill in creating lively dialogue for his characters.

The *Troy Book* of John Lydgate was commissioned by Henry, Prince of Wales, in 1412, the year before his accession to the throne as Henry V, and it was completed in 1420. In a poem of 30,177 lines written in rhymed couplets, Lydgate uses extensive rhetorical adornment of every kind to expand the narrative of Guido while at the same time diligently maintaining his fidelity to it. Lydgate regarded Chaucer as his master, and he surely derived the sense of history that has been praised in the *Troy Book* from his reading of *Troilus and Criseyde* (circa 1382–1386), Chaucer's contribution to Middle English Troy literature. As in most English literature of the fifteenth century, a central concern of Lydgate's version of the fall of Troy is the theme of Fortune. While his attitude seems to waver in various parts of the poem, at the fall of Troy Lydgate succumbs to an almost overwhelming acceptance of the wretchedness of the human condition, the inevitability of the destruction of human grandeur and glory. (*The Sege of Troy* [circa 1425] is a brief prose summary of Lydgate's *Troy Book,* thirteen pages in a modern edition, apparently made during the second quarter of the fifteenth century by an unknown writer.)

The earliest of the Middle English Troy books is *The Seege or Batayle of Troye,* a 2,066-line poem in four-stress couplets written early in the fourteenth century. Unlike the works that derive from Guido, this poem seems to derive from several sources, including Benoit's *Roman* and a version of Dares. While the poet follows the usual narrative represented in Guido's version, he adds material from classical sources concerning the childhoods of Paris and Achilles, who become the heroes of this romance.

The last of the Middle English Troy books are three works translated into English and printed by William Caxton, England's first printer. *The Recuyell of the Historyes of Troy* is a translation of several sources, including a version of Guido's *Historia.* Printed in Bruges in 1473–1474, this prose work of some seven hundred pages in a modern edition was made over several years at the command of Margaret, Duchess of Burgundy, sister of Edward IV, when Caxton was governor of the English Merchant Adventurers at Bruges. Preceding the standard account derived from Guido's narrative are redactions of classical myths associated with Troy and taken mainly from Giovanni Boccaccio's *De Genealogia deorum gentilium* (circa 1375) by Raoul Lefèvre for his *Recueil des histoires de Troyes* (1464), which was popular in Burgundy at the time that Caxton translated it for the duchess of Burgundy. Soon after he set up his printing press in Westminster, Caxton published a companion piece, *The History of Jason* (1477). This translation of Raoul Lefèvre's *Jason and Medee* (circa 1460), which tells the story of the Golden Fleece and of the marriage of Jason and Medea, was dedicated to the Prince of Wales, but it was meant to honor Edward IV, who was a member of the Burgundian Order of the Golden Fleece. In 1490 Caxton printed his *Eneydos,* a translation of a fourteenth-century French romance, which retold the story of Virgil's *Aeneid.* The work was dedicated to Arthur, Prince of Wales, the eldest and ill-fated son of Henry VII. The work is best known for its prologue, in which Caxton complains of the difficulty of writing in English: "And certainly our language now used varieth far from that which was used and spoken when I was born. For we Englishmen are born under the domination of the moon, which is never steadfast, but ever wavering, waxing one season, and waneth and decreaseth another season. And that common English that is spoken in one shire varieth from another."

The second major subject of the Matter of Rome narratives is the life of Alexander. The Monk in Chaucer's *Canterbury Tales* (circa 1375–1400) states that the story of "worthy, gentil Alisandre" was so common "That every wight that hath discrecioun / Hath herd somwhat or al of his fortune." From the later years of the thirteenth century, when the metrical romance *Kyng Alisaunder* was written, and continuing into the third decade of the sixteenth, when a reworking of it was printed by Richard Faques, English vernacular writers seem to have been feeding an enduring taste for stories of Alexander.

The Middle English lives of Alexander derive mainly from one of two recensions of the so-called Pseudo-Callisthenes Alexander Romance that was composed in Alexandria sometime after 200 B.C. and perhaps as late as the second century of the modern era. The first of these is a Latin translation, dated 320–330 and attributed to Julius Valerius; an abbreviated form of this translation, known as the *Zacher Epitome* and made no later than the ninth century, is the ultimate source of *Kyng Alisaunder* (circa 1300). The other Middle English romances derive

from one of the several recensions of the *Historia de Preliis.* While on a mission to Constantinople around 950 the archpriest Leo of Naples discovered a Greek text of the Pseudo-Callisthenes Romance and transcribed it. On returning to Naples, Leo translated it for his master, Duke John III of Campania, and entitled it *Nativitas et Victoria Alexandri Magni.* While this text has been lost, a version known as the *Historia de Preliis* and containing much interpolated material was composed during the eleventh century and before about 1150 was independently revised twice, with further interpolations in each case.

In all the Middle English versions the general outline of the story is the same: the mysterious conception of Alexander during the absence of his father Philip of Macedon; his tutelage by Aristotle; his taming of the wild and, in some versions, man-eating horse, Bucephalus; his early conquests culminating in the defeat of Darius and victory over Persia; his lengthy travels and conquests in the East; and finally his seduction by Candace and his death by poison.

Often thought to be the best of the Middle English Alexander romances, *Kyng Alisaunder* consists of 8,021 lines in four-stress couplets. Of significance is the fact that the earliest copy of this version is preserved in the famous Auchinleck manuscript (National Library of Scotland, MS. Advocates 19.2.1). Compiled in London between 1330 and 1340, this important miscellany of Middle English romance was probably a commercial enterprise. As it was in London at the time Chaucer was writing, and as he was familiar with works it contains, the idea that he might have read them in this volume is an attractive one. It has also been argued that the author of *Kyng Alisaunder,* who freely adapted the French *Roman de Toute Chevalerie* to create his romance, might be the author of other Auchinleck romances, but this idea does not seem likely. Though the narrative moves along in a lively manner, the author skillfully adds rhetorical adornment, most notably in his much-praised seasonal headpieces which mark important breaks in the action and which find their closest parallels in medieval love lyrics.

At least two other complete Middle English accounts of the life of Alexander were written, though they are extant only in fragmentary condition: the alliterative *Wars of Alexander,* still undated but perhaps from the early fifteenth century, and the *Prose Alexander,* probably from the second quarter of the fifteenth century. The *Wars of Alexander,* consisting of about 5,800 long alliterative lines, breaks off just before Alexander's death. As a close translation of its source, the poem has an episodic structure; nevertheless, the narrative style is economical and at the same time, thanks to effective use of familiar detail and imagery, concrete and vivid. Two other alliterative fragments, known as *Alexander A*, or *Alisaunder of Macedoine* (1,247 lines), and *Alexander B*, or *Alexander and Dindimus* (1,139 lines) — both circa 1350 — are possibly, but not necessarily, parts of one chronicle account of Alexander's life. The former has a somewhat lively narrative, but neither work offers a fully mature and successful handling of alliterative verse. A brief fragment from a now-lost manuscript gives evidence of perhaps another alliterative version of the life of Alexander.

The second nearly complete Middle English life of Alexander, the *Prose Alexander*, begins imperfectly because of the loss of several leaves from the unique copy preserved in the famous Thornton Manuscript (Lincoln Cathedral MS. 91). With no apparent precedent for his attempt, the author of this work introduced the prose romance, currently fashionable on the Continent, into fifteenth-century England, and he achieved at least modest success in presenting his narrative in a fluent, idiomatic, and at times skillful prose style. The *Prose Alexander* was copied into an important manuscript miscellany by a member of the minor gentry in Yorkshire; this scribe, Robert Thornton of East Newton, was a man of limited education, modest means, considerable piety, and esteem for the written word.

Still another, brief prose life of Alexander appears in several versions of *The Dicts and Sayings of the Philosophers*, a collection of mainly apocryphal sayings of ancient sages, compiled in Arabic in the eleventh century. These translations were made in the second half of the fifteenth century, one by Stephen Scrope, that was revised by William Worcester, a second by an anonymous translator, and the third by Anthony Woodville, Earl Rivers, brother-in-law to Edward IV. The Rivers translation was one of the first books printed by William Caxton, in 1477; the demand for it was apparently great enough to warrant a second edition in 1480. In the modern printed edition of the Scrope and anonymous translations about 20 percent of the book is devoted to the prose life of Alexander (nineteen pages), along with wise sayings attributed to Alexander (five pages) and others of Aristotle, many of them directed to Alexander (eleven pages).

Some late-medieval writings treat Alexander with moral disapproval, and the question arises as to whether that is the tone of the Middle English accounts of the conqueror's life. What is clear is that

they present Alexander as an exemplary character from whose life later ages might draw learning. The claim of the author of *Kyng Alisaunder* is representative of statements found in these works: "Othere mannes lijf is oure schewer." That is, the lives of other men who have gone before are exemplars or mirrors. It is not easy to see how the writers would have their readers use Alexander's life as an exemplar, for they do not always offer straightforward explanations of their purposes. Nevertheless, it is clear that, like Chaucer's Monk, these writers see Alexander as a tragic figure, whose rise through world conquest and subsequent fall from glory attest to the untrustworthiness of the mutable world.

In the three lives that are complete or nearly complete, Alexander repeatedly speaks of his knowledge of the uncertainty of fortune and his mortality, and he does so with remarkable equanimity. As he is a pagan, all the implications of that knowledge are not clear to Alexander, though he does at least see in his life a larger plan whose design he discovers, bit by bit, through prophecies and dreams. Furthermore, this knowledge makes him a man of restraint and, for a conqueror of all the world, surprising modesty. As least once in *Kyng Alisaunder* and more often in *Wars of Alexander* and the *Prose Alexander*, it is explicit that his destined greatness is an act of divine grace, and it is implied that Alexander earns this grace because he accepts his mortality and his role in a larger plan that he does not understand. In other writings that view Alexander in an unfavorable light, the reason for the criticism is arrogance and an accompanying lack of restraint resulting from a failure to recognize and accept his mortality.

Besides these major narrative topics, the siege of the city of Thebes seems to have been another popular subject of Matter of Rome narratives. In Chaucer's *Troilus and Criseyde* (circa 1382–1386) there is a domestic scene in which the heroine, Criseyde, sits with two other ladies within a paved parlor, and the three "Herden a mayden reden hem the gest / Of the siege of Thebes." Surprisingly, only one Middle English narrative of that famous story survives — John Lydgate's *Siege of Thebes*, a 4,716-line poem in decasyllabic couplets begun in 1420 and completed in 1422. The work may have been thought a companion piece to his *Troy Book*, which he had completed in 1420. His master Chaucer was certainly on his mind when Lydgate wrote his account of Thebes, for he cast it into a frame as a Canterbury tale told on the homeward journey. Indeed, in the sixteenth century it was several times published in collections of Chaucer's writings. The narrative begins with the founding of Thebes and tells the story of Oedipus, with inappropriate moralizing about the need to honor one's parents. The greater part of the story, however, concerns the wars between the sons of Oedipus over the succession to the throne of Thebes. In the concluding portion of the poem Lydgate speaks out against war and prophesies a time of peace and quiet, concord and unity among realms. In doing so, Lydgate had in mind the Treaty of Troyes, which promised to bring an end to nearly a century of war between England and France. Unfortunately, with the death of Henry V in 1422, such prophecies went unfulfilled. As with Lydgate's *Troy Book,* his *Siege of Thebes* was condensed and retold in a prose version, the *Sege of Thebes* (circa 1450). (For a full discussion of *The Siege of Thebes,* see the essay on John Lydgate in this volume.)

When Chaucer wrote of antiquity, he did so with some awareness that the events occurred in a world unlike his own. His contemporaries and successors largely lacked such a historical perspective, and in writing about ancient events they treated them as they would have treated contemporary ones. For these writers the importance of the past was as an exemplar or mirror for the present. They set their stories in a world governed by the providential order of a Christian God, and they considered the stories of antiquity as illustrative of the workings of that order. Of course they understood that the ancients did not enjoy the grace of Christian enlightenment; consequently, the ancients' understanding of the mutability of fortune and the transitory nature of human glory was far less than theirs. The stories medieval writers told of the destruction of Troy and Thebes, the fall of Alexander, and hapless loves of the lovers reminded their contemporaries of the uncertainties of their mortal existence. This is not to suggest, however, that these narratives present an unrelentingly gloomy vision of human life. On the contrary, at the same time as they remind that human glory fades, they also demonstrate the brilliance of that glory and extol the ideals that the unenlightened ancients upheld as they strove to achieve glory.

Bibliographies:

R. M. Lumiansky, "Legends of Alexander the Great," "Legends of Troy," and "Legends of Thebes," in *A Manual of the Writings in Midde English, 1050-1500,* edited by J. Burke Severs (New Haven: Connecticut Academy of Arts and Sciences, 1967), pp. 104-119, 268-277;

Alain Renoir and C. David Benson, "John Lydgate," in *A Manual of the Writings in Midde English, 1050-1500,* volume 6 (New Haven: Connecticut Academy of Arts and Sciences, 1980);

A. S. G. Edwards, *Middle English Prose: A Critical Guide to Major Authors and Genres* (New Brunswick N.J.: Rutgers University Press, 1984);

Joanna A. Rice, *Middle English Romances: An Annotated Bibliography. 1955-1985* (New York: Garland, 1987).

References:

W. R. J. Barron, "The Matter of Rome," in *Medieval English Romance* (London: Longman, 1987), pp. 109-131;

Albert C. Baugh, "The Romance: I-ii. The Matter of Rome," in *A Literary History of England* (New York: Appleton-Century-Crofts, 1948), pp. 181-184;

C. David Benson, *The History of Troy in Middle English Literature* (Cambridge: Brewer, 1980);

John M. Bowers, "*The Tale of Beryn* and *The Siege of Thebes:* Alternative Ideas of *The Canterbury Tales,*" *Studies in the Age of Chaucer,* 7 (1985): 23-50;

G. H. V. Bunt, "Alexander's Last Days in the Middle English *Kyng Alisaunder,*" in *Alexander the Great in the Middle Ages* (Nijmegen: Alfa Nijmegen, 1978), pp. 202-225;

Bunt, "An Exemplary Hero: Alexander the Great," in *Companion to Middle English Romance,* edited by Henk Aertsen and Alasdair A. MacDonald (Amsterdam: VU University Press, 1990), pp. 29-55;

George Cary, *The Medieval Alexander,* edited by D. J. A. Ross (Cambridge: Cambridge University Press, 1956);

John Clark, "Trinovantum – The Evolution of a Legend," *Journal of Medieval History,* 7 (1981): 135-151;

Hoyt N. Duggan, "The Source of the Middle English *The Wars of Alexander,*" *Speculum,* 51 (October 1976): 624-636;

Duggan, "Strophic Patterns in Middle English Alliterative Poetry," *Modern Philology,* 74 (February 1977): 223-247;

John M. Ganim, "Mannerism and Moralism in Lydgate's *Siege of Thebes,*" in his *Style and Consciousness in Middle English Narrative* (Princeton: Princeton University Press, 1983), pp. 103-122;

Richard Jenkyns, *The Legacy of Rome: A New Appraisal* (London: Oxford University Press, 1992);

David A. Lawton, "The Middle English Alliterative *Alexander A* and *C:* Form and Style in Translation from Latin Prose," *Studia Neophilologica,* 53 (1981): 259–268;

Lesley Lawton, "The Illustration of Late Medieval Secular Texts, with Special Reference to Lydgate's 'Troy Book,' " in *Manuscripts and Readers in Fifteenth-Century England,* edited by Derek Pearsall (Cambridge: Brewer, 1981), pp. 41–69;

William Matthews, "Arms and the Man," in his *The Tragedy of Arthur* (Berkeley: University of California Press, 1960), pp. 68–93;

A. J. Minnis, *Chaucer and Pagan Antiquity* (Cambridge: Brewer, 1982);

Peter Noble, Lucie Polak, and Claire Isoz, *The Medieval Alexander Legend and Romance Epic: Essays in Honour of David J. A. Ross* (Millwood, N.Y.: Kraus, 1982);

Lee Patterson, *Chaucer and the Subject of History* (Madison: University of Wisconsin Press, 1991);

Derek Pearsall, *John Lydgate* (Charlottesville: University of Virginia Press, 1970);

Gert Ronberg, "The Two Manuscripts of *The Wars of Alexander:* A Linguistic Comparison," *Neophilologus,* 69 (October 1985): 604–610;

A. C. Spearing, "Lydgate's Canterbury Tale: *The Siege of Thebes* and Fifteenth-Century Chaucerianism," in *Fifteenth-Century Studies: Recent Essays,* edited by Robert F. Yeager (Hamden, Conn.: Archon, 1984), pp. 333–364;

Sharon Stevenson, "Aeneas in Fourteenth-Century England," in *The Classics in the Middle Ages,* edited by Aldo S. Bernardo and Saul Levin (Binghamton, N.Y.: Medieval & Renaissance Texts & Studies, 1990);

Paul Strohm, "*Storie, Spelle, Geste, Romaunce, Tragedie:* Generic Distinctions in the Middle English Troy Narratives," *Speculum,* 46 (1971): 348–359;

McKay Sundwall, "The *Destruction of Troy,* Chaucer's *Troilus and Criseyde,* and Lydgate's *Troy Book,*" *Review of English Studies,* new series 62 (1975): 313–317;

J. S. P. Tatlock, *The Legendary History of Britain* (Berkeley: University of California Press, 1950);

Thorlac Turville-Petre, *The Alliterative Revival* (Cambridge: Brewer, 1977);

Turville-Petre, "A Lost Alliterative Alexander Romance," *Review of English Studies,* new series 30 (1979): 306–307;

Turville-Petre, "Nicholas Grimald and *Alexander A,*" *English Literary Renaissance,* 6 (Spring 1976): 180–186.

The Middle English Lyric

(twelfth century – fifteenth century)

Edmund Reiss

Manuscripts: Middle English lyrics can be found in a multitude of manuscripts, including British Library MS. Harley 2253, a well-known miscellany dated circa 1340. Facsimile: *Facsimile of British Museum MS. Harley 2253,* with an introduction by N. R. Ker, EETS, 255 (1965).

Standard editions: *English Lyrics of the XIIIth Century,* edited by Carleton Brown (Oxford: Clarendon Press, 1932); *Religious Lyrics of the XVth Century,* edited by Brown (Oxford: Clarendon Press, 1939); *Religious Lyrics of the XIVth Century,* edited by Brown, revised by G. V. Smithers (Oxford: Clarendon Press, 1952); *Secular Lyrics of the XIVth and XVth Centuries,* edited by Rossell Hope Robbins, second edition (Oxford: Clarendon Press, 1955); *Cambridge Middle English Lyrics,* edited by Henry A. Person, revised edition (Seattle: University of Washington Press, 1962); *The Harley Lyrics: The Middle English Lyrics of MS. Harley 2253,* edited by G. L. Brook, fourth edition (Manchester: Manchester University Press, 1968); *The Early English Carols,* edited by Richard Leighton Greene, second edition (Oxford: Clarendon Press, 1977).

Of all forms of medieval literature, the lyric has been said to strike the most modern note and to be the easiest for a modern reader to appreciate. Given the difficulties of the Middle English language, it is understandable that these shorter pieces would tend to be more accessible than the longer romances and dramas. But, more important, the lyrics, often witty and ironic, purposely ambiguous, compellingly reflective, and dramatic to the point of being shocking, possess qualities readers tend to associate with the modern spirit and with much more recent literature.

At the same time, these poems are rather different from what is today regarded as lyric poetry. They are not primarily about love – no substantial body of love poetry exists in English until the late fourteenth century; they lack the melodiousness characterizing lyric poetry since the Elizabethans; and they are without the personal feelings considered by the Romantics as essential to the lyric. In fact, the term *lyric* was not used in English until the late sixteenth century. Those poems now known as medieval secular lyrics were viewed by their creators as songs and dances – carols were ring dances – and those called religious lyrics were often referred to as meditations, prayers, and even treatises.

The poems that have survived may not offer an accurate reflection of the English lyric as it existed from the twelfth through the fifteenth century. Although thousands of didactic and reflective lyrics remain, relatively few secular pieces have been found – more than half of those dating from before the end of the fourteenth century are preserved in a single manuscript, Harley 2253. It has been estimated that for each secular lyric about four religious poems exist. Significantly, the religious lyrics are frequently preserved in multiple copies, while most of the secular poems are unique. The Harley compilation offers a pertinent illustration. Of the thirty-two lyrics collected in the manuscript, twenty-four are clearly religious or moral, and of these the great majority are found elsewhere. Each of the eight remaining secular pieces, on the other hand, exists only in this manuscript.

Whereas religious lyrics were composed in English as a way of bringing piety to the unlettered, the purpose of vernacular secular lyrics is not so clear. Notwithstanding the view of medieval moralists that these lyrics were designed to lead to sin and sacrilege – as Robert Mannyng of Brunne wrote in *Handlyng Synne* (circa 1303–1317), "Daunces, karols, somour games, / Of many swych come many shames" – it is clear that, no matter what their particular form, they were trivial and ephemeral. Lacking the seriousness of religious lyrics, as well as the monumentality of longer narrative poems, they might well have seemed too slight or insignificant to be preserved. And given their na-

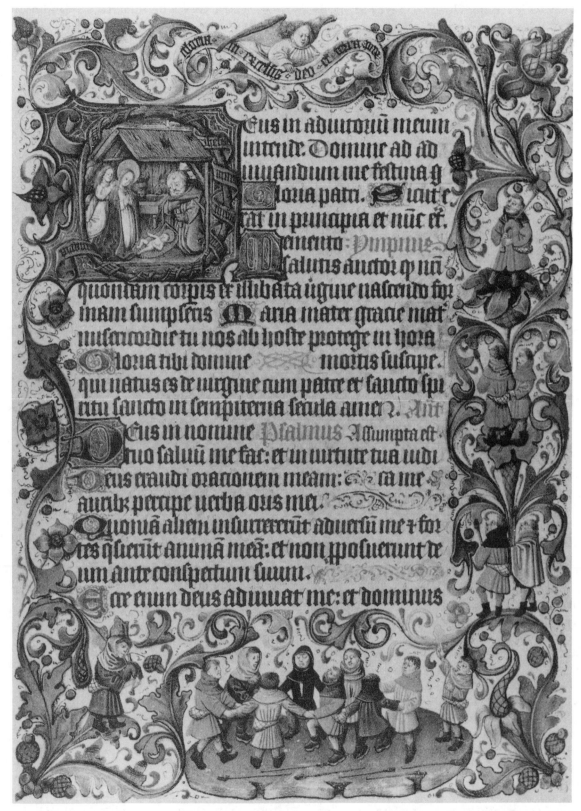

A carol, or ring dance, of shepherds at the Nativity, from a fifteenth-century manuscript. The dance is illustrated at the bottom of the page (Bodleian Library, Oxford, MS. Douce 93, fol. 28ʳ).

ture, they were far more likely to have been transmitted orally than to have been memorialized in manuscripts. If monastic scribes were going to use expensive parchment to preserve lyrics in English, they would certainly have given preference to those that were explicitly devotional, moral, and didactic. Readers might well conclude that the extant Middle English lyrics are by and large religious and didactic precisely because these are the sort most likely to have been written down and preserved.

The wonder is not that so few Middle English secular lyrics exist today but rather that so many have survived across the centuries. At the end of the fourteenth century Geoffrey Chaucer noted in the "Retraction" at the close of his *The Canterbury Tales* (circa 1375-1400) that he had composed "many a song and many a leccherous lay," but fewer than twenty of his secular lyrics are extant. If the poems of an author as celebrated as Chaucer have been lost, the compositions of lesser, earlier figures can hardly be expected to have fared better.

Although scholars will never know how many secular pieces once existed, they may be sure that those preserved represent a very small fraction of the total. Fragments of lost secular lyrics appear throughout medieval writings. As early as the twelfth century Thomas of Ely included in his Latin chronicle four lines of English verse attributed to King Canute (died 1035): "Merrily sang the monks of Ely / When King Cnute rowed thereby: / 'Row, knights, near the land, / And let us hear these monks' song.' " According to the chronicler, these lines and others – presumably the song of the monks by the river – were frequently cited and were sung publicly in dances. Another twelfth-century chronicler, Gerald of Wales, told of a priest kept awake all night by dancers in the churchyard. At mass the next morning, instead of uttering the customary "Dominus vobiscum" (Lord be with you), he echoed the refrain he recalled from the night before, "Swete leman, thin are" (Sweet love, your mercy). When Chaucer depicted in his *Canterbury Tales* the Pardoner pilgrim setting out for Canterbury singing "Come hider, love, to me," he was doubtless quoting a popular song. Although the poems from which these lines come are now lost, the fact that they were cited may indicate something of their popularity. Also their condemnation by churchmen – the eminent mystic Richard Rolle of Hampole in his *The Form of Living* (circa 1342) called it a sin of the mouth "to syng seculere sanges and lufe tham" – offers a further indication of their popularity, for moralists do not waste their time condemning unpopular activities.

Not only is the number of Middle English secular lyrics in doubt, so is their precise nature. After the Norman Conquest, Continental traditions were received in England as never before. The mid-twelfth-century court of the Angevin king Henry II and his wife Eleanor of Aquitaine provided a notable center of culture, where native poets and visitors from the continent retold the old stories of Paris and Helen and created the new stories of Tristan and Isolt. They worked with the new techniques of rhyme, octosyllabic couplets, refrains and burdens, and intricate stanzaic patterns; and, employing the image of the lover languishing for his lady, they fashioned not only complaints and dialogues of love, but songs of spring and amorous adventures.

Notable as they were, the poems created by these court poets were in French, not English, for the latter did not become a respectable literary language until the late fourteenth century. Neither they nor the sophisticated, artful lyrics found in twelfth-century France, Provence, and Germany were models for the earliest English lyrics. Rather, these tended to follow dance songs – as did the piece attributed to King Canute – or Latin hymns, as did three very early prayers attributed to Saint Godric (died 1170), who, according to a contemporary, was taught words and music by the Blessed Virgin herself.

When not simple devotions, early English lyrics were concerned with the pleasures of daily life, such as drinking and making love, and associated more with folk festivals than with life at court. Before Chaucer – who introduced ballades, roundels, and the rhyme royal stanza into English – the lyrics, secular and religious alike, tended to be short, couched in homely language, and deceptively simple. Even though no direct line exists between Old and Middle English poetry, these lyrics show the influences of native tradition. They employ the alliterative language, verbal formulas, and rhythms of Old English poetry in general, and they express the spirit found in the meditative and elegiac poems in particular.

The fact that many lyrics – both secular and religious – exist in a musical setting raises an additional question about their precise nature. Were they designed to be sung (perhaps also to accompany dancing), or were they intended to be recited? The image of medieval minstrels wandering through the countryside, singing their songs and reciting their poems, is not reliable. In medieval England no accounts exist of minstrel performances, and no manuscript collection has been clearly shown to be a minstrel repertoire. Moreover, the wandering minstrels that actually existed may have been instrumentalists, not singers.

Although some devotional lyrics represent paraphrases and translations of Latin hymns and others are recorded in songbooks and choir repertoires, the words and the music are frequently not in accord. Sometimes the evidence suggests that they are not by the same person, and, moreover, that the rhythm has probably been determined by the language rather than the music. What may be the best known of all Middle English lyrics, "Sumer is icumen in," exists, accompanied by music and Latin instructions for singing, in a commonplace book compiled over several years by the monks of Reading Abbey. Although this lyric – probably written in the manuscript around 1240 and the only English poem among several French and Latin pieces – may be the first English song for six voices, the music, with its liturgical affinities, does not fit the words very well and may actually be a later addition.

The relationship between the words and the accompanying music is further complicated by the desire of churchmen to transform preexisting secular pieces. Immediately before "Sumer is icumen in" an alternative text in Latin appears in the manuscript, probably included by the same scribe as a pious substitute for the English. The most widespread effort at transforming the secular lyric is doubtless that of the fourteenth-century bishop of Ossory, Richard de Ledrede, who so disapproved of his clergy's delight in vernacular songs that he replaced the lyrics of some sixty of them with pious Latin words. As his re-created religious poems exist in manuscript, several are preceded by a line or two of the vernacular to indicate the original popular tune. Problems also exist even when lyrics are not actually accompanied by music. Although the well-known Harley Lyrics are without music in manuscript, the fact that they are in stanza forms that were customarily set to music in France may indicate that they were meant to be sung.

The point is that the relationship between Middle English lyric and song is not at all clear. On the one hand, the music may represent a way to bring out deeper significances of the words, or a way to legitimize them. On the other hand, the lyric may be popular verse humorously set to serious music, or serious religious verse designed to transform trivial popular music. Except for approximately one hundred fifteenth-century carols that have survived with their musical settings, it seems best to consider the lyrics apart from the music.

Although the extant Middle English lyrics are found in manuscripts of all sorts, the great majority appear in those created for institutions or for public use: miscellanies compiled by friars and belonging to abbeys (Reading Abbey, for instance); collections of sermon materials designed for preachers (especially the extensive alphabetized compilation of John of Grimestone) and of hymns, generally from the Latin and intended for public worship (notably by the Franciscan friars William Herebert and James Ryman); and collections of mystical and devotional pieces (especially by the school of Rolle). Manuscript collections for private use – prayer books, song books, art lyrics – do not appear before the mid fifteenth century.

Although lyrics have been discovered on the fly leaves of manuscripts, as well as in the margins and in odd corners, most of those extant are included in the manuscript proper, mixed in with prose and verse and with various writings in Latin and French. Some lyrics are clearly translations from the Latin, others from the French – the original text may be included with the English; and still others are macaronic poems, mixing words and lines from Latin and French with the English. In most instances the scribe or compiler of the manuscript is not the author of the lyric. The Harley Lyrics, for instance, are a collection of pieces from different parts of England made about 1340. Though in a West Midland transcription, they reflect several different Middle English dialects, suggesting not only that the poems predate the manuscript and that they are by different authors, but that there existed many other lyrics, not chosen for inclusion in the collection.

Most of the lyrics are anonymous, not because their authors' identities have been lost, but because it was not thought important at the time of their composition to know who wrote them. Unlike more-modern poems, these were not composed to advance the particular views or feelings of their authors or to demonstrate their skills of composition. The religious lyrics, growing directly from a devotional movement rather than in imitation of a secular art form, were by and large traditional celebrations of the glory of God, expressions of dedication, and exhortations to piety. The fact that these lyrics do not appear in quantity in manuscripts until the middle of the thirteenth century suggests that they were related to the specific attempt by the new orders of friars to use the vernacular in bringing piety to the laity.

Similarly, the secular pieces employed stock language, conventional figures of speech, and such familiar characters as the wily clerk and the serving maid to celebrate new love, lament lost love, and praise or scorn women. Play of all sorts

— ambiguity, paradox, irony — is a significant feature of this poetry. An antifeminist lyric once attributed to Chaucer exhibits its author's interest in the play of language, as its opening lines indicate:

> O wicket wemen, wilfull, and variable,
> Richt fals, feckle, fell [fierce], and frivolus,
> Dowgit [Obstinate], dispytfull, dour, and dissavable.

The diatribe continues in this manner for another eighteen lines, piling alliterative adjective upon adjective until the author runs out of words. The creator of this frenzy of insult is using a conventional subject to indulge his interest in language. The result is more amusing than serious.

Often lyrics employ a common refrain — perhaps a variation of "Lullay, lullay" or "Merry it is" — or use the same initial line. "Summer is come" begins several celebrations of spring; and "As I rode out the other day" is a popular opening for songs of amorous adventure. Three lyrics beginning "I have a . . . " are grouped together in a fifteenth-century manuscript. Using wordplay and sexual innuendo — male in "I have a gentle cock" and female in "I have a new garden" — these lyrics employ techniques of riddling to create enigmas. The third, "I have a young sister," speaks of the nature of love through the paradox familiar in nursery rhyme and ballad of the cherry without any stone and the dove without any bone.

Certain subjects and themes were particularly popular in the lyrics. The *reverdie* (greening again), a celebration of nature coming back to life, was a form common in Continental lyrics and much used in the English. In "Sumer is icumen in," after stating that spring has arrived, the poet not only focuses on the song of the cuckoo ("Lhude [loudly] sing cuccu!"), but includes the sight of wood and meadow in bloom and the sounds of barnyard animals and their newly born offspring. All of nature is seen as vibrantly alive, and man is asked to participate in the celebration of new life, as the exuberant refrain makes clear: "Sing cuccu nu, sing cuccu! / Sing cuccu, sing cuccu nu!"

Frequently man is shown as an isolated creature, apart from the renewal of the natural world, as in a thirteenth-century *chanson d'aventure* (song of amorous adventure) which begins:

> Nou sprinkes [blooms] the sprai [sprig] —
> Al for loue icche [I] am so seeke [sick]
> That slepen i ne mai!

Nature is joyful, alive; man is melancholy, so sick with love longing that he cannot sleep. The motif is common in the Harley Lyrics. In "Bytuene Mersh and Aueril / Whan spray biginneth to springe," the speaker, who lives "in loue-longinge," is out of sorts with the rest of nature. And in "Lenten [Spring] ys come with loue to toune," the blossoming trees and song of birds are not enough to cure man of his love longing. Instead of participating in the universal joy, he exists as an outcast.

Notwithstanding how the lovesick speakers regard themselves, their situation is not tragic or even poignant but ridiculous, and they (never to be confused with the creators of the lyrics) are ludicrous in their lamentations. Moreover, they are conventional, as are their situations and the language used. The effectiveness of these lyrics is often due not only to the ironic juxtaposition of the general state of nature and the particular condition of the speaker, but also to an incongruity between the lamentable situation and the cheerful language and rhythms used to depict it.

The language of the lovesick narrators may also be used in religious lyrics. "In a tabernacle of a tour," a very popular piece from the end of the fourteenth century — extant in eight manuscripts — transforms the situation and complaint of the secular *chanson d'aventure* into something sacred and mystical. Mary, as Queen of Heaven, appears to the narrator in a nocturnal vision and complains of man's inadequate love of her and her son. Using the refrain "Quia amore langueo" (Because I languish for love), which concludes each of the twelve stanzas, the poem effectively explores the nature of divine love and its ideal human counterpart.

Another kind of springtime celebration is more overtly religious and concerns either the Nativity or the mystery of the Virgin Birth. The best known of these is probably the fifteenth-century lyric "I syng of a myden," which, without any direct scriptural reference, asks its audience to consider both the paradox of Mary as "moder and mayden" and the mystery of the conception of Christ, who came to his mother as quietly "As dew in Aprille / That fallyt on the flour." "I syng of a myden" acts both as a *reverdie* and as a poem of adoration. Such poems of adoration may function as worship of the Virgin Mary, whose several attributes are praised, or as an account of the beauties of an earthly love. In the celebration of spring beginning "Bytuene Mersh and Aueril" the narrator goes on to praise in detail the physical attractions of his love, Alysoun, a name that may function not only as that of a woman but also as a parody of "eleison" (God's grace).

Another subject common in the lyrics celebrating spring is the Passion of Christ — more than twenty are included in John of Grimestone's preaching book (circa 1375). Focusing on the suffering and pathos, these poems ask their audience to meditate about Christ's sacrifice, to grieve, and to love. Several open with the phrase "When I see on the cross" and include a speaker who presents the Crucifixion as though it is at hand. In others the speaker is Mary, asking the reader why he or she will have no pity on her child, or Jesus presenting himself as a knight – "I am Jesus who comes to fight / Without shield and spear." These Passion lyrics often focus on Jesus's agony and vividly describe his wounds. In one the speaker wishes to take on Christ's role – "I wolde ben clad in Cristes skyn / That ran so longe on blode"; and in another, "Loue me broughte," Christ speaks and, through repetition of the word *love,* defines the Passion in terms of his love for man.

A well-known early-thirteenth-century piece on the Crucifixion may be quoted in its entirety:

> Nou goth sonne vnder wod:
> Me reweth, Marie, thi faire rode [countenance].
> Nou goth sonne vnder tre:
> Me reweth, Marie, thi sone and the.

Far more oblique and less bloody than the Passion poems in John of Grimestone's collection, this lyric employs a speaker who describes the events to Mary, not to the reader. She, apparently at the foot of the cross, is his ostensible subject. The poet effectively employs the conventional wordplay of *sun/son* to join *sunset* and *Crucifixion,* and likewise uses the ambiguity of *rode* meaning both countenance and cross. Moreover, the repetition with variation makes it clear that while beginning as an apparent description of nature, the lyric changes to a lament for Mary, a reflection on her grief, and finally becomes a realization of suffering and of the coming of night and death to the world. *Sunset* and *Crucifixion* are made to parallel and give implications about each other.

Many poems on the subject of death focus on the coming of night and winter in the world. One short piece, beginning as a *reverdie* and changing to a complaint about winter and death, survives complete with music. Dating from the early thirteenth century, it may well be the oldest known song in the English language:

> Myrie it is while sumer ilast [lasts],
> With fugheles [birds'] song;
> Oc [But] nu necheth [draws near] windes blast
> And weder strong.
> Ei! ei! what this nicht is long;

And ich, wid well michel [very much] wrong,
Soregh [sorrow] and murne and fast.

Here the pleasures of summertime give way to the bitterness of winter, and the sorrowful cry of the speaker replaces the melodious song of birds. With his recognition that the joy of the world, including the celebration of spring, comes to nothing, the feeling of gladness that once was his is changed to sorrowing, mourning, and fasting. A similar realization is the basis of a Harley lyric:

> Wynter wakeneth al my care,
> Nou this leues [these leaves] waxeth bare.
> Oft y sike [sigh] and mourne sare [sorely]
> 　Whan hit cometh in my thoht
> 　Of this worldes ioie [joy], hou hit geth [goes] al to noht.

Although the focus in this first of three stanzas is on the change of season, the speaker sees in this mutability the need to prepare for his death.

Other lyrics are concerned with the imminence of actual death. These detail the signs of death, reflect on what will happen to the corpse when it is food for worms; ask the reader to consider what has happened to those who lived before; insist on an awareness of the transitoriness of the world, including its beauties and riches; and demand that the reader reflect on his or her fate before it is too late. Other poems represent considerations of the four last things (death, judgment, hell, and heaven) and the state of the soul. Reflecting motifs in art and drama, including the dance of death, these poems are often striking in their bluntness, grim humor, and sense of drama.

One pervasive image is of three sorrowing things. Short lyrics beginning "When I think things three" appear in several manuscripts, including two as early as the thirteenth century:

> Wanne i thenke thinges thre
> Ne mai i neuere blithe [happy] be:
> The ton [one] is that i sal awei [shall (go) away],
> The tother is i ne wot wilk dei [don't know which day].
> The thridde is mi moste kare [greatest concern] –
> I ne wot wider [where] i sal fare [go].

Although the speaker knows he will die, he does not know when, or what will happen to his soul. The combination of his certainty of the first and his uncertainty of the second and the third (the most important concern) gives the poem a sense of urgency. Although the systematic listing may give the impression of calm, ordered thinking, this tone belies the real concern of the speaker, who is contemplating the death of his body and the state of his soul.

The recognition of his state of sin may lead man to remorse and to awareness of the way to his salvation. Thus as his focus on death leads to his anticipation of rebirth, so the sadness of the Crucifixion leads to the joy of the Resurrection, and the reader is back again to the renewal of life and to celebrations of springtime. As one thirteenth-century lyric announces, "Somer is comen and winter gon." Along with the new joy that fills the world, the speaker of this poem feels concern for the Christ child and in the rest of the poem details his life, death on the cross, and Resurrection.

Even though the distinction between religious and secular lyrics – and between popular and courtly lyrics – can hardly help but be made, it is inadequate for speaking of many, including the best, of the Middle English lyrics. Among the artful Harley Lyrics are two pieces that purposely play on the distinction. The first, known as "The Way of Christ's Love," begins:

> Lutel wot [Little knows] it any mon
> How loue hym haueth ybounde [has bound],
> That for us on the rode ron [Cross bled]
> And boghte us with his wounde.

The companion piece, "The Way of Woman's Love," intentionally parallels it:

> Lutel wot it any man
> Hou derne [secret] loue may stonde,
> Bote [Unless] hit were a fre wymmon [immodest woman]
> That muche of loue had fonde.

Whatever the precise relationship between these two pieces – whether the first, urging love of God, provides a basis for understanding the earthly love of the second, or whether the complaint of earthly love is a parody of the overtly religious poem, simultaneously calling up ideal love and making clear the inadequacy of earthly passion – it is clear that the two together offer two perspectives on an issue, both of which must be taken into account. Together, with their parallel language and verses, they create a purposely ambiguous statement on love that demands solution or reconciliation.

Whereas the oft-cited fourteenth-century piece "Maiden in the mor lay" is probably the best-known example of an ostensibly secular lyric that is essentially religious, many other pieces blend to no less an extent the sacred and secular in their language, imagery, and themes. A four-line poem following "Maiden in the mor lay" in manuscript illustrates something of this blend and demonstrates how a so-called popular lyric can be quite artful:

> Al nist [night] by the rose, rose –
> Al nist bi the rose i lay;
> Darst ich noust [Dared I not] the rose stele
> Ant yet i bar the flour [flower] awey.

The imagery is familiar, the language colloquial, and the techniques conventional; but out of the most ordinary ingredients a final product is created that is surprising, compelling, and even demanding. Its paradox may resemble that of the popular riddle, but the reader is asked to do other than make an identification or find a solution. One may feel the need to go beyond the literal level of the poem – a reader will hardly take at face value the narrator's claim that he spent the night alongside a rose – and even beyond the obvious suggestion of an amorous encounter – is the poem merely the report of a successful seduction?

While employing the common erotic image of the lover picking a rose, "Al nist by the rose, rose" also calls up the familiar religious image of the rose as type of the Virgin Mary and of divine love. How these two images work together is complex and purposely unclear in this lyric, but their joining, or perhaps clashing, is a major reason for the poem's success. Rather than be concerned with classifying this lyric as secular or religious, readers need to see how it mixes the natural and supernatural, the human and divine. Pondering this poem does not yield an easy answer for the reader but something unknown, a sense of mystery. What initially seems so simple, familiar, and ordinary becomes on reexamination increasingly complex, strange, and extraordinary; and this poem, like the best of Middle English lyrics, religious or secular, stays in the reader's mind. Likewise, to conclude that this lyric reveals a sophisticated use of popular materials is to show the inadequacy of that distinction. Its artistic manipulation of the familiar has not only resulted in intensity and complexity but has given it an appeal that reaches across almost seven centuries.

"Al nist by the rose, rose" is one of a half-dozen lyrics on a single leaf, perhaps accidentally bound up in manuscript with different material. These poems compare well with the more famous Harley Lyrics, which, along with using the homely language and alliterative formulas of native tradition, also employ elaborate stanza structures and rhetorical formulas associated with French and Latin lyrics. Though in their sophistication the Harley Lyrics are not typical of the early English lyric and often more closely resemble the later medieval art lyric, they should be viewed not as aberrations but as examples of what the best of the Middle English lyrics, secular and religious, were like.

Although for years considered a poor relation of the splendid lyrics written on the Continent and a rudimentary stage in the development of the lyric in English, the Middle English lyric is now viewed as a body of literature valuable in its own right and properly belonging not to antiquarians and philologists but to lovers of good literature. From humble beginnings, through the artful Harley Lyrics to the elegant and intricate lyrics composed by poets, from Chaucer in the fourteenth century through William Dunbar at the end of the fifteenth century, the Middle English lyric in fact leads to the sixteenth-century lyric, its direct descendant.

References:

Peter Dronke, *Medieval Latin and the Rise of European Love-Lyric,* 2 volumes, second edition (Oxford: Clarendon Press, 1968);

Dronke, *The Medieval Lyric* (London: Hutchinson University Library, 1968);

David L. Jeffrey, *The Early English Lyric and Franciscan Spirituality* (Lincoln: University of Nebraska Press, 1975);

Stephen Manning, *Wisdom and Number: Toward a Critical Appraisal of the Middle English Religious Lyric* (Lincoln: University of Nebraska Press, 1962);

Arthur K. Moore, *The Secular Lyric in Middle English* (Lexington: University of Kentucky Press, 1951);

Raymond Oliver, *Poems Without Names: The English Lyric 1200–1500* (Berkeley & Los Angeles: University of California Press, 1970);

Daniel J. Ransom, *Poets at Play: Irony and Parody in The Harley Lyrics* (Norman, Okla.: Pilgrim Books, 1985);

Edmund Reiss, *The Art of the Middle English Lyric: Essays in Criticism* (Athens: University of Georgia Press, 1972);

William Elford Rogers, *Image and Abstraction: Six Middle English Religious Lyrics* (Copenhagen: Rosenkilde & Bagger, 1972);

Sarah Appleton Weber, *Theology and Poetry in the Middle English Lyric: A Study of Sacred History and Aesthetic Form* (Columbus: Ohio State University Press, 1969);

Siegfried Wenzel, *Verses in Sermons: Fasciculus Morum and Its Middle English Poems* (Cambridge, Mass.: Mediaeval Academy of America, 1978);

Rosemary Woolf, *The English Religious Lyric in the Middle Ages* (Oxford: Clarendon Press, 1968).

Morality Plays:
Mankind
(circa 1450 – 1500)

and

Everyman
(circa 1500)

Zacharias P. Thundy

Mankind (circa 1450–1500)

Manuscript: *Mankind* comprises thirty-eight leaves (fols. 154–191) of Folger MS. V.a.354 (formerly MS. 5031, circa 1440–1465) in the Folger Library, Washington, D.C. Facsimile: *Mankind,* Tudor Facsimile Texts (London & Edinburgh: T. C. & E. C. Jack, 1907).

First publication and standard edition: In *Specimens of the Pre-Shakespearean Drama,* volume 1, edited by John M. Manly (Boston: Ginn, 1897).

Standard editions: In *Quellen des weltlichen Dramas in England vor Shakespeare,* edited by Alois Brandl (Strasbourg: Trübner, 1898); in *The Macro Plays,* edited by Mark Eccles, EETS, o.s. 262 (1969).

Everyman (circa 1500)

Manuscript: The work does not survive in manuscript.

First publication: *Here begynneth a treatyse how the hye fader of heuen sendeth dethe to somon euery creature to come and gyue a counte of theyr lyues in this worlde and is in maner of a morall playe* (London: Printed by John Skot, [1528–1529]).

Standard edition: *Everyman,* edited by A. C. Cawley (Manchester: University Press, 1961).

Medieval drama is immense in scope, from musical drama to vernacular plays. Though David Bevington's *Medieval Drama* (1957) includes Latin church drama, most anthologies used in classrooms are limited to vernacular plays, which are usually divided into three groups: mystery cycles, miracle plays, and morality plays.

Mystery plays, or biblical plays, enact salvation history ranging from Creation to Judgment Day. The best-known English members of this group are the four complete mystery cycles (York Cycle, Wakefield or Towneley Plays, N-Town Plays, and Chester Plays); on the Continent mystery plays take the popular form of passion plays, for instance the Oberammergau Passion Play.

Miracle plays are primarily plays about saints, but they are called miracle plays because they include a miraculous central element. Though over one hundred saint or miracle plays survive in Europe, there are today only three extant miracle plays in England: *Mary Magdalene* and *The Conversion of St. Paul* in the Digby Manuscript and *The Play of the Sacrament.* Most English saint plays did not survive the Reformation, but miracle plays share significant features with mystery plays and morality plays; for instance, *Mary Magdalene* includes scenes from Christ's life and morality characters (World, Flesh, and the Devil).

The third genre is the popular morality play, or didactic drama. Whereas God is the central figure in mystery cycles and the saint is in miracle plays, humankind is the main character in morality plays with emphasis on the various phases of life, such as youth, old age, and death. Further, the moral play dramatizes the battle of vices and virtues for the human soul, a battle that leads to the repentance of the sinner. Thus the morality play emphasizes the topos of the rite of passage from sinfulness to sanctification. On the other hand, morality plays complement mystery plays just as a sermon complements the Mass and other Christian liturgical worship services. The themes of morality plays are about the same as those of the Corpus Christi mystery cycle: conflict between good and evil, the fall of humankind, and its redemption by Christ. One significant difference between mystery plays and morality plays is that the latter emphasize salvation through the reception of Christ-given sacraments such as penance and the Eucharist in the Church.

The most frequently studied of the morality plays are *Mankind* (circa 1450–1500) and *Everyman* (circa 1500). Though both are called morality plays, they are different in the sense that *Everyman* stands apart from *Mankind* and other morality plays, which generously mix levity with gravity. As such, the latter are sometimes called interludes.

The key to defining *interlude* lies in the Latin word *ludus* from which it is derived. *Ludus* was used by the Romans to signify any kind of recreational activity. This kind of activity could be fun or serious; it is in this sense that the English word *play* (the equivalent of the Latin *ludus*) is used for drama. Originally interludes (*inter* meaning "between" and *ludus* meaning "play") were performed between courses of meals during Roman times, and the word was later translated into Italian as *intermezzo,* into Spanish as *entremet,* and then into English. It is possible that during the fifteenth and the sixteenth centuries *interlude* meant a dramatic form that was simultaneously serious and playful. It is interesting to note that one medieval play devoted to a secular subject is called *The Interlude of the Student and the Girl* and that John Wyclif warned in his *Tretis on Miriclis* (circa 1385) that it was inappropriate for priests to play in "entrelodies." In the sixteenth century interludes became a popular pastime in England. While both the medieval interludes and Reformation interludes are moral and funny, the latter tend to contain much anti-Catholic polemic as in the case of John Bayle's Tudor interludes such as *King Johan* (circa 1530–1538) and *The Temptation of Our Lord* (1538).

Mankind was written in an East Midland dialect with East Anglian *x* in *xall* (shall) and *xulde* (should), and the play was performed in Cambridgeshire and Norfolk, both in East Anglia. The author paid close attention to meter and rhyme: for instance, Mercy and Mankind speak sixty-four four-line stanzas rhyming *abab.*

Though the play is about Mankind, a personified Mercy has an equally important role in the play: he begins the dialogue of the play and concludes it. Mercy appears in the play not as the daughter of God, as the audience might expect, but as Mankind's father confessor who preaches repentance. As Mercy speaks, Mischief appears ridiculing him; after a gap in the manuscript, three rogues called New Guise (latest fashion or pride of life), Nowadays (the carpe diem philosophy of instant gratification), and Nought (vanity) appear and dance around Mercy and mock his preaching style. After they are forced to leave, Mankind asks Mercy for spiritual counsel and receives it: resist the temptations of the flesh, the world, and the devil; fight against God's enemies with courage as a

knight of Christ should; and practice moderation in everything. Inspired by Mercy's advice, Mankind fends off his adversaries with his spade and then goes to fetch seeds for sowing. Meanwhile Mischief advises the scorned worldlings to call on the devil Titvillius for help. Immediately the devil makes his entry, jokes with his clients, and sends them away to steal horses and money. Invisible to Mankind, the devil plants a board under the soil to deter the protagonist from tilling the field; mixes weeds with seeds; distracts Mankind from praying; and whispers that Mercy is a horse thief, a fugitive from justice, a convicted criminal, and a renegade married priest. Titvillius also urges Mankind to find a whore and to seek forgiveness from New Guise, Nowadays, and Nought for his having hit them with the spade. In the next scene New Guise dresses Mankind in the latest fashion while the murderer Mischief sets up a mock court and makes Mankind swear to rob, steal, and kill. Mankind falls into despair and prepares to hang himself, but Mercy rescues him and counsels Confession and Reconciliation.

There is no one single identifiable source for the play. Though some critics have pointed out affinities between it and William Langland's *Piers Plowman* (circa 1360–circa 1390), many of the play's motifs and ideas seem to be derived from the Old Testament Book of Job and the New Testament. Barring the unlikely discovery of a Latin play in some monastic library, it is safe to conclude that *Mankind* is an original play with complex intertextual and oral traditions. It seems that the playwright has combined traditional Christian doctrine with the style of Franciscan and Dominican preachers of the fifteenth century.

Five main ideas emphasized in traditional Christian preaching stand out in the play: the devil is everywhere trying to drag mankind to hell, it is important for the soul to control bodily desires, the idle mind is the playground of the devil, human beings will be judged by their deeds rather than by their words, and God's mercy knows no bounds provided humans freely choose to seek God's forgiveness.

Unlike the other medieval plays, *Mankind* was never popular on the stage – for three centuries it lay in total oblivion. Even today it is seldom performed. The reason for this neglect seems to be the obscene language found in much of the play's dialogue as well as its overt Catholic bias. Recently, however, it was revived in three productions – at the University of Toronto, at Ohio State University, and at the Bristol Old Vic Theatre School. These productions have rekindled interest in the staging potential of the play. In sum, in spite of its extensive moralizing, *Man-*

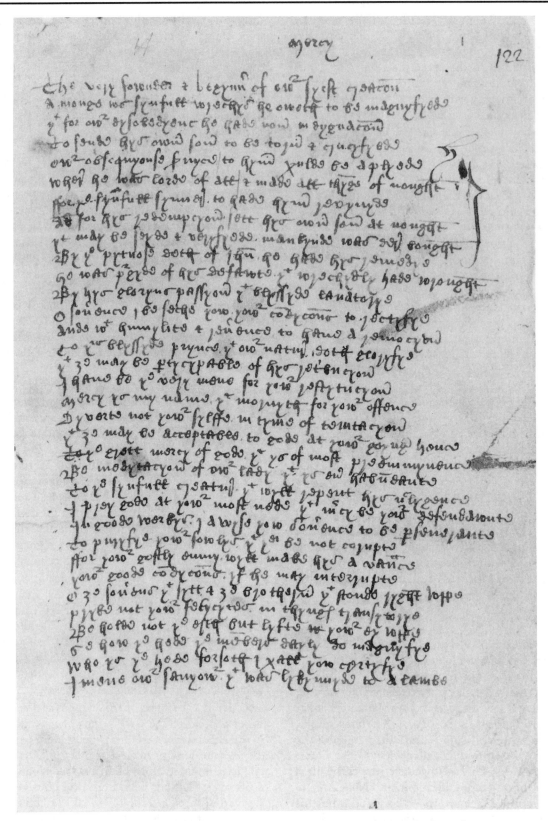

First page of Mankind *in the only extant manuscript for the work (Folger MS. V.a.354)*

kind is fun to read, and recent theatrical productions show that it is funnier on the stage.

The plain, clear diction of *Everyman,* written in the popular dialect of the fifteenth century, resembles the language and style of Geoffrey Chaucer. Like Chaucer, the playwright eschews the extremes of flowery style and colloquial dialect. In this sense, it is different from *Mankind,* which uses "Englysch Laten" in the speech of Mercy and vulgar words in the speech of the villains. The author of *Everyman* prefers, like William Caxton, a style "not ouer rude ne curyous, but in suche termes as shall be vunderstanden." On the other hand, the stanza forms, the verse length, and the rhymes used in *Everyman* are irregular, unlike *Mankind.*

Careful analyses of the language and versification of the play indicate that it is more likely a translation of Vorsterman's printed edition of the Dutch *Elckerlijc* (circa 1518–1525) than an English original. In line 463, the end words "make my mone" correspond to the Dutch rhyme word *claghen* (427), found only in Vorsterman's edition, whereas all the other editions and manuscripts of *Elckerlijc* have *ghwaghen* (plead). The conclusion that the English *Everyman* is a translation of the *Elckerlijc* is strengthened by the fact that in the early sixteenth century Antwerp was the center of the Anglo-Dutch book trade, and thus Dutch printers regularly printed English-language books translated from Dutch.

The main feature that distinguishes *Everyman* from other morality plays is that, whereas the latter give practical advice for living, *Everyman* gives practical advice for dying. Two other medieval English morality plays – *The Castle of Perseverance* (circa 1400–1425) and *The Pride of Life* – also deal with death, but they emphasize the conflict of good and evil forces for the human soul rather than the two points *Everyman* is stressing: the psychological process of dying, in which Everyman is abandoned by all his faculties in the play; and the preparation for death, which involves the reception of sacraments.

There are two major sources corresponding to the two emphases of the play. As for the actual preparation for the death of the Christian, the popular treatise called *Ars Moriendi* (early fifteenth century), translated into English as the *Book of the Craft of Dying* (circa 1490), was well known in the fifteenth century. Caxton published two abridged translations of *Ars Moriendi* in 1490 and 1491, in which the fifth temptation a dying person faces is attachment to temporal things such as wealth, family, and fellowship, similar to Everyman's temptations in the play. Further, Everyman's call to judgment is similar to the same motif found in the judgment plays of the mystery cy-cles. The play's overall dependence, however, on the teachings of the Bible can be seen in Revelation 14:13: "And I heard a voice from heaven saying, 'Write this: Blessed are the dead who die in the Lord henceforth.' 'Blessed indeed,' says the Spirit, 'that they may rest from their labors, for their deeds follow them.' "

The story element of *Everyman* is ultimately based on Oriental sources. Besides the ancient popular Sanskrit proverb "Wealth, friends, and relatives abandon you at the grave, but your good and bad deeds do not," the Indian parable of the faithful friend seems to have served as a major source of the play. Popular versions of the Indian faithful friend story can be found in the medieval European Barlaam and Josaphat, with Josaphat as the Europeanization of the Sanskrit word *bodhisatva* (Buddha), Petrus Alphonsi's twelfth-century *Disciplina clericalis,* and Caxton's English translation of Jacobus de Voragine's Latin *Legenda aurea* (circa 1260). Summarily, the popular faithful friend story narrates how two allegorical friends, Riches and Kindred, abandon an accused man, while the third friend, identified as Faith, Hope, and Charity, agrees to plead his case before the king.

The plot of *Everyman* is fairly simple and straightforward. Everyman, an allegory for the individual human being, is summoned to his final judgment by Death, the messenger of God; Everyman calls upon Fellowship, Kindred, and Goods to accompany him on his journey to meet his Master and Judge, but they forsake him one after another. Lastly, he begs Good Deeds to go with him; she would gladly go with him if she could, but she lies cold and in chains in the ground, unable to get up and walk. Instead, Good Deeds asks her sister Knowledge to accompany Everyman. Knowledge conducts him to the holy man Confession in the church. As soon as Everyman receives forgiveness for his sins in the sacrament of penance, Good Deeds rises from the ground as though she is rising from the dead. At this point Strength, Beauty, Discretion, and Five Wits join Knowledge and Good Deeds in escorting Everyman to his death and judgment; however, as Everyman is expiring, all these companions with the exception of Good Deeds leave him, and finally his soul is welcomed to heaven by the angels.

Thematically speaking, *Everyman* is a dramatic presentation of the medieval Catholic teaching on holy dying: that dying persons should not place their trust in worldly goods, friends, and relatives but rather only in God's grace and their own good works. Since all human beings are often guilty of mortal sins, they lose grace and merits (good deeds), which, therefore, are incapable of helping them on their final pilgrimage. The only way grace and merits can be regained is through the sacrament of penance administered by the priests in the holy church.

The most intriguing problem raised by the play concerns why Good Deeds is presented in the play as unable to help Everyman in his need. The solution is that Good Deeds is mortally ill on account of the mortal sins committed by Everyman – that is, Everyman is a sinner who is guilty not only of venial sins but also of mortal sins. Everyman could thus be consigned to hell upon God's judgment if his good deeds or merits were not revived and restored by the sacrament of confession. However, in order to make a good confession and avoid further sins, Everyman needs God's special help, known in Catholic theology as actual grace, which he receives. The Catholic doctrine of the reviviscence of grace and merits is the key in the interpretation of the play and for the identification of its allegorical characters. In the case of Everyman, as soon as he receives absolution for sins in confession, his merits and grace are restored; this restoration is symbolized in the revivification of the character of Good Deeds. Similarly, according to traditional Catholic teaching, actual grace is always available to every human being, whether he or she is in a state of grace or not. The characters of Knowledge, Beauty, and Five Wits are aspects of actual grace – a special divine help available to all human beings to perform meritorious deeds or to seek forgiveness for sins.

The theological identification of Good Deeds, Knowledge, and the other characters complement the moral and psychological dimensions of the play. On the moral-dramatic plane, the same characters of Strength, Beauty, Discretion, and Five Wits are bodily or spiritual powers of Everyman. The playwright reminds his audience that these faculties are as unreliable and incapable of saving Everyman as Fellowship, Kindred, and Good Deeds are in the first part of the play. The moral emphasis, then, is on the instability of all earthly entities – physical and spiritual. Though ultimately it is God alone who saves Everyman, he does so at least partly through the revivified Good Deeds or merits, that is, faith in God should be supplemented by good deeds.

There is no evidence that *Everyman* was performed in England after 1600 until William Poel revived it for the Elizabethan Stage Society in 1901. Since then it has been staged with some regularity in London, at Oxford, at Rugby, and at other schools. Under the guidance of Charles Frohman, the play was performed from October 1902 to May 1903 in New York and later in Boston, Philadelphia, Chicago, and Baltimore. Since *Everyman* does not include the dy-

namic elements of dance, procession, and secular music that liven drama and delight spectators, it is less frequently performed today on college campuses than other morality plays such as *Mankind, Wisdom* (circa 1460), and *The Castle of Perseverance.*

The importance of *Everyman*, however, lies not so much in its stageability as in its theological teaching. It is above all a profoundly theological play. On this level the different characters of the play have a deeper meaning and a saving function in the drama of redemption, according to medieval Catholic preaching.

Bibliographies:

W. W. Greg, *A Bibliography of the English Printed Drama to the Restoration,* 4 volumes (London: Bibliographical Society, 1939–1959);

Carl J. Stratman, *Bibliography of Medieval Drama* (Berkeley & Los Angeles: University of California Press, 1954);

Peter J. Houle, *The English Morality and Related Drama: A Bibliographical Survey* (Hamden, Conn.: Archon, 1972).

References:

David Bevington, ed., *Medieval Drama* (Boston: Houghton, 1957);

E. K. Chambers, *The Medieval Stage* (Oxford: Clarendon Press, 1903);

Mary P. Coogan, *An Interpretation of the Moral Play, 'Mankind'* (Washington, D.C.: Catholic University Press, 1947);

Hardin Craig, *English Religious Drama of the Middle Ages* (Oxford: Clarendon Press, 1955);

G. R. Owst, *Literature and Pulpit in Mediaeval England* (Cambridge: Cambridge University Press, 1933);

L. V. Ryan, "Doctrine and Dramatic Structure in *Everyman,*" *Speculum,* 32 (1957): 722–735;

Martin Stevens, "Medieval Drama: Genres, Misconceptions, and Approaches," in Richard K. Emmerson, *Approaches to Teaching Medieval English Drama* (New York: MLA, 1990), pp. 36–49;

Zacharias P. Thundy, "Good Deeds Rediviva: *Everyman* and the Doctrine of Reviviscence," *Fifteenth-Century Studies,* 17 (1990): 421–437;

Glynne Wickham, *English Moral Interludes* (Totowa, N.J.: Rowman, 1975);

Wickham, *The Medieval Theatre* (Cambridge: Cambridge University Press, 1987);

Arnold Williams, *The Drama of Medieval England* (East Lansing: Michigan State University Press, 1961).

N-Town Plays

(circa 1468 – early sixteenth century)

Theresa Coletti
University of Maryland

Manuscript: The only extant manuscript, written by a main scribe and containing work by three other hands, is British Library MS. Cotton Vespasian D.viii (1468). Facsimile: *The N-Town Plays: A Facsimile of British Library MS Cotton Vespasian D. VIII,* edited by Peter Meredith and Stanley J. Kahrl, Leeds Texts and Monographs, Medieval Drama Facsimiles 4 (Ilkey, U.K.: Scolar, 1977).

First publication: *Ludus Coventriae: A Collection of Mysteries Formerly Represented at Coventry on the Feast of Corpus Christi,* edited by James Orchard Halliwell (London: Shakespeare Society, 1841).

Standard editions: *Ludus Coventriae: or The Plaie Called Corpus Christi,* edited by K. S. Block, EETS, e.s. 120 (1922; reprinted, 1960); *The N-Town Play,* edited by Stephen Spector, EETS, supplemental series 11 and 12 (1991).

Edition in modern English: *The Corpus Christi Play of the English Middle Ages,* edited by R. T. Davies (Totowa, N. J.: Rowman and Littlefield, 1972).

Of the four complete mystery cycles that comprise a major portion of the extant corpus of early English biblical drama, the N-Town Plays are surely the most enigmatic. Indeed, they probably do not constitute a mystery cycle at all, if that term is taken to mean a narrative sequence of discrete plays dramatizing biblical history and originating in a civic environment in late-medieval England. Like other issues basic to a consideration of the group of plays preserved in British Library MS. Cotton Vespasian D.viii, the question of exactly what the N-Town Plays are has been the focus of much detailed scholarly scrutiny and speculation; relatively little is known with certainty about this group of plays. The institutional auspices and precise geographical origins of the plays remain hidden, as do the circumstances that led to the composition of this remarkable and eclectic collection. Even the name "N-Town," derived from the proclamation text that opens the collection, withholds more than it delivers. That it has only recently emerged as the preferred designation for a group of plays previously known under other aliases – Ludus Coventriae, Lincoln plays, Hegge cycle – provides eloquent testimony to the compelling and complex problems that the N-Town Plays present to modern readers.

In the single manuscript in which the N-Town group survives, the date 1468 appears at the ending of the purification play. This date is consistent with the hand of the main scribe, as well as with that of the scribe who wrote the interpolated play of the Assumption of Mary; both are generally assigned to the third quarter of the fifteenth century. Two other late-fifteenth- or early-sixteenth-century scribal hands also contributed to the manuscript with interpolated folios, marginal revisions, and other additions. Supported by the approximate dates of the watermarks of the many varieties of paper comprising the manuscript, the dates of the scribal hands indicate that the N-Town codex was transcribed and most likely compiled between the mid fifteenth and early sixteenth centuries.

Although the sequence of plays contained in the N-Town manuscript follows the general pattern of dramatized biblical episodes appearing in other extant cycles, the N-Town Plays in many respects stand apart from the dramatic mainstream of the northern cycles. One example of N-Town's singularity may be found in the departure of its Christ and the Doctors play from the four other extant versions in the York Cycle, the Chester Plays, the Towneley Plays, and the Coventry Miracle Plays, which are remarkably similar. The N-Town Plays also include several unique scenes as well as other features unparalleled in the York, Chester, and Towneley cycles. According to the inventory provided by Stephen Spector in his 1991 edition of N-Town, only this cycle dramatizes Lamech's killing of Cain, the prophets as a Jesse tree, the story of Anne and Joachim, the presentation of Mary in the temple, the Parliament of Heaven, the trial of Joseph and Mary, the cherry tree episode, Death's killing of Herod, the appearance of Veronica, the division of the harrowing of hell into two plays, and the appearance of the risen Christ to the Virgin Mary. Still more noteworthy is N-Town's singular incorporation into its historical frame of what clearly were once discrete works: an independent, multi-episode play on the life of Mary and a two-part Passion play. Compared to the other extant cycles, the individual plays or dramatic episodes of N-Town do not always divide as easily into discrete pageants. Rather, as Martin Stevens has pointed out, they sometimes constitute clusters of dramatic action, with scene blending into scene — for example, the episodes of Cleophas and Luke and the appearance to Thomas. Relatively few of the individual N-Town pageants are announced by specific titles, as is *Hic de muliere in adulterio deprehensa* (folio 121^r). Consequently, the editorial habit of providing titles for the plays, as in the most recent edition, makes N-Town look more like the complete civic cycles and gives to the plays the appearance of a greater structural coherence and regularity than they in fact possess.

It is rather the many irregularities of the N-Town manuscript that have received by far the most attention from scholars of medieval drama, who now agree that the plays contained in British Library MS. Cotton Vespasian D.viii are a compilation of texts, probably from distinct origins and disparate auspices. Many scholars believe that the main scribe of the N-Town Plays was also their compiler. Detailed studies of bibliographical and textual features of the N-Town manuscript — its collation, types of paper, handwriting, stanzaic forms, prosody, stage directions, and patterns of textual alteration and interpolation — have shed much light on the process of its compilation. These studies clearly show how the scribe-compiler went about constructing the cycle. Among the many signs indicating the work's composite nature, some of the most important involve the banns or proclamation, spoken by three vexillators who appear at the beginning of the text. The proclamation describes a numbered series of pageants that do not correspond completely to the dramatic episodes and plays of the N-Town codex. Some plays included in the manuscript are not mentioned in the proclamation, or the proclamation describes versions of the episodes that are different from those preserved in the manuscript. Additionally, the numbers of the pageants in

the proclamation do not fully correspond with the order of the plays and episodes as they appear in the manuscript, notwithstanding the efforts of the scribe to stress this correspondence by providing in the margins large red numerals denoting the beginning of new plays.

These disjunctions between proclamation and play texts and other features of the N-Town manuscript lead Peter Meredith (1991) to conclude that the process of compilation was rather haphazard; he suggests that the scribe continued to change his plans as he went along, even as he attempted to give the collection a unified appearance. It is impossible to determine, though tantalizing to speculate about, what the scribe-compiler's larger intentions may have been. It appears that he was engaged in an effort to make a partially independent proclamation describe a group of play texts that were being brought together for the specific occasion of the collection. Was he aiming to create a collection of plays analogous in content and form to Corpus Christi civic cycles from other locales? Did he, as Meredith suggests, have in mind a grand production or even a text suitable for printing? What is most important about the N-Town manuscript and text, however, is that, despite their patchwork character, scholars have frequently found the collection to bespeak unities of theme and design. Configured in these terms, the debate about the N-Town Plays opposes those who would argue for N-Town as an integrated whole characterized by distinctive artistic value, to those who would see its "unfinished" state as a barrier to any assessment of literary or theatrical merit.

Postmodern theory shows how this opposition, as several scholars of medieval drama have put it, between the text as "product" and the text as "process" is fundamentally misleading. Such an opposition wrongly assumes both that a text can achieve a status as finished product whose full intentions are completely manifest, and that any textual state short of that goal is deficient. In contrast, postmodern theory recognizes all texts as fundamentally unstable and "unfinished," a function of their being in language, their social production, and their dialogic and variable reception. Within this framework, the instability of medieval texts, whose production and circulation in manuscript defined their constant involvement in the process of becoming that Paul Zumthor terms *mouvance,* figures as a special historical instance of textuality generally. From this perspective the N-Town collection must be seen neither as a roughly hewn, deformed dramatic codex nor as a fully accomplished artifact, but rather as a text that reveals the dynamic process of its own creation, subject to all the accidents of circumstance and to the material and social conditions that would prompt a compiler to undertake a project of this sort at the end of the Middle Ages.

The multiplicity and dynamism of the N-Town codex invite questions about these material and social circumstances. Unfortunately, the manuscript itself yields only the barest traces of evidence that might disclose its history, and these reveal nothing about a specific provenance. Notations on the flyleaf and other manuscript pages indicate the N-Town Plays belonged in the early seventeenth century to Robert Hegge of Durham, and were eventually acquired by Richard James, librarian of Sir Robert Bruce Cotton and a member of Hegge's college at Oxford, Corpus Christi. The first record of the manuscript appears in the catalog of Cotton's collection drawn up between 1631 and 1638. By contrast, for the cyclic texts from Chester, York, and Coventry copious records documenting civic and guild participation in play production still survive; and the manuscript of the Towneley plays provides several rubrics that link those dramas with the town of Wakefield in the West Riding of Yorkshire. But the N-Town Plays are still in search of a local habitation, if not a name. For many years they were misattributed to the city of Coventry because of the label (Ludus Coventriae) given to them by James on the manuscript's flyleaf. They were also mistakenly supposed to have originated in Lincoln, where surviving records of dramatic celebrations of St. Anne's Day had suggested connections with the Marian emphases of the N-Town Plays. Though references to Coventry and Lincoln occasionally still appear in discussions of N-Town's origins, there is now a clear consensus, based on detailed dialectal evidence, that the N-Town Plays are East Anglian plays and that their main scribe hailed from Norfolk, most likely the south-central region near the Suffolk border.

To be sure, dialectal evidence alone yields nothing definitive in a search for the precise origins of the N-Town Plays. The dialect of a scribe does not necessarily identify the geographical origin of the text copied, and the case of N-Town is further complicated by the fact that its four distinct hands have been assigned to different East Anglian locales. But dialectal evidence confirming an East Anglian origin for the N-Town text nevertheless has major implications. First, it points up N-Town's important participation in a larger corpus of dramatic literature unique texts – including the Digby plays of *Mary Magdalene* (circa 1500–1525), the *Conversion*

of St. Paul (circa 1500–1550), and the *Killing of the Children of Israel* (circa 1512); the Macro plays of the *Castle of Perseverance* (circa 1400–1425), *Mankind* (circa 1450–1500), and *Wisdom* (circa 1465–1470); and the Croxton *Play of the Sacrament* (circa 1461–1500) – are also assigned to East Anglia on the basis of linguistic, codicological, and other types of evidence. N-Town's addition to this corpus makes it possible to recognize late-medieval East Anglia as an important center for the creation of dramatic texts whose relationship to each other highlights the shared dramatic traditions of the region. Even more important, dialectal evidence reinforces the need to examine the N-Town manuscript and text in light of the dominant economic, demographic, and cultural characteristics of late-medieval East Anglia.

H. R. L. Beadle and Gail McMurray Gibson have each detailed how East Anglia's rich social and cultural fabric informed patterns of religious expression and the production of religious art. These scholars have made clear that late-medieval East Anglia, including the counties of Norfolk and Suffolk and neighboring portions of Cambridgeshire and the Isle of Ely, possessed a density of both population and wealth large enough to inspire the creation of a regional culture that inscribed its prosperity and its distinctive spiritual style in monuments of glass and stone, in image and text. Beadle's research uncovering the extensive amount of vernacular literary activity in late-medieval East Anglia reinforces the increasingly well-developed image of a regional culture fully capable of producing the rich variety of dramatic texts that were at some moment in their shadowy history gathered together in the N-Town codex.

Looking more specifically at patterns of local activity that link East Anglian dramatic manuscripts, literary production, evidence of dramatic performance, and internal features of the N-Town Plays themselves, Gibson has argued the provocative hypothesis that the N-Town collection originates from the great Benedictine abbey of Bury Saint Edmunds. Although impossible to prove conclusively, her thesis has the advantage of identifying areas of cultural activity that surely must be brought to bear on any consideration of N-Town's auspices in light of East Anglian culture. Of paramount significance here is the connection drawn between N-Town and the ecclesiastical establishment of Bury Saint Edmunds. Ever since William Dugdale, interpreting Cotton librarian James's description of the codex, mistakenly attributed the N-Town Plays to the Grey Friars of Coventry, scholars have endorsed the proposition that the collec-

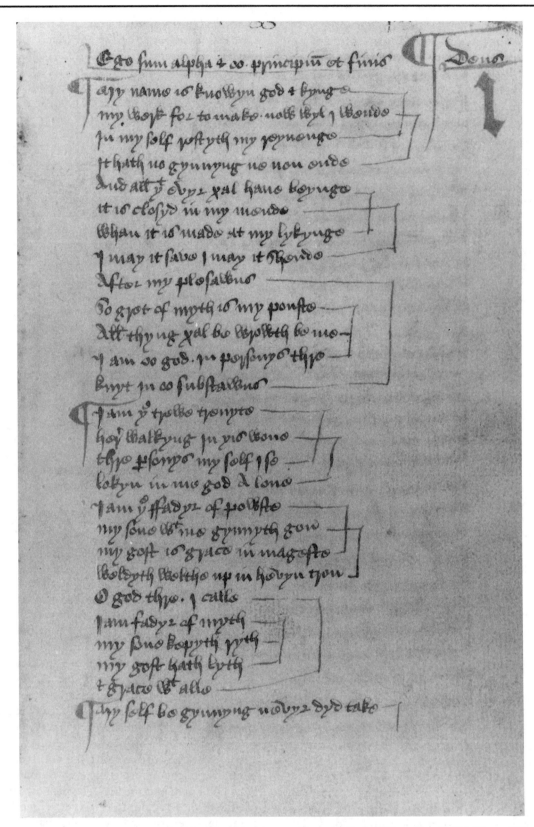

Page from The Creation, and Fall of Lucifer *in the only extant manuscript for the N-Town Plays (British Library, MS. Cotton Vespasian D. viii, fol. 10)*

tion, or at least portions of it, was affiliated with some sort of religious institution. Among the features of the manuscript prompting this attribution are its marginal notations in a liturgical hand, its extensive use of liturgical music, and what has seemed to some its preoccupation with theological learning.

Ultimately, determining the precise character and location of the probable ecclesiastical auspices of all or part of the N-Town Plays is of less importance than recognizing that the ecclesiastical environment of late-medieval East Anglia afforded many institutional and communal occasions in which the plays of N-Town could have been nurtured. Late-medieval East Anglia provides ample evidence of the predominance of and interaction between the multiple spheres of cultural activity – religious houses and foundations, towns, parishes, and religious guilds – which most likely furnished the plays and sequences of plays amalgamated in the N-Town manuscript. While it is true that, in tracing the auspices of the extant East Anglian play texts and manuscripts, many roads lead to Bury Saint Edmunds, it is also important to recognize that other East Anglian ecclesiastical centers could just as easily have provided the collocation of piety, ingenuity, and substantial material resources that would probably have characterized the institutional auspices of the N-Town Plays.

For example, the town of Thetford, on the Norfolk-Suffolk border, furnishes a telling illustration of the kinds of drama-related activities that played an important role in the late-medieval East Anglian culture in which the plays of N-Town once flourished. A manuscript now in Cambridge University Library from the Cluniac Priory at Thetford includes for the early decades of the sixteenth century lists of expenditures for entertainment that attest to a monastic taste for players and minstrels at all seasons. The priory hosted a diverse group of entertainers, many of them under royal and noble patronage, and it regularly made payments to parish games in and around Thetford. The surviving records of dramatic activity associated with Thetford Priory support the portrait of East Anglia as an area rich in parish and community-based theater. Thetford was also the home of a wealthy and influential ecclesiastical establishment, the College of Saint Mary at Baily (or Bailey) End, which has left few traces of its important contributions to the life of that late-medieval town. Scholars do know, however, that the collegiate church sponsored a guild whose membership comprised the governing body of the town and other prominent citizens and was dedicated to the Virgin Mary.

The religious foundation of the collegiate church has been largely unstudied in relation to late-medieval dramatic activity, primarily because these institutions were completely eliminated at the time of the dissolution, when their activities were halted and their records and church fabric destroyed; as a result, there are significant gaps in what is known of the activities of these institutions and their allied religious guilds and the roles they played in late-medieval religious culture. Occupied by secular canons and a complement of chaplains, priests, and choristers, the main employment of the collegiate church was the celebration of mass in conformity with the founders' wishes. But as the focal point of the life of a prominent religious guild, as was the case in Thetford, the collegiate church also suggests itself as a likely site for dramatic activity. Despite the fact that not a scrap of evidence links the N-Town Plays to a collegiate church, institutions such as the College of Saint Mary at Baily End, Thetford, provide one of the most provocative unexplored areas for further speculation about N-Town's auspices. Several scholars have already linked portions of the N-Town collection, such as its unique Mary play, to possible production by East Anglian religious guilds; it thus seems appropriate to consider whether a play as textually elaborate and as theatrically complex as the Mary play might not in fact be the product of the collaboration of religious-guild and collegiate foundation rather than of a simple parish guild. Hypothesizing auspices of this sort provides a meaningful context for some of the signal features of the N-Town Mary play. Celebrating their annual feast on the Sunday after the nativity of Mary, the guild and college at Baily End certainly had the occasion and probably the capability to produce a sequence of plays that called for liturgical music, liturgical prayer, and a large role for priestly actors and that emphasized the ecclesiastical establishment in both the figure and the edifice of the "Temple," prominent in the several scenes of the Mary play. Considering these features, it may also be significant that N-Town's Marian sequence concludes with the singing of *Ave regina celorum,* an antiphon used in processions on the Nativity of Mary, the feast day of the Virgin to which the College at Baily End allied its annual celebration.

Contributing to the discourse of inconclusiveness that attends all discussion of the N-Town Plays, speculations such as these serve nevertheless to sketch in some of the blank spaces in the still-unfinished portrait of late-medieval East Anglian dramatic activity. Still other segments of that portrait and aspects of the N-Town manuscript prove mutually illuminating. One prominent feature of N-Town's banns or proclamation, for example, may signal patterns of activity specific to East Anglian play production. For many years scholars assumed that the inclusion of a proclamation in the N-Town manuscript meant that the plays described therein were the repertory of a touring company. This assumption was based on the proclamation's notice that the plays will be played in "good aray" for those who come to see them "A Sunday next" at six o'clock "in N-town." But rather than announce a touring play for which N-Town is one of many venues, it is just as likely that the proclamation refers to a dramatic production in a central location to which audiences were summoned by the crying of the banns. This hypothesis advantageously offers an alternative to the unlikely possibility that a compilation of plays as ambitious as N-Town could ever have even been intended for production in multiple locales. More important, it fully accords with a pattern of organizing and presenting plays that appears to have prevailed in East Anglia in the decades before the Reformation. Investigations into East Anglian rural theater have revealed that dramatic production in the region was commonly a multicommunity effort; evidence points to the existence of dramatic centers in villages or townships, around which clustered neighboring communities that contributed to plays performed at the center or performed their own plays there.

Whether or not the extant N-Town Plays were ever actually performed in this format, their proclamation's announcement of the apparently familiar playing place at "N-Town" suggests that at some point in its invisible history the N-Town manuscript, or portions of it, may have been associated with production for a dramatic center and its neighboring communities. Distinct from the civic-production model of the other cycles, this scenario might thus explain the unusual composite character of the manuscript as well as provide a plausible context for the work of the compiler. It also emphasizes the important ways that understandings of local context may shed light on the unique features of extant dramatic texts.

Another facet of N-Town's relation to its local context worthy of mention involves the numerous correspondences with Continental drama that the plays exhibit. N-Town declares its kinship with the medieval dramas of France and the Low Countries, for example, through an emphasis on the Virgin Mary, generally more characteristic of Continental drama, and the inclusion of scenes and motifs, such as the Parliament of Heaven, the Lamech episode,

and the depiction of the prophets as a Jesse tree, all of which appear in Continental drama but in no other extant English play. While these similarities need not suggest N-Town's direct borrowing from Continental plays, they probably do reflect an important aspect of the East Anglian climate in which the N-Town collection was written and compiled: the region's strong economic and cultural ties to northern Europe. Not only did the East Anglian cloth industry, staffed in part by Flemish workers, provide ample opportunities for many forms of economic, social, and religious exchange between England and Continental markets, but wealthy East Anglian merchants and feudal magnates such as John Fastolf and William de la Pole, Duke of Suffolk, through their commercial, political, and diplomatic contacts with northern Europe and the example of their own patronage, served as conduits for Continental culture, enhancing opportunities for artistic interaction between the East Anglian counties, France, and the Low Countries.

Among all of the N-Town collection's resemblances to Continental drama the most noteworthy is its use of a fixed stage requiring action in a *platea,* or playing place, and various loci, or stations. Employed by French and German Passion plays, for instance, this manner of staging distinguishes N-Town's interpolated two-part Passion sequence, and, as several scholars have argued, it may have been the mode of staging for other segments of the cycle as well. Indeed, after the compilation and auspices of the manuscript, the staging of the N-Town Plays is the aspect of the collection most subject to scholarly debate, which has focused on the multiple possibilities for staging the plays. Differences in stage directions among various parts of the collection suggest that at least some of the plays may have been presented on the sequential pageant model typical of the northern cycles, while still other features of the manuscript point to the possibility that whole groups of plays were revised to accommodate a *platea* and loci stage.

Still, as is the case with other important aspects of the N-Town collection, precise determinations about its manner of staging remain inconclusive. On this understandably elusive topic, however, several points should be borne in mind. First, in spite of the evidence that the N-Town compiler was sensitive to the exigencies of staging and that specific plays bear signs of being tailored for performance, the extant manuscript collection was probably never staged wholly and entirely in the manner in which it survives. Second, the fixed stage that was prominent in Continental drama and remains such a memorable aspect of the N-Town collection was apparently a staple feature of East Anglian dramatic production, as the texts of plays such as the Macro *Castle of Perseverance* and the Digby play of *Mary Magdalene* indicate. Third, and most important, the fixed-staging techniques of plays such as N-Town's two-part Passion enable some of the most dramatic and spectacular effects known to the medieval English stage.

The N-Town Plays contain more stage directions than any of the other extant cycles. In the Passion sequence particularly these directions frequently draw astonishingly precise portraits of the visual details and choreography of the dramatic scene, as in this example describing Christ's entrance into Jerusalem: "Here the iiii ceteseynys makyn hem redy for to mete with oure Lord, goyng barfot and barelegged and in here shyrtys, savyng thei xal [shall] have here gownys cast abouth them. And qwan thei seen oure Lord thei xal sprede ther clothis beforn hym, and he xal lyth and go therupon. And thei xal falle downe upon ther knes all atonys, the fyrst thus seyng. . . . " An equally striking account of stage business appears in the direction occurring immediately after Satan announces his hastily hatched plot to stop the Crucifixion in order to keep hell free from the conquering Christ. He decides to send a dream to Pilate's wife so that she may persuade her husband not to kill Christ: "Here xal the devyl gon to Pylatys wyf, the corteyn drawyn as she lyth in bedde; and he xal no dene make, but she xal sone after that he is come in makyn a rewly noyse, comyng and rennyng of the schaffald, and here shert and here kyrtyl in here hand. And sche xal come beforn Pylat leke a mad woman."

The copious and detailed stage directions of N-Town's two-part Passion Play also make clear how the techniques of the fixed stage, calling for action in and between the various stations marked off from the *platea,* allow for rapid juxtapositions of scene, simultaneity of multiple dramatic actions, and the deliberate use of theatrical space to articulate and reinforce dramatic meaning. In fact, the interpolation of several folios into the N-Town manuscript suggests that the compiler worked deliberately to take advantage of the potential for juxtaposition and simultaneity that a fixed stage invites. For example, N-Town stages the Last Supper at one station as the conspiracy to capture Christ is being plotted at another: "Here Cryst enteryth into the hous with his disciplis and ete the paschal lomb; and in the menetyme the cownsel hous befornseyd xal sodeynly onclose schewyng the buschopys,

prestys and jewgys syttyng in here astat lych as it were a convocacyon." This call for dramatic action "in the meantime" occurs regularly in the scenic requirements of the N-Town Passion; thus, Christ is led away by his capturers "with gret cry and noyse, some drawyng Cryst forward, and some bakward," while Mary Magdalene, having witnessed the spectacle from afar, runs to the Virgin Mary to "telle here of oure Lordys takyng." Satan plays in the "place in the most orryble wyse," as Christ is dressed in white after his scourging and led about the place and "than to Pylat be the tyme that hese wyf hath pleyd." The intense and frenetic image of the Passion that results from its enactment on a multistation fixed stage is reminiscent of the panoramic and shifting perspective found in late-medieval northern European paintings of the Passion narrative that foreground the Crucifixion, which vies for the viewer's attention with other Passion episodes represented on different picture planes.

Besides the exceptional features of its material existence, its late-medieval social and cultural context, and its formal characteristics and theatrical requirements as text and drama, the N-Town collection also solicits the attention of scholars because of the provocative and, in many instances, unique ways that it represents the narrative of sacred history. Chief among N-Town's distinctive traits in this regard is its previously noted Mary play, comprised of a sequence of episodes ultimately derived from the apocryphal gospels of Pseudo-Matthew and the *De Nativitate Mariae* as they were filtered through Jacobus de Voragine's *Legenda aurea* (circa 1260) and the pseudo-Bonaventuran *Meditationes Vitae Christi* (circa 1300–1350). Beginning with the story of Anne and Joachim in the Conception of Mary, this sequence includes Mary's presentation in the temple, her betrothal and marriage to Joseph, the Parliament of Heaven and Annunciation, and, after the intervening play of Joseph's troubles, the visit to Elizabeth. Although all the cycles contain plays that call for extended representations of Mary, notably during the scenes of Christ's birth and death, only N-Town provides so much attention to her. This Marian focus is strong enough to prompt Martin Stevens to observe that N-Town's interest in the life of Mary constitutes a strategic dramatic move that makes Mary's story a secondary plot of the entire cycle, subsumed within the main plot of the life of Christ.

While N-Town's Marian focus is most evident in the episodes dramatizing her early life, the cycle takes advantage of many other opportunities to represent Mary's role in and responses to sacred history. For example, N-Town includes an unusual scene in which Mary Magdalene announces to the Virgin Mary the arrest of her son, as well as the scene, popularized in Franciscan devotion, in which the risen Christ appears to his mother. N-Town and York are the only extant cycles to preserve plays of the Virgin Mary's Assumption, and N-Town alone dramatizes the episode of the trial of Joseph and Mary – extremely rare in all of medieval European drama. Based on the apocryphal account of Mary's life in Pseudo-Matthew, the play depicts an open challenge to Joseph and Mary's claim that their marriage is chaste: her obvious pregnancy provokes accusations that either the two of them are lying or she is an adulteress. Joseph and Mary are made to submit to a purgation ritual by drinking from the "botel of Goddys vengeauns," which harkens back through the apocryphal account to the bitter waters of Numbers 5. In adapting the apocryphal story of the trial, however, the N-Town play introduces an important innovation: it transports the scene of Joseph and Mary's accusation to that of a late-medieval ecclesiastical court, making the holy couple the subject of scurrilous defamation on the part of two characters designated as "detractors." Joseph and Mary, of course, are found innocent of all charges against them, as the play takes advantage of the opportunity to emphasize Mary's uniquely pure body, here deployed to critique excesses of ecclesiastical court proceedings.

With its scurrilous language and sexual innuendo, N-Town's play of the trial of Joseph and Mary departs from the solemn tone that otherwise characterizes the Marian portions of the cycle. Yet, its prevailing interest in Mary as the "clean tabernacle" of the deity is thoroughly consistent with the capacious yet finely nuanced figurations of Mary that predominate in the N-Town collection. The Mary of the N-Town Plays is only intermittently the pious and humble Madonna; instead, she is more consistently imaged as the glorious and immaculate virgin and queen whose purity the cycle declares and dramatizes at every available occasion. In the N-Town plays Mary occupies many overlapping special roles: she is an exemplary Christian, an interpreter of redemptive promise, and the conduit of salvation. Whether pledged to a life of "holy prayere," as she is at the end of the Crucifixion, or commenting on the virtues of saying the psalter, as she does after her betrothal to Joseph, or explaining the meaning of Christ's sacrifice, as she declares after her risen Son's appearance to her, Mary is a central figure in N-Town's version of the redemptive drama of human history. The risen Christ's ex-

pression to Mary of her essential role in that drama also summarizes her importance in the drama of the N-Town Plays: "had I not of yow be born, / Man had be lost in helle."

These aspects of Marian representations in the N-Town Plays also accord with the prevailing emphases of the cycle as a whole. Although the suggestion that any text as manifestly eclectic as N-Town could reveal a coherent and deliberate design should be made with great caution, it is possible nevertheless to identify patterns that emerge from its representation of sacred history. To do so is not to make a formalist argument for N-Town's unity as a work of art; it is, rather, to acknowledge that N-Town is in this respect no different from the other extant cycles, all of which exhibit distinctive differences of tone, theme, and emphasis. Given the extraordinary duplication of subject matter, character, and plot that the cycles inevitably engage, the differences are all the more remarkable. Basically, N-Town's distinction is to be found in what numerous scholars have identified as its concern with redemptive promise, grace, and mercy. More specifically, the N-Town Plays realize this concern through their notable attention to Christ's hypostatic nature and his kinship with humankind.

Through such features as the inclusion of the Parliament of Heaven, repeated declarations that Christ is both God and man, and serial attestations of Mary's special humanity, the N-Town Plays expound the meaning of the Incarnation as the central act of mediation between the deity and humanity and depict the Christian story so as to highlight the ever-present and immediate benefits resulting from that singular act. On the level of dramatic subject matter and technique, N-Town's particular interest in redemptive promise is manifested in a tendency throughout the cycle to render the scriptural story in terms of the rites and customs of contemporary Christian belief and worship and to present its characters and events in light of devotional habits cultivated by the late-medieval Christian community. The N-Town Plays variously dramatize the means by which redemptive grace is made continuously and presently available through the ceremonies of the church and the informal, noninstitutional forms of Christian worship; the plays are concerned with the practical ways that the decisive mediation between God and man effected in the Incarnation is constantly renegotiated for the day-to-day benefit of humankind through prayer, liturgy, sacrament, and devotional image.

N-Town's Mary play furnishes one important focal point of these thematic concerns and dramatic techniques. As noted earlier, these plays are peopled by ecclesiastical characters – bishops, ministers, and so on – who participate in biblical and liturgical rites. The betrothal play, for instance, includes the only marriage ceremony dramatized in the English cycles. All of the Marian episodes include a high incidence of liturgical music – in fact, of all the cycles N-Town is richest in liturgical music, and it nearly always fits the context in which it occurs. The betrothal play includes hymns from the English marriage ceremony; in the play of the death and Assumption of Mary, songs from the liturgy of the dead accompany the funeral procession and burial of Mary. N-Town's liturgical hymns and sequences thus help to represent as cultic acts of worship the scenes in which they occur. The Mary plays also contain noteworthy observations on the efficacy of prayer. Not only does Mary elaborate on the importance of reciting the psalter, but she concludes her antiphonal singing, with Elizabeth, of the Magnificat by noting that the song is "evyr to be songe and also to be seyn / Every day amonge us at oure evesong." Her brief but specific reference to the recitation of the Magnificat during vespers service, which may also point to the play's affiliation with a religious house, casts her own praise of God in terms of a contemporary form of worship.

The emphasis shown by the Mary play on the priesthood's performance of mediating rites and ceremonies is equally pronounced in other parts of the N-Town cycle, figuring prominently in the Passion sequence. Thus, in an episode unique to the N-Town cycle that concludes the Agony in the Garden, an angel descends to Christ with a chalice and host and says that these shall be offered to God the Father by "thi dyscipulis and all presthood." This iconographic motif of the Eucharist serves as a fitting conclusion to the first part of the Passion play, which dramatizes the Passover meal that Christ shares with his disciples as a eucharistic service. In this episode Christ instructs his disciples on the responsibility of the priesthood to consecrate and distribute the Eucharist.

The attention to the Eucharist in the N-Town Plays must be seen as part of their larger interest in the sacraments as a whole. The angel who announces the birth of Christ to the shepherds makes that moment an occasion to announce the sacramental benefit that will redound to humankind as a result: "Sacramenys ther xul be vii / Wonnyn tho[r]we that childys wounde." Like several of the other cycles, N-Town dramatizes the Baptism of Christ, but it is the only one to depict a marriage

ceremony and the celebration of the Eucharist. It also uniquely focuses on the sacrament of penance. At the entry into Jerusalem, Peter urges the necessity of redressing "be mowthe" mortal sins.

In still other instances the N-Town Plays draw upon the habits of worship and of social organization in the late medieval Christian community. N-Town appropriately depicts the Entry into Jerusalem, for example, as a Palm Sunday procession; by contrast, the treatment of the episode in the York cycle is more civic, suggesting rather the aura of a royal entry. N-Town's play of the raising of Lazarus departs from the conventions of the other three cyclic versions to make that episode an object lesson on the benefits of mutual aid. It presents a cast of *consolatores* who help bury Lazarus and provide emotional support to his sisters. It highlights the social dimension of mourning, emphasizing the brotherhood and friendship experienced by Lazarus and his survivors. The *consolatores* also praise Lazarus for his generous acts of charity as friend and neighbor. The values the play espouses are remarkably similar to those of late-medieval religious guilds, whose members were committed to mutual aid and to assistance and support of their deceased brothers and sisters. N-Town's interest in attesting, even at the most difficult and pathetic moments of the Passion sequence, to the ever-present efficacy of Christ's sacrifice, is also apparent in its treatment of the Veronica episode on the way to Calvary. When Veronica interrupts that journey to wipe Christ's face with her cloth, his response to her gesture configures that event in terms of its practical role in late-medieval devotion: "I xal them kepe from al mysese / that lokyn on thi kerchy and remembyr me." His reference to the benefits associated with the devotional image of the vernacle contrasts significantly with the handling of this same episode in the York cycle, where the vernacle is presented as a sign bearing witness to "Howe goddes sone here gilteles / Is putte to pereles payne."

Although the scholarly scrutiny of the N-Town Plays has been dominated by suppositions, hypotheses, and speculations, the collection itself has withstood its singular reputation as a locus of literary historical uncertainty to remain a compelling object of study for persons interested in early English biblical drama. The intricacies of N-Town's text and the power of its spectacle mitigate the disappointment modern readers may forever be destined to experience in the search for its lost origins and auspices. The continued study of N-Town's text and spectacle and pursuit of its origins may not bring the N-Town Plays home; but these efforts surely will extend knowledge of the rich cultural imagination that created East Anglian biblical drama at the end of the Middle Ages.

References:

H. R. L. Beadle, "The Medieval Drama of East Anglia: Studies in Dialect, Documentary Records and Stagecraft," Ph.D. dissertation, University of York, 1977;

Beadle, "Plays and Playing at Thetford and Nearby 1498–1540," *Theatre Notebook,* 32, no. 1 (1978): 4–11;

Beadle, "Prolegomena to a Literary Geography of Later Medieval Norfolk," in *Regionalism in Late Medieval Manuscripts and Texts,* edited by Felicity Riddy (Woodbridge, Suffolk: Brewer, 1991), pp. 89–108;

Kenneth Cameron and Stanley J. Kahrl, "Staging the N-Town Cycle," *Theatre Notebook,* 21 (Spring 1967): 122–138; (Summer 1967): 152–165;

A. C. Cawley, Marion Jones, Peter F. McDonald, and David Mills, *Medieval Drama,* volume 1 of *The Revels History of Drama in English,* edited by Lois Potter (London & New York: Methuen, 1983);

Theresa Coletti, "Devotional Iconography in the N-Town Marian Plays," *Comparative Drama,* 11 (Spring 1977): 22–44;

Coletti, "Purity and Danger: The Paradox of Mary's Body and the Engendering of the Infancy Narrative in the English Mystery Cycles," in *Feminist Approaches to the Body in Medieval Literature,* edited by Linda Lomperis and Sarah Stanbury (Philadelphia: University of Pennsylvania Press, 1993), pp. 65–95;

Coletti, "Sacrament and Sacrifice in the N-Town Passion," *Mediaevalia,* 7 (1981): 239–264;

Hardin Craig, *English Religious Drama of the Middle Ages* (Oxford: Clarendon Press, 1955);

Joanna Dutka, *Music in the English Mystery Plays,* Early Drama, Art, and Music (EDAM) References Series 2 (Kalamazoo: Medieval Institute Publications, 1980);

Sister M. Patricia Forrest, "Apocryphal Sources of the St. Anne's Day Plays in the Hegge Cycle," *Medievalia et Humanistica,* 17 (1966): 38–50;

Forrest, "The Role of the Expositor Contemplacio in the St. Anne's Day Plays of the Hegge Cycle," *Medieval Studies,* 28 (1966): 60–76;

Gail McMurray Gibson, "Bury St. Edmunds, Lydgate, and the N-Town Cycle," *Speculum,* 56 (January 1981): 56–90;

Gibson, *The Theater of Devotion: East Anglian Drama and Society in the Late Middle Ages* (Chicago: University of Chicago Press, 1989);

Peter Meredith, "Manuscript, Scribe and Performance: Further Looks at the N. Town Manuscript," in *Regionalism in Late Medieval Manuscripts and Texts,* edited by Felicity Riddy (Woodbridge: Brewer, 1991), pp. 109–128;

Meredith, *The Passion Play from the N-Town Manuscript* (London & New York: Longman, 1990);

Meredith, ed., *The Mary Play from the N. town Manuscript* (London & New York: Longman, 1987);

Martial Rose, "The Staging of the Hegge Plays," in *Medieval Drama,* edited by Neville Denny, Stratford-upon-Avon Studies 16 (London: Edward Arnold, 1943), pp. 196–221;

Stephen Spector, "The Composition and Development of an Eclectic Manuscript: Cotton Vespasian D VIII," *Leeds Studies in English,* 9 (1977): 62–83;

Spector, "The Provenance of the N-Town Codex," *Library,* 6th series, 1 (March 1979): 25–33;

Martin Stevens, *Four Middle English Mystery Cycles: Textual, Contextual and Critical Interpretations* (Princeton: Princeton University Press, 1987);

Esther Swenson, *An Inquiry into the Composition and Structure of the Ludus Coventriae,* University of Minnesota Studies in Language and Literature 1 (1914);

Richard Wright, "Community Theatre in Late Medieval East Anglia," *Theatre Notebook,* 28, no. 1 (1974): 24–39;

Paul Zumthor, *Essai de poétique médiéval* (Paris: Seuil, 1972).

The Owl and the Nightingale
(circa 1189 – 1199)

Laurel Boone
University of New Brunswick

Manuscripts: There are two extant manuscripts of *The Owl and the Nightingale:* British Library, MS. Cotton Caligula A.ix and Bodleian Library, Oxford, MS. Jesus College 29. Facsimile: *The Owl and the Nightingale: Facsimile of Jesus College Oxford MS. 29 and British Museum MS. Cotton Caligula A. ix,* with an introductory essay by N. R. Ker, EETS, o.s. 251 (1963 [i.e. 1962]).
First publication: *The Owl and the Nightingale,* edited by Josephus Stevenson (London: Printed by S. Bentley for the Roxburghe Club, 1838).
Standard editions: *The Owl and the Nightingale,* edited by John Edwin Wells (Boston: Heath, 1907); *The Owl and the Nightingale,* edited by Eric Gerald Stanley (London: Nelson, 1960; republished, Manchester: Manchester University Press, 1972); in *Medieval English Literature,* edited by Thomas J. Garbáty (Lexington, Mass.: Heath, 1984), pp. 556–602.
Edition in modern English: *The Owl and the Nightingale,* edited and translated by J. W. H. Atkins (Cambridge: Cambridge University Press, 1922).

Few medieval works in English have been read with so much pleasure yet analyzed to so little effect as *The Owl and the Nightingale.* Although the poem exists in two good manuscripts and its language and style make it easily accessible, no one knows precisely when the poem was written, who wrote it, or what it is about.

The Owl and the Nightingale consists of 1,794 lines written in iambic tetrameter couplets. Many anomalous word forms and the two systems of spelling in the Cotton manuscript complicate dialect analysis, but the original dialect could have been that of Guildford, in Dorset. The poem tells the story of a debate between a serious owl and a more romantic nightingale – a debate ranging over so many topics that scholars have argued for more than a century over the poem's central theme. At last, a wren intrudes to quiet the disputants, and they agree to take their cause before Nicho-las, formerly of Portesham and now of Guildford, who will judge between them. The poem ends as the birds set off peacefully for Guildford.

Although several arguments to the contrary exist, it seems likely that *The Owl and the Nightingale* was written between 1189 and 1199, during the reign of Richard I (the Lion-Hearted). The lines "þat under þe king Henri – / Iesus his soule do merci!" and their context set 1189 as the earliest date for the poem, the year in which the courtly Henry II died. The latest possible date, soon after 1216, is established by the Cotton manuscript, which also contains a French prose chronicle that ends with the accession of Henry III.

Three pieces of evidence suggest that *The Owl and the Nightingale* was written in King Richard's reign rather than in King John's. A. C. Cawley's study of the astrological references in the poem indicates a date after 1186, when a conjunction of Saturn and Mars terrified people in all stations of life. The commotion over this celestial event fueled debate over the validity of astrology, a debate which the Owl and the Nightingale enter. Cawley also demonstrates that all of the disasters the Owl predicts are Martian or Saturnian and that some were among the miseries actually blamed on the planetary conjunction. When *The Owl and the Nightingale* was written, the events of 1186 were a fairly recent memory.

Similarly, the Owl helps men to repent, encourages them to weep for their sins, and boasts, "Ne singe ich hom no foliot." *Foliot* is an Old French word for a trap or snare used in fowling, and this is its only recorded appearance in English. It may therefore be a pun on the name of Bishop Foliot of London, who died in 1187. If so, the poem must have been written when the memory of the bishop's reputation was still fresh.

Finally, at the end of the poem, the Wren intrudes to quiet the dispute, saying, "Hwat! wulle ʒe þis pes tobreke, / An do þan [kinge] swuch schame? / ʒe! nis he nouþer ded ne lame." The king who is "nouþer ded ne lame" (neither dead nor lame) may

First page of The Owl and the Nightingale *in a thirteenth-century scribal copy (British Library, MS. Cotton Caligula A. ix, fol. 233)* well be Richard. During his ten-year reign, Richard spent only a few months in England, trusting his ministers to maintain the "king's peace." While he pursued his continental adventures, these ministers, many of whom had learned their craft under his father's rule, managed England in an orderly fashion. When the Wren asserts that the king is neither dead nor lame, she means that even though he may be abroad, he is still able to exercise his authority; in fact, since the Wren partakes of the wisdom of men, her speech may even be taken as a report on King Richard's health. John, Richard's successor, is certainly not the king to whom the Wren refers, for after this cruel and capricious man came to the throne in 1199, not even a wren could call the state of affairs "þis pes" (this peace).

Debate over authorship of *The Owl and the Nightingale* is closely tied to debate over its subject, its theme, and its moral content. That the poem has extra-narrative significance is clear. It is didactic: the birds distinguish good behavior from bad and prescribe worthy actions for one another, and readers have consistently believed that the poem contains lessons for them, too, although they cannot agree on what they are. But unlike comparable English works, such as the earliest body-and-soul debates and the prose vice-and-virtue debates, *The Owl and the Nightingale* is secular, and the ratio of entertainment to instruction is much higher in *The Owl and the Nightingale* than in this other debate literature. Scholars have tried to establish the theme by attempting to identify the one main issue of the debate. But while their arguments illuminate parts of the poem, they ignore or twist so much of it that ultimately they cannot be considered keys to the whole work.

Kathryn Huganir and R. M. Lumiansky point out that none of the single-issue readings considers the purpose of the poem. Both scholars identify the poet as Nicholas of Guildford, the intended arbiter of the dispute, and they propose that this identification explains the purpose of the poem. Nicholas wrote *The Owl and the Nightingale* to advertise himself for preferment, and the incompatibility of this purpose with most interpretations of the theme shows the improbability of those interpretations. Huganir and Lumiansky suggest that the birds discuss many of the most hotly disputed questions of the day in order to demonstrate Nicholas's understanding of the issues and his skill in handling them. This demonstration constitutes the true theme of the poem. Presenting both sides of each question in an appealing way, and showing the debaters considering their arguments and planning their strategy, the poet displays his understanding of the problems, his readi-

ness to give ear to more than one opinion, and his ability to respect people of diverse viewpoints – all in hopes that these attributes would persuade his prospective patron to favor him.

Although Huganir's and Lumiansky's conclusions about the author and the purpose of *The Owl and the Nightingale* may be debated, they remain the most reasonable and inclusive yet proposed. They also open up the poem in useful directions. Since Nicholas's prospective patron was his immediate audience, identification of the kind of position Nicholas was seeking tells what kind of person this man was and points to Nicholas's wider audience. Nicholas is an educated man and a cleric, but he has only one benefice. The obvious conclusion would be that Nicholas seeks advancement in the church and that this poem is therefore addressed to a bishop. But the Wren's blunt remarks about the folly of bishops and the Owl's scathing agreement with these observations weigh against this interpretation. The poet's lenient attitude toward fornication and adultery further discourages the idea that he sought advancement in the church. He does not condone either of these sins, but, even if he is mocking the debaters' sophistry, his compassion for such sinners might not impress a bishop in his favor.

It is much more likely that Nicholas used this poem to advertise his qualifications as an itinerant judge. Writing from a strong ecclesiastical background, he was seeking secular advancement. In their translation of the *Lais* of Marie de France, Robert Hanning and Joan Ferante explain why men like Nicholas found themselves in such a situation. In the twelfth century cities and cathedral towns had grown rapidly, flourishing as centers of learning and art. Intellectuals, highly trained but "often only minimally involved with or controlled by ecclesiastical authority," spread out from these new centers to "the burgeoning courts of France and England, where they formed a civil service and also found an outlet for their literary abilities."

Although the author of the *The Owl and the Nightingale* was obviously very knowledgeable about church teachings and church politics, the poem's frame of reference is neither biblical nor patristic nor homiletic, but legal. At the end of the twelfth century canon law began to impinge upon English law to the extent that "exceptions" became common in court procedure. In earlier practice, no opportunity existed to explain extenuating circumstances – the accused was either completely guilty or completely innocent. The practice of permitting *exceptiones,* as in Roman law, began to develop early in Henry II's reign, and by the end of the century it was well established. Frederick Pollock and Frederic William Maitland cite records contemporary with *The Owl and the Nightingale* that show long, loose, irregular debates in which "an exception may be met by a replication, the replication by a triplication and so on ad infinitum," and they note that "The pleaders . . . are guilty of argumentativeness and duplicity." Pollock and Maitland might have been describing *The Owl and the Nightingale;* these contentious birds never answer charges and countercharges plainly but make each answer as complex and discursive as possible. The argument is not a mock trial; its function is to show how skillfully Nicholas can handle cases complicated by digressive exceptions.

Anne W. Baldwin points out that the poet's familiarity with legal procedures is certified by his ability to parody them. M. Angela Carson demonstrates that, on three different levels, *The Owl and the Nightingale* conforms to the classical oratory practiced by lawyers. In his 1960 edition of the poem Eric Gerald Stanley identifies the Latin debate poems, composed and used in law schools to train lawyers, as the closest relatives of *The Owl and the Nightingale.* "In this type of fictitious litigation," he notes, "the disputant who used language best, and who could blind his opponent by tricks of logic, was the victor." The constant concern of the Owl and the Nightingale for clever argument rather than for truth connects the poem to the law-school exercises. Although the Owl loses the debate on a rhetorical technicality, the dispute is not over, for Nicholas has yet to judge between the birds; their argument has been a kind of legal exercise or rehearsal.

Nicholas is showing his understanding of how cleverly people can devise their arguments and how they ought to settle their differences. If he can arbitrate this dispute between the Owl and the Nightingale, he could certainly settle the disputes that come before a circuit judge. Indeed, he is already famous for his wise judgment – even the birds know all about him. *The Owl and the Nightingale* makes a complete and entertaining plea for Nicholas's advancement to a judgeship.

It is not possible to determine exactly who the recipient of the poem might have been, any more than it is possible to ascertain who Nicholas was. However, the power of appointing judges was ultimately held by the king, and during Richard's reign it was exercised by his deputies. Some such man was Nicholas's intended patron, and people of similar social position, intellectual ability, and interests made up the poem's wider audience.

Identification of this purpose and audience addresses another perennial question about *The Owl and the Nightingale:* why was it written in English rather than in French or Latin? Since men trained in Henry II's English-speaking court operated Richard's government, English was known in influential circles during Richard's reign. A brilliant poem written in English might well intrigue a powerful patron, especially an English one. Indeed, Ralph V. Turner's 1976 survey shows that a large proportion of the long-term itinerant justices around the turn of the century had English names. The efficacy of Nicholas's self-advertisement would depend on how accurately it imitated the kind of complicated cases he would judge. Since English was commonly used in the local courts over which itinerant justices presided, this complexity was fittingly expressed in English.

There is likely a close connection between *The Owl and the Nightingale* and the *Lais* and *Fables* of Marie de France. These works were probably all written within a period of thirty years, and they appealed to an audience that was cultivated, appreciative of learning, interested in the relationships between men and women but not adherents of courtly love, and curious about but not involved with the lives of the lowly. Marie's prologues and epilogues reveal an audience craving entertainment that included moral instruction, although hidden lessons fulfilled the need adequately; this very quality remains at the heart of scholarly interest in *The Owl and the Nightingale.* Marie and Nicholas were not only fascinated by legal procedures, but so aware of the roots of these procedures in human nature that their imitations remain fresh and lively eight hundred years later. The two poets used the same literary conventions, they told some of the same anecdotes, and they drew from a common literary environment. *The Owl and the Nightingale* is the first English poem written in an anglicized version of French octosyllabic couplets; Marie believed she would gain credibility by pretending to a greater knowledge of English than she possessed; and Marie and Nicholas tell several of the same stories in a similar way and remain the earliest sources for the fable contrasting the cat, who has only one trick, with the fox, who has many.

Speculation about the relationship between *The Owl and the Nightingale* and Marie's *Lais* and *Fables* is intriguing when considered in the light of J. Eadie's and Alexandra Barratt's arguments that the author of *The Owl and the Nightingale* was a woman. Grammatically, *owl* and *nightingale* are feminine nouns, and the author and scribes of *The Owl and the Nightingale* usually (though not always) observe this convention; John Leyerle's objections to modern acceptance of the birds as females seem constrained by custom and prejudice. Furthermore, generally (though not invariably), the poet treats the Owl and the Nightingale as females. Barratt's and Eadie's conjectures that the author was female call into question not just the poem's authorship, but its purpose as well. Eadie believes that the author may have been a lover of Nicholas; that her praise of him is extravagant to the point of absurdity for this reason; and that the subject and themes of the poem all relate to "the pain suffered by lovers, above all by women, who are separated . . . from their sweethearts or husbands." Barratt agrees that the poet sees the world from a female perspective (although for her the subject of the poem is the triumph of law over force). She concludes that the author may have been a nun or a group of nuns at Shaftesbury Abbey, in Dorset, presided over from about 1181 until about 1216 by Henry II's half sister, who is commonly thought to have been Marie de France.

It is conceivable that *The Owl and the Nightingale* poet and Marie de France were acquainted, at least with one another's work. But their most significant similarity is that they shared an attitude toward language and literature that transcended their differences in tongue. Students of English literature often believe that when Nicholas (or his lover, or the nuns of Shaftesbury) and Marie were writing, intellectuals and nobility did not use English among themselves. But the interest of these two poets in the same material, at least some of which was in English, adds to the evidence against that belief, and their adoption of the literature in each other's language makes it even less tenable. *The Owl and the Nightingale* and the works of Marie de France should be viewed as literary expressions of a bilingual vernacular culture; English and French were beginning to meet in what would become the literature of England. Perhaps readers might let this linguistic experimentation suffice as the "lesson" hidden in *The Owl and the Nightingale* and yield themselves to the entertainment that the poet, whoever he or she was, so richly provides.

Bibliography:

Eric Gerald Stanley, *The Owl and the Nightingale* (London: Nelson, 1960).

References:

J. W. H. Atkins, *English Literary Criticism: The Medieval Phase* (Gloucester, Mass.: Peter Smith, 1943);

Anne W. Baldwin, "Henry II and The Owl and the Nightingale," *Journal of English and Germanic Philology*, 66 (1967): 229;

Alexandra Barratt, "Flying in the Face of Tradition: A New View of *The Owl and the Nightingale*," *University of Toronto Quarterly*, 56 (Summer 1987): 471–485;

Laurel Boone, "The Relationship Between *The Owl and the Nightingale* and Marie de France's *Lais* and *Fables*," *English Studies in Canada*, 11 (June 1985): 157–177;

M. Angela Carson, "Rhetorical Structure in The Owl and the Nightingale," *Speculum*, 42 (January 1967): 92–103;

A. C. Cawley, "Astrology in 'The Owl and the Nightingale,'" *Modern Language Review*, 46 (1951): 161–174;

J. Eadie, "The Authorship of *The Owl and the Nightingale*: A Reappraisal," *English Studies*, 6 (1986): 471–477;

Jane Gottschalk, "*The Owl and the Nightingale*: Lay Preachers to a Lay Audience," *Philological Quarterly*, 45 (1966): 657–667;

Robert Hanning and Joan Ferante, trans., *The Lais of Marie de France* (New York: Dutton, 1978);

C. Warren Hollister, "Normandy, France, and the Anglo-Norman Regnum," *Speculum*, 51 (April 1976): 236;

Kathryn Huganir, *The Owl and the Nightingale: Sources, Date, Author* (New York: Haskell, 1931);

Kathryn Hume, *The Owl and the Nightingale: The Poem and its Critics* (Toronto: University of Toronto Press, 1975);

John Leyerle, "The Text and the Tradition," *University of Toronto Quarterly*, 32 (January 1963): 205–216;

R. M. Lumiansky, "Concerning the Owl and the Nightingale," *Philological Quarterly*, 32 (1953): 411–417;

G. R. Owst, *Literature and Pulpit in Medieval England* (Cambridge: Cambridge University Press, 1933);

Douglas L. Peterson, "*The Owl and the Nightingale* and Christian Dialectic," *Journal of English and Germanic Philology*, 55 (1956); republished in *Middle English Survey*, edited by Edward Vasta (Notre Dame, Ind.: Notre Dame University Press, 1965), pp. 35–56;

Frederick Pollock and Frederic William Maitland, *The History of English Law Before the Time of Edward I*, 2 volumes (Cambridge: Cambridge University Press, 1899);

Ralph V. Turner, "The Judges of King John: Their Background and Training," *Speculum*, 51 (July 1976): 447–461;

Karl Warnke, ed., *Die Fabeln der Marie de France*, Bibliotheca Normannica, 6 (Halle: Niemeyer, 1898; republished, Geneva: Slatkine, 1974).

The *Paston Letters*

(1422 – 1509)

Anthony J. Ouellette
University of South Carolina

Manuscripts: Most of the nearly 1100 extant manuscript *Paston Letters* are in the British Library; others are at the Bodleian Library, Oxford, the Pierpont Morgan Library (New York), and Pembroke College (Cambridge).

First publication: *Original Letters,* 5 volumes, edited by John Fenn (London: Robinson, 1787–1823).

Standard editions: *The Paston Letters 1422–1509 A.D.,* 4 volumes, edited by James Gairdner (Westminster: Constable, 1900–1901); republished in 6 volumes (London & Exeter: Chatto & Windus, 1904); *The Paston Letters,* edited by John Warrington (London: Dent, 1956); *Paston Letters and Papers of the Fifteenth Century,* 2 volumes, edited by Norman Davis (Oxford: Clarendon Press, 1971, 1976).

The *Paston Letters* are a collection of over one thousand letters, memorandums, state papers, and legal documents – the majority of which were written either by or to members of three generations of the Paston family of Norfolk during the fifteenth century and early on in the sixteenth. Although, as Norman Davis points out in his 1971 edition of the letters, the series is not the earliest collection known in English, it is "far more numerous and more varied in interest than any of the other fifteenth-century series." The Paston material covers a span of almost ninety years (1422–1509) and is a valuable source for English political and social history during that period.

The forms of the manuscripts are diverse. The assorted watermarks on the sheets show the paper to be of foreign origin. The size of the sheets varies from 10 to 12 inches wide and from 16 to 18 inches long. Because of the practice of cutting off the paper at the end of a letter, many short letters have no watermark, and others have it cut through. If the letters were being sent, and not merely drafts, they were folded into small oblong packets about 3 to 4 inches long and from 1 1/2 to 3 inches wide. They were then fastened by the insertion of a narrow piece of paper or stitches of string through the thicknesses, after which they were sealed with wax, sometimes covered by a paper wafer, and the address added. (Seal impressions and watermarks are reproduced in John Fenn's 1787–1823 edition.)

The form of the writing varies greatly throughout the letters, and often the same writer changes the format in different letters. Some are divided into paragraphs, but the majority show continuous writing, often lacking consistent capitalization or punctuation. When punctuation occurs it is most often a single stroke, or a double stroke at decisive divisions. Corrections appear both in drafts and final copies. Many of the *Paston Letters* are dated by reference to the day and month only. A great number of them are dated according to the ecclesiastical calendar, with reference to Sundays, religious festivals, and saints' days. Letters written on days not specified by the church calendar are dated in reference to a previous or upcoming feast day.

The *Paston Letters* descended through several generations to William, second Earl of Yarmouth – the last male heir of the Pastons – after lying in neglect for over two centuries. After his death in 1732 some of the family papers came into the possession of Tom Martin of Palgrave, and others were acquired by Francis Blomefield, who used them for his *History of Norfolk* (after 1735). Part of Blomefield's papers were collected by the Bodleian Library, while Martin's collection was eventually purchased by Fenn in 1775. Encouraged by Horace Walpole and others, Fenn printed a selection in two quarto volumes (dedicated, by permission, to George III). He was knighted on 23 May of the same year for his service by the king, to whom Fenn presented the originals. In 1789 Fenn published two more volumes. After Fenn's death in 1794, his nephew, William Frere, published a fifth volume from his uncle's transcripts in 1823.

All of the originals to the five volumes were lost, and it was not until 1865 that the manuscripts

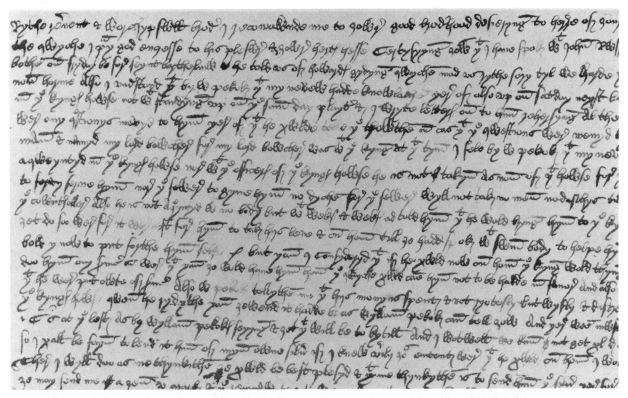

Part of a letter from Clement Paston to John Paston, dated 25 August 1461 (British Library, MS. Add. 34888, fol. 191)

of volume five, together with some unprinted documents, were found at Frere's home at Dungate, in Cambridgeshire. They were sold to the British Museum in 1866. In 1875 the originals of the third and fourth volumes, together with ninety-five new letters, were found at Roydon Hall near Diss, and these were sold to the British Museum in 1896. Another group found at the Hall was purchased by the museum in 1904. The manuscripts of Fenn's first two volumes were rediscovered in 1889 at Orwell Park in Suffolk and bought by the British Museum in 1933. Apart from this main collection the museum (now the British Library) possesses minor groups as well as a single Paston letter purchased in 1964. A few other items are located in the Bodleian Library at Oxford, the Pierpont Morgan Library in New York, and Pembroke College, Cambridge.

The history of the *Paston Letters* begins with William Paston, who was appointed a judge of the Common Pleas in 1429. He established the family fortunes by marrying Agnes, daughter of Sir Edmund Berry, and afterward by purchasing lands in and around Norfolk. Although few of the letters come from this period (the few documents relating to the private affairs of William), the correspondence greatly increases after 1444 with the death of Judge Paston. William Paston's eldest son and heir,

John, had married a lady, Margaret Mauteby, and became a respected gentleman with a wide circle of political acquaintance. It is around John Paston that the main historical interest of the letters is based. Three-fifths of the whole collection belongs to the period from 1440 to 1466 (the year of John Paston I's death). Thus, although the majority of the *Paston Letters* are private correspondence, they often contain discussions of public affairs of the fifteenth century. In fact, several of the letters are written solely to provide the recipient with updated information about political and public affairs.

In 1448 the Pastons were dispossessed of their manor at Gresham by Lord Moleyns, and in 1449 a John Hauteyn claimed right of ownership to family property at Oxnead. Although both claims were ultimately lost or abandoned, the affairs continued for more than three years. The letters relate these and further private occurrences among numerous references to public disorders of the period – the outrages of Charles Nowell, the bailiff of Bradeston; Cade's rebellion; and the principal events in the period of discord known as the Wars of the Roses (1455–1485) – many of which were especially serious in Norfolk.

Political interest in the letters begins during the ministry of the duke of Suffolk around 1447.

Paston, although not actively involved in politics, closely followed the public events of the disquieted later half of the fifteenth century. Besides carefully filing his private correspondence, John Paston saved numerous letters and documents despite the request of their writers that they should be destroyed as soon as read. Thus the articles of Suffolk's impeachment were carefully preserved, as was a copy of a farewell letter that Suffolk addressed to his son before his departure from England on 30 April 1450. On 5 May 1450 William Lomner writes to Paston of Suffolk's execution on board a small ship, where a member of the crew "smotte of his hedde withyn halfe a doseyn strokes."

The letters of the subsequent twelve years contain many references to the political upheaval during, and leading up to, the Wars of the Roses. Paston was of enough importance to be courted on the Yorkist side by the duke of Norfolk. In the summer of 1454 several letters mention the movements of the Yorkist lords and the continual imprisonment of the duke of Somerset. In 1455 Paston received a letter telling of Henry VI's slow recovery from his illness during 1454 that seemingly had left him an utter idiot. Henry's recovery led to the outbreak of war and to the first battle of Saint Albans, news of which Paston was informed in a brief note written three days afterward. Succeeding letters provide invaluable details of the events of 1454–1455.

The principal influence on the correspondence between 1440 and 1466 is Paston's connection with Sir John Fastolf, the cousin of John's wife, Margaret, and an extremely wealthy veteran of the French wars. By 1450 John Paston I was actively involved in Fastolf's business transactions. In 1456 he was even made one of a body of Fastolf's trustees. Between 1455 and 1459 many letters discuss Fastolf's business affairs and lifestyle while he resided at his newly constructed Caister Castle.

When Fastolf died in 1459, Paston, in return for a payment of four thousand marks, was left all Fastolf's estates in Norfolk and Suffolk (including Caister, Drayton, Hellesdon, and Cotton) in which he was to be responsible for the foundation of a college at Caister. The difficulty for Paston was that the claim was based on a nuncupative will and was disputed by influential rivals, including eight other executors of whom William Worcester (Fastolf's secretary and agent) is the most notable because of his frequent correspondence with Paston. The letters sent by him and other writers include some of the most valuable historical information of the collection.

Following Fastolf's death Worcester allied himself with William Yelverton (an executor and justice) to contest Paston's claims. In 1461, when Henry VI was deposed and Edward IV was proclaimed king, the duke of Norfolk took possession of Caister, while Drayton and Hellesdon were seized by the duke of Suffolk. When John Paston died in 1466, these and other contentions continued. During this period, when John was away from home, he left the management of the property to Margaret and his estate servants. The letters from him are infrequent and mostly concerned with instructions for care of the estate. The majority of the letters are replies to him during the difficult years after Fastolf's death.

Much of the remainder of the letters focuses around the activities of John II (Sir John) and John III. Although John II succeeded his father in 1466, the litigations which had consumed John Paston I's life were far from over. Still, as early as July 1466, John II was given recognition from King Edward IV of his right to Caister. During 1466–1468 both brothers involved themselves with the care of the estate. This preoccupation was interrupted in the summer of 1468 when both brothers attended Princess Margaret's retinue to Bruges, where she married the duke of Burgundy. On this trip John II met Anne Haute, a cousin of Anthony Woodville, Lord Scales, brother of the queen, and to whom he became engaged some two years later.

Because of the disputed possession of Caister, the manor was sold in 1468 (while still occupied by the Pastons) by two trustees of Fastolf to the duke of Norfolk. In 1469, after the king had been taken prisoner and law and order had decayed, the duke was determined to take the castle by force. At the time, John II was in London and thus put John III in command. The duke laid siege with an army of three thousand men, and he forced a surrender on 26 September 1469. In addition, the social position of the Paston family was dealt a blow when, despite family opposition, Margery Paston married the Pastons' head bailiff, Richard Calle. Calle was never accepted into the family, and both he and Margery are never mentioned in Margaret Paston's will.

In 1470 the lawsuit to determine the execution of Fastolf's will was compromised, and John Paston II was allowed to retain, among some other holdings, Caister, Hellesdon, and Drayton. Still, because of long negotiations and political events such as the restoration of Henry VI (including the alliance of the eldest Paston brothers to the Lancastrian restoration), Caister was not recovered until after

Norfolk's death in January 1476. In 1477 Sir John's engagement to Anne Haute was finally canceled, and in 1479 John II became ill in London and died.

The letters during the period from 1471 to 1478 consist mainly of the correspondence between the two brothers, John II and John III. For the most part, besides the frequent political allusions, they discuss Sir John's dealings in Calais, where he served as one of the council, and with general family affairs and court news. With John III's succession to head of the family, the letters become fewer. Some deal with John III's uncle William II and his claims to manors near Newgate. After the death of Margaret Paston in 1484 the majority of the letters are concerned less with family affairs and more with business transactions. After the death of his first wife, Margery Paston, John III married Agnes, daughter of Nicholas Morley. John III died on 28 August 1504. The last survivor of this generation was William III, who continued to write occasionally, under the service of the earl of Oxford, until 1492. He inevitably was discharged in 1503 or 1504 because he was "so troubled with sickness and crazed in his mind."

Although the letters have long been regarded as an invaluable resource of the political history of the fifteenth century, they likewise serve as an important link to an understanding of the social aspects of the period. In *The Pastons and Their England* (1932) H. S. Bennett comments, "a study of their many-sided activities allows us to form a clear idea of the conditions under which they live, while the letters of their friends and many correspondents help to complete and to widen the view-point. They receive letters from Bishops or serving-men, prisoners or Dukes, priests or ribald companions; and all help to construct the social history and life of their times."

One of the most valuable aspects of the letters is their importance as examples of the English written language at a significant stage in its history (before and immediately after the introduction of printing into England), for the study of which, as Davis argues in his edition, "they are scarcely less valuable than they are for the wider field of social history." In an essay written in 1954 Davis discusses an added value of the collection in that it displays correspondence from four generations of Paston men – Judge Paston; his four sons, John, Edmond, William, and Clement; John's sons, John II, John III, Edmond II, Walter and William; and John III's son, William IV, of whom a single, short letter is representative. The third generation is the best represented in that the two younger Johns' letters over-

lap their father's and uncles' correspondence by several years. Likewise, three generations of women also appear in the collection: Agnes, the wife of Judge Paston; Margaret, the wife of John I; Elizabeth, John I's sister; and Margery, the wife of John III. One peculiarity of the letters is that only about half of them are in the handwriting of the authors, since the Paston women employed numerous clerks to whom they presumably dictated their letters.

Since several of the Paston men were brought up in Norfolk yet educated in London and then at either Oxford or Cambridge, several letters show a combined use of provincial dialect with cosmopolitan forms. The letters from the third generation of Pastons also clearly demonstrate that in the latter half of the fifteenth century it was possible to choose among numerous variations in written form. In a letter of John Paston II, the word *ground* is spelled three different ways in the space of two lines.

Many of the letters are written by servants, business acquaintances, stewards, domestic chaplains, and friends of the Pastons, demonstrating that a variety of people from different classes were able to write with adequate ability. Calle frequently wrote about business affairs. Often the nobility were the worst writers. The letters suggest that the state of education among the people of the fifteenth century was fairly well distributed – seemingly any person of rank or station above laborer was at least partly literate. The letters written by abbots and priors, in particular those of Friar Brackley, show the style of writing used by ecclesiastics of the period, as well as the rhetorical manner in which sermons were constructed.

The multiple hands involved in the writing of the women's letters suggest that they could write only with great difficulty. Three of the letters of Margery have subscriptions "Be yowre servaunt (and bedewoman) Margery Paston," all in the same uncontrolled hand. Although it appears Margery could not have written a whole letter, she is the only one of the women who seems to have been able to write her own name. In any respect it is apparent that the Paston women were not wholly literate. This does not mean that none could read, however, for Anne Paston had her own copy of John Lydgate's *Siege of Thebes* (1420–1422).

Despite the fact that the letters of the Paston women may not preserve the exact language of their authors, they presumably preserve the basic messages the women dictated. In this respect the letters provide some insight into the life of women in the period. In his survey of contemporary documents

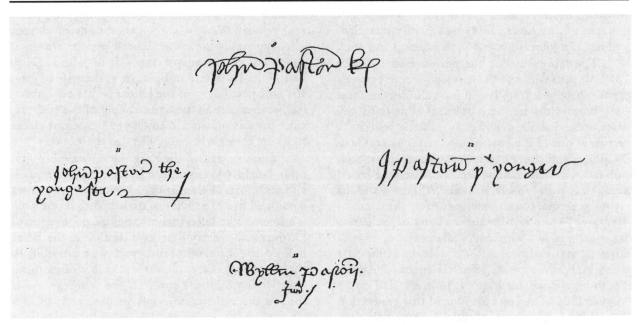

Signatures of four Pastons (clockwise, from top): John Paston; John Paston, the Younger; Wylliam Paston, Junior; John Paston, the Youngest (from Original Letters Written during the Reigns of Henry VI, Edward IV, and Richard III, *volume two, 1787)*

Bennett finds that "for the rich as well as the poor, a wife was essentially a house-wife. Her real function was the ordering and proper management of the house. Devotion to her husband in medieval thought necessarily implied that she would be concerned for his well-being and comfort, and anxious that everything in his house should be well ordered." The letters of Margaret Paston correspond with Bennett's statement – it appears that she was always attempting to keep the Paston household supplied. A continual difficulty was the making of clothes – not only the spinning and weaving, but the actual cutting and creation of the garments – and the major necessity was the providing of food. A few of the letters refer to the plan of large fifteenth-century houses, showing that provision was needed for a variety of buildings, including the brew house, the bake house, and the dairy.

The stores of food for the Paston household came largely from the surrounding countryside or from nearby towns such as Yarmouth and Norwich. But, as with cloth, foreign goods of all kinds seem to have come from London. There are constant requests in the *Paston Letters* for such goods, and often Margaret Paston asks someone to get her provisions from London because of the poor quality or lack of items she wanted in Norwich. Even in the middle of the troublesome events of 1454–1455, Margaret writes to her husband, John, requesting "I pray yow that ye woll vowchesawf to remembr to

purvey a thing for my nekke, and to do make my gyrdill."

Still, it must be remembered that the Paston women were often left at home to manage the estates while the men were away. They were quite capable, especially Margaret and Agnes, of maintaining any and all matters of business – from arranging marriages to preparing the agreements for new tenants. As the correspondence shows, often it was the Paston women who made crucial decisions that saved the family from assured loss.

One aspect of the fifteenth-century social structure, often alluded to in the letters, is that of arranged marriages. The Pastons, like many others of their class, were strongly interested in increasing their lands and possessions. A marriage was perhaps the easiest and most lucrative way to take a prominent place among the Norfolk gentry. Many of the letters detail the proceedings at length. In most of these there is an insistence on the monetary value of the marriage, much along the lines of a business transaction. In others there is no direct reference to the individuals to be betrothed.

Despite the Pastons' frequent references to public affairs in London and elsewhere, their livelihood and social position depended on the business dealings on their estates – the Pastons, like many others of their class, were dependent on their lands as a source of revenue and food. From time to time, as mentioned throughout the letters, they were in need of money (particularly when the estates were under the incompetent guidance of John Paston II). The Pastons had to take every step to see that their rents were paid and at times were forced to take extreme measures in order to do so. Frequently in such cases they seized the household goods or agricultural tools of a tenant. John Russe, an agent of John Paston I, wrote: "As to Skilly, fermour of Cowhaugh, we enteryd therre, and seyd we wold have payment for the half yeer past, and sewrete for the half yeer comynge, or else we wold distreyne and put hym out of pocession, and put in a newe fermoure." In one letter the Paston finances had become so low that Margaret implores her husband to come home; otherwise she would have to borrow money as she only had four shillings. Not only were the Pastons economically tied to the lands, so too were the actual tenant farmers; John Paston III writes to his brother, "I have spok with Barker, and he hathe no moneym, nor can get tyll harvest, when he may dystreyn the cropp upon the ground; he seyth there is no owyng past v. mark." Several of these letters make reference to manor courts, or Halmotes, which existed on each manor so that estate litigations could be resolved. They were conducted several times a year by the lord of the manor or by his agent.

Within the pages of the vast collection of the *Paston Letters* there can be found information about many other areas – politics, travel, law, religion, pilgrimages, education, houses, and books in fifteenth-century England. Yet, as John Warrington mentions in his 1956 edition, there are no references within the series to several major events that occurred within the period: the invention of printing; the capture of Constantinople by Mahomet in 1453; the movement of Turkish advance guards in the west from 1471 to 1480; or the taking of Granada and the discovery of America in 1492. Thus, while the *Paston Letters* may cover a limited area of fifteenth-century life, they are nevertheless archives of a vast store of details and facts that help to augment the broad descriptions of the period found elsewhere.

References:

H. S. Bennett, *The Pastons and Their England* (Cambridge: Cambridge University Press, 1932);

Norman Davis, "The Language of the Pastons," in *Middle English Literature,* edited by J. A. Burrow (Oxford: Oxford University Press, 1989), pp. 45–70;

Charles Kingsford, *English Historical Literature in the Fifteenth Century* (New York: Burt Franklin, 1962);

Colin Richmond, *The Paston Family in the Fifteenth Century* (Cambridge: Cambridge University Press, 1990).

The *South English Legendary*

(circa thirteenth – fifteenth centuries)

Katherine G. McMahon
Mount Union College

Manuscripts: The work survives in sixty-three manuscripts; two of the most important are Corpus Christi College, Cambridge, MS. 145 and British Library MS. Harley 2277.

First publication and standard edition: *The Early South English Legendary,* edited by Carl Horstmann, EETS, o.s. 87 (1887; reprinted, Kraus, 1973).

Standard edition: *The South English Legendary,* 3 volumes, edited by Charlotte D'Evelyn and Anna J. Mill, EETS, 235, 236, 244 (1956, 1959).

Carl Horstmann, in his 1887 edition of *The Early South English Legendary,* introduces the text as "one of the most important works of mediaeval literature." His comment probably surprised his readers, because up to that time very few scholars or other readers had devoted much attention to this legendary. While Frederick J. Furnivall and other scholars of the nineteenth century had explored small parts of this collection, the complex textual history of the whole work as well as the inadequately studied saint's-life genre probably discouraged many scholars, critics, and readers from considering it at all. Horstmann's statement has turned out to be prophetic, however, as the work has steadily gleaned attention and reputation throughout the twentieth century. This work, known today simply as the *South English Legendary,* is a rich body of material not only for those interested in medieval literature, but also for those interested in saints' lives, textual studies, dialect studies, historical linguistics, popular culture, and other related literary areas. Most recently, in addition to significant textual efforts, it is being examined as a literary work whose styles, themes, and structural handling are important to our understanding of English literary developments during the early medieval period.

The *South English Legendary* is a collection of Christian saints' lives and homiletic pieces written in Middle English verse. The collection has sur-

vived in several extant manuscripts, no two of which are alike. Because of this diversity, the contents and number of legends vary from manuscript to manuscript, from approximately 55 to 135 legends in the more complete versions. These legends tell the stories of many men and women whose lives were important to the dissemination and evolution of the Christian Church and Christian doctrine. In fact, the saint's legends had long been an effective way of articulating and realizing that doctrine. Early audiences of saints' legends were both informed and inspired by the stories that they heard, especially when the depiction of a saint's faith involved a test of moral character or modeled an ideal of Christian behavior. Two different prologues to the collection are found in the extant *South English Legendary* manuscripts, differing for the most part in length and not in actual information, but neither provides a satisfactory introduction to the full intent or breadth of the work as it finally evolved. The prologue, entitled "Banna Sanctorum" in some manuscripts, primarily indicates that the book is made of holy days and holy men's lives which should be read on the appropriate feast day or anniversary of the saint:

Of apostles & martyrs þat hardy kniȝtes were
þat studeuast were in bataille & ne fleide noȝt for fere
þat soffrede þat luþer men al quik hare lymes totere
Tell ichelle be reuwe of ham as hare dai valþ in þe ȝere
Verst bygynneþ at ȝeres day for þat is þe uerste feste
And fram on to oþer so areng þe wile þe ȝer wol leste

(Of apostles and martyrs who were hardy knights
who were steadfast in battle and fled not in fear
who endured that wicked men tear apart their limbs all
    alive
I shall tell in pity of them as their day falleth in the year
First begin at New Year's Day, for that is the first feast day
and from one to another so in order while the year will
    last).

The contents of the *South English Legendary* include *sanctorale* and *temporale* material. Most texts of the collection contain the lives of early Christian martyrs, such as Saint Sebastian, Saint Valentine, and Saint Katherine; the lives of exemplary Christian figures, such as Saint Benedict, Saint Jerome, and Saint Gregory; the lives of biblical figures, such as Saint John the Baptist, Saint Andrew, and Saint Martha; and the lives of many English saints whose lives are important to the development of Christianity on the British Isles, such as Saint Kenelm, Saint Thomas Becket, and Saint Wulfstan. In addition, some of the texts contain additional material – homiletic pieces, Old Testament history, the Life of Christ, and Moveable Feasts. Yet the principal concern, as the prologue indicates, is a presentation of a year's worth of holy lives.

As it evolves, the story of each saint's life usually becomes loosely connected to the events surrounding the historical figure who inspired it in the first place, and the lives found in the *South English Legendary* are no exception. Although much source work is yet to be done, most scholars agree that many of the texts of these legends most likely have their ultimate sources in earlier Latin versions. The stories were probably known to the audience, often simply as a part of their general cultural experience. A similar situation exists today in the way that many people are familiar with various fairy tales even though they may not be familiar with the actual texts of the Brothers Grimm or the Andrew Lang versions. In the transmission of these legends even those saints' lives originally based on historical evidence begin to take on recurrent hagiographical formulas and begin to share details with one another. The *South English Legendary* versions of many of the narratives often reflect such an unfolding, blending historical material with legend.

Saint Agnes (died circa 305), for instance, is one of the most popular of the early Christian martyrs, whose life became well known. Interest in her story is indicated by the proliferation of the tellings of her life and the versions of her martyrdom. Saint Jerome, later in the fourth century, wrote about her fame, which had spread throughout many countries in the hymns and homilies of many languages. This proliferation continued for centuries; her legend occurs in every major Christian legendary from Bede's through Mombritius's, from the early through the later Roman martyrologies.

Traditional information about her life reveals simply that she was a young girl who was martyred for being a Christian. Early historical accounts are vague about details concerning her family, her trial, the particular tortures that she underwent, and the manner of her death. Those aspects of Agnes's life

concerning miracles after her death – most notably the story of Emerentiana and that of Constantina (Emperor Constantine's daughter), neither of which are reliably documented in their connection with Agnes – are most likely part of the legendary (as opposed to the historical) aspects of her story. In the earlier versions Agnes's admission that she is a Christian is apparently spontaneous, and she is characterized by a faith-driven eagerness for martyrdom. Later versions, including that of the *South English Legendary,* involve a pagan suitor who sees her walking home from school and falls in love with her. Her refusal to marry him leads to her arrest and trial, and finally to her being forced to choose between marriage and a career in a brothel. She, of course, chooses death. What began as the story of a religious passion that exemplifies the cultural tension between the rejection of an older pagan religion and the acceptance of a newly emerging and powerful Christianity has evolved in theme and content. The story of Agnes in the *South English Legendary,* representative of the resulting hagiographical evolution as well as reflecting thematic interests of its own, connects the idea of Agnes's Christian choice with her virginal purity and her rejection of a pagan religion with her refusal of a pagan suitor. This important shift demonstrates the way historical material in a legend can bend to accommodate developing doctrinal purposes.

The Christian ideal of physical chastity as evidence of spiritual purity, which developed in the early centuries of the Christian Church, is reflected in the lives of many of the saints. Mary Byrne, in *The Tradition of the Nun in Medieval England* (1932), notes that in early Latin patristic writings, the idea of virginity was the great Christian antithesis to paganism and eventually became synonymous with Christian asceticism. Virginity, symbolically and literally, represented purity of body and spirit as well as rejection of the desires of this world. As Marina Warner suggests in *Alone of All Her Sex: The Myth and the Cult of the Virgin Mary* (1976), "concupiscence, as Augustine defined it, was the root of sin, and one of its principal manifestations was lust. Virginity and martyrdom became complementary ideas and the physical subjugation of the body to the pains and ordeals of ascetic discipline was an integral part of sanctity." Chastity and virginity became important aspects, even requirements, of sanctification. Most of the women's saints' lives accepted by the early Catholic church were stories of martyrdoms that connected an acceptance of Christianity and virginal purity with a rejection of paganism, marriage, and worldly concerns. While the *South English Leg-*

endary includes stories of both men and women martyrs, as did many legendaries, its selection of women strongly reflects a bias towards virginal purity. Very few of its women saints are not virgin martyrs. Most of the legends of men martyrs, on the other hand, while stressing the denial of the flesh through scenes of pain and torture, do not make a connection between virginity (and rejection of marriage) and affirmation of faith.

The lives of these early Christian women martyrs often share many themes and aspects, demonstrating the development of hagiographical patterns and formulas. The Saint Agnes legend in many ways suggests the standard story – a young girl of pagan parents who refuses to marry a pagan and is thus martyred for her Christianity. Saint Juliana's story also follows this pattern. Like Saint Agnes and others, she refuses to marry a pagan suitor; like Saint Katherine, she is tortured on a razor-spiked wheel, and like many others, she is tempted by the devil disguised as an angel.

The legends of men also reflect this tendency to use patterns and stock motifs, although the virginity and chastity emphasis is found less frequently. Like other legendaries, the *South English Legendary* has a wider range of possibilities for the lives of sanctified men. The collection contains many holy virtuous men and church men as well as martyred men, and all of the legends echo and retell the stories of real lives, miracles, torture, and conversion or commitment to faith. In her 1966 article "Saints' Lives" Rosemary Woolf describes the atmosphere usually found in a martyr's story, where "the historical world is heightened and distorted in order to magnify the hero. Every emperor is a persecutor of the Christians and local governors execute imperial edicts with malignant ferocity. . . . No martyr is simply put to death, but undergoes spectacular tortures which are related zealously and in detail." In the *South English Legendary* the male martyrs follow this pattern, but there are also as many stories of holy men who lived in Jerusalem, in Rome, in Sicily, in France, in Ireland, and in England, and whose lives became associated with miracles that occurred during their lifetimes or shortly thereafter. Saint Benedict, for instance, was a man who chose to live a holy life. As his community heard of his commitment to Christian ideals – he retreated and meditated in the mountains – his reputation as a holy man grew. By the time he developed and experimented with his ideas about monastic living, he already had great respect and was associated with various miracles.

In *A Literary History of England* (second edition, 1967) A. C. Baugh states that "what goes by the name of the *South English Legendary* could almost be described as a group of similar works having certain parts in common." Despite this variety and complexity, most scholars today agree that this collection coheres as a single work. Manfred Görlach, in his 1974 work *The Textual Tradition of the South English Legendary,* insists that "the *South English Legendary* must obviously be considered as a whole." The question of whether there is indeed a single work or several related works has to be addressed before issues and inquiries about individual legends or the collection as a whole can be satisfactorily investigated.

Perhaps the question of completeness and textual integrity arises from the very nature of the *South English Legendary* and from the obvious popularity of the work. A collection of legends, or *liber festivalis,* like any anthology of smaller pieces, allows variation in a way that a continuous piece of writing, such as a novel, cannot. Each time the *South English Legendary* was copied by a scribe, the opportunity for making alterations was present. Perhaps the material needed to be organized in a different way, or the local favorite saints needed to be added, or certain lives needed to be shortened or lengthened. Adapting the text to the language needs of a particular audience's dialect might have determined whether a scribe copied word for word or changed the vocabulary. The scribe's copying habits might have been precise or casual, good or bad, heavily editorial or simply secretarial. His exemplar text (the text from which he copied) itself might have been flawed or might have diverged from the original. Since the complex textual variety of the extant manuscripts demonstrates complicated relationships and extensive revisions in the transmission of the texts, and since the dates and geographic distribution of the extant manuscripts also vary, several different circumstances have obviously affected the shape and condition of the extant versions of this work.

Current knowledge about the *South English Legendary* is based on sixty-three known manuscripts, which contain almost all or only parts of this collection. The discovery of other manuscripts containing the work is always an exciting possibility. Horstmann mentioned fifteen extant *South English Legendary* manuscripts when he was at work in the late nineteenth century. Carleton Brown listed thirty-four manuscripts in his *A Register of Middle English Religious and Didactic Verse* (1916). In 1957 Charlotte D'Evelyn and Anna Mill, having just com-

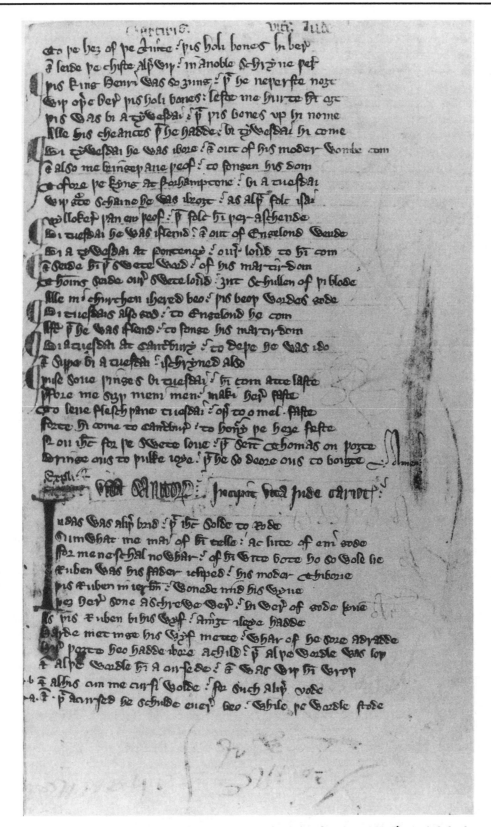

Page from the South English Legendary, *in a transcription dating from circa 1300. The text includes the beginning of the story of Judas (British Library, MS. Harley 2277, fol. 227ᵃ).*

pleted their edition of the collection, listed fifty-one manuscripts. Rossell Hope Robbins and J. L. Cutler listed fifty-four in the 1965 *Supplement to The Index of Middle English Verse*. A newly discovered manuscript (the Takamiya) was sold in England in 1980, bringing the total number of extant manuscripts, including fragments and single legends, to sixty-three.

None of these manuscripts is exactly like another: no two have exactly the same range of legends or order of those legends. The texts of the lives that appear in more than one version are never exactly alike, although they are usually closely related. For instance, the collection's legend of Saint Agnes has survived in two versions, differing in length by almost fifty lines. The legend of Saint Benedict, however, exists in two completely different versions, representing two different source traditions. Because each saint's life is associated with a particular anniversary date or a feast day, the order in which the legends are presented is essentially chronological. For many of the manuscripts the chronology is based on the calendar year, January to December, yet other manuscripts follow the liturgical year, which begins in late November. The organization of the earliest known manuscript, a conflated and textually confused collection that was obviously not the original *South English Legendary* text, is a mixture of both calendars in sections, and in other sections it has a thematic order. The collection's prologue occurs almost in the middle of this text.

This earliest known manuscript, Laud Misc. 108, now residing in the Bodleian Library, Oxford, dates from the mid to late thirteenth century. Several other important manuscripts are dated as very early fourteenth century. The latest of the known manuscripts are generally dated late fifteenth century; however, most of the manuscripts seem to have been written between 1350 and 1450. Thus the dates of the extant manuscripts range from about 1270 to about 1500, a range during which the English language was undergoing significant changes. The geographical domain of the manuscripts ranges throughout the south and midland area of England, yet through dialect differences, script analysis, and other evidence in the manuscripts, it appears that the earliest texts come out of southwestern England, suggesting that area as a possible place of origin.

Thus, scholars can surmise that the *South English Legendary* originated in southwestern England in the thirteenth century and, based on the number of extant manuscripts, that it was a popular work. Little else is verifiably known about its origins. Its author, its original audience, its original purpose, and the details of its subsequent history are unknown. This lack of information is not unusual, as the background of many medieval works remains obscure. The Venerable Bede's *Martyrology* is a good example. Bede certainly compiled this work at some time in the eighth century. It apparently was the basis for several martyrologies that followed, but most scholars have concluded that it is now impossible to distinguish accurately what part or layer of the *Martyrology* is in fact Bede's. On the other hand, the *Legenda aurea,* an important and influential Latin collection of saints' lives, has a much clearer and more substantiated history. It was written by Jacobus de Voraigine in approximately 1260 as a service book – to be read in churches – or as a religious book. The *Legenda aurea* was clearly an important and popular work, as evidenced by the many extant copies of it and the many references to it.

Because it seems to have predated the *South English Legendary* by only a few years, the *Legenda aurea* has been examined by a number of scholars as a potential source. During the nineteenth century the theory that Robert of Gloucester, a thirteenth-century monk, was the author of the *South English Legendary* as well as of the *Chronicle of Robert of Gloucester* was advanced, accepted, and finally rejected. Concern in the twentieth century shifted from an examination of possible authorship of the collection by the mendicant orders to an examination of the possible connection between the *South English Legendary* and the *Legenda aurea.* Whether or not the *Legenda aurea* was the inspiration for or the source of the later collection has been discussed ever since Horstmann asserted that it was neither. Minnie Wells argues that the *Legenda aurea* was the source; Warren Manning argues that parts of the *South English Legendary* are derived from the *Legenda;* Görlach and others continue to examine a possible relationship but are cautious about conclusions. Much work remains to be done with this work in the way of textual clarification and definitive editions before anything conclusive about authors or sources can be resolved. However, many are reading the available editions and finding the *South English Legendary* a rich source for discussion about England, language, and literature during the medieval period.

References:

Albert C. Baugh, ed., *A Literary History of England,* second edition (New York: Appleton-Century-Crofts, 1967);

Beverly Boyd, "A New Approach to the *South English Legendary*," *Philological Quarterly,* 47 (October 1968); 494–498;

Carleton Brown, *A Register of Middle English Religious and Didactic Verse* (Oxford: Oxford University Press, 1916);

Mary Byrne, *The Tradition of the Nun in Medieval England* (Washington, D.C.: Catholic University of America, 1932);

Manfred Görlach, "The *Legenda Aurea* and the Early History of the *South English Legendary*," in *Legenda Aurea: Sept Siecles de diffusion,* edited by Brenda Dunn-Lardeau (Montreal & Paris: Bellarmin Vrin, 1986);

Görlach, *The Textual Tradition of the South English Legendary,* Leeds Texts and Monographs, new series 6 (Leeds: University of Leeds, 1974);

Görlach and O. S. Pickering, "A Newly Discovered Manuscript of the *South English Legendary*," *Anglia,* 100, nos. 1–2 (1982): 109–123;

Thomas J. Heffernan, "Additional Evidence for a More Precise Date of the *South English Legendary*," *Traditio,* 35 (1979): 345–351;

Klaus Jankofsky, ed., *The South English Legendary: A Critical Assessment* (Tübingen: Francke, 1992);

Warren F. Manning, "The Middle English Verse Life of St. Dominic: Date and Source," *Speculum,* 31 (January 1956): 82–91;

Rossell Hope Robbins and J. L. Cutter, *Supplement to the Index of Middle English Verse* (Lexington: University of Kentucky Press, 1965);

Marina Warner, *Alone of All Her Sex: The Myth and the Cult of the Virgin Mary* (New York: Knopf, 1976);

Minnie Wells, "The *South English Legendary* in its relationship to the *Legenda Aurea*," *PMLA,* 51 (June 1936): 337–360;

Rosemary Woolf, "Saints' Lives," in *Continuations and Beginnings: Studies in Old English Literature,* edited by E. G. Stanley (London: Nelson, 1966).

The Towneley Plays

(fifteenth and sixteenth centuries)

Clifford Davidson
Western Michigan University

Manuscript: The unique manuscript is Huntington Library MS. HM 1. While many scholars continue to believe that this manuscript was copied in the late fifteenth century (with sixteenth-century additions), an early date has been disputed on the basis of the strap-work initials that have been said to point in the main to a compilation copied in the sixteenth century in the West Riding of Yorkshire. Facsimile: *The Towneley Cycle: A Facsimile of Huntington MS HM 1,* with an introduction by A. C. Cawley and Martin Stevens, Medieval Drama Facsimiles 2 (Leeds: University of Leeds School of English, 1976).

First publication: *The Towneley Plays,* Surtees Society 3 (London: J. B. Nichols, 1836).

Editions: *The Towneley Plays,* edited by George England, with an introduction by Alfred W. Pollard, EETS, e.s. 71 (1897; reprinted, Kraus, 1973); *The Wakefield Pageants in the Towneley Cycle,* edited by A. C. Cawley (Manchester: Manchester University Press, 1958).

In its most spectacular form English religious drama, which flourished in the later Middle Ages and survived into the reign of Queen Elizabeth I, was presented in great civic cycles that staged biblical history from the Creation to doomsday. The presentation of such a cycle at York is fully documented; the texts of the plays are extant, and the dramatic records from the late fourteenth century through 1580 not only provide much information about production of individual pageants but also reveal the nature of the civic patronage that supported the plays. York's plays, presented "for the glory of God and the honor of the city," were the most famous in the north of England and perhaps second in all of England only to the mysteries at Coventry in the Midlands before their suppression under pressure from the Protestantism favored by the government and church. The Towneley manuscript

(Huntington MS. HM 1) contains what had long been believed to be a second Yorkshire cycle of plays associated with the West Riding town of Wakefield. While there are Wakefield connections to be observed in the manuscript, the entire cycle of plays that it contains may no longer be identified with the "Corpus Christy play" — a play or series of pageants nowhere described and almost certainly more like the Creed Play at York than the Creation to Doom cycle of that city — recorded in the Wakefield burgess court rolls in 1556 and 1559 and a York commissioners' injunction in 1576.

The Towneley manuscript is so named because it was in the possession of the Towneley family of Towneley Hall, near Burnley in Lancashire, prior to its being sold in 1814. It was most likely acquired in the early seventeenth century by the antiquarian Christopher Towneley, who apparently had it rebound, replacing its earlier sixteenth-century binding. Nothing is known about its previous history that would connect the entire cycle with a specific city or town, though the place-name Wakefield was written at the head of two plays by the rubricator, and there is one verifiable reference in the text — to Goodybower, a quarry near this town — in addition to a few other references to nearby places that seem right (for example, "Horbury shrogys," possibly referring to the chapel at Horbury, a short distance to the southwest). Formerly, scholarly speculation concerning the production of these plays at Wakefield was based on some spurious records published by the local historian and promoter John Walker, who is now known to have forged references indicating a Corpus Christi play of the Creation to doom type. In fact, the town demographics and lack of adequate guild structure would have made such a massive dramatic effort impossible, at least if only the local citizenry were involved. The identification of the plays in the Towneley manuscript as the "Wakefield cycle" and hence as pageants presented by the local people at

Wakefield at the feast of Corpus Christi in the fifteenth and sixteenth centuries, though still insisted upon by some scholars, must now be rejected.

The exact nature of the pageants in the Towneley manuscript must also remain something of a mystery. Recent searching of the Yorkshire–West Riding dramatic records by John Wasson and Barbara D. Palmer has produced no clues, though some towns have turned out to be better candidates than Wakefield for extensive theatrical activity by the local people. The two plays identified with Wakefield by the rubricator may, to be sure, have originated with a Wakefield troupe; further, there seems to be no reason to set aside the name Wakefield Master, coined early in the twentieth century by Charles Gayley to refer to the author of six of the plays and of revisions to others. As for the collection as a whole, however, the best suggestion has been J. W. Robinson's hypothesis that it may be an example of "clerks' plays," a manuscript from which individual pageants could be chosen for production. There is precedent for such collections in the Netherlands, and also presentation of individual plays by local troupes would seem to be consistent with what is currently known about playacting in the West Riding of Yorkshire, where these plays are verifiably located by their dialect. The manuscript shows signs of heavy use, a factor that also would argue for its use as a playbook lent out to different acting companies or guilds for productions in various locales around the West Riding. It is safe to assume that the plays were intended for acting and, in the case of the Wakefield Master's plays, were written with a specific troupe in mind. Evidence of tampering with the text for purposes of performance is provided in a post-Reformation marginal note to play 19, which specifies that a stanza referring to the seven sacraments, described in terms of the sacramental doctrine of the "Old Religion," was "corectyd & not playd" (fol. 66^{r}). No hint is provided, however, of a town or city where this pageant, which dramatizes the baptism of Jesus by John the Baptist, might have been staged. However, some have suggested that the collection in MS. HM 1 might have been copied to function primarily as a meditative or mnemonic aid for readers who thus might use it to bring to mind the events of salvation history. The references to guilds, which are not identified convincingly with any specific town (for example, the naming of the Fishers in connection with play 27, the *Peregrini*), should, however, clinch the connection between the manuscript and the physical presentation of the pageants for audiences.

In any case, someone of Protestant persuasion attempted either to protect future audiences from Roman Catholic pageants such as the *Assumption* or *Coronation of the Virgin* or to shield readers from contact with reading matter that was not considered consistent with the official theology of the reformed Church of England. Though mutilated when these plays were excised and also lacking a quire at the beginning containing a portion of *The Creation* and possibly the banns, the Towneley manuscript still contains thirty-two pageants or portions thereof, the last two – *Lazarus* and the incomplete *Suspencio Jude* – being added on at the end:

1. *The Creation* (incomplete; the ending of the pageant is missing)
2. *Mactacio Abel (The Killing of Abel)*
3. *Processus Noe cum Filius*
4. *Abraham* (incomplete; the ending is missing)
5. *Abraham and Isaac* (incomplete; only the final seventy lines remain)
6. *Jacob*
7. *Processus Prophetarum* (incomplete; unfinished)
8. *Pharao*
9. *Cesar Augustus*
10. *Annunciatio*
11. *Salutacio Elezabeth (The Visitation)*
12. *Prima Pastorum (First Shepherds' Play)*
13. *Secunda Pastorum (Second Shepherds' Play)*
14. *Oblacio Magorum (The Gifts of the Magi)*
15. *Fugacio Joseph & Marie in Egiptum (The Flight to Egypt)*
16. *Magnus Herodes (Herod the Great)*
17. *Purificacio Marie (The Purification* – incomplete; the text following line 141 is missing)
18. *Pagina Doctorum (The Doctors* – incomplete; the beginning is missing)
19. *Johannes Baptista (John the Baptist)*
20. *Conspiracio (The Conspiracy)*
21. *Coliphizacio (The Buffeting)*
22. *Flagellacio (The Scourging)*
23. *Processus Crucis (The Way of the Cross)*
24. *Processus Talentorum (The Talents)*
25. *Extraccio Animarum (The Harrowing)*
26. *Resurreccio Domini (The Resurrection)*
27. *Peregrini (The Pilgrims)*
28. *Thomas Indie (Thomas of India)*
29. *Ascencio Domini (The Ascension* – the text is incomplete following line 411)
30. *Judicium (The Last Judgment* – incomplete; the beginning is missing)
31. *Lazarus*
32. *Suspencio Jude (The Hanging of Judas* – incomplete).

Five of these plays are direct borrowings from the York cycle: *Pharao* (the Exodus, including the crossing of the Red Sea), *Pagina Doctorum* (Jesus at age twelve in the temple), *Extraccio Animarum, Resurreccio Domini,* and the incomplete *Judicium,* which has additions by the Wakefield Master. Similarities may also be noted between the parallel York plays and the pageants of the betrayal of Jesus (*Conspiracio*), the Emmaus story (*Peregrini*), and the death of Judas (*Suspencio Jude*).

The six plays that are entirely the work of the Wakefield Master are *Mactacio Abel* (a Cain and Abel play), *Processus Noe cum Filiis* (the Great Flood), *Prima Pastorum, Secunda Pastorum, Magnus Herodes* (including the Slaughter of the Innocents), and *Coliphizacio*. This playwright also revised and added portions to the *Flagellacio, Processus Crucis, Processus Talentorum,* and *Ascencio Domini.* His work is distinctive in its handling of language and verse form, both of which have been claimed as signs of his genius. On the basis of his hand in the Towneley collection Martin Stevens has argued for seeing the Wakefield Master not only as a "playwright-poet of extraordinary genius" but also as the author of the entire cycle, though it is more likely that his plays and revisions were a core around which a different compiler (not the scribe) added other pageants from various sources to make up the compilation. Thus to search for a single principle of unity in the collection would seem to be a misguided effort. On the other hand, the Old Testament stories are closely connected by analogy and contrast to New Testament events that are also dramatized. As in the *Biblia Pauperum,* Old Testament types foreshadow New Testament antitypes (for example, the Wakefield Master's flood in the time of Noah looks forward to the Last Judgment, the final deluge which will destroy the world); yet, as Jeffrey Helterman demonstrates in his *Symbolic Action in the Plays of the Wakefield Master* (1981), there is a considerable "tension between type and antitype . . . responsible for much of the action in the drama." Such tension is especially noticeable in the figure of Noah's wife, whose shrewishness involves the inversion of the divine order – an example of the "world-upside-down" topos frequently illustrated in late-medieval wood carvings, such as misericords showing wives beating or dominating over their husbands and thus reversing the feminine-masculine roles that normally require male mastery.

The distinctive verse form of the Wakefield Master appears in modern editions as a nine-line stanza, of which the following from the opening of the *Secunda Pastorum* is an example:

> Lord, what these weders ar *cold!* and I am yll happyd.
> I am nerehande *dold,* so long haue I nappyd;
> My legys thay *fold,* my fyngers ar chappyd.

It is not as I *wold,* for I am al lappyd
In sorow.
In stormes and tempest,
Now in the eest, now in the west,
Wo is hym has neuer rest
Mydday nor morow!

The opening section of four lines (the *frons*) is marked by internal rhyme (indicated above by the italicized words), followed by the bob (the short line, here of three syllables) and wheel. As described by Alfred W. Pollard in his introduction to the 1897 Early English Text Society edition, the form is written *a/b a/b a/b a/b cdddc.* However, Martin Stevens argues that this nine-line schema may be more a convenient way of displaying the text on the page than a sign of metrical originality. Some editors henceforth may prefer to display these stanzas as thirteen-line units.

The contribution of the Wakefield Master also involves not only sharp social criticism but additionally a much-admired sense of high comedy, though this latter characteristic has been regarded as controversial by Eleanor Prosser and others because of its placement in the biblical stories being dramatized. Marxist critics and those influenced by their methodology, on the other hand, have approvingly seen the comedy as subverting the sacred meaning of the plays. However, audience response to individual plays, though complicated, is highly unlikely to come down ultimately on the side of such subversive characters as the torturers in the *Coliphizacio* or King Herod in the *Magnus Herodes.* Herod certainly is designed as a character to be both feared and laughed at; he is in fact identifiable as an *alazon,* an impostor figure commonly appearing in comedy. A fully comic structure is present only in the *Second Shepherds' Play,* which conforms to the requirements for comedy as codified by Northrop Frye; it begins in rebelliousness, then moves through its triumph, followed by an order-restoring conclusion. In the pageant the trickster and impostor Mak – whose name suggests Scotland, hated on account of border raids, and whose fake accent affects a southern dialect, also disliked by Yorkshiremen – successfully succeeds in stealing a sheep, but his deception even at the moment of his triumph is foiled by the shepherds, whose insistence upon giving gifts to the false "child" foreshadows the giving of symbolic gifts – a bob of cherries (foreshadowing the Passion), a bird (signifying Christ's spiritual nature), and a ball (symbolizing his kingship) – to the true Child, the Son of God, in the latter part of the play. Mak, appro-

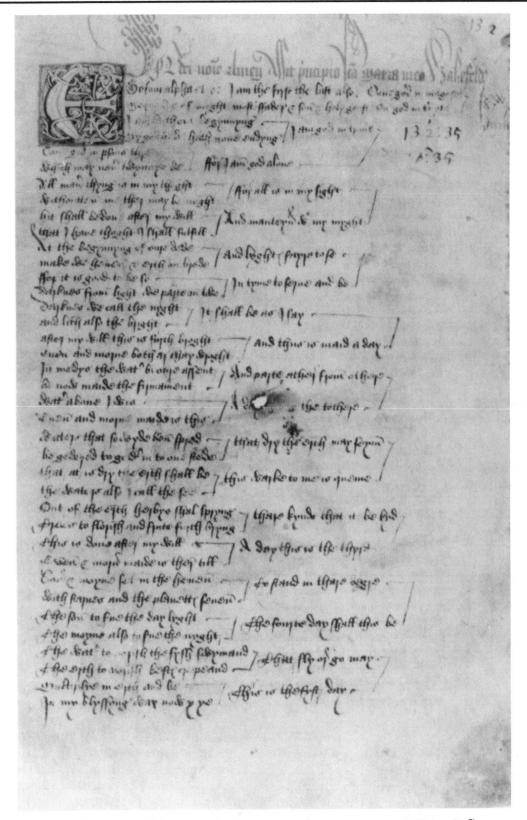

First page of The Creation *in the Towneley Manuscript (Huntington Library, MS. HM 1, fol. 1ʳ)*

priately for comedy, is given only a mock punishment, and the jest culminates in the Nativity scene, which is also the point at which eternity and time intersect.

The Wakefield Master tends to mix jest with earnest and, utilizing the rhetorical principle of *ridendo dicere verum* (revealing truth through the use of laughter), achieves effects that are stunningly effective. When Cain counts out his sheaves in the *Mactacio Abel,* his selfishness reflects his audience's natural selfishness but at the same time demonstrates the inherent absurdity of his acts. It is the idea of autonomous man that is depicted as comic. Ugly and self-defeating actions are signs of the post-lapsarian condition, but they are also worthy of exorcizing laughter that points to the harmony and perfection beyond earthly existence.

For the Wakefield Master the drama itself is like a game, both serious and inherently based in an as-if situation. Its depictions reveal humanity in both its potential despair and its hope – reflecting both the wide road to the everlasting bonfire that is the way of Cain and the narrow path to spiritual perfection that is the way of Abel. The re-creative principle, rehabilitated by the Dominican saint Thomas Aquinas and likewise by the Franciscans, could thus function as a means of enlightening an audience and of communicating scenes of the greatest spiritual significance. The Wakefield Master's aesthetics are thus diametrically opposed to the staunch antitheatricalism of the writers of *A Tretise of Miraclis Pleyinge* (late fourteenth or early fifteenth century) the most extended piece of drama criticism of the late Middle Ages from England but also a text hostile to all forms of play, which is regarded as the work of the devil. As a cleric (proven by his familiarity with various aspects of the religious tradition) the Wakefield Master wrote for laymen and, presumably, amateur actors of considerable skill, whose purpose would be broader than either mere amusement or social criticism, though both these elements are present in his plays.

The Wakefield Master's additions to the doomsday pageant, which lost its beginning when signatures S_2 through T_5 – containing the plays of the Assumption and Coronation of the Virgin – were removed, provides an appropriate conclusion to the collection of plays. The twenty-eight or more stanzas borrowed from the York pageant are transformed into a different kind of drama from the original upon which he grafted his embellishments. The solemn and powerful York text

probably received the most spectacular theatrical treatment among the York plays since it was staged under the patronage of the rich Mercers Guild. In the Towneley collection the Judgment play is expanded by extensive scenes of demons featuring the devil Tutivillus and his cohorts, who are shown becoming aware of the end of time, which is signaled by one of the fifteen signs of doomsday – the death of all the living, hell now holding its full complement of souls prior to being released for their appearance before the Judge. Tutivillus was a popular devil in folklore, sermon, literature, and art, where he was normally depicted as the recording demon who writes down the words misspoken or missed at mass. Here, however, he is given a larger role and also is depicted with a horn, an instrument with which the devil is elsewhere identified. It is hard to believe that a devil such as Tutivillus could have any musical ability.

Against the comedy and satire of the devils is the spectacle of the descent of Christ from heaven to judge all of humankind – an event that culminates in the separation of good and evil humans by the archangel Saint Michael, who uses his sword (no psychostasis with scales to weigh good and bad deeds seems to have been present) to divide those who have done the Corporal Acts of Mercy specified in Matthew 25 from those who have not. The test required for those entering bliss is not so much a quantitative one as it is a qualitative determination in the Augustinian sense: the selfishness of humans such as Cain and Judas is the principle of evil opposed to generosity and concern for others. Ultimately such selfishness is self-defeating at the bar of divine justice. The York doomsday play, for which an inventory of properties from 1433 as well as later records are extant, demanded a complex staging technology utilizing a pageant wagon with an upper level, a lowering mechanism for the descent of Christ, puppet angels, a display of the signs of the Passion, and graves out of which the saved and the damned rose. The scenic form involved in the Judgment was universally familiar, and it was represented in the West Riding by stained glass in the church at Thornhill, near Wakefield, and in the upper portion of the east window at Selby Abbey; formerly at Wakefield and elsewhere in England the Judgment scene appeared in wall paintings over the chancel arches of churches. However, the staging demanded in the Towneley Judgment play is not made entirely clear by either text or stage directions, and the lack throughout the collection of coherent staging directions, either specified or implied, has been noted by those who have set out to present the entire set of Towneley plays as a cycle.

Nevertheless, it is clear that a different kind of staging from the pageant-wagon stages used in the York Corpus Christi productions would have been needed for many of the pageants in the Towneley collection. The Wakefield Master's *Secunda Pastorum* is a prime example of a play that could not be staged on a single pageant wagon built to negotiate the narrow streets of a medieval city. Three loci are needed: the countryside where the shepherds are tending their sheep, Mak's house, and the ruined stable of the Nativity. Judging from the evidence of Continental staging and iconography, Mak's house was perhaps on the left (the side associated with hell, the powers of darkness, and evil) and the stable on the right (the side associated with goodness and the powers of goodness); even if the countryside was represented in the *platea,* or "place," rather than on a scaffold, a single pageant wagon would hardly have been sufficient for both indoor locations. The logical conclusion is that instead of wagons the staging was intended to be of the place-and-scaffold type, with a higher scaffold for the angelic song announcing the Incarnation to the shepherds.

More elaborate staging effects are required by other plays. Among plays by the Wakefield Master, a team (possibly utilizing representations of animals from the "hobby horse" tradition) and a plow are needed for the *Mactacio Abel,* and two loci, a hill for Noah's wife and a place for the construction of a prefabricated ark, as well as rising sea (possibly provided by cloth waves or more realistic effects) in the *Processus Noe cum Filiis.* Other plays in the cycle have diverse staging requirements. For example, while play 1 demands a complex vertical arrangement with heaven (a raised platform for the Creator fitted with a throne), hell (opening for the fall of Lucifer), and a middle space or platform for the creation of earth and its creatures, play 8, recounting the story of the Exodus from Egypt, is mainly horizontal in its organization, with the conflict between Pharaoh and the Israelites culminating in passage through the Red Sea, in which the Egyptian tyrant and his army are drowned as they pursue Moses in their "chariottis." (Chariots are, it should be noted, a borrowing from the York text; they appear invariably in medieval visual representations of the crossing of the Red Sea, where Pharaoh's vehicle is a two-wheeled cart overturned in the waves, as in a roof boss at Norwich Cathedral.) In the

Towneley *Pharao,* a spectacular effect involving some kind of fireworks display represents God within the burning bush, an effect probably best carried out on ground level on the *platea* rather than on a platform.

Analogous scenes from the visual arts can help modern readers understand how the playwrights of the Towneley collection saw various events, including not only such aspects as costumes but also very specific actions and gestures. In the *Resurrection* the soldiers describe in wonderment what happened when Jesus rose from the dead; though they were as if sleeping, the second soldier comments that he "sagh myself when that he yede." In the examples of medieval alabaster carvings published by W. L. Hildburgh, the "sleeping" soldiers have eyes open to see the event of Christ's Resurrection as he steps out of the coffer tomb in which he has been confined. In the play the fourth soldier reports that the risen Christ had placed his foot upon him in his departure from the tomb: "Alas, hard hap was on my hede. . . ." One of the alabasters illustrated by Hildburgh shows Christ's foot on the torso of a soldier in armor beside the tomb, and examples of iconography from the West Riding show a similar detail. An early-fourteenth-century alabaster panel from an altar retable at Ripon shows Jesus, wearing the crown of thorns, his side bleeding, placing his right foot on one of the soldiers, while at Elland, a village approximately fifteen miles west of Wakefield, is a panel of painted glass circa 1490 that also portrays Christ with his right foot resting on a soldier.

Jesus's long speech when he arises in the Resurrection play also places him in a pose that was frequently depicted in the visual arts. The emphasis of the speech is on the soteriological work that Jesus has performed in his Passion and on the cross through his suffering and shedding of his blood:

> Behold my body . . .
> All to-rent and all to-shentt,
> Man, for thy plight.

The suffering body that sustained the terrible blows shown in the pageant dramatizing the buffeting (*Coliphizacio*) and scourging (*Flagellacio*) – and that by the time of his death had been wounded from the top of his head to the bottom of his feet – was the object of deep devotion in the religious practice of the time. Such devotion expressed itself through recognizable images in the visual arts and apparently also in the drama. Sometimes those who looked upon the Passion in the visual arts were moved to tears, and there is documentation that people were likewise affected by the religious theater, particularly at scenes of the suffering of Christ or the saints. Thus it is not only the mechanics of gesture and movement that may be explained by reference to the visual arts, but also the visual aesthetics of religious experience of the time. Both drama and the visual arts participated in a variety of piety that stressed emotion and devotion to the crucified Christ and risen Savior, whose blood was a sign of his sacrificial act on the cross and which, since it was especially venerated, was depicted in stage effects that did not shrink from holy gore. In the case of the Chester Whitsun cycle, attendance at the plays with devotional intent was said to have resulted in indulgences, meriting relief from future suffering in purgatory.

The representation of Christ's suffering in the *Coliphizacio, Flagellacio,* and *Processus Crucis,* though abbreviated when compared to the more extensive series in the York cycle, nevertheless is indicative of the emphasis in the religious life of the late medieval West Riding on the events of Holy Week, culminating on Good Friday. But these events look forward to the subsequent events of the harrowing in the *Extraccio Animarum* (a play which, though mainly borrowed from a pageant in the York cycle, nevertheless adds such touches as the identification of a particularly lively devil as "Rybald") and of the *Resurrection, Ascension,* and *Judicium,* or Last Judgment. The *Extraccio Animarum,* based on apocryphal writings that reveal the activities of the Soul of Jesus during the Descent into Hell mentioned by the Creed, is a drama of deliverance in which the souls of the righteous who had lived previously – Adam, Eve, Moses, David, Simeon, John the Baptist – were released from limbo. The scene is a familiar one in the visual arts of the period: the gates of hell are broken down by Christ, who holds the same cross staff in his hand that is held in representations of the Resurrection; often a devil is pinned painfully beneath the fallen gates of hell. At the end of the pageant the devils, who should be imagined as the ugly, furry, dirty creatures depicted in the visual arts (costumes and masks for these characters are noted in the records at such centers of dramatic activity as York and Coventry), have been humiliated, while the good people who lived before the Crucifixion are released from their captivity in darkness and the *Te Deum laudamus* is sung. The event foreshadows the happy judgment of the just at the last day in the *Judicium,* when again the *Te Deum* is sung while the righteous

make mirth and offer praise as they enter into bliss. This musical item also had provided the symbolic closure of the liturgical musical dramas (for example, the *Visitatio Sepulchri* at Easter) designed for presentation at Matins, and, although scholars no longer claim that plays such as those in the Towneley collection evolved out of the sung church drama, the *Te Deum* forms an appropriate conclusion for a play on the end of time and the moment when further preparation for that event is no longer possible since the time of grace has passed.

The two final plays in the Towneley collection – *Lazarus* and the incomplete *Suspencio Jude* – are out of order, and the second of these was added in a later sixteenth-century hand. The play of *Lazarus,* though it presents a vivid description of hell by one who has experienced it and returned – perhaps an extension of the warning to sinners implied in the *Judicium* – is nevertheless, except for *Johannes Baptista,* the sole representative of Jesus's ministry in the Towneley collection. The *Suspencio Jude* is a monologue in which the betrayer of Christ confesses that he "was born with owtyn grace"; as one who is "of Camys kyn," he will share the despair that characterized the first permanent resident of hell. The story of Judas's birth and rejection by his parents, his exposure at sea, and his miraculous landing on an island where he is adopted by a king and queen hardly suggests drama at all; in spite of a connection with the York *Remorse of Judas,* it is more likely a fragment of a poem entered into the manuscript for readers rather than for potential production.

Obviously in a gathering of pageants such as the Towneley collection the quality of the individual pageants as both literature and theater will vary, with the best – including the *Prima Pastorum* with its astounding, fabulous (imaginary) feast, and the *Secunda Pastorum,* which regularly appears in anthologies that survey English literature – having been long ago inducted into the literary canon. But even the weakest from a literary standpoint are capable of being surprisingly successful when staged.

References:

M. D. Anderson, *Drama and Imagery in English Medieval Churches* (Cambridge: Cambridge University Press, 1963);

David Bevington and Pamela Sheingorn, "'Alle this was token domysday to drede': Visual Signs of Last Judgment in the Corpus Christi Cycles and in Late Gothic Art," in *Homo, Memento Finis: The Iconography of Just Judgment in Medieval Art and Drama* (Kalamazoo, Mich.: Medieval Institute Publications, 1985), pp. 121–145;

A. C. Cawley, Marion Jones, Peter F. McDonald, and David Mills, *Medieval Drama* (London: Methuen, 1983);

Theresa Coletti, "Theology and Politics in the Towneley *Play of the Talents*," *Medievalia et Humanistica*, new series 9 (1979): 111–126;

John P. Cutts, "The Shepherds' Gifts in *The Second Shepherds' Play* and Bosch's 'Adoration of the Magi,'" *Comparative Drama*, 4 (Summer 1970): 120–124;

Clifford Davidson, "From *Tristia* to *Gaudium*: Iconography and the York-Towneley *Harrowing of Hell*," *American Benedictine Review*, 28 (September 1977): 260–275;

Davidson, "An Interpretation of the Wakefield *Judicium*," *Annuale Mediaevale*, 10 (1969): 104–119;

Davidson, "Jest and Earnest: Comedy in the Work of the Wakefield Master," *Annuale Mediaevale*, 22 (1982): 65–83;

Davidson, ed., *A Tretise of Miraclis Pleyinge* (Kalamazoo, Mich.: Medieval Institute Publications, 1993);

Hans-Jürgen Diller, *The Middle English Mystery Play: A Study in Dramatic Speech and Form* (Cambridge: Cambridge University Press, 1992);

E. Catherine Dunn, "The Medieval 'Cycle' as History Play: An Approach to the Wakefield Plays," *Studies in the Renaissance*, 7 (1960): 76–89;

JoAnna Dutka, *Music in the English Mystery Plays* (Kalamazoo, Mich.: Medieval Institute Publications, 1980);

Grace Frank, "On the Relation Between the York and Towneley Plays," *PMLA*, 44 (March 1929): 313–319;

Harold C. Gardiner, *Mysteries' End: An Investigation of the Last Days of the Medieval Religious Stage* (New Haven: Yale University Press, 1946);

Charles Gayley, *Plays of Our Forefathers* (New York: Duffield, 1907);

Cherrell Guilfoyle, "The Staging of the First Murder in the Mystery Plays in England," *Comparative Drama*, 25 (Spring 1991): 42–51;

Jeffrey Helterman, *Symbolic Action in the Plays of the Wakefield Master* (Athens: University of Georgia Press, 1981);

W. L. Hildburgh, "English Alabaster Carvings as Records of Medieval Religious Drama," *Archaeologia*, 93 (1949): 55–101;

Margaret Jennings, C.S.J., *Tutivillus: The Literary Career of the Recording Demon*, Studies in Philology 74, no. 5 (Chapel Hill: University of North Carolina Press, 1977);

Alexandra F. Johnston, "Evil in the Towneley Cycle," in *Evil on the Medieval Stage*, edited by Meg Twycross (Lancaster: Medieval English Theatre, 1992), pp. 94–103;

V. A. Kolve, *The Play Called Corpus Christi* (Stanford, Cal.: Stanford University Press, 1966);

Marie Caroline Lyle, *The Original Identity of the York and Towneley Cycles* (Minneapolis: University of Minnesota Press, 1919);

Walter E. Meyers, *A Figure Given: Typology in the Wakefield Plays* (Pittsburgh: Duquesne University Press, 1968);

William F. Munson, "Typology and the Towneley Isaac," *Research Opportunities in Renaissance Drama*, 11 (1978): 129–139;

Barbara D. Palmer, "Corpus Christi 'Cycles' in Yorkshire: The Surviving Records," *Comparative Drama*, 27 (Summer 1993): 218–231;

Palmer, *The Early Art of the West Riding of Yorkshire: A Subject List of Extant and Lost Art Including Items Relevant to Early Drama* (Kalamazoo, Mich.: Medieval Institute Publications, 1990);

Palmer, "'Towneley Plays' or 'Wakefield Cycle' Revisited," *Comparative Drama*, 21 (Winter 1988): 318–348;

Eleanor Prosser, *Drama and Religion in the English Mystery Plays* (Stanford, Cal.: Stanford University Press, 1961);

J. W. Robinson, *Studies in Fifteenth-Century Stagecraft: The Nativity and the Passion in the Yorkshire Cycles* (Kalamazoo, Mich.: Medieval Institute Publications, 1991);

Martial Rose, trans., *The Wakefield Mystery Plays* (Garden City, N.Y.: Doubleday, 1962);

Lawrence J. Ross, "Symbol and Structure in the *Secunda Pastorum*," *Comparative Drama*, 1 (Summer 1967): 122–143; republished in *Medieval English Drama*, edited by Jerome Taylor and Alan H. Nelson (Chicago: University of Chicago Press, 1972);

Edgar Schell, "The Limits of Typology and the Wakefield Master's *Processus Noe*," *Comparative Drama*, 25 (Summer 1991): 168–187;

Martin Stevens, *Four Middle English Mystery Cycles* (Princeton: Princeton University Press, 1987);

Stevens, "The Manuscript of the *Towneley Plays:* Its History and Editions," *Papers of the Bibliographical Society of America,* 67 (1973): 231–244;

Stevens, "The Missing Parts of the Towneley Cycle," *Speculum,* 45 (1970): 254–265;

Stevens, "The Towneley Plays Manuscript (HM 1): *Compilatio* and *Ordinatio,*" *Text,* 5 (1991): 157–173;

Peter W. Travis, "The Social Body of the Dramatic Christ in Medieval England," *Acta,* 13 (1985): 17–36;

Cynthia Haldenby Tyson, "Noah's Flood, The River Jordan, the Red Sea: Staging in the Towneley Cycle," *Comparative Drama,* 8 (Spring 1974): 101–111;

Donna Smith Vinter, "Didactic Characterization: The Towneley Abraham," *Comparative Drama,* 14 (Summer 1980): 117–136; republished in *Medieval English Drama,* edited by Peter Happé (London: Macmillan, 1984), pp. 71–89;

Robert Weimann, *Shakespeare and the Popular Tradition in the Theater,* edited by Robert Schwarz (Baltimore: Johns Hopkins University Press, 1978);

Arnold Williams, *The Characterization of Pilate in the Towneley Plays* (East Lansing: Michigan State College Press, 1950);

Glynne Wickham, *Early English Stages 1300 to 1600,* volume 1 (London: Routledge & Kegan Paul, 1959);

Rosemary Woolf, *The English Mystery Plays* (Berkeley & Los Angeles: University of California Press, 1972).

The York Cycle

(circa 1376 – circa 1569)

Perry T. Patterson
University of South Carolina

Manuscript: The York Cycle is preserved in British Library MS. Add. 35290, sometimes called the Ashburnham manuscript. Facsimile: *The York Play: A facsimile of British Library MS Additional 35290 together with a facsimile of the Ordo Paginarum section of the A/Y Memorandum Book,* edited by Richard Beadle and Peter Meredith (Leeds: University of Leeds Press, 1983).

First publication: *York Plays: The Plays Performed by the Crafts or Mysteries of York on the Day of Corpus Christi in the 14th, 15th and 16th Centuries. Now First Printed from the Unique Manuscript in the Library of Lord Ashburnham,* edited by Lucy Toulmin Smith (Oxford: Clarendon Press, 1885).

Standard editions: *The York Cycle of Mystery Plays: A Complete Version,* edited by J. S. Purvis (London: SPCK, 1978); *The York Plays,* edited by Richard Beadle (London: Arnold, 1982).

Edition in modern English: *York Mystery Plays: A Selection in Modern Spelling,* edited by Richard Beadle and Pamela M. King (Oxford: Clarendon Press, 1984).

When the Belgian nun Juliana of Mount Cornillon set out in pursuit of her lifelong dream to create a feast day in celebration of the Eucharist, she never considered that her efforts in creating a religious holiday would in turn create a new form of medieval dramatic expression. After Juliana's death in 1258, Pope Urban IV supported her cause, as did Pope Clement V after him. Ultimately the celebration of the Eucharist was sanctioned at the Council of Vienne in 1311. The event was to fall in midsummer on the first Thursday after Trinity Sunday, which could occur anytime between 23 May and 24 June depending on the year. It was called the Feast of Corpus Christi (Body of Christ), and from this religious occasion was born a drama unique to the Middle Ages. This drama was made up of a group of separate plays that transcended their individuality to contribute to the didactic aim of a unified whole.

These groups of Corpus Christi plays were referred to as cycles because they depicted, in a series of chronological dramas, the history of man from the Creation to the Last Judgment. Unlike medieval miracle plays, which dramatized the life of a saint, or medieval morality plays, which focused on the conflict between good and evil forces for the possession of man's soul, Corpus Christi or cycle plays were based on stories from the Old and New Testaments of the Bible, the Apocrypha, and legend. Since the dramas were primarily drawn from Scripture, the playwrights were able to produce an array of plays on such diverse subjects as the Fall of Man, Noah and the Flood, the Nativity, the Crucifixion, the Resurrection, and the Last Judgment. The York Cycle particularly emphasizes the importance of Christ's Nativity and Passion as opposed to his teachings. It seems that the cycle's anonymous playwrights wanted to concentrate initially on the joyous birth of their savior and subsequently show how, through great suffering, Jesus sacrificed his life to save the world from sin and death. Consequently, in addition to one play entitled *The Nativity,* there are six others dramatizing events related to Christ's birth: *The Annunciation and Visitation, Joseph's Trouble about Mary, The Shepherds; Herod* and *The Magi* (two plays interconnecting and performed simultaneously), *The Flight into Egypt,* and *The Slaughter of the Innocents.* On the other hand, there are nine plays dramatizing the Passion of Christ, including *The Last Supper, The Agony in the Garden and the Betrayal, Christ before Herod, The Road to Calvary, The Crucifixion,* and *The Death of Christ.*

From the late fourteenth century to the late sixteenth century, roughly a span of two hundred years, the Corpus Christi plays were in their heyday in England. They enjoyed immense popularity;

when the plays were performed annually during the Feast of Corpus Christi, thousands of people would come to watch them. There are similarities between the existing cycles along the lines of structure, character, theme, and diction; however, a city with a sizable population would be inclined to have cycle plays of its own which, on the whole, would have been artistically distinct from the cycle plays of other English towns. At one time as many as twelve different cycles existed in such places as Preston, Kendall, Norwich, and Newcastle upon Tyne, and the highest concentration of cycle plays tended to be in cities located in the northern and eastern sections of England. To date, only four complete cycles have survived from the Middle Ages, and they are from the towns of Chester, Wakefield, York, and an unknown location possibly in East Anglia that scholars refer to as N-Town.

Of the four extant cycles, the York Cycle is the oldest, with records mentioning it as early as 1376, and it is the largest, too, in that it tells the story of man in forty-eight separate plays which total over fourteen thousand lines of verse. The entire cycle survives in a single manuscript, the Ashburnham manuscript (British Library MS. Add. 35290). Even though the plays were undoubtedly written by various dramatists, most of this particular manuscript seems to have been transcribed from craft-guild copies by an anonymous scribe during the 1460s or 1470s. This copy of the York Cycle exists in fairly good condition, suggesting that it was not used as a performance copy. Most certainly, the manuscript is the city of York's master copy of the plays and is commonly referred to as the Register.

The York plays were not written in final form and left untouched; instead, these dramas were in a constant state of flux during the two hundred years they were performed. Many changes were made to the York Cycle text, new plays were added on occasion, existing plays were frequently revised, and sometimes plays were dropped entirely depending on changing social attitudes or financial hardships experienced within the city of York.

The purpose of the York Cycle was twofold — to entertain and to teach. Capturing and holding the audience's attention was an ever-present challenge for the play's director. Lavish sets and beautiful costumes were used to attract the eye of the onlooker. With respect to stagecraft, in *The Building of the Ark* an abbreviated version of Noah's great vessel is actually erected onstage during the action, which would have awed the audience. Also, the dramatists injected comic lines and characters into some of the plays to provide relief from so much solemn religious subject matter and doctrine. Yet the comedy of the York Cycle does not center around laughter as much as it focuses on a feeling of joy at such events as Christ's Nativity and Resurrection. Moreover, the length of the plays helped to prevent boredom. Only occasionally was an individual York play over 500 lines long. In fact, the cycle's first play, *The Fall of the Angels,* is only 160 lines in length, and another play of great theological importance, *The Fall of Man,* is only 176 lines.

The principal purpose of the York Cycle was to help the people develop spiritually, and the York playwrights accomplished their task, in part, through the use of single characters delivering scripturally based speeches or through the interplay and dialogue of various biblical figures. Whatever the methods of the dramatists, the plays usually proved to be grand and spectacular experiences that helped further the didactic aim of the cycle as a whole.

The York dramatists used God/Christ frequently to teach the audience about the nature of the Holy Father and Son. God is shown as all-powerful and glorious, and there is no doubt in the audience's mind that he is in complete control of the universe. In fact, *The Fall of the Angels* opens with an awesome God who states, "Ego sum alpha et O, Vita, Via, / Veritas, Primus et Novissimus" (I am Alpha and Omega, the life, the way, the truth, the first and the last). The tone is set, and the magnificence and power of God permeate the rest of the cycle, literally from the first to the last play. Even if God is not physically present on the stage, his presence looms over the cycle and moves through each play because of his status as ubiquitous creator. God is the supernatural essence of the York Cycle, and he ends these forty-eight plays just as dynamically as he began them — the final play, *The Last Judgment,* emphasizes Christ's swift and uncompromising judgment of the damned souls. The wicked quake as Jesus declares the final damning:

Ye cursed caitiffs, from me flee,
In hell to dwell without an end.
There shall ye nought but sorrow see,
And dwell by Satanas the fiend.

If the York playwrights showed God/Christ's unbridled power or unbending judgment in one play, they were quick to focus on his love and mercy in another. For example, *The Death of Christ* portrays a Jesus who possesses such a deep-rooted love for man that he willingly gives his life on the cross in order to pay the price for human sin. He suffers and sacrifices himself so that man can overcome death and live eternally. As Christ hangs on

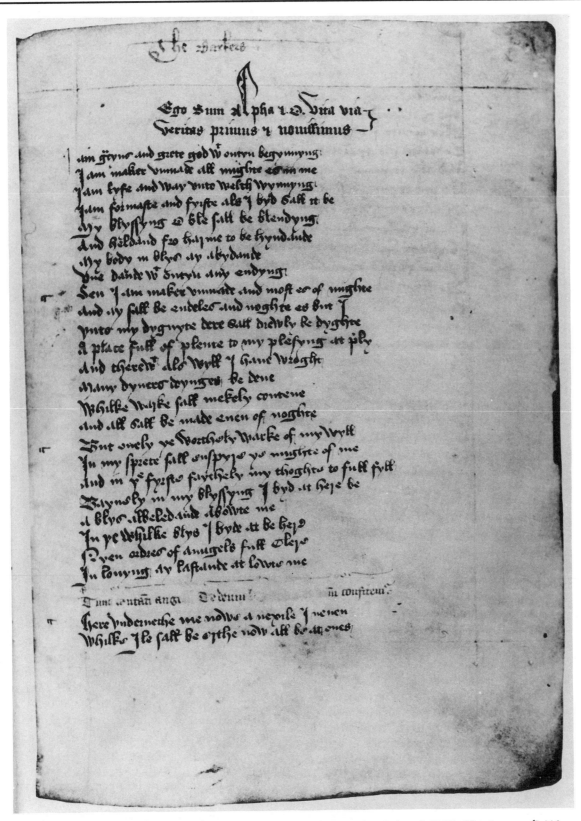

First page of the York Cycle in the only extant manuscript, a scribal transcription from the latter half of the fifteenth century (British Library MS. Add. 35290)

the cross, he delivers a moving speech filled with love and a hope that man will repent:

> Thou man that amiss here has meant,
> To me tent entirely now take
> On the rood am I ragged and rent,
> Thou sinful of soul, for thy sake.
> For thy misdeed amends will I make;
> I bide here, my back to bend low.
> This woe for thy trespass I take
> Who could thee more kindliness show
>   Than I?
> Thus for thy good
> I shed my blood.
> Man, mend thy mood
> For full bitter thy bliss must I buy.

By watching forty-eight plays depicting the entire history of humankind, average villagers would be able to see God's movement through time, but more specifically, they would come to understand their role in God's overall plan for the world. Consequently, it was the hope of the playwright that an audience would feel a part of the grand design and would realize the spiritual significance of their descent from the first humans, Adam and Eve. But most important, by concluding the series of plays with a drama on the Last Judgment, the York Cycle would force spectators to come to terms with their own salvation. Medieval onlookers could not walk away from this production without thinking about their own relationships to God.

The cycle's didactic power was firmly embedded in a typological framework where figures or events of the Old Testament prefigured parallel episodes in the New Testament. For example, a medieval audience nurtured by the Roman Catholic church would certainly understand that the Flood of the Old Testament foreshadowed the Last Judgment of the New Testament or that Abraham's near sacrifice of Isaac was a mere prelude to God the Father's sacrifice of his Son, Jesus, on the cross, and that Jonah's three days inside the great fish prefigured Jesus' three days within the tomb before his Resurrection. During the York drama called *The Flood* this typology is apparent as Noah (Noye) reminds the audience that God's destruction of earth by water will be followed by his destruction of the world by fire in the end times. In a dialogue with his second son, we hear Noah speak of the Doomsday yet to come:

2 SON	Sir, now since God our sovereign sire
	Has set his sign thus in certain,
	Then may we wit this world's empire
	Shall evermore last, for that is plain.

NOYE	Nay, son; that shall we not desire,
	For if we do we work in vain;
	For it shall once be waste with fire,
	And never work to world again.

In fact, the play entitled *Abraham and Isaac* emphasizes the typological significance of the episode by portraying Isaac not as a boy but as a man in his early thirties — an age very close to that of Christ when he was crucified. This inclusion of Old and New Testament parallels gives the cycle a distinct cohesiveness. The thread of typology runs through enough of the plays to provide a unity for the forty-eight-play group as a whole.

The production of the York Cycle was not controlled by the church at all. In fact, it was York's city government that kept the Register and made sure that all the events on feast day went smoothly. But the production of specific plays was left in the hands of the city's fifty or so craft guilds. Each guild practiced a certain trade such as carpentry, tailoring, or shipbuilding, and they existed as a kind of fraternity. The Glovers, for example, lived in close proximity to each other, attended the same church, had the same patron saint, and, of course, performed the same trade. The guilds operated in this fashion and became so powerful that members made up York's city government. During the Middle Ages the guilds were sometimes called mysteries, a term which referenced the skills of a given craftsman and that carried over many years later to the plays themselves. Hence the York Cycle is sometimes referred to as the York Mystery Cycle.

Each guild was assigned a play by the city's administrators, but how these officials decided which play went to which guild is not fully known. Of course, in some instances, one can speculate that certain guilds were allowed to produce certain plays because the drama, in some way, reflected that guild's profession. For example, the Shipwrights were responsible for performing *The Building of the Ark,* the Bakers were allowed to stage *The Last Supper,* the Goldsmiths put on *The Magi,* and the Fishers and Mariners teamed up to produce *The Flood.* But on occasion a guild might be assigned a play because it had the wealth and power to sway the minds of city officials. The Barkers or Tanners guild, perhaps, used its influence to secure the right to perform the first play of the cycle, *The Fall of the Angels.* Certainly this was a reflection of the Barkers' prestige to be allowed to start the feast day's activities. Another very wealthy guild in York, the Mercers, probably exerted its influence in order to produce *The Last Judgment,* the cycle's climactic ending.

Producing a play was very expensive; sometimes it became a financial burden. But each craft guild took pride in its assigned play and would stage it to the best of its ability. The responsibility for managing the finances needed for production was given to each guild's elected pageant masters, who collected money from the other guild members and who spent it on necessary items such as costumes or on the maintenance and storage of their pageant wagon – the movable stage upon which the play was performed.

The guilds maintained high standards by hiring professional actors for the more demanding roles and custom building their pageant wagons in order to accommodate the action of their specific play. However, most of the roles were played by the guild members themselves, and because the entire responsibility of production was placed in the hands of the common man, this unique situation made the York Cycle a source of great civic pride. Each guild not only felt a spiritual obligation to produce the best play possible but also felt a civic one.

Most guilds performed the same plays year after year, and this situation caused the organizations to develop a profound sense of ownership concerning their particular dramas. In most cases, a guild would stop producing a play only if it no longer had the finances to cover production. In such a case the play probably would not have been discarded but would have been reassigned to a more financially stable guild.

The production of these plays was a logistic feat. A. M. Kinghorn cites an account from the *Collectanea Bradfordiana,* which claims that in 1415 there were fifty-four plays performed during the feast of Corpus Christi. At least seven hundred actors and extras were required to perform the cycle, and the total number of people helping with the plays and the other festivities amounted to more than one thousand. The feast day was a grand affair with thousands of people present to watch the various productions and to immerse themselves in an atmosphere of celebration.

The presentation of the plays took the form of a single-file procession through the streets of York. There was a set route to be followed, and on it there were twelve different stations where each guild would stop and perform its particular play. Consequently, each drama was acted twelve times during the course of the day, creating an exhausting schedule. The city's administrators were faced with the task of cramming all the plays into the length of one

day. Their solution was to start the first drama at 4:30 A.M. with the last play ending about twenty hours later, when the Mercers performed *The Last Judgment* in the Pavement – the twelfth and final stop.

To make their job easier, the guilds did not walk with their props and sets to each of the twelve performance stations. Instead, they built curious contraptions called pageant wagons on which their plays were acted. To say that these movable stages were merely wagonlike platforms on wheels would not be altogether true. Even though information is sparse on the various aspects of pageant wagons, it is known that they were custom-built to accommodate the guilds' particular dramas and that they were, in some instances, multileveled stages where God could be seen enthroned in heaven or Satan seen descending into the fiery mouth of hell. The pageant wagons had curtains used on the stage and also employed as a kind of bunting around the playing area in order to hide the wheels of the wagon. Moreover, these moving theaters were not pulled by horses but were moved to each and every station by a team of able-bodied men.

The proper use of costuming and music in these dramas was considered an important part of a successful production. In fact, medieval stained glass showing assortments of biblical characters provides a quick and easy visual aid when trying to find out how the York players were dressed. For example, the windows of York Minster Cathedral depict biblical figures in various kinds of attire, helping scholars a great deal in determining cycle costumery. A medieval audience could easily relate to the minor characters of a given drama because these players were usually dressed in the fashion of the day. However, some play directors used certain types of costumes to distance the audience from the supernatural characters such as God and Satan. Consequently, these two figures, along with angels and demons, wore masks and wigs to accentuate their visual appearance onstage. The mask, with its fixed expression, emphasized the otherworldliness of these beings. Moreover, in an age where all the parts for women were played by men, wigs were often used to create a more believable female persona.

With respect to music, the dominant practice was to sing the songs a cappella. Music helped to create certain moods during the play's performance, and many songs were sung in praise of God's awesome power and in appreciation for his divine mercy. In the York play entitled *Moses and Pharaoh,* God empowers Moses to part the Red Sea in order for the Israelites to escape the wrath of Pharaoh and his army (Exodus 14). In appreciation for God's protection and guidance, the First Jew in the drama announces that they will all sing praises to God, their deliverer. This man says at the play's end, "Now are we won from woe, / And saved out of the sea. / Cantemus domino: / To God a song sing we." A song follows this declaration, and the drama ends on a joyful note of praise.

As an audible symbol, music was employed to reveal the harmony among the inhabitants of heaven, for it is God's ordered world, not Satan's hell, that is filled with the beauty of song. When God entered or exited the stage area, he would often be surrounded by beautiful music. It seems as though these two entities were inseparable.

On a bright, clear summer day in fifteenth-century England, it would have been exciting to see the York Cycle performed in all its splendor. The feasting, the streets and alleyways packed with people, and the plays would have stressed the celebration of Corpus Christi as an important day in the life of the church. Troops of lay actors would have exuded pride not only in their particular productions but also in their professions and city. The Feast of Corpus Christi was a day when people could reexamine their relationship with God and come to understand their part in the grand scheme of the universe. But also this day of activity provided the city of York with the opportunity to show off its great wealth. In a sense, it is as if the city used the Corpus Christi celebration to boast its prosperity to the surrounding towns of northern England.

In the sixteenth century the York Cycle, with its Catholic leanings, began to die at the hands of the Reformation. Zealous Protestant reformers detested the idea of dramas linked to the notion of transubstantiation, and York plays dealing with the Virgin Mary (*The Death of the Virgin, The Funeral of the Virgin, The Assumption of the Virgin,* and *The Coronation of the Virgin*) further aroused the anger of Protestants, who considered her prominent place within the Catholic church a form of idolatry. To these Reformers the cycle plays did not elevate but demeaned the beauty and the sanctity of scriptural events. Protestant extremists also fought against the fact that men were playing women's roles – a situation that was perverse in their eyes. By the close of the sixteenth century the lavish procession of the York Cycle and the plays that had been seen by so many thousands of people were quietly put to rest. In fact, after 1569 the cycle was not performed again for almost four centuries.

In the second half of the twentieth century the York Cycle has been revived. There was a production of the cycle in 1951 for the Festival of Britain, and subsequent performances were staged in Leeds in 1975 and in Toronto in 1977. Also, every three years or so, the city of York stages the cycle in the open courtyard of Saint Mary's Abbey. These revivals have proved popular and have helped develop the public's appreciation for this grand contribution to the dramatic arts. Audiences can still learn from and be entertained by these plays, for they teach about biblical history and explore the timeless theme of humanity's relationship to God.

References:

Richard Beadle, "The Origins of Abraham's Preamble in the York Play of *Abraham and Isaac,*" *Yearbook of English Studies,* 11 (1981): 178–187;

Beadle, "The Shipwrights' Craft," in *Aspects of Early English Drama,* edited by Paula Neuss (Totowa, N. J.: Barnes & Noble, 1983), pp. 50–61;

Beadle, "The York Cycle: Texts, Performances, and the Bases for Critical Enquiry," in *Medieval Literature: Texts and Interpretation,* edited by Tim W. MacHan (Binghamton, N.Y.: State University of New York Press, 1991), pp. 105–119;

Richard J. Collier, *Poetry and Drama in the York Corpus Christi Play* (Hamden, Conn.: Archon, 1978);

Hardin Craig, *English Religious Drama of the Middle Ages* (Oxford: Clarendon Press, 1955), pp. 199–238;

Clifford Davidson, *From Creation to Doom: The York Cycle of Mystery Plays* (New York: AMS Press, 1984);

Peter Holding, "Stagecraft in the York Cycle," *Theatre Notebook,* 34, no. 2 (1980): 51–60;

Richard L. Homan, "Ritual Aspects of the York Cycle," *Theatre Journal,* 33 (October 1981): 303–315;

R. D. S. Jack, *Patterns of Divine Comedy: A Study of Mediaeval English Drama* (Cambridge: Brewer, 1989);

Alexandra F. Johnston, "The York Cycle and the Chester Cycle: What do the records tell us?," in *Editing Early English Drama: Special Problems and New Directions,* edited by A. F. Johnson (New York: AMS Press, 1987), pp. 121–143;

A. M. Kinghorn, *Mediaeval Drama* (London: Evans, 1968), pp. 61–87;

V. A. Kolve, *The Play Called Corpus Christi* (Stanford, Cal.: Stanford University Press, 1966);

D. Levey, " 'Nowe is Fulfillid all my For-Thoght': A Study of Comedy, Satire, and Didacticism in the York Cycle," *English Studies in Africa,* 24, no. 2 (1981): 83–94;

Peter Meredith, "John Clerke's Hand in the York Register," *Leeds Studies in English,* 12 (1981): 245–271;

Richard Rastall, "Music in the Cycle Plays," in *Contexts for Early English Drama,* edited by Marianne G. Briscoe and John C. Coldewey (Bloomington: Indiana University Press, 1989), pp. 192–218;

Martin Stevens, "The York Cycle: City as Stage," in *Four Middle English Mystery Cycles: Textual, Contextual, and Critical Interpretations* (Princeton: Princeton University Press, 1987), pp. 17–87;

Sarah Sutherland, " 'Not or I see more neede': The Wife of Noah in the Chester, York, and Towneley Cycles," in *Shakespeare and Dramatic Tradition: Essays in Honor of S. F. Johnson,* edited by W. R. Elton and William B. Long (Newark: University of Delaware Press, 1989), pp. 181–193;

Meg Twycross, " 'Apparell comlye,' " in *Aspects of Early English Drama,* edited by Neuss (Totowa, N.J.: Barnes & Noble, 1983), pp. 30–49;

Arnold Williams, *The Drama of Medieval England* (East Lansing: Michigan State University Press, 1961);

Paul Willis, "The Weight of Sin in the York *Crucifixio*," *Leeds Studies in English,* 15 (1984): 109–116;

Rosemary Woolf, *The English Mystery Plays* (Berkeley: University of California Press, 1972).

The English Language: 410 to 1500

Bruce L. Pearson
University of South Carolina

English was not the original language of the British Isles. The first inhabitants of England were Stone Age people who had migrated from the mainland, probably taking advantage of a lowered sea level during the Ice Age. They were established on the islands now known as Great Britain more than ten thousand years ago and of course brought with them their language, but we have no idea what that language was or what they called themselves. Later arrivals from the Continent in the years from 8000 to 3000 B.C. brought with them domesticated cattle and sheep, pottery making, and simple agriculture. Even if these people were related to the first inhabitants, the passage of time without contact would have made the languages of the two groups mutually unintelligible. The second wave of migration must therefore represent a second language that presumably displaced the first.

Still-later arrivals, about 2000 B.C., brought weaving and began making bronze tools. These people built Stonehenge and similar monuments. Their identity also is unknown – as is the language they spoke. It is safe to suppose, whatever their affinity to the earlier arrivals, that their language represented something new and unintelligible – a third major language to reach the islands. By about 700 B.C. various Celtic tribes from northwestern Europe began invading the island. The indigenous population was dominated and completely absorbed, making the Celts – the fourth known population to settle the island – the first about whose language we know anything. The Gaels were probably the first Celtic tribe to arrive, and they, in turn, were pushed on to Scotland and Ireland by the Britons, another Celtic tribe that arrived later and claimed the parts of Great Britain now known as England and Wales. The Britons were familiar with iron and maintained trade with their kinsmen on the mainland – the Gauls.

Toward the middle of the first century B.C. the Gauls, living in what is now France, were subdued by Julius Caesar, who then led his legions on a brief tour across the Channel to reconnoiter Britain. Why he undertook this expedition is unclear. Perhaps he feared the Britons would aid the Gauls in rebelling against Roman rule. Possibly he had heard exaggerated tales of mineral wealth. At any rate, he returned to Britain the following year, traveled as far as the Thames, overcame a Celtic army, exacted promises of tribute – which was never paid – and sailed back to Gaul. Caesar's foray into Britain did not result in permanent conquest. It was left to the emperor Claudius in 43 A.D. to establish firm control of Britain and incorporate it into the Roman Empire.

Roman control brought economic benefits to the island, along with an influx of Latin-speaking administrators and merchants. But Latin, probably the fifth major language to be spoken in the British Isles, was largely confined to the cities. Some of the Celts must have learned enough Latin to deal with Roman officials, but in the villages and countryside the Celtic dialects remained in popular use. To safeguard their British colony the Romans relied chiefly on the natural barrier of the sea. In 122 the emperor Hadrian had a seventy-mile wall built across the island "to divide the barbarians from the Romans." A second wall, farther north, where the island is only thirty miles across, was built in 142 on orders from the emperor Antoninus. For nearly 300 years these walls were adequate protection against the Celtic tribes to the north, a people known to the Romans as Picts – painted warriors whose homeland was too desolate to tempt the Roman impulse to colonize.

By the year 410 Rome needed its legions on the mainland to resist incursions by restless Germanic tribes who were now facing pressures from hostile groups migrating westward from eastern Europe and Asia. Rome's withdrawal from Britain left the island in Celtic hands, but the Celts had lived under Roman protection for nearly four hundred years and now found themselves no match for the Picts, who came swarming over the walls with their eyes on the prosperous villages and fertile fields to the south. To protect themselves, the Celts sought help from Germanic tribes on the Continent, already known to them because these tribes had made sporadic raids on Britain even before the Roman withdrawal.

These tribes – the Jutes, Angles, and Saxons – were only too happy to accept an invitation to help the Britons restore order. Their idea of restoring order,

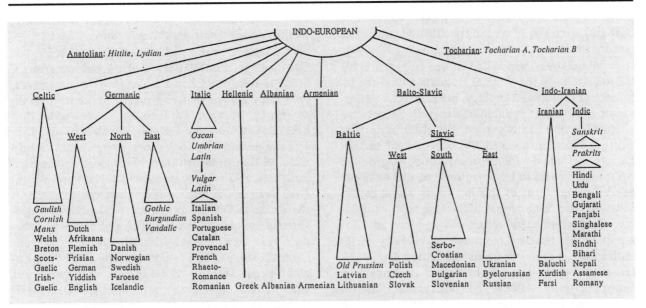

Figure 1. The Major Indo-European Languages. *The chart shows the the ten major branches of the Indo-European language family, with names of the branches underlined. Extinct languages are printed in italic type; those still being spoken are printed in roman type. Lines indicate presumed descent from an earlier language, and triangles are used where several languages have developed from an earlier language. The left-to-right placement of languages corresponds roughly to the distribution of the languages from west to east. Lesser-known modern languages, especially those sometimes regarded as dialects of better-known languages with established literary traditions, are omitted. Also omitted are three sparsely documented ancient languages — Illyrian, Thracian, and Phrygian — whose exact positions in the family are uncertain.*

however, was to take over the land for themselves. According to later chronicles, the Jutes began their influx in 449, settling south of the Thames in what is now Kent. The Saxons were the next to arrive, staking claim to the territories around London. The Angles, apparently the last to arrive, settled along the coast north of London in the region still known as East Anglia. This last group eventually gave their name to both the land and the language. Although 449 is the traditional migration date given by the Venerable Bede in his *Historia ecclesiastica gentis Anglorum* (*Ecclesiastical History of the English People,* completed in 731), it seems likely that invasion and settlement began almost as soon as the Romans withdrew.

The Jutes, Angles, and Saxons came from adjacent parts of Denmark and northern Germany and spoke closely related Germanic dialects. Their language had diverged from Celtic, Latin, and Greek some two thousand years earlier and from Balto-Slavic and Indo-Iranian earlier still. These languages, together with Armenian and Albanian and the now-extinct Tocharian and Hittite, had all sprung from an ancestral language spoken in eastern Europe or west-central Asia possibly in the fifth millennium B.C. (see figure 1). The ancestral language, known to us as Indo-European, must have had still-earlier forerunners, but it is impossible to know anything about these

predecessors with any degree of certainty. Some scholars have suggested a relationship between Indo-European and the languages that were ancestral to the Finno-Ugric, Semitic, or Turko-Altaic families, but these suggestions are speculative and far from established fact.

It is known that the original Indo-Europeans were successful farmers and herders in their own homeland, possibly located in eastern Europe. Their numbers increased, and tribal groups wandered off in different directions, eventually colonizing most of the vast territory between India and northwestern Europe. In the process they either displaced or absorbed the indigenous populations in the areas they occupied, leaving only scattered remnant languages such as Finno-Ugric, Basque, and the now-extinct Etruscan. With the passage of time the various Indo-European groups lost touch with each other, and what had begun as related dialects evolved into mutually unintelligible languages. Although Sanskrit, Greek, and Latin preserved many features of the original language with only slight modifications, in the case of Germanic the changes, perhaps influenced by contact with indigenous populations, were more far-reaching.

Most notable was a shift in the pronunciation of major classes of consonants, which had the effect of preserving the original phonological system while changing each sound within the affected categories (see figure 2).

Word stress, which had shifted from one syllable to another in the original language under the influence of inflectional endings, became fixed in Germanic on the first syllable of the root. Before this change became firmly settled, the older pattern of shifting stress influenced the outcome of certain changes in consonant pronunciation to produce what would seem to be "irregular" results once the conditioning factor of shifting stress disappeared. Likewise, the original grammatical system with numerous categories of tense was reduced in Germanic to two tenses. One tense, specifically designating past, was marked by a distinctive dental suffix, either -d or -t, while the other, an unmarked "nonpast" tense, was used for both present and future. Categories such as perfective and progressive were eliminated from the system at this stage. Perhaps most distinctive — and most indicative of contact with an unknown indigenous population — was the emergence of numerous words common to the Germanic languages but lacking cognates in other Indo-European languages. Such was the language carried to Britain by the Jutes, Angles, and Saxons.

Although writing had been known in the Middle East and Mediterranean for some three thousand years by the time the Germanic invaders reached Britain, the practice had not been widely adopted among Germanic people. Consequently, our knowledge of common Germanic as it must have existed before the various tribes went their separate ways depends entirely on inferences drawn from a comparison of shared features documented in the later languages. The earliest extant manuscript in a Germanic language is a fourth-century translation of the Bible into Gothic. In Britain itself the written record does not begin until after 597, when missionaries from Rome arrived to introduce Christianity. Christianity was already established in Ireland, and, indeed, Irish missionaries had preceded those from Rome in carrying the gospel to England and eventually joined forces with them. Within the next hundred years monasteries had sprung up throughout England, and British learning was gaining a reputation on the continent.

By the time Roman missionaries made their appearance, the Germanic tribes had become dominant throughout what is now England and spoke of themselves as English. The Celtic people they encountered had been faced with unpleasant choices since the arrival of the English. They could fight for their lands and risk losing life as well as property,

they could accept the dominance of the newcomers, or they could flee to outlying regions.

Many Britons did in fact flee to Wales or Cornwall to join friendly Celtic-speaking groups. Some crossed the Channel, carrying their language, later known as Breton, to Brittany in the western tip of France, where it is still spoken. In the lands that became Scotland and Ireland, the Celtic languages and the people who spoke them were so sufficiently isolated that pressure from the ascendant English left them relatively unmolested for several centuries. Despite the efforts of English kings to extend their rule to Scotland, the Scots maintained a precarious independence until the end of the Elizabethan era. Ties between Ireland and England were much looser, and it was not until the 1500s that England began serious efforts to control the Emerald Isle. In Scotland, and to a somewhat lesser extent in Ireland, the English language has almost completely displaced the Celtic dialects.

The idea that everyone in a society might aspire to literacy is a modern notion fueled by a technology that has made printing and the mass production of books possible, created the need for a literate work force, and generated enough wealth to make widespread education possible. In Anglo-Saxon England, only those in the service of the church needed to be literate. Their needs were met by Latin translations of the Scriptures and other church-related documents. Since to be literate was to read and write Latin, it followed that even much of the writing done by English monks for the use of other English monks was in Latin.

When the Scriptures were eventually translated into Old English, the scribes simply took the Latin alphabet, using the familiar letters to represent the English counterparts of Latin sounds. Thus the Old English vowels *i, e, a, o,* and *u* have the same phonetic value associated with these letters in Latin — or modern descendants of Latin such as Spanish. The scribes contrived an additional letter *æ,* called "ash," to represent the vowel sound contained in the name of the letter, a sound that did not occur in Latin. They used *y* to represent a vowel similar to *i* but with the lip rounding associated with *u.* This was a distinctive sound in Old English — for example, in *cyng* (king), although it is clear from the modern form of the word that the sound eventually merged with *i.* Diphthongs were spelled *ea* and *oa.* Each vowel in English could be either long or short in duration, with no appreciable change in quality. Modern editors mark long vowels with a macron, but the original manuscripts depended on the reader's understanding of the language and used no

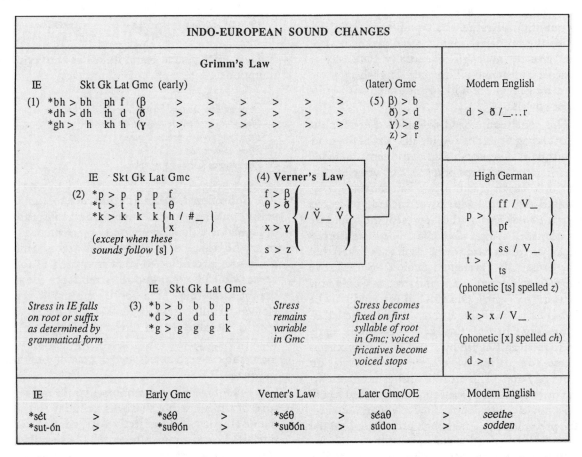

IE		Early Gmc		Verner's Law		Later Gmc/OE		Modern English
*sét	>	*séθ	>	*séθ	>	séaθ	>	seethe
*sut-ón	>	*suθón	>	*suðón	>	súdon	>	sodden

Figure 2. Indo-European Sound Changes. *The chart shows a widely accepted analysis of the principal sound changes that set the Germanic languages apart from the other Indo-European languages. The left-to-right dimension represents the passage of time. In Step 1 of the sound changes described by Jacob Grimm (hence "Grimm's Law"), IE *bh, *dh, *gh retain most of their complexity in the classical languages (Sanskrit, Greek, Latin) but ultimately become b, d, g in the Germanic languages (Step 5). The parenthesized intermediate stage was not identified by Grimm although it must be posited to account for "irregular" developments noted by Grimm. (In this intermediate stage the IE sounds become Gmc voiced fricatives *ß, *ð, *γ.) In Step 2, IE *p, *t, become Gmc f, θ while IE *k becomes h in initial position and x elsewhere. In Step 3, IE *b, *d, *g become Gmc p, t, k. The changes must have taken place in this order; reversal of Steps 1–3 would have merged all distinctions.*

In Step 4, the sound changes described by Karl Verner (hence "Verner's Law") operate to modify the outcome of Grimm's Law by changing voiceless fricatives in Germanic (f, θ, x, s) to voiced fricatives (ß, ð, γ, z) under certain circumstances, for example, when following an unstressed vowel and preceding a stressed vowel. Note that stress in Indo-European (and early Germanic as well as the classical languages) could fall on either the root or a suffix depending on the grammatical form of the word in question. Accordingly, related forms of the same word might have either a voiceless or voiced fricative as a consequence of Verner's Law. Voiced fricatives resulting from Verner's Law now merge with the identical voiced fricatives that must be posited as the intermediate stage between Steps 1 and 5. These sounds (ß, ð, γ) then become voiced stops b, d, g in Step 5 (the final part of Grimm's Law), while z becomes s.

As Step 5 was taking place, word stress in Germanic became fixed on the first syllable of the root. Thus the environment that had conditioned Verner's Law was effectively concealed. The history of English seethe/sodden is traced at the bottom of the chart to show the operation of Verner's Law. Other Old English words with similar variation as a result of Verner's Law have since been lost from the vocabulary.

Subsequent changes occurred in both English and High German — the "standard" dialect spoken in the highland region as opposed to the coastal lowland German dialects, which continue to bear a closer resemblance to English. Thus Old English d became ð in certain words preceding r. The changes were more sweeping in German, where p became ff following a vowel and pf elsewhere. Similarly, t became ss after a vowel and ts elsewhere; k became x after a vowel; and d became t in all environments. As a result of these sound changes, Old English fæder becomes father, while the corresponding German word is Vater (where v is phonetically f and nouns are customarily capitalized). Other English/German word pairs illustrating these sound changes are pepper/Pfeffer, street/Strasse, tide/Zeit and book/Buch.

distinguishing marks. Even though length was originally quantitative rather than qualitative, comparison with the modern vowel system makes it clear that differences of length eventually gave way to qualitative differences. Thus Old English *sittan* (to sit) and *mis* (mice) are now pronounced with quite different vowels.

The consonants of Old English were for the most part recognizable as sounds still part of the modern consonant inventory. The consonants included voiceless and voiced stops *p, t, k; b, d, g;* voiceless fricatives *f, s, h;* nasals *m* and *n;* and continuants *l, r, w.* The sound associated with *k* was spelled *c* as in *corn* (grain), but *c* was also used to represent the sound we would now spell *ch* as in *cild* (child). The letter *g* represented the so-called hard sound, as in *græs* (grass), but in some contexts it represented a voiced velar fricative as in *sagu* (saw, saying) or a sound that we would now spell *y* as in *gear* (year). Old English *sc* would now be spelled *sh* as in *fisc* (fish), and *cg* would be spelled either *j* or *dge* as in *brycg* (bridge). The sounds represented in modern English by *v* and *z* did not occur as distinctive sounds but were merely pronunciation variants of *f* and *s* when these sounds occurred between vowels. Similarly, the sound now spelled *ng* did not exist as a distinctive unit; final *g* was pronounced, and the preceding nasal (although pronounced *ng*) did not acquire its distinctive status until the *g* that followed it was lost in the Middle English period. The sound now spelled *th* had no counterpart in Latin, and scribes used either *ð* (called "eth," or "edh," a manuscript form of *d* with a cross through the ascender) or *þ*, a letter borrowed from the runic alphabet and known as "thorn." The *th* spelling, used occasionally in the Old English period, eventually became standard after the Norman Conquest.

In grammatical structure the language depended as much on inflectional endings (morphology) as it did on word order (syntax). Even though the most common word order within the sentence was subject-verb-object, it was always possible to vary this order because each noun was marked for case. If the subject happened to follow the verb or if the object happened to precede the verb, an inflectional ending was always present to specify the noun's grammatical role. Only as inflectional endings became indistinct and finally disappeared altogether after the Norman Conquest did speakers of the language come to depend on word order itself as the primary signaling device. Even today we occasionally invert subject and verb, as the preceding sentence demonstrates. A simple sentence in Old English about a man killing a white bear might take the familiar subject-verb-object order:

Se	mann	slog ðone	hwitan	beran.
the-NOM	*man*-NOM	*slew* *the*-ACC	*white*-ACC	bear-ACC

But the arrangement could follow several other permutations:

Se mann ðone hwitan beran slog.
Slog se mann ðone hwitan beran.
Slog ðone hwitan beran se mann.
Ðone hwitan beran se mann slog.
Ðone hwitan beran slog se mann.

The inflectional suffix (or absence of any overt suffix) attached to each noun clearly indicated the grammatical role of the noun in the sentence. Moreover, the article or adjective that accompanied the noun was also inflected (that is, varied in form) to agree with the noun and thus reinforce the noun's grammatical role. As a result, the major sentence elements could occur in almost any order. Poetry tended to take greater liberties with word order than prose, but even in prose, variation in the common subject-verb-object order was by no means unusual.

The foregoing examples also illustrate a feature of the adjective that was peculiar to the Germanic languages. An adjective preceded by the definite article or demonstrative took the so-called weak form, as in the above sentences. An adjective that stood alone assumed a strong form:

Se	mann	slog	hwitne	beran.
the-NOM	*man*-NOM	*slew*	*(a) white*-ACC	bear-ACC

Adjectives therefore had separate sets of endings to distinguish strong and weak declensions and to agree with the gender of the accompanying noun (see figure 3).

Nouns were divided into three arbitrary gender classes — masculine, feminine, and neuter — although these classes did not correspond to what we now consider natural gender. Thus *mann* (man) was masculine, but so also was *wifman* (woman) because it was a compound containing a masculine root as its final element. Similarly, *cild* (child) was grammatically neuter regardless of the gender of the child referred to, and *glof* (glove) was arbitrarily feminine. Within each class there were subclasses based on phonological characteristics as well. Although each class of words had many different inflectional suffixes, there was a certain amount of overlap among classes, suggesting that already the forms were not as functionally distinct as they might once have been.

		Strong Declension			Weak Declension		
		masc.	*fem.*	*neut.*	*masc.*	*fem.*	*neut.*
Sg.	Nom.	hwit	hwit(u)	hwit	hwita	hwite	hwite
	Acc.	hwitne	hwite	hwit	hwitan	hwitan	hwite
	Gen.	hwites	hwitre	hwites	hwitan	hwitan	hwitan
	Dat.	hwitum	hwitre	hwitum	hwitan	hwitan	hwitan
	Inst.	hwite	hwitre	hwite	hwitan	hwitan	hwitan
Pl.	Nom./Acc.	hwite	hwita[1]	hwit	hwitan	hwitan	hwitan
	Gen.	hwitra	hwitra	hwitra	hwitra[2]	hwitra[2]	hwitra[2]
	Dat.	hwitum	hwitum	hwitum	hwitum	hwitum	hwitum

[1]or *hwite*   [2]or *hwitena*

Figure 3. Strong and weak declension for the Old English adjective hwit, *"white"*

Modern English has stripped the inflectional apparatus of the noun to the bare essentials. Arbitrary gender has been replaced by natural gender, but this is evident only when a noun is replaced by a pronoun and not from the form of the noun itself. We have an unmarked singular form and a plural marked by the addition of *-s*. This suffix is the modern development of the *-as* ending that marked nominative and accusative plural for one class of Old English masculine nouns, but it has displaced other Old English plural suffixes and is the only form that remains productive in modern English. Nouns that preserve other Old English plural formations such as vowel mutation (*foot/feet*) seem "irregular" by modern standards. Mutated plurals, however, were once a productive class at a fairly early stage of Germanic:

	sing.	*pl.*	
(1)	gos	gos-i	*plural is formed by addition of suffix*
(2)	gos	ges-i	*anticipation of suffix causes umlaut (vowel mutation)*
(3)	goose	geese	*suffix is lost, leaving vowel change as only mark of plural*

Stage 3, although illustrated by modern English forms, is essentially the stage that had already been reached by Old English. The process is fairly natural when one considers that both *o* and *e* are mid vowels; *o* is back whereas *e* is front, and it is easy to slip from a back to front articulation as one prepares to pronounce the front vowel *i*. Even though the suffix that conditioned umlaut was lost during some stage of early Germanic, the process of umlaut

itself remains productive in modern German: for example, *Ball/Bälle* (ball/balls), where *ä* is the orthographic representation of a front vowel corresponding to the back vowel *a*.

The other "irregular" plural to survive into modern English is the *-en* ending of *brethren, oxen,* and *children*. This too was a common ending in Old English. In *brethren* it survives only in religious or fraternal usage, having lost out to the regular formation *brothers* in everyday usage. *Oxen* has survived into the twentieth century because oxen were being used as draft animals into the early years of the century. The term is now little used by an increasingly urban population, and the niche formerly occupied by the animal itself has been taken over by mechanized tractors. Consequently, oxen are likely to be mentioned now only with reference to things of the past, and when the term comes up at all it is not unusual to hear people speak of "oxes." The term *children* persists because it is part of the everyday vocabulary, and it has never become unfamiliar enough that anyone could be unsure of the standard form. The word actually belonged to a small class of Old English nouns that formed their nominative/accusative plural by adding *-ru: child/childru*. By Middle English times this formation had lost its plural force and, since the *-en* suffix was still productive, speakers began adding this suffix to the existing form to reinforce the notion of plurality. In the process the two vowels coalesced, but the modern word technically is a double plural: *child-r(u)-en*.

The only other noun inflections in modern English are the possessive (genitive) singular marked by *-'s* and the genitive plural marked by *-s'*.

The suffixes are graphically distinct although pronounced the same. Thus, in terms of pronunciation most nouns in modern English have only two forms: an unmarked singular and an inflected form with -s (although often pronounced like z) which marks plural as well as both possessive singular and possessive plural.

For nouns, modern English lacks distinct forms for different cases such as nominative (subject), dative (indirect object), or accusative (direct object). The language relies instead on word order or prepositions:

> *The director gave her assistant the assignment.*
> *The director gave the assignment to her assistant.*

For pronouns, however, a distinction between subject and object forms survives – although the object forms no longer maintain a distinction between dative and accusative:

> *He saw him* (ACC). *He gave him* (DAT) *the assignment.*

Even in Old English, first- and second-person pronouns were losing the distinction between dative and accusative. The distinction was at least partially preserved in third-person forms. A three-way gender distinction also prevailed in third-person singular forms, as in modern English. Third-person plurals, then as now, made no gender distinction:

Third Person	Masc.	Fem.	Neut.	Plural
Nominative	he	heo	hit	hie
Accusative	hine	hie	hit	hie
Dative	him	hiere	him	him
Genitive	his	hiere	his	hiera

Although dative and accusative are distinct if third-person categories of masculine, feminine, neuter, and plural are considered individually, similarities across categories are great enough that the resulting ambiguities eventually led to extensive restructuring, especially in the feminine, neuter, and plural forms.

First- and second-person pronouns have also undergone restructuring over the years. Old English, in addition to the expected singular and plural, had a dual category – 'we two,' 'you two.' Although not widely used even in Old English times, it provided a useful way to refer to married couples or battle companions.

First Person	Singular	Dual	Plural
Nominative	ic	wit	we
Accusative	me, mec	unc	us
Dative	me	unc	us
Genitive	min	uncer	ure

Second Person	Singular	Dual	Plural
Nominative	þu	git	ge
Accusative	þe, þec	inc	eow, eowic
Dative	þe	inc	eow
Genitive	þin	incer	eower

Already in Old English the contrast between dative and accusative was weakening as the distinctive forms for accusative *mec, þec, eowic* lost out to *me, þe, eow.* Other developments can easily be inferred from a comparison with modern forms. Nominative *ic* lost its final consonant and the vowel became lengthened, eventually developing into a diphthong. The genitive *min* was eventually differentiated into modern *mine/my.* In the second-person forms the distinction between singular and plural was lost for most English speakers in the seventeenth century, but the Old English singular forms are recognizable as forerunners of the *thou, thee, thine* that remained in use until that time. Plural *ge* is recognizable as nominative *ye,* familiar from the 1611 translation of the English Bible. This form eventually gave way to objective *you* and genitive *your,* which have taken over as the all-purpose pronouns for second person.

Old English verbs, although simpler in structure than the Indo-European verbal system from which they developed, were still complex by modern standards. The so-called strong verbs exhibited vowel alternation in different parts of their conjugation. Thus the present tense conjugation of *helpan* (to help) was *ic helpe* (I help), *þu hilpst* (you [sing.] help), *he hilþð* (he helps), *we, ge, hie helpað* (we, you [pl.], they help). The past-tense conjugation used different vowels: *ic healp* (I helped), *þu hulpe* (you [sing.] helped), *he healp* (he helped), *we, ge, hie hulpon* (we, you [pl.], they helped). The present participle took the form *helpende,* and the past participle was *geholpen.* In addition, there were separate forms for singular and plural in the imperative and for different categories of person in both the present and past subjunctive. The weak verbs exhibited no vowel alternation. Their endings were the same as those for the strong verbs. In the present tense these endings were attached directly to the invariable verb root, and in the past tense they followed the -t or -d suffix that denoted tense.

The earliest literature in Old English reflects the oral tradition of the preliterate era and commonly takes the form of poetry. Stories composed in metered lines involving rhyme or alliteration fit readily into one's memory and are easily retold.

Rhyme, however, was not a device of Old English poetry for a fairly simple reason. Stressed syllables were followed by several unstressed syllables in Old English, a pattern that severely limited the possibilities for end rhyme. Patterns of alliteration were preferred – a kind of initial rhyme involving only consonants and disregarding vowels. The other characteristic feature of Old English poetry was special diction – in particular, the use of kennings, metonymic compounds used to identify familiar objects in picturesque ways. Examples are *ban cofa* (bone den) for body and *hron rad* (whale road) for sea.

The prose of the Old English era, some of it translated from Latin and some composed in Old English, often shows traces of the same literary elegance seen in the poetry. As might be expected in an era when for all practical purposes to be literate was to be a monk, much of the prose was religious in nature. Portions of the Bible were translated into Old English (the first seven books of the Old Testament, some of Psalms, and the Gospels), *Ecclesiastical History of the English People,* as was Bede's originally written in Latin. Other surviving prose works include sermons, histories, some riddles, and a few fragments of fiction and fantasy, including *Apollonius of Tyre, Alexander's Letter to Aristotle,* and *Wonders of the East.*

Although Bede (673–735) is sometimes called the father of English learning, the bulk of Old English literature belongs to a somewhat later period, from the early 700s through the Norman Conquest of 1066. The golden age, in the judgment of many, came during the time of Alfred the Great, who reigned from 871 to 899. He unified England, bringing peace and stability to a turbulent era. Many of the monasteries, the principal centers of learning, had been sacked in Viking raids, and many of their treasures and manuscripts had been destroyed. Under Alfred the monasteries were rebuilt and learning revived. Much of the literature that has survived is, therefore, in Alfred's West Saxon dialect of Old English. This dialect is probably not the direct ancestor of the London dialect that eventually acquired prestige as the national standard, but the differences are small enough that the surviving manuscripts give a reasonably clear picture of what Old English was like.

We usually think of the Norman Conquest as marking the break between Old English and Middle English, but the historical events leading to the conquest go back to the Viking invasions of King Alfred's time and, arguably, were an outgrowth of events set in motion in the 400s by the arrival of the first Germanic tribes. By 787 the Angles, Saxons, and Jutes were firmly in control of the island nation and had exchanged their individual tribal identities for a new identity as Englishmen. Seven English kingdoms had been carved from the former Celtic lands of Britain. The relative prosperity of these kingdoms attracted the attention of other Germanic tribes from Denmark and what is now Norway, people known today as Vikings.

A raiding party of these people, called Danes by the English, appeared in Dorsetshire on the English Channel in 787. In 793 another party sacked the Holy Island Priory in Northumberland. In 865 a large Viking army landed in East Anglia and within years controlled most of northeast England. King Alfred assumed the throne of Wessex in 871. He defeated a Danish army that year and in 878, a century after the first Viking raid, subdued the Danes entirely. In the ensuing treaty the Danes agreed to adopt Christianity and to confine themselves to an area north and east of a line running roughly from London to modern Liverpool; Alfred controlled the remainder of England.

This arrangement left Alfred free to revive learning in his kingdom. The monasteries were rebuilt, and Alfred arranged for learned works to be translated from Latin into English. He established schools and instituted *The Anglo-Saxon Chronicle,* a historical record that was maintained in some parts of England for nearly a century after the Norman Conquest.

In the region under Danish control – known as the Danelaw – the Vikings rather easily came to terms with their English neighbors. Old English and Old Norse were similar enough, especially in their word roots, that speakers in the region may have hastened the decline of the Old English inflectional system by focusing their attention on roots and overlooking differences in the English and Norse inflectional endings.

In time numerous words of Old Norse origin found their way into northern English, and many of these worked their way southward and became a standard part of the language. The list includes common words such as *law, take, want,* and *window.* Most words pronounced with an initial *sk* come from the Vikings – *scathe, scrape, scrub, skill, sky,* and many others. The word *skirt* was introduced in the north and took its place alongside English *shirt,* with the two words eventually differentiated to refer to different parts of the common tunic type of garment. Even common words such as *sister* and *wagon* are of Viking origin, displacing the Old English cognate forms *sweostar* and *wain.* Place names ending in *-by, -thwaite* and *-thorpe* betray Old Norse origin, as do family names ending with *-son*.

In the year 991, after a century of tranquility, raiders from Norway and Denmark renewed their attacks on England, meeting much less resistance than they had in the days of King Alfred. Indeed, from 1016 to 1042 the English throne was occupied by Danish kings. The first of the Danish line, King Canute, ruled effectively for nineteen years; but his sons, who succeeded him, were less successful, and in 942 the royal council recalled Edward, the son of the last English king, from Normandy, where he had gone into exile as a child after his father's death. Normandy at this time was ruled by descendants of the same Vikings ("northmen") who had raided and eventually ruled England. These Normans, now thoroughly French in language and outlook, had ties through both kinship and marriage with the royal families of Denmark and England. It was not inconceivable that they could be claimants to the throne of either land, although even the most ambitious and determined of feudal lords would have difficulty imagining a set of circumstances auspicious enough to make good on such a claim.

Edward the Confessor, as he came to be known, was about forty years old when he was recalled to the English throne. In many ways a foreigner in his own land, he remained close to a handful of Norman friends who had come to England with him. For political guidance he depended at first on a trusted adviser, Godwin, who had previously served Canute, and later on Godwin's son Harold. When Edward died in January 1066 without an heir, the council that had brought him back from France elected his adviser Harold as king.

William, the duke of Normandy, was infuriated when the news reached him. A second cousin of Edward, William claimed he had been promised the support of both Edward and Harold as heir to the English throne. William appealed to the pope for the justice of his cause and, armed with the pope's blessing, set about raising an army and building a fleet to enforce his claim. Meanwhile, Harold Hardraade (whose understated nickname means "hard bargainer"), a Norseman who had tried for fifteen years to take the Danish throne by force, saw an opportunity to extend his claim to England as well. On 19 September Harold of England learned that Harold Hardraade had landed in the north of England. Gathering an army as he marched northward, Harold of England decisively defeated the Viking invaders on 25 September. At the victory feast a week later, word reached Harold that

William's forces had landed near Hastings, in the south of England, on 28 September.

Weary as he must have been, Harold was back in London on 5 October planning his response to this new invasion. The armies of William and Harold met at Hastings on 14 October. The battle lasted from early morning till sundown. By nightfall the English army had been devastated, and Harold, along with his two brothers and much of the English nobility, were dead. Among the English there was some talk of continued resistance, but it was only talk. William's army plundered the villages around London without hindrance while the royal council reconciled itself to the inevitable. On Christmas Day William was crowned king of England. It had been just 355 days since the death of Edward.

Some changes took place at once. The English earls who had survived the Battle of Hastings were deposed, and in their place French-speaking followers of William were installed. The laws were now made by the Normans and published in French. English-speaking peasants who were hauled into court found themselves outcasts in their own land.

Other developments took place more gradually. The Normans who took over the estates of deposed English earls still thought of themselves as French and had little need to learn English. But their tenants, servants, and nursemaids found themselves required to learn enough French to understand orders and communicate with their masters. The same was not true in dealing with the master's children, however. In time these children, born in England, grew up learning English from their nursemaids before they learned French from their parents. Gradually the Normans began to think of themselves as English rather than French. By the 1300s English began to replace French as the language of the courts, government proclamations, and Parliament.

But by the time English reemerged as an official language after more than two hundred years of underground status, it no longer bore any similarity to the language of Alfred the Great. The elaborate system of inflectional endings attached to nouns and verbs was reduced to little more than the present-day system, which retains few inflections beyond the *-ed* for past tense and *-s* or *-es* to mark plurality or possession in nouns.

The loss of the inflectional system no doubt was reinforced by changes in pronunciation. With a heavy stress on the first syllable of the root, all remaining syllables in a word tended to have reduced stress. Stressed vowels would naturally be pronounced distinctly, but unstressed vowels tended to be neutralized as ə (schwa), the sound that occurs in both syllables of the modern English word *above*. Some confusion in the spelling of inflectional endings was already evident in the late Old English period, and by the time literature began to reappear in English in the late 1300s almost all that remained of the earlier inflectional system for nouns was the *-es* ending used for both plural and possession. For a while the Old English nouns that had once had plural suffixes in *-a* or *-u* reduced these endings to *-e* (pronounced ə), but this remnant of the older system eventually yielded to the prevailing *-es* ending. The vowel of this ending was pronounced ə, and the *s* was voiceless. Eventually the vowel was dropped except after sibilants (the *s*-type sounds at the end of words such as *bush, rose, church, judge, wish,* and *mirage*). In the process the *s* frequently became voiced (that is, pronounced as *z*) although the spelling continues to represent the earlier voiceless pronunciation. Voicing came about in the surviving *-es* endings under the influence of the preceding vowel, which of course was voiced. In the *-s* variants, voicing occurred if the *s* was preceded by a voiced sound. Thus *hands* and *reasons* are pronounced with final *z* while *books* retains the voiceless sound. This development was complete by Sir Thomas Malory's time.

The past-tense suffix *-ed* continued to be pronounced as a separate syllable until at least the fifteenth century. By William Shakespeare's lifetime (1564–1616) omission of the vowel in this syllable was apparently optional except after words ending in *t* or *d*, and the Bard was able to exploit this option for metrical purposes.

With the blurring of vowel distinctions in unstressed final syllables and the eventual loss of these syllables, the distinction between strong and weak adjectives (see figure 3) gradually became blurred. The weak endings *-an* (singular) and *-um* (plural) initially fell together as *-en*. Then, with the loss of final *n*, the weak form survived for a time as an *-e* suffix with no effective distinction between singular and plural. Thus *min greete lord* (my great lord) displayed the weak ending, while the absence of a suffix in *greet lord* (a great lord) continued the strong form. But the *-e* suffix also marked plural for both strong and weak forms as in *greete lordes* (great lords [strong]) and *min greete lordes* (my great lords [weak]). By the time of Malory the unstressed final vowel had disappeared entirely, leaving modern English with adjectives that display no inflectional variation at all.

The final *n* that was part of the verbal infinitive survived through most of the Middle English period, although the vowel of the infinitive ending

was reduced from *a* to *e* (ə) . The infinitive ending thus became homophonous with the present-tense plural suffix *-en,* which was still in use in Midland and Southern speech at the time of Geoffrey Chaucer. By this time, however, the infinitive was accompanied by the preposition *to:*

> Than longen folk to goon on pilgrimages,
> and palmeres for to seken straunge strondes . . . [.]

In the above passage *longen,* the present-tense plural form, retains the final *n,* as do the infinitives *goon* and *seken*. Eventually these instances of final *n* disappeared entirely, leaving only the vowel *-e* (ə), which was unstressed and soon disappeared as well. As for infinitives, once the preposition *to* became redundantly associated with the infinitive, it was the infinitive suffix itself that came to be seen as redundant. This, combined with the weakened pronunciation of the final syllable, doomed the suffix to disappearance:

Old English – Middle English – Modern English
(ge)-fyllan >   fillen >to fillen >to fille >   to fill

The development of the infinitive illustrates other pronunciation changes that were taking place and, at the same time, shows how structural changes can have far-reaching consequences for the grammatical structure of a language. The Old English phoneme *y,* a high-front rounded vowel comparable to modern German *ü,* lost its distinctive lip rounding and became indistinguishable from *i,* a high-front vowel without rounding. Thus *fyllan* developed into *fillen* (ultimately *fill*). The merger of *y* and *i* resulted in a structural change, namely a reduction in the vowel inventory. Meanwhile, the loss of the infinitive ending, which began as a simple pronunciation change, led to structural change of a different kind. The infinitive structure itself was not lost, but it eventually was signaled in a different way as the preposition *to* replaced the earlier suffix.

The loss of the Old English verbal prefix *ge-* (pronounced [y], with *y* representing the familiar consonant sound of Modern English) also involves a combination of pronunciation and grammatical change. In Old English the prefix often accompanied the past participle and was used with verb roots either as an intensifier or without clearly discernible meaning. In Middle English it became *y-* or *i-* (pronounced [i]) and was gradually used less and less although it was still in use by Chaucer's contemporaries. Thus we find *yscolded* (scalded) in a version of *Ancrene Riwle* dating from about 1375, and such forms as *y-clept* (called) in Chaucer's *The*

Canterbury Tales, dating from the period circa 1375–1400 – although one suspects Chaucer uses the construction sometimes for its intentional quaintness and sometimes for its metrical qualities. The construction then fell into disuse. Spenser resurrected it in the *Faerie Queene* (1596) as a conscious archaism.

Other pronunciation changes in the Middle English period led to the simplification of initial consonant clusters *hl, hn,* and *hr.* Thus Old English *hnutu* became Middle English *nute* and Modern English *nut.* Similarly, Old English *hlæfdige* and *hrafn* became Middle English *ladi, raven* and Modern English *lady, raven* respectively. From the foregoing examples it is evident that medial clusters (as in *hlæfdige*) undergo simplification as well and that Old English *f* becomes differentiated as *f* and *v.* The initial cluster *hw* eventually followed the other *h* clusters, at least in some dialects (thus the similarity of pairs such as *what/watt, which/witch* for many speakers), but not all dialects have adopted this change even today. The initial *kn* cluster survived well into the 1500s, and the spelling *gh* represented a voiceless velar fricative as in modern German *Buch.* Thus Chaucer's spelling of *knight* was a fairly accurate phonetic representation of pronunciation in the fourteenth century.

The pronunciation changes that eventually separated English spelling from the phonetic values of the Latin alphabet did not come about until after 1500, but the stage for these sweeping changes was nonetheless set during the Middle English period. Old English vowels, as already noted, had contrasted on the feature of length. That is, each vowel in Old English could be either long or short in duration, with no appreciable change in quality. This dimension of contrast persisted in Middle English, but in certain phonetic environments vowels that had been short were now lengthened while other vowels that had been long in Old English were now shortened. Thus Old English *bindan* (to bind), *mild* (mild), and *yeldan* (to yield) developed long vowels in Middle English: *binden, milde,* and *yelden* (although spelling did not always indicate this). Early in the Modern English period the highest of these long vowels (such as *binden, milde*) began to diphthongize. A slightly different environment for lengthening is found in words such as Old English *bacan* (to bake). Its Middle English development as *baken* led speakers to syllabify the word *ba-ken* – as though the root were *ba-* instead of *bak-.* This led to lengthening of the vowel in the root syllable as *baken.* The lengthened vowel did not diphthongize in modern English but instead developed into a higher vowel, one that would

have been spelled *e* in Old English or Latin – or in the phonetic alphabet, which is based on Latin.

While some vowels were being lengthened, others that had been long in Old English were shortened. Thus *hidde* (hid) from Old English *hydan* (to hide) was shortened because the past tense inflection created a consonant cluster that shortened preceding vowels. In Middle English the qualitative difference between the long and short vowels in these related words would have been slight indeed. But early in the Modern English period speakers seemingly added greater tension to the long vowels as a redundant feature to enhance their contrast with the short vowels. This feature eventually led to the qualitative differences already noted. Long vowels were raised to a higher place of articulation, and vowels that were already articulated in the highest position became diphthongs.

As a result, the system that came to characterize Modern English is based on differences of vowel quality rather than vowel length, although vowels in most cases are still spelled as they were in Middle English. Thus *hide* and *hid,* cited above, are pronounced with different vowels today although the vowel in both forms is spelled the same. The plain form, unmarked for tense, developed from a Middle English long vowel inherited from Old English while the form marked as past developed from a Middle English vowel that was shortened under the conditions described above. The upheaval in English vowels, although it dates from the period after 1500, cannot be separated from the changes in vowel length that occurred during the Middle English period. This upheaval, commonly known as the Great Vowel Shift, has led to a large number of related words in Modern English that are now pronounced with different vowels although still spelled as though the same: *wise/wisdom, keep/kept, break/breakfast, Spain/Spanish, south/southern, move/motion, cone/conical,* and many others.

In the verbal system the most notable development was the loss of many strong verbs, those that marked past tense (and various other categories) by vowel change. Even in Old English the weak verbs had far outnumbered the strong verbs, and after the Norman Conquest virtually all verbs added to the lexicon entered the language as weak verbs, forming their past tense with the addition of *-ed* or its phonetic equivalent. Although some strong verbs like *sing/sang/sung* have survived into Modern English, these verbs are commonly regarded as "irregular." The vowel changes are now confined to the principal parts – that is, they distinguish past-tense forms and the past participle from present-tense

	Northern	Midland	Southern	meaning
	lok	loke	loken	to look
I	lok, loked	loke, lokede	loke, lokede	I look, looked
ðu	lokes, loked	lokest, lokedest	lokest, lokedest	thou lookest, looked
he/sche/hit	lokes, loked	lokeð, lokede	lokeð, lokede	he/she/it looks, looked
we	loke, loked	loken, lokeden	lokeð, lokeden	we look, looked
ye	loke, loked	loken, lokeden	lokeð, lokeden	you look, looked
hi	loke, loked	loken, lokeden	lokeð, lokeden	they look, looked

Figure 4. *Northern, Midland, and Southern forms for* look *in Middle English*

forms and the past participle from present-tense forms. We no longer find vowel alternation for different person categories within the same tense, as was the case in Old English.

It is difficult to generalize about Middle English verb forms because different forms were used in different dialect areas, and writers often drew from two or more of these areas in a single text. However, it appears that northern England tended to be an innovative area, and northern innovations gradually worked their way southward, where they found acceptance in the speech of London. Thus if we compare typical Northern, Midland, and Southern forms for the word *look,* we sense that the Southern forms appear the oldest and the Northern forms the most modern (see figure 4).

In addition to the present and past tense forms illustrated, there was a past participle, *loked* in the north and *loked* or *yloked* in the Midlands and south, and two competing forms of the present participle, *loking* and *lokend,* both of which have survived into Modern English – the first as the usual written form *looking* and the second as the common spoken form often written as *lookin'.* Separate imperative and subjunctive structures remained in use, but they were no longer distinct from forms used in other categories.

The examples given above to illustrate verb forms also show the development of the Middle English nominative pronouns. Missing by this time are the dual forms of Old English. The second-person singular *þu* and plural *ye* remained in use although by Chaucer's time the choice of pronoun depended as much on social status as it did on number. Thus one might address an intimate or subordinate using the singular form but use the plural form to address an individual of higher status. The rules were complex, however, and people of different social classes followed different rules. It was not until the seventeenth century that the object form *you* displaced the others to become the all-purpose second-person pronoun.

Toward the end of the Middle English period the third-person singular pronouns acquired a modern look although there was still a great deal of regional variation. The neuter *hit* lost its initial *h* whenever the word occurred without full stress, and this must have happened often enough that the form without *h* eventually became standard. The plural form *hi* continued Old English *hie,* and the corresponding object form was *hem.* Both forms were enough like the masculine singulars *he* and *him* that London speakers eventually replaced them – first with the Northern nominative *they* and somewhat later with the objective *them,* also introduced from the north.

If pronunciation and grammatical changes in Middle English are noteworthy, even more striking are the vocabulary differences. Old English had relied heavily on native roots to form new words. Thus the Christian concept of the holy triad was expressed by the compound "three-ness." In post-Conquest England this was replaced by the French (ultimately Latin) borrowing *trinity.*

In other cases French terms took their place alongside English words of the same meaning, and these word pairs became differentiated, drawing on English to designate the everyday article and French to specify the more elegant counterpart associated with the Norman rulers. The most obvious pairs are *cow/beef, swine/pork, sheep/mutton,* and *deer/venison.* But in the same class are *house/mansion, stool/chair,* and *doom/judgment.*

The language was enriched by the addition of numerous terms reflecting French culture and the French system of government, a system that was at first imposed from outside but eventually blended with the native culture to produce something having greater vigor than either culture from which it had sprung. Although French borrowings permeated every area of life, they are especially conspicuous in government, religion, law, military terminology, fashion, and the arts and sciences.

With government in the hands of the Normans after the Conquest, it is only natural that French terms should abound in this area. Terms introduced from French include *government* itself (and the related verb *govern), crown, state, realm, administer, authority, majesty, court, council, parliament, assembly, treaty, repeal, adjourn, tax, reign, royal, noble, nobility, public,* and *liberty.* Also notable is the usage applied to offices such as *attorney general* (that is, general attorney), which keeps the modifying adjective after the noun, as in French.

Church officials were political appointees, therefore French, so it is no surprise that French terminology would be prominent in the religious vocabulary. Examples include *religion, theology, sermon, sacrament, baptism, communion, confession, prayer, lesson, crucifix, incense, chapter, sanctuary, creator, savior, saint, faith, reverence, pastor, miracle, mystery, devotion,* and numerous others. Many of these terms, while originating in the context of religion, have of course passed into the general vocabulary — an indication of the role religion has played in English culture.

Law, like government and religion, was in the hands of the Norman ruling class and therefore conducted in French for more than two hundred years after the conquest. Although the term *law* itself is of Old Norse origin, many other terms are drawn from French: *plea, suit, plaintiff, defendant, judge, advocate, attorney, bill, petition, complaint, inquest, summons, indictment, jury, juror, panel, evidence, bail, verdict, sentence, award, punishment, prison, jail, sue, arraign, arrest, seize, pardon, felony,* and *assault.* The terms *grand jury* and *petit jury* use the French adjectives meaning *big* and *little.*

The armed forces were led by French-speaking noblemen, and much of the fighting took place in France as the Normans tried to maintain or extend their holdings on the Continent. Henry II (1133–1189) acquired extensive territory in southern France through his marriage to Eleanor of Aquitaine in 1152. Meanwhile the English lost control of

Normandy in 1204. During the Hundred Years War (1337–1453) English fortunes on the mainland alternately rose and fell, with the victory of Henry V at Agincourt the high point. The exploits of Jeanne d'Arc in 1429, although brief, marked the turning point. By the end of the war, which actually lasted 116 years with intermittent truces, the English held only the city of Calais, which they eventually lost in 1558. French military terms from this period – such as *army, navy, soldier, enemy, peace, battle,* and *combat* – remain part of the language. Terms for certain military ranks – *sergeant, lieutenant,* and *captain* – entered the language at this time. Titles of all other army ranks (except for *major,* taken directly from Latin) were also furnished by French but belong to later periods.

Norman taste in food, clothing, and household furnishings set the standards for fashion and added to the vocabulary in the process. The terms *fashion* and *dress* are themselves French, together with *gown, robe, buckle, button,* and *boot.* (*Shoe* is native English.) The basic color term *blue* was added during the Middle English period. (*Black, white, red, yellow, green, brown,* and *grey* were already part of the Old English vocabulary.) The term *jewel* is French, along with *diamond, ruby, emerald, pearl,* and the names of several other precious stones. Both *dinner* and *supper* come from French, as well as *plate, platter, roast, boil, stew, fry,* and the names of many specific foods. *Couch* and *chair* belong to this period, along with *blanket, quilt, towel, closet, wardrobe, pantry,* and many similar words.

The terms *art* and *science* are both from French, though ultimately from Latin. *Beauty, color, image,* and *figure* belong to this period, as do *painting, sculpture,* and *music.* The last three are ultimately from Latin or, in the case of *music,* from Greek via Latin. French was also the conduit for *physician, surgeon, balm, malady,* and *pain,* although these terms also derive from Latin and in some cases Greek via Latin.

The influence of Latin remained as strong as ever. In addition to its indirect influence through French, many Latin words entered English directly as a result of the continuing use of Latin among scholars and educated laypersons. Latin words introduced at this time include *allegory, history, index, script, scripture, submit, subscribe,* and *testimony.* In some cases Latin borrowings joined preexisting English-French doublets to form triplets of related meaning, with the native English word having connotations of familiarity, the French term suggesting greater refinement, and the Latin form associated with a learned or legalistic setting. Examples are *ask-question-interrogate* and *house-mansion-domicile.*

The good life for Englishmen after the conquest was probably not too different from what it had been before. The food supply was still plentiful. The population remained stable, and there was work for all. War was not a serious threat. Society was organized from the top down, but that had been the case before the conquest as well. People knew their place in society and were generally satisfied that arrangements were just. The feeling of servitude no doubt increased for a time, but the Normans after all were not barbarians. Trial by jury came into common use after the conquest. Landlords offered protection and security in exchange for the services required of peasants. If the landlord benefited more than the peasant, that was accepted as the natural order of things. By and large, the country continued its tradition of government by consultation and consent.

The Magna Carta of 1215 was not so much a demand for new rights as it was for an affirmation of rights to which the upper classes already supposed they were entitled. But the Magna Carta certainly reinforced the notion that even the king was bound by requirements of law and decency and that those in subordinate roles also had rights that were protected by law. Kings continued to exercise arbitrary power when they could, and the upper classes resisted the extension of basic rights to peasants; but human nature is such that privileges once achieved are seldom relinquished.

In 1348 the Black Death – strains of bubonic and pneumonic plague that had already ravaged Europe – spread through England. The disease affected all classes; but the peasants, who lived in the most crowded conditions, were especially hard hit. Something close to one-third of the population died. A direct consequence was a labor shortage and a sudden ability on the part of workers to command higher wages. Peasants now had options; they could leave their master's land in search of better wages and working conditions elsewhere. Parliament enacted legislation in 1351 to place an upper limit on wages. Enforcement was impossible, but the effort stirred popular resentment. With coordinated planning the peasants could have taken over the country at any time; but while the peasants were in the most unfavored position in society and therefore might have had the greatest desire for reform, they had no means to organize a coordinated uprising. And the teachings of the church reinforced acceptance of one's lot in life. The church was not altogether a disinterested party. Clerics had large landholdings and were among the harshest landlords. The clergy thus became a target for agitation that church lands be confiscated and distributed among the peasants.

Finally in 1381 the peasants of Essex and Kent, led by Wat Tyler, rebelled and marched on London to demand reforms. The immediate cause of the Peasants' Revolt was a poll tax instituted that year. The peasants succeeded in winning promises of reform from Richard II, but these promises were quickly forgotten once the peasants returned to their homes. Tyler himself was killed in the uprising. The tax, however, was not collected, nor was any other poll tax attempted.

Discontent with the church remained an undercurrent from the 1300s onward. John Wyclif, known for his translation of the Bible into English, became disillusioned with the worldliness of the church and argued that no priest – the pope included – could legitimately administer sacraments unless he was in a genuine state of grace. This kind of disillusionment was by no means isolated. Chaucer's unflattering portrayal of clerics in *The Canterbury Tales* suggests that he expected a portrait of a worldly, money-minded churchman to strike a responsive chord with his readers. Perhaps even more significant is the fact that he could present such descriptions with impunity.

Much of the literature of Middle English is poetry rather than prose, and the poetry is now well suited for end rhyme, although the older alliterative style is still found in works such as *Sir Gawain and the Green Knight* (circa 1350–1400). Chaucer, however, favored rhymed couplets in iambic pentameter for his *Canterbury Tales*. Latin remained the vehicle of serious prose writing, but Latin and French works were often translated into English. Other prose works that have survived include letters, legal documents, handbooks, and of course much religious writing. Drama grew in popularity during the period. A collection of mystery plays based on Bible stories dates from about 1400, and the morality play *Everyman,* in which abstract qualities such as Fellowship and Discretion are personified, dates from about the year 1500.

If *Beowulf* seems like it is in a foreign language to the modern reader, the language of Chaucer seems almost like modern English. In his "General Prologue" to *The Canterbury Tales* the poet comments on the eagerness people feel in the spring to go on pilgrimages:

> And specially from every shires ende
> Of Engelond to Caunterbury they wende
> The hooly blisful martir for to seke
> That hem hath holpen whan that they were seeke.

Everything in these four lines makes sense to the modern reader who is willing to take the spelling in stride and tolerate a few peculiarities of word use. It may take shrewd guessing to figure out that *seke* represents *seek* and *seeke* represents *sick,* but the only word in these lines that is really mystifying to the modern reader is *hem*. Third-person pronouns in Chaucer's time were undergoing change. The usual subject and object forms for singular were *he* and *him*. Scandinavian *they* for plural subjects was firmly established in the north of England, where so many Vikings had settled. *They* had been adopted in London speech as a subject form by Chaucer's time, but *hem* (or *'em*) remained in use as the object form. *Hem* eventually gave way to Scandinavian *them* to avoid confusion with *him,* but this final development took place after Chaucer.

By the end of the 1400s life in England was quite different from what it had been at the time of the Norman Conquest. Peasants were drifting away from farming communities and finding their way to towns, where the manufacture of woolen cloth offered better wages. Printing had been introduced, and new lands far to the west had been discovered. Change was in the air. The Renaissance was working its way to England, and the Protestant Reformation would soon divide Christendom. People were growing dissatisfied with life as it had been and were coming to feel that something better was possible. What this would mean no one could tell, but England was soon to become a world power. The English language would soon be opened to unexpected new influences, and in the process it would have an opportunity to make its own influence felt in a much wider realm than even William might have dreamed in 1066.

References:

Philip Baldi, "Indo-European Languages," in *The World's Major Languages,* edited by Bernard Comrie (New York: Oxford University Press, 1987), pp. 31–67;

Albert C. Baugh and Thomas Cable, *History of the English Language,* third edition (Englewood Cliffs, N.J.: Prentice-Hall, 1978);

W. F. Bolton, *A Living Language: The History and Structure of English* (New York: Random House, 1982);

Karl Brunner, *An Outline of Middle English Grammar* (Cambridge, Mass.: Harvard University Press, 1963);

David Burnley, *A Guide to Chaucer's Language* (Norman: University of Oklahoma Press, 1983);

Alistair Campbell, *Old English Grammar* (London: Oxford University Press, 1959);

Robert E. Diamond, *Old English Grammar and Reader* (Detroit: Wayne State University Press, 1970);

Robert J. Kispert, *Old English: An Introduction* (New York: Holt, Rinehart & Winston, 1971);

C. M. Millward, *A Biography of the English Language* (New York: Holt, Rinehart & Winston, 1989);

Bruce Mitchell and Fred C. Robinson, *A Guide to Old English* (London: Blackwell, 1986);

Fernand Mossé, *A Handbook of Middle English*, translated by James A. Walker (Baltimore: Johns Hopkins University Press, 1952; sixth printing, corrected and augmented, 1968);

Thomas Pyles and John Algeo, *The Origins and Development of the English Language,* third edition (New York: Harcourt Brace Jovanovich, 1982).

The Celtic Background to Medieval English Literature

Elissa R. Henken
University of Georgia

Although history textbooks and literature anthologies list the Anglo-Saxon conquest as circa 450, the Anglo-Saxons did not simply arrive in a land vacated by the Roman Empire, drive out a few remaining earlier inhabitants, and establish their own independent culture. Apart from the fact that Germanic peoples had first arrived long before the supposed conquest, coming in as early as A.D. 43 as Roman recruits, it also took a couple of centuries after 450 for the new settlers to gain supremacy in southern Britain. The people who inhabited the land before, during, and after the Roman occupation were the Britons, a Celtic people who had arrived in the islands by the fourth century B.C.

While each language and culture may develop its own distinct traditions and literature, none develops totally untouched by its neighbors, whether in cultural conflicts or in cultural borrowings. As with any cultural analysis, examination of the literature of the Anglo-Saxons and later English people must begin with some understanding of their cultural contacts, of their neighbors and foes. The Anglo-Saxons continually interacted with the Celts – Britons and Irish – on the battlefield, in the court, and in the scriptorium.

The Celts, who occupied vast areas of Europe in the third and fourth centuries B.C., from Ireland and Spain in the west to Hungary and Turkey in the east, were not a single unified people, but they were culturally and linguistically linked. At the time of the Anglo-Saxon invasions, the Celts in Ireland spoke "q-Celtic" and those in Britain spoke "p-Celtic" or Brittonic, which developed into Welsh, Cornish, and Breton. The earliest known literature in both Irish and Welsh dates to the sixth century A.D., making them the oldest vernacular literatures in Europe.

The Britons were not readily dismissed by the Anglo-Saxon intruders; indeed, Brittonic was still spoken in eastern England as late as 700. In the fifth century Irish raiders were probably at least as problematic to the Britons as were the Saxon raiders established in southeastern Britain. Between 550 and 650, however, the Saxons greatly expanded their territories in a period of intense warfare between Britons and Saxons. British territory was divided into three parts – the North (currently southern Scotland and northern England), a larger form of present-day Wales, and a southern region covering Cornwall and Devon, which sent mass migrations to northwest France to establish Little Britain or Brittany. Out of this period of strife, the loosely associated Brittonic kingdoms and tribes of the North and Wales emerged with a sense of themselves as one people, the *Cymry,* the plural of *Cymro* (together in one border, that is, fellow countrymen); *Welsh* is a Saxon term meaning *foreigners.* Together they fought the Angles, Jutes, and Saxons, all of whom were referred to without distinction as *Saeson* (*Saxones* in Latin) or Saxons. Through Welsh literature we see a fuller picture of the centuries of conflict, the picture from the other side, and we see the sources for certain themes in English history and literature.

The battles between the Cymry and the Saxons are recorded in the earliest Welsh poetry, in the works of the sixth-century poets Aneirin and Taliesin. Taliesin wrote most of his extant poems (preserved in a fourteenth-century manuscript) for Urien, king of Rheged, one of the Northern kingdoms. Urien and his son Owain were renowned for fighting the Saxons. Taliesin gives us glimpses of those battles in such works as *Gwaith Gwên Ystrad* (Battle of Gwên Ystrad):

Gweleis wyr gwychyr yn lluyd.
A gwedy boregat briwgic.
Gweleis i twrwf teirffin traghedic.
gwaed gohoyw gofaran gochlywyd.

yn amwyn gwen ystrat y gwelit
gofur hag a gwyr llawr lludedic.
Yn drws ryt gweleis y wyr lletrudyon.
eiryf dillwg yrac blawr gofedon.
Vn ynt tanc gan aethant golludyon
llaw yg croes gryt ygro garanwynyon.
kyfedwynt y gyrein kywym don.
gwanecawr gollychynt rawn eu kaffon.

(I saw savage men in war-bands:
And after morning's fray, torn flesh.
I saw border-crossing forces dead,
Strong and angry the clamour one heard.
Defending Gwen Ystrad one saw
A thin rampart and lone weary men.
At the ford I saw men stained with blood
Downing arms before a grey-haired lord:
They wished peace, for they found the way barred,
Hands crossed, on the strand, cheeks pallid.
Their lords wondered at Idon's rich wine:
Waves washed the tails of their horses.)
– translation by Joseph P. Clancy (in his *The Earliest Welsh
    Poetry,* 1970)

and *Gwaith Argoed Llwyfain* (Battle of Argoed
Llwyfain):

E bore duw sadwrn kat uawr a uu.
or pan dwyre heul hyt pan gynnu.
dygrysswys flamdwyn yn petwar llu.
godeu a reget y ymdullu.
dyuwy o argoet hyt arvynyd.
ny cheffynt eiryos hyt yr vn dyd.
Atorelwis flamdwyn vawr trebystawt.
A dodynt yg gwystlon a ynt parawt.
Ys attebwys. Owein dwyrein ffossawt.
nyt dodynt nyt ydynt nyt ynt parawt.
A cheneu vab coel bydei kymwyawc
lew. Kyn as talei o wystyl nebawt.
Atorelwis vryen vd yr echwyd.
o byd ymgyfaruot am gerenhyd.
dyrchafwn eidoed oduch mynyd.
Ac am porthwn wyneb oduch emyl.
A dyrchafwn peleidyr oduch pen gwyr.
A chyrchwn fflamdwyn yn y luyd.
A lladwn ac ef ae gyweithyd.
    A rac gweith argoet llwyfein
    bu llawer kelein.
        Rudei vrein rac ryfel gwyr.
    A gwerin a grysswys gan einewyd.
    Armaf y blwydyn nat wy kynnyd.

(Saturday morn a great battle there was
From the time the sun rose till it set.
Fflamddwyn came on with four war-bands;
Goddau and Rheged were marshalled in
Dyfwy, from Argoed to Arfynydd:
They were given not one day's delay.
Shouted Fflamddwyn, big at boasting,
'Have the hostages come? Are they ready?'
Answered Owain, bane of the East,

'They've not come, are not here, are not ready.
And a cub of Coel's line must be pressed
Hard before he'd render one hostage.'
Shouted Urien, lord of Yrechwydd,
'If a meeting for concord's to come,
Let our banners rise on the mountain
And let our faces lift over the rim
And let our spears rise over men's heads
And let us charge Fflamddwyn amid his men
And let us kill both him and his comrades.'
    Before Argoed Llwyfain
        There was many a dead man.
            Crows were crimsoned from warriors.
And the tribe charged with its chieftain!
For a year I'll shape song to their triumph.)
– translation by Clancy

Aneirin's work, *Y Gododdin*, preserved only in the
thirteenth-century manuscript *Llyfr Aneirin*, com-
memorates a battle otherwise lost to history.
Around 600 Mynyddog Mwynfawr, leader of the
Gododdin kingdom, gathered a war band composed
of men of Gododdin and allies in his capital Din
Eidyn (Edinburgh). After a year of preparation,
during which he feasted them on mead, the traditional payment for a warrior's service, he sent them
off to fight the Angles of Deira and Bernicia at
Catraeth (Catterick in York). The Britons met overwhelming forces, and of the three hundred who set
out, only one (or three, depending on the variant)
survived. Aneirin's lengthy poem (103 verses) is in
the form of an elegy, praising and remembering the
individuals and groups of comrades who went off to
battle and did not return.

Caeog, cynhorog men ydd elai,
Diffun ymlaen bun, medd a dalai;
Twll tâl ei rodawr yn y clywai awr,
    Ni roddai nawdd maint dilynai.
Ni chiliai o gamawn oni ferai waed,
Mal brwyn gomynai gwŷr ni dechai.
Neus adrawdd Gododdin ar llawr mordai,
Rhag pebyll Madog pan atgoriai
Namyn un gŵr o gant ni ddelai.
. . . .
Caeog, cynhorog, arfog yng ngawr,
Cyn no'i ddiwedd gŵr gwrdd yng ngwriawr,
Cynran yn rhagwan rhag byddinawr,
Cwyddai pum pymwnt rhag ei lafnawr.
O wŷr Deifr a Brynaich dychïawr
Ugain cant yn nifant yn un awr.
Cynt i gig blaidd nogyd i neithiawr,
Cynt i fudd brân nogyd i allawr,
Cyn no'i argyfrain ei waed i lawr.
Gwerth medd yng nghyntedd gan lliwedawr
Hyfaidd Hir edmygir tra fo cerddawr.
. . . .
Gwŷr a aeth Gatraeth, buant enwawg:
Gwin a medd o aur fu eu gwirawd

464

Blwyddyn yn erbyn urddyn ddefawd,
Trywyr a thri ugaint a thrychant eurdorchawg.
O'r sawl yd grysiasant uch gormant wirawd
Ni ddiengis namyn tri o wrhydri ffosawd,
Dau gatgi Aeron a Chynon daerawd,
A minnau o'm gwaetffrau gwerth fy ngwenwawd.
....

Cywyrain cedwyr, cyfarfuant,
I gyd yn un fryd yd gyrchasant.
Byr eu hoedl, hir eu hoed ar eu carant,
Saith gymaint o Loegrwys a laddasant.
O gyfrysedd gwragedd gwyddw a wnaethant,
Llawer mam a'i deigr ar ei hamrant.

(Wearing a brooch, in the forefront wherever he went,
Breathless before a maiden, he earned his mead;
Shattered was the front of his shield when he heard the
　　battle-cry,
　He gave no quarter to as many as he pursued.
He did not retreat from battle until blood flowed,
Like rushes he cut down men who did not flee.
The men of Gododdin relate on the floor of the hall
That before Madog's tent when he returned
There would come but one man from a hundred.
....

Wearing a brooch, in the forefront, armed in the fight,
Before his death a mighty warrior in combat,
A princely leader charging before armies,
Five fifties fell before his blades.
Of the men of Deira and Bernicia there fell
A hundred score into oblivion in one hour.
Quicker to a wolf-feast than to a nuptial,
Quicker to the raven's gain than to the altar,
Before his burial his blood flowed down.
In return for mead in the hall with the hosts
Hyfaidd Hir will be praised while there is a minstrel.
....

Warriors went to Catraeth, they were renowned:
Wine and mead from gold vessels was their drink
For a year according to honourable custom,
Three men and three score and three hundred, gold-
　　torqued.
Of those who hastened forth after plentiful drink
Only three escaped through prowess in battle,
The two battle-hounds of Aeron and Cynon returned,
And I from my blood-shedding on account of my fair
　　song.
....

The warriors arose, they assembled,
Together with one accord they attacked.
Short were their lives, long their kinsmen's grief for
　　them,
They slew seven times their number of the English.
By fighting they made women widows,
Many a mother with her tear on her eyelid.)

The poem, which has the same cumulative, tragic effect as reading the individual names on the Vietnam War Memorial, expresses the heroic code that loyalty is a prime virtue and that death is acceptable as long as it leads to everlasting fame, attitudes

recognizable in later English works such as *Beowulf* (circa 900–1000 or 790–825) and *The Battle of Maldon* (circa 1000), but here again Welsh literature provides an early record and from the other side.

　　Aneirin and Taliesin both appear in a list of people "famed in British verse" in the *Historia Brittonum* compiled by the author known as "Nennius" (circa 800). Nennius, probably a Welsh monk in northern Wales, drew on documents and traditions from many parts of Britain. He too recorded those early centuries of conflict between Britons and Saxons, including lists of the English kings and the Britons who fought against them.

　　Welsh poetry continued to record the fighting and destruction. Among the best known of the ninth-century works are *Canu Llywarch Hen* (The Song of Llywarch Hen) and *Canu Heledd* (The Song of Heledd). Set against the background of ninth-century border warfare between north Wales and England, these *englynion* (the plural of *englyn,* the oldest known Welsh form of metrical stanza) present views of sixth- and seventh-century events. *Canu Llywarch Hen* shows Llywarch sending each of his twenty-four sons in turn to battle. First he taunts them:

> Maen wynn tra vum yth oet.
> ny sethrit vy llenn .i. a thraet.
> nyt erdit vyn tir .i. heb waet.
> ....
> Maen wynn tra uum .i. efras.
> oedwn i dywal galanas.
> gwnawn weithret gwr kyt bydwn gwas.

> (Maenwyn, when I was your age,
> No feet trampled my mantle,
> None ploughed my land without bloodshed.
> ....
> Maenwyn, when I was strong-limbed,
> I was savage in slaughter.
> I did a man's work, though a lad.)
> – translation by Clancy

Then he praises their accomplishments:

> Kyt delei gymry ac elyflu [lloeger]
> a llawer o bell tu.
> dangossei byll bwyll udu.

> (Though Welshmen and hordes of English should come
> 　　And many from afar,
> Pyll would show them what skill meant.)
> – translation by Clancy

Only after the death of the last, Gwen, does Llywarch recognize the tragedy of events:

Gwen wrth lawen yd welas neithwyr
[yr] athuc ny techas.
oer adrawd ar glawd gorlas.
. . . .

Pedwarmeib ar hugeint yg kenueint lywarch
o wyr glew galwytheint.
[cwl] eu dyuot clot trameint.

Pedwarmeib ar hugeint a ueithyeint vyg knawt
drwy vyn tauawt lle<de>sseint
da dyuot [bychot] colledeint.

(Gwên by the Llawen stood guard last night:
    Hard pressed, he did not flee,
    Sad the tale, at Clawdd Gorlas.
. . . .
Four and twenty sons in Llywarch's household
    Of brave men, fierce in rage.
    A sin is excess of fame.

Four and twenty sons, bred of my body:
    Because of my tongue they're slain.
    Small fame is best: they are lost.)
– translation by Clancy

Canu Heledd laments the deaths of Heledd's
brothers, especially Cynddylan (a seventh-century
Powys ruler), and the destruction of the land:

Stauell gyndylan ys tywyll heno
heb dan heb wely.
wylaf wers. tawaf wedy.

Stauell gyndylan ys tywyll heno.
heb dan heb gannwyll.
namyn duw pwy am dyry pwyll.
. . . .

Stauell gyndylan neut athwyt heb wed.
mae ym bed dy yscwyt.
hyt tra uu ny bu dollglwyt.
. . . .

Stauell gyndylan am gwan y gwelet.
heb doet heb dan.
marw vy glyw. buw mu hunan.

(The hall of Cynddylan is dark tonight,
    No fire, no pallet.
    I'll keen now, then be quiet.

The hall of Cynddylan is dark tonight,
    No fire, no candle,
    Who but God will keep me tranquil?
. . . .
The hall of Cynddylan, your beauty's gone,
    In the grave's your buckler.
    While he lived, not a fissure.
. . . .
The hall of Cynddylan, the sight stabs me,
    No rooftop, no fire.

Dead my lord, myself alive.)
– translation by Clancy

These works are full of desolation, a mood that
appears in the Old English lyrics which, as in *The
Wanderer* (circa 970) and *The Seafarer* (circa 970),
also deal with the speaker's emotional response to a
situation, and which may show Welsh influence.

With all the years of conflict and loss and seeing their territories dwindle, the Welsh naturally
questioned why and tried to make some sense of
their history. Gildas (circa 495–circa 570), a Bry-
thonic monk, gave the first clear answer in his *De excidio Britanniae* (On the Destruction of Britain, circa
547), where he deplored that "Britain has been un-
gratefully rebelling, stiff-necked and haughty, now
against God, now against its own countrymen,
sometimes even against kings from abroad and their
subjects." He depicted Britain's losses to the Saxons as being God's chastisement of the people for
their waywardness and sin; British unfaithfulness to
Rome and God had left them open to the barbarian
instruments of God's justice. Gildas, as well as providing important, almost contemporaneous information on an ill-recorded time, also set patterns of
historicity for both the English and the Welsh. He
applied the biblical notion that history is a record of
God's dealings with peoples (*gens*), and that peoples,
like individuals, have certain moral characteristics.
Subsequent writers may not have picked up
Gildas's task of setting his people on the right moral
path, but they took on other themes appropriate for
their own concerns. Gildas had described the blind
and stupid plan devised by British leaders by which
"the ferocious Saxons (name not to be spoken!),
hated by man and God, should be let into the island
like wolves into the fold, to beat back the people of
the north" and compared the Saxons to the Assyrians.

In contrast, Bede, a Northumbrian monk writ-
ing his *Historia ecclesiastica* in the eighth century, put
his own people, the English, in the role of latter-day
Israelites and rejoiced in their finding God's favor
while the British were condemned for their sins. On
the Welsh side, however, Saxon victories were not
seen as a final condemnation by God, but rather as
correctives and tests before God restored the British
to their rightful glory – it would have been unbear-
able to live with that other idea of history – and the
significance of events lay not in victory by the Saxons (who were simply tools) but in the loss of sovereignty by the Welsh. The Britons once had sovereignty over the whole island, but they lost it. Why
they lost it was subject to interpretation, but the fact

of it was well established. Throughout the literature and into the present, the Welsh refer to themselves as the British and the island Prydein/Britain as theirs.

The theme of sovereignty and the theme of future hope became entwined in Welsh mythology, so that by the ninth century Nennius includes in his *Historia Brittonum* the prophecy of restored sovereignty. Nennius tells the story of the coming of the Saxons. Instead of the "proud tyrant" who arrogantly brought them in he depicts Vortigern as a foolish man anxious for help against the Irish and Picts and tricked by his German guests Hengist and Horsa. Nennius relates events known to the Welsh as *Brad y Cyllyll Hirion* (Treachery of the Long Knives), when the English took hidden daggers into a peace conference and then slew all the unarmed Welsh except for King Vortigern, who ransomed himself by giving them Essex, Sussex, and Middlesex. (With its explanation of county names this story must have been an English one that was adapted by the Welsh.) In addition to acknowledging the loss of Britain, Nennius holds out a clear promise for future Welsh victory through the prophecies of the fatherless boy Ambrosius (Emrys), who explains to Vortigern the actions of a red worm and a white worm hidden beneath the king's fortress. They watch the worms fight until finally the red one drives off the white one. The boy explains, "The cloth represents your kingdom, and the two worms are two dragons. The red worm is your dragon, and the lake represents the world. But the white one is the dragon of the people who have seized many peoples and countries in Britain, and will reach almost from sea to sea; but later our people will arise, and will valiantly throw the English people across the sea."

Prophecies became important expressions of hope in medieval Wales – the Britons would rise again and, led by a deliverer (Cynan and Cadwaladr primarily, but later Arthur and Owain), would regain sovereignty of their island. The prophecies included instructions on who would aid in the battle. We see the prophecies and historical events come together in the poem *Armes Prydein* (Prophecy of Britain), written circa 930. It prophesies the return of Cynan and Cadwaladr, who will lead a confederation of the Welsh, Irish, Dublin Danes, Cornish, Bretons, and men of Strathclyde to drive out the Saxons and their high king.

Kynan yn racwan ym pop discyn.
Saesson rac Brython gwae a genyn.
Katwaladyr yn baladyr gan y unbyn.

trwy synhwyr yn llwyr yn eu dichlyn.
. . . .
Atui pen gaflaw heb emennyd.
Atui gwraged gwedw a meirch gweilyd.
Atui obein vthyr rac ruthyr ketwyr.
A lliaws llaw amhar kyn gwascar lluyd.
Kennadeu agheu dychyferwyd.
pan safhwynt galaned wrth eu hennyd.
Ef dialawr y treth ar gwerth beunyd.
ar mynych gennadeu ar geu luyd.
Dygorfu Kymry trwy kyfergyr.
yn gyweir gyteir gytson gytffyd.
. . . .
ymgetwynt Gymry pan ymwelant.
nyt ahont allmyn or nen y safant.
hyt pan talhont seithweith gwerth digonsant.
Ac agheu diheu yg werth eu cam.
. . . .
Dysgogan derwydon meint a deruyd.
o Vynaw hyt Lydaw yn eu llaw yt vyd.
o Dyuet hyt Danet wy bieiuyd.

(Cynan striking foremost in every attack;
the Saxons will sing their lamentation before the Britons,
Cadwaladr will be a shaft of defence with his chieftains,
skillfully and thoroughly seeking them out.
. . . .
There will be heads split open without brains,
women will be widowed, and horses riderless,
there will be terrible wailing before the rush of warriors,
many wounded by hand; before the hosts separate
the messengers of death will meet
when corpses stand up, supporting each other.
The tribute and the daily payments will be avenged –
and the frequent expeditions and the wicked hosts.
The Cymry will prevail through battle,
well-equipped, unanimous, one in word and faith.
. . . .
When they come face to face with each other, the Cymry will take care
that the foreigners shall not go from the place where they stand
until they repay sevenfold the value of what they have done,
with certain death in return for their wrong.
. . . .
Wise men foretell all that will happen:
they will possess all from Manaw to Brittany,
from Dyfed to Thanet, it will be theirs.)

The battle called for here almost took place in 937 when the kings of Dublin, Scotland, and Strathclyde, but not the southern Britons, united against and were badly defeated by the English King Athelstan in the Battle of Brunanburh. Once again we see the same political situation described from opposite sides in the literature (*Armes Prydein* versus *The Battle of Brunanburh*). As Brynley F. Roberts points out in his article "Geoffrey of Monmouth and Welsh Historical Tradition" (1976), "Early English history is the story of attempts to create unity and establish sovereignty: Welsh history recounts the loss of sovereignty and consequent fragmentation."

The themes of Welsh history are pulled together and given new impetus with Geoffrey of Monmouth's *Historia regum Britanniae* (circa 1138). Combining traditional themes and his own imagination, he tells the history of the Welsh people from their beginnings with the fall of Troy to their loss of sovereignty to the Saxons in the seventh century. The themes of unity, sovereignty, and loss run throughout the book; indeed it opens with the statement, "the Britons once occupied the land from sea to sea, before the others came. Then the vengeance of God overtook them because of their arrogance and they submitted to the Picts and the Saxons." Geoffrey presents a succession of kings, under some of whom the kingdom is divided or lost, but under some of whom it prospers, as is appropriate under a just king and as it does under Arthur. Though Arthur's rule is glorious, he too fails and is carried off to Avalon to have his wounds attended while the Welsh are left with Merlin's prophecies that "Cadwallader shall summon Conanus" and drive out the foreigners.

Geoffrey simultaneously provided the Normans with knowledge of their new domain and a place in the long line of rulers over the land and gave the Welsh a coherent history of themselves which confirmed their inherent worth, honored their often-glorious past, and held out the possibility of a future British golden age. His creative history so suited people's needs that it was immediately accepted on all sides. The Welsh effectively adopted it as their own official history; its popularity is indicated by its being translated into Welsh three times in the thirteenth century alone. Geoffrey's summing up of Welsh history, the combination of defeat and a promised redeemer, was important for the Welsh, but it became important for the Anglo-Normans as well. Geoffrey gave new shape and added importance to the figure of Arthur and helped make him the model of the redeemer-hero even for the English. Arthur, the concept of the loss of Britain, the prophecies all existed before Geoffrey, but he gave them a literary shape which caught the imagination of the rest of Europe and became one of Wales's most cherished contributions to English literature.

Arthur had been established in Welsh tradition long before Geoffrey spread his name. The earliest reference is in *Y Gododdin*, where the sixth-century poet praises one of the warriors who went to Catraeth for doing great deeds, *cyn ni bei ef arthur* (although he was not Arthur). In the ninth century Nennius described Arthur's victories in twelve battles against the Saxons ("Then Arthur fought against them in those days, together with the kings of the British; but he was their leader in battle"), culminating with the twelfth battle on Badon Hill: "and in it nine hundred and sixty men fell in one day, from a single charge of Arthur's, and no one laid them low save he alone; and he was victorious in all his campaigns." Nennius also included in the list of the Wonders of Britain the tomb of Arthur's son Amr and a stone in which Arthur's dog Cafal left his footprint when they were hunting the boar Twrch Trwyth, clear indications of Arthur's place in the popular imagination. A few Arthurian poems of uncertain date exist (possibly tenth century, certainly before 1250), including *Pa gur yv y porthaur?* (What man is the gatekeeper?), in which Arthur and Cei hold dialogue with a gatekeeper and review their past accomplishments, and *Preiddeu Annwn* (The Spoils of Annwn), in which Arthur leads a raid on the Otherworld. In *Culhwch ac Olwen*, the oldest extant native Welsh prose tale (text circa 1100), in the triadic literature known as *Trioedd Ynys Prydein* (Triads of the Isle of Britain), and in the Welsh saints' *Vitae* (eleventh- and twelfth-century compositions), Arthur was already established as a great king, complete with a court to which people resort for help, a group of companions (Cei, Bedwyr, Gwalchmei), a wife (Gwenhwyfar), a hero's prized possessions (arms, steed, hound, ship, magic cloak), and the story of his death at Camlan. A series of stanzas (possibly ninth century) on the graves of Welsh heroes (*Englynion y Beddau*) includes the line *Anoeth bid bet y arthur* (difficult of finding in the world is a grave for Arthur), which shows him already established as a deliverer in Welsh tradition. The motif of the unknown grave was certainly well established by 1125 when the Englishman William of Malmesbury reported in *De gestis regum Anglorum*, "Arthur's tomb is nowhere to be seen, whence the ancient sorrowful songs tell the story that he is yet to come."

Geoffrey of Monmouth's influence on English literature can be directly traced through Wace, who rendered Geoffrey's *Historia regum Britanniae* into Norman dialect, and then Laȝamon, who rendered Wace's *Roman de Brut* into his own Middle English *Brut* (circa 1185–1216). Laȝamon probably also drew more directly (through translators) on the Welsh prophecies, especially Merlin's and *Armes*

Prydein, and possibly on the Triads. However, Geoffrey's influence can also be seen generally in the shape he gave to the Arthurian story, transferring Arthur's court from Celliwig in Cornwall to Caerleon in Wales, where knights gathered to perform heroic deeds and win each his lady, assigning conquests in distant lands, and dooming Arthur's kingdom through infidelity and ill-founded battle. In addition to a certain Arthurian ambience, he also confirmed the names which remained everafter at the center of Arthur's court – Cei (Kai, Caius), Bedivere (Bedoier, Beduerus, Bedwyr), Gawain (Gauvain, Gwalchmei, Gualganus), Guenevere (Guenièvre, Gwenhwyfar, Guenhumare), Owain ap Urien (Yvain fiz Uriens).

Apart from Geoffrey's work, twelfth-century Norman-Welsh contacts, especially in south Wales, allowed for an exchange of ideas and narratives so that, for instance, the French could learn the tales of the Welsh heroes, write their own texts as Chrétien de Troyes did, and influence later forms of the Welsh tales, as with the romances of *Owein* (Chrétien's *Yvein*), *Geraint* (*Erec et Enide*), and *Peredur* (*Perceval*). In the meantime, these and other French forms of the Welsh tales were taken into English literature, as when Thomas Malory sought sources for his *Le Morte Darthur* (1451–1470). Thus, routed through the Normans as well as more directly from the Welsh, Arthurian themes, legends, and specific heroes were passed into English literature.

Moreover, in addition to the specifically Arthurian traditions, a variety of traditional, originally non-Arthurian, material found its way from Welsh or Irish into English literature. The transmission may have been an effect of Arthur's pulling everything into his orbit or it may have been helped by English assumptions that anything with Celtic ambience was Arthurian. The three most striking examples are the beheading game, the loathsome lady, and the tragic love triangle. The beheading game of *Sir Gawain and the Green Knight* (circa 1350–1400) has its earliest analogue in the eighth-century Irish text *Fledh Bhricrenn* (Bricriu's Feast). Three of the Ulster warriors compete to determine which deserves the Champion's Portion. They are tested in various ways, but the final, conclusive test comes when an enormous, uncouth, strangely clad figure appears in the hall one night demanding a favor – a beheading game to be repaid the next night. Three warriors in turn behead the churl, watch him walk out carrying his head, and then fail to appear for the return blow, before Cú Chulainn makes and keeps the bargain. The churl taunts Cú Chulainn several times before finally delivering the blow with the ax

blunt side down, whereupon he releases the hero and, returning to his true form as the (semi-mythological) king Cu Roi mac Dairi, declares Cú Chulainn the greatest champion.

Another motif drawn from Celtic materials into English is that of the loathsome hag who transforms into a beautiful young woman. Rather than a hag, the woman may appear first as a white hart who must be captured by the hero. In either case the motif is tied to Celtic concepts of sovereignty, by which the king is mated with the land (through its tutelary goddess), and the land's fruitfulness and prosperity depend on the justice of the king's rule. The motif plays itself out in various forms, but one of the fullest examples appears in the Irish text *Echtra mac nEchach Muigmedoin* (The Adventures of the Sons of Eochaid Mugmedón). Five brothers out hunting go in turn to seek water, and each is put off by the hideous hag (a gray bristly mane, a sickle of green teeth, "a middle fibrous, spotted with pustules, diseased, and shins distorted and awry") guarding the well until the last, Niall, lies with her. She turns into the most beautiful of women, introduces herself as Sovereignty, and explains, "as thou hast seen me loathsome, bestial, horrible at first and beautiful at last, so is the sovranty; for seldom it is gained without battles and conflicts; but at last to anyone it is beautiful and goodly."

Yet another Celtic theme is the tragic love triangle of an older king, his (promised) bride, and his young friend/kinsman. The best known examples in Irish are Conchobar, Derdríu, and Noísiu in "The Exile of the Sons of Uisnech" and Fionn, Grainne, and Diarmuid in "The Pursuit of Diarmuid and Grainne"; in Welsh there are Arthur, Gwenhwyfar, and Melwas (the earliest known reference is in Caradoc of Llancarfan's *Life of Gildas*) and March, Essyllt, and Drystan. In "The Celtic Inheritance of Medieval Literature" (1965), Rachel Bromwich suggests that the tales of boyhood deeds leading to the hero's awkward initiation at court, which, along with "magic springs and caldrons of plenty, sword-bridges and revolving castles, hunts for a white doe or hart are among the recurrent or 'inconstant' elements of Arthurian romance," are taken from one or another of the Celtic cultures. She points out too that the mere fact of having more extant analogues in Irish manuscripts does not mean that the motifs and themes were particularly Irish rather than Welsh.

As the absorption of the Arthurian materials and various Celtic motifs into English literature indicates, despite the centuries of warfare, there must also have been close, peaceful contacts between the

English and their Celtic neighbors, whether British or Irish. This intermingling must have been especially prevalent in the North, where the peoples would have united on occasion in mutual defense against the Picts and where, more particularly, they had religious contacts. First the British (third and fifth centuries) and then the Irish (fifth century) were Christianized, and they then helped Christianize the Saxons. Rhun, one of the sons of Urien (the British king praised by Taliesin for his wars against the Saxons), was reported by Nennius as having baptized King Edwin of Northumbria, a point contradicted by Bede (who despised the British). The suggestion of friendly contact, nonetheless, remains. In Northumbria Edwin's successor, Oswald, established Celtic Christianity, with its emphasis on ascetic monasticism, in which he had been trained at Iona. The monastery of Lindisfarne was founded in 634–635 on the Irish model. These contacts meant not just sharing an approach to Christianity but also aesthetics in art and literature. The links are strikingly visible in illuminated manuscripts such as the *Book of Durrow,* the *Lindisfarne Gospels,* and the *Lichfield Gospels* (*Book of St. Chad*), which are in the same, though less fully developed, style as the *Book of Kells.* In Mercia, too, there were close contacts, with the Irish influence introducing Hisperic Latin and with the British bards possibly affecting themes and tone in some of the *Exeter Book* poetry. In Wessex, King Alfred made a Welshman, Asser, his teacher and adviser, and it is Asser who has left the fullest account of Alfred's reign in his *Life of Alfred.* Commenting in her article "The Celtic Background of Early Anglo-Saxon England" (1964) on the rapid flowering of Anglo-Saxon culture, Nora K. Chadwick concludes, "It is initially to the influence of the Celtic peoples, first the Britons within northern England and southern Scotland, and later the Irish from Iona and Ireland, that I would attribute the swift development of the Anglo-Saxons of Northumbria from barbarism to a lofty civilisation, especially in intellectual matters."

The complications of disentangling Celtic, as well as Germanic, Roman, Mediterranean, and then later Norman, influences from Anglo-Saxon literary and cultural developments are great. Scholars have found British or Irish influences in early English prayer books, in Old English homiletic literature, in the Harley lyrics, and in gnomic literature. The influences may take the form of using loricas, enumerative tropes, or a peculiarly analytical style. The influences are not necessarily wholesale borrowings but – in attitudes, themes, motifs, and style – are often subtle, intricate, and accomplished over long periods of time, and they are effected sometimes directly and sometimes through intermediaries, as one would expect when cultures come into close contact, in both competition and cooperation, across centuries.

References:

Rachel Bromwich, "The Celtic Inheritance of Medieval Literature," *Modern Language Quarterly,* 26 (1965): 203–227;

Bromwich, ed., *Trioedd Ynys Prydein* (Cardiff: University of Wales Press, 1978);

Bromwich, A. O. H. Jarman, and Brynley F. Roberts, eds., *The Arthur of the Welsh* (Cardiff: University of Wales Press, 1991);

Nora K. Chadwick, "The Celtic Background of Early Anglo-Saxon England," in *Celt and Saxon: Studies in the Early British Border* (Cambridge: Cambridge University Press, 1963; reprinted with corrections, 1964), pp. 323–352;

T. M. Charles-Edwards, "Bede, the Irish and the Britons," *Celtica,* 15 (1983): 42–52;

Joseph P. Clancy, *The Earliest Welsh Poetry* (London: Macmillan, 1970);

Tom Peete Cross and Clark Harris Slover, eds., *Ancient Irish Tales* (New York: Holt, 1936; reprinted, with a revised bibliography, New York: Barnes & Noble, 1969);

John Davies, *A History of Wales* (London: Allen Lane/Penguin, 1993);

Geoffrey of Monmouth, *The History of the Kings of Britain,* translated by Lewis Thorpe (Harmondsworth: Penguin, 1966);

Robert W. Hanning, *The Vision of History in Early Britain* (New York: Columbia University Press, 1966);

Kathleen Hughes, "Some Aspects of Irish Influence on Early English Private Prayer," *Studia Celtica,* 5 (1970): 48–61;

Jarman, ed., *Aneirin: Y Gododdin,* Welsh Classics 3 (Landysul: Gomer Press, 1988);

Jarman and Gwilym Rees Hughes, eds., *A Guide to Welsh Literature,* volume 1 (Swansea: Davies, 1976);

Gwyn Jones and Thomas Jones, eds. and trans., *The Mabinogion* (London: Dent, 1968);

Françoise H. M. Le Saux, *Laȝamon's Brut: The Poem and Its Sources* (Cambridge: Brewer, 1989);

I. C. Lovecy, "The Celtic Sovereignty Theme and the Structure of *Peredur,*" *Studia Celtica,* 12/13 (1977/1978): 133–146;

John Morris, ed. and trans., *Nennius: British History and the Welsh Annals* (London: Phillimore, 1980);

Brynley F. Roberts, "Geoffrey of Monmouth and Welsh Historical Tradition," *Nottingham Mediaeval Studies,* 20 (1976): 29–40;

Roberts, *Studies on Middle Welsh Literature,* Welsh Studies 5 (Lewiston: Edwin Mellen Press, 1992);

Jenny Rowland, *Early Welsh Saga Poetry* (Cambridge: Brewer, 1990);

Patrick Sims-Williams, "Gildas and the Anglo-Saxons," *Cambridge Medieval Celtic Studies,* 6 (Winter 1983): 1–30;

Sims-Williams, "Thought, Word and Deed: An Irish Triad," *Eriu,* 29 (1978): 78–110;

Whitley Stokes, ed. and trans., "Adventure of the Sons of Eochaid," *Revue Celtique,* 24 (1903): 190–207;

William of Malmesbury, *De Gestis Regum Anglorum,* edited by William Stubbs, 2 volumes, Rolls Series 90 (London, 1887/1889);

Ifor Williams, *The Beginnings of Welsh Poetry* (Cardiff: University of Wales Press, 1972);

Williams, ed., *Armes Prydein,* translated by Bromwich (Dublin: Dublin Institute for Advanced Studies, 1972);

Williams, ed., *The Poems of Taliesin* (Dublin: Institute for Advanced Studies, 1968);

Michael Winterbottom, ed. and trans., *Gildas: The Ruin of Britain and Other Works* (London: Phillmore, 1978);

Charles D. Wright, "The Irish 'Enumerative Style' in Old English Homiletic Literature, Especially Vercelli Homily IX," *Cambridge Medieval Celtic Studies,* 18 (1989): 28–74;

Wright, *The Irish Tradition in Old English Literature,* Cambridge Studies in Anglo-Saxon England 6 (Cambridge: Cambridge University Press, 1993).

Anglo-Norman Literature in the Development of Middle English Literature

Jane Dick Zatta
University of Georgia

It is perhaps necessary to justify an entry on Anglo-Norman literature in a volume dedicated to English literature in the Middle Ages. In spite of the fact that scholars such as William Henry Schofield, Paul Studer, M. Dominica Legge, and, most recently, Susan Crane have shown that both the Anglo-Norman literature and language are the product of distinctively English conditions and concerns, it is not often recognized that the English literature of the fourteenth century is a progression and development of the large and extremely varied body of literature of high quality either written in England, or under English patronage, or preserved earliest only in English manuscripts between the twelfth and the fourteenth centuries. Anglo-Norman literature develops a range of literary subjects, attitudes, and forms that directly foreshadow the explosion of Middle English literature in the fourteenth century. In 1906 Schofield noted that no significant work was produced in English from the Norman Conquest to the time of Chaucer that was not an imitation of, or at least prefigured by, an Anglo-Norman work. Anglo-Norman writers repeatedly used an English theme or historical figure to create an original literary work in the French language, which would then generate imitations or translations in Middle English as well as Anglo-Latin. This phenomenon can be seen in the explosion of works in a variety of new genres including history, lais, miracles of the Virgin, romance, and hagiography. Not only did new literary genres develop for the first time in England, such as the *Brut* chronicles, the romance, and the drama, but translations and adaptations of Latin originals such as saints' lives and miracles of the Virgin show characteristically insular treatment. The particular conditions in England were to favor the treatment of themes and figures from the English past as well as the development of a variety of literary styles that embraced everyday realism, allegory, psychological complexity, and emotional intensity. The purportedly didactic intent of much Anglo-Norman literature and the large number of works of religious character have to some extent prevented the appreciation of the lyricism, imagination, and psychological realism, as well as the unmistakable Englishness, of Anglo-Norman literature.

Leaving aside writing in fields such as natural science, medicine, and law, Anglo-Norman literature includes a wide array of genres: chronicles, history, lyrics, pseudohistory, hagiography in prose and verse, miracles of the Virgin, lais, romances, sermons and religious treatises, satires and fabliaux, proverbs, debates, and glosses and translations of the Bible. The most complete survey of Anglo-Norman literature is that of Legge, although the studies of Johan Vising, C. B. West, Schofield, and Studer are still useful. The most complete examination of the position of the French language in England from 1000 to 1600 is that of Douglas A. Kibbee. In an overview as brief as the present one, it is impossible to represent the range of Anglo-Norman literature adequately. The aim of this survey therefore is to identify a few of the most typical characteristics of Anglo-Norman literature and illustrate them with representative works from several genres.

A remarkable fact about the Normans, in England as well as in Sicily, is their early appreciation of the value of literature in the legitimization of a new political order. Literary patronage was a characteristic of Norman royalty and aristocracy, and the French literature produced for the French-speaking court was designed to appeal to the non-Latin-literate Norman nobility. The Norman barons constituted a new aristocratic class. Many had been mere swordsmen before the Conquest, while others were the cadets of families who still considered their primary residence to be France. For this reason the Normans required works of literature that would not only justify their subjection of England, but also enhance the stature of the English royal titles that they had come to hold. Native traditions were magnified and utilized to praise the importance of England and her rulers; Anglo-Norman kings repeatedly invoked the authority of Alfred, Athelstan, and Edward, whose heirs and descendants they claimed to be. The genre most intensely cultivated by Anglo-Norman royal and aristocratic patrons was history writing, and it is a well-known fact that the beginnings of history writing in French lie in England. Historians in the twelfth century were still influenced by classical historians such as Virgil, Lucan, and Sallust, and the purpose of history as they saw it was to provide moral instruction by furnishing examples of good and bad behavior. William of Malmesbury considered history as the noblest branch of ethics, "which, by an agreeable recapitulation of past events, excites its readers, by example, to frame their lives to the pursuit of good, or to aversion from evil." From the first half of the twelfth century, Geoffrey of Monmouth's *Historia regum Britannie* (History of the Kings of Britain, circa 1138) and later the vernacular *Brut* chronicles of Geffrey Gaimar, Robert Wace, and Benoit de Sainte-Maure popularized the myth, already suggested by official Latin histories from the reign of William I, that the Britons (and thus the Normans) were the descendants of Brutus and the Trojans. By identifying the descendants of Brutus with the line of King Arthur, Geoffrey of Monmouth created, alongside the cowardly Britons of Gildas, Nennius, and Bede, a noble race that had not vanished but had rather been exiled to Armorican Britain from whence they would one day return to vanquish the usurpers. It was not hard to see in William's conquest of England the final, just revenge of the line of Arthur over Mordred and his Saxon allies. Furthermore, as Schofield has observed, in Arthur the Normans had a king who had ruled not only all England at a date prior to the arrival of the Saxons, but who had also conquered the Normans' archrival, France.

An important type of history writing that developed in the twelfth century was the vernacular chronicle. One popular form was the *Brut* chronicle, first suggested by Geffrey Gaimar. Gaimar, author of a now-lost *Estoire des Bretuns* and the *Estoire des Engleis,* integrated Geoffrey of Monmouth's mythical "history" of the Britons drawn from legend, imagination, and classical sources (such as Virgil's *Aeneid*) with a factual, annalistic record of English kings drawn from Bede and the *Anglo-Saxon Chronicle* and with his own account of the events of his day, thus forging a continuum stretching from the mythological past to his time. Gaimar's *Brut* formula, consisting of a history of the Britons, a history of the English, and a continuation, gave rise to numerous adaptations and sequels. Gaimar broke with his Norman contemporaries and predecessors by writing his history in the vernacular and in verse rather than Latin prose, and his reason, as he states in his epilogue, seems to have been his wish to expose the widest possible audience to his version of English history. Under the patronage of Henry II, Wace and Benoit further expanded Gaimar's formula to include a history of the Norman dukes.

As a literary genre, the *Brut* chronicles (extremely popular through the fifteenth century) had several particular characteristics. They were in effect anthologies containing a variety of tales, ranging from dragon fights to battles to courtly love romances. Although the *Brut* chronicles achieved their maximum literary development with Wace and Benoit, they remained a popular form of history through the fifteenth century. In the fourteenth century the ratio of space dedicated to current politics in comparison to the *Brut* adventures and the Anglo-Saxon past greatly increases, and fourteenth-century chronicles usually employ the mythological *Brut* story to justify English rights over Scotland. Chronicles of the times of Arthur, which were regarded as factual accounts, were relevant to the political ambitions of the Plantagenet kings, who used them to justify their policies. John Taylor has noted that Edward I cited arguments from the *Brut* to sustain his right to dominion over Scotland in the case he made before the pope in 1301. From the beginning of the fourteenth century survives *The Anglo-Norman Prose Brut*. This history exists in an earlier form that ends in 1272 (written circa 1300) and a later version that carries the chronicle to 1333. *The Anglo-Norman Prose Brut,* which was translated into English as the *Chronicles of England* and printed by Caxton in 1480, had become by the fifteenth century the most popular history of the day and remained, until the seventeenth century, the most authoritative history of England. One indication of the enormous popularity of this work is the fact that it survives in over two hundred manuscripts in French, English, and Latin. *The Anglo-Norman Prose Brut,* which was eventually carried up to the year 1461 and the coronation of Edward IV, was the closest English equivalent to a national chronicle in late-medieval England. Despite the fact that numerous English versions of the work dating from the fourteenth century exist, French versions continued to be written, such as those of Peter de Langtoft (1307), later translated into English by Robert Mannyng of Brunne, and the Anglo-Norman prose chronicle entitled *Le Petit Bruit,* written in 1310 by Meistre Rauf de Boun at the request of Henry de Lacy, Earl of Lincoln, one of the most eminent barons of Edward I and the king's closest counselor.

The story matter of the chronicles projects into the mythological past the political concerns of the Norman barons. An episodic plot is held together by a series of repeating patterns that emphasize some constant themes: the inevitable emergence of the hero or nation aided by God, the obligation of the king to protect the rights of his subjects, fear of the loss of inheritance, the importance of producing legitimate offspring to receive the inheritance of their parents. The basic plot of many *Brut* episodes is the same: the lawful inheritance of land from one generation to another is disrupted by foreign aggression, a usurping relative or regent, or "disseisin" (dispossession) by a dishonest king. In the *Brut* story of Gormund, sovereignty is threatened by aggression from foreign pagans. More often, however, the threat to lawful succession comes from a jealous uncle, brother, or regent who tries to usurp the rights of the lawful heir. This is the case in the story of Belinus and Brennius, Edwin and Cadwallo, Leir and his daughters, and Ferrex and Porrex. Other events include battles, treachery, tournaments in order to win the hand of an heiress, marriages that seal political alliances, imprisonment, land seizure, journeys to a foreign land in search of allies, the repentance of a hero, the birth of heirs, and reconciliation with former enemies. Restoration of the legal heir to his inheritance is brought about by battle, the outcome of which is determined by God. The many long and complex battle-episodes are often resolved by clever ruses. Often wars conclude in reconciliation and alliance between former enemies, as in the *Brut* stories of Brennius and Belinus and Edwin and Cadwallo. Sometimes the new alliance is sealed by a marriage pact. After Claudius surrenders to Arvirigus in the *Anglo-Norman Brut,* not only do they make peace ("Ore sunt ensemble cum pere e fiz"), but they also affirm their new friendship by the marriage of Claudius's daughter, Genuissa, to Arvirigus. The peace between Brutus and the Greeks concludes with the marriage of Brutus to Ignogen, the daughter of the Greek king Pandrasus.

The propagandistic value of the vernacular histories in enhancing the stature of Henry II was increased by stressing the didactic and moral purpose that they claimed and by attempts to heighten their appeal to the French-speaking nobility. Already in Geffrey Gaimar's early chronicle (1136–1137) are several attempts to make the narrative more interesting by exploiting bizarre or unexpected plot developments, by elaborate and detailed descriptions of court customs and trappings, and by the portrayal of emotions such as love and pity.

Gaimar's treatment of the story of the death of King Aella and his nephew Orin (foretold by a mysterious, blind soothsayer), or the mixture of pathos and outrage in his story of the rape of Buern Bucecarle's wife, the daring rebellion of the outlaw Hereward, or the delicate description of the love between King Edgar and Elftroed, assuredly one of the earliest descriptions of courtly love, are clearly meant to heighten reader interest. Thus, before the middle of the twelfth century the first indications of what will become the most characteristic trademarks of Anglo-Norman romances surface in the chronicle of Geffrey Gaimar: pretense to high moral purpose; emphasis on plot, event, and episode; detailed and realistic descriptions of court environments; celebration of courtly pastimes and values such as hunting, feasting, and gift giving; literary exploitation of emotions such as love and pathos; and the glorification of English history and its heroes.

The romance is without doubt the Anglo-Norman genre that produced the largest number of translations and adaptations in Middle English, including, from the second half of the twelfth century, Thomas of England's *Tristan,* Béroul's *Tristan* (1150–1195), the *Romance of Horn* (circa 1180), the *Lai d'Haveloc, Ipomedon* by Hue de Rotelande (circa 1185), *Amis e Amillyoun,* the *Roman de Toute Chevalerie* by Thomas of Kent, *Waldef,* and, at the turn of the century, *Amadas et Ydoine* (1190–1220). The remaining romances of English heroes date from the thirteenth century: *Gui de Warewic, Boeve de Haumtone,* and *Fouke le Fitz Waryn.* The strong resemblance between the *Brut* chronicles and the romances of native English heroes suggests that the latter may have originated as an attempt to imitate the former. Like the chronicles, the romances present themselves as works of moral didacticism. The romance hero, no less than the national heroes of the chronicles, is one destined for success by God, and his identity is made known by prophetic dreams, magical objects, and supernatural encounters. His typical enemies (besides usurping uncles or unjust kings) are Saracens, and his military victories usually result in the conversion of large numbers of pagans; he normally undergoes a process of repentance and penance (as do Gui, Boeve, and Fouke) in his progression from knightly to Christian perfection.

The so-called Matter of England romances, *Horn* (circa 1170), *Lai d'Haveloc* (circa 1175), *Boeve de Haumtone* (circa 1200), *Gui de Warewic* (circa 1230), *Waldef* (circa 1200–1220), and *Fouke* (circa 1280), all of which gave rise to Middle English versions (although the Middle English versions of *Waldef* and *Fouke* have been lost), were first and foremost

Anglo-Norman creations. The romances of native heroes promote the fiction that Normans participated in Anglo-Saxon history. *Gui de Warewic* gives a Norman hero a crucial role at one of the central events in Anglo-Saxon history, the Battle of Brunanburg. Likewise, the story of Havelok, which appears first in Geffrey Gaimar's *Estoire des Engleis* and next in the *Lai d'Haveloc,* gives the English a Danish king who ruled over both England and Denmark long before the arrival of the Saxons. That both of these episodes were taken as fact is evident from their reappearance in several chronicles in the fourteenth century. Other romances adopt Anglo-Saxon names for the principal characters; for example, Waldef is the son of King Bede. Other characters in the same romance are Swein, Hardacunut, and Merlin, and King Edgar plays a role in *Boeve de Haumtone.*

To a great degree the typical literary features of Anglo-Norman literature result from the political aims that shaped the early chronicles. A characteristic of Anglo-Norman literature is its pretense to didactic intent. Not only religious works, but satires, fabliaux, romances, and chronicles all claim to be works of moral instruction. At the same time, in order to secure the widest possible readership for a body of literature unusually attuned to promoting the stature of the political class that sponsored it, great care was taken to engage the reader and produce works that would be read with enjoyment. Anglo-Norman literature develops a high degree of narrative skill and a wide range of subjects and styles. Finally, Anglo-Norman literature gives great attention to native English sources, figures, and themes. Idealization of the subject matter and literary form, didactic pretenses, as well as the exploration of complex and subtle emotional situations are strategies that were extended to a variety of stories, a fact that makes Anglo-Norman romance hard to classify. *Le Roman de Toute Chevalerie* (circa 1173) by Thomas of Kent, a treatment of the long-popular Alexander story, has a heavy tone of pious moralism yet gives the episode of Alexander's ensnarement by Candace – described as "bele, blanche cum flur d'espine" (beautiful and fair as a hawthorne blossom) – a courtly treatment. Both *Amis e Amillyoun* (late twelfth century) – the Anglo-Norman version of a favorite medieval story, *Amis et Amiles* (late twelfth century) – and the courtly love romance *Amadas et Ydoine* (circa 1190–1220) present themselves as works of moral instruction, the first representing the ideal of friendship, the second representing the ideal pair of lovers whom love held united all their lives "without deceit, villainy, or pride." At the same time, however, Anglo-Norman romances

develop great emotional intensity and extreme psychological subtlety, as does Thomas's *Tristan* (that also includes an epilogue claiming didact intent), written probably between 1155 and 1160, of which only five short middle fragments and the entire ending survive. Notable in Thomas's *Tristan* are the imaginative force and psychological complexity behind his descriptions of the personal conflicts of the principal characters, such as Tristan's decision to marry Ysolt of the White Hands and his subsequent inability to consummate the marriage; the impossible position of King Mark; the fight between Brengvein and Ysolt; and the jealousy of Ysolt of the White Hands. Perhaps Thomas's most memorable invention is the Hall of Statues that Tristan has built. The building houses lifelike statues of Ysolt and Brengvein, to which Tristan resorts in order to vent the various emotions caused by the memories of his love affair. Béroul's version – composed in England between 1150 and 1195, according to Guy R. Mermier – of which only the second half survives, is somewhat more brutal than Thomas's. Béroul's *Tristan* gives a larger role to the love potion (hardly mentioned by Thomas), and has generally been considered the less courtly treatment. The *Lais* of Marie de France, compiled for an English audience and written under English patronage, are equally surprising fusions of fantasy and emotion, characterized, as Barbara Schonwald Brookes has pointed out, by a limited but intense emotional range, emphasizing melancholy and suffering.

Humorous and satirical pieces, as well as lyrics on love, also claim pious intent. The unexpected juxtaposition of secular and pious themes can produce startling emotional effects. "Ferroy chaunson que bien doit estre oye" (I'll make a song that must be heard), a lover's complaint on being abandoned by his mistress, describes in three stanzas her betrayal of her lover in spite of her lover's blameless behavior, yet each stanza ends with a prayer to God and Saint Thomas for her forgiveness, thus revealing, in a surprisingly touching manner, the depth of the emotion he still feels for her as well as his own hopelessness. The "Débat entre Mère et Fille," a lyric whose subject is a debate between mother and daughter over whether to choose a wealthy husband (favored by the mother) or one whose kisses are like spiced wine (the daughter's choice), puts forth the usual arguments on both sides in a tone of good-natured satire, and then neatly switches from humor to homily as the daughter tells her mother that whatever may happen to wealth, honor and goodness endure, and the one who understands moderation is the one who is truly wealthy. "En

May," a macaronic *pastourelle*, begins with the description of a young girl walking alone one May morning when she is espied by a young man, who addresses her with an invitation to love. Instead of proceeding as a debate between two lovers as the tone of the poem thus far suggests, the poem quickly and deftly ends with the girl's response, a prayer to the Virgin to maintain her virginity. The "Lai du Cor" (Lay of the Horn) by Robert Biket, a twelfth-century burlesque of Arthurian themes involving a chastity test, ends with the claim that the tale has been told under instructions of an abbot.

An extremely large and varied body of literature is religious in nature. Besides Bible stories, passions, treatments in verse and prose of the childhood of Christ, sermons in verse, lyrics, and miracles of the Virgin, there was also an Anglo-Norman prose translation of both testaments of the Bible (incomplete) in existence by the fourteenth century. Just as secular narrative literature asserts a seriousness on a par with religious works, pious literature appeals to the literary tastes of a courtly audience. A genre particularly close to romance and historical narratives was hagiography. Saints' lives were, like heroic literature, considered works of moral didacticism of an exemplary nature. Benedeit's *Voyage of St. Brendan* (the earliest known Anglo-Norman work, written circa 1121, according to Edwin G. R. Waters) is, as Legge calls it in *Anglo-Norman Literature and Its Background* (1963), "a full tale of wonders" whose best-known episode is probably the Easter feast on the back of the sleeping whale, mistaken for an island. The tale reflects its courtly audience's taste for adventure narratives, and Waters notes in his edition of the poem Benedeit's attempts to make the narrative coherent and to avoid tedium, his frequent insertion of realistic touches, and his fondness for descriptions of costly and luxurious ornament.

Saints' lives show many of the characteristics of secular literature. They can exalt courtly life and describe emotions close to the heart of a feudal noble. In the Anglo-Norman *Vie de St. Alexis* (circa 1150), possibly based on a French original composed a century earlier but possibly composed in England around the middle of the century, Alexis's father expresses his anguish over his son's death in terms that any feudal lord could understand: "Oh, son, for whom was my great inheritance, my wide lands of which I had so many, my great palaces in the city of Rome? For you I went to all this trouble, so that after my death you would be honored." Gui de Warewic's father and mother lament his departure in much the same terms: "Who will govern, after our days, our castles and our honors?"

In addition, the subject matter of saints' lives often reflects the Anglo-Norman interest in promoting the belief in the Anglo-Saxon descent of the Norman royalty, as do Denis Pyramus's *Life of St. Edmund* and Clemence of Barking's *St. Edward,* composed most likely between 1163 and 1169. An adaptation of Ailred's Latin *Life,* this anonymous work stresses the relationship of Henry II to Edward through the marriage of Henry I to Matilda, greatniece of Edward the Confessor. Clemence of Barking's *St. Catherine,* also from the late twelfth century, is an adaptation of an earlier French translation of a standard Latin life that adds a courtly dimension that Legge notes is not to be found anywhere else in a saint's life. According to Legge, the influence of Thomas's *Tristan* is suggested by the emotional tone of the emperor's lamentation over the defection of his wife, whom Catherine has converted: "I cannot help but slay you; my life afterwards will be nothing but death. How can you die without me? How can I live without thee?" and "In sadness I will lead my life, when I lose you, beloved friend."

Running through Anglo-Norman religious literature is a strain of mysticism, allegory, and lyricism. Courtly love is one of the main models for religious literature. Bishop Robert Grosseteste's famous sermon, the *Chasteau d'Amour* (circa 1200–1250), is an allegory in praise of Mary, described as the castle of love that sheltered Christ. Its four towers represent the four cardinal virtues; the bailies represent maidenhood and chastity; the barbicans represent the opponents of the Seven Deadly Sins. Miracles of the Virgin were an extremely popular genre, apparently intended to counter the appeal of secular literature by appropriating Mary as the ideal of feminine virtue. Anglo-Norman miracles of the Virgin, which date from the end of the twelfth century, are short verse or prose narratives compiled from various sources, often chronicles and histories as well as hagiography, that relate how Mary helped someone who was particularly devoted to her, often a sinful monk or nun. Miracles of the Virgin portray her in tenderly human terms. One popular theme regards the healing power of Mary's milk. The miracle of a monk who was healed by the milk of the Holy Virgin (number 39 in Hilding Kjellman's *La Deuxième Collection Anglo-Normande des Miracles de la Sainte Vierge,* 1977) offers a characteristically tender portrayal. After Mary addresses the monk who was dying of a throat cancer as "duz ami" and lovingly reassures him that not only will he be entirely cured, but that he will be with her in Paradise after his life is over, the narrative continues:

With these words the sweet Mary
Embraced his neck and caressed it.
Then she did much more, the beautiful girl.
She uncovered her sweet breast
And put it in the monk's mouth,
And he sucked the holy milk
That ran down his throat in the midst of the illness,
With great sweetness, right into his heart,
So that he did not want to let go for any reason.
The glorious one by her great virtue
Caressed him where the pain was.
So much joy did the lady give him
That all the swelling of the neck subsided:
The hand without, the milk within
Healed him so that all his body was healthy.

Anglo-Norman lyrics, dating for the most part from the second half of the thirteenth century, were often parts of collections compiled by various orders of friars and used for devotional purposes. One well-known lyric by Nicholas Bozon, "Coment le fiz Deu fu armé en la croyz" (How the Son of God was armed on the Cross), announces that it contains a tale of high chivalry and narrates how a knight took to the field of battle in order to win back his estranged beloved held in thrall by sin. The knight is forced to disguise his identity, and Christ's human incarnation is compared, in an elaborate allegory, to a knight being armed for battle by a beautiful damsel who furnishes him with the armor of flesh and blood. Likewise, many lyrics and other works portray Christ the Savior-Knight addressing the soul in the language of courtly love. The lyric "Eya ore, ma duce amie" (Listen now, my sweet friend) is the address by Christ to his beloved, the human soul, describing Christ's sacrifices in terms of courtly love service to an ungrateful mistress. Likewise, the twelfth-century Anglo-Norman drama, the *Mystère d'Adam,* which can be considered the first drama in England since it was not performed as a part of the liturgy, mixes realistic detail and dialogue, secular themes such as disagreement between husband and wife, and courtly love with high religious seriousness. Satan tempts Eve by telling her that she and Adam are mismatched, and he does so in the language of a courtly lover:

You are a delicate and tender thing,
And fresher than the rose;
You are whiter than crystal,
Than snow that falls on ice in the valley.
    – translation by David Bevington (in his *Medieval Drama,*
      1975)

The *Wooing of Our Lord* is an address to Christ by a woman who claims Christ as her natural lover, beginning:

Jesu, sweet Jesu, my love, my darling, my Lord, my Saviour, my honey nectar-drop, my balm! Sweeter is the remembrance of Thee than honey-dew in the mouth. Who is there that may not love Thy lovely face? What heart is there so hard that may not melt at the remembrance of Thee? Ah! who may not love Thee, lovely Jesu? For within Thee alone are all the things united that ever may make any man worthy of love to another. ... Jesu my precious darling, my love, my life, my beloved, my most worthy of love, my heart's balm, my soul's sweetness, Thou art lovesome in countenance, Thou art altogether bright.
    – translation by William Henry Schofield (in his *English Literature from the Norman Conquest to Chaucer,* 1968)

Norman interest in vernacular literature no doubt began in the effort to produce a body of writing that would dignify the background and culture of the new Norman aristocracy in England, and many of the characteristics of the literature, such as the attention given to English subjects and the interest in widening the literary audience by appealing to ever-more-popular segments of the population, are ascribable to this background. Throughout the thirteenth century, Anglo-Norman literature continued to be extremely vital, and only in the fourteenth century does English literature begin to rival Anglo-Norman. The renewed energy of English literature in the fourteenth century clearly shows the continuity with Anglo-Norman. Not only are English works often translations or imitations of Anglo-Norman originals, but the many new genres embraced by Middle English literature are the inheritance of the Anglo-Norman past. A glance at the genres of the works in the Auchinleck Manuscript is indicative of the debt that Middle English literature owes to Anglo-Norman, since they were all foreshadowed by Anglo-Norman writers. Besides the romances for which it is famous, the manuscript contains, among other things, legends of the Virgin, various saints' legends, a variety of religious literature, a debate between the body and the soul, a dispute respecting women, one fabliau, and a chronicle of the kings of England based on the *Brut* tradition. The creation of a recognizably national English literature owes a large debt to Anglo-Norman writers between the twelfth and the fourteenth centuries.

References:

Amadas et Ydoine, edited by C. Hippeau, Collection des Poètes Français du Moyen Age 6 (Geneva: Slatkine Reprints, 1969);

Amis e Amillyoun, edited by Hideka Fukui, Plain Text Series 7 (London: Anglo-Norman Text Society, 1990);

Benedeit, *Voyage of St. Brendan,* edited by Edwin G. R. Waters (Slatkine Reprints, 1974);

Benoit de Sainte-More, *Chronique des Ducs de Normandie,* 3 volumes, edited by Carin Fahlin (Uppsala, Sweden: Almqvist & Wiksells, 1954);

Béroul, *Tristan and Yseut,* edited and translated by Guy R. Mermier (New York: P. Lang, 1987);

David Bevington, *Medieval Drama* (Boston: Houghton Mifflin, 1975);

Rauf de Boun, *Le Petit Bruit,* edited by Diana B. Tyson, Plain Text Series 4 (London: Anglo-Norman Text Society, 1987);

Susan Crane, *Insular Romance: Politics, Faith, and Culture in Anglo-Norman and Middle English Literature* (Berkeley: University of California Press, 1986);

Fouke, le Fitz Waryn, edited by E. J. Hathaway, P. T. Ricketts, C. A. Robson, and A. D. Wilshere (Oxford: Anglo-Norman Text Society, 1975);

Geffrey Gaimar, *The Anglo-Norman Metrical Chronicle of Geoffrey Gaimar,* edited by Thomas Wright (1850; New York: Burt Franklin, 1967);

Gaimar, *L'Estoire des Engleis,* edited by Alexander Bell, Anglo-Norman Text Society 14–16 (Oxford: Blackwell, 1901);

Gui de Warewic, 2 volumes, edited by Alfred Ewert (Paris: Champion, 1932);

David L. Jeffrey and Brian J. Levy, *The Anglo-Norman Lyric: An Anthology* (Toronto: Pontifical Institute of Mediaeval Studies, 1990);

Douglas A. Kibbee, *For To Speke Frenche Trewely* (Amsterdam & Philadelphia: Benjamins, 1991);

Hilding Kjellman, ed., *La Deuxième Collection Anglo-Normande des Miracles de la Sainte Vierge* (Genève: Slatkine Reprints, 1977);

Pierre Langtoft, *The Chronicle of Pierre de Langtoft,* edited and translated by Thomas Wright (London: Longmans, Green, Reader & Dyer, 1866–1868);

M. Dominica Legge, *Anglo-Norman Literature and Its Background* (Oxford: Clarendon Press, 1963);

The Romance of Horn, 2 volumes, edited by Mildred K. Pope, Anglo-Norman Text Society 9–10 (Oxford: Blackwell, 1955);

William Henry Schofield, *English Literature from the Norman Conquest to Chaucer* (New York: Haskell House, 1968);

Paul Studer, *The Study of Anglo-Norman* (Oxford: Clarendon Press, 1920);

John Taylor, *English Historical Literature in the Fourteenth Century* (Oxford: Clarendon Press, 1987);

Thomas of Kent, *The Anglo-Norman Alexander (Le Roman de Toute Chevalerie),* 2 volumes, edited by Brian Foster (London: Anglo-Norman Text Society, 1976);

Diana B. Tyson, "Patronage of French Vernacular History Writers in the Twelfth and Thirteenth Centuries," *Romania,* 100 (1979): 180–222;

La Vie de Saint Alexis, edited by Christopher Storey (Geneva: Librairie Droz, 1968);

Johan Vising, *Anglo-Norman Language and Literature* (Westport, Conn.: Greenwood Press, 1970);

William of Malmesbury, *William of Malmesbury's Chronicle of the Kings of England,* edited and translated by J. A. Giles (London: H. G. Bohn, 1847).

Checklist of Further Readings

Old English
compiled by Jonathan Evans, University of Georgia

Anderson, George K. *The Literature of the Anglo-Saxons*. Princeton: Princeton University Press, 1949.

Bately, Janet. *Anonymous Old English Homilies: A Preliminary Bibliography of Source Studies*. Binghamton, N.Y.: Center for Medieval and Early Renaissance Studies, 1993.

Beale, Walter H., ed. *Old and Middle English Poetry to 1500: A Guide to Information Sources*. Detroit: Gale Research, 1976.

Bessinger, Jess B. Jr., and Stanley J. Kahrl, eds. *Essential Articles for the Study of Old English Poetry*. Hamden, Conn.: Archon, 1968.

Blair, Peter Hunter. *Anglo-Saxon England*. Cambridge: Cambridge University Press, 1956.

Blair. *Roman Britain and Early England, 55 B.C.–A.D. 871*. Norton Library History of England. New York: Norton, 1963.

Bradley, S. A. J. *Anglo-Saxon Poetry*. London: Dent / Rutland, Vt.: Tuttle, 1982.

Brooke, Stopford A. *English Literature from the Beginning to the Norman Conquest*. New York & London: Macmillan, 1898.

Bruce-Mitford, R. L. S. *Aspects of Anglo-Saxon Archaeology: Sutton Hoo and Other Discoveries*. New York: Harper, 1974; London: Gollancz, 1974.

Bruce-Mitford. *The Sutton Hoo Ship Burial*, 3 volumes. London: British Museum Publications, 1975.

Cassidy, Frederic G., and Richard N. Ringler. *Bright's Old English Grammar & Reader*, third edition. New York: Holt, Rinehart & Winston, 1971.

Chaney, William. *The Cult of Kingship in Anglo-Saxon England*. Berkeley: University of California Press, 1970.

Colgrave, Bertram, and others, eds. *Early English Manuscripts in Facsimile*, 19 volumes to date. Copenhagen: Rosenkilde & Bagger, 1951– .

Collingwood, R. G., and J. N. L. Myres. *Roman Britain and the British Settlements*. Oxford History of England, volume 1. London: Oxford University Press, 1936; second edition, 1937.

Fry, Donald K. "Old English Formulaic Themes and Type-Scenes," *Neophilologus*, 52 (1968): 48–54.

Garde, Judith N. *Old English Poetry in Medieval Christian Perspective: A Doctrinal Approach*. Cambridge: Brewer, 1991.

Gardner, John. *The Construction of Christian Poetry in Old English*. Carbondale: Southern Illinois University Press, 1975.

Garmonsway, G. N., and Jacqueline Simpson. *Beowulf and Its Analogues*. London: Dent / New York: Dutton, 1968.

Gatch, Milton McC. *Preaching and Theology in Anglo-Saxon England: Ælfric and Wulfstan*. Toronto: University of Toronto Press, 1977.

Godden, Malcolm, and Michael Lapidge, eds. *The Cambridge Companion to Old English Literature*. Cambridge: Cambridge University Press, 1991.

Göller, Karl Heinz. *Geschichte der altenglischen Literatur*. Berlin: Erich Schmidt, 1971.

Greenfield, Stanley B. *The Interpretation of Old English Poems*. London & Boston: Routledge & Kegan Paul, 1972.

Greenfield and Daniel G. Calder. *A New Critical History of Old English Literature*. New York: New York University Press, 1986.

Greenfield and Fred C. Robinson, eds. *A Bibliography of Publications on Old English Literature to the End of 1972*. Toronto: University of Toronto Press, 1980.

Grein, C. W. M., and Richard P. Wülker, eds. *Bibliothek der angelsächsischen Poesie,* 3 volumes. Kassel: G. H. Wigand, 1883–1898.

Grein and Wülker, eds. *Bibliothek der angelsächsischen Prosa,* 13 volumes. Kassel: G. H. Wigand, 1872–1933.

Heusinkveld, Arthur H. *A Bibliographical Guide to Old English*. Iowa City: University of Iowa Press, 1931.

Hill, David. *An Atlas of Anglo-Saxon England*. Toronto: University of Toronto Press, 1981.

Howarth, David. *1066: The Year of the Conquest*. New York: Viking, 1978.

Howe, Nicholas. *The Old English Catalogue Poems*. Anglistica 23. Copenhagen: Rosenkilde & Bagger, 1985.

Huppé, Bernard F. *Doctrine and Poetry: Augustine's Influence on Old English Poetry*. Albany: State University of New York Press, 1959.

Huppé. *The Web of Words: Structural Analyses of the Old English Poems*. Albany: State University of New York Press, 1970.

Isaacs, Neil D. *Structural Principles in Old English Poetry*. Knoxville: University of Tennessee Press, 1968.

Kaske, Robert E. "*Sapientia et Fortitudo* as the Controlling Theme of *Beowulf*," in *Old English Poetry: Fifteen Essays,* edited by Robert P. Creed. Providence: Brown University Press, 1967, pp. 285–310.

Ker, N. R. *Catalogue of Manuscripts Containing Anglo-Saxon*. Oxford: Oxford University Press, 1957.

Krapp, G. P., and E. V. K. Dobbie, eds. *The Anglo-Saxon Poetic Records,* 6 volumes. New York: Columbia University Press, 1931–1953.

Magoun, Francis P. Jr., "Oral-Formulaic Character of Anglo-Saxon Narrative Poetry," *Speculum,* 28 (1953): 446–467.

Malone, Kemp. *The Nowell Codex: British Museum Cotton Vitellius A.xv, Second Manuscript.* Early English Manuscripts in Facsimile 12. Copenhagen: Rosenkilde & Bagger, 1963.

Malone. "The Old English Period (to 1100)," in *A Literary History of England,* edited by Albert C. Baugh. New York: Appleton-Century-Crofts, 1948; second edition, 1967.

Malone. "Words of Wisdom in *Beowulf,*" in *Humaniora: Essays in Literature, Folklore, Bibliography Honoring Archer Taylor,* edited by Wayland D. Hand and Gustav. O Arlt. Locust Valley, N.Y., 1960, pp. 180–194.

Newton, Sam. *The Origins of Beowulf and the Pre-Viking Kingdom of East Anglia.* Cambridge: Brewer, 1993.

Nicholson, Lewis E., and Dolores Warwick Frese, eds. *Anglo-Saxon Poetry: Essays in Appreciation for John C. McGalliard.* Notre Dame: Notre Dame University Press, 1975.

Niles, John D., ed. *Old English Literature in Context.* Totowa, N. J.: Rowman & Littlefield / Cambridge: Brewer, 1980.

Robinson, Fred C. *Old English Literature: A Select Bibliography.* Toronto: University of Toronto Press, 1970.

Robinson. "Understanding an Old English Wisdom Verse: *Maxims II, Lines 10ff,*" in *The Wisdom of Poetry,* edited by Larry D. Benson and Siegfried Wenzel. Kalamazoo, Mich.: Medieval Institute, 1982, pp. 45–51, 270.

Sanders, W. B., ed. *Facsimiles of Anglo-Saxon Manuscripts,* 4 volumes. Southampton: Ordnance Survey, 1878–1884.

Scholtz, H. van der Merwe. *The Kenning in Anglo-Saxon and Old Norse Poetry.* Utrecht & Nijmegen: Dekker & Van de Vegt, 1928.

Short, Douglas D. *Beowulf Scholarship: An Annotated Bibliography.* New York: Garland, 1980.

Stenton, F. M. *Anglo-Saxon England.* Oxford History of England 2, second edition. Oxford: Clarendon Press, 1971.

Tolkien, J. R. R. "*Beowulf:* The Monsters and the Critics," *Proceedings of the British Academy,* 22 (1936): 245–295; republished in *The Monsters and the Critics and Other Essays,* edited by Christopher Tolkien. Boston: Houghton Mifflin, 1984.

Tolkien. "The Homecoming of Beorhtnoth Beorhthelm's Son," *Essays and Studies,* new series 6 (1953): 1–18.

Wallace-Hadrill, J. M. *Early Germanic Kingship in England and on the Continent.* Oxford: Clarendon Press, 1971.

Whitelock, Dorothy. *The Beginnings of English Society.* Pelican History of England. Harmondsworth & New York: Penguin, 1952.

Williams, Blanche Colton. *Gnomic Poetry in Anglo-Saxon.* New York: Columbia University Press, 1914.

Wilson, David M. *The Anglo-Saxons.* New York: Praeger, 1960; revised edition, Harmondsworth & New York: Penguin, 1971.

Wilson. *The Archaeology of Anglo-Saxon England.* London: Methuen, 1976.

Wrenn, C. L. *A Study of Old English Literature.* New York: Norton, 1967.

Middle English
compiled by William Provost, University of Georgia

Ackerman, Robert W. *Backgrounds to Medieval Literature*. New York: Random House, 1966.

Atkins, J. W. H. *English Literary Criticism: The Medieval Phase*. New York: Peter Smith, 1952.

Baugh, Albert C. "The Middle English Period (1100–1500)," in *A Literary History of England*, edited by Baugh. New York: Appleton-Century-Crofts, 1948; second edition, 1967.

Bennett, H. S. *Chaucer and the Fifteenth Century*. New York & Oxford: Oxford University Press, 1947.

Bennett. *Six Medieval Men and Women*. Cambridge: Cambridge University Press, 1955.

Bennett, J. A. W. *Middle English Literature*. Oxford: Clarendon Press, 1986.

Benson, Larry D., and Theodore M. Andersson, eds. *The Literary Context of Chaucer's Fabliaux: Texts and Translations*. Indianapolis & New York: Bobbs-Merrill, 1971.

Berrigan, Joseph. *Medieval Intellectual History*. Lawrence, Kans.: Coronado Press, 1974.

Bloomfield, Morton W. *The Seven Deadly Sins*. Lansing: Michigan State College Press, 1952.

Böker, Uwe, Manfred Markus, and Rainer Schöwerling, eds. *The Living Middle Ages: Studies in Medieval English Literature and Its Tradition: A Festschrift for Karl Heinz Göller*. Stuttgart: Belser, 1989.

Brewer, Derek. *Chaucer and His World*. New York: Dodd, Mead, 1978.

Burrow, J. A. *The Ages of Man: A Study in Medieval Writing and Thought*. Oxford: Clarendon Press, 1988.

Chambers, E. K. *English Literature at the Close of the Middle Ages*. Oxford: Clarendon Press, 1945.

Coulton, G. G. *Chaucer and His England*. London: Methuen, 1908.

Coulton, *Medieval Panorama: The English Scene from Conquest to Reformation*. Cambridge: Cambridge University Press, 1938.

Craig, Hardin. *English Religious Drama of the Middle Ages*. Oxford: Clarendon Press, 1955.

Doob, Penelope B. R. *Nebuchadnezzar's Children: Conventions of Madness in Middle English Literature*. New Haven & London: Yale University Press, 1974.

Dunn, Charles W., and Edward T. Byrnes, eds. *Middle English Literature*. New York: Harcourt Brace Jovanovich, 1973.

Esch, Arno, ed. *Chaucer und seine Zeit: Symposion für Walter F. Schirmer*. Tübingen: Max Niemeyer, 1968.

Heer, Friederich. *The Medieval World*, translated by Janet Sondheimer. New York: New American Library, 1961.

Kane, George. *Middle English Literature: A Critical Study of the Romances, the Religious Lyrics, Piers Plowman*. London: Methuen, 1951.

Lewis, C. S. *The Allegory of Love: A Study in Medieval Tradition.* Oxford: Clarendon Press, 1936.

Loomis, Roger Sherman, ed. *Arthurian Literature in the Middle Ages: A Collaborative History.* Oxford: Clarendon Press, 1959.

Loomis and Rudolph Willard, eds. *Medieval English Verse and Prose in Modernized Versions.* New York: Appleton-Century-Crofts, 1948.

Miller, Robert P., ed. *Chaucer: Sources and Backgrounds.* New York: Oxford University Press, 1977.

Mossé, Fernand. *A Handbook of Middle English,* translated by James A. Walker. Baltimore: Johns Hopkins University Press, 1952.

Oakden, James P. *Alliterative Poetry in Middle English: A Survey of the Traditions,* 2 volumes. Hamden, Conn.: Archon, 1968.

Owst, G. R. *Literature and the Pulpit in Medieval England.* Cambridge: Cambridge University Press, 1933.

Patch, Howard R. *The Tradition of Boethius: A Study of His Importance in Medieval Culture.* Oxford & New York: Oxford University Press, 1935.

Powell, James M. *Medieval Studies.* Syracuse: Syracuse University Press, 1976.

Rickert, Edith. *Chaucer's World,* edited by Clair C. Olson and M. M. Crow. New York: Columbia University Press, 1948.

Robertson, D. W. Jr., *The Literature of Medieval England.* New York: McGraw-Hill, 1970.

Robertson. *A Preface to Chaucer: Studies in Medieval Perspectives.* Princeton: Princeton University Press, 1962.

Speirs, John. *Medieval English Poetry: The Non-Chaucerian Tradition.* London: Faber & Faber, 1957.

Utley, Francis Lee. *The Crooked Rib: An Analytical Index to the Argument about Women in English and Scots Literature to the End of the Year 1568.* Columbus: Ohio State University Press, 1944.

Wilson, R. M. *Early Middle English Literature,* third edition. London: Methuen, 1968.

Wilson. *The Lost Literature of Medieval England.* London: Methuen, 1952; revised, 1970.

Zesmer, David M. *Guide to English Literature from Beowulf through Chaucer and Medieval Drama.* New York: Barnes & Noble, 1961.

Contributors

Elizabeth Psakis Armstrong...*University of Cincinnati*
Laurel Boone..*University of New Brunswick*
Elizabeth J. Bryan...*Brown University*
Joy L. Cafiero...*University of South Carolina*
Nancy Coiner..*Middlebury College*
Theresa Coletti..*University of Maryland*
Edwin D. Craun..*Washington and Lee University*
Clifford Davidson..*Western Michigan University*
Denise L. Despres..*University of Puget Sound*
Anthony S. G. Edwards..*University of Victoria*
Deanna Delmar Evans..*Bemidji State University*
Jonathan Evans..*University of Georgia*
Carol Falkenstine..*Berea College*
Allen J. Frantzen..*Loyola University of Chicago*
Joel Fredell..*Southeastern Louisiana University*
Maureen Fries............................*State University of New York College at Fredonia*
Shearle Furnish..*West Texas A&M University*
Rosanne Gasse..*Brandon University*
Thomas A. Goodman..*University of Miami*
Eugene Green..*Boston University*
Jeffrey Helterman..*University of South Carolina*
Jolyon Helterman...*Columbia, South Carolina*
Elissa R. Henken...*University of Georgia*
Iain Higgins..*University of British Columbia*
Sarah Lynn Higley...*University of Rochester*
John C. Hirsh..*Georgetown University*
Arthur G. Holder................................*Church Divinity School of the Pacific*
Sally C. Hoople..*Maine Maritime Academy*
George R. Keiser...*Kansas State University*
Katherine E. Krohn...*Texas A&M University*
John Felicien Lorio, Jr..*University of South Carolina*
Phoebe A. Mainster..*Wayne State University*
Kathleen Gaines McCarty..................................*University of South Carolina*
William McColly..*University of South Carolina*
Katherine G. McMahon...*Mount Union College*
Douglas J. McMillan..*East Carolina University*
Jerome Mitchell..*University of Georgia*
Margaret Pyne Monteverde...*Belmont University*
Toni J. Morris...*University of Indianapolis*
Marie Nelson..*University of Florida*
Timothy D. O'Brien..*United States Naval Academy*
Alexandra Hennessey Olsen...*University of Denver*
Anthony J. Ouellette...*University of South Carolina*
Perry T. Patterson..*University of South Carolina*
Bruce L. Pearson...*University of South Carolina*
Russell A. Peck..*University of Rochester*
Daniel F. Pigg...*The University of Tennessee at Martin*
William F. Pollard..*University of Evansville*

William Provost .... *University of Georgia*
Edmund Reiss .... *Durham, North Carolina*
Judith Davis Shaw .... *University of Georgia*
R. A. Shoaf .... *University of Florida*
Sharon Stevenson .... *Mount Pleasant, Michigan*
Zacharias P. Thundy .... *Vienna, Austria*
Andrew Welsh .... *Rutgers University*
Richard David Wissolik .... *Saint Vincent College*
Jane Dick Zatta .... *University of Georgia*

Cumulative Index

Dictionary of Literary Biography, Volumes 1-146
Dictionary of Literary Biography Yearbook, 1980-1993
Dictionary of Literary Biography Documentary Series, Volumes 1-11

Cumulative Index

DLB before number: *Dictionary of Literary Biography*, Volumes 1-146
Y before number: *Dictionary of Literary Biography Yearbook*, 1980-1993
DS before number: *Dictionary of Literary Biography Documentary Series*, Volumes 1-11

D

F

G

T

Cumulative Index

ISBN 0-8103-5707-0

90000

9 780810 357075

(Continued from front endsheets)

Documentary Series

Yearbooks